To Beverly!
Love XOXOXO
Thank you

DREAMS –
THE 60TH PART OF PROPHECY

DEBORAH M. MILLER

BALBOA.
PRESS

A DIVISION OF HAY HOUSE

Interior Graphics/Art Credit: Deborah Miller

Balboa Press books may be ordered through booksellers or by contacting:

Balboa Press
A Division of Hay House
1663 Liberty Drive
Bloomington, IN 47403
www.balboapress.com
1 (877) 407-4847

ISBN: 978-1-9822-1043-4 (sc)
ISBN: 978-1-9822-1044-1 (e)

Library of Congress Control Number: 2018911186

Print information available on the last page.

Balboa Press rev. date: 10/09/2018

Images And Words in the Night

In a dream, in a vision of the night, when deep sleep falls upon men, while slumbering on their beds, when He opens the ears of men, And seals their instruction (Job 33:15-16 NKJV)

Until you get to the place, where you have extracted certain behaviors from your system one needs God to have something to put in your face.

Many times God has to go outside of our capacity spiritually and connect us to something psychologically or scare us with some kind of threat in order to keep us until we can walk, as He wants us to walk

He uses consequences and deterrents that catch us quickly. They catch you on the way, so you don't get too deeply into something that is going to take half of your mind to get out of it

You don't want to go the edge of your mind to change your mind in order to do different behavior

Within the context of this reference those catalysts, consequences, and deterrents are your dreams

----

There is in sleep something mysterious, which seems from the earliest of times, to have impressed man and aroused his curiosity. (CHARLES SOUVA)

There, are all the stimuli and experiences we know from real life –sights and sounds; thoughts and actions; exhilaration and dread. However, everything is all over the place; distorted, opposing all logic.

In a dream, one might look into a mirror and be headless, or fly out of a building, through the sky and beyond. What we believe in our dreams to be negative may possibly be quite positive. A mother might be younger than her daughter, a dish may run away with a spoon, or you may literally help the little old lady who lived in a shoe who didn't know what to do. When the axe came into the forest, the trees said, "The handle is one of us".

Dreams...perception without the discipline of reason

This book is dedicated to my friend, my confidant,
to the one who ministered deeply to my soul
My very beautiful mother, so wise, so loving, so strong, so real
Mrs. Vinie Mae Wright Miller
July 16, 1919 – July 24, 2009

During a dark time in my life, my mother,
at eighty-five years young, called and left this message…

"Deb, this is your mother. I just wanted to talk to you. I wanted to hear your voice and to let you know that whatever you're feeling, whatever you're going through, I'm going through with you. I'm praying for you every day. This is your mother, and I love you sooo very much. Daughter be strong, and read the 3rd and 27th Psalms. The Lord is your light and salvation. The Lord is your strength and remember, your sisters and I have been through it all, and you will make it through this. I love you Deb". 8/05

Her enduring words that she spoke over my life everyday
"Deborah, a good name is rather to be chosen than many riches"
Thank you mama

Thank you
To all who allowed me to publish their personal dreams, and
to all who encouraged and sponsored me in this endeavor

Contents

DREAMS –
THE *60TH* PART OF PROPHECY

DEBORAH M. MILLER

IN THE NIGHT SEASONS WHILE SLEEPING ON
MY BED VISIONS OF PEACE, LOVE,
JOY AND DREAD DANCE IN MY HEAD. O' WHAT A NIGHT, O'
WHAT A DREAM, TELL ME, WHAT DOES IT ALL MEAN.

I SEE THE OCEAN'S WAVES SO BLUE, WHITE CAPS TOSSED;
I EMBRACE MY LOVER WITH PASSIONS SO TRUE. O'
WHAT A NIGHT, O' WHAT A DREAM, TELL ME,
WHAT DOES IT ALL MEAN.

I'M RUNNING; I'M FALLING, I SUDDENLY HAVE WINGS; I'M
FLYING PEACEFULLY IN MY DREAM. O' WHAT A NIGHT, O'
WHAT A DREAM, TELL ME, WHAT DOES IT ALL MEAN.

FIRE FROM HELL, DEMONS OF DREAD, SOMEBODY WAKE
ME FROM THIS DREAM IN MY HEAD. O' WHAT A NIGHT,
O' WHAT A DREAM, PLEASE, PLEASE, SOMEONE,
TELL ME WHAT DOES IT ALL MEAN.

DEBORAH MILLER

EDGAR ALLEN POE

**A DREAM
WITHIN A DREAM**
YOU ARE NOT WRONG,
WHO DEEM THAT MY
DAYS HAVE BEEN
A DREAM;
YET IF HOPE HAS
FLOWN AWAY IN A
NIGHT, OR IN A DAY,
IN A VISION, OR IN NONE,
IS IT THEREFORE
THE LESS GONE?
ALL THAT WE SEE OR SEEM
IS BUT A DREAM
WITHIN A DREAM.

I STAND AMID THE ROAR
OF A SURF-TORMENTED
SHORE, AND I HOLD WITHIN
MY HAND GRAINS OF THE
GOLDEN SAND-HOW FEW!
YET HOW THEY CREEP
THROUGH MY FINGERS
TO THE DEEP,
WHILE I WEEP-
WHILE I WEEP!
O GOD! CAN I NOT
GRASP THEM WITH A
TIGHTER CLASP?
O GOD! CAN I NOT SAVE
ONE FROM THE PITILESS
WAVE? IS ALL THAT WE SEE
OR SEEM BUT A DREAM
WITHIN A DREAM?

DREAMS – THE 60TH PART OF PROPHECY
COPYRIGHT 2018, DEBORAH M. MILLER

For more information, please contact:

Deborah M. Miller
dreamweaverministries@yahoo.com

Chalom: A Dream

....the mystery of sleeping is enhanced by the phenomenon of dream that accompanies it. (Souvay, C. 1909)

If you do dream, and I believe we all do, then you too have wondered about a dream and the mystery of its origin, makeup, and purpose. Internally inconsistent and disordered, dreams, oftentimes, enter and leave the life of the dreamer, meaningless. How should we consider our dreams? Are they all simply electrical activity in the brain, or, was it something you ate? Should we seek to understand them as a form of prophecy, a sort of heavenly posts, or should we disregard them due to our inability to understand them? What is a dream? In order to gain some perspective on the phenomenon of dreams, and to properly understand their purpose in this world, we must first delve (briefly) into the inner dimensions of dreams.

GENESIS OF DREAMS

In the beginning, we understand that everything emanates from one supreme creative force, Elohim (Genesis 1:1; John 1:1-3). There is no single substance existing in the universe, whether it is that which we experience through the senses, or that which we perceive through the mind, and that, which is unknown, which did not exist first in our Creator. No matter what is out there in our vast universe, it did not come into existence without the Creator. The beginning of all reality takes place first in the heavens, gradually descending into this world (whether through divine will, faith, hope, love), and is govern by Almig hty God. Dreams are a branch of this divine order.

Picture a tree. The spiritual and corporeal worlds may be compared to a tree. From bottom to top, a tree is composed of a root system, a trunk, branches, leaves, and fruit. The root system of the tree, which is unseen, serves as its' source. T he trunk is the main stem of the tree. We know the type of tree by the revealed branches, leaves, and fruit of the tree. Think of branches as miniature versions of trunks, with the leaf connected to the branch. Most leaves have two parts: the petiole and the blade. The petiole connects the blade to the branch. It carries sap, supports the leaf, and directs it towards the light.

Pulling all this together, God in His governance from the heavens (the unseen world) is symbolically the root, the source of all that is. That which emanates from the root manifests itself in the visible world, via a symbolic trunk, branches, leaves, and fruit. Thus, the visible (or physical) world is an expression of the spiritual world (Romans 11:16-18).

Our dreams figuratively operate pretty much like branches. Thus, our dreams are symbolic branches. The leaf (or blade) is symbolic of knowledge. The petiole is that which connects knowledge (the leaf) to our dreams (the branches). The branche s connect us to the main source (God) by way of the trunk, supplying us with "life giving" wisdom (the meaning of our dreams), which directs us towards the Light (aka Yeshua). Further, what our dreams reveal to us in our material world is, also referred to as fruit.

Dream interpreters employ the names of the branches of this physical world to explain their spiritual counterparts. For the processes in creation often, parallel realities within the spiritual realm. This is what I term, The Language of the Branches, The Language of Dreams (see Chapter Three). One principle of interpretation supports this: When the symbol is in the heavenly realm, its meaning is in the human realm. For example, when Joseph dreamt of the sun, moon, and eleven stars bowing to him (the heavenly realm), his family immediately knew the meaning as referring to his father, mother, and brothers (Genesis 37: 9-11). On the other hand, when the symbol is in the corporal realm, as in *Daniel 7:8, "... in this horn were eyes like the eyes of a man and a mouth speaking great things (KJV)"*. Its interpretation is in the spiritual realm. For example, within the context of this dream (Daniel 7:8), these symbols and images of animal horns, human eyes and mouth (the human realm), signify the embodiment of evil, the principal agent of the antichrist and the source of his power and strength. Dreams, as with all, phenomenon, have laws and principles, which were, established by God, and are subject to His decrees. Moreover, if you are so incline, as with any discipline, the rules are available for you to discover, to your benefit or dismay, depending upon the particular discipline, and the tendencies of the student.

Supporting Premise

Within Abrahamic religions, dreams are, believed to be divine communications (Numbers 12:6). One view of dreams as a means of communication by God with man is, based on a Talmudic quote, "Although I have hidden my face from Israel, I will communicate with him through dreams". In another place it is written, *"For God speaks again and again, though people do not recognize it. He speaks in dreams, in visions of the night, when deep sleep falls on people as they lie in their beds. He whispers in their ears and terrifies them with warnings". (Job 33:14-16 NLT)*

Approximately one third of the Bible chronicles stories and actions, which came about because of dreams. Actually, all the dreams recorded in Holy Writ came from 'out of the blue', thus confirming their cause as from God. The divine origin of the dream is evident by its strangeness, its exclusive one of a kind quality, and the suddenness with which it burst forth in our sleep, shining forth like a beacon of light. The biblical writers, as well as, the early church fathers, have all acknowledg ed the divine providence and prophetic significance of dreams without controversy. Every major writer in the first four centuries of Christianity regarded dreams as one way that God offered healing and guidance to humanity. Judeo-Christian belief acknowledges dreams and recognizes that they can be used of God for divine revelation.

With over seven billion people on earth (2012 census), at least six billion dreams occur all over the planet every night; it is not inconceivable to believe that Creator God is instrumental in at least five billion dreams per night. Our Creator has dealt with humankind through dreams in our distant past, and God has declared that He would continue to use dreams in the last days.

> *"And, it shall be in the last days," the God says. "That I will pour fourth of My Spirit on all mankind; and your sons and your daughters shall prophesy, and your young men shall see visions, and your old men shall dream dreams" (Acts 2:17 NASB)*

No one can question God's power, nor His prerogative, to introduce His purpose and His will into our dreams, if He so desires. Once, accurately interpreted and wisely applied, your dreams can be used to rectify yourself and/or affect actual events that take place in your life. They can remove all fear to recreate yourself, thus becoming more of whom, you are, purposed to be. Your dreams can be a transformational force in your life.

A Dream

Most of the time the information acquired within dreams exceeds that which we could obtain during our normal, analytical, waking state of mind. Throughout history, most cultures believed that humans could obtain knowledge from their dreams. From biblical covenants bestowed upon men within dreams, to divine warnings given pagan kings, to Generals receiving battle plans in their dreams, prior to the day of attack by their enemies, to famous musicians hearing arrangements within their dreams, to modern scientific breakthroughs; humankind has received life changing insight and guidance from their dreams. The spiral slicer for holiday hams was, inspired by a dream[1]. Dreams can have a powerful effect on anyone who dares to acknowledge them as significant insight within their life. People from all lifestyles can benefit from their dreams, as they explore deeper into understanding them.

Prophecies, healings, instructions on how to handle our various affairs reflect some of the wisdom given within our dreams. Sometimes the most meaningless dream will help change your life in ways you would have never thought. One day I decided to write a book. What I initially wanted to write and what I eventually wrote were very different. After deciding the title of my initial thoughts, I dreamt that a writing instrument (a quill) was taken (or lifted) out and away from my fingers. I decided not to write those initial thoughts. Several months later, another title and different inspirations came to me, so I began writing. The latter inspirations were very instrumental in helping me overcome a long and arduous grieving process. Dreams have played a major role in the human experience in many ways, for they are direct links to the inspirational and prophetic undercurrents that flow through you, from heavenly places.

On the other side

Never make a major decision in your life based solely on a dream. It would be dangerous to center your entire life on dreams, for dreams may lead men astray, as with any spiritual discipline taken to extreme – out of balance, above and beyond boundaries set by God (Ecclesiastes 10:8). However, that does not negate the fact that God speaks to us through our dreams. We, humankind, are standing on the threshold of a new dawn. The Creator of this world is speaking to His children through dreams. God confirms promises and pledges through our dreams. He leads and directs us in our dreams. He sheds light on our talents within our dreams. Life can be somewhat of a mystery at times, but God graces us with favor by allowing us to experience, and I hope comprehend, through our dreams, His purposes.

Dreams (and visions) are significant links through which God have chosen to connect with us, thus they must be given serious consideration. They are one essential tool, amongst many, for anyone who wants to know what God is trying to tell them. If you were to interview Joseph (Genesis 41:41) or Daniel (Daniel 2:46-49), both will tell you that there is much benefit from exploring the phenomenon of dreams.

CHALOM

The noun Chalom[2], translated dream, has two basic meanings. The first are those ordinary dreams associated with sleep–your emotions and thoughts visualized in sleep. The second are prophetic dreams — or the elevated parts of dreams, most familiar to us from the story of Joseph, Genesis 37:5-11. Between the ordinary and the prophetic, there are many facets to dreams. Further, not all dreams are equal in significance, thus the diverse kinds of dreams calls for regard in differing degrees. Case in point, amid the class ordinary dreams, is natural dreams.

Ordinary Dreams

This category of dreams is, influenced by natural stimuli such as foods, physical needs and desires, or atmospheric conditions. All of these corporal influences have some bearing on the body, so that your dreams may bear a close resemblance to your physical state. For example, you may dream that you have an uncontrollable urge to go to the restroom, when in actuality there is a physical need to do so. These dreams are not significant, and do not warrant special attention, other t han, to perhaps, highlight the necessity, desire to take care of some physical need.

The sentiments, which we indulge throughout the day often, mingle with the grateful slumbers of the night. (Claudian)

Other ordinary dreams (causative dreams) that come because of man's thoughts, are usually about the anxieties that overwhelm the mind during the day. For instance, a not so healthy senior citizen may have dreamed that his or her deceased father or mother approached them in their dreams, asking the dreamer to come with him or her. For the most part, the dreamer has caused this sort of dream, having become weary of living, due to health related issues, coupled with the fears and frustrations that overwhelm the mind because of the aging process. On another vein, selfish and money oriented pursuits will also be the source of causative dreams. The prophet Jeremiah spoke of this type of dream as a dream, which you caused to be (Jeremiah 29:8).

Yet another ordinary dream: A "Real-Time" Dream

On occasion, one may have what I term a *Real-Time Dream*. Attributes of real-time dreams, consists of events actually happening within your space while you are asleep dreaming of those same events. When the body is in slumber, your spirit is sometimes cognizant of your surroundings, and it will hear or pick-up on activity that is going on around you in real time — the actual time it is happening. Disquieting the senses, these observations are, filtered down to the mind's eye, where they take the form of a dream. This type of ordinary dream catches sight of very real experiences exactly as they are happening around you at that moment. It is very common to be woken up in the middle of this type of dream, acting-out the dream, just to realize the events that were happening in your dream, are actually happening now! This type of dream is not to be confused with sleepwalking or any other altered state of consciousness. The events in this type of dream are actually happening in real time.

The following real-time dream was, related to me one evening:

The young man was dreaming of a stranger creeping up on him while he was sleeping. As the stranger entered his bedroom, the stranger began tiptoeing towards the dreamer, with a very hard shoe in his hand. The stranger's purpose was to bash the dreamer's head with the shoe, murdering him. In the young man's dream, the dreamer rose up to protect himself, shouting some very fiery and violent words, startling the intruder. Fortunately, in real time, the dreamer suddenly awoke, rising up shouting the same words he was actually screaming in his dream, and with the same intensity. The dreamer then realized that there really was a stranger in his bedroom, coming towards him, with a shoe in his hand. The dreamer's aggressive words and actions startled the intruder and he fled. The dreamer later found out that the intruder was a neighbor who had just been released from prison, diagnosed with bi-polar tendencies, and who just happened to be in love with the dreamer's girlfriend. The dreamer attributes this real-time dream to God protecting him during his sleep and to the prayers of others, especially his parents. (A. P. Church, Jr.)

Whereas most all ordinary dreams are for the most part influenced by substantive stimuli, or are the result of man's thoughts, there are ordinary dreams that are not so ordinary, because of their prophetic overtones, for example, nightmares. Herein, they are termed, Prophetically Ordinary dreams.

Prophetically Ordinary

These types of dreams, although aroused because of fears, anxieties, and thoughts that overwhelm our mind, they do reveal (or prophesy) a debilitating physical or spiritual condition. Mark Virkler, co-author of *Hear God through Your Dreams*, shares that in his own life, a recurring nightmare of fifteen years disappeared immediately and completely when he had a demon cast out of him (an exorcism) which was the underlying fear being portrayed in his recurring nightmares. Virkler, "nightmares are the screams of an unhealed heart's cry for inner healing". For more on recurring dreams, see chapter one, section entitled, "Still yet, another Prophetic Dream".

It is, said of King David, that he was a man of extraordinary spiritual character. Whenever he experienced a terrifying nightmare, he was able to glean the message from it and make the necessary spiritual corrections in his life [3].

Prophetic Dreams - The Elevated Parts of Sleep

Dreams also have a prophetic nature and prophetic significance. This level of dream, referred to as the elevated parts of sleep is rarely forgotten.

THE 60ᵀᴴ PART OF PROPHECY

"But there is a God in heaven who reveals secrets, and He has made known... what will be in the latter days. Your dreams, and the visions of your head upon your bed, were these..." (Daniel 2:28 NASB)

Our Creator, at times, permits us to see partly into His intended plan for our life, or that of another, through that which is, called prophecy. Prophecy is one entryway into the revelation of God's will. It occurs when God reveals Himself and His Wor d to an individual by affecting his or her thought processes, causing the person to hear or see someth ing in the spiritual realm. The most common expression amongst those who have this experience is "I saw or I heard" (1 Kings 22:17, 19; Job 4:16; Psalm 62:11; Isaiah 6:1, 8; Ezekiel 1:1, 4, 15, 27, 28; 2:2, 9; 3:12, 17; 8:5, 7,10,14; 9:1, 2; 43:6; Daniel 8:13, 16; 12:7, John 8:40, Acts 11:7; 26:14, et al). Your dreams have the capacity to give you access to this kind of revelation. When this happens, within our dreams, it is 1/60ᵗʰ of what is called prophecy. For a dream, as is declared within ancient texts is the sixtieth part of prophecy[4].

Moreover, as with all prophecy, the revelation, and the interpretation thereof, it belongs to God, this includes our dreams and their interpretations. Joseph, rhetorically asked, *"Do not interpretations belong to God (Genesis 40:8 NASB)?"* Joseph boldly declared to Pharaoh and his servants, *"... it is not in me (Genesis 41:16 NASB)"*. See chapter two, "Do Not Interpretations Belong to The Lord?" Daniel made it clear, *"It is He who reveals the profound and hidden things; He knows what is in the darkness, and the light dwells with Him" (Daniel 2:22 NASB)*. This is true even if the dream interprets itself. Yes, there are dreams that are "self-interpreting". Meaning the dream reveals its meaning within the dream. This is also of God.

The nuances of the class, prophetic dreams, are varied. They have the ability to convict, encourage, guide, instruct, make known future events, promote self-awareness, restrain from evil, startle, warn, and to reveal God's will. They do not abolish or substitute His revealed will per sacred texts, nor replace the work of the Holy Spirit, but are an accessory. Even more, while prophetic dreams primarily are filled with symbols, there are prophetic dreams that are pretty much straightforward and plain. Herein, they are termed, Prophetically Simple dreams. Prophetically simple dreams are not to be confused with prophetically ordinary dreams.

Prophetically Ordinary dreams are ordinary dreams because they are a result of the fears, anxieties, and thoughts that overwhelm the mind, and they have prophetic overtones. On the other hand, Prophetically Simple Dreams are purely prophetic.

Prophetically Simple

Prophetically Simple Dreams always have a message; they are clear-cut, and directive. A few of the most common directives within these types of dreams are, "come", "do not", "go", "it is done", "leave". Even more, this type of dream, w hile affecting the dreamer's life, spiritually and literally, will oftentimes reveal circumstances of another's life. Most importantly, the message speaks to those who have the wherewithal to do something with the information. So it is with all forms of prophecy.

As evidenced in Matthew 1:20, Joseph was instructed within a prophetic dream to not be afraid to wed Mary. Although Joseph's dream was prompted because of his anxieties, and his overwhelming thoughts and concerns, which would seemingly categorized his dream as an ordinary dream (something that he caused to be dreamt, due to his disconcert over Mary's pregnancy); the message was clearly prophetic, directive, and from God. Moreover, Matthew 2:12, 13 tells of dreams given the Magi (as we know them), directing them to not go the way by King Herod when leaving town, so as to not, unknowingly, participate in Herod's evil schemes against the child Jesus. Joseph received another dream, to get up and leave town. As then, God can give you a straightforward dream to warn you of the enemy's plots ahead of time that you may avoid or thwart those plans. The primary purpose of this sort of dream is to lead and guide, as other prophetic dreams are given for their purpose. Additionally, this type of dream should closely resemble real life situations, with the dream events actually being capable of happening. For example, Joseph was actually engaged to a woman named Mary. The magi were actually leaving for their homes, with plans to stop by Herod's palace.

Oneirovatic or an OV Dream

Oneirovatic [o·nei·ro·vatic (ō nī rō váttik)], or an OV dream: To see and prophesy by dreams. On occasion, one may have a vision within a dream. For example, Job 33:15-18, Jeremiah 30:1-31:26; and Daniel 7:1-28. This type of dream, herein termed, Oneirovatic or an OV dream, should be regarded a vision (hazon[5]). Hazon is a Hebrew word for vision, which means, in sum and substance, to see via dream or vision and prophesy. Within the scriptures cited, did you notice the close similarity between a dream and a vision? While, it is impossible to draw a sharp line of demarcation between dream and vision, the two words are almost the same, often used interchangeably within the Bible. Both involve the viewing of images on the screen of one's mind. A dream is the flow of those images while sleeping; a vision is the flow of those images while awake. Notwithstanding, as with most disciplines, there are always exceptions to the rule, and visions within dreams are one of thos e exceptions. I credit this extraordinary anomaly (an OV dream) to the prophetic gifting one has, allowing them direct access into prophetic insight, via dreams.

Ninety percent of your dreams are about, and for, you. Ten percent are about, and for, another. However, visions within dreams are prophecy, about and for others, 100% of the time. Visions, for the most part are given that God may reveal His truth to the seers in pictorial form. Their messages often affect people and communities, usually a body of people sharing some common interest. This type of dream bares insight into the present day or near future events of others. Most people, who experience OV dreams, are usually found consulting and/or supporting local police crime units. One may plainly see homicides, larceny, or other assaults taking place in their neighborhood or town before or after they happen, and soon thereafter, notice the violation reported in the news. On some level, this type of dream will affect the dreamer's life, req uiring action on the part of the seer. This type of dream should closely resemble real life situations, with the dream events actually being capable of happening. For example, was a crime actually committed? If you saw Alvin take Amanda's car; the question is does Amanda own a car?

Oneirovaticicritica or an OVC dream

Oneirovaticicritica [o·nei·ro·vati-ci·crit·i·ca (ō nI row və tíss'n kríttik'a)], or an OVC dream: To decipher or interpret and prophesy by dreams. While this dream shares common qualities with its previous counterpart, an OV dream, or visions within a dream, and is considered a vision as well, it is not as clearly lit (a great deal of symbolism). This is, illustrated within Daniel 7:1-8:27.

...Daniel saw a dream and visions in his mind as he lay on his bed; then he wrote the dream down and related the following summary of it. Daniel said, "I was looking in my vision by night, and behold the four winds of heaven were stirrin g up the great sea. Four great beasts were coming up from the sea, different from one another. The first was like a lion and had the wings of an eagle. I kept looking until its wings were plucked, and it was lifted up from the ground and made to stand o n two feet like a man; a human mind also was given to it". (Daniel 7:1-4 NASB)

When dreams are this intricately symbolic, even the most experienced dream interpreter, such as Daniel, will seek another with ability, skill, and experience in interpretation (vs. 15-28). This sort of dream prophesies of distant future events, and the times and seasons of that future era. The events are usually of great historical significance. While this type of dream will affect the dreamer on some level, it is most definitely for those of a distant future. The vision, although accurate an d true, is oftentimes beyond the dreamer's contemporary understanding, but he or she is compelled to journal what they've seen as best they can. As well, as this type of dream is considered a vision in that it is for and about others. The dreamer is usu ally led to secure his or her writings that those of the distant future may read the vision at the appropriate time. These dreams are usually dreamt by prophets (aka seers) or great visionaries, those with the necessary understanding and wherewithal to do something with the information. Hence, I attribute this rare dream experience to one, the dreamer, who is a great prophet, as Daniel was a great prophet of God. Unfortunately, since the dream speaks of future events, there is no direct way, to immediately tell, if the prophecy will prove, without controversy, accurate and true. For the prophecy will not unfold, for the most part during the dreamer's lifetime. However, if the prophecy is so accurate that critics of the future era, question the authorship and time of the writing, this prophet's dreams' authenticity, and his or her reckonings were remarkably clear. On another vein, if the prophecy shadows great concerns as to its accuracy and clarity, per the readers of that distant time, th is prophet of dreams, may have use other means to conjure his or her vision (see chapter two section entitled, "Level Two, Other Interpreters").

Oneirocritica Excelsus

Oneirocritica Excelsus [o·nei·ro·crit·i·ca ex·cel·s·us (ō nī rō kríttik'a ik sélsee uss)], or an OE dream: to decipher or interpret and rise above. This is the highest, or most elevated, of prophetic dreams. One more type of prophetic dream that bares insight into the future, herein, termed *Oneirocritica Excelsus* or an OE dream. This sort of dream prophesy life and/or earth changing events that are going to happen in the near future, and possibly the changes needed, at present, to survive or victor over those coming events. Since what is revealed usually effects a great number of people, possibly a nation, these types of dreams are usually dreamt by ruling dignitaries, high officials, notable visionaries, great leaders, and/ or others who are well able to handle great responsibility; endowed with tremendous potential for achieving and effecting far-reaching ideas and policy. This leader's dream, for the most and major part, will unfold during the dreamer's lifetime. This type of dream may be straightforward, with no symbolism and requiring no dream interpreter (King Solomon, 1 Kings 3:5-15). However, if an OE dream contains a great deal of symbolism (e.g. Pharaoh's dream), it will require the ability and skill of an experienced dream interpreter; a God appointed dream interpreter, one who is brought forth for such a time as that. The interpreter will appear and be made available, to interpret the dream of the leader and, if applicable, to offer wisdom as to the direction one may possibly pursue. This type of dream will not only affect the dreamer's life, and those under his or her authority tremendously, but may very well affect the life of the dream interpreter, via an increase in authority, power, and wealth, because of his or her interpretation.

An OE dream reveals a couple of matters. (1) It reveals future events, usually of historical importance, giving the dreamer time to strategically prepare for what's coming, maximizing the moment. Here, *recurring dreams[6] will often occur. This is what happened when Pharaoh had two dreams back-to-back (Genesis 41:1, 5), as well as, Joseph's two dreams (Genesis 37: 5, 9). Also note, the recurring dreams of each person validated the prophetic nature of their dreams, for one dream bore witness in support of the other (Deuteronomy 19:15, John 8:17, 18). (2) This sort of dream reveals how you; the dreamer, in your everyday life, may have set aside wisdom and went your own way. You may not be aware of the actual condition of your relationship with those you are leading, perhaps because of pride (Daniel 4:27). As well, you are so often focused on your outer world that oftentimes the outer does not match the inner. The Holy Spirit or your conscience, by way of your dreams, places into the forefront that which you've been avoiding and

7

reveals the truth of your heart. He convicts you of your current path, gives you a peek at some hidden motives you may have, and provides you with new direction, if you would but heed the warnings (Daniel 4:24-37). This kind of prophetic dream is a sign of God's nearness and concern that He is still there with you to build up or tear down, and to comfort. His illuminating grace (the free and unmerited favor and beneficence of God), gives you another opportunity to hear and act on the message within your dream.

Recurring Dreams

In addition to recurring dreams validating one another as prophetic, when a dream is not interpreted, not interpreted properly, or if the message within the dream is not understood or readily accepted, the "memorandum" is sent again, and again. By this, recurring dreams lets us know that there is a side of our behavior that may not be spiritually healthy and our habits of doom are echoing within our lives. If, however, some aspect of our disposition does change, our dream will repeat itself, except there will be some new information in it with respect to the change. That new information may be used as a type of feedback to gauge your progress of transformation. If a complete change has occurred, as with Mr. Virkler and his nightmares (see chapter one section entitled, "Prophetically Ordinary"), those particular recurring dreams will cease. The beautiful aspect of recurring dreams is that they are very good examples, amongst many, of God's love, grace and long- suffering towards us.

FAMOUS PROPHETIC DREAMS

Joseph's Dream

The most famous prophetic dream is from the story of Joseph (Genesis 37). Joseph had a dream (*Chalom — prophetic in nature*), and he told it to his brothers. *He said to them,*

> *"Please listen to this dream which I have had; for behold, we were binding sheaves in the field, and lo, my sheaf rose up and also stood erect; and behold, your sheaves gathered around and bowed down to my sheaf." Then his brothers said to him, "Are you actually going to reign over us? Or are you really going to rule over us?" So they hated him even more for his dreams and for his words. Now he had still another dream, and related it to his brothers, and said, "Lo, I have had still another dream; and behold, the sun and the moon and eleven stars were bowing down to me". He related it to his father and to his brothers; and his father rebuked him and said to him, "What is this dream that you have had? Shall I and your mother and your brothers actually come to bow ourselves down before you to the ground?" His brothers were jealous of him, but his father kep t the saying in mind. (Genesis 37:6-11 NASB).*

The supposition of Joseph's arrogance implied by his brothers, coupled with Joseph's feelings of rejection by his brothers, and his father having put Joseph in that precarious position, could have conceivably affected Joseph's dreams, exposing unethical aspirations (e.g. those who snubbed and hurt him, and he who put him in harm's way, will plead and bow before him one day). Even if Joseph's brothers assumptions of pride were correct, coupled with his feelings of rejection, and thus a possible "I'll show you one day" attitude, and youthful naiveté, I am quite confident that Joseph's thirteen years of slave labor affected humility, wisdom, and sense of purpose, within him like nothing else could.

Much of Joseph's life story revolves around dreams. He comes from a family of dreamers and interpreters, namely his brothers and his father Jacob (aka Israel). Jacob knew the

Dream interpretation is an innate and hereditary ability.

power of dreams. For many years before, he too dreamt a prophetic dream. Of a stairway set up on the earth and whose top reached heavenward (Genesis 28:12). Joseph's great-grandfather Abraham also knew dreams[7]. This supports the premise that the knack for dream interpretation is an innate ability that is oftentimes hereditary within families. Joseph was the eleventh son of Jacob and he, as did his brothers, had a God-given talent to interpret dreams. Joseph became highly skilled in the discipline of dreams and their meanings. Actually, his ascent to eminence is characterized by six prophetic dreams: two of his own, referencing his future glory, and his interpretation of four others - the dreams of a butler and baker, and a pharaoh's two dreams about cows and corn.

The repetition of Joseph's personal two dreams validated that they were prophetic, again, for one dream witnessed in support of the other (Deuteronomy 19:15, John 8:17, 18). To boot, while both dreams were prophetic, one contained a symbol that did not readily correspond to reality. Joseph dreamt that the sun and moon, symbolic of his father and mother, respectively, would pay obeisance to him; but as the entire family knew, Joseph's biological mother (figuratively of the moon) had died. In spite of this detail, Joseph's father kept these things in mind. Israel was aware that this discrepancy did no t cancel out the whole dream. For even if most of a dream comes true, at times, not all of it will [8]. Notwithstanding, Joseph's surrogate mothers, counted as one whole, would come to represent the moon. It should also be mentioned that within Joseph's dreams, the symbols of grain, the sun, moon and stars, were all closely connected to the work his family did. These symbols are everyday images to shepherds and other agricultural workers. Additionally, it would be grain, which caused Joseph's family to come before him. Giving reverence and honor due him as Prime Minister of Egypt.

Joseph's brothers, focusing only on the action of bowing, and what it represented, took offense to his dreams. Even Jacob reprimanded him when he insisted, perhaps boastfully, on telling his second dream of the sun, moon, and stars bowing down to him. While his father pondered the question, what will cause him, the family patriarch, and his sons to bow before Joseph? His brothers have no doubt as to the validity of dreams, so they schemed to prevent Joseph's dreams from coming to pass (Genesis 37:19, 20). Moved by jealously, his brothers decided; "Let's kill this master of dreams". The plot, quelled by two of his brothers, Reuben and Judah, thickened even more. Instead of murdering their brother, they all agreed to throw Joseph in a pit and to tell their father some wild animal killed him. Then they decided to sell him as a slave to some Ishmaelite merchants from Midian passing by, for twenty pieces of silver. At seventeen, Joseph's life transitioned drastically (Genesis 37:2). Unknowingly, that which would bring his dreams to pass began to play out.

The merchants took Joseph into Egypt, and there he became the slave of a wealthy Egyptian official named Potiphar. Because of Joseph's excellent service and hard work, as demonstrated throughout his entire ordeal, Potiphar promotes him to be in charge of his entire household. Subsequently, Potiphar's wife accused Joseph of rape and he is thrown into prison.

During Joseph's prison stay, two distinguish prisoners were put in his charge - Pharaoh's chief wine butler and chief baker (Genesis 40). During a moment in time, they both have startling dreams. Joseph now stepped into the last leg of his journey. He is intended to interpret those dreams. Joseph's accurate interpretations inevitably brought him before Pharaoh, to deal with Pharaoh's recurring dreams (Genesis 41).

Pharaoh's magicians could not interpret his dreams, because, his dreams were preordained to be interpreted by a specific interpreter. Only messengers selected by God can properly interpret the specific dreams meant for them to interpret (see Chapter Two, "Dream Interpreters — Carriers of the Message"). Therefore, according to divine providence in a dramatic turn of events, Joseph finds himself in front of Pharaoh to interpret his dreams. The survival of an entire empire was at stake. These dreams had to be interpreted correctly. God gave Joseph favor and wisdom to do what he did best, interpret dreams.

Joseph developed into an insightful and wise dream interpreter, and he was known as such. He proves this by not only interpreting a dream, but also suggesting a proper and sensible course of action.

The Chief Wine Butler's Dream

"Behold, in my dream a vine was before me, and in the vine were three branches; it was as though it budded, its blossoms shot forth, and its clusters brought forth ripe grapes. Then Pharaoh's cup was in my

hand; and I took the grapes and pressed them into Pharaoh's cup, and placed the cup in Pharaoh's hand". (Genesis 40:9-11 NKJV). Joseph's interpretation of the dream: The growing vine, the butler will live; three branches, three days; and the cup in Pharaoh's hand, indicative of the butler's restoration to his previous position as Pharaoh's head cupbearer.

Further elaborations: the branches that budded and blossomed, the butler would not only live, but will prosper in his reinstated position; and the grapes pressed into Pharaoh's cup, the butler would remain as Pharaoh's head cu pbearer until his retirement. This dream also indicated that the butler was innocent of the charges against him.

The Chief Baker's Dream

"I also was in my dream, and there were three white baskets on my head. In the uppermost basket were all kinds of baked goods for Pharaoh, and the birds ate them out of the basket on my head". (Genesis 40:16-17(NKJV). Joseph interpretation of the baker's dream was this, three baskets, three days. Joseph told of the baker's death in three days by hanging. He will be left for birds to eat of his flesh.

Further elaborations: A basket is a symbol of wickedness. Three white baskets on the baker's head, unscrupulousness on several levels. (1st basket): some type of thievery, and the mischievousness also included the nefarious rich, represented by white baskets, who were just as greedy and crooked as the baker was, thus birds eating out of the basket. Moreover, birds, within the context of this dream, symbolize an ignominious death. Judgment is approaching and death is imminent. The method of death will involve the baker's head, thus baskets on head also. Hanging was within the cultural context of that period. (2nd basket): the baker chiefly masterminded the wickedness; thus, ownership of baskets belongs to baker. (3rd basket): the baked foods were eaten up by birds, symbolic of the baker's loss of employment due to dishonorable acts. No doubt, Joseph knew according to this dream that the baker was guilty of embezzlement, intrigue, and other fraud.

Pharaoh's Dreams

Then it came to pass, at the end of two full years, that Pharaoh had a dream; and behold, he stood by the river. Suddenly there came up out of the river seven cows, fine looking and fat; and they fed in the meadow. Then behold, seven other cows came up after them out of the river, ugly and gaunt, and stood by the other cows on the bank of the river. And the ugly and gaunt cows ate up the seven fine looking and fat cows. So Pharaoh awoke. He slept and dreamed a second time; and suddenly seven heads of grain came up on one stalk, plump and good. Then behold, seven thin heads, blighted by the east wind, sprang up after them. And the seven thin heads devoured the seven plump and full heads. So Pharaoh awoke, and indeed, it was a dream.
(Genesis 41:1-7 NKJV)

And Pharaoh said to Joseph, "I have had a dream, and there is no one who can interpret it. But I have heard it said of you that you can understand a dream, to interpret it." So Joseph answered Pharaoh, saying, "It is not in me; God will give Pharaoh an answer of peace."
(Genesis 41:15, 16 NKJV)

Then Joseph said to Pharaoh, "The dreams of Pharaoh are one; God has shown Pharaoh what He is about to do: The seven good cows are seven years, and the seven good heads are seven years; the dreams are one. And the seven thin and ugly cows which came up after them are seven years, and the seven empty heads blighted by the east wind are seven years of famine. This is the thing which I have spoken to Pharaoh. God has shown Pharaoh what He is about to do. Indeed seven years of great

plenty will come throughout all the land of Egypt; but after them seven years of famine will arise,
and all the plenty will be forgotten in the land of Egypt; and the famine will deplete the land.
(Genesis 41:25-30 NKJV)

Further elaborations: The east wind is symbolic of unprecedented ruin, grievous damage, and great pain. It is also indicative of God's judgment, and to a season of late spring.

The repetition of Pharaoh's dreams, very much like Joseph's earlier two dreams, substantiated their prophetic significance. By this, Joseph sensed that God had given Pharaoh a warning that he may prepare for the coming calamity. Therefore, Joseph gave Pharaoh some advice, a sensible and practical course of action (Genesis 41:31-37). Let Pharaoh appoint commissioners over the land to collect one-fifth of the produce of the land of Egypt during the seven years of abundance that the land may not perish during the famine. This food should be held in reserve for the country, to b e used during the seven years of famine that will come upon Egypt. Pharaoh should select a discerning and wise man to oversee this endeavor. The plan seemed good to Pharaoh and to all his officials.

And Pharaoh said to his servants, "Can we find such a one as this, a man in whom is the Spirit of God?"
Then Pharaoh said to Joseph, "Inasmuch as God has shown you all this, there is no one as discerning and
wise as you. You shall be over my house, and all my people shall be ruled according to your word; only in
regard to the throne will I be greater than you." And Pharaoh said to Joseph, "See, I have set you over
all the land of Egypt." Then Pharaoh took his signet ring off his hand and put it on Joseph's hand; and he
clothed him in garments of fine linen and put a gold chain around his neck. And he had him ride in the
second chariot which he had; and they cried out before him, "Bow the knee!" So he set him over all the land
of Egypt. Pharaoh also said to Joseph, "I am Pharaoh, and without your consent no man may lift his hand or
foot in all the land of Egypt." (Genesis 41:38-44 NKJV).

Question: Why did Pharaoh have such confidence in Joseph's interpretation of his dream?

When a dream has been correctly interpreted, there is usually a deep sense of certainty of the accuracy of the message, and a spirit of gratitude.

Pharaoh's dreams happened as predicted and within the second year of this far-reaching famine (Genesis 45:6); Joseph's brothers came to Egypt to buy food. Joseph recognized his brothers, as they bowed face down before him. At that moment, Joseph was taken back twenty-two years. He realized that this is the bowing down of the grain that he dreamt about so long ago, thus fulfilling the first of his two prophetic dreams. The arrival of his entire family (the sun, moon, and eleven stars) a short while later fulfilled the second dream. It was twenty-two years ago, when Joseph told his dreams to his family. Hence, his journey set the following precedent; it is, said that it can take up to twenty-two years before a dream comes true [9]. The length of time before manifestation does not invalidate the entire dream. A good dream should be kept in mind and not forgotten so that it will be fulfilled [10]. Joseph always anticipated the fulfillment of his dreams. Moreover, he achieved power and influence above, and beyond, because of the dreams of others and his wise interpretation of their dreams.

Others Who Dreamt Prophetic Dreams

Although the story of Joseph is most familiar to us, when on the subject of prophetic dreams, there are others. Others who dreamt prophetic dreams were Abimelech (Genesis 20:3); Jacob (Genesis 31:10); Laban (Genesis 31:24); an unnamed person (Judges 7:13, 14); Solomon (1 Kings 3:5-15); Job (Job 7:14); Nebuchadnezzar (Daniel 2:1-13); Joseph (Matthew 1:19, 20); wise men (Matthew 2:12); and Pilate's wife (Matthew 27:13,19). There is also mention of prophetic dreams in relation to false prophets (Deuteronomy 13:1, 3, 5; Jeremiah 23:27, 28, 32). Moreover, see Chapter Two, section entitled Syncretism [28].

The dreams of biblical persons from long ago certainly played an important role in their personal lives, as well as the development of nations. Stories like these fill our Holy Bible. There are many occurrences in the Bible where God communicated with people in dreams and gave them messages. However, what about our dreams in the twenty-first century? Do the dreams in the Bible have anything to do with our dreams today? If so, what should we glean from them? Is symbolism of old, relevant today?

ARE THE DREAMS IN THE BIBLE MODELS FOR OUR DREAMS TODAY?

Remove not the ancient landmark, which thy fathers have set. (Proverbs 22:28 KJV)

Boundary Markers, Landmarks, and Property Lines: Foundationally Speaking

An ancient boundary marker or old landmark is a conspicuous, fixed object. For example, a marked tree, a ditch, a stone or heap of stones, was used to designate the boundary of land, marking out and identifying an owner's property. It's always good to know your boundaries. According to the article, "How to Determine Your Property Line"; knowing the boundary lines of your property can help you avoid being forced to alter or remove structures that extend over the property line. Sometimes property owners assume (incorrectly) that their lines extend to the same distance as their next-door neighbor's line. Property lines are not always straight. For instance, lines on an arc can be hard to define. To determine exactly where your property lines are located, you will need a licensed land surveyor. The surveyor will review the original tract maps filed with the county when your home was constructed; then use a variety of tools to measure the exact boundaries of your property. My father, Mr. Anthony Miller, Sr., was an assistant land surveyor. One of his duties was to determine and mark out property lines. He proudly marked out the property lines of his first home. I can remember once using the neon tape he used as a line for hair ribbon.

Boundary markers, landmarks, and property lines helped people of old, and of today, understand their boundaries, property rights, and inheritance. For someone to remove or alter boundary markers was a violation of the Law of Moses. So sacred did Moses consider boundary markers that he pronounced a curse against any Hebrew who moved their neighbor's landmark (Deuteronomy 27:17). In another place and time, this prohibition against the removal of the ancient landmarks was reiterated (Proverbs 22:28). On a darker, more sinister note, (as was then, so it is now), thieves would move the boundary markers and alter property lines, in order to impinge on somebody else's land. All of this is also true within the spiritual realm.

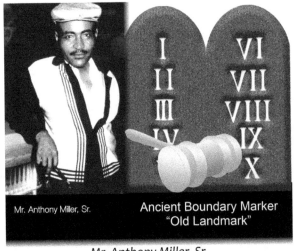

Mr. Anthony Miller, Sr.

Ancient Boundary Marker "Old Landmark"

Mr. Anthony Miller, Sr.
Ancient boundary marker "old landmark"

Spiritualizing Boundary Markers, Landmarks, and Property Lines

Spiritually, ancient boundary markers, landmarks, and property lines, are the commandments, principles, precepts, laws, statutes, and teachings marked out within our sacred record. These guidelines help us understand our spiritual inheritance and rights and how to live within the boundaries of our heritage. They reveal to whom we belong and what He has required of us from time immemorial.

Unfortunately, as it is literally, so it is spiritually. Thieves (unwise and foolish persons) have moved, and still do move; holy landmarks of old and alter sacred boundary markers, and property lines. These persons also are disfavored.

At this point, you may be wondering, what does ancient boundary markers, landmarks, and property lines, have to do with the question, "Are dreams in the Bible models for our dreams today?" I wanted to lay a foundation, so hang in there, and keep reading; we'll get there soon.

Since God created and owns, both the physical and spiritual worlds, it is logically correct to conclude that all principles and methodologies are intrinsically set in order according to His universal laws; fixed laws set as boundaries to guide our lives, as well as, all that is connected to the universe (Job 38:4-39:30). Symbolism plays a major part in communicating those fixed laws to human beings. God unveiled this "language of the branches", and then acted as a sort of exegete, interpreting this symbolic language for us, via inspired men. Those God-led sages of long ago, acting as "assistant surveyors", marked out, and set in place within Holy Writ, this symbolic language and its boundaries (Deuteronomy 4:1, 2). Hence, the dynamics of symbolism and its interpretations are inherently rooted in God's Word, which is a constant, fixed object, and an ancient boundary marker.

Within Judaism, the sages worried about conflicts between dream interpretations. Since it was not an option to disregard this form of prophecy, they said, "A dream un-interpreted is like an unopened letter from God"[11], and so used the Torah to interpret the meaning of a dream. Validating it will be within scripture that you will find the unmodified and maximal meaning of symbols within your dreams.

As we investigate further the dynamics of symbolism and its contemporary relevance, it is valuable to know the divine margins set in place, to avoid altering or exaggerating the meaning of a symbol. As previously stated, it's always good to know your boundaries. Example: had not the writers of old clearly declared within scripture that the twelve stars within Joseph's dream represented him and his brothers, and the sun and moon his parents; thereby, revealing a divine set boundary. One might assume as apparent that twelve stars, a sun, and moon within a dream represented some type of astrological sign or religious symbol, instead of ones' literal (or spiritual) siblings and parents. In so doing, some have mutated these symbols and their actual meanings.

Expositional Constancy[12]

The Hebrew Bible is a book full of concrete images and symbols. One principle that bears this out is the principle of expositional constancy. This principle holds that symbols, especially within scripture, tend to be constant and thus fixed and perpetual. The first time a thing (or, as in this case, a symbol) is dealt with in the Bible, it displays certain characteristics or qualities, which cling to it throughout the Holy Record. Essentially, the meaning of the word is most often defined by its first use in the Bible, which is another term of biblical interpretation called Law of First Mention. This frequently aids us in understanding other passages in which that subject is once again raised. Additionally, the idea that we can use scripture to interpret other scripture is a common theme throughout hermeneutics.[13].

Case in point: If a rock or stone means something in one part of the Bible, namely the Old Testament, it will mean the same elsewhere, though the context may change. Had not Isaiah use the imagery of a rock and stone as the Messiah (Isaiah 8:14, 28:16), had not Daniel interpreted the stone (or rock) within King Nebuchadnezzar's dream as the Kingdom of God, the world to come (Daniel 2:44, 45), as would be established by His Anointed One. Had not Jesus used the symbol of a stone in Matthew 21:42, referencing Psalm 118:22, to explain why the Jewish leaders had rejected Him. One might conclude as certain that a rock or stone, symbolically represents a large gem, or someone or thing that is firm, hard, stable, strong, and/or dependable, instead of it referring to Jesus Christ, His teachings and His Father's Kingdom, (which are by the way firm, hard, stable, strong, and dependable). All scriptures regarding a rock or stone collectively endorse this meaning. This is an ancient boundary marker, landmark, and property line, and we are charged not to move (or change) the ancient boundary markers. God's meanings are the boundary markers, and property lines, set in place before the foundations of the world.

> *Every Word of God is flawless; he is a shield to those who take refuge in him. Do not add*
> *to his words, or he will rebuke you and prove you a liar. (Proverbs 30:5, 6 NIV)*

Old Boundary Markers, Landmarks, and Property Lines

Had not David metaphorically link the symbol of a horn to God's power of deliverance (Psalm 18:2), and to His strength (Psalm 112:9). Had not Jeremiah draw upon the symbol of a broken horn (Jeremiah 48:25), to illustrate a ruler's power and strength being broken. Or, had not the angel Gabriel explicitly interpreted Daniel's dream symbols of horns (Daniel 8:16-27) as the rise and fall of powerful empires, one might assert as probable that horns signify the hardening of one's mind to new concepts, instead of power and strength, prominence, and worth in a person's life. Hence, a dream of horns (human or animal) could very well mean a display of strength or superiority. FYI: To dream of blowing your own horn (car or wind instrument) exposes a prideful, arrogant, and boastful mind-set regarding your own power, authority, or importance. Warning: When pride comes, then comes disgrace, haughtiness draws destruction (Proverbs 16:18).

Another example, Christ refers to bread as representative of Himself; as the manna of the past in John 6:31, 41; as the heavenly bread of the present in John 6:32-35; and as the eternal bread of the future in John 6:47-51. This constancy establishes a symbol's meaning as set and permanent - an ancient boundary.

Symbolic Property Lines

Great caution is necessary in the interpretation of these type symbols, which I will refer to here, as "property line" symbols. For, unlike symbols that are constant, fixed, and straightforward in meaning, the meanings of property line symbols are not always clear-cut, straight, or direct. For instance, while stars represent the literal descendants of Abraham, the patriarch of the Hebrews, stars also represent all who will come to believe God, via His Messiah, according to the Abrahamic order, aka spiritual descendants of Abraham (Romans 4:1-25; Galatians 3:6-25). As well, those stars were also Joseph's literal siblings. Thus, stars within a dream may very well represent the dreamer's literal siblings. The dream's context will play a major part in its meaning. For it will depend on the way the symbols are contextually put together and the background of which they appear. Hence, a rock star within a dream could possibly mean you are a joint-heir with Jesus, the Son of God (Luke 8:21; Galatians 4:1-7). Rock=Jesus, star=sibling (literal or spiritual). On another vein, a star may represent a person above average in wisdom, and formidable in strength and power. Contrarily, on a darker, more sinister note, again depending on the context, stars may denote a dealer in astrology, or one who is participating in some type of demonic, antichrist activity. *Adam's Clark Commentary:* For, in the process of time there stood up false prophets among the sons of Adam. Which said that God had commanded and said unto them, worship such a star, or all the stars, and do sacrifice unto them thus and thus; and build a temple for it, and make an image of it, that all the people, may worship it. The false prophet showed them the image, which he had feigned out of his own heart, and said it was the image of such a star, which was made known unto him by prophecy. This is one root of idolatry. Hence, such stars as a pentagram, which is a star-shaped figure with five points, popularly known as an occult symbol, used in witchcraft and occult rituals to conjure up evil spirits. Thus, this dream could very well denote one, who is the direct opposite of a born-again, aka a believer, the antithesis of Christ.

Another instance, how can a snake (or serpent) represent a kingdom, a philosophy, wisdom, a healer, your enemy, and something deceptive and cursed of God? How can one snake be holy and another profane? Is that not confusing? Your deductive reasoning is understandable, but the meaning we give to the symbol is inadequate. The symbol of the serpent, as with all animals, is figurative of personality traits, characteristics, our basic nature, and endowments. The essence of the serpent is that of chief headship, aggressiveness, astuteness, authoritative, healer, influencer, prophetic, razor sharpness, and resourceful. These character traits are based on biblical references (Genesis 3:1, 14-15; 49:17, Numbers 21:6, 8, Psalm 58:4, Isaiah 14:29, Matthew 10:16, John 3:14-16, Revelation 20:2). Interpreted, within context of your dream, this type of symbol helps us to comprehend what God wants us to focus on, namely our conduct or that of another, specifically a chief leader. Accordingly, a serpent can represent positive or negative personality traits.

Symbolic Property Lines on an Arc

Like property lines on an arc, a number of property line symbols can be very hard to interpret due to their esoteric, indirect, or many layered nature. For example, wrinkled clothing within a dream (Ephesians 5:25-29). This dream interprets as repeated hateful and provoking behavior in the dreamer's life due to a hormonal imbalance, especially within women or a repeated cycle of wicked and insulting behavior within a man's' life. To discover the crux of the meanings of these type symbols, and avoid misinterpretation or alterations, one will need a dream interpreter (see chapter two, "Dream Interpreters - Carriers of the Message"). Using a variety of theological resources and divine insight, the interpreter ascertains, as close as possible, the original meaning of the symbol to determine its divine set boundaries, coupled with context, to give you an accurate interpretation of your modern-day dream.

Another Example of Property Line Symbols on an Arc

God's Word is often portrayed as, fire, a hammer, bread, meat, milk, solid food, a sword, a mirror, a seed, a lamp, or light illuminating your path. While all these symbols are to be taken as, "Thus says the Lord", type messages, they can be very hard to interpret due to, for example, food means food, a sword is weapon. Nevertheless, dreams of this nature confirm that God will use symbols as pointers to direct you towards what He's trying to communicate to you specifically, via the Bible (e.g. fire or hammer, see Jeremiah 23:25-32) and it is up to you to dig deep enough through the layers to get to that meaning.

As God has often assigned three or more layers of interpretation to His Word, this method takes into account how we all read the same passage of scripture and each grasp something different. This occurs because people are uniquely different; we are endowed differently, we live life differently, and we are at different levels spiritually. Moreover, during our spiritua l journey, at one point scripture will mean one thing, and at another juncture in our life, that same passage will mean some thing else because it is to meet our specific individual need at a particular moment in time. This is due largely to the progressi veness of our spiritual journey. The original meaning and intention of the passage has not changed, but God will use it to speak to each one of us according to our understanding at a certain moment, thus many layered.

Taking all of this into account, the evidence supports that our dreams of the twenty-first century are connected deeply to the biblical dreams of long ago. The voice of God in our dreams, the validity of our dreams, the purpose, and response to our dreams are all, modeled within the Bible. Therefore, when interpreting your dreams you should always examine them from the perspective of Holy Writ first. For, unless we have the expressed authority of the sacred writers themselves, we cannot conclude with certainty that the imagery and symbols in our dreams figuratively represent this or that person, place, thing o r event because of the resemblance, which we may perceive between them, but we may perhaps admit it as probable. Probable: I'll leave that there for now (see following paragraph entitled "Probables"). Nevertheless, if we assert, that a person or thing was designed symbolically to represent another person or thing, where divine authority has declared no such meaning, we make an assertion for which we don't have a very good basis. You perhaps are attempting to move boundary markers.

Do Not Move the Boundary Markers...

Down through the years, assertions, assumptions, and modifications of symbols and their meanings by some have oftentimes mutated the symbol into something profanely exaggerated, leading into an illicit syntheses. This world's systems have crept in and put a stranglehold on the realm of symbolism, trespassing upon God's system of symbols and their meanings, very much like a thief having moved the boundary markers of old. To such an extent, that dreams and their interpretations ar e not, taken seriously anymore, but for entertainment purposes only. Yet, God's ways and means holds a high place in countless hearts. Many people regard their dreams as serious insight because of God's Word. Still today, His Word has a significant bearing upon how billions of individuals view their dreams. So, whether a person views dreams as ninety-eight percent nonsense, irrelevant, or perhaps deems them as neither here nor there, it cannot be argued that dreams, as well as symbolism, are fixed within scripture, and dreams and symbolism are fixed within us. In light of this reality, we ought to embrace fresh paradigms regarding dreams and their significance.

It cannot be argued that the Spirit of God, to reveal God's purposes in this world, often transmits prophetic dreams and their symbols to us. Consequently, humanity carries a common storehouse of symbols and meanings that transcends time, culture, race, or creed, in our collective unconscious. Every symbol contains meaning for the individual and for humanity at large. In this, dreams and their symbols operate in the same way as signs and symbols in waking life. Their meaning depends on the way they are contextually put together, and the background of which they appear. For example, to dream of driving a car sitting on the left or passenger side (as in the USA), would represent the taking control of, or impingement upon, another's lifestyle. This same dream in another country or culture (sitting on the left side, which is the driver's side) represents y ou are in control of your lifestyle.

A female once dreamt that someone named Moses was driving her car and she was in the backseat. Moses led God's chosen people out of bondage and slavery, and gave them the law of God, and he was a type of Christ. Thus, this may indicate three situations, either the dreamer is being led out of some manner of bondage, or is following the law and forfeiting grace (see John 1:17, Romans 6:14, Galatians 5:18), or this dream is a good indication that you have given control over your lifestyle to Jesus Christ and His principles. As well, it indicates that you're in very good hands spiritually, as far as leadership, within your life (e.g. Jesus, husband, pastor). While on the subject of cars, I guess this would be a good place to share this stor y: A Christian man was driving home one evening. He began to ecstatically, praise the Lord in his car and ended up running off the road. An inebriated driver pulled up next to his car and asked the man was he all right? The man cheerfully replied, "Yes, I've got Jesus in the car with me". The intoxicated fellow hiccupped and said, "You'd better put him in here with me, cause you're gonna kill him".

Probables (remember about four paragraphs ago...)

It's necessary to say that a few assertions have proven, over time, to be good probables for some symbols. This is because symbols will at times become coined due to their frequent usage in one particular way within our diverse cultures and individual lives. Even here, divine margins and boundaries should still be respected. An example of this would be a fish ca ught by someone. This dream is usually a probable for a literal pregnancy, especially within the African American culture. While dreams of catching fish has referred to literal pregnancies within this culture since time immemorial, this interpretation is still well within divine set margins; for fish are symbolic of births, albeit spiritual; those predestined to, become born again within the Kingdom of God (see John 3:1-17). Moreover, the meaning of fish will vary within cultures, viz. a seafaring people or an aquatic community. For this person, a dream of fish may simply prove to be an ordinary dream. For more information on ordinary dreams, see chapter one, "Chalom".

We will learn how to interpret our dreams and unravel their messages to us, when we declare, as Joseph declared, "It is not in me; God will give...an answer" (Genesis 41:16 KJV).

Because of the biblical dreams of old, we can know with surety that our dreams have the capacity (but are not limited):

To Encourage (Judges 7:13-15)

In the Old Testament, a prophetic dream and its interpretation by a foreigner encouraged Gideon. As the Israelites were preparing to attack the Midianites, the Lord urged Gideon to go down against the camp of his enemies, for He had given it into his hands. Recognizing the apprehension within Gideon, the Lord counseled him to go, under cover of night, with his servant, down to the camp of his enemies and listen to what they were saying, and subsequently his hands would be strengthened.

> *When Gideon came, behold, a man was relating a dream to his friend. And he said, "Behold, I had a dream; a loaf of barley bread was tumbling into the camp of Midian, and it came to the tent and struck it so that it fell, and turned it upside down so that the tent lay flat". His friend replied, "This is nothing less than the sword of Gideon the son of Joash, a man of Israel; God has given Midian and all the camp into his hand". When Gideon heard the account of the dream and its interpretation, he bowed in worship. He returned to the camp of Israel and said, "Arise, for the Lord has given the camp of Midian into your hands" (Judges 7:13-15 NASB)*

The loaf of barley represented Gideon to the Midianite dream interpreter, because Gideon was a miller by trade; so, supporting the belief that dreams can be specific to you with regard to your job-related activities[31]. Judges 7:15 credits the victory to the Lord; thereby, acknowledging another layer of the meaning of the loaf of barley bread, Gideon's God. As bread represents the Lord (John 6:33-35, 41, 48-51, 58), this would be a more proper interpretation.

To Reaffirm (Genesis 28:10-22)

This type of dream is to engender an awareness of impending turn-arounds, changes, and ups-and-downs within the dreamer's life. God wants the dreamer to know that He is aware of your circumstances, He is with you, and that He is working a work within you for the betterment of you, your Christian walk, and everyday life. God's Spirit will lead and guide you into all truth, pointing you towards the good and wise way, the way that will eventually lead to peace and life more abundantly. The decisions will be yours regarding how less strenuous you want to get to that good way, and how long it will take.

To See the Future (Daniel 2:1-49)

Nebuchadnezzar, king of Babylonia, was a man noted for his strange and alarming dreams. Once, troubled by a dream, so much so, he refused to tell it to anyone. He threatened his dream interpreters with death and destruction of their property if they did not tell him his dream and the interpretation of it.

> *The astrologers answered the king, "There is no one on earth who can do what the king asks! No king, however great and mighty, has ever asked such a thing of any magician or enchanter or astrologer. What the king asks is too difficult. No one can reveal it to the king except the gods, and they do not live among men" (Daniel 2:10, 11 NIV).*

Suspect of all his wise men, the king ordered that a genuine dream interpreter come forward to recall and interpret his dream or all the wise men in Babylon would be killed. This decree included Daniel and his friends. How could anyone know what he had dreamt? Daniel went to the king and asked him for a chance to reveal his dream to him and the interpretation of it. That day Daniel and his friends prayed to God for revelation. That night in a dream, God revealed the king's dream and its interpretation to Daniel. Daniel explained to the king that his dream depicted what is going to take place in the future, in the last days.

Daniel begins, *"You, O king, were looking and behold, there was a single great statue; that statue, which was large and of extraordinary splendor, was standing in front of you, and its appearance was awesome" (Daniel 2:31 NASB).* Daniel then described a large, brilliant statue standing before the king in his dream. This statue had a head made of fine gold, a chest and arms of silver, a belly of brass, legs of iron, and feet made partly of iron and partly of clay. Then a stone, cut out of a mountain, without the use of hands, entered the dream. It struck the statue at its feet, smashing the entire idol to pieces until it was dust. As the wind blew the dust away, the stone became a great mountain that filled the whole earth. After telling the king what his dream was, Daniel proceeded to interpret it.

Daniel tells Nebuchadnezzar that the God of heaven had given him dominion, power, might, and glory. He was made ruler over man, beast and birds. Nebuchadnezzar, and thereby Babylon, was represented by the symbol of the head of gold. After Babylon, there will come another empire that is of inferior quality to his, represented by the chest and arms of silver. After this empire will come a third one of brass, followed in turn by the fourth empire of crushing iron, which crushes all others. However, this fourth empire will later be divided between a mixture of peoples that will not remain united, and end up as the feet and toes that are partly clay and partly iron. While these kingdoms exist, God will set up a Kingdom that will never be destroyed. It will crush all the other kingdoms and end them, but not by human hands. This will be accomplished by miraculous means. This is the meaning of the stone, cut from the mountain without hands, which smashes the idol to pieces. This dream's timeframe is from the time of King Nebuchadnezzar to a future day when God's eternal Kingdom is established. King Nebuchadnezzar fell on his face, prostrate before Daniel. After commanding offerings be given Daniel, he acknowledged, *"Surely your God is the God of gods and a Lord of kings, and revealer of mysteries, since you have been able to reveal this mystery" (Daniel 2:47 NASB).* Then the king promoted Daniel and his friends.

To Warn (Genesis 20:3, 6)

> *But God came to Abimelech in a dream of the night, and said to him, "Behold you are a dead man because of the woman whom you have taken, for she is married". (Genesis 20:3 NASB)*

This dream message was one of grace (the free and unmerited favor and beneficence of God). God warned this king of the evil he was about to commit.

> *Then God said to him in the dream, "Yes, I know that in the integrity of your heart you have done this, and I also kept you from sinning against Me; therefore I did not let you touch her. (Genesis 20:6 NASB)*

This is another instance of the protective care, which the Lord gives His people via dreams. This dream is also one more example of a simple prophetic dream.

To Restrain from Wickedness (Daniel 4:4-37 NIV)

This type of dream comes that God may withdraw mankind from his (or her) purpose, and hide pride from him or her. Here again, Nebuchadnezzar, a man troubled by a series of nightmares. *I, Nebuchadnezzar, was at home in my palace, contented and prosperous. I looked, and there before me stood a tree in the middle of the land. Its height was enormous. The tree grew large and strong and its top touched the sky; it was visible to the ends of the earth. Its leaves were beautiful, its fruit abundant, and on it was food for all. Under it, the beasts of the field found shelter, and the birds of the air lived in its branches; from it, every creature was, fed. I looked, and there before me was a messenger, a holy one, coming down from heaven. He called in a loud voice, "Cut down the tree and trim off its branches; strip off its leaves and scatter its fruit. Let the animals flee from under it and the birds from its branches. However, let the stump and its roots, bound with iron and bronze; remain in t he ground, in the grass of the field. Let him be drenched with the dew of heaven, and let him live with the animals among the plants of the earth. Let his mind be changed from that of a man, and let him be given the mind of an animal, until seven times pass by for him. The decision is announced by messengers, the holy ones declare the verdict, so that the living may know that the Most High is sovereign over the kingdoms of men and gives them to anyone he desires and sets over them the lowliest of men".*

Daniel was shocked and had to re-group. He has to gather his thoughts and form his words carefully. Not only was he interpreting the dream of a king exposing his wickedness but also needed was counsel. The king responded to Daniel's obvious alarm by assuring him, "It's OK". Daniel reacted, as most interpreters do, desiring the meaning of the dream to be turned around in some way to affect the meaning for good. So he starts with, *"My lord may the dream concern those who hate you and its interpretation concern your enemies (Daniel 4:19 NKJV)*. Daniel's thinking may have followed along these lines, since the king was sort of like a spectator within the dream, this dream could possibly be about others, and secondly, dreams do "go according to the mouth"[14], meaning dreams are fulfilled according to the interpretation or "mouth" of the interpreter. However, angelic messengers revealed that the dream was about and for Nebuchadnezzar, as well as, what had been decreed regarding the king. An angelic decree rescinds the dream interpreter's "mouth".

As an interpreter, I know firsthand the dread that comes when a dream presented to you is of this nature. The first thought that comes to mind is, how can I turn this thing around? What can I say to help avert this tragedy? Especially when it appears that, the dreamer is not going to rectify his or her ways because their dream does not depict any particulars that present that such recourse will be taken by the dreamer to ward off the coming tragedy. Notwithstanding, the unadulterated truth is always appropriate and necessary when interpreting a dream for someone. Therefore, Daniel's suggested course of action to the king was for him to restrain from wickedness and start treating his subjects righteously by showing mercy to the poor. Then, perhaps God will extend grace to him and pardon his injustices that he might continue to prosper.

Nonetheless, as the dream gave no inkling that Nebuchadnezzar would change his ways, true to form, he did not. One year later, God's grace was removed from over Nebuchadnezzar. As a result, Nebuchadnezzar began experiencing some serious mental health issues. Supposing himself an animal, he went out in the wild and started living like a wild animal. H e stayed in this condition for seven years. At the end of that period, Nebuchadnezzar raised his eyes toward heaven and his reason returned to him, and he blessed the Most High, praised, and honored Him who lives forever.

If your dreams depict heavy judgment (divine reprimand for folly and sin) or feature unusual loss or reduction, your dreams are warning you to act, to commit to some type of positive and righteous change so calamity will not befall you. Firs t repenting to Jesus can diminish a tragic outcome. A genuine, "I'm sorry", and a changing of one's ways towards r ighteousness and a refraining from nefarious actions in the future will often suffice. As a result, fruits of said change will begin to manifest, via actions and good deeds. If you do not respond appropriately, the tragedy will come.

To Guide (Matthew 1:18-24; 2:12-13; 19-23)

As with warning dreams, guidance dreams are pretty much straightforward, simple prophetic dreams. Five dreams of guidance are, found in Matthew. Four are, attributed to Joseph, the husband of Mary, the mother of Jesus, and the o ther to wise men.

Joseph's dreams of guidance included the pregnancy of Mary, his family's flight into, and return from, Egypt, and their subsequent dwelling in a city called Nazareth.

Joseph wanted to divorce Mary, quietly, on the grounds of infidelity.

> *But after he had considered this, an angel of the Lord appeared to him in a dream and said, "Joseph son of David, do not be afraid to take Mary home as your wife, because what is conceived in her is from the Holy Spirit. She will give birth to a son, and you are to give him the name Jesus, because he will save his people from their sins." When Joseph woke up, he did what t he angel of the Lord had commanded him and took Mary home as his wife (Matthew 1:20, 21, 24 NIV).*

> *After Herod died, an angel of the Lord appeared in a dream to Joseph in Egypt and said, "Get up, take the child and his mother and go to the land of Israel, for those who were trying to take the child's life are dead". So he got up, took the ch ild and his mother and went to the land of Israel. But when he heard that Archelaus was reigning in Judea in place of his father Herod, he was afraid to go there. Having been warned in a dream, he withdrew to the district of Galilee, and he went and lived in a town called Nazareth (Genesis 2:19-23 NIV).*

The fifth dream of guidance, was that of three wise men (aka the magi) visiting Jerusalem from the East, seeking Him who was born King of the Jews. When they came into the house and saw the Child, they worshiped Him; and presented gifts to Him. Subsequently, that evening, all the magi had the same dream. Guided by God, they were, via their dreams, directed not to return to Herod, so they departed for their own countries by another way.

These are a few biblical dreams sent by God that have contemporary relevance. For just like men of old, we too deal with apprehension, discouragement, pride, little to no self-awareness, and a lack of direction and guidance. Dreams then, were, as dreams are now, were very practical, prophetic, contain real spiritual power, and can be catalysts for change.

There are many symbols within scripture and searching for their meanings within the Bible will reveal God's ubiquitous wisdom within your dreams. Even more, while not all of our dreams are prophetic, God has declared that He will counsel us at night through our dreams. He has in the past and He does so today.

Do You Dream?

For thousands of years humankind has closed their eyes and beheld mysteries. These breathtaking sights have caused scientists, philosophers, theologians, and other great thinkers to ponder the meaning of what he or she is seeing and why.

Scientifically Speaking [15]

There are two distinct phases of sleep: non-rapid eye movement (NREM) and rapid eye moment (REM). NREM sleep is the quiet, restful, recuperative phase of sleep, also referred to as slow wave sleep. It is divided into four stages of progressively deepening sleep. In NREM sleep, the body is active and the brain inactive. No eye movements occur, and dreaming is very rare during this stage. However, sometime during the night, while you slept, you went into the REM phase of sleep and climbed aboard the dream weaver's train. You may not remember dreaming, but all healthy humans enter into REM sleep and dream every night. REM sleep is the phase of sleep in which the brain is active and the body inactive. This is when most dreaming occurs; it is also known as dream sleep. When this dreaming stage of sleep occurs, our muscles become paralyzed and more relaxed than they are during the deepest levels of non-REM sleep. This alpha level stage of sleep is where one has rapid eye movement (REM). Our eyes flutter and the depth of our breathing increases.

When we first go to sleep, the brain waves (the electrical activity normally produced in the brain) slow from a frequency of ten cycles per second, which usually occur while we are awake, to about six cycles per second as our alertness decreases and we fall asleep. Then after about an hour, there is a sudden increase in brain wave activity. For a few minutes, the electrical activity in the brain speeds up. The waves sent to the brain closely resemble those of an awake and active person. This is REM sleep. During REM, sometimes the dreams will appear so real that the person will question whether it took place while he or she was awake or asleep. Then the electrical activity of the brain slows down, again entering into a NREM stage of sleep. This cycle may be repeated several times during one night's sleep. Total REM sleep for the night is about twenty percent of the total sleep time. Therefore, we spend about a fifth of our sleeping time dreaming.

Neuroscientists have done sleep studies, which concluded that five to ten percent of people woken during the NREM stage of sleep remembered a memory of a dream, while seventy to ninety-five percent of people woken during REM sleep remembered their dreams, and that both groups were affected by their ability to remember. This suggests that both NREM and REM are essential in the sleep process and its many functions. A lack of restful and recuperative sleep that comes from NREM sleep deepens depression, and intensifies feelings of hopelessness and fatigue. In addition, persons deprived of the opportunity to dream, due to a lack of REM sleep; during sleep studies, have often developed psychological symptoms such as hallucinations, paranoia, and neurotic tendencies very quickly. The REM state is the mechanism that connects us with reality. Some scholars have long believed that the Hebrew verbs *halom*, 'to dream', and *halam*, 'to be in good health', are related [16]. Dreaming is vital to our mental health, as well as stress reduction.

Fortunately, for us the unhealthy effects resulting from an improper amount of both phases of sleep are reversible. For, both NREM and REM sleep are homeostatically driven; that is, if a human is selectively deprived of one of these, he or she wi ll recover once they are allowed to sleep. Similarly, once a person is allowed to sleep again, upon enterin g the dream stage, one may experience the occurrence of having a dream continue, a part two. On another vein, dreams that occur during the same night, are usually dealing with the same subject matter.

Although, science hasn't yet adequately explained the experience of dreaming, or why we need to sleep, scientific observations concerning dreams have proven that under normal circumstances everyone dreams one to two hours each night. If you sleep a full eight hours, the entire last hour is essentially spent in alpha level sleep. Thus, the average person sleeping for eight hours a night will dream about one to two hours of that time.

Theologically Speaking

> *A dream that is not remembered might as well have not been dreamed, And therefore, a dream forgotten and gone from the mind is never fulfilled* [17].

If you think that you do not dream, or you cannot recall a dream, there are reasons for that. Aside from stress, physical and mental health issues, pharmaceutical and other drugs and alcohol use or abuse, and other sleep difficulties, many dreams associated with sleep, namely, ordinary dreams are not significant; consequently, they are easily and are often forgotten. Remembrance of these types of dreams, are not always compulsory. The words of the prophet Jeremiah illustrates this point, "*...neither hearken to your dreams which ye caused to be dreamt*", (*Jeremiah 29:8 KJV*). Everything in these dreams (ordinary dreams) is borrowed from our central memory, our waking lives, or is simply wishful thinking. Here a person dreams only of his or her thoughts and/or carnal, sensual urges. Ninety percent of the time you will not remember dreaming, just have a memory of dreaming, or you will remember only a fragment of your dream, and spending a lot of time trying to understand the fragment might not get you anywhere. In this, your dreams are, basically, guardians of your mental, emotional, and/or physical well-being.

Another forgotten dream; is one associated with what is called *Déjà Vu* (already seen).[18] This is the experience of feeling that you have witnessed or experienced a new situation previously, a sensing of having done that, or been here, before. This is the occurrence of remembering a dream forgotten. This type of dream, although at present forgotten, is brought to mind later to arouse appreciation that your life is on an intended course. Eighty percent of the population has had these types of dreams at one time or another.

A more challenging and confrontational rationale for not dreaming, or not remembering your dreams: It is written that if a person fails to have a dream for seven days or more, it is because he or she is consumed by selfish desires, and tremendous negative forces are now controlling him or her [17]. Their negative deeds far outweigh their positive deeds each day. Dreams that occur during this season of one's life, tend to be hellish and extremely terrifying, often resulting in denial of ever h aving dreamt (intentional or not); conceivably the matters may be too hard to face. Spiritual help by way of clergy, or perchance, psychological help, is highly recommended. Moreover, a character and lifestyle change can occur through prayer and heartfelt repentance to Jesus and to individuals affected by your actions, in the form of an apology (if possible). Repentance is seeking pardon and expressing sincere feelings of regret and brokenness for having done something awry and/or for having hurt someone, see 2 Corinthians 7:10, 11. To individuals, a phone call or a letter of apology is a good place to start. To Jesus pray, Psalm 51, this, coupled with prayer and fasting, followed by appropriate application of wisdom, can conceivably avert some of the repercussions of your choices. This is what is called leaving a blessing behind. When a man or woman genuinely return to God in love and surrender, your deliberate transgressions become like actual merits (also see Luke 7:37-50). Because, the realization of your distance from God, resulting from your transgressions (Isaiah 59:2), becomes the motivating force to return to God with a passion even greater than that of someone who has never sinned in such a manner (or never left the Father's house, Acts 9:1-30).

RECOGNIZING GOD'S VOICE IN YOUR DREAMS

For God does speak, now one way, now another, though man may not perceive it. In a dream, in a vision of the night, when deep sleep falls on men as they slumber in their beds. He may speak in their ears and terrify them with warnings, to tu rn man from wrongdoing and keep him from pride, to preserve his soul from the pit (or grave, which is a symbol of death), his life from perishing by the sword (or crossing the River, another death symbol). (Job 33:14-18 NIV)

All who have wondered about their dreams can testify that dreams are not often easy to figure out. They can be very complex, and do have a language all their own, a language of imagery, symbolism, and sometimes strange goings -on. It is these very attributes, which make them at times difficult to understand. Yet, what we know as vague or contrary bits and pieces in our dreams, will often come together to communicate instruction from God, make known intended destiny and purpose, and most importantly, reveal the true intents of our heart. This is the voice of God within dreams.

Insight, coupled with the veracity of my findings, supports that collectively the following principles will assist you in recognizing God's voice in your dreams.

Prayer

On top of everything, humbly ask Jesus for the interpretation, allowing Him to grant you the u nderstanding of your dream (Daniel 2:16-19). In a solitary place, you can perceive His voice, via the Holy Spirit. The Holy Spirit will guide your thoughts, bringing the bits and pieces together into a logical story that you will be able to relate too. For, it is written, *"My sheep hear my voice, and I know them, and they follow me" (John 10:27 KJV)*. You can learn to distinguish God's voice through prayer.

Journal

To help sort things out and get some clarity, it is suggested that you write your dreams down (Daniel 7:1). Include people, animals, places, things, and colors, taking into account the smallest details. Whatever you remember write it down. It is a good thing and is highly recommended that you journal your dreams. Your journal will help you track, and make sense of, the various symbols and activities within your dreams. You will begin to recognize patterns in your dreams, and to compile symbols that have personal significance to you.

Contemplate

Think about what the symbols mean to you, at that particular time, and journal those thoughts. Although most all symbols have the origin of their meanings within the Bible, some credence attached to those symbols will come from your everyday life. For example, a candle, within scripture represents God's word and the illumination thereof. However, worry over an electrical bill, may prompt a prophetically ordinary dream, whereas a candle may be a warning, revealing a lack of li ght and electricity if something is not done, and this in itself is a type of illumination, pay the electric bill. Therefore, always bear in mind the matters you were dealing with the day before you had the dream.

Ask questions

You can bring to light the meaning of your dream if you think about it and pose the right questions. Ask, "Why am I dreaming about this or that, now?" Did your dream have something to do with you living life on God's terms? Are your dreams bringing to light a prophetic gifting that can be developed and used to help others? Your dreams oftenti mes will confirm God-given longings that were placed in your heart.

Reflect

Consider the emotional state you are in when you awake from your dreams. Do you most times have a sense of urgency to accomplish or finish something? Are you happy, relieved, encouraged, bewildered, scared, or broken for the most part? Are you always disappointed and sad?

A young woman dreamt that she was running from the police (symbolic of ministers "administrators of the law"). The law being the revealed will of God within an individual's life. For he (or she) who knows to do good or right, and does not, it is an offense within his (or her) life (James 4:17). While she was running (figurative of running away from someone or thing), she hid behind a rock (symbolic of the Logos), and other places (contextually within this dream, places, coupled with the law and rock, would represent principles, precepts, and statutes). The woman had just been presented with an opportunity to pursue a God - given desire to minister in a certain area within the Body of Christ. As the ministry deals with face-to-face spiritual warfare, she had become a bit apprehensive and began backing off because of the newly acquired knowledge she was obtaining. It was suggested that concealing her fears, viz. running from the opportunity and hiding behind the Word of God (the hiding behind rocks and other places), rather than facing and dealing with them, would not be advantageous. God knowing her heart included no rebellion symbols within her dream, so it is assumed that the dreamer really is apprehensive, and not out-and-out disobedient.

Validate

God counsels, let everything be established by two or three witnesses. Coupled with your dream, which is one witness, allow the counsel of wise friends (Daniel 2:17, Proverbs 11:14, 15:22, 23) to bear out your reckonings, along with other additional confirmations from the various ways God speaks to, and guides us. Noting too, hold your dream up against the immutable light of Holy Scripture, and the changeless nature of God Almighty. Prophetic dreams will never conflict with either; as they are always within context of God sanctioned covenants with humankind.

For instance, you will never have a divine sent dream that undeniably directs you to pursue, praise, worship, and/or serve God in any way that is in direct conflict with His Nature and His Word. Example, dreams requiring child sacrifice, molestation, incest, adulterous affairs, ritual harlotry, prostitution, or homicide, to name a few, or a dream declaring that you are god, requiring worship of you, angels or demons. This is confusion on so many levels. Not every dream is divinely sent, but when they are, there is usually a sense of certainty of the accuracy of the message and a spirit of gratitude that follows (Daniel 2:19-23). If the conclusion of your dream is not within the context of the changeless nature of God Almighty, and in full accord with it, via scripture, your dream may prove deceptive, and will quite likely prove misleading, or false.

False Dreams

It is written that an unjust person will regularly be shown a happy dream (albeit an untruthful one), to lead him or her further astray from the path of truth[3]. When a person strongly desires to believe something, he or she may very well have a dream that supports what they want to believe. If you deeply and earnestly want to embrace a delusion, a lying spirit will come to convince you of what you want to accept as truth, is truth, as is evidenced in 1 Kings 22:5-28, Job 12:16, Daniel 11:32. This seems to be the fundamental basis for false dreams and false prophesy.

> *Whoever sets out to purify himself is purified from above, and whoever sets out to defile himself is similarly defiled from above. The more veracious an individual is, the more dependable his or her dream messages will be*[19].

Your dreams will never violate your right of choice or your right to be self-governed (taking counsel within your own mind). Nor, will they violate your right to be in denial, much the same way the conscious and subconscious mental activities work together, processing information that you do not want to deal with —they will hide or cover it. When people are inclined to selfish behavior, imprisoned to their own ego, and have no sincere intent or desire to change or experience spiritual growth or truth, the symbols, and messages within their dreams will be much harder to detect. Noted, while a few of our dreams will contain illogical or parodic type symbols within them, these particular dreams, false dreams, will be subject to great exaggeration and contain excessive and extreme nonsensical, cartoonish, mythological, *"Alice in Wonderland"*, *"Clash of the Titans"*, Xbox 360 games- type elements. People who are predominantly pretenders, self-seeking, and/or materialistic will often experience this level of dream. Falsehoods, fiction, illusions, inventions, fabrications, untruths, or drama within your life, often cause one to open up to lies. The more callous, deceptive, or secretive a person bears out to be the more likely; his or her dreams will present ambiguous and/or illusory particulars.

Imagery that is cartoonish, caricaturized, mythological, or an entity with two faces, are all ways your dreams will hide or cover the truth you choose to deny. Double dealing in a card game, acting out some form of cheating, embracing, returning to, and/or moving in with a dead spouse or an ex-spouse who has in all honesty moved on, or a dream of someone taken hostage, to name a few, are also other ways your dreams will support your willingness to be in denial. These symbols are warnings of the imminent arrival of a lying spirit that comes to draw men and women away from truth and perchance from God. For more information, see index or relevant category for specific action, activity, person, animal, place, or organization primary within your dream.

Given, the symbols themselves represent an attitude of denial of truth within the heart of the dreamer, the message the symbols reveal is truth. Thus, the truth is revealed to you, via your dreams, beforehand. Therefore, these types of dreams may be considered forewarnings, giving the dreamer ample time (a grace period), to change his or her mind and ways. How does a man or woman embrace truth inwardly, when they don't want to know the truth, or when they do not know the path to truth, or are unable to embrace truth? Taking ownership of what your warning dream is revealing to you about you, and working from that point, via prayer, fasting, diligent self-examination, persistent practice of truthfulness, candid support from family and friends, and/or Christian counseling, will help truth inwardly begin to emerge; at a pace, you'll be able to "wrap your mind around" comfortably. This followed by appropriate application of wisdom, can conceivably avert self-deception and the repercussions thereof. This is what is called leaving a blessing behind.

Are You Ready To Hear The Messages In Your Dreams?

...when men still listened for the voice of God in the still of the night.• J. Trachtenberg, *The Dream in Human Affairs*

In order to hear the messages intended for you in your dreams, there is one important truth to acknowledged, ninety percent of the time; your dreams are for you. The dream is for and about the dreamer; I can't say that enough. Of the thousands of dreams, I've interpreted through the years; no less than 30% of the dreamers have assumed or felt that their dream was for someone else, and when told their dream was for them, many have departed embittered or a bit rebuffed to say the least. Nonetheless, a dream is primarily for the dreamer.

As simple and obvious as that may sound, again many dreamers assume that a very large percentage of their dreams are messages for other people, rather than messages intended for self. The tendency to mistake one's dream subject matter as information you need to pass on to those depicted within your dream or to others is very common. Either the issue here is one's particular prophetic gifting, a misunderstanding of the purpose and function of dreams, or there is a distortion within one's heart regarding you. Thus, it is always easier to point out the speck in another's eye, than to deal with the plank in our own. If you just happened to dream of a plank or speck in your eye or in the eye of another, do refer to Matthew 7:1-5, this is the interpretation of that dream, and it is for, and about, the dreamer.

Universal Principal

Any recipient of a divinely sent communication should always glean and apply the wisdom of it, to his or her life first. You can't go wrong applying this principle first.

Due to the very nature of humankind, in our passions to suppose, reason, justify, or validate. We sometimes mistake the word (or wisdom) God has given us, for us, to be for someone else. The static of our lives, the condition of our relationship with Christ, coupled with our emotional faculties oftentimes drown out the warning signals for us, sending us into a state of denial. So much so, that we begin to lean to our own understanding, pronouncing our personal opinions, as prophecy from God for others, declaring, "thus says the Lord", when the Lord has not said thus; while ignoring or dismissing the hints that come to warn us of the error of our own way. As a result, our spiritual lives become in such disorder that we can't hear, or aren't listening anymore, to divine wisdom sent to us personally, be it through our dreams or other words sent through other means.

In spite of this, compassionately, because of His great love and faithfulness towards us, the Lord with patience persistence, helps us keep the frequency clear. Our dreams serve as one of His ways of getting through to us if we would but listen. Conscientiously looking into the messages within your dreams, as applicable to yourself, your eyes will open to a clearer picture of who you really are. For the majority of your dreams are about your inner self, so your dream is probably about something you are or should be dealing with in your own life right now.

In an interview with JUF News, Cindy Sher, Managing Editor Author, Poet Rodger Kamenetz shared the following

Why should we listen to our dreams?

"I (Kamenetz) once dreamed that I was on my deathbed and I was reciting my resume. That one didn't require interpretation; it required action. I thought all of the stuff I was doing was important, but I was being foolish and [the dream] was a wakeup call. That's an example of how you can learn from dreams and how they are worth paying attention to. They can be so blunt and so uncompromising. Dreams have an honesty that we don't get anywhere else. We're wasting this incredible resource".

If we do not respect the messages conveyed via our dreams, we may miss pivotal points of correction or paths that God would have us to take that would affect rectification within our lives. That point of correction could be a conflict that needs to be resolved between you and a family member, friend, or foe. The cause of the conflict could be your own stubbornness or rebelliousness, frequently revealed as witchcraft within dreams. For example, if you are the person practicing witchcraft within your dream, you are self-aware of your own negative deeds. If you are truly unaware of the part you've played within a conflict, your dream will depict someone else practicing the witchcraft. If you know the person practicing the witchcraft, deep down you recognize your own stubbornness, but are unwilling to own up to it. If you do not know the person practicing the witchcraft, you are genuinely unaware of your own obstinacy.

A dream of witchcraft exposes a need of refinement of character, namely in the area dealing with the deeds of the flesh. For example, dishonesty, adultery, sensuality, hostility, feuding, vendettas, grudges, unfriendliness, strife, jealousy, outbursts of anger, disputes, dissensions, discord, factions, cliques, envying, drunkenness, carousing, idolatry (idolatry is "foreign service", any act that expresses devotion or fanatical admiration to something or someone other than Adonai Elohim), or any traits of these sorts (see 1 Corinthians 6:8-11). This also includes a possible belief in, and/or practice of, necromancy.

If we miss, or do not regard, the messages conveyed in our dreams as for us, and our character remains unchanged, a door is left, wide-open for more chaos and negativity to manifest in our lives. This is sometimes, portrayed within a dream (including, but not limited to): As you suddenly realizing that one, or all, doors of your home are open and people you may or may not know are living in your personal space.

Our dreams will address the issues we are wrestling with in our body, in our mind, and in our spirits. They have the capacity to reveal health, psychological, and spiritual related issues. They will articulate the state of your relationship with God, with others, and the circumstances and events that surround your life, ministry, and work, for these are important to your heart and spirit. They will make known the pressures of life that makes us want to run and hide; the frustrations and aggravations, the trying times. Dreams will expose the serious problems, unrest, and disquiet within your soul, when you're so weary that you're unable to fight spiritually anymore. They will counsel you on how to allow the Lord to comfort you and give you rest. It is these concerns that our dreams will address. Should you not hear what thus says the Lord via your dreams?

Ninety Percent of the Times, Your Dreams Are For You. The Other Ten Percent is for another

Approximately ten percent of your dreams will be about, and for, others. These dreams will include important information about significant others, and is usually dreamt by those who has the wherewithal to do something with the information. Visions within dreams and the revelations within those dreams are not given haphazardly to any individual, but only to those with the ability and influence to truly, do something with the information. These types of dreams bear insight into the present day or near future events of another who seriously needs your help. Thus, on some level, these dreams will also affect the dreamer.

Unique Prophetic Gifting

Prophecy comes to you by way of your dreams. I credit this extraordinary anomaly to the unique prophetic gifting one may have been endowed with, allowing you direct access to prophetic insight, via your dreams (Deuteronomy 13:1). As a result, the percentage of your dreams for others will be higher. Usually one will have a vision, which is usually for, and about, others within a dream. God revealed Nebuchadnezzar's dream to Daniel in a dream (Daniel 2:19, and other instances of visions within dreams elsewhere in Daniel). This dream is considered a vision; thus, it is for others (see *Oneirovatic* dreams). Here also is where visions differ from dreams. Ninety percent of the time, a vision is prophecy for, and about, another.

Is your dream for you or another?

Consider the following: Were you a spectator only within your dream? Were you a partaker of the things going on within your dream? Were you both, part spectator, part partaker? Did the Lord or someone speak directly to you in your dream?

Your answers are possible clues as to whether your dream was for you or another.

SPECTATOR DREAM: If the dreamer was a spectator only (a close observer; someone who looks at something, but does not participate), perhaps this dream is for another. However, some type of action is required of the dreamer on behalf of another. This is also true if the dreamer was mostly a spectator and then at some point became a partaker. Thus, this dream of both, part spectator, part partaker, may also be considered a spectator's dream.

PARTAKER DREAM: If you are a partaker (one who has, gives, or receives a part or a share) of the activity within your dream, this is a good indicator that the dream is for, and about, the dreamer. If the dreamer were mostly a partaker than spectator, this dream of both, would be considered a partaker's dream.

If the Lord, or someone, spoke directly to you within your dream, their words will lead the way.

The following dreams best bear out the principle of spectator and partaker:

Spectator Dreams

Gideon, upon instructions from God, secretly goes down into the enemy's camp. He arrived just as a man was telling his dream to a friend. "I had a dream. A loaf of barley bread tumbled into the camp, and struck the tent with such force that t he tent overturned and collapsed". His friend interpreted the dream, as representing the sword of Gideon. Gideon hears the interpretation of the dream and is encouraged, and goes away worshipping the Lord (see Judges 7:13-15). The dreamer was a spectator only; hence, the dream was about, and for, another, who happened to be Gideon who was secretly listening to the dream and its interpretation. The interpreter also affirms that the dream is for, or about, another. For, he says, "That can only be the sword of Gideon, son of Joash, from Israel. God is going to hand Midian and the whole camp over to him". Further, the dreamer unknowingly fulfilled the requirement of a spectator dream, which obliges the dreamer, on some level, to act on behalf of another. He encouraged Gideon, although unwittingly.

In Pharaoh's two dreams, Genesis 41:1-7, he stood and beheld (spectator) the happenings within his dreams. These two dreams were one and it was for the entire nation of Egypt. The action required of the dreamer, on behalf of his nation, was to use wisdom to lessen the effects of the coming famine.

If the dreamer was mostly a spectator, and then at some point became a partaker, on some small level, this dream of both, mostly spectator, part partaker, would also be considered a spectator's dream. Consider the following dreams:

Genesis 15:12-18. Abraham has fallen into a deep sleep, when intense dark horror comes upon him (he's terrified, making him a partaker, on a small level). The Lord then speaks to Abraham, establishing a covenant with him; subsequently Abraham notices (spectator) a smoking firepot with a blazing torch. Although the Covenant and a promise of long life is made to Abraham, thus fulfilling the condition of a partaker dream, this dream is primarily for Abraham's descendants, this fulfils the duty of a spectator dream.

In Daniel 7:2-16, Daniel looked and watched (spectator) and there before him were four winds, four great beasts, horns, thrones, and the Ancient of Days. Then in verse 16, Daniel asked (making him a partaker on a small level). Because of him asking, a guide begins to interpret his dream. Without doubt, Daniel was predominantly a spectator within this dream. Although, verse 16 makes him a partaker in that he asks another for the interpretation, his dream plainly states that its purpose is for others.

In Daniel 8:1-26, Daniel observes (spectator); he saw himself in Susa, and he looks up and before him was a ram and goat, he hears holy ones speaking, and Gabriel interprets his dream. Daniel becomes terrified and faints, and then is raised to his feet (partaker). While Daniel's dreams clearly depicts him as an onlooker for the most part. Note Daniel faints, is raised to his feet, and is asked to write and seal up the prophecies of both dreams. The act of writing and sealing up what he saw for a future generation fulfills a condition of a partaker dream (he has to seal up and write something). So, while primarily a spectator dream, there is an action required of the dreamer. Daniel is to veil the prophecy in his writings. As this prophet's dreams exalts God's omniscience by foreseeing future world events, he is instructed to seal up the prophecies, as they will benefit the future generation they are intended for.

A couple of important observations of the Spectator Dreams: The spectator dreams were prophetic in nature and anyone can have a spectator dream. If you sense that your dream is for, or about, another, the question as to why you have been made privy to this information, and how do you factor into the equation, should be seriously considered along with necessary actions. Gideon's anonymous dreamer, although unbeknownst to him, was a key factor in Gideon's victory over the Midianites. Moreover, it is quite plausible that this mysterious person could very well have alarmed his fellow comrades of the imminent defeat of their camp by Gideon, thus triggering an unprecedented spirit of fear to come over the camp. So when they heard the loud noise and seen the many lights, they automatically went into hysteria. Once again, dreams that are for others and the revelation within those dreams (as with all prophecy) are not given haphazardly to any individual, but only to those with the ability, and influence to truly do something with the information. Divine communications are never sent for gossip purposes, or simply as an FYI. You are asked, via divine inspiration, to act on behalf of another. You will not hear from God about people over whom you have no influence or bearing upon, nor about events you are powerless to impress upon, avert, or lessen the consequential effects.

Dreams for, or about others, are given us as they pertain to our particular area of responsibility. You are required to do something with the information you receive. The action required on the part of the dreamer maybe as simple as re-telling the dream to another, writing a letter, or making a phone call. The action may be as intense as initiating the investigation of child molestation, exposing the perpetrator, or as complicated as initiating the re-investigation of a cold case file or exposing major offenses in the life of another and the subsequent judgment (divine reprimand for folly and sin). This type of prophetic insight may require you revealing a critical sickness or disease in the life of another. Do you have the godly wisdom and/or wherewithal to tend to, teach, guide, encourage, nurture, help, comfort, aid, or support the individual hands-on and empathically? Could God have chosen you because you have prophetic abilities, e.g. spiritual watchman, seer, prophet, or prophetess? One thing is for sure, if you failed to do what is required, the spiritual implications will be required at your hand s (see Ezekiel 3:17-21; 33:7-20).

A wife may observe within her dream that her head is cut off, and is floating away. Wisely interpreted, she will find that this dream is about the approaching death of her husband. The wife should pass on this information to her husband, aggressively encouraging him to seek medical attention, averting a serious illness, having been caught in time. This was my dream two years before that grave event took place. As my husband was not a man given to any illness, except the common cold, he never went to doctors. His health was taken for granted. Because of not acting on the message within my dream due to denial, medical attention was never suggested until it was too late. I was not willing to hear the message within that dr eam, thus I did not act. Although his soul is with Heavenly Father, it took a very long time, and many bitter tears trying to get my house in order without his wisdom, thus my first book, *Bitter Anguish.*

Other dreams of this vein can and do occur. A mother may find out within a dream that her adult child is returning home sick. In her dream she realizes that her child has come home, looking smaller in stature and emaciated, and gets into the bed with her. Then suddenly the child is out of bed and regular size again. Within her dream, the mother is told that her child is ill and the nature of the illness. The mother did not want to know the nature of the illness, so she woke herself up out of the dream. Upon recalling the dream, she does not remember the name of the infirmity. This dream revealed an emotional problem or physical condition of another and exposed the mother's unwillingness to hear the message within her dream. The child did come home for healing, rest, and recuperation for a long while. Fortunately, according to the dream, the child recovered fully.

Partaker Dreams

King Abimelech, in Genesis 20:3-8, has a serious conversation with God (partaker), within a dream, regarding Abraham and Sarah's deception. God tells him not to touch Sarah. This dream was about, and for Abimelech.

Although Jacob watched angels ascend and descend upon a stairway, the Lord spoke to Jacob, reaffirming the Abrahamic covenant through which Jacob's seed will fulfill, Genesis 28:12-16. The Lord spoke, so for this reason the dream was about, and for Jacob.

The cupbearer and baker in Genesis 40:5-23 were in every respect participants within their dreams. As was interpreted, one was restored and the other executed.

Pilate's wife, in Matthew 27:19, sent word to him saying, *"Have nothing to do with that just Man, for I have suffered (partaker) many things today in a dream because of Him"*. Despite the fact, she acted on behalf of another, by speaking-out, on the righteousness of Jesus because of her dream. Her dream depicted her suffering (partaker); thus, her dream was for her. No doubt, this dream foretold of the inevitable great pain and despair she would endure because of her love for her husband and because of the love and respect, she had for Jesus. Tradition has it that Jesus healed her son Pilo's crippled foot. It is also believed, that she became a Christian and is honored to this day as Saint Procula. Her husband, Pilate, as tradition has it, after a series of downturns and bad choices, eventually committed suicide while in exile [21].

In summary, a larger part of the dreams revealed within the Bible was for the dreamer. In addition, every biblical dreamer, spectator, and partaker alike, proved him or herself ready to hear the message within their dreams, by acting on them.

Oneirocritica: Dream Interpretation

CHAPTER TWO

Why Symbols And Images?

It is the glory of God to conceal a matter, but the glory of kings is to search out a matter
(Proverbs 25:2 NKJV)

That deeper matter is one hidden by God that we might seek Him out for an answer.

The Symbol

The Ancient of Days has His own language (and ideals) that are high and above. Hence, "For my thoughts are not your thoughts, neither are your ways my ways," declares the Lord. "For as the heavens are higher than the earth. So are my ways higher than your ways, and my thoughts than your thoughts..." (Isaiah 55:8, 9 ESV). Thus, we cannot communicate with God on His level in a direct manner (face to face). We are not His equal; although He is nearby and very open to our human desire for relationship, which He instigated. Further, it is not in man to experience the intangible, without some measure of tangible attached to it. So, in order to lend a measure of concreteness to our very human need to experience God, an intermediary was needed. God provided a "go-between" accessible to all, the symbol. Even more, while God's language is invariable, change, variety, beginnings, and endings are continuous elements in our earthly languages. Human language evolves from a combination of feelings and ideals, and the human influence ties it to specific cultures and times in history. The symbol is different, in that it will always mean, what it was at first meant to mean, until the sands of time run out. In addition, it will always speak in the language of all men, and remain user-friendly to all, for all times. C. S. Lewis, "Symbols are the natural speech of the soul, a language older and more universal than words".

Symbols are visible representations, images of the abstract or unseen. They are but thoughts and ideals, copies and shadows, according to Hebrews 8:5; set forth in visual form. Using visual representations of people, places, things, animals, attributes, ideals, and actions of this world, our Heavenly Father imparts to us some knowledge of His world. He is able to reach out to us, to aid our entrance into His Kingdom, and to shed light on His vision and objectives. Wonder and deep mysteries, are hidden within symbols and within the dreams they comprise. There is no branch of wisdom, secular or divine, that is not contained within their depths. To this end the dream and its symbol has both an esoteric and an exoteric quality. In their own unique way, they embrace depths and heights within human nature, fulfilling a need, a hunger, and a thirst that God knows to exist in man. For thousands of years humanity has appreciated dreams and symbolism because of the insight that accompanies their revelation.

If this were your dream, what would it mean? How would you tell this dream to someone?

Do drying clothes on a clothesline have anything to do with you? What about the apartments; is this something from your past? Is the location important? What about the well-manicured lawn, and/or palmetto trees, do they effect an emotion? Where would you find this kind of scene? If this were your dream, what would all of this have to do with you? What would this dream mean to someone who lived in this area in the past? Could there be any possible spiritual significance to a dream of this sort to the dreamer?

Why symbols and images?

By use of symbols, God through your dreams can softly admonish, as well as smuggle alarms into your heart. In this capacity, symbols are disguises for referents, for the main purpose of sanctification, purging, and/or preparation. Because of our moral fiber, warnings and oftentimes His Ways are objectionable to our mind and spirit. Of which, the mind and spirit have the power to suppress anything objectionable. To possibly prevent this, a more tolerable and endearing language is used. For instance, one may dream of a broken gold vessel (or ceramic pottery of this sort). While a ceramic vessel is a beautiful accessory to any home, this broken piece of earthenware, refers to approaching death. The broken bowl (the disguise) is easier on the spirit, while the actual words, "You may have six months to live", can be stark and hard to accept. This dream is one of God's ways of breaking it to you gently, preparing you for one of life's common denominators, and if heeded, can prevent you from being emotionally blindsided by physical loss. This type of dream gives the dreamer time to seek medical attention, to make peace with his or her Maker, to seek forgiveness, and to forgive, and to get his or her home in order.

FAQ: Could not God have made His directives plain, instead of using symbols and dreams?

Of the many that God gave simple instructions to, Adam to multiply, Noah to build, Abraham to leave, Joseph to marry, Saul to go and ask for a man, there is only one person within scripture that it is spoken of that God spoke face to face and plainly, and that person is Moses.

Per, The Handbook of Jewish Thought referencing Numbers 12:6-8 the revelations of Moses were unique. Unlike other prophets, Moses received his revelations clearly, not masked by symbolism. Thus, it is written, God said, "I speak to Moses mouth to mouth, manifestly, and not in allegory". Only Moses spoke with God direct, without the use of symbols, dreams, visions, or enigmas. Moses would receive his revelations while wide-awake and in full command of his senses. Of other prophets and men of old, even until today, God has declared, "When I speak through one of you, I will speak with you in a dream (or vision). Not so with my servant Moses". Moses revelations were therefore plainly spoken to him. God spoke to Moses face to face, as a man speaks to his friend, because he found favor in God's sight (see Exodus 33:11, 17).

Moses in the Midrash: Even of his birth, it is said; he (Moses) was good. Midrashic teachings states that when the biblical text of Exodus 2:2 described the baby (Moses) born as good, by using the word *tov*, the Hebrew word for good, it heightened the superhuman, spiritual qualities of Moses. In that when Moses was born, the whole house became flooded with light, a phenomenon enhanced when the text connects the word *tov* with Genesis 1:4, God saw the light and it was good. Rabbi Judah's comment that Moses was fit for prophecy even before birth elevates Moses to a level of pre-natal spirituality not found in the biblical narrative about any other prophet. Moses was born with the ability to effect great spiritual accomplishments. He made use of his inherent spiritual gifts to negate himself completely before God. So it is written, *"Now the man Moses was very humble, more than all men who were on the face of the earth" (Numbers 12:3 NASB)*, the epitome of humility. Since Moses' personality was completely nonexistent before God, his physical nature no longer acted as a barrier between him and the Creator, so he was able to obtain revelation from God, at any time and in any place[22].

Moreover, in his mysterious death and burial, Moses' body did not descend into the "captivity", as did all before and after him (Matthew 17:3, Jude 9), up until Jesus' resurrection. This was the destination of all, from Adam until the descending of Jesus, and His subsequent taking of the keys of death and Hades, preaching to those held captive, and to His resurrection leading the "captivity" captive (Matthew 27:53; Ephesians 4:8-10, 1 Peter 3:18-20; Revelation 1:18). It is; therefore, a foundational truth that Moses was the greatest of all prophets, both past, present, and future. Hence, it is written, *"there has not risen a prophet in Israel like Moses, whom God knew face to face" (Deuteronomy 34:10 KJV).* The essence of this verse is that there will never again emerge a prophet like Moses anywhere, allowed to communicate with God on such a level. Moses is second only to Jesus Christ, as Paul testifies,

> *"...who was faithful to Him who appointed Him, as Moses also was faithful in all His house. For this One has been counted worthy of more glory than Moses, inasmuch as He who built the house has more honor than the house. For every house is built by someone, but He who built all things is God".*
> *(Hebrews 3:2-4 NKJV)*

Let's unpack this…

Unlike others, whose revelations were, and still are, limited to symbols, dreams, visions, and enigmas, Moses' revelations were of a direct nature; he, having had a closer relationship with God than the average human. Therefore, God said, "Moses is trusted in all My house" (see Numbers 12:7). Likewise, God promised Moses, "I will make all my benefits pass before you" (see Exodus 33:19). In this, God opened Moses' understanding, permitting him access to all the gates of wisdom (knowledge regarding spiritual truths and concepts, most often far deep and esoteric). He was given full access to delve into the most hidden treasures and secrets of God's wisdom, being fully entrusted to explore and inquire at will. God, having miraculously enlarged Moses' capacity for knowledge, allowed Moses to gain the highest level of understanding possible, thus, he was able to speak to God face to face, as a man speaks to his friend. R. Aryeh Kaplan states, "Nobody has ever been given this privilege since, and it is understood that the reason for this awesome privilege was that God chose to reveal His Torah to Israel, and to the entire world, through Moses". It is for these reasons Moses did not experience God's revelations via symbols or dreams, nor did he experience them as an overpowering occurrence, like others before and after him [23].

Gates of Wisdom

Regarding gates of wisdom, mentioned a minute ago. If you dream of walking through a gate, you will increase in wisdom and knowledge, regarding spiritual truths or concepts you may be wrestling with presently. This increase will happen through personal experience and a miraculous impartation, primarily communicated via the Holy Spirit. The gates, as with all symbols, should be interpreted within the context of your dream. For instance, if a dark foreboding ominous place is on the other side of that gate, you will gain a dark and erroneous knowledge, the devil's so-called deep secrets (Revelation 2:20, 24). You will gain this knowledge also through personal experience and supernatural imparting. This knowledge; however, is primarily, demonically communicated. The knowledge gained will lead you to that dark ominous place on the other side, emotionally, spiritually, and if not aborted, eternally. Moreover, see dream symbol categories: Entryways, Enclosures. Kept within context of your dream and of the interpretation, this may be an area (or situation) of relevance.

Why symbols and images?

Illumination according to our capacity for knowledge

"For we know in part, and we prophesy in part, but when that which is perfect is come, then that which is in part shall be done away. When I was a child, I spake as a child, I understood as a child, I thought as a child; but when I became a man, I put away childish things. For now we see through a glass, darkly; but then face to face: now I know in part; but then shall I know even as also I am known"
(1 Corinthians 13:9-12 KJV)

Paul, in his letter to the Corinthians, is literally shedding light on why God reveals His revelations to us in the way that He does, namely symbols.

When I was a child (nēpios), I spoke as a child; I understood as a child, I thought as a child ...

Because the human race is the youngest of created beings, we are considered but children: *Nēpios* meaning wordless, referring to one too young to talk, a babe (without any definite limitation of age) as to ignorance and simplicity, immature, unskilled[24]. It is within this context that Paul refers to himself, and to humankind, as a child. As children, just like newborn babes and toddlers, our faculty for divine illumination is limited. Our best knowledge and our greatest abilities are, at present, like our spiritual condition, narrow and temporary. Therefore, spiritual truths have to be processed bit by bit to make them understandable to man. The means to the end of this process is symbolism in all of its facets.

Our human understanding of, and reaction to, spiritual realities is oftentimes crudely green. This type of simplicity is compared to *"springs without water, and mists driven by a storm"* (2 Peter 2:17 ASV). We mouth empty and boastful words that appeal only to the lustful desires of our human nature, very much like Saul's mentality, prior to his name change to Pau l. The spiritual truths he thought he knew, and what was eventually revealed to him (how blind he really was) during his personal enlightenment, led him to acknowledge that his understanding of spiritual realities was childish at best, and perilously dangerous to others. Fortunately, he went into the desert to deprogram and re-program himself (Galatians 1:12-24). At this crossroads in his life, he counted all that he knew to be worthless (Philippians 3:3-9). Now known as Paul, he began to walk and grow into a mature spiritual being, going on towards perfection, enabled to see into the spiritual realm more clearly (figurative of the scales falling from his eyes and the regaining of his eyesight). No matter his hardships, and they were grievously many (2 Corinthians 11:23-33), Paul never again looked back, but he genuinely, in words and deeds, put away childish things. As a result, his capacity for greater illumination, intellectually and spiritually, was enlarged giving him access to more than a few of the gates of wisdom (2 Corinthians 12:2-7). Moreover, as God gave Moses the responsibility of the Torah, in addition to leading His people out of bondage, likewise, He entrusted Paul with writing approximately forty-five percent of the New Testament, along with the colossal task of proselytizing the gentile world, leading them out of bondage.

When mankind (individually and as a whole) matures enough to handle all of God's benefits and can prove trustworthy in all of His wisdom, without becoming conceited, prideful, self-aggrandizing, running amok, or trying to kill somebody because of differences (1 Corinthians 12:7). At that time, that which is imperfect shall make way for that which is perfect (*teleios*, finished), describing that which has achieved or reached its goal, objective, purpose, limit, end, completion, mature, or full - grown. The child will put away childish things and understand as a mature spiritual being and shall know even as he or she is, known (Psalm 139). That is, to understand as you are understood, so as, to present before God without pride or prejudice. To do as Moses did, genuinely decrease in order that God may increase. In this, our personalities will become invisible before God, so that our humanness will no longer act as a barrier between us and our God, enabling us to communicate face to face with our Maker without the use of symbols, dreams, visions, riddles or parables. Our half–knowledge will become full knowledge in the radiant light of heaven.

(However) for now, we see through a glass, darkly...

Paul explains that we will, one day receive God's Word plainly, face-to-face, like Moses. However, in the mean time we will all continue to see through a glass that is not so clear, opaque. Therefore, we all see through a glass that is darkly. The phrase 'darkly' figuratively means that humans have an imperfect perception of spiritual realities; for we know only in part, (e.g. dreams are a 60ᵗʰ part of prophecy). We are, individually given pieces of the puzzle that we might look interdependently to one another for the other pieces. Which piece of the puzzle are you, entrusted? Moses saw the entire picture, with all of its many parts, thus, Moses saw through a clear brightly polished glass. He understood what he was looking at, and was meek enough to receive it (1 Corinthians 13:12).

Note, a dream of looking through some type of glass, be it a looking glass, eye glasses, a transparent drinking glass or windows, and the glass is cloudy, murky, dirty, foggy, or shadowy. This is, interpreted to mean that the dreamer does not ha ve a clear or correct understanding of spiritual truths and/or spiritual realities, especially of that which articulates the true nature of God.

The Creator, in His mercy, shows us some of the Light of His Glory, by way of the dream; for dreams are a level of prophecy that anyone can receive. God is being seen in dreams but He is hidden from the eye, for Divinity is not, personified in visual imagery. He shows us an image of His Divine Presence, and this is the Shekinah (a glow of the Light of God's Goodness; God's presence in and throughout the world). After having ascertain a more excellent spirit and a greater facility for spiritual ideals, we will no longer need the 'covering' of symbolism to protect us from the lethal majesty of God's Light —as it is written, *"No man shall see Me and live" (Exodus 33:20 KJV)*. Until then, the Creator illuminates us according to our understanding and maturity level, as well as our aptitude for knowledge. At present, this human condition is not yet refined and purified to the point where we are able to receive perfect knowledge and wisdom, and not send it back void. Therefore, God sets forth symbols, via dreams, visions, to humankind, for God knows all things. The symbol is therefore; essentially, perfect, and requires no further external evidence for the truths it represents.

I have discussed the use, and on the other hand, the non-use, of symbolism and dreams at length, because I believe they are too often limited in their application, merely to minor preaching and teaching of parables. How often do you hear of anyone teaching on the deeper meanings of symbols and dreams? There is a deeper meaning behind them. Perhaps with a broader understanding of symbols and dreams, a unique forum will develop through which the deeper qualities of their spiritual implications maybe exchanged.

Do Not Interpretations Belong To The Lord?

*Dreams and their interpretations, both ascribe to the greatness of
the One who so graciously, guides us by way of them.*

Joseph's outspoken faith in his belief that dream interpretations belong to the Lord God could have cost him his life in the presence of an Egyptian king who was himself regarded as a god. When in Genesis, Joseph categorically declared that his God would give the interpretation of Pharaoh's dream. It is at this moment in time that the master of dreams set in stone a precedent that the interpretation of dreams belonged to God. The Creator fashioned the dream with its use of symbolic language and compelling images to shape our understanding of Him and His ways. Then He serves as translator, a sort of exegete of this pictographic language. In this, interpretations belong to Him and interpreters are merely carriers of His message.

Dreams allow you to receive God-intended instructions; and the Lord is gracious enough, intelligent enough, and flexible enough to make sure you understand the message He wants delivered especially to you. Dreams are trustworthy mediators. They reveal the condition of your heart and mind, including the wisdom of God regarding that condition. Hence, there are ample enough types and shadows (symbols) for us to, reasonably draw some conclusions as to the meaning of some of the imagery within our dreams and how God wants that imagery interpreted.

Dream Interpreters: "Carriers Of The Message"

The true power of a dream is only realized once it has been interpreted. -Chanan Morrison

God is uncovering His dream interpreters, as in the days of Joseph and Daniel because dreams are an important part of the latter-day outpouring, according to Joel 2:28. The dream interpreter is wrought to make known, "What says the Lord", as is communicated within your dreams. Those that are endowed with the ability to "hear" and interpret a dream are able to understand the messages that are hidden within them. In addition, the dream interpreter articulates this message by not only interpreting your dream but, also by advising wise and appropriate counsel. It is for this purpose that a spirit of wisdom is bonded to, or comes with, the gift of dream interpretation. The dream interpreter will help you maneuver through critical transitions and guide you through significant changes within your life, per the insinuations of your dreams. For dreams, do expose profound and far-reaching truths about you in order to enlighten and influence your heart. The crux of what an interpreter will try to express is that anyone can transform their life by taking into account the meaning of their dreams, since judicious wisdom is not in having dreams, but in waking up and knowing their true meaning.

Wisdom in using dream interpreters

Objectivity

Of course, objectivity is the canvas used when trying to render the meaning of a dream. Oftentimes, individuals cannot (or will not) objectively interpret their own dreams. Our perception, for the most part, is bias. I have found it wise to seek other interpreters to figure out my dreams. The interpreter should be insightful and understanding. He or she will need to discern the possible impact the dream may have on the dreamer's life. Once a dream is explained, its symbols and images are more clear and meaningful because the dream's influence is deepened. The effect on the dreamer is powerful and the dreamer is more prepared for the subsequent outcome.

Manifestation

The act of interpreting significantly effects the manifestation of your dream; it can determine how your dream will "play - out" in your life. Hence, the interpretation of a dream is literally more important than the dream itself. If you have a go od dream, and you do not tell it to an interpreter, the dream remains in a state of potential[25]. It becomes much harder for the positive elements of the dream to manifest in your life.

Additionally, a negative dream can be interpreted from the perspective of the positive that could come because of change. Illustration, a man is running hard from someone he can't see, only to reach a high fence. His only way out is to c limb it. As he attempts to climb and jump over the fence, his pursuer grabs his leg. When he turns and looks his pursuer in the face, he saw or sensed that it was Jesus. The positive side of this dream is that Love is running hard after the dreamer. If the dreamer will allow himself to be caught (the change needed), he will find that God loves, need and wants him, just as much as he needs God in his life. Therefore, the dreamer is counseled to flee evil desires and pursue righteousness, faith, love, and peace, along with those who call on the Lord out of a pure heart. The negative aspect of this dream is that the dreamer is running from genuine Love. He is literally running from God. Knowledge of God's true nature and character, and the extent o f His love for humankind is the key to overcoming the fear within the dreamer.

So to you, be encouraged not to view your negative dreams, as if they truly are hopeless, fatalistic, or final, but rather view them as a God-given siren. For God will never ask you to do something that you absolutely cannot do at that specific moment in your life. He will always give ample enough support and time for rectification and transformation to take place, for He is truly faithful, gracious, kind, and long-suffering, and so has He been with all of us.

In view of this, it would be very beneficial for you to make every effort to find the right person to interpret your dream. He or she should respect the sacredness of God and possess a love for God's people. A person who loves you will always interpret an unpromising dream in a more positive light. This is extremely important because the interpretation will color the dream's influence in your life. Moreover, you should not tell more than one person your negative dream, so say other interpreters that have gone before me, and I agree, as well.[26, 27]

AUTHORITY

Dreams are used to transmit ideals concerned with mankind's relationship to a most sacred and holy God, and mankind's relationship with mankind. This belief is in harmony with the Creator's wisdom in establishing the office of dream interpret er. Ask yourself, did the interpretation of your dream foster a better understanding of God? Did it encourage you to draw closer to Him? For, like all the ways and means of God, prophetic dreams are also meant to lift men to God. Any interpretation tha t falls short of this objective should be considered unauthorized. *Unauthorized, I'll leave that there for now. Only divine sanctioned dream interpreters are authorized to handle these particular posts (dreams) sent from up above, via interpretations. This dream interpreter is given authority to bring to fruition the genuine strength of your dream.

Revered wise men of old made an extraordinary claim regarding an interpreter's authority; dreams are fulfilled according to the interpretation. These authorities believed that speaking a dream's interpretation made that interpretation true; and so declared, "Dreams go according to the mouth"[27]. How seriously this proclamation was taken, we may conclude from Scripture via the words of the head cupbearer, *"And it came to pass, just as he interpreted for us, so it happened" (Genesis 41:13 NKJV)*. Although the butler was a long time coming in revealing his experience while in jail, he remained convinced of Joseph's God-given authority within the arena of dream interpretation. So much so that he put his own life at risk when he recommended Joseph to his king, when one night that king had some very disturbing dreams and desired the meaning of them.

*BACK TO UNAUTHORIZED...

With any inborn gift given men from the hand of the ascended Christ, comes some level of authority. Unfortunately, when people have influence they don't always use it responsibly. The prophets Jeremiah and Zechariah realized humanity's tendency to deceive and to be deceived, as is evidenced by their words. *"Let not your prophets and your diviners that be in the midst of you deceive you...." (Jeremiah 29:8, 9 KJV)*. Moreover, *"For the idols have spoken vanity, and the diviners have seen a lie, and have told false dreams; they comfort in vain" (Zechariah 10:2 KJV)*. Since humankind may be easily misled, it was necessary that God should make known evidences, as would make His interest clearly identifiable. The criterion established i s not if what was interpreted (or prophesied) "came to pass", or is true. The higher standard is whether the dream interpreter points you towards faithfulness in God plus whether their prophetic words prove true. This "boundary marker" is illustrated in the book of Deuteronomy, and to move it, is known as syncretism.

SYNCRETISM[28]

> *"If there arises among you a prophet or a dreamer of dreams, and he gives you a sign or a wonder, and the sign or the wonder comes to pass, of which he spoke to you, saying, 'Let us go after other gods'--which you have not known--'and let us serve them,' you shall not listen to the words of that prophet or that dreamer of dreams, for the Lord your God is testing you to know whether you love the Lord your God with all your heart and with all your soul. (Deuteronomy 13:1-3 NKJV)*

In Deuteronomy 13, prophecy and dreams are to be tested in the same way. If a prophet, or dreamer of dreams whose predictions (or in this case interpretations) are true, contrarily follows and attempts to sway you contrary to the teachings of God's revealed Word, and whose beliefs are possibly akin to spiritists, mediums, or secular humanism, or some other type of syncretism, he or she should be considered an inferior substitute (Jeremiah 23:25-32). Authoritative and authorized prophecy is indicated by whether or not the prophesied event actually comes to pass (or is true), coupled with whether or not the dream interpreter (or prophet) is vested in the Kingdom of the One True Living God and into His higher spiritual principles. A sur e sign of a renegade dream interpreter is if he or she attempts to persuade you to engage in any form of worship that does not guide you into a covenant relationship with Yeshua HaMashiach, entered into via faith, by means of grace (the free and unmerited favor and beneficence of God). Most call Yeshua HaMashiach, Jesus, Wonderful Counselor, Mighty God, Everlasting Father, Prince of Peace, our atonement, advocate, liberator, propitiator, and our salvation. Any dream interpreter, who promotes worship of other gods or adulation of dreams must, of necessity be deemed insubordinate no matter how accurate their interpretations might be.

Adulation of dreams: A young person was becoming overly captivated by their dreams. They began devoting an excessive amount of time to them, heeding their images and symbols, more than God's Word. The person was using their dreams more as a fortune-telling tool, than for wisdom, and unsuspectingly, I was the fortune-teller! I got a call one evening, and as usual, they had a dream. However, instead of talking about a dream, this particular evening, I was guided to relate to the person that their excessive dependence upon dreams could be liken to idolatry (idolatry is "foreign service", any act tha t expresses devotion or fanatical admiration to something or someone other than Adonai Elohim), if they did not balance their tendency to extreme. They got balanced!

To you the reader, no resource available to humankind (prophetic or otherwise) is to be esteemed as above God and His revealed Word, per Holy Writ. Moreover, it is always wise to stay within mainstream Judeo-Christianity. Privately study your bible and let your understanding of it be known to others. Believe nothing, especially religious or sacred, you cannot express in its entirety openly and sensibly to the whole world, don't lie to hide your beliefs or the beliefs and/or actions of others. Reject any sort of beliefs that put forth, "we are gods", and aspire to be worshipped as such. Reject any isolated groups or denominations that claim only their small group alone will be "saved". Jesus died for the entire world and not exclusively for any one sect or western denomination. For although, narrow is the gate and straight is the way (Matthew 7:13), there is approximately seven billion people on earth, according to a 2012 census, if three and half billion are saved, that's bigger than your group. Most importantly, do not die (lay your life down), emotionally, spiritually and/or physically, for no one person or group, Jesus did that on Calvary for all our sins.

That syncretism is encouraged by dream interpreters, when they say, "Let us follow other gods and let us serve them"; affirms that these deceptive and misleading interpreters are not authorized carriers of God's message. They are advocates of a type of worship that is in direct conflict with the inspired written Record. Their manner of service is the use of witchcraft in some form or another, for they hard-press people to believe what they say, and compel individuals to follow other gods.

This also suggests that there is no direct way to, immediately tell an unauthorized dream interpreter from a genuinely authorized one. For with contemporary society being as it is, you may never know who, what, and/or how one truly worships. Moreover, as history has proven repeatedly through the years, people can be deceived, and sometimes are willingly deceived. Nonetheless, God's counsel within dreams is available and profitable to anyone who sincerely attempts to understand His workings within their life, via their dreams. Dreamer, if you accept your Heavenly Father's Words and store up His commands within you, turning your ear to wisdom and applying your heart to understanding, calling out for insight and crying aloud for discernment. Looking for it as for silver and searching for it as for hidden treasure, then you will know the fear of the Lord and find the knowledge of God you seek. For the Lord gives wisdom and from His mouth comes knowledge and understanding.

Then you will understand what is right and just and fair – every good path. When wisdom enters your heart and knowledge becomes sweet to your soul, discretion will protect you, and understanding will guard you. To deliver you from the ways of wickedness, and from people whose words are perverse, who leave the straight paths to walk in darkness gladly, whose paths are crooked and who are devious in their ways (Proverbs 2:1-6, 9-15). This is one of God's covenant promises to you and it will help you discern authorized interpreters, prophets, teachers, preachers, pastors, from illegal ones, as well as the many other various forms of syncretism.

WHY DO DREAM INTERPRETERS AND INTERPRETATIONS DIFFER FROM ONE ANOTHER?

There are three levels of answers to this question.

Level One: (Judeo-Christian Interpreters)

Anyone who has had their dream interpreted by more than one person has asked or wondered why do different dream interpreters give so many possible meanings for the imagery we see in our dreams? Each dream interpreter combines signs and symbols in his or her own way, according to their own "knack". God has made each interpreter, as with all his children, unique for a purpose. One interpreter's innate inclination might be to focus primarily on the colors within a dream; another may master numbers as they relate to time, while another's concentration will predominantly be on the image portrayed, while not considering colors, numbers. All the uniqueness of each interpreter is important and needed. If you can picture a specialist, you can get this analogy. If you had a heart problem, you would go to a cardiologist, if cancer an oncologist, for female matters, an ob-gyn; for stomach and intestinal issues, a gastroenterologist, for general issues, your primary physician, who may refer you to a specialist if need be. All the specialists are very important; however, each specialist is only required at the time when their specialty is needed. Even more, consider the gospel writers, they all told the same story, but from different standpoints. God has given us all individual tendencies that we may work together interdependently (Romans 12:4-8). Julie Ackerman, so eloquently put it, "We shine the brightest not when we see our own likeness reflected in others, but when each of us performs the distinct functions that God designed for us to do".

Having then gifts differing according to the grace that is given us (Romans 12:6-8), let us use them, distributing to the necessity of all. Note, while Romans 12:6-8 is speaking of many distinctively different gifts; within this context, the different methods of dream interpretation, e.g. an interpreter's understanding of colors, of periods of time, or of images, are also distinctively different gifts. If you are before a dream interpreter whose specialty is colors or "times frames", then their particular gifting and expression is required to interpret your dream. If you are before me, or referencing this guide regarding a dream, then my particular area of interpretation and style of expression is required. You can confidently trust that God has led you to the right interpreter for the interpretation of your dream. God sent the dream; and it is a small thing for Him t o direct you to an interpreter. By God's wise designing, all are wonderfully made, every part essential, and in perfect balance laid (Anonymous). These words are as beautiful, as they are true. However, the question remains.

"IF THEY DIFFER THEN WHO'S RIGHT?"

It is believed that there were twenty-four interpreters of dreams in Jerusalem during the time of the Second Temple. If a person told his dream to all twenty-four interpreters, the dreamer might very well receive twenty-four different interpretations.[29] Remarkably, rabbinical sages teach that all twenty-four interpretations could actually play themselves out in the physical world. If they differed, then how could they all have been right? I know, just keep reading and it'll straighten itself out, hopefully.

LET'S DEMYSTIFY THIS, FOR CONTEMPORARY RELEVANCE SAKE

Example, if you tell one interpreter your dream of being naked, he or she may very well tell you that this dream symbolizes exposure of a shameful secret. If you tell another interpreter the same dream, he or she might state, "Your dream implies that you will be stripped of everything". A third could tell you that some form of spiritual adultery has taken place within the life of the dreamer. A fourth, "You are found unprepared and thus lacking". A fifth interpreter may summarize yo ur dream as such: Exposure of the bleak and desolate condition of your spiritual life will result in great loss. Yet another, especially if you've given him or her a gift, may interpret your dream from a very positive light, "You will walk humbly before the Lord". They are all right! Since nakedness is defined as a lack of any kind of "covering", naturally and spiritually. To find yourself in such a state is sure to bring some manner of corrective admonishment.

Since they are all right, my question to you is, how do you need to hear your truth?

Case in point, Joseph's interpretation of the butler and baker's dreams (Genesis 40) focused primarily on moments of time because time was of the essence to them, so fate would have them presented to Joseph for his style of interpretation and his way of communicating that. Joseph's mastery of "time frames" within dreams is extraordinary. In addition, his interpretations and expression tended to be short and to the point, (most men communicate in this way naturally); "in three days you will be restored as pharaoh's cupbearer", and to the other, "in three days you will die". If further details or counsel was required, he gave it, nothing more, and nothing less. Another interpreter's preference might have been to focus primaril y on the colors within the dreams of the cupbearer and baker. His or her interpretation might have been of this nature: The green vines and the white baskets, respectively, denote some kinds of spiritual privileges and some manner of a complete purification process. The interpreter may have expounded on the type of privileges or process, as they related contextually to each dream. The dreamer, guided to this interpreter, may have needed to hear the interpreter's full elaborations on their dream, especially wanting to hear the why, of the life granted, or the sentenced of death.

Reader, how do you need to hear your truth, short and to the point, or more clarifying details and additional illustrations? It is obvious that dates and times were of the utmost importance to both the butler and baker and Joseph's specialty and style was what they needed at that time. A discussion on the meaning of all the symbols within their dreams, and possible answers as to why one lives, and the other dies was not necessary. More than likely, they knew those answers already. Hence, God directed the butler and baker to Joseph; one who specialized in what He wanted communicated at that time. Thus, it is only within the interpreter's style of unfolding a dream that interpretations may differ, if they do differ. Each interpreter, whether his or her concentration is on colors, symbols, or something else, can actually be right. OK, it's according to the interpreter's style.

Level Two: Other Interpreters (not Judeo-Christian)

Interpreters that are not of the Judeo-Christian belief, but are of some other Abrahamic, or monotheistic, religious influence, will interpret your dream from the perspective of their spiritual belief systems. Resulting in interpretations th at will oftentimes, differ from a Judeo-Christian dream interpreter. The difference is primarily due to particular persuasions. For instance, a dream of Jesus may mean one thing to a Jewish interpreter, another thing to a Muslim interpreter, and another thing to a Christian interpreter. Dream interpreters, as with all spiritual guides, will oftentimes attract people who have the same or similar belief systems as they do. Like kind will attract like kind, and their interpretations will contain meaning for that individual. I may not agree with the interpretation, as well, they may not agree with my take on a dream. Thus, individuals drawn to this dream interpreter, namely interpreters (not Judeo-Christian), according to my observations, are usually of similar beliefs and religious persuasion. However, as with all things, there are exceptions. Pharaoh, a non-believer in the Hebrew

God, attracted Joseph, a follower of Elohim, to interpret his dreams, as with Daniel and Nebuchadnezzar. The implications of these two examples are clear, again, humanity carries a common storehouse of symbols and meanings that transcends time, culture, race, or creed, in our collective unconscious, and this implies that God is not constrained or limited—the Creative Force is limitless (Ayn Sof). God is all possibility. He can communicate with any human He chooses, by any means He chooses, and still get His truth expressed.

Level Three: Other Interpreters

Then there are those who...

While it is true that God endows all humankind with natural abilities, and skills and these are irrevocable. In that He does not take them back once, He has bestowed them within you; they are yours to keep in the interim. There are those who do not have a distinct proclivity towards their Benefactor, Jehovah God, nor of His ways. Their gifts, presented at the altars of demons, are for sensual benefit only.

To this, I quote Moses, *"When they say, 'let us go after other gods, which you have not known — and let us serve them, you shall not listen to the words of that prophet or that dreamer of dreams".* (Deuteronomy 13:1-3 ESV)

This type of dream interpreter view dreams and their symbols from a secular, dark perspective; the source of their knowledge is limited to tools instigated by devils. They use books containing incantations and other dark sinister means to conjure up demons to extrapolate the meanings of dreams. This dream interpreter is of the same kind as conjurers, mediums, sorcerers, and witches. They say, *"Let us go after other gods and follow them".* It is their belief that all symbols presented to you, whether in dreams, fantasy, meditation, or guided imagery are coded messages from self to self. They are unable to acknowledge God's providence on any level. It is also their belief that the meaning of symbols is what you want or need them to be hence a more favorable interpretation. They often herald peace when there is none, pointing the dreamer down a road of possible catastrophe. This interpreter's interpretations will differ greatly and to the highest degree from all interpreters. In addition, as they follow no God sanctioned principles for dream interpretation, but pursue occult practices, their interpretations ought not, be compared to Judeo-Christian interpreters, as to differences. This dream interpreter's way is the very antithesis of Christ and His interpreters.

They are so not divinely sanctioned as is proven by the words contained within Daniel 2:2-12. The occasion recorded, tells of a time when a king ordered his magicians, conjurers, sorcerers, soothsayers, and astrologers to tell him his dream and its interpretation, upon threat of death. This undertaking forced upon the diviners by their king, was beyond their means an d tools, per their own acknowledgement, *"There is not a man on earth who could declare the matter for the king inasmuch as no great king or ruler has ever asked anything like this of any magician, conjurer or Chaldean (soothsayer or astrologer). Moreover the thing which the king demands is difficult, and there is no one else (no man) who could declare it to the king except gods, whose dwelling place is not with mortal flesh"* (Daniel 2:10, 11 NASB).

This task was impossible to those types of dream interpreters because they were limited to paraphernalia and knowledge instigated and influenced by demons. However, it was not impossible for the Most High's dream interpreter, Daniel, "a man on earth who could declare the matter", via prayer and faith in Yahweh. After this wondrous event, namely the revealing of the dream by God to Daniel, and the declaring of the king's dream by Daniel, I'm quite sure that at least one or two of those interpreters turned to Daniel's God, renounced their gods, and learned a thing or two from the teachings of Daniel. For, Daniel's teachings did have the capacity to turn them away from the obvious pitfalls of their occult practices to the lawful functions of genuine wise men. Furthermore, it is my belief, per the biblical narrative cited, that God ordained dream interpreters, might even be called upon in these last days to carry out the charge of recalling dreams forgotten (or intentionally not revealed) by the dreamer, and to interpret them.

A woman, referred to me by a common friend, called me one evening to share her dream experience. She expressed, "Before I went to sleep, I prayed that my god would show himself to me". That night she dreamt that as she was swinging on a swing, she noticed that the ground beneath her and all around her was desolate and barren, and then a dog with large red eyes, shaped like saucers was coming out of the sky towards her. She wanted to know what it meant. As this dream presented great desolation and an animal of folklore or myth, I wondered was I the interpreter for her. Nonetheless, I gave her what I knew. Namely, this was her god and the desolation she observed is the inheritance of those who worshipped that god. How it is worship or why, I don't know. According to folklore, this is Black Shuck, a devil dog or hellhound, with black shaggy hair and enormous fiery red eyes the size of saucers. He seeks lost souls, and is an indication of doom. I believe that this dreamer would have heard a more favorable interpretation had she sought a dream interpreter similar to the level three interpreters.

In light of all the different interpretations that do come about from the many dream interpreters upon this earth, prophetic dreams are from YHWH and are always within the context of His covenant with humankind, per Holy Writ. If the interpretation you receive is not within that context and in accord with it; it may prove misleading. Even to the separation of your soul from heaven. The higher principle is always whether or not the interpretations of your dream encourages a greater intimacy with, and obedience to, Jesus Christ (John 14:6), as well as promote spiritual maturity, faith in God, and in His truths.

The Language of the Branches: The Language of Dreams

the words which I have said to you are spirit and they are life (John 6:63 BBE)

Billions of symbols speak on behalf of their spiritual counterparts, and the links that connect both realms are branches (see Chapter One, Genesis of Dreams). While this knowledge is far wide and deep, and does express God's infinite wisdom, I will do my best; according to the knowledge, I have innately and through study, to interpret this special language of the branches just for you.

Your Responsibility

To you, who have taken this challenge to explore the significance of your dreams, a dream is like a puzzle in which each piece is connected and vital to the big picture. So do,

1. Pray for truth and wisdom inwardly, and for the courage to apply it, God will grant wisdom. If, by just asking, you might get wisdom, one may suffer needlessly, because he or she will not ask Jesus for it. Ask Jesus as often as you need to, regarding all of your emotional concerns, considering how personal His promises are, He will meet you in your need.

2. Share with someone your dream interpretation; an objective opinion will always help keep your deductions unbiased.

3. Keep in remembrance; your dreams are primarily for you.

4. Write down (journal) your dreams.

5. The following is a list of 21 categories of dream topics. All categories include a short description of each topic, subcategories, and their referents, plus a suggested course of action and a specific meaning section. This list is not comprehensive, but it is a good tool to help you get started on discovering the meaning of your dreams.

6. Read the entire introduction of the category, before selecting a symbol. A category may be broad and wide, including many subcategories, e.g. Actions and Activities category. All Symbols and Referents + Notes (1, 2, 3, etc.) + Notes relevant to a particular category + Suggested Course of Action or Specific Meaning = a more comprehensive interpretation.

7. Take into account your entire dream's context, highlighting all the individual symbols, noting key symbols. For it will be the sum of those key symbols, the surrounding conditions, the activity, background settings, circumstances, emotions, events, perspectives, situations, people, places, things, and words that will help explain your dream's meaning.

8. Note key symbols: Search index for relevant category. For example, key symbol: Hotel or Kitchen – relevant category, BUILDINGS, STRUCTURES; key symbol: Puppy or Meat – relevant category, ANIMALS; key symbol: Spoiled Fruit – relevant category, AGRICULTURE, key symbol: Seven Sisters – relevant categories: PEOPLE and NUMBERS; key word: Love – relevant category: EMOTIONS, and so on, do search index.

9. Most all symbols have dual, triple or more, meanings. Example, interpretation may read: This dream has two meanings (choose one). Dreamer will be asked, to choose one meaning or one, two, or all meanings may apply. Additionally, there are also, one, two, or three parts to a choice (e.g. a, b, c). It is suggested that dreamer choose the interpretation that is closest to your dream symbols and/or most relevant to your life situation.

10. Consider any biblical significance your symbols may personally mean to you, include scripture and commentary (e.g. blood on a piece of wood, may represent the passion of Christ to you, and the redemptive work of His cross), journal the scripture and commentary. At this point, your dream is interpreted there is no need to proceed any further with the particular interpretation.

11. As some symbols are very personal to our lives, dreamer may also consider your own personal, special, or cultural associations with symbols. These symbols are referred to as probables. As long as the interpretation is kept within the principles of spiritual boundary markers, landmarks, and property lines, (see Chapter One, section entitled, Spiritualizing Boundary Markers, Landmarks, and Property Lines).

12. Journal and Interpret your symbols chronologically (or the last first); for it will be in that order that your interpretation will begin to unfold, and perhaps events or situations will play out.

13. Many symbols will have the same meaning.

14. All Suggested Courses of Action will end the same, See "PRAYER OF DELIVERANCE"[30], page 897.

15. Notes (1, 2, 3, etc.): Note (1) of each category will always read as such. Unless "Otherwise noted", if, in your everyday living, your awaked state, as part of your lifestyle, work, or ministerial activities, or a special event, you have a very real connection to the particular symbol, skip interpretation and go to Specific Meaning at the end of the category. "Otherwise noted", will give more information on the symbol. Note (2) of most categories will have you consider Probables. Note 3 of each category will help determine who your dream is for; you or another. Note 4 of most categories will read as such. Consider all the people, places, backgrounds, and activity highlighted within your dream; this is to help you discover a part of yourself on some level or another. Other additional information is included in Notes (5, 6, and so on). Subcategories have their own notes.

16. Specific Meaning[31]: When assigning significance to symbols, be careful to distinguish between general and specific meanings of symbols. General meanings are those meanings that are primarily common to that symbol. Specific meanings are those meanings that are specifically relevant to the dreamer's life. For example, all buildings within dreams generally reveal the varied conditions of one's spiritual and/or physical person. However, to a person who is an architect, real estate developer, or anyone connected to the design of, building of, or whose work is construction, this symbol will quite often be specifically related to your literal life's work and/or activity, and not your spiritual life; thus the section, Specific Meaning. This section is an addendum at the end of each category. If your dream is specific to you, skip interpretation and go to Specific Meaning, at the end of that category. Examples of "specifics" are included within the introduction of each category. The specifics should be relevant to your lifestyle and closely resemble your real-life situations. Meaning it can actually occur during your awaked state.

17. In addition to the varied interpretations of a specific symbol, other common words, expressions, usages, (e.g. slang or clichés), or a 'probable' that are metaphorically represented by that symbol are also considered (primary source: Encarta ® World English Dictionary © & (P) 1998-2004 Microsoft Corporation). This section is an addendum at the end of each category or subcategory. For other idioms, refer to other sources available to you, e.g. a Bible, a dictionary, encyclopedia, or the internet.

18. Since the following list of symbols is not extensive, dreamer is encouraged to seek biblical guidelines for recognizing the metaphorical meaning of your particular symbols within your dreams. See also, other relevant research to determine the metaphorical meaning of your symbols, depicted within your dream, via a Bible concordance, Bible illustrated dictionary, encyclopedia, or internet. Having done your research you should be able to determine some basic behaviors or attributes your Lord and Savior wants you to focus on.

19. Do not be prone to take one symbol that may seem negative, and run with it upset and crying. Consider the entire dream, and remember your dreams are primarily warnings. People and situations can, and often do, change for good, even in one day.

20. Ask yourself, "What did I experience the day or evening before the dream?" Consider your emotions and thoughts the day or evening before the dream. Perhaps that evening you were reading the short story, *Bitter Anguish*, and then later that night you dreamt that you were standing at the pearly gate. This would not be as significant as if you "out of the blue" without prior influence had a dream about being at the pearly gate one night. That may be a good time to be prone to running and crying. Breathe, I'm only kidding.

21. Ask yourself, have you dreamt this dream or a similar one before? What did it mean then? It will probably have the same meaning now. If so, there is no need to proceed any further with the particular interpretation.

22. It is very important to know that dreams are not written in stone. The beneficial or influential effects of dreams within our lives are primarily subject to the power of free choice and application. For example, had Pharaoh chose to disbelieve Joseph's interpretation of his dreams or decided against Joseph's suggested course of action, Egypt too, would have suffered the grave effects of the coming famine. Had Joseph, the husband of Mary, freely chose not to believe the message within his dream, *"do not be afraid to take Mary home as your wife" (Matthew 1:19 NIV)* more than likely he would not have married her.

23. Any health care information contained herein is for informational purposes only. The interpretations, or suggestions, are not meant to diagnosis the nature or cause of any illness, or disorder, nor to treat, cure, or prevent any disease. You should not use the information contained within for self-diagnosing, or self-treating a health problem or disease, or for prescribing any medication. Before considering any medical process, physical activity, medication, or diet, always consult your physician first or other appropriate professional health care providers. If you have, or suspect that you have a medical problem, promptly contact your professional health care provider. The primary resource referenced within this work, regarding health suggestions is "Healthy Aging: Keeping Mentally Fit as You Age", The Geriatric Mental Health Foundation.

24. These principles, in addition to all presented thus far, will almost certainly cause the prophetic implications of your dreams to speak to you.

25. If your appreciation of dream symbols and your interpretations differ from those given here, just know that our Heavenly Father will meet you in your dreams according to your expectations. For dreams, do take into account the veracity of the inner person.

I pray that you find God's goodness and faithfulness in a new way, and that you benefit from your exploration.

Sample dream:

Two females were leaving a home. The older female stopped at the fence to observe something. They both were dressed very casual.

Highlighted symbols within this dream: Home, fence, two females, sunny day

All Symbols and Referents + Suggested Course of Action or Specific Meaning = a more in depth interpretation

First, consider if this dream is specific or general. How would the interpretation of this dream differ if the dreamer was a real estate agent, home assessor, or was moving into an area similar to the one depicted? If dreamer is a real estate agent, he or she may skip the interpretation and go directly to Specific Meaning of that category. See examples of "specifics" included within the introduction of each category.

Try interpreting the sample dream yourself. Review all symbols (e.g. home, fence, two females, and sunny day). For more information, see index or relevant category for the particulars within your dream (e.g. Buildings, People, and/or Weather). Read introduction to each category. Pull together all the information and summarize. If relevant, include the suggested course of action. What is this dream conveying, if anything, to the dreamer?

INTERPRETING CHILDREN AND TEENS DREAMS

One day some parents brought their children to Jesus so He could touch and bless them, but the disciples scolded the parents for bothering Him. When Jesus saw what was happening, He was angry with His disciples. He said to them, "Let the children come to Me. Don't stop them! For, the Kingdom of God belongs to those who are like these children. I tell you the truth, anyone who doesn't receive the Kingdom of God like a child will never enter it." Then He took the children in His arms, and placed His hands on their heads and blessed them. (Mark 10:13-16 NLT)

The disciples supposed that the children were too young to understand and experience spiritual things. Nonetheless, these children could receive from the Lord, and they did receive, for Jesus took them in His arms and blessed them. There have been children brought to Christ at an extremely young age (1 Samuel 1:22; 2:18; Luke 2:22, 23). That, children even as young as two or three years of age, may have an unusually early spiritual development or maturity of the knowledge of God, and of His grace, is not altogether unbelievable.

Thus, God commands parents to bring up their children in the way in which they should go (according to their naturally unique talents, often manifested within their play, e.g. orator, leader, teacher, doctor, scientist, lawyer, activist, preacher. To prepare them for what they are truly designed for), and when they are old they will not depart from it (Proverbs 22:6). Ordinarily the vessel retains the savor with which it was first seasoned. (Matthew Henry Commentary)

Children are their calling in the making, and their dreams, often at very early ages, will at times reflect their purpose.

A beautiful example of this,

She (Hannah) said to her husband, *"After the boy is weaned, I will take him and present him before the Lord, and he will live there always. So now, I give him to the Lord. For his whole life he will be given over to the Lord"*. And, he worshiped the Lord there (1 Samuel 1:22, 28 NIV). Some years later, via a *vision within a dream, Samuel, at approximately 12 years of age, was summoned by God to prophesy (the Jewish Historian, Josephus).

* In 1 Samuel 3:1, the word vision in the Hebrew is hazon[5], which means to see via dream or vision and prophesy (see: Other prophetic dreams, Oneirovatic).

... and while Samuel was lying down, that the LORD called Samuel. And he answered, "Here I am!" So he ran to Eli and said, "Here I am, for you called me." And he said, "I did not call; lie down again." And he went and lay down. (Now Samuel did not yet know the LORD, nor was the word of the LORD yet revealed to him.) And the LORD called Samuel again the third time. Then he arose and went to Eli, and said, "Here I am, for you did call me." Then Eli perceived that the LORD had called the boy. Therefore Eli said to Samuel, "Go, lie down; and it shall be, if He calls you, that you must say, 'Speak, LORD, for Your servant hears.' "So Samuel went and lay down in his place. (1 Samuel 3:2-5, 7-9 NKJV)

The young teen Samuel, before he knew God, had a prophetic revelation in the form of a vision while sleeping. The Lord called Samuel in such a way that Samuel awoke several times, thinking that his mentor, Eli, was calling him. Eli kept telling the boy to go back to sleep. Eli, finally realizing that God was calling the boy, counseled him to go and lie back down, and whe n he heard his name called again, answer, "Speak, Lord, for your servant is listening". God revealed to Samuel, Eli's personal failure as a father and of coming judgment. Reluctantly, he prophesied to his mentor. Afterward, Samuel went on to become a great prophet of God (1 Samuel 3:1-19).

I still remember a dream of Jesus coming down to me and giving me a message about the end of the world. Recalling the neighborhood my family was living in at that time, I was no more than 12 years of age when I dreamt that. This stirred my interest in dreams. From that moment on, I became drawn to books, workshops, and any information that pertained to dreams. Thus, some 50+ years later, here I am writing about a "calling" that began with a dream when I was a very young child.

I can also remember my younger sister having a dream, and while dreaming she spoke out that she was Nefertiti, the queen of the Nile. This is my earliest childhood memory. She was in kindergarten and I was in the second grade. I know for a sure fact, we had absolutely no knowledge of who Nefertiti was or of Egypt at that time. Both, my sister and I are dream interpreters, and yes, she has a look of that of Queen Nefertiti, beautiful. Many adults will attest to the fact that a coup le of their childhood dreams echoed some of their life choices as adults.

The preceding duly noted, for the most part, children and teens, dream about human relationships, standards of behavior, and/or what they are experiencing now. As their lives involve significant changes and major adjustments, their dreams will often mirror their daily concerns, symbolically. Children and teens deal with the same spiritual and emotional issues as adults, but on a different level, using different tools, as they lack experience; thus their dreams will take into account this lack of experience and knowledge. Be that as it may, if they do not understand the messages in their dreams, they may miss, the 'rod and staff' of God, aka His correction and guidance. By learning to interpret their dreams from an early age, children will have a better chance of figuring out what they want from life, and what 'life' wants from them.

PARENTS ARE GOD'S INTERPRETERS FOR THEIR CHILDREN'S DREAMS

As Eli was to Samuel, when a child first becomes aware of his or her dreams, and can relate it to their parent(s), until approximately 16 years of age (+ or – a couple of years), depending on the maturity level of the teen. Interpretation of children and teens dreams should be rendered by their parents and given as serious consideration as adult dreams. It can be as simple as, what Eli told Samuel, "Go and lie back down, and when you hear your name called again, answer, "Speak, Lord, for your servant is listening", or as intricate as interpreting a nightmare.

Interpreting children and teens dreams can be intricate, and those anointed by God, to 'hear' and understand their dreams are, primarily, their parents or guardians. Parents are God's authorized interpreters of their children's dreams. Parents are, divinely enabled, to understand the messages hidden within their child's dreams. By helping your child interpret their dreams, the parent will gain further insight into what their fears are, and any trouble they may be having at school, w ith friends, or at home. Parents can teach their children helpful dream interpretation skills early. In addition, if you equip them with a few helpful tips on how to figure out what their dreams are expressing, it will go a long way in easing their fears. Once they realize that dreams are messages from God, sent to help them figure out solutions to their problems, the mystification of dreams will go away.

Children Nightmares

Parents need to be mindful of what is said around their young children, as they take comments such as "I should have killed you before you were born", "the devil is going to get you if you are bad", or "you are good for nothing", or "I don't believe Reverend Wood did that to you", more literal than adults. These types of statements may create confusing visuals in their minds, which are then, turned into nightmares that wake them up screaming. So too, the turn-arounds, changes, and ups and downs, within a child's life can unquestionably be frightening. The child's dreaming mind takes any fear and automatically turns it into something terrifying. In addition, character traits from ancestors, namely genetic codes and traits, will often trouble, and taunt children in their dreams, especially generational issues. These spirits attempt to "bend" the child's personality towards a certain direction, oftentimes towards a way that is desolate and wicked, for it is Satan's scheme to kill and make desolate all children; thus, to keep them from raising up and leading their generation to Christ (see the birth of Moses, Exodus 1:15-2:10). Question, is there one person that triggers your child nightmares frequently? Consider, and react appropriately, perhaps "hide" the child from that person. Do not think to protect or cover a possible predator, at the expense of your child's safety and sanity, those choices never end good for the child or for the parent.

Parent, although a child's articulation skills may be limited due to their small vocabulary, simple pictures, drawn by the child, can often explain to their parents what has frightened them. Discerning the symbol and its' meaning, the p arent can decide the best steps to take in handling the fears of the child.

Tips for interpreting children, teens' dreams

1. If your child does not remember his or her dream, do not coerce, push, or pressure them to remember. For children dreams, most often result from their daily activities. These sorts of dreams are usually about their routine and mundane activities or the anxieties that overwhelm their mind during the day. Very much like ordinary dreams, see Chapter One, Chalom, these dreams are an inner release mechanism, which helps provide children with emotional balance. These dreams are not significant, and do not warrant special attention; therefore, are oftentimes forgotten.

2. Get the child to write down as much as they can remember about their dream. For younger children, pictures will do. This may be a good time for your child to start a journal, even one with pictures.

3. Name (or draw) all persons, places, things, animals, attributes, and actions in the dream, e.g. mommy, daddy, friend, uncle, monster, avatar, teacher, stranger, dog, airplane, spaceship, car, train, horse, running, laughing, scared, dead, crying, dark, fire.

4. Ask your child to label how they feel about each. Example: Dad is safe, strong, bad, scary, or mean. Have child explain why, in simple terms. For example, airplane is high in the sky, helps me get away, vacation. My friend makes me happy, someone to play and talk with. Bobby is a bully. Monster is scary. Avatar is a killer. Teacher is nice, or not nice. What makes teacher good or bad? A stranger is danger. Did a stranger talk to them at school? Dog is good, bad, or a protector.

5. Write the labels according to the order, which they appear in the dream, to tell a story. Example: With (dad) I was going away in the (airplane). We got away from the (monster) that looked like the scary bully at school. In the airplane, a stranger or an avatar gave me an ugly doll or nasty candy.

6. Give each dream a title, e.g. "Safety with dad", "Vacation in the airplane", or "Ugly doll"

7. What does being safe with dad mean to your child? Is he or she out of danger? What does vacation mean to your child, getting away from someone or some place? What does spaceship in the sky mean to your child, rising above his or her fears? What was the name of the avatar? Describe the ugly doll, or who did the doll look like?

8. What possible dealings did the child have with each person, place, thing, or animal that day?

9. If applicable, what are some action steps, the parent and/or child can take to help the child?

10. Pray with your child for God to help them with whatever they need.

11. If a violation has occurred, call and involve the appropriate authorities.

Teaching your child to glean from their dreams is like having an extra godparent on board, for children's dreams can be supportive, and enlightening.

Symbols and Referents

CHAPTER FOUR

ACTIONS AND ACTIVITIES

"Yet, wisdom is proved right by its actions"
(Matthew 11:19 GW)

Remember your Creator when you are young, before the days of trouble come and the years catch up with you. They will make you say, "I have found no pleasure in them." Remember your Creator before the sun, the light, the moon, and the stars turn dark, {and} the clouds come back with rain. Remember your Creator when those who guard the house tremble, strong men are stooped over, the women at the mill stop grinding because there are so few of them {and} those who look out of the windows see a dim light. Remember your Creator when the doors to the street are closed, the sound of the mill is muffled, you are startled at the sound of a bird, {and} those who sing songs become quiet. Remember your Creator when someone is afraid of heights and of dangers along the road, the almond tree blossoms, the grasshopper drags itself along, {and} the caper bush has {no} fruit. Mortals go to their eternal rest, and mourners go out in the streets. Remember your Creator before the silver cord is snapped, the golden bowl is broken, the pitcher is smashed near the spring, and the water wheel is broken at the cistern. Then the dust {of mortals} goes back to the ground as it was before, and the breath of life goes back to God who gave it.
(Ecclesiastes 12:1-7 GW)

This category deals with behaviors, proceedings, dealings and interplay, all carried out to achieve personal goals, hopes, and desires. This category, although not comprehensive, includes domestic, economic, labor, leisure, social needs, and other actions and activities that are connected to human life and its' performances.

For some short descriptions of types, phrases, and/or other processes and particulars, connected in some way to this category, see category content list, or index.

All Symbols and Referents, Notes (1, 2, 3, etc.), Suggested Course of Action, and Specific Meaning offer guidance toward a more comprehensive interpretation.

Notes

1. Unless otherwise noted elsewhere, if, in your everyday living, your awaked state, as part of your lifestyle, work, or ministerial activities, or a special event, you have a very real connection with the specific activity within your dream (see content list for this category), skip referent, and go to Specific Meaning of that particular category.

    Otherwise noted, this dream may be a Prophetically Simple Dream (see Chapter One: The 60th Part of Prophecy). Whereas, the dreamer is warned to stop any unwise, reckless, or dangerous actions or activities, e.g., you should cease any daredevil or impetuous activity, especially if this is a thing within the dreamer's life. If any of the preceding is happening, or was depicted within your dream, this dream is a first step intervention and an alarm. Skip interpretation and re-consider your activity as harmful, hurtful, or life threatening, at present. Handle the situation wisely, b y first thanking God for the warning, for Adonai Elohim knows all. Also, see Specific Meaning at the end of the category, section entitled, Note (Specific Meaning).

    Otherwise noted, per your lifestyle, if your dream closely resembled real life situations, meaning it can actually occur (or has occurred) during your awaked state; this dream may be an Ordinary Dream, resulting from your daily activities (see Chapter One, Chalom). These sorts of dreams are usually about your routine and mundane activities or anxieties that overwhelm your mind during the day. They are an inner release mechanism, which helps provide you with emotional balance and the maintaining of your sanity. These dreams are not significant, and do not warrant special attention.

2. Probables: As actions and activities are frequently demonstrated in many, and very personal ways; for example, does a particular action or activity remind you of a particular person, place, thing, or environment? Thus, could the action or activity depicted be a possible probable (see Chapter One, section entitled, Probables)? Hence, dreamer may also consider your own personal and special associations with various actions and activities, as long as the interpretation is kept within the principles of spiritual boundary markers, landmarks, and property lines, (see Chapter One, section entitled, Spiritualizing Boundary Markers, Landmarks, and Property Lines).

3. Determine who your dream is for you or another. Always, considering yourself first, reflecting on your present behaviors. Ask yourself, why am I dreaming about this now? What is this dream revealing about me? Have I taken on new attributes? What about my beliefs, doctrine, or philosophy, are they still based on Holy Writ? Is there something I need to know about those I am ministering to or serving?

Remember your actions and activities within your dream. Were you the only participant within your dream? Did you play a major role? For example, did you initiate the action or activity? Did you try to encourage someone else to do something; did you take over the action or activity? Unless otherwise noted elsewhere, an answer of yes, to one or more of these, or similar questions, is a good indicator that your dream is about the dreamer. Dreamer what symbolic "actions or activities" are you sowing? This sowing can be of a sacrosanct or sacrilegious doctrine or philosophy; thus, this dream. On another vein, could you be reaping the results of good choices, during this season within your life? Are you in a process of renewal, sanctification, or transformation? Are you judgmental, self-righteous, or intolerant of others? In light of your dream, via the relevant interpretation, do you believe that your behavior will enhance or endanger your well-being, safety, and/or happiness, if so, how and why? Do you believe that your belief system will strengthen or weaken you spiritually in any way, if so, how and why? Is death a possibility, perhaps because of lifestyle? See following relevant subcategory, the interpretation is about and for you.

Did someone else initiate the action or activity? Did someone else try to encourage you to do something; did another take over the action or activity? Unless otherwise noted elsewhere, an answer of yes, to one or more of these, or similar questions, is a good indicator that your dream is about another and their role, and/or influential effects, within the life of the dreamer. Consider, is someone greatly influencing your physical, spiritual, or mental health, your understanding, perspective, and reasoning regarding spiritual issues? Are they enhancing your spiritual and/or literal prosperity, or are they responsible for the dwindling thereof? Could they be influencing your ministry, on some level? Do you know someone whose life activities or physical being is similar to that which stood out the most within your dream? Could it be that person? If you sense that your dream is for or about another, the question as to why you have been made privy to this information, and how do you factor into the equation, should be seriously considered along with necessary actions. Perhaps the dreamer is being made aware of the plight of someone, and you are to get involved (see Chapter One, Are You Ready to Hear the Messages in Your Dreams, section entitled, The 10% for others).

If your dream is for, or about another: Dreams that reference others and the revelation within those dreams, is not given haphazardly to any individual, but only to those with the ability, and influence to do something with the information; this is also prophecy. With that, journal the following questions, and if unable to answer the questions now, this denotes that the person, represented within your dream, will enter your life shortly. Are you entering into a personal relationship with someone? Do you not know or understand what you're looking at, especially certain behaviors, when learning about this person? Has someone new entered your life or maybe you've just begun opening up to someone not so new, and have started listening to their advice, accepting their assistance, or are you supporting or enabling someone? Are you in denial regarding the toxicity of one of your present relationships, particularly a spouse, family member, or friend? Are you anxious, concerned, frightened, and/or troubled by recent changes in your behavior, especially because of someone's influence upon your life at present? Have you allowed someone to convince you to deceive another? Have you recently become aware of (or is being made aware of, via your dream) certain undesirable behaviors within you towards another? Are you trying to cut ties with one that is bad company? Have you just joined (or re-joined) a church, fellowship, or social group?

Note: If your dream has attributes that indicate that your dream is about you, and other attributes that indicate that your dream is about another, dreamer should consider that your dream is about you and another. For example, while you may have participated in the action or activity, thus indicating that the dream is about the dreamer, someone else may have initiated the action or activity, thus indicating that your dream is about another. Therefore, while your dream is about the dreamer, the dreamer should expect the role and/or influential effects of another, also plays a part in your interpretation. For example, dreamer may have been emotionally wounded, violated, hurt, by another, and now that hurt has bred bitterness and an unforgiving spirit within the dreamer, again, see relevant interpretation.

More questions to consider. Why has the person been allowed within your life, and/or how did they get there? Again, if unable to answer the questions now, this denotes that the person, represented within your dream, will enter your life shortly. If their activity, within your dream, has proven positive, via the interpretation, this someone will prove, unwittingly, to be a very strong ally, benefactor, defender, and supporter. God has sent this someone into your life to help you carry out your next endeavor by enlarging your spiritual capacity. Allow the strength of that person's character to guide, help, and support you. On the other hand, if his or her presence and/or activity, within your dream, proved negative, via the interpretation, for sure, this person will prove to be a very strong and formidable challenge for you, perhaps unto death. If negative, your dream is a dire warning. Take steps accordingly to struggle against, or to cut off, adverse and unfavorable relationships. Remember certain personalities are all encompassing, affecting everything, cataclysmic, contagious, deadly, harmful, infectious, predatory, and/or venomous. Symbolically meaning that if allowed to continue or prosper within your life, serious harm or devastation to the dreamer may result. Idolize no one, especially beyond the warning of the Lord, and we are definitely not to lay our lives down for no one. No longer, allow that particular person's influence within your life to continue or thrive. Then again, this person maybe allowed within your life because of the dreamer's unwillingness to abstain from immorality after having been asked to abstain from such by God, see 1 Corinthians 6:9-20, Galatians 5:19-21, or the dreamer's self-righteous behavior, or a lack of a balanced and honest view of your own personality. In this case, this person will affect self-awareness within the life of the dreamer, exposing the negative traits of your personality, especially those traits, which cause you to follow, or to be so easily misled, and/or your wrong beliefs; no matter, this type of mentality needs reckoning with. Graciously, all of this will restore the dreamer to his or her right place with God, opening your eyes to see how far you've strayed from God (1 Corinthians 5:4-7; James 5:20). The lesson is, no matter how personable, powerful, or difficult a person, or how uncertain or unpopular the choices and issues, always take the next biblical and ethical step, for obedience to God's principles will always prove safer and stronger foundationally. Although, you will need all kinds of outside support to recover from this person's domination, again no longer allow that particular person's influence within your life, to continue or thrive, especially if negative, end it abruptly.

4. Consider all the people, places, backgrounds, and activity highlighted within your dream.

Known (in your awaked life) person, animal, place, or organization within your dream: Unless otherwise noted elsewhere, people, animals, places, backgrounds that are actually known by the dreamer in your awaked life, indicates a part of you that you recognize within yourself on some level or another. Question to journal, if dreamer seriously considers all the particulars, what stood out the most, what features, or character traits stood out the most. For example, age, color, height, size, happiness, considerate, loving, let you be yourself, peacefulness, encourager, irrational, leader, liar, mentor, passionate, personable, neglected, poor, run-down, sage, shyster, unwise, upscale, vengeful. Write down (journal) the particular highlighted within your dream. The attribute or activity highlighted is for a reason. Since the attribute written down is a part of you, namely the dreamer's nature, demeanor, and/or lifestyle, an honest and unbiased assessment is very important for truth sake. Happy note, considering that other people's attributes, within dreams, also represent attributes of your own personality, causes one to look at another in a better light. According to your capacity to embrace self-awareness and a rectification of mind, body, and spirit, God will begin to enhance, make better, more attractive, sanctify, diminish, and make pure and free from sin and guilt, this part of you.

Otherwise noted, if the person, animal, place, or background within your dream is actually known by the dreamer, in your awaked life, this person, animal, place, or background may represent him or herself, or itself.

Unknown in your awaked life or although known, was unseen, invisible, or only talked about - person, animal, place, or organization within your dream: Unless otherwise noted elsewhere. If you did not recognize, the person, place, thing, they, or it, was not seen, invisible, or only talked about within your dream, this indicates an attribute or activity within your life that you are unfamiliar with, or are in denial about, or you refuse to acknowledge it, but it does exists. Question to journal: what character trait, feature, action, or activity, stood out the most? For example, age, color, height, size, happiness, considerate, loving, let you be yourself, peacefulness, encourager, irrational, leader, liar, mentor, passionate, personable, neglected, poor, run-down, sage, shyster, unwise, upscale, vengeful. Although, on some conscious level, you are aware of a certain behavior or attribute within you, you have chosen to filter out or simply ignore certain information about yourself that contradicts your view of yourself and/or your preconceived notions of others and of the world around you. Possibly protecting yourself, emotionally and psychologically, from a situation, which you are unable to cope with at this time, or you lack control over; then again, perhaps the dreamer has an exaggerated or unrealistic view of yourself. No matter the reason, right now a question is before you, via your dream. Do you want to know this part of yourself? According to your ability to handle self-awareness, God will begin to reveal this side of you to you. Why, He wants to balance your understanding of things; thus, effecting wholeness within your life, so that the enemy will no longer be able to manipulate your emotions so easily. The Holy Spirit is with you to help you throughout this entir e process, listen to Him. Now, in your life, this activity or attribute needs reckoning with, somehow or some way.

Otherwise noted, (known or unknown), if the person, place or thing that initiated (or was a recipient of) the action or activity within your dream was not seen, invisible, or only talked about within your dream, this may indicate that the dreamer does not recognize the influential effects another has within your life, or upon your attitude.

If more than one person (known or unknown): Consider what the group had in common. What behavior, character trait, feature, action, or activity, stood out the most? For example, were they argumentative, authoritative, beautiful, criminal minded, dancing, difficult, dressed unusual, enigmatic, fighting, focused, flirty, helpful, hurtful intentions, powerful, promiscuous, quiet, secretive, seemed unreal, unassuming? That which was highlighted and noted is what you need to focus on at present.

If the attribute or quality is a desirable or positive one, allow the strength of that attribute to help you overcome some manner of immorality or irreverence within your life and/or to help you to become better, productively, for the Kingdom of God in some manner. If the attribute is an undesirable or negative one, take steps accordingly to struggle against the growing desires of the carnal side of you. If applicable, get help and support via prayer, fasting, and a Christian based support group.

For dreams of the dead see following note.

How did someone die? While the dead has nothing to do with the living (Ecclesiastes 9:4-6), it may be considered what character trait did that person represent to the dreamer, while the person was actually alive, what character feature stood out the most. With that trait noted, dreamer may consider that the trait noted, is within the dreamer, and that trait is no longer useful or needed for the progression of your spiritual walk, on this side of heaven. Dreamer, it is suggested that you render that trait (good or bad) obsolete, and began anew attempting to move forward, using different tactics to overcome unproductive habitual life cycle choices, and for maneuvering through this thing we call life in a more, better way. See category, Death, and/or other relevant categories.

5. In addition to the following interpretations, see index or relevant categories for more information. For example, if an animal was involved in some way, see category, Animals; if a building was highlighted, see category, Buildings, Structures. If a particular person was highlighted, see category, People. Kept within context of your dream and the interpretation, the additional symbols are perhaps relevant. It will be within the sum of all the symbols that you will find a more thorough interpretation.

6. Since the following list is not extensive, dreamer is encouraged to seek biblical guidelines and other relevant research to determine the metaphorical meaning of your particular action and activity, depicted within your dream, via a Bible concordance, Bible illustrated dictionary, encyclopedia, or internet. Having done your research you should be able to determine some basic behaviors or attributes your Lord and Savior wants you to focus on.

7. Suggested Course of Action is a postscript at the end of each Actions and Activities subcategory.

Symbols and Referents

Most dreams of actions and activities generally imply, coupled with the relevant interpretation, the status of your spiritual life, as well as the intents and purposes of your heart regarding your spiritual life.

In addition to the varied meanings of actions and activities, other common words, expressions, usages, (e.g. slang or clichés), or a 'probable' that are metaphorically represented by any of the following are also considered (this section is an addendum at the end of the subcategory). If needful, also see suggested course of action.

Category Content - If not listed see index, perchance, for your specific type of action and/or activity type dream.

- Abating
- Accidents
- Ascending or Expanding (moving upward, getting ready to, or planning, scheduled to, ascend in some manner, or to increase or cause something to increase in capacity, scope, size, or stature)
- Ascending and Descending (moving upward and then downward, to rise and descend, to go up and down, to fall and get back up, and these actions are repeated and/or 'stand-out' within the dream)

- Blood, Bleeding
- Bowing or Kneeling or Prostrated or Stooping
- Chasing, Running, Following, Seeking, or Stalking
- Cheating, Thievery
- Clapping
- Cleaning, Washing, Decorate, Remodeling, Repair (bathing, cleansing, showering, scrubbing, straightening-up, vacuuming, or being reconstructed)
- Cutting (carving, chop, hack, shave, haircut, engrave, sculpt, as well as, hacking into a system, e.g. computer) (pgs. 115-121)
- Dancing
- Divorce
- Drinking, Smoking (wine, alcoholic or fermented drinks, or any kinds of pharmaceutical or street drugs, or cigarettes, cigars, chewing tobacco)
- Falling into or Sinking or Sliding Downward or Lowered down or March Downward or Taken Down from (Abyss, Altar, Basket, Cloth, Clouds, Ditch, Downstairs, Fabric, Fence, Heaven, Hell, Hill, Hole, Ladder, Mountain, Pit, Pulpit, Rope, Sky, Wall, Well)
- Fighting, Killing, Struggling, Violence, Conflict, Contestation, Dispute, or Accusations
- Flying: To travel through the air using wings or an engine, or to be capable of flight
- Frozen, Frost, Refrigeration, Cold, Thaw
- Games
- Parades
- Pregnancy or Giving Birth
- Sitting, Reclining, or Leaning on in some way
- Sleeping (preparing, make ready to sleep)
- Standing (to be in an upright position; or put something in an upright position)
- Swimming
- Talking
- Vacation
- Walking
- Working, Work Places

ABATING - To lessen or make something lessen gradually; also to suppress or end

Some short descriptions of types, phrases, and other processes and particulars, connected in some way to this category are, for example, abandonment, aging, coupon discounts, dwarf, to fade away, to be held or kept back, riches to rags, retreat, or terminate. Abating can apply to a person, animal, place, or organization.

Unless otherwise noted elsewhere, if, in your everyday living, your awaked state, as part of your natural stature, lifestyle, work, or ministerial activities, or a special event, you have a very real connection with any type of abating activity. For example, you are literally a person, who is markedly small (e.g. midget), discount store, geriatrics, illness, loss of wages, (also see content list for this category), your dream is not significant and does not warrant special attention.

Otherwise noted, see Note 1 at the beginning of Actions and Activities category.

To determine who your dream is for you or another, see Note 3 at the beginning of Actions and Activities category.

Symbols and Referents: Dreams of some form of abating generally implies a lack of, or diminishing of, spiritual qualities within one's life. These types of dreams also point to the natural process of aging, the changes, and challenges endured.

Category Content - If not listed see index, perchance, for your specific type of abating dream activity.

- To decrease in degree, force, intensity or grow tired
- To discount in value or amount or cheap, cheapen (e.g. coupon discounts or a sale of some sort)
- To fade away
- To be held or kept back
- From prosperity to poverty or riches to rags or homelessness
- To put an end to or terminate something
- To shrink, or be markedly small in stature or Dwarf or Midget
- To abandon, leave, to hide, pull out or retire or retreat (as in pull back)

To decrease in degree, force, intensity, or grow tired: The natural process of aging, the changes, and challenges endured has begun to make you feel as though life is passing you by or has already. You feel a need to take a more pro-active and forceful role in your life; yet you have little strength. As a result, you feel angry, a silent frustration, and have become very ill- tempered and hasty with your words. Dreamer, have faith in God, which is a resolute trust in the integrity of God and in His Word, for He has promised good things to you, His servant. Now, He is pleased to bless your house that it may continue in His sight, and it will be blessed. From this day, forward God's blessings will flow abundantly, producing spiritual growth within you. God's blessings: Gifts of God's grace, anything God freely gives you, absolution, the Holy Spirit, salvation, regeneration, eternal life, health, children, love of family, longevity, necessities, prosperity, and dominion over all that is yours; and all are parts of the supply of grace, and all are sanctified by the Lord, and technically belongs to Him. The result of this supply in your life will be peace.

To discount in value or amount or **cheap, cheapen (e.g. coupon discounts or a sale of some sort):** This dream has two meanings (choose one). (1) This type of dream of discount in value indicates a loss of self-respect, due to a cheapening of one's self-value and talents, as well as a loss of respect from others. Dreamer, the following is necessary to say, you have failed to elevate or promote the righteousness of Christ to those around you, due primarily to a lack of purity within your o wn life and low self-esteem. As a result, you are in an evil state of affairs. Thus, your dream is to engender an awareness of impending turn-arounds, changes, and ups and downs within the dreamer's life. Favorably that which will affect good self- esteem, humility, and a level of purity within your life has come. Because of you receiving Jesus as your personal Savior and have begun embracing His teachings and principles, your lack of purity and low self-esteem issues will now begin to be healed. For this is one thing that Christianity promises, and that is a better you. Nevertheless, whatever "will be, will be"; things will get worse, and then you will get relief. See suggested course of action. (2) To a father-in-law or mother-in-law: Your dream counsels the dreamer to demonstrate respect and honor to your child's spouse as your own child. Do not express preju dice, treat with contempt, or speak ill of them to others. Today, do not harden your heart to this, but sincerely make a complete turnaround in your actions towards your child, children's spouse, especially if you are guilty of this at present. You will be judged unsympathetically, when mercy will be needed most, if this counsel is not heeded. See suggested course of action.

To fade away: You have replaced faithfulness and humility with greed, pride, and spiritual murder (a premeditated attempt to destroy someone's personal relationship with Christ, or a cruel destruction of someone's reputation). You are tearing down and wounding others to hide your own unfaithfulness to the true and living God and to hide thievery. See suggested course of action.

To be held or kept back: You have become defiled; therefore, your offerings are not received or blessed of the Lord. Never bring gifts or money earned by prostitution (the spiritual or literal selling of one's mind, body, or soul for money or favors) into the House of the Lord as an offering you vowed to give. These earnings are not acceptable to the Lord your God (also see Deuteronomy 23:18). See suggested course of action.

From prosperity to poverty or **riches to rags** or **homelessness:** Your dream is a final warning of the futility of self- confidence that God may withdraw you from your purpose and hide pride from you. You boast in your own self-perceived strength, which, in reality, is non-existent. Arrogance, self-reliance, poisoning of any sense of justice, exchanging righteousness for bitterness, and rejoicing in this, has reached a pinnacle. Your confidence will be shattered because it is groundless, via trouble, distress, worry, and/or health problems. You will begin to experience need and want. Respect and heed this warning from the Lord (also see Psalm 119:67, 68; Proverbs 3:11-18). Righteous humility will cause you to eat again in prosperity. See suggested course of action.

To put an end to or terminate something: Your present troubles are diminishing. Spiritual cleansing has taken place. Within five months, stability will return within your home, family, and finances.

To shrink, or be markedly small in stature, or Dwarf or Midget: This dream has two meanings (choose one). (1) Your dream comes to counsel the dreamer. Your belief system has changed or is presently changing. When the heart turns from the Lord, the beliefs of the world's systems are quickly adopted. You are actively involved in the immorality of your surroundings, which has its primary focus on spiritual separation from the Lord and His truth. You have become weak-willed, and in so doing, you are no longer faithful to the Creator of this world. Having turned, you now look to heretical ideology and fame to be your strength and satisfaction, rather than the Lord God. This is done, in spite of the fact that God has dealt with you according to His grace (the free and unmerited favor and beneficence of God). He chose you and covered you with His protection and riches. You will be rejected and shown disapproval by the ones with whom you have committed spiritual fornication. You bribe them to come to you from everywhere; but no one runs after you for your favors, and no compensation is given you. Instead of receiving pay, you give payment and none is given to you. After many days, you will be reinstated into God's favor. At that time, you will become ashamed of your past contempt, because of the things you would have suffered, and will be saved. See suggested course of action. (2) Your spiritual immaturity, sin, and other fleshliness, are hindering what God has purposed for you (your individual, personal ministry). Your carnality is such that others are unable to speak to you as a spiritual person. At this stage in your spiritual development, your attitude is embarrassing. Read Hebrews 5:11-14. See suggested course of action.

To abandon, leave, to hide, pull out, or retire, or retreat (as in pull back): You and/or your children have forsaken godliness, and now believe in something akin to Spiritism. You and/or your children worship with spiritists and witches (see Chapter Two, Dream Interpreters – Carriers of the Message, section entitled – ²⁸ Syncretism). Even more, you and/or your children have attributed your prosperity to the power of demons. Thus, you (they) give to those whom the Lord disapproves of. The prosperity God has provided you will begin to abate and your anarchy will be exposed. Turn back to Jesus, seek forgiveness, and tangibly, if applicable, participate in the turning back of your children to Jesus that He may leave a blessing. See suggested course of action.

Suggested Course of Action

Question to consider and journal, did your dream depict any symbols that alludes to, the dreamer will make the necessary changes, spiritually, emotionally, and/or physically to affect a more positive outcome? If changes are initiated, your dreams will change.

Notwithstanding, these types of dreams, challenges the dreamer to appreciate that Yahweh chastens every son, daughter whom He receives (Hebrew 12:5-13). If you are without chastisement, then you are not a legitimate child of the King. Those who will enjoy His great blessings will at times experience His chastening. These times of correction are a sign of both His displeasure and love towards you. Humble submission is essential in this process of spiritual growth. Wisdom suggests that if we reverence the Lord and endure correction with patience and understanding, we will be delivered from evil.

Consider and journal the following questions. In view of your dream's context, namely abating, what choices are you making that may cause a diminishing with your spiritual and/or physical life? The questions will help you determine; the issue at hand, how you feel about it, and what may have instigated it. What kind of abating activity was it? Why was there diminishing activity? Were others involved? If yes, who and in what manner were they involved? Keep in mind that the others represent a character trait, quality, or talent within you. Did anyone get hurt emotionally, physically, or was disturbed in any way? How did you feel, and what did you do, because, of your feelings, regarding the abating and/or the place where it happened? Was it agitating, confusing, dangerous, disturbing, frustrating, peace with the situation, happy, joyful, life threatening, safe, scary, o r unsure? Where were you? Was the place unfamiliar to you? Were you coherent? Your answers, coupled with the interpretation, and any additional information, should begin to unfold the subject matter and issue at hand, if not now, mull over things a few days. For more information, see index or relevant category and subcategory for other particulars within your dream.

Now, pray (See Prayer of Deliverance, pg. 897)

Specific Meaning

If, you have a very high chance that you will be dealing with some form of abating action or activity (e.g. foreclosure of mortgages, store clerk, mental health, or some other form of work that involves diminishing activity). Dreams of this sort, for the most part, are ordinary dreams, resulting from your daily activities (see Chapter One, Chalom). These sorts of dreams ar e usually about your routine, mundane activities or anxieties that overwhelm your mind during the day. They are an inner release mechanism, which helps provide you with emotional balance and the maintaining of your sanity. These dreams are not significant, and do not warrant special attention. However, if specific action is relevant, e.g. foreclosure, then dreamer should respond to the issue at hand prudently.

ACCIDENTS - Events that happen by chance, by coincidence, fortuitously, inadvertently, by mistake, 'out of the blue', unintentionally

Some short descriptions of types, phrases, and other processes and particulars, connected in some way to this category are, for example, break, bump into, crack, crash, collision, to drop something, to fall off, industrial accident, run into, smash into, smash-up, shatter, spill, tear, trip over, tumble or over.

Unless otherwise noted elsewhere, if, in your everyday living, your awaked state, as part of your lifestyle, work, or ministerial activities, or a special event, you have a very high propensity for accidents, (also see content list for this category), skip referent, and go to Specific Meaning at the end of this category.

Otherwise noted, a dream of an accident may be a Prophetically Simple Dream (see Chapter One: The 60th Part of Prophecy). Whereas, the dreamer is warned to be extra cautious regarding situations that have a high chance for accidents, or is warned to stop any unwise, reckless, or dangerous behavior that may incur accidents. Example, you should cease any daredevil, or impetuous activity, especially if this is a thing within the dreamer's life. If any of the preceding is happening, or was depicted within your dream, this dream is a first step intervention and an alarm. Your dream should be received as a precautionary warning. Skip interpretation and re-consider your activities as harmful, hurtful, or life threatening at present. Refrain from such activities at present. Handle the situation wisely, by first thanking God for the warning, for Adonai Elohim knows all. Skip referent, and go to Specific Meaning at the end of this category.

Otherwise noted, to see another in an accident within this type of dream, dreamer should receive this dream as a precautionary warning. Skip referent, and go to Specific Meaning at the end of this subcategory, section entitled, Note (Specific Meaning). Perhaps the dreamer is being made aware of the plight of someone, and you are to get involved (see Chapter One, Are You Ready to Hear the Messages in Your Dreams, section entitled, The 10% for others).

Otherwise noted, see Note 1 at the beginning of Actions and Activities category.

To determine who your dream is for you or another, see Note 3 at the beginning of Actions and Activities category.

Unless otherwise noted elsewhere, if you were an observer, minor participant, or the person, place or thing that initiated (or was a recipient of) the action or activity, was not seen, invisible, or only talked about within your dream, or is actually deceased, or no longer in existence, (known or unknown). See Note 3 at the beginning of Actions and Activities category.

Otherwise noted, to see, and respond, in some manner, see: To see (or hear of) an accident from a distance)

Symbols and Referents: Accidents within most dreams are dire warnings regarding spiritual or literal lifestyle choices of the dreamer.

Category Content - If not listed see index, perchance, for your specific type of accident dream activity.

- Accidents
- To see (or hear of) an accident from a distance or dreamer was one of the first persons to arrive at the accident scene; and gave aide, as a first responder, or assistance, to the injured or incapacitated (no matter the accident)
- Airplane or Helicopter crashed (to be in one, caused one)
- Accident involving a baby or children (any kind of accident involving children)
- Automobile Accident (hit by a car)
- Broken glass, bottles, drinking glass, lenses, mirror, window, see category, Buildings (Windows)
- Dropped someone or thing (e.g. a bible, money)
- Dropped a dime, see category, Numbers (#10)
- Fire or Explosion or Bomb (or any kind of explosives)
- "Burning Bush"
- "Ball of Fire"
- Warm yourself by a fire, or to be near a fire
- To be far from the fire
- Walking through fire, see category, Walking (Fire)
- Smashed, smash-up, shatter (to break something into pieces, as by striking or knocking over)
- Spilled something
- To topple, trip, stumble
- Window washing on a scaffold and you fall off

To see (or hear of) an accident from a distance or dreamer was one of the first persons to arrive at the accident scene; and gave aide, as a first responder, or assistance. To the injured or incapacitated (no matter if a spacecraft, crash, boat, or ship, capsized, car accident, explosion, fire, a person fallen, or stumble): This dream has three meanings (choose one). (1) Dreamer you have been found by God, willing and obedient to Him and to His cause. Because of this, you will recover all that was lost because of your youth and/or bad, unwise, and foolish decisions and choices (e.g. family, fertility, finances, friends, health, honor, job, respect, or reputation). Question to journal: what have you lost, and desire God to rectify or restore? The righteous desires of your heart will now begin to manifest within your life. You will receive double, and you will live your life more peaceful and abundant than before and to its fullest (financially, happiness, love, and respect). If illness is a concern at present, you will recover from this, and live; all this because of your sense of duty and respect to others. You are one who voluntarily offers help or sympathy in times of trouble, one who demonstrates mercy, and truly loves his or her neighbor.

You are the proverbial "Good Samaritan" (Luke 10:25-37). You have learned to handle much; therefore, much will be given you. You will live to testify of God's great love, everlasting kindness, and of His great faithfulness. (2) If victims of crash were known, dreamer will witness with your own eyes, divine retribution upon those who are belligerent, who instigate confusion, are angry, who has contended with you. Those who are misleading, out of order, untrue, who secretly practice immoral, impure, and unchaste conduct, as well as, those who are weak, spiritually and/or physically. For example, addictions, cheating, exposing confidences to others, greedy, gossiping, jealously, lying, stealing, or any other sinful attribute (see 1 Corinthians 6:9- 20, Ephesians 5). This behavior has caused their anointing to fade and spiritual authority to wane. All of this is the reward of disobedience, hypocrisy, or an uncommitted life. Questions to consider, why are you being made privy to such insight, what does any of the information regarding others have to do with you, can you perhaps change things, is there a need for you to warn of a coming "crash" or collapse of their ministry, or to advise, or mentor? You have been instilled with a sense of duty to others because you understand that every right implies a responsibility; every opportunity, an obligation; every possession, a duty. Therefore, you will be instrumental in the spiritual recovery of another(s). (3) If crash victims were unknown, dreamer has not fully acknowledge to yourself the damage another has done to you emotionally. You are still hurting inwardly. It is suggested that you go to a quiet place and earnestly do the psychological and emotional "work" it takes for you to release all past hurts that you may progress peacefully into a place of restoration that God has for you. Amen.

Airplane or Helicopter crashed (to be in one, caused one): This indicates a severe warning of divine discipline (the Lord's chastening, correction that leads to instruction and reformation). With that, the following are a few possible reasons for such a severe warning (choose one). (1) For dreamers (15 years of age to 29): This choice has two parts (choose one). (a) Dreamer, you are internally inconsistent and disordered, because of a violent violation in your past or recent present; examples of the violation are abuse, assault, bullying, kidnapping, molestation, rape, stalked, or being held prisoner. The diabolical entity, having possessed the person(s) who committed the literal act, was sent to rob, steal, and destroy a quality of life that has been destined you, to keep you from living that life abundantly, happily, and in peace. The demon's mission is to get you to entertain, embrace, and live out the negative results, of your particular violation, to oppress, persecute, and bring you into bondage of an ungodly and/or unprofitable lifestyle. With hopes that unfavorable consequences will cost you your emotional sanity, possibly your life, and ultimately your soul. Thus, instead of you moving towards, and thus fulfilling, your divine purpose, and reaching a pinnacle in your life, thereby with, you will prosper, you have begun to listen to, and be fooled by, demons. Having listened and embraced their lies, you have begun to decrease and fall, eventually running amok your life, literally crashing, when you should be clear and focused mentally, emotionally, and spiritually. Dreamer; oftentimes, bad things happen to innocent and good people. A bad thing happened to you, and you are good and innocent. Compassionately, the Lord is creating a miracle in your life. This miracle will stop the effects of your violation from playing a significant role in your life, enabling you to move forward with your life and to make good decisions. However, the miracle's success depends upon your willingness to be healed and set free; for one will always have the choice to say no, or perhaps sabotage their progress. First, recognize and respect your time of visitation from the Lord, for it is upon you, as well as the work of His Hand upon your life. If you lack wisdom ask God for wisdom; and He will give you wisdom. For the Lord gives wisdom and from His mouth comes knowledge and understanding. Then you will understand what is right and just and fair, every good path. When wisdom enters your heart and knowledge becomes sweet to your soul, discretion will protect you, understanding will guard you, and His Truth will lead you. To deliver you from the ways of wickedness, and from demons whose words and ways are perverse, who causes you to walk in darkness gladly, whose paths are crooked and devious, causing you to leave straight paths (Proverbs 2:1-6, 9-15). This is one of God's covenant promises to you. Have faith in this. Further, with much fortitude choose not to be a victim, nor to perpetuate the desolation. Dreamer, go and separate yourself from anyone and anything that hinders your clarity and emotional stability; literally stop what you're doing. Moreover, and if applicable, go, and continue your education, the Lord will help you in your endeavors. Dreamer, if you do not respect the work of the Lord within your life, and the opportunities He is offering you, to be set free, spiritually, emotionally and physically. You will have nothing to work with, but your body, namely deviant sexual promiscuousness, and all that comes with it, including diseases, and/or physical devastation; having forfeited purpose, reasonable resources, and wise counsel that has surrounded you. For, your kind of choices, at present, leads to begging, early death, homelessness, homosexuality, imprisonment, poverty, and/or prostitution. Working with and using your intellect (mind) and/or strength, and good ethics, for your livelihood, will always out last the use of your body immorally for sustenance, and these choices makes life easier. Dreamer is counseled to seek all kinds of spiritual support now, to possibly avert or turn things around. Again, if you are in a negative place, again, move away from your present environment, definitely, you should run away from all negativity abruptly, God will provide, trust Him. If you do not genuin ely seek help and change, for sure ruin will be your destiny. Utilizing the powerful resources of prayer and heartfelt repentance to Jesus is needed. Repentance is seeking pardon and expressing sincere feelings of regret and brokenness for having done something awry and/or for having hurt someone. To Jesus pray, Psalm 51, this followed by appropriate application of wisdom, can conceivably avert some of the repercussions of your choices. This, coupled with a lifestyle of fasting, perhaps twice a week, a changed mindset, serious re-consideration of God's ways and means, and an honest acknowledgement of God's hand within your life, then the severe impact of your choices and actions upon your life, can be reversed and damages repaired (also see Ezekiel 33:12-19). This is what is called leaving a blessing behind. (b) If you are an unbeliever (one who has no religious beliefs, a non-religious person, or one who has no religious faith or belief in Jesus Christ, or one who does not embrace a personal relationship with Jesus Christ, at present). Jesus loves you, thus, He is petitioning you to accept Him as your personal Savior, for you are valuable in His eyes. The first step in receiving Him as your personal Savior is repentance (see in the Holy Bible, Acts 2:37-41). Then you will know the Messiah, Jesus Christ, intimately, and find the knowledge of God you seek. See suggested course of action. (2) For dreamers (30+ years of age), a few general causes for this kind of dream, are as follows: Dreamer, you have ceased to abide in Christ, having trusted in your own righteousness. For example, adopting a more legalistic viewpoint (a belief that strict adherence to the commandments, the law, is requisite for entrance into Heaven). The Bible issues urgent warnings concerning self-righteousness, designed both to alert us to the deadly peril of abandoning grace (the free and unmerited favor and beneficence of God), thus, our union with Christ, and to motivate us to persevere in faith and love. This will keep you from becoming enslaved again to sin and immorality (see Romans 3:21-4:16). Another cause, in judging others, via condemnatory, critical, derogatory, disapproving, harsh, negative, scornful, or uncomplimentary in your thoughts or speaking aloud, you have set a precedent over your own life, discharging a universal law. The Universal Law: With the same judgments, you judge others, so will you be judged (see Matthew 7:1-5). Examples of judging, have you thought or said, "They're life is not holy, or they're not Christian, because I know they behave this way, or do that", or thought to yourself, "They need to sit down with all the emotional or physical hardship they're going through; they're not a super person". "How can they witness about God one moment, and then beg for money the next?" Or, "They have mental health issues". Have you never been in a fallen state, or had a material need, at the same time, you were required to testify of the Kingdom of God, t he world to come or, did you just disobey the commission because of a preconceived notion or pseudo-image? Have you not been under such pressure emotionally or physically that you could have experienced an emotional or mental breakdown, and yet you were still required to witness, or to preach, on behalf of the Kingdom of God? With that said, dreamer, now you're judged as an offender, in that you have violated your own standard, the one you've held up, so high, for others to follow, fo r he or she who knows to do right and do not, to him or her it is a sin. You should have done what you expected of others or at least remembered from where you've come. While Christ does not deny the necessity of exercising a certain degree of discernment, or of making valid judgments with respect to sin in others. Jesus condemns the habit of criticizing others, while ignoring your own faults.

A believer must first submit him or herself to God's righteous standard before attempting to examine and influence the conduct of others, which is often done in an unjust or unloving manner if you haven't judged yourself first. Another cause includes condemning a wrongdoer without a genuine desire to see the offender return to God, but to be condemned to hell. Here again, discharging a preset law within this type of offense, which is to not see you, as an offender, return to God, but to be condemn to hell also. Dreamer, genuinely deal with why you are so judgmental or critical, and repent over judging others, this will remove such severe and unsympathetic standards from over your own life, and your dreams will change. Also, by so doing, a more compassionate, understanding, empathic and loving spirit will begin to manifest within you. Other reasons for such a severe warning are an unforgiving attitude towards someone, or literally rejecting the teachings of Christ and His apostles (Hebrews 6:4-8). See suggested course of action.

Accident involving a baby or children (any kind of accident involving children): This sort of dream is exposing the true circumstances surrounding a ministry (or ministries) you're involved with or is trying to launch. Most of the meaning of the dream may be obtained by considering the following questions. Who caused the accident? What happened to the baby, children? Dreamer, now ask yourself the following questions, journal the answers. What would you do if a literal baby, child were in the condition, as they appeared in your dream? If you physically caused the accident, what would you do? Would you try to hide the accident? Should the situation be handled without getting authorities involved? If someone else caused the accident, would you call the police? Would you take the baby from those responsible for the accident? Would you call child protective authorities? What were your actions within your dream? To determine the symbolic equivalent to your response, examples of symbolic equivalents to responses, examples of symbolic equivalents to responses: You hiding the incident would be spiritually equivalent to you pretending that your ministry is something that it is not. Calling the police is figurative of intercessory prayer for a ministry. Taking the baby denotes taking over a ministry. Handling the situation without involving authorities is equivalent to you attempting to get a ministry off the ground according to your own ideas, understanding, perspective, and reasoning abilities, without dependence upon God. Just observing is equivalent to you doing nothing with a ministry. Journal your answers, and then determine the ministry this dream is referring to, considering any new ministry you are involved with or you are trying to help get underway, and react appropriately. If necessary, see suggested course of action. May also, see category, People (Children).

Automobile Accident (hit by a car): This dream has two meanings (choose one). (1) Your way of life, modus operandi "MO" (mode or state of operating, living, or lifestyle), as you know it, is about to "come to an end". There will be major changes (significant in scope, extent, and effect) in your normal, everyday habits, and in your way of operating and functioning. The changes are a result of your prayers. You've asked God for a change; a change is coming. Pay close attention to shifts within your relationships with others. Keep what is good, toss what is bad, know the difference, and understand God's hand within all your situations. Dreamer, resolve to vigorously and quickly release hurts, pains, disappointments, disillusionments, and a reluctance to change. Quickly forgive and move on to prevent being stuck in a negative and self-sabotaging mind-set for many years. Choose good deeds and habits that will lead to the fulfilment of your God given purpose. While it is easier said than done, it is necessary to say; one cannot grow or go forward stuck in the past. Do not lose today holding on to yesterday; let it go. (2) Hit by a car: Because of someone else's lifestyle changes and/or choices your lifestyle at present (with or without your consent) will be seriously impacted. Some examples of lifestyle changes and/or choices are an un-consenting separation or divorce from your spouse. A diagnosis of a serious illness of a family member or significant friend, resulting in you becoming primary caretaker, or elderly parents needing primary care, all of these can change your life drastically. Your children or grandchildren needing to come live with you, or any job related adversity, whatever the cause, major adjustments (significant in scope, extent, and effect) in your everyday living is approaching. Dreamer, resolve to vigorously and quickly release hurts, pains, disappointments, disillusionments, and a reluctance to change. Quickly forgive and move on to prevent being stuck in a negative and self-sabotaging mind-set for many years. An unforgiving heart is the single most popular poison that the enemy uses against God's people and it is; one of the deadliest poisons a person can take spiritually, recommended reading, "Deliverance in Forgiveness, through obedience to the Holy Spirit, A. M. Perry". Dreamer, while it is easier said than done, it is necessary to say; one cannot grow or go forward stuck in the past. Do not lose today holding on to yesterday; let it go. See suggested course of action.

Dropped someone or thing (e.g. the Bible, or money): This dream has two meanings (choose one). (1) Your behavior is haphazard and/or reckless, specifically in the area, concerning the item (or individual) dropped. Kept within context of your dream, other references highlighted will also point to the area where you have acted haphazardly. See suggested course of action. (2) Bible drops on the floor: You are careless with the Word of God; this is a very serious matter. Your recent interpretations of God's standards are erroneous. Seek help via a faith based bible study group, Sunday school, and church service. See suggested course of action.

Fire or Explosion or Bomb (or any kind of explosives): This dream has two meanings (choose one). (1) Explosion or Bomb (or any kind of explosives): This choice has two parts (choose one). (a) You will experience extreme grief over the loss of a love one. Grieving is a natural process, allow the process, no matter the duration. Dreamer, under no circumstances, d o you allow yourself to medicate (or be prescribed medication for) the pain of grief; it will only hinder the natural process of grieving. This experience will prove useful. You will draw upon your experience and present more empathically and compassionately when ministering to others who are experiencing grief and great pain. (b) Dreamer, you have a serious medical issue. Depending where the explosion was located, determines what part of your body is in need of medical attention (e.g. in a hallway, could mean, especially for females, your pelvic cavity, fallopian tubes, or uterus, or for males abdomen area. In a kitchen could mean heart problems, or in a bedroom could mean your reproduction area). If applicable, see index for relevant category. Kept within context of your dream, other references highlighted may also be points of relevance, see index or relevant category for other particulars within your dream. If necessary, see suggested course of action. (2) Fire: Fire is a common figure of God's presence and it denotes a purifying of some kind. However, that purifying can vary greatly. Question, what was on fire? This choice has three parts (choose one). (a) If any parts of your body were on fire or if an animal was on fire. Your dream denotes purification by means of divine discipline (the Lord's chastening, or correction that leads to instruction and reformation). There will come a season of time when God will come down in a dramatic way to deal with your contemptuous, rebellious, and disobedient attitude and behavior. If body was on fire, it will be the characteristics attributed to the body part, it will be these attributes of your behavior that will be affected; thus see category, The Body. If animal was on fire, it will be the negative characteristics attributed to the animal that will be chastened, thus see category, Animals. It is hoped that this experience will lead to the reformation that it is intended to effect, rescuing the dreamer from error and causing a return to a rightful course. Moreover, utilizing the powerful resources of prayer and heartfelt repentance to Jesus is needed. To Jesus pray, Psalm 51, this followed by appropriate application of wisdom, can conceivably avert some of the repercussions of your choices. This coupled with fasting, a changed mindset, serious re-consideration of God's ways and means, and an honest acknowledgement of God's hand within your life, then the severe impact of your choices and actions, upon your life, can be lessen. This is what is called leaving a blessing behind. See suggested course of action. (b) If a building was on fire, your dream denotes divine judgment, via some manner of suffering via a sickness, if sinfulness, arrogance, and/or oppression of God's people, does not cease. Please note, there will always be divine vengeance against God's people oppressors, and you are considered an oppressor. See category, Buildings, for possible area that will be judged and/or seriously affected. Dreamer, utilizing the powerful resources of prayer and heartfelt repentance to Jesus and to others is needed. To Jesus pray, Psalm 51, this followed by appropriate application of wisdom, can conceivably avert some of the repercussions of your choices. An apology to others, perhaps in the form of a letter is advised. This coupled with fasting, a changed mindset, serious re-consideration of God's ways and means, and an honest acknowledgement of God's hand within your life, then the severe impact of your choices and actions, upon your life, can be lessen. This is what is called leaving a blessing behind. See suggested course of action. (c) If bushes, trees, or nature was on fire, your dream denotes God's presence. Dreamer, although you are in the midst of hard trails, and tribulations, you are being purified spiritually. Whatever is going on, wherever you are, God's presence is there with you. You are not alone; neither should you feel that way. Do no t falter, for He is there at all times. Learn from your experience and mature. There will come a season of time when God, in a dramatic way, will bring deliverance and restorations for you, for you have been deemed righteous. This deliverance speaks of hope, prosperity, and unprecedented blessings; there is a "breaking of day" for you and there will be joy.

In addition, the following are common words, expressions, usages, (e.g. slang or clichés), or a 'probable' that are metaphorically represented by fire:

- **"Burning Bush"**: Your dream denotes that the fundamental assumptions from which something was (or has) begun within you, developed or calculated by you or another, or been explained to you, is based on God's divine will. Therefore, the position the dreamer has taken on a topic at hand is holy and rational; this includes your motives. Dreamer, your heart is pure, your stance is holy, and you may move on from there, wherever or whatever "there" is to you, today. God will lead the way. Moreover, you will accomplish your divine ordained purpose, and inherit eternal life.
- **"Ball of Fire"**: Your dream denotes the healing power of God within the "hand" of the dreamer. Dreamer, you are anointed to become a healer. You will begin to sense a feeling of "fire" or heat within your hands, and have probably experience this heat once or twice before, when you've prayed for another. With that said, dreamer your ministry of healing is being taken to another level. That ball of fire is a sign to you that any person before you, who is in need of healing, can and will be healed by the laying on of your hands in Jesus' Name. However, please note, only lay hands when you sense the "fire or heat" in your hand, and give God the glory. You will not sense the fire or heat all the time, but onl y when God has deemed it so. Warning, if you begin to swell-up with pride because of your gift, and begin laying hands without waiting upon the Lord, God's anointing will be removed, and you will be left pretending that you still have the healing anointing when you actually do not. Hypocrisy is a heavy burden to bear.
- **Warm yourself by a fire; or to be near a fire:** Dreamer, be encourage for your dream denotes, closeness to God; God is very close to you and you are very close to God.
- **To be far from the fire:** Denotes dreamer is far from the Kingdom of God. Your beliefs are not based on the teachings of Christ. You have corrupted the one true religion, with syncretistic [28] ideas. See suggested course of action.

Smashed, smash-up, shatter (to break something into pieces, as by striking or knocking over): Question, what was smashed, if needful see index or relevant category, for the particular that was smashed, couple with this interpretation. Then dreamer will fully understand the beautiful work the Lord has completed in your life. Your dream was sent to encourage and to warn. With that this dream has two meanings (choose one). (1) Dreamer, be encouraged, God has broken into pieces, within your life, self-righteousness, self-confidence, self-wisdom, and self-help, via a refining process, see Proverbs 17:3, 27:21; thus, dreamer is now able to welcome fully the Gospel of grace. With its message of a Savior who came into the world, not to condemn, but that through Him we all might be saved (John 3:18). In another way, our Savior patiently bears the contradictions of mankind. He is given to gentleness to those who are oppressed with doubts and fears; He will not despise them, nor lay upon them more work or more suffering than they can bear. By the power of His gospel, grace, and a long course of miracles, He fixes principles in the minds of men and women that are intended to make them wise and just. He came not to break the bruised reed, nor to quench the smoking flax, but to preach glad tidings to the poor, to heal the broken - hearted, and to grant forgiveness of sins to all the captives (Isaiah 42:3, Matthew 12:20). Therefore, let your soul rely on Him, and rejoice in Him; then the Father will be well please with you. With that said, dreamer, God used your sufferings (the smashing) to instill His principles into your mind, and make His ways penetrate your heart. He or she who has suffered in the flesh has ceased from sinning (1 Peter 4:1) that the sacrificial offerings of your worship, service, and financial support to the ministry, might be a sweet smell unto the Lord. Now, you're under new management, you are the redeemed. Moreover, having been refined via the "crucible" of suffering and adversity, you are humbled and made ready and prepared to render your gifts unto the Lord properly. You will now, emerge suddenly, and become productive and go forth, bearing spiritual fruit that you might be counted amongst those who are sagacious; whose character is faithful, law-abiding, moral, open, scrupulous, sincere, straightforward, trustworthy, upright, reasonable in many situations, and submissi ve to God. Moreover, blessings, joy, protection, and prosperity will be yours. Dreamer, God will raise you up and sit you amongst His people for the benefit of a ll within your sphere, help God's people by doing good deeds. There will be quick turnovers in your interests and relationships, and perhaps jobs; fortunately along with these changes will come business, power, and money, people will elect you to lead. As well, these changes will give you a multi-dimensionality that will befriend you to people of every "walk of life". The warning, dreamer, unfortunately, because you learn so quickly you have little patience with those whose mental processes are somewhat slower; thus, you could become supercilious or somewhat a "know it all" in your attitude, becoming intolerant and critical of others, quick to argue and to dominate situations. This characteristic is called pride. After being puffed up with pride and arrogance, you could experience falling flat on your face, again. In other words too much arrogance and self-pride are sure to bring bad and disappointing results. However, dreamer, if you are diligent in subduing this negative quality you can turn bad situations into a good overnight; people can and do change, and sometimes overnight, e.g. Apostle Paul. Thus, dreamer you are urged to heed this warning. See Proverbs 16:18. Additionally, it is suggested that perhaps dreamer may consider a humanitarian effort, some effort that promotes human welfare and/or social reforms, with a primary focus on God's love towards His people. (2) If broke something by dropping it: This choice has two parts (choose one). (a) Your dream suggests that in your secret intentions and wrongful motives for material or positional gain, you have wronged so meone within the Body of Christ. Repentance is seeking pardon and expressing sincere feelings of regret and brokenness for having done something awry and/ or for having hurt someone, see 2 Corinthians 7:10, 11. To individuals, a phone call or a letter of apology is a good place to start, coupled with restoration of those wronged. To Jesus pray, Psalm 51, this, coupled with prayer and fasting, followed by appropriate application of wisdom, can conceivably avert some of the repercussions of your choices. This is what is called leaving a blessing behind. (b) Male: if your wife is pregnant, she could lose the pregnancy. It is suggested that you encourage your wife to seek medical attention as soon as possible.

Spilled something: Your unwillingness to accept, and make use of, God's fresh revelation given you unequivocally is costing you greatly. You have said, "The old way is good enough", when God has said, "It is not and needs to be done away with". This old way, you insist continuing in, has caused God's people to stumble, err, and be unable to recover. Because of your noncompliance, stubbornness, and pride, God is becoming adversarial towards you (also see Isaiah 66:4). See suggested course of action.

To topple, trip, stumble: Dreamer, you have become offended, either because of God's Word, the preaching, teaching of Jesus Christ, the preaching, teaching of the cross, or of Christians liberties. Due to this offense, you are behaving very unwisely. Moreover, because of their prosperity, you envy the arrogant and wicked. Dreamer, understand and respect that all things will end; nothing earthly lasts forever. Thus, you must take time and consider your final destiny, hopefully heaven, as well as t hat of the arrogant and wicked (see 1 Corinthians 6:9-20, Ephesians 5). Eternal life is the greatest of all things, for it does not end. Questions to consider from an eternal perspective, if non-Christians live more successful lives than Christians do, then why bother being a Christian? Moreover, if the world's standards are the same as yours, perhaps are yours are too low? The perfection our King demands of us, will accomplish a far greater thing than what you are stumbling over today. You should seek a God led wise man or woman for counsel and follow through on their counsel, no matter how simple it may seem to you. Further, only speak the words given you by God's messenger, and think on those things. See suggested course of action.

Window washing on a scaffold and you fall off: The dreamer is in denial about something. Your dream was sent that your spiritual eyes might be open that you may know the true intents of your actions and behavior that spiritual (or literal) devastation within your life may be averted. See suggested course of action.

Suggested Course of Action

Question to consider and journal, did your dream depict any symbols that alludes to, the dreamer will make the necessary changes, spiritually, emotionally, and/or physically to affect a more positive outcome? If changes are initiated, your dreams will change.

Nonetheless, most dreams of accidents generally warn of some type of 'heart felt' change; thus deep spiritual work needs to happen within the dreamer's life. One should view these warnings as communicating the certainty of a probationary period placed upon you and regard the warnings with sincere alarm. This probationary period decreed might be a proving by trial (e.g. a wilderness experience); by humiliation and servitude (Judges 13:1; Acts 13:21, 22); or by waiting (Acts 7:23-30). This probationary period points to grace, leads to repentance, and ends in revival and renewal. During this season, you are counseled to begin implementing godly principles that will move you toward discipline and humility, while embracing faith and love of God. Regularly thank God for His patience, long-suffering, and grace (the free and unmerited favor and beneficence of God), while you get things decent and in order. Further, spiritually and materially bless the people of God (those belonging to "The Way", as we were called in the early church, Acts 9:2) with your words and actions, and not disfavor.

Consider and journal the following questions. The questions will help you determine; the issue at hand, how you f Samuel 3:1, the word vision in the Hebrew is hazon5 eel about it, and what may have instigated it. What kind of accident was it? Why was there an accident? Were others involved? If yes, who and in what manner were they involved? Keep in mind that the others represent a quality of you, see Note 3 at the beginning of Actions and Activities category. Did anyone get hurt emotionally, physically, or was disturbed in any way? How did you feel, and what did you do, because, of your feelings, regarding the accident and/or scene where the accident took place? Where were you? Was the place unfamiliar to you? Were you coherent? In view of your dream's context, namely accidents, what choices are you making that may impair your spiritual growth, judgment, health, or that will encourage immorality and/or are you reacting out of fear? If so, what can you do to combat the paralyzing emotion of fear? Your answers, coupled with the interpretation, plus any additional information, should begin to unfold the subject matter and issue at hand, if not now, mull over things a few days. For more information, see index or relevant category and subcategory for other particulars within your dream.

Now, pray (See Prayer of Deliverance, pg. 897)

Specific Meaning

If, you have a very high propensity for accidents, because of driving, including racecar, or motor cross, construction work, or some other form of accident prone or dare devil activity. A dream of this sort should be received as a precautionary warning, to prevent serious harm to yourself, and/or others, due to an accident, mishap, misunderstanding, or disgruntle persons. Be careful. Do not assume that you're safe or it's ok, caution should be heeded at this time. The accident, kept within context of the dream, should be relevant to your everyday working life and/or closely resemble real life situations. Meaning it can actually occur during your awaked state. This will help you narrow down the specifics, and steer clear, of an accident.

Note: If another had the accident, you are being made aware of the plight of someone, the person highlighted within your dream, and you are to get involved (see Chapter One, Are You Ready to Hear the Messages in Your Dreams, section entitled, The 10% for others). There may be potential for a serious accident. Did you know the individual within your dream? If not, God will bring them to your attention. Where did the accident occur? What kind of accident was it? Dreamer, the details, kept within context of your dream, should be relevant to the person's life, and/or closely resemble real life situat ions. Meaning it can actually occur during your awaked state. If you sense your dream is for or about another, namely the person highlighted within the dream, the question as to why you have been made aware of this information, and how do you factor into the equation, should be seriously considered, along with necessary actions. Call the person, and warn them of your concerns. Your warnings will help them narrow down the specifics needed to steer them clear of possible trouble.

However, if your dream was inundated with symbols that are not easily linked to your life activities, then the spiritual implications (the interpretation) should be heeded.

ASCENDING OR EXPANDING - moving upward, getting ready to, or planning, scheduled to, ascend in some manner, or to increase or cause something to increase in capacity, scope, size, or stature

Short Description of "positive types" of ascending or expanding: Someone or something brings you up, lifts you up, or pulls you up, climbing, rising, soaring, raptured-up into heaven, or body becomes larger, in size.

Short Description of "negative types" of ascending or expanding: Bringing or lifting you up, climbing or stepping, on top of others, or rising of smoke.

Unless otherwise noted elsewhere, if, in your everyday living, your awaked state, as part of your lifestyle, work, or ministerial activities, or a special event, you have a very real connection with any type of ascending or expanding activity. For example, circus ride operator, flight, hot air balloon operator or rider, promotional activity, re-construction, especially expansion plans, (also see content list for this category), skip interpretation and go to Specific Meaning at the end of this category.

Otherwise noted, see Note 1 at the beginning of Actions and Activities category.

To determine who your dream is for you or another, see Note 3 at the beginning of Actions and Activities category.

Category Content - If not listed see index, perchance, for your specific type of ascending or expanding dream activity. Positive aspects of ascending or expanding: Positive aspects of ascending or expanding dreams generally imply, coupled with the relevant interpretation, the dreamer will be strengthened and established in the Body of Christ. As well, your dream implies spiritual growth, divine illumination, or some type of promotion or confirmation on a prophetic level. Note, although the following referents are true, they are conditional; according to your faith and obedience, will "it" be done.

- Airplane or Helicopter ascending, see category, Flying (Airplane or Helicopter)
- Body or Baby is rapidly growing bigger or taller
- Body in Heaven or Clouds (to be suddenly up in the heavens, paradise, in the clouds, raptured, and/or to be before God, Jesus in heaven)
- Church or Altar (walking within a church or to approach or bow down at an altar)
- Cord, Rope, or Fabric used to pull you, someone, or something up
- Elevator (going up)
- Hand pulling or lifting you, someone, or something, up
- Ladder
- Lower elevation to a higher one (climbing upward, traveling upward, or walking upward) or Floating upward

- Up out of (or coming out of) a pit, tunnel, or well
- Poverty to Prosperity or "Rags to Riches"
- Scaffold (to be up on one)
- Stairs, staircase or Fire Escape (at top of)
- Wall or Fence (to be up on a wall or fence)

Negative aspects of ascending or expanding: Negative aspects of ascending or expanding dreams generally imply, coupled with the relevant interpretation, sinful ambition in the heart. This will cause God to relent on His promises to approve you in any of your endeavors that would have come with ascending. Take great care and heed God's warnings. We are called to exhibit faith by steadfast obedience, determination, confidence, fortitude, thanks, and love. The genuineness of your faith is judged by your response to hardships and opposition engendered by your identification with Christ, and by your inner temptations to sin. We must exhibit courage under trials, and not take lightly God's disciplinary instructions.

- Climbing up on top of others or Hurting others in any way while ascending in any manner (e.g. causing others to cry while smashing or stepping on others)
- Hot air balloon
- Rising of smoke
- Pulling oneself up by sheer will or using some type of pulley
- Stairs, staircase

Positive aspects of ascending or expanding

Body or Baby is rapidly growing bigger or taller: This dream has two meanings (choose one). (1) Dreamer, God is rapidly maturing you spiritually, intellectually, and emotionally. He has need of you within the Kingdom. Focus and obedience are the key words for you right now. You will need to become passionate, unwavering, and single-minded about your beliefs and never doubt them. Make sure you know the foundational principles of Christianity, as taught by Jesus Christ and His disciples (also see John 3:1-21; Acts 2:37-39), as these should be the overarching theme of your personal ministry – the Gospel of Jesus Christ, the Messiah. When you hear from God, take immediate and dramatic action. Dreamer, fear not, strengthen, and established, you will rise to the occasion. (2) Baby's body is rapidly growing bigger or taller: Dreamer, your hurts, disappointments, lack of friends, loneliness, and separateness, most through no apparent cause of your own, were all ways that the Lord used to mature you; your many challenges have made you a fighter by nature. Your life fraught with fighting, you are now directing your aggressiveness toward positive aims. Dreamer, the anguish and humiliation you've borne has ended; you can safely "bury your weapons in the ground, for you are truly knocking on heaven's door". Be encouraged, your storm is over. God has shaped you into a very sagacious minister. You are now prepared, and is chosen, and anointed for such times as these. Now, entering into this season of your life, amazingly, yours will be a voice of a great leader, respected by many, a nd you will be known by your kindness and eloquence. Dreamer, you are one who is deemed righteous, and a beloved servant o f God. Go forth in confidence, you will be successful, sagacious, and strong. Someone(s) has need of your unique way of presenting truth. Because of the way you distinctively present the gospel and the teachings of Jesus and His disciples, they will receive Christ. Be prepared, for the opportunity, to reach many for Christ, and always be prepared. Moreover, as you continue to mature in Christ, you will be confirmed on a prophetic level. Remember to always listen for God's soft voice and stay humble. Be blessed.

Body in Heaven or Clouds (to be suddenly up in the heavens, paradise, in the clouds, raptured, and/ or to be before God, Jesus in heaven): Dreamer, God will rescue, or has rescued, you from a powerful enemy, one who is/was too strong for you. This person confronted you during a very hard time in your life, but the Lord was your support (2 Samuel 22: 17-25). Now, you will begin to experience a miraculous increase in divine knowledge, and wisdom. This knowledge and wisdom will be imparted to you to be used exclusively for interpreting the gospel of Jesus Christ to others, and for the edifying of the Body of Christ; the body of believers. Your dream also confirms that you're in order for heaven.

Church or Altar (walking within a church or to approach or bow down at an altar): According to the context of your dream, this dream implies one of three issues. It implies spiritual growth, divine illumination, and some type of promotion or confirmation, on some level or another. Your height of spiritual progress and promotion will be according to your faith and obedience to God's will over your life personally. The following is necessary for you to hear, understand, and heed. If you want to approach and worship the Holy One by way of inspirational music, praise and worship ministry, teaching, or preaching, you should come before Him in a sense of appropriateness. Meaning you should aspire for some level of truthfulness, modesty, and reliability. No other is responsible for this in your life but you; therefore, deal with an existing situation that hinders your approach to God with some level of purity (Leviticus 11:45, 1 Peter 1:13-2:3). With that said, some questions; was dreamer already inside the church walking around, or, did you walk into a church, or did you remained outside? Did you bow before the altar? (1) If dreamer was already inside the church walking around, this denotes one who is spiritually prepared for spiritual growth, divine illumination, and some type of promotion or confirmation. Therefore, prepare your mind for action; be self-controlled; set your hope fully on the grace to be given you when Jesus Christ is revealed, and no longer conform to your carnal desires (see 1 Peter 1:13-16). Moreover, your dream is additional proof of something you have believed God for is correct (e.g., for a spouse, rectification of an attitude of anger, frustration, discontent, or for a healing of unbelief, or a healing of your faith level, or a healing of physical health, or for any hindrances to your spiritual clarity that you have recognized). In addition, a promotion or confirmation ceremony will be held in a church, and/or you will meet a potential spouse in about 50 days. (2) If dreamer walked into a church, entering into a church denotes one who has purified him or herself in preparation for ministry. Now that you have purified yourself by obeying the truth, so that you have sincere love for other Christians, and love deeply from your heart (see 1 Peter 1:22-24). Your height of spiritual progress and promotion will be according to your faith and obedience to God's will over your life personally. (3) To remain outside of the church, remaining outside of the church denotes one who, rather than choosing to approach and enter into (or embrace) God's righteousness, is opting to refrain from the process of sanctification and/or ministering. Dreamer this choice will surely be unprofitable for you. Therefore, rid yourself of all malice and all deceit, hypocrisy, envy, and slander of every kind, and crave that which will help you mature spiritually in the Lord (see 1 Peter 1:24-2:3). See suggested course of action.

Cord, Rope, or Fabric used to pull you, someone, or something up: You have access to prophetic wisdom because you have the capacity to discern truth from false. Nurture your gift of discernment; developing it that others may spiritually grow by your words of wisdom. For you is truly a prophet, prophetess. Do not suppress the prophetic nature of your gifting out of fear or laziness; this may prove detrimental to your spiritual and financial life. Your efforts will be a revolutionary force in other people's lives. For this reason, you will be delivered from your present predicament. Someone has been sent by God to help you. Receive, and allow their help; they are qualified. By helping you get free, they will be helping you go towards your divine destiny. Remember them in the day of your prosperity.

Elevator (going up): Your optimistic and generous personality, coupled with your strong desire to uplift humanity is leading you into situations where you will be able to express your desire to serve others. You will be provided with the resources to carry out your vision, and will become established, expect it.

Hand pulling or lifting you, someone, or something, up: A promotion is within reach, at hand. Moreover, admission or entrance into a place or association will happen very easily (e.g. go to college, join that club, apply for that job, or start that ministry), wherever you are trying to gain entrance, it will be granted you.

Ladder: Your dream was sent as a word of encouragement and one confirmation that the dreamer is maturing spiritually properly.

Lower elevation to a higher one or Floating upward (climbing upward, traveling upward, or walking upward): In your present business or personal dealings, you will be satisfied and take delight in your goals. If you are involved in any situ ation that is competitive, you will triumphant. Additionally, the pace and/or distance depicted (e.g. running, walking, or already there) will often refer to a "time frame", the length of time before manifestation. For example, one already at their destination refers to the present, or denotes that dreamer is already at destined place, while running, or walking, both refer to a future time. Moreover, one running, will reach their destination in approximately one-fourth the time quicker than walking. Note: one city block will often refer to approximately six months to one year. Moreover, if mode of travel was highlighted, see category, Vehicles, Modes of Transportation. Note: if the "mph" is highlighted within your dream, see category, Numbers. No matter the pace or distance, your dream denotes that you're on your way to manifestation.

Up out of (or coming out of) a pit, tunnel, or well: Because of your humble respect towards your relationship with

Christ, God has made a way for you or a loved one to escape from, or leave, a place of confinement or desolation. Be it prison, a bad relationship, or a place of spiritual barrenness (e.g. a cult or a spiritually dead ministry).

Poverty to Prosperity or "Rages to Riches": Because of a spirit of humility, God will begin to cover you with His protection and riches. You will now begin to experience God's favor, coupled with abundance. Dreamer, from this day forward God's blessings will flow abundantly, producing spiritual growth within you. God's blessings: Gifts of God's grace, anything God freely gives you, absolution, the Holy Spirit, salvation, regeneration, eternal life, health, children, love of family, longevity, necessities, prosperity, and dominion over all that is yours; and all are parts of the supply of grace, and all are sanctified by the Lord, and technically belongs to Him. The result of this supply in your life will be peace.

Scaffold (to be up on one): Your spiritual eyes will be open to a spiritual truth you have not known or they will be open to one you have believed to be untrue. Accept God's truth and reject man's traditions. For the traditions are no longer relevant or applicable. If necessary, see suggested course of action.

Stairs, staircase or Fire Escape (at top of): Whatever you have set out to do, do your best with it, for you will be successful within your endeavor, and will be highly esteemed. God has promised to make known to you His presence, His guidance, and protection. Be encouraged. Additionally, the pace and/or distance depicted (running, walking, or already upstairs) will often refer to a "time frame", the length of time before manifestation. For example, one already upstairs refers to the present, or denotes that dreamer is already at destined place, while running or walking upstairs, both refer to a future time. Moreover, one running, will reach their destination in approximately one-fourth the time quicker than walking. No matter the pace, your dream denotes that you're on your way to manifestation.

Wall or Fence (to be up on a wall or fence): Your state of affairs is before God. Any condition that is upon you at present that seems hopeless and/or extremely frustrating; you will overcome it. For instance, if you have been diagnosed with a serious or incurable illness, you will be healed and survive to declare the glories of the Lord. Go through your circumstances hopeful and optimistic (Psalm 27:5). Yes, you will experience loss materially and possibly physically, but all will be repla ced. Do not be dismayed, nor lose courage. Faith is a keyword for you at present.

Negative aspects of ascending or expanding

Climbing up on top of others: This dream has two meanings (choose one). (1) You are evidencing traits of an abusive leader, who mistreats those appointed to serve within the realm of your authority. Your ill treatment of others and misuse of your authority will cause your divine given anointing to cease and you will lose the respect of those you've been leading. Others see you as egotistical, wickedly ambitious, and lacking in authentic love for God's people. Their instincts are not far off the mark. You have become blind to the things of God and the care of His people. You are also raising offspring with the same attitude. Dreamer, you need to seriously re-think things and do change your behavior towards others. Go and request an audience of Jesus, and then take immediate and dramatic actions to rectify existing negative state of affairs. Moreover, if relevant, rectify the behavior of your children, which they have modeled after you. As well, seek honest advice from other leaders if necessary. Dreamer, the more God allows you to see your emptiness, it is suggested that you be more earnest to repent, for your dream is to warn a rebellious person, in the spirit of grace. To see if you will yet be worked upon, and change your mindset, or else to leave you inexcusable, in your accusations against God, because of your ruin (e.g. continually plundered, seized, and disfavored, also see Jeremiah 9:7-9; Zechariah 13:9; Matthew 23:37-39; Revelation 3:15-21). See suggested course of action. (2) Hurting others in any way while ascending in any manner (e.g. causing others to cry while smashing or stepping on others): Dreamer, you have insurgent, anarchist, and/or coup intentions towards the established church of God and towards the leadership within your ministry, and/or towards some other God ordained authority over your life (e.g. spouse, parents, the law). Your thoughts are demonically influenced and will be demonically led. Any kind of rebellious actions, at present, will be exposed publicly, and your behavior and actions will certainly result in a denial of admission or entrance into some important place, or denial of a promotion or a confirmation; you will surely fall into our own trap. Correct your existing negative mind-set. Dreamer, the more God allows you to see your rebelliousness, it is suggested that you be more earnest to repent, for your dream is to warn a rebellious person, in the spirit of grace. See suggested course of action.

Hot air balloon: This is a symbol of a physical devastation, of the one riding in the balloon. If the one riding in the balloon continues on their present path, embracing their life choices, which are primarily negative, they will pass away within five years. You walk unwise and foolish, thus you will die before your time. An immediate and dramatic change in your way of thinking and acting, your behavior, is of utmost importance right now, that you might live beyond what is intended you because of your present choices and way of living. See suggested course of action.

Rising of smoke: The dreamer portrays a false image of him or herself, for glory and praise purposes. Such an attitude of great hypocrisy will cause God to relent on His promises to approve you in any of your endeavors. Any genuine praise you would receive because of service to the King's Kingdom will be halted. Hence, presenting a more realistic and truthful image of yourself will gain you the respect and support you need to go forward in your endeavors, as well as, diminish the embarrassment that comes when the masquerade is over. God, and God alone is to be worship", for God has said, "*I am the Lord: that is My name: and My glory will I not give to another*" (Isaiah 42:8 NKJV). Therefore, dreamer you are warned to be careful lest you become so prideful that there creeps into you the idea that you can be deified. Self-deification is of Satan. God can dwell in the human, via the Holy Spirit, but forever the human is the human, and Adonai Elohim is forever God. See suggested course of action.

Pulley (pulling oneself up by sheer will or using some type of pulley): You are promoting your own personal agenda, and your motive is self-exaltation. If no immediate and dramatic actions are taken to subdue your greed for power, formidable adversaries will rise up against you, and it will allowed. You will not be able to withstand them. Stop, pray, and listen f or God's agenda. Only within His will for your life, will you attain genuine power, security, and promotion. An immediate and dramatic change in your way of thinking and acting, your behavior, is of utmost importance right now, that you might live beyond what is intended you because of your present choices and way of living. See suggested course of action.

Stairs, staircase: This dream has three meanings (choose one). (1) To see someone creeping upstairs: Your behavior is asinine and your lifestyle is profoundly burdened with envying, covetousness, lusts and sinful desires. You are blinded by l ust. Your justifications are weak excuses, unstable, leading to trouble. The more God allows you to see your emptiness, it is suggested that you be more earnest to repent that you may find Him to be grace and healing. Hence, your dream is to warn a rebellious person, in the spirit of grace, to see if you will yet be worked upon, and change your mindset, or else to leave you inexcusable, in your accusations against God, because of your ruin. If no immediate and dramatic actions are taken to subdue the wickedness within your life, formidable adversaries will rise up against you, and it will allowed. You will not be able to withstand them. See suggested course of action. (2) Unmarried dreamer (male or female): If you are involved in a potentially serious relationship with someone, do not be deceived, this person has a "Machiavellian" nature — deceitful, tricky, scheming, sneaky, and underhanded, although he or she considers him or herself Christian. Dreamer, you are in a weaken state sexually, and can easily to be preyed upon by this person. The enemy creeps as a thief and robber, he comes to rob, steal, and destroy. This relationship (you and the person creeping) is a ploy from the enemy to cause an offense within you against your God, leaving you thinking that God has forgotten you or does not care about your present state of affairs. Truth: Your Heavenly Father has not forgotten you, and He does care. It is your impractical, unrestrained behavior, and refusal to sacrifice temporary pleasure for long-term gain, that has caused this breech in character. Go no further with this relationship. (3) Searching for, or seeking, someone upstairs: New and bleak information will be revealed about someone significant in your life. More than likely, the person, you were searching for or seeking. If applicable, withdraw all of your financial support from this person. Duly heed the warning, and proceed with caution with this relationship, to spare your emotions from serious hurt, for you are a possible victim of this person, and of many. Learn to guard your heart with all diligence, and learn what a victimization mentality is. For after a while, your victimization will begin to infuriate you, breeding bitterness.

Suggested Course of Action

Question to consider and journal, did your dream depict any symbols that alludes to, the dreamer will make the necessary changes, spiritually, emotionally, and/or physically to affect a more positive outcome? If changes are initiated, your dreams will change. With that, see the following.

As this dream was sent to demonstrate grace, via a warning, a change that may affect positive results in your life is still possible. It is not too late to re-group and re-gather. Sincerely, amend the true intents and purposes of your actions; and if applicable, bring to an end the abusing of your authority, status, or connections. You are expected to respect your fellow m an, hence, running over or even crowding others, and especially stepping on others is to be avoided emphatically. Never aggressively take, push, or toil for any position, promotion, place, or seat of honor, or wealth. Allow God to provide the w ay, knowing exaltation comes from the Lord.

Positive aspects of ascending: In view of your dream's context, namely ascending (positively), spiritual growth, divine illumination, or some type of promotion is in sight. Do not make any major decisions or act untypical during this time in yo ur life. Your choices may hinder the positive influences coming your way. Be patient, in due time you will reap if you faint not.

Negative aspects of ascending: The negative aspects of ascending are warning or precautionary dreams. In view of your

dream's context, namely ascending (negatively), what choices are you making or have made, that are hindering your success spiritually and/or literally. What are doing that may impair your spiritual growth, judgment, health, or that will encourage immorality and/or are you reacting out of fear? If so, what can you do to combat the paralyzing emotion of fear?

Consider and journal the following questions. The questions will help you determine; the issue at hand, how you feel about it, and what may have instigated it. What kind of ascending activity was it? Why was their ascending? Were others involved? If yes, who and in what manner were they involved? Keep in mind that the others represent a quality of you, see Note 3 at the beginning of Actions and Activities category. Did anyone get hurt emotionally or physically? How did you feel, and what did you do, because, of your feelings, regarding ascending and/or where you ended up or was going? Was it agitating, confusing, dangerous, disturbing, frustrating, peace with the situation, happy, joyful, life threatening, safe, sc ary, or unsure? Where were you? Was the place unfamiliar to you? Were you coherent? Your answers, coupled with the interpretation, plus any additional information, should begin to unfold the subject matter and issue at hand, if not now, mul l over things a few days. For more information, see index or relevant category and subcategory for other particulars within your dream.

Now, pray (See Prayer of Deliverance, pg. 897)

Specific Meanings

Positive aspects of ascending: Unless otherwise noted elsewhere, if, in your everyday living, your awaked state, as part of your lifestyle, work, or ministerial activities, or a special event, you have a very high propensity for flight, window washing, o r some other form of upward activity, a dream of this sort is encouragement and assurance in the physical realm. The ascension, kept within context of the dream, should be relevant to your everyday working life and/or closely resemble real life situations. Meaning it can actually occur during your awaked state. This will help you narrow down the specifics needed to help you let go of your fears, and bring encouragement.

Negative aspects of ascending: Unless otherwise noted elsewhere, if, in your everyday living, your awaked state, as part of your lifestyle, work, or ministerial activities, or a special event, you have a very high chance that you will direct others (e.g. supervisory responsibilities in some form or another or in dealing with the public, within the human resource arena). A drea m of this sort should be heeded as a warning in the physical realm, to prevent serious emotional harm to others by you, and/or physical harm to you, due to a disgruntle person. Your dream kept within context, should be relevant to your lifestyle and closely resemble your real-life situations. Meaning it can actually occur during your awaked state. This will help you narrow down the specific areas of concern with regard to your attitude and dealings with others.

ASCENDING AND DESCENDING - **moving upward and then downward, to rise and descend, to go up and down, to fall and get back up, and these actions are repeated and/or 'stand-out' within the dream**

Who hath ascended up into heaven, and descended? (Proverbs 30:4 ASV)
Some short descriptions of types, phrases, and other processes and particulars, connected in some way to this category. For example, someone or something lifts you up and then down, to climb up and go back down, to grow and shrink, to mount and dismount, to offer up and retract, to be put on a pedestal, or wall, and to be taken down.

Unless otherwise noted elsewhere, if, in your everyday living, your awaked state, as part of your lifestyle, work, or

ministerial activities, or a special event, you have a very real connection with any type of ascending and descending activit y.

For example, circus-ride operator, construction, flight, hot air balloon operator, or rider, drone activity, promotional activity, or up on a scaffold, (also see content list for this category). Your dream is not significant and does not warrant special attention.

Otherwise noted, this dream may be a Prophetically Simple Dream (see Chapter One: The 60th Part of Prophecy).

Whereas, the dreamer is warned to stop any unwise, reckless, or dangerous actions or activities, you should cease any daredevil or impetuous activity, especially if this is a thing within the dreamer's life. If any of the preceding is happening, or was depicted within your dream, this dream is a first step intervention and an alarm. Skip interpretation and re-consider your activity as harmful, hurtful, or life threatening, at present. Handle the situation wisely, by first thanking God for the warning, for Adonai Elohim knows all. Also, see Specific Meaning at the end of this category, section entitled, Note (Specific Meaning).

Otherwise noted, see Note 1 at the beginning of Actions and Activities category.

To determine who your dream is for you or another, see Note 3 at the beginning of Actions and Activities category. *Symbols and Referents:* Primarily these types of dreams reference the blessings promised to you and your lineage. **Category Content** - If not listed see index, perchance, for your specific type of upward, downward dream activity.

- Baptize or Lowered down, Fell, Leaped, or Walked down into an Abyss, Cavity, Crater, Depression, Ditch, Hole in the ground, Hollow, Pond, Pool, Spring, Trench, Water hole, Waterless Pit, or Well, and then brought up out of, or came back up again
- Circus Rides & Playground Equipment (e.g. Roller Coaster, Sea Saw, Sliding Board, Swings)
- Elevator (up and then down)
- Going up and down (from a low place to a high place, back to a low place, e.g. going up and down a fire escape, stairs, or up a peak, mountain, hill, in the sky, and above, and then back down again)

Baptize or Lowered down, Fell, Leaped, or Walked down into an Abyss, Cavity, Crater, Depression, Ditch, Hole in the ground, Hollow, Pond, Pool, Spring, Trench, Water hole, Waterless Pit, or Well, and then brought up out of, or came back up again: This dream has two meanings (choose one). (1) Water (baptism) or to be sprayed, sprinkled, or doused with water: This dream was sent to encourage. Dreamer be encourage, you have fulfilled all requirements for righteousness and you have a clear conscience. In addition, you have access to prophetic insight, enabling you to discern between true and false. This wisdom will be a transformational force in many people's lives. Dreamer, you have been found of good reputation, full of the Spirit, and wise. Your dream is also one confirmation that the dreamer has been chosen by God, and approved by man, to be set aside and ordained as a ministerial leader. If not already, you will be officially ordained. Dreamer, the way the ordination will be carried out may not be to your liking; nonetheless, do not attribute (or call) that which is of God, unclean (e.g. confusion, erroneous, out of order, unlawful, weak, wicked, or any other attributes of the unregenerate). Do not consider yo ur ordination as unofficial or a small thing, for it is of God and His kindness towards you. You are to carry out an official role (e.g. bishop, deacon, deaconess, elder, evangelist, pastor, preacher, superintendent, or teacher). (2) Lowered down, fell, leaped into, or walked down into, an abyss, cavity, crater, depression, ditch, hole in the ground, hollow, lake, trench, waterless pit, well, and then brought up out of, or came back up again: You will experience, or is experiencing, intense mental health issues because of some form of demonic oppression. Favorably, you will endure and will rise to a preeminent level that you may accomplish your divine destiny in a timely manner. God is sending someone to help you get free from your present predicament. This person is very capable. Allow him or her to fulfill their God given mission. See suggested course of action.

Circus Rides & Playground Equipment (e.g. Roller Coaster, Sea Saw, Sliding Board, Swings): There is a level of spiritual immaturity within your life, because of a shallow, superficial demeanor when dealing with yourself and others. You also lack depth and insightfulness when it comes to the knowledge of God, and His Word. Notwithstanding, God will accomplish through you, whatever He has asked of you. This accomplishment of His Will, by you, can be done easy or with many hardships, depending on your willingness to mature and level of obedience. Nonetheless, His will, will most assuredly be done. See suggested course of action.

Elevator (up and then down): Someone is praying on your behalf (interceding) to the Ruler of rulers. They are reminding Him of your courageous good works towards them on behalf of the Kingdom of God. At present, you are at a critical moment in your life, a crisis of your faith. Although you have fallen, you will rise. Although you sit in darkness, the Lord will be your light. Own up to your wrongdoings to Jesus and others, and make amends to those you've hurt or offended. As God has delivered you in the past because of His faithfulness, so He will deliver you now, only repent. If necessary, see suggested course of action.

Going up and down (from a low place to a high place, back to a low place, e.g. going up and down a fire escape, stairs, or up a peak, mountain, hill, in the sky, and above, and then back down again): This dream has two meanings (choose one). (1) Dreamer, as it is written, in Isaiah 30:18-21, so it will be with you. You will come to know and experience grace (the free and unmerited favor and beneficence of God). Moreover, because of your faith, humility, strong leadership, and your courageous and optimistic spirit, you will be greatly honored. You will rise to a level the Anointing of God and your acumen deem you should be. God is with you and He will keep you wherever you go. Even more, you have the miraculous power to change history on some level or another. For example, family generational curses can stop with you (Exodus 20:5, 7; Psalm 112:2), or by introducing radically new fundamental concepts, far beyond the norm (Acts 13:14-52). Whatever the miraculous history change is, be it on a small-scale, via practicing what you preach, or by facilitating some specialize workshops, or by becoming a great leader and orator, you are equipped to handle large-scale undertakings. Dreamer, a large part of your mission in life centers on raising the spirits of your fellow mankind; thus changing history in the lives of those, you touch. The driving force behind all this is your support of others. Your first step is to start by recognizing and thanking Jesus fo r the small blessings that are before you now and for the miraculous endowment of history changing vision and courageous leadership. Do you want your miracle? Then prepare yourself mentally for it. This is not to say there will not be a lot of twists an d turns, and fear, but you will get to your destined place to carry out your divine ordained purpose, if you are willing, prudent, and obedient. Additionally, the pace and/or distance depicted (traveling speed, running, walking, or driving, or already the re or in place) will often refer to a "time frame", the length of time before manifestation. For example, one already at their destin ation refers to the present, or denotes that dreamer is already at destined place, while traveling speed, running, or walk ing, all refer to a future time. Moreover, one running, one will reach their destination in approximately one fourth the time quicker than walking, and depending upon the means of travel and speed, one will reach their destination in one half to three fou rths the time quicker than running. Note: one city block will often refer to approximately six months to one year. Moreover, if mode of travel was highlighted, see category, Modes of Transportation. Note: if the "mph" is highlighted within your dream, see category, Numbers. Nevertheless, no matter the pace or mode of travel, you're on your way to manifestation, and things may happen quickly. For more information, see index or relevant category for other particulars within your dream. Kept within context of your dream and the interpretation, this highlighted reference is an area (or situation) of relevance. (2) Up and down stairs, staircase, or Fire Escape: You have an open connection to divine revelation, which should be use on a prophetic platform, as a prophet or prophetess. Properly developed, your link to prophetic revelation can and should be used to help others. Freely received, freely give. Moreover, you will inspire others to dream and to make their dreams come true. Unfortunately, you have a problem with partiality; you show favoritism. This will undoubtedly cause division within your family and/or ministry.

Suggested Course of Action

Question to consider and journal, did your dream depict any symbols that alludes to, the dreamer will make the necessary changes, spiritually, emotionally, and/or physically to affect a more positive outcome? If changes are initiated, your dreams will change.

Nonetheless, the promises intrinsic to ascending and descending dreams, requires obedience for their continuance. Acknowledgement of the error of your way to yourself and to Jesus is requisite, hence making your way (ascension) easier, with less hardships and loss. Dependence upon your own ingenuity to survive and succeed; essentially, should give way to you finally accepting the command and the will of the Lord.

Consider and journal the following questions. The questions will help you determine; the issue at hand, how you feel about it, and what may have instigated it. What kind of ascending and descending was it? Why was there ascending and descending activity? Were others involved? If yes, who and in what manner were they involved? Keep in mind that the others represent a character trait, quality, or talent within you. Did anyone get hurt emotionally, physically, or was disturbed in any way? How did you feel, and what did you do, because, of your feelings, regarding the ascending and descending and/or the place where it happened? Was it agitating, confusing, dangerous, disturbing, frustrating, peace with the situation, happy, joyful, life threatening, safe, scary, or unsure? Where were you? Was the place unfamiliar to you? Were you coherent? In view of your dream's context, namely ascending and descending, what choices are you making that may impair your spiritual growth, judgment, health, or that will encourage immorality and/or are you reacting out of fear? If so, what can you do to combat the paralyzing emotion of fear? Your answers, coupled with the interpretation, plus any additional information, should begin to unfold the subject matter and issue at hand, if not now, mull over things a few days. For more information, see ind ex or relevant category and subcategory for other particulars within your dream.

Now, pray (See Prayer of Deliverance, pg. 897)

Specific Meaning

If, you have a very high propensity for flight, or some other form of upward and then downward activity, a dream of this sort should be received as a precautionary warning, or assurance, in the physical realm, depending upon the context of your dream. There is potential for an accident, however, you will recover and regain the ability to continue with (or be restored to) you r job. Your dream specifics should be relevant to your everyday working life and/or closely resemble real life situations. Meaning it can actually occur during your awaked state. This will help you narrow down the specifics of a possible accident.

BLOOD, BLEEDING

Some short descriptions of types, phrases, and other processes and particulars, connected in some way to this category are, for example, to see blood loss from any parts of the body, to draw blood, blood transfusion, or blood shed by violence, slay, or murder. Blood, sweat, perspiration, and tears, blood from a wound or surface, blood on your hands, dried blood, hemophiliac, hemorrhage, internal bleeding, the bleeding heart plant, pouring of, gushing, oozing, or spurting of blood, stigmata, tainted or contaminated blood, a woman's time of "uncleanness".

Unless otherwise noted elsewhere, if, in your everyday living, your awaked state, as part of your lifestyle, work, or ministerial activities, or a special event, you have a very real connection with any type of loss of blood activity. For exa mple, blood donations or drives, blood diseases, lab work, or medical field, (also see content list for this category), your dream is not significant and does not warrant special attention.

Otherwise noted, this dream may be a Prophetically Simple Dream (see Chapter One: The 60th Part of Prophecy). Whereas, the dreamer is counseled to cease any impetuous or suicidal activity, especially any actions or activities that invo lve the "cutting" or killing of yourself; dreamer, although your emotional pain that set off this kind of activity is real, the "cutting" of yourself, or the suicidal intents, is demonically led, deliberately marked by a violent force. The voices you hear, now, are not your own. Trust this. The act is carried out in undue haste and lacks forethought, e.g. "pain can and will end, especially with appropriate change of people, places, things, actions, and/or activities; change is possible via prayer to Jesus. Ask Jesus to take it all away, giving you enough time to make an intelligent decision, to walk away and start over. For a wise person, when he or she falls, can and should get back up. There is a future for you; this is not the end of your story (Jeremiah 29:10 -14). If any of the preceding is happening (cutting activity or suicidal intents), or if this was depicted within your dream, this dream is a first step intervention and an alarm. Skip interpretation and re-consider your activity as harmful, hurtful, or life threatening, at present. Handle the situation wisely, by first thanking God for the warning, for Adonai Elohim knows all. Also, see Specific Meaning at the end of this category, section entitled, Note (Specific Meaning).

Otherwise noted, this dream of bleeding may be a Prophetically Simple Dream (see Chapter One: The 60th Part of Prophecy). Whereas, the dreamer is warned to seek emergency medical attention due to health issues related to bleeding (e.g. blood transfusion, hemophiliac, hemorrhaging, internal bleeding, stigmata, or sweating blood), especially if this has been an issue within the dreamer's life or within the life of someone connected to the dreamer. This dream is a first step intervention and an alarm. Skip interpretation and go get emergency medical attention.

Otherwise noted, this dream may be an ordinary "real-time" dream (see Chapter One, Chalom), whereas the dreamer is physically bleeding in real time (e.g. nosebleed, bandage need changing, or woman's monthly cycle). Skip interpretation and go attend to your situation, if appropriate.

Otherwise noted, see Note 1 at the beginning of Actions and Activities category.

Symbols and Referents: Loss of blood usually denotes literal or spiritual life passing away, due to a physical or spiritual weakness, illness, erroneous ideology, or forgiveness, on some level, needs to take place.

Category Content - If not listed see index, perchance, for your specific type of bleeding dream activity.

- Baby, Children bleeding
- Bleeding Heart plant
- Blood on, bubbling, gushing, oozing, running down, spurting, or heavily flowing from any part of the body
- Blood Sacrifice (animal or human) or Donated Blood
- Blood Transfusion or Blood Bank
- Contaminated or Tainted blood
- Buildings, Structures, Walls with blood bubbling, oozing, running down, or heavily flowing from any parts of the edifice
- Clothing soaked with blood
- Dried blood (to see it anywhere)
- Drinking Blood
- To enjoy looking at Bloodshed
- Hematidrosis (aka Sweating Blood)
- Hemophiliac (blood clotting disorder resulting in extensive bleeding, from even minor injuries)
- Hemorrhaging (excessive internal bleeding)
- Man or woman covered with blood
- Money with blood on it, "blood money"
- Pouring blood out of a container
- To see blood bubbling, oozing, spurting, or flowing from a rock or stone. Or, to see Jesus bleeding
- Shedding of innocent blood
- Stigmata (bleeding wounds corresponding to the crucifixion wounds of Jesus)
- Tears mixed with blood
- To see the flow of blood stopped
- Woman's monthly cycle (menstruation, period) or monthly accessories (e.g. kotex, tampon)
- Wood, tree: To see blood bubbling, oozing, spurting, or flowing from a piece of wood or a tree

Baby, Children bleeding: A dream involving a baby or children bleeding from any parts of their body is a dire warning to the dreamer. This dream has two meanings (choose one). (1) On occasion, one may have an Oneirovatic or "OV" dream (see Chapter One: The 60th part of prophecy, other prophetic dreams). This type of dream bares insight into the present day or near future events of another who seriously needs your help. Concerning children, one may plainly see abuse, assaults, accidents, or molestation taking place. This type of dream should closely resemble real life situations, with the dream events actually being capable of happening. For example, if you dreamt your child is bleeding and the child says within the dream, "Rev. Woods did it!", then Rev. Woods realistically needs to be able to have committed the crime or offense. Has Rev. Woods ever had access to your child? Does your child know a Rev. Woods? If you sense that your dream is for or about another, namely a child, the question as to why you have been made aware of this information, and how do you factor into the equation, should be seriously considered, along with necessary actions. Dreamer, you are sent to get involved immedi ately (see Chapter One, Are You Ready to Hear the Messages in Your Dreams, section entitled, The 10% for others). Are you the parent, grandparent, a relative, or close family friend? If this is your child, take earnest heed to the warning and be caut ious of abuse, assaults, accidents, or any violations perpetrated against the child. Have authorities been notified? Are you able to stop the violation? Establishing a safe environment, alerting law officials and other pertinent individuals is highly recommended. Dreamer, actually calling the police and involving child protective services needs to happen without consideration of the abuser, especially if child is bleeding from private parts. If the abuser didn't respect your child and you enough, to stop him or herself from violating your child, then do not respect them enough, not to call the appropriate authorities. Your dream is a first step intervention and an alarm. Skip further interpretation and call the police. (2) Baby, Children bleeding: This choice has two parts (choose one). (a) Baby, child belonged to dreamer: This sort of dream is revealing the loss of a ministry (or ministries) due to serious neglect or spiritual immaturity on the part of the dreamer. Most of the meaning of the dream may be obtained by considering the following questions. What happened to the baby, children to cause the bleeding? What part of their body was bleeding? What condition was the baby, children in during the bleeding? Who was responsible for the incident? Dreamer, now ask yourself the following questions. What would you do if your literal baby, child was bleeding, as the baby, children were in your dream? If you physically caused the bleeding, what would you do? Would you try to hide the incident? Should the situation be handled without getting authorities involved? If someone else caused the bleeding, would you call the police? Would you take your baby from those responsible for the bleeding? Would you call child protective authorities? Were you just staring at your baby, children? (b) Baby, child belonged to someone else: Your dream is about another who may possibly need your help. Ask yourself, what would you do if a literal baby were in that condition (bleeding)? For example, if you saw or sensed, someone so neglect or abused a baby or children to the point of bloodshed, would you try to hide the incident? Would you call the police or other appropriate authorities? Would you handle the situation without involving the authorities? Would you take the baby? What were your actions within your dream?

For (a) and (b): To determine the symbolic equivalent to your responses, see following examples: You hiding the incident would be spiritually equivalent to pretending that your ministry is something that it is not. Calling the police is figurative of intercessory prayer for a ministry. Taking the baby denotes taking over a ministry. Handling the situation wi thout involving authorities is equivalent to you attempting to get a ministry off the ground according to your own ideas, understanding, perspective, and reasoning abilities, without dependence upon God. Just observing is equivalent to doing nothing. Journal your answers, determine the ministry your dream is referencing, considering any ministry you are involved with or is trying to help get underway, and react appropriately. If necessary, see suggested course of action.

Bleeding Heart plant: Highlighted within your dream or remembered, refers to a person who shows extreme sympathy, especially towards those who are the objects of suspected persecution or oppression, and/or is depressed. The missionary field calls out for you, even if only in your neighborhood or community, go start a mission, and God will give you the resour ces to build and maintain. Start your own ministry without consideration of support from anyone. The reason for this principle is that when you look for support from others, and there is none, this may, and often does, hinder your initial response to the call, and/or progress. Look to God for your sufficiency, for He will provide.

Blood on, bubbling, gushing, oozing, running down, spurting, or heavily flowing from any part of the body: *Note:* If your dream closely resembles, real life situations this dream of blood may be a Prophetically Simple Dream, see Note 1 at the beginning of this category. With that, this dream has two meanings (choose one). (1) Dreamer is seeking to cruelly, destroy someone spiritually or physically, one who has helped you and/or your family. This is spiritual murder (a premeditated attempt to destroy someone's personal relationship with Christ, or a cruel destruction of someone's reputation). The evil you do to others will come back to haunt you. You will be ensnared by your own evil. Additionally, from where was the blood flowing? For example, was it an arm, ear, eye, hand, leg, mouth, nose, or stomach? For specific body part bleeding, see category, The Body. Was person known? Kept within context of your dream and the interpretation, other references highlighted may also be points of relevance, pointing to why you are cruelly treating others. See suggested course of action. (2) To see blood on, bubbling, oozing, or flowing from any part of somebody's body: Dreamer, you are going to be made aware of the plight of someone that is being falsely slandered and spiritually murdered. You have the resources and/or the God given authority to stop what is happening (see Chapter One, Are You Ready to Hear the Messages in Your Dreams, section entitled, The 10% for others). Did you know the individual within your dream? If not, God will bring them to your attention. From where was the blood flowing? For example, was it an arm, ear, eye, leg, mouth, nose, or stomach? For specific body p art bleeding, see category, The Body. Kept within context of your dream and the interpretation, other references highlighted may also be points of relevance.

Blood sacrifice (animal or human) or Donated Blood: This dream has three meanings (choose one). (1) To sacrifice a clean animal upon an altar or to see one bleeding on an altar: Your wrongdoings will be covered for a short while and consequences temporarily deferred. Deal with your indulgences immediately, for judgment will come. Kept within context of your dream and the interpretation, other references highlighted may also be points of relevance, such as kind of animal. For specific animal, see category, Animals. See suggested course of action. (2) To sacrifice an unclean animal upon an altar or to see one bleeding on an altar: Extreme pride and refusal to repent will cause you to lose your God given ministry and/or life by slaughter. Grace will be shown you, via a probationary period, and regard this period with sincere alarm. This probationary period decreed might be a proving by trial (e.g. a wilderness experience); by humiliation and servitude (Judges 13:1; Acts 13:21, 22); or by waiting (Acts 7:23-30). This probationary period points to grace, leads to repentance, and ends in revival and renewal. During this season, you are counseled to begin implementing godly principles that will move you toward discipline and humility, while embracing faith and love of God. Regularly, thank God for His patience, long-suffering, and grace (the free and unmerited favor and beneficence of God), while you get things decent and in order. One should regard the warning of this dream with sincere alarm. This warning must not be undermined by notions that presuppose the warning is real, but the possibility of an actual loss of a God-given ministry, your prosperity, or even life itself is not. See suggested course of action. (3) To sacrifice a human being upon an altar or to see one bleeding on an altar or donate blood: An individual is being spiritually crushed, dishonored, humiliated, or tortured by the dreamer, or by someone the dreamer has authority over; putting this person's relationship with Christ in harm's way. With that said, this choice has three parts (choose one). (a) If dreamer does not know the person upon the altar, then the act of spiritual murder is being committed by someone you lead. If you do not know who the culprit is, expose the atrocity, via preaching or teaching. (b) If you know the person, in your awaked life, then you are the culprit. Stop what is happening to the specific individual who is on the altar. You have the power to do so, for this act of murder is accounted to you within the spiritual realm. See suggested course of action. (c) Dreamer was sacrificed upon an altar or donated blood: Dreamer, you are allowing yourself to be handled abusively, emotionally, physically, mentally, and/or spiritually by another namely the one who was responsible for the altar or the one drawing the blood. One thing is for sure; you recognize the abusive tendencies, and they are real, you are in harm's way, and you are warned. If you do not stand up for yourself, you will draw harm and violence to yourself, resulting in destruction of family and/or loss of life. This warning must not be undermined by notions that presuppose the possibility of actual loss of life is not real. Moreover, you are to reject people, places, and circumstances that hinder spiritual clarity, growth, and stability. Dreamer, exalt no one, or your public image of well-being, above God, especially to the point of devastation emotionally or spiritually. To lie down your life for someone, something, or image, especially as a ritual offering, is idolatry. In time, through the workings of grace, there will be deliverance, freedom, and rest for you. Regularly thank God for His patience, long- suffering, and grace (the free and unmerited favor and beneficence of God), while you get things decent and in order. One, who does understand your situation, is near you. Seek them out, as well as, a program for abused persons. If necessary, see suggested course of action.

Blood Transfusion or Blood Bank: This dream has two meanings (one or two may apply). (1) Dreamer received a blood transfusion: Your dream denotes a spiritual change, in the form of deliverance, restoration, or salvation for the dreamer, a spiritual revival. (2) Someone else received a blood transfusion: The dreamer will be a source of spiritual revival for others. Dreamer, start planning a series of revivals, to be carried out in many different places; God will give you the resources to fulfill this mission.

Contaminated or Tainted blood: This dream has two meanings (choose one). (1) Dreamer received, contaminated or tainted blood: A destructive resurrection is occurring within the dreamer, spiritually. A renewal of interest in something that was rendered spiritually dead long ago, this revival is due to you embracing erroneous ideology and your pride. One thing is for sure, this new belief and your pride have corrupted you. If not checked, this resurrection will lead to open shame. (2) Someone else received contaminated or tainted blood: The dreamer is attempting to get others to believe or behave as you do. Dreamer, you are counseled, do not attempt to contaminate or taint others with your erroneous thoughts and prideful behavior; and/or do not attempt to ruin somebody's reputation by linking him or her with something reprehensible, simply because they will not follow you and your wrong ideas. If you insist on going this way, go alone, that the blood of others may not call out against you; adding extra to your coming desolation. See suggested course of action.

Buildings, Structures with blood bubbling, oozing, running down, or heavily flowing from any parts of the edifice: This dream has two meanings (choose one). (1) Your soul is not upright within you. Your aggression, antagonism, belligerence, cruelty, hostility, immorality, prejudice, offensive and/or violent behavior towards others has come up to God because of their prayers. You are being judged by the divine council. This coupled with other references highlighted, such as the particular part of the building. See category, Buildings, and relevant subcategory. See suggested course of action. (2) Walls with blood on them: Your dream was sent to rebuke and make known deception. Dreamer, your life is before God, and mayhem is your modus operandi "MO" (mode or state of operating, living, or lifestyle). Thus, a door has been opened for you to be deceived. Dreamer, the matter at hand that you desire of God to make happen on your behalf will not happen. The big event you are expecting to happen will not. Illustration: If you are lead to believe that a specific person will marry you, you are deceived; they will not. If you are expecting to receive a lump sum settlement, you will not. Dreamer, thank God for His patience, long- suffering, and grace (the free and unmerited favor and beneficence of God), while you get things decent and in order. See suggested course of action.

Clothing soaked with blood: This dream has two meanings (choose one). (1) Clothing soaked with blood represents the self-sabotaging of your covering of grace (the free and unmerited favor and beneficence of God). Simply put, you're using grace as a 'cloak for vice', the grace given you by God to veil your indiscretions; enabling you to live without shame. Beca use of your un-repented ill behavior, arrogance, and/or untruths told against honest people. All coverings will become transparent; you will be exposed. Any status of leadership you may have; will cruelly be taken away. Favorably, after a period-of-time, you will be restored. Dreamer, submit to your leaders rulings. Take the step down, knowing that you will be restored later. During this season, begin to embrace humility, holiness, and honesty again. See suggested course of action. (2) To see another's clothing soaked with blood: You are being made privy to someone's shame or embarrassment (see Chapter One, Are You Ready to Hear the Messages in Your Dreams, section entitled, The 10% for others). They have sabotage their covering of grace given them by God to hide their indiscretions. You have the God given authority to stop what is happening, or at least try. Pray for them, and a subtle rebuke from you, may alarm them to their wrongdoings. Did you know the individual within your dream? If not, God will bring them to your attention; remain attentive to hear His guiding.

Dried blood (to see it anywhere): This dream has three meanings (choose one). (1) The dreamer has not dealt with a past insult, or offense committed (or presumed committed) against you. First consider, dreamer what part did you play in causing the insult, offense? Did you not repay a loan, perhaps forgotten by you, but not the other person? Did you slight the person in any way? Nevertheless, the insult, offense is related to a real life situation, committed when the dreamer was at your lowest or most vulnerable point, and needed help emotionally or financially. For example, dreamer's parents were drug abusers, severely neglecting you as a child, or a family member would not help you, financially, to attend a family member's funeral, when they had it within their means to do so. Your dream reveals within it, some indication as to who committed the insult, offense against you; thus, consider the background images and other symbols. They all point to someone or somewhere significant (e.g. dried blood on the steps of the person's home or at a place of business or church). Dreamer, forgiveness and a letting go needs to happen, in order for you to go forward properly. Without forgiveness, there can be no forgiveness of your trespasses and indiscretions. See Matthew 6:12, 8:21-35. An unforgiving heart is the single most popular poison the enemy of our soul uses against God's people, and it is the deadliest poison a person can take spiritually. There may or may not be a need to approach the individual; this issue is primarily within the dreamer and need not be made public, only to the Lord. Moreover, recommended reading, Deliverance in Forgiveness, through obedience to the Holy Spirit, A. M. Perry. See suggested course of action. (2) To clean up dried blood: In light of the preceding, dried blood, your dream denotes spiritual cleansing from unrighteousness. The dreamer recognizes and agrees with God that your unforgiving spirit against a particular person, no matter how justified, is sin, and you're making the effort to change your heart. There may or may not be a need to approach the individual during this process; this issue is primarily within the dreamer and need not be made public. You are basically, cleaning up your attitude and/or opinion of the other person; they need not know this process. If you go back to your old way regarding this person or situation, the Holy Ghost will bring the sin back to your remembrance. If necessary, see suggested course of action. (3) To refuse to clean up dried blood: Your dream is warning the dreamer that there is an urgent need for forgiveness. Forgiveness and letting go, needs to happen in order for the dreamer to go forward properly. Without forgiveness, there can be no forgiveness of your indiscretions. See Matthew 6:12, 8:21-35. An unforgiving heart is the single most popular poison that the enemy uses against God's people and it is one of the deadliest poisons, a person can take spiritually. Your dream indicates that the dreamer may not choose forgiveness but will continue to embrace that which will possibly lead to a weakening of your core beliefs, namely a rejection of all or some of the original foundational teachings of Christ and His apostles. Dreamer; choose to no longer feed into, or give power to, the negative situation. The situation is dried up; it is over. As believers, our struggles, our fights, are not against our fellow brother or sister, but it is with the enemy of your soul, the devil, or within. See suggested course of action.

Drinking Blood: Dreamer has murdered someone, literally or spiritually, due to envy and deep hatred within you. Spiritual murder is a premeditated attempt to; cruelly destroy someone's reputation or an attempt to destroy someone's personal relationship with Christ, because of jealously. You will be exposed, for Adonai Elohim knows all. From then on, you will be referred to as one who is unrighteous. As well, you will no longer prosper, no matter how hard you work, and you will become homeless and a wanderer. See suggested course of action.

To enjoy looking at Bloodshed: You take pleasure in your thoughts of someone being falsely slandered and spiritually murdered. Spiritual murder is a premeditated attempt to; cruelly destroy someone's reputation or an attempt to destroy someone's personal relationship with Christ, because of jealously. You will be given over to mayhem in the form of slander and discredit of reputation, because of your very bad thought life. This will pursue you. On the other hand, this type of chastisement will cause you to know the Lord and affect a deep genuine love for others within your heart. Regrettably, this is what it takes for you because you have not heeded other warnings. You have only feigned changed. See suggested course of action.

Hematidrosis (aka Sweating Blood): The dreamer is under extreme duress because of your labor and sacrifices within Christendom. Very soon, your diligence will be recompensed according to your capacity to handle prosperity. You will be comforted and ministered to by others. Do continue to allow your Heavenly Father's will to be done in your life's state of affairs.

Hemophiliac (blood clotting disorder resulting in extensive bleeding, from even minor injuries): This dream has three meanings (choose one). (1) Male dreamer: This dream implies a male's refusal to embrace the fact that Jesus is the only reason why Christians are Christians, and why they endure all that comes with being a Christian. Your attitude is primarily due to your unforgiving spirit, because of a wrong done you by one considered pious, but was not, nor was this person a Christian. Now, you suppose that all Christians are like that person, and have disdained them as such. An unforgiving heart will cause you to miss an opportunity to have a genuine relationship with Jesus, and an unforgiving heart is the single most popular poison that the enemy uses against God's people, and it is one of the deadliest poisons, a person can take spiritually. This wrong, hurt, or harm was allowed, because you have honored people or celebrity more than God. Do not exalt anyone (or thing) before God, for this is idolatry. Idolatry is "foreign service", any act that expresses devotion or fanatical admiration to something or someone other than Adonai Elohim. Dreamer, release the hurt and push forward to forgive, seeking God at every step, and never again esteem any one or thing above Jesus; your happiness will return to you and you will be set free. Moreover, recommended reading, Deliverance in Forgiveness, through obedience to the Holy Spirit, A. M. Perry. See suggested course of action. (2) Female dreamer: You have allowed the rejection of men (father, brother, husband, lover, and/or friend) to turn your heart away from men and to damage you spiritually. You have allowed this rejection to be a banner over your life. Thus, you have attracted certain types of men to you; those who abuse and reject you or you have rejected relationships with men for other kinds. Somehow, if you will no longer allow the rejection of certain men to be a banner over you, you will begin to attract positive change within your life. This change can happen with the help of your Heavenly Fathe r. Although He's figuratively a male figure, He will not hurt or reject you. Seek Jesus now while He may be found by you. Know thou self and allow the changes needed. See suggested course of action. (3) To see another with this condition: You are a witness, or will be made one, to a male or female's dilemma. Their plight is similar to the preceding male or female dream interpretation of hemophiliac. You will be sent to minister to someone in their weakness, to tell of God's grace (the free a nd unmerited favor and beneficence of God), words of wisdom, guidance, and truth.

Hemorrhaging (excessive internal bleeding): This dream has two meanings (choose one). (1) You are deceitful and speak falsehoods. Results of your behavior, namely your devious and fraudulent ways, have come up to God. Your life and flesh will be turned over to wickedness that your soul may be restored, due to you having come to yourself. Resist pride and He will deliver you from a lying spirit. Seek the power of God through Jesus, and He will leave a blessing behind. To be blessed: Gifts of God's grace, anything God freely gives you, absolution, the Holy Spirit, salvation, regeneration, eternal life, health, children, love of family, longevity, necessities, prosperity, and dominion over all that is yours; and all are parts of the supply of grace, and all are sanctified by the Lord, and technically belongs to Him. The result of this supply in your life will be peace. See suggested course of action. (2) To see another with this condition: You are a witness, or will be made one, to another's dilemma. Their plight is similar to the preceding interpretation of hemorrhaging. You will be sent to minister to someone in his or her weakness, to tell of God's grace, words of wisdom, guidance, and truth.

Man or woman covered with blood: This denotes that the dreamer is devious and guilty of cruelly destroying someone spiritually, because of your uncontrolled anger. One with an unrelenting vendetta against you will pursue you, and yes, it will be allowed. If the person covered with blood, is someone you do not know, the dreamer is blind to this part of your character, but it does exists. Acknowledge that this is a part of your character, you do not know. Seek help, via prayer, fasting, and an anger management program. If you do know the person, the person is you. Dreamer is aware of this part of your character; but you are unwilling to acknowledge it, challenge, and/or change. See suggested course of action.

Money with blood on it, "blood money": Your dream implies that the dreamer exhibits character traits of a conspirator, conniver, traitor, or schemer, especially when it comes to money and people. Further, you will call upon one or more of these negative traits to obtained money by any means necessary, sinister, or criminal. Even to the cost of t he spiritual life of another, friendships, and/or damaging your personal relationship with Christ (Matthew 27:5-7). Recognition of your damnable behavior, and a genuine desire to change, will be profitable at this time. For what does it profit to gain th e world, and while doing so, lose the aspiration of heaven? See suggested course of action.

Pouring blood out of a container: Your dream implies a great lack of respect towards the lives of others. Don't be deceived, you will reap what you have sown. Even to the cost of your own life, especially if no attempts to make amends and seek forgiveness because of your wrongdoings are made. See suggested course of action.

To see blood bubbling, oozing, spurting, or flowing from; a rock or stone, or to see Jesus bleeding: Your dream denotes that Jesus Christ has made reparation for you. Your life will be spared and there will be a refraining from others treating you harshly, releasing you from possible trouble or devastation. You have passed the worst. You are out of danger. You will be treated leniently from this moment on. Began to apply God's principles in your life and you will begin to prosper, even as your soul prospers (also see, Proverbs 4:5-13). Make sure to turn back and thank Jesus for His grace, favor, and consideration given you, by way of a testimony of praise for His works in your life. Go and sin no more. Embrace the Word earnestly and this new chapter in your life.

Shedding of innocent blood: You are using the influence God has afforded you, to turn a whole nation away from the truth of, and obedience to, Jesus Christ. You have turned from righteousness and are teaching others to do so. Your thought s are continually on wickedness because of your antagonism towards God. A change in the way you view God, His ways and means, needs to happen, your paradigm needs a shift. Dreamer, love the people enough to relinquish your leadership role. In your resignation, encourage the people to go and seek out truth on their own, without your influence and then become unreachable (disappear) to all. God will deal with you in your exile; grace is available. See suggested course of action.

Stigmata (bleeding wounds corresponding to the crucifixion wounds of Jesus): God is bringing about His pre-arranged appointment with you, in spite of the fact that you have not yet believed on His Messiah. You will receive all the encouragement, help, and support needed for your conversion to the faith, which is in Jesus Christ, via the Paraclete, and a Christian counselor advocate. Accept His invitation for eternal life. The granting of eternal life to individuals, because of their acceptance of, and submission to, the Son of God, as Lord over their life, and His blood sacrifice, is a fact. Your appointment is neigh. Set your house in order. If done properly, your comfort will be abundant in Christ. See suggested course of action.

Tears mixed with blood: Your dream was sent to encourage the dreamer. It implies that the dreamer is a hard worker concerning your duties, missions, and responsibilities. You devote yourself to work, as well as show concern for the betterment of your community at large; and with your organized, efficient approach, things will be done resourcefully. You radiate security, and often forfeit your own desires for your family and anyone else you consider a responsibility, as well as, for any worthy cause. You will now reap the rewards of such diligence, including rest and graceful surroundings.

To see the flow of blood stopped: How was the blood flow stopped? From whom, what, or where was the blood flow stopped? Did blood stop flowing from an arm, leg, or stomach? Was an animal or building involved? You may see index or relevant category for other particulars within your dream. The person, animal, place, or organization will reveal the specific area of uncleanness (impurity). With that, this dream has three meanings (choose one). (1) Dreamer, although you have grown worse spiritually and/or physically, you can be healed via your faith, prayer, and heartfelt repentance to Jesus and to individuals affected by your actions, in the form of an apology (if possible). Repentance is seeking pardon and expressing sincere feelings of regret and brokenness for having done something awry and/or for having hurt someone, see 2 Corinthians 7:10, 11. To individuals, a phone call or a letter of apology is a good place to start. To Jesus pray, Psalm 51, this follo wed by appropriate application of wisdom, can conceivably avert some of the repercussions of your choices. This is what is called leaving a blessing behind. Seek God's strength through His Christ for encouragement and/or salvation. If warning is heeded, dreamer you will be set free and/or healed from a specific uncleanness in your life. (2) Symbolically, uncleanness personifies one of two states regarding human behavior. (a) Within the life of a believer, it denotes anger, animosity, confusion, out of order, an unforgiving spirit, and/or other weaknesses, are present within your heart, as well as, immoral, impure, and unchaste conduct, or any other sinful attribute (see 1 Corinthians 6:9-20, Ephesians 5). This behavior causes one's anointing to fade and spiritual authority to wane. Favorably, you are now one, whom the body of believers should, and will, help restore back to God, in the spirit of empathy, mercy, leniency, and kindness, until the issue is cleaned up or rendered lifeless, and allow t his. See suggested course of action. (b) Symbolically, uncleanness also personifies one who is not re-born spiritually and not repentant. A non-believer (one who has no religious beliefs, a non-religious person, or one who has no religious faith or belief in Jesus Christ, or one who does not embrace a personal relationship with Jesus Christ, at present). (3) Dreamer is embracing views and practices that are erroneous, unlawful, toxic, and spiritually and/or physically deadly. The purpose of your dream is to encourage the dreamer. God will save you from all your uncleanness that you might know God is God, and honor and glorify Him whose power is the power, and whose rule will endure eternally, and that you might know your God ordained destiny. Dreamer, He does as He pleases; and choose whom He please, with the powers of heaven and the peoples of the earth. Once you recognize your true destiny, and that being in Christ Jesus, your outlook on life will change. Then use your abilities and talents exclusively for the Kingdom of God. If you are careful to submit to His ordinances, you will be His people, and He will be your God and you will be made clean.

A woman's monthly cycle (menstruation, period) and/or monthly accessories (e.g. Kotex, tampon): This dream has four meanings (choose one). (1) Female or male dreamer: If a female has, or saw, evidence of her cycle, or if a male was made privy to a woman's cycle, within a dream: Your familiarity with the anointing and power of God in the midst of you has bred a self-assurance or over-confidence. This has caused you to become morally and spiritually unclean. Symbolically, spiritual uncleanness, within the life of a believer, denotes anger, animosity, confusion, out of order, self -condemnation, sexual impropriety, an unforgiving spirit, or some form of immoral, impure, unchaste conduct, or weakness, is present within your heart or life, or any other sinful attribute (see 1 Corinthians 6:9-20, Ephesians 5). This behavior causes one's anointing to fade and spiritual authority to wane. Favorably, you are now one, whom the body of believers should, and will, help restore you back to God, in the spirit of empathy, mercy, leniency, and kindness, until the issue is cleaned up or rendered lifeless; all ow this. If you do not check your attitude, and allow divine wisdom, via the help of another, to restore within your heart and mind, a respect and reverence for the manifestations of God's glory and presence, your indiscretions, no matter how slight, w ill be exposed publicly that you might remember to approach the Lord with great caution and reverence. If issue was not cleaned up, see suggested course of action. (2) If issue was cleaned up, in some way, e.g. pad thrown away or flushed, under clothes washed or changed, this denotes that you will allow the wisdom and the help of the body of believers to restore you back to God, in the spirit of empathy, mercy, leniency, and kindness, until the issue is cleaned up or rendered lifeless. By this, you will be restored, promoted, and seated in a high place. (3) If a women or male saw, a women's period stopped, this choice has two parts (choose one). (a) Female dreamer experienced your monthly cycle stopping, this denotes that the dreamer is being delivered and made complete spiritually. You will be delivered from your repeated cycles of hateful, wicked, insulting, and provoking behavior, towards others. Dreamer, you will no longer take pleasure in your thoughts of someone being falsely slandered, demeaned, and spiritually murdered. As well, you will be restored to your divine ordained place within a ministry. (4) Unmarried male: If an unmarried male was made privy to evidences of a female's period being stopped, and the dreamer is a significant other to the female (e.g. fiancée), grace is shown in order for you two to marry. Note, female must be actually known by dreamer in your awaked life, and must be depicted within dream.

Wood, tree: To see blood bubbling, oozing, spurting, or flowing from a piece of wood or a tree: Your dream indicates idolatry. Idolatry is "foreign service", any act that expresses devotion or fanatical admiration to something or someone other than Adonai Elohim), or any traits of these sorts (see 1 Corinthians 6:8-11). This enslavement has made you spiritually irrational and demonically influenced. See suggested course of action.

Suggested Course of Action

Question to consider and journal, did your dream depict any symbols that alludes to, the dreamer will make the necessary changes, spiritually, emotionally, and/or physically to affect a more positive outcome? If changes are initiated, your dreams will change.

Nevertheless, take into account your entire dream's context and remember, dreams are, for the most part, warnings. People and situations do, and can, change for the good, especially with the help of God. Change is the key word. There is a lesson to learn, please be attentive, and give ear to what God is trying to convey to you, and encourage yourself.

Consider and journal the following questions. The questions will help you determine; the issue at hand, how you feel about it, and what may have instigated it. What kind of bleeding or blood was it (light or heavy, spurting, flowing, oozing, or dried)? Why was there bleeding or blood? Where was the blood? Were others involved? If yes, who and in what manner were they involved? Keep in mind that the others represent a quality of you, see Note 3 at the beginning of Actions and Activities category. Did anyone get hurt emotionally, physically, or was disturbed in any way? How did you feel, and what did you do, because, of your feelings, regarding the blood, bleeding? Was it agitating, confusing, dangerous, disturbing, frustrating, peace with the situation, happy, joyful, life threatening, safe, scary, or unsure? Where were you? Was the pla ce unfamiliar to you? Were you coherent? In view of your dream's context, namely bleeding, what choices are you making that may impair your spiritual growth, judgment, health, or that will encourage immorality and/or are you reacting out of fear? I f so, what can you do to combat the paralyzing emotion of fear? Your answers, coupled with the interpretation, plus any additional information, should begin to unfold the subject matter and issue at hand, if not now, mull over things a few days. For more information, see index or relevant category and subcategory for other particulars within your dream.

The following will help you determine the approximate length of time you have thus far dealt with the matter and how much longer you will have to deal with the issue. If you started bleeding at the beginning of the dream, you are dealing with this issue right now. If somewhere in the middle onward, you will encounter the issue shortly. Did you stop bleeding at som e point? This is indicative that you've completed the process that will heal the issue your dream is referencing. If you did not stop bleeding, the matter at hand will not end soon, if you continue avoidance, complaining, faithlessness in God's Word, and murmuring. Dreamer, deal with the issue without evasion or compromise, in other words head-on. All of these questions should pull together for you your dream. They summarize the issue at hand and what changes the dreamer should make within your attitude or life.

Now, pray (See Prayer of Deliverance, pg. 897)

Specific Meaning

If, your chances are very high that you will come in contact with blood flow, for example, healthcare, crime scene investigat ion, veterinary services, blood bank, dreams of this sort, for the most part, are ordinary dreams, resulting from your daily activities (see Chapter One, Chalom). These sorts of dreams are usually about your routine, mundane activities or anxieties that overwhelm your mind during the day. They are an inner release mechanism, which helps provide you with emotional balance and the maintaining of your sanity. These dreams are not significant, and do not warrant special attention.

Note: However, on another vein, the dreamer may consider his or her (specific) dream as a clue given to assist in finding facts, needed to support a prevailing or pressing investigation. Example, crime investigator might consider blood from rocks, money, or clothing as a clue pointing towards the direction of the crime scene and/or the perpetrator. Heath care professionals might consider an inability to stop blood flow within a dream, as a clue pointing to possible hemophiliac type symptoms within a patient. Dreamer, the details, kept within context of your dream, should be relevant to your life, and closely resemble your real-life situations. Meaning it can actually occur during your awaked state. This will help you narrow down the specifics needed to support and steer you clear of possible mishaps. However, if your dream was inundated with symbols not easily linked to your life activities, then you should heed the spiritual implications (the interpretation).

BOWING OR KNEELING OR PROSTRATED OR STOOPING: To bend the head forward, or to bend forward from the waist, as a sign of respect, greeting, consent, submission, or acknowledgment, also to rest on, or get down on, one or both knees.

Some short descriptions of types, phrases, and other processes and particulars, connected in some way to this category are, for example, to bend the knee, curtsy, fall, genuflect, or rest on the knees, prostrate yourself, stoop over.

Unless otherwise noted elsewhere, if, in your everyday living, your awaked state, as part of your lifestyle, work, or ministerial activities, or a special event, you have a very real connection with any type of bowing, kneeling, prostration, or stooping activity. For example, head servant of a household, cultural, or religious rites, ordinations, dealings with royalty, physical therapist, or having to lay face down, (also see content list for this category), your dream is not significant and does not warrant special attention.

Otherwise noted, see Note 1 at the beginning of Actions and Activities category.

To determine who your dream is for you or another, see Note 3 at the beginning of Actions and Activities category.

Symbols and Referents: Dreams of bowing, kneeling, prostration, or stooping, generally deal with blessings from God, or submission to, and/or worship of, God, or someone or something else. As well as, one who has perhaps stumbled spiritually, or has been offended or hindered.

WARNING: Bowing, kneeling, prostrated, stooping: No angel, or any other created being, including humans, who is godly, never ever accepts worship from mankind, even if the angel, any other created being, or human, is mistaken to be worthy of such worship. The Bible teaches that worship is due to God alone (Exodus 20:3-6). The first commandment "Thou shalt have no other gods before me" emphasizes the fact that there is but one God, in protest against the worship (e.g. bowing, kneeling, prostrated, stooping) of many gods.

Examples of this is as follows,

- The devil said to Jesus in his temptation. All these things will I give you, if you will go down on your face and give me worship (Matthew 4:9-10 BBE).
- As Peter was coming in, Cornelius met him, and fell down at his feet and worshiped him. But Peter lifted him up, saying, "Stand up; I myself am also a man" (Acts 10:25, 26 NKJV).
- When Paul and Barnabas were in Lystra, and did miracles there. When the people saw these things, the people raised their voices, "The gods have come down to us in the likeness of men!", and they started to worship Paul and Barnabas. Paul and Barnabas tore their clothes and ran in among the multitude, crying out and saying, "Men, why are you doing these things?

We also are men with the same nature as you, and preach to you that you should turn from these useless things to the living God, who made the heaven, the earth, the sea, and all things that are in them (Acts 14:11-15 NKJV).

- And I (John) fell at his (an angel) feet to worship him. But he said to me, "See that you do not do that! I am your fellow servant, and of your brethren who have the testimony of Jesus. Worship God! For the testimony of Jesus is the spirit of prophecy" (Revelation 19:10 NKJV)

God appeals to us to put Him before all else, to put Him first in our affections, and in our lives; we owe wholehearted allegiance and devotion to God, via Jesus, to whom it is an honor and privilege to have a personal relationship with, to know, to love, and to trust. Therefore, to bow, kneel, prostrate, or stoop before anyone or anything but God, or to desire that anoth er bow before you; is a sin equal to murder, adultery, or lying. To worship something else, in the place of God, whether it is, wealth, knowledge, position, or persons, places us in jeopardy. With that said, keep the previous in mind when considering the following:

Category Content - If not listed see index, perchance, for your specific type of bowing, kneeling, prostration, or stooping dream activity

- Genuflect, Curtsy (to bend the knee or curtsy)
- Fall and rest on one or both knees
- Forced to bow, kneel, prostrate yourself, or stoop over
- To prostrate yourself (to lie flat with the face down)
- To stoop over (to bend the head or body forward and down)
- To not bow, kneel, prostrate yourself, or stoop over

Note: All of the bowing, kneeling, prostration, or stooping dream activity subcategories will deal with the following four subdivisions:

Bowing, Kneeling, Prostrated, or Stooping:

- Before God, Jesus, or Heavenly Throne
- Before an angel, a man, or woman
- Before an adversary, devils, demons, altars, idols, mirror image of yourself or another, wooden images (or any inanimate object, iconic image, effigy, picture, or representation that is a sign or likeness that stands for an object or entity, by signifying or representing it either concretely or by analogy)
- Someone bows, kneels, or stoops before the dreamer

Genuflect, Curtsy (To Bend The Knee Or Curtsy):

Genuflect (bend the knee): Male dreamer, see the following

To bend the knee before God, Jesus, or Heavenly Throne: Because you have demonstrated humbleness of heart, an offense is pacified, anger is appeased, and grace (the free and unmerited favor and beneficence of God) is extended.

To bend the knee before an angel or a man: You will serve as a role model to men, to teach the proper way to conduct oneself righteously. Do not hide but reveal your righteousness for the sake of young men within you sphere of influence.

To bend the knee before a woman: Your dream expresses a call for remorse and an apology to a female, because of an offense committed by the dreamer against a female, possibly the person within your dream. If unknown, the opportunity to apologize will present itself shortly, by a female you did not know that you had offended. See suggested course of action.

To bend the knee before an adversary, devils, demons, altars, idols, mirror image of yourself or another, wooden images (or any inanimate object, iconic image, effigy, picture, or representation that is a sign or likeness that stands for an object or entity, by signifying or representing it either concretely or by analogy): Your dream is to convey disapproval and warning. In practicing Christian liberties, you are cautioned to beware of temptation and unbelief, and to be conscious of affiliation with demons. Dreamer, you sit and eat at the tables of demons. You cannot have part in both the Lord's Table and the table of demons. Those who advocate the belief that all beings will be reconciled to God, including the devil and the fallen angels are mistaken (Matthew 25:41). As well as those who hold to the belief that Jesus, as one's Lord and Savior, has little or no impact on your personal lifestyle and values; that God has little interest in the way we live our lives. They are rejecting Christianity's core system of beliefs and practices (see John 3:16-21; 1 Corinthians 10:1-23; Hebrews 12:14; Revelation 20:1-15). The dreamer is advised to make a decision as to who (or what) you will follow and worship, at this time. See suggested course of action.

Someone bends the knee before the dreamer: Due to the dreamer's nit-picking, trivial objections, and/or errors in your belief system, a significant other has moved to get away from you. However, because they have not been forthright, your dream is revealing the true motive of their move, your trifling attitude. Understanding and accepting that others have their own viewpoints, which will at times differ from yours, creates peace, respect, and a congenial atmosphere. In addition, the dreamer needs to respect other's personal space and do not encroach upon it, for this will also cause others to run from your presence. See suggested course of action.

Curtsy: Female dreamer, see the following

To curtsy before God, Jesus, or Heavenly Throne: Your dream is to urge the dreamer to bless the God of heaven. To bless God: To have genuine faith in, and to give heartfelt thanks for, His gifts of grace. Gifts of God's grace, anything God freely gives you, absolution, the Holy Spirit, salvation, regeneration, eternal life, health, children, love of family, longevity, necessities, prosperity, and dominion over all that is yours; and all are parts of the supply of grace, and all are sanctified by the Lord, and technically belongs to Him. The result of this supply in your life will be peace. Moreover, because of your prayers, praise and thanks to God, a secret will be uncovered. You will be strengthen and enlighten because of this revelation.

To curtsy before an angel or a man: You are about to receive your just recompense. Because you have demonstrated wisdom within your choices, and submission and humbleness of heart toward your spouse and/or leader, you will be granted the primary desire of your heart.

To curtsy before a woman: You will serve as a role model to females, to teach the proper way to conduct oneself righteously. Do not hide but reveal your righteousness for the sake of women within your sphere of influence.

To curtsy before an adversary, devils, demons, altars, idols, mirror image of yourself or another, wooden images (or any inanimate object, iconic image, effigy, picture, or representation that is a sign or likeness that stands for an object or entity, by signifying or representing it either concretely or by analogy): The dreamer practices legalism and is self-righteous. You reject the doctrine of grace (the free and unmerited favor and beneficence of God), thus you've chosen to be under the law. Your spirituality is one of outward show and hypocrisy. You love to give alms, pray, and appear righteous publicly, but inwardly you are lifeless, and lawlessness prevails. Your lack of love towards others has contributed to your lack of grace towards, understanding, receiving, and giving. See suggested course of action.

Someone curtsies before the dreamer: Two things, (1) God has sent an apprentice to you, to be taught by you, the prophetic nature of God. This person will remain within your life for at least one year, not more than three. Train him or her well, for he or she is your replacement. Read and understand 1 Kings 19-21, for this is to you. Note, dreamer, you are not getting ready to die physically, God's plans for you are to prosper you financially and health wise, and to cause you to rest peacefully, with everything you will need and desire. Only accept that it is your time to retire, therefore, retire gracefully, and give your best to the coming apprentice. Additionally, allow God to give you what He chooses to give you, and if He gives you more than you need, then be a good steward over that. The following is a suggested prayer to keep one balanced, "Jesus, I don't want any more than God wants me to have. Give me my portion, don't give me too much so that I worship my wealth instead of God, and become self-sufficient, and don't give me too little so that I'll steal and dishonor God's name" (Proverbs 30:8.9). (2) Additionally, a nefarious leader, (perhaps the one fallen upon his or her knees before you within your dream), annoyed at you because of your spiritual purity and righteous words, is seeking to harm you. When asked to come before this leader, and you will be asked to come before a religious leader of some kind, you are to relay God's message to this leader. The message — this leader will not recover from an illness that is upon him or her, because of their immorality. Allow your apprentice to accompany you for this word will come to past.

Fall and rest on one or both knees, see the following

To fall and rest on one or both knees before God, Jesus, or Heavenly Throne, or before a church altar: Dreamer, they that trust in the Lord God will not be ashamed. Your life will be spared and there will be a refraining from treating you harshly, releasing you from possible trouble, because of the intercession of an elder of a church. Trust God in this. You will also begin to experience the powerful and unseen Hand of God within your life's circumstances.

To fall and rest on one or both knees before an angel, a man, or woman: An immoral leader, seeking to harm a man or woman of God, will ask you, the dreamer, to contact this person of God, and ask them to have an audience with the immoral leader. Go, and approach this man or woman of God respectfully and in humility. However, make known that you suspect the immoral leader means harm to him or her. Out of respect for you, they will go with you before this leader. Their message from God to this leader; is that the leader will not recover from the illness that is upon him or her, because of their immorality. As for the dreamer, because of your wisdom and humility demonstrated towards God's man or woman, when you came before him or her, you will be delivered from your illness and live long afterwards.

To fall and rest on one or both knees before an adversary, devils, demons, altars, idols, mirror image of yourself. Or, other wooden images (or any inanimate object, iconic image, effigy, picture, or representation that is a sign or likeness that stands for an object or entity, by signifying or representing it either concretely or by analogy): Dreamer, you have high regard for, and abide by, the doctrines of demons. Your belief system is idolatrous (image worship; worship or fanatical admiration given to anyone or anything but the one true God). You are of those who advocate the belief that all beings will be reconciled to God, including the devil and the fallen angels. As well as those who hold to the belief that Jesus, as one's Lord and Savior, has little or no impact on our personal lifestyle and values; that God has little interest in the way we live our lives. You are mistaken. You are rejecting Christianity's core beliefs and practices (also see John 3:16-21; 1 Corinthians 10:1-23; Hebrews 12:14-29; and Revelation 20:1-15). Therefore, you are warned to sever affiliation with demons and the demonically possessed, to be aware of temptations, and to pray that your unbelief be healed. If warning is not heeded, you will be given over into the hands of those who are high priests of such doctrines. They will belittle, disgrace, and humiliate you, and it will be allowed. By this, you will understand the importance of seeking God's truth, especially when facing conflict or transition. Seeing that all Scripture is God-breathed and is useful for teaching, rebuking, correcting, and training in righteousness, so that the man (or woman) of God may be thoroughly equipped for every good work. The context of your dream will suggest if you are willing to accept God's truth. For example, did you get up and walk, or run away, rejecting who or what you knelt before? Alternatively, did you remain at their feet? See suggested course of action.

Someone fall and rest on one or both knees before the dreamer: Your dream was sent to encourage and to warn the dreamer. You are valued within the Kingdom of God and of man. Further, someone loves, respect, and holds you in high esteem, possibly the person bending the knee before you, within your dream. One thing is for sure, you have had a powerful affect upon someone who has entered your life. However, although you are held in high esteem by some, let them know immediately, "Don't worship me, I too am just a man or woman like yourself, God, and God alone is to be worship", for God has said, "I will not give my glory to another" (Isaiah 42:8). Therefore, dreamer you are warned to be careful lest you become so prideful that the idea creeps into you that you can be deified. Self-deification is of Satan. God can dwell in the human, via the Holy Spirit, but forever the human is the human, and Adonai Elohim is forever God.

Forced to bow, kneel, prostrate yourself, or stoop over, see the following

Forced to bow, kneel, prostrate yourself, or stoop over before God, Jesus, or Heavenly Throne: Your dream comes as a warning to the dreamer. You have allowed something or someone to stand in your way of coming to Christ. It may be pride, position, family, friends, sin, or even wealth. Even more, your resistance to bow also indicates an unwillingness to become a follower of Jesus (aka an authentic believer or Christian). Recognition of your damnable behavior will be profitable at this time. For what does it profit to gain the world, and while doing so, lose the aspiration of heaven (Matthew 6:24)? What will a man or woman give in exchange for their soul? Dreamer, is it wise to forfeit the eternality of heaven, for that which lasts and gratifies only a short time, especially after having been warned? Receive God's message in simple childlike faith, trusting that by it you will be saved (Matthew 18:3-5, 7-9). In doing this, you will be justified solely based on grace (the free and unmerited favor and beneficence of God) and faith. Even more, having accepted Jesus, your desires will also change and be more satisfying. See suggested course of action.

Forced to bow, kneel, prostrate yourself, or stoop over before an angel, a man, or woman: This is a hard way to learn a lesson. You will be humiliated and made ashamed publicly because of your personal weaknesses. Dreamer, you have chosen to override and thus, make ineffective, your God given innate instinct to survive. In that, you have allowed another to kill you spiritually, and possibly abuse you physically, rather than speak and act forthright and live (defend yourself). Your choices and actions are parallel to those who are easy prey for predators or cults, those with "victim" mindsets. Consequently, you will be given over into the hands of those you hate. They will humiliate, disgrace, and belittle you, and it will be allowed. By this, you will understand the importance of speaking God's truth, and yours, in a direct and straightforward manner, when in the face o f abuse, molestation, opposition, or any form of persecution, oppression, or harassment. As well, never do you ever, adore or worship anyone, image, personality, or rank, to the peril of health and safety. Do not put anyone on a pedestal above your God given right to live in peace and safety. Expose the violations and/or seek help. The context of your dream will suggest if you are willing to love yourself enough to live. For example, did you eventually bow? Did you remain adamant at not bowing? If you remained adamant at not bowing, you will seek justice for yourself and prevail. See suggested course of action.

Forced to bow, kneel, prostrate yourself, or stoop over before an adversary. For example, devils, demons, altars, idols, mirror image of yourself or another, wooden images (or any inanimate object, iconic image, effigy, picture, or representation that is a sign or likeness that stands for an object or entity, by signifying or representing it either concre tely or by analogy): Your dream is an admonition to the dreamer. You are about to receive your just recompense. God will not ignore wrongdoers in His midst. He is aware of your secret, that hidden thing. You will be judged and corrected for those hidden things. The dreamer should not think because you have not been caught, God condones your behavior; justice will be done. See suggested course of action.

Someone forced to bow, kneel, or prostrate them self, or stoop over before dreamer: Your dream marks a transition within the dreamer's life. Your life's circumstances will begin to change; state of affairs will be in favor of the dreamer, and this is nearer than you could possibly imagine, even at the door. As to why, because someone has moved violently against the dreamer, causing you much anguish, simply because you would not praise or flatter him or her. They will no longer prevail in their struggle against you, and they will be deeply humiliated, full of remorse and sorrow. Do accept their apology, for one will be forthcoming.

To prostrate yourself (to lie flat with the face down), see the following

To prostrate yourself before God, Jesus, or Heavenly Throne: Because of your adoration, dependence, and submission to Christ, God will abundantly bless the dreamer. Dreamer, from this day forward God's blessings will flow abundantly, producing spiritual growth within you. God's blessings: Gifts of God's grace, anything God freely gives you, absolution, the Holy Spirit, salvation, regeneration, eternal life, health, children, love of family, longevity, necessities, prosperity, and dominion over all that is yours; and all are parts of the supply of grace, and all are sanctified by the Lord, and technically belongs to Him. The result of this supply in your life will be peace. As well, you will experience a divine visitation, sent from the Lord that will deliver you from the evil and wickedness that has surrounded you. Desolation will be before you, you will see it with your o wn eyes, but it will not affect you.

To prostrate yourself before an angel, a man, or woman: Two things, (1) your dream warns of a weakness within the dreamer. You are obsessed with a fake image of purity, thus you find impurity in all things, because your conscience and mind are defiled. Therefore, lest you be found powerless and ineffective, and become disqualified, because of a lack of doctrinal soundness and genuine moral purity, judged unfit for service, re-think your beliefs on what is genuinely clean and unclean spiritually, according to the Word of God and not your opinions. (2) With that said, your dream counsels the dreamer to begin seriously contemplating your spiritual qualifications for an upper headship position within ministry. This level of leadersh ip demands great personal sacrifice of rights and freedoms and requires the subduing of your appetites and passions. For, to whom much is given, much is required. At times, in order to fulfill your commission, to reach all for Christ, you will even need to forgo your dietary liberties and decline compensation (e.g. fulfill numerous fasts, eat what's put before you, only at the time it's put before you, and putting right back into a ministry your wage). God will lead the way. See suggested course of action.

To prostrate yourself before an adversary, devils, demons, altars, idols, mirror image of yourself or another, wooden images (or any inanimate object, iconic image, effigy, or picture. Any representation that is a sign or likeness that stands for an object or entity, by signifying or representing it either concretely or by analogy): You will gain dark and erroneous knowledge, through personal experience and through a supernatural imparting, which is demonically communicated. The knowledge gained will not allow you to praise the Lord, only to exalt one's self. You are abandoning the faith and is now worshipping false gods and images, and adhering to lies. You hold to beliefs, views, and practices that are erroneous, unlaw ful, toxic, and spiritually and/or physically deadly. Your attitude is leading to a mental and spiritual breakdown, and corruption, opening the door for demons to run havoc within your life and to bring you down to desolation. Demonic influences will swarm around you, ready to help you in your wicked, evil, despicable, immoral, reprehensible, disreputable, degenerate, infamous, and/or perverse choices. Your kind of choices leads to prostitution, poverty, homelessness, begging, imprisonment, and/or early death. Your lifestyle choices are, or will become, offensive and repulsive (abominable) in the sight of God and humanity. You are forfeiting purpose for foolishness and ruin. Dreamer, demons have had thousands of years to master human weaknesses and can rival men and women of God if we are not careful. Compassionately, because of grace (the free and unmerited favor and beneficence of God) and the many mercies of God extended to you, your dream is only a warning and not an official declaration. Dreamer is counseled to seek all kinds of spiritual support now, to possibly avert or turn things around, and perhaps move away from your present environment, definitely walk away from all negativity abruptly. Utilizing the powerful resources of prayer and heartfelt repentance to Jesus and to individuals affected by your actions, in the form of an apology (if possible), is needed. Repentance is seeking pardon and expressing sincere feelings of regret and brokenness for having done something awry and/or for having hurt someone, see 2 Corinthians 7:10, 11. To individuals, a phone call or a letter of apology is a good place to start. To Jesus pray, Psalm 51, this followed by appropriate application of wisdom, can conceivably avert the repercussions of your choices. This coupled with fasting, a changed mindset, serious re-consideration of God's ways and means, and an honest acknowledgement of God's hand within your life, then the severe impact of your choices and actions upon your life, can be reversed and damages repaired (also see Ezekiel 33:12-19). This is what is called leaving a blessing behind. If you do not genuinely seek help and change, for sure ruin will be your destiny's declaration. See suggested course of action.

Someone prostrates him or herself before the dreamer: The dreamer will begin to see the omnipotent Hand of God within your life's circumstances. Those that hindered you will now go from before you. You will gain the respect of a leader in upper management, because of your faith in God (a resolute trust in the integrity of God and in His Word). As a result, y ou will be promoted to an upper management position within the employment arena, and/or to an upper headship position within ministry. This leader will cause benefits and favors to flow towards you, and he or she will acknowledge, and revere the power of your God. One thing is for sure; you are highly favored and blessed of God. To be blessed: Gifts of God's grace, anything God freely gives you, absolution, the Holy Spirit, salvation, regeneration, eternal life, health, children, love of family, longevity, necessities, prosperity, and dominion over all that is yours; and all are parts of the supply of grace, and all are sanctified by the Lord, and technically belongs to Him. The result of this supply in your life will be peace. You are expected to promote qualified friends to leadership positions at work and/or within ministry also. Do not underestimate anyone. In this, you will show yourself faithful to God and man.

To stoop over (to bend the head or body forward and down), see the following

To stoop over before God, Jesus, or Heavenly Throne or at an altar: Your dream indicates your attitude of humility, respect, and reverence, toward God and His messengers. Because of your prayer, heartfelt repentance to Jesus, and an apology to man or woman, your humility, and your servant's attitude towards God, His laws and order, and to His Word, God will bless you with tremendous recompense. Now, He will send an angel to rescue you out of an extremely severe situation, because of your faith. Be aware that the stranger within your midst may be that angel. He comes to lead the way. Further, because of your deliverance, your oppressor will respect your God, acknowledge His Power, and respect you.

To stoop over before an angel, a man, or woman: This dream has two meanings (choose one). (1) Dreamer, you have esteemed a particular person, or organization above God. You worship created beings, in the place of your Creator. The person, or organization, you were stooped over, or before, in your dream represents, or is the object of your inordinate desires right now; thus, the reason for your dream. Your dream comes to warn the dreamer that God is displeased with your excessive adoration of this person, or organization. You have them in an exalted place. The dreamer is counseled to prioritize that, which is more important. Will it be man or God? Dreamer, take inventory of what you believe, and why, and become clear about that. You cannot worship man and God; this is a conflict of interest. This new attitude should drive you to take inventory, regularly, of your sense of right and wrong, and religious principles and beliefs, to make sure that they are based on the infallible Word of God and not on sensual desires. See suggested course of action. (2) Your dream denotes poverty and bondage. Both of which is the result of a recently adopted bourgeois mentality. This mentality is concerned only with your personal comfort, material wealth, and status, at any expense. Now, having in yourself nothing that you respect more than power and greed, you are willing to sacrifice all, God, principle, family, and friend, to the image or idol of vanity. Your new way is based on exploring alternatives to God's righteous principles, as well as, creating a sense of unity with the wickedness around you. This mentality sacrifices children, family, and morality, to the hollowness of satisfying immoral desires and appetites. All carried out, with the hope of finding happiness by pacifying jealously and covetousness. The selling-out of yourself over to immorality, allowing wickedness to prevail in your home, devaluing those you should be protecting and nurturing, while closing your eyes to it all, are all principles based on values that are not only vile, but also increasingly unstable. This way cries out against godly ethics, and its' end offends any sense of godliness. Your recklessness can be remedied by prayer and heartfelt repentance to Jesus and to individuals affected by your actions, in the form of an apology (if possible). Repentance is seeking pardon and expressing sincere feelings of regret and brokenness for having done something awry and/or for having hurt someone, see 2 Corinthians 7:10, 11, also see Deuteronomy 6:10-15; 11:10-28. To individuals, a phone call or a letter of apology is a good place to start. To Jesus pray, Psalm 51, this coupled with prayer and fasting, and followed by appropriate application of wisdom, can conceivably avert some of the repercussions of your choices. This is known as leaving a blessing behind. See suggested course of action.

To stoop over before an adversary, devils, demons, altars, idols, mirror image of yourself or another, wooden images (or any inanimate object, iconic image, effigy, picture, or representation that is a sign or likeness that stands for an object or entity, by signifying or representing it either concretely or by analogy): You have opened a door for serious demonic activity. Demonic oppression, demons running havoc within your life, or demonic possession, is at hand. Along with prayer and fasting, you will now need to seek professional help from a Christian counselor, a Christian based support group, and there is a need to set up an accountability system, and earnestly commit to that help. If you do not seek help, within one year, God's covering will be removed from over you. As a result you will begin to experience serious mental health issues and will have to be restrained, against your will, if needs be. Dreamer, if urged by God, declare a one, two, or three day fast for sanctification purposes; also, wash (bathe) and make yourself, clothing, and personal surroundings clean. Nonetheless, you will need to declare some kind of fast and commit to it, for a period-of-time, to abate this coming influence. Refrain from wickedness and do no one harm, physically, sexually, emotionally, and/or spiritually, any longer. Start treating God's people, your family, and others, with respect. By this, God will pardon your injustices. The context of your dream will suggest if you are willing to rectify your ways to ward off the coming tragedy. For example, did you discontinue stooping over, and walked or ran away; rejecting who or what you stooped over before? Did you remain at their feet? To remain at their feet denotes that you will resist the counsel God is sending your way and embrace the demonic. See suggested course of action.

Someone stoops over before the dreamer: See subcategory, someone prostrates him or herself before the dreamer.

To not bow, kneel, prostrate, or stoop over, see the following

To not, bow, kneel, prostrate, or stoop over before God, Jesus, or Heavenly Throne: Within one year, God's covering and favor will be removed from over you, until you acknowledged that the Most High Go d rules over all humans, and appoints whomever He chooses, over whatever. When God removes His protection, you will begin to experience some mental health issues. To avoid this, it is suggested that the dreamer refrain from wickedness and start treating people with respect; showing mercy to the unfortunate. By this, God will pardon your prejudices that you may continue to prosper. The context of your dream will suggest if you are willing to rectify your ways to ward off the coming tragedy. For example, did you eventually bow or kneel before God? Did you remain resistant before Him? If you submitted, you will rectify your behavior. If you remaine d resistant, you will remain resistant to submitting to change; thus, reaping the coming tragedy. See suggested course of action.

To not bow, kneel, prostrate, or stoop over before an angel, a man, or woman: Although you are totally committed to righteousness, you desire God to exercise His vengeance on all idolaters (those worshipping anyone or anything b ut the one true God, Job 40:8-14). You have forgotten that God's true and innermost essence is love, grace (the free and unmerited favor and beneficence of God), rescuing, and preserving. It really is His will that none should perish (see Matthew 18:12-13), and although most have broken the covenant of grace, God still maintains His covenant and remains faithful, enduring, and long - suffering. The spiritual state of affairs you observe in others; is a thousand times better than you think.

To not bow, kneel, prostrate, or stoop over before an adversary, devils, demons, altars, idols, mirror image of yourself or another, wooden images, or any inanimate object, iconic image, effigy, or picture. Any representation that is a sign or likeness that stands for an object or entity, by signifying or representing it either concretely or by analogy: Your dream was sent to encourage the dreamer. You are highly favored and blessed of God. To be blessed: Gifts of God's grace, anything God freely gives you, absolution, the Holy Spirit, salvation, regeneration, eternal life, health, children, love of family, longevity, necessities, prosperity, and dominion over all that is yours; and all are parts of the supply of grace, and all are sanctified by the Lord, and technically belongs to Him. The result of this supply in your life will be peace. Withhold not your hand in the day of your prosperity, but receive and keep all that God has ordained for you and your family (implying good stewardship). As well, you are a righteous person, with a strong desire to uplift humanity. You will now be led into situations where you can express your desire to serve others. You will show up when most needed, and then disappear without a thought of compensation. Many will be inspired by your faith in Christ and humility.

Someone does not (or will not) bow, kneel, prostrate, or stoop over before the dreamer: Your dream marks a transition within the dreamer's life. Your life's circumstances will begin to change; state of affairs will not be in favor of the dreamer, and this is nearer than you imagine. The dreamer has moved violently against one of God's chosen (perhaps one depicted within your dream), causing them much anguish, simply because they would not praise or flatter you. The desire to be put on a pedestal is to covet God's glory (Isaiah 42:8, 48:11). You will never be worshipped, nor should you continue to desire to be worshipped. You will no longer prevail in your struggle against whomever, and will be deeply humiliated, full of remorse and sorrow. Fortunately, people and state of affairs can, and do, change for the good, sometimes in one day. Dreamer, utilizing the powerful resources of prayer and heartfelt repentance to Jesus and to individuals affected by your action s, in the form of an apology (if possible), is needed. Repentance is seeking pardon and expressing sincere feelings of regret and brokenness for having done something awry and/or for having hurt someone, see 2 Corinthians 7:10, 11. To individuals, a phone call or a letter of apology is a good place to start. To Jesus pray, Psalm 51. This, coupled with fasting, a changed mindset, serious re- consideration of God's ways and means, and an honest acknowledgement of God's hand within your life, followed by appropriate application of wisdom, will lessen the severe impact, or avert the repercussions of your choices, actions, upon your life (also see Ezekiel 33:8-19. This is what is called leaving a blessing behind. If you do not genuinely seek help and change, for sure ruin will be your destiny. See suggested course of action.

Suggested Course of Action

Question to consider and journal, did your dream depict any symbols that alludes to, the dreamer will make the necessary changes, spiritually, emotionally, and/or physically to affect a more positive outcome? If changes are initiated, your dreams will change.

Notwithstanding, if urged by God, declare a one, two, or three day fast for sanctification purposes; wash and make yourself clean. During the fast, diligently get an understanding of, and embrace, the doctrine of grace (the free and unmerited favor and beneficence of God) and of Jesus Christ. God will lead and enable you. You will need to declare some kind of fast and commit to it, for a period-of-time, to abate this coming influence. Afterwards, go before Jesus petitioning for help. You will begin to see, significantly, the unseen hand of God. See also Isaiah 1:16-17, Hebrews 5:7-10.

Consider and journal the following questions. The questions will help you determine; the issue at hand, how you feel about it, and what may have instigated it. What kind of bowing was done? Why was there bowing? Were you forced to bow? Were others involved? If yes, who and in what manner were they involved? Keep in mind that the others represent a quality of you, see Note 3 at the beginning of Actions and Activities category. Did anyone get hurt emotionally, physically, or was disturbed in any way? How did you feel, and what did you do, because, of your feelings? Especially, regarding the bowing and/or whom or what was being bowed before. Was it agitating, confusing, dangerous, disturbing, frustrating, peace with the situation, happy, joyful, life threatening, safe, scary, or unsure? Where were you? Was the place unfamiliar to you? Were you coherent? In view of your dream's context, namely bowing, what choices are you making that may impair your spiritual growth, judgment, health, or that will encourage immorality and/or are you reacting out of fear? If so, what can you do to combat the paralyzing emotion of fear? Your answers, coupled with the interpretation, plus any additional information, should begin to unfold the subject matter and issue at hand, if not now, mull over things a few days. For more information, see index or relevant category and subcategory for other particulars within your dream.

Now, pray (See Prayer of Deliverance, pg. 897)

Specific Meaning

If, there is a very high chance that you will be bowing or kneeling, in some form (e.g. butler, royal duties, ministerial ordination, or some other manner of activity that involves bowing, kneeling). Dreams of this sort, for the most part, are ordinary dreams, resulting from your daily activities (see Chapter One, Chalom). These sorts of dreams are usually about your routine, mundane activities or anxieties that overwhelm your mind during the day. They are an inner release mechanism, which helps provide you with emotional balance and the maintaining of your sanity. These dreams are not significant, and do not warrant special attention.

CHASING, RUNNING, FOLLOWING, SEEKING, OR STALKING: An act or situation in which something or somebody is being pursued, either dreamer is pursuer or someone is pursuing dreamer.

Some short descriptions of types, phrases, and other processes and particulars, connected in some way to this category are, for example, to be chased, run after, or followed. Competitive running (e.g. foot race), run after, hunted, hounded, jogging or running as exercise or recreational (a fitness or recreational activity that involves running at a moderate pace, often over long distances for exercise), followed, trailed, tracked, looked for, searched for, to go after, to cause to flee, run away, to dr ive or hurry away, or to put to flight.

Unless otherwise noted elsewhere, if, in your everyday living, your awaked state, as part of your lifestyle, work, or ministerial activities, or a special event, you have a very real connection with any kind of chasing or running activity (e.g. athletics, exercise, recreational, or law enforcement), also see content list for this category. Your dream is not significant and does not warrant special attention.

Otherwise noted, this dream may be a Prophetically Simple Dream (see Chapter One: The 60th Part of Prophecy). Whereas, the dreamer is warned to stop chasing after any and all illegal or illicit activity, especially if this is going on within your life (e.g. illegal or illicit affairs, handling of drugs, money, or weapons, stalking, or any other criminal minded, under- handed activity). You should surrender to the appropriate authorities, especially if this has been an issue within the dream er's life, or submit or yield to other relevant persons if this is appropriate. If any of the preceding is happening, this dream is a first step intervention and an alarm. Skip interpretation and re-consider your activity as harmful, hurtful, illegal, or life threatening, at present. Handle the situation appropriately by surrendering, first to God, for Adonai Elohim knows all, and then to appropriate authorities or relevant others.

Otherwise noted, see Note 1 at the beginning of Actions and Activities category.

To determine who your dream is for you or another, see Note 3 at the beginning of Actions and Activities category.

Symbols and Referents: To chase, be chased, jogging, running, followed, or stalked within a dream generally implies one of two meanings: (1) Someone's accusations have resulted in intense harassment, hounding, maltreatment, persecution, or a singling out of someone and/or a loss of favor. Either the dreamer is the perpetrator, depicted by the dreamer doing the chasing or following; or another is responsible, portrayed by someone else doing the chasing or stalking. This intense harassment activity will often represent spiritual realities; e.g. the enemy of your soul instigating others (or the dreamer) to do his dirty work, thus vigorous pestering and serious aggravation by the demonically used. In this, dreamer, your struggle is not with man, but is spiritual. Read, understand, and embrace, Ephesians 6:10-18, for this is to you now. Therefore, worldly or carnal dealings are not advantageous. Godly wisdom is your best bet. Listen to that still small voice; it will guide you, for it is of God. (2) The positive or unwise aspects of a certain way of life, is in pursuit of you or you in pursuit of it. Your attention and time given to the positive or unwise aspects of the lifestyle chasing or following you or you chasing it will change your way of living. For example, the dreamer is running from drug addicts. Potentially, the dreamer is rejecting the negative tempta tion to use drugs or to allow drugs within your environment; thus, changing your way of living to a drug free lifestyle. Another example: a prodigal Christian is following the dreamer. A spirit of recklessness and wasteful extravagance is following the dreamer. There is a potential of dreamer becoming reckless in your spirituality, and embracing a lack of faith and respect regarding your spiritual benefits and inheritance in Christ.

Category Content - If not listed see index, perchance, for your specific type of chase, pursuit, running, or following dream activity.

- Animal chasing, running, following, seeking, stalking, or pulling on you
- Clergy chasing, running, following, seeking, stalking, or pulling on you
- Criminal chasing, running, following, seeking, stalking, or pulling on you (e.g. drug dealer, gangster, killer, mobster, molester, murderer, pimp, pusher, player, prostitute, rapist, thief, or any kind of violator)
- Demon, Enemy, Monster, or Ghost, chasing, running, following, seeking, stalking, or pulling on you
- Doctor chasing, running, following, seeking, stalking, or pulling on you
- Ex-spouse is chasing, running, following, seeking, stalking, or pulling on you
- Friend or Neighbor chasing, running, following, seeking, stalking, or pulling on you
- Giants chasing, running, following, seeking, stalking, or pulling on you
- God, Jesus or celestial beings chasing, running, following, seeking, stalking, or pulling on you
- Illicit lover or Fatal Attraction chasing, running, following, seeking, stalking, or pulling on you
- Invisible entity was chasing, running, following, seeking, stalking, or pulling on you
- Officer of the law chasing, running, following, stakeout, stalking, or pulling on you (e.g. judge, detective, parole officer, police, probation officer)
- Person, People chasing, running, following, seeking, stalking, or pulling on you
- Racing (e.g. competitive running)
- Rats racing, running "rat race"
- Revenge (someone seeking revenge)
- Running (e.g. running fall down, getting back up, stealthily running and hiding)
- Scurrying or hurrying about (darting, dashing about, fleeing, hustle and bustling, moving quickly, or speeding)
- Spouse or fiancée chasing, running, following, seeking, stalking, or pulling on you

- Vehicle (someone in any mode of transportation) pursuing you
- Witch or Hag chasing, running, following, seeking, stalking, or pulling on you
- You chasing, running, following, seeking, stalking, or pulling on you

Animal chasing, running, following, seeking, stalking, or pulling on you: Animals, within our dreams, for the most part, are anthropomorphized or given human characteristics. Thus, animals denote our personality traits, our basic nature, behavioral patterns, and endowments. This type of dream helps the dreamer to know what your divine Counselor wants you to focus on; namely, your particular behaviors. The character trait and/or specific action and activity figurative of the animal within your dream is overtaking your life or if dreamer is chasing the animal, the dreamer is absorbed in the pursuit of identity void of foundation (e.g. pretending to be someone you are not; and not knowing what it takes to be that what you are chasing). This type of identity pursuit will not withstand your storms of life. You will begin to crack in your personality. The only foundation upon which humankind should wisely establish his or her identity, are the principles within the Word of God. For specific animal, see category, Animals. If necessary, see suggested course of action.

Clergy chasing, running, following, seeking, stalking, or pulling on you: This dream has two meanings (choose one). (1) If cleric was chasing, running, following, seeking, stalking, or pulling on you, dreamer you are running from a particular calling upon your life. The type of actions, activities, duties associated with that particular cleric chasing, running, following, stalking you should be explored as a possible ministry or full time profession (e.g. bishop, deacon, elder, evangelist, minister, overseer, pastor, pope, preacher, priest, rabbi, speaker, superintendent, teacher, or writer). (2) If the dreamer was doing the chasing this choice has two parts, (choose one). (a) If you did not clearly see, or know, the cleric, the dreamer is on the right track, pursuing, growing, and going towards your purpose God has destined for you. You are the cleric; thus, you are, purposed to do whatever the cleric was doing (e.g. casting out demons or an exorcist, laying-on-of-hands for divine healing, preaching, leading). Alternatively, you are purposed to be whatever that particular cleric represented to you within your dream (e.g. pope, bishop, pastor, preacher, elder, minister, or teacher). Patiently and contentedly continue on the track you are on, you will get there. If you've gotten off track, consider your dream a warning, and do your first acts of love and obedience towards Christ. (b) If you clearly recognized or knew the cleric, then that particular clerics' image, finances, reputation, and/or title, you covet. Failing to recognize covetousness within your heart may give you a false sense of "calling" with regard t o God's purpose for your life. If that cleric is in good standing, with men and God, glean from that person, and if applicable allow their mentorship within your life, but be who God has called you to be including your own unique ministry and style. If t hat cleric is not a reputable leader, e.g. an adulterer, greedy, imposter, molester, or violator of the flock, do not pursue, nor engage in the activities of that leader. At best, you can learn what not to do, from this immoral cleric and flee! See suggested course of action.

Criminal chasing, running, following, seeking, stalking, or pulling on you (e.g. drug dealer, gangster, held hostage, kidnapper, killer, mobster, molester, murderer, pimp, pusher, player, prostitute, rapist, thief, or any kind of vio lator): This dream has two meanings (choose one). (1) Your dream was sent to demonstrate grace, via a warning. Dreamer, due to your challenging life activities, personal illness, and/or the wearying of others, you have become very exhausted emotionally. Overcome by profound discouragement and a sense of being alone in your conflicts, coupled with exhaustion, an old familiar lifestyle has reared (or will rear) up its' ugly head to try to take advantage of your physical weakness. Dreamer stand still, cease from your work and take a rest; know that God is God. He is able to care for you, to care for His ministry He has assigned to you, and He knows where you are. He alone will deliver you out of the snares of the enemy. Go take a long vacation, atleast eight weeks. Schedule it within two months at the latest. If you do not take a sabbatical, you will be forced into one via a serious illness. This illness may be avoided if you will rest. During your rest, your Heavenly Father will heal your discouragement in a caring and understanding manner. He will allow you to sleep, and He will nourish and visit you with inspiring revelations of His Power and Presence and give additional revelation regarding direction for your life. The hope, labor, love, and struggle of your life's work are not in vain. You are not alone; neither should you feel that way. (2) You chasing criminal, killer: You are attempting to resolve your conflicts with the ungodly and their activities against you, in your own strength and carnal knowledge, according to your sense of street knowledge, without seeking the help and strength of God (Isaiah 30:15, 16, 18). Let go, and let God. See suggested course of action.

Demon, Enemy, Monster, or Ghost, chasing, running, following, seeking, stalking, or pulling on you: This dream has two meanings (choose one). (1) You are internally inconsistent and disordered, because of a violent violation in your past or recent present. The violation (e.g. abuse, assault, bullying, kidnapping, molestation, rape, stalked, or being held prisoner) is the demon, monster, ghost, or hag within your dream. This diabolical entity, having possessed the person(s) who committed the literal act, was sent to rob, steal, and destroy a quality of life that has been destined you, to keep you from living life abundantly, happily, and in peace. The demon's mission is to get you to entertain, embrace, and live out the negative results of your particular violation, to oppress, persecute, and bring you into bondage of an ungodly and unprofitable lifestyle. With hopes that unfavorable consequences will cost you your emotional sanity, possibly your life, and ultimately your soul. Dreamer; oftentimes, bad things happen to innocent and good people. A bad thing happened to you, and you are good and innocent. Compassionately, the Lord is creating a miracle in your life. This miracle will stop the effects of your violation from playing a significant role in your life, enabling you to move forward with your life. However, the miracle's success depends upon your willingness to be healed and set free; for one will always have the choice to say no, or perhaps sabotage their progress. Firstly, recognize and respect your time of visitation from the Lord, for it is upon you, as well as the work of His Hand upon your life. With fortitude, choose not to be a victim, nor to perpetuate the desolation. For example, you are verbally abused, and allowing it, now you're angry with others with little or no cause. Loving your brother or sister is becoming a growing problem within you; thus, the internally inconsistent and disordered issue. Perhaps, long ago, someone you loved was murdered, and you find yourself unable to forgive the murderer, thus, the internally inconsistent and disordered issue.

Another example, you are (or were) sexually violated, now you no longer desire anyone of the opposite sex; thus, the internally inconsistent and disordered issue. Dreamer, no longer entertain or embrace the bad or negative results of your particular violation. If successful, you will be able to empathically, understand situations that violate others, and subsequently devote yourself to this type of ministry in a specialist type position. You will become renowned for your expertise and passion. First step to success is forgiveness. An unforgiving heart is the single most popular poison that the enemy uses against God's people; and it is the deadliest poison a person can take spiritually. Further, an unforgiving heart is a most subtle thing that steals its way into your heart almost unknown, but in the sight of God, it is the greatest hindrance to your spiritual fellowship and communion with a Holy God who answers prayer. This is the one thing spoken of in the Word that if found in the heart of a believer will hinder answered prayer. The very first sign that this spirit is manifesting in your heart, is continual anger towards that person's actions toward you. Pastor Alma M. Perry, "What I found out experientially was that an unforgiving heart will bring the consequences of judgment (divine reprimand for folly and sin); which I know we have heard that it opens the door to all kinds of sicknesses, even premature death"[32]. Dreamer, deliberately develop habits of holiness, prayer, fasting, theological study, abstinence, sobriety, and separation from people, places, and circumstances that are contrary to your development of clarity, cleanness, and stability. Then you will be healed emotionally, physically, and spiritually. (2) You chasing (and killing) a demon or monster: You are powerful and strong and are able to do mighty works for the Kingdom of God. God has given you a rare sense of purpose from birth. Ultimately, that purpose is inherent in the Word of God. For you, a purposeless existence will cause only frustration and despair within you. Therefore, you must choose a lifelong commitment to sowing "seeds" that will ultimately uproot and replace the wicked seeds planted by demonic forces some time ago. The seeds you must sow are intentional development of habits of holiness, prayer, fasting, theological study, abstinence, sobriety, and separation from people, places, and circumstances that are contrary to your development of holiness, clarity, and stabili ty. These wise choices will in due course, bring you authentic joy, happiness, divine purpose, and miraculous knowledge and power.

Doctor chasing, running, following, or stalking: Dreamer, you are spiritually, physically, or psychologically sick. The sick are in need of a physician. If you are doing the chasing, you are clearly aware of the need for change, spiritually, physically, or psychologically. With that, this dream has three choices (choose one). (1) Spiritual aspect: You have need of an up close and personal experience with Jesus, the Great Physician. For your dream denotes an unhealed heart's cry for inner healing. This very personal experience will effect spiritual and emotional healing, and lead to a closer, more spiritual relationship with God. Consequently, there will be a regeneration of your life's' spiritual fruitfulness. This release will affect comfortable and pleasant effects in your heart, even to the point of physical healing. (2) Physical aspect: Your dream was sent to demonstrate grace, via a warning of possible serious health issues. The physical weakness or ailments you've been experiencing as of late will need medical attention as soon as possible. Note, the progress of your up close and personal relationship with Christ Jesus resulting in emotional healing, will be beneficial to your physical healing during this time as well. (3) Psychological aspect: Dreamer, you are embracing behaviors that lead to great disillusionments, emotional breakdowns, and/or breaks with reality. Thus, your dream comes as a very harsh warning. Dreamer, you are not in harmony with the will of God for your life, nor with the particular objectives that are intended to ensure the fulfillment of that will. Your behavior contradicts practicality, basic reality, and deviates from the morality of God. Yours is a life full of unnecessary words and activities, which have no basis in fact or reality, and they are not rooted in faith in God. Reality is understood to be what God says it to be via His Word. For example, we are saved by grace through faith, not by works (Ephesians 2:5-10). Hence, anyone who does not correspond with His truth, in a levelheaded and practical manner, is deceived and erroneous in your thoughts and ideas; thus, exposing your rejection of the certainty of God's word. See suggested course of action.

Ex-spouse is chasing, running, following, seeking, stalking, or pulling on you: Your dream denotes anger and fear. Question to journal: Who was doing the chasing? The one doing the chasing is angry with the other. Therefore, your dream was sent as a warning. The one doing the chasing is devious and guilty of cruelly destroying the other, spiritually, emotionally, and possibly physically, because of their uncontrolled anger and serious fear issues. This person, being demonically influenced, has come (will come) to rob, steal, and destroy the peace afforded the other via Christ Jesus. With that said, nonetheless, the one being chased also has anger problems and serious fear issues. Your dream is challenging you, the dreamer, whether you were the chaser, or the one being chased, to confront your dysfunction, one way, or another. One primary sign that anger is manifesting in your heart is a continual unforgiving heart towards another or a group of persons, a place, or circumstance. An unforgiving heart is a most subtle thing that steals its way into your heart almost unknown, but in the sight of God, it is the greatest hindrance to your spiritual fellowship and communion with a Holy God who answers prayer. This is the one thing, spoken of in the Word that if found in the heart of a believer it will hinder answered prayer and it opens the door to all kinds of sicknesses, even premature death. Fear is akin to idolatry; for you exalt that spirit above God's promised word of protection from all hurt, harm, and danger. Dreamer, deliberately develop habits of holiness, prayer, fasting, theological study, abstinence, sobriety, and separation from people, places, and circumstances that are contrary to your development of clarity, cleanness, and stability. You will be healed emotionally, physically, and spiritually. Acknowledging that anger and fear are parts of your character, and seeking help, via prayer, fasting, and/or an anger management program, will help determine the root cause of your anger, and possibly your fears. If you are unwilling to acknowledge, challenge, and/or change you, you will be pursued by one with an unrelenting vendetta against you, and yes, it will be allowed. See suggested course of action.

Friend or Neighbor chasing, running, following, seeking, stalking, or pulling on you: This dream has two meanings (choose one). (1) Friends or neighbor was chasing dreamer. You will become estranged from forbidden relationships and restored to correct relationships. This will happen because of God's great love and devotion toward you. Respond positively to the Lord's love, respect His precepts, principles, statutes, and acknowledge that He is your Lord and Savior and that He restores (also see Hosea 2:14-3:5). (2) You chasing friends, see Hosea 4:1-3. See suggested course of action.

Giants chasing, running, following, seeking, stalking, or pulling on you: Two things, choose one. (1) If you were running from the giant or prevail over the giant in some way, the dreamer has power over others as to be able to burden, distress, and/or oppress them (e.g. bully). Fortunately, you are running from, or fighting against, the temptation to intimidate and/or to be offensive to others. You will render that side of you dead. (2) If you were chasing the giant, or was captured by the giant; the dreamer has ridiculed or snubbed at, the honor obtained by godly virtues, and is choosing to make a great name for yourself by actions that actually ruin good names. For example, you burden, distress, and/or oppress others. They that have power over others as to be able to oppress them, rarely have power over themselves to refrain from such choices. Power and authority is a very great snare to many, and you are one of the many. See suggested course of action.

God, Jesus, or Celestial Beings chasing, running, following, seeking, stalking, or pulling on you: Two things (choose one). (1) Chased or being chased by God, Jesus, or celestial beings: This choice has two parts (choose one). (a) To the believer: Dreamer, God is earnestly, and vigorously, pursuing you, with an emphasis on a lifelong commitment to His way of life. This means that all that is true and faithful, spiritually, will now began to follow and press hard after you. Literally to pursue you as one does a fleeing enemy. There will be one coming in the name of Jesus, testifying of God's Truth. Recognize your time of visitation, and do not harden your heart against their words, provoking God. Dreamer, you have been running from God too long (see Psalm 68:1). See suggested course of action. (b) To the unbeliever (one who has no religious beliefs, a non-religious person, or no religious faith or belief in Jesus Christ), Jesus loves you; thus, He is petitioning you to accept Him as your personal Savior, for you are valuable in His eyes. The first step in receiving Him as your personal Savior is repentance (see in the Holy Bible, Acts 2:37-41). Repentance is seeking pardon for having done something awry, and for having hurt someone, and expressing sincere feelings of regret and brokenness. To Jesus pray, Psalm 51:1-19. To individuals, a phone call or a letter of apology is a good place to start, if appropriate. Moreover, if you will accept the Heavenly Father's Words, via the Bible, and store up His principles, and His ways and means within you, turning your ear to wisdom and applying your heart to understanding, calling out for insight and crying aloud for discernment, Jesus will meet you. This, coupled with a lifestyle of prayer and fasting, followed by appropriate application of wisdom, and you will know the Messiah, Jesus Christ, intimately, a nd find the knowledge of God you seek. For the Lord gives wisdom and from His mouth comes knowledge and understanding. Then you will understand what is right and just and fair, every good path. When wisdom enters your heart and knowledge becomes sweet to your soul, discretion will protect you, understanding will guard you, and His Truth will lea d you. To deliver you from the ways of wickedness, and from demons whose words and ways are perverse, who causes you to walk in darkness gladly, whose paths are crooked and devious, causing you to leave straight paths (Proverbs 2:1-6, 9-15). This is one of God's covenant promises to you. Have faith in this. (2) To pursue God, Jesus, or celestial beings: Your dream indicates one whose spirit is upright within him or her, and one who is diligent and faithful.

Illicit lover or Fatal Attraction chasing, running, following, seeking, stalking, or pulling on you: This dream has three meanings (choose one). (1) Unmarried dreamer, to chase, run after, follow, or stalk an illicit lover is akin to following a fter other gods. Just as you have chased after other lovers, so have you chased after other gods, and dishonored the covenant between you and God. Your Heavenly Father has commanded that you have no other gods before Him; therefore, be earnest and repent. Rethink your last actions, thoughts, and/or plans, and consider your attitude, perhaps your behavior, as akin to idolatry, and your thoughts subliminally suggested by demons. Dreamer read, understand, respect, and embrace Exodus 34:14-15, Deuteronomy 6:5, Matthew 22:37, Mark 12:30. Repentance is seeking pardon and expressing sincere feelings of regret and brokenness for having done something awry and/or for having hurt someone, see 2 Corinthians 7:10, 11. To Jesus pray, Psalm 51, this followed by appropriate application of wisdom, can conceivably avert some of the repercussions of your choices. This is what is called leaving a blessing behind. See suggested course of action. (2) If married and dreamer is involved in any illicit sexual activity in your awaked life: If you, dreamer, was chasing, running, following, seeking, stalking, or pulling on an illicit lover or fatal attraction within your dream, let's begin with some questions: If you found out that your spouse was sexually involved with another, would you forgive him or her? Imagine that the unfaithfulness was not a one-night stand, but a long affair. Imagine further that your spouse wasn't very repentant and was rather open about what he or she was doing. Would you still love your spouse? If your spouse left you, and then wanted to return, would you receive him or her back? Just as you have chased after other lovers, so have you chased after, and dishonored the covenant between you and your spouse, even within your heart. In the same way you have sincerely answered the exploratory quest ions, from your heart, so it will, be done unto you. See suggested course of action. (3) Illicit lover or fatal attraction is chasing, running, following, seeking, stalking, or pulling on you: Dreamer wants a change in your life. Fortunately, people and state of affairs do change for the good, via prayer and heartfelt repentance to Jesus and to individuals affected by your actions, in the form of an apology (if possible). To individuals, a phone call or a letter of apology is a good place to start. From this moment on, you will begin to notice the "fruit" of sagacious choices, actions, behaviors, and desires.

Invisible entity was chasing, running, following, seeking, stalking, or pulling on you: The wicked flees when no one pursues (Proverbs 28:1). Dreamer, you are not in harmony with the will of God for your life, nor with the particular objectives that are, intended to ensure the fulfillment of that will. Your behavior contradicts practicality, basic reality, and deviat es from the morality of God. Yours is a life full of unnecessary words and activities, which have no basis in fact or reality, nor are your activities God sanctioned. With you, fantasy and reality oftentimes become intermingled, causing you to become very impractical. All this suggests a way of life that is going contrary to God's call. Dreamer, reality is, understood to be what God says it to be via His Word. Hence, anyone who does not correspond with His truth, in a levelheaded and practical manner, is deceived and erroneous in your thoughts and ideas; thus, exposing your rejection of the certainty of God's word. See suggested course of action.

Officer of the law chasing, running, following, seeking, stakeout, stalking, or pulling on you (e.g. judge, detective, parole officer, police, or probation officer): This dream has two meanings (choose one). (1) If officer was doing the chasing, running, following, stakeout, or stalking, the dreamer is being watched, very closely, by servants, ministers of God, as well as other Christians. Dreamer is under close observation, by ministers of God and other Christians, in anticipation or expectancy of any evil act, or any morally objectionable behavior committed by the dreamer. Therefore, walk circumspectly, behaving discreetly, with discretion, prudently, and with wise self-restraint. Your reputation is on the line, and some may become disappointed and disheartened within their spirituality, because of your actions. (2) If dreamer was doing the chasing, this dream is to urge the dreamer to pursue holiness from the perspective of God's grace (the free and unmerited favor and beneficence of God) and love. Attempting holiness under the law is spiritually disastrous (see Galatians 4:21 -5:1-14; James 2:12, 13). See suggested course of action.

Person, People chasing, running, following, seeking, stalking, or pulling on you (known or unknown): Question to journal, how did dreamer react to the chasing? Couple this with one of the following four (choose one). (1) If circumstances were pleasant and friendly, this person is a hindrance to the dreamer's ministry or purpose, under the pretense of friendship. Dreamer, be aware of a certain person who will enter your life soon. They are to be considered an obstacle, distracting and drawing your attention away from your time of ministry. They will be entertaining, provoking your interest, with words and activities that are pleasing to your flesh. They may appear as a person of light, friendly, loving, or expressing some manner of interest in you, possibly intimate. They will be allowed, due to dreamer's own carnal desires. Dreamer, forsake not your time of service to Adonai and to His Kingdom, for, if you do neglect your service, it will prove very unprofitable for you and cau se much pain, heartache, distress, depression, and illness. If you think you're lonely now, wait until that person(s) get through with you. Dreamer, it's all right to be lonely, as long as you have peace inwardly, and know that you are free spiritually. Having been forewarned let your actions go according to wise counsel. (2) If person(s) behavior of chasing, running, following, seeking, or stalking was troubling and frightening, this denotes that intense harassment activity that vexes even to the soul, and causes physical illness, has come against the dreamer. The enemy of your soul has instigated others to do his dirty work, thus vigorous pestering and serious aggravation by the demonically used against you, with intentions on robbing, stealing, an d destroying you, spiritually, emotionally, and physically. Your struggle is not with man, but is with dark spiritual powers. Read, understand, and embrace, Ephesians 6:10-18, for this is to you now. Worldly or carnal dealings will not be advantageous, especially at this time. Godly wisdom and obedience is your best bet. Listen to that still small voice that is speaking to you at present; He speaks of peace. He will guide you, for He is of God. (3) If dreamer was friendly person, who was chasing, running, following, seeking, or stalking another, then you are the distraction to another. Yes, you are just that distracting. See suggested course of action. (4) If dreamer was doing the troubling and frighteningly chasing, running, following, seeking, or stalking another, you are intensely harassing someone to the same degree as (#2), see choice #2. Moreover, your issues are within. Deal with your own attitude, and why you are allowing dark spiritual powers to influence you, by this, you will get relief spiritually and mentally. See suggested course of action.

Racing (competitive running): This dream has two meanings (choose one). (1) Competitive running, racing (athletically): Your dream is a notification and warning to the dreamer. Your time of action on behalf of the Kingdom of God is quickly approaching. However, you have need of discipline. You lack commitment, dependability, determination, and drive. Your days of preparation and grounding are upon you. Your choices will make your time of grounding a dvantageous or wearisome. It will be up to you. You are free to do as you please; you still have personal liberty. Nevertheless, you are not free fro m the consequences of your choices. If your true intent is on doing God's will, reaping prosperity, experiencing genuine joy, and most importantly inheriting eternal life, you will have to practice restricting yourself in all things (weaning yourself from sensual appetites). This includes your diet, activities, relationships, associations, friendships, partying, and your lack of Christian fellowship. Dreamer, in order to reach your level of proficiency in ministry, you must bring your appetites and sensual desires under subjection, sacrificing fleshy satisfaction, during your days of preparation and ground ing. You will need to lay aside every obstacle that hinders you and causes you to forfeit God's principles, including laziness; that you might r each the point where you are capable of accomplishing your mission. See suggested course of action. (2) To see others competitively run or race: Although, you do not possess the qualities of one who is determined and steadfast; you want to be respected as one who is. The desire is there because of a God ordained undertaking that you're destined to achieve. Ho wever, you give up too easily and quit too soon. You can no longer pretend to have a determined and steadfast quality; you must actually possess it within, in order to complete your purpose and to prosper. Prayer and fasting is the first step in this p rocess. This will help you see yourself and your issues more realistically. You are counseled to accept yourself just as you are, yo ur weaknesses and flaws and your strengths. Afterward, develop specific and reachable goals, and some manner of accountability that will help lead you to your desired goals, and help you develop a disciplined and determined spirit, also set "times frames" for major choices. For example, do not move from your present place of worship for at least seven years, and make it happen, come what may. Reading God's Word, coupled with wise application, will keep things in perspective, real, and balanced. As well as, allow for God's purposes and plans for you personally, to come to the forefront. By genuinely applyin g these qualities to your life, you will be respected as one who is purposeful and persevering. If necessary, see suggested course of action.

Rats racing, running, aka "rat race": Your struggle to survive and make progress in the competitive environment of modern life, is dehumanizing you. It is taking away your individuality, namely the creative and interesting aspects of your personality. As well, your compassion, friendliness, and sensitivity toward others are disappearing. You no longer desire t o enhance other people lives. Your attitude will ultimately lead to a fruitless, futile, pointless, and useless purpose. You will feel the emptiness within. Change, prayer, and heartfelt repentance to Jesus are powerful resources, even to the point of suicide prevention. To Jesus pray, Psalm 51, this followed by appropriate application of wisdom, can conceivably avert some of the repercussions of your choices. This is what is called leaving a blessing behind. See also category, Animals (Rodents). See suggested course of action.

Revenge (someone seeking revenge): This dream has two meanings (choose one). (1) The dreamer has wounded or crushed someone spiritually with your words; thus, a "righter of wrongs" is after you, someone with a vendetta. If you are n ot guilty, because you sincerely did not know the effects of your words, seek refuge in the House of God, around His people, and you will be covered. Use wisdom in the future. If you are guilty, a great need to ask for forgiveness is necessary now; or you will be brought before the court of the people, exposed, and judged righteously. See suggested course of action. (2) The dreamer was seeking revenge: Vengeance is mine says the Lord. God will fight against those who fight against you. Let it go, and let God handle it. You will receive justice in due time. If necessary, see suggested course of action.

Running (e.g. running fall down, getting back up, stealthily running and hiding): This dream has three meanings (choose one). (1) In your present business or personal dealings, you will be satisfied and take delight in your goals. If you are involved in any situation that is competitive, you will triumphant. Additionally, the pace and/or distance depicted (running, traveli ng speed, walking, or already there or in place) will often refer to a "time frame", the length of time before manifestation. For example, if you were "already there" this refers to the present time, while running, traveling speed, and walking, all refer to a future time. Note: one city block will often refer to approximately six months to one year. Moreover, running, one will reach their destination in approximately one fourth the time quicker than walking, and depending upon the means of travel and speed, one will reach their destination in one half to three fourths the time quicker than running. Moreover, if mode of travel was highlighted, see category, Modes of Transportation. Note: if the "mph" is highlighted within your dream, see category, Numbers. No matter the pace, your dream denotes that you're on your way to manifestation. (2) Running, falling down, getting back up, and running: Dreamer read, embrace, and be encouraged via Proverbs 24:16. For, you have proven yourself righteous and upright. Thus, because of your faith, humility, strong leadership, and your courageous and optimistic spirit, you will be greatly honored. You will rise to a level the Anointing of God and your acumen deem you should be. God is with you and He will keep you wherever you go. Even more, you have the miraculous power to change history on some level or another. For example, family generational curses can stop with you (Exodus 20:5, 7; Psalm 112:2), or by introducing radically new fundamental concepts, far beyond the norm (Acts 13:14-52). Whatever the miraculous history change is, be it on a small- scale, via practicing what you preach, or by facilitating some specialize workshops, or by becoming a great leader and orator, you are equipped to handle large-scale undertakings. Dreamer, a large part of your mission in life centers on raising the spirits of your fellow mankind; thus changing history in the lives of those, you touch. The driving force behind all this is your support of others. Your first step is to start by recognizing and thanking Jesus for the small blessings that are before you now and for the miraculous endowment of history changing vision and courageous leadership. Do you want your miracle? Then prepare yourself mentally for it. You're on your way to manifestation, and things may happen quickly. This is not to say there will not be a lot of twists and turns, and fear, but you will get to your destined place to carry out your divine ordained purpose, if you are willing, prudent, and obedient. (3) Stealthily Running and/or Hiding from a person, animal, place, or organization: This choice has two parts (choose one). (a) The dreamer is running away and/or hiding from a difficult predicament or trouble. You've gotten to the point where you're spiritually weak and feel discouraged, feeling that your faith has been in vain. Dreamer, when things go awry and you're overly worried, Jesus is waiting for you to come to Him in prayer. For it will be by His Power that a way out of no way will be made for you, and your state of affairs will be turned around and worked out as you have believed God for all these years. You can pray, "Lord I don't know how I'm going to make it. I can't see my way, come, and see about me. I'm down here trying to do what's right, because I think your cause is right. But Lord, I must confess, I'm weak now, I'm faltering, and I'm becoming discouraged". You can tell Him what you want Him to know. Somehow, God will make a way for you. Jesus will come and see about you, keep your faith regarding what you've believed God for; He has promised never to leave you alone. You are not alone; neither will you be made ashamed. You will experience a miracle. (b) Dreamer, although you do not act so discreetly right now, do not be overly critical of yourself, but wholly embrace God's grace now, for, it is sufficient. You need this. As well, allow patience to prevail within you, and continue to wait on, and seek after, the Lord for He is faithful, just, and a rewarder of them that diligently seek Him (Hebrews 11:6). On another vein, you are in danger of putting forth your hands to iniquity, because the rule of the wicked has impeded upon your living too long (Psalm 125:3). The dreamer is aggressively running towards difficulty or trouble and is hiding so as not to be recognized. Moreover, did you recognize any persons, places, or things within your dream? If necessary, see suggested course of action.

Scurrying or hurrying about (darting, dashing about, fleeing, hustle and bustling, moving quickly, or speeding): Your dream is to trigger a rational and sincere examination of your feelings, thoughts, and motives at present, due to your overwhelming hardship. Dreamer, it is often true that the righteous is in danger of putting forth their hands to iniquity, w hen the rule of the wicked impedes upon their living too long (Ecclesiastes 7:7; Psalm 125:3, 4). Even to the point of resentmen t toward his or her religious beliefs that seem powerless to help during their time of crisis. Even more, overwhelming hardshi ps that are long in endurance, and cumbersome, makes a wise man (or woman) very frustrated. For when even, wise men or women have unreasonable burdens put upon them, they struggle to keep their temper and to keep their place, if they are oppressed too much and too long, he or she is very apt to speak and act unwise and foolishly. Oftentimes, to their own peril, the righteous and wise alike, will openly voice harsh complaints against God and man, and seek secular remedies for a little relief; exposing him or herself to the dangers of transgressing. Dreamer, although you do not act so discreetly right now do not be overly critical of yourself, but wholly embrace God's grace (the free and unmerited favor and beneficence of God) now. Yo u need this. As well, allow patience to prevail within you, and continue to wait on the Lord for He is faithful, just, and a rewarder of them that diligently seek Him (Hebrews 11:6). See suggested course of action.

Spouse or Fiancée chasing, running, following, seeking, stalking, or pulling on you: If you were being chased, this implies God's love for you, and someone else love for you, with his or her emphasis on a lifelong commitment to love and faithfulness. If you were doing the chasing, this denotes your love for someone you care about just as much as you love God, with emphasis on marriage and fidelity. Be confident, you will fulfill your God given responsibility within your marriage, a s will they, and both of you will fulfill your covenant relationship with Jesus.

Vehicle (someone in any mode of transportation) pursuing you: two things (choose one). (1) If another was pursuing you, someone is trying to impose his or her lifestyle and opinions on you, by means of intense harassment, hounding, maltreatment, persecution, and/or a singling out. Dreamer, know whom you are and stand up for your right to be you and stand up for your convictions. (2) If you were doing the pursuing: Live and let live, and your health will improve. Life is too brief to try to control someone for no other reason than to feed an evil desire within your flesh. There is only one Creator, and He has designed everyone individually unique and for a particular purpose. The way God has allowed one person to live their life, although different from yours, is for a purpose. For example, not everyone is meant to be married. One may not marry whom you think they should. Another may take life a little more lightly and humorous than another. She may be prudent, it may be a chore for you to budget, or he may have a major flaw, so do you. Choose to celebrate others uniqueness and teach others, to do so as well. You'll find that others will love you freely, without reservation, and your place in this world will be friendlier and happier. See suggested course of action.

Witch or Hag chasing, running, following, seeking, stalking, or pulling on you: Rebelliousness is pursuing you or you are chasing it (1 Samuel 15:23). You do not pursue by faith, the righteousness that only comes from the Lord. A change has come. This transition can be an easy one, if obedience to God is adhered to, or it can get rough and rugged, if there is open defia nce. One thing is for sure, you can no longer pursue waywardness nor allow it to pursue you, and continue as before. D reamer, resist unruliness within your nature, and it will flee. See suggested course of action.

You chasing, running, following, seeking, stalking, or pulling on you: The dreamer is agitated because your soul is buried underneath the pain of unproductive, vain, and worthless pursuits, your choices are negative and have harmful effects. Compassionately, God has extended His mercy and forgiveness towards you, because He knows why you do what you do, even if you don't. Pray and ask Jesus to help you look reflectively within, into why you do what you do, and then seek out available resources for help, support, and accountability. Know yourself; and resist those detrimental urges via a serious commitment to a lifestyle of prayer and fasting. In addition, humbly submit your negative inclinations to Christ and to His principles, and those urges will abate. Dreamer, the strength and resistance you draw upon to resist those dark ways when you're before people, use that same level of resistance and control when no one is looking or suspects you. Be patient in doing well, coupled with faith in God (a resolute trust in the integrity of God and in His Word), and you will overcome! See suggested course of action.

Suggested Course of Action

Question to consider and journal, did your dream depict any symbols that alludes to, the dreamer will make the necessary changes, spiritually, emotionally, and/or physically to affect a more positive outcome? If changes are initiated, your dreams will change.

Nevertheless, consider seriously the chase or hiding, then ask yourself, is what you are chasing or hiding from, or is what is chasing, running, following, stalking you, more important than what you'll be leaving behind, forfeiting, or are in denial about? If allowed within your life, will it build or destroy, strengthen or weaken, enlighten or blind? If you lack wisdom, ask Jesus for wisdom. He gives wisdom to all men generously, no matter who you are and what you've done; wisdom will be given you (James 1:5-8).

Consider and journal the following questions. The questions will help you determine; the issue at hand, how you feel about it, and what may have instigated it. What kind of chase was it? Why was there chasing or hiding? Why were you running and/or hiding? Who were you running towards or from within your dream? Were you hiding, if so from whom? Were they, or it, dangerous or insignificant to you? Were you investigative or undercover? Were others involved? If yes, who and in what manner were they involved? Keep in mind that the others represent a quality of you, see Note 3 at the beginning of Actions and Activities category. Did anyone get hurt emotionally, physically, or was disturbed in any way? How did you feel, and what did you do, because, of your feelings, regarding the chase and/or where you ended up or was going? Was the experience confusing, dangerous, happy, joyful, or life threatening, safe, scary, or unsure? Where were you? Was the place unfamiliar to you? Were you coherent? In view of your dream's context, namely chasing, running, following, or stalking, what choices are you making that may impair your spiritual growth, judgment, health, or that will encourage immorality and/or are you reacting out of fear? If so, what can you do to combat the paralyzing emotion of fear? Your answers, coupled with the interpretation, plus any additional information, should begin to unfold the subject matter and issue at hand, if not now, mul l over things a few days. For more information, see index or relevant category and subcategory for other particulars within your dream.

The following will help you determine the approximate length of time you have thus far dealt with the matter and how much longer you will have to deal with the issue. If you started chasing, running, following, seeking, or stalking at the beginning of the dream, you are dealing with this issue right now. If somewhere in the middle onward, you will encounter the issue shortly. How far or long did you chase, run, follow, or stalk? Every ½ mile is approximately five years of time. Did you go in circles within the same area? Was it a familiar place? This would indicate some type of cycle within your life that need s to be broken in order for you to progress forward. If area was familiar, you know the cycle within you very well. If unfamiliar, you are now, made aware of a cycle within you. Dreamer, did you stop chasing, running, following, stalking, and/or hiding at some point? This is indicative that you've completed the process that will heal the issue your dream is referencing. If, you did not stop chasing, running, following, stalking, and/or hiding, the matter at hand will not end soon, if you continue avoidance, complaining, faithlessness in God's Word, and murmuring. You are counseled to deal with the concern without avoidance or compromise, in other words head-on. All of these questions should pull together for you your dream. They summarize the issue at hand and what changes need to be made within the dreamer's attitude or life. All of these things will help you pinpoint what you're running and/or hiding from.

Now, pray (See Prayer of Deliverance, pg. 897)

Specific Meaning

If, your chances are very high you will chase, run, follow, or stalk someone (or vice versa), e.g. law enforcement, bounty hunting, detective, undercover, spy, or illegal activity, or some other type of chasing, running, following, seeking, or stalking activity. Dreams of this sort, for the most part, are ordinary dreams, resulting from your daily activities (see Chapter One, Chalom). These sorts of dreams are usually about your routine, mundane activities or anxieties that overwhelm your mind during the day. They are an inner release mechanism, which helps provide you with emotional balance and the maintaining of your sanity. These dreams are not significant, and do not warrant special attention.

Note: On the other hand, the dreamer may consider chasing, running, following, stalking, or hiding activity as an indication that you may be exposed, especially if some manner of law enforcement, detective, undercover, or spy activity is actually relevant within the dreamer's life. Dreamer, the details, kept within context of your dream, should be relevant to your life, and closely resemble your real-life situations. Meaning it can actually occur during your awaked state. This will help you narrow down the specifics needed to support and steer you clear of possible life threatening or major issues. However, if your dream was inundated with symbols that are not easily linked to your life activities, then the spiritual implications (the interpretation) should be heeded.

CHEATING, THIEVERY: Someone uses deceit or trickery to gain an unfair advantage.

Some short descriptions of types, phrases, and other processes and particulars, connected in some way to this category are, for example, breaking and entering, burglar, burglary, cheater, decoy, dupe, embezzlement, hoodwink, larceny, lure, pinch or squeeze someone, pull a fast one, pull the wool over somebody's eyes, red herring, robbery, sweet-talk, swindle, or thief.

Unless otherwise noted elsewhere, if, in your everyday living, your awaked state, as part of your lifestyle, work, or ministerial activities, or a special event, you have a very real connection with any type of cheating, thievery activity. For example, criminal activity, or law enforcement, (also see content list for this category), skip interpretation and go to Specific Meaning at the end of this category.

Otherwise noted, if the cheater, thief, burglar was not seen, invisible, only talked about, (known or unknown), in your dream; the cheater is the dreamer. What was said or done regarding the cheater? What was said or done; is what the divine council in heaven, regarding the dreamer, is officially deciding upon. This official decision will be according to your own actions, thoughts, or words within your dream (see Ezekiel 33:12-20); this in addition to the following interpretation that relates to your dream.

Otherwise noted, see Note 1 at the beginning of Actions and Activities category.

To determine who your dream is for you or another, see Note 3 at the beginning of Actions and Activities category.

Symbols and Referents: Cheating, Thievery generally implies one of two meanings for the dreamer: (1) A soul that is not upright due to greed, false impressions, or some form of character exaggeration, or (2) A leader who sabotages positive ministry ideas and opportunities presented by others, because of covetousness, ignorance, jealously, or spite.

Category Content - If not listed see index, perchance, for your specific type of cheating dream activity.

- If someone else instigated or provoked, in any way, the cheating, thievery - no matter if a defense was put up
- Cheating (swindling or defraud by deceitful means)
- Con (to dupe, hoodwink, lure, pull a fast one, pull the wool over somebody's eyes, sweet-talk)
- Deception (decoy, pinch, squeeze someone, red herring, or engage in deceitful behavior)
- Dishonesty (lying, untruthfulness)
- Embezzlement (misappropriation, misuse of money for your own use or profit, in violation of a trust)
- Fraud (defeat someone through trickery, hoax, practical joke, pretense)
- Scam (devious, deceptive design, plan, plot, proposal, racket, set-up, sham)
- Scheming (calculating, crafty, sleight of hand, sly, sneaky, wily)
- Shoplifting (stealing merchandise)
- Stolen ID or Identity Theft
- Thievery (burglary, larceny, robbery, stealing)
- Treacherous (to deal treacherously with others by holding back wages, loan sharking, usury, double-crossing)

If someone else instigated or provoked, in any way, the cheating, thievery - no matter if a defense was put up. Questions to journal, known or unknown, who or what do they represent to you personally, or who or what did they represent within your dream? For example, authority figure, burglar, helper, favorite, fighter, leader, liar, mentor, minister, pastor, rebel, sage, shyster, teacher, thief, unwise, vengeful, or violators. Consider the background and activity, where were you, what was going on. For example, a cab driver in NYC, stealing your credit card information, may represent someone connected to you in that place. A burglar attempting to break into your home may represent someone sent to attempt do harm, to rob, steal, and/or destroy a certain lifestyle intended the dreamer. Nonetheless, it is this person, with that title, or within that sphere, who will come against you, and they will suppose they're doing God's will by coming against you, and they will come against you, if not already. Although, your abusers and accusers suppose they're doing God's will by coming against you, they don't know Him, nor His will, regarding why they are coming against you, they are in error. But for you, (Matthew Henry's Commentary): Our Lord Jesus by giving us notice of trouble, is designed to take off the terror of it, that it might not be a surprise to us. Of all the adversaries of our peace, in this world of troubles, none insult us more violently, nor put our troops more into disorder, than disappointment does; but we can easily welcome a guest we expect, and being fore-warned are fore- armed, Praemoniti, praemuniti. Regrettably, you are mistreated by some, dodged, and victimized by others. Although not a majority, some hostility is so great, you are considered as one with a psychiatric disorder, and your inspirations, to those few, are considered the words of a fool. They are adversarial and contentious towards you. They will attempt to lead you to believe something that is not true, and/or to defeat you through some fraudulent scheme or manner of trickery or deceit. They engage in deceitful behavior, practice trickery, and fraud. Your dream comes to forewarn you of one who would dare come against you, to cheat you, in some manner. Your dream also cautions the dreamer that their behavior will, or has, caused a spirit of alarm within you. Whatever your reaction was, within your dream, to their cheating, thievery, will be your same reaction, and to the same degree, towards one who has cheated you. For example, if you caught them in the act, and took back what was deprived you by deceit, your reaction to someone cheating you, will be the same. If you called the police, you will expose the cheater in some way. Moreover, you need (or will need) restoration from feelings of distrust and/or an unforgiving heart. How do you feel knowing that someone, or others, is scheming against you in this way? Are you offended or fearful? Are there feelings of weariness, discouragement, embarrassment, hostility, rage, resentment, and/or revenge? You may feel a bit discombobulated, or perhaps you may shrug your shoulders as to say, "it's neither here or there", then again, you may feel a need to dissimulate. Unfortunately, their feelings or thoughts will be directly expressed to you; therefore, being warned beforehand, is meant to take some of the sting out of their words. For you, dreamer, take the "fear, revenge, or figh t" out of your feelings, as well as any other negative emotion that may arise because of someone else foolishness. Simply take the "high road", and visualize yourself presenting the negativity to the feet of God as an enemy of His Kingdom (Psalm 110:1, Matthew 22:44), as an enemy of your spiritual work, and of your purpose, via prayer. Dreamer, you have divine protection, you have no need to worry, only worship before the Lord (see 2 Chronicles 20:15, 17-19). This is what the Lord says, "Yes, I will contend with those who contend with you" (Isaiah 49:25, 2 Chronicles 20:17, Matthew 5:39). Rest from defending yourself against the demons that want to defeat you, and rest assured God, is, and will be, a defense for you, see Psalm 91. Dreamer, you have in Christ, grace and healing, refreshment, and a refuge. Don't forfeit these graces. Embrace the help your Heavenly Father is offering you, via a sabbatical, and the effects of their negativity will no longer hold sway over your heart.

Cheating (swindling or defraud by deceitful means): Implies character attributes that are unethical, dishonorable, and corrupt. The Lord does not approve of your actions. See suggested course of action.

Con (to dupe, hoodwink, lure, pull a fast one, pull the wool over somebody's eyes, sweet -talk): Your dream implies character traits of one who is arrogant, deceptive, and very angry; one who subverts the way of the Lord, by using known agitators, hotheads, stirrer-ups of things, or troublemakers. Dreamer, an unrelenting soldier of the Lord will become an agitator, a stirrer-up of issues, and troublemaker within your life, affecting the same degree of aggravation and hurt you have caused others. This warrior is sent to put into effect the law of reaping and sowing. This is their present mission and the y will not stop until God says, "Stay your hand". See suggested course of action.

Deception (decoy, pinch, squeeze someone, red herring, or engage in deceitful behavior): You are laughing and lying in someone's face. Seeking to cause them to embrace you as a friend, to gain advantage over them, to do them harm because of revenge. Taking revenge into your hands by lying or misrepresenting your words and motives is a defilement of the soul. You r Heavenly Father is watching you. You will cause His name to be profane amongst those not very familiar with the one true God. The noose you have prepared for another will ensnare you. See suggested course of action.

Dishonesty (lying, untruthfulness): Your self-serving actions and/or choices are affecting others in a very negative way. You are putting others in harm's way, especially those that you, are put here to love, and watch over, as a spiritual leader; thus, making it easy for them to be seriously violated by someone else, even more, causing the violator, although unaware, to collide with God, because of their actions towards His chosen. You will have to give an account for your actions to God, the victim, and the violator. See suggested course of action.

Embezzlement (misappropriation of money for your own profit, in violation of a trust): Dreamer, hurling insults, you've proven to be a bully and braggart, with tyrannical tendencies. Further, you have violated a trust, a confidence communicated to you. Ruthlessly aggressive, you harbor wicked thoughts, using half-truths, twisting confidences, to gain advantage over some. In doing so you have tainted the faith, which is in Jesus Christ, of him or her whose confidence was violated, you wil l be found out. Confession to God and seeking forgiveness is required, by this you will be forgiven for all you've done. See suggested course of action.

Fraud (defeat someone through trickery, hoax, practical joke, pretense): You have instigated one sibling turning against another (blood or spiritual siblings), because of your deceptive and dishonest ways. You have provoked jealously and grudges, resulting in division within your family or church family. In this, you have brought damage and ruin upon yourself, instead of blessings. You will be replaced by another, in some aspect of your life. See suggested course of action.

Scam (devious, deceptive design, plan, plot, proposal, racket, set-up, sham): You have distorted true religion, because of covetousness, greed, and selfishness. You have led people astray, causing the people of God to err in the things of God. Your cupidity will be uncovered, and evil will be brought upon you that will send you away from your place. Humble yourself with fasting before the Lord to lessen the harshness of your days to come. See suggested course of action.

Scheming (calculating, crafty, sleight of hand, sly, sneaky, wily): Dreamer, does God pervert justice? Does the Almighty pervert what is right? Those who are within the Body of Christ will expose your deception. You will be removed from your position and subject to humbler unassuming service until you go home to be with the Lord. Favorably, one day in paradise, and you'll thank the Lord for allowing you to serve Him in that humbling capacity. See suggested course of action.

Shoplifting (stealing merchandise): Implies a getting of gain unjustly, or a desire of ill-gotten gain, because of greed, and signifies a need of restoration of your spiritual life. See suggested course of action.

Stolen ID or Identity Theft: Dreamer, you are allowing the spirit of fear to cause you to lose your psychological and spiritual identity (the individual characteristics by which the dreamer is known or is recognized by), and to terrorize you. It, the spirit of fear, has become your own personal terrorist. Read and understand Romans 8:15, 2 Timothy 1:7. This demon terrorizes you in your thoughts, when you are paranoid, when you are afraid, when you hesitate, when you are insecure, when you are impatient, when you are confused, when panic comes, when your thoughts are filled with worry, when you are uneasy and unsure, when despair and depression find you, when stress comes, when you are full of apprehension, when your thoughts forecast only doom and gloom, when you are restless, when you are frightful, when you are full of dread, when you are anxious, when you are nervous, and when you feel hopeless. You will find this demon in every phobia. Question to journal: What would it feel like if all of your fears were suddenly released from you at one time? Pause and feel that. Bible story, there was that herd of pigs that Legion was cast into, and these pigs found their thoughts to be so unbearable that they all ran off a cliff to commit suicide, because they could not bear what had been unleashed upon them (Matthew 8:28-34, Mark 5:1-20, Luke 8:26-39). This is what the spirit of fear oftentimes leads to, if embraced wholly. On the other hand, the man whom, the devils were suddenly released from, was found sitting, clothed, healed, and in his right mind, and all this done without medication. The spirit of fear is adversarial to the Word of God that says all things will work together for good, to those who love God, and are called according to His purpose. For, if you truly can believe the Word of God, it will change all the rules that darkness has established in your heart and mind. Now I say to you that before you can move forward, fear must be cast out, and renounced, and not medicated. Therefore, dreamer, earnestly renounce the insidious voice of the devil. If you will daily come away and pray, then God will heal you of all things, only come with much prayer and spiritual fasting. The spiritual fast is that time of waiting when you are praying and asking the Lord to come and perform that which only He can perform. Similar to a literal fast, during this time you must abstain. But this fast you must refrain from any counsel or thoughts that tempt you to put your hand on the matter, or to turn you away from waiting on, and having faith in, the Lord. During this time of waiting, you simply need to continue in prayer and be still. Then you will know that only God's love is able to break the curse of darkness from over your mind, body, and spirit. Warning, it will be during your spiritual fast that weaknesses, such as unbelief, doubt, fear, pride, arrogance, will come forth to tempt you to eat the counsel of their lies, rather than to wait for the Lord to come to deliver, heal, help, save, reveal, and/or guide. Wait on the Lord, for He is faithful to come, and again I say wait on the Lord. Moreover, if urged by God, declare a one, two, or three day fast without food.

Thievery (burglary, larceny, robbery, stealing): The fruit of your behavior is akin to false teachers or deceivers who, by pretending they care about the underprivileged, lead men away from the truth. Your ideas have opened a dark gate that will lead to hard press demonic oppression, or demon possession, and possible suicide. Change your mind that you may have life, and it will be abundant, even as your soul prospers. Repent, and God will deliver you from devastation and your feet from stumbling, that you may walk before God in the light of life (Psalm 56:13). See suggested course of action.

Treacherous (to deal treacherously with others by holding back wages, loan sharking, usury, or double-crossing): Dreamer, the cries of an innocent person against you, has reached the ears of the Lord Almighty. You are an oppressor of God's people. You have lived in luxury and self-indulgence, using the money of those who do not dispute your words. Your money will testify against you. You will weep and wail because of the misery that is coming upon you. See suggested course of action.

Suggested Course of Action

Question to consider and journal, did your dream depict any symbols that alludes to, the dreamer will make the necessary changes, spiritually, emotionally, and/or physically to affect a more positive outcome? If changes are initiated, your dreams will change.

Notwithstanding, if cheating was emphasized within your dream, dreamer seek clarity and understanding from the Lord, regarding your decision-making processes and/or identity issues, and apply His wisdom vigilantly. During this season within your life, there will be some very dark hours and major conflict (significant in scope, extent, or effect); this is primarily for the purifying of your faith, the perfecting of patience, and/or spiritual maturity. Encouragingly, this can be replaced with a b eauty or handsomeness that radiates brilliance and righteousness via diligent obedience to God through His Word and endurance. By this, grace and faith will once again be made manifest in your life. Further, rather than allow bitterness or resentment to take root due to the discomfort of change, choose to recognize, acknowledge, and accept that spiritual development and progress is indeed happening within you, and it is for your betterment.

Consider and journal the following questions. The questions will help you determine; the issue at hand, how you feel about it, and what may have instigated it. What kind of cheating was it? Why was there cheating? Against whom (or what) was the cheating? Were others involved? If yes, who and in what manner were they involved? Keep in mind that the others represent a quality of you, see Note 3 at the beginning of Actions and Activities category. Did anyone get hurt emotionally, physically, or was disturbed in any way? How did you feel, and what did you do, because, of your feelings, regarding the cheating? Was it confusing, dangerous, happy, hurtful, insignificant, joyful, life threatening, safe, scary, or unsure? Where were you? Was the place unfamiliar to you? Were you coherent? In view of your dream's context, namely cheating, what choices are you making that may impair your spiritual growth, judgment, health, or that will encourage immorality and/or are you reacting out of fear? If so, what can you do to combat the paralyzing emotion of fear? Your answers, coupled with the interpretation, plus any additional information, should begin to unfold the subject matter and issue at hand, if not now, mull over things a few days. For more information, see index or relevant category and subcategory for other particulars within yo ur dream.

Now, pray (See Prayer of Deliverance, pg. 897)

Specific Meaning

If, your chances are very high that you will be tempted to act in a criminal manner (e.g. handling large amounts of money, driving an armored truck, banking activities, cashier, or any fiscal responsibilities). Dreams of this sort are warnings. There is a chance you will be exposed and criminal charges brought against you because of your actions. Your dream kept within context, should be relevant to your lifestyle and closely resemble your real-life situations. Meaning it can actually occur during your awaked state. This will help you narrow down the specifics of a devious plan and reveal possible consequences.

CLAPPING - clapping the hands together, and/or to strike the hands together with an abrupt, loud sound. Clapping hands to the rhythm of a beat. To slap someone with an open hand or a sudden, loud, explosive sound (e.g. a clap of thunder).

Some short descriptions of types, phrases, and other processes and particulars, connected in some way to this category are, for example, clap (the hands), applaud, pat, slap, smack, give a standing ovation, strike together, tap to a beat, or a loud nois e.

Unless otherwise noted elsewhere, if, in your everyday living, your awaked state, as part of your lifestyle, work, or ministerial activities, or a special event, you have a very real connection with any type of clapping activity. For example, critic, entertainment field, or a ruler, (also see content list for this category), your dream is not significant and does not warrant special attention.

Otherwise noted, see Note 1 at the beginning of Actions and Activities category.

To determine who your dream is for you or another, see Note 3 at the beginning of Actions and Activities category.

Symbols and Referents: Clapping within a dream generally implies joy and peace, divine discipline (the Lord's chastening, correction that leads to instruction and reformation), or pleasure over another's pain.

Category Content - If not listed see index, perchance, for your specific type of clapping dream activity.

- Applaud, cheering (applauding or receiving applauds, a demonstration of approval, no standing ovation)
- Clapping hands very slowly and deliberately (as in a demonstration of disapproval)
- Clapping hands to the rhythm of a beat
- Noise (loud or explosive sound, e.g. a clap of thunder)
- Slap a person or animal (a sharp blow with the open hand)
- Standing Ovation (cheering you on, enthusiastic recognition, especially one accompanied by loud applause)
- Strike hands together (as in to give an order)

Applaud, cheering (applauding or receiving applauds, a demonstration of approval, no standing ovation): This dream has two meanings (choose one). (1) You delight over another's painful experience, because of jealously. See suggested course of action. (2) Being applauded or cheered: Dreamer, you will be released from your spiritual bondage. Groaning will be removed from your lips, and your mouth will be filled with laughter once more. There will be freedom from worry, and there shall be a regeneration of your life's spiritual fruitfulness. This release will affect comfortable and pleasant effects in your heart, even to the point of physical healing. It will also bring blessings of salvation, joy, and peace to your household. You shall go out with joy, and others will rejoice with you (also see Isaiah 55:12). Dreamer, from this day forward God's blessings will flow abundantly, producing spiritual growth within you. God's blessings: Gifts of God's grace, anything God freely gives you, absolution, the Holy Spirit, salvation, regeneration, eternal life, health, children, love of family, longevity, necessities, prosperity, and dominion over all that is yours; and all are parts of the supply of grace, and all are sanctified by the Lord, and technically belongs to Him. The result of this supply in your life will be peace.

Clapping hands very slowly and deliberately (as in a demonstration of disapproval): This dream has two meanings (choose one). (1) You are sad and/or stressed out, because it seems as though nothing is going right for you now. Your reaction to your present state of affairs is due to discontentedness and unbelief (see Philippians 4:11-13). Dreamer, holding on to faith in God, and persevering in your service to His Kingdom, is sometimes the hardest thing to do; however, your curtain is worth waiting for. Your life will be on display, thus patience is vital right now. You're moving from where you are, to where you're supposed to be, and there are principles that God has ordained, in order for you to be successful in your new place. It is those principles that you're being exposed to right now, gain wisdom from your present experience. Consider the bigger picture. For, when you stop and think about, what the Lord has already done for you, and how far He's brought you; think about His goodness. Think about His hedge of protection around you; the provisions and ways He's made for you, the doors He's open for you. Think about you're in your right mind, and how the Lord is blessing you right now. As well, you've been given the honor of knowing that you can boldly come before His Throne with prayer, and that He takes joy in you, let this be your contentment; a sweet sound in your ear. Pray for Jesus to heal your unbelief, and wait on the Lord, and again I say wait. (2) Another is clapping (slowly): The disapproval of you by another has affected you to the point of discontent and unbelief. The question is how much do you believe in God's goodwill and His approval of you and your actions, as oppose to others approval of you. If you know He's benevolent, then you can never give up hoping that a change for the better is neigh, no matter how grim the circumstances or how dismal others opinions are of you. God's salvation can arrive from anywhere in an instant, and deliverance will come to you (see Jeremiah 29:11).

Clapping hands to the rhythm of a beat: This dream has two meanings (choose one). (1) Because you expressed satisfaction and excitement, and not concern and care, when wickedness was revealed amongst the people of God and, sternly dealt with by the Lord, now the Lord's hand will be upon you to expose and deal with your wickedness. Judge properly your brothers and sisters in Christ (Matthew 7:1-3). Reflection, dreamer always love as though another is one of your love ones, by this you will prove more empathic, understanding, and compassionate. See suggested course of action. (2) To see another clapping their hands to the rhythm of a beat: You will end up amongst those who are literally perishing and don't know it. You will be given over to sin, because of the lustful deeds of your flesh; fortunately, your soul will be restored. This "giving over" will cause you to know that the Lord is Lord. You will also grow in compassion, empathy, and understanding towards God's people when He is dealing with them. See suggested course of action.

Noise (loud or explosive sound, e.g. a clap of thunder): This dream has two meanings (choose one). (1) Your dream denotes some form of hysteria. Dreamer is experiencing a state of violent mental agitation, or excessive uncontrollable fear. (2) Your dream is an alarm to assemble yourself to God at the door of the church. Simply put, you need to go to church. Every Christian should be faithfully attending and supporting a fundamental Holy Bible believing church. Revelation 2:1, 8, 12, 18, 3:1, 7, 14, references churches, thus this lets us know that God has ordained churches, and not without purpose. Hebrews 10:25, sheds light on the reasons for participation in the local church. The church is a place of edification, protection, a nd fellowship. The ultimate reason why we should participate in a local church, it is specifically charged by God for us to do so. Allow God's wisdom to supersede your own. See suggested course of action

Slap a person or animal (a sharp blow with the open hand): This dream has three meanings (choose one). (1) Your dream was sent to demonstrate grace, via a warning. To slap a person is to emotionally and/or spiritually conquer, defeat, overpower, overcome, crush, or suppress another because of vengeance or anger within you, possibly the person you slapped in your dream. Do not take vengeance into your own hands. If person was known, you do not respect the literal person. If person was unknown, this points to another, who the dreamer will take vengeance out on, or disrespect violently, in the near future. Dreamer, if you attempt to take judgment into your own hands, you will need to go in exile (e.g. incarceration, leave town, go underground), for a period of seven (days, months, or years), depending upon the nature of the assault. As well, the potential victim has prayed, or will pray, to God to be delivered from your hand, because they fear you. God will deliver them and frustrate your plans. Two witnesses (e.g. persons or evidence) will testify publicly of your evil plans. See suggested course of action. (2) Someone slaps the dreamer: Oftentimes, as with this dream, people represent characteristic traits of the dreamer. Thus, it follows to say that you slapped your own self. You are a victim of your own state of mind and/or choices. See suggested course of action. (3) To slap an animal: You are the animal. The dreamer is in a process of renewal, sanctification, or transformation, thus a conquering over the animalistic behavior within you, which are traits typical of th e animal depicted within your dream. See category: Animals (type of animal slapped).

Standing Ovation (cheering you on, enthusiastic recognition, especially one accompanied by loud applause): This dream has two meanings (choose one). (1) If you were the one receiving the ovation, you are getting ready to reap your due recompense, for God rewards those who diligently served Him. You have been judged righteous, thus you will reap equity. Further, for your sake, those who have fought against you and have made your way hard will be judged. Don't rejoice over their hardships, just stay your course, for many will rejoice with you, namely, they that are rich and powerful and those who are full of faith. You shall go out with joy and be led forth with peace. (2) Another is receiving the ovation: Dreamer, rejoice and be happy for another, namely one who is being acknowledged as a diligent servant of the Lord, at present. They are receiving their due rewards for diligent service. There is a need for you to, reflectively look, within, as to why you would need to be encouraged to graciously applaud another. Something is there, perhaps covetousness, jealously, or hatred? See suggested course of action.

Strike hands together (as in to give an order): This dream has three meanings (choose one). (1) There is a conflict, which needs to be resolved, between the dreamer and another, be it a family member, friend, or foe. The core cause of the conflict is your own stubbornness and/or rebelliousness. There is a necessity to be reconciled with another, rather than to, always be in opposition and/or contrary. Dreamer, you simply need to take the higher ground. Dreamer, if you are truly unaware of the part you've played within the conflict, you are being made aware via your dream. However, deep within, you recognize your own stubbornness, but are unwilling to own up to it. Nonetheless, this conflict really needs to be resolved; you need to heal the wounds that you've made, the war within you and without has to cease. In this, you will learn principles an d Christian values that will encourage you to reach out and touch others in a loving and graceful manner; ultimately finding yourself promoting the genuine cause of Christ and the good of others. See suggested course of action. (2) Dreamer, an unforgiving spirit, and animosity are present within your heart. The fruits thereof are feelings of doubt, guilt, and unworthiness, questioning whether God or anybody really cares. Ask yourself why an unforgiving spirit and animosity, or why the feelings of doubt, guilt, and unworthiness, are present within me? Dreamer, it's time to own up to, and deal with, your issues and their resulting fruit. The fruits of doubt, guilt, and unworthiness, are betrayal, deceitfulness, spitefulness, faithlessness, irrational beliefs, and eventual rebelliousness. If not dealt with now, you will soon reap the consequences of said fruit and are possibly feeling some of the effects at present (e.g. inability to sleep, unrest, no quietness within, and/or anointing and spiritual authority are abating). Dreamer, mend your broken heart and/or offended feelings, via genuine forgiveness that the forgiveness offered you by Jesus, will stand (also see Matthew 18:21 -35). See suggested course of action. (3) You striking your hands together denote that you, the dreamer, have adopted a form of worship that is akin to syncretism[28]. In doing so, you have abandoned the people of God and God Himself. Your ideas collide with God's word; they will be exposed in the open sight of others, and your peers will deal with you accordingly. See suggested course of action.

Suggested Course of Action

Question to consider and journal, did your dream depict any symbols that alludes to, the dreamer will make the necessary changes, spiritually, emotionally, and/or physically to affect a more positive outcome? If changes are initiated, your dreams will change.

Nevertheless, ask yourself, what is keeping you from experiencing genuine joy, laughter, and peace? Clapping dreams oftentimes indicate a need of joy and laughter within one's life and they suggest a reason for the lack thereof. Joy means being in touch with the bigger picture, and the beauty of joy is that it has the power to rescue you from your stresses. Laughter in its highest and holiest expression is our reaction to the realization that the world is so much bigger, deeper, and more beautiful than we ever give it credit. God will cause you to laugh again.

Consider and journal the following questions. The questions will help you determine; the issue at hand, how you feel about it, and what may have instigated it. What kind of clapping was it? Were others involved? If yes, who and in what manner were they involved? Keep in mind that the others represent a character trait, quality, or talent within you. Did any one get hurt emotionally, physically, or was disturbed in any way? How did you feel, and what did you do, because, of your feelings, regarding the clapping and/or who or what was being applauded? Was it confusing, dangerous, happy, hurtful, insignificant, joyful, life threatening, safe, scary, or unsure? Where were you? Was the place unfamiliar to you? Were you coherent? In view of your dream's context, namely clapping, what choices are you making that may impair you emotionally and spiritually? Your answers, coupled with the interpretation, plus any additional information, should begin to unfold the subject matter and issue at hand, if not now, mull over things a few days. For more information, see index or relevant categ ory and subcategory for other particulars within your dream.

Now, pray (See Prayer of Deliverance, pg. 897)

Specific Meaning

If, your actions or words may cause applause or clapping or a, thumbs-up or hold back applause, clapping or a thumbs-down (e.g. CEO, Critic, director, entertainment, inspirational acting, preaching, singing, or teaching). Dreams of this sort, for the most part, are ordinary dreams, resulting from your daily activities (see Chapter One, Chalom). These sorts of dreams are usually about your routine, mundane activities or anxieties that overwhelm your mind during the day. They are an inner release mechanism, which helps provide you with emotional balance and the maintaining of your sanity. These dreams are not significant, and do not warrant special attention.

Note: On the other hand, the dreamer may consider applause as an indication to promote or approve others, ideas, or things, rather than disapprove or vice versa. Dreamer, the details, kept within context of your dream, should be relevant to your life, and closely resemble your real-life situations. Meaning it can actually occur during your awaked state. This will help you narrow down the specifics needed to support and steer you clear of possible mishaps. However, if your dream was inundated with symbols that are not easily linked to your life activities, then the spiritual implications (the interpretation) should be heeded.

CLEANING, WASHING, DECORATE, REMODELING, REPAIR (bathing, cleansing, showering, scrubbing, straightening- up, vacuuming, or being reconstructed)

Some short descriptions of types, phrases, and other processes and particulars, connected in some way to this category are, for example, bathing, cleaning, scrubbing, vacuuming, or washing a/an animal, automobile, building, church, dish es, house, floors, wound or sore, to clean from physical stains and dirt, to be clean, to sprinkle water upon, freshness, neatness, order, unclutteredness.

Unless otherwise noted elsewhere, if, in your everyday living, your awaked state, as part of your lifestyle, work, or ministerial activities, or a special event, you have a very real connection with any type of cleaning activity. For example, car wash, deacon, launderer, house cleaner, homemaker, janitorial, (also see content list for this category), your dream is not significant and does not warrant special attention.

Otherwise noted, this type of dream may be a natural dream (see Chapter One, Chalom). If so, the dreamer needs to perform some type of cleaning, cleansing, or washing for sanitary or medicinal purposes (especially if that which was highlighted within your dream is actually unclean, soiled, or unkempt). This dream is a first step intervention and an alarm. Skip interpretation and go clean up.

Otherwise noted, see Note 1 at the beginning of Actions and Activities category.

To determine who your dream is for you or another, consider one of the following (relevant interpretation) first, as well as, see Note 3 at the beginning of Actions and Activities category.

Symbols and Referents: Bathing, cleaning, cleanliness, showering, scrubbing, vacuuming, or washing within a dream generally express, coupled with the relevant interpretation, the seriousness of sin and the great lengths God goes to, in removing our sin, as well as, one having a moral flaw so as to make impure according to God's righteous principles. Thus, some type of spiritual purification or refinement is happening, will happen, or needs to happen.

Category Content - If not listed see index, perchance, for your specific type of cleaning dream activity.

- To do no cleaning
- If dreamer was cleaning for another (e.g. hired help, house cleaner, any manner of domestic service), see category, Working (Butler, housemaid)
- Bathing, Showering, Cleaning (incl. cleaning-up a baby, washing face, hands, feet, or footwear)
- Cleaning, Washing a/an:
- • Animal; Bathroom, Lavatory, Restroom (Bathtub, Shower, Sink, Washbasin, Basin, or Toilet); Bedroom or Bed or Sleeping Quarters; Building; Church; Dishes (all tableware); Drinking glass, see category, Buildings (Windows); Dressers, Cabinets (any furniture shelves and/or drawers for storage); Dusting, Wiping something clean; Mopping or Sweeping a Floor; Hair (washing), see category, The Body; House; Kitchen; Motored Vehicle, Toys, Wound, Sores
- Decorate or Beautify or Remodeling or Repair
- Soaked (very wet)
- Water was unclean, see category, Body of Water (Condition of water)

To do no cleaning: The extent of the messiness represents the extent of disorderliness in a particular area of your life. Your dream intent is to persuade the dreamer to choose to do the things that promote devotion, love, and togetherness towards God and others. Dreamer is counseled to choose to do the "righteous" and "gracious" thing. With that said, couple this with one of the following three (choose one). (1) If you are actually, in your awaked life, an employer, CEO, supervisor, or someone who is in authority: You have decided not to give someone, something asked or applied for (e.g. a job, raise, or membership to an organization), because of your issues with your rejection experience and the resulting pains and defense mechanisms. Out of selfishness, you refuse to accept them, justifying that they're not good enough or not the right person, none of which is true. See suggested course of action. (2) If dreamer did no cleaning: If dreamer saw or sensed a person, animal, place, or organization in need of cleaning or messy, and to, not clean them, or it up, but left things as they were. This indicates the dreamer is hesitant or unwilling to clean-up a particular area within your life or straighten out a relationship issue with someone, because of personal rejection issues. While it is true that you have not been accepted by most, your issues wi th rejection, and the resulting pains and defense mechanisms, has caused you to behave in an unkind and unfriendly way toward someone, before you at present, who expects, or has a right to expect, love, kindness, and friendship from you. You have put aside cordiality and forgiveness, and out of selfishness, you have refused to accept someone who will prove to be a very good ally, and one who will not reject you, but accept you, just as you are; this may very well be a significant someone. You hav e begun justifying to yourself that they are not good enough, not the right person, or they just do not like you anyway. None of which is true. Dreamer, although, deep down within, you're frighten by your fears, if you're not careful, those hurts and pa ins, in your heart, will make you blind to the real thing once it comes along; thus your dream. Dreamer, Jesus is there with you, this moment, to help you get things together, because He knows you've been hurting a long time. If allowed, God will hold yo u and anoint you that you might see your way. Moreover, your dream also points to a particular area that needs cleaning up. Example, if the main living area of a house was messy. The living room, lounge, or sitting area of a home represents your family and friends, and love of family and friends. You are possibly losing the respect of significant others in that area. The dreamer needs to clean up relevant relationships for the sake of the Kingdom, for your namesake and to, not be a hindrance to others. If the kitchen was messy, then an emotional issue needs reckoning. Additionally, dreamer, an unforgiving heart is the single most popular poison that the enemy uses against God's people; it being one of the deadliest poisons a person can take spiritually. See index or relevant category for specific action, activity, person, animal, place, or organization that was messy or highlighted. See suggested course of action. (3) If another did no cleaning, when cleaning was needed: This signify that the dreamer is hesitant or unwilling to help another cleanup a particular area or matter within their life or straighten out a relationship issue with that someone, possibly person depicted within your dream, if known. Nevertheless, known or unknown, dreamer has assumed that you know what another's response will be to you helping them. Dreamer, you do not know. The true reason why you have chosen to remain indifferent towards that person reveals your lack of love towards that person. Your dream is to persuade the dreamer to choose to do the things that promote love, togetherness, and devotion towards God, and others. You have the opportunity to help another according to your gifting, look beyond their faults, and yours, and see the need. The dreamer needs to help clean up the issue, and not be a hindrance to others. See index or relevant category for specific action, activity, person, animal, place, or organization that was messy or highlighted. See suggested course of action.

Bathing, Showering, Cleaning (incl. cleaning-up a baby, washing face, hands, feet, or footwear): This dream has nine meanings (choose one). (1) Your dream was sent to encourage. To dream of taking a bath, showering, or cleaning oneself implies one who is purifying him or herself morally, by dealing with the sin issues in your life, no matter how seemingly insignificant. You have begun, again, to listen to the Paraclete within you, instead of relying on your emotions and opinions. This is good. Dreamer, the state of affairs in your life at present, may not be to your liking; but God allows them. God is using your situations to work things out for your good. Therefore, do not attribute (or call) that which is of God, unclean (e.g. confusion, disfavored, erroneous, out of order, unlawful, weak, wicked, or any other attributes of the unregenerate). No matter how difficult or how uncertain the issues continue to always take the next biblical, ethical, and most informed step, for obedience is better than sacrifice. See suggested course of action. (2) To bathe someone: The dreamer is (or will be) instrumental in helping someone come to Christ, supporting them in their born again experience (see John 3:1-17), and in their process of sanctification, via mentoring or teacher student relationship. Both of you will benefit from the relationship. (3) To need a bath or shower (or to be dirty and/or smelly): Denotes a necessity to deal with the moral impurities within your life, no matter how seemingly insignificant. It is essential that you purify yourself by rejecting the influence, the sin that so easily overwhelm you. There is a need to be clean morally, and of a clear conscience; for God is calling you now, recognize and respect your time of visitation and hear Him. See suggested course of action. (4) To be already clean (you or someone else): What God has cleansed, sanctified, and blessed, do not discredit, bring into dispute, disbelieve, disrepute, or call unholy, nor should you question the work of the Holy Spirit, or call His work unholy. It is blasphemous t o accredit the work of the Paraclete to devils (Matthew 12:31, 32, 36, 37). See suggested course of action. (5) Bathing or cleaning-up a baby: Your dream denotes a maturing process is happening within the dreamer, due to you embracing ethically prudent principles. This increase in wisdom, reliability, and sensibleness will prepare you for your destined ministry within the Kingdom of God. (6) Baby's diaper (changing one or cleaning one): This choice has two parts (choose one). (a) If dreamer is an ordained minister (meaning, you have the priestly responsibilities of ordained clergy). Although the dreamer is unaware of the positive spiritual effects you're having upon Christians; be encourage, you are making a difference in people's lives, your ministry, and its uniqueness in presenting the gospel, is what they need at present. These persons are members of other ministries or churches; just know that you are reaching and touching others you know not of and that you are worthy of your wage (1 Timothy 5:18, 1 Corinthians 9:13, 14). (b) If dreamer is not a minister, but part of the laity, the dreamer needs to make amends, to one hurt by your arrogance. The dreamer is also encouraged to surrender to a more mature and humble attitude and choices. See suggested course of action. (7) Washing face: Because of your adoration, dependence, and submission to Christ, God will abundantly bless the dreamer. Dreamer, from this day forward God's blessings will flow abundantly, producing spiritual growth within you. God's blessings: Gifts of God's grace, anything God freely gives you, absolution, the Holy Spirit, salvation, regeneration, eternal life, peace, health, children, love of family, longevity, necessities, prosperity, and dominion over al l that is yours; and all are parts of the supply of grace, and all are sanctified by the Lord, and technically belongs to Him. The result of this supply in your life will be peace. As well, you will experience a divine visitation, sent from the Lord that will deliver you from the evil and wickedness that has surrounded you. You will now begin to see the manifestation of divine vengeance against those who trouble you. Be encourage, the wicked will cease from troubling. God will validate you and, if applicable, your children. You will get relief from those who oppress you, and if pertinent, you or a loved one, will get release from imprisonment. The dreamer or a close family member will return to a place or state of safety and plenty and will return to Christ and to His church. Accordingly, your soul and lifestyle will begin to bear fruit of positive choices, resulting in spiritual strength and power within the dreamer's life. An increase in spiritual knowledge and mastery of an innate gift will begin. (8) Washing feet or footwear (e.g. sandals, shoes, sneakers): This choice has two parts (choose one). (a) Dreamer's feet or shoes were being washed: Dreamer you are clean; therefore, no longer suppose yourself as unclean or unsaved. For in doing so, you reckon God a liar. If you persist in your accusations, insisting that you are guilty, charging that the atoning work of Christ is insufficient for one like you, you make yourself unclean (John 13:10, 11). If necessary, see suggested course of action. (b) If dreamer was washing, someone else's feet or shoes: Dreamer once a person is forgiven by God they are clean. Therefore, do not call anyone impure that God has made clean (Acts 10:15). While no one is saved whose sins against God are not forgiven by Jesus, God rules no one out of His favor of forgiveness. Christians should never look down on anyone and say they are unfit (or too unclean), or have too many offensive habits, to be told the good news of the Kingdom of God and the gospel of Jesus Christ. Forgiveness comes through believing in Jesus, and in His Name. Once you are forgiven, this is salvation, you are clean, you are saved (Acts 2:37-41). After that initial act of repentance, forgiveness, and acceptance, all that is necessary is the daily cleansing of sins from our lives (1 Corinthians 15:31-34). (9) Washing hands: This dream can denote either disdain or respect for materialism; thus, this choice has parts (choose one). (a) To wash your hands after an activity (no matter the activity): This points to growing feelings of intense dislike and lack of respect for the serious, sometimes fatal, contagion of materialism. This growing disdain is a direct result of the dreamer having sought satisfaction and happiness through the obtaining of objects, only to find an illusion of happiness. Dreamer, as you become less materialistic, your wellbeing (good relationships, autonomy, sense of purpose) will boost; finding peace with who you are, what you have, and what you can share. (b) To wash your hands before an activity (no matter the activity): Dreamer, you feed the flesh by wanting more and more, by wanting to obtain things others have, and by wanting to become someone respected; rather than attempting to conquer the evil within. This bourgeois mentality is concerned only with your personal comfort, material wealth, and status, at any expense. Now, having in yourself nothing that you respect more than power and greed, you are willing to sacrifice all, God, principle, family, and friend, to the image or idol of vanity. This way is based on exploring alternatives to God's righteous principles, as well as, creating a sense of unity with the wickedness around you. This mentality sacrifices children, family, and morality, to the hollowness of satisfying immoral desires and appetites. Dreamer, the selling-out of yourself over to materialism, and allowing wickedness to prevail in your life and in your home, is based on principles and values that are not only immoral and vile but also increasingly unstable. Materialistic people are more susceptible to disorders; as you become more materialistic, your wellbeing (good relationsh ips, autonomy, sense of purpose) diminishes. This way cries out against godly ethics, and its' end offends any sense of godliness. Prayer and heartfelt repentance to Jesus can remedy this. Repentance is seeking pardon and expressing sincere feelings of regret and brokenness for having done something awry. To Jesus pray, Psalm 51, this coupled with prayer and fasting, and followed by appropriate application of wisdom, can conceivably avert some of the repercussions of your choices. This is known as leaving a blessing behind. See suggested course of action.

Cleaning, washing a/an (animal; bathroom, bathtub, shower, sink, washbasin, basin, toilet, bed, bedroom, building, church; dishes, all tableware, dressers, cabinets, dusting, mopping, sweeping a floor; wiping something clean, house, kitchen, motored vehicle, toys, wound, sore). See one of the following.

Animal: Your strong convictions and positive attitude regarding spiritual issues is a transformational force in the life of someone. The specific animal being cleaned, points to the person's character. For specific animal, see category, Animals. It is this part of their character, primarily the negative aspects, which are being transformed. This information will help you to continue mentoring and ministering to this person in a more caring, effective, and positive manner, as they transition into a more intimate relationship with Christ Jesus. This person is before you now. Moreover, for you dreamer, continue your stand against any negativity that would encroach upon your lifestyle, it will abate.

Bathroom, Lavatory, Restroom, Toilet (Bathtub, Shower, Sink, Washbasin, Basin, or Toilet): This dream has four meanings (choose one). (1) Your dream was sent to encourage the dreamer. It implies you are taking responsibility for your physical health, and/or you are purifying yourself morally, by dealing with the sin issues in y our life, no matter how seemingly insignificant. You have begun, again, to listen to the Paraclete within you, instead of relying on your emotions and opinions. This is good. Dreamer, the state of affairs in your life at present, may not be to your liking; but God allows them. God is using your situations to work things out for your good. Therefore, do not attribute (or call) that which is of God, unclean (e.g. confusion, erroneous, out of order, unlawful, weak, wicked, or any other attributes of the unregenerate). No matter how difficult or how uncertain the issues always take the next biblical, ethical, and most informed step, for obedience is better than sacrifice. See suggested course of action. (2) Bathtub, Shower: This choice has two parts (choose one). (a) Your dream denotes some manner of detoxification, removal of poison toxins from the physical body is necessary; by this, a physical healing will occur. (b) Cleaning or washing fecal matter in bathtub, shower: Your dream suggests a physical illness is due to an abomination within the life of the dreamer. It is suggested that you seek medical attention. Dreamer there is healing in the name of Jesus, pray Psalm 38:1-22. Genuine repentance will bring healing within your body. Have faith in this. Repentance is seeking pardon for having done something awry, and for having hurt someone, and expressing sincere feelings of regret and brokenness. Further, pray Psalm 51:1-19. To individuals, a phone call or a letter of apology is a good place to start, if appropriate. Moreover, if you will accept the Heavenly Father's Words, via the Bible, and store up His principles, and His w ays and means within you, turning your ear to wisdom and applying your heart to understanding, calling out for insig ht and crying aloud for discernment, Jesus will meet you. This, coupled with a lifestyle of prayer and fasting, followed by appropriate application of wisdom, and you will know the Messiah, Jesus Christ, intimately, and find the knowledge of God you seek. For the Lord gives wisdom and from His mouth comes knowledge and understanding. Then you will understand what is right and just and fair, every good path. When wisdom enters your heart and knowledge becomes sweet to your soul, discretion will protect you, understanding will guard you, and His Truth will lead you. To deliver you from the ways of wickedness, and from demons whose words and ways are perverse, who causes you to walk in darkness gladly, whose paths are crooked and devious, causing you to leave straight paths (Proverbs 2:1-6, 9-15). This is one of God's covenant promises to you. Have faith in this. (3) Sink, Washbasin, Basin, this dream denotes, a spiritual or physical condition of the heart. Thus, this choice has two parts (choose one): (a) Dreamer, within your heart, a spiritual condition is beginning that will lead to you acting in such a way that is vicious and vile. Your behaviors will instigate unwarranted disgust and abhorrence towards you by others, and will cause a separation between you and God, for sin separates, see Isaiah 59:1, 2. Therefore, you are urged, with the help of the Paraclete, prayer, and possibly fasting, to put your whole heart into making a go of subduing your mood, mental state, and frame of mind with courage and determination. By this, you will change your character and rectify your heart. (b) Your dream denotes that there is actually a literal physical heart problem. If so, dreamer is encouraged to seek medical attention, as any heart problem can be potentially serious. (4) Toilet: This choice has four parts (choose one). (a) Physically, a toilet may also point to literal health issues within the excretory system, indicating possible issues with the alimentary canal, bile, bladd er, kidneys, intestine, liver, skin, or urethra, this system deals with egestion, body waste, any discharges from the body. If so, dreamer is encouraged to seek medical attention, as any excretory system problem can be potentially serious. (b) A toilet generally denotes a feeling of deep and bitter anguish, and consequent bitterness and ill will towards a person, place, or organization. Question, did you clean or flush the toilet or no? (c) Cleaned or Flushed, the toilet of whatever: This denotes some manner of uncleanness within the life of the dreamer is being purged; thus, a spiritual or physical healing is taking place. Moreover, dreamer please note, your human understanding of, and reaction to, spiritual realities is oftentimes crudely green. You mouth empty and boastful words that appeal only to the lustful desires of your human nature, which, amongst other things, has led, or will lead, to a physical illness within your excretory system. The spiritual truths you think you know, and what will eventually be revealed to you, via a personal enlightenment season, will lead you to acknowledge that your understanding of spiritual realities was childish at best, and perilously dangerous to others to say the worst. Favorably, you will go through a de-programing and re-programing of your beliefs, thus a personal enlightenment and physical healing. During this crossroads in your life, all of your "crudely green" thoughts and beliefs will be eliminated. Subsequently, you will begin to walk and grow into a mature spiritual being, going on towards perfection, enabled to see into the spiritual realm more clearly, and no matter your hardships, you will never again look back, but genuinely, in words and deeds, continue to progress forward. Moreover, your capacity for greater illumination, intellectually and spiritually, will become enlarged giving you access to more than a few of the gates of wisdom. (d) To, not clean, wash, or be unable to flush the toilet of whatever: Dreamer, in your most, inner deepest feelings, there is deep anger and ill will towards a person, place, or organization that represented God to you. Unfortunately, due to a vicious violation inflicted upon you, you blame God, although that person has, or will, receive their just punishment, and you will see justice. You have never admitted to yourself that the violation prospered due to your victim mindset, and your unwillingness to stand up for yourself, this needs to be acknowledge also. Notwithstanding, in blaming God for everything, you now mouth that Adonai Elohim creates imperfect beings and then forces them to rise up to a level of perfection, which by design, they are unable to attain, by torturing them, causing millions to suffer in body and soul. You reason that this is God's only way, a path of pain, torture, and then death. You ask what human being aspires to evolve through this endless agony. You proclaim that God's promises are no more than vague words of doubtful happiness, and implacable laws that promise remote and unknowable joy, under the mask of love of humanity. You say His ways are nothing more than a profound indifference and a hardened selfishness. Further, you believe that God's intolerance of sin and the inherent results of sin, mainly separation from Him, as written within Holy Writ, and expressed in Christian dogma, are the picture of an angry god, conjured up by angry, unwise, and foolish men. You boast of philosophies, which appeal to the lustf ul desires of human nature, condoning rebellious, unhealthy, immodest, immoral, indecent, lewd, and lascivious, behavior. Desires that if not checked, can and often do lead to early death, as you have personally witnessed. This is what you call l ove. You exalt your wisdom above the Creator. While you discredit the Creator's wise and sensible guidelines for living life, on this side of eternity, as healthy, humanly, and sanely as possible; and in harmony with His provision for life on the other side o f eternity, in heaven. You respect your truth, while never acknowledging, it is delivered without grace; thus, it is never enough to fill an emaciated soul. Read, understand, and embrace Galatians 5:13-25. Favorably, your dream is only a warning and is sent in the spirit of grace. If you continue on this path, your behaviors will become so vicious and vile; your actions will arouse distaste and/or hate of you by others, and you will feel the brunt of those feelings of others towards you. There will be no response of love, sympathy, or tenderness toward you.

Moreover, you will expose your physical body to illnesses, from which you will be unable to recover without divine help, via Jesus. Dreamer, forgiveness of that person, place, or organization that viciously violated you, and heartfelt repentance to Jesus, coupled with a renunciation of your spiritually poisonous words and ways are the antivenin to the venomous attack of that old serpent, the devil, upon your life. Further, if urged by God, decl are a one, two, or three day fast, coupled with studying the teachings of Jesus Christ. You will again begin to experience God's truth, and see the demonic for what it is - a lie. If relevant, avoid personal isolation and isolated groups that teach something different from the gospel of Jesus Christ. Additionally, if not practiced regularly, go to church, join a church, a faith based bible- believing community, commit to that ministry, and don't leave, no matter what, for three years. Forsake not the gathering of yourself together with other mainstream Christians. A prophecy will be given you, via someone within that ministry, during this season, write it down for it will happen. Even more, entering the House of God should be done reverently rather than carelessly. Cease from many words but rather humbly learn, and let your words be sprinkled with empathy. For, in spite of what we do not know about the many mysteries of God and life, one thing remains eternally true: God is our loving Father. He does not desire that any one perish; great effort is exercised to save us, even in the moment of our death. Hence, do not call anyone impure (e.g. unsaved, hypocrite, unregenerate, ignorant) that God alone has made clean (read Acts 10:15, Ephesians 4:17-5:21).

Bedroom, Bed, or Sleeping Quarters: Your dream suggests a cleaning up of one's sexual habits, or dreamer will be granted the opportunity to get some rest, and should anticipate, and take full advantage of this. With that, if bedroom or bed was clean, straighten, made-up a bed: Dreamer, due to your challenging life activities, personal illness, and/or the wearying of others, you have become very exhausted emotionally. Overcome by profound discouragement and a sense of being alone in your conflicts, coupled with exhaustion, an old familiar lifestyle has reared (or will rear) up its' ugly head to try to take advantage of your physical weakness. Dreamer stand still, cease from your work and take a rest; know that God is God. He is able to care for you, and He knows where you are. He alone will deliver you out of the snares of the enemy. Go take a long vacation, at least eight weeks. Schedule it within two months at the latest. If you do not take a sabbatical, you will be forced into one via a serious illness. This illness may be avoided if you will rest. During your rest, your Heavenly Father will heal your discouragement in a caring and understanding manner. He will allow you to sleep, and He will nourish and visit you with inspiring revelations of His Power and Presence and give additional revelation regarding direction for your life. The hope, labor, love, and struggle of your life's work are not in vain. You are not alone; neither should you feel that way. Dreamer, you have no need to worry, only worship before the Lord (see 2 Chronicles 20:15, 17-19). Rest from defending yourself against the demons that want to defeat you, and rest assured God is and will be a defense for you, see Psalm 91. Dreamer, you have in Christ, grace and healing, refreshment, and a refuge. Don't forfeit these graces. Embrace the help you r Heavenly Father is offering you, via a sabbatical, and the effects of their negativity will no longer hold sway over your heart.

Building: Suggests a cleaning up of one's spiritual person via the application of the Word of God within your life. The condition of the building, dwelling reveals the state of your inner person. The amount (or intensity) of cleaning hints to the effort required on your part, regarding your spiritual progress. Dreamer, be encouraged, you are growing spiritually, even i f at times when you're not aware of it.

Church: Your dream denotes that your spiritual life is being cleaned up; a personal revival is happening within you and you are being called upon to participate in that purification process. The context of your dream, especially your willingness or unwillingness to clean, and your attitude regarding it, exposes your level of participation and submissiveness to the leading and guiding of the Holy Spirit. Dreamer, you are being prepared and set aside for the priesthood, to carry out the official role, position, or office of a priest (e.g. prophet, pastor, minister, or some type of a very visible cleric). Further, chosen, yo u are to show forth the praises of Him who has called you out of darkness into His marvelous light (also see 1 Peter 2:9, 10). At present, continue to allow the Paraclete to complete the work of purification and sanctification within you. For those who go forth in tears, shall return rejoicing

(Psalm 126:5, 6). Be diligent and patient, everything will be done proper, and in its own time; you will be ordained to this office, and if earned, honored in some respect in another area. If necessary, see suggested course of action.

Dishes (all tableware): Dreamer, you've reached a turning point in your life that will lead to success, and you've been in this space before, within one of your positive life cycles. Seize the moment, and attempt to learn of, and then maneuver around, your self-sabotaging life cycle, this time, that you might go on to prosperity and success. Question to journal, where was dreamer washing dishes, if in a particular room within a building was highlighted, e.g. kitchen, see following subcategory, House (Kitchen), and/or see category, Building, Structures. If necessary, see suggested course of action.

Dresser, Cabinets (any furniture shelves and/or drawers for storage): Where they filled with stuff? If so, dreamer, learn to be content with what you have and where you are, for God knows where you are, and He knows what you need. Moreover, in the words of Jesus, "Stop storing up treasures for yourselves on earth, where moths and rust destroy, and where thieves break in and steal. But keep on storing up treasures for yourselves in heaven, where moths and rust do not destroy and where thieves do not break in and steal, because where your treasure is, there your heart will be also" (Matthew 6:19-21 ISV). Moreover, "Bring the entire tithe into the storehouse that there may be food in my house. So, put me to the test in this rig ht now", says the Lord of the Heavenly Armies, "and see if I won't throw open the windows of heaven for you and pour out on you blessing without measure. And, I'll prevent the devourer from harming you, so that he does not destroy the crops of your land. Nor will the vines in your fields drop their fruit", says the Lord of the Heavenly Armies. "Then all the nations will call you blessed, for you will be a land of delight," says the Lord of the Heavenly Armies". (Malachi 3:10-12 ISV)

Dusting, wiping something clean: This denotes one who is sorrowful through loss or deprivation (e.g. widowhood, loneliness, financial decrease, or some disadvantage that resulted from lost, in some form or another). Fortunately, a change from one place, state, subject, or stage to another is happening within the life of the dreamer. Your part is to make an earnest go of freeing yourself from the residuals of grief, by freeing yourself from thoughts, behaviors, and places that hinder clarity, and rid your atmosphere of things like shrines, mementoes, memorials that sorrowfully remind you of past events. Free yourself of all stuff, words, and talk that keeps you from enjoying the goodness of the Lords' favor today, allow this by faith and gratitude. The extent of the messiness within your dream is the amount of change that needs to happen within your life. To know the extent of the process is to be prepared for the amount or degree of change needed. The dreamer is counseled to obey the lead of the Paraclete and to once again make an earnest go at enjoying life and to go on from this space, stage, or subject.

Mopping or Sweeping a Floor: Dreamer, you are undergoing a thorough purging from worthless dogma, irrelevant ideas, and self-conceited talk against God, namely any ungodliness. Whatever is currently going on in your life, anticipate a spiritual cleansing taking place in those specific areas, e.g. people, places, things and/or issues, within your life. This will produce a level of purity within your life that is requisite for ministry and will affect humility within you. Your emotions will become intense and situations will become more volatile, but your agenda will be thoroughly purged. Take a seat and hold t ight, it's going to get bumpy. If necessary, see suggested course of action.

House: This dream has two meanings (choose one). (1) Your dream marks a transition within the dreamer's life. One starts the house cleaning process through faith in God and gratitude for the provisions He has provided for you. The condition of the house, and/or what was being cleaned, reveals what will undergo a change within the dreamer. For example, cleaning a fireplace, hearth reveals the emotional condition of the heart. Cleaning furniture, e.g. sofa, or sitting and lounging areas, reveals the need to be about spending quality time enjoying your family, and delightfully enjoying the goodness of the Lords' peace and favor upon your life. The amount (or intensity) of cleaning hints to the effort required on the part of the dreamer, regarding your spiritual progress. Dreamer, be encouraged, you are growing spiritually, even if at times when you're not awa re of it. To know the extent of the process is to be prepared for the amount or degree of change needed. The dreamer is, counseled to obey the lead of the Paraclete, and to once again, enjoy life and go on from this space, stage, or subject. See also category, Buildings, for specific room that was messy and its symbolic meaning. This area possibly needs rectifying that the refinement process might be complete. (2) If dreamer is a non-believer (one who has no religious beliefs, a non-religious person, or one who has no religious faith or belief in Jesus Christ, or one who does not embrace a personal relationship with Jesus Christ, at present): Your dream is a prelude to the infilling of the Holy Spirit within the dreamer. One starts the house cleaning process through prayer and heartfelt repentance to Jesus and to individuals affected by your actions, in the form of an apology (if possible). Repentance is seeking pardon and expressing sincere feelings of regret and brokenness for having done something awry and/or for having hurt someone, see 2 Corinthians 7:10, 11. To individuals, a phone call or a letter of apology is a good place to start. To Jesus pray, Psalm 51, this followed by water baptism, and you shall receive the gift of the Holy Spi rit (see Acts 2:38-40). The action of cleaning symbolically anticipates the Holy Spirit, by preparing a place for the Lord to dwell in. The Holy Spirit then enters into you and begins to clean you up, via the process of sanctification. That is one of His jobs, housekeeper. This cleaning will influence the dreamer, begin to change your lifestyle, and it will affect those connected to you. Question to journal: In what condition was the house in? Was it very messy, run-down? This is a clue to the scope of your spiritual condition. The extent of the uncleanness is the amount of change that will happen within your life, not all at once of course. This is a process. Dreamer, to know the extent of the process is to be prepared for the amount or degree of change you will experience; so you will not be surprised or taken aback from all the changes happening within and around you, and from the reactions of those connected to you, because of your new life and different choices. Obey the lead of the Holy Spir it, adhere to the principles within the Bible, and join a church if you're not already a member of one. See suggested course of action.

Kitchen: Your evil is taken away, and you are made clean from sin, via the Cross of Jesus and grace. God therefore has no call to remember your sins, for they are irrelevant. Additionally, go and make an offering of $20.00 to your church, and consider this money an offering to the Lord.

Motored Vehicle: Indicates a cleaning up of one's regular manner of operating, living, dealing, talking, as there is a need for change in that area at present. Dreamer is counseled to apply wise principles to all aspects of your life, and you will experience the positive results of those choices in due time. Consequently, a new standard of living will become the essence of your identity. If necessary, see suggested course of action.

Toys: The dreamer feels that you, your emotions, and feelings are insignificant or unimportant to God and others. You've felt your heart squeezed tight, mind played with, pride thrown up against a wall, and you've experienced your name being scandalized. All this has been hard for you to bear and has hurt you miserably. Nonetheless, these experiences have affected spiritual purification and refinement within you, like nothing else could. You have put childish ways behind you and now follow the way of love (ref. 1 Corinthians 13:11-13; 14:1). Moreover, dreamer you have never been insignificant or unimportant to God or to your significant others.

Wound, Sores: You have been led astray from those of The Way (Acts 9:2). After a seven day fast of purification from things unclean (e.g. addictions, hatred, an unforgiving spirit, or any unrestrained lustful indulgences), go and present yourself to your spiritual leader. Remain within that faith-based community and remain innocent and free from things that defile. By this, you will be made clean, and restored. See suggested course of action.

Decorate, Beautify, Remodeling, or Repair: Any space, structure, or building within your dream that was in the process of being decorated, beautified, remodeled, or repaired (by dreamer or another). Your dream denotes a transition within the life of the dreamer, and good health and strength to make the changeover. This transition will affect within you a far -reaching hope, profoundly greater faith, and a more intense love for all things Jesus, including His people; allow it. Dreamer, as you have done well serving your present place of worship, the leadership, and members, especially by making them better and greater qualitatively. By this you have open the door for you to become a leader, namely a CEO of your own ministry. God will send someone to help you along the way. He or she will lead and guide you to where you need to be. This relationship will be an "equal partner" or "friendship" type relationship, in other words they will not be head over you. You will always be respected as a lead person. Moreover, dreamer you have been blessed with a great understanding of spiritual knowledge, and not without reason. One who is given the means to study and teach and has access to prophetic wisdom, is purposed to be a transformational force in people's lives. Your power of speech and wisdom will convert souls to the Kingdom of God. Your time of missions is upon you. You are sent to those who are spiritually "asleep". You are counseled to focus your ministry on God's providence over life. Primarily, the wisdom, care, and guidance He has provided His people, for He always guards over His chosen; thus, He watches over His people. You must continue to encourage others, and encourage yourself too, that the feeling of rest and serenity that comes with trust in God's divine providence is available right now, and that it would be wise of them to put their trust in God now. This, coupled with, contentment, and theirs, and your, peace will overflow. Those who will listen and adhere will begin to experience the blessings spoken of in Leviticus 26:4-13, tell them this. In particular, (verse 6 GW), "I will bring peace to your land. You will lie down with no one to scare you" (Leviticus 26:6 GW). Moreover, you (the dreamer) will be leaving your present church, and you will experience a mega-ministry. You will become friends with major leaders, but not covenant partners with them. You will (or should) remain attached to your present church and come back to rest there. Shortly thereafter, because of your diligence and honorable service, you will be given the opportunity to take a sabbatical rest, covered by the Lord's grace.

Soaked (very wet): Your dream of getting soaked; denotes that the dreamer will accumulate large losses on a business transaction, or an investment, and will suffer a severe financial setback.

Suggested Course of Action

Question to consider and journal, did your dream depict any symbols that alludes to, the dreamer will make the necessary changes, spiritually, emotionally, and/or physically to affect a more positive outcome? If changes are initiated, your dreams will change.

Nevertheless, while cleansing makes it possible for imperfect believers to enjoy close fellowship with a Holy God; and is primarily for the purifying of your faith, the perfecting of patience, and/or spiritual maturity; this sort of dream suggests a definite need to prepare emotionally and mentally for the coming turbulence that accompanies change and pro motion (e.g. haughtiness, pride, smugness). These changes must not be undermined by notions that presuppose God accepts us just as we are; therefore, there's no need for change. Instead, one should view these changes as the certainty of God's grace (the free and unmerited favor and beneficence of God) and long-suffering towards us. Further, rather than allow bitterness or resentment to take root due to the discomfort of change, choose to recognize, acknowledge, and accept that spiritual development and progress is indeed happening within you, and it is for your betterment.

Consider and journal the following questions. The questions will help you determine; the issue at hand, how you feel about it, and what may have instigated it. What kind of cleaning was it, and who, what, or where needed cleaning? Were you able to do the cleaning? Did you volunteer? Did it eventually get clean? Was it clean enough for you? Were others involved? If yes, who and in what manner were they involved? Keep in mind that the others represent a quality of you, see Note 3 at the beginning of Actions and Activities category. Did anyone get hurt emotionally, physically, or was disturbed in any way? How did you feel, and what did you do, because, of your feelings, regarding the cleaning? Was it confusing, dangerous, happy, hurtful, insignificant, joyful, life threatening, safe, scary, or unsure? Where were you? Was the place unfamiliar to you? Were you coherent? Your answers, coupled with the interpretation, plus any additional information, should begin to unfold the subject matter and issue at hand, if not now, mull over things a few days. For more information, see index or relevant categ ory and subcategory for other particulars within your dream.

In view of your dream's context, namely cleaning, what choices are you making that may impair your spiritual growth, judgment, health, and/or will encourage immorality and/or are you reacting out of fear? If so, what can you do to combat the paralyzing emotion of fear? What choices are you making that would lead to God replacing you, and Him rising up another to stand in your stead?

Now, pray (See Prayer of Deliverance, pg. 897)

Specific Meaning

If, you have a very good chance that you'll be cleaning or washing someone or something that day (e.g. health care services, house cleaning services, janitorial services, or launderer). Dreams of this sort, for the most part, are ordinary dreams, resulting from your daily activities (see Chapter One, Chalom). These sorts of dreams are usually about your routine, mundane activities or anxieties that overwhelm your mind during the day. They are an inner release mechanism, which helps provide you with emotional balance and the maintaining of your sanity. These dreams are not significant, and do not warrant special attention.

CUTTING (carving, chop, hack, shave, haircut, engrave, sculpt, as well as, hacking into a system, e.g. computer)

Some short descriptions of types, phrases, and other processes and particulars, connected in some way to this category are, for example, axe, blades, knives, body piercing, carving, cut, chop, engrave, gash, lacerate, nick, pierce, sculpt, scythe, sickl e, to cut and set stones, and hacking into a computer system.

Unless otherwise noted elsewhere, if, in your everyday living, your awaked state, as part of your lifestyle, work, or ministerial activities, or a special event, you have a very real connection with any type of cutting activity or computer activity. For example, butcher, sculptor, tool and dye person, hacking into computer systems, (also see content list for this category), skip interpretation, and go to Specific Meaning at the end of this category.

Otherwise noted, this dream may be a Prophetically Simple Dream (see Chapter One: The 60th Part of Prophecy). Whereas, the dreamer is counseled to cease any impetuous or suicidal activity, especially any actions or activities that invo lve the "cutting" or killing of yourself; dreamer, although your emotional pain that set off this kind o f activity is real, the "cutting" of yourself, or the suicidal intents, is demonically led, deliberately marked by a violent force. The voices you hear, now, are not your own. Trust this. The act is carried out in undue haste and lacks thoughts of, e.g. "pain can and will end, especially with appropriate change of people, places, things, actions, and/or activities; change is possible via prayer to Jesus. Ask Jesus to take it all away, giving you enough time to make an intelligent decision, to walk away and start over. For a wise person, when he or she falls, can and should get back up. There is a future for you; this is not the end of your story (Jeremiah 29:10 -14). Additionally, if dreamer is illegally hacking into computer systems, God is watching you; therefore, consider your actions as hurtful to humankind. If any of the preceding is happening (cutting activity, suicidal intents, or system hacking), and this was depicted within your dream, this dream is a first step intervention and an alarm. Skip interpretation and re-consider your activity as harmful, hurtful, illegal, or life threatening, at present. Handle the situation wisely, by first thanking God for the warning, for Adonai Elohim knows all. Also, see Specific Meaning at the end of this category, section entitled, Note (Specific Meaning).

Otherwise noted, see Note 1 at the beginning of Actions and Activities category.

To determine who your dream is for you or another, see Note 3 at the beginning of Actions and Activities category.

Symbols and Referents: Dreams of cutting generally deal with one of two situations (cutting may be intentional or accidental): (1) A setting right by the Lord of spiritual behavior, or (2) one who makes and enacts laws, religious or civil leadership.

Category Content - If not listed see index, perchance, for your specific type of cutting dream activity.

- Axe, Knife, Blade, any kind of cutting instruments
- Body piercings, see category Body
- Carving (to disjoint, slice, and serve meat or poultry)
- Chopped or Hacked into pieces or Butchery (person, animal, place, or hacked into a system, e.g. computer)
- Castrated or Circumcision, see category, The Body
- "Cutting" oneself (to penetrate, stab, slash, wound, or mutilate)
- Shave, Haircut, or Receding hairline
- Suggested Course of Action For: Shave or Haircut (ONLY)
- Engrave (to impress deeply as to write or draw into a surface, cut in, etch, incise, score, or scratch)
- Lacerate (to cut, divide roughly by ripping or tearing with a tool or by hand)
- Sculpt (Effigy, Statuette, or Bust, any three dimensional figures or forms made by Chiseling Marble, Stone, Ice, Wood)
- Scythe, Sickle, Lawnmower, or Edger (any cutting instruments used for cutting crops, flowers, or grass)
- Cut and set stones, gems

Axe, Knife, Blade, any kind of cutting instruments: Dreamer, there is a need to renounce religious beliefs that are based on faithless ritualistic practices, customs and traditions, as well as pride. Your dream is a second witness and warning. God has sent someone to you, calling for you to repent, in preparation for an unadulterated personal relationship with Christ. Heartfelt repentance to Jesus and to individuals affected by your actions, in the form of an apology (if possible) is required of the dreamer at this time. Repentance is seeking pardon and expressing sincere feelings of regret and brokenness for having done something awry and/or for having hurt someone, see 2 Corinthians 7:10, 11. To individuals, a phone call or a letter of apology is a good place to start. To Jesus pray, Psalm 51, this followed by appropriate application of wisdom, can conceivably avert some of the repercussions of your choices. This is what is called leaving a blessing behind. Dreamer, you are chosen; hesitate not to answer the call. If no abandonment of such practices occurs, as well as pride, your choices will possibly lead you to be counted amongst those illustrated in Matthew 7:21-23. See suggested course of action.

Carving (to disjoint, slice, and serve meat or poultry): Dreamer, you have been graciously endowed with wisdom, understanding, and resources to fulfill your purpose in life. You are intended to be an appointed ruler, judicially, within a religious or civil system. If you are not there, your dream is to engender an awareness of your untapped potential and to encourage you to develop toward this purpose. Make this happen, that you may be found a good and faithful servant on your day of the Lord (Matthew 25:14-30), the day of your reckoning. One way humanity praises the Lord is by reaching his or her potential. If you are already there allow your dream to rekindle the truth that it is God who has given you power to get wealth. Even more, understand that as a religious judicial or political leader, you are still a minister of God, and you are first accountable to Him. Meat: For kind of mean, and if necessary, may see category, Animal.

Chopped or Hacked into pieces or Butchery (person, animal, place, or hacked into a system, e.g. computer): Unless otherwise noted elsewhere, this dream has five meanings (choose one). (1) Dreamer chopped or hacked into pieces someone or something, or hacked into a system, e.g. computer: This choice has two parts (both apply). (a) Your dream is more than a warning; it is a siren. The results of a self-indulgent life are poverty, spiritual emptiness, and/or devastation. (b) Dreamer is attempting to overcome the weaknesses of your flesh, and desire to break wicked alliances you have made with certain people, places, and/or things. Dreamer, your weaknesses of the flesh will be exposed, and very hurtful emotions and many tears will follow, that you might make wiser choices regarding relationships in the future. It is suggested that you declare, and began practicing, a lifestyle of prayer and fasting, abstaining from people, places, and circumstances that trigger your unrighteous desires, at least two days a week. Additionally, allow yourself to be accountable to leadership and to significa nt others. By this you will began to live a victorious life. See suggested course of action. (2) Dreamer (or dreamer's belongings) was chopped or hacked into pieces, or system was hacked into, e.g. computer: You are too easily led astray from God and from what is spiritual by the lust of your flesh, and is willing to give up eternal happiness for temporary relations of today. As a result, the enemy is able to use your fleshly desires in an attempt to destroy you. A group of believers, doing the will of God, will come against you, to expose your sin, which is a disgrace in the sight of God, your family, and others. Instead of becoming angry become convicted and repent. If you have never taken time to reflect on the lust of the flesh in relation to your life, you need to do so now. Do you see a godly oriented focus; a focus on integrity, character, right, and wrong, living your life today in light of eternity? Do you care? You need to ask yourself before God, "Am I living in the world or is the world living in me?"

Deal with your issues via prayer, fasting, anonymous groups, and/or in-patience programs for addictions, psychological help, or education, with emphasis on a greater commitment to God. See suggested course of action. (3) Cut-off or severed body parts: Your dream denotes that the dreamer has allowed greed and covetousness to drive you. You, the dreamer, deeply desire, gain and material possessions, by unrighteous, dishonest, and violent means. You boast of having gained some of your heart's desires and how you bless those whose behavior the Lord hates (Proverbs 6:16-19), and have neglected those whom the Lord loves. You have wounded the righteous and destroyed right relationships. Question to consider: what is the hope of the hypocrite, though he or she gains, when God takes away his or her soul (ref: Job 27:8-23)? If no change of attitude, behavior, and some kind of restraint occur, your choices will lead you to be counted amongst those who are considered murderers, and/or counted amongst those illustrated in Matthew 7:21-23. You will lose your life too. We are not asked or required to do what we cannot do; therefore, you are able to reject this wickedness and live. See suggested course of action. (4) Dreamer cut in half a person or animal: The dreamer will be called upon to decree hard decisions. Your destiny is that of a leader enacting judicial decisions. However, this type of leadership requires more wisdom and courage than any one person has. Graciously, your Heavenly Father has bestowed you with wisdom, understanding, and resources sufficient to fulfill your purpose. Even more, you must understand that as a leader you are a minister of God and that you are first accountable to Him. If you trust in human wisdom, you will be persuaded into doing the wrong thing or the politically correct thing. It will be hard to know what is right, and even harder to do what is right! If you abide in Him, and His Word abide in you then you sha ll ask what you will and it will be done. See index or relevant category for specific action, activity, person, or animal that was cut or highlighted. If necessary, see suggested course of action. (5) Dreamer was cut in half: In your heart, you have mistaken the adversity and uncertainty of your life's state of affairs, for a certainty that God is unfaithful, impotent, or just don't care. You no longer believe that He is able to make happen for you what you need to happen, nor can He control the time factor. You have judged Him as mere folklore. Without faith, it is impossible to please God (Hebrews 11:6 NIV); your faithlessness will be exposed. However, this exposure may literally be the deliverance you need. Consider your dream a warning, and ask Christ to heal your unbelief, to create within you a clean heart, and to restore an upright spirit within you. It is not too late; never give up on Christ. See suggested course of action.

"Cutting" oneself (cut, penetrate, mutilate, slash, or wound): This dream has three meanings (choose one). (1) Self- inflicted gash, slash, wound, or mutilation (no suicidal intent): You are concerned with understanding only the superficial knowledge of a matter. This attitude has caused a shallowness of heart and leanness of spirit. Your thoughts and words have very little substance. As a result, the dreamer flagrantly violates God's law and distorts rightfulness and truth on every level, without fear of divine intervention. Although you have been repeatedly warned to repent and genuinely make efforts to change, you have stubbornly and hardheartedly refuse. God is rising up individuals against you, similar in nature to you, but stronger in spirit and tenacity. They will come against you swiftly, violently, and completely. You will be helpless before them. After this, the Lord will come again to you. Resolve to remain repentant that deliverance will quickly come again because of diligent prayer and corresponding obedience. See suggested course of action. (2) Self-inflicted gash, slash, wound, or mutilation (suicidal intent): You are spiritually weak, because you lack knowledge that leads to power, strength, and eternal life. You have chosen rituals and regimented rules supposing you are worshipping and serving God. Your ways and means do not promote confidence and security in salvation, only condemnation. You have made your own way hard, believing God to be a hard taskmaster. There is a need to renounce religious beliefs that are based on faithless ritualistic practices, customs, and traditions. Make it your habit to speak and act like those who shall be judged by the law of liberty, see James 2:12, 13. Honesty with yourself and God, realistically admitting your limitations, trusting in Christ's redemptive work, and accepting that His grace (the free and unmerited favor and beneficence of God), alone, is sufficient, can change things around for the best. Choose to live for Him, and not die. Choose the path of truth and liberty. If no abandonment of present religious practices occurs, your choices will lead you to be counted amongst those illustrated in Matthew 7:21-23. See suggested course of action. (3) Dreamer had a gash, slash, wound, or mutilation, and not knew how it got there: A setting right by the Lord of your behavior is taking place. You have been made aware, via the Holy Spirit, of your extreme bitterness, offensive behavior, unforgiving spirit, and subsequent sins. Moreover, because you're a leader within your ministry, your attitude has affected others as well. The Lord is asking you to genuinely deal with your bitterness, offenses, and unforgiving spirit that are due to grave offenses committed against you by others. Your Lord and Savior will hold you accountable for your actions. A definite and noticeably change in your attitude really needs to happen now, and you know this right well. By so doing, God will again restore favor upon your life. This is called, leaving a blessing behind. To be blessed: Gifts of God's grace, anything God freely gives you, absolution, the Holy Spirit, salvation, regeneration, eternal life, health, children, love of family, longevity, necessities, prosperity, and dominion over all that is yours; and all are parts of the supply of grace, and all are sanctified by the Lord, and technically belongs to Him. The result of this supply in your life will be peace. See suggested course of action.

Shave, Haircut, or Receding hairline: The overall impression of your dream is voluntary submission to divine established authority, as well as, a possible loss of glory (glory in this sense is divine admiration, praise, prosperity, success, triumph, and/or respect from others) within your life, if specific issue is not dealt with. This type of dream may also denote mourning. With that, this dream has three meanings (choose one). (1) To shave: This choice has three parts (choose one). (a) Male or female dreamer: Shaving (any part of your body): Your dream warns of serious problems within your home or finances, and internal frustration. However, if you manage to stay put, and maintain through this storm, help will come from an unlikely source. See suggested course of action, specifically for this subcategory: "Shave or Haircut", at the end of this subcategory. (b) To shave and then dress up: Male or female dreamer: To shave and then dress up: A high-ranking leadership promotion is at hand. You will attain great prosperity and respect. Important: in the day of your prosperity, make provision for your fami ly (spouse, children, parents, siblings, in-laws, significant others), be joyful, and forgive all pass transgressions against you. For, an unforgiving heart is the single most popular poison that the enemy uses against God's people, and it is one of the deadliest poisons, a person can take spiritually[32]. (c) To see another being shaved or getting a haircut (male or female dreamer): If dreamer actually knows the person depicted within your dream, describe one attribute or quality that stands out the most when you think or talk of that person. For example, are they believable, lifeless, devoted, encouraging, faithful, fanatical, hypocritical, or vengeful? If person is literally unknown, considering the person's behavior, describe one attribute or qual ity that stood out the most within your dream. If more than one person consider, what did the group have in common (e.g. ministers, pastors, rebels, or teachers). Write down (journal) the attribute(s). This is the attribute or behavior the drea mer is embracing, needs to embrace, or if negative, needs to refrain from embracing that the promises of God to you may be manifested at this time. See suggested course of action, specifically for this subcategory: "Shave or Haircut", at the end of this subcategory. (2) Haircut or Receding hairline: This choice has five parts (choose one). (a) Male dreamer: If the dreamer normally styles long hair (shoulder length or longer) in your awaked life, and dream your hair is cut off or receding: Your dream marks a transition within the dreamer's life. Dreamer, while you faithfully sustain the outward signs of appearing to be blessed and sanctified, your spirit is outrageously out of control. You have allowed your sexual desires to run rampant. As a result, Christ will now begin to deal with your unruly and egotistical tendencies. Do not spurn the rectifying of you by the Lord. He is getting you in order, resulting in a greater commitment to your family, ministry, and to Christ. Your life's circumstances will begin to change; state of affairs will spiritually be in favor of the dreamer in a very short while, that you might be highly blessed. To be blessed: Gifts of God's grace, anything God freely gives you, absolution, the Holy Spirit, salvation, regeneration, eternal life, health, children, love of family, longevity, necessities, prosperity, and dominion over all that is yours; and all are parts of the supply of grace, and all are sanctified by the Lord, and technically belongs to Him. The result of this supply in your life will be peace. (b) Male dreamer: If the dreamer normally styles a closely cropped haircut, in your awaked life, and dream your hair is cut off or is receding: Your dream warns of great weeping, mourning, and bitter anguish of heart because of someone within your family. That someone is in bondage, which may lead to jail time or devastation. There has been a lack of discipline and/or leadership by the dreamer, concerning your family, particularly this family member. Open your eyes to the reality of your family's social and emotional problems and seek professional support, if necessary. As well, pray and fast. If urged by God, declare a one, two, or three day fast without food. See suggested course of action, specifically for this subcategory: "Shave or Haircut", at the end of this subcategory. (c) Unmarried female dreamer: To dream that your hair is cut off, or receding implies one of two states (choose one). (I) Dreamer, dethroning God's providential sovereignty (the wisdom, care, and guidance provided by God) from over your life, which has started within your thoughts, coupled with your hasty and inconsiderate verdicts on His divine procedures, denies His Power. You are beginning to hijack God's authority within your life, and are replacing faith in Him, with your own set of beliefs and opinions, rendering your faith in God's omnipotence as pretense. It is by your own beliefs and opinions that you are shaping the way you think, understand, and believe God. Thus, you have an image of godliness, but deny its power; as well, your love for Jesus has dwindled to little or nothing. If not corrected, you will begin to experience a loss of glory (glory in this sense is divine admiration, praise, prosperity, success, triumph, and/or respect from others) within your life. See suggested course of action, specifically for this subcategory: "Shave or Haircut", at the end of this subcategory. (II) Your dream denotes that you are a fighter and quick-tempered person naturally, either by generational, family inheritance or because of the hardships of "life" over the years. Unfortunately, a familiar or kindred combative "spirit", has come, in the form of a person, to stir-up your contentious nature, which earlier has been laid dormant (inactive but capable of becoming active). Consequently, you are now inclined to disagree and argue; you frequently engage in and seem to enjoy arguments and disputes. It does not matter to you if you are accurate, as long as you feel in control. Opposite of mediator or person of unity, you are likely to cause disagreements and disputes between people with differing views, provoking strong disagreements and disapproval of you, within others. Deal with the source of the "familiar spirit" by removing that person or situation from your domain, repent for damage done, and render again, dead, your "fighting" spirit. See suggested course of action, specifically for this subcategory: "Shave or Haircut", at the end of this subcategory. (d) Married female dreamer: To dream that your hair is cut off, or receding, signifies that you are angry, antagonistic, and domineering. You have aligned yourself, with your male superiors, especially your husband, and have thrown off submission. You take on authority, which God has bestowed on men; and display mannerisms customarily appropriate for men only. Your actions are that of a woman desirous of changing sexes. The Lord your God forbids the confusing of the relationships of the sexes, men must not be effeminate or figuratively emasculated by a female, nor must women be virile, masculine, or domineering. As disobedience in small matters shows great contempt of God's principles, so obedience in small matters shows a very great regard for them. Daughter, obey him that has rule over you, especially your husband. Like Sarah, who obeyed Abraham and called him her master. You are her daughters if you do what is right and do not give way to fear (1 Peter 3:6 NIV). Dreamer, if you do not gain control over your antagonistic and domineering attitude, standing before the Lord improperly, you will begin to experience a loss of glory (glory in this sense is divine admiration, praise, prosperity, success, triumph, and/or respect of your husband and of others) within your life. See suggested course of action, specifically for this subcategory: "Shave or Haircut", at the end of this subcategory. (e) To cut another's hair (male or female dreamer): The dreamer is attempting to do the work of the Lord within someone's life, putting yourself in the place of God within another's life; this, may possibly be the person's hair you were cutting. This is not wise (Isaiah 14:13, 14). See suggested course of action, specifically for this subcategory: "Shave or Haircut", at the end of this subcategory.

Suggested Course of Action for: Shave or Haircut (ONLY)

If you are here, since hair figuratively denotes glory, glory in this sense is divine admiration, praise, prosperity, success, triumph, and/or respect from others within one's life; it goes to say that hair loss denotes loss of glory on some level of another. The following questions, to consider and journal will help you determine why the loss of glory, possible issues as to why the loss, how you feel about it, and what may have instigated the decline. Questions to journal: What kind of haircutting was it? Why was haircut? Were others involved? If yes, who and in what manner were they involved? Keep in mind that the others represent a quality of you, see Note 3 at the beginning of Actions and Activities category. Did anyone get hurt emotionally, physically, or was disturbed in any way? How did you feel, and what did you do, because, of your feelings, regarding the cutting of your hair or shaving? Was it agitating, confusing, dangerous, disturbing, frustrating, peace with t he situation, happy, joyful, life threatening, safe, scary, or unsure? Where were you? Was the place unfamiliar to you? Were you coherent? In view of your dream's context, namely shaving or haircutting, what choices are you making that may impair your spiritual growth, judgment, health, or that will encourage immorality and/or are you reacting out of fear? If so, what can you do to combat the paralyzing emotion of fear? Your answers, coupled with the interpretation, plus any additional information, should begin to unfold the subject matter and issue at hand, if not now, mull over things a few days. For more information, see index or relevant category and subcategory for other particulars within your dream. Nonetheless, did your dream depict any symbols that alludes to the dreamer will make the necessary changes, spiritually, emotionally, and/or physically to affect a more positive outcome? If changes are initiated, your dreams will change. Notwithstanding, seek clarity and understanding from the Lord, regarding your decision-making processes and/or identity issues, and apply His wisdom vigilantly. During this season within your life, there will be some very dark hours and major conflict (significant in scope, extent, or effect). Encouragingly, this can be replaced with a beauty or handsomeness that radiates brilliance and righteousness via diligent obedience to God through His Word and endurance. By this, grace (the free and unmerited favor and beneficence of God) and faith will once again be made manifest in your life. Also, see prayer, at end of Suggested Course of Action within this category.

Engrave (to impress deeply as to write or draw into a surface, etch, incise, score, or scratch) : This dream has three meanings (choose one). (1) The dreamer was the engraver: This type of dream is to bring about an awareness of an appointed inheritance of abundant peace, comforts, and sufficient wealth for the dreamer. At some point in the undisclosed future, honor and wealth will be bestowed upon the dreamer, if not already. You are becoming self -sufficient and unrelenting, capable of handling much responsibility, especially when required to make major decisions. Many will be inspired by your wisdom, confidence, and blameless actions, while others will feel threaten by it. Those who plot evil against you (family, friend, or foe) will not prevail, but will yield willingly to your authority. A warning: At present, keep quiet and appear speechless or deaf; take on an unassuming disposition (also see Deuteronomy 8:6-20). (2) To the unmarried male or female dreamer In addition to the preceding interpretation, a dream of you engraving also implies that God has appointed a spouse for you, a religious or civil leader (e.g. politician, representative, or an official of some kind), and that person is very near you at present. As they are sensitive to God's leading right now, so should you be sensitive to God's leading. Moreover, seek out the true and practical meaning of unequally yoked, and you will better understand relationships. If you seek truth, truth will come, by this God is showing His loving kindness towards you. (3) To see images or words already engraved on something: Question, what was the image depicted, or word(s), engraved. Dreamer may consider the image or word(s) engraved as direction or helpful suggestions regarding a decision, or future course of action. Couple the image or word(s) engraved with the following. Your dream was sent to remind the dreamer of your charge and of God's promises to you. Dreamer, remember your charge. You are sent to a rebellious people, a group of people who are obstinate. You are not to be in awe of them. God has long ago describe to you the type of people you would be working with (or ministering to), and that He would make you just as unrelenting as they are. Those that cast you aside will think they're doing the will of the Father, but they have never known Him. Dreamer, an ingratiating demeanor, before those you are sent to minister to, will "backfire on you", and cause you to fall into their evil ways and to forsake God's charge. Forsaking God's will and purpose leads to unfaithfulness and will bring disgrace upon you, resulting in loss of divine favor. Additionally, you will lose most of your finances by the unethical means of one you revere so greatly. Favorably, you will receive divine help; fear not. God will never leave you alone, nor forget you. Only let your desires be without covetousness; and be content with such things as you have. If you obey and fulfill His purposes the Lord shall command His blessings upon you in all that you find to do. God's blessings: Gifts of God's grace, anything God freely gives you, absolution, the Holy Spirit, salvation, regeneration, eternal life, health, children, love of family, longevity, necessities, prosperity, and dominion over all that is yours; and all are parts of the supply of grace, and all are sanctified by the Lord, and technically belongs to Him. The result of this supply in your life will be peace. Dreamer, you are to, always keep in the forefront, your primary mission, for it is upon you now. Do this no matter whom you meet, what they have, or what they believe about the God who chose you. For it is only through Christ, you have entered into your wealthy place, and it is only through Christ that you will remain there. If necessary, see suggested course of action.

Lacerate (to cut, divide roughly by ripping or tearing with a tool or by hand): This dream has two meanings (choose one). (1) Dreamer, promotion of all kinds of indecent practices, sexual perversions and other odious traditions, under the guise of Christianity, dishonors God, His truth, and His church. Those who truly love Him, regards certain actions, characteristics, and behaviors as destructive to the church, family, and society. Consequently, the dreamer will begin to experience a loss of divine favor. Note, a third of the people that adhere to such practices as you do, will all die of the same illness, a third will fall away (becoming apostates) because of a lack of saving knowledge, and a third will "pull up stakes" with a stigma attached to their name. The dreamer will find him or herself within one of these three categories. When these things begin to happen, if not already, you will know that the Lord has spoken. Dreamer, dump your darken ideology, and enlighten and encourage others to do so as well that you, and they, might live. See suggested course of action. (2) To you who have not promoted any kinds of indecent practices, sexual acts of perversions or other horrible traditions. Your dream was sent to demonstrate grace, via a warning of a dark generational issue, hereditary within your family line (e.g. maternal and/or paternal, grandparents, siblings, aunts, uncles, cousins). Dreamer, character traits from ancestors, namely genetic codes and traits, will often trouble and taunt the offspring of a given progenitor, especially generational issues (Exodus 20:5-7). The demons that have so plague your family line, are now visiting (re-visiting) you. Your issue is demonically instigated and it is spiritually perverse, perhaps sexually perverse as well (e.g. adultery, fornication, homosexuality, prostitution, or whorishness). These spirits attempt to "bend" the personality, as early as possible with regards to age, towards a certain direction, oftentimes towards a way that is desolate and wicked, for it is Satan's scheme to kill and make desolate all; thus, to keep some from rising up and leading their generation to Christ (see the birth of Moses, Exodus 1:15-2:10). Favorably, generational curses and issues can stop with you (Jeremiah 31:29, 30; Ezekiel 18:2-14, 20-23). Thus, your Heavenly Father is requiring that you overcome and subdue negative and dark emotions, feelings, behaviors, and/or ideas that would influence you, before they overcome you. Dreamer, God is not asking you to do something you cannot do. For a surety, vanquishing of the coming influence can be done. By faith, you will need to declare some kind of fast and commit to it, for a long period-of-time, to abate the demonically instigated circumstance, you find yourself in now, Matthew 6:16-18. Try abstaining from food and drink (midnight to 6 PM), twice a week, and refrain from words, attitudes, people, places, and things, including music, magazines, videos, TV, or any such things that fuel anger and discontent, and stir up lustful feelings. This is also known as, faith with works, read, understand, and embrace James 2:14-26. Nonetheless, earnestly pray, God will guide, enable, and answer you as to the type of fast. Additionally, if relevant, forgive your mother and/or father for the darkness (aka curse) they may have perpetuated, for they knew not what they done. Forgiveness is important to your success (Matthew 6:12-15, 8:21-35). See suggested course of action.

Sculpt (Effigy, Statuette, or Bust, any three dimensional figures or forms made by Chiseling Marble, Stone, Ice, Wood): This dream has four meanings (choose one). (1) Male dreamer: A dream of you sculpting speaks of two matters (both apply). (a) Your dream implies some form of forbidden worship, extreme devotion to a person, animal, place, or organization within your life. This is also known as idolatry. Idolatry is "foreign service", any act that expresses devotion or fanatical admiration to something or someone other than Adonai Elohim. This is due to your superstitious and fearful nature. Dreamer is urged to flee idolatry. Read, understand, and embrace 1 Corinthians 10:14. (b) You boast in your own abilities, intuitiveness, and strength. You do not consider the Lord's Hand within your life anymore. You credit the favor upon your life to irrational things or to the work of your own hands. You have become contrary. You have gone out from the presence of the Lord, that is, you willingly renounced God, and have become content to forego the privileges He offers, namely eternal life, that you might not be under His precepts. Your dream was sent from God as a message of grace (the free and unmerited favor and beneficence of God), and you are advised to deal with the fears that so easily overwhelm you. Upon your prayer and heartfelt repentance to Jesus and to individuals affected by your actions, in the form of an apology (if possible), His harshness will turn away from you. Repentance is seeking pardon and expressing sincere feelings of regret and brokenness for having done something awry and/or for having hurt someone, see 2 Corinthians 7:10, 11. To individuals, a phone call or a letter of apology is a good place to start. To Jesus pray, Psalm 51, this followed by appropriate application of wisdom, can conceivably avert some of the repercussions of your choices. This is what is called leaving a blessing behind. The Lord will heal your waywardness and you will find compassion. Afterwards, never again credit God's providential care to the work of your own hands or to irrational theories. See also Jeremiah 1:16; Acts 17:22-31; 1 Corinthians 10:14-23. See suggested course of action. (2) Female dreamer: A dream of you sculpting something implies that you are arrogant and openly immoral. Dreamer is counseled to seek wisdom from the Lord through prayer, fasting, and the reading of His Word, and apply it vigilantly. Seek also help (professional and spiritual) regarding your identity issues and unsafe choices. Darkness and major conflict within can be replaced with a beauty that radiates brilliance and righteousness via diligent obedience to God through His Word and a commitment to good healthy principles. See suggested course of action. (3) To see someone else sculpting something: Because of God's mercy, your life will be rebuilt. God's favor will once again be upon your life; it is coming your way. There are those, at present, who are considering harm against you, because they do not know the way of peace. They who gather against you shall utterly fall. The Lord is also causing irresponsible gossip about you to be stopped. Thus, while, people may complain and talk about your inadequacies there shall be no formal accusations that shall stand against you. Dreamer, also seize the God given opportunity that is before you, to advance in some manner, no matter how humble, and remember your reputation and life was given back to you because of His grace (the free and unmerited favor and beneficence of God), mercy, and love for you. Give God all the glory, and glorify not yourself this time. Contemplate: Self-righteousness will never enable you to come into the presence of God, for it only produces pride, and pride goes before a fall (see Proverbs 16:18). Therefore, dreamer you are warned to be careful lest you become so prideful that the idea that you can be deified creeps into your mindset. Self-deification is of Satan. God can dwell in the human, via the Holy Spirit, but forever the human is the human, and Adonai Elohim is forever God. If necessary, see suggested course of action. (4) To see figures already formed (e.g. an effigy, statuette, or bust): Your dream implies freedom or imprisonment, deliverance or divine discipline (the Lord's chastening, correction that leads to instruction and reformation). Whatever situation the dreamer finds him or herself in at present (ethical or scandalous), regarding a business pursuit, enterprise, or undertaking. The words, actions, and deeds you have said and done to others, shall come back to you, honorable or shameful. Example: have you spoken liberty or libel to those who have fallen in their undertakings? Have you judge those who have made bad business judgments as unworthy stewards or have you offered help, kindness, and understanding? What you have judged in others, those things you also do. Thus, in judging others, you have set a precedent over your own life – discharging a universal law, with the same judgments you judge others, so will you be judged. If deliverance or freedom is upon you, because of words of empathy, acts of compassion, and/or alms given in secret, God is ordaining peace for you now. If judgment or imprisonment is upon you, do not quarrel with God or blame others. It is you, who have turned things around. Jesus condemns the habit of criticizing others, while ignoring your own faults. Allow the experience to effect wisdom within your life. When you begin to sanctify His name, and respect Him; a more compassionate, understanding, empathic, and loving spirit will begin to manifest within you. This will remove such severe and unsympathetic standards from over your own life. See index or relevant category for other particulars within your dream. See suggested course of action.

Scythe, Sickle, Lawnmower, or Edger (any cutting instruments used for cutting crops, flowers, or grass): This dream typifies a divine harvest of souls, as well as health care concerns: With that, this dream has two meanings (choose one). (1) To cut grass or flowers: Typifies failing health, coupled with the following. This choice has two parts (choose one). (a) Male dreamer: A female relative within your immediate family (e.g. wife, daughter, mother, sister, niece, or other significant female) is not in good health, and requires medical attention (see Chapter One, Are You Ready to Hear the Messages in Your Dreams, section entitled, The 10% for others). The dreamer will need to help in a very hand's on kind of way until.

Accordingly, this dream deals with your attitude in giving to others, especially your family. Charity begins at home. You s hould be very available, and your attitude should be one of caring, cheerfulness, generous, gentleness, and thoughtfulness. See suggested course of action. (b) Female dreamer: Seek medical attention as soon as possible, and call for the elders of your church, for it is through their prayers of faith and anointing of oil upon you that sin is forgiven and healing is bestowed[36]. Have faith in this, for it will be by your faith that you will be healed wholly. This is a true saying. God has appointed someon e, possibly a male relative (e.g. husband, son, father, brother, nephew, or other significant male), to help you t hrough this difficult time. See suggested course of action. (2) To see grass, or flowers already cut or being cut by another (male or female dreamer): Your dream is one of God's ways of breaking it to you gently. Preparing you for one of life's common denominators, and if heeded, can prevent you from being emotionally blindsided by loss, as your dream is a notice; it symbolizes shortness of life. For someone who has met Jesus, we experience Him in the little graces, the big miracles, the ordinary days, and the curious moments. He is with us, leading us onward, even sharing our tears. This same Jesus trustworthy in life, even when we are not, can be trusted at the ending of life, for He is the resurrection (John 11:25, 26). If we love Jesus and love our neighbor as we love ourselves, there is nothing in this world or the next to fear. Love is what we take with us, and love is what awa its us when we have finally arrived. Nonetheless, dreamer seek medical attention as soon as possible, and call for the elders of your church, for it is through their prayers of faith and anointing of oil upon you that sin is forgiven and "spiritual" healing bestowed, and perhaps physical healing[36]. This is a true saying, thus it is time to have faith in God. Additionally, it is always a good time to get your house and papers in order (e.g. insurances, bequeaths, untold truths that need to be said), and always a good time to gather family together for prayer, support, wisdom, and truthfulness (Ecclesiastes 12:6). Moreover, if flowers were highlighted, see category, Agriculture (Flowers), for type of flower and "time frame". If necessary, see suggested course of action.

Cut and set stones, gems (the dreamer or someone else doing the cutting): This type of dream is to bring about an awareness of an appointed inheritance of abundant peace, comfort, and sufficient wealth for the dreamer, and greatness. At some point in your near future, wealth will be bestowed upon the dreamer, if not already. A warning: Don't forget the lessons of the past when you come into your prosperity. There is danger in wealth and ease. Your children may turn from God because of a lack of appreciation of things given them liberally. Continue to teach your children the pure ways of Jesus. If you lack wisdom, ask Jesus for wisdom. He gives wisdom to all men generously, no matter who you are and what you've done; wisdom will be given you (James 1:5-8). Further, it is counsel that you embrace a down-to-earth, unpretentious disposition (also see Deuteronomy 8:6-20).

Suggested Course of Action

Question to consider and journal, did your dream depict any symbols that alludes to, the dreamer will make the necessary changes, spiritually, emotionally, and/or physically to affect a more positive outcome? If changes are initiated, your dreams will change.

Nevertheless, cutting within dreams are primarily warnings to those who are spiritually weak, yet are in line to be prosperous. Seek clarity and understanding from the Lord, regarding your decision-making processes, unsafe choices, and identity issues, and apply His wisdom vigilantly. In quietness and patience, you will find the wisdom to live unpretentiousl y and the strength to embrace a re-making season within your life (also see James 1:5, 6). A prophecy will be given you, during this season, write it down for it will happen. Go to church and forsake not the gathering of yourself together with other mainstream Christians. Avoid isolated groups that teach something different from the gospel of Jesus Christ. Jesus died for the world, and not exclusively for any one sect or western denomination. Even more, entering the House of God should be done reverently rather than carelessly. Cease from many words and let your works speak for you. In spite of what we do not know about the many mysteries of God and life, one thing remains eternally true: God is our loving Father. He does not desir e that any one perish; great effort is exercised to save us, even to the moment of our death. Therefore, cast your burdens upon the Lord, for He genuinely cares for you. Again, run with endurance the race set before you.

Consider and journal the following questions. The questions will help you determine; the issue at hand, how you feel about it, and what may have instigated it. What kind of cutting was it? Why was there cutting? Were others involved? If yes, who and in what manner were they involved? Keep in mind that the others represent a quality of you, see Note 3 at the beginning of Actions and Activities category. Did anyone get hurt emotionally, physically, or was disturbed in any way? How did you feel, and what did you do, because, of your feelings? Regarding the cutting and/or who or what was cut. Was it agitating, confusing, dangerous, disturbing, frustrating, peace with the situation, happy, joyful, life threatening, safe, scary, or unsure? Where were you? Was the place unfamiliar to you? Were you coherent? In view of your dream's context, namely cutting, what choices are you making that may impair your spiritual growth, judgment, health, or that will encourage immorality and/or are you reacting out of fear? If so, what can you do to combat the paralyzing emotion of fear? Your answers, coupled with the interpretation, plus any additional information, should begin to unfold the subject matter and issue at hand, if not now, mull over things a few days. For more information, see index or relevant category and subcategory for other particulars within your dream.

Now, pray (See Prayer of Deliverance, pg. 897)

Specific Meaning

If, your chances are very high that you will participate in some type of cutting (e.g. a chef, diamond, gem cutter, landscaper, lumberjack, meat handler, medical examiner, sculpture, or surgeon, dreams of this sort are ordinary dreams, resulting from your daily activities (see Chapter One, Chalom). These dreams are usually about the anxieties that overwhelm your mind during the day. They are an inner release mechanism, which helps provide you with emotional balance and the maintaining of your sanity. These dreams are not significant, and do not warrant special attention.

Note: If an accident was highlighted within your dream, this is a precautionary warning. There may be potential for an accident. Dreamer, the details, kept within context of your dream, should be relevant to your life, and closely resemble your real-life situations. Meaning it can actually occur during your awaked state. This will help you narrow down the specifics needed to support and steer you clear of possible mishaps. However, if your dream symbols are not easily, linked to your life activities, heed the spiritual implications (the interpretation).

DANCING: To move the feet and body rhythmically, usually in time to music, to jump up and down, to leap or skip, especially in an emotional manner. To make violent twisting, rolling, and squirming movements with the body.

Some short descriptions of types, phrases, and other processes and particulars, connected in some way to this category are, for example, to choreograph a dance, to dance about, skip or thrash about, tremble, to wait anxiously, or writhing in agony.

Unless otherwise noted elsewhere, if, in your everyday living, your awaked state, as part of your lifestyle, work, or ministerial activities, or a special event, you have a very real connection with any type of dancing activity. For example, dancer, dance instructor, dance school, entertainment, (also see content list for this category), your dream is not significant and does not warrant special attention.

Otherwise noted, this dream of dancing may be a Prophetically Simple Dream (see Chapter One: The 60th Part of Prophecy). Whereas, the dreamer is encouraged, for example, if a new dance move was introduced to you within your dr eam, to adopt the dance as your own signature move or learn the dance. Did you invent something? Skip interpretation and go do or learn the dance.

Otherwise noted, see Note 1 at the beginning of Actions and Activities category.

To determine who your dream is for you or another, see Note 3 at the beginning of Actions and Activities category.

Symbols and Referents: Dreams of dancing generally deal with joy or evil within the life of the dreamer, and the varied emotional changes (depression, happiness, laughing, mourning, or weeping) experienced because of one thing or another.

Category Content - If not listed see index, perchance, for your specific type of dancing dream activity.

- Ballet
- Choreograph a dance
- Dancing before altars, idols, wooden images (or any inanimate object, iconic image, effigy, picture, or representation that is a sign or likeness that stands for an object or entity, by signifying or representing it either concretely or by analogy
- Dancing (as if at a party or in a playful type manner; alone or with others)
- Sacred Praise Dancing
- Slow dancing (close partner dance, to dance in a sensuous manner)
- Tango (a ballroom dance)
- Thrash about (turn round, sway, and wiggle)
- Tremble (shiver, shake, shudder, quake, or quiver)
- Wait anxiously (nervously, restlessly, or worriedly)
- Writhing in agony (make violent twisting, rolling, and squirming movements with the body, especially because of severe pain)

Ballet: Dreamer, you will be led out of your present bondage or affliction by a miraculous intervention of God. You will begin to praise the Lord, when you see His Powerful Hand in your situation. You will be restored; thus be encouraged.

Choreograph a dance: You desire freedom from restrictions in order to pursue your own aspirations, it will be granted you. Many will be inspired by your ideas and confidence, while others will resent them, or be threaten by them, and will walk away from you, namely a few older brothers and/ or sisters in Christ, but just a few. Dreamer, know who you are in Christ, and do not be swayed by good or bad reports, or by others opinions of you. God's favor is upon you and your time of rejoicing is now, for God has made all things beautiful in their own time. You are enabled to accomplish your goals. You will be given the opportunity, in an executive leadership capacity, to plan, coordinate, implement, and supervise a highly esteemed venture. You will need to compose, calculate, and account all the costs prior to this undertaking, including your family qu ality time, if applicable. You are able to capably balance and accomplish all your objectives, if you wisely plan and involve pertinent one s, especially family members, in your decision making process, at the beginning. Carefully consider your family's input. Further, you need only ask counsel of Jesus, and it will be given you, somehow or some way. On another note, it is counseled that you still respect your elders (spiritual or not), lest prideful bitterness take root within you.

Dancing before altars, idols, wooden images (or any inanimate object, iconic image, effigy, picture, or representation that is a sign or likeness that stands for an object or entity, by signifying or representing it either concretely or by anal ogy): Your dream denotes one who is powerful, full of pride, and insolent. You trivialize the honor your ancestors obtained by worshipping and honoring Jesus, and His righteousness, and have made, or are making, yourself a renowned name by that which perpetually ruins good names. You have chosen low or base standards, morals, ethics, ideas, principles, tenets, and beliefs; thus, there is a defection of the faith, which is in Jesus Christ. You are abandoning the faith, and is now worship ping false gods and images, and adhering to lies; holding to beliefs, views, and practices that are erroneous, unlawful, toxic, and spiritually and/or physically deadly. Dreamer, because of your unwise and foolish passions, the sharp reproofs of the Word, and the severe censures of men, you are allowing a weakening of your core beliefs, namely a rejection of all or some of the original foundational teachings of Christ and His apostles, to take root within you spiritually. You are listening to and be ing fooled by demons. Moreover, your lack of an objective critical analysis and judgment of a belief system's infrastructure, its foundation, existence, deity, nature of worship, sacred text, values, attitudes, earthly and eternal benefits and recompense; and whether its beliefs are worthy of consideration or not, is leading you towards dark and erroneous knowledge, the devil's so-called deep secrets. This knowledge is gained through personal experience and through supernatural imparting, which is demonically communicated (1 Timothy 4:1-5). The knowledge gained will not allow you to praise the Lord, only to exalt one's self. This counterfeit image of godliness is excessively concern with outward forms and appearances, especially in religious matters. Your lifestyle choices are, or will become, offensive and repulsive (abominable) in the sight of God and humanity, for your kind of choices leads to prostitution, poverty, homelessness, begging, imprisonment, and/or early death. You are forfeiting purpose for foolishness and ruin. Demonic influences will swarm around you, ready to help you in your wicked, evil, despicable, immoral, reprehensible, disreputable, degenerate, infamous, or perverse choices. Dreamer, demons have had thousands of years to master human weaknesses and can rival men and women of God if we are not careful. Favorably, because of grace and the many mercies of God extended to you, your dream is only a warning and not an official declaration. Utilizing the powerful resources of prayer and heartfelt repentance to Jesus and to individuals affected by your actions, in the form of an apology (if possible), is needed. As well, fasting, a changed mindset, serious re-consideration of God's ways and means, and an honest acknowledgement of God's hand within your life, then and only then, can the severe impact of your choices and actions, upon your life, be reversed and damages undone and restored as before (see Ezekiel 33:8-19). Repentance is seeking pardon and expressing sincere feelings of regret and brokenness for having done something awry and/

or for having hurt someone, see 2 Corinthians 7:10, 11. To individuals, a phone call or a letter of apology is a good place to start. To Jesus pray, Psalm 51, this followed by appropriate application of wisdom, can conceivably avert some of the repercussions of your choices; this is what is called leaving a blessing. Dreamer is counseled to seek all kinds of spiritual support now, to possibly avert or turn things around, and perhaps move away from your present environment, definitely walk away from all negativity abruptly. If you do not genuinely seek help and change, for sure ruin will be your destiny. See suggested course of action.

Dancing (as if at a party or in a playful type manner; alone or with others): This dream has three meanings (choose one). (1) See Psalm 30:11-12. Your dream is to guide the dreamer that you may be found with your purpose complete when standing before the Throne of the Almighty; as well as, to affect a happier, more contented you. You are gifted with multipl e talents that may be expressed through inspirational acting, preaching, teaching, or writing. Dreamer, do not bury your gifts (see Luke 19:12-26); for many will be drawn to God because of your loving disposition and positive attitude; others will be dramatically changed by your example. Moreover, you have insight into prophetic wisdom by this you are able to discern truth from false. (2) To the unmarried: You will very soon get married, if not already engaged. Do not be afraid; you will not suffer shame. Do not fear disgrace; you will not be humiliated. If germane, to this union there will be children born of your own body or seed. (3) To the married male or female without children: Dreamer, God has granted mercy to you and has deemed your marriage worthy to merit children. If desired, you will very soon give birth to your own children. To the female, God will give you the miraculous strength and knowledge, as well as a door, to the right physicians to help you bear and birth your children. Your husband will be a great support to you during this time. On another note, dreamer, you should no longer feel ashamed because of something you've done wrong in your past (e.g. seriously bad, unalterable, or life damaging actions, due to uninformed choices, and/or ruinous relationships). The reproach of your past actions is put behind you. Therefore, don't lose the authentic good that is before you, looking back at the past; do not try to revive old grievances; forget about past conflicts. Go on from there, "let the dead bury the dead".

Sacred Praise Dancing: This dream has two meanings (choose one). (1) Your dream is an expression of the joy and happiness you have experienced serving the Lord. You are encompassed about with righteousness and purity. The intents and motives of your heart are pure and righteous. You are honorable in the eyes of God. Many will be inspired by your faith and unpretentiousness. Consequently, you are prepared for any spiritual conflict or evil activity that may come your way b ecause of the pride, criticism, and littleness of mind of others. Do not allow others to dampen your joy, for no weapon will prosper against you (Isaiah 54:17). (2) To the unmarried: A potential spouse is looking carefully at you at present. Your faithfulness and unpretentiousness is beautiful in their sight. An introduction will present itself shortly. The question of the possibi lity of relocation may be asked.

Slow dancing (close partner dance, to dance in a sensuous manner): This dream has three meanings (choose one). (1) Married person dancing with someone other than your spouse or an unmarried person: Dreamer, you are a dangerous seducer. Vindictively you seductively lure those who are already ensnared by their uncontrollable lustful desires into compromising, dangerous, and/or deadly situations. You hide your purpose; using your beauty, charm and sexuality. In some situations, you use lying or coercion rather than charm; thus, the purpose of your dream, unfortunately, you have erroneously charged and maliciously wronged a genuine man or woman of God. One who has done nothing but tell you the truth. This person believed your lies; thus, they entered into a relationship with you naively. Now he or she is a victim, caught in an asymmetrical or lopsided relationship with you, from which they cannot walk away, without much bitter anguish and regret. Surely, the heartbreak you have caused will come back to you. Heartfelt repentance to Jesus and to individuals affected by your actions, in the form of an apology (if possible), is required on the part of the dreamer, as well as a ceasing of your cruel and spiteful ways immediately. Repentance is seeking pardon and expressing sincere feelings of regret and brokenness for having done something awry and/or for having hurt someone, see 2 Corinthians 7:10, 11. To an individual, take words with you, and say to this person as before God,

134

"Forgive all my scandalous behavior and wrongdoings toward you". Then just walk away; they will heal. To Jesus pray, Psalm 51, this followed by appropriate application of wisdom, can conceivably avert the repercussions of your choices. This is what is called leaving a blessing behind. Dreamer, repentance to Jesus and man will turn God's displeasure away from you. The Lord can and is willing to heal your waywardness and love you freely. Vow to yourself, and to God, to never again hurt anyone intentionally and keep that vow (see Numbers 30:2-4; Deuteronomy 23:21-23). Moreover, developing a lifestyle of fasting and prayer will bring about a cleansing of the soul and cause that malicious spirit to abate, and effect a personal revival within you. It is also suggested that you seek help and counseling from clergy. Jesus will strengthen you emotionally, psychologically, and physically, to go get help for your issues, He will lead the way. If necessary, see suggested course of action. (2) Married person dancing with your spouse: Dreamer, your marriage will prove to be a time of "jubilee" for you. Celebrate for God's blessings are upon you; thus, you should participate in the various social celebrations that you may be invited to. Additionally, dreamer you will be led out of your present bondage or affliction by a miraculous intervention of God. You will begin to praise the Lord, when you see His Powerful Hand in your situation. You will be restored. For, your dream implies that a bad situation, within the dreamer's life, will begin to change quickly, because, those who wanted to harm you have been put to confusion and shame. Dreamer, when God reverses this tragedy, you will testify that the Lord has done great things for you, and you will be glad, joyful, and thankful, and you will praise Him for His faithfulness. Moreover, you are the object of God's care, guidance, loving kindness, righteousness, strength, and wisdom. These graces coupled, with God's divine intervention, will comfort you, and will again, cause your mouth to be filled with laughter, and your tongue with singing. You will now, begin to noticeably experience the miraculous wonders of divine providence — the wisdom, care, and guidance provided by God that you might fulfill your mission, your purpose. Moreover, your past experiences and lessons learned will be used to strengthen your witness. Take care that you become sensitive to and respect the continuous acts of God's providential care. For, there is a promise that you will eat and do very well, on this side of eternity, and inherit eternal life. As well, the feeling of rest and serenity that comes with trust in God's divine providence is available to you right now. Dreamer, embrace and celebrate God's love towards you and His providential care over you. (3) Dreamer was a spectator (watching someone else dancing): This is a good indicator that the meaning of (#1) is about another, who has been risen up, and is sent to, seduce the dreamer, because of the dreamer's uncontrollable lustful desires. Which have been 'hyped-up" or awaken. Your dream was sent to warn the dreamer and to give the dreamer a chance to subdue and bring under control your lustful inclinations, via repentance, fasting, and prayer. If no attempt is made, one who is a dangerous seducer and very vindictive will seduce you and your pain will be great. See suggested course of action.

Tango (a ballroom dance): There is an old saying, "It takes two to tango". This is used to indicate that both persons involved in an awkward or unpleasant situation are both responsible and to blame. Thus, it goes to say that you, dreamer, are part to blame in the unpleasant situation that is before you. See suggested course of action.

Thrash about (turn round, sway, and wiggle): Again, God will build you up, and turn your mourning into gladness and joy. Lessons learned have caused you to see your doctrinal errors, and to get the better of your personal weaknesses, and overcome pride, via the power of God. The intents and motives of your heart are purified and correct. Promotion is at hand. Further, when you are troubled, ask counsel of Jesus. Counsel will be given you somehow or some way. See also: Psalm 30:11, Jeremiah 31:13.

Tremble (shiver, shake, shudder, quake, or quiver): Give careful thought to this, from this day forward. Dreamer, from this day forward, God's blessings will flow abundantly, producing spiritual growth within you. God's blessings: Gifts of God's grace, anything God freely gives you, absolution, the Holy Spirit, salvation, regeneration, eternal life, health, children, love of family, longevity, necessities, prosperity, and dominion over all that is yours; and all are parts of the supply of grace, and all are sanctified by the Lord, and technically belongs to Him. The result of this supply in your life will be peace.

He will cause people to reverence you greatly. This respect will go deep. Keep in mind your motives and that God desires diligence, integrity, and that you love and obey Him above all, as well as love others.

Wait anxiously (nervously, restlessly, or worriedly): Your dream instructs the dreamer to not murmur and to remain silent. There is something the Lord wants you to learn, a lesson. Do not complain when others prosper around you. Sincerely acknowledge that God is in complete control of your state of affairs, and earnestly wait for Him to work it out for your good and for His glory. Harmonize your life with His agenda and you will learn this lesson well. See suggested course of action.

Writhing in agony (make violent twisting, rolling, and squirming movements with the body, especially b ecause of severe pain): This dream has three meanings (choose one). (1) Your waiting has not been in vain, those within your family who are spiritually and emotionally dead shall live, those whom you've been praying for, they will rise and increase in r ank, status, and position in life, especially employment wise, and move on to a better quality of life. Expect this in a spirit o f excited anticipation- sing for joy! For, Jesus loves you and you are valuable in His eyes. (2) The following is specifically for the dreamer. If you will accept the Heavenly Father's Words, via the Bible, and store up His principles, and His ways and means within you, turning your ear to wisdom and applying your heart to understanding, calling out for insight and crying alou d for discernment, Jesus will meet you, regardless of wherever you find yourself, emotionally, spiritually, and physically, at the moment. This, coupled with a lifestyle of prayer, followed by appropriate application of wisdom, and you will know the Messiah, Jesus Christ, intimately, and find the knowledge of God you seek. For the Lord gives wisdom and from His mouth comes knowledge and understanding. Then you will understand what is right and just and fair, every good path. When wisdom enters your heart and knowledge becomes sweet to your soul, discretion will protect you, understanding will guard you, and His Truth will lead you. To deliver you from the wickedness that is before you, from demons whose words and ways are perverse, (Proverbs 2:1-6, 9-15). This is one of God's covenant promises to you. Have faith in this. (3) Regrettably, a close friend, one who gives you sound advice, will betray, or has betrayed, you before those who hate you. This friend is one who has been treated lovingly and trusted explicitly. This betrayal will grieve you very deeply. You will experience embarrassment, shame, great fear, and internal stress because of the vicious lies told against you. Although your anger is justifiable (rig hteous indignation), remain silent and watch things play out. Jehovah will cause a rift amongst the group, and stop their lies, via an ally of yours sent by God to join the group. This ally's mission is to confuse, divide, and separate. So, know that not everyone in the group is one with the group. Do not return evil for evil. Pray and cry aloud evening, morning, and at noon. Only, let your prayers come from a right heart that loves God, and not from angry vengeful motives. See your deliverance as a present fact, and know, without a doubt that God hears you, and will turn things around. They will reap what they have sown. If necessary, see suggested course of action.

Suggested Course of Action

Question to consider and journal, did your dream depict any symbols that alludes to, the dreamer will make the necessary changes, spiritually, emotionally, and/or physically to affect a more positive outcome? If changes are initiated, your dreams will change.

Consider and journal the following questions. The questions will help you determine; the issue at hand, how you feel about it, and what may have instigated it. What kind of dancing was it? Why was there dancing? Were others involved? If yes, who and in what manner were they involved? Keep in mind that the others represent a quality of you, see Note 3 at the beginning of Actions and Activities category. Did anyone get hurt emotionally, physically, or was disturbed in any way? How did you feel, and what did you do, because, of your feelings, regarding the dancing and/or your dance partner or group? Was it confusing, dangerous, enjoyable, fun, happy, joyful, life threatening, safe, scary, or unsure? Where were you? Was the p lace unfamiliar to you? Were you coherent? Your answers, coupled with the interpretation, plus any additional information, should begin to unfold the subject matter and issue at hand, if not now, mull over things a few days. For more information, see index or relevant category and subcategory for other particulars within your dream.

The following will help you determine the approximate length of time you have thus far dealt with the matter and how much longer you will have to deal with the issue. If you started dancing at the beginning of the dream, you are dealing with this issue right now. If somewhere in the middle onward, you will encounter the issue shortly. Did you stop dancing at some point? This is indicative that you've completed the process that will heal the issue your dream is referring to, within your life. If you did not stop dancing, the matter at hand will not end soon, if you continue avoidance, complaining, faithlessness in God's Word, and murmuring. You are counseled to deal with the issue without evasion or compromise, in other words head-on. All of these questions should pull together for you your dream. They summarize the issue at hand and what changes need to be made within the dreamer's attitude or life.

In view of your dream's context, namely dancing, what attributes are you embracing that may hinder your happiness or bring about sadness and the practice of habits of doom? What qualities do you need to embrace, to affect happiness, joy, and the manifestation of God's blessings? God's blessings: Gifts of God's grace, anything God freely gives you, absolution, the Holy Spirit, salvation, regeneration, eternal life, health, children, love of family, longevity, necessities, prosperity, and domi nion over all that is yours; and all are parts of the supply of grace, and all are sanctified by the Lord, and technically belongs to Him. The result of this supply in your life will be peace. There is purpose and wisdom in every situation; be it joy and happiness or mourning; thus give careful thought to the instructions or coaching within your dream interpretation, and allow a sp irit of humility, gratefulness, and submissiveness to lead the way.

Now, pray (See Prayer of Deliverance, pg. 897)

Specific Meaning

If, your chances are very high that you will participate in some type of dancing activity (e.g. dancer or teach dance). Dreams of this sort, for the most part, are ordinary dreams, resulting from your daily activities (see Chapter One, Chalom). These sor ts of dreams are usually about your routine, mundane activities or anxieties that overwhelm your mind during the day. They are an inner release mechanism, which helps provide you with emotional balance and the maintaining of your sanity. These dreams are not significant, and do not warrant special attention.

Note: If a dancing accident was highlighted with your dream, this is a precautionary warning. There may be potential for an accident. Dreamer, the details, kept within context of your dream, should be relevant to your life, and closely resemble your real-life situations. Meaning it can actually occur during your awaked state. This will help you narrow down the specifics needed to support and steer you clear of possible mishaps. However, if your dream symbols are not easily, linked to your life activities, heed the spiritual implications (the interpretation).

DIVORCE: The ending of a marriage by an official decision in a court of law

Some short descriptions of types, phrases, and other processes and particulars, connected in some way to this category are, for example, 1st Divorce, 2nd Divorce +, annulment, dismissed, private, public, separation.

Unless otherwise noted elsewhere, if, in your everyday living, your awaked state, as part of your lifestyle, work, or ministerial activities, or a special event, you have a very real connection with any type of divorce activity. For example, judicially, or advocacy, (also see content list for this category), skip interpretation and go to Specific Meaning at the end of this category.

Otherwise noted, this dream of divorce may be a Prophetically Simple Dream (see Chapter One: The

60th Part of Prophecy). Whereas, the dreamer is warned to do, or do not, instigate a divorce; or you are or are not getting a divorce; or something of that nature. This dream is a first step intervention and/or an alarm. The Lord is a witness to the covenant made between you and your spouse. The Lord desires godly offspring, figurative of love and fear of the Lord. So take heed to yourself, and do not be found disloyal. "I hate divorce", says the Lord God (Malachi 2:14-16 NIV). This dream is a first step intervention and warning.

Otherwise noted, see Note 1 at the beginning of Actions and Activities category.

To determine who your dream is for you or another, see Note 3 at the beginning of Actions and Activities category.

Symbols and Referents: Divorce within a dream generally implies one of three meanings: A callused, cynical, resistant attitude towards a known directive of God, spiritual faithlessness, or an act of deceitfulness and violence against someone emotionally or physically.

Category Content - If not listed see index, perchance, for your specific type of divorce dream activity.

- Causes of Divorce (Abandonment, Adultery, Indignant Estrangement, Cruel and Inhumane treatment, Irreconcilable Differences, or to follow Jesus)
- Persons Concerned (claimant, defendant, children, e.g. child custody)
- Types of Divorces (Annulment, Dismissed, 1st Divorce, 2nd Divorce, and on, Private, Public, Separation)

Abandonment, Adultery, Indignant Estrangement, Cruel, and Inhumane Treatment, Irreconcilable Differences, or to follow Jesus - only applicable if primary within the dream, e.g. if seen written on a document or spoken of within your dream): This dream has five meanings (choose one). (1) Abandonment (desertion, rejection): Dreamer, covetousness has caused you to defile yourself, even to the point of sexual immorality to satisfy your lusts. Consequently, t he dreamer eyes are closed to spiritual realities. You do not see the miraculous wonders of divine providence within your life. You have chosen not to see God's unfailing love, but instead have chosen to trust in fallacy. You have rejected authentic worship of God, and no w participate in a simulated worship of humanistic or superstitious ideas that are in direct conflict with the inspired written Word. Neglect not the purity of your covenant relationship with Christ, for God desires to bring you back into a right relationship with Him. Return to ideals that are holy, wise, well judged. This will lead you back to Christ. Your dream is one of God's ways of calling you back unto Him that you might be saved. See suggested course of action. (2) Adultery (infidelity): Behind closed doors, you violate the innocent. The innocent are suffering anguish, affliction, misery, and sa dness at the seemingly success of your ungodly practices. Woe to you; who has caused the Spirit of the Messiah to leave. When the Spirit of Messiah leaves, the spirit of holiness, wisdom, understanding, counsel, might, knowledge, and of the fear of the Lord, also, departs. You have made the Word of God dry and dark, when God has said, "He is Living Waters", and "Let there be Light". Your coming judgment (divine reprimand for folly and sin) will bring about a rectification and exposure of your atrocities. Those violated will be compensated and justified. You will also be assigned ignoble works within the Kingdom. See suggested course of action. (3) Indignant estrangement, cruel and inhumane treatment (emotional, literal, and/or verbal abuse): Your frustration over your limited ability to cope with life's trials, tribulations, and the obligations expected of you by God, has resulted in intentional rebellion against God. Your soul is ensnared by the forces of evil, and you do not know how to distinguish between the sacred and the profane. You are bitter, angry, and self-absorbed. Therefore, you rail against God in torment, "Why have you made my life so miserable?" You want "freewill", yet you do not want the consequences that come with your own free choices. The dreamer will need to resolve to stop hindering the display of godliness within your own life and others by your rebellious attitude and deeds. You will soon realize that God's behavior toward you (past, present, and future) has always been for your best interest, and that the consequences of your bad behavior, is your wrong. See suggested course of action. (4) Irreconcilable differences (opposing belief systems): The wrongdoing that you've consented to or have allowed to prosper around you and/or within your household has come up before God. The consequences of your choices are on the way. You will lose your place within your community, as well as respect amongst those who are respected. Favorably, because you do have a spiritual inheritance within the Kingdom of God, grace (the free and unmerited favor and beneficence of God) will be shown you. You will be restored after a while, and not to the heights from which you have fallen. See suggested course of action. (5) To follow Jesus: A recent decision you've made; although, you thought you were courageous and righteous by your action, it was not done for the Lord. Your decision did not in any way glorify God or make His Kingdom come earlier. You made that decision for yourself, because of your hardened, cynical, and resistant attitude towards a known directive of God. As well as, to avoid presumed future sufferings. With that said, in the future, reason your decisions, especially regarding relationships, with a practical wisdom. This time, the grace of God will help you get pass your difficulty, and His grace (the free and unmerited favor and beneficence of God) will make all things new. In the near future, you will be elevated to a high and prosperous condition, a state of honor, dignity, and authority within business and/or ministry and it will be God's grace that will enable you to remain there. See suggested course of action.

Persons Concerned (claimant, defendant, children-only applicable, if primary within your dream, if seen written on a document, spoken of, or if child custody was determined): This dream has three meanings (choose one). (1) Claimant, Petitioner, or Plaintiff: This choice has two parts (choose one). (a) Male dreamer: The sin of hypocrisy must be acknowledged and forsaken. Dreamer, you have neither loved, nor walked close to the Lord, you have proven yourself insincere. Hence, His care and protection given you will no longer cover you. The face of the Lord is against them that do evil, to cut off the remembrance of them from the earth (see Psalm 34:16-18). Thus, repentance is necessary at this time. Because of God's mercy and grace (the free and unmerited favor and beneficence of God), He desires to bring you back into a right relationship with Him. Heartfelt repentance to Jesus and to individuals affected by your actions, in the form of an apology (if possible), is required. Repentance is seeking pardon and expressing sincere feelings of regret and brokenness for having done something awry and/or for having hurt someone, see 2 Corinthians 7:10, 11. To individuals, a phone call or a letter of apology is a good place to start. To Jesus pray, Psalm 51. Dreamer, repentance followed by appropriate application of wisdom, can conceivably avert some of the repercussions of your choices. This is what is called leaving a blessing behind. See suggested course of action. (b) Female dreamer: You have lost your way, your identity, and you do not know who you are spiritually. Superstition and unfaithfulness to God and His ways has caused this. You trusted in your beauty and pursued immorality. Favorably, because of His grace, God desires to bring you back into a right relationship with Him; prayer and heartfelt repentance to Jesus and to individuals affected by your actions, in the form of an apology (if possible), is needed. Repentance is seeking pardon and expressing sincere feelings of regret and brokenness for having done something awry and/or for having hurt someone, see 2 Corinthians 7:10, 11. To individuals, a phone call or a letter of apology is a good place to start. To Jesus pray, Psalm 51. As well, the sin of hypocrisy must be acknowledged and forsaken. This followed by appropriate application of wisdom, can course of action. (2) Defendant, Respondent: This choice has two parts (choose one). (a) Male dreamer: Evil has come against you, although you have behaved wisely. The Lord has not, and will not, forsake you. You will see the guaranteed reward of the wicked. An expectation they're not expecting. For it is their own child they've sacrificed to evil. Let them know about the child, if possible. To the dreamer, appreciate again the sweetness of wisdom to the soul. For wisdom, also offers a guaranteed recompense and an expectation that shall not disappoint. Men and women of honor will seek your wisdom, which God has or will put in your heart. (b) Female dreamer: The Lord is calling you back with great compassion, and with a love and kindness that will last. His loving kindness will remain and His promise of peace will not be shaken. In righteousness, you will be established. You will be far from oppression. Your boundaries are to obey God's call and His principles. Be encouraged. (3) Children: Primary custody of a child granted to either party within a dream is figurative of two primary emotions, love, and fear of the Lord. Thus, charge of a child, or children, within this context is the ultimate realization and embodiment of your attitude regarding devotion to God. This choice has three parts (choose one). (a) Gaining custody of a son or male child: A son (or male child) is symbolic of love of the Lord. Love within this context is the practice of living life on God's terms for no other reason or benefit than to be close to God, this is called holiness. Be encouraged, God will raise you up and sit you amongst His people. You will receive the benefits of participating in a local church (community, support, proper ordination, burial, honor, respect, edification, and accountability). Moreover, visit and fellowship with those who are glad and sincere of heart. (b) Gaining custody of a daughter or female child: A daughter (or female child) is symbolic of fear of the Lord. Fear within this context is the practice of living life on God's terms in order to receive recompense, meaning while hoping for some benefit from your efforts. You respect God but your love for Him is conditional. A tenacious faith in, and acceptance of, all of the Word of God, the good and the not so easily received, and prayer, will lead you into the Light of His Love. A conscienti ous and diligent effort on the part of the dreamer to deal with your emotional fears and scars and some type of Christian counseling is needed at this time. See suggested course of action. (c) Gaining custody of both, boy and girl represents the Light within your life is refining and purifying you, effecting holiness. The works and responsibilities assigned you at present are for those purposes. Your participation in the service and work of the Lord will also cause the emergence of wisdom. It will be through these works that the wisdom of harmonizing love and fear will be imparted to you.

Types of Divorces (Annulment, Dismissed, 1ˢᵗ Divorce, 2ⁿᵈ Divorce, and on, Private, Public, Separation, only applicable if primary within your dream, e.g. if seen written on a document, or spoken of): This dream has seven meanings (choose one). (1) Annulment: Some uncleanness has been found in you; a pollution of doctrine, immoral sexuality, or an unforgiving spirit; causing the spirit of wisdom to leave. Further, uncleanness, within the life of a believer, denotes anger, animosity, confusion, out of order, an unforgiving spirit and/or weakness, are present within your heart, as well as, immoral, impure, and unchaste conduct. For example, addictions, cheating, exposing confidences to others, greedy, gossiping, jealously, lying, stealing, or any other sinful attribute (see 1 Corinthians 6:9-20, Ephesians 5). Your behavior has led to a resistance of God's ordinances. The dreamer needs to once again embrace the Holy Scriptures as the genuine work of God, via His chosen writers, and apply its' wisdom to your life. Favorably, you are now one, whom the body of believers should, and will, help restore back to God, in the spirit of empathy, mercy, leniency, and kindness, until the issue is cleaned up or rendered dead, allow this. See suggested course of action. (2) Dismissed: Dreamer, if divorce case was dismissed, it is now time to return to the place of worship where you first met God, and there is a need to give an account of your actions to the leaders. Rejoice together with those of the assembly, and get on one accord with the fellowship, offering up prayers of thanksgiving. If you are already in that place o f worship, or never left: There is a need to get on one accord with the fellowship, to defeat that spirit of division that is upon you right now. An attitude of thankfulness for your life and all it encompasses will most definitely help things. See suggested course of action. (3) 1ˢᵗ Divorce: Your heart is subtly drifting away from Christ. The first danger sign for any believer is to grow cold toward Christ. In spite of all your commendable qualities, meticulous care with doctrine and discipline, your love and desire for the presence of God has decline. Repent or you will be replaced. See suggested course of action. (4) 2ⁿᵈ Divorce and on: Your dream speaks of a callused, cynical, resistant attitude towards a known directive of God. A spirit of humility will prevent the fall resultant of your attitude. If necessary, see suggested course of action. (5) Private divorce: This choice has two parts (choose one). (a) You have passed your test, thus God has chosen not to reveal your sins. You will be allowed to fulfill your mission. Only remain obedient to God's directives. Go, and sin no more. If necessary, see suggested course of action. (b) To the unmarried person: You are getting married very soon. Do not be afraid to marry. The union will produce godly offspring. If no children are desired, "godly offspring" is also figurative of love and fear of the Lord, especially within the relationship. (6) Public divorce: God is bringing to light the hidden things of darkness within your life and is making known the motives of your heart. This process will allow you to, freely praise God for all his blessings to you. God's blessings: Gifts of God's grace, anything God freely gives you, absolution, the Holy Spirit, salvation, regeneration, eternal life, health, children, love of family, longevity, necessities, prosperity, and dominion over all that is yours; and all are parts of the supply of grace, and all are sanctified by the Lord, and technically belongs to Him. The result of this supply in your life will be peace. See suggested course of action. (7) Separation: This choice has two parts (choose one). (a) Formal agreement to separate (legal): Although the spirit of the leader has risen up against you, causing an offense within you, do not leave your place, stay right where you are, things will pan out. Begin serving God with fasting, prayer, and quietness. If urged by God, declare a one, two, or three day fast. God will give you a door to leave after things have calmed down, and He will be glorified. (b) Informal separation (no legal agreement): Luke warmness has led to spiritual faithlessness within the dreamer's life. Choose whom or what you will serve, if God, commit resolutely and wholeheartedly. See suggested course of action.

Suggested Course of Action

Question to consider and journal, did your dream depict any symbols that alludes to, the dreamer will make the necessary changes, spiritually, emotionally, and/or physically to affect a more positive outcome? If changes are initiated, your dreams will change.

Nonetheless, there is wisdom in every situation; be it joy and happiness or mourning; thus give careful thought to the instructions or coaching within your dream. Allow the change and choose wisdom instead of speaking foolishness. As a result, the spirit of humility will lead the way. Prayer, courage, and obedience are the key words right now. Pray every day for wisdom, and, if needed, for the courage to change, and for obedience to allow what God is trying to effect within your life a t present.

Consider and journal the following questions. The questions will help you determine; the issue at hand, how you feel about it, and what may have instigated it. What kind of divorce was it? Was the divorce granted? Who divorced whom? Were others involved? If yes, who and in what manner were they involved? Keep in mind that the others represent a quality of you, see Note 3 at the beginning of Actions and Activities category. Did anyone get hurt emotionally, physically, or was disturbed in any way? How did you feel, and what did you do, because, of your feelings, regarding the divorce and/ or how it ended? Was it confusing, dangerous, insignificant, life threatening, painful, or releasing? In view of your dream's context, namely divorce, what choices are you making that may impair your spiritual growth, judgment, health, or that will encourage immorality and/or are you reacting out of fear? If so, what can you do to combat the paralyzing emotion of fear? Your answers, coupled with the interpretation, plus any additional information, should begin to u nfold the subject matter and issue at hand, if not now, mull over things a few days. For more information, see index or relevant category and subcategory for other particulars within your dream.

Now, pray (See Prayer of Deliverance, pg. 897)

Specific Meaning

If, your chances are very high that you will counsel couples regarding divorce concerns or judicially grant divorces. Dreams of this sort are ordinary dreams, resulting from your daily activities (see Chapter One, Chalom). These dreams are usually about the anxieties that overwhelm your mind during the day. They are an inner release mechanism, which helps provide you with emotional balance and the maintaining of your sanity. These sorts of dreams, are not significant, and do not warrant special attention.

Note: If a specific situation is before you, namely divorce proceedings and its particulars, and you dreamt of an outcome. This may be taken as a guide towards the direction the ruling and/or counseling may go. Dreamer, the details, kept w ithin context of your dream, should be relevant to your life, and closely resemble your real-life situations. Meaning it can actually occur during your awaked state. This will help you narrow down the specifics needed to support and steer you clear of possible mishaps. However, if your dream symbols are not easily, linked to your life activities, heed the spiritual implications (the interpretation).

DRINKING, SMOKING (wine, alcoholic or fermented drinks, or any kinds of pharmaceutical or street drugs, or cigarettes, cigars, or chewing tobacco)

Some short descriptions of types, phrases, and other processes and particulars, connected in some way to this category. For example, the various alcoholic beverages, beer, cocktail, liquor, martini, red and white wine, whiskey, or pharmaceutical or street drugs, amphetamines, barbiturates, cocaine, meth, OxyContin, cannabis, cigarettes, or any type of natural or artificial substance that changes your behavior and perception, often addictive, mostly illegal. Drugging, drunkenness, getting high, inebriated, intoxicated, smashed, smoked, smoking, spaced-out, to be thirsty, under the influence, wasted, or to refuse to drink or use drugs.

Unless otherwise noted elsewhere, if, in your everyday living, your awaked state, as part of your lifestyle, work, or ministerial activities, or a special event, you have a very real connection with any type of drinking wine, alcoholic or fermented drinks, or drugs, or cigarettes. For example, connected with substance abuse counseling, legal matters, medical doctor, AA, NA, in-patience, out-patience substance abuse clinic or recovery program, or with the Bureau of ATF, tobacco industry, or you are using a nicotine patch. Bartender, distillery, distribution or sell of alcohol, drugs or tobacco, vineyard, winery, or wine tasting, (also see content list for this category), skip interpretation and go to Specific Meaning at the end of this category.

Otherwise noted, as drinking, drugging, or smoking could result in some serious health related issues, health concerns might be highlighted within your dream. If so, please cease drinking, drugging, and/or smoking, and see a physician immediately. If someone else was the participant, consider a possible intervention of some sort. Further, if your dream of craving drinks, drugs, or smoke, closely resembled real life situations, with the dream events actually being capable of happening, see Note 1 or Note 3 of this category. See also Specific Meaning at the end of this category.

Otherwise noted, see Note 1 at the beginning of Actions and Activities category.

To determine who your dream is for you or another, see Note 3 at the beginning of Actions and Activities category.

Symbols and Referents: Is your dream an intervention or stern warning? Your dream of craving or thirsting after pharmaceutical or street drugs, wine, other alcoholic or fermented drinks or cigarettes; or of being under the influence of alcohol or drugs and operating a motored vehicle; or of open, public, or secret drunkenness, drinking, or drugging; may be a warning. Whereas, the dreamer is urgently warned to stop drinking, drugging, or smoking because of possible addiction, health related issues, illegal operation of a motored vehicle while under the influence, possibl e endangerment of the lives of others, or anything of this nature; especially if this is an issue within the dreamer's life at present. This dream is a first step intervention and a warning. Dreamer is counseled to immerse yourself into the cleansing Word of God and abide there, via prayer and fasting. Pray and ask Jesus for help, emotionally, mentally, and physically, with your "flesh" issue, earnestly asking your Heavenly Father to help you deal with your strong dependence upon and cravings for that, which is detrimental to life and soul, and wait patiently for His answer, for He will answer you. Coupled with spirituality, you will need ministerial and/ or professional help, and other supports, to affect a personal revival within you, and possible medical attention. Jesus will strengthen you, to go get help with your addiction. Skip interpretation and go get help.

Persons in recovery or rehabilitation (aka rehab) or those who are dealing with their addiction "cold turkey" will oftentimes experience what is called "User Dreams". You will dream of drinking or drugging, sometimes many years after sobriety. As long as you remain focused, in your program and continue doing whatever keeps you clear, and sober, these dreams are ordinary dreams. They are usually about your routine, mundane activities, or the anxieties that overwhelm your mind during the day. These dreams are not significant, and do not warrant special attention. However, if you've stopped your sobriety process, this dream is a first step intervention and an alarm. Hence, your dream should be viewed as a warning, exposing the coming consequences of forfeiting your sobriety. Jesus will strengthen you to go get help for your relapse back into negative behavior. Prayer and fasting are powerful tools at this time.

Otherwise, a dream of drinking wine, drinking other alcoholic or fermented drinks, using any kinds of pharmaceutical or street drugs, smoking cigarettes or drunkenness, or to refuse to drink, drug, or smoke, generally imply, an encounter with the blessings and promises of God, because of obedience and wisdom, or to experience His harshness because of waywardness. It also denotes spiritual purification, rectification of chaos, a refinement process, and/or restoration, within the li fe of the dreamer. Take great care and heed God's warnings. We are called to exhibit faith by steadfast obedience, determination, confidence, fortitude, thanks, and love. The genuineness of your faith is judged by your response to hardships and oppositi on engendered by your identification with Christ, and by your inner temptations to sin. We must exhibit courage under trials, a nd not take lightly God's disciplinary instructions.

Category Content - If not listed see index, perchance, for your specific type of wine or alcohol drinking, drug use, or refusal to drink or use drugs, dream activity.

- Alcoholic or Fermented Drinks or Pharmaceutical or Street Drugs (not cannabis)
- Cigarettes, Cigars, Cannabis, Chewing Tobacco
- Wine
- Abstinence or Refuse to drink, wine or other alcoholic or fermented drinks, or refuse to use pharmaceutical or street drugs, or refuse to smoke
- DWI or DUI (intoxicated on wine, or other alcoholic or fermented drinks, or pharmaceutical or street drugs, and operate a motored vehicle or walk
- Intoxicated or Sober and you do not know what was drunk or taken
- Intoxicated on or Purchased, Drugs, Pharmaceutical or Street Drugs (e.g. Amphetamines, Barbiturates, Cocaine, Marijuana, Meth, OxyContin, or whatever your drug of choice)
- Intoxicated on or Purchased, Wine, or other Alcoholic or Fermented Drinks at a:
    - Bar, Nightclub; Bathroom; Church; Closet; Home; Work; Unknown or Strange place
- Sober (to drink wine or other alcoholic or fermented drinks, or take pharmaceutical or street drugs (e.g. cannabis), and not be intoxicated)
- Wine or other Alcoholic or Fermented Drinks (thrown in your face, or poured over you (to have wine, or other alcoholic or fermented drinks, poured or thrown on you)
- Winepress, Distillery, Brewery, Pharmacy, Smoke Shop, Tobacco Factory (any place where wines, liquors, drugs, or cigarettes are made and/or sold)
- Be off, or on, the wagon
- Bitter pill (to swallow)
- Tobacco Road
- Wine and Dine

Alcoholic or Fermented Drinks, or Pharmaceutical or Street Drugs (not cannabis): This dream suggests that strife and envying has led the dreamer to agree to a potential commitment that should be avoided. You are not quiet internally; there i s much unrest and drama. Your dream was sent in an effort to rectify chaos and waywardness within your life. The Lord can deliver you from bondage, if you would but, with bold faith, seek Him while He may be found, and call upon Him while He is near. Dreamer, recognize and respect your time of visitation from the Lord, for it is upon you. Attend church and appreciate your current place of worship, for you are in the right place at the right time. By doing this, your soul will be satisfied, made quiet, and the chaos will subside.

Cigarettes, Cigars, Cannabis, Chewing Tobacco: Dreamer, you've recently encountered something that appears spiritual, yet the teaching rejects authentic worship of Yeshua. The teaching is a simulated worship of humanistic and superstitious ideas, in direct conflict with the inspired written Word of God, rejecting Christianity's core system of beliefs; thus, leading you into giving praise and thanks to a false god. This wisdom only leads to shadows, and an encounter with something that is not God's Shekinah (a glow of the Light of God's Goodness). Therefore, choose not to go out from the presence of the Lord that is to willingly, renounce God, e.g. relegating Him to a lower position; reduced in rank, perhaps to some alien visitation, but n ot Creator God in all of His Power. Dreamer, choose this moment, to go no further with this dissidence. Do not be content to forego the privileges Elohim offers, that you might not be under His precepts; make things right. See suggested course of action.

Wine: This dream has two meanings (choose one). (1) Dreamer, your hunger for holiness, has set-off a process, whereupon your old belief system is being challenged. When your heart turned from the world's system to living life on God's terms, you began experiencing a spiritual awakening, taking you to another level emotionally and intellectually. This is what you're experiencing at present. This process will be complete, only after the dreamer has gone through a season of great difficulty, hardship, and/ or distress. Be encourage and patient, this process will improve you inwardly, making you wiser, more effective for the Kingdom causes, and more refined. Blessed are you, if you suffer these hardships now, and with a good conscience and hope in God. For you will see justice and right, taking place. You will also be delivered from those who are a source of stress, trouble, and/or worry. Quietly plead your cause to Jesus, and in due time you will be abundantly satisfied, in the wisdom given you, and the kindness shown you, by Jesus. (2) If the color of the wine was highlighted within your dream or remembered, e.g. dreamer literally requested red or white wine, or commented on the color. With that, this choice has two parts (choose one). (a) To drink red wine: Dreamer, you have prophetic abilities, which you should develop and u se to help others at this time in your life. Commissioned, you will have to give an account of the fulfilling of this purpose. If necessary, see suggested course of action. (b) To drink white wine: You will begin to experience the blessings that come with wisdom, positive choices, and helping others. Dreamer, from this day forward God's blessings will flow abundantly, producing spiritu al growth within you. God's blessings: Gifts of God's grace, anything God freely gives you, absolution, the Holy Spirit, salvation, regeneration, eternal life, health, children, love of family, longevity, necessities, prosperity, and dominion over all that is yours; and all are parts of the supply of grace, and all are sanctified by the Lord, and technically belongs to Him. The result of this supply in your life will be peace

Abstinence or Refuse to drink, wine or other alcoholic or fermented drinks, or refuse to use pharmaceutical or street drugs, or refuse to smoke: *Note:* This dream of refusing to drink, do drugs, or smoke, may also be a prophetically simple dream, (see Chapter One: The 60th Part of Prophecy). Whereas, the dreamer is able, and willing, to say no to addiction, especially if this has been an issue within the dreamer's life. God will strengthen you as you go forward, on to clarity. This type of dream should closely resemble real life situations, with the dream events, actually being capable of happening. For example, does the dreamer drink or smoke? Moreover, this dream may also be an intervention, see at the beginning of this category, Symbols and Referents: Is your dream an intervention or stern warning. With that, this dream has three meanings (choose one). (1) To refuse to drink wine: Your dream denotes self-restraint in the face of desire and/or temptation. The dreamer has exemplified temperance. You will now encounter the blessings and promises of God, because of your obedience to His directives over your life. God's blessings: Gifts of God's grace, anything God freely gives you, absolution, the Holy Spirit, salvation, regeneration, eternal life, health, children, love of family, longevity, necessities, prosperity, and dominion ove r all that is yours; and all are parts of the supply of grace, and all are sanctified by the Lord, and technically belongs to Him. The result of this supply in your life will be peace. (2) To refuse to drink other alcoholic or fermented drinks or use pharmac eutical or street drugs: The dreamer is encouraged to embrace a more hopeful view of your life from this day forward. This hope will give you the strength needed to hang-on during the tough times that are approaching. Your innate qualities are those of a righteous person. These qualities will only be made perfect through your tough times. These tough times will be the cleansing agents used to create within you a clean heart and to restore an upright spirit within you (Psalm 51). No longer, doubt your inner strength, and ability to handle any challenge, and never doubt God's ability and willingness to help you. Put your trust in Him. He knows where, and who, you truly are. He knows that you desire a more self-controlled and balanced way of living, and that you have a great deal of loyalty to those you love and respect. Even more importantly, He knows that your obedience to Him is becoming sincere. Again, be hopeful and have faith in God, which is a resolute trust in the integrity of God and i n His Word. (3) To refuse to smoke anything: In His mercy, the Creator will reveal to you some of the light of His glory, and you will genuinely experience His Divine Presence. Glory in this sense is a state of honor, spiritual beauty, and greater illuminatio n. You will be healed of a present sickness, as well as experience instantaneous knowledge, according to your aptitude for knowledge, understanding, and maturity level. This experience will create within you a greater capacity for spiritual ideals, and a better spirit. Moreover, a lifestyle cycle needs to be broken within your life, experiencing the glory of God's Shekinah (a glow of the Light of God's Goodness) will heal this too.

DWI or DUI (intoxicated on wine, or other alcoholic or fermented drinks, or pharmaceutical or street drugs, and operate a motored vehicle or walk: This dream has two meanings (choose one). (1) This choice has two parts (choose one). (a) To be intoxicated on wine and operate a motored vehicle: In earlier times, you have been lifted up in honor, joy, and prosperity. At present, it appears, as though you've been cast down and forsaken. Dreamer, you are experiencing a spiritual refinement. This process is transforming your lifestyle, as well as, maturing your understanding of grace (the free and unmerited favor and beneficence of God). With that said, dreamer, a good man, or woman, such as yourself, may be overwhelmed because of your hardships and perhaps be ready to faint under them. Dreamer in all this, do not sin by charging God with wrongdoing (Job 1:6-22). The Lord gave and the Lord took way, nevertheless, blessed be the name of the Lord. When your spirit is overwhelmed, it is to your advantage that you humbly unburden your grievances and grief before the Lord. He gives us all the liberty to be free with Him, talking openly and direct. Dreamer, you have access to your Advocate, Jesus Christ. After this process, you will encounter, once again, the blessings and promises of God, if you faint not. (b) To be intoxicated on alcoholic or fermented drinks or under the influence of pharmaceutical or street drugs (e.g. cannabis), while operating a motored vehicle: You are experiencing, or will experience shortly, the Lord's harshness because of unreasonably stubborn disobedience, and your perverse ways and practices. Although you appear happy and smiling, your enslavemen t has made you spiritually irrational and demonically influenced. You will be exposed and known by an extremely bad reputation, namely as the instigator of something extremely offensive. You will be known as an instigator, causing others to follow your ways, practicing false religion, and all sorts of lewdness and wickedness, and filthy conversations. You are as one who has figuratively shed blood and murdered in an abundant manner, spiritually much blood is on your hands. Read and understand, Ezekiel 13:3-23, 33:6, and then repent. There is a need to purify your character, namely in the area dealing with the deeds of the flesh, dishonesty, adultery, sexuality, hostility, feuding, vendettas, grudges, unfriendliness, strife, jealousy, outburs ts of anger, disputes, dissensions, discord, drunkenness, carousing, traits of these sorts. If your character and choices remain unchanged, the door will be left wide-open for even more chaos and negativity to manifest in your life. Dreamer, your ways are due primarily to a wrong done you by one considered pious but who was not. Now, you suppose that all Christians are like that person, and have disdained them as such and have spoken lies from this place of pain. Not all Christians are like that. There are those who genuinely and successfully deal with their issues. There is one near you, who does understand your situation and the mentality behind the madness, he or she can help you, and you do need help, for you are in serious trouble. Seek them out, as well as, professional Christian counseling. See suggested course of action. (2) This choice has two parts (choose one). (a) To be intoxicated on wine while walking: Be encouraged, your dream is a good indication that the dreamer will be provided the opportunity to increase in wisdom and knowledge, regarding a spiritual truth or concept you may be wrestling with now. This increase will happen through personal experience and a miraculous impartation. You will be blessed because of the clarity this increase of wisdom will bring. Your honesty has brought you here. (b) To be intoxicated on alcoholic or fermented drinks, or under the influence of pharmaceutical or street drugs (e.g. cannabis), while walking: Dreamer, Christianity is a meaningful belief system based on biblical values, views, thoughts, ideas, attitudes and opinions that shape the way you think, act, and understand this world. Following godliness is aimed at making you not only wiser, but also better. Thus, you are encouraged to think soberly and be honest and open with yourself that you may be on the alert against spiritual dangers, those sins that set you back so easily and often when demons come pushing. Be temperate and modest in apparel, business, drinking, eating, recreation, and in all your behavior, demonstrating humility in your opinions and in practice. You must learn to discipline your mind, inner man, and affections, to restrain from extravagances, and let your strength and quickness of mind be used, fulfilling your obligations to God and His cause. Walk soberly and holy that you may be ready and on time regarding the business of God you've been destined to handle (1 Peter 1:13-25). Separate yourself from all that would hinder you and go on unwavering in obedience to God. Dreamer, you have a journey to go on, a walk-to-walk, spiritual warfare to fight, and a great work to do. By prudently embracing the principles and precepts of Jesus Christ, the One who has made you holy, via His blood sacrifice, all may be accomplished. See suggested course of action.

Intoxicated or Sober and you do not know what was drunk or taken: See Isaiah 29:9-16. See suggested course of action. **Intoxicated On or Purchased, Drugs, Pharmaceutical or Street Drugs (e.g. Amphetamines, Barbiturates, Cocaine, Marijuana, Meth, OxyContin, or whatever your drug of choice):** This dream has three meanings (choose one). (1) Although you've been found slacking, you will be rectified, via the Paraclete who resides in you. God will use this season in your life to fortify you spiritually that you may be complete, wanting nothing, having broken your negative life cycle of self-sabotaging spiritual and ministerial progression. For, He has said, "My grace is sufficient for you, for my power is made perfect in weakness" (2 Corinthians 12:9 NIV). You are now ready for promotion. (2) Dreamer, you are being made aware of the spiritual state of things within your church, via confidences, gossip, and personal experiences. You have been told so much and seen so much that your spirit has become drugged. Dreamer you have begun to falter and become discouraged and weak. If you are not careful, the enemy can use any one of these openings to snare you into immorality that will cause you to forfeit purpose for foolishness. Note (for consideration only) when a church's major focus is within the confines of a building, the congregation may morph into a religious country club, with morality dropping to an all-time low. Dreamer; therefore, resolve to continue serving Jesus, and not use men's weaknesses to justify waywardness. Moreover, although you've seen others living unholy, determine, with firmness of purpose, to be, and present, like those who will be judged by the law of liberty (James 2:12). If the dreamer chooses to allow the fortifying work of Jesus to continue within you, keeping in mind, now is the time, God, will surely open doors of opportunity for you to do so. If not, a very bleak future is before you. (3) Dreamer very recently (within a day or so, or perhaps hours ago) you adhered to knowledge, which was demonically based. For example, if you are a writer or songwriter, and are in the process of writing a publication of some sort, or song, go now and re-write your last pieces of writing. The information used was from an unholy source. If you are a counselor, mentor, or an advisor of some sort, your last bit of guidance given another was erroneous, your conversation was not of God, go now, and make things right with that person. Reverse your counsel, and give another counsel. See suggested course of action.

Intoxicated On or Purchased, Wine, or other Alcoholic or Fermented Drinks at a (Bar, Bathroom, Church, Closet, Home, Nightclub, Work, or an Unknown or Strange place): This dream has two meanings (choose one). (1) To see another intoxicated or take drugs or smoke: The person you saw was you; see Note 3 at the beginning of Actions and Activities category. Dreamer, you have esteemed others above God. This is idolatry (idolatry is "foreign service", any act that expresses devotion or fanatical admiration to something or someone other than Adonai Elohim). You've allowed other people, places, and/or things to become discouraging factors in your effectiveness within the Kingdom of God, because you lack faith in God. You've given their opinions and comments too much power over you. Thus, you have begun to falter and become discouraged and weak; losing focus. If the dreamer chooses to re-discover your purpose, keeping in mind, now is the time, God will, surely open doors of opportunity for you to do so. For, you have naturally been given big goals that involve building a better world and giving back to it what it has given you. Additionally, write your vision down, that you may articulate it to others prop erly, for the vision will happen, suddenly and quickly. Prepare a good proposal, name your ministry, and write down all the details and specifics. Give it your best that it may be acceptable to any reputable financial entity, benefactor, or merit a grant o f some kind. Perhaps, hire a grant writer. That which you will need to fulfill your aims, surely, you will have. If you choose no t to seize the opportunity, at this time, you will remain drunk-and-disorderly (spiritually and/or physically), forfeiting purpose for foolishness. See suggested course of action. (2) See one of the following.

Bar, Nightclub: Dreamer, you are in a state of complete disorder and confusion. You present your talents and offerings at the altars of demons. A change needs to come. There is a need to re-evaluate your ideas from a less worldly perspective. Your dream was sent to spotlight that rectification of chaos and waywardness within your life is needed. The Lord can deliver you from bondage, if you would but, with bold faith, seek Him while He may be found, and call upon Him while He is near. As well, commit to a judicious study of the Holy Scriptures, via a bible study group or Christian school, with emphasis on accep ting all that is written within Holy Writ and reconciling that, which seemingly appears to contradict, embracing all of it. Dreamer, separate truth from false, wisdom from foolishness, and choose purposefully. If no change occurs, you will experience an absence of blessings (absence of divine support, help, backing, approval, sanction, consent, exaltation, promotion, or sanctification), due to the harshness of the Lord. See suggested course of action.

Bathroom: Dreamer is being warned to remember life lessons and negative experiences learned from previous "self- sabotaging" behaviors, from which God has delivered you. Unconsciously you yearn (or perhaps have attempted) to destroy your own reputation without cause. You feel as though you will mislead God's people, condemning your own individual character flaws, via deliberate exaggerations and lies about yourself. If you do not stop this self-condemnation, you will begin to implode. Your "self-sabotaging" behavior from the past is being "triggered" by a spirit of fear. Read and understand Romans 8:15, 2 Timothy 1:7. You are on the brink of success, happiness, and prosperity, and your sensing or knowing that you are becoming a celebrated man or woman of God has triggered your "self-sabotaging" behavior that has been dormant for some time, and has open the door for a spirit of fear to gain power over your emotions. You will find this demon (the spirit of fear) in every phobia. Question to journal: What would it feel like if all of your fears were suddenly released from you at one time? Pause and feel that. Jesus will come and see about you, keep your faith regarding what you've believed God for; you will experience a miracle. Joy shall then be revealed, rest shall appear, and healing shall descend, disease shall withdraw, anxiety, anguish and crying shall pass from you; gladness will happen. Learn not to be afraid of darkness, but to stand bold in its face, for the greater one lives within you, and that spirit of fear that has intimidated you will flee. Dreamer, while y our weaknesses maybe legitimate, you unknowingly deny the truth of His report, there is therefore now no condemnation to them that are in Christ Jesus (Romans 8:1); as well, His grace is sufficient (2 Corinthians 12:9). There is a difference between conviction and condemnation. Dreamer, think on these things (see Romans 7:7-8:17; 2 Corinthians 12:7-10; Philippians 1:6; 4:8). Take great care and heed God's warnings. Dreamer, you are on the brink of promotion and celebrity, and you are being watched by heaven and others. Thus, you are called to exhibit faith by steadfast obedience, determination, confidence, fortitude, thanks, and love. The genuineness of your faith is judged by your response to hardships and opposition engendered by your identification with Christ, and by your inner temptations to sin. Be encouraged, take comfort, and believe (see John 14:1-4). No other affirmation will be sent.

Church: This dream has two meanings (choose one). (1) If wine was consumed for spiritual reasons (e.g. Holy Communion, Eucharist): This implies that the dreamer is clear and has the spiritual capacity to handle and maintain appropriately an encounter with the blessings and promises of God, because of obedience and wisdom. God's blessings: Gifts of God's grace, anything God freely gives you, absolution, the Holy Spirit, salvation, regeneration, eternal life, health, children, love of family, longevity, necessities, prosperity, and dominion over all that is yours; and all are parts of the supply of grace, and all are sanctified by the Lord, and technically belongs to Him. The result of this supply in your life will be peace. (2) Dreamer, you are in denial about an offense, or you are resistant, unclear, and/or superficial regarding your religious convictions. Whichever the issue, you are not pure within your heart. This state of being will prove detrimental to you. In this state, your pride and stubbornness will lead to irrational thinking, adoption of erroneous ideas, and some mental health issues.

Dreamer, if you have a serious offense against someone, humble yourself enough to relinquish your ministry (if germane), and go and make things right that you may be open enough to hear and receive God when He speaks. If there is no offense, dreamer needs to become resolute about your dedication to the Lord Jesus Christ. It's one thing or another. Since your dream also denotes restoration, after you've taken care of the issue, go and revive your ministry again. If necessary, see suggested course of action.

Closet: Secretly the dreamer believes that you will live in peace and merit divine protection, despite the fact that you walk in stubbornness, twist, and then attempt to justify, your distortions of God's principles. Your vain imaginations will not lead to peace. The dreamer lacks wisdom in your choices. You either, do not have enough knowledge, or life experience, or you are deliberately choosing to remain immature, regarding utilizing your ability to form sound opinions and make sensible decisions. Go no further with your erroneous ideas and seek advice from others. The Bible says in many ways that in the multitude of counsel there is safety (see Proverbs 11:14, 13:10, 20, 14:15, 15:22). Choose to walk in the way of understanding, and you will live. If you continue to walk according to your own foolishness, you will experience some form of misfortune, which should be regarded as divine punishment for folly or sin. See suggested course of action. *Note:* This dream (intoxicated in a closet) may also be an intervention, see at the beginning of this category, Symbols and Referents: Is your dream an intervention or stern warning. Whereas, the dreamer needs to admit that he or she has a secret addiction, and possibly needs to seek help via prayer, fasting, a Christian based support group, Christian counseling, healthcare, NA, AA, especially if this is an issue within the dreamer's life, a hidden addiction. This type of dream should closely resemble real life situations, with the dream events actually being capable of happening. For example, does the dreamer addictively drink or use pharmaceutical or street drugs, or smoke cigarettes? If so, your dream is a first step intervention and an alarm. Dreamer, immerse yourself into the cleansing Word of God and abide there, via prayer and fasting. Coupled with spirituality, you may also need professional help, and will need spiritual support to affect a personal revival within you. Jesus will strengthen you emotionally, psychologically, and physically, to go get help with your addiction. Skip interpretation and go get help.

Home: Your dream refers to a rectification of chaos and a spiritual purification process happening within the life of the dreamer, as well as your entire household. This season of cleansing will draw you away from personal pursuits, and allow time for you to devote yourself, and all that you are, to God's glory (e.g. by perfecting your inborn talent in some way for the glory of God, or by starting or enhancing a ministry). It will also perfect a quietness within your soul, and a more compassionate and obedient spirit, leaving you more open to divine influence. You will gain knowledge on how to be moderate in all things, just and fair. This will take some time, be patient, and allow the process. Moreover, as a house reveals the condition of your inner person and physical well-being, and each room is significant, see index or relevant category for other particulars within your dream. For example, rooms in a house see category, Buildings, Structures. If necessary, see suggested course of action.

Work: The quality of your spiritual efforts, are poor and has led to cynicism. There is no one to blame but yourself. For it is written, we are to work out our own salvation with fear and trembling (Philippians 2:12-16). Favorably, your dream denotes deliverance from sins and restoration. God will redeem you with His Power, once you've wholeheartedly returned to Christ, via prayer and heartfelt repentance to Jesus and to individuals affected by your actions, in the form of an apology (if possible). See suggested course of action. *Note:* This dream (intoxicated at work) may also be an intervention, see at the beginning of this category, Symbols and Referents: Is your dream an intervention or stern warning. Whereas, the dreamer is warned not to be intoxicated at work, especially if this has been an issue within the dreamer's life. Dreamer may possibly need to seek he lp via prayer, fasting, a Christian based support group, Christian counseling, healthcare, NA, AA, especially if this is an issue within the dreamer's life. This type of dream should closely resemble real life situations, with the dream events actually being capable of happening. For example, does the dreamer drink or use pharmaceutical or street drugs, before or during work hours? If so, your dream is a first step intervention and an alarm. Dreamer, immerse yourself into the cleansing Word of God and abide there, via prayer and fasting. Coupled with spirituality, you may also need professional help, and will need spiritual support to affect a personal revival within you. Jesus will strengthen you emotionally, psychologically, and physically, to go get help with your addiction. Go get help!

Unknown or strange place: You are not in harmony, spiritually, due to carnality. The Kingdom of God has need of you now and you have been found wanting. Grace (the free and unmerited favor and beneficence of God) will be shown you, via a probationary period, and regard this period with sincere alarm. This probationary period decreed might be a proving by trial (e.g. a wilderness experience); by humiliation and servitude (Judges 13:1; Acts 13:21, 22); or by waiting (Acts 7:23-30). This probationary period points to grace, leads to repentance, and ends in revival and renewal. During this season, you are counseled to begin implementing godly principles that will move you toward discipline and humility, while embracing faith and love of God. Thank God for His patience, long-suffering, and grace, while you get things decent and in order. Moreover, you are in need of a personal tutor or mentor. Presently, one is available and prepared, all you need do is ask and diligently apply yourself. No teacher should be asked to tolerate a lack of application or diligence; and this one will not. Moreover, repentance to God and man (a godly sorrow for hurting God and others, see 2 Corinthians 7:10, 11) is also needed. If you do not seize the opportunity that is afforded you because of the Lord's grace, you will experience His harshness because of waywardness. See suggested course of action.

Sober (to drink wine or other alcoholic or fermented drinks, or take pharmaceutical or street drugs (e.g. cannabis), and not be intoxicated): This dream has two meanings (choose one). (1) To drink wine, and not be intoxicated (sober): Your dream denotes forgiveness of sins and spiritual purification. Dreamer, because of past offenses, some are treating you with disrespect and hatred. Attempting to prevent you from succeeding, they cause much frustration and humiliation. God will handle them. However, as for you, because you have received forgiveness of your sins from God, only ask for forgiveness from those you've sinned against, forgive those who've sinned against you, and you will experience having your whole person renewed, emotionally, physically, and spiritually, becoming a new man or woman, bearing the image of Christ Jesus. This is righteousness. (2) To drink other alcoholic or fermented drinks, or take pharmaceutical or street drugs (e.g. cannabis), and not be intoxicated (sober): Your dream denotes a grave disrespect towards God, which has serious consequences, and therefore needs to be thought about more carefully. Because of past offenses, committed by others considered pious, yo u are treating God, Christians, and others with disrespect and hatred. Your profaneness has led you to embrace a false doctrine, which view s spirituality from a darker perspective that does not lift men to God. This belief system follows a sensual, secular wisdom, a syncretic [28] mixing and mingling of truth and error. You will now experience the Lord's harshness because of waywardness and disrespect. See suggested course of action.

Wine or other Alcoholic or Fermented Drinks (thrown in your face, or poured over you (to have wine, or other alcoholic or fermented drinks, poured or thrown on you): Your dream denotes an arrogant person. Dreamer, God is wrathful against the arrogant. Boast no more, and no longer use you influence to manipulate or persuade others according to your carnal desires. Moreover, do not attempt to force or exalt your prideful agenda against God's plans, He will frustrate your wisdom. You do not have the power to exalt, nor bring down anyone; only God has that power. See suggested course of action.

Winepress, Distillery, Brewery Labs, Pharmacy, Smoke Shop, Tobacco Factory (*any place where wines, liquors, drugs, or cigarettes are made and/or sold*): See one of the following.

Winepress: This dream has two meanings (choose one). (1) If dreamer is a spiritual leader (e.g. e.g. bishop, deacon, deaconess, elder, evangelist, minister, overseer, pastor, pope, preacher, priest, rabbi, superintendent, teacher, or any cleric or ecclesiastical type role), your dream denotes that the dreamer is a respected spiritual leader, who is looked upon as a sagacious and understanding leader, and whose instructions, reproofs, and corrections are heeded. With that said, dreamer, you too must heed instruction, as well as, reproof and correction from those who are considered your leaders. For your leaders love you, as you love those you are over, thus, both, you, and your leaders, are embracing godly wisdom. Therefore, dreamer, heed the wisdom that is before you that happiness may be your end. Continue desiring to embrace God wholly and to subdue your carnal nature, putting an end to (or controlling) negative desires and passions, for religious purposes. For the principles of discipline and abstinence, helps to control and put an end to ungodly desires and passions, and your present situation, is calling for godly wisdom. He or she, who will humble them self shall be exalted. It is counseled that you use (if not already doing) the principles of discipline and abstinence, via fasting, prayer, and reading and meditating on the Holy Bible in solitude, daily for about 3 hours. Not for study only, or to fill your head with trivia, but that you might as a believer an d a spiritual leader, observe to do according to what is written therein; and that you might understand the deeper meanings within the Word of God, and have it in you when occasion calls for you to know the Word. Additionally, read Proverbs 4:1-13. (2) Your dream also denotes one who has stolen money, property, or a title from the rightful owner, the one who inherited those things rightfully. As you have made one impoverish and poor, evicting them from what's rightfully theirs, so it will be unto you. You will reap what you've sown. See suggested course of action.

Distillery, Brewery, Liquor Store, Labs, Pharmacy, or Drugs bought at any Venue (legal or illegal venue): This dream has three meanings (choose one). (1) Your dream denotes one who will shortly experience the harshness of God, because of waywardness. Notwithstanding, because of His loving kindness, you will not be utterly brought down. His Spirit will not be taken from you, nor will His faithfulness fail. See suggested course of action. (2) Your dream is figurative of spirits ha ving been summoned to a place (angelic or demonic), by the dreamer. Their purpose (the spirits) will emerge slowly, if angelic, for help spiritually, or if demonic, for instigating chaos. If demonic, you are urged to renounce witchcraft, or you will reap the devastation that comes with embracing darkness. See suggested course of action. (3) Brewery: Your dream is figurative of something forming, being concocted, or developing that is dark, ominously, and threatening in nature, to all involve, includi ng the dreamer. If necessary, see suggested course of action.

Smoke Shop or Tobacco Factory: Your dream denotes false worship. Dreamer, you have rejected authentic worship of God, and now participate in a simulated worship of humanistic or superstitious ideas that are in direct conflict with the inspired written Word of God. You are rejecting Christianity's core system of beliefs and practices (also see John 3:16 -21; 1 Corinthians 10:1-23; Hebrews 12:14; Revelation 20:1-15). Because of your beliefs and practices, you are unable to overcome your present predicament, for your wisdom only leads to shadows and desolation. See suggested course of action.

In addition, the following are common words, expressions, usages, (e.g. slang or clichés), or a 'probable' that are metaphorically represented by drinking, drugs, or smoking:

- **Be off, or on, the wagon:** To dream of being on, or getting off a wagon: Denotes one who has resumed drinking alcoholic beverages after a period of abstinence, or one who has abstained from drinking any alcoholic beverages.
- **Bitter pill (to swallow):** To dream of swallowing a bitter pill, denotes something that is difficult or painful to accept.
- **Tobacco Road:** To dream of a road with such a name, denotes a shabby, poverty-stricken rural community or physical or spiritual condition.

- **Wine and Dine:** To dream of drinking fine wine at an expensive restaurant: This denotes enjoyment, to entertain someone lavishly, and/or to be treated, or to treat somebody, to an expensive meal out.

Suggested Course of Action

Question to consider and journal, did your dream depict any symbols that alludes to, the dreamer will make the necessary changes, spiritually, emotionally, and/or physically to affect a more positive outcome? If changes are initiated, your dreams will change.

Nevertheless, the following questions will help you determine; the issue at hand, how you feel about it, and what may have instigated it. What kind of drinking, drugging, or smoking was it? Were others involved? If yes, who and in what manner were they involved? Keep in mind that the others represent a quality of you, see Note 3 at the beginning of Actions and Activities category. Did anyone get hurt emotionally, physically, or was disturbed in any way? How did you feel, and what did you do, because, of your feelings, regarding the intoxication and/or where you ended up because? Was it curious, dangerous, depressive, funny, insignificant, joyful, life threatening, or happy? Did you or anyone need medical attention or was diagno sed with a medical condition? If so, what kind of medical attention was given (see Note 1 at the beginning of this category)? In view of your dream's context, namely drinking, drugging, or smoking, what choices are you making that may cause you to be unprepared for an encounter with the blessings and promises of God, or to experience His harshness because of waywardness? Your answers, coupled with the interpretation, plus any additional information, should begin to unfold the subject matter and issue at hand, if not now, mull over things a few days. For more information, see index or relevant category and subcategory for other particulars within your dream.

Now, pray (See Prayer of Deliverance, pg. 897)

Specific Meaning

If, you have a very real connection with any type of wine, alcoholic, fermented drinks, drugs, or cigarettes, e.g., any connection with substance abuse counseling, legal matters, medical doctor, AA, NA, in-patience, out-patience substance abuse, or recovery program, or with the Bureau of ATF. Is there a connection with the distillery, distribution, or sell of alcohol, drugs, or tobacco? Do you own a vineyard, winery, or wine tasting establishment, or are you a bartender? Dreams of this sort, for the most part, are ordinary dreams, resulting from your daily activities (see Chapter One, Chalom). These sorts of dreams are usually about your routine, mundane activities or anxieties that overwhelm your mind during the day. They are an inner release mechanism, which helps provide you with emotional balance and the maintaining of your sanity. These dreams are not significant, and do not warrant special attention.

Note: If any illegal activity was within your dream or if dreamer is involved in any illegal activity, this dream is a precautionary warning. There may be potential for an accident, homicide, or incarceration. Dreamer, re-consider your activities as harmful, hurtful, illegal, and/or life threatening, at present. Handle your business by surrendering, first to Jesus, and then to appropriate authorities. The details, kept within context of your dream, should be relevant to your life, and closely resemble your real-life situations. Meaning it can actually occur during your awaked state. This will help you narrow down the specifics needed to support and steer you clear of possible mishaps. If dreamer is ill, or is experiencing health related issues, seek medical attention immediately, your dream is a first step intervention and an alarm. However, if your dream symbols are not easily, linked to your life activities; then heed the spiritual implications (the interpretation).

FALLING INTO OR SINKING OR SLIDING DOWNWARD OR LOWERED DOWN OR MARCH DOWNWARD OR TAKEN DOWN FROM (Abyss, Altar, Basket, Cloth, Clouds, Ditch, Downstairs, Fabric, Fence, Heaven, Hell, Hill, Hole, Ladder, Mountain, Pit, Pulpit, Rope, Sky, Wall, Well, or an Unknown or strange place)

Some short descriptions of types, phrases, and other processes and particulars, connected in some way to this category are, f or example, to descend from, enter into, to go down, to lower down, or to be taken down off a high place.

Unless otherwise noted elsewhere, if, in your everyday living, your awaked state, as part of your lifestyle, work, or ministerial activities, or a special event, you have a very real connection with any type of descending or entering into activity. For example, cave exploration, diving, mining, underground maintenance, or some other type of descending activity, skip interpretation and go to Specific Meaning at the end of this category.

Otherwise noted, see Note 1 at the beginning of Actions and Activities category.

To determine who your dream is for you or another, see Note 3 at the beginning of Actions and Activities category.

Symbols and Referents: Dreams of descending generally deal with irresponsible behavior of some kind and the consequences of such actions.

Category Content - If not listed see index, perchance, for your specific type of descending dream activity.

- Abyss or Hell (fall, sink, or march, or descend downward)
- Altar, Fence, Mountain, Pulpit, or Wall (taken down off a high place)
- Ditch, Pit, Well, or Hole in the ground
- Heavens, Clouds, or Sky
- Hill or Downstairs (fall, sink, or march, or descend downward
- Ladder (going down one)
- Rope, Basket, Cloth, or Fabric (to b, lowered down by)
- Sink or Slide down (in an unknown or strange place)

Abyss or Hell (fall, sink, or march, or descend downward): This dream has three meanings (choose one). (1) You have stolen (allegedly borrowed with the intent of never returning) belongings from a trusting and innocent person. He or she is asking God, why have you lied to, and/or stole from, them. You also handle people, whom you judge as unimportant or insignificant, very haphazardly, imprudently, recklessly, and unwisely. You have judged them incorrectly, for all are precious in the Lord's sight. You have come in the spirit of the devil, to rob, steal, and destroy. Your attitude has led to a criminal mindset. Return all things to their rightful owners, with an appropriate apology and humbly make amends to those you've slighted. Subsequently your prayer and heartfelt repentance to Jesus will be received. To Jesus pray, Psalm 51, this can conceivably avert some of the repercussions of your choices. See suggested course of action. (2) Dreamer, you have settled for a voluptuary type philosophy and desire to propagate your beliefs. How can you say, "I have great desire, thus my physical enjoyment, luxury, and sensual gratifications are my primary concerns? This is a characterization of the ungodly or spiritually immature. Weigh: The child thinks that all that appears pleasant and tasty belongs to them and that he or she has the right to partake of any and everything. Consideration of others, and/or of the resulting outcome is unfamiliar to him or her. They will never consider the results of their behavior, nor how their behavior will affect others. This type of consideration is not w ithin a child's mind-set, because he or she is a child. As the immature child takes what they want, when they want it, and believes that it's theirs, and that they do have a right to whatever it is, so does the spiritually immature, do what they want, when they want, and believe that it's OK, using grace as a cover for sin. Unfortunately, spiritual change cannot begin with this kind of expectation and mind-set. Dreamer, I invite you to consider the following: Accepting Jesus Christ as your Savior, on His terms and not yours, and where there would be chaos emotionally and spiritually, genuine peace will abide. Moreover, believing and encouraging others to approach God the Father, without the essential provision He has provided for humankind, to approach Him properly; that provision being Jesus, is not safe. Some call God's provision, Wonderful Counselor, Mighty God, Everlasting Father, Prince of Peace, our atonement, advocate, liberator, propitiator, and our salvation. It is only through this channel that you may hope through faith to conciliate with your Creator (see Acts 2:37-42; 1 Timothy 2:4-7). Choose not to go out from the presence of the Lord, that is to, willingly renounce God, and to be content to forego the privileges He offers, that you might not be under His precepts, make things right. You will shortly, have to give an account of the fulfilling of your purpose for which you was design, as well as, of your philosophy and words. Dreamer, no authority, bravery, greatness, riches, or strength wil l be able to support you when your earth is shaken, when your time of divine discipline (the Lord's chastening, correction that leads to instruction and reformation) is approaching. Additionally, there are many bitter and poisonous consequences of sexual encounters without the commitment of holy matrimony. Flee sexual immorality; this principle is a hedge of protection, against STDs, HIV, and another four-letter word that can take you to your final resting place AIDS. Your behavior is irresponsible, and if not diligently avoided, will usher you into the path of darkness. See suggested course of action. (3) To you who have not promoted any kinds of indecent practices, sexual acts of perversions or other horrible traditions. Your dream was sent to demonstrate grace, via a warning of a dark generational issue, hereditary within your family line (e.g. maternal and/or paternal, grandparents, siblings, aunts, uncles, cousins). Dreamer, character traits from ancestors, namely genetic codes an d traits, will often trouble and taunt the offspring of a given progenitor, especially generational issues (Exodus 20:5-7). The demons that have so plague your family line, are now visiting (re-visiting) you. Your issue is demonically instigated and it is spiritually perverse, perhaps sexually perverse as well (e.g. adultery, fornication, homosexuality, or prostitution, whorishness). These spirits attempt to "bend" the personality, as early as possible with regards to age, towards a certain direction, oftentimes towards a way that is desolate and wicked, for it is Satan's scheme to kill and make desolate all; thus, to keep some from rising up and leading their generation to Christ (see the birth of Moses, Exodus 1:15-2:10). Favorably, generational curses and issues can stop with you (Jeremiah 31:29, 30; Ezekiel 18:2-14, 20-23). Thus, your Heavenly Father is requiring that you overcome and subdue negative and dark emotions, feelings, behaviors, and/or ideas that would influence you, before they overcome you. God is not asking you to do something you cannot do. For a surety, vanquishing of the coming influenc e can be done. By faith, you will need to declare some kind of fast and commit to it, for a long period-of-time, to abate the demonically instigated circumstance, you find yourself in now, Matthew 6:16-18. Try abstaining from food and drink (midnight to 6 PM), twice a week, and refrain from words, attitudes, people, places, and things, including music, magazines, videos, TV, or any such things that fuel anger and discontent, and stir up lustful feelings. This is also known as, faith with works, read, und erstand, and embrace James 2:14-26. Nonetheless, earnestly pray, God will guide, enable, and answer you as to the type of fast. Moreover, command all unclean spirits to leave you, and to go into an unclean thing or into outer darkness, in the name of Jesus, and renounce any generational curse (or morally objectionable behavior) that is affecting your life. Claiming the propitiatory sacrifice of Jesus on the cross, having been made a curse, Christ has made us free from curses (Galatians 3:13). Such provision has the just God made to fulfill the curse, which He pronounced on the earth, bearing the punishment, Himself, due to sin. H e died in our place, on our account, that He might bring us near, reconciling us to Himself. Additionally, if relevant, forgive your mother and/or father for the darkness (aka curse) they may have perpetuated, for they knew not what they done. Forgiveness is important to your success (Matthew 6:12-15, 8:21-35). See suggested course of action.

Altar, Fence, Mountain, Pulpit, or Wall (taken down off a high place): This dream has two meanings (choose one). (1) Your place of honor and respect, coupled with your pride has deceived you. You believe that you are untouchable. You are presently committing or have committed a grave violation against someone, namely a child of God. Did you not consider that God would take it as an offense to Him, if you offended one of His people? Your actions are/were utterly heartless. The provocation or violation will not be allowed, hidden, or covered. God will not allow it. You will lose honor and no longer will you be respected at the level you are accustomed. Moreover, publicly disgraced, you will become stressed to the point of becoming ill. Nonetheless, because of God's great mercies, you can be forgiven, pray Psalm 51; and, an apology in the form of a letter is a good place to start with the offended person. See suggested course of action. (2) An attitude of insubordina tion and waywardness has led to a more secular and worldly mind-set. The comfort, security, and over all ease afforded you by Christ, will now have to be worked for with difficulty. In addition, hidden secret sins will be exposed in a very public way. He humbles the high-minded that your paths might be made righteous. It is suggested that you concern yourself with the spiritual well-being of others. Listen, you will hear their cry, by this a more submissive and compassionate attitude towards God and others will begin to emerge. See suggested course of action.

Ditch, Pit, Well, or Hole in the ground: This dream has two meanings (choose one). (1) Ditch or Pit: He (or she) who has committed murder (spiritual or literal), though you flee, you shall be continually haunted with terrors, you will run int o a pit, betray yourself, and torment yourself. You will become a fugitive and a vagabond, and tremble continually (Proverbs 28:17). The Lord is calling your attention to, and wants you to, understand that not only the outward act of iniquity shall be dealt with accordingly by the Lord, but your injurious words towards others, and evil passions, will also meet their just recompense and reward. Dreamer, you will reap what you have sown very soon (see also Psalm 51:1-19). See suggested course of action. (2) Well or Hole in the ground or unknown or strange place: This dream was sent to open wide the eyes of, and disconcert, a secure and careless person (the dreamer) who proclaims peace to him or herself. With a calm resignation, you say you are godly and will inherit paradise, yet you have no genuine love for Christ Jesus, the Door into paradise (see John 5:39). Dreamer, the excuse of good intentions is often used to support bad actions. This mindset has become a cycle within your life, and you have abused this cycle of justification far too long. Your attitude has led to your criminal mindset. Dreamer is involved in, and guilty of, criminal activity. Dreamer you will experience some level of public exposure, for open shame shortly, or possible incarceration. Therefore, a quick and resolute change is vitally needed in the way you believe and behave. With that said if, no authentic change occurs, it is just of God to bring down those to poverty and restraint who have abused their life, liberty, and prosperity. Thus, you will be forced to endure a place of confinement. Although your place of confinement is the place God has appointed for you, for a time of change and preparation, in that desolate place, great sin c an be connived under the pretense of cheering up your spirits. In a place of confinement, people that dwell together, especially in solitary (separated from the general public) need to carefully watch and guard against the least of evil thoughts, lest Satan get an advantage. You must break your cycle of justification and change your mindset. The danger of not breaking your cycle will prove the breech or opening the enemy needs to instigate the worst and most unnatural sins you can do, and this will be a perpetual wound and dishonor to you, especially publicly. This great sin will defile, dishonor, profane, and pollute you. Justifying yourself to be weak; or whatever your pretense is, one thing is for sure, your scheme is very wicked and vile, and an affront to the very Light and Law of God. It is an abomination. Subsequently, you will become sick and/or diseased, a physical rottenness in your flesh. You are counseled to stop being careless, for this principle is a hedge of protection against addictions, STDs, HIV, and other diseases that can take you to your final resting place. Dreamer, right now God is giving you understanding. Now, you have been granted wisdom, and you are in line to reap the rewards of both, freedom and the fullness of life. You can have perfect deliverance, via faith in Jesus Christ. This suggests that if you stand humble before God, you will stand upright in the final day. Humble yourself in the sight of the Lord, and He will lift you up (James 4:10 NKJV). The context of your dream will suggest if you are willing to rectify your ways to ward off the coming tragedy (sickness and disease). Pray Psalm 38:1-22. For example, did you come out of the abyss, ditch, hole, opening in the ground, pit? If yes, you are willing to overcome your issues. If no, your chance to make the correct decision to go on with God is available to you right now (see John 11:44). He will miraculously strengthen you, for you are also a prophet or prophetess. However, the decision to allow the wisdom of God to direct your life will not be forced upon you. You must choose. It is suggested that if urged by God, declare a one, two, or three day fast without food for purification purposes; wash and make yourself clean. During the fast, diligently get an understanding of, and embrace, the doctrine of grace and of Jesus Christ. Refrain from wickedness, physically, sexually, emotionally, and/or spiritually. Afterwards, go before Jesus petitioning for help. You will begin to see, significantly, th e unseen hand of God. Start treating your relationship with God and all the freedoms He has allowed you with respect. By this, God will pardon your transgressions. This is called leaving a blessing behind. To be blessed: Gifts of God's grace, anything God fr eely gives you, absolution, the Holy Spirit, salvation, regeneration, eternal life, health, children, love of family, longevity, necessities, prosperity, and dominion over all that is yours; and all are parts of the supply of grace, and all are sanctified by the Lord, and technically belongs to Him. The result of this supply in your life will be peace. See suggested course of action.

Heavens, Clouds, or Sky (fall, sink, or march, or descend downward, from above the sky): This dream has two meanings (choose one). (1) Dreamer, you have insulted one of God's servants. Consider who it is you've insulted. Were you not afraid to speak against God's servant? How dare you abuse any servant of God, especially one who has been a friend, and a confidant to you, and an excellent steward of the House of God? Did you not expect that God would resent it, and take it as an affront to Himself personally? Your dream is to warn you. You take great risk, when you have no fear of saying or doing anything against the servants of the Lord; you put yourself in harm's way, for Jesus will plead their cause, and consider those who touch them as touching Him likewise. It is a dangerous thing to offend Christ's servants. You show yourself presumptuous, when you do not fear to speak evil of the Lord or His servants. Your character is one of extreme haughtiness, presumptuousness, pride, and self-assuredness in the very negative sense of the word. All are signs that your heart is hardened. If this disposition is not let go, it will lead to a great fall (Proverbs 11:2; 16:18, 19; 29:23). Even now, the harshness of the Lord is kindled against you; thus, you will begin to experience a change in your anointing, authority, and favor given from the Lord. Moreover, as He knows your thoughts afar off, repent, and ask Jesus for wisdom, and for the courage to apply it. Other than heartfelt repentance to Jesus, no other excuse or weak justification will be heard. Repentance is seeking pardon and expressing sincere feelings of regret and brokenness for having done something awry and/or for having hurt someone, see 2 Corinthians 7:10, 11. To individuals, a phone call or a letter of apology is a good place to start. To Jesus pray, Psalm 51, this followed by appropriate application of wisdom, can conceivably avert some of the repercussions of your choices. This is what is called leaving a blessing behind. See suggested course of action. (2) Your dream is a critical alarm. Due to hatred an d an unforgiving spirit, deep within the heart of the dreamer, so as to hide it from yourself, a severing of your personal relationship with Christ is probable (see Matthew 6:14, 15). Consequently, you have slowly abandoned all or some of the original foundational teachings of Christ and His apostles, especially the doctrine of grace (the free and u nmerited favor and beneficence of God). This has resulted in a corrupt doctrine and perverse bondage (1 Timothy 4:1-16). You have ceased to abide in Christ, and instead have become enslaved again to sin and immorality, trusting in your own righteousness. Evil and depravity is your guiding force, thus sin has separated you from God. Dreamer, the beginning, development, arrival, or manifestation of something large (significant in scope, extent, or effect) is about to happen within your life, in a threaten ing way. Favorably, the One True Living God can change things. However, this may be your last alarm or warning regarding this issue. Dreamer, declare a three day fast without food or water, coupled with studying the teachings of Jesus Christ and His disciples, and God's relation to it. You will experience God's truth again, and see the demonic for what it is - a lie. Renounce corrupt teachings and accept all of God's truth and ways, including grace, and His truths you do not prefer. See suggested course of action.

Hill or Downstairs (fall, sink, or march, or descend downward): This dream has two meanings (choose one). (1) Downhill: Your place of honor and respect, coupled with your pride has deceived you. You believe that you are untouchable. You are presently committing or have committed a grave violation against someone, namely a child of God. Did you not consider that God would take it as an offense to Him, if you offended one of His people? Your actions are/were utterly heartless. The provocation or violation will not be allowed, hidden, or covered. God will not allow it. You will lose honor and no longer will you be respected at the level you are accustomed. Moreover, publicly disgraced, you will become stressed to the point of becoming ill. Nonetheless, because of God's great mercies, you can be forgiven, pray Psalm 51; and, an apology in the form of a letter is a good place to start with the offended person. See suggested course of action. (2) Downstairs: God is sending you to a place you do not want to go, and to a people you are not fond of, for they are a rebellious people. You have taken a sabbatical because you do not want to go where God is sending you. Your rest will be unpleasantly interrupted. The sooner you do your job, the sooner you will be able to leave. Someone is assigned to you, in that place, to help you in your endeavor. You will be fond of this person.

Ladder (going down one): Beginnings and endings, diversity, and growth, are constant elements in your life. Albeit, you are able to let go of anything or anyone in order to further your growth. Because of this ability, coupled with your knack f or persuading and, by persuading, to convince others to act or to identify with given values, you are gifted to become a remarkable religious teacher and writer. Uncover, practice, and become skilled in the talents you were born with, lest you b e found fruitless in the Kingdom of God, and be cast aside or replaced. Neither of which is profitable for you. See suggested course of action.

Rope, Basket, Cloth, or Fabric (to b, lowered down by): This dream has three meanings (choose one). (1) In a basket: Your difficult state of affairs, at present, is a result of your own malicious plots against innocent persons. You are reaping what you have sown. Although your way may seem hard, you are more than able to endure the repercussions of this universal law, go to a quiet place, re-think your ideology, and align it with faithful biblical values and love. This study may take up to three years. Invest the time. You are a chosen one, and will do great works for the Kingdom of God. (2) By cloth, fabric: Your present difficult state of affairs is a result of your own conceit; handling people indiscriminately and unwisely. Practice the golden rule, the rule of conduct that advises people to treat others in the same manner as they wish to be treated themselves. See suggested course of action. (3) By rope: Low self-esteem and feelings of insignificance has caused you to act very corruptly. Your present difficult state of affairs bears witness of this. Not caring about your physical and spiritual well -being, coupled with your suggestive behavior will always leave you humiliated and in bondage. You will be held accountable for all your actions, before God and man. Go to a quiet place and study your bible. Go to church and forsake not the gathering of yourself together with other mainstream Christians. Avoid persons, places, or things that do not promote moral living or self- esteem. You personally, must learn to choose the good over the bad. See suggested course of action.

Sink or Slide down (in an unknown or strange place): This dream has two meanings (choose one). (1) You have neglected to carry out a charge given you by the Lord. Consequently, someone else is performing it for you at present, accordingly he or she will receive the wage that is connected to the charge. Favorably, because of them, God will let you ge t by with that particular. For He, is dealing with you according to His grace (the free and unmerited favor and beneficence of God). However, you are still required to fulfill your mission. He chose you; and has covered you with His protection. On another note, you will be rejected by some and shown disapproval by others, you will never be alone. Dreamer cast your burdens upon the Lord for He genuinely cares for you. See suggested course of action. (2) Slide down: Your dream implies covetousness. Just know, by paying the same price as another, you can have the same thing too. If you're not willing to pay the costs, desire those things, you are willing to pay for. See suggested course of action.

Suggested Course of Action

Question to consider and journal, did your dream depict any symbols that alludes to, the dreamer will make the necessary changes, spiritually, emotionally, and/or physically to affect a more positive outcome? If changes are initiated, your dreams will change.

Consider and journal the following questions. The questions will help you determine; the issue at hand, how you feel about it, and what may have instigated it. What kind of descending was it? Were others involved? If yes, who and in what manner were they involved? Keep in mind that the others represent a quality of you, see Note 3 at the beginning of Actions and Activities category. Did anyone get hurt emotionally, physically, or was disturbed in any way? How did you feel, and wh at did you do, because, of your feelings, regarding the descending and/or where you ended up? Was it agitating, confusing, dangerous, disturbing, frustrating, peace with the situation, happy, joyful, life threatening, safe, scary, or unsure? Where were you? Was the place unfamiliar to you? Were you coherent? In view of your dream's context, namely descending, what choices are you making that may impair your spiritual growth, judgment, health, or that will encourage serious immorality? Your answers, coupled with the interpretation, plus any additional information, should begin to unfold the subject matter and issue at hand, if not now, mull over things a few days. For more information, see index or relevant category and subcategory for other particulars within your dream. Whatever predicament you find yourself in, allow God to ma ke your steps correct. Cry aloud, "O Lord, you are my God. I will exalt you and praise your name, for in perfect faithfulness you have done these things". Crying does help ease the pain and repentance restores.

Now, pray (See Prayer of Deliverance, pg. 897)

Specific Meaning

Another suggestion, ask yourself, "What did I experience the day or evening before the dream?" Consider your emotions and thoughts the day or evening before the dream. If you had or have concerns regarding the safety of your j ob or leisure activities, this dream could simply reflect your fears. Precaution is still suggested.

Note: If, there's a very high chance for you descending or entering into some place, for example, caves, diving, mining, underground maintenance, or some other type of descending activity, a dream of this sort should be received as a precautionary warning, to prevent serious harm to yourself and/or others, due to a mishap. The mishap, kept within context of the dream, should be relevant to your life, and closely resemble your real-life situations. Meaning it can actually occur during your awaked state. This will help you narrow down the specifics of the mishap, and possibly prevent a mayday type of situation.

FIGHTING, KILLING, STRUGGLING, VIOLENCE, CONFLICT, CONTESTATION, DISPUTE, OR ACCUSATIONS: To make vigorous efforts to oppose, resist, or overcome something or somebody, or the act of causing the death of a human being or an animal.

Some short descriptions of types, phrases, and other processes and particulars, connected in some way to this category are, for example, accusations, arguing, assassination, attack, battle, boxing, brawl, butchery, clash, exchange blows, execute, homici de, murder, scrap, slay, struggle, to take life, war, wrestling.

Unless otherwise noted elsewhere, if, in your everyday living, your awaked state, as part of your lifestyle, work, or ministerial activities, or a special event, you have a very real connection with any type of fighting, killing, struggling, or violence activity. For example, advocacy, attorney, boxing, chaplain services, death row, hired assassin, homicide detective, judicial system, law enforcement, murderer, private eye, protestor, soldier, suicide, victim, vigilante, warfare, wrestling, (also see content list for this category), skip interpretation and go to Specific Meaning at the end of this category, unless otherwise noted.

Otherwise noted, this dream of fighting, killing, struggling, violence, conflict, contestation, dispute, or accusations may be an Oneirovatic "OV" dream, or an Oneirovaticicritica "OVC" dream, (see Chapter One: The 60th Part of Prophecy, The Elevated Parts of Sleep). One may plainly see homicides, larceny, or other assaults taking place in their neighborhood or town before or after they happen, and soon thereafter, notice the violation reported in the news. On some level, this type of dream will affect the dreamer's life, requiring action on the part of the seer. Most people, who experience "OV" or "OVC" dreams, are usually found consulting and/or supporting local police crime units. This type of dream should closely resemble real life situations, with the dream events actually being capable of happening.

Otherwise noted, this dream of fighting, killing, struggling, violence, conflict, contestation, dispute, or accusations, may be a Prophetically Simple Dream (see Chapter One: The 60th Part of Prophecy). Whereas, the dreamer is being warned not to accuse, fight, struggle, or initiate violence, and/or to surrender to the appropriate authorities, especially if this is an issue within the dreamer's life at present. For example, the dreamer is actually involved, engaged in some kind of accusations, fight, homicide, struggle, or violence, be it argument, gang related, hate group, illegal activity, legal debate, sports, or war. Thus, this dream is a first step intervention and an alarm. Dreamer, Jesus will strengthen you emotionally, psychologically, and physically to go get help for your issues. Skip interpretation and perhaps contact the police with the truth, or go get help via an attorney, Christian counseling, a Christian based support group, and prayer, or fasting. Also, see Specific Meaning at the end of this category, section entitled, Note (Specific Meaning).

Otherwise noted, see Note 1 at the beginning of Actions and Activities category.

To determine who your dream is for you or another, consider one of the following (relevant interpretation) first, as well as, see Note 3 at the beginning of Actions and Activities category.

Symbols and Referents: Most dreams of this sort are grave warnings to the dreamer. For, dreams of violence generally imply, coupled with one of the following interpretations, some kind of spiritual or emotional conflict, the taking up again o f internal turmoil because of anger, deeds of the flesh, and/ or the imminent termination of your spiritual life (and possibly temporal life). The righteousness of one turning to wickedness will no longer be remembered. Your righteousness will be reckoned as the superficial righteousness of an unregenerate person (see Ezekiel 33:12-20). Take great care and heed God's warnings. We are called to exhibit faith by steadfast obedience, determination, confidence, fortitude, thanks, and love. Th e genuineness of your faith is judged by your response to hardships and opposition engendered by your identification with Christ, and by your inner temptations to sin. We must exhibit courage under trials, and not take lightly God's disciplinary instructions.

Category Content - If not listed see index, perchance, for your specific type of fighting, killing, struggling, violence, conflict, contestation, or dispute dream activity.

- Break-up or stop words or blows from being exchanged any further, see category, Abating (to put an end to something, terminate)
- Grow tired or lose strength while fighting, struggling, disputing, see category, Abating (To decrease in degree, force, intensity, or grow tired)
- Held, kept back, or prevented from fighting, struggling, violence, conflict, contestation, or dispute (no words or blows were exchanged), see category, Abating (to be held or kept back)
- Slap someone, see category, Clapping (Slap a person)
- If someone else instigated or provoked, in any way, the fighting, killing, struggling, violence, conflict, contestation, dispute, or accusations - no matter if a defense was put up or if dreamer witnessed any kind of violence
- Argument, Contestation, Dispute (badgering, confrontation, conflict, threats, or any encounter with words)

- Assassination (the killing of a political leader or other public figure by a sudden violent attack, especially gunfire, shooting)
- Attack (battering, beat-up, fighting, physical attack)
- Boxing or Fighting Match, Knocked-out, or Punched (contest, competition, "extreme-fighting", come to blows, spar, or punch)
- Execution (Death Sentence, Facing a Firing Squad, a putting to death)
- Fighting, Dispute, Struggling with
   - God, Jesus, Spirit Beings or Animal; Angel; Demon or Dark spirit, The Dead; Animal
- Genocide, Mass Murder, Massacre, or Slaughter
- Guilty or Not Guilty of Fighting, Killing, Struggling, Violence, Conflict, Contestation, Dispute, or Accusations (e.g. declared guilty or not guilty in a court of justice)
- Homicide (attempted homicide, accidental or premeditated killing, murder, or pulling a gun on someone, shooting someone)
- Sadism or Abuse (e.g. brutality, cruelty, sadism, spit on you or in your face; or any manner of abuse, viciousness, or violence)
   - Your father and/or mother spit on you or in your face, or vice versa ; If a sick or elderly person (or someone unknown), spits on you or in your face, or vice versa
- Slay (to strike or beat with an object to cause death, strike a fatal blow)
- Stab, Wound, or Nick (with a sharp instrument, e.g. knife, or sharp pick, stabbed)
- War (to do battle, combat, campaign, crusade, warfare)
- Wrestle, Wrestling Match (to fight back, kick, move violently, resist, struggle, tussle, contest, competition in wrestling)
- Weaponry (any weapon or armament, or any device used with intent to inflict damage or harm to living beings, structures, or system, legal or illegal)
- Whipping, Walloping, Thrashing, Licking, or Corporal Punishment (the act of inflicting punishment as a form of discipline)

If someone else instigated or provoked, in any way, the fighting, killing, struggling, violence, conflict, contestation, dispute, or accusations - no matter if a defense was put up or if dreamer witnessed any kind of violence: This dream has two meanings (choose one). (1) If dreamer witnessed any kind of violence or if dreamer gave no defense in any way, did not return word for word, like for like, did not make a counterattack, did not strike back, did not retaliate, or respond to their aggressor(s), was held back due to someone restraining you, or no matter the reason. Your dream comes to forewarn you of those who would dare come against you, to contend with you, and it comes to caution you that their behavior will, or has, caused a spirit of animosity or fear within you, to the same degree of your reaction to their actions within your dream. You need (or will need) restoration from this offense. Regrettably, you are mistreated by some, dodged, and victimized by others. Although not a majority, a few are so great, you are considered as one with a psychiatric disorder, and your inspirations, to those few, are considered the words of a fool. They are the antagonist in your present-day life's story. Your abusers or accusers, those within your dream or who or what they represent to you personally, for exa mple, authority figures, helpers, favorites, fighters, leaders, liars, mentors, ministers, pastors, rebels, sage, shyster, teacher, unwise, or vengeful, violator. Although, they suppose they're doing God's will by coming against you (and they will come against you, if not already), they don't know His will, with regards as to why they are coming against you, but for you, dreamer, consider the following. (Matthew Henry's Commentary): Our Lord Jesus by giving us notice of trouble, is designed to take off the terror of it, that it might not be a surprise to us. Of all the adversaries of our peace, in this world of troubles, none insult us more violently, nor put our troops more into disorder, than disappointment does; but we can easily welcome a guest we expect, and being fore- warned are fore-armed, Praemoniti, praemuniti. How do you feel knowing that some feel this way about you? Are you offended? Are there feelings of weariness, discouragement, embarrassment, hostility, rage, resentment, and/or revenge? You may feel a bit discombobulated, or perhaps you may shrug your shoulders as to say, "it's neither here or there", then again, you may feel a need to dissimulate. Unfortunately, their feelings or thoughts will be directly expressed to you; therefore, being warned beforehand, is meant to take some of the sting out of their words. For you, dreamer, take the "fight" out of your feelings, as well as any other negativity within you. Visualize yourself presenting the negativity to the feet of God as an enemy of His Kingdom (Psalm 110:1, Matthew 22:44), as an enemy of your spiritual work, and of your purpose, via prayer. Dreamer, you have divine protection, you have no need to fight, only worship before the Lord (see 2 Chronicles 20:15, 17-19). This is what the Lord says: "Yes, I will contend with those who contend with you" (Isaiah 49:25, 2 Chronicles 20:17, Matthew 5:39). If applicable; additionally, your children will be saved. Rest from defending yourself against the demons that want to defeat you, and rest assured God is and will be a defense for you, see Psalm 91. Dreamer, you have in Christ, grace and healing, refreshment, and a refuge. Don't forfeit these graces. Embrace the help your Heavenly Father is offering you, via a sabbati cal, and the effects of their negativity will no longer hold sway over your heart. Additionally, to help determine the characteristics of the person(s) who would come against, see one of the relevant subcategories within this category. (2) If dreamer retaliated in any way, e.g. returned word for word, like for like, made a counterattack, struck back, or called for help. The dreamer is fighting or struggling against, perhaps violently, something within you (e.g. anger, fear, loneliness, negative thinking, self-sabotage, vanity, worry, or insecurity about what others think of you). You are the antagonist in your own life's story. Dreamer, be confident and rest assured, you have in Christ, grace (the free and unmerited favor and beneficence of God), healing, refreshment, and a refuge. Don't forfeit these graces by condemning yourself (see Romans 8:1, 5-39). There is a difference between conviction and condemnation. Dreamer, think on these things (see Romans 7:7-8:17; 2 Corinthians 12:7-10; Philippians 1:6; 4:8). Moreover, be warned, if you begin embracing self-condemnation, unable to forgive yourself, or accept Jesus forgiveness of your sins, you will open the door for the enemy to come in to "rob, steal, and destroy". See suggested course of action.

Argument, Contestation, Dispute (badgering, confrontation, conflict, threats, or any encounter with words): Your dream was sent to demonstrate grace, via a warning. It denotes God's displeasure at the dreamer's rebellion and disobedience. You say, "How can this be?" Dreamer, you grumble inside yourself and say, "The Lord hates me". You say, "God has brought me to this place, into the hands of 'lovers of themselves only', fools, those who I hate. God has brought ruin unto me. Where can I go, I'm beginning to lose heart" (also see Isaiah 40:27-31). Dreamer, considering anyone a fool is spiteful and this stems from hatred deep within you. You have become angry, judgmental, and unforgiving (e.g. condemnatory, critical, derogatory, disapproving, harsh, negative, scornful, or uncomplimentary in your thoughts or speaking aloud). You are (or is becoming) disrespectful, ill-mannered, impolite, insolent, mouthy, rude, presumptuous, and sassy, possibly towards the person(s) you were angry with within your dream or what they represent to you personally (e.g. authority figures, helpers, favorites, fighters, leaders, liars, mentors, ministers, pastors, rebels, sage, shyster, teacher, unwise, vengeful, or violators). Anyone who is angry with another, seeking their hurt, with desires leading to no good conclusion, without just, reasonable, and appropriate cause, or if you are angry due to your intolerance of differences and lack of understanding, hate group mentality, your anger is then sinful, and is subject to judgment (divine reprimand for folly and sin, Matthew 5:22). Question to journal, what was the intensity of your anger, and who or what was your anger directed. This is who or what you are judging unforgivingly. Consequently, you are in danger of being judged likewise by God, and with the same intensity expressed within your dream. If no change, you will find yourself in the middle of a heated crisis that will hurt you deeply, because of your anger and judgmental attitude. Fortunately, as your dream is only a warning of impending crisis, trouble maybe averted if you carefully persevere in Christian love and peace. Make every effort to live in peace with all men and women and to be holy; without holiness no one will see the Lord (Hebrew 12:14). If at any time a violation happens, strive for reconciliation, as much as is possible, making restitution or offering some kind of satisfaction for wrong done in word or deed. "When they go low, you go high" -Michelle Obama. Humble yourself to God, to yourself, and to others and acknowledge your faults, weaknesses, and/or offenses. Moreover, resolve things quickly, until then, the carrying out of your ministerial obligations are not acceptable, for they are performed with envy, malice, wrath, and un-charity, in your heart; thus, performed with an unclean heart and incorrect spirit. Moreover, you are lacking in genuine intimacy and fellowship with God in the spirit of holiness. There is nothing you can do, outside of reconciliation, that will please God when these sins are dominant within your heart (Matthew 5:23, 24). Moreover, you are not, asked to do something you cannot do at this time. If necessary, see suggested course of action.

Assassination (the killing of a political leader or other public figure by a sudden violent attack, especially gunfire, shooting): Secretly you yearn (or have attempted) to coldheartedly destroy a particular individual's reputation without cause before whom you will now begin to implode. You have misled people (Christians, community leaders, judicial authorities, and/or others) about this individual's character flaws, via deliberate exaggerations, lies. You are being watched, as well, you have not fooled God. You will be found out and appropriate actions will be taken. Your community, be it your family, friends, co-workers, or some faith based community you're involved with, will expose you. Your life will implode and you will be unable to recover on your own; that is without the guidance of the Paraclete. On another vein, your plans will literally make a clear-cut path for that individual to succeed, and indeed, they will succeed. S/he has divine favor and protection. On your part, you will be exposed. Your dangerous and negative thoughts and actions toward this particular individual need to end now; your thoughts are of your own imagination and bitterness, due to personal hurts and an unforgiving spirit. Favorably, even in this, there is nothing too hard for God. Grace (the free and unmerited favor and beneficence of God) is extended that you may change your heart and mind. Unless you end this, there can be no forgiveness of your sins, only judgment (divine reprimand for folly and sin). See Matthew 6:12, 8:21-35. Don't know who this person is? Kept within context of your dream, it is the person being assassinated, or who and what that person may represent to you. For example, a presidential assassinatio n may represent your supervisor or any type of top leadership. This may also be one, who has been appointed to take charge of meetings or formal gatherings. Somebody who holds the top official position in a company, club, organization, or society; a man or woman who is a member of the church's governing board, a pastor, a first lady, elder, minister, teacher, or deacon; the head of an educational or governmental establishment, or the head of state.

Attack (battering, beat-up, fighting, physical attack, hurtful or criminal intentions): Moreover, see Wrestle, if wrestling was involve in some way. This dream has three meanings (choose one). (1) Physically attacked: Your dream denotes that your perspective on the nature of God is in the process of change and you will begin to experience a paradigm shift; subsequently, your life and/or ministry will be as though you have run amok, this will cause you to view God differently. Not as a God of curses and blessings, but as a righteous and just God who is full of mercy and grace (the free and unmerited favor and beneficence of God). Too, never again ponder over your increase, peace, and other favorable conditions within your life, without first acknowledging God as the true benefactor. Even more, do not exalt any personality or allow charm to override wisdom or your better judgment. If necessary, see suggested course of action. (2) Dreamer overcomes your attacker: Your dream marks a transition within the dreamer's life. Your life's circumstances will begin to change; state of affairs will spiritually, and materially, be in favor of the dreamer. At present, because of your struggles against sin and the challenges endured to live righteously, you have little strength. However, your spiritual resolve is strong; you are resilient. This i s a good thing, for much is required to whom much is given. God is your champion and favors your cause. He understands you and is on your side to do you good. You have the power of heaven at your disposal. Have faith in God (a resolute trust in the integrity of God and in His Word). (3) Dreamer is the attacker: Your dream is an admonishment to the dreamer. God's providential blessing (the wisdom, care, and guidance provided by God) is upon you to increase. However, because of your struggles against sin and the challenges endured to live righteously you stopped looking to God and started lookin g at others; taking into account rich persons and how their wealth may benefit you, or how others may have hurt you. Unfortunate ly, bitterness is beginning to take root and hurtful intentions towards others will be the fruit. At this point, you do not kn ow the way of peace. See suggested course of action.

Boxing or Fighting Match, Knocked-out, or Punched (contest, competition, "extreme-fighting", come to blows, spar, or punch): This dream has four meanings (choose one). (1) Boxing Match or Sparring (contest, competition): The dreamer is in a grounding stage of your spiritual walk. You are being prepared to reach your personal level of proficiency in ministry, thus you are, advised to discipline your body, and your sensual desires and to bring them under control. Temperance in all things is your key word. Adopt a determined resolve: a made up mind, steadfastness, doggedness, tenacity. Go no further with an attitude of uncertainty about God, His Word, and Christianity. This way of behaving causes one to become ineffective. Rather, become intense and convicted when it comes to defending your beliefs. As well, steel your emotions and thoughts against all that wi ll come against your God, and against all demonic abuse. If necessary, see suggested course of action. (2) "Extreme-Fighting", if dreamer was fighting another, dreamer there are those who called themselves Christian but they are not. One or two have deceitfully charmed their way into your life. They have come to destroy the liberty you have in Christ Jesus that you might be brought into bondage causing you to trust in oppression. Do not listen to them, not even for one hour that the truth of the gospel might continue with you. Your charge is to strive in defense of the faith, which is in Jesus Christ, against all objections, and to expose the lies that are set up to bring other Christians into bondage. Always base your defense of Christianity on t he Holy Record, historical evidence, philosophical arguments, scientific investigation, rhetorical persuasion and other disciplines. For it is written, carefully study to present yourself approved unto God, a workman that need not be ashamed, rightly handlin g the word of truth (2 Timothy 2:15). In another place, Christians must always be prepared to make a defense to anyone who asks you for a reason for the hope that is in you, with gentleness and respect (1 Peter 3:15). (3) Knocked-out, if dreamer was knocked down, your dream implies that alleged difficulties or hindrances to your spiritual growth; and limits on your freewheeling; have given rise to frustration, resentfulness, and bitterness within you. You have become intolerant of God's principles; demeaning those things you do not understand, or consider too challenging; thereby, imposing stress on your relationship with the Lord, as well as with others. Because of your attitude, you are being ostracized. See suggested course of action. (4) Punched (a blow with the fist): This choice has three parts (choose one). (a) If dreamer received the blow, dreamer will be accused or condemned openly and/or formally because of the cries of your victims. You will experience a stat e of extreme dishonor, and incur an evil public reputation. You will be classified or describe as disgraceful. (b) If dreamer gave the blow, God will use you to expose someone who is dishonorably, of ill repute because of the cries of his or her victims. (c) Punch (and punch had no power behind it): If dreamer gave a blow with no power behind it or received a blow with no power behind it, although you are under extreme pressure, there is a way of release for you, if you would but adhere to wise counse l. Firstly, acknowledge that pressure is a mark of good service. Second, acknowledge that you are under great pressu re, and is without strength now. Dreamer, to be without strength during a life season is ok. Third, drop the "god" complex, and stop, if I may use a cliché, "trying to be everything to everybody", and just say no, to any extra work, or extra anything tha t would add to an already high-pressured situation that really needs to be released. What cannot or will not be worked out via prayer or counsel, lay it all at God's throne, along with the people who are attached to "it", whatever "it" is and leave it there. Next, take a sabbatical, for even God rested after creating (making things happen). For, you are now entering into (or you are already experiencing) a sabbatical, and it's your due time. Your heavenly Father is protecting you by allowing you to rest from your work; in order to avoid overly cruel and oppressive pressure from the enemy, via those he uses. They that have vexed you wil l now go far from you, for God will make you a threat to them without any effort on your part. During this sabbatical, peace will again hold sway over your life. Moreover, Jehovah Jireh will provide for all your needs. Put your trust in Him and His prov ision, coupled with contentment with His provisions, and your peace will overflow. You may have to downsize during this sabbatical;

this will affect humility, which is, needed now also. Notwithstanding, go and refresh yourself mentally, physically, and spiritually. If necessary, see suggested course of action

Execution (Death Sentence, Facing a Firing Squad, a putting to death): Whether the dreamer or another is executed or committing or participating in an execution, the dreamer's anger against a relative, Christians, Jesus, or God, is without cause. In your dream, the depiction of a family member will represent a relative; thus, the dreamer's anger is against a relative. If someone else is portrayed, this will represent Christians; thus, the dreamer's anger is against Christians, if Jesus or God is portrayed, this will represent Jesus or God; thus, the dreamer's anger is against Jesus or God. The dreamer has spiritually crushed or killed someone, either by self or proxy. The prayers of those affected by your anger testify against you. Guilt has been determined and consequences ordained by God, within the spiritual realm. Accordingly, you will be dealt with as a spiritual murderer. Spiritual life will be cut short. Your righteousness will be reckoned as the superficial righteousness of an unregenerate person (see Ezekiel 33:12-20). Favorably, even in this, there is nothing too hard for God; grace is extended that you may change your heart. You must personally respond, repent, and genuinely commit to some type of righteous change to have life, with primary emphasis on life after this present life. See suggested course of action.

Fighting, Dispute, Struggling with God, Jesus, angel, demon, dark spirit, the dead, or animal: See one of the following: God: While in defiance against God and the teachings of Christ, you exalt your wisdom above the Creator. A bold and daring seducer, you mouth empty, boastful words; discrediting the Creator's wise and sensible guidelines for living life, on this side of eternity, as humanly and sanely as possible; and in harmony with His provision for life on the other side of eter nity, in heaven. You have become contrary to God's righteous precepts, for darkness has blinded you to truth. Your dream was sent as a message of grace, and to encourage the dreamer to choose not to go out from the presence of the Lord, that is, to willingly renounce God, and to be content to forego the privileges He offers, that you might not be under His precepts; make things right, check yourself. Pray for divine truth, for one should never exalt their thoughts, ideas, feelings, above God's truth, for, every house is built by someone, but the builder of all things is God" (Hebrews 3:2-4). See suggested course of action.

Jesus: Your secret hatred of believers in Christ is becoming more apparent, to the point of a hate group mentality. You have now taken it upon yourself to pass judgment upon all who believe in the name of Jesus, His Power, His glory, His Kingdom, and His word. A prestigious elder will rise to counsel you, to wait and see, before boldly and openly condemning believers; thus, exposing your hatred of the Lord and Savior. Listen to him, receiving and abiding by his advice, lest you find yourself on the wrong side of God. Pray for divine truth, for one should never exalt their thoughts, ideas, feelings, above God's truth, for, every house is built by someone, but the builder of all things is God (Hebrews 3:2-4). If urged by God, declare a one, two, or three day fast without food for sanctification purposes, during which, diligently get an understanding of, and embrace, the doctrine of grace (the free and unmerited favor and beneficence of God) and who is Jesus Christ. Afterwards, go before Jesus petitioning Him for forgiveness and help. You will begin to see, significantly, the unseen Hand of God. See suggested course of action.

Spirit Beings or Animal: Read, understand, and embrace, Ephesians 6:10-18, for this is to you now. Also, see one of the following.

Angel: Your dream is a sign of God's efforts to reconcile you unto Him; thus, it is one of grace (the free and unmerited favor and beneficence of God). He has sent His servants to you with His gospel of love, and you've rejected that. Other servants have come with a message of reaping hell, and you've rejected that. Dreamer, will you not repent and receive His gi ft of eternal life, while grace is here? Dreamer, the issue of eternal life will not be forced upon anyone. Favorably, even in this, there is nothing too hard for God; grace is still available that you may change your heart. You must personally respond, by repenting and genuinely committing to some type of righteous change, to have life; with primary emphasis on life after this present life (see Acts 2:37-42). If necessary, see suggested course of action.

163

Demon or Dark spirit: You are fighting or struggling against the carnal side of your nature; thus, you're engaged in some type of spiritual warfare. Questions to journal, how did the fight, struggle start and/or end? Did you walk away unscathed or slightly beaten? Were you badly beaten and defeated? Did you run away and/or hide? Did you just wake up, possibly out of fear? Your answers will expose your level of preparation for spiritual warfare, internally, and your passion for holiness. Considering your answers, are you prepared for spiritual warfare? See also: Hebrew 12:3-13, James 1:2-18. See suggested course of action.

The Dead: There is a sense of urgency attached with this message. Dreamer, there is a conflict between grace and corruption of the heart, going on within you. You must contend for the faith, which is in Jesus Christ, which has been, entrusted to you. Dreamer, embracing legalism (the belief that good deeds, via the law, are required for entrance into Heaven), is to fight and struggle with a dead person. See Romans 7:7-8:17, Galatians 5:1-6:10. Self-righteous, you reject the doctrine of grace (the free and unmerited favor and beneficence of God), thus you've chosen to be under the law. Your spirituality is one of outward show and hypocrisy. You love to give alms, pray, and appear righteous publicly, but inwardly you are lifeless, and lawlessness prevails. Your lack of love towards others has contributed to your lack of, understanding, receiving, and giving genuine grace. Questions to journal, how did the fight or struggle start and/or end? Did you walk away unscathed or slightly beaten? Were you badly beaten and/or defeated? Did you run away and/or hide? Did you just wake up, possibly out of fear? Your answers will expose your level of preparation for spiritual warfare and you r passion for holiness, via the righteousness of Christ only. Considering your answers, are you prepared for internal spiritual warfare? Are you ready to embrace grace, leaving the dead works of legalism behind you? See suggested course of action.

Animal: Animals, within our dreams, for the most part, are anthropomorphize or given human characteristics or personality traits, behavioral patterns, basic nature, and endowments. This type of dream helps the dreamer to know what your divine Counselor wants you to focus on; namely, your particular behaviors or character. The positive character traits figurative of the animal within your dream conflicts with the negative; this sheds light on your emotional or spiritual confl ict. Your dream also warns that you are in the company of those who feed your negative side (or war against your positive side). Do not be deceived, bad company distorts, corrupts good character. Dreamer, stand in direct opposition of evil men and women, and against your negative behaviors. Additionally, those who deny Jesus are false teachers, according to the Holy Bible. For specific animal, see category, Animals. This will reveal the particular behaviors you are fighting. If necessary, see suggested course of action.

Genocide, Mass Murder, Massacre, or Slaughter: This dream has two meanings (choose one). (1) Dreamer committing the massacre, slaughter: You are attempting to overcome the weaknesses of your flesh, and to sever wicked alliances you have made with certain people, places, or things, in your own strength and carnal knowledge. Declare and began practicing a lifestyle of prayer and fasting, abstaining from people, places, or things that trigger your unrighteous desires, for at leas t two days a week. Allow yourself to be accountable to your spiritual leadership and significant others. By this, you will begin to spiritually, live again. See suggested course of action. (2) Someone else committing the genocide, massacre, or slaughter: Although, the dreamer desires to cut off wicked alliances that have led you astray from God, you will not. Someone has easily led the dreamer astray from God and from what is spiritual, because of the lust of your flesh. The enemy is able to use your fleshly desires in an attempt to destroy you. You are too willing to give up eternal happiness for temporary relations of today. You are counseled to, not forfeit the benefits of serving Christ, for temporary pleasures that will lead to bareness. Your unwillingness to end the relationship will cause you much pain. The results of a self-indulgent life are poverty, spiritual emptiness, and/or death. A focus on integrity, character, uprightness, and living your life today in light of eternity; with emphasis on a greater commitment to God is advised See suggested course of action.

Guilty or Not Guilty of Fighting, Killing, Struggling, Violence, Conflict, Contestation, Dispute, or Accusations (e.g. declared guilty or not guilty in a court of justice): Only if highlighted within your dream, (e.g. if dreamer was declared guilty or not guilty in a court of some kind). Was the dreamer declared guilty or innocent of an offense within your dream? With that, this dream has two meanings (choose one). (1) Guilty: If dreamer was declared guilty, your dream is a grave warning. You are being watched by servants of the Most High. You are abusive, and have no respect for the lives of your family. You have tyrannically and greedily taken over your family's lifestyle, especially those who are elderly, in order to control their assets. Even more, you have accepted bribes that devalue the life of those you should treasure, for favors. In doing so, you have defiled the land which God was going to give to you as an inheritance (see Jeremiah 18:9, 10). Your temporal life is also at stake. A tragic outcome can be diminished by first repenting to Jesus. Taking ownership of what your warning dream is revealing to you about you, and working from that point, via diligent self-examination and conversion should bring about truth inwardly and divine clemency. See suggested course of action. (2) Not guilty (e.g. self-defense, accidental homicide): If dreamer was declared not guilty, you are conflicted within, regarding someone who is using the influence God has afforded them, to turn people, including the dreamer, away from the truth of, and obedience to, Jesus Christ. They have turned from righteousness and are now teaching others to do so. Your intuition is correct; this person regards neither life nor principle and they are now demonically led. Your spiritual life and that of your family, as well as others, is at stake. Consider the per son injured within your dream, without regard to title, place, or status. This person may very well be the perpetrator, or a ministry connected to this person. You will need to separate yourself from this person and/or ministry. Because you are the instrument, God may use to expose the truth of this person and/or a ministry. Prepare yourself for this task; document y our facts. They will retaliate, but you will overcome them. The cause you will represent is right; therefore, stand up for trut h, justice, and righteousness and God will be with you. If you do not stand up for truth, damages done to others will be accounted to you as one who is guilty of spiritual homicide. See suggested course of action.

Homicide (attempted homicide, accidental or premeditated killing, murder, or pulling a gun on someone, shooting someone): This dream has two meanings (choose one). (1) It highlights the critical need to value life and liberty, which is made in the image of God, especially the lives of your family (spouse, children, parents, siblings, other relatives, and sign ificant others), and more importantly your own life. See suggested course of action. (2) Dreamer, you have mixed feelings within, supposing that someone, possibly a spiritual leader, is using their influence God has afforded them, to turn people, includin g the dreamer, away from the truth of, and obedience to, Jesus Christ. Dreamer, you need to reconsider your suppositions. For, perhaps you've chosen to serve Christ in a manner of your own choosing, and in doing so have disobeyed God's directives for you, and His purpose, thus, the spirit of the ruler has risen up against you. Subsequently, their actions or behaviors have caused animosity, anger, perhaps rebellion within you against God. Dreamer, if the spirit of the ruler rise up against thee, leave not thy place; for yielding pacifieth great offences, (Ecclesiastes 10:4). See suggested course of action.

Sadism or Abuse (e.g. brutality, cruelty, sadism, spit on you or in your face; or any manner of abuse, viciousness, or violence): This dream has three meanings (choose one). (1) If dreamer initiated the sadism or abuse, dreamer, you are one who encourage brutality, cruelty, sadism, viciousness, and perpetuate it. Your bad behavior needs a transformation (also see Romans 12:1, 2). See suggested course of action. (2) If someone else initiated the sadism or abuse, the dreamer is, surrounded by violent people, and needs to separate from those associations (also see Matthew 26:52). See suggested course of action. (3) Spit on you, or in your face, or vice versa: This choice has three parts (choose one). (a) Dreamer, you are putting your attitudes, ideas, opinions, thoughts, and views, on the same level as the authoritative Word of God. Thus, you are exhibiting antichrist attributes. Moreover, that which you are complaining about is pretense to cover your jealously. God will make you an example to others. You will be treated contemptuously by some and scorn by others. Your contemporaries will reject you.

There will be attitudes of disgust towards you, powerful feelings of dislike. You will be considered undeserving of respect until you truly recognize; who are you to, judge another's servant. To his own master he stands or falls [and not before you, or at your word or whim, does anyone fall or stand], and he [they] will stand, for the Lord is able to make him [her] stand (Romans 14:4). This example of you will continue, until you acknowledge that, you were wrong. See suggested course of action. (b) Your father and/or mother spit on you or in your face, or vice versa: Two parts (choose one). (i) If parents are living, dreamer, shame is coming upon you, because of your disrespect to a god ordained leader. You will publicly bear this shame for seven days. (ii) If parents have passed on, dreamer has no need to bear the shame any longer; you bear the shame now, because of an inability to forgive yourself. You only need to forgive yourself. If necessary, see suggested course of action. (c) If a sick or elderly person spit on you, or vice versa: This dream exposes spiritual uncleanness on some level. Symbolically, uncleanness personifies one of two states regarding human behavior (choose one). (i) Within the life of a believer, it denotes anger, animosity, confusion, out of order, self-condemnation, sexual impropriety, an unforgiving spirit, and/or other weaknesses, are present within your heart, as well as, immoral, impure, and unchaste conduct. For example, addictions, cheating, exposing confidences to others, greedy, gossiping, jealously, lying, stealing, or any other sinful attr ibute (see 1 Corinthians 6:9-20, Ephesians 5). This behavior causes one's anointing to fade and spiritual authority to wane. Favorably, you are now one, whom the body of believers should, and will, help restore back to God, in the spirit of empathy, mercy, leniency, and kindness, until the issue is, cleaned up or rendered dead, allow this. (ii) Uncleanness also personifies one who is not re-born spiritually, not repentant, and/or a non-believer (one who has no religious beliefs, a non-religious person, or one who has no religious faith or belief in Jesus Christ, or one who does not embrace a personal relationship with Jesus Christ, at present). You may also hold to views and practices that are erroneous, unlawful, toxic, and spiritually and/or physically deadly. Jesus loves you, thus, He is petitioning you to accept Him as your personal Savior, for you are valuable in His eyes. The first step in receiving Him as your personal Savior is repentance (see in the Holy Bible, Acts 2:37-41). Repentance is seeking pardon for having done something awry, and for having hurt someone, and expressing sincere feelings of regret and brokenness. To Jesus pray, Psalm 51:1-19. Moreover, if you will accept the Heavenly Father's Words, via the Bible, and store up His principles, and His ways and means within you, turning your ear to wisdom and applying your heart to understanding, calling out for insight and crying aloud for discernment, Jesus will meet you. This, coupled with a lifestyle of prayer and fasting, followed by appropriate application of wisdom, and you will know the Messiah, Jesus Christ, intimately, and find the knowledge of God you seek. For the Lord gives wisdom and from His mouth comes knowledge and understanding. Then you will understand what is right and just and fair, every good path. When wisdom enters your heart and knowledge becomes sweet to your soul, discretion will protect you, understanding will guard you, and His Truth will lead you. To deliver you f rom the ways of wickedness, from demons whose words and ways are perverse, who causes you to walk in darkness gladly, whose paths are crooked and devious, causing you to leave straight paths (Proverbs 2:1-6, 9-15). This is one of God's covenant promises to you. Have faith in this.

Slay (to strike or beat with an object to cause death, strike a fatal blow, intentional or unintentional): This dream has three meanings (choose one). (1) Your dream implies the ending of a union, friendship, or other significant relationship, spiritually and emotionally. As well, it denotes a literal separation and distance, a departing or fleeing to another place. (2) If you or another slayed someone: Your union (marriage, friendship, or other relationship) has ended, or will end, as all your relationships end. You, the dreamer, fly into a narcissistic rage, hurling accusations you know are untrue. Betraying the heart of the union, you inflict, and have inflicted this time as well, the fatal blow ending the relationship. See suggested cours e of action. (3) If someone slayed you: Too much time apart and distance has had an unfavorable impact upon your union (marriage, friendship, or other relationship). The separation is the result of the other party's choices. They were advised to return and they would not. The relationship is dissolved. It is suggested that you remain where you are at and wait for a promise given you by God. It shall happen shortly. See suggested course of action.

Stab, Wound, or Nick (with a sharp instrument, e.g. knife, or sharp pick, stabbed): This dream has three meanings (choose one). (1) Dreamer, deeply cut, stabbed, or wounded someone (intentional or accidental): This choice has two parts (choose one). (a) You have before, and will again shortly, offend someone who sincerely cares about you. You do not know the way of peace, nor is there fair dealing in your behavior. Your spiteful behavior bears record of this, as well as, your present illness. Your extreme bitterness has led to your very nasty behavior, and this is the underlying cause of your present illness. No amount of medications or doctors can heal this; that is why doctors have been unable to give you a definite diagnosis. Yo ur attitude has affected others as well. An authentic and drastic change in your attitude really needs to happen now, for your health sake. By so doing, you will be healed physically. For why should you die before your time? Yes, you, dreamer, can d ie before your time. Therefore, genuinely deal with your bitterness and unforgiving spirit due to a grave offense committed against you by another, as well as your own offensiveness. Notwithstanding, your offensive behavior will not be tolerated th is time. You will be confronted by one you've offended. Therefore, repentance and an earnest change are requisite now, namely, in your course of conduct, ways, deeds, thoughts, and attitude. If psychological, emotional, and spiritual change occurs, dreamer, God will again restore favor upon your life. This is called, leaving a blessing behind. To be blessed: Gifts of God's grace, anything God freely gives you, absolution, the Holy Spirit, salvation, regeneration, eternal life, health, child ren, love of family, longevity, necessities, prosperity, and dominion over all that is yours; and all are parts of the supply of grace, and all are sanctified by the Lord, and technically belongs to Him. The result of this supply in your life will be peace. See suggested course of action. (b) Dreamer will (or has) hurt someone deeply. If person was unknown in y our dream, you are unaware of the emotional pain you have caused someone. It will be made known to you, and an apology will be appropriate at that time. As well, your behaviors and motives should be evaluated as to why you act in such an insensitive, petty, and malicious manner. The type and severity of the cut, stab, or wound, equals the degree of emotional hurt you've caused another, as well as the extent of your disrespectful and rude behavior. If the person, within your dream, is known, the dreamer is well aware of your spiteful behaviors towards another. The Lord is not pleased with your offensive behavior, any disobedience continued in, after being warned by God. A setting right of your spiritual behavior by the Lord is in process. Hence, you can no longer prosper under the anointing and authority of God, there will be loss and setbacks. Please note that there is a difference in spiritual blessings and prosperity and material prosperity. Dreamer, you cannot have spiritual bles sings without material prosperity, but you can have the material without the spiritual. Choose not to go out from the presence of the Lord, that is, to willingly renounce God, and to be content to forego the privileges He offers, namely eternal life, so that you might not be under His precepts; make things right. Heartfelt repentance to Jesus and man or woman is needed, with a sense of urgency. Repentance is seeking pardon and expressing sincere feelings of regret and brokenness for having done something awry and/or for having hurt someone, see 2 Corinthians 7:10, 11), to individuals affected by your actions, in the form of an apology (if possible). A phone call or a letter of apology is a good place to start. See suggested course of act ion. (2) Someone, deeply cut, stabbed, or wounded the dreamer (intentional or accidental): This choice has two parts (choose one). (a) Hypocritical men, those that despise you are plotting evil against you, supposing you do not have the covering of God. They that cast you aside (or out), have reasoned amongst themselves that they're doing the will of the Father, but they have never known Him, or at least do not know His will in what they are planning against you. The same wicked deeds attempted against you will fall upon those who are guilty. Keep silent and hold your peace. Cease from talking, the Lord will fight this battle. God, will avenge you. He will fight for you. (b) Someone, demonically influenced, is intentionally trying to rob, steal from, kill, and/or destroy you, the dreamer, spiritually, or your reputation, with hopes of causing an offense within you against God. This is the enemy's effort to turn you away from the One True God. Consider the person in your dream, without regard to place or rank; if known in your awaked life, this person, may very well be the perpetrator. Take a step back, if applicable, and carefully consider their actions towards you. If deemed necessary, God will remove you from where this person is prominent within your life (e.g. example, church, friend, home, spouse, or work). Do not despair because of your removal, or how it is brought about, you will prosper wherever you go. Because of your move, relief from the evil schemes and lies of th e enemy, in that particular place, will end. Most importantly, because of your move, you will find the peace and rest needed, physically, emotionally, and spiritually. Note, your dream is not an encouragement to forfeit fellowship with church or fami ly, or to quit your employment, nor is it meant to engender strife. Simply put, you will be moved or rescued from that which is potentially dangerous to your personal relationship with Christ and your health, by Christ Himself. Allow God, not you, to handle His business of keeping His promises to you, namely, "I will give you rest" and "My peace I leave with you". (3) To nick or inflict a surface wound upon someone (a cut that does not noticeably wound or penetrate deeply): Dreamer, you do not know the way of peace; there is no justice in your tracks. You are making your paths crooked because of bitterness, an unforgiving spirit, and/or an inability to let others go when they have fulfilled their time or purpose with you. Additional ly, the moral guilt of a righteous person killed (spiritually or physically) by someone in your immediate family will fall upon you publicly. However, an earnest change in your course of conduct, and you will not be blamed, or pardoned from the guilt. Moreover, an earnest change in your ways, deeds, thoughts, and attitude, and you will be healed from your present illness. See suggested course of action.

War (to do battle, combat, campaign, crusade, warfare): Your dream comes to alert the dreamer. You are caught up in serious spiritual warfare right now. There is a struggle between your old nature and your new nature, the leftovers of sin and the beginnings of grace (the free and unmerited favor and beneficence of God). The carnal part of you is struggling against the spiritually renewed you. Your carnal nature is resisting everything that is spiritual and is opposing all the suggestions of the Holy Spirit and the ethical urgings of your conscience. As the law of grace within you will not allow you to do all the evil which your carnal nature would prompt you to do, so neither can you do all the good that you would. Hence, you cannot do the things you want to do, now, due to the intense oppositions within you. It is in your best interest to ; seriously focus, on your struggle and to side with your convictions and godly principles against your lusts at present. Couple this with one of the following (choose one). (1) If you prevailed or conquered: You are choosing to side with godly principles and your convictions. God's providential blessings are upon you to increase. However, always be alert that you are in spiritual warfare and the enemy of your soul is real and present. Be mindful of your words and do not boast of your increase. Furthermore, due to the intensity of your struggle, one of God's messengers is sent to give you the support needed at this time. Be aware that the new person within your midst may be that messenger. It may very well be the person, at present, you don't quite take a liking to o. Too, deal wisely with your allies (associates, friends, followers, or partners) lest they join your enemies and fight against you, and you become unable to overcome the many. If necessary, see suggested course of action. (2) If you were defeated: Dreamer, the Kingdom of God will always be a better choice than serving the enemy of your soul, who reigns over the kingdom of darkness. Your carnal side is getting the best of you. Your choices will delay spiritual progress and make your way hard. As well, if not already, shortly, two people (a couple or two distinct individuals) will enter your life; they will charm their way in. These people do not know the way of peace. They harbor hurtful intentions. If allowed, these people will introduce to you a get-tough policy to be used against those who have no issue with you or you with them. Example of their policy; reward hard work with more hard work, with no acknowledgement, appreciation, pay, or rest. You will become so enchanted with these individuals; you may allow this. If you continue listening to them and following their advice, where there was peace, unity, and favorable conditions; your life and/or ministry will be consumed by a season of mistrust, suspicion, concern, and re- consideration; resulting in upset and division within your family and/or ministry. See suggested course of action.

Wrestle, Wrestling Match (to fight back, kick, move violently, resist, struggle, tussle, contest, competition in wrestling):

Dreamer, what you are experiencing now, is serious spiritual warfare. You are intense and convicted when it comes to defending your beliefs, as you never doubt your inner strength and ability to handle any challenge, and although, many are inspired by your confidence, others are threaten by it. Those that feel threaten often instigate some of the opposition you face. Notwithstanding, continue striving, to win the prize of the high calling of God in Christ Jesus; and on their part, Jesus is evil spoken. Moreover, due to your intense struggle, one of God's messengers is sent to support you and to give you the assistance needed at this time. Be aware that the stranger within your midst may be that messenger. It may very well be the person, at present, you don't quite take a liking too.

Weaponry (any weapon, or armament, or any device used with intent to inflict damage or harm to living beings, structures, or system, legal or illegal): There is a dizzying array of weapons available, however, no matter the weapon, question to journal is, was the weapon used for legal or illegal purposes? With that, this dream has two meanings (choose one). (1) Legal Purposes: If weapon was used for legal purposes (meaning, purposes that are established by or founded upon law or official or accepted rules; lawfulness by virtue of conformity to a legal statute, one exercising self-defense, or showing good judgment): If dreamer or another used a weapon, legally, this dream has two parts (choose one). (a) Your dream denotes one who is set aside for the priesthood. Dreamer, you are being prepared to carry out the official role, position, or office of a priest (e.g. prophet, pastor, minister, or some type of a very visible cleric). With this office comes spiritual growth and divine illumination. Dreamer, if you have genuinely sought after truth, truth will continue to be revealed to you, and lead, and guide you. With that said, the following is necessary to say. First, your promotion is predicated upon your understanding of, and continued obedience to, God's directives over your life. Second, pray to God for divine t ruth, for one should never exalt their thoughts, ideas, feelings, emotions, above God's truth, for, every house is built by someone, but the builder of all things is God (Hebrews 3:2-4). Further, chosen, you are to show forth the praises of Him who has called you out of darkness into His marvelous light (also see 1 Peter 2:9, 10). At present, continue to allow the Paraclete to complete the work of purification and sanctification within you. For those who go forth in tears, shall return rejoicing (Psalm 126:5, 6). Be diligent and patient, everything will be done proper, and in its own time; you will be ordained to a priestly office, and if relevant, your request in another area of your life will be granted. Again, your height of spiritual progress and promotion will be according to your faith and obedience to God's will over your life personally. (b) Your dream denotes one who is in the process of being made whole, emotionally, psychologically, physically, and financially, because of your reverence for God. You are entering into a process of being purified and purged, examined, proven and tested, spiritually and emotionally cleansed. Everything that's unusable within you will give way to that which is beneficial and profitable, and that which is undesirable will become brightly polished, according to God's good pleasure. Your pride will soon give way to humbleness, dignity, honor, and righteous self - esteem, your foolishness to peace and wisdom. This process will also heal the animosity within you resulting in a physical healing you've believed God for, for some time now. Allow the process without complaining or murmuring for it is preparing you for a great journey. Be as one who gets satisfaction from embracing good habits. (2) Illegal Purposes: If weapon was used for, illegal purposes (meaning, purposes that are not conforming to legality, moral law, or social convention; contrary to, or prohibited by, or defiant of, law; not morally right or permissible; prohibited by law or by official or accept ed rules). If dreamer or another, used a weapon, illegally, this dream has two parts (choose one). (a) Dreamer, you have abandoned the faith, and is now adhering to lies; thus a breakdown in communication, with the Heavenly Father. You are embracing be liefs, views, and practices that are erroneous, unlawful, toxic, and spiritually and/or physically deadly. Your choice of lifestyle will not withstand your storms of life. Your conscience will haunt you. Weakened by frequent panic attacks, brought on by your own guilt and the fear of God's retribution, you will begin to crack in your personality. He, who carries his or her own acc user, and their own tormentor, always in their bosom, cannot but be afraid on every side

(Matthew Henry's Commentary on Job 18:11-21). The only foundation upon which one should wisely establish his or her identity is the principles within the Word of God. Your attitude is leading to a mental and spiritual breakdown, opening the door for demons to run havoc within your life and to bring you down to desolation. You are forfeiting purpose for foolishness and ruin. Demonic influences will swarm around you, ready to help you explore all manner of wickedness, and evil, immoral, reprehensible, disreputable, degenerate, and perverse choices. Your lifestyle choices will become offensive and repulsive (abominable) in the sight of God and humanity. Dreamer, demons have had thousands of years to master human weaknesses and can rival men and women of God if we are not careful. Favorably, while your dream is a seriously severe rebuke and warning, because of grace and the many mercies of God extended to you, it is not an official declaration. Dreamer is counseled to seek all kinds of spiritual support now, to possibly avert or turn things around, and perhaps move away from your present environment, definitely walk away from all negativity that is the antithesis of Christ, abruptly. Utilizing the powerful resources of prayer and heartfelt repentance to Jesus is a good place to start. To Jesus pray, Psalm 51, this followed by appropriate application of wisdom, can conceivably avert some of the repercussions of your choices. This coupled with fasting, a changed mindset, serious re-consideration of God's ways and means, and an honest acknowledgement of God's hand within your life, then the severe impact of your choices and actions upon your life, can be reversed and damages repaired (also see Ezekiel 33:12-19). This is what is called leaving a blessing behind. If you do not genuinely seek help and change, for sure ruin will be your destiny's declaration. See suggested course of action. (b) This type of dream exposes a need of refinement of character, namely in the area dealing with the deeds of the flesh. For example, dishonesty, adultery, sensuality, hostility, feuding, vendettas, grudges, unfriendliness, strife, jealousy, outbursts of anger, disputes, dissensions, discord, factions, cliques, envying, drunkenness, carousing, or any traits of these sorts (see 1 Corinthians 6:8-11). This dream comes to warn an immoral believer that your choices are spiritually forbidden, and/or your activities are illegal. You have deliberately chosen to become enslaved to that which is forbidden by the One True and Living God. Dreamer, refrain from wickedness and no longer do harm to anyone, physically, sexually, emotionally, and/or spiritually. Start treating God's people, your family, and others, with respect, as well as yourself. By this, God will pardon your injustices. Dreamer, if urged by God, declare a one, two, or three day fast for sanctification purposes; also, wash (bathe) and make yourself, clothing, and personal surroundings clean. If not a day fast, you will need to declare some kind of fast and commit to it, for a long period-of-time. See suggested course of action.

Whipping, Walloping, Thrashing, Licking, or Corporal Punishment (the act of inflicting punishment as a form of discipline): Your dream is sent as a warning of divine discipline, the Lord's chastening and correction that leads to instruction and reformation. Dreamer, God will, in a dramatic way deal with your contemptuous, rebellious, and disobedient attitude. It is hoped that the experience will lead to a character and spiritual reformation, which it is intended to effect, rescuing the dreamer from error and causing a return to a rightful course. Moreover, heartfelt repentance to Jesus is needed. To Jesus pray, Psalm 51, this followed by appropriate application of wisdom, can conceivably avert some of the repercussions of your choices. See suggested course of action

Suggested Course of Action

Question to consider and journal, did your dream depict any symbols that alludes to, the dreamer will make the necessary changes, spiritually, emotionally, and/or physically to affect a more positive outcome? If changes are initiated, your dreams will change.

Nevertheless, since, most fighting, killing, struggling, violence, conflict, contestation, dispute, or accusations dreams are dealing with some kind of spiritual warfare; the dreamer is, counseled to embrace an unwavering determination in favor of God's ways and in opposition of wickedness and ungodliness. Further, do not allow anyone or anything to effect dissension within your Christian life, your ministry, or home. Do not allow any issue to cause you to walk away from your Christian and/or family duties. The quality and usefulness of your spiritual life is at stake. Notions, which presuppose the possibility of an actual loss of a God-given ministry, your prosperity, or even life itself is not real, must not undermine these warnings, the warnings are real. Moreover, spiritually and materially bless the people of God, those belonging to "The Way", as we were called in the early church (Acts 9:2) with your words and actions, and not curse.

Consider and journal the following questions. The questions will help you determine; the issue at hand, how you feel about it, and what may have instigated it. What kind of fighting was it? Why was there fighting? Were others involved? If yes, who and in what manner were they involved? Keep in mind that the others represent a quality of you, see Note 3 at the beginning of Actions and Activities category. Did anyone get hurt emotionally, physically, or was disturbed in any way? How did you feel, and what did you do, because, of your feelings, regarding the fighting and/or how or where it ended? Was it agitating, confusing, dangerous, disturbing, frustrating, peace with the situation, happy, joyful, life threatening, safe, sc ary, or unsure? Where were you? Was the place unfamiliar to you? Were you coherent? In view of your dream's context, namely fighting, killing, struggling, violence, conflict, contestation, dispute, or accusations, what choices are you making that may impair your spiritual growth, judgment, health, or that will encourage immorality and/or are you reacting out of fear? If so, what can you do to combat the paralyzing emotion of fear? Your answers, coupled with the interpretation, plus any additional information, should begin to unfold the subject matter and issue at hand, if not now, mull over things a few days. For more information, see index or relevant category and subcategory for other particulars within your dream.

The following will help you determine the approximate length of time you have thus far dealt with the matter and how much longer you will have to deal with the issue. If you started fighting, killing, struggling, violence, conflict, contesta tion, dispute, or accusations at the beginning of the dream, you are dealing with this issue right now. If somewhere in the middle onward, you will encounter the issue shortly. Did you stop fighting at some point? This is indicative that you've completed the process that will heal the issue your dream is referencing. If you did not stop fighting, the matter at hand will not end soon, if you continue avoidance, complaining, faithlessness in God's Word, and/or murmuring. You are counseled to deal with the issue without evasion or compromise, in other words head-on. All of these questions should pull together for you your dream. They summarize the issue at hand and what changes need to be made within the dreamer's attitude or life.

Now, pray (See Prayer of Deliverance, pg. 897)

Specific Meaning

If, your chances are very high that the dreamer is, or will be involved in some kind of violent activity (e.g. advocacy, legal representative, social work on behalf of the underprivileged, debate, professional fighting, war, executioner, law enforcemen t, or some other kind of activity akin to this category). Else, if you have a love one engaged in some type of violent activity (e.g. war, gang related, or matters before the courts). Dreams of this sort, for the most part, are ordinary dreams, resulting from your daily activities (see Chapter One, Chalom). These sorts of dreams are usually about your routine, mundane activities or anxieties that overwhelm your mind during the day. They are an inner release mechanism, which helps provide you with emotional balance and the maintaining of your sanity. These dreams are not significant, and do not warrant special attention.

Note: If there were any illegal matters within your dream, this is a precautionary warning. There may be potential for an accident, homicide, or incarceration. Dreamer, the details, kept within context of your dream, should be relevant to your life, and closely resemble your real-life situations. Meaning it can actually occur during your awaked state. This will help you narrow down the specifics needed to support and steer you clear of possible mishaps. However, if your dream symbols are not easily, linked to your life activities, heed the spiritual implications (the interpretation).

FLYING: To travel through the air using wings or an engine, or to be capable of flight

Some short descriptions of types, phrases, and other processes and particulars, connected in some way to this category are, for example, airborne, soaring in the air, sky, on the wings or back of someone or something, "fly in the face of".

Unless otherwise noted elsewhere, if, in your everyday living, your awaked state, as part of your lifestyle, work, or ministerial activities, or a special event, you have a very real connection with any type of flying activity. For exampl e, aerodynamics, aeronautics, balloons, blue angels, or sky diving, (also see content list for this category), your dream is not significant and does not warrant special attention.

Otherwise noted, this dream of flying may be a Prophetically Simple Dream (see Chapter One: The 60th Part of Prophecy). Whereas, the dreamer is warned to be extra cautious regarding situations that have a high chance for accidents; especially if this is an issue within the dreamer's life at present. This dream is a first step intervention and an alarm. It should be received as a precautionary warning. Skip interpretation and re-consider your activities as harmful or life threatening at present. Refrain from such activities at present. Also, see Specific Meaning at the end of this category, section entitled, Note (Specific Meaning).

Otherwise noted, see Note 1 at the beginning of Actions and Activities category.

To determine who your dream is for you or another, see Note 3 at the beginning of Actions and Activities category.

Symbols and Referents: Dreams of flying generally imply, coupled with the relevant interpretation, a warning that some manner of accountability is approaching, regarding the fulfilling of your specific purpose within the spiritual scheme of thi ngs. As well, an extremely important event going on presently or very shortly within your life, will affect how you fulfill your purpose. Wisdom, courage, and obedience are key words right now.

Category Content - If not listed see index, perchance, for your specific type of flying dream activity.

- Airplane or Helicopter
- Flying through the Air or Floating Upward (Building, Carpet, Person, Rug, Paper flying through the air, Flying Scroll)
- Hand Gliding or Wings (riding on the wings or back of someone or something or given assistance to fly, e.g. angel, bird's wings, hand gliding, or any cartoon, fictional, or mythological character)
- Unable to fly (e.g. broken wings)
- Airplane or Helicopter crashed, see category, Accidents (Airplane or Helicopter)
- "Fly a kite" (flying a kite should be highlighted)
- "Fly-by-night" (flying at night should be highlighted)
- "Fly in the face of" (something or someone flying in front of your face should be highlighted)
- "Fly-off-the-handle" (a handle and flying should be highlighted)
- "High as a kite" (a kite and someone or something flying higher than the kite should be highlighted)
- Out of body experience, see category, The Body (Soul)

Airplane or Helicopter: This dream has three meanings (choose one). (1) Airplane or Helicopter ascending, taking off, or scheduled to take off: Dreamer, because of your faith, humility, strong leadership, and your courageous and optimistic spirit, you will be greatly honored. You will rise to a level the Anointing of God and your acumen deem you should be. Even more, in your present business or personal dealings, you will be satisfied and take delight in your goals. If you are involved in any situation that is competitive, you will triumphant. (2) Ascending and descending (taking off and then landing): Dreamer, the Spirit of Truth is coming to you. That is to say, one who has the Spirit of Truth abiding within them is coming. He or she will testify of Jesus; a side of Him you don't know. This new truth will usher you into a personal revival, affecting restoration of better and happier times (e.g. improved health, economic security, improved family relations) or a new birth experience for one needing to be born again (see John 3:1-17). Believe and you will receive the promise of eternal life, and you will be set free. (3) Flying an Airplane or Helicopter: Dreamer, you are prepared to meet Christ, you genuinely believe and love Him; you have fulfilled all righteous requirements. Your dream is to reaffirm that you are going to heaven, trust God in this and not man's words (no matter how bleak your situation). Dreamer, while your weaknesses maybe legitimate, and the report and whispers are true, you unknowingly deny the truth of His report, "Therefore, there is now no condemnation for those who are in Christ Jesus"; as well, "His grace is sufficient". There is a difference between conviction and condemnation. Dreamer, t hink on these things (see Romans 7:7-8:17; 2 Corinthians 12:7-10; Philippians 1:6; 4:8). Be encouraged, take comfort, and believe (see John 14:1-4). No other affirmation will be sent.

Flying through the Air or Floating Upward (Building, Carpet, Person, Rug, Paper flying through the air, Flying Scroll): This dream has five meanings (choose one). (1) Building: Your love of, and devotion to, the teachings of the Bible, and your, heart's aspiration to understand its inner truths, is lifting you above your preoccupation with earthly things, and is connec ting you to Divine insight. (2) Carpet, Rug: Your love of money and material things, and the accumulation of such, coupled with crooked business and the attempted assassination of character of Christians; has provoked a pronouncement of judgment (divine reprimand for folly and sin) upon you. You have been measured and found wanting. Someone stronger than yourself, with more power, authority, and wealth will come against you, to the aid of God's people. This person's schemes have been well thought out and they will succeed. God has declared it so. See suggested course of action. (3) Paper flying through the air: This choice has two parts (choose one). (a) You, the dreamer, are being (or will be) made aware of information concerning certain individuals (see Chapter One, Are You Ready to Hear the Messages in Your Dreams, section entitled, The 10% for others). It has been made known (or will shortly be made known) to you of individuals that are deceiving God's people, lying on others, dealing in dirt, and stealing, all in the name of the Lord. The names of these actual individuals may have possibly been depicted within your dream on the papers. Notwithstanding, when the time presents, you will have to make known to each of them that deceiving and lying violates mans' obligation to God. And, stealing violates mans' obligation to man, those who are engaging in such acts, God's judgment (divine reprimand for folly and sin) is being poured out against them, even as you speak to them, and they will not escape. They will no longer be allowed to hinder God's work. Their time is complete they will be removed. Their only hope is to repent and desire eternal life in heaven. Their souls are at stake. If you failed to do what is required, the spiritual implications will be required at your hands (also see Ezekiel 3:17-21, 33:7-20). Dreamer; if you are a partaker, in any of these acts; eat this word first, for it also includes you, and then take it to othe rs. Don't delay. If necessary, see suggested course of action. (b) If dreamer has a legal issue before the courts, the success of the court's decision is out of your hands now, you've prayed about it, thus, let go, let God, go and rest, and whatever will be w ill be. (4) Flying Scroll (a roll of parchment, leather, or papyrus): Dreamer is one who is involved with others who express gross and obscene disrespect for God and sacred things. You swear falsely by His name; and you are a thief. Thus, there will be an ecclesiastical pronouncement of censure against you and perhaps ex-communication. You will be deemed a heretic or hireling, especially if thievery is an issue. This divine ordained official declaration shall remain in your house and consume it. Fa vorably, utilizing the powerful resources of prayer and heartfelt repentance to Jesus and to individuals affected by yo ur actions, coupled with, fasting, a changed mindset, serious re-consideration of God's ways and means, and an honest acknowledgement of God's hand within your life. Then the severe impact of your choices and actions, upon your life, can be reversed and damages repaired (see Ezekiel 33:12-19). Repentance is seeking pardon and expressing sincere feelings of regret and brokenness for having done something awry and/or for having hurt someone, see 2 Corinthians 7:10, 11. To individuals, a phone call or a letter of apology is a good place to start. To Jesus pray, Psalm 51, this, followed by appropriate application of wisdom, can conceivably avert some of the repercussions of your choices. This is what is called leaving a blessing behind. See suggested course of action. (5) Dreamer flying through the air or floating upward: This choice has two parts (choose one). (a) Flying with others: Dreamer needs to go to church, commit to a ministry, and then spread your ministry abroad. Every Christian should be faithfully attending and supporting a fundamental Bible believing church. Revelation 2:1, 8, 12, 18, 3:1, 7, 14, lets us know that God intended churches, and Hebrews 10:24, 25 sheds some light on the reason for participation in the local church. We provoke one another to good works, and exhort one another to live consistent lives worthy of God. This is best done within the context of a local church, so we, as believers, are commanded not to forsake the assembling of ourselves together. You will shortly, have to give an account of the fulfilling of your specific ministry, and the excuse of somebody or something else was standing in your way will not fly. Consider your dream a sufficient warning. If your ministerial call, a s purposed by God, is not fulfill, you will lose the opportunity that would prosper you in that area. See suggested course of action. (b) Dreamer you may feel busy with the daily routines of life; and desire freedom, or an escape, from a set of regimented rules and restrictions imposed upon your physical and/or spiritual life by an organization, or freedom from a person, or place. Whatever you are involved in, whomever you're involved with, or wherever you are, that has initiated the desire to leave, be encouraged, you have asked for, prayed for, and desired the right thing. Your desires will be granted you, and your prayers will result in your freedom, literally, emotionally, and spiritually. Very soon, you will break free and follow your dreams and goals; you are going to create a beautiful, purpose-filled life that will inspire many. You are endowed with a warrior soul and you will make it big, you are going to live an incredible life. You will rise above your present circumstances, and to a position within a ministry, to the level God's anointing and your intuitiveness deems you should be; deficiency, lack, basically the state of needing something that is absent or unavailable, will no longer be a problem. With that said; the following three issues are needful that the issue may be dealt with and rectified; hence, a release, choose one. (i) Female dreamer: Your dream indicates that the dreamer is in a dark place, space emotionally, spiritually, and/or financially. Resentment toward your religious beliefs that seem powerless to help you at this moment has begun to fester inside of you. The dreamer is in a crisis of her faith. Dreamer, never trade your wisdom for foolishness and lies, and diligence for lazine ss and a beggar mentality and lifestyle. This will only lead to you, blindly, self-sabotaging potentially successful endeavors. When our hearts are painfully torn apart, broken, or troubled, God can take those disappointments, those trials and tragedies, and mak e them door of hope. For no, one has an experience to give to another until God has given them their own experience. Dreamer, set your face steadfastly toward God; look beyond your circumstances, and see Jesus high and lifted up through your trouble, pain, and tears. Only then, will you began to say, "I'm going on with God". Shift your paradigm. See suggested course of action. (ii) Male dreamer: Your dream is a strong word to the dreamer: You have lost your place of authority within the sacred scheme of things; having exalted your wisdom, above the Creator's, and settled for an earthy, secular, sensual type of philosophy. The glory you once encountered and experienced personally cannot return, since the doctrine of demons does not lend itself to genuine glory. Glory in this sense is a state of high honor, spiritual beauty, and great illumination. Dreamer, will you not completely abandon your anti-Christ philosophy and begin again to hope for eternal life in heaven? Your soul is at stake. Re-shift your paradigm. Pray for divine truth, for one should never exalt their thoughts, ideas, feelings, above God's truth, for, every house is built by someone, but the builder of all things is God" (Hebrews 3:2-4). See suggested course of action. (iii) Male or female dreamer: Dreamer, never short-change yourself in your own mind, according to your own dark and obscure reasoning. For, as your words and thoughts have the power to cause happiness, they also have the power to cause physical pain, emotional, and psychological suffering, and great unhappiness, and, yes, you have spoken and thought some issues into existence; see Proverbs 18:21. Moreover, your words and thoughts have revealed what is in your heart; and those words are a result of a deep emotional wound. Dreamer, albeit, from the depth of your deep emot ional pain, make a personal introspection of your words and deeds and fully return to God, admitting also your disregard and pride, and turn to the Almighty in prayer, crying, remember me, oh Lord, in all of my suffering. God will hear your prayers. Sudd enly, there will be comfort, and inspiration. God is good to those who trust in Him and seek Him out. One must never give up hope and always wait for God's salvation that will eventually come. God's kindness and mercy never ends. If necessary, see suggested course of action.

Hand Gliding or Wings (riding on the wings or back of someone or something or given assistance to fly, e.g. angel, bird's wings, hand gliding, or any cartoon, fictional, or mythological character): This dream has three meanings (choose one). (1) Bird's wings: This choice has two parts (choose one). (a) Female dreamer: You are being attacked relentlessly, due to the schemes of wicked persons. There is no rest. God is getting ready to move you from where you are currently residing, worshiping, or working. Have faith God will lead the way. Because of your move, relief from the evil schemes and lies of th e adversary in that particular place (e.g. home, church, or work) will end. Most importantly, because of your move, you wi ll find the peace and rest needed physically, emotionally, and spiritually. This is not an encouragement to forfeit fellowship with church or family, or resign from your place of employment, nor is it meant to engender strife. Simply put, you will be rescued from that which is potentially dangerous to your personal relationship with Christ and your health. Allow God, not you, to handle His business of keeping His promises to you, namely, "I will give you rest" and "My peace I leave with you". (b) Male dreamer: You are commissioned to preach the gospel of Jesus Christ, through evangelism, outreach efforts, or a pastorate. You are sent to many, of every nation and tongue. You should already know by now who you are in Christ, an evangelist, outreach organizer, or pastor. Do you love Jesus? If so, then feed His flock (figuratively and literally). You love Him when you obey Him. Write your vision that you may articulate it to others properly. On the other side, a wicked servant would bury h is or her gift, blaming their lack of faithfulness, commitment, and stewardship on God or others. When in reality, he or she has actually chosen to remain spiritually immature. Upon facing your Maker, there will be no one else to blame but you. No one can ever claim he or she has not been sufficiently warned. You will have to give an account of the fulfilling of your specific purpose. Consider your dream as sufficient warning. If necessary, see suggested course of action. (2) Hand gliding: Deliverance from drifting back and forth in a sin that has so easily beleaguered you has been accomplished. Respect, protect, and value, your deliverance. Moreover, remember it is God and by His Grace (the free and unmerited favor and beneficence of God) alone that you are delivered; it is not by anything that you've done so good, perfect, or righteous. See suggested course of action. (3) Riding on the wings or back of someone or something (e.g. angel, bird, or any cartoon, fictional, or mythological character): This choice has three parts (choose one). (a) Angel: In response to God hearing your prayer, Jehovah Jireh is going to help you through your storm, even to the shaking up of things for your benefit. Figuratively, God will move mountains; He will create the opportunity for you to walk in His perfect will. It is up to you to be ready to seize the opportunities He is putting before you. Have faith, be perceptive, be prepared, and remain humble. You will begin to experience His benevolence speedily. (b) Bird: You are a great and faithful leader, who is in distress. Righteous indignation is what you're experiencing. The attacks of wicked persons has deeply grieved and caused you much agony. Go boldly to the throne of grace with your request, with your offense, and God will hear your prayers. He will be there, God has not forsaken you, and He will champion your cause. No weapon, wicked plots, plans, or actions instigated against you shall prosper, no not this time. You shall be at rest. Also, see category, Animals (Birds), to learn the collective characteristics of the persons who have attacked you and caused you much grief, as indicated by the type of bird. Knowledge replaces fear, and better prepares you to handle persons with understanding and skill, see Matthew 10:16-42. (c) Cartoon, Fictional, or Mythological Character: Your dream is a strong warning to the dreamer. Your heart is hardened, and you have chosen to remain spiritually immature. Your dream speaks of a defection of the faith, which is in Jesus Christ. The experience of those who lack faithfulness, a love of God, and do not endure; those who have fallen away, they will not reign in the Kingdom (also see Hebrews 3:12, 13; 6:4-7). Powerful, prideful, and insolent, your haughtiness and your subsequent fall will cause astonishment, mourning, and great grief. Notwithstanding, God is to be seen as just, in doing what is necessary to stop the arrogance that was spreading amongst His people, because of you r propaganda. Another has taken your place. For other attributes of the character highlighted within your dream, see category, Animals (Monsters, Mythological or Legendary Creatures, or other Abominable Creatures). See suggested course of action.

Unable to fly (e.g. broken wings): This dream has two meanings (choose one). (1) The dreamer lacks faith in spiritual realities, thus you are trapped by the illusions of things tangible. This is akin to the spirit of agnostic, a religious orientation of doubt; a denial of ultimate knowledge of the existence of God, namely a person who claims that they cannot have true knowledge about the existence of God, but does not deny that God might exist. This attitude will result in unfulfilled potential within your life (John 20:29; 1 Peter 1:8). See suggested course of action. (2) Broken wings: The dreamer needs healing spiritually. Ask Jesus to take your brokenness and once again restore wholeness within your life. Have faith that God is willing and is able to do just that. If necessary, see suggested course of action.

In addition, the following are common words, expressions, usages, (e.g. slang or clichés), or a 'probable' that are metaphorically represented by flying:

- **"Fly a kite" (flying a kite should be highlighted):** This denotes one who does something or speak about something in order to test public opinion on it, or to issue a fraudulent financial document such as a check without having enough funds to cover it. See suggested course of action.
- **"Fly-by-night" (flying at night should be highlighted):** This alludes to one who is unscrupulous, especially in his or her business dealings, or one who is not creditworthy in business or commerce. This symbol also denotes something not lasting long, ephemeral. See suggested course of action.
- **"Fly in the face of" (something or someone flying in front of your face should be highlighted):** Your dream denotes one who has defied someone or something deliberately and/or recklessly. Dreamer, no matter how powerful or difficult a person or how uncertain or unpopular the choices and issues, always take the next biblical, ethical, and most informed step, for obedience to God's principles is safer. See suggested course of action.
- **"Fly-off-the-handle" (a handle and flying should be highlighted):** Your dream hints to one who loses his or her temper, without cause or justification. See suggested course of action.
- **"High as a kite" (a kite and someone or something, flying higher than the kite, should be highlighted):** This denotes one who is extremely excited or elated, or extremely intoxicated or drug-affected. If applicable, some manner of addiction support is suggested, e.g. AA, NA. See suggested course of action.

Suggested Course of Action

Question to consider and journal, did your dream depict any symbols that alludes to, the dreamer will make the necessary changes, spiritually, emotionally, and/or physically to affect a more positive outcome? If changes are initiated, your dreams will change.

Nonetheless, there is wisdom in every situation; be it joy and happiness or mourning; thus give careful thought to the instructions or coaching within your dream. Allow the change and choose wisdom instead of speaking foolishness. As a result, the spirit of humility will lead the way. Prayer, courage, and obedience are the key words right now. Pray every day for wisdom, and, if needed, for the courage to change, and for obedience to allow what God is trying to effect within your life a t present.

Consider and journal the following questions. The questions will help you determine; the issue at hand, how you feel about it, and what may have instigated it. What kind of flying was it? Why was there flying? Were others involved? If yes, who and in what manner were they involved? Keep in mind that the others represent a quality of you, see Note 3 at the beginning of Actions and Activities category. Did anyone get hurt emotionally, physically, or was disturbed in any way? How did you feel, and what did you do, because, of your feelings, regarding the flying and/or where you ended up or was going? Was it confusing, dangerous, happy, joyful, insignificant, life threatening, relaxing, safe, or scary? In view of your dream's context, namely flying, what choices are you making that may hinder you from changing? What choices, if applicable, are you making that may impair your spiritual growth, judgment, health, or that will encourage immorality and/or are you reacting out of fear? If so, what can you do to combat the paralyzing emotion of fear? Your answers, coupled with the interpretation, plus any additional information, should begin to unfold the subject matter and issue at hand, if not now, mull over things a few days. For more information, see index or relevant category and subcategory for other particulars within your dream.

Now, pray (See Prayer of Deliverance, pg. 897)

Specific Meaning

If, you have a very high propensity for flying (e.g. aerodynamics, aeronautics, balloons, blue angels, hand gliding, sky diving, or some other type of flying activity). Dreams of this sort, for the most part, are ordinary dreams, resulting from your daily activities (see Chapter One, Chalom). These sorts of dreams are usually about your routine, mundane activities or anxieties that overwhelm your mind during the day. They are an inner release mechanism, which helps provide you with emotional balance and the maintaining of your sanity. These dreams are not significant, and do not warrant special attention.

Note: If an accident was highlighted within your dream, this is a precautionary warning, especially if assistance was needed within the dream, or you were unable to fly. There may be potential for an accident. Dreamer, the details, kept with in context of your dream, should be relevant to your life, and closely resemble your real-life situations. Meaning it can actually occur during your awaked state. This will help you narrow down the specifics needed to support and steer you clear of possible mishaps. However, if your dream symbols are not easily, linked to your life activities, heed the spiritual implications (the interpretation).

FROZEN, FROST, REFRIGERATION, COLD, THAW: **Depicted by extreme cold or covered by ice or snow, to be preserved by freezing, or to thaw**

Some short descriptions of types, phrases, and other processes and particulars, connected in some way to this category are, for example, to be frozen, to see someone or thing frozen, frost, ice, or snow, refrigerate.

Unless otherwise noted elsewhere, if, in your everyday living, your awaked state, as part of your lifestyle, work, or ministerial activities, or a special event, you have a very real connection with any type of frozen activity. For example, cryogenics, cryonics, refrigeration, snow removal, meteorology, laboratory work, (also see content list for this category), your dream is not significant and does not warrant special attention.

Otherwise noted, this dream of being very cold may be a real time ordinary dream (see Chapter One, Chalom); whereas the dreamer's sleeping environment is physically very cold. These dreams are not significant, and do not warrant special attention, except to encourage the dreamer to get warm.

Otherwise noted, see Note 1 at the beginning of Actions and Activities category.

To determine who your dream is for you or another, see Note 3 at the beginning of Actions and Activities category.

Symbols and Referents: Dreams of ice, frost, refrigeration, snow, or anyone or thing frozen; generally suggest a gaining of control over a difficult situation, God's favor, His recompense for diligence; and/or ensnarement of foes.

Category Content - If not listed see index, perchance, for your specific type of frozen dream activity.

- To be Frozen or Very Cold or Lowered Body Temperature
- Coldness

- Freeze up
- Ice figures, see category Cutting (Sculpt)
- Frost Covered
- Ice
- Break the ice
- Cut no ice (to want to cut ice, but do not or cannot)
- Ice (aka jewelry, ice connected to jewelry in some way)
- Ice (dream associated with drugs)
- Ice (dream associated with death)
- On ice (to be on top of a thick block of ice)
- On thin ice (to be on top of a thin layer of ice)
- Refrigeration, Refrigerator, or Freezer (icebox, to refrigerate, cool, chill, preserve by chilling)
- Thaw, Thawing, Melting, or Unfreeze

To be Frozen or Very Cold or Lowered Body Temperature: This dream has three meanings (choose one). (1) Male dreamer: Your greatest adversary is your lack of learning, especially in the area of reading and writing. In order to, rightly understand God's word, you will have to discipline yourself to sit down and read, get a dictionary, and really understand what you're reading; write it down, and clearly state to others your understanding of things. For it is written, carefully study to present yourself approved unto God, a worker that need not to be ashamed, rightly handling the word of truth (2 Timothy 2:15). Dreamer, invest in you, invest in some type of adult education; a man or woman cannot learn without a teacher, and most times, a teacher is summoned and hired. This type of diligence will cause you to; properly finish your course God has destined for you. Moreover, by this, an adversary will go from before you, namely illiteracy, and your words will give birth, spiritually, to many. See suggested course of action. (2) Dreamer, fear not, your greatest enemy will go from before you. The sin of their mouth, the words of their lips, has (or soon will) caused their pride to be dealt with publicly. As a result, t hey will no longer be able to bother you. Even more, God will abundantly supply your needs, for He has promised to bless you. To be blessed: Gifts of God's grace, anything God freely gives you, absolution, the Holy Spirit, salvation, regeneration, eternal life, health, children, love of family, longevity, necessities, prosperity, and dominion over all that is yours; and all are parts of the supply of grace, and all are sanctified by the Lord, and technically belongs to Him. The result of this supply in your life will be peace. (3) Lowered Body temperature: This choice has three parts (one or two may apply). (a) Forsake not the assembly of yourself with other people of like faith, and develop Christian friendships, and relationships. This keeps your soul sensiti ve to all things Christian. Extend a warm and eloquent greeting to all fellow Christians. Often, we isolate from the very people we need spiritually. Isolation oftentimes happens because you're not comfortable within the context of the Christian community anymore, due to rejection, betrayal, or feelings of low self-confidence. Thus, you begin establishing relationships that are not connected to any faith-based community, and perhaps are even hostile to most things Christian. Dreamer must prepare mentally and emotionally to get out of your comfort zone, for you are becoming one whom believers will interact with socially on very personal levels (e.g. business partner, friendship, marriage, and/or other mutual relationships). (b) Your innocence and righteousness before the sight of God has caused you to be closely watched. Speak good things of the Lord's grace poured out upon you. You will also be healed from some malady or sickness as you pray for mercy. See one of the following regarding your present dilemma, especially where you need God's mercy, so that divine healing will be affected. (c) Dreamer, does anyone feel as though you owe him or her something, or do you feel you owe someone? Reason to make good on any obligatory relationships, somehow, for, if taken for granted or lingered too long, they can become bad for the soul, creating feelings of awkwardness. They clog your spiritual arteries, preventing warm, healthy feelings from circulating through your spirit and your consciousness, creating those awkward and contentious feelings, and sometimes divide within relationships

In addition, the following are common words, expressions, usages, (e.g. slang or clichés), or a 'probable' that are metaphorically represented by frozen or very cold:

- **Coldness:** Your dream denotes animosity towards someone. See suggested course of action.
- **Freeze up:** Your dream denotes that the dreamer is blocking or preventing something from moving forward. See suggested course of action.

To see someone or thing frozen: This dream has two meanings (choose one). (1) Unfortunately, the dreamer's actions, attitude, and/or words have provoked a grievous offense within another. Thus, dreamer needs to check your attitude and behavior towards others. Fortunately, the wicked plans of someone against the dreamer, because of the dreamer's insulting ways, will be brought out into the open, but this is primarily due to that person's own vindictive nature. That person will be made humbled before you. The same trap they have set for you will trap them. However, is there anythin g the dreamer can do to help lighten the situation, out of a spirit of love? For, it is the dreamer's own condescendingly disrespectful and pe rhaps boastful attitude that instigated the offense within the person; you cannot say you've done nothing. For example, a frozen car does refer to the dreamer's lifestyle and activities. For more information, see index or relevant category and subcategory f or specific action, activity, person, animal, or place frozen or highlighted. See suggested course of action. (2) To see persons or things frozen together: This choice has three parts (choose one). (a) Your praise will cause you to, completely overcome your situation, and to be victorious. Yes, your praise will cause you to overcome your present darkness for He rewards them that diligently serve Him. Additionally, and only if unmarried, couple this interpretation with one of the following (choose one). (b) Unmarried male dreamer only: Because of your diligence, you will receive the approval of a great leader to marry his daughter, if you so choose. (c) Unmarried female dreamer only: Someone will be specially introduced to you, and you two will connect. This is your future husband, if you so choose. He will be a wise leader.

Frost Covered: Your dream is figurative of God's power, as well as the frailty of the dreamer. There is a physical weakness or ill health, due to a vice, or shortcoming, within the life of the dreamer. Do not be dismayed, but celebrate God's control over your state of affairs. Have faith, for He will impart life, healing, health, strength, and wisdom to you. For grace employs health and its wages is wholeness and prosperity. God will abundantly supply your needs, for He has promised to bless you. To be blessed: Gifts of God's grace, anything God freely gives you, absolution, the Holy Spirit, salvation, regeneration, eternal life, health, children, love of family, longevity, necessities, prosperity, and dominion over all that is yours; and all are parts of the supply of grace, and all are sanctified by the Lord, and technically belongs to Him. The result of this supply in your life will be peace. For more information, see index or relevant category and subcategory for specific action, activity, person, animal, or place covered with frost or highlighted. Kept within context of your dream and the interpretation, other references highlighted may also be points of relevance, regarding the dreamer's vice, weakness, ill health, and/or present dilemma. See suggested course of action.

Ice: Your dream speaks to an imbalance in, your intellect, spirituality, and faith in God; contributing directly to your depression. The breach is so deep it seems impossible to restore. You're in need of a revival; specifically, a renewal of i nterest concerning the existence, nature, and worship of God, and of His divine involvement in the universe and human life. By way o f your dream, God is letting you know there will be a renewal and restoration within your mind, body, and soul, anticipate this. Do you trust that God can effect a revival within you? He can and will. There will be a flash of insight, a sudden awareness, recognition, or realization of all these concerns, the imbalance, breach, depression, prayerlessness, faithlessness. This p ersonal revival will reconnect and unify, again, your intellect to your spirituality, as well as revive and restore faith and prayer within your life. Instead of worshiping God from the perspective of your head (intellect), you will again worship Him with your whole heart, mind, body, and soul.

In addition, the following are common words, expressions, usages, (e.g. slang or clichés), or a 'probable' that are metaphorically represented by ice:

- **Break the ice (to dream of breaking or crushing ice):** Your dream suggests that the dreamer and/or someone you've just met will overcome the initial uneasiness felt under awkward circumstances.
- **Cut no ice (to want to cut ice, but do not or cannot):** Your dream suggests that the dreamer will fail to impress or make a difference.
- **Ice (aka jewelry, ice connected to jewelry in some way):** Your dream denotes stolen merchandise, especially diamonds or jewelry in general. Elohim knows all, you have not gotten away; justice will prevail.
- **Ice (dream associated with drugs):** Your dream denotes a concentrated form of the drug methamphetamine, "meth". This is deadly to the dreamer.
- **Ice (dream associated with death):** Your dream suggests that the dreamer or another will actually kill somebody. Elohim knows all, you will not get away; justice will prevail.
- **On ice (to be on top of a thick block of ice):** Your dream denotes something is in abeyance or in a state of being postponed, as well, that something is in a place of safekeeping.
- **On thin ice (to be on top of a thin layer of ice):** Your dream denotes you're in an unsafe, difficult, or vulnerable situation.

Refrigeration, Refrigerator, or Freezer (icebox, to refrigerate, cool, chill, preserve by chilling): This dream has four meanings (one or all may apply). (1) Dreamer prepare for "the" change. What is "the" change? Dreamer has been made aware of the imminence of some level of advancement (e.g. a raising in rank or position, a furtherance of some enterprise, gradual improvement, growth or development, be it spiritual, physical, emotional, or financial). Dreamer, must prepare mentally and emotionally to get out of your comfort zone, for you are becoming one whom believers will interact with socially on very personal levels (e.g. business partner, friendship, marriage, and/or other mutual relationships). (2) Your home will be identified as one who serves the Lord, extending a very warm and eloquent invitation to all fellow Christians. You will say of your home, here you are welcome; here it is safe to come in and eat, make yourself at home. Moreover, you will say with pleasure, as for me, and my household, we are serving the Lord, according to the proper spirit of the Word. (3) Dreamer, do not exalt your wisdom over God's wisdom based on your own feelings, thoughts, and ideas, especially those feelings, thoughts, and/or ideas that are dark, and not proper or legitimate, according to God's word, and that can be easily refuted, within scripture. For error will not lead you to where God has purpose for you to be, it will put a stain on your purpose. (4) If refrigerator was not clean, or in bad condition, this may allude to a health issue with your skin. The extent of the condition of the refrigerator will determine the "majorness" of the skin problem. If condition of refrigerator was very bad, this is a good indicator that your skin problem is major, requiring medical attention. If minor condition, e.g. a small stain, this is a go od indicator that your skin problem is minor, requiring minor medical attention. Nonetheless, if there is a skin problem, it is recommended that you do see a medical professional, before tending to any health issues yourself or attempting to self - diagnosis.

Thaw, Thawing, Melting, or Unfreeze: Your dream was sent to encourage. God's power has made a way out of no way for you, and your state of affairs is turning around. Dreamer, there will be a relaxation or slackening of tension in your l ife, stop, and feel the tension leaving. Those who have charged you falsely, with malicious intent, attacking your good name and reputation will be far from you. Others will become less hostile, as will you. You will be more relaxed, easygoing, and genial. The necessity to be reconciled with others than to always be in opposition has been resolved. Dreamer, you have simply taken the higher ground. You have re-evaluated your life, learned from your mistakes, found new directions in solving problems, pursued healing, sought out encouragement, and figured out what God would like you to change in order to bet ter fulfill His purpose. Moreover, you have learned the principles and Christian values that encourage one to reach out and touch others in a loving and graceful manner; ultimately finding yourself promoting the genuine cause of Christ and the good of others. Spiritually mature, you are a very peaceful and poised individual; now, prepared, you will be honored publicly. Caution, you should not think that your accomplishments are purely of your own volition. Truthfully, it is God, who gives you the capabi lity and strength to achieve success. This is especially true of your struggles with your sinful tendencies, whether they manifest as a lack of concern or interest in the things of God, a stubborn resistance to the will of God, or laziness. If it had not been for God's efforts on your behalf, you would not have been able to overcome any negative tendencies. He delivered you. Any achievements you will accomplish, or have accomplished, any good deeds you've done, any fulfillment of God's will, was, and still is, dependent upon divine aid and guidance. One merely places his or her hand under the weight carried exclusively by God. Therefore, do not claim credit for your achievements. Nevertheless, your words have pleased the Lord, for they are words of wisdom. Thus, He has done according to your words; go forward with purpose, looking for results, for you are headed towards your chosen destiny. You will experience a miracle very soon, "it" (whatever "it" is to you personally) will happen, and you will be blessed. All of these promises will begin now. Even now, Jesus is coming to see about you, keep your faith, regarding what you've believed God for, because He has promised and He will fulfill His promise. Moreover, God will grant you both riches and honor, and "if" (if refers to "conditional") you continue to walk in His ways, diligently and obediently, you will have long life too. This is His promise to you, and He will do according to His promise. Additionally, use your cr eative passion to inspire others, via inspirational preaching, teaching, acting, or some other medium of expression. For you are gifted in many areas, and you have access to prophetic wisdom, thus, you are required to be a transformational force in people's lives, via not neglecting the gift that is within you. You will now be led into situations, where you will show up when most needed, and then disappear without a thought of compensation. You will be dispatched on missions, to help believers who are facing urgent needs during a crisis, and/or in an emergency, and to give instant help, as well as, to express God's loving kindness, His grace, mercy, and compassion. You are sent to protect and defend those who obediently love God, and who is loved by God. Altruistic, goodhearted, and generous service to God and others is beneficial at this time. Dreamer, love God so completely that you will never forsake His service for any reason. One last thing, respect cautionary advice about something imminent (especially imminent danger or other unpleasantness), remain thankful, and become aware and tap into the intuitive insight you are (or will be) receiving. Read, understand, and embrace Psalm 147:12-20.

Suggested Course of Action

Question to consider and journal, did your dream depict any symbols that alludes to, the dreamer will make the necessary changes, spiritually, emotionally, and/or physically to affect a more positive outcome? If changes are initiated, your dreams will change.

Nevertheless, dreamer, do not be distressed; celebrate God's control over your state of affairs. Have faith, for He will impart life and wisdom to you, and He will give you the primary desire of your heart. Further, dreamer needs to remember that in gaining control over your difficult situations, remember, it is, and has always been God, who has given insight and favor that you might overcome. Be aware of His provisions, acknowledge His authority over them, and the authority granted you as His child. A spirit of humility will cause you to continue to prosper. Prayer and humbleness are the key words right now. Pray every day for wisdom, and if needed, for the courage to not sabotage your blessings from God. God's blessings: Gifts of God's grace, anything God freely gives you, absolution, the Holy Spirit, salvation, regeneration, eternal life, health, children, love of family, longevity, necessities, prosperity, and dominion over all that is yours; and all are parts of the supply of grace, an d all are sanctified by the Lord, and technically belongs to Him. The result of this supply in your life will be peace.

Consider and journal the following questions. The questions will help you determine; the issue at hand, how you feel about it, and what may have instigated it. What was frozen, frost, refrigerated, or snow covered? What caused the freeze? Were others involved? If yes, who and in what manner were they involved? Keep in mind that the others represent a quality of you, see Note 3 at the beginning of Actions and Activities category. Did anyone get hurt emotionally, physically, or was disturbed in any way? How did you feel, and what did you do, because, of your feelings, regarding the frozen, frost, refrigerated, or snow-covered situation? Was it agitating, confusing, dangerous, disturbing, frustrating, peace with the situation, happy, joyful, life threatening, safe, scary, or unsure? Where were you? Was the place unfamiliar to you? Were you coherent? In view of your dream's context, namely frozen, what choices are you making that may contribute to your harsh state of affairs? What choices, if applicable, are you making that may impair your spiritual growth, judgment, health, or th at will encourage immorality and/or are you reacting out of fear? If so, what can you do to combat the par alyzing emotion of fear? Do you know why you behave or believe as you do? Your answers, coupled with the interpretation, plus any additional information, should begin to unfold the subject matter and issue at hand, if not now, mull over things a few days. For more information, see index or relevant category and subcategory for other particulars within your dream.

Now, pray (See Prayer of Deliverance, pg. 897)

Specific Meaning

If, you have a very high chance to deal with things frozen (e.g. cryogenics, cryonics, ice cream, refrigeration, snow removal, meteorology, laboratory work, or some other kind of frozen activity). Dreams of this sort, for the most part, are ordinary dreams, resulting from your daily activities (see Chapter One, Chalom). These sorts of dreams are usually about your routine, mundane activities or anxieties that overwhelm your mind during the day. They are an inner release mechanism, which helps provide you with emotional balance and the maintaining of your sanity. These dreams are not significant, and do not warrant special attention.

GAMES: Something played for fun or competition. The activity has specific rules.

Some short descriptions of types, phrases, and other processes and particulars, connected in some way to this category are, for example, athletics games, board games, card games, children games, educational games, hi-tech games, gambling games, party games, puzzles, quizzes, video games.

Unless otherwise noted elsewhere, if, in your everyday living, your awaked state, as part of your lifestyle, work, or ministerial activities, or a special event, you have a very real connection with any type of game activity. For example, ath lete, coach, casino operator, gambler, game show host, team player, participant, (also see content list for this category), your dream is not significant and does not warrant special attention.

Otherwise noted, see Note 1 at the beginning of Actions and Activities category.

To determine who your dream is for you or another, see Note 3 at the beginning of Actions and Activities category.

Symbols and Referents: Dreams of games generally deal with spiritual immaturity, moral weaknesses; ways based on exploring alternatives to God's righteous principles, as well as, creating a sense of unity with the wickedness around you. The intentions of the dreamer may be found in the objective of the game, its' rules, and how you played. For example, what is th e objective of the game? Did you play fair? Did you win or lose? How did you feel during and after the game? Rate your sportsmanship, coupled with the interpretation.

Category Content - If not listed see index, perchance, for your specific type of game dream activity.

- Cheerleader
- Children Games or Game Rooms or Playgrounds (Jump Rope, Hopscotch, Marbles, Skating, or any place where child's play may occur)
- Gambling Games
- Mazes, Puzzles, or Riddles
- Musical Chairs
- Sports (all athletic and obstacle games, including any place where athletic activities may occur, e.g. Athletic, Sport Facilities or Fields, Arenas, Dugouts, Gyms, Stadiums, Swimming pools)
- Tabletop Games (Cards, Checkers, Chess, Dominoes, and other board and card games)
- Video, Hi-tech Games (arcade, computer, console, handheld, mobile, online games)
- Other Games (Educational, Party, Parlor, and Q & A)

Cheerleader: Your dream was sent to encourage. Dreamer, God is getting ready to restore you, and you will reap your due recompense, for God rewards those who diligently serve Him. You have been judged diligent in your efforts. Many will rejoice with you, they that are rich and powerful and those who are full of faith. You shall go out with joy and be led fort h with peace.

Children Games or Game Rooms or Playgrounds (Jump Rope, Hopscotch, Marbles, Skating, or any place where child's play may occur): This dream has two meanings (choose one). (1) While your dream points to spiritual immaturity, it presupposes Jehovah's restoration of the dreamer. Although you should be relatively mature by now, you still show signs of immaturity. Signs of immaturity include, but are not limited to, a tendency to be easily misled, an inability to tell right from wrong. Suing others over relatively minor financial disputes; coveting and swindling; vicious and violent in selfishness; so committed to your own personal rights that you don't genuinely care about the cause of Christ and the good of others, and yet you pride yourself as being more spiritual than others. Those who are mature have trained themselves to recognize the difference between right and wrong and then do what is right; dreamer, seriously press towards the mark of the high calling of God. This interpretation will also be alluded to by a prophecy that will be given you. With that said, favorably, in spite of some behavioral issues, your dream assumes that your identity has changed. It supposes that you will earnestly put forth the effort to do the right thing, and that you have been completely forgiven, sanctified, and declared righteous and justified in God's eyes. Your restoration will not only be marvelous in the eyes of people, but also in the eyes of the Lord. A beautiful future awaits you. If relevant, there will be an abundance of your descendants, and you will be blessed of God. To be blessed: Gifts of God's grace, anything God freely gives you, absolution, the Holy Spirit, salvation, regeneration, eternal life, health, children, love of family, longevity, necessities, prosperity, and dominion over all that is yours; and all are parts of the supply of g race, and all are sanctified by the Lord, and technically belongs to Him. The result of this supply in your life will be peace. (2) To see others playing children games: Your dream suggests that the dreamer will be delivered from a phobia and develop an ability to help others grow and go forward spiritually in Christ, you will be a mentor. You will be able to enjoy the fellowship of family and friends openly, without fear or pretense. You will grow to a good old age; in perfect peace and safety, and will be bles sed of God, because of a right relationship with Jehovah who dwells in your midst.

Gambling Games: This dream has three meanings (choose one). (1) Because of emotional or spiritual immaturity, the dreamer pretends to be a particular type of person, acting deceptively. Example, you avoid agreeing (or disagreeing) with a suggestion, invitation, or proposal, with the intention of appearing tolerant. You want to be received in a particular way t o make an impression that is not true to the God you serve. It is always better to be true to God, than to appear "politically correct" or to be liked or received by everybody. It is by this others will respect and understand you better. See suggested course of action. (2) Dreamer, consider your shift in thinking. You now, having in yourself nothing that you respect more than greed, you are willing to sacrifice all, God, principle, family, and friend, to the ideologies of those who newly surround you, without inquiring as to whether their beliefs are worthy of consideration or not. Your new way is based on exploring alternatives to God's righteous principles, as well as, creating a sense of unity with the wickedness around you. Thus, God's name is contemptuously reproached by some because of you. You are in a strange land, a great way from love of God and your own principles. This way cries out against godly ethics, and the end results, offends any sense of godliness. This evil will not be remedied until a change comes by way of prayer and heartfelt repentance to Jesus. To Jesus pray, Psalm 51, this followed by appropriate application of wisdom, can conceivably avert some of the repercussions of your choices. This is what is called leaving a blessing behind. See suggested course of action. (3) To see others playing gambling games: You are entering into or live in a precarious neighborhood, can be urban or suburban; where the wisest of heart, can be led by deception to explore alternatives to God's righteous principles, and to create a sense of unity with wickedness. Being a foremost leader amongst people, if you truly are, you should not take a chance on degrading yourself or of profaning the name of the Lord. You are to remain holy unto the Lord, set apart from the wicked games people play. Consider your surroundings and determine what you will include in your life and what you won't, set godly standards, and then stand by them. See suggested course of action.

Mazes, Puzzles, or Riddles: Your dream was sent to arouse awareness of your prophetic ability, which you have not yet, accessed. Dreamer, your prophetic gifting is beginning to awaken. You may now begin to assess your prophetic abilities, practice, and use your abilities confidently, to help others. As you are naturally endowed with this ability, freely help others, without thought of recompense.

Musical Chairs: Dreamer, consider your shift in thinking. Things are not as good as you claim. You are extravagantly wasteful in your spending, to a degree bordering on recklessness. You have recently adopted a bourgeois mentality. A bourgeois mentality is concerned only with material wealth, prosperity, and comfort, at any expense. It sacrifices children, family, and morality to the hollowness of greed, and satisfaction of immoral desires and appetites. You now, having in yourself nothing that you respect more than greed, you are willing to sacrifice all, God, principle, family, and friend, to the ideologies of those who newly surround you, without inquiring as to whether their beliefs are worthy of consideration or not. Your new way is based on exploring alternatives to God's righteous principles, as well as, creating a sense of unity with the wickedness around you. Thus, God's name is contemptuously reproached by some because of you. You are in a strange space, a great way from love of God and His principles, which you respected some time ago. Sanctify your sorrows and tears in a correct and proper way, with your heart towards God. Fasting and praying before the God of heaven who sees in s ecret. This will result in spiritual renewal. See suggested course of action.

Sports (all athletic and obstacle games, including any place where athletic activities may occur, e.g. Athletic, Sport Facilities or Fields, Arenas, Dugouts, Gyms, Stadiums, Swimming pools): This dream has two meanings (choose one). (1) Your dream is a notification to the dreamer. There is a God ordained undertaking that you're destined to achieve. Your time of action on behalf of the Kingdom of God is quickly approaching. Your days of grounding and preparation are over. Your attitude and choices during your time of grounding and preparation were either advantageous or are proving wearisome. If advantageous, you are prepared to go forward. You have become one who is determined and steadfast, and is respected as such. You are counseled, now, to develop specific and reachable objectives, and some manner of accountability that will help lead you to your desired goals and ministry. As well, dreamer, accept yourself just as you are, your strengths, and your weaknesses and flaws. You will fulfill your purpose, receive your desires, reap prosperity, and inherit eternal life. If yo ur time of grounding has proven wearisome, there remains a lack of preparedness (see next choice). (2) To see others participating in sports games (or if your time of grounding has proven wearisome): Your time of grounding and preparation has proven wearisome to you. Dreamer, if you continue in your mindset, your attitude will cause you to not, possess the qualities of one who is determined and steadfast. You give-up too easily and quit too soon. A change of mind is needed, for there is power in a changed mind. Dreamer, if your true intent is on doing God's will, reaching a level of proficiency in ministry, reaping prosperity, experiencing spiritual joy, and most importantly inheriting eternal life, you will have to practice restricting y ourself in all things. You must bring your appetites and sensual desires under subjection, sacrificing personal comforts. You will need to lay aside every obstacle that hinders you and causes you to forfeit God's principles, including laziness; that you might r each the point where you are capable of accomplishing your mission. This type of discipline will also help you see yourself and your issues more clearly; affecting a paradigm shift. It will be up to you. You are free to do as you please; you still have personal liberty. However, you can no longer pretend to have a determined and steadfast quality; you must actually possess it within, in order to complete your purpose and to prosper. Prayer and fasting is the first step in this process towards clarity. You ar e also counseled to accept yourself just as you are, your weaknesses and flaws and your strengths. Afterward, develop specific and reachable objectives, and some manner of accountability that will help lead you to your desired goals, and help you develop a disciplined and determined spirit, set "times frames" for major choices. For example, do not move from your present place of worship for at least seven years, and make it happen, come what may. Reading God's Word, coupled with wise application, daily, will also keep things in perspective, real, and balanced. As well as, allow for God's purposes and plans for you personally, to come to the forefront. See suggested course of action.

Tabletop Games (Cards, Checkers, Chess, Dominoes, and other board and card games): This dream has four meanings (choose one). (1) Generally, these types of games allude to the old cliché "playing mind games" with yourself or with people. Suggesting that dreamer is in denial of certain negative behaviors within you. You are unaware of the deepest innermost part of your feelings and emotions, which are provoked by the actions of others. For example, your deeply hidden feelings of rejection, often stir-up your "fight nature", when others make you feel rejected, or cause a reclusive type attitude. No matter the behavior or feelings, your emotions run deep, and dreamer needs to become more self-aware of your defense mechanism that you might be genuinely free and at peace within. Couple this with one of the following. (2) If dreamer was playing a tabletop game alone, or did not see the others who were playing, or did not know or remember who was playing, this suggest that there is some anger issues and discontent within the heart of the dreamer that needs to be dealt with. Core issue, dreamer, bad things do happen to innocent people and a bad thing happened to you. However, you no longer have to be the bad thing that happens to others. Ask your Heavenly Father to forgive you of your sins, as you forgive those who violated yo u, and forgive yourself, and no longer will the bad thing hold sway over your entire life. For whom Jesus sets free, is free. By grace (the free and unmerited favor and beneficence of God), prayer, and change, your life will begin to transform and you wi ll be restored to the person you was intended to be. (3) If dreamer was playing a tabletop game with others and you knew them: This choice has two parts (choose one). (a) Dreamer, you are in line for a celebrity status type of position on some level, exercise your office with humility, love, faith, compassion, and empathy, not domineering over those within your sphere of influence, but being an example to those you are allowed to influence. Please read 1 Peter 5:1-11, and make this your anthem. (b) Unfortunately, at present, the dreamer is attempting to manipulate a family member, friend, job, or perhaps those you were playing with. Do you see this characteristic within yourself? For sure, you have been made aware of your "fight" nature, "takeover" personality, or extreme competitiveness, from a very young age. Dreamer, if this "base" part of your nature is not checked, and is allowed to reign, and it can reign with demonic influence, you will become, spiritually, a bad person, seducer, with tyrannical tendencies. See suggested course of action. (4) To see others playing tabletop games. This suggests an adversary is in the dreamer's midst, and is in unity with another. They're very calculating in their efforts aga inst you, very busy stirring up jealousies, misrepresenting you, and causing many people to be angry with you. Favorably, God has given you authority to trample on snakes and scorpions and to overcome all the power of the enemy; nothing will harm you (Luke 10:19). Pray for wisdom and a strategy; praising God for His support, then do what you need to do to defend yourself against the onslaughts of your enemy. Have faith and confidence that God is with and for you.

In addition, the following is a common word, expression, or usage (e.g. slang or cliché), or a 'probable' that is metaphorically represented by this subcategory

It's **"in the cards"** for you to be whatever your dreams, acumen, and anointing deems you can be. Depending on whom you were playing cards with (e.g. playing cards with a celebrity), then maybe it's "in the cards" for you to become a celebrity.

Video, Hi-tech Games (arcade, computer, console, handheld, mobile, online games): This dream has two meanings (choose one). (1) Your inheritance (money, property, and/or a title) is waiting on you to heal and forgive. You profane that which is holy, because you have been wounded by one considered pious, who is not. Dreamer, this is wisdom, no one person, hypocrite, or not, is the full representation of God or of the Kingdom of God, the world to come; therefore, no longer allow the enemy to rob you of your intended destiny. For, from you, a ministry will be born, from which men and women, who have never considered God, will begin to call upon the name of the Lord from their brokenness and pain. In this, you will find your heritage, your legacy, your family. You will cause a people to become one, and nothing will be restrained from them. Only, do not allow the power of the oneness, your ability to lead, and pride to corrupt you spiritually and cause you to revert to profaning that, which is holy. Upon stepping into your destiny, remember you have been wounded, and if not dealt with holistically, via prayer, fasting, Christian counseling, and support, the sacrilegious, irreverent, and disrespectful acting out you did (is doing) because of your wounds, will come back to haunt you. See suggested course of action. (2) To see others playing video, hi-tech games: You are well aware of your destiny, and how great it is, but you do not know how to accomplish that which you know to do. Your first objective should be to, fast and pray. If urged by God, declare a one, two, or three day fast without food. Second, seek professional Christian counseling, and other supports, to deal with your wounds holistically. Wr ite your vision down, along with your goals and reachable objectives. By way of diligent prayer, fasting, Christian counseling, and other supports, you will find ways to accomplish your goals and objectives, one at a time, one day at a time. You will reach your destiny. See suggested course of action.

Other Games (Educational, Party, Parlor, and Q & A): This dream has three meanings (choose one). (1) Most social games are designed to test skill and/or intelligence. These types of games will often suggest that there is a need to learn facts and skills, as they relate to your life, ministry, and/or purpose, and to apply those facts and skills wisely. As well, the intentions of the dreamer can be found in the objective and rules of the game, as well as, how you played the game. For example, what i s the objective of the game? Did you play fair? Did you win or lose? How did you feel during and after the game? Rate your sportsmanship, journal your observations. In view of your dream's context, what are the life lessons to be learned that you may go on to spiritual maturity and live life wisely. If necessary, see suggested course of action. (2) Your dream was sent to demonstrate grace, via a warning of a dark generational issue, hereditary within your family line (e.g. maternal and/or paternal, grandparents, siblings, aunts, uncles, cousins). Dreamer, character traits from ancestors, namely genetic codes and traits, will often trouble and taunt the offspring of a given progenitor, especially generational issues (Exodus 20:5-7). The demons that have so plague your family line, are now visiting (re-visiting) you. Your issue is demonically instigated and it is spiritually perverse, perhaps sexually perverse as well (e.g. adultery, fornication, homosexuality, prostitution, whorishness.). These spirits attempt to "bend" the personality as early as possible, with regards to age, towards a certain direction, oftentimes towards a way that is desolate and wicked, for it is Satan's scheme to kill and make desolate all; thus, to keep some from rising up and leading their generation to Christ (see the birth of Moses, Exodus 1:15-2:10). Favorably, generational curses and issues can stop with you (Jeremiah 31:29, 30; Ezekiel 18:2-14, 20-23). Thus, your Heavenly Father is requiring that you overcome and subdue negative and dark emotions, feelings, behaviors, and/or ideas that would influence you, before they overcome you. Dreamer, God is not asking you to do something you cannot do. For a surety, vanquishing of the coming influence can be done. By faith, you will need to declare some kind of fast and commit to it, for a long period-of-time, to abate the demonically instigated circumstance, you find yourself in now, Matthew 6:16-18. Try abstaining from food and drink (midnight to 6 PM), twice a week, and refrain from words, attitudes, people, places, and things, including music, magazines, videos, TV, or any such things that fuel anger and discontent, and stir up lustful feelings. This is also known as, faith with works, read, understand, and embrace James 2:14-26. Nonetheless, earnestly pray, God will guide, enable, and answer you as to the type of fast. Moreover, command all unclean spirits to leave you, and to go into an unclean thing or into outer darkness, in the name of Jesus, and renounce any generational curse (or morally objectionable behavior) that is affecting your life. Claiming the propitiatory sacrifice of Jesus on the cross, having been made a curse, Christ has made us free from curses (Galatians 3:13). Such provision has the just God made to fulfill the curse, which He pronounced on the earth, bearing the punishment, Himself, due to sin. He died in our place, on our account, that He might bring us near, reconciling us to Himsel f. Additionally, if relevant, forgive your mother and/or father for the darkness (aka curse) they may have perpetuated, for they knew not what they done. Forgiveness is important to your success (Matthew 6:12-15, 8:21-35). See suggested course of action. (3) To see others playing other types of games: Although, you are known to take on the biggest challenges in order to make the longest strides, at this moment, during this season in your life, don't go chasing big ideas. Your biggest challeng e, right now, is your moral weaknesses. There is an old saying that goes, "Your gifting may take you, where your character can't keep you". In order to fulfill your commission, to reach many for Christ, you will need to, seriously begin reflecting upon your moral weaknesses. How you might bring them under subjection to Christ's principles, and how you might aspire for a certain level of purity. Try abstaining from food and drink (midnight to 6 PM), and refraining from words, attitudes, people, places, and things, including music, internet, videos, TV, magazines, or any such things that fuel anger and discontent, and stir up lustful feelings, fast at least twice a week until. Earnestly pray, God will guide, enable, and answer you as to the type of fast. Moreover, command all unclean spirits to leave you, and to go into an unclean thing or into outer darkness, in the name of Jesus, and renounce any generational curse (or morally objectionable behavior) that is affecting your life. Claiming the propitiatory sacrifice of Jesus on the cross, having been made a curse, Christ has made us free from curses (Galatians 3:13). Nonetheless, God will lead the way. However, if your moral weaknesses are not brought under subjection, you will become an object of scorn, derision, laughter, a joke to all who encounters you. See suggested course of action.

Suggested Course of Action

Question to consider and journal, did your dream depict any symbols that alludes to, the dreamer will make the necessary changes, spiritually, emotionally, and/or physically to affect a more positive outcome? If changes are initiated, your dreams will change.

Notwithstanding, remember your identity in Christ and attempt to live consistent with it. How you view yourself, is what you will value. If you view yourself primarily as a sexual object, you will value sexual immorality. If you view yourself as a financial survivor, you will value material gain. If you view yourself as a child of God, one who is secure in Christ, whom God promises to care for in this life, and in the life to come, as one who is called to the high honor of representing God in this world, then you will value God, family, and others. Along with prayer and fasting, seek counsel from spiritual leaders.

Consider and journal the following questions. The questions will help you determine; the issue at hand, how you feel about it, and what may have instigated it. What kind of game was played or action performed? Were others involved? If yes, who and in what manner were they involved? Keep in mind that the others represent a quality of you, see Note 3 at the beginning of Actions and Activities category. Did anyone get hurt emotionally, physically, or was disturbed in any way? How did you feel, and what did you do, because, of your feelings, regarding the game? Did you know how to play? Di d you win, lose, or tie? Rate your sportsmanship. Was it agitating, confusing, dangerous, disturbing, frustrating, peace with the situ ation, happy, joyful, life threatening, safe, scary, or unsure? Where were you? Was the place unfamiliar to you? Were you coherent? In view of your dream's context, namely games, what choices are you making that may impair your spiritual and/or physical growth, judgment, or that will encourage immorality and/or are you reacting out of fear? If so, what can you do to combat the paralyzing emotion of fear? Do you esteem your reputation, your name? Do you know why you behave as you do? See also Ephesians 5. Your answers, coupled with the interpretation, plus any additional information, should begin to unfold the subject matter and issue at hand, if not now, mull over things a few days. For more information, see index or relevant category and subcategory for other particulars within your dream.

Now, pray (See Prayer of Deliverance, pg. 897)

Specific Meaning

If, in your everyday living, your awaked state, as part of your lifestyle, work or ministerial activities, or a special event, your chances are very high that you will participate in some type of games (e.g. professionally or some other level). Dreams of t his sort, for the most part, are ordinary dreams, resulting from your daily activities (see Chapter One, Chalom). These sorts of dreams are usually about your routine, mundane activities or anxieties that overwhelm your mind during the day. They are an inner release mechanism, which helps provide you with emotional balance and the maintaining of your sanity. These dreams are not significant, and do not warrant special attention.

PARADES: An organized procession or display of people celebrating a special occasion and often including decorated vehicles or floats, a marching band, people twirling batons and carrying banners, and/or people on horseback.

Some short descriptions of types, phrases, and other processes and particulars, connected in some way to this category. For example, arts festival, Christmas, commemorating famous leaders, Easter, Flower, Halloween, Independence Day, Labor Day, Mardi Gras, Memorial Day, military victory, New Year's Day, President's Day, pride, protest, rain on your parade, St. Patrick's Day, sports, victory, techno, Thanksgiving Day, ticker-tape, Veteran's Day, World Olympic Games.

Unless otherwise noted elsewhere, if, in your everyday living, your awaked state, as part of your lifestyle, work, or ministerial activities, or a special event, you have a very real connection with any type of parade activity. For example, parade organizer, participant, (also see content list for this category), your dream is not significant and does not warrant special attention.

Otherwise noted, see Note 1 at the beginning of Actions and Activities category.

To determine who your dream is for you or another, see Note 3 at the beginning of Actions and Activities category.

Symbols and Referents: Dreams of parades are primarily warning dreams. They generally suggest a change is vital in the way the dreamer believes and behaves, for the purposes of sanctification, purging, and preparation, getting the dreamer ready for some level of public exposure for honoring or open shame. If there is no change, prepare for open shame.

Category Content - If not listed see index, perchance, for your specific type of parade dream activity.

- Carnival, Festival Parade (usually with amplifiers, loudspeakers, techno, themed attire, people wearing masks, with flamboyant and flaunting exhibitions, highly colorful, showy and ostentatious)
- Pride Festival, Mardi Gras Carnival
- Celebratory, Pageantry Parade (held for special or triumphal occasions, usually with confetti, and an honoree, e.g. Ticker Tape)

- Commemorative Parade (usually with a historical or traditional flavor, Flag Day, Independence Day, Labor Day, Martin Luther King's Day, President's Day, Washington's Birthday, St. Patrick's Day)
- Holiday Parade (Christmas, Easter, Good Friday, New Year's Day, Thanksgiving, or Valentine's Day)
- Military Parade (Cinco de Mayo, Memorial Day, Patriot's Day, Veteran's Day, Military Victory)
- Soldiers, see category, People (Soldier)
- Parade Participants (Band Member, Chauffeur, Drum Major, Majorette, Observer, Organizer, Processional Member, or Sponsor)
- Parade Procession of (Airplanes, Animals, Flowers, Marching bands, People Twirling Batons, People Walking, or Decorated Vehicles, Parade Floats)
- Protest Parade (public demonstration of opposition or disapproval of contemporary social issues or for propaganda purposes)
- Sports, Victory Parade (high school, youth, Olympics, World Olympic Games, any professional games, usually with a sport activity theme)
- Cliché (Rain on your Parade)

Carnival, Festival Parade (usually with amplifiers, loudspeakers, techno, themed attire, people wearing masks, with flamboyant and flaunting exhibitions, highly colorful, showy and ostentatious): Your dream comes to strongly and earnestly urge the dreamer to embrace a more practical godliness (functional, mainstream, plain, and suitable for everyday use), as a guard against extremism, separatism, and false teachers. Do not embrace views well outside those of conventional Christianity. It is wise to stay within mainstream Judeo-Christianity. Privately study your bible and let your understanding be known to others. Believe nothing you cannot express, in its' entirety, openly and sensibly to the whole world, don't lie to hide your beliefs or the beliefs and/or actions of others. Reject any sort of isolated groups or beliefs that put forth, "we are the only ones", or that "the expected Messiah is here with us in this secret place". Jesus died for the whole world, and not exclusiv ely for any one sect or western denomination. His teachings are universal, far-reaching, and too deep for any one person or sect to grasp in its entirety (Psalm 92:5, 145:3, Romans 11:33). Most importantly, do not die, emotionally, spiritually and/or physically, for nobody or group. You have been called unto liberty, and you should stand fast in that liberty, by means of which Christ has made you free. Yet be very careful not to use this liberty as an occasion to indulge yourself in corrupt desires and practices; especially those that create alienation, contention, division, and falling out between you and family, friends, and/or fellow believers. Any minor differences that might be amongst you and others, deal with the issues with kindness, respect an d truthfulness; you should not strive with other believers but love one another with a selfless spiritual love felt by Christians for their fellow human beings. The Christian faith requires you to do so. See also 1 Timothy 6:3- 6. See suggested course of action.

Pride Festival, Mardi Gras Carnival: You are greatly conflicted and divided within. On the one hand, you desire to honor Jesus Christ as Lord and Savior. On the other, you are willing to renounce God that you might not be under His precepts because your lifestyle does not concur with His principles morally. The dreamer embraces a licentious liberty; you pursue your desires aggressively and egoistically, unchecked by morality. Although Christ has redeemed us from the curse of the law, yet He has not freed us from the obligation or wisdom of it, in that the gospel of Jesus Christ is a doctrine according to holiness, and is so far from blatant immorality and shamelessness that it compels us to avoid and/ or subdue such. Dreamer, per your dream, you are being asked to remember the ugly decadence of the lifestyle you're so willing to forfeit Christ for; to re-think your stance, and to decline the temporary relations of darkness that you might inherit a more enduring pleasure, and that being an entrance into paradise having answered God's call upon your life. Favorably, a person (e.g. associate, friend, old acquaintance, possible spouse) will enter your life as a messenger of God's grace. This person has come to guide you into wholeness and into a better understanding of Christ and His ways and means. Grace is, extended that yo u might change your heart. For, a new healthy, happy, prosperous lifestyle awaits you on this side of heaven, emotionally and physically. However, you must personally respond, repent, and genuinely commit to some type of righteous change to have this new life; with primary emphasis on life after this present life (see Acts 2:37-42). See suggested course of action.

Celebratory, Pageantry Parade (held for special or triumphal occasions, usually with confetti, and an honoree, e.g. Ticker Tape): While the dreamer may be a leader who is intensely bold, impressive, successful, prosperous, and versed in various religions. You flatter yourself too much to look deeply within, thus your dream. Your dream speaks of your narcissistic tendencies, your excessive and irrational beliefs in your own abilities and attractiveness in the eyes of others. It points towards fake pride, foolishness, pompousness, pretentiousness, and other superficial characteristics. You use your influence as an occasion to behave toward others as though they are less important or intelligent than you are; arrogantly inciting arguments, controversies, or strife, especially amongst Christians, who may be of a different mind than you. We should not engage ourselves to act arrogantly and to provoke or envy each other (Galatians 5:26). The dreamer should always maintain an attitude of love and service towards others; for all the law is fulfilled in you loving your fellow man as yourself. Love is the sum of the whole law and it is not arrogant or rude (see 1 Corinthians 13:1-13). See suggested course of action.

Commemorative Parade (usually with a historical or traditional flavor, Flag Day, Independence Day, Labor Day, Martin Luther King's Day, President's Day, Washington's Birthday, St. Patrick's Day): Your dream is a summons; an authoritative demand to appear at a particular place for a particular purpose, as this is your appointed time for change. Dreamer, your time to be about your heavenly Father's business is now. He has need of you; it is time for you to start your ministry. With that said, dreamer, there is a set assembly, designated to help you fulfill your purpose, therefore, find your church, and abide there, until, as well, heed the counsel of the overseers of the ministry. By heeding counsel, you will gain God's favor and be a light unto others. Dreamer, the counsel of the Lord makes wise, and pleases the sincere of heart and converts the soul (Psalm 19:7-14). God will cause you to be well known, celebrated, and full of joy, and if relevant happily married. Thus, do not be indecisive about the matter or long in deciding a church. Moreover, dreamer, refrain from all boasting or you will experience a downfall, which will "arduously" lead you to your destined place. On another vein, dreamer, you speak and/or write arrogantly about your accomplishments, possessions, and pilgrimages (see Proverbs 16:18). This is what the Lord says (to male or female), "Let not the wise man boast of his wisdom or the strong man boast of his strength or the rich man boast of his riches. But let him who boasts boast about this: That he understands and knows me, that I am the Lord, who exercises kindness, justice, and righteousness on earth, for in these I delight", declares the Lord (Jeremiah 9:23, 24; 1 Corinthians 1:31). Unfortunately, if you continue without change, expecting different results, you will be made a fool of, resulting in you acting insanely. Choosing to remain powerless, in spite of spiritual help, makes it easier for the enemy of our soul to subjugate. Evil spirits always lie-in-wait for those who are willing to be in denial, or even slightly deceived, just to remain justified in purposelessness. The specific type of commemorative parade may suggest the type of ministry that needs to be initiated by the dreamer in that particular assembly. For example, an Independence Day parade could suggests a ministry primarily focused on freedom from dependence upon, or control by, a person, animal, place, or organization. A Labor Day parade could suggest a resource ministry, primarily focused on assisting working people or pre-employment help. New Year's Day could possibly be a new beginnings ministry, geared towards the misguided, or those whose choices have led them down a negative life path. Pray, God will guide you as to what He has need of from you. See suggested course of action.

Holiday Parade (Christmas, Easter, Good Friday, New Year's Day, Thanksgiving, or Valentine's Day): Your dream suggests that the dreamer must become skilled at analyzing, discerning, and judging truth, so that little escapes your observation and deep understanding. A greater development of your mind for searching out truth is needed. Get involve in a search for wisdom and become a leader on whatever it is you are focusing on. Pursue knowledge with vigor. Dreamer, you are well capable to study and learn really deep and difficult subjects, and to search for hidden fundamentals. It will be through your mastery of illustrating God's truths that many will come together in unity; worshipping Jesus as Messiah. Your ministry will be anointed to reach and save multitudes of people from uncomfortable situations; circumstances where they feel confused, overwhelmed, or desolate. You will expose extreme and irrational beliefs, counterfeits, and perversions within Christendom that are being introduced by all venues of public communications; effecting reformation, refreshing, reconciliation, and reunions. Prepare for public honoring. Failure to make lifestyle adjustments to prepare for this great mission you've been call to, will cause you to be dishonored and ostracize, for a long period-of-time, due to you aggressively and selfishly pursuing sensual desires. See suggested course of action.

Military Parade (Cinco de Mayo, Memorial Day, Patriot's Day, Veteran's Day, Military victory): Your dream comes to encourage the dreamer. There is a struggle within you, between your old nature and your new nature, the leftovers of sin and the beginnings of grace (the free and unmerited favor and beneficence of God). The carnal part of you is struggling against the spiritually renewed you. Your carnal nature is resisting everything that is spiritual and is opposing all the suggestions of the Holy Spirit and the ethical urgings of your conscience. Fortunately, you are choosing to side with godly principles and your convictions. Consequently, God's providential blessings are upon you to increase. Be mindful of your words and do not boast of your increase. Furthermore, due to the intensity of your struggle, one of God's messengers is sent to give you the support needed at this time. Be aware that the new person within your midst may be that messenger. Dreamer, all things will be made beautiful in their own time. If necessary, see suggested course of action.

Parade Participants (Band Member, Chauffeur, Drum Major, Majorette, Observer, Organizer, Processional Member, or Sponsor): This dream has four meanings (choose one). (1) Drum Major: You have the power to change history. Your path is that of becoming a forerunner for change, freedom, justice, and intellectual and spiritual illumination. It is by this you will find genuine pu rpose and hear the words, "Well done my good and faithful servant". (2) Observer: To see a parade, do not be afraid you will not suffer shame. Do not fear disgrace you will not be humiliated. (3) Organizer: This choice has two parts (choose one). (a) Question, what type of parade was you organizing. See relevant subcategory, for interpretation. It will be within that interpretation that you will find what you are orchestrating within your life, and as a spiritual guide or leader, in the lif e of others. If necessary, see suggested course of action. (b) Because of your selfishness, greed, and disloyalty, you have grievously let down, betrayed, and/or hurt someone deeply. Someone you have authority over. God has promised to fight their battle for them; thus, your actions will be exposed publicly. See suggested course of action. (4) All other types of roles (sponsor, band member, chauffeur, majorette, processional member): Dreamer, you will be made a public example, for the good or wicked deeds done by you within a group setting. It will be done unto you, graceful favor, or dishonor; it will be as you have done unto others. If necessary, see suggested course of action.

Parade Procession of (Airplanes, Animals, or Flowers, Marching bands, People Twirling Batons, People Walking, or Decorated Vehicles, Parade Floats): The dreamer has with much thought and inner turmoil, chosen to commit to a certain lifestyle. Either you have chosen to honor Jesus Christ as your Lord and Savior, or you have forfeited the privileges that come with serving His Kingdom that you might not be under His precepts, because your lifestyle and choices do not concur with His principles morally. In addition, as you are a natural born leader, you have the power to lead others towards God, or away from the truth of His word, and you will influence others to do according to your choice. Hence, your dream comes to alert the dreamer of the approaching consequences of your choices. Fate will put you in a position for some level of public exposure, either for honoring, because you have chosen to support the truths of God's word, or for open shame. Dreamer, no matter your circumstances, the Kingdom of Light has always guaranteed a better you, and a promise of eternal life in heaven. The kingdom of darkness leads to desolation and emptiness and subsequently, eternal damnation. If you have chosen to follow God, you will become a great leader, leading many to Christ, and the favor of the Lord is upon your life to cause men to honor and respect you; the blessings of the Lord will rise upon you (see Isaiah 60:1-22). Blessings; in this sense, is a state of high honor, spiritual beauty, and great illumination. This is your time for the Lord's favor to be upon your life. This is the benefit of having served God. If you have chosen to serve the kingdom of darkness, and to worship at the altar of demons, get ready for open shame, for your particular habits, especially the lewd and lascivious, will be exposed. Even now, you're still unable t o control the foulness you find within yourself, and no spiritual help or grace (the free and unmerited favor and beneficence of God) has come. This is the recompense for serving the kingdom of darkness. See suggested course of action.

Protest Parade (public demonstration of opposition or disapproval of contemporary social issues or for propaganda purposes): Your dream speaks of pettiness and immaturity. Dreamer, the excuse of good intentions is often used to support bad actions. Your complaints and objections, display of disagreement and contention, and refusal to submit to righteous principles, are bad actions. You are not rejecting mankind; you're rejecting God. This mindset has become a cycle within your life, and you have abused this cycle of justification far too long. Your offensive behavior will no longer be tolerated. Your dream comes as a warning that a change is vitally needed in the way you behave and believe. Your limited degree of trust in people and your tendency to be self-righteous, overly critical, and intolerant of others, needs to transform; your petty bickering needs to stop. There is a necessity to be reconciled with others than to always be in opposition. One simply needs to take the higher ground. With that said, unfortunately, in judging others (e.g. condemnatory, critical, derogatory, disapproving, harsh, negative, scornful, or uncomplimentary in your thoughts or speaking aloud), you have set a precedent over your own life, discharging a universal law. The Universal Law: With the same judgments, you judge others, so will you be judged. Examples of judging, have you thought or said, "They're life is not holy, or they're not Christian, because I know they behave this way, or do that", or thought to yourself, "They need to sit down with all the emotional or physical hardship they're goi ng through; they're not a super person". Or, "They have mental health issues". Have you never been in a fallen state, at the same time, you were required to testify of the Kingdom of God, did you just disobey the commission because of a preconceived notion or pseudo-image? While Christ does not deny the necessity of exercising a certain degree of discernment, or of making valid judgments with respect to sin in others. Jesus condemns the habit of criticizing others, while ignoring your own faults. You should have done what you expected of others. Therefore, humbly ask Jesus for wisdom to help you understand the simplicity of His love and His nature. In this, you will learn principles and Christian values that will encourage you to re ach out and touch others in a loving and graceful manner; ultimately finding yourself promoting the genuine cause of Christ and the good of others. At full maturity, you will be a very peaceful and poised individual. The sooner you mature spiritually and emotionally the sooner you will be restored and prepared to, be honored publicly. Fate has put you in a position for some level of public exposure, either for honoring, because you have chosen to support the truths of God's word, or for open shame. Therefore, a change is needed. See suggested course of action.

Sports, Victory Parade (high school, youth, Olympics, World Olympic Games, any professional games, usually with a sport activity theme): Your dream is a notification that your time of action on behalf of the Kingdom of God is quickly approaching. There is an ordained undertaking that you're destined to achieve. However, you do not possess the qualities of one who is determined and steadfast. You give-up too easily, quit too soon, and never take projects to the finish. You lack drive, determination, commitment, and dependability; you have need of discipline. Your days of training, preparation and grounding are upon you. Your choices will make your time of grounding advantageous or wearisome. It will be up to you. You are free to do as you please; you still have personal liberty. But if your true intent is on doing God's will, reaping prosperity, experiencing genuine joy, and most importantly inheriting eternal life, you will have to practice restricting yourself in all things. This includes your diet, activities, associations, friendships, sensual desires, and your lack of quality fellowship with other believers. In order to reach your level of proficiency in ministry, you must bring your appetites and sensual desires under subjection, sacrificing personal comforts, during your days of preparation and grounding. You will need to lay aside every obstacle that hinders you and causes you to forfeit God's principles, including laziness. You can no longer pretend to have a determined, principled, and steadfast quality; you must actually possess it within, in order to complete your purpose and to prosper. In genuinely acquiring and applying these qualities, you will be respected and honored publicly, as one who is purposeful and persevering. Prayer and fasting is the first step in this process. This will help you see yourself and your issues more realistically. You are counseled to accept yourself just as you are, your weaknesses and flaws and your strengths. Afterward, develop specific and reachable objectives, and some manner of accountability that will help lead you to your desired goal, and help you develop a disciplined and determined spirit. Set "times frames" for major choices, e.g., do not move from your present place of worship for at least seven years, and make it happen, come what may. Daily prayer, reading God's Word, coupled with wise application, will keep things in perspective, real, and balanced. As well as, allow for God's purposes and plans for you personally, to come to the forefront. See suggested course of action.

Rain on your parade (cliché): This dream has two meanings (choose one). (1) This cliché of a dream warns the dreamer of someone who is attempting to spoil something for you. They are trying to mess up your plans and/or pleasure. Stay focus and consider very carefully whom you receive gifts or advice from regarding important projects and/or plans. (2) Rain on someone else's parade (you're just an observer): This cliché of a dream points to the dreamer having spoiled (or is spoiling) something for someone. You are messing up someone's plans and/or pleasure. See suggested course of action.

Suggested Course of Action

Question to consider and journal, did your dream depict any symbols that alludes to, the dreamer will make the necessary changes, spiritually, emotionally, and/or physically to affect a more positive outcome? If changes are initiated, your dreams will change.

Nevertheless, the following questions will help you determine; the issue at hand, how you feel about it, and what may have instigated it. What kind of parade was it? Were you a participant or observer? If participant, what role did you play? Were others involved? If yes, who and in what manner were they involved? Keep in mind that the others represent a quality of you, see Note 3 at the beginning of Actions and Activities category. Did anyone get hurt emotionally, physically, or was disturbed in any way? How did you feel, and what did you do, because, of your feelings, regarding the parade? Was it confusing, dangerous, entertaining, happy, joyful, life threatening, safe, scary, unsafe, or insignificant? In view of your dream's context, namely parade, what choices are you making that may impair your spiritual growth, judgment, health, or that will encourage immorality and/or are you reacting out of fear? If so, what can you do to combat the paralyzing emotion of fear? Your answers, coupled with the interpretation, plus any additional information, should begin to unfold the subject matter and issue at hand, if not now, mull over things a few days. For more information, see index or relevant category and subcategory for other particulars within your dream.

Now, pray (See Prayer of Deliverance, pg. 897)

Specific Meaning

If, you have a very high chance that you will be participating in, or organizing, some type of carnival, festival, parade, or pageant type activity. Dreams of this sort, for the most part, are ordinary dreams, resulting from your daily activities (see Chapter One, Chalom). These sorts of dreams are usually about your routine, mundane activities or anxieties that overwhelm your mind during the day. They are an inner release mechanism, which helps provide you with emotional balance and the maintaining of your sanity. These dreams are not significant, and do not warrant special attention.

Pregnancy Or Giving Birth

> *She was pregnant and cried out in pain as she was about to give birth. She gave birth*
> *to a son, a male child, who will rule all the nations with an iron scepter. Her child was*
> *snatched up to God and to His throne. Satan tries to kill the child, but fails to do so.*
> *-The Woman of the apocalypse (Revelation 12:1-13:1)*

Short description of types and experiences of pregnancy and giving birth: This includes multiple babies, normal pregnancy, old age pregnancy, or an unnatural, contrary pregnancy, miscarriage, stillbirth, termination of pregnancy.

Unless otherwise noted elsewhere, if, in your everyday living, your awaked state, as part of your lifestyle, work, or ministerial activities, or a special event, you have a very real connection with any type of Pregnancy or Giving Birth activity, from fertilization to delivery. For example, abortion, OBGYN office, Planned Parenthood, pregnant, surrogate, or if you or someone close to you is pregnant, your dream is not significant and does not warrant special attention.

Otherwise noted, one may experience, an Oneirovatic or "OV" dream (see Chapter One: The 60th part of prophecy, other prophetic dreams). This dream bares insight into the life of another who seriously needs your help. The dreamer may have plainly saw or sensed in his or her dream, a dangerous, harmful, or irregular pregnancy, or a medical emergency birth, taking place. The dreamer is urged to strongly advise, insist upon, or warn, another to seek medical attention due to possible health issues related to a pregnancy, or other resources for an unwanted pregnancy, especially if this is an issue within the life of someone connected to the dreamer. Your dream should closely resemble real life situations, with the dream events actually being capable of happening.

Otherwise noted, an "OV" dream may reveal molestation, rape, or any unwanted sexual crime, forced or threatened, upon a child, teen, or a psychological, physically weaker, incapacitated adult (consensual or not), which can lead, or has led, to an unwanted pregnancy. If the dreamer saw or sensed, within his or her dream, a child, teen, or adult, being molested, raped, or pregnant; first, the victim within your dream, should realistically be, or have been, in a situation where that criminal act could happen (e.g. adult care facility, class room, day care, hospital, neighborhood playground, nursery room, nursing home, at home, outside play area at home, school, summer camp, Sunday school class, in the care of foster parents, or in your own home, by a natural or step parent). As well, the victim will actually show signs of a violation, no matter how subtle.

If you sense that your dream is for or about another, possibly a child, sibling, parent, friend, or significant other, the question as to why you have been made aware of this information, and how do you factor into the equation, should be seriously considered, along with necessary actions. Dreamer, you are sent to get involved immediately. This dream is a first step intervention and an alarm. Is someone too young to be pregnant? Is adult abuse, molestation, or rape suspected in the life of someone close to you? If possible, how can you stop the violation? Have authorities been notified? Establishing a safe environment, alerting the law and other pertinent individuals is strongly recommended. Prophecy within dreams, and the revelation within those dreams, is not given haphazardly to any individual, but only to those with the ability and influence to, truly do something with the information. Skip interpretation, call the police, and go help the person seek medical attention. Jesus will strengthen you emotionally, psychologically, and physically to go get help.

If you or someone you know is being molested, or you suspect abuse, you must contact the appropriate authorities. Remove yourself or the victim from the unsafe environment and contact the proper authorities immediately (e.g. police, child, and/or adult protective services). If you were abused as a child and now, you have placed your child in harm's way, often the identical situation; feigning denial, go talk to God, and ask Him to help you emotionally and psychologically, to do what it takes to keep your child safe, from the same violation. Allow the darkness of the violation to stop with you. Moreover, if you suspect that your abuser is still harming others, please report it. You may also check with your local department of human services for reporting procedures. Medical, legal, and psychological intervention, are likely necessary. Children should never be left in abusive situations. Sex with a child, teen, or incapacitated adult is never justifiable; it is always wrong. Jesus says, it's better for you to sink to the bottom of the sea, tied to cement (Mark 9:42-48), than for anyone to perpetrate such acts against others.

Molestation, rape, or any unwanted sexual activity or attention forced upon a child, teen, or a psychological, physically weaker, incapacitated adult (consensual or not) is a sad reality, but it is not beyond God's ability to overcome. God can redeem and restore. We praise Him "who is able to do immeasurably more than all we ask or imagine, according to His power that is at work within us" (Ephesians 3:20 NIV). The "more than we can imagine" includes forgiveness and healing.

Can I be forgiven if I have sexually abused a child or if I knowingly allowed my child to be sexually abused? [34] Yes, God is gracious and merciful. No sin is beyond His ability to forgive (Romans 5:20). Jesus came to cleanse all sin: "Truly I tell you, people can be forgiven all their sins" (Mark 3:28 NIV). When you recognize your sin, acknowledge that it is evil, and then genuinely and deeply cry out to God for deliverance, with much fasting and prayer, He will hear you, forgive you, and sanctify you. Often, abusers have been abused themselves. In addition to God's forgiveness, you may require professional help and accountability support for, stopping certain behaviors, healing from past wounds, and seeking forgiveness from those, you have injured.

Otherwise noted, a dream of medical issues regarding a pregnancy may be a Prophetically Simple Dream (see Chapter One: The 60th Part of Prophecy). Whereas, the dreamer is warned to be extra cautious, regarding a literal pregnancy that has a high chance for some kind of irregular pregnancy. The dreamer may have plainly saw in her dream, a dangerous, harmful, or irregular pregnancy, or a medical emergency birth, taking place, the dreamer is warned to seek medical attention, due to possible health issues related to your pregnancy, especially if this is an issue within the dreamer's life. Skip interpretation and go seek medical attention for your condition.

Otherwise noted, see Note 1 at the beginning of Actions and Activities category.

To determine who your dream is for you or another, see Note 3 at the beginning of Actions and Activities category.

Symbols and Referents: Pregnancy and/or giving birth within most dreams generally imply one of the following two meanings, coupled with the applicable interpretation: (1) A pregnancy represents some type of ministry that will be birth from within you. You will become, responsible for a few young men and women being born again into the Kingdom of God (see John 3:1-17). You know how to nurture and accept anyone; therefore, many will be drawn to you, including those, others call "ne'er-do-wells", via your ministry. Under your tutelage, those newly born into the Body of Christ will become strong and active, for the cause of the Kingdom of God. They will be known as persons who speak and does that which is good, counted amongst those who are faithful and submissive to God. Dreamer, be willing, obedient, prepared, and in place (accountable to a specific house of worship, church), for the birthing of your ministry and for those who will become born again because of your ministry. (2) If giving birth within your dream, the fruit of your natural talents, pursuits, and morality is coming into full fruition. Your conduct towards others (for benefit or harm) will be openly manifested before all. You will reap what you ha ve sown. Further, that which you have begotten emotionally, mentally, and/or spiritually will also arise within your children and/or within those you aid, comfort, encourage, guide, help, minister to, nurture, support, teach, or tend to.

Category Content - If not listed see index, perchance, for your specific type of pregnancy and/or giving birth dream activity

- Birth Pains, Contractions, or Labor (birth with no labor pains, labor and birth nothing)
- Infant Loss (abortion, abuse, miscarriage, neglect, SID, stillborn, the death of a baby, or child was in jeopardy or unresponsive)
- Membrane or Veil over babies faces (a thin tissue that covers)

- Mother dies in child birth
- Normal Pregnancy or Birth
- Old Age Pregnancy or Birth (age 50+)
- Twins or Siamese Twins or Multiple Babies (pregnancy or birth)
- Unnatural, Contrary Pregnancy or Birth (particularly that which goes against nature, e.g. male pregnancy, a young child or baby, human birthing an animal, monster, mythological or legendary creature, or other abominable creatures)

Birth Pains, Contractions, or Labor (birth with no labor pains, labor and birth nothing): This dream has five meanings (choose one). (1) If you are a preacher, educator, prophet, or praise leader, in your awaked life, God is getting ready to deal with you, if not already; He will mark you with a sign of His displeasure, by way of a trial. Your works and words will testify against you, for you have proven proud, covetous, false, and oppressive. He will strip you of your anointing, you will no lo nger inspire. You will become despairingly overwhelmed with anxiety; and will reach a point of losing hope, resulting in drastic and reckless choices. Extremely desperate, because of difficult times and great need, your wickedness will go beyond hope of recovery. Dreamer, if you pretend to be a spiritual leader of some sort, be it preacher, educator, prophet, spiritual singer, and are immoral, your immorality exposes your pretensions for what they are, false. See Philippians 3:18, 19. Pray Psalm 51. See suggested course of action. (2) If dreamer is actually ill, at present, in your awaked life, your dream was sent as an alert. Dreamer, although you may be currently suffering or will soon enter a season of suffering, suffering has a purifying effect in our life so that after we have suffered we will cease (stop, restrain, refrain, quit, desist) from sin (1 Peter 4:1-9), especially the sin that chronically assails you. This should be your attitude toward sin and it should be so intense that even in your suffering, your determination remains, I'm done with sin! Wisdom: when a believer has wandered off into sin and remained in sin and God chastens him or her by bringing sickness into their life to bring them back to Himself. When the believer recognizes that God has brought the trial or severe illness to incapacitate them, he or she is to call for the elders of the church[36]. The elders are to come; the believer openly confesses sin, afterwards, the elders anoint the person with oil and pray over him or her. If sin is the cause of the trial or sickness, which is the case here, and sin is taken care of via confession (Pray Psalm 38:1-22), there will be no need for further chastisement, and God will raise you up. God takes away the chastisement and the believer is restored to physical health. Thank God for His patience, long-suffering, and grace while you get things decent and in order. Therefore, be earnest to repent. Moreover, keeping in mind that dreams are primarily warnings, dreamer know that a person, can go from bad to good in one day, if wisdom is adhered to. This is known as the power of a changed mind. The key here is to stop sinning via a complete change of lifestyle choices and God will deliver you from devastation and your feet from stumbling, that you may walk before God in the light of life (Psalm 56:13). If necessary, see suggested course of action. (3) Dreamer, your advisers, and friends are scoffers, in that they are contemptuous, cynical, distrustful, mocking, sarcastic, suspicious, nega tive, and misanthropists. They hate people in general, and dislike and distrust others. They are ordinary men and women, who choose not to make the leap of faith that changes the ordinary into the extraordinary. Unfortunately, you are giving their words power, thus, you are now liken to those who worship idols, for you have exalted their words, and them, above Christ. This is your downfall, hence your dream was sent to expose the evil within the life of the dreamer, and to bring awareness of the coming circumstances of sin. Consequently, you will become very sick and frail, leading, perhaps, to an ongoing chronic illness (e.g. cancer, diabetes, heart disease, HIV), which may continue for a long time. You are strongly advised to careful ly consider, and heed the Word of God, as oppose to men's opinions. Pray Psalm 38:1-22. See suggested course of action. (4) Birth with no labor pains: This choice has two parts (both apply); it implies a ministerial calling and deliverance. (a) Ministerial calling: Dreamer, progressive thinking, especially along the lines of apologetics (a branch of religious study that is concerned with proving the truth of Christianity) should be the focal point of your ministry. A ministry geared toward a plain and sim ple critical study of religious truths; e.g. a beginner's bible study group on apologetics. This will endow you with a multi-dimensionality that will enable you to understand, appreciate, and greatly benefit the lives of many kinds of people, even so me whom others call "ne'er-do-wells". (b) Deliverance: Your dream implies deliverance from bondage. This deliverance will be easy, without pain or struggle, and confidentially done, because there is a genuine love of the Lord within your heart.

Dreamer, you are also advised that an increase in patience will create a greater sense of order within your life and help you to better accept changes as they come along. In addition, God will make you fruitful, and, if applicable, your offspring will b uild churches. Began preparing them now and let them know that God will set them up for Himself, to replenish His churches. (5) In labor and birth nothing: At present, you have not heeded the Word of God. He has warned you of the dangers of your interests, but you have not regarded His words, nor the counsel of His servants sent to you. All that has been said has been regarded as a fairy-tale, rumor, or gossip, by you. Further, you have not allowed the discipline you've rec eived thus far to calm, control, and bring order to your life. You have been presumptuous in committing shameful offenses, and downright malicious. How can those who will not hearken to the Word of God, but do wickedly? God has told you your duty and what is required of you; yet, there remains, at present, a serious disregard of God's business within you. You have not been a witness, on any level, for the cause of Christ for some time now; nor are you producing anything of eternal value within the lives of those you are purposed to usher into the Kingdom of God. Your purpose has returned unto you void. Dreamer, the achievement, admiration, distinction, and/or honor given you in the past, because of praising God, will now begin to abate, a s it is done with all who will not hearken to Him (Ezekiel 33:12, 13). Pray Psalm 51. See suggested course of action.

Infant Loss (abortion, abuse, miscarriage, neglect, SID, stillborn, the death of a baby, or child was in jeopardy or unresponsive): This dream has five meanings (choose one). (1) Abortion or Termination of pregnancy: Your dream is an alarm to the dreamer. You have aborted your purpose (also see Ezekiel 33:11-16). Let sin; therefore, be repented of and forsaken, before it destroys you. Dreamer that which would teach and persuade you to do well, you have rejected. He or she who comes in Jesus' name, you also reject, and you wonder why there is wicked doings amongst you and yours? In your own heart you lust after, thus is tempted by, that which corrupts; "but each one is tempted when, by his (or her) own evil desire, he or she is dragged away and enticed" (James 1:14). Little by little, your sinful desires have carried you far away from the Lord, Jesus Christ. The power and dominion of sin within your life will prove to be your destroyer. See suggested course of actio n. (2) Baby was neglected, abused, or was in any kind of jeopardy: This choice has two parts (choose one). (a) Your dream was sent to demonstrate grace. The dreamer needs to consider your own well-being emotionally, mentally, and spiritually. Think about what personal life cycles, denials, fears, failures, experiences, hang-ups, hindrances, lies, and/or rejections, have prevented you from developing, growing, expanding, increasing, or becoming all that you can be. What exactly is holding you back? Because, something pertaining to the dreamer's individual ministry is lifeless, or is in jeopardy or unresponsive. It is a wicked servant who would neglect his or her gifting, blaming their lack of faithfulness, commitment, and stewardship on God, others, or transitory circumstances (Matthew 25:24-30). If no action, commitment, or obligation to ministry, is heeded at this time, you may find yourself similar to the guest spoken of in the parable, who attended the King's wedding without proper wedding clothes, and when Jesus asked why, he was speechless (Matthew 22:11-14). Moreover, if your designated service is given to another, so will the prosperity that is attached to that service, be given to that person also, and for you, jealous ly will be your recompense. (b) This is indicative of deliberate spiritual immaturity or serious neglect concerning taking care of God's business (also see following subcategory, Termination of pregnancy). Those who are diligent and prudent in nurturing the opportunities they have before them, God will enlarge their territory, and will set before them an open door (Revelation 3:8). Those who do not respect the opportunities placed before them shall have the things that support their peace taken away (also see Matthew 25:14-30; 1 Timothy 4:14-16). What did you do regarding the neglect, lost, or unresponsiveness? This is how you feel about the neglect of a ministry. See suggested course of action. (3) Miscarriage (baby died at birth):

Your dream is an alarm to the dreamer. You are warned to restrain and get your flesh under control. For, before you are the possible loss of distinction, honor, and reputation. To whom much is given, much is required. Dreamer if you, in anything, set a bad example (e.g. adultery, addiction, arrogance, envious, liar, maliciousness, sexual immorality, shyster), you do not know the great deal of harm you will do (or are doing) by your acts and choices, particularly to your family; and for sure, to those t o whom you minister. One bad act or choice of a good man or woman may be more damaging to others than twenty acts of the wicked. As well, one bad act or choice is hurtful to a good name; not only spoiling the goodness of it, but making it now, a name of ill-repute; base, disgraceful, low, scandalous, wicked (Ecclesiastes 10:1). Dreamer, even a good reputation and great wisdom can be easily lost or counted foul by others. Resentfulness, unhappy feelings, and/or wanting somebody else's success, qualities, or possessions will cause you to make mistakes that will lead to the mishandling of those you aid, comfort, encourage, guide, help, minister to, nurture, support, teach, or tend to, and to failure (miscarriage). Your attitude and/or unwise choices will prove to your disadvantage, even to the point of being exposed openly. Dreamer, you have made a genuine and public profession of following Christ Jesus; thus, you need to walk cautiously, refraining from all forms of evil, and approaches towards it, because many eyes are upon you. They watch your character, for error, faltering, stumbling; for any type of dishonor or violation, and surely, you have a great deal to lose. See suggested course of action. (4) SID or Baby died after birth: Your dream is an alarm to the dreamer. This type of dream is revealing the loss of a ministry (or ministries) due to serious neglect and/or spiritual immaturity, as well as the loss of honor and respect. Dreamer, it is a wicked servant who would discount, disregard, or spurn their talents, skills, and/or ministerial responsibilities, blaming their lack of commitment, faithfulness, knowledge, and stewardship on God, others or transitory circumstances (Matthew 25:24-30). If no action, commitment, or obligation to ministry, is heeded at this time, you may find yourself similar to t he servant spoken of in the parable who buried his gift (Matthew 25:15). If your designated service is given to another, so will the prosperity that is attached to that service, be given to that person also, and for you, jealously will be your recompense. You have been appointed to do certain things within your present fellowship, this is a small thing; do what is expected of you. For God is sending you to preach the gospel, to set up a church for Christ, to bring people to the obedience of faith, and to build them up in it. You have received power and the tools to do this. Now, earnestly, be about your Father's business, utilizing your ta lents and skills for the Kingdom of God, and stick to it. Determine within yourself to do all the good you can for people, and to lead them to Christ. All Christians have business to do for Christ in this world. You were not called to be idle. You will have to give an account of what service you have done for Christ, what eternal good have you done for men and women, and what other use you made of the talents and skills you were endowed with. Those that are called to do business for Christ, He equips wit h gifts necessary for their business; and, further, to those He equips, He expects service. If necessary, see suggested course of action. (5) Stillborn (baby died in the womb): This choice has two parts (choose one). (a) To dream your baby is stillborn (or dead): Your dream is a dire warning and comes to rectify behavior, and to hopefully, change the dreamer's d irection of ministry. Although dreamer is participating in some kind of ministry, it is not the primary ministry of service God has orda ined for you to do. While many people are multi-talented, God has a primary ministry for all, while not neglecting other gifting's or ministries. Dreamer, for one reason or another, you have chosen to believe that you may select what kind of service you want to do, how you want to do it, and who you want to be of service too, especially regarding unbelievers and the indi gent. Dreamer, since all babies symbolically represent a ministry and those predestined to be born again within the Kingdom of God. It is your Christian's duty to do what you are called to do, so that those whom you are called to minister too may become born again, live, and prosper, even as their soul prospers (see Luke 17:10, 3 John 1:2). Unfortunately, if souls perish, (symbolically represented by a stillborn baby), because of your neglect of duty, you bring guilt upon yourself, (Ezekiel 33:1 -9, Acts 18:5, 6). That is to be responsible, spiritually, for someone's death (or many deaths). Dreamer, your lack of Christian service comes down to indifference. The level of indifference you have towards the commands of God, and for the destiny of the lost, has caused many to perish, spiritually and/or physically. Even more, the risks you take in disappointing the One who shed His blood for you is unwise. Those that follow the choices of their own hearts, feelings, emotions, rather than the dictates of the divine will, oftentimes, find themselves far from peaceful shores. Stop yourself from walking down the path of destruction. Be willing to release those things that are in conflict with, or hinder, what God has called you to do. Your carnal mind may fight you on it, but your heart and mouth can still agree and defeat any thought of doubt, unbelief, or fear. When working to eliminate negative thoughts and feelings, pray, and think before you act! When you practice this, you will see that God will meet all your needs and you will be better able, emotionally and spiritually, to meet the needs of those God has sent you to (see Ezekiel 37:7). See suggested course of action. (b) To dream of seeing a stillborn (known or unknown): Dreamer, because of trials, tribulations, and/or transitory circumstances, corruption has entered into your heart. Your dream is an alarm to you. You have begun to think upon, imagine, and fantasize about lustful experiences (unhealthy, immodest, indecent desires, erotic, lewd, and lascivious, behavior, or voyeurism). When lust has conceived, it brings forth sin. Sin, allowed to excite desires in us, will soon develop those desires into consent; strengthened by frequent acts, into a habit, resulting in devastation (spiritua l, literal, and possibly eternal). Although, at present, the sin is in your mind, when it has grown to its full size in the mind, it will manifest openly and in full operation. Bring to an end the beginnings of sin, within your mind now; or else, all the evils it produces will prove very detrimental to you. Blessed is the man or woman who perseveres under trial, because when he or she has stood the test, he or she will receive the crown of life that God has promised to those who love Him. When tempted, no one should say, "God is tempting me". For God cannot be tempted by evil, nor does He tempt anyone; but each one is tempted when, by his or her own evil desire, he or she is dragged away and enticed (James 1:12-15). Don't be deceived dreamer. Every good and perfect gift is from above, coming down from the Father of the heavenly lights, who does not change like shifting shadows. He chose to give us birth through the Word of Truth that we might be a kind of first fruits of all He created. See suggested course of action.

Membrane or Veil over babies faces (a thin tissue that covers): This dream has two meanings (both apply). (1) It represents some type of ministry that will be birth from within the dreamer. You will become, responsible for a few young men and women being born again into the Kingdom of God (see John 3:1-17). You know how to nurture and accept anyone; therefore, many will be drawn to you, including those, others call "ne'er-do-wells", via your ministry. Under your tutelage, those newly born into the Body of Christ will become strong and active, for the cause of the Kingdom of God. They will be known as persons who speak and does that which is good, counted amongst those who are sagacious; whose character is faithful, law-abiding, moral, open, and submissive to God, scrupulous, sincere, straightforward, trustworthy, upright, and reasonable in many situations. Blessings and prosperity will be theirs, and yours, because of your guidance. Dreamer, be willing, obedient, prepared, and in place (accountable to a specific house of worship, church), for the birthing of your ministry and for those who will become born again because of your ministry. (2) Your dream also denotes that the ministry birth from within the dreamer will be marked by its prophetic depth, will be in essence esoteric, will operate beyond the ordinary, and will be confined to, and understood only, by those within its inner circle, and they will be called end -time prophets. Although these end-time prophets will, in their early stages, be under the dreamer's tutelage, their ministry and those connected to the ministry, will go beyond the dreamer's understanding, and will appear confusing and perplexing to many, but the welding of their authority emanates from God, and is according to divine providence. Nonetheless, the prophetic purpose of their ministry will become clearer to the dreamer, and you will understand most of its operations, "by and by".

Mother dies in childbirth: Your dream has a threefold meaning. It speaks of a wisdom no longer valid, turning sorrow into joy, and it acknowledges a prophetic gifting within the dreamer and, if applicable, your offspring. Dreamer, old, archa ic forms and traditions of teaching and worship, those that are no longer useful or efficient, will be (are) superseded by a newer adoration of, devotion to, delight in, passion for, and worship of, the Lord Jesus Christ. This new beginning, new wisdom, fresh revelation, will turn (or is turning) your heaviness and sorrow into joy, influence, strength, and favor. Additionally, dreamer, you are, by special counsel, chosen and designed for the work of a prophet, prophetess, or minister. What God has designed you for; He has also fashioned and fitted you for it too. God destined you for a unique type of ministry, when He first formed your spirit within you. Natural endowment, as well as education, makes a well-versed prophet, prophetess, or minister. Moreover, if applicable, expose and prepare your offspring for this type of office as well, f or they will inherit your ministry. If necessary, see suggested course of action.

Normal Pregnancy or Birth: This dream has five meanings (one, two, or three may apply). (1) It speaks of a ministerial calling and it is sent to encourage the dreamer to have faith in God, which is a resolute trust in the integrity of God and in His Word. Dreamer, you are under the special protection of the Lord. Have faith in God, and not in state of affairs or people. God is promising that no hurt shall be done you, if you respect His principles and precepts, and most importantly reverence Him. Moreover, God has persuaded others to be very compassionate, sensitive, and to take care, when dealing or speaking with you. (2) A dream of pregnancy is symbolic of a ministry being birth within the dreamer. A ministry is the line of work and livelihood of a religious minister for a particular season. Dreamer, greatness is germinating inside you, for you are called for such times as these. Seize all the opportunities that are put before you to progress emotionally and spiritually. For out of a cooperative and diligent spirit, your ministry will be born. Moreover, out of a sense of duty to God, humankind, and self, y ou should be willing to help others, especially those around you. He or she that is useful to others is considered beneficial to the Kingdom of God and to the common good of humanity. As well, a level of moral purity is expected. (3) Birth a daughter: Th e birth of a daughter suggests that the focal point of your ministry should be geared towards faith, testimony, miracles, empowerment, encouraging positive self-esteem, or uplifting others in some way. At least one of these qualities should be a part of your mission statement. Your dream also suggests that while the dreamer has a genuine fear or reverence of the Lord, it is conditional (based on or contingent upon, determined or influenced by what God does, or has done, for you). For example, you love the Lord because He has delivered you from something. However, if you were not delivered, your love or respect of God would be affected. Fortunately, because of His love and work within your life, you admire, have a high opinion of, look up to, respect, and reverence the Lord, as well as His people. (4) Birth a son: The birth of a son suggests that the focal point of your ministry should be geared towards working with the elderly, the young, the sick, and the underprivileged. Atleast one of these qualities should be a part of your mission statement. Moreover, your dream suggests that the dreamer has a genuine unconditional (not contingent, nor determined or influenced by what God does, or has done, for you) love of the Lord and for His people. You have a deepness that is the source of much generosity, kindness, and understanding. Hence, you have the capacity to spearhead a philanthropic type ministry successfully. (5) Birth both daughter and son: Your dream suggests that the dreamer has a balance of love and respect for the Lord. You are multi-talented and are very inspirational. A variety of venues will become open to you that you may demonstrate your desire to benefit humanity. One thing is for sure, you will inspire others to make their dreams come true.

Old Age Pregnancy or Birth (age 50+): Your dream indicates great change. You are called to exhibit faith by steadfast fortitude, thanks, and love. The genuineness of your faith has been judged by your recent response to hardships and opposition engendered by your identification with Christ, and by your inner temptations to sin. You have exhibited courage under trials. You have not taking lightly God's disciplinary instructions. As a result, a renewing and reworking of your fe elings, ideas, and perceptions is happening within you (e.g. going from a menial mentality to a proficient mentality, from looking at your state of affairs with a negative mind-set, to viewing them as God's disciplining of His child). Your capacity to understand and reason is becoming enlarged. A new state of mind, a new pattern of thinking and feeling, a paradigm shift, will emerge because of peace and great joy. This new dawn will have an effect on your behavior, desires, intentions, and health. God wi ll renew your life and sustain you in your old age, because of your loyalty (allegiance, commitment, dedication, trueness). There will be a time and place of laughter, the charm of celebrations will return. Are you ready for another measure, another level, of God's love? Are you ready for a better you? Humility is the key for sustainment; pride is a robber and destroyer. Counsel: from time to time reflectively check your pride level.

Twins or Siamese Twins or Multiple Babies (pregnancy or birth): If highlighted, also consider the number of babies; see category, Numbers. With that, this dream has two meanings (choose one). (1) The dreamer has the capacity to spearhead a new dawn, giving birth to a new generation that will usher in an age of mass revivals, with a primary emphasis on a personal and saving relationship with Christ Jesus. However; the dreamer has begun to grow careless in your worship of the one true God, in that you, irresponsibly, humor others in their search for religious rationale by allowing foreign and outlandish opin ions concerning the existence, nature, and worship of pseudo-deities, within your study group. While unwisely believing that a state of spiritual conflict; will result from the contradiction, between their simultaneously held beliefs, ending in a choice for Christ, a doctrine familiar to them. You ask, what harm is there in allowing other beliefs to be looked at and reasoned within a Christian group? (Jamieson-Fausset-Brown Bible/Bible History): Old Testament: Consider Israel during the reign of King Solomon. He was considered a very wise man. Yet, Solomon's extraordinary gift of wisdom was not sufficient to preserve him from falling into grievous and fatal errors. For he allowed his wives to practice their superstitions, worshipping images of wood or stone in sight of the very temple which, in early life, he had erected to the true God, and he allowed these foreign ideas to spread throughout the country (1 Kings 11:1-11). Moreover, reference 1 Corinthians 10:18-22. Consider the people of Israel: Do not those who eat the sacrifices participate in the altar? Am I implying then that a sacrifice offered to an idol is anything, or that an idol is anything? No, but the sacrifices of pagans (the spiritually unenlightened), are offered to demons, not to God, and I do not want you to be participants with demons. You cannot drink the cup of the Lord and the cup of demons too; you cannot have a part in both the Lord's Table and the table of demons. Are we trying to arouse the Lord's jealousy? Are we stronger than He is? Dreamer, if those that are in reputation for wisdom, honor, and for perpetuating the teachings of Christ, in anything set a bad example, they know not what great deal of harm they may do by it, particularly to those you minister too. One bad choice of a good person, may be more damaging to others than, twenty of a wicked man or woman. As well, one bad choice is hurtful to a good name; not only spoiling the goodness of it, but making it now, a name of ill-repute; base, disgraceful, low, scandalous, and wicked (see Ecclesiastes 10:1). See suggested course of action. Further, a multiple pregnancy is hereditary. In that, this attitude is capable of being passed on or handed down from one generation to the next. (2) Siamese twins or Babies bodies joined at some point: At times of great change in our life, babies may appear in our dream, in an irregular manner. This type of birth, specifically babies bodies joined at some point, represents Syncretism[28] of religious beliefs on some level, within your ministry. Dreamer, your attempt to fuse or cause a union between different systems of thoughts or beliefs (especially in religion or philosophy), within your ministry, will be publicly manifested in your life, and dreamer m ay or may not be able to handle the "fall out". You will definitely be an outcast and possibly labeled a heretic by many. Thus, your dream is a dire warning to the dreamer, it is to warn a rebellious person, in the spirit of grace (the free and unmerited favor and beneficence of God), to see if you will yet be worked upon, and change your mindset. Or else to leave you inexcusable, in your accusations against God, because of your ruin (e.g. continually plundered, seized, and disfavored). With that said, dreamer, the following is grace: you are a people holy to the Lord your God. The Lord your God has chosen you out of all the peoples on the face of the earth to be His people, as His treasured possession. The Lord did not set His affection on you and choose you because you were better than other peoples, but it was because the Lord loved you and kept the oath He swore to your forefathers (Deuteronomy 7:1-8). Therefore, choose this day, "this moment", who you will serve. God has set before you this day, this moment, life and good, and death and evil. Thus, you are beckoned this day to love the Lord your God, to walk in His ways, to embrace His commandments, statutes, and judgments, that you may live and multiply properly; and the Lord your God will bless you in your land. However, if in your heart you turn away so that you will not hear nor heed this dire warning, but be drawn away, and worship other gods, and serve them, it is denounced unto you this day, this moment, that you will not fare well. Dreamer, if it seems evil to you to serve the LORD, choose for yourself this day, this moment, whom you will serve (Deuteronomy 30:16-20, Joshua 24:15). Again, this type of dream is an alarm. It is time for the dreamer to restrain or get yourself under control morally (also see 1 Corinthians 6:9, 10). See suggested course of action.

Unnatural, Contrary Pregnancy or Birth (particularly that which goes against nature, e.g. male pregnancy, a young child or baby, human birthing an animal, monster, mythological or legendary creature, or other abominable creatu res): This dream has five meanings (one, two may apply). (1) At times of great change in our life, a baby may appear in our dream, in a way contrary to the physical laws of nature, extremely unusual, or perhaps even monstrous. This baby represents, emotionally, mentally, and spiritually that which can develop and be publicly manifested in your life in a bad sense. That which can develop, is attributed to negative activities, habits, or mannerisms practiced by the dreamer. This type of dream is an alarm. It is time for the dreamer to restrain or get yourself under control morally (also see 1 Corinthians 6:9, 10). Couple this with one of the following, to see more fully the meaning of unnatural, irregular pregnancies or birth. (2) Male pregnant or birthing a baby: You are powerful and strong and are well able to do mighty works for the Kingdom of God. God has given you a rare sense of purpose from birth. Ultimately, that purpose is seriously tied to the Word of God. For you, a purposeless existence will cause only frustration and despair. Therefore, you must choose a lifelong commitment to sowing "seeds" that will ultimately uproot and replace the wicked seeds planted by demonic forces some time ago, at an earlier age. Your seeds should be intentional development of habits of holiness, prayer, fasting, theological study, abstinence, sobriety, and separation from people, places, and circumstances that are contrary to your development of holiness, clarity, and stability. Dreamer, w ise choices will bring you authentic joy, happiness, divine purpose, and miraculous knowledge and power, in due time. (3) One too young to be pregnant or give birth (e.g. a young child or baby): This choice has two parts (choose one). (a) If there is one connected to the dreamer in any way that is too young to be pregnant, and there are obvious signs of molestation, e.g. a pregnancy, or other signs. This type of dream may be an Oneirovatic or "OV" dream (see Note 1 at the beginning of this category), otherwise. (b) Your dream is revealing a lack of depth and maturity regarding your, the dreamer's, emotional and spiritual development; for the dreamer is the one too young to be pregnant or giving birth, no matter your age in your awaked life. Although you should be relatively mature by now, you still show signs of emotional, psychological, and spiritual immaturity. Signs of emotional, psychological, and spiritual immaturity include, but are not limited to, a tendency to be ea sily misled, easy to fool, or naive. An inability or deliberate choice, not to be able to tell right from wrong, suing others over relatively minor financial disputes, caught up in coveting and swindling, vicious and violent in selfishness, verbal aggression, adultery or fornication, drunkenness, condemning others, or so committed to your own personal rights that you disdain the cause of Christ and the good of others. These are all indicators that you are still living like an unbeliever. Motivated by their same values, and handling your problems in the same way as they, unbelievers, do. Dreamer, you have chosen to remain immature and unskilled in the things that pertain to God and to living life ethically and strongly. Those who are mature hav e trained themselves to recognize the difference between right and wrong and then do what is right. See suggested course of action. (4) Human birthing an animal or vice versa: The dreamer is the animal, as well as that which was birthed. The birth of an animal within a dream implies spiritual backsliding and confusion, on so many levels. He (or she) who is pregnant with evil and conceives trouble gives birth to disillusionment (Psalm 7:14 NIV). Thus, your dream alludes to a way of life that is going contrary to God's call. Dreamer, you are not in harmony with the will of God for your life, nor with the particular objectives that are intended to ensure the fulfillment of that will. Your behavior contradicts practicality, basic reality, and deviate s from the morality of God. Yours is a life full of unnecessary words and activities, which have no basis in fact or reality, and they are not rooted in faith in God. Reality is understood to be what God says it to be via His Word. For example, we are saved by grace through faith, not by works (Ephesians 2:5-10). Hence, anyone who does not correspond with His truth, in a levelheaded and practical manner, is deceived and erroneous in your thoughts and ideas; thus, exposing your rejection of the certainty of God's word. (5) Human birthing a monster, mythological or legendary creature, or other abominable creatures or vice versa: The dreamer is symbolically the monster, as well as that which was birthed. Meaning you embrace the characteristics of that which was birth, also see category, Animals (Monsters, Mythological or Legendary Creatures, or other Abominable Creatures). The birth of a creature within your dream implies spiritual wickedness and confusion, on so many levels. Even from birth, th e wicked go astray; from the womb, they are wayward and speak lies (Psalm 58:3). The dreamer is involved in unnatural lusts; sins not to be mentioned without horror, and surely acts that will result in great open shame and/or devastation. Your foul behavior, on all levels, is to the highest degree appalling and offensive in the sight of God and others. It is an abomination. Additionally, that which the dreamer has begotten emotionally, mentally, and/or spiritually will also arise within those you aid, comfort, encourage, guide, help, nurture, support, teach, or tend to. Even now, some are wayward and speak lies, and this is your doing. Suggested course of action: Dreamer, you need to reverse the situation by exposing the negative influence of your wickedness to relevant others. If you failed to do what is required, and they are not warned of their wickedness and told the truth; they will die because of their iniquities, but the spiritual implications will be required at your hands (see Ezekiel 3:17-21; 33:7-20).

Suggested Course of Action

Question to consider and journal, did your dream depict any symbols that alludes to, the dreamer will make the necessary changes, spiritually, emotionally, and/or physically to affect a more positive outcome? If changes are initiated, your dreams will change.

Nevertheless, to determine the symbolic equivalent to your literal responses, see the following. Some examples of symbolic equivalents to literal responses: You hiding the incident would be spiritually equivalent to pretending that your ministry is something that it is not. Calling the police is figurative of intercessory prayer for a ministry. Taking the baby denotes taking over a ministry. Handling the situation without involving authorities is equivalent to you attempting to get a ministry off the ground according to your own ideas, understanding, perspective, and reasoning abilities, without dependence upon God. Just observing is equivalent to doing nothing. Anger insinuates complaining, deception, disobedience, disrespect, harsh treatment, jealousy, sexual violations or unrighteous dealings. Feelings of confusion or fright are typical of evil, and are types of great disorder; replacing reason with foolishness, not knowing your own mind. These feelings suggest demonic influence is somewhere close around. Embarrassment is symbolic of one needing to reflect upon his or her own inconsideration in not making a way for others sooner. As well as one who obliges others to keep their distance. This emoti on also suggests shame and humiliation. Happiness suggests that there is a reverence of God, a trust in God, and obedience to God. Happiness also implies one who is using wisdom to control and guide his or her conduct. This is abundant living. Sadness, sorry, sorrow is sometimes better than laughter (Ecclesiastes 7:3, 4). That which is best for the soul, is best for us, although it is unpleasant to our feelings at the time. Sadness is often a happy means of seriousness, for it inspires reverence or godly fear towards our Lord and Savior, Jesus Christ. Suicidal feelings are indicative of, one who has control issues, self- centeredness, and selfishness, thus, one who is rebellious. You hiding the incident would be spiritually equivalent to you aborting your ministry or pretending that your ministry is something that it is not. Pro-life implies taking initiative spiritually, and making a vow to accept the call to ministry, with no excuses. Pro-choice implies an attempt to get a ministry off the ground according to your own understanding, perspective, and reasoning abilities, without dependence upon God. If your emotion or action is a desirable or positive one, allow the strength of the trait within you to help rectify your conduct, relationships, and benefit to others; that you and your works may be deemed respectable in the sight of God and others. If your emotion or action is an undesirable or negative one, take steps accordingly to struggle against the growing desires of the carnal side of you. Determine your ministry, considering any ministry you are, or were, involved with, and react appropriately. Additionally, get help and support via prayer, fasting, and a Christian based support group.

Consider and journal the following questions. The questions will help you determine; the issue at hand, how you feel about it, and what may have instigated it. Taking into account the entire context of your dream and the interpretation thereof, reflect on your emotional state when you awoke from your dream. Were you happy, relieved, encouraged, bewildered, or broken? You should begin to see a story unfold. Having read the interpretation for your type of dream, do you now have a sense of urgency regarding a ministry? Are you guilty of neglect of ministerial duties? Did your dream bring to light a ministerial or prophetic gifting that should be developed and used to help others? On another vein, using your imagination, how do you think you would feel if you experienced, although not humanly possible, birthing an animal, or if a male, you experienced an actual pregnancy or birth? Would you try to hide or expose the incident? By answering the questions regarding your actions and feelings, are you angry, confused, embarrassed, frighten, happy, sad, or sorry?

Now, pray (See Prayer of Deliverance, pg. 897)

Specific Meaning

If, you have a very real connection with any type of Pregnancy or Giving Birth activity, e.g. example, abortion, midwife, OBGYN, Planned Parenthood, pregnant, or surrogate). Ask yourself why are you dreaming about this now, or what would you do or how would you feel, physically, if during this season of your life, you experienced a real pregnancy, birth, or infant loss? Are you pro-life or pro-choice? Does this choice have anything to do with your life now? Dreams of this sort, for the most part, are ordinary dreams, resulting from your daily activities (see Chapter One, Chalom). These sorts of dreams are usually about your routine, mundane activities or anxieties that overwhelm your mind during the day. They are an inner release mechanism, which helps provide you with emotional balance and the maintaining of your sanity. These dreams are not significant, and do not warrant special attention. With the exception of an actual pregnancy or abortion, then some manner of action is expected. Having been forewarned let your actions go according to wise counsel.

SITTING, RECLINING, OR LEANING ON IN SOME WAY

Some short descriptions of types, phrases, and other processes and particulars, connected in some way to this category are, for example, recline, take a seat, be seated, or squat.

Unless otherwise noted elsewhere, if, in your everyday living, your awaked state, as part of your lifestyle, you have a very real connection with any type of sitting or reclining activity, for example, builder of chairs, clerk, orchestra, receptionist, secretary, typist, or writer. Also see content list for this category, or if you have, a health related issue that has you resigned you to sitting or reclining, or you're actually waiting for someone to return from a long absence (armed forces, incarceration, or college), your dream is not significant and does not warrant special attention.

Otherwise noted, see Note 1 at the beginning of Actions and Activities category.

To determine who your dream is for you or another, see Note 3 at the beginning of Actions and Activities category.

Symbols and Referents: This type of dream was sent to encourage the dreamer to progress towards your appointed place, spiritually and physically. On the other hand, this type of dream is to bring about an awareness that the dreamer is already at your appointed place, if someone or thing is sitting or reclining on your lap, or on you, somehow. No matter the one, going there or already there, your set place is before you, with a primary emphasis on abiding there contentedly and resting.

Category Content - If not listed see index, perchance, for your specific type of sitting or reclining dream activity.

- Sitting, Reclining Upon, or Leaning On, in some way, an (Animal, Bench, Chair, Couch, Chaise, Lounge Chair, Ottoman, Pew, Shoulder, Sofa, Heels, Lap, or Throne)
  - Animal; Bench or Pew; Chair, Couch (including Chaise, Lounge Chair, Ottoman, Sofa); Heels (sitting on your heels) ; Lap or Shoulder (sitting on someone's lap or shoulder); Throne
- Forced to Sit Down, Recline, or Lean, in some way
- Place where you were Sitting, Reclining, Leaning, or Squatting on or at
  - Building or Dwelling; Church; Courtroom, Judge's Seat; Feet (including Christ's Feet) ; Floor, Ground, Valley, Hell; Garden, Lea; Mountain or higher; School; Tables (Coffee Table, Counter Tops, Dinettes, Kitchen-Island); Tree; Vehicle; Work
- Sit and Wait
- Waiting to sit down or Unable to sit down
- Whom were you Sitting or Reclining or Leaning upon
  - Alone; Dead People; Leadership, Ruler, CEO, Celebrities; Others (known or unknown)

Sitting, Reclining Upon, or Leaning On in some way, an:

Animal: This dream has three meanings (choose one). (1) Dreamer, you have the power and means, now, to have dominion over behavioral patterns of which the animal you sat upon represents. These behaviors are within you. You are at a crossroads within your life, use what your dream is revealing about your abilities and means, to help prepare yourself wholly ; emotionally, physically, and spiritually, for your destiny is upon you. If the characteristics ascribed to the animal are desirable or positive, allow the strength of the traits to help you seize the opportunities that are before you, to multiply and prospe r, and to fulfill your divine destiny. If the behaviors are undesirable or negative, take steps accordingly to struggle against the growing desires of the carnal side of you that would thwart your purpose. For specific animal, see category, Animals. If necessary, see suggested course of action. (2) If animal was sitting upon your lap, or you carried the animal around in your arms: Dreamer, you are allowing someone to lead you who have the character traits of the animal depicted within your dream. Moreover, you are beginning to embrace and mimic their behavior or personality. For specific animal, see category, Animals. If necessary, see suggested course of action. (3) To see an animal sitting, reclining upon, or leaning on someone, or something: The trying times that have brought much frustration, aggravation, and were so troublesome will (or have already) begin to decrease. You've weathered a great storm, suffered enormous difficulties, and have not gotten any relief. God has seen your troubles. You are now entering into (or you are already experiencing) a sabbatical. Your heavenly Father is protecting you by allowing you to rest from your work; in order to avoid overly cruel and oppressive pressure from the enemy, via those he uses. They that have vexed you will now go far from you, for God will make you a threat to them without any effort on your part. During this sabbatical, peace will again hold sway over your life. Moreover, Jehovah Jireh will provid e for all your needs. Put your trust in Him and His provision, coupled with contentment with His provisions, and your peace will overflow. You may have to downsize during this sabbatical; this will affect humility, which is, needed now. Moreover, there is a positive trait, this animal represents, within you. Embrace it and nurture it, you will need it. Use this 'you' time to cultivate your strengths and discipline your weaknesses. For specific animal, see category, Animals.

Bench or Pew: This dream has two meanings (choose one). (1) This sort of dream is considered a symbolic milepost, and it speaks of a physical and/or spiritual transition, within the life of the dreamer; thus, this choice has two parts (choose one). Note, if dream contains aspects of both, physical and spiritual, then both are possibilities: (a) Physical transition: If the place and/or person(s) sitting or reclining next to you, within your dream are actually known, in your awaked life, or the place is open or active, and/or the person(s) is alive. You will be leaving your present place of worship and/or ministry to embark upon a new direction, in a new place. Consider the place where you were sitting or the person(s) sitting next to you in your dream. That place or person(s) is the milepost. When you see this place or person(s) physically becoming more a part of your waking life, you will know you are approaching a milepost within your life. As your dream and its symbols are figurative of mileposts, it is understood that there is some distance between one post and another, the in-between time, the time between your present place and new place. This in-between process may take years and perhaps will be very demanding. One thing is for sure, the interval will be busy with restrictions on your freedom, obstacles to your progress, and turnovers in your jobs, ministerial responsibilities, and/or relationships. The changes are meant to prepare you for your destination. Unfortunately, the frustrations may cause you to feel resentful and perhaps rebellious. Fortunately; you have a natural ability to get what you need, and want for your survival, so persevere optimistically and remain obedient to God's directives over your life, you will get there. Having reached your new place, your journey getting there will have enriched you with a multi-dimensionality that befriends you to people of every lifestyle. This attitude will enlarge you spiritually to handle more, prudently and sagacio usly. Journal your dream, you will need to recall it later. See suggested course of action. (b) Spiritual transition: If the place depicted, or the person sitting next to you, within your dream, is not applicable in your waking life, meaning the literal pl ace is closed down or non-operational, or the person is not alive, and one or both are literally unknown to the dreamer. You will very shortly begin to experience, if not already, a paradigm shift in your core beliefs and spirituality. You are approaching new and deeper dimensions. This transition will affect within you a far-reaching hope, profoundly greater faith, and a more intense love for all things Jesus, including His people; allow it. Consider the place where you were sitting or the person you were sitti ng next to in your dream. Using a one-word answer, answer the following questions. What condition was the place or person in (e.g. beautiful, clean, dirty, friendly, hostile, run-down, tired, unattractive)? What did the place or person mean to you within your dream (e.g. dangerous, faithfulness, loyalty, love, offensive, safety)? Kept within context of your dream and the interpretation, this is a spiritual matter. Your answers are indicative of your present spiritual state; thus, honesty with yourself is essential. The condition of your present state, as represented within your dream, will be the stimulus to i nstigate change within your life. For example, if the place was run-down. This means, you are depleted emotionally and physically. If the person was your deceased mother, your wisdom is now considered irrelevant, or obsolete. With that said, this condition is the catalysts that will press you higher spiritually. If change comes easy, and is welcomed by the dreamer, this transition will be full of exciting new subject matter and experiences. If change is arduous to the dreamer, the transformation will prove very demanding, difficult, and frustrating. The frustrations may cause you to feel resentful and even rebellious. It is counseled that you keep an optimistic outlook and remain obedient to God's directives over your life. The change is needed. Jo urnal your dream, you will need to recall it later. See suggested course of action. (2) Bench or pew is on top of you: You are at your 'sat' place. Remain where you are. Having reached your sat place, your journey getting there has enriched you with a multi- dimensionality that befriends you to people of every lifestyle, thus, reach out, and touch others. Your transition has enlar ged you spiritually to handle more, prudently and sagaciously. You have experienced, or will experience, a paradigm shift in your core beliefs and spirituality, and will approach new and deeper dimensions, to go with this shift. Moreover, the experiences you've endured, getting to where you are now, has affected within you a far-reaching hope, profoundly greater faith, and a more intense love for all things Jesus, including His people.

Chair, Couch (including Chaise, Lounge Chair, Ottoman, or Sofa): This dream has two meanings (choose one). (1) Your dream expresses a necessity to deal with the moral impurities within your life, no matter how seemingly insignificant they may seem. Right behavior results in good feelings. The dreamer is counseled to recognize the connection between your present depression and your anger. You've been here before. This is one of your negative life cycles. This cycle can be broken by prudent choices and appropriate follow through. If you purify yourself by rejecting the influences that arouse the sin that so easily overwhelmed you. You can have mastery over your silent rage and frustrations. If you choose to communicate honestly and clearly in the beginning with others, and choose strongly, meaning doing that which is principally sound and ethically go od, God promises to give you the success you seek. He will cause you to lie down in peace, and nothing shall make you afraid. Dreamer, there is a need to be clean morally and of a clear conscience, for God is calling you now, hear Him. If you do not respond appropriately, sin is waiting for the opportunity to devour completely. Your rage will have mastery over you, and the carnal side of your nature will cause you to do and/or say some things that you will regret the rest of your life or may even cost you your freedom or life. See suggested course of action. (2) If chair, couch was on top of you or you are carrying the chair, couch around in your arms: You have dealt with the immoral impurities within your life. You have completed the task of purification, and have rejected the negativity in your life. Begin, now, the ministry, mission, or task Jesus has set before you. You are anointed, blessed, and will receive what you need, to complete the call.

Heels (sitting on your heels): Your dream reveals a cowardly drawback spirit (also see Luke 9:57-62). The dreamer needs to re-consider the cost of following Jesus and its true value, eternal life in heaven (John 14:2-6). Doing the will of the Father is far more important than the opinions of others, public image, or any other self-satisfying trait or vanity, one may have. See suggested course of action.

Lap or Shoulder (sitting on someone's lap or shoulder): This dream has two meanings (choose one). (1) You will be taught the deeper things of God from one of His preferred or model teachers. Remain under their tutelage and never discr edit their appointment as a teacher sent to you. A wise man or woman will increase their learning; the unwise and foolish is opposite. If necessary, see suggested course of action. (2) If someone was sitting on your lap or shoulder: You are, at present, teaching someone the deeper things of God, for you are one of God's preferred or model teachers. Never discredit your appointment or gifting as a teacher sent by God. Dreamer, no matter your emotional, physical, or spiritual state; remai n where you are and continue to teach, for this is your present assignment, your sat place at this time. By remaining and continuing, deliverance will be affected within your life. You will be delivered from your present negative attitudes and th e overwhelming hurts and pains that have caused your negative attitudes and state of affairs. Additionally, dreamer, a wise man or woman multiply their talents by teaching and/or passing on the knowledge gained by use of those talents, to others; thus, prospering emotionally, financially, physically, and spiritually. The wicked will quit or bury their gift, blaming their hesitancy on God, circumstances, situations, or others, bringing great loss upon themselves. This is necessary to say, sanctification is from God and not by your own efforts or will; therefore, do your job and allow God to do His. Who was sitting, reclining upon, leaning on your lap or shoulder (e.g. an adult, a baby, someone dead, your husband, wife, a stranger, a teen)? What were they doing (e.g. asleep, awake, crying, feeding)? This person represents the attributes and/or spiritual condition of the student you're teaching; thus, teach compassionately, emphatically, and wisely. If necessary, see suggested course of action.

Throne: Dreamer is held in high honor by many. Dreamer, God puts His servants in situations where they are responsible to usher His Presence into the mentality of the situation. We usher His Presence in, and magnify the Lord, when we proclaim His goodness, His truth, harmonize with His word, and exalt His Mighty Name. Our adoration of God, in all of its many forms, causes us to become more aware of His awesome power and authority. This enables us to handle the situation at hand by faith. The dreamer is one such servant and you have been put in a situation such as that mentioned. You are a vessel of God's glory, and a possessor of the truth needed for the situation at hand, the greater the truth, the greater your authority, the greater your success. You are equipped to handle your, and God's, business. However, although you are held in high esteem by many, immediately let them know, "Don't worship me, I too, am just a man or woman like yourself, God, and God alone is to be worship", for God has said, "I will not give my glory to another" (Isaiah 42:8). Therefore, dreamer you are warned to be careful lest you become so prideful that there creeps into you the idea that you can be deified. Self-deification is of Satan. God can dwell in the human, via the Holy Spirit, but forever the human is the human, and Adonai Elohim is forever God.

Forced to Sit Down, Recline, or Lean, in some way: This dream has two meanings (choose one). (1) Your dream reveals; that the dreamer will be given land to live on, it is counseled that you remain there. You are in this situation as a sort of "kinsman redeemer". This property will be a place of refuge for you and all those connected to your family for many years to come. Take care not to sell it, and to be prudent with this inheritance. (2) If unmarried, you will be getting married very soon. In addition, land will be given you to be a place of refuge for you and all those connected to your family for many years to come. Remain there. Take care not to sell it, and to be prudent with this inheritance.

Place where you were Sitting, Reclining, Leaning, or Squatting (Building, Church, Christ's Feet, Courtroom, Dwelling, Feet, Floor, Garden, Ground, Hell, Judge's Seat, Lea, Mountain, School, Tables, Tree, Valley, Vehicle, Work)

Building or Dwelling: Your dream suggests that the direction of spiritual and emotional growth for the dreamer will be in embracing the positive attributes that you may impute to the building, dwelling and/or particular room you were sitting in, with emphasis on an earnest resolve towards betterment. For example, if an educational facility, then dreamer needs to, earnestly embrace some manner of education. On the other hand, if negative feelings are associated with the place, take steps accordingly to struggle against the growing desires of the carnal side of you that would hinder growth. See suggested course of action.

Church: Keyword for the dreamer is abiding. You are in your set place spiritually and physically. Spiritually, because you are abiding in Jesus, and His Word is abiding in you; thus, you are in a position to ask what you will and it shall be given you. Physically, your present place of worship is your appointed place for now; abide there that all may go well with you during this season of your life.

Courtroom, Judge's Seat: This dream has three meanings (choose one). (1) Dreamer, Christian believers, clergy, or ministers are not exempt from the authority and powers of the law. You, as with all citizens, are subject to them. Moreover, if you are guilty of a real crime, you should submit to the official verdict. If innocent, submit to their formal investigation for information to clear yourself. See suggested course of action. (2) Sitting in the judge's seat in a courtroom: Dreamer, resolve your disagreement with another believer via church counsel and godly advice. Taking your problem before non-believers or the unjust and not before the saints exposes your antagonistic, reckless, and thoughtless behavior. While you pretend to be a person of peace and wisdom, and a follower of the Prince of Peace, your actions are likely to bring a reproach upon Christianity within your sphere of influence. Matters of little consequence are better to be forgiven. If you have said, it's not about "this or that" it's about the principle of the matter; the matter is too small, and a greater principle is forgiveness, especially of our brothers and sisters in Christ. See suggested course of action.

Feet (including Christ's Feet): This dream has two meanings (choose one). (1) Christ's Feet: Your dream denotes one who is in the process of being made whole, emotionally, psychologically, physically, and financially, because of your reverence for God. You are entering into a process of being purified and purged, examined, proven and tested, spiritually and emotionally cleansed. Everything that's unusable within you will give way to that which is beneficial and profitable, and that which is undesirable will become brightly polished, according to God's good pleasure. Your pride will soon give way to humbleness, dignity, honor, and righteous self-esteem, your foolishness to peace and wisdom. This process will also heal the animosity within you. Allow the process without complaining or murmuring for it is preparing you for a great journey. Be as one who gets satisfaction from embracing good habits. (2) To sit at someone's feet: This denotes one who is teachable.

There is an old saying, "When the student is ready, the teacher will appear". Dreamer, you are the student, another is your teacher, and you are ready. Although, you may be very accomplished, prosperous, and/or wise, you have need of a teacher at present. God is sending someone into your life to help you carry out your next undertaking, by enlarging your spiritual capacity. This person is modest and unassuming in attitude, behavior, and dress. Notwithstanding, great respect towards them is appropriate and required, as well as some form of compensation. You will need to be honest, open, and transparent, to get what you need from him or her. Your undivided attention is required, thus you may need to take a vacation from your normal business and/or ministerial activities. Your dream is to bring about an awareness of this person's coming, and to prepare you to meet them sagaciously.

Floor, Ground, Valley, or Hell: This dream has three meanings (choose one). (1) If dreamer was on a floor (the inside lower horizontal surface, as of a room, hallway, tent, or other structure), your dream is a critical warning to the dreamer. The dreamer needs to start showing kindness to all alike, including animals. For you will entertain an angel shortly. The purpo se of the angel's visit is to stop you from doing evil against God's people and/or to stop you from abusing children, adults, and/or animals. If you do not change your mean and vicious ways, the Lord will not spare you. His harshness will be incense against you. Thus, all the kinds of evils and the breadth of evil effects that may befall a human, because of reaping what has been sown, when one is not covered with mercy, will come upon you. See suggested course of action. (2) If dreamer was on the ground (the land surface), dreamer, your place of honor and respect, coupled with your pride has deceived you, causing you to act very irresponsibly. Thus, you have lost honor and will no longer be respected at the level you are accustomed to by many; however, not all. The consequence of your irresponsible behavior has deeply distressed you, and now you've nea rly given up hope for future blessings. Dreamer, although you're in a low place, it's only a lesson. You are humbled. Before a person's dishonor, his or her heart is prideful. Favorably, humility comes before honor and grace has always been available. Your soul has deeply prospered because of your humbling. You will again obtain a measure of honor within your life; for humility and the fear of the Lord will bring wealth, honor, and life once more (Proverbs 15:33, 18:12, 22:4). Be encouraged. (3) Valley, Hell, dreamer you are slipping into darkness, listening to flattery and smooth words, from those without knowledge, who surrounds you. Their ideas or arguments are illogical, non-mainstream, and without favorable conclusions. Demonically lead, they are passionate regarding their arguments and beliefs, and they angrily justify sinfulness. It is this attitude that you are embr acing, having lost your equilibrium within the sacred scheme of things. You have also become blasé regarding the treasure of truth you have been given. Dreamer, you no longer respect, nor acknowledge that the precepts, principles, statutes, as well as the rites and other liturgical services that are considered to have been established by Jesus Christ, brings grace (the free and unmerited favor and beneficence of God) to those participating in or receiving them. These undertakings include, but are not limited to, water baptism, repentance, which is seeking pardon and expressing sincere feelings of regret and brokenness for having done something awry and/or for having hurt someone, see 2 Corinthians 7:10, 11, receiving of the Holy Spirit, fellowship with others, communions, confirmations, ordinations, anointing of the sick, holy matrimony. Once again, respecting the sacredness of these things will affect within you, a personal revival. Additionally, a servant of the Lord will visit you, and instruct you on how to get out of your negative situation. Recognize and respect your time of visitation and respect the servant of the Lord. Further, you are destined to be a spiritual leader; thus, your direction of growth should be toward maintaining a greater level of purity. Your mentor, the servant of the Lord will guide you in that direction. Moreover, do not speak lies, neither shall a deceitful tongue be found in your mouth. Having set these things in order, physical sustenance, and spiritual restoration will result. Then you will no longer be outside in a low place. Your dream also speaks of marriage and prosperity. As well as abiding in the set place of worship, that is before you presently. If necessary, see suggested course of action.

Garden, Lea: Your dream speaks of rest and work. The dreamer will experience a good balance between rest and work. You will have a deep experience with God that can only be accomplished by time spent with Him in quietness and rest. As for work, your dream is also indicative of travel, for evangelistic purposes. As you travel from one venue to another, lifting up the Name of Jesus, you will be provided, not only, physical sustenance, but spiritual restoration as well. When your body becomes weak, God will revive it. When your soul becomes sorrowful, God will restore, and when your spirit becomes weary, He will reinvigorate it. Be encourage and strong.

Mountain or higher: Your dream denotes spiritual recklessness and foolishness. You have tempted the Lord God and will now begin to reap the consequences of your actions. See suggested course of action.

School: The dreamer is one who will be (or already is) instructed in divine knowledge by the immediate inspiration of the Paraclete, and by a teacher sent to you by God. You will personally, be taught some of the great truths found within scripture; that are of great value. Esteem the teacher that God sends to you, for he or she is highly qualified to do their job. This teacher is there to lay the groundwork for you to become the great teacher you are destined to be. This meeting and experience is fa st approaching. If necessary, see suggested course of action.

Tables (Coffee Table, Counter Tops, Dinettes, Kitchen-Island): Your dream denotes God's provision, as well; it encourages the dreamer to strive for a more intimate fellowship with your Savior, your family, and with other believers. If necessary, see suggested course of action.

Tree: Your dream is to bring to remembrance the abundant comfort the dreamer has had with Jesus Christ, as well as to reiterate that the dreamer is known (or will be known) for your wisdom, prophetic abilities, and great usefulness to the public. As God's mouthpiece, you will correct abuses and deal with wrongs, especially amongst those who worship God. People will come to you from everywhere for advice on improvement and restoration of things pertaining to Christ and life. You are one who is extraordinarily knowing and wise, and so, you will come to be very important, and well known. You are already intimately acquainted with God and devoted to the service of His Kingdom. Dreamer, with great delight put your entire confidence in the protection and wisdom of the Lord, for He knows you, and He will give you the desires of your heart.

Vehicle: If vehicle was moving, this type of dream was sent to encourage the dreamer that your wait is over, and you are progressing towards your appointed place spiritually and/or physically. If vehicle was not moving, waiting will become a lar ge part of your lifestyle, because you are in need of endurance. Whichever one, your set place is before you, with a prima ry emphasis on abiding there contentedly and resting. See also category, Vehicles, Modes of Transportation.

Work: This type of dream was sent to encourage the dreamer to progress towards your new appointed place, ministerially. This new place is before you, or will be introduced to you shortly. Join and abide there, with a primary emphasis on abiding there contentedly that you may offer unto the Lord your rightful duties in righteousness. Many need to be touched by your wisdom. Additionally, dreamer, letting go of people and places when you have fulfilled your role with them, when the season is over, is an important lesson for you to learn. If necessary, see suggested course of action.

Sit and Wait: Your dream is to remind the dreamer of God's supreme providence over humanity state of affairs, including the circumstances and duration a person will remain in a situation. The dreamer needs to, solemnly acknowledge that righteousness belongs unto the Lord and that the turmoil that is before you at this time is of your doing; a trespass you have committed against God. Repentance is necessary. Pray Psalm 51. See suggested course of action.

Waiting to sit down or Unable to sit down: Dreamer, unanswered prayer cannot be traced to the unfaithfulness of God. God does not refrain from delivering, helping, or healing because He lacks the power to do so. In His loving plan, your pray er was not answered. Whether the Mighty One chooses to heed our prayers or not, the Lord Jesus is still Holy and omniscience. You should not be concerned with God's faithfulness in hearing you, for He hears you. You may not like His answers, but He hears you. If you will begin to express the very real reality of inheriting heaven to others, you will begin to understand a nd appreciate that which goes beyond the natural realm, including God's wisdom in unanswered prayer. See suggested course of action.

Whom were you Sitting or Reclining or Leaning upon (Alone, Dead People, Leadership, Ruler, CEO, Celebrities, others). See one of the following.

Alone: Your dream was sent to encourage the dreamer and to bring about an awareness of an appointed inheritance. Dreamer; although, you've seriously applied yourself to the duty of your religious office, wholly to the business o f the Lord, allowing nothing to divert you from your work, forfeiting much, even permissible activity; of late, you've had little satisfa ction. You've sat alone, because the hand of the Lord is strong upon you to carry out His work. You are becoming self-sufficient and unrelenting, capable of handling much responsibility, especially when required to make major decisions. The life of a useful man or woman is beautiful, dignified, elegant, and poised. Many will be inspired by your wisdom, confidence, and blameless actions, while others will feel threaten by it. Those who plot evil against you (family, friend, or foe) will not prevail against you, but will yield willingly to your authority. Dreamer, be attentive and approachable, your set inheritance, of abundant peace, comfort, and sufficient wealth is upon you, now. Further, at some point in your future, high honor will be bestowed upon you. This will be the Lord's doing and it will be marvelous in your sight.

Dead People: Dreamer, you are known for being spiritually alive, but you are spiritually dead. Outward you appear well to others, but inwardly there is only the form of godliness, not the power of God. There is great deadness in your soul, and in your service to the Lord. Your works are hollow and empty; your prayers are not filled with holy desires, your giving is not with true love, and your day set aside for worship of the Lord, is not filled with suitable devotion of your soul to God, your spiritual expressions are just ritualistic acts. Your inward affections, feelings, and desires, do not match your outward acts. Your outward acts are primarily hypocritical, disordered, and spiritually lifeless. When the inward spirit is lacking genuine int imacy with the Lord and is, conflicted, the outward will begin to show it through your actions, choices, and words, which lead only to desolation within. Although you are in a declining state, dreamer, the Lord is calling you to endeavor once again to become dependent on the Holy Spirit and the grace of God that the faith and spiritual affections you once had for God, will become revived and strengthen. You are counseled to, from your whole heart and being, become active and earnest in your duties for the Kingdom of God that you may be humbled and revived, and able to hold fast to that which remains, that your name might be found in the Book of Life on your "great day". He or she that overcomes shall be clothed in white raiment. See Revelation 3:1-3, 5, 6. Dreamer, remember God has given you His Spirit, the spirit of wisdom, understanding, counsel, strength, knowledge, and the spirit of the fear of God (see Isaiah 11:3) that you may be equipped to overcome, for He is not asking of you something He has not equipped you with the ability to complete. Therefore, be earnest and diligent to return to God in the spirit of genuineness, love, and obedience that He may graciously receive you, on your appointed day, as a loving Savior and not as a wrathful Judge. Please note, while a portion of this interpretation counsels a "getting right of the soul" before you meet the King of kings, your dream is not implying that the dreamer will die anytime soon. See suggested course of action.

Leadership, Ruler, CEO, Celebrities: This dream implies two things (both apply). (1) The dreamer will become a great leader sometime in the near future. (2) Notwithstanding, the dreamer is to consider carefully what is being offered or presented to you, at this moment, by someone in an influential position. Although the offer is pleasing and very tempting, it is deceptive. The temptation is stronger and dangerous, to one who is not use to such activity, distractions, diversions, or pursuits. Dreamer, you will regret entering into an agreement with them, as it is a snare to you. You are unable, emotionally, to pay the hidden costs, as you are not yet ready to deal with what is called "the swelling (or thickets) of Jordan" (Jeremiah 12:5). It is counseled that you consider yourself in danger, and just say no, to this offer, until you have matured more as a sagacious and tenacious leader, especially who is wise as a serpent and innocent as a dove (Matthew 10:16). If necessary, see suggested course of action.

Others (known or unknown): The Lord is calling you back to Himself with compassion, and with a loving kindness that will last. His loving kindness will remain and His promise of peace will not be forgotten. In righteousness, you will be establi shed. You will be far from oppression. You will see the guaranteed justice of the wicked, and an outcome they're not expecting. However, your boundaries are to obey God's standards for you exclusively. Namely, disrespect, on any level, towards those in authority over you is forbidden. Disrespect on any level towards any of God's children, especially the least of them, as well as prejudice and hatred is forbidden. Your expressed disapproval of justice handed down by God will not be tolerated. Since yo u will see justice handed down, do not say, "God is not fair by allowing this or that to happen". Letting go of negativity, and the people, places, and/or things that fuel it, and appreciating the justice and grace (the free and unmerited favor and benefice nce of God) afforded you, will bring sweetness to your soul. Embrace again the sweetness of wisdom to the soul, for wisdom offers a guaranteed recompense and an expectation that shall not disappoint. Then will men and women of honor seek your wisdom, which God has put in your heart. Additionally, consider those you were sitting with. Are they the men and women who fuel the negativity? Could they possibly be the men and women of honor seeking your wisdom? If necessary, see suggested course of action.

Suggested Course of Action

Question to consider and journal, did your dream depict any symbols that alludes to, the dreamer will make the necessary changes, spiritually, emotionally, and/or physically to affect a more positive outcome? If changes are initiated, your dreams will change.

Nevertheless, as the Lord has not rejected you; do not walk out of your service or ministry to His people, nor turn from following Him. Consider what great things He has done for you (see 1 Samuel 12:22, 24) and continue progressing and maturing within yourself and in the Lord. Yes, your wrongdoing has offended the Lord, and your thoughts and ways were not His, but these things have not thrown you out of covenant with Him. Therefore, His righteous warnings should not run you away from hope in His mercy, but draw you near to Him. God is pleased to make you His people. Dreamer, be pleased to be His people.

Now, pray (See Prayer of Deliverance, pg. 897)

Specific Meaning

If you have a very real connection with any type of sitting or reclining activity, for example, builder of chairs, court stenographer, clerical, secretarial, handicapped, judge, orchestra, transit services, or some recent health related issue that has you resigned to sitting. Maybe you're waiting for someone, due to a college term, military duty, prison term, or some other separation. Dreams of this sort, for the most part, are ordinary dreams, resulting from your daily activities (see Chapter One, Chalom). These sorts of dreams are usually about your routine, mundane activities or anxieties that overwhelm your mind during the day. They are an inner release mechanism, which helps provide you with emotional balance and the maintaining of your sanity. These dreams are not significant, and do not warrant special attention.

SLEEPING (preparing, make ready to sleep)

Some short descriptions of types, phrases, and other processes and particulars, connected in some way to this category, are. For example, to be asleep, catnap, dead sleep, doze, fall asleep, have a lie-down, have a siesta, forty winks, nap, put someone to sleep, sleep late, to wake up.

Unless otherwise noted elsewhere, if, in your everyday living, your awaked state, as part of your lifestyle, work, or ministerial activities, or a special event, you have a very real connection with any type of sleeping activity. For example, mattress maker or salesman, expertise in the assessment, diagnosis, and management of clinical conditions that occur during sleep, that disturb sleep or that are, affected by disturbances in the wake-sleep cycle, or you are affected by sleep disorders (e.g. insomnia, narcolepsy, sleepwalking), your dream is not significant and does not warrant special attention.

Otherwise noted, to see another asleep, if person was unknown or unseen the person is the dreamer. If person is, known dreamer, you are being made aware of another's issues (see Chapter One, Are You Ready to Hear the Messages in Your Dreams, section entitled, The 10% for others). The issue can be found within the interpretation of the relevant sleep symbol.

Otherwise noted, see Note 1 at the beginning of Actions and Activities category.

To determine who your dream is for you or another, consider one of the following (relevant interpretation) first, as well as, see Note 3 at the beginning of Actions and Activities category.

Symbols and Referents: Dreams of sleep figuratively deal with aging, or a loss of, or decrease of, faith on some level, or a state of devastation in some form (spiritual or physical). Additionally, sleep also has two meanings. The first is associated with any unconscious state that is inactive or dormant for a time. The second is that which is figuratively referred to as death; biblically, most commonly known to us from the story of Lazarus (John 11:11-15; also see Psalm 90:5). Question, did dreamer wake up within your dream? If so, see subcategory, to awake out of sleep. The interpretation of your dream will largely depend on the way the elements of your dream are contextually put together, and the background, which they appear. Kept within context of your dream and the interpretation, other references highlighted may also be points of relevance. It will be the sum of those surrounding conditions (e.g. the activity, background settings, circumstances, emotions, events, perspective s, situations, and words), that will help to explain your dream's meaning.

Note: Most all of the following sleeping dreams, are metaphorically represented by common words, expressions, and other usages (e.g. slang or clichés), or a 'probable'. It will be those meanings considered.

Category Content - If not listed see index, perchance, for your specific type of sleep dream activity.

- To awake out of sleep, to wake up (within your dream)
- Can't find a place to sleep, looking for a place to sleep, or no place to sleep, "no place in the end" (hotel, house, or anywhere)
- To be asleep completely under covers (e.g. blankets, comforters, sheets)
- Unable to sleep, scared to go to sleep, or uncomfortable sleeping somewhere
- Asleep or preparing to sleep in a (see one of the following):
    - Bizarre, strange, or surprising place (e.g. in another's bed, on a bench, in a box, a casket, a church, a garbage dump, a graveyard, at someone's home, at a homeless shelter, homeless on the street, in places of ill-repute, amongst ruins); Comfortable place, or common position, usual for sleeping (e.g. in your bed, eyes closed, peaceful, reclining, relaxed, tranquil, or in a state of intimacy associated with being in bed with a spouse- the marriage bed); Foreign place, far-off, overseas, remote, strange land, unknown or outside; Outside, exposed to the elements, countryside, field, forest, on the ground, meadow, park, to be asleep in the dust; Uncomfortable or uncommon position, not usual for sleeping (e.g. eyes wide open, holding something, sitting up, standing up, suspended above, from, or over something, driving in a car, unclean, on the floor, or on/in any uncomfortable position)
- Dead sleep or sleeping with the dead (to appear as dead should be highlighted)
- Dozing off, drowsy, falling asleep (to nod off, letting the head fall forward, almost asleep, or sluggish should be highlighted should be highlighted)
- Napping
- Catnap (a cat sleeping should be highlighted)
- Have forty winks (the number 40 should be highlighted)
- Have a siesta (time of the day between noon and early part of the day should be highlighted)
- Nightmare (to awake in a state of terror and disorientation, oftentimes screaming)
- Put someone to bed (bedding down someone should be highlighted)
- Sleep around (to be in a circle or circular motion should be highlighted or to have casual sexual relationships with different people)
- Sleep in (asleep at place of employment should be highlighted)
- Sleep face down (face downward should be highlighted)
- Sleep on someone's lap or rocked to sleep
- Sleep late (lateness should be highlighted)
- Sleep it off (something falling off you while you are asleep should be highlighted)
- Sleepwalking, see category, Walking

To awake out of sleep, to wake up (within your dream): Your dream denotes some type of conquering, and a spiritual awakening, renewing of your strength, see Isaiah 40:29-30, is happening within the life of the dreamer, particularly, a completely new awakening regarding your relationship with Christ, Jesus. You are opening your eyes to what it means to be "one on one", with Christ. Moreover, Jesus will strengthen you emotionally, psychologically, and physically to deal with your issues, whatever they might be. You will overcome your situation. Question, where was dreamer asleep? If relevant, see subcategory, Asleep.

Can't find a place to sleep, looking for a place to sleep, or no place to sleep, "no place in the end" (hotel, house, or anywhere): Your way of life, modus operandi "MO" (mode or state of operating, living, or lifestyle), as you know it, is about to end. There will be major changes (significant in scope, extent, and effect) in your normal, everyday habits, and in your way of operating and functioning. Responsibilities that are attached to, and are major parts of, your ministerial purpose wi ll increase. The changes are a result of your prayers, plus, your sabbatical is over. You've asked God to heal your faith, and to heal you, that you might be a healer to others in some way, and you've asked for change; healing and change is here. Dreamer, this is necessary to say, you are not too old. Anyone who wants to follow Jesus has to understand that discipleship requires total commitment (Matthew 8:19-22). Therefore, now, begin to choose good deeds and habits that will lead to the fulfilment of your God given purpose, and strengthen your resolve. Pay close attention to shifts within your relationships with others. K eep what is good, toss what is bad, know the difference, and understand God's hand within all your situations. Your boundaries are to obey God's standards for you exclusively. Namely, your expressed disapproval of justice handed down by God will not be tolerated. Since you will see justice handed down, do not say, "God is not fair by allowing this or that to happen". Dre amer, resolve to vigorously and quickly release hurts, pains, disappointments, disillusionments, and a reluctance to change. Quickly forgive and move on to prevent being stuck in a negative and self-sabotaging mind-set for many years. While it is easier said than done, one cannot grow or go forward stuck in the past. Do not lose today holding on to yesterday; let it go. Disrespect, on any level, towards those in authority over you is forbidden. Disrespect on any level towards any of God's children, especially the least of them, as well as prejudice and hatred is forbidden. As you have opportunity, do well to all people, especially to those who belong to your family, and to the family of believers. Without also neglecting to consider how you treat the homeless or the poor, (see Ben Sira 29). Do you give to the unknown stranger who asks alms of you? When asked, "Do you have any change?" do you say, "No, I don't have any change", because you are too busy to go get it out of your car or purse? Do you have change? Have you made a way for that homeless person to have dinner in that restaurant? Do you not greet someone, with a kind, "greeting", because of his or her dress or physical condition, appearance? See, Matthew 25:31-46. As a servant of humanity, consider yourself a humble servant, and not one to be served or adored. Dreamer you are endowed with the power of God, to cause some to become alive again, to restore others from a depressed, inactive, and unused state, and others to return from the dead (spiritually). Therefore, elevate and promote the righteousness of Christ to those around you. Lead people to pray to Jesus personally, embrace God personally, and come to know and love God from whatever situation they find them self. If necessary, see suggested course of action.

To be asleep completely under covers (e.g. blankets, comforters, sheets): Dreamer, although you are growing weary and tired of waiting on someone or something, feeling "too old", your expectancy will be delayed, for a little while longer, you have need of perseverance. However, do not cast away your faith, hope, and your spirit of expectation, for in due time, you will reap what you have desired most, and you will rest, deeply and soundly, emotionally, physically, and spiritually, a ll will be well with you. A couple of things, during this delay season, do not depend so heavily on others, as to look about anxiously when you need them the most. God knows exactly what you need, and He will provide. Therefore, keep your hope alive, an d be on the lookout for that which is expected from God. It is counseled that you stay in place, particularly your present pla ce of worship, until something happens, and it will. Within a month, Christianity will provide you with a ministerial position t hat will yield a living. You will also be the legal recipient of a monetary benefit or compensation, from some kind of public administration. Moreover, you will be leaving your church, and you will experience a mega-ministry. You will become friends with major leaders, but not covenant partners with them. You will (or should) remain attached to your present church and come back to rest there. Shortly thereafter, because of your diligence and honorable service, you will be given the opportunity to take a sabbatical rest, covered by the Lord's grace (the free and unmerited favor and beneficence of God).

Unable to sleep, scared to go to sleep, or uncomfortable sleeping somewhere: This implies that some type of gratitude and recompense needs to be considered. The dreamer is advised to be particularly grateful to someone. One whom you may possibly consider an aide, amateur, assistant, attendant, congregant, dependent, green, junior, laymen, nonprofessional, novice, outsider, unbeliever, uninitiated, unskilled, unversed Their services to you has indebted you to them. Two rules of gratitude (1) Better to honor than not at all. If you are unable to make financial recompense to those who have been kind to you, do them honor by acknowledging their kindness and owning your obligations to them. (2) If you have neglected to acknowledge, with gratefulness, good done you by another, do it now, it's better late than never. If necessary, see suggested course of action.

Asleep or preparing to sleep in a (see one of the following):

Bizarre, strange, or surprising place (e.g. in another's bed, on a bench, in a box, a casket, a church, a garbage dump, a graveyard, at someone's home, at a homeless shelter, homeless on the street, in places of ill-repute, amongst ruins). This dream has two meanings (choose one). (1) This refers to a clear visible loss of Christian identity and a loss of faith in God (a resolute trust in the integrity of God and in His Word), in His Power of deliverance, and in His miracles. You are aware of what is causing the loss of your Christian identity and of the critical condition of your relationship with Christ. See suggested course of action. May, also see category Death. (2) To see another asleep, within this context: This choice has two parts (choose one). (a) If person was unknown, the person is the dreamer. You intentionally deny the grave condition your relationship with Christ is in, having chosen to close your eyes to your spiritual issues. See suggested course of action. (b) Did you know the individual within your dream? If so, you are being made aware of this person's backsliding. They have openly relapsed back into a shameful and embarrassing lifestyle; having sabotage their covering of grace given by God (the free and unmerited favor and beneficence of God) to hide their indiscretions and/or have lost their faith in God, in His Power of deliverance, and in miracles. Dreamer, you have the God given authority to pray for this person, coupled with a biblical based, no-nonsense, straight talking rebuke. This may wake them up to their wrongdoings. You will be given the opportunity to privately, and seriously, talk with them.

Comfortable place, or common position–usual for sleeping (e.g. in your bed, on a couch, eyes closed, peaceful, reclining, relaxed, tranquil, or in a state of intimacy associated with being in bed with a spouse-the marriage bed): Your dream was sent to counsel the dreamer to focus your attention on God's providence over your life. For, this type of dream speaks of the dreamer's ability to release stress by putting confidence in God's support; it would be wise of you to put your trust in Him at present. This, coupled with, contentment, and your peace will overflow. Dreamer, focus on the wisdom, care, and guidance He has provided you thus far, as you grow older, for He always guards over His chosen; hence, He watches over you. Dreamer, the feeling of rest and serenity that comes with trust in God's divine providence is available to you right now. You will begin to experience the blessings spoken of in (Leviticus 26:4-13 GW). In particular, (verse 6 GW), "I will bring peace to your land. You will lie down with no one to scare you".

Foreign place (e.g. distant, far-off, overseas, remote, strange land, unknown): This dream has two meanings (choose one). (1) Your dream alerts the dreamer that you will soon experience an unwilling separation from your home and/or church, as a correction for the dreamer's extreme behaviors, tactics, political, quasi-religious or jihad activities. For example, violent condemning of, and/or physical attacks upon those connected to abortions, homosexuality, or any denomination or religion different from yours Your protests are very closely akin to hate groups, if not deemed one already. You have no love for others, have lost faith in God (a resolute trust in the integrity of God and in His Word), and in His providential powers. A literal and spiritual exile has been officially decided upon by the divine council in heaven regarding the dreamer and this will be enforced by a civil, criminal, and/or religious court on earth. See suggested course of action. (2) To see another asleep, in a foreign place: This choice has two parts (choose one). (a) If person was unknown, the person is the dreamer. You're in denial concerning the total wrongness of your extremist ideas and action, having chosen to close your eyes to your own hatred, and your resulting condemnatory, judgmental, and overall negative actions and behaviors. See suggested course of action. (b) Did you know the individual within your dream? If so, you are being made aware of this person's heretical ideas and actions. Th ey have openly and violently protested alongside hate groups; having lost their faith in God and love for others. Dreamer, you have the God given authority to pray for this person, coupled with a biblical based, no-nonsense, straight-talking rebuke. This may wake them up to their wrongdoings. You will be given the opportunity to privately, and seriously talk, with them.

Outside, exposed to the elements, countryside, field, forest, on the ground, meadow, park, to be asleep in the dust): This dream has two meanings (choose one). (1) Your dream warns the dreamer that you have chosen (or is choosing) not to believe that God's loving care, guidance, and wisdom are provided for you. God is no longer perceived by you as a caring for ce bestowing foresight, and guiding humans towards good judgment in the management of their affairs and resources. Dreamer, in actuality, you are reaping the consequences of a condemnatory, judgmental, and overall negative attitude towards others. Since your eyes are closed, you do not see His wonders. You have closed your mind to the miraculous wonders of divine providence; the wisdom, care, and guidance provided by God, because of your own attitude, disappointments, and mental health concerns. You're in denial concerning the total wrongness of your behaviors. Thus, you have become insensitive to th e continuous acts of God's loving care. See suggested course of action. (2) To be asleep in the dust (fine powdery material such as dry earth that can be blown about in the air): See Daniel 12:2, 3. Wisdom suggests that if we reverence the Lord and endure correction with patience and understanding, deliverance from evil will come. See suggested course of action.

Uncomfortable or uncommon position, not usual for sleeping (e.g. eyes wide open, holding something, sitting up, standing up, suspended above, from, or over something, driving in a car, unclean, on the floor, or on/in any uncomfortable position): Your dream is attempting to draw your attention to a lifeless or dead faith that you have begun to embrace. It is a faith without passion (James 2:14-26); thus, your faith is asleep (or is going to sleep). While believing that God is able to do, you have chosen to not actively, take part in believing Him for anything. Your attitude is one of coldness, disinterest, dispiritedness; usually letting situations just happen and decisions be made regarding you, without any active participation on your part. This way you do not have to exercise your faith, nor hope for anything. While this attitude is seemingly safe an d may prevent some emotional difficulties, it does not produce a faith sufficient to support the advancement of the Kingdom of God (Matthew 17:20, 21:21; Luke 7:9; John 14:12). Dreamer, you are advised to pray, "Lord increase (or heal) my faith", and to wake up to the fullness of life this kind of faith offers. See suggested course of action.

Dead sleep or sleeping with the dead (to appear as dead should be highlighted): Your dream is to warn the dreamer. It implies that you are in a backsliding downward spiral. See also Isaiah 29:10. Your activities and attitude will lead to spiritual and/or literal death. Favorably, via your dream, Jesus Christ is demonstrating grace (the free and unmerited favor and beneficence of God) by offering you a resurrection from dead works, people, places, and things. Consider your dream an intervention. Coupled with your spirituality, via prayer and fasting, you may also need professional help, and will need spiritual support to affect a personal revival within you. Jesus will strengthen you emotionally, psychologically, and physically, to go get help for your backsliding, via a Christian based support group, Christian counseling, healthcare, inpatient Dreamer, have faith in this, followed with works (James 2:17). See suggested course of action.

Dozing off, drowsy, falling asleep (to nod off, letting the head fall forward, almost asleep, or

sluggish should be highlighted should be highlighted): This dream is to warn the dreamer, for it denotes spiritual or physical devastation. This dream has three meanings (choose one). (1) Dreamer, you say, peace and safety, when there is none. You do not realize the great danger you are in spiritually. Although, you have a reputation of being alive, you are spiritually lifeless. God know s your deeds and the foolishness of your heart. Wake up! Strengthen what remains and is about to die, for your deeds have been found incomplete in the sight of God. Remember, therefore, what you have received and heard; obey it, and repent. If you do not wake up, Jesus will come like a thief, and you will be caught off guard (Revelation 3:2, 3). At that time, your personal day of reckoning would have come. See suggested course of action. (2) Your dream implies a spiritual indifference. You express a lack of care, concern, or interest regarding your preparation for the return of Messiah and the subsequent judgment (divine reprimand for folly and sin). You have no more thought or care about heaven and the cause of the Kingdom of God than those who are literally asleep. This is unimportant or insignificant to you. Instead, you have chosen to indulge yourself in idle dreams, forfeiting the moments on which your eternity depends (see Isaiah 56:10). Dreamer, you are too careless of your Christian duty; spending too much time lazily. See Proverbs 6:6, 9-11, 19:15. See suggested course of action. (3) The dreamer is counseled to become aware of your spiritual and/or physical condition. After your spiritual evaluation, you are advised to practice self-control and to begin implementing godly principles that will affect discipline, while embracing faith and love of God. For God has not appointed you to suffer wrath, but to receive salvation through the Lord, Jesus Christ. He died for you so that whether you are awake or asleep you may live together with Him (1 Thessalonians 5:10). See suggested course of action.

Napping: Your dream generally comes to encourage or warn the dreamer that you should not be secure and careless, nor indulge in spiritual laziness and idleness. You are to be attentive and on guard, because you are surrounded with many temptations to indulge in excess. Unless you be attentive and consider that your enemy roams about, seeking whom he may devour, you will not endure to the end.

Catnap (a cat sleeping should be highlighted): This applies if dreamer saw a literal cat, feline taking a nap in your dream, see category, Animals. Your dream is to, greatly encourage the dreamer, and it implies two things. (1) It implies healing and/or deliverance, as well as one who is a healer, namely the dreamer. You may lay hands on one who is sick. Have faith and they will be healed. (2) Your dream implies one who is a just and righteous person; you exemplify the religious ideals of Jesus. You also take joy in justice (Proverbs 21:15). You are also disciplined, educated, refined, and sophisticated. If a leader, you rule justly and righteously. Take comfort and rest in this.

Have forty winks (the number 40 should be highlighted): This dream applies only if the number forty was highlighted within your dream. Your dream was sent to encourage the dreamer. It implies that profound and insightful wisdom, previously unknown to you, will begin to flow from deep within you outward like a flowing stream; living waters. The dreamer has the capacity to spearhead a new dawn, giving birth to a new generation that will usher in an age of mass revivals, with primary emphasis on a personal and saving relationship with Christ Jesus. However, the dreamer has begun to grow careless in your worship of the one true God. Favorably, grace will be shown you, via a probationary period. During this period, you are counseled to begin implementing godly principles that will move you toward discipline and humility, while embracing faith and love of God.

Have a siesta (time of the day between noon and early part of the day should be highlighted): This dream applies only if the time of noon was highlighted within your dream. Your dream is to warn the dreamer. It implies the downfall of a wealthy powerful person. This fall is a result of a weakness that will be exposed, because of your activities. Most will be quick to make remarks about your ruin. They will say, "Nothing good could have come of your life, since you took the wrong methods of establishing yourself in your wealth and power". Nonetheless, through the grace of God, you will and can recover. See suggested course of action.

Nightmare (to awake in a state of terror and disorientation, oftentimes screaming): This type of dream implies that there is some type of underlying fear, possibly demonically influenced, within the dreamer's life; for nightmares are the screams of an unhealed heart's cry for inner healing. These types of dreams are primarily warnings. Dreamer, you are in a crisis of your faith. Listen, consider, and understand, no evil spirit, or human being, has any authority over your life unless you give it, him, or her, permission. God did not give anyone the right to stop you. What you believe about yourself doesn't line up with the Word of God. It may be hard to believe what God is saying about you because everything and everyone in your experiences, past and present, has told, or is telling, you the exact opposite; thus, the demonic influence. It doesn't matt er what is happening in your life now or what has been happening up until now. If it's not what God has said about you, especially within His Word, it isn't you and it is not for you. Dreamer, God is trying to get your heart and mouth to change. By this, your life will change. You might be saying, "I just want to tell the truth". The Word of God is the truth. What you see in your life may be a fact, but the power of the truth of the Word to change that condition is the same power that silences the screams of an unhealed heart. When you consider and understand the Word, and keep on saying it, it will get down into your heart. You can have doubt in your head, but not in your heart. Your carnal mind may fight you on it, but your heart and mou th can still agree and defeat any thoughts of doubt or unbelief. When you practice this, you will see that God will meet all your needs and then you will be better able to meet the needs of others. God cannot lie. Furthermore, what God says about you in His words is a done deal. He's just waiting for you to believe it and say it so you can have it. Find the verse of scripture you need for your situation, put it in your heart, and out of the abundance of the heart, you say the truth about yourself and your situation. Also see, Romans 3:3-31, Ephesians 2:10, Philippians 4:13, 2 Peter 1:3. See suggested course of action.

Put someone to bed (bedding down someone should be highlighted): Your dream implies that your old attributes are no longer appropriate, important, relevant, or useful to the dreamer. Fortunately, the dreamer's abstinence from pleasure, hardship, or self-imposed discipline, has put an end to the desires and passions associated with the particular person put to bed. This was done for religious purposes. Behaviors or character traits associated with the person being put to sleep, have changed and are now opposite of what they were within the life of the dreamer. The dreamer will need to identify the antonyms of the attributes associated with the person within your dream. For example, faithfulness is the opposite of faithlessness; wisdom is the antonym of foolishness. Thus, faithfulness and wisdom are now the new attributes within the dreamer's life; having replaced the old ones. If needful, may also see category People. Whatever the attributes, a change has been effected within the dreamer's life. If necessary, see suggested course of action.

Sleep around (to be in a circle or circular motion should be highlighted or to have casual sexual relationships with different people). Your dream implies character attributes that are unethical, dishonorable, and corrupt. The Lord does not approve of your actions. As well, the dreamer is not a good friend, loyal to no one. See suggested course of action.

Sleep in (asleep at place of employment should be highlighted): This dream interpretation applies only if the dreamer was asleep in your place of employment, no matter the type of place or business (e.g. entertainment, home based business, ministry, self-employed, sports, any type of industry). Your dream implies that the dreamer is refusing to pay attention to the alarms, danger signs, warning bells you have been receiving, forewarning of imminent danger, physically or spiritually. You have previously been extensively warned, and now warned via your dream. Dreamer, the beginning, development, arrival, or manifestation of something large (significant in scope, extent, or effect) is about to happen within your life, in a threaten ing way. Your place of employment is a dangerous place to be. If you do not leave, you will experience a downfall, along with others. See suggested course of action.

Sleep face down (face downward should be highlighted): This dream applies only if the dreamer was asleep face down. Your dream denotes some type of conquering. Coupled with your prayer and fasting, Jesus will strengthen you emotionally, psychologically, and physically to deal with your issues, whatever they might be. You may become ill a few days, but you will rise and be about your Heavenly Father's business. You will overcome your situation, rise up, and embrace a strong commitment to Jesus Christ, His cause, His philosophy, and an appropriate lifestyle for such endeavors. By this, you will avoid the wrath of God coming upon those who are committed to the kingdom of darkness and practice the deeds of such. If necessary, see suggested course of action.

Sleep on someone's lap or rocked to sleep: Sleeping on someone's lap or rocked to sleep reveals that the dreamer's sense of entitlement has led you to disobey God's revealed will for your individual life. You are carelessly confident and s ecure in yourself. You live in excess, mischievousness, and unruliness, to the point of recklessness. Someone demonically led particularly one who takes part in your secret activities or undertakings, has lulled you into a false sense of security and trusts. Although this person feigns kindness and friendship, they have great harm in mind for you. How he or she is able to defer your mind from purpose is unknown. They are, and you are, forfeiting purpose for ruin. Ruin is the fatal consequence of carelessness and sureness. You will now experience a downfall. God's anointing, favor, and strength that has been a part of your life will begin to abate. You will experience the consequences of your choices. Favorably, after a while, you will be restored, but not to your former glory. Glory in this sense is a state of high honor, spiritual beauty, and great illuminati on. Dreamer, immerse yourself into the cleansing Word of God and abide there, via prayer and fasting. Pray and ask Jesus for help, emotionally, psychologically, and physically, with your "flesh" issue, earnestly asking your Heavenly Father to help you deal with your strong dependence upon and cravings for that, which is detrimental to life and soul, and wait patiently for His answer, for He will answer you. Couple this with one of the following. (1) Did you know the individual whose lap you laid upon, or who rocked you to sleep? If so, you are being made aware of this person's intents towards you. (2) If unknown in your awaked, you are in denial regarding an undercover friend. Dreamer, Satan ruins men and women by rocking them to sleep, flattering them into a good opinion of their own safety, and so bringing to mind, there is nothing to worry about; then he robs them of their honor and strength and leads them captive at his will. See suggested course of action.

Sleep late (lateness should be highlighted): This dream applies only if sleeping late or too long was highlighted in your dream. Your dream implies that the dreamer has been living too long in excess, mischievousness, and unruliness, to the point of recklessness. As a result, you are now becoming increasingly bitter, irritated, and resentful; blaming your lack of faithfulness, commitment, and stewardship on others. Actually, you have given the enemy of your soul an advantage; seizing the moment to benefit from your spiritual poverty, making you poorer and needier. Dreamer, you should be teaching, at present. However, you are still considered an infant spiritually; not fully acquainted with the teachings about righteousness. You are spiritually, emotionally, and perhaps physically, weak, because you have not submitted to the teachings of the basic truths of God's word. Dreamer, like those you should be teaching, crave pure spiritual word; the direct words of God imparted to us through the words of others, such as a preacher in a worship service, a Sunday school teacher, and other bible studies, so that by it you may grow up in your salvation. See suggested course of action.

Sleep it off (something falling off you while you are asleep should be highlighted): Your dream implies that an illness will be healed through rest and quietness. Heartfelt repentance to Jesus and to individuals affected by your actions, in the form of an apology (if possible) is also needed. Repentance is seeking pardon and expressing sincere feelings of regret and brokenness for having done something awry and/or for having hurt someone, see 2 Corinthians 7:10, 11. To individuals, a phone call or a letter of apology is a good place to start. To Jesus, pray Psalm 38:1-22, this followed by rest, will be your salvation; and in quietness and trust, you will find strength and healing (Isaiah 30:15). Will you trust God in this?

Suggested Course of Action

Question to consider and journal, did your dream depict any symbols that alludes to, the dreamer will make the necessary changes, spiritually, emotionally, and/or physically to affect a more positive outcome? If changes are initiated, your dreams will change.

Nevertheless, in view of your dream's context, namely sleeping, what choices are you making that may impair or cause you to neglect your spiritual growth, good judgment, health, and/or earthly responsibilities? Whatever predicament you find yourself in, it's not too late to wake up and allow God. Allow God, to handle His business of keeping His promises to you, namely, "I will give you rest" and "My peace I leave with you". Do this, understanding the present time. The hour has come for you to wake up from your slumber, because our salvation is nearer now than when we first believed (Romans 13:11 NIV). Have nothing to do with the fruitless deeds of darkness, but rather expose them. For it is shameful even to mention what the disobedient do in secret. However, everything exposed by the light becomes visible. For it is light that makes everything visible. This is why it is said, "Wake up, O sleeper, rise from the dead, and Christ will shine on you". Be very careful, then, how you live, not unwise, but wise, making the most of every opportunity, because the days are evil. (Ephesians 5:11-16 NIV)

Consider and journal the following questions. The questions will help you determine; the issue at hand, how you feel about it, and what may have instigated it. What kind of sleeping was it? Were others involved? If yes, who and in what manner were they involved? Keep in mind that the others represent a quality of you, see Note 3 at the beginning of Actions and Activities category. How did you feel, and what did you do, because, of your feelings? Especially regarding the sleeping activity, and how things ended up, was it confusing, dangerous, happy, insignificant, joyful, life threatening, relaxing, safe, or scary? Your answers, coupled with the interpretation, plus any additional information, should begin to unfold the subject matter and issue at hand, if not now, mull over things a few days. For more information, see index or relevant category and subcategory for other particulars within your dream.

Now, pray (See Prayer of Deliverance, pg. 897)

Specific Meaning

If, you have a very real connection with any type of sleeping activity, e.g. mattress maker or salesman, expertise in the assessment, diagnosis, and management of clinical conditions that occur during sleep, that disturb sleep or that are affected by disturbances in the wake-sleep cycle. Perhaps, you are affected by sleep disorders (e.g. insomnia, narcolepsy), or take sleeping pills. Dreams of this sort are ordinary dreams, resulting from your daily activities (see Chapter One, Chalom). These dreams are usually about the anxieties that overwhelm your mind during the day. They are an inner release mechanism, which helps provide you with emotional balance and the maintaining of your sanity. These sorts of dreams, are not significant, and do no t warrant special attention.

Note: If disciplinary actions are before you, due to sleeping (e.g. sleeping on the job, falling asleep in a car) and you dream of an outcome. This may be taken as a guide, towards the direction the ruling and/or counseling may and/or should go. Dreamer, the details, kept within context of your dream, should be relevant to your life, and closely resemble your real-life situations. Meaning it can actually occur during your awaked state. This will help you narrow down the specifics needed to support and steer you clear of possible mishaps. However, if your dream symbols are not easily, linked to your life activities, heed the spiritual implications (the interpretation).

STANDING: To be in an upright position; or put something in an upright position

Some short descriptions of types, phrases, and other processes and particulars, connected in some way to this category. For example, unable to stand, standing alone, standing apart, standing army, stand aside, stand by, or to stand with. To stand f ace to face, stand fast, stand your ground, stand guard, standing in, stand in front of, standing in line, stand in the way, standoff, stand on, stand out, standing ovation, standing still, standing stone, stand up, stand up to, stand up for, standing water.

Unless otherwise noted elsewhere, if, in your everyday living, your awaked state, as part of your lifestyle, work, or ministerial activities, or a special event, you have a very real connection with any type of standing activity. For example, standing guard, cashier, cook, dancer, medical doctor, nurse, teaching, (also see content list for this category), your dream is not significant and does not warrant special attention.

Otherwise noted, to see another standing in your dream, if known, the dreamer is aware of the non-support or support you're giving to another or of the extra trouble, you've been. If support was given, you will be gratefully acknowledged and recompense will be given. If non-supportive or troubling, dreamer will be shamefully reprimanded in the near future. The particular matter of care, neglect, or imposition, is within the interpretation. If person standing was unknown, the dreamer will soon, be made aware of the help, or hindrance, you've given or shown another.

Otherwise noted, see Note 1 at the beginning of Actions and Activities category.

To determine who your dream is for you or another, consider one of the following (relevant interpretation) first, as well as, see Note 3 at the beginning of Actions and Activities category.

Symbols and Referents: Dreams of standing are generally warnings. They are sent to alert the dreamer, about the enemy's stand against him or her. That you might stand bold against the enemy, preparing you to become a good leader within the Kingdom of God. The dreamer is counseled to not yield to the enemy's allurements and assaults, but to oppose them.

Note: Most all of the following walking dreams, are metaphorically represented by common words, expressions, and other usages (e.g. slang or clichés), or a 'probable'. It will be those meanings considered.

Category Content - If not listed see index, perchance, for your specific type of standing dream activity.

- Unable to Stand
- Standing Alone or Stand Aside or Stand Out or Standing and Waiting on someone
- Standing Apart from or Stand Guard or Standing Still
- Standing Army or Stand Side by Side to someone or Standoff or Standing In the Way (as to block the way)
- Stand Face to Face or Stand Up To
- Stand Fast (to get up very quickly should be highlighted)
- Stand your Ground (standing on your own grounds or property should be highlighted)
- Standing in the Way
- Stand On (standing on something should be highlighted)
- Standing Ovation, see category, Clapping
- Standing Stones or Monument (any large stone set upright in the ground, single or part of a larger structure, ancient or modern)
  - Cornerstone; Tombstone; Memorial Stone; Large Stone Faces (e.g. Easter Island Stone Faces, La Venta Monument, Mt. Rushmore); Large Stones Grouped Together
- Stand Under (to stand under something should be highlighted)
- Stand Up (to get up from a sitting or prostrate position should be highlighted)

Unable to Stand: Your dream implies that the dreamer needs to be particularly grateful to someone of a lower status or rank than yourself (e.g. an aide, assistant, attendant, dependent, or junior). Their services to you has indebted you to them. Two rules of gratitude are: (1) Better to honor than nothing. If you are unable to make recompense at this time to those wh o have been kind to you, do them honor by acknowledging their kindnesses and owning your obligations to them. (2) If you have neglected to acknowledge, with gratefulness, good done to you by another, it's better late than never.

Standing Alone, Stand Aside, Stand Out, or Standing and Waiting on someone: This dream has four meanings (choose one). (1) Standing alone: Your dream implies one who is definite in your ideas, independent, and self-governing; yet, isolated and alone. You have separated yourself from others, and have hidden yourself within yourself. You do this well. Others unkind remarks have caused a "reclusive" type behavior to emerge within you. This is a subtle "trick" of the enemy to keep you away from society; causing you to seek solitude; thus, hindering you from progressing forward within your very public ministry. The devil is whispering lies to you, such as people do not like you or will not receive you, or that you don't look good enough, and any other lie that engenders low self-esteem and breeds a drawback spirit. Dreamer, it is not good for anyone to be alone, especially intentional. You need others and others need you. Moreover, believe that God has made you wonderfully and beautifully. If necessary, see suggested course of action. (2) Stand aside (standing out of the way should be highlighted): Your dream implies a resignation of some kind. You are either, giving up, stepping down, or quitting. However, the dreamer is counseled to think again, before acting. The reason for the reconsideration is you are choosing to ignore, overlook, or disregard the true reasons for your resignation. It is you who have chosen to let things ride (concerning a particular situa tion), in a sense, giving your approval. Dreamer, you should be willing to step up and be fairly heard and/or protest; because, you are viewed as accepting things just as they are when that may not be necessarily true. If you are unwilling to make yourself be heard, your next steps are to forgive, step aside, and allow another who will take a stand. If another was standing aside (known or unknown), this implies that the dreamer may not protest; thus, you will need to prepare to step aside. See suggested course of action. (3) Stand out (to be outside of, or to appear different, should be highlighted): Yo ur dream implies that the difficult situation the dreamer finds him or herself in right now, is of God. It is designed to open wide the eyes of, and disconcert, a careless person, namely you. Dreamer, you're being deprived of the power to do mischief. If you would question yourself, you would soon find out that what you know is nothing, compared to what you do not know. Why then presume that the wisdom of providence be changed in order to accommodate your carelessness. God makes His counsel a minister of His justice as well as of his mercy. See suggested course of action. (4) Standing and waiting on someone: Blessed, are all who wait on Adonai. Your dream denotes that this is the season of the Lord's favor upon your life. Dreamer, although the Lord has given you the bread of adversity and the water of affliction, you waited on the Lord, and you have completed the process of spiritual and emotional cleansing. This process has healed your animosity and healed you emotionally and physically. However, as feelings go, because of your questionable behavior and deeds, you are discouraged, and feel unfit and unworthy of God's favor and restoration. Nonetheless, promises of deliverance, restoration, and fruitfulness are before you, because of God's grace. God has by His grace, prepared and qualified you for mercy and then bestowed it on you. Your process and waiting, has also instilled within you an appropriate and balanced confidence in your own merit as an extraordinarily gifted prophet, minister, evangelist, teacher, or pastor. Your path, now, should be towards developing your mind at searching out the deeper truths of the Word of God; and at becoming a skilled "watchman or watchwoman", on guard always, keeping watch, and keeping to heart the word of the Lord. Now your ears will hear a voice behind you, saying, "This is the way; walk in it", obey the voice, for it is of God.

Standing Apart from, or Stand Guard or Standing Still: This dream has three meanings (choose one). (1) Standing apart from: Your dream implies a spiritual indifference. You present as one who does not care, or is not concern or interested in fellowship with others of like belief. Dreamer, you are confused and illogical in your thinking. Although you blame others for your disinterest, lack of stewardship, faithfulness, and friendliness, actually it's you to blame. It is you, who is unconcerned for, and uninterested in, the things of Christ; thus, you have chosen to become disconnected and removed from others and from a personal relationship with Christ. See suggested course of action. (2) Standing Guard: This choice has two parts (choose one). (a) Dreamer, if you were standing guard, you are to protect someone from danger or loss. Perhaps the one you were guarding within your dream (known or unknown). If unknown, this person will be made known to you shortly. If a weapon is within context of your dream, the danger is high, but God's love is near. Consider, what can you do to help heal another, emotional ly, physically or spiritually? However, if you say, you know nothing about this; does not He who weighs the heart perceive it?

Does not He who guards your life know it? Will He not repay each person according to what he (or she) has done (Proverbs 24:12). (b) If another was standing guard, you will kindly be saved from danger or loss, by someone (known or unknown). If known, dreamer will be aware of the good deed. If unknown, this good deed will be a secret. (3) Standing still (to stand a t attention or very still should be highlighted): Your dream implies that the dreamer should seriously consider what God is doing in your life. God is trying to tell you something. Now then, stand still and see this great thing, the Lord is about to do before your eyes (1 Samuel 12:16). If necessary, see suggested course of action.

Standing Army, Stand Side by Side to someone, or Standoff or Standing in the Way (as to block the way): This dream has three meanings (choose one). (1) Standing Army or Standing side by side: Dreamer, wherever you find yourself, one is always oblige to, wisely and discerningly abide by the laws of the land. Especially laws that promote godliness and orderliness that you may take possession of the land you are entering, and become powerfully established, and remain there permanently (also see Deuteronomy 4:5, 6). Do not be afraid, for the Lord is your salvation, and He is the strength of your life (Psalm 27:1-3). Moreover, your dream speaks of one, the dreamer, who is commissioned to edify those who are within the Body of Christ, first within your local church and then abroad. Your endeavors should be along the lines of progressive thinking; aimed at presenting a rational basis for the Christian faith, which is in Jesus Christ; and to defend the faith against objections, and misrepresentation; exposing perceived error within religious and worldviews. You will be upheld within your endeavors by the King of kings. If dreamer saw or sensed someone else standing, this implies that it is another who is commissioned, and that the dreamer will be an assistant to this person. If necessary, see suggested course of action. (2) Standoff (some type of defensive stand should be highlighted): Your dream implies that there is a contest of sort between dreamer and another. Because both parties are equally unyielding in this situation, there will be no resolution. Dreamer, graciously remove yourself from the situation. If necessary, see suggested course of action. (3) Stand in the Way (as to block the way): This choice has two parts (choose one). (a) Dreamer, due to your argumentative, disagreeable, and overall, difficult to work with attitude, you are not accepted by others easily (e.g. family, friends, particular community, and/or a Christian based support group). You block, contradict, disallow, forbid, refute, refuse, reject, prevent, and all this activity is done unnecessarily and/or with out cause. Your actions will reap divine reprimand if continued. You are, via your dream, clearly warned and reproved; take care to bring a stop to your never-ending complaints and childish behavior. See suggested course of action. (b) Your dream implies that you are about to replace someone or someone will replace you. Question to journal; was the dreamer st anding in for someone, or was someone standing in for you? If dreamer was standing in for another, you will replace another or vice versa.

Stand Face to Face or Stand Up To: This dream has two meanings (choose one). (1) Standing Face to Face: The dreamer has first-hand knowledge of an unpleasant fact and/or situation. The dreamer needs to honestly deal with the unpleasant fact and/or situation, and involve all pertinent individuals. This matter should not be covered, kept secret, or denied. It n eeds reckoning with, seriously, and as soon as possible, even to the point of confrontation, if necessary. The matter is before y ou, at present. Question, whom was you standing face to face with? The issue may very well be with that person. If standing face to face with yourself, the issue is within you. Listen to the Paraclete, He will lead and guide you into all truth. Dreamer, although, you may have challenged, confronted, and tackled this matter in dispute, before; the matter has proven to be of g reater difficulty than you previously had imagined, thus, it powerfully prevails. Again, confront it, with a new strategy, and you will succeed this time. See suggested course of action. (2) Standing up to someone or for someone: Your dream implies one, who will be called upon to defend another, so that this person may keep their family, home, and/ or place within a ministry, for t he sake of the Kingdom. Although, greatly challenged, by this person's opponents, be encouraged, for God is standing up for you.

Stand Fast (to get up very quickly should be highlighted): Your dream implies that the dreamer is a disciplined and matter-of-fact type person. You take life seriously and are loyal. Those connected to you know they can rely on you. However, someone, near, is attempting to take advantage of your loyalty and reliability. Dreamer, you've built your home, family, and living on a solid foundation, based on common sense and hard work. You must allow others to build their livelihood also, according to their own choosing. They too must stand fast (or not). For the same price you've paid for your livelihood, they can have the same too. Just say no.

Stand your Ground (standing on your own grounds or property should be highlighted): This dream has two meanings (choose one). (1) Your dream implies one who is being true to him or herself, and/or to another, but is not true to God's Word. To be true to self or another, is to seek affirmation with respect to condoning your particular sin, while basin g your ideas, arguments, and/or beliefs on something that is sacrilegious, profane, illogical, and non-mainstream doctrine or philosophy. Your ideology is without favorable conclusions, thus this dream. You are full of pride. Moreover, your interpretation of the Word of God has become unrecognizable to those you influence. When those who seek truth, ask Jesus why they do not recognize your teachings, the words spoken of you are that you are true to yourself and sacrilegious. Your offerings are not acceptable (Genesis 4:3-8), and if you persist on perpetuating your self-serving ideology and calling it divinely ordained, you will be stripped and humiliated publicly, and replaced because of shameful acts. See suggested course of action. (2) If another was standing on your ground, the dreamer has begun to embrace the teachings of one whose beliefs are illogical, and without foundation. This person, is, or will be replaced because of shameful acts. If the dreamer does not t urn back from such doctrines of demons, you will also experience the consequences of such beliefs, none of which are favorable. Dreamer, re-think your views and attitude, regarding the doctrine you are adhering to, and your philosophy, and decline the temporary relations of darkness that you might inherit an entrance into paradise having sincerely answered God's request upon your life, and seriously re-consider how you are being true to yourself or to another. Dreamer set your heart towards understanding godly knowledge. See suggested course of action.

Stand On (standing on something should be highlighted): Your dream implies that the dreamer insistently imposes his or her own ideas upon others, adamantly wanting things done your way. Although your desires or ideas may seem important or correct to you, when dealing with others, it is always wise to consider both sides of a situation. Developing an ability to see both sides will endow you with a quiet, non-judgmental wisdom that will endear you to some, and invite others needing advice and an objective point of view, to be open with you. See suggested course of action.

Standing Stones or Monument (any large stone set upright in the ground, single or part of a larger structure, ancient or modern): All types of stones represent the quality of your relationship with Jesus Christ, on some level, as well as, your perspective, and your level of understanding and reasoning of His Word. Standing stones will denote your acceptance or rejection of Jesus, your attitude regarding His cause, your beliefs. As each stone will vary; accordingly, the interpretation will differ also. The interpretation of your dream will largely depend on the type of stone. What kind of stone was in your dream? Was there writing on the stone, if so, what did it mean? What is the stone primarily known for, and what characteristics stood out the most? The meaning may prove to be a probable for you, see Note 2 at the beginning of this category, Actions and Activities. What was the color, location, shape, size, or other outstanding features of the stone? The stone's earliest meaning, any activity associated with the particular stone (even contemporary activity), and the context of the stone within your drea m, should be noted. To determine the ancient and/or symbolic meaning associated with your stone, see a bible concordance, bible illustrated dictionary, encyclopedia, or internet. All this consideration will reveal the meaning of your dream, and that meaning, in sum and substance, will either, reveal a spirit of acceptance or rejection of Christ, boldness or the lack thereof, for the cause of Christ. It will reveal if Christ is head of your life, or it will expose contempt, desolation, or forgetfulness of the benefits of God towards you. It will reveal expose who, or what, do you consider the source of your blessings. Further, the meaning should make known the foundation of the church you're a member of, the foundation of your faith, and your good or sinful works. It can point towards a place of refuge or renewal, or reprobation. It can disclose if Christ's teachings are an obstacle for you. See one of the following.

Cornerstone: Your dream denotes where, and when did the foundation of your beliefs start, and the basis for those beliefs. Questions to journal, what was written on the cornerstone? Was it attached to a church, school, home, or a club of some sort? Answering these questions will point the dreamer towards what the Lord wants you to focus on, namely the core and/or beginnings of your spiritual foundation, and if your foundation is based on wise and godly principles, or other secular principles. See suggested course of action.

Tombstone: Your dream denotes spiritual death on some level. Read and understand Galatians 5:19-21, for this speaks of spiritual death. See suggested course of action.

Memorial Stone: Your dream speaks of honoring the memory of somebody or something in a ceremony, usually associated with some form of ritual idolatry, which is equivalent to spiritual rebellion. See suggested course of action.

Large Stone Faces (e.g. Easter Island Stone Faces, La Venta Monument, or Mt. Rushmore): Your dream denotes judgment, divine reprimand for folly and sin, and a time of difficulty is imminent, due to anxiety (fear), impulsiveness, and intolerance. Dreamer, utilizing the powerful resources of prayer and heartfelt repentance to Jesus and to individuals affect ed by your actions, in the form of an apology (if possible), is needed. Repentance is seeking pardon and expressing sincer e feelings of regret and brokenness for having done something awry and/or for having hurt someone, see 2 Corinthians 7:10, 11. To Jesus, pray Psalm 38:1-22. To individuals, a phone call or a letter of apology is a good place to start. This followed by appropriate application of wisdom, can conceivably avert some of the repercussions of your choices. See suggested course of action.

Large Stones Grouped Together: Your dream represents boundary markers; this usually indicates the dreamer has gone too far towards one extreme or another, either, extreme left or extreme right. See suggested course of action.

Stand Under (to stand under something should be highlighted): This dream has two meanings (both apply). (1) Your dream implies that the dreamer is known (or will be known) for your wisdom, prophetic abilities, great usefulness to the public, and as a peacemaker. As God's mouthpiece, you will correct abuses and deal with wrongs, especially amongst those who worship God. People will come to you from everywhere for advice on improvement and restoration of things pertaining to Christ. Dreamer, with great delight put your entire confidence in the protection and wisdom of the Lord, for He knows you, and He will give you the desires of your heart. However, now you are in need of a teacher. (2) There is an old saying, "When the student is ready, the teacher will appear". Dreamer, you are the student, another is your teacher, and you are ready. Although, you may be very accomplished, prosperous, and/or wise, you have need of a teacher at present. God is sending someone into your life to help you carry out your next undertaking, by enlarging your spiritual capacity. This person is mod est and unassuming in attitude, behavior, and dress. Notwithstanding, great respect towards them is appropriate and required, as well as some form of compensation. You will need to be honest, open, and transparent, to get what you need from him or her. Your undivided attention is required, thus you may need to take a vacation from your normal business and/or ministerial activities. Your dream is to bring about an awareness of this person's coming, and to prepare you to meet them sagaciously. Additionally, they will not feed your vanity; therefore, do not be, conceited in your attitude.

Stand Up (to get up from a sitting or prostrate position should be highlighted): The ordeal you think will destroy you is, intended to elevate you, proving you; causing you to stand up and become an anointed and powerful force for the Ki ngdom of God. Surely, at present, you don't feel elevated while going through your making season. Yet, this is when you can expect God to come and show Himself, strong on your behalf. Someone, a prayer warrior, will come to pray for you. This person is someone you least expect to be so powerful in the realm of prayer; more than likely a male who is very humble and unassuming. During the prayer, you will see yourself, spiritually, getting up from a sitting or prostrate position. Dreamer, your adversity is affecting a dependable, faithful, loyal, reliable responsible, resourceful, upright, and upstanding spirit within you. Let your dream, and the vision during prayer, be your comfort for the endurance. To see another (known or unknown) getting up, you are the prayer warrior that the Lord will send to another, possibly the person getting up. See suggested course of action.

Suggested Course of Action

Question to consider and journal, did your dream depict any symbols that alludes to, the dreamer will make the necessary changes, spiritually, emotionally, and/or physically to affect a more positive outcome? If changes are initiated, your dreams will change.

Nevertheless, dreamer, you, have the potential for leadership; it just awaits the right time and place to manifest itself that you may stand established. Your hour awaits the timing of Jesus the Messiah and the quality of your preparation. Thus, these types of dreams challenges the dreamer to not be slack regarding your time of preparation for ministry, and to not be condescending, disrespectful, or rude to any person; for everyone, including you, has his or her hour, for good and for bad (also see Ecclesiastes 3:1-8). Dreamer, when another makes a mistake and/or let others down, instead of being critical and faultfinding show love. Consider what you can do to help heal another (or yourself), emotionally, physically or spiritually. Let your words be filled with grace. Question to consider, when you're talking with people, do you speak words o f grace; do your words empower people? Do others leave your presence feeling strengthened, wanting to stand on their convictions? Dreamer, always look for ways to build up the people around you. You do, what you think others should be doing. For, when you sow grace and mercy, you will reap the same in return. As well, one whose speech is gracious will have the King for a friend (Proverbs 22:11). However, if you say, you know nothing about this; does not He who weighs the heart perceive it? Does not He who guards your life know it? Will He not repay people, according to what he (or she) has done, per their purpose (Proverbs 24:12). Become clear about this.

Now, pray (See Prayer of Deliverance, pg. 897)

Specific Meaning

If, you have a very real connection with any type of standing activity, for example standing guard, cashier, cook, dancer, medical doctor, nurse, teaching, dreams of this sort should be received as ordinary dreams, resulting from your daily activit ies (see Chapter One, Chalom). These dreams are usually about the anxieties that overwhelm your mind during the day. They are an inner release mechanism, which helps provide you with emotional balance and the maintaining of your sanity. These sorts of dreams, are not significant, and do not warrant special attention.

Note: If you're unable to stand, due to an accident, receive your dream as a precautionary warning. There may be potential for an accident. Dreamer, the details, kept within context of your dream, should be relevant to yo ur life, and closely resemble your real-life situations. Meaning it can actually occur during your awaked state. This will help you narrow down the specifics needed to support and steer you clear of possible mishaps. However, if your dream was, inundated with symbols not easily linked, to your life activities, then heed the spiritual implications (the interpretation).

SWIMMING: **The action or activity of moving yourself through water (lake, ocean, pond, pool, sea, or spring) unsupported, using your arms and legs, or scuba equipment, usually for pleasure, exercise, or sport.**

Some short descriptions of types, phrases, and other processes and particulars, connected in some way to this category. For example, aqua-aerobics, aquanaut, bather, deep-sea diver, diver, drowning, to float, go for a dip, lifeguard, plunge, scuba diver, skinny-dipper, snorkeler, swim against the tide, swim with the tide, swimmer, swimwear, swim in the head.

Unless otherwise noted elsewhere, if, in your everyday living, your awaked state, as part of your lifestyle, work, or ministerial activities, or a special event, you have a very real connection with any type of swimming activity. For example, aqua-aerobics, aquanaut, deep-sea diver, lifeguard, professional swimmer, scuba diver, designer, or selling of, swimwear, snorkeler, (also see content list for this category), your dream is not significant and does not warrant special attention.

Otherwise noted, this dream may be a Prophetically Simple Dream (see Chapter One: The 60th Part of Prophecy). The dreamer is warned to be extra cautious regarding situations that may present a high chance for accidents or drowning, especially if this was highlighted within your dream. This dream is a first step intervention and an alarm. Skip interpretation and re-consider your activity as harmful or life threatening at present. Refrain from such activities for now. Also, see Specific Meaning at the end of this category, section entitled, Note (Specific Meaning).

Otherwise noted, see Note 1 at the beginning of Actions and Activities category.

To determine who your dream is for you or another, see Note 3 at the beginning of Actions and Activities category.

Symbols and Referents: Dreams of swimming or of anything connected to swimming generally implies help is available for overcoming difficulties and shortcomings, usually related to adultery, affliction, barrenness, cowardice, doubting, excessive indulgence, lack of self-control, peace, phobia, regeneration, slavery, spiritual growth, stubbornness, and, for understanding the deeper things of God, for restoration. This dream also refers to a spiritual watchman.

Category Content - If not listed see index, perchance, for your specific type of swimming dream activity.

- Afloat (floating on water, e.g. in or on some type of floatation cushion)
- Deep-Sea or Scuba Diving
- Drowning or Underwater not drowning or Rescued from Drowning or Water up to your Neck
- Grow tired or lose strength while swimming, see category, Abating (To decrease in degree, force, intensity, or grow tired)
- Held or kept back from swimming, see category, Abating (To be held or kept back)
- Lifeguard
- Skinny-Dipper (swimming nude)
- Swim with, or against, the Tide
- Swimming (leisurely or competitively)
- Swimwear
- Swim in the Head (dizzy feeling in your head while swimming, should be highlighted)

Afloat (floating on water, e.g. in or on some type of floatation cushion): Now, He (Jesus) is pleased to heal you and bless your house that it may continue in His sight, and it will be blessed. Dreamer, from this day forward God's kindness and blessings will flow abundantly, producing spiritual growth within you. God's blessings: Gifts of God's grace, anything God freely gives you, absolution, the Holy Spirit, salvation, regeneration, eternal life, health, children, love of family, longevity, necessities, prosperity, and dominion over all that is yours; and all are parts of the supply of grace, and all are sanctified by the Lord, and technically belongs to Him. The result of this supply in your life will be peace.

Deep-Sea or Scuba Diving: This dream has two meanings (both apply). (1) Your dream denotes the love of money. People who strenuously strive to get rich falls into temptation, a trap, and into many unwise, foolish, and harmful desires that plunge men (and women) into ruin and destruction. For the love of money is a root of all kinds of evil. Some people, eager for money, have wandered from the faith, which is in Jesus Christ, and inflicted upon themselves many pains. However you, child of God, flee from all this, and pursue righteousness, godliness, faith, love, endurance, and gentleness. Fight the good fight of the faith, which is in Jesus Christ. Take hold of the eternal life to which you were called when you made your good confession in the presence of many witnesses (1 Timothy 6:3-12). Do you eat and live well, thank God and live truthfully before Him, and before your family. Dreamer, it is time for you to, qualitatively enjoy your family and the prosperity you already have, and to abandoned strenuously striving to get rich. Make sure your family is spiritually happy that you may rest emotionally, physically, and spiritually, and when the time comes that you may have a proper burial. This should be your focus. For, one thing is sure, we brought nothing into the world, and we can take nothing out of it. (2) Dreamer, if anyone teaches false doctrines, and does not comply with the sound instructions of our Lord Jesus Christ, and to godly teaching, he or she is conceited and understands nothing. Dreamer, you have an unhealthy interest in controversies and quarrels about words that result in envy, strife, malicious talk, evil suspicions, and constant friction between people of corrupt minds, who have been robbed of the truth and who think that godliness is a means to financial gain. Thus, you do not know that godliness with contentment is great gain. Therefore, live wisely, discerning between what's really, important, to love and family and what is not so much. See suggested course of action.

Drowning or Underwater not drowning or Rescued from drowning or Water up to your Neck: This dream has four meanings (choose one). (1) To be underwater (not drowning): Your dream is one confirmation that you have fulfil led all requirements for righteousness and you have a clear conscience. In addition, you have access to prophetic insight; enabling you to discern between true and false. This wisdom will be a transformational force in many people's lives. The dreamer has been chosen by God, and approved by man, to be set aside and ordained as a ministerial leader. You are to carry out the official role and position of that office (e.g. bishop, deacon, deaconess, elder, evangelist, pastor, preacher, superintenden t, or teacher). You have been found of good reputation, full of the Spirit, and wise; thus, you will be officially ordained. Dream er, the way the ordination will be carried out may not be to your liking; nonetheless, do not attribute (or call) that which is o f God, unclean (e.g. confusion, erroneous, out of order, unlawful, weak, wicked, or any other attributes of the unregenerate). Do n ot consider your ordination as unofficial or a small thing, for it is of God. If necessary, see suggested course of action. (2) Drowning, the dreamer has been continually changed, converted, improved, rehabilitated, renewed, and transformed. As well, the Lord has destroyed your enemies from before you, even unto this time; yet, you continue to embrace excessive indulgences, a lack of self-control, lack of knowledge, and spiritual uncleanness. Symbolically, spiritual uncleanness, within the life of a believer, denotes anger, animosity, confusion, out of order, self-condemnation, sexual impropriety, an unforgiving spirit, and/or other weaknesses, are present within your heart, as well as, immoral, impure, and unchaste conduct. For example, addictions, cheating, exposing confidences to others, greedy, gossiping, jealously, lying, stealing, or any other sinful attribute (see 1 Corinthians 6:9-20, Ephesians 5). This behavior causes one's anointing to fade and spiritual authority to wane. Your dream is to warn a rebellious person, in the spirit of grace. To see if you will yet be worked upon, and change your mindset, or else to leave you inexcusable, in your accusations against God, because of your ruin (e.g. continually plundered, seized, and disfavored, also see Jeremiah 9:7-9; Zechariah 13:9; Matthew 23:37-39; Revelation 3:15-21). Favorably, you are now one, whom the body of believers should, and will, help restore back to God, in the spirit of empathy, mercy, leniency, and kindness, until the issue is cleaned up or rendered dead, allow this. The more God allows you to see your emptiness, it is suggested that you be more earnest to repent that you may find Him to be grace and healing, refreshment, and a refuge. See suggested course of action. (3) To be rescued from drowning: Dreamer, you have been very obstinate, and there has been excessive indulgences, a lack of self-control, lack of knowledge, and spiritual uncleanness. You have proven yourself rebellious, deceitful, and unwilling to listen to the Lord's instructions. You no longer want to hear what is right and just; only what is pleasing and satisfying to the flesh. In spite of all this, as soon as the Lord hears your voice of prayer and heartfelt repentance to Jesus and to individuals affected by your actions, in the form of an apology (if possible), He will answer you, for the Lord, longs to be gracious to you. Repentance is seeking pardon and expressing sincere feelings of regret and brokenness for having done something awry and/or for having hurt someone, see 2 Corinthians 7:10, 11. To individuals, a phone call or a letter of apology is a good place to start. To Jesus pray, Psalm 51, this followed by appropriate application of wisdom, can conceivably avert some of the repercussions of your choices. This is what is called leaving a blessing behind. Favorably, your dream indicates that you will genuinely repent. Thus, God will show you compassion during this time, because He is a God of justice. Blessed are all who wait for Him. Dreamer, although the Lord gives you the bread of adversity and the water of affliction, your ears will hear a voice behind you, saying, "This is the way; walk in it". You will be one, whom the body of believers should, and will, help restore back to God, in the spirit of empathy, mercy, leniency, and kindness, until the issue is cleaned up or ren dered dead, allow this. Then you will be renewed and transformed. See suggested course of action. (4) Water up to your neck: Your dream comes as an alarm. Dreamer, you are well respected, at a high elevated state, for all to see. You are the head and not the tail, above only and not beneath, a very powerful individual. However, the pride that corrupts because of power, is becoming a stronghold in your life, thus, danger is imminently approaching, even near your doors. The beginning, development, arrival, or manifestation of something large (significant in scope, extent, or effect) is about to happen within your life, in a threatening way. Someone within your life, powerful and capable of doing much harm, one who is too strong fo r you, is contemplating to destroy you. This person once confronted you with foolishness during a very hard time in your life, but the Lord was your support (2 Samuel 22: 17-25). Now they are back, and will be allowed because of your pride. If pride is repented of now, and you choose to humble yourself, God will rescue you from this enemy; they will no longer do you harm. There will be no need to fear, nor to be shaken, or look anxiously about you; they will not be able to overcome you. You wil l be given miraculous help; angels will be at your deposal, even now. As well, you will be given words as a defense against those who would put you and yours in danger. Do not fear, you and your household will be spared, and your reputation enlarged. God will take care of you, because He delights in you. However, these promises are conditional; you must repent of pride, oppressive and tyrannical behavior, remain humble before the Lord, and obedient to His ways. If necessary, see suggested course of action.

Lifeguard: Dreamer, the servant of the Lord must always be prepared to serve his (or her) present generation, thus your dream. You are appointed a spiritual "watchman" to the people of God. A watchman's religious duties are to pronounce future events, which you will see in prophetic visions, give timely warnings of danger to God's people, especially where none is suspected, warn the wicked to turn from their way, from danger, that they may live (Ezekiel 3:17-21; 33:1-20). You are to warn of the enemies' approach, strategies, and to comfort, and sympathize with, those who need comforting. As you receive the Word of the Lord, you are to present it faithfully to His people, and to see that it is accepted, observed, and obeyed. You are to keep your finger on the pulse of the people. To see what people have to answer for, to see who makes excuses for sin, to see who flatter sinners, and who encourages wrongdoers to believe they shall have peace, though the misery of their soul is at stake. If souls perish through the neglect of your duties, you will bring guilt upon yourself. If you warn the wicked, you are not chargeable with their ruin. There will be those, not most, who are offended at ministers who obey their Master's command, and give faithful warnings. They are those who would rather perish, listening to smooth things. Whosoever hears you hear God, and whosoever despises you despises Him who sent you. Dreamer, be encourage, the God who sends you, does have the power to keep you safe.

Skinny-Dipper (swimming nude): Your dream denotes that the dreamer has listened to another word, independent of God's Word. When the enemy said to you, you shall not surely die, that was another word. Because God said, the wages of sin is death, and when you partake of sinful things, you will die, if not physical, surely spiritual. Dreamer, it is astonishing that you've so quickly deserted the One who called you by the grace of Christ Jesus, and is turning to a different gospel, which i s really no gospel at all. Now that your nakedness and shame has been exposed, revealing the real you, what shall be done. Consider Psalm 139. Pray and repent, knowing that God has a perfect knowledge of who you are, for Adonai Elohim knows all. Trust God again. See suggested course of action.

Swim with, or against, the Tide: This dream has two meanings (choose one). (1) Swimming with the tide: Your dream denotes one who follows the opinions and attitudes of other people. Dreamer, no matter how powerful or difficult a person or how uncertain or unpopular the choices and issues always take the next biblical, ethical, and most informed step, for obedience to God's principles is safer. See suggested course of action. (2) Swimming against the tide: Your dream denotes one taking a stance that is different from, or opposite to, that taken by others. Dreamer, no matter how difficult or how uncertain the issues, always take the next biblical, ethical, and most informed step, for obedience is better than sacrifice. See also Psalm 133. If necessary, see suggested course of action.

Swimming (leisurely or competitively): Your dream denotes one who is approaching spiritual maturity, or if appropriate, one predestined to become born again within the Kingdom of God (see John 3:1-17). Only take care to do your rightful duties (obligation to God, family, and if applicable, to country), offering mature service and exercising mature judgment. As well, you are undefiled according to biblical standards, down-to-earth, fair, humble, just, unpretentious, not rude, or obscene, and one whom a believer may interact with socially on very personal levels (e.g. business associate, friendship, ministry, and spouse). Moreover, the floodgates of heaven are open to you. Those floodgates are fullness in your spirituality, the blessings of God, and the glory of God in the midst of your life. Glory in this sense is a state of high honor, spiritual beauty, and great illumination. The blessings of God, anything God freely gives you, absolution, the Holy Spirit, salvation, regeneration, ete rnal life, health, children, love of family, longevity, necessities, prosperity, and dominion over all that is yours; and all are parts of the supply of grace, and all are sanctified by the Lord, and technically belongs to Him. The result of this supply in your life will be peace.

Swimwear: This dream has two meanings (choose one). (1) Properly dressed for swimming: Your dream denotes that the dreamer; is ready for Christ's blessings. Dreamer, from this day forward God's blessings will flow abundantly, producing spiritual growth within you. Gifts of God's grace, anything God freely gives you, absolution, the Holy Spirit, salvation, regeneration, eternal life, health, children, love of family, longevity, necessities, prosperity, and dominion over all that is yours; and all are parts of the supply of grace, and all are sanctified by the Lord, and technically belongs to Him. The result of this supply in your life will be peace. Further, these blessings will cause you to soften your expression towards God and others. (2) Improperly dressed for swimming: Dreamer, you will be exposed, as one who has gone too far in your attitude of disharmony, and is now considered rebellious. Because of your rebellious attitude, you have allowed yourself to enter a spiritually precarious situation. One that is dangerously unstable, unsteady, and uncertain. There is a loss of innocence. You will never be the same, since sin is pleasant to you now. However, your dream is only a warning, you can let go of this rebellion and emerged spiritually fortified, one who is able to withstand temptation. When this happens, you will wear appropriate clothing, befitting God's blessings. See suggested course of action.

In addition, the following is a common word, expression, or usage, (e.g. slang or clichés), or a 'probable' that is metaphorically represented by swimming:

- **Swim in the Head (dizzy feeling in your head while swimming, should be highlighted):** Your dream denotes dizziness or confusion. Dreamer, it is astonishing that you are so quickly deserting the One who called you by the grace of Christ, and is turning to a different gospel, which is really no gospel at all. Evidently, some people are throwing you into confusion and are trying to pervert the gospel of Christ. Fortunately, your dream presupposes that you will take no other view, other than that of Christ and His grace. The one who is throwing you into confusion will pay the penalty, whoever they may be (Galatians 1:6, 7; 5:10). See suggested course of action.

Suggested Course of Action

Question to consider and journal, did your dream depict any symbols that alludes to, the dreamer will make the necessary changes, spiritually, emotionally, and/or physically to affect a more positive outcome? If changes are initiated, your dreams will change.

Nevertheless, a dream of swimming or of anything connected to swimming generally implies help is available for overcoming difficulties and shortcomings, usually related to adultery, affliction, barrenness, cowardice, doubting, excessive indulgence, lack of self-control, peace, phobia, regeneration, slavery, spiritual growth, stubbornness, and, for understanding the deeper things of God, for restoration. Dreamer, you have the potential to emerge spiritually fortified, one who is able to withstand temptation. Leading, to you being considered, righteous, well respected, and with much authority. Your hour awaits the timing of Jesus the Messiah and the quality of your preparation. Thus, these types of swimming dreams challenges the dreamer to not be slack regarding your time of preparation for ministry, and to not be condescending, disrespectful, or rude to any person; for everyone, including you, has his or her hour, for good and for bad (also see Ecclesiastes 3:1 -8).

Consider and journal the following questions. The questions will help you determine; the issue at hand, how you feel about it, and what may have instigated it. What kind of swimming was done? Why was there swimming? Is the process from bad to good or vice versa, unpleasant to the dreamer, if so why? Were others involved? If yes, who and in what manner were they involved? Keep in mind that the others represent a quality of you, see Note 3 at the beginning of Actions and Activities category. Did anyone get hurt emotionally, physically, or was disturbed in any way? How did you feel, and what did you do, because, of your feelings, regarding the swimming? Was it agitating, confusing, dangerous, disturbing, frustrating, peace wi th the situation, happy, joyful, life threatening, safe, scary, or unsure? Where were you? Was the place unfamiliar to you? Were you coherent? In view of your dream's context, namely swimming, what choices are you making that may impair your spiritual growth, judgment, health, or that will encourage a desertion of the faith, which is in Jesus Christ? Your answers, coupled with the interpretation, plus any additional information, should begin to unfold the subject matter and issue at hand, if not now, mull over things a few days. For more information, see index or relevant category and subcategory for other particulars within your dream.

Now, pray (See Prayer of Deliverance, pg. 897)

Specific Meaning

If, you have a very real connection with any type of swimming activity, e.g., aqua-aerobics, aquanaut, deep-sea diver, lifeguard, professional swimmer, scuba diver, designer, or selling of, swimwear, snorkeler. Dreams of this sort should be received as ordinary dreams, resulting from your daily activities (see Chapter One, Chalom). These dreams are usually about the anxieties that overwhelm your mind during the day. They are an inner release mechanism, which helps provide you with emotional balance and the maintaining of your sanity. These sorts of dreams, are not significant, and do not warrant special attention.

Note: If an accident was highlighted within your dream, especially if you're drowning, this is a precautionary warning. There may be potential for an accident. Dreamer, the details, kept within context of your dream, should be relevant to your life, and closely resemble your real-life situations. Meaning it can actually occur during your awaked state. This will help you narrow down the specifics needed to support and steer you clear of possible mishaps. However, if your dream symbols are not easily, linked to your life activities, heed the spiritual implications (the interpretation).

TALKING - **To speak, or to express something, using speech, to communicate in a way other than by speaking.**

Some short descriptions of types, phrases, and other processes and particulars, connected in some way to this category. For example, arrogantly talking, arguing, babbling, boasting, bragging, chatter, command, complaining, compliments, counsel, declare, dispute, gossiping, God talking, growl, moan, question, or preaching. Sign language, singing, speaking another language, or speaking lies. Thought transference or telepathy, talking book, talking head, talking point, talking-to, teaching, to declare, to moan or growl, to plot, to promise, to repeat something, to threaten or be threaten, to warn or be warned, or whispering.

Unless otherwise noted elsewhere, if, in your everyday living, your awaked state, as part of your lifestyle, work, or ministerial activities, or a special event, you have a very real connection with any type of talking activity, or if dreamer uses sign language as a form of communication. For example, communication services, counseling, deaf, entertainment industry, facilitator, human resource worker, mediator, teaching, telemarketing, preaching, public speaker, use of sign language, voiceover, (also see content list for this category), your dream is not significant and does not warrant special attention.

Otherwise noted, if, you dreamt of someone else doing the talking and the person was unknown, the dreamer, is unaware of the effect, good or bad, you're having upon another. It is made known to you, via your dream. If positive things were ta lked about, this is a person you should possibly mentor, for your ministry and its uniqueness in presenting the gospel, is what they need. If bad things were talked about, you are having a negative effect upon another; your conversation is not of God. See dream interpretation, if needed, to help determine if meaning is positive or negative.

Otherwise noted, see Note 1 at the beginning of Actions and Activities category. To determine who your dream is for you or another, consider one of the following (relevant interpretation) first, as well as, see Note 3 at the beginning of Actions and Activities category.

Symbols and Referents: Dreams of some sort of talking generally imply, coupled with the relevant interpretation, some type of promise, warning, command to go somewhere, subdue, or a need to meditate, take account of, reckon. Take great care and heed God's warnings. We are called to exhibit faith by steadfast obedience, determination, confidence, fortitude, thanks, and love. The genuineness of your faith is judged by your response to hardships and opposition engendered by your identification with Christ, and by your inner temptations to sin. We must exhibit courage under trials, and not take lightly God's disciplinary instructions.

Category Content - If not listed see index, perchance, for your specific type of talking dream activity.

- Arguing, see category, Fighting (Argument)
- If someone else was doing the talking, instigated or provoked, in any way, the talking
- Boasting, Bragging, Arrogantly Talking
- Complaining or Whining or Murmuring
- Compliments
- Conspire or Plot or Scheme or Talked into or Talked out of (persuading somebody to do something should be highlighted)
- Cussing or Name Calling (e.g. Bullying, Defamation, Slander, Utter Obscenities, Profanities, Verbal Abuse; Crassness)
- Discussion (a civil discussion with another regarding a specific subject or topic in an effort to work things out, should be highlighted)
- Echo or Repeating
- God, Jesus Talking
- Gossiping
- Language (speaking another language)
- Lying or Cursing (speaking lies, or wishing harm upon; invoking evil upon)
- Oath or Promising (to promise)
- Preaching, Eulogist or to Declare loudly (any address of a religious nature or announce something loudly, should be highlighted)
- Rebuttal or Talk back (replying in an impertinent or defiant way)
- Reprimand or "Talking-to" (a disciplinary conversation should be highlighted)
- Sign Language or Telepathy (e.g. thought transference, signing, or communication from one mind to another without using sensory perceptions)
- Singing, see category, Music, Musical Instruments (Singing)
- Talk Show (a talk show should be highlighted)
- Talking Head (a head, without a body, is talking should be highlighted)
- Teaching see category, Working, Work Places (Educator)
- Whispering
- "Talk a blue streak" (you literally see a thin blue line while talking should be highlighted)

- "Talk a mile a minute" (distance was highlighted in some way while talking)
- "Talk round" (something circular, spherical, shaped like a circle, while talking, e.g. round table was highlighted in some way while talking)
- "Talk through your hat" (talking, while some type of hat is in front of your mouth should be highlighted)
- "Talk trash" (garbage or trash was highlighted in some way while talking)
- "All talk and no trousers" (talking, with no pants on should be highlighted)
- "Talk turkey" (a turkey was highlighted in some way while talking or to mimic gobbling)

If someone else was doing the talking, instigated or provoked, in any way, the talking, no matter if a rebut was put up, or if dreamer heard talking: This dream has two meanings (choose one). (1) If person talking is actually known by dreamer in your awake life, the dreamer is unaware of the effects, good or bad, that another is having upon you. If positive things were talked about, you should listen to this person in your awaked life, for their words or conversation is of God. If immoral, bad things, lies, were talked about or gossiping, you are counseled to not listen to that person in your awaked life, any longer, because their words or conversation are not of God. Questions to consider, how do you feel knowing God has made you aware of the effects of this person's words upon you? What manner of talking was going on (e.g. gossiping, complaining, compliments)? Per the manner of conversation, also see one of the following subcategories. May also, see category, People. (2) If person talking is literally unknown by dreamer in your awake life, the dreamer, is unaware of the effects, good or bad, you're having upon another. It is made known to you, via your dream. If positive things wer e talked about, this is a person you should possibly mentor, for your ministry and its uniqueness in presenting the gospel, is what they need. If immoral, bad things, lies, were talked about, or gossiping, dreamer, you are having a negative effect upon another; your words and conversation are not of God. Questions to consider, how do you feel knowing God has made you aware of the effects your words are having upon someone? What manner of talking was going on (e.g. gossiping, complaining, compliments)? P er the manner of conversation, also see one of the following subcategories. May also, see category, People. If necessary, see suggested course of action.

Boasting, Bragging, or Arrogantly Talking: Dreamer, the Lord intensely dislikes the arrogant, conceited, egotistical overconfident, pompous, self-important, and self-righteous. Be sure of this, the proud of heart will reap a fall in some manner (Proverbs 16:18, 18:12). Thus, do not keep talking so proudly or let your mouth speak such arrogance, for the Lord is a God who knows, and by Him, deeds (and words) are weighed. See suggested course of action.

Complaining, Whining, or Murmuring: Dreamer, do your rightful religious duties, professionally minded and complete, without murmurings. Do them all, and do not find fault with doing. For the enemy of your soul is devising and plotting evil against you, to create an offense within you against God and His cause, thus an offense against you by God. Therefore, mind your work, and do not quarrel with it. God's expectations were given to be obeyed, not to be disputed. The service you do, in Jesus name, leads to freedom, and the work for His cause, has its own rewards. Cheerfully willing to do God's service, also greatly adorns you. As well, dedication to His cause, without complaining, testifies to the world that you serve a good Lord. Further, learn to not injure anyone, in word or deed, and give no occasion for offense that you may be blameless and harmless, a child of God, without rebuke. If necessary, see suggested course of action.

Compliments: Your dream references some type of business deal or work related activity, possibly a claim that's in dispute or some type of deeds. You will be approved or awarded, according to your desires.

Conspire, Plot, Scheme, Talked into, or Talked out of (persuading somebody to do something should be highlighted): This dream has three meanings (choose one). (1) Conspire, Plot, or Scheme: This choice has two parts (choose one). (a) I f dreamer conspired, plotted, or schemed against another within your dream, you have distorted true religion, because of covetousness, greed, and selfishness.

233

You have led people astray, causing the people of God to err in the things of God. Yo ur cupidity will be uncovered, and evil will be brought upon you that will send you away from your place. Humble yourself with fasting before the Lord to lessen the harshness of your days to come. See suggested course of action. (b) If another conspired, plotted, or schemed against the dreamer within your dream, see Proverbs 24:1, 2, your dream denotes hostility and harm are plotted against the dreamer. A plan decided on in secret, to cause the dreamer to act in a wildly rebellious manner. Therefore, do not envy the demonically used, the backslider, or the non-believer (one who has no religious beliefs, a non- religious person, or one who has no religious faith or belief in Jesus Christ, or one who does not embrace a personal relationship with Jesus Christ, at present). Do not even think that they are happier than you are. Moreover, do not be covetous of their supposedly prosperity, namely the illusion of them prospering in their wickedness, for their end is neigh, and possible eternal, or else you will grow weak and falter in your spirituality. (2) If dreamer talked or persuaded somebody to do something: Your dream implies that the dreamer is very influential regarding a certain person's decisions. You are attempti ng to persuade them to do something by talking to him or her. Whatever the decision at hand, it should be made by the person, and not by the dreamer. Especially, do not use any undue pressure on another, thus the purpose of your dream. If necessary, see suggested course of action. (3) Talked out of: This choice has two parts (choose one). (a) If dreamer talked another out of doing something negative (e.g. suicide), the following interpretation is for another (see Chapter One, Are You Ready to Hear the Messages in Your Dreams, section entitled, The 10% for others). If person was known by the dreamer, the dreamer is asked to relay the interpretation to the person within the dream. If person was unknown then the dream is for, and about, th e dreamer. The dreamer is not self-aware regarding this part of you. Your dream was sent to talk you out of something bad, especially bad choices you are contemplating at present. (b) If dreamer talked another out of something good (e.g. their righteous belief and faith in God, their money), or another talked the dreamer out of som ething good, the following words are about, and for, the dreamer. Dreamer, you are headstrong, stubborn, rebellious, obstinate, wayward, noncompliant, unruly, unmanageable, disobedient, uncontrollable, and one who greatly desires power. You are unwilling to submit yourself to the discipline necessary for church order, disrespectful of good church government and of sound doctrine. A vain talker and deceiver, believing yourself to be wise, you are arrogant enough to believe your own lies, and diligent enou gh to draw others into the same foolishness. Pretending to be Christian, you are a false teacher. Self-righteous, you reject the doctrine of grace (the free and unmerited favor and beneficence of God), thus you've chosen to be under the law. Your spirituality is one of outward show and hypocrisy. You love to give alms, pray, and appear righteous publicly, but inwardly you are lifeless, and lawlessness prevails. Your lack of love towards others has contributed to your lack of, understanding, receiving, and giving genuine grace. You shatter the peace of the church, and corrupt other churches. You undermine whole households, teaching things you ought not, namely, legalism, and that good deeds are required for entrance into Heaven, distorting the gospel a nd sabotaging the souls of men, even whole families. False teachers draw many from the true faith to their ruin; thus, the mout h of the deceiver will be stopped. The root cause as to why you do what you do is money, serving your fleshly lust, under the pretense of religion. For the love of money, people will deceive, defraud, and swindle, and they don't care who they hurt or beat. A man or woman will sell his or her body, a Christian his or her soul. This attitude has separated you from God (Mark 8:36-37). This is how you will be dealt with from this day forward, your mouth will be stopped, by someone proving you wrong, and by that person, exposing that the doctrine you are adhering to is false, invalid, and/or faulty. That someone, se nt by God, will do this by presenting sound doctrine and reasons, from the scripture, as evidence, exposing you, and they will not give place to you even for an hour to rebut. As well, there will be an official disapproval of you, by a vote of the elders and other leadership of your ministry. Dreamer, faithful ministers will oppose you, as they do all seducers that your foolishness may go on no further, having been exposed. See also Titus 1:10-16. See suggested course of action.

Cussing or Name Calling (e.g. Bullying, Defamation, Slander, Utter Obscenities, Profanities, Verbal

Abuse; Crassness): The words spoken within your dream are about you, and who and what you are. Dreamer, your words against others is rash, harsh, and uncharitable judgments. Perhaps dreamer has contrarily judged another as neglectful, lazy, or as one who is dishonoring God. Dreamer, you do not personally know their situation, you are truly on the outside looking in, judging by sight. Your words are just opinions, which happened to be very judgmental. Dreamer, in judging others, via condemnatory, critical, derogatory, disapproving, harsh, negative, scornful, or uncomplimentary in your words and thoughts, you have set a precedent over your own life, discharging a universal law. The Universal Law: With the same judgments, you judge others, so will you be judged (see Matthew 7:1-5). Thus, the words spoken within your dream are about you. This revelation of, who you are, the names you called others, is meant to strongly convict you within; do not ignore the strong alarm of the Holy Ghost and of your conscience. The following is loosely based on Matthew Henry Concise of Matthew 7:1-5: We must not judge rashly, nor pass judgment upon our brethren (or sisters), e.g. our family, friends, or foes, without any solid grounds. We must not make the worst of people. Thus, Matthew 7:1-5, is a just reproof to those who quarrel with their brethren for small faults, while they allow themselves in greater ones. That which charity teaches us to call but a splinter in our brother's eye, true repentance, and godly sorrow will teach us to call a beam in our own. It is as strange that a man (or woman) can be in a sinful, miserable condition, and not be aware of it, as that a man should have a beam in his eye, and not consider it; but the god of this world blinds their minds. Here is a good rule for reproves; first reform thyself. See suggested course of action.

Discussion (a civil discussion with another regarding a specific subject or topic in an effort to work things out, should be highlighted): This dream has three meanings (choose one). (1) Dreamer, there is a need to resolve or settle a difference of opinion with another, civilly and quickly. It is OK to disagree. If necessary, see suggested course of action. (2) Your dream implies that some form of legislation is being blocked, to prevent the passage of a piece of legislation, by prolonging the discussion of it until it is too late to vote on it. If you, the dreamer, are using your position to block such legislation, you will bear the repercussions of not supporting the people you governed, justly. See suggested course of action. (3) Dreamer, you will begin to experience the promises the Lord God has in store for you, just as He promised you. Be careful to obey His directives over your individual life, as you've been taught these past years that you may increase greatly, and that it may go well with you as you walk into your prosperity. Love the Lord your God with all your heart, with all your soul, and with all your strength, and studiously teach your children, to do so as well (Deuteronomy 6:3-7).

Echo or Repeating: Your dream denotes an argument of some kind between the dreamer and another. Dreamer, hold back or restrain yourself from this argument or debate. This conversation does not edify God's cause, nor will it usher His Kingdom back to earth any quicker. Thus, your conversation is a bunch of meaningless disputes and bickering, words that do not lead to answers, salvation, truth, or wisdom; they are words that are meant to keep up foolishness. See suggested course of action.

God, Jesus Talking: This dream has two meanings (both apply). (1) Anyone inquiring of the Lord should go to church and participate in your local assembly. (2) Dreamer, God is challenging you by asking some very penetrating questions. For instance, can God be trusted to do you good? Do you believe in the goodness of the Lord for your life or is His goodness only for a select few, which does not include you? Can God do immeasurably more than you can ask or imagine? Do you have faith in Him? Do you know your divine purpose and/or gifting? Do you like the things that your life is showing you? Are you content? Have you've gotten what you've been hoping for, or gotten your heart's desire? Are there any open doors for your desire? Your capacity to answer these questions honestly, and not in an expected manner, reveals your level of understanding of God, your depth of spirituality, and self-awareness. If you answered no, to three or more of these questions, it is counseled that the dreamer, go and pray, taking these words with you, "Dear Jesus, if you are pleased with me, teach me your ways so I may know you and continue to find favor with you. Remember that I am your people". If you answered yes to seven or more of these questions, your dream is revealing to you that God's Presence will go with you, and He will give you rest. He will do the very thing you've asked for, because He is pleased with you and knows you by name; have faith in this. Therefore, dreamer, embrace God's love towards you and His providential care over you.

Gossiping: Dreamer, you have betrayed confidences, and by this, you have separated close friends, and deeply hurt others. You are one who causes division amongst your fellow brethren and sisters in Christ (Proverbs 16:28). You will experience a visitation from the Lord, may He find you as He wants you to be; therefore, you must discontinue causing division amongst the saints. Moreover, check excessive carnal desires, lest an illness come upon you that will consume your flesh, causing a skeletal like appearance (Pray Psalm 38:1-22). See suggested course of action.

Language (speaking another language): This dream denotes one of two situations (choose one): (1) The Holy Spirit has entered into the dreamer, thus, you are sealed unto the day of redemption (see Ephesians 4:30). (2) The dreamer is not clear internally, and is conflicted within. Moreover, your conversation and words expose this to all who come within your sphere. It is said of you that you do not communicate rationally, and you have heard this personally. Dreamer, you are in denial about an offense, or you are resistant, unclear, and/or superficial regarding your religious convictions. Whichever the issue, you are not pure within your heart. This state of being will prove detrimental to you. In this state, your pride and stubbornness has l ed to irrational thinking, adoption of erroneous ideas, and some mental health issues. Dreamer, if you have a serious offense against someone, humble yourself enough to relinquish your ministry (if germane), and go and make things right that you may be open enough to hear and receive God when He speaks. If there is no offense, dreamer needs to become resolute about your dedication to the Lord Jesus Christ. See suggested course of action.

Lying or Cursing (speaking lies, or wishing harm upon; invoking evil upon): Your truths are deceitful and worthless, leading to destruction. Your justifications are weak excuses, unstable, leading to trouble. The Lord detests lying lips, but He delights in men (and women) who are truthful (Proverbs 12:22 NIV). Dreamer, although you've committed something immoral and shameful, even horrible, and yes the Lord disapproves, genuinely owning up to your offenses, without justifications, will allow healing and restoration to begin in your life. Your dream is to warn a rebellious person, in the spirit of grace (the free and unmerited favor and beneficence of God). To see if you will yet be worked upon, and change your mindset, or else to leave you inexcusable, in your accusations against God, because of your ruin (e.g. continually plundered, seized, and disfavored, also see Jeremiah 9:7-9; Zechariah 13:9; Matthew 23:37-39; Revelation 3:15-21). The more God allows you to see your emptiness, it is suggested that you be more earnest to repent that you may find Him to be grace and healing, refreshment, and a refuge. Question to ponder, dreamer, if after God has examined you, would it turn out well for you? Make it so. See suggested course of action.

Oath or Promising (to promise): Your dream denotes that promises have been made by the dreamer to others. Someone is waiting, in a spirit of expectation, for those promises to be fulfilled, for they view them as having come from God also. Broken promises can lead many away from Christ. Dreamer, it is always better not to promise, than to promise and not made good on it (Ecclesiastes 5:4-6). Moreover, there are promises of God yet to be fulfilled within the dreamer's life. However, there are expectations, placed upon the life of the dreamer by God that must be fulfilled, by the dreamer, in order to obtain your promise. Dreamer, God is a promise keeper and so must you be. Go and fulfill your promises to others, and then come back to Jesus to inquire into the fulfillment of His promises to you. See suggested course of action.

Preaching, Eulogist or Declare loudly (any address of a religious nature or announce something loudly, should be highlighted): This dream has two meanings (one or both may apply). (1) Your dream denotes that your voice will be used as an instrument of righteousness; uplifting those who are spiritually dead; and coming against those who would attempt to oppress you and others. The dreamer's spiritual strength, tenacity, and knowledge, will be used of God; penetrating the soul of those who listen, affecting conversion. By all this, you will be remembered by the Lord your God and rescued from your enemies. For, your words will cause your enemies to turn on themselves. Your dream comes as a message of affirmation. You have been called to a high calling; withdraw not your spirit when that day is officially upon you. Question to con sider, how do you feel knowing God has made you aware of this ahead of time? Dreamer, embrace God's love towards you and His providential care over you. (2) Dreamer your prayers are especially effective now, what you decree, God will fulfill. Only remember to seek first the Kingdom of God, via His Son. Yeshua is the key to activate all that comes with seeking the Kingdom of God. For, He is our righteousness required to access the Kingdom blessings, then will God give you the keys of the Kingdom of Heaven; whatever you bind on earth will be bound in heaven, and whatever you loose on earth will be loosed in heaven (ref Matthew 16:19). Dreamer, be who God made you to be, use your God given talents, as best you can, to make the world a better place; take your past and use it to teach those whom God has purposed you to reach. Additionally, no matter who you are and what the situation, the words of the Psalms will speak the words of your heart and those words will be heard on High. Thus, began singing a new song, see Psalm 96:1-13. Start listening to inspirational music, music that praises our Lord and Savior.

Rebuttal or Talk back (replying in an impertinent or defiant way): This dream has two meanings (choose one). (1) Rebuttal, your dream denotes that the dreamer has judged someone's character as boastful or complaining. In doing so, it is also acknowledge that you are guilty of the same thing. Dreamer, see Matthew 7:1-5. See suggested course of action. (2) Talk back (replying in an impertinent or defiant way should be highlighted): You are impolite and rude, showing a lack of respect for elders and those who have authority over you. Moreover, you are excessively presumptuous, so much so, you lack modesty. Dreamer, your soul is buried underneath the pain of violations, and this has distorted your reasoning. Your truths are deceitful and worthless, leading to destruction. Your justifications are weak excuses, unstable, leading to trouble. Therefore, repentantly pray Psalm 51, looking reflectively within, as to why you do what you do, and then seek support and accountability. Know yourself; and resist those detrimental urges via a serious commitment to a lifestyle of prayer and fast ing; humbly submitting your negative inclinations to Christ and to His principles. Dreamer, the strength, and resistance you draw upon to resist those dark urges when you're before certain others, use that same level of resistance and control when you disrespect your elders, and your attitude will eventually abate. See suggested course of action.

Reprimand or "Talking-to" (a disciplinary conversation should be highlighted): See Proverbs 3:11, 12, Hebrews 12:5-29. Dreamer, despise not the correction of Jehovah, neither be weary of His discipline, for whom He loves, He admonishes. You are also to respect any other godly and/or wise authority figure in your life, in like manner, when admonished. See suggeste d course of action.

Sign Language or Telepathy (e.g. thought transference, signing, or communication from one mind to another without using sensory perceptions): If dreamer is deaf and/or uses sign language, see introduction of this category, for this is an ordinary dream. Otherwise, it is recommended that dreamer read, understand, pray, and embrace Psalm 38. Dreamer, you are in the same state, therefore, glean from this scripture, and use the same words as King David did, for this is wisdom for you during this time. See suggested course of action.

Talk Show (a talk show should be highlighted): At present, the negativity of your current behavior warrants deep consideration, for you will be exposed publicly, and to great extent. A conscientious and diligent effort on the part of the dreamer to deal with your emotional fears and scars, which are the cause of your present negative behavior, is needed. Moreover, some type of Christian counseling should bring about truth inwardly, and at a pace, you'll be able to handle comfortably. Dreamer, you are counseled to break your heartaches, pains, anxieties, worries, and concerns in half and give some to Jehovah-Rapha (Psalm 147:3), for you cannot bear them alone; lest you find yourself gagging and choking on pieces of your sin, forfeiting the peace that comes with humbly asking for help from God and others. All this, coupled with the refining and purifying work of the Paraclete, and a greater service to others, will cause the emergence of a divine led wisdom. See suggested course of action.

Talking Head (a head, without a body, talking should be highlighted): Your dream denotes one who has the potential to be a leader, but is unwilling to embrace your purpose. Dreamer, you are lazy, prideful, and/or live unwise and foolishly, because you have been taught desolation. Notwithstanding, without purpose, and detached from the Body of Christ, you will physically die before your time. Dreamer, pray for truth and wisdom inwardly, and for the courage to apply it, ask and it sh all be given you (James 1:5). One may suffer needlessly, because he or she will not ask Jesus for wisdom. Ask Jesus as often as you need to, regarding all of your emotional concerns, considering how personal His promises are, He will meet you in your need. See suggested course of action.

Whispering: Your dream denotes one who is a true gossiper, you have secretly, and maliciously, carried rumors from house to house, telling stories not fit to be told. Although, the stories had some truth in them, you twisted and misrepresented the truth. All this was done with the motive to damage people's reputation, to break-up friendships, and to cause division and trouble amongst family members and friends, setting each one against the other. You pretended to be overly concern and very troubled over another's misfortune; appearing as if you were personally wounded by it, when you really rejoiced over their misfortune, and were glad to hear of it. You visited to get all the information needed to satisfy your wickedness, and then you went to tell it with pride and pleasure, twisting and misrepresenting truths. Dreamer, your words have seriously wounded one of whom they were spoken of. Moreover, to the one you spoke them to; you have destroyed their love and care of another, as well as of you. You have caused an offense within one who had no offense, now they hate when they ought to love. They will be reconciled with those they love. You have been exposed as the culprit, and will be ostracized by many. See suggested course of action.

In addition, the following are common words, expressions, usages, (e.g. slang or clichés), or a 'probable' that are metaphorically represented by talking:

- **Talk a blue streak (you literally see a blue line while talking should be highlighted):** Your dream denotes the dreamer is moving too fast, and really needs to slow down and contemplate some things. As cliché as this may sound, you really do need to judge the tree by its' present fruit, and then choose. See suggested course of action.
- **Talk a mile a minute (distance was highlighted in some way while talking):** Dreamer, you are talking too much, and not listening enough. Even a fool is thought wise if he (or she) keeps silent, and discerning if they holds their tongue (Proverbs 17:28). See suggested course of action.
- **Talk round (something circular, spherical, shaped like a circle while talking, e.g. round table was highlighted in some way while talking):** Dreamer, either, you are persuading someone, or is being persuaded, to agree with an opinion that will cause confusion on many levels in your life. You are always learning but never able to acknowledge the truth of God, never dealing with the core issues, always talking in circles. A deeper depth of spirit, mind, and soul, is needed and is available to you right now, if you would but ask Jesus for wisdom, and you should. This will cause you to understand more clearly the things of God and His Nature. See suggested course of action.
- **Talk through your hat (talking, while some type of hat is in front of your mouth should be highlighted):** Your dream denotes one who is talking nonsense. See Ephesians 5:4-17, and adhere carefully to what this scripture text is teaching you. See suggested course of action.
- **Talk trash (garbage or trash was highlighted in some way while talking):** Your dream denotes one who tries to intimidate others, through boasting and insults, a braggart and bully, with tyrannical tendencies. You harbor wicked thoughts, and are ruthlessly aggressive. These are some of the characteristic of the most horrendous leaders throughout history (e.g. Edi Amin, Hitler, Mussolini, Nero, and others). You are an enemy of God's people. You conspire and plot, and speak devastation, against His people, those whom He cherishes. It is said of you, may you be ashamed, dismayed, and perish in disgrace. Dreamer, your dream is sent to a rebellious person, in the spirit of grace (the free and unmerited favor and beneficence of God), to see if you will yet be worked upon, and change your mindset, or else to leave you inexcusable, in your accusations against God, because of your ruin (also see Jeremiah 9:7-9; Matthew 23:37-39). Jesus is petitioning you to

cleanse the evil from your heart, and from the horribleness of it all, and be saved. Dreamer, many lacking courage, boldness, or enthusiasm, weak in spirit and unfit for service, are healed, restored, and strengthened by the grace of God. If you are ready to acknowledge that you are weak, and remain mindful of your weaknesses, God will in an extraordinary way, increase your strength. He is willing to help you, if you are willing to be helped, and to do your best, with a humble dependence upon Him. The more God allows you to see your garbage, and the horribleness of it all, it is suggested that you be more earnest to repent that you may find Him to be grace and healing, refreshment, and a refuge. See suggested course of action.

- **All talk and no trousers (talking, with no pants on should be highlighted):** Someone who is doing a lot of talking, with no pants on denotes one who talks about doing big, important things, but doesn't take any action. See suggested course of action.
- **"Talk turkey" (a turkey was highlighted in some way while talking; or to mimic gobbling):** Your dream denotes one who talks honestly and bluntly. You will eat the words you speak, and they will be presented, back to you, in the same manner you've presented words to others (e.g. words spoken to others, without compassion, sympathy, and understanding, will be spoken to you without compassion, sympathy). You will reap what you sow; therefore, say unto others, as you would have others say unto you, under the same or similar circumstances, for empathy and compassion begets empathy and compassion. Dreamer, counsel, and conversation are better received when your words are carefully thought out and presented empathically. See suggested course of action.

Suggested Course of Action

Question to consider and journal, did your dream depict any symbols that alludes to, the dreamer will make the necessary changes, spiritually, emotionally, and/or physically to affect a more positive outcome? If changes are initiated, your dreams will change.

Nevertheless, these types of dreams, challenges the dreamer to appreciate that Yahweh chastens every son/daughter whom He receives (Hebrew 12:5-13). If you are without chastisement, then you are not a legitimate child of the King. Those who will enjoy His great blessings will at times experience His chastening. These times of correction are a sign of both His displeasure and love towards you. Humble submission is essential in this process of spiritual growth. Wisdom suggests that if we reverence the Lord and endure correction with patience and understanding, deliverance from evil will come.

Therefore dreamer, revere God and consider your actions, words, and thoughts, especially when you go to the House of God. Go to listen and learn rather than to act as those, who do not know that they do wrong, pretending to be blind. Do not be quick with your mouth; do not be hasty in your heart to utter anything before God. God is in heaven and you are on earth, so let your words be few. As a dream comes when there are many cares, so the speech of a fool when there are many words. Do not let your mouth lead you into sin (Ecclesiastes 5:1-3, 6). What kind of talking activity was it? Were others involved? If yes, who and in what manner were they involved? Keep in mind that the others represent a character trait, quality, or talent within you. That trait has gotten you here. Did anyone get hurt emotionally, or was disturbed in any way? If so, your actions are affecting others as well. How did you feel, and what did you do, because, of your feelings, regarding the talking activity that went on? Was it agitating, confusing, dangerous, disturbing, frustrating, peace with the situation, happy, joyful, life threatening, safe, scary, or unsure? Coupled with the interpretation, in view of your dream's context, namely talking, what choices are you making, what words are you uttering, which are grieving the Holy Spirit and that the Lord Jesus has no pleasure in?

Now, pray (See Prayer of Deliverance, pg. 897)

Specific Meaning

If, you have a very real connection with any type of talking activity, e.g., communication services, counseling, entertainment industry, facilitator, human resource worker, mediator, teaching, telemarketing, preaching, public speaker, voiceover, or use of sign language as a form of communication. Dreams of this sort should be received as ordinary dreams, resulting from your daily activities (see Chapter One, Chalom). These dreams are usually about the anxieties that overwhelm your mind during the day. They are an inner release mechanism, which helps provide you with emotional balance and the maintaining of your sanity. These sorts of dreams, are not significant, and do not warrant special attention.

Note: If a medical issue was highlighted within your dream, especially if you're unable to talk, or if legal issues, or any other troubles, were highlighted because of something said or exposed, this is a precautionary warning. There may be potential for a health issue or legal ramifications. Dreamer, the details, kept within context of your dream, should be rele vant to your life, and closely resemble your real-life situations. Meaning it can actually occur during your awaked state. This will help you narrow down the specifics needed to support and steer you clear of possible mishaps. However, if your dream was inundated with symbols that are not easily linked to your life activities, then the spiritual implications (the interpretation) should be heeded.

Vacation: A scheduled season, during which the activities of work, school, or other regular businesses are suspended, and a period-of-time devoted to rest, travel, or recreation.

Some short descriptions of types, phrases, and other processes and particulars, connected in some way to this category are, for example, visit a beach, day trip, take a break, hiatus, holiday, resort, respite, retreat, sabbatical, travel, tourist, trip, vacationing, and/or visiting.

Unless otherwise noted elsewhere, if, in your everyday living, your awaked state, as part of your lifestyle, work, or ministerial activities, or a special event, you have a very real connection with any type of vacation activity. For examp le, cruise ship employee, hotelier, travel agent, tour guide, or any leisure activity agent, employee, owner, your dream is not significant and does not warrant special attention.

Otherwise noted, this dream of vacationing may be a Prophetically Simple Dream (see Chapter One: The 60th Part of Prophecy), whereas, the dreamer needs to take a vacation, or is warned not to take a vacation, especially if danger was highlighted within your dream. If an accident or tragedy was highlighted within your dream, this is a precautionary warning. There may be potential for trouble. Dreamer, the details, kept within context of your dream, should be relevant to your life, and closely resemble your real-life situations. Meaning it can actually occur during your awaked state. This will help you narrow down the specifics needed to support you or to steer you clear of possible danger. If applicable, cancellation of tri p may be considered.

Otherwise noted, on occasion, one may have an Oneirovatic or "OV" dream (see Chapter One: The 60th part of prophecy, other prophetic dreams). This type of dream bares insight into the present day or near future events of another. One may plainly see, or hear of, accidents or trouble happening within your dream. This type of dream should closely resemble real life situations, with the dream events actually being capable of happening. If you sense that your dream is for or about another, the question as to why you have been made aware of this information, and how do you factor into the equation, should be seriously considered, along with necessary actions. Dreamer, you are sent to get involved. The person in your dream should either, be encouraged to take a vacation, or warned not to take a vacation, especially if danger was highli ghted within your dream. If an accident or trouble was highlighted, this is a precautionary warning. There may be potential for trouble, cancellation may be considered.

Otherwise noted, see Note 1 at the beginning of Actions and Activities category.

To determine who your dream is for you or another, see Note 3 at the beginning of Actions and Activities category.

Symbol and Referent: Dreamer, you have in Christ, grace (the free and unmerited favor and beneficence of God), healing, refreshment, and a refuge. Embrace the help your Heavenly Father is offering you, via a vacation.

Vacation: God has seen your plight. You've weathered a great storm, suffered enormous difficulties, and have not gotten any relief. The trying times that have brought much frustration, aggravation, and were so troublesome will now begin to abate. Those that have vexed you will now go far from you, for God will make you a threat to them without any effort on your part. You are entering into a rest. Your heavenly Father is protecting you by allowing you to rest from your work; in order to avoid overly cruel and oppressive pressure from the enemy, via those he uses. The dreamer will be favored with a vacation, including pay. Jehovah Jireh will provide for all your needs. During this vacation, peace will again hold sway over your life. Put your trust in Him, and your peace will overflow. Rest, be encouraged, recoup, and strengthen yourself that you may go on to perfection, spiritually, being built up in your faith and complete, lacking nothing. This vacation will take some time, perhaps seven weeks, allow it, for it will perfect quietness within your soul, restoring a more pleasant and peaceful concentration o f the mind on spiritual matters, leaving you more open to divine influence. Moreover, use this "you" time to cultivate your strengths and discipline your weaknesses.

This vacation should be used exclusively for the purpose it was intended, rest, encouragement, recouping, and strengthening. Dreamer, have faith in God, which is a resolute trust in the integrity of God and in His Word that He will provide for you and protect you. Moreover, if applicable, God will oversee His ministry, you've been given charge over, while you're on vacation.

Specific Meaning

If, you have a very real connection with any type of vacation activity, e.g. cruise ship employee, hotelier, travel agent, tour guide, or any leisure activity agent, employee, owner, dreams of this sort should be received as ordinary dreams, resulting from your daily activities (see Chapter One, Chalom). These dreams are usually about the anxieties that overwhelm your mind during the day. They are an inner release mechanism, which helps provide you with emotional balance and the maintaining of your sanity. These sorts of dreams, are not significant, and do not warrant special attention.

Note: If an accident or any other tragedy was highlighted within your dream, this is a precautionary warning. There may be potential for a tragedy of some sort. Dreamer, the details, kept within context of your dream, should be relevant to your life, and closely resemble your real-life situations. Meaning it can actually occur during your awaked state. This will help you narrow down the specifics needed to support and steer you clear of possible mishaps. However, if your dream symbols are not easily, linked to your life activities, heed the spiritual implications (the interpretation).

WALKING: **When walking, as opposed to running, to travel along or through something on foot, to lead or exercise an animal, usually on a leash.**

Some short descriptions of types, phrases, and other processes and particulars, connected in some way to this category. Are for example, do not walk sign, just learning to walk, not able to walk, sleep walking, pacing, walk off, walkover somebody, walking aid (cane, crutches, stick, and walker), walking out, walking papers, or window-shop.

Unless otherwise noted elsewhere, if, in your everyday living, your awaked state, as part of your lifestyle, work, or ministerial activities, or a special event, you have a very real connection with any type of walking activity. For example, armed forces, athletic endeavors, exercise regiment, handicapped, hiker, medical profession, parade participant, par k keeper or ranger, police enforcement, postal worker, protestor, surveyor, walking competition, walker of animals, or other kinds of walking activity, also see content list for this category, your dream is not significant and does not warrant special attention.

Otherwise noted, this dream of walking may be a Prophetically Simple Dream (see Chapter One: The 60th Part of Prophecy); whereas, the dreamer is encouraged to walk somewhere or with someone, or is warned not to walk somewhere or with someone. If an accident or any other tragedy was highlighted within your dream, because of you walking somewhere or with someone, this is a precautionary warning. There may be potential for a tragedy of some sort. Dreamer, the details, kep t within context of your dream, should be relevant to your life, and closely resemble your real-life situations. Meaning it can actually occur during your awaked state. This will help you narrow down the specifics needed to support and steer you clear of possible mishaps. However, if your dream symbols are not easily, linked to your life activities, heed the spiritual implications (the interpretation).

Otherwise noted, see Note 1 at the beginning of Actions and Activities category.

To determine who your dream is for you or another, see Note 3 at the beginning of Actions and Activities category.

Symbols and Referents: Dreams of walking generally indicate a potentially strong, and possibly legal, commitment to an agreement, covenant, philosophy, or lifestyle; thus, the dreamer is encouraged, or forewarned, about a decision you have made (or is making) regarding a particular commitment, possibly a long-term commitment. The dreamer has, with much thought and inner turmoil, chosen to commit to a certain lifestyle. Either you have chosen to honor Jesus Christ as Lord and Savior, or you have forfeited the privileges that come with His Kingdom that you might not be under His precepts, because your lifestyle and choices do not concur with His principles morally. These types of dreams are primarily warnings.

Category Content - If not listed see index, perchance, for your specific type of walking dream activity.

- Walk up and down, see category, Ascending and Descending (Going up and down)
- Walk upstairs, or up to someplace, or up something, see category, Ascending or Expanding (Stairs)
- Walk out a door, see category, Buildings, Structures (Walk out a door)
- Walking on Broken Glass (broken glass should be highlighted), see category, Buildings, Structures (Windows)
- Walking through a gate, see category, Buildings, Structures (Gates)
- Alone or With Others
- Animal (walking an animal)
- Baby Steps, Just Learning to Walk, Walking with another until they are able to walk on their own, or To Force to Walk (to help or cause somebody to walk by supporting them somehow, or to force someone to walk, e.g. pushing, dragging)
- Barefoot (walking)
- Cane or Crutch or Staff (any walking stick) or Injured, Hurt, or Wounded (walking injured)
- Children (walking with)
- Footsteps (Christ's Footsteps or another) or Walk One Mile in Someone Shoes
- City (walking around in a city)
- Competitively Walking (competitions based on walking, e.g. cakewalk or competitive walking, as in a race)
- Danger or Darkness (walking in the midst of danger, distress, trouble, or in the dark)
- "Do Not Walk" Sign
- Fast or Quickly or Determined
- Fire or Hot Coals (walking through fire or on hot coals)

- Hiking, Leisurely Walking, Mall Walking, Rambling, Strolling or Window Shopping (e.g. walking for amusement, bliss, contentment, diversion, delight, enjoyment, fun, gratification happiness, joy, leisure, pleasure, recreation, or relaxation)
- House (walking in or outside a house)
- Intoxicated, see category Drinking
- Inspecting or Measuring (walking over or along to measure or inspect, e.g. using a walking measure)
- Lost or Wandering (walking around lost, wandering)
- Maze or Walking in a Circle (walking through or in a maze of some kind)
- Pacing (walk back and forth)
- Pathway, Walkway, or Route for Walking or Primrose Path (e.g., Alley, Boardwalk, Causeway, Catwalk, Corridor, Footpath, Platform, Passageway, Pathway, or Sidewalk)
- Patrolling ("Walk the Beat" or patrol)
- Single File (walking single file)
- Sleepwalking or Blindly Walking or Walking in "Fog" (finding your way around obscurely)
- Staggering or Unsteady or Wobbling (walking as if about to fall)
- Tightrope or "Walking a Thin Line"
- Torch (walking with a torch)
- Trampling or Treading (walking on others)
- Trap (walk into a trap)
- Unable to Walk
- Walk By, Pass By, or Sail By
- Walk Away, Walk Off, or Walk Out of (e.g. Desert, Leave, Quit, Turn your Back On)
- "Walking Papers" (to see the words "walking papers" on papers should be highlighted)
- "Walking Tall" (appeared taller than what you literally are)

Alone or With Others: This dream has two meanings (choose one). (1) Walking alone: Your dream comes to encourage or warn, depending on what you saw or sensed, and/or how the dreamer was feeling in the dream; thus, this choice has two parts (choose one). (a) If dreamer was not afraid or accepting of the circumstances, be encouraged, in the Eyes of the Lord, you are committed to the way of holiness, living life on God's terms, as humanly as possible. Dreamer, you are the redeemed, and know that this is who you are. You are not considered a fool, nor a wicked and lazy servant, nor unclean, by the Lord, Jesus Christ. Further, any present evil and/or wickedness that have caused you to fear and/or be troubled, will suddenly disappear. It will be as though it was never there. Take courage and be strong, knowing that the Lord knows who you are, where you are, what's going on, and He will take care of you, for you are His and He cares. (b) On the other hand, if dreamer was afraid, apprehensive, worried, did not like what you was looking at, was not comfortable with, or disturb by, the situation, be warned. An event or situation that will cause intense fear is coming to discourage and terrify you. This will be in the form of an annoying, difficult, and unpleasant person, if applicable, possibly a child of yours. This person is a slick spokesperson who can turn any criticism to the advantage of his or her employer, the devil. Moreover, this person will begin to exhibit bizarre behavior, characterized by extreme agitation, delirious words, and profound paranoia; this person may even have delusions of super human strength. Possessed and sent by Satan, this person will attack you with intense adverse criticism, publicly. The trouble this person will cause will become so overwhelming, you may possibly need to stop working for a short while, or postpone some commitments, or perhaps even take a temporary leave from ministerial duties. Compassionately, although this spiritual battle will be great, and will demand your full attention, you won't fight this battle. Instead, take your stand, control your inner person to go "tit for tat", and stay where you are, leave not your place, and you will see the salvation of the Lord, which He will work for you. Thus, have no fear and do not be troubled. Then, suddenly, unexpectedly, and without any warning, all the evil and wickedness that caused you to fear and be troubled, will disappear, and you will not see that kind of intense adverse criticism and spiritual warfare again. It will be as though it was never there. Take courage and be strong, knowing that the Lord knows who you are, where you are, what's going on, and He cares; for you are His. Only, learn the wisdom from this situation, and keep faith in God. Read, understand, and embrace, Ephesians 6:10 -18, for this is to you now. Dreamer, yours is not a wrestling match against a human opponent. You are wrestling with rulers, authorities, the powers who govern the world of darkness, and spiritual forces that control evil in the heavenly world. However, this battle was not waged between equal foes. Therefore, our God, the Almighty, is the supreme Conqueror, and those who have been washed in the blood of His Lamb, will not be overcome but will emerge victoriously. Hence, as others have done, dreamer, bow your head; and fall down before Jehovah, worshipping Jehovah, and praise Jehovah, the God of Israel, with an exceeding loud voice. (2) Walking with others: This choice has two parts (choose one). (a) If person(s) dreamer was walking with, is actually known by dreamer, in your awaked life, this person(s) represents him or herself. As your dream indicates a potentially strong, possibly legal, commitment to an agreement, covenant, philosophy, lifestyle, person, place, or organization, the dreamer is encouraged or forewarned, about a decision you have made, is making, or will make, regarding a particular commitment, possibly a long- term commitment. This commitment is, tied to the person(s) in your dream. Moreover, while the dreamer has, with much thought and inner turmoil, chosen, is considering choosing, or will choose to commit to something. You must also consider if, along with your commitment, you have chosen to honor Jesus Christ as Lord and Savior, or are you forfeiting the privileges that come with His Kingdom that you might not be under His precepts, because your choices do not concur with His principles morally. As well, are you willing to live, or deal, with all the aspects of the potential commitment? For sure, whomever yo u were walking with, you are considering, or will have to consider soon, committing to that person and/or attribute of that person. Question to journal: what features stood out the most in your dream, regarding the person(s)? For example, age, color, height, size, happiness, considerate, loving, let you be yourself, peacefulness, sad, crying, upset, irrational, leader, follower, estranged, hated, or greatly loved spouse, liar, mentor, passionate, neglected you, poor, run -down, sage, shyster, unwise, upscale, or vengeful. If more than one person was walking with you, consider, what did the group have in common, e.g. classmates, family, ministers, pastors, rebels, teachers, or theologians? One or more of these characteristics will color the commitment relationship. The dreamer is also asked to consider where were you walking to, and/or what was being discussed, if anything? Again, the features highlighted, is (will be) major facets of that commitment. If necessary, see suggested course of action. (b) If dreamer was walking with an unknown person(s), your dream concerns your present sadness, the primary features highlighted, are a major part of your downheartedness. Dreamer, Jesus is concerned about your well-being, He truly cares for you; and is troubled over your discouraged and unhappy state of mind, for you are truly one of His. Your dream denotes that you have given up (or is giving up) on the cause of Christ, because of so many personal disappointments regarding your expectations of Christ Jesus and of others in leadership over you. One residual of this, is now you find yourself not knowing which way to go or what to do. Dreamer, comfort is being offered to you, but, due to your weakness in the faith, which is in Jesus Christ, you are unable or unwilling to receive it, possibly due to the attribute highlighted. Nonetheless, because of God's great faithfulness towards you, you are sent your dream. You are counseled to surround yourself with good company and good conversation. This is an excellent remedy against your current sadnes s and disappointments. Dreamer, when Christ's followers are disappointed and sad, they are encouraged to reach out to one another, in open and honest dialogue, and not to isolate, for two are better than one, especially in times of great sorrow. Venting will ease the pain, and by talking it over with others, you will find yourself having talked yourself, and perhaps others, into a better frame of mind. Moreover, you will find that when two or more share jointly in sorrow, they can become mutual comforters. Also, meditate upon Psalm 10 and other Psalms. Use the Psalms, to vent your frustration because of your enemies, as a form of supplication, as a venue to express your regret over sin, and to offer praise and thanksgiving to God. Additionally, one of God's messengers will be sent to you. They will lead and guide you through this time of downheartedness, make good use of this opportunity. Be aware of the stranger in your midst, and readily embrace him or her, for him or her ma y be that messenger. If necessary, see suggested course of action.

Animal (walking an animal): Your dream denotes that the dreamer is embracing the characteristics and is beginning to commit to a lifestyle associated with the animal depicted; see category: Animals, e.g. type of animal walked. Kept within context of your dream and the interpretation, other references highlighted may also be points of relevance. If necessary, see suggested course of action.

Baby Steps, Just Learning to Walk, Walking with another until they are able to walk on their own, or To Force to Walk

(to help or cause somebody to walk by supporting them somehow, or to force someone to walk, e.g. pushing, dragging): This dream has three meanings (choose one). (1) Baby Steps or Just learning to walk: Your dream denotes one, learning by experience that you may go on to perfection. Dreamer, there will be a strengthening of you, by Jesus, that you may be successful in your Christian walk and work, as well as, for spiritual warfare. You will be given strength and power for spiritual performances, above what you can do naturally, and against what you were in your past. It will be through Christ strengthening that you will be able to do all these things (also see Zechariah 10:12); therefore, be encouraged. (2) Walking with another until they are able to walk on their own: It is God, who has taught you these years to feel and display self-respect and esteem in your achievements. He has enabled you to walk in purpose. The person needing support to walk was you. If, within your dream, you recognized the person needing support to walk, or the person was indeed you, you sincerely realize that had it not been for God's support, you would not be the person you are today. If, however, the person was unknown, you do not acknowledge that it was God, who healed you (spiritually, emotionally, and/or physically). It would be beneficial for yo u to, honestly acknowledge to yourself that had it not been for God, who was there when you could not help you rself; you would not be where you are today. Your dream also denotes one who should explore the area of healing and evangelizing, especially to the poor, (see Ben Sira 29). You are gifted to be a healer, via an evangelistic ministry of some sort. Now that you are able to commit to something, consider embracing and learning from a healing ministry that you may learn, further, how to walk within your purpose. See suggested course of action. (3) To Force somebody to walk, e.g. pushing, dragging: Dreamer, you are encouraging another to embrace either the positive or the negative aspects of a certain way of life. With that, this choice has two parts (choose one). (a) If you were helping, or cause somebody to walk by supporting, bracing, or holding them in any way, this denotes you are encouraging someone to embrace the positive aspects of a certain lifestyle. Encouraging another to embrace the positive qualities of a certain lifestyle, this implies that the dreamer shows concern for the betterment of your community at large. You will (or already do) take part in teaching and helping others to reach for deeper, more spiritual and valuable things in life; improving their existence and inspiring them to make their dreams come true. You will now reap the rewards of such diligence, including rest and graceful surroundings, and some type of promotion is in sight. (b) If you were forcing someone to walk, by pulling, dragging, or pushing them along, this denotes you are encouraging someone to embrace the negative aspects of a certain lifestyle, even against their will. Your attention and time given to encouraging someone to embrace the unwise aspects of a lifestyle will change your way of living from this moment on. Encouraging another to embrace the negative traits of a certain lifestyle, your dream is a warning. Dreamer, you have a great lack of respect towards the lives of others. Don't be deceived, you will reap what you have sown. Your choices are hindering your success spiritual ly and literally. You are impairing your own spiritual growth, judgment, and health. Even to the cost of your own spiritual life, especially if no attempts to make amends and seek forgiveness because of your wrongdoings are made. Favorably, as your dream is a warning, a change that may affect positive results in your life and others is still possible. It is not too late to re- group and re-gather. Sincerely, amend the true intents and purposes of your actions. Bring to an end the abusing of your authority, influence, status, or connections. You are expected to respect your fellow man, hence, forcing others to do anything should cease. For, it is God, who leads and guides, and He does not impose Himself on individuals. Moreover, never aggressively take, push, or toil for any position, promotion, place, or seat of honor, or wealth, especially at the expense of others. Allow God to provide the way, knowing exaltation comes from the Lord. See suggested course of action.

Barefoot (walking): Dreamer, Christianity is a belief system that follows godliness, and is aimed at making you not only wiser, but also better. Thus, you are encouraged to walk soberly and holy that you may be ready, on time, and quick -minded regarding the business of God you've been destined to handle (1 Peter 1:13-16). Moreover, think soberly and be honest and open with yourself that you may be attentive, cautious, and on the alert against your spiritual triggers, those sins that set you back so easily and often, when demons come to push you. Be temperate and modest in appa rel, business, drinking, eating, and recreation, and in all your behavior demonstrate humility in your opinions and in practice. You must learn to discipline your mind, inner man, and affections, to restrain from extravagances, and allow your strength and quickness of mind to be used, fulfilling your obligations to God and His cause. Separate yourself from all that would hinder you, and go on, unwaver ing in obedience to God. Dreamer, you have a journey to go on, a walk-to-walk, spiritual warfare to fight, and a great work to do. By prudently embracing the principles and precepts of Jesus Christ, the One who has made you holy, via His blood sacri fice, all may be accomplished.

Cane or Crutch or Staff (any walking stick) or Injured, Hurt, or Wounded (walking injured): This dream has two meanings (choose one). (1) To dream of walking with some kind of stick, or to see one, refers to the difficult hardship you find yourself in at present. You've been in this situation before. Dreamer, be encouraged, God worked it out for your good in the past; He will do the same for you now. Providence would have your faith put on trial that God may be glorified in your relie f. Fear no evil, for God is with you. (2) Walking hurt, injured, or wounded: You have been offended, hurt, and/or upset over a violation inflicted upon you by someone. Moreover, there has yet to be any justice. Thus, you continue to be affected by gr eat emotional pain and internal conflict. This offense was demonically influenced. This is the enemy's efforts to turn you away from the One True God. Favorably, you are still able to commit to, and embrace, God's purposes for you, despite your emotional, physical, or spiritual injury. Dreamer, know that justice is being rendered, and God will remove this abominable offense from before you. God can, and will, check the violence of those who injure His people. As a result, you will find t he peace and rest needed, physically, emotionally, and spiritually; you will be comforted and healed. For he o r she who goes out weeping (hurt) carrying seed to sow, will return with songs of joy, carrying sheaves with them (Psalm 126). Sheaves figuratively imply the blessings of the Lord are coming into full fruition, bundled together, and will rest upon your life. The Lord your God will bless you in all the works of your hands. To be blessed: Gifts of God's grace, anything God freely gives you, absolution, the Holy Spirit, salvation, regeneration, eternal life, health, children, love of family, longevity, necessities, prosperity, and dominion over all that is yours; and all are parts of the supply of grace, and all are sanctified by the Lord, and technically belongs to Him. The result of this supply in your life will be peace. Your joy will be complete, be encouraged.

Children (walking with): Dreamer, parents that love the Lord God is primarily responsible for the religious education of their children (also see Deuteronomy 6:7). It is your ministry, and responsibility to encourage your children, to partici pate and get involved in activities that will draw them to Christ Jesus, His cause, and His Kingdom, that your Christian legacy might continue on to your generations (also see Proverbs 13:22; Ecclesiastes 7:11). That which is so graciously given unto us, we must pass on to those that come after us. Frequently and repeatedly, tell and teach God's principles, precepts, and statues to your children, and not your children only, but their friends, and all those that are in anyway under your care, mentorship, and/or teaching. God's word and ways are so very easy and straightforward that every parent, guardian, or mentor can instruct children in it. Try all ways of instilling His principles into their minds, and making His ways penetrate their hearts. God will enlighten you in your endeavors to perpetuate your Christian heritage.

Footsteps (Christ's Footsteps or another) or Walk One Mile in Someone Shoes: This dream has three meanings (choose one). (1) Walk in Christ's Footsteps (Jesus should be highlighted): Your dream denotes that the dreamer is teachable, and the lessons learned will enable the dreamer, through Christ Jesus, to defeat an enemy, and to overcome a personal issue. (2) Walk in someone else's shoes or in their footsteps: Dreamer, do not center or found your righteousness, or the lack thereof, on a baseless set of regimented rules and empty ritualism. Wearying yourself with the vanity of external performances, of which scripture calls works of the flesh will not merit God's acceptance of you (Philippians 3:3-9). Are you attempting to indebt God to you? God will be indebted to no man. See also Romans 4:4-25. Dreamer, we are justified not by works, but by grace (the free and unmerited favor and beneficence of God). Walk in this truth. See suggested course of action. (3) Walk one mile in someone shoes (one mile should be highlighted): The dreamer is counseled to adopt and practice a spirit of empathy and compassion, before judging anyone (e.g. condemnatory, critical, derogatory, disapproving, harsh, negative, scornful, or uncomplimentary in your thoughts or speaking aloud). For with the same judgment you have judged others, so it will be rendered back unto you (Matthew 7:1-5). See suggested course of action.

City (walking around in a city): Dreamer, your prosperity and adversity, as well as persons within your life, are set one over against the other that your arrogance and pride may not be secure, nor your unhappiness be overly despairing. Thus, there is a time set for your barrenness, despondency, emptiness, obscurity, and/or unhappiness to end. God's providence shall again smile upon you, He shall cause His indignation towards you to cease, and things will run their course as before, or as is predestined. Dreamer, you are encouraged to begin rebuilding, using your best skills to recover. It is counseled that you make better use of your skills, than you have formerly. Make sure your activities are allowable, innocent, ethical, moderate, mod est, and sober. Moreover, your increase shall be devoted to God, to His honor, and used for His service. Do not hoard up prosperity, as you've done in the past, to be the subject of your pride and the support of your carnal doings. Additionally, two questions to weigh and journal. (1) What city were you walking about, where were you? How do you feel about that particular place in your awaked life (e.g. do you like or dislike the place)? Were you angry, comfortable, frighten, lost, s ecure about being in the place within your dream? It will be those feelings you will experience throughout your process of rebuilding. (2) What pleasure could you have had in you sabotaging your relationship with Christ and/or His people, thus causing a memorial that was intended as a remembrance of you, as a celebration of your life and work, to perish with it? Favorably, this too will be restored.

Competitively Walking (competitions based on walking, e.g. cakewalk or competitive walking, as in a race): This dream has two meanings (choose one). (1) Your dream was sent to demonstrate grace, via a warning and notification; thus, this choice has two parts (both apply). (a) The warning: Your attention and time given to a certain lifestyle will change your way of living. You have recently adopted a bourgeois mentality. This mentality is concerned only with your personal comfort, material wealth, and status, at any expense. Now, having in yourself nothing that you respect more than power and greed, you are willing to sacrifice all, God, principle, family, and friend, to the image or idol of vanity. Your new way is based on exploring alternatives to God's righteous principles, as well as, creating a sense of unity with the wickedness around you. This mentality sacrifices children, family, and morality to the hollowness of satisfying immoral desires and appetites. All carried out, with the hope of finding happiness by pacifying jealously and covetousness. The selling-out of yourself over to immorality, allowing wickedness to prevail in your home, and devaluing those you should be protecting and nurturing are all principles based on values that are not only vile, but also increasingly unstable. This way cries out against godly ethics, and the end results, offends any sense of godliness. Your recklessness can be remedied by prayer and heartfelt repentance to Jesus and to individuals affected by your actions, in the form of an apology (if possible). Repentance is seeking pardon and expressing sincere feelings of regret and brokenness for having done something awry and/or for having hurt someone, see 2 Corinthians 7:10, 11, Deuteronomy 6:10-15; 11:10-28, Galatians 5:7-26. To individuals, a phone call or a letter of apology is a good place to start. To Jesus pray, Psalm 51, this followed by appropriate application of wisdom, can conceivably avert some of the repercussions of your choices. (b) The notification: Your time of action on behalf of the Kingdom of God is quickly approaching. Your days of preparation and grounding are upon you. Your choices will make your time of grounding advantageous or wearisome. It will be up to you. You are free to do as you please; you still have personal liberty. But if your true intent is on doing God's will, reaping genuine prosperity, experiencing authentic joy, and most importantly inheriting eternal life, you will have to practice restricting yourself in all things (weaning yourself from sensual appetites). This includes your activities, associations, friendships, partying, and your lack of Christian fellowship. See suggested course of action. (2) Cakewalk: It is suggested that the dreamer offer God a "first-fruit" offering of your finances, and give an offering of acknowledgment (financial) to the senior priest of your church. This is symbolically acknowledging your dependence upon God for your daily bread. Moreover, this offering, by faith, is expressly meant to open streams of income for you personally that you may again prosper, as well as cause the blessings of the Lord to rest upon your house (Ezekiel 44:30). God's blessings: Gifts of God's grace, anything God freely gives you, absolution, the Holy Spirit, salvation, regeneration, eternal life, heal th, children, love of family, longevity, necessities, prosperity, and dominion over all that is yours; and all are parts of the supply of grace, and all are sanctified by the Lord, and technically belongs to Him. The result of this supply in your life will be peace.

In addition, the following are common words, expressions, usages, (e.g. slang or clichés), or a 'probable' that are metaphorically represented by cakewalk:

- There is something that is very easy to do or to achieve
- There is something that should be free of ceremony, unofficial, and casual

Danger or Darkness (walking in the midst of danger, distress, trouble, or in the dark): This dream has two meanings (choose one). (1) Walking in the midst of danger, distress, or trouble, dreamer, although, you are a good and great person, your spirit is ready to sink and fail, because of the storms of life you've encountered lately. Dreamer, know that God takes care of His children when they are oppressed, and you are His child. Hold on, God will revive and comfort you, and make things le ss oppressive, and more cheerful. "Divine consolations have enough in them to revive us even when we walk in the midst of troubles and are ready to die away for fear" (Matthew Henry Commentary). Dreamer, better days are before you. Encourage yourself with this hope. (2) To walk in darkness: Your dream comes as a stern rebuke and as a message of grace. Dreamer, there are many bitter and poisonous consequences of your irresponsible behavior. Your ways are perverse and wicked, paths that are devious. Ways that have caused you to walk in darkness gladly. While in defiance against God and the teachings of Christ, you exalt your wisdom above the Creator. A bold and daring seducer, you mouth empty, boastful words; discrediting the Creator's wise and sensible guidelines for living life, on this side of eternity, as humanly and sanely as possible; and in harmony with His provision for life on the other side of eternity, in heaven. You have become contrary to God's righteous precepts, for darkness has blinded you to truth. Dreamer, after all this time, still you hesitate to give God you heart, mind, and soul. If you love, and need Him then why won't you give Him you? Yes, He understands and can handle all your doubts and fears. When wisdom enters your heart and knowledge and truth becomes sweet to your soul, discretion will pro tect you, and understanding will guard you. Favorably, although you walk in darkness, the Lord will be your light. Own up to your wrongdoings to God and others, and make amends to those you've hurt and/or offended. As God has delivered you in the past because of His faithfulness, so He will deliver you now, only repent and allow His Word to be a light unto your path that the work of purification and sanctification may be complete within you. Prayer and repentance is the first step. Repentance is seeking pardon and expressing sincere feelings of regret and brokenness for having done something awry and/or for having hurt someone. To Jesus pray, Psalm 51. To individuals, a phone call or a letter of apology is a good place to start, if appropriate. This coupled with prayer and fasting, and followed by appropriate application of wisdom and Jesus will meet you. Have faith in this.

Otherwise, unfit for Kingdom business, you will become disqualified for the prize (Matthew 22.1-14, 1 Corinthians 9:27). If necessary, see suggested course of action.

"Do Not Walk" Sign: Dreamer, your dream is to be taken as a warning; there is a need to change your mind about a binding commitment at this time. There is potential for a tragedy of some sort, due to a strong commitment to a particular philosophy, lifestyle, person, place, or organization. Thus, the dreamer is forewarned about a decision you are making regarding a particular commitment. Moreover, see Proverbs 11:15, 17:18, and Ecclesiastes 5:1-6. See suggested course of action.

Fast or Quickly or Determined: Dreamer, although, with much thought and inner turmoil, you are choosing to embrace a certain lifestyle, and you are strong-minded and fixed regarding your decisions, you do not know or have all the facts necessary to make an informed decision regarding that commitment. Thus, your dream is a warning to the dreamer, you are moving too fast regarding this commitment. Questions, are your choices honoring Jesus Christ as your Lord and Savior? Is your lifestyle, ethical, morally clean, honorable? If you are not embracing Jesus, so that you might not be under His precepts, because your decisions do not concur with His principles morally then you are forfeiting the honor and privileges that come with His Kingdom. Dreamer, re-think fully your decisions, looking deeper into the spiritual implications of your decisions. Seek wise and honest advice from others if necessary. Plans fail for lack of counsel, but with many advisers, they succeed (Proverbs 15:22 NIV). See suggested course of action.

Fire or Hot Coals (walking through fire or on hot coals): This dream has two meanings (choose one). (1) Fire (walking through or in the midst of fire): Fire denotes purification by means of divine discipline (the Lord's chastening, correction that leads to instruction and reformation); as well, it denotes God's presence. Dreamer, although you are in the midst of hard trials and tribulations, you are being purified spiritually. Whatever is going on, wherever you are, God's Spirit is there with you. You are not alone; neither should you feel that way. Do not falter, for He is there at all times. Learn from your experience and mature. All things will be made beautiful at the proper time. See suggested course of action. (2) To dream of walking on Hot Coals, rocks: Your dream is a dire warning to the dreamer. Dreamer, it is imperative that you govern your desires, lusts, and passions with wisdom. You have a journey to go on, a walk-to-walk, spiritual warfare to fight, and a great work to do. There is a possible threat of physical devastation if you continue pining after that which is forbidden and potentially deadly. Dreamer, you have settled for a more voluptuary lifestyle. How can you say, "I have great desires and needs, thus my physical enjoyment and sexual gratification are my primary concerns? The child thinks that all that appears pleasant and tasty belongs to them and that he or she has the right to partake of any and everything. Consideration of others, and/or of the resulting outcome is unfamiliar to him or her. They will never consider the results of their behavior, nor how their behavior will affect others. This type of consideration is not within a child's mind-set, because he or she is a child. As the immature child takes what they want, when they want it, and believes that it's theirs, and that they do have a right to whatever it is, so does the spiritually immature, do what they want, when they want, and believe that it's OK, using grace as a cover for sin. Dreamer, change cannot begin with this kind of mind-set. Rather say, "I have great desire but what can I do, since my Father in Heaven forbids me from involving myself in such acts". Whenever you partake of anything you are required to pause and ask yourself if that particular activity is permitted or not; and even if it is permitted, you must inquire whether you should participate or involve yourself in it at that moment. This will help train you to pause briefly between the moment that your desire demands to be satisfied and the moment that you literally satisfy it or not. For you already know that desire causes you to act compulsively even when you know you will regret your actions later. Thus, that pause is the decisive moment. It will transform your tendency, your desire, into an act of will. The will is what leads to action after your desire passes through the filter of your thought. By prudently embracing the principles and precepts of Jesus Christ, the One who has made you holy, via His blood sacrifice, all may be accomplished. As well, wisdom is necessary for managing and improving your life; ask and it shall be given you (James 1:5). For it is the answer, antidote, cure, medicine, remedy, solution to your particular life's issue. Wisdom will not allow you to conceal, cover up, explain away, gloss over, misrepresent, sweep under the carpet, or suppress God's truth regarding your lifestyle choices and the obvious outcome of such activity. Wisdom will prolong your life. Dream er, it is understood that life is not fair concerning a million issues. For example, it's not fair that baby molesters and killers are allowed to prosper in their wickedness. It's not fair that many people who do evil seem to thrive while the righteous o ften are trampled down. It's not fair that some people are born much better looking and popular than others are. It's not fair that dictators can commit heinous acts on innocent citizens of their country and not be held legally accountable; nor is it fai r that some people are very rich, while others are very poor, and the list can go on forever. Dreamer, do not be covetous of the wicked supposedly prosperity, namely the illusion of them prospering in their wickedness, for their end is neigh, and possibl e eternal. God wants to purify you that you may fulfill the righteous purpose, for which, you are designed. Consider your dre am as sufficient warning. See suggested course of action.

Hiking, Leisurely Walking, Mall Walking, Rambling, Strolling, or Window Shopping (e.g. walking for amusement, bliss, contentment, diversion, delight, enjoyment, fun, gratification happiness, joy, leisure, pleasure, recreation, or relaxation): First, dreamer, anticipate with confidence and joyful pleasure, an expectation of eternal salvation. Second, as well, being full of faith, know that the evil and fear you've experienced recently (within the last three years) has affected a better you, an d if you have not experience any evil or fear, you will very shortly, and the experience will effect a better and stronger you spirituality. Example of the evil and an example of fear are as follows. (1) Examples of the evil are, broken relationship, suffering from grievous physical pain, threat of death, mental health issues, intense affliction, troubled by loss, very unhappy, full of misery, or you've had to put up with something or somebody very unpleasant. You've gotten to the point where you feel discouraged, feeling that your faith has been in vain. (2) Examples of the fear are, when you are afraid, insecure, impatient, confused, filled with worry, uneasy and unsure. When you hesitate, is full of apprehension, when your thoughts forecast only doom and gloom, when panic and stress comes, and despair and depression find you, when you are restless, frightful, full of dread, anxious, nervous, and when you feel hopeless. You will find this demon (the spirit of fear) in eve ry phobia. Read and understand Romans 8:15, 2 Timothy 1:7. Question to journal: What would it feel like if all of your fears were suddenly released from you at one time? Pause and feel that. Dreamer, by God's power, a way out of no way will be made for you, and your state of affairs turned around. Somehow, God will make a way for you. Jesus will come and see about you, and keep your faith regarding what you've believed God for; you will experience a miracle. Joy shall then be revealed, rest shall appear, and healing shall descend, disease shall withdraw, anxiety, anguish and crying shall pass from you; gladne ss will happen. Learn not to be afraid of darkness, but to stand bold in its face, for the greater one lives within you, and that sp irit of fear that has intimidated you will flee. Have faith and hope in Jesus Christ, who is the source of the things you' re hoping for and the author of your faith. For, when God reverse your drama, misfortune, or tragedy, you will testify that the Lord has done great things for you, and you will be glad. Your situation will change and He will give you a new song in your h eart. You will sing a new song. Wait on the Lord, for He is faithful to come, and again I say wait on the Lord.

House (walking in or outside a house): Dreamer, be careful to live a blameless life, with a pure heart, acting conscientiously and with integrity, with all sincerity. Do not create or adopt a false appearance, feigning purity before God and/or people, this is spiritual suicide. Although you've been met with much hardship on the one hand, yet on the other, you've had many wonderful deliverances and favors bestowed upon you. Your dream is one of them. Dreamer, joy and pain, are like sunshine and rain, one is set over against the other, for balance. Therefore, testify gratefully of God's beneficen t hand upon your life, sing of His mercy and grace (the free and unmerited favor and beneficence of God) shown you, and be content wherever you find yourself now. This too shall pass. So make the best of it, and learn from it.

Inspecting or Measuring (walking over or along to measure or inspect, e.g. using a walking measure): Dreamer, you will receive a gracious visit from one of God's messengers, possibly a stranger.

250

Be hospitable to him or her. This person has co me to confirm a promise made to you by God. Your assets and revenue will become enlarged, and it's time for you to purchase land and/or to build. If the land or place you walked over or along to measure or inspect, is actually known by you in your awaked life, God is giving you that land. If the land or place was unknown, it's time for you to choose a piece of property for sale, and to build on it, for God is giving it to you.

Lost or Wandering (walking around lost, wandering): Your dream denotes one who is a spiritual vagabond; you wander from place to place, having no permanent place of worship, no shepherd looking out for your soul, no accountability from the Body of Christ, and no close fellowship with other Christians. Dreamer there needs to be a transformation, a complete reversal, in your behavior, via prayer and heartfelt repentance to Jesus, and a reclamation of your thinking and beliefs. Repentance is seeking pardon and expressing sincere feelings of regret and brokenness for having done something awry and/or for having hurt someone, see 2 Corinthians 7:10, 11. To Jesus pray, Psalm 51, this followed by appropriate application of wisdom, can conceivably avert some of the repercussions of your choices. Additionally, your dream comes to alert the dreamer of a definite probationary and testing period decreed within your life. This can be a testing by trial (e.g. a wilderness experience); by humiliation and servitude (Judges 13:1; Acts 13:21, 22); or by waiting (Acts 7:23-30). This probationary and testing season points to grace, leads to repentance, and ends in revival and renewal. Dreamer, when you have settled in one place, allowing yourself to be accountable to the leaders of that ministry, give yourself completely to the cause and Kingdom of God, via that ministry, and having made good friends with other Christians, especially of that fellowship, your probationary period will end. It is suggested that you remain within that ministry, and committed to service, for at least seven years, n o matter your circumstances. Compassionately, God's provisions for you will not cease during this time, and His miracles and mercies are to be an everlasting testimony, as encouragement for you to trust in Him at all times. If necessary, see suggested course of action.

Maze or Walking in a Circle (walking through or in a maze of some kind): This dream has two meanings (choose one). (1) If dreamer was walking through or in a maze of some kind: Dreamer, your purpose is to teach others how to walk a walk o f faith in Christ Jesus. If you sincerely do not know that you have teaching abilities, your dream comes to effect awareness within the dreamer as to who and what you are purposed to be. Your teaching ministry should be in operation at this moment in time. You have been (or should have been) well instructed in the doctrine of the gospel, to be reasonably proficient in teaching others by now. God takes notice of the time and help you have been given for gaining knowledge of His Word. Those who have a good understanding of the gospel and of spiritual knowledge should be teachers to others. To whom much is given, much is expected. If necessary, see suggested course of action. (2) If dreamer was walking around in a circle, your dream suggests that there is reason to think that you have missed your way, your direction. Choices you are making at present are not based on wisdom, but on irrational and rash thinking. The dreamer is advised not to proceed rashly. You are counseled to pause and seek wisdom, and carefully find other means to proceed in a wiser manner. Ponder the paths of yo ur feet, and seek out well-proven guiding principles and strategies that guarantee you reaching your journey's end. Seek out the wisdom, the observations, and experiences of those who have proven themselves wise, and with fruit to prove it, especially in the area of concern. It is recommended that you consult your elders (e.g. parents, pastor, church elders, other Christian leaders within a ministry, a counselor). Utilize every opportunity to discourse with those about yourself, your beliefs, mor ality. Stay away from dialogue not based on the revealed Word of God, and any secret or veiled mysteries, or matters of conflict, controversy, disputation, or strife, but talk of the plain truths and laws of God, and the things that belong to peace. Be u neasy until you have reached satisfaction. See suggested course of action.

Pacing (walk back and forth): Dreamer, if the Lord has strengthened you, physically, emotionally, and spiritually, then you must be busy about your Father's business. Start doing something that will edify the Kingdom of God and His cause. Dreamer, you must be active and busy in the work of the Lord, walking back and forth as diligent, hardworking, conscientious, and energetic people do, losing no time, and letting no opportunity slip by. Moreover, whatever you do in word or deed, you must do in the name of the Lord Jesus, that you receive not your strength in vain. Doing all that you do in dependence upon Him. Whoever claims to live in Him must walk as Jesus did (1 John 2:6).

Pathway, Walkway, or Route for Walking, or Primrose Path (e.g., Alley, Boardwalk, Causeway, Catwalk, Corridor, Footpath, Platform, Passageway, Pathway, or Sidewalk): The path, walkway, route, denotes your manner of life. Was the path well-manicured, kept up; or was it dirty, littered with garbage or trash? Was it covered with graffiti, if so what did the graffiti depict? The condition of the pathway or route, coupled with one of the following, will give you a better understand ing of what your dream is implying. See one of the following:

To make a path, walkway, or route, no matter how (e.g. walking, running, driving, or plowing): Your dream advises the dreamer to make very good use of the opportunity that is presented before you, and to be responsible. This is an opportunity for you to become a trailblazer. Further, you are counseled to regulate your lifestyle and to conduct yourself in a way that will leave an honorable legacy of your life. See suggested course of action.

Walking down a straight and narrow path, walkway, route, or one that was well manicured and/ or kept up: Your dream symbolizes the dreamer's walk of righteousness and obedience to God; as well, you've come through great trials and tribulations. God has bottled up every one of your tears. You will be recompensed accordingly for your diligent work towards the Kingdom of God. Things are going to get easier and better.

Walking along, or on, a crooked path, walkway, route, or one that was dirty, littered with garbage or trash, or covered with graffiti: Dreamer, you have made your paths crooked because of bitterness and an unforgiving spirit. Your thoughts are thoughts of iniquity, you do not know the way of peace, and there is no justice in your tracks. With you come conflict, confrontation, drama, and hostilities. You create confusion and havoc wherever you go. You are bitter, brutal, unforgiving, and an enemy of righteous people. The guilt of many righteous persons injured (emotionally or spiritually) by you, requires justice, thus your dream. You will now begin to experience divine discipline (the Lord's chastening, correction that leads to instruction and reformation). That your soul might be saved, peace will be taken from you, you will lose your place (e.g. assignment, dwelling, job, locality, opportunity, position, rank, responsibility, seat, or status), and people will be allowed to destroy your reputation and to create havoc within your life. Conflicts, confrontations, difficulties, and hostilities will become constant elements in your life. Dreamer, it is counseled that you take each change, turnaround, and up and down, as a stern rebuke of you by God, that you might become wiser and made clean (also see Proverbs 9:8-12). This rebuke is only a precursor of even worse judgments that will come later, if you do not abandoned and change your ways. God is not condemning you, He's holding out His Hand of Hope, giving you an opportunity to start anew. Let the wicked forsake his way, God wants to pardon (Isaiah 55:7-13, Matthew 7:17-23, Luke 6:43-45). Dreamer, if you earnestly change your ways, you will be healed from your present condition and pardoned from the guilt previously mentioned. Prayer and repentance is the first step.

Repentance is seeking pardon and expressing sincere feelings of regret and brokenness for having done something awry and/or for having hurt someone. To Jesus pray, Psalm 51. This coupled with prayer and fasting, and followed by appropriate application of wisdom and Jesus will meet you. Have faith in this. See suggested course of action.

Primrose Path (to walk down): To walk down or lead someone down the primrose path denotes a course of action, option, or way, considered to be the route to ruin or degeneration. Although your choices seem to make for a more enjoyable, easy way of life, or a more pleasurable lifestyle, they will inevitably lead to ruin, deterioration, collapse, falling apart, worsening, or relapse. See suggested course of action.

Patrolling ("Walk the Beat" or patrol): If dreamer was patrolling in some manner, you already know that you are a teacher of righteousness. If you choose not to teach, your dream comes as an alert. For sure, bitterness and jealously will cover you, for, they cover all who choose not to walk in their gifting competently. Those who do not respect the opportunities placed before them shall have the things that support their peace taken away. If no action, commitment, or obligation to ministry, is heeded at this time, you may find yourself similar to the servant spoken of in the parable who buried his gift (Matthew 25:15). If your designated service is given to another, so will the prosperity that is attached to that service, be given to that person also, and for you, jealously will be your recompense. You are forfeiting purpose for foolishness, blaming your slackness on God or on others, believing that others are standing in your way. This is not true; the fulfillment of your pur pose is your responsibility. Moreover, it is a sin for Christians that are mature in age, and standing, in the church, to be spiritual children and babes in understanding. It is not good to continue in a spiritual childish state; you should endeavor to pass t he infant state. No one who lives on milk, being still an infant, is acquainted with the teaching about righteousness. See Hebrews 5:11-6:2. Repent, and God will deliver you from that which is wicked, that you may walk before God in the light of life (Psalm 56:13). If necessary, see suggested course of action.

Single File (walking single file): Your dream was sent to encourage the dreamer. There is no need to worry over a matter. You have lived in an orderly fashion, and you will go on prosperously. Moreover, a particular situation, namely a very close relationship, will turn out well. Additionally, if applicable, the things you (or a close significant other) are now considered guilty of will be counted as nothing.

Sleepwalking, Blindly Walking, or Walking in "Fog" (finding your way around obscurely): Your dream was sent to demonstrate grace, via a warning. Dreamer, the man or woman who walks obscurely, does not understand, does not know, or is not clear, where he or she is going spiritually (see 1 John 1:5-2:17). It is necessary of you to answer the following questions. Where am I going? What is my purpose? What is wrong and what is right as they relate to morality? Do you desire to acquire, do, get, or receive things in an appropriate manner and ethical way? Are you governed by what benefits you, your own interest, and not by reason or justice? Am I in line for heaven? Dreamer, this sort of dream denotes that you know not, desire not, and do not, because you will not understand. There is none so blind, as those that will not see. Spiritual blindness and deception, go hand in hand, and have deadly, eternal consequences. Do you care to understand your God given responsibility? Then you must put forth effort to study it? You have confused your own conscience, and so you walk on in darkness, not knowing, nor caring, what you do or where you go. This kind of mentality is concerned only with your personal comfort, material wealth, and status, at any expense. Now, having in yourself nothing that you respect more than greed, you are willing to sacrifice all, God, principle, family, and friend, to the image or idol of vanity. Your new way is based on exploring alternatives to God's righteous principles, as well as, creating a sense of unity with the wickedness around you. This way sacrifices children, family, and morality to the hollowness of satisfying immoral desires and appetites. All carried out with the hope of finding happiness by pacifying jealously and covetousness. The selling-out of yourself over to immorality, allowing wickedness to prevail in your home, devaluing those you should be protecting and nurturing, while closing your eyes to it all, are all principles based on values that are not only vile, but also increasingly unstable. This way cries out against godly ethics, and the end results, offends any sense of godliness. Those that walk on in darkness are walking on into everlasting darkness. Your recklessness can be remedied by prayer and heartfelt repentance to Jesus and to individuals affected by your actions, in the form of an apology (if possible). Repentance is seeking pardon and expressing sincere feelings of regret and brokenness for having done something awry and/or for having hurt someone, see 2 Corinthians 7:10, 11, Deuteronomy 6:10-15; 11:10-28). To individuals, a phone call or a letter of apology is a good place to start. To Jesus pray, Psalm 51, this followed by appropriate application of wisdom, can conceivably avert some of the repercussions of your choices. This is what is called leaving a blessing behind. See suggested course of action.

In addition, the following is a common word, expression, or usage (e.g. slang or cliché), or a 'probable' that is metaphorically represented by blindly walking:

- **"Blind Leading the Blind":** Denotes that the person in charge of the situation, possibly the dreamer, knows no more about it than those whom he or she is leading. Uninformed and incompetent people are leading those who are similarly incapable (Matthew 15:14). It is suggested that you seek competent people to guide you into the best way to go, and not surround yourself with those who agree with your thoughts and careless decision. See suggested course of action.

Staggering, Unsteady, or Wobbling (walking as if about to fall): The fruit of your behavior is akin to talebearers, slanderers, false teachers, and/or deceivers who, by pretending they care about the underprivileged, lead men away from the truth. Your ideas have opened (or will open) a dark gate that will lead to demonic oppression, demon possession, or possible suicide. For sure, bitterness and jealously will cover you, for, they cover all who choose not to walk in their gifting competently. Those who do not respect the opportunities placed before them shall have the things that support their peace taken away. If no action, commitment, or obligation to ministry, is heeded at this time, you may find yourself similar to the servant spoken of in the parable who buried his gift (Matthew 25:15). If your designated service is given to another, so will the prosperity that is attached to that service, be given to that person also, and for you, jealously will be your recompense. You are forfeiting purpose for foolishness, blaming your slackness on God or on others, believing that others are standing in your way. This is not true. Change your mind that you may have life, and it will be abundant, even as your soul prospers. Repent, and Jesus will deliver you from death and your feet from stumbling, that you may walk before God in the light of life (Psalm 56:13). See suggested course of action.

Tightrope or "Walking a Thin Line": This represents one who needs to deal cautiously with a dangerously unstable, unsteady, uncertain, or insecure situation. The information presented is not well founded, having been based on uncertain premises and unwarranted assumptions. This situation involves a choice or compromise. See suggested course of action.

Torch (walking with a torch): To dream of walking with a torch, dreamer, your dream is a stern warning to the dreamer. See Isaiah 50:11. You no longer trust in God. Arrogantly bold, and conceited, you trust in your own righteousness; and have begun embracing erroneous teachings. Thus, you place your happiness in your worldly possessions and enjoyments, and not in the favor of God. Dreamer, those that make this world their comfort, and their own righteousness their confidence, will certainly meet with bitter disappointment. A godly person's way may be melancholy, but his or her end shall be peace and everlasting light. A wicked man's way may be pleasant, but his end will be utter darkness. Your choices will lead you to be counted amongst those illustrated in Matthew 7:21-23. Dreamer, at this crossroad in your life, it is counseled that you do as the apostle Paul, and count all that you know, all that has brought you to this point, to be worthless (Philippians 3:8). Favorably, there is still hope and time for you to recognize the immorality you've embraced, and go on from here. Dreamer, seize this opportunity to sincerely repent, and to denounce trusting in your own righteousness and erroneous teachings. See suggested course of action.

Trampling or Treading (walking on others): You are without a doubt a born leader. However, as with power comes the opportunity to abuse that power. Thus, your dream was sent to warn and counseled the dreamer to; "in no uncertain terms", tolerate ill treatment or abuse of those under your leadership by you or others. If dreamer begins to evidence traits of an abusive leader, one who mistreats those appointed to serve within the realm of your authority, tyrannically. Your ill treatment of others and misuse of your authority will cause your divine given anointing to cease, and you will lose the respect of those you've been leading. They will leave your ministry. Others will see you as egotistical, unethical, and wickedly ambitious, and they will not be far off the mark. Hence, dreamer, you need to, seriously consider who you are as a leader, do you have traits, at present, that present as abusive, egotistical, and unethical, and possibly make the changes, now, in your behavior towards others and to subdue those negative traits. Dreamer, know your dark side and reject embracing it. For, when in a rut, you are abusive, enraged, and out of control. You then become unpleasant, intolerant of others, demeaning and very sarcastic in your expression; imposing stress on your relationship with the Lord, as well as, with others. Seek Jesus truth, and honest advice from other godly leaders, otherwise, although appointed as leader over God's people, you will shipwreck. See 1 Samuel 11-28, the story of King Saul. See suggested course of action.

In addition, the following is a common word, expression, or usage (e.g. slang or cliché), or a 'probable' that is metaphorically represented by treading, trampling, or walking on someone:

- One who is ignoring another's rights or feelings, see suggested course of action.

Trap (walk into a trap): Your dream is to make known to the dreamer that others have secretly set snares for you. God knows who they are, and He knows where you are. Because of others, you may be quite overwhelmed within, and at a loss. Possibly, your spirit has grown faint, and you're ready to sink under the burden of despair, fear, and grief, becaus e of the tricks and games people have played. Dreamer, take comfort in knowing that deliverance is being worked out for you. God knows your sincerity of heart, the rightful way you have walked, and that you are not like those who would hurt or trouble yo u. The same traps others have set for you will ensnare them, and their wickedness will be exposed for all to see.

Unable to Walk: Your dream implies some form of idolatry within the life of the dreamer. Idolatry is "foreign service", any act that expresses devotion or fanatical admiration to something or someone other than Adonai Elohim. You worship money and image, in all of its forms (e.g. desiring to be someone you're not, worship of materialistic things, personalities, self, vanity, and/or a literal statue). The dreamer's extreme or obsessive admiration or fanatical devotion to a person, animal, place, or organization is idolatrous. You even attribute your prosperity to the power of demons. With that said there is a great need for prayer and heartfelt repentance to Jesus and to individuals affected by your actions, in the form of an apology (if possible). Repentance is seeking pardon and expressing sincere feelings of regret and brokenness for having done something awry and/or for having hurt someone, see 2 Corinthians 7:10, 11. To individuals, a phone call or a letter of apology is a good place to start. To Jesus pray, Psalm 51. Dreamer, God is a forgiving God; therefore, grace (the free and unmerited favor and beneficence of God) is extended and repentance is possible at this moment. Moreover, with persistent hard work and effort in correcting your dangerous mindset and lifestyle, you can again remember Jesus, and once more respect His principles. Seek counsel from godly individuals, you will find wisdom with them. Dreamer, without repentance and change, your mindset will cause you, eventually, to forget God, and you will forget, only to remember Him again, with regret, on your deathbed. Your dream was sent to encourage remembrance. God wants you to consider, and remember from this day forward, as a preservative against future idolatry the following. Of all the things you've done to acquire wealth, and/or to remain youthful or popular, did any of it, bring you freedom within, authentic and lasting happiness, exemption from accusations, blame, harm, reproach, or unpleasant consequences? Omitting God and His ways from your life is to omit true happiness, health, joy, and peace. Now, having gone through, and experienced, the repercussions of covetousness, greed, vanity, and the worship of materialism, your mindset should have changed. Beware; therefore, that you no longer imitate the doings of others, and do not fear them, lest the fear of them be allowed to seize you. When you see them lifted-up and praised by others, say in your heart, only the Lord should be adored, and remember God is watching you and only He can demand an account of your soul. Dreamer, have no other gods before God (see Matthew 22:37-40). If necessary, see suggested course of action.

Walk By, Pass By, or Sail By: Your dream suggests that the dreamer set aside ten days, and those ten days are to be to you a time of sacrifice, a time of sacrificial fasting, a giving of yourself, and an offering. Concerning, sacrificial fasting, do not eat any breads, pasta, or potatoes for ten days straight. Regarding, giving of yourself, visit the elderly, sick, and/or wid ows, a total of ten days. About, an offering, you are to give a part of your increase to the designated leader of your church as a sacrificial offering unto the Lord, within ten days. By these, after completion, within ten days you will be freed from a specific bondage within your life. Specifically that which has attacked, harassed, or troubled you for a very long time. Not only freed, you will never have to deal with that particular issue again, and you will be able to embrace your new freedom with a humbled heart, and a fresh perspective.

Walk Away, Walk Off, or Walk Out of (e.g. Desert, Leave, Quit, Turn your Back On): Your dream denotes you are leaving a space, or letting go of someone or something that you may go forward to a place where you will be used to minister to others. Dreamer you are entering into a season within your life that will prepare you spiritually for the visitation of the Lord in your individual life. During this time, you will experience His love and presence, as you've never known it before. For, He is saying to you, "I will teach you godly wisdom". You will receive direct insight of divine truth. You will come to know, without a doubt, that God is the true source of your strength and wisdom, and He is your sufficiency. As a result, a greater love for self, family, and others will begin to manifest, affecting wholeness within your life. Be available to Him and seize the moments and opportunities as they are presented, especially an opportunity for you to advance your education, with a focus on teaching.

In addition, the following are common words, expressions, or usages (e.g. slang or cliché), or a 'probable' that is metaphorically represented by walking:

- **"Walking Papers" (to see the words "walking papers" on papers should be highlighted):** Your dream points to one who will be formally discharged, fired from a job, or dismissed from military service. See suggested course of action.
- **"Walking Tall" (appeared taller than what you literally are):** Dreamer, those who walk in pride God is able to humble, and He will humble you. Until you sincerely and humbly remember that God alone worked deliverances within your life.

It was not any deeds through your own efforts. For any effort that you may have put forth, the strength to perform that effort was given you by God. Unfortunately, God is planning a disaster against you, a calamity. He will use someone that you will not be able to overcome, until you confess your sins of arrogance, pride, and self-righteousness to Him and admit it to yourself, and turn from those ways completely. Fortunately, this disaster will effect within you humility that you might be saved. On the other hand, if you recognized, now, your transgressions and repent, calamity can be averted. The choice is up to you, you can do it easy (choosing to repent and change now), or you can do it hard (repentance and change being worked within you, at the cost of great loss and pain). Those who walk humbly and uprightly will enter into peace; they will find rest. Choosing how to walk is up to you. See suggested course of action.

Suggested Course of Action

Question to consider and journal, did your dream depict any symbols that alludes to, the dreamer will make the necessary changes, spiritually, emotionally, and/or physically to affect a more positive outcome? If changes are initiated, your dreams will change. Notwithstanding, God's prophets, who gave you fair warnings of approaching judgment, via preaching, teaching, and prophesying, told you only what they had received from the Lord. The warnings of God approaching judgments, were not in vain or to amuse you. Oftentimes, God prepares trouble to deal with sin in our lives, and usually it is with our own hands that we are entangled. Nothing, but prayer and heartfelt repentance to Jesus and to individuals affected by your actions, in the form of an apology (if possible), can disentangle you. Note; God will not remove the affliction He has sent until it has done its work and accomplished that for which He sent it. However, if you humble yourself, confess and forsake your sins, then th at which He sent, namely the affliction, will have accomplished its purpose, and then, and not until then, will the afflictions be removed from your life, and you delivered in love and mercy.

Dreamer, what does the Lord your God ask of you but to fear the Lord your God, and no one or nothing else; to walk in all His ways, to love Him, to serve the Lord your God with all your heart and with all your soul. Teach His ways, His principles and precepts to your family, cause your family table, in your home, to be one of prayer and bible study, talking about Jesus when you sit at home, when you walk, when you lie down, and when you get up. If you carefully follow His wisdom and His instructions, that is given to you this day, to love the Lord your God, to walk in all His ways and to hold fast to Him, the Lord will establish you as His holy people, and you shall have what you ask. Only declare from this day forward that the Lord is your God and that you will walk in and keep His ways, and that you will obey Him with all your heart. Love the Lord your God, then you will live and increase, and the Lord your God will bless your land. Note, you will be tested to see whether you keep the ways of the Lord and walk in them (Deuteronomy 10:12, 11:19, 22, 19:9, 26:17; Joshua 22:5; Judges 2:22).

Now, pray (See Prayer of Deliverance, pg. 897)

Specific Meaning

If, you have a very real connection with any type of walking activity; for example, an animal walker, armed forces, athletic endeavors, daycare provider, exercise regiment, handicapped, hiker, medical profession, parade participant, park keeper or ranger, police enforcement, postal worker, professional shopper, protestor, surveyor, walking competition. This sort of drea m should be received as an ordinary dream, resulting from your daily activities (see Chapter One, Chalom). These dreams are usually about the anxieties that overwhelm your mind during the day. They are an inner release mechanism, which helps provide you with emotional balance and the maintaining of your sanity. These sorts of dreams, are not significant, and do not warrant special attention.

Note: If an accident or any other tragedy was highlighted within your dream, this is a precautionary warning. There may be potential for a tragedy of some sort. Dreamer, the details, kept within context of your dream, should be relevant to your life, and closely resemble your real-life situations. Meaning it can actually occur during your awaked state. This will help you narrow down the specifics needed to support and steer you clear of possible mishaps. However, if your dream symbols are not easily linked to your life activities, heed the spiritual implications (the interpretation).

WORKING, WORK PLACES: **The duties or activities that are part of a job or occupation, employed and the places those activities are carried out.**

Some short descriptions of types, phrases, and other processes and particulars, connected in some way to this category are, for example, artisan, blue-collar, engineering, entertainer, industrial work, manual worker, manufacturing, pink-collar, place of work, white-collar, or volunteer.

Unless otherwise noted elsewhere, if, in your everyday living, your awaked state, as part of your lifestyle, work, or ministerial activities, or a special event, you have a very real connection with any type of employment, work activity, or work place. For example, business owner, employment specialist or trainer, employment referral resource, human resource worker, job fair representative, owner, operator, unemployment specialist, (also see content list for this category), your dream is not significant and does not warrant special attention.

Otherwise noted, this dream may be a Prophetically Simple Dream (see Chapter One: The 60th Part of Prophecy). If an accident or any other tragedy was highlighted within your dream, this is a precautionary warning. There may be potential for a tragedy of some sort. Dreamer, the details, kept within context of your dream, should be relevant to your life, and closely resemble your real-life situations. Meaning it can actually occur during your awaked state. This will help you narrow down the specifics needed to support and steer you clear of possible mishaps. Dreamer is warned to be extra cautious regarding situations that have a high chance for accidents, especially if this is an issue within the dreamer's life at present. This dream is a first step intervention and an alarm. Skip interpretation and re-consider your activities as harmful or life threatening at present. Refrain from such activities at present.

Otherwise noted, see Note 1 at the beginning of Actions and Activities category.

To determine who your dream is for you or another, see Note 3 at the beginning of Actions and Activities category.

Symbols and Referents: Dreams of working generally imply, coupled with the relevant interpretation, that one is effective, gifted, productive, and/or one who is responsible for certain events and the consequences of that event. Moreover, it can denote the presence of a very powerful angel in your midst, for some important reason, primarily life threatening reasons.

Category Content - If not listed see index, perchance, for your specific type of working dream activity.

- Accountant, Banker, Bookkeeper, Broker, Cashier, Cash Handler, CFO, Economist, Financial Consultant, Fiscal Operations, Moneychanger, Stock Market, Tax Preparer, Wall Street, or any business involved in the handling or exchange of money, currency
- Agricultural Work (e.g. farmer, fieldworker, gardener, nursery, harvester, migrant or seasonal worker) see category, Agriculture and Forestry
- Bodyguard
- Butler or Maid or Maintenance or Janitorial (anyone employed to clean and maintain a building); additionally, if dreamer was connected in any way to one of the following
  - Attic, Loft; Bedroom, Bed, Sleeping Quarters; Jail; Kitchen, Dining area; Lounge, Living Room, Family Room, Sitting Room (e.g. employee's lounge, breakroom, TV room, a recreation room, a relaxation room in a private residence)
- CEO or Administrator or Executive or Landlord or Business Management or Office Managerial Position or Secretary or Clerk
- Co-Worker(s)
- Criminal (illegally working, e.g. any white, blue, pink collar crime, drug dealer, embezzlement, illegal immigrant, insider trading, prostitution, stealing, or any criminal activity)
- Doorkeeper or Gatekeeper (Door Guard, Doorman, Hall Porter, Usher, or guarding any entryway)
- Educator, Facilitator, Technician, Expert, or Student (e.g. Professor, Reader, Researcher, Seminar or Training Facilitator, Teacher, Technician, Expert, Tutor, including any Facility or Residence connected to Education in any way, include Boarding Schools, Bookstore, Classroom, College, Dormitory, Gymnasium, or High School); and/or connected in any way to one of the following
  - Kindergarten-5th grade, Middle or Junior High, High School, College, University; Hallway; Lunchroom; Principal's Office; Reading Room, Reader; Restroom; Teacher's Lounge, or Breakroom
- Foodservice (Baker, Caterer, Chef, Cook, Restaurateur, any food service related job)
- Going to work or leaving from work ("out to lunch")
- Judicial or Law Enforcement Officials (e.g. Judge, Advocacy, Attorney, Police Officer, Investigator, Detective, Spy, PI, or Operative; anyone connected to an establishment, facility, or place concerned with the law, courts, government)
- Manufacturing, Work Places (any place where work is done)
  - Archaeological Sites, Architectural Work, Assembly Plant, Barber Shop, Beauty Salon, Brewery, Bricklayer, Cannery, Construction. Excavation, Fabrication, Factory, Foundry, Machine Shop, Mail, Mailbox, Mailperson, Manicurist, Masonry, Mill, Mining, Nail Technician, Painter, Plant, Postal Clerk, Post Office. Potter, Pottery, Refineries, Saw Mills, Steelworks, Sweatshop, Water Mill, and Windmill)
  - Brewery, Distillery, see category, Drinking
  - Dry cleaner, see category, Clothing
  - Salt Mine, see category, Agriculture (Salt)

- Physician or Psychiatrist or Healer or Health Aides (any health care provider)
- Plumbers, Plumbing
- Religious Leaders, see category (People)
- Soldiers, see category, People (Soldier)
- Volunteer (working without compensation)
- Worker's Compensation (paid for injury at work)
- Working Late, Double Shift, or Overtime

Accountant, Banker, Bookkeeper, Broker, Cashier, Cash Handler, CFO, Economist, Financial Consultant, Fiscal Operations, Moneychanger, Stock Market, Tax Preparer, Wall Street, or any business involved in the handling or exchange of money, currency: Dreamer, God is completely restoring things materially and spiritually within your life. As well as in, the lives of those connected to you. Because of your brokenness over your past sins, you have opened the door to contriteness and humility. It is through this door that an act of kindness will come very soon. With that said, the following is necessary to say, that you might continue to prosper spiritually and sagaciously as God has fated you. Dreamer there is a need to understand the unadulterated and full meaning of divine providence, get a bible dictionary, and respect the meaning. For, there is also a need to recognize, acknowledge, and respect divine providence, God's absolute control over the affairs of humankind, and to renounce the belief that humans are in complete control (see Job 9:12, Isaiah 14:27; 43:13). Dreamer, there is a difference between divine providence and the will of humankind. Although you have the power of free choice, you should not think that your accomplishments are purely of your own volition. It is God, who gives you the capability and strength to achieve succes s. This is especially true of your struggles with your sinful tendencies, whether they manifest as a lack of concern or interest in the things of God, a stubborn resistance to the will of God, or laziness. If it had not been for God's efforts on your behal f, you would not have been able to overcome any negative tendencies. He delivered you. Any achievements you've accomplished, any good deeds you've done, any fulfillment of God's will, was, and still is, dependent upon divine aid and guidance. One merely places his or her hand under the weight carried exclusively by God. Just say and truly believe, "I will exalt you, God, for you have lifted me up". In addition, there is a need to check your theology. There is something missing in your belief system that has affected someone who is very close to you. It has caused them to seek God in other teachers, in other faces, and most are evil. Fortunately, that love one lead astray, because of you, will come home, embracing Jesus. Altruistic, goodhearted, and generous service to God and others is beneficial at this time.

Bodyguard: Question to journal, was the dreamer a bodyguard, or was the dreamer escorted and protected by a bodyguard? If dreamer was a bodyguard, your dream denotes one, the dreamer, whose calling is to become, if not already, an adjunct (e.g. associate, friend, personal assistant, secretary) to a very prominent Christian leader. An adjunct is one who escorts and protects the one they are divinely directed to defend. If dreamer had a bodyguard, a new person, or old acquaintance, is allowed within the dreamer's life as a helper and/or protector. Allow the person into your life (e.g. adjun ct, associate, friend, personal assistant, secretary, possible spouse). This person is under God's protection. For, he or she, who honors Jesus Christ, is under God's protection and has been made clean. This person is down-to-earth, fair, humble, just, unpretentious, not rude or obscene, and one whom a believer may interact with socially on very personal levels.

Butler or Maid or Maintenance or Janitorial (anyone employed to clean and maintain a building): This dream has two meanings (one or both may apply). (1) Your dream represents a cleric of some kind (e.g. bishop, evangelist, minister, missionary, parson, pastor, preacher, priest, rabbi, or teacher). You are one whose calling is to give sermons, spread the gospel, and conduct religious services. Dreamer, a large part of your mission should center on, you raising the spirits of your fellow mankind, and establishing yourself as an inspirational person spreading hope. Your gift is to inspire and motivate. (2) Was dreamer connected in any way to one of the following?

Attic, Loft: Dreamer you are multidimensional. This natural endowment gives you an inner strength and awareness that makes you an excellent advisor, philosopher, and teacher. Only do not be habitually careless, irresponsible, or guilty of fa iling to, properly prepare for the charge you have to keep, and to glorify God.

Bedroom, Bed, Sleeping Quarters: Your dream was sent as a warning. Dreamer, do not bury your prophetic gifts (see Luke 19:12-26); for many will be drawn to God because of your loving disposition and positive attitude; others will be dramatically changed by your example. Do not be negligent now, for your slackness will cause those you are purposely sent to, to become non-productive, and this will prove very unprofitable for you spiritually, physically, and financially (Ezekiel 13:3-23, 33:6). See suggested course of action.

Jail: See Genesis 40, Pharaoh's chief wine butler and baker

Kitchen or Dining area: Your dream denotes that your voice will be used as an instrument of righteousness; coming against those who would attempt to oppress you and others. The dreamer's spiritual strength, tenacity, and knowledge, will be used of God; penetrating the soul of those who listen, affecting conversion. By all this, you will be remembered by the Lord your God and rescued from your enemies. For, your words will cause your enemies to turn on themselves. Your dream comes as a message of affirmation. You have been called to a high calling; withdraw not your spirit when that day is officially up on you.

Lounge, Living Room, Family Room, Sitting Room (e.g. employee's lounge, breakroom, TV room, a recreation room, a relaxation room in a private residence): The dreamer will be responsible to, empathically usher God's presence into the mentality of situations. Your responsibility is to usher God's Presence in and magnify the Lord. This you do, when you proclaim His goodness and His truth. You are a vessel of God's glory, and a possessor of the truth needed for the place and situation at hand, the greater the truth, the greater your authority, the greater your success.

CEO, Administrator, Executive, Landlord, Business Management, Office Managerial Position, Secretary, or Clerk: This dream has two meanings (choose one). (1) CEO, Administrator, or Landlord represents Elohim within a dream. (2) Your dream is figurative of ministerial service, daily prayers, and a formal assignment given to the dreamer. Dreamer you have a responsibility to your "set house" of God. Therefore, it is expected, as you would any job assignment, to be there, to be th ere on time, and to perform your assigned duties, as unto the Lord; for God (not man) is a rewarder of them that diligently serve Him, (Hebrews 11:6). Moreover, if you have found yourself slack in this area of ministry, it is suggested that for the next 10 days you pray, daily, seeking God guidance and wisdom, regarding your service within your church, your individual ministry, and to encourage a more intimate prayer life. See suggested course of action.

Co-Worker(s): This dream has two meanings (choose one). (1) Your dream denotes that the dreamer has learned the Christian values and principles that leads one to reach out and touch others in a loving and graceful manner; ultimately find ing yourself promoting the genuine cause of Christ and the good of others. You have an open connection to divine revelation, which will at times be used on a prophetic platform. Properly developed, your link to prophetic revelation can and should be used to help others. If not already, you will inspire others to dream and to make their dreams come true. Mor eover, dreamer, you are gifted in many areas, and your access to prophetic wisdom, will be a transformational force in people's lives, via not neglecting the gift that is within you. You will now be led into situations, where you can express your desire to help. You will show up when most needed, and then disappear without a thought of compensation. You will be dispatched on missions, to help believers who are facing urgent needs during a crisis, and/or in an emergency, and to give instant help, as well as, to express God's loving kindness, His grace, mercy, and compassion. You are sent to protect and defend those who obediently love God, and who is loved by God. An angel (perhaps disguised as human, or one, who is a true servant of God, with the Spirit of Truth within) will lead the way. Read, understand, and embrace Psalm 147:12-20. Altruistic, goodhearted, and generous service to God and others is beneficial at this time. Freely received, freely give. Dreamer, love God so completely that yo u will never forsake His service for any reason. (2) To the married male or female without children: Dreamer, God has granted mercy to you. You will no longer feel ashamed because of something you've done wrong in your past (e.g. seriously bad, unalterable, and life damaging actions, due to uninformed choices, and/or ruinous relationships). The reproach of your past will be put behind you. Additionally, if desired, you will very soon give birth to your own children. To the female, God will give you the miraculous strength and knowledge, as well as a door to the right physicians to help you bear and birth your own children. Your husband will be a great support to you during this time.

Criminal (illegally working, e.g. any white, blue, pink collar crime, drug dealer, embezzlement, illegal immigrant, insider trading, prostitution, stealing, or any criminal activity): This dream has two meanings (choose one). (1) You are one who has found a way to profit off unsuspecting Christians, those who trust you. Your thoughts and intents are on ways you can rob the people of God of their finances. You're in it for the money. If you're in some type of head "cleric" leadership position, y ou're a "hireling". Your end will be disastrous. See suggested course of action. (2) Prostitution wages (male or female): Your dream denotes that your oblation, offerings, and/or sacrifices are misguided and are not acceptable in the eyes of the Lord. For it is written, "Never bring gifts or money earned by prostitution [of a female prostitute or of a male prostitute] into the house of the LORD your God as an offering you vowed to give. These earnings are disgusting to the LORD your God" Deuteronomy 23:18 (GW). See suggested course of action.

Doorkeeper or Gatekeeper (Door Guard, Doorman, Hall Porter, Usher, or guarding any entryway): This dream has three meanings (choose one). (1) If another was keeper of door or gate, dreamer determine what character trait(s) stood out the most regarding that doorkeeper, gatekeeper, within your dreamer, journal those traits. It is those traits, if positive, that will usher you into another dimension of living, or it will be those traits, if negative, that will hinder your progression into a nother dimension of living. (2) This type of dream is to bring about an awareness of an appointed inheritance of abundant peace, comfort, and sufficient wealth for the dreamer, if you have been positive and diligent regarding God's business, namely the ministry He has entrusted you with, or have just been positively diligent about your Heavenly Father's business. If you have indeed been faithful of little, you are becoming self-sufficient and unrelenting, capable of handling much responsibility, especially when required to make major decisions. At some point in the undisclosed future, honor and wealth will be bestowed upon the dreamer, if not already. Moreover, many will be inspired by your wisdom, confidence, and blameless actions, while others will feel threaten by it. Those who plot evil against you (family, friend, or foe) will not prevail, but will yield willingly to your authority. A warning: at present, keep quiet and appear speechless or deaf; take on an unassuming disposition (see Deuteronomy 8:6-20). (3) Unmarried dreamer: In addition to the preceding interpretation, your dream also implies that God has appointed a spouse for you, a religious or civil leader (e.g. politician, representative, or an official of some kind), and that person is very near you at present. As they are sensitive to God's leading right now, so should you be sensitive to God's leading. Moreover, seek out the true and practical meaning of unequally yoked, and you will better understand relationships.

Educator, Facilitator, Technician, Expert, or Student (e.g. Professor, Reader, Researcher, Seminar or Training Facilitator, Teacher, Technician, Expert, Tutor, including any Facility or Residence connected to Education in any way, include Boarding Schools, Bookstore, Classroom, College, Dormitory, Gymnasium, or High School): See one of the following.

Educator, Facilitator, Technician, or Expert: This dream has two meanings (choose one). (1) If another was educator, facilitator, technician, or expert, this represents the Holy Spirit, our spiritual helper. Note; whatever was said or done by the educator, this is what is being said about the dreamer. If necessary, see suggested course of action. (2) Other than that, your dream generally implies spiritual growth, divine illumination, and some type of promotion or confirmation on a prophetic level. Dreamer now you will begin to experience a miraculous increase in divine knowledge and wisdom. This knowledge and wisdom will be imparted to you to be used exclusively for interpreting the gospel of Jesus Christ to others, and for the edifying of the Body of Christ; the body of believers. Your height of spiritual progress and promotion will be according to your fait h and obedience to God's will over your life personally. If desired, you will also get married soon.

Student: Recalling your dream, what level of education was depicted? Were you about to begin that level, already there at that level, or had you just finished and/or graduated? Answering one of these questions, coupled with one of the following grade levels, should shed light on what God wants you to focus on, namely where you are at spiritually, mentally, and/or emotionally, be it just beginning, at present, or ending.

Kindergarten-5th grade (beginning level of education): Your dream denotes spiritual infancy. Spiritual infancy is lack of spiritual growth after your new birth experience. The spiritual infant is concerned with self rather than service. The spiritual infant is concerned with argument rather than action. The spiritual infant looks to people rather than the Messiah. Thus, dreamer has not readied yourself for "solid" teaching of the Word of God. There is still jealously, strife, and insecurity within you. You are still carnal minded (see 1 Corinthians 3:1-3). Favorably, because of God's grace, you will be starting all over again, with some kind of learning experience, be it a life experience, person, people experience, or work experience; this experience is meant to affect a spiritual maturity within you, leading to a better walk with God. Yes, you've been through this lesson, experience before; hopefully, you will learn from this second experience, what you did not get the first time, and then progress forward, to the next level. God wants you to leave the elementary principles of Christ - to leave, to progress forward (not abandon), the elementary principles about Christ. He wants you to progress beyond them. What are the elementary principles? They are mentioned as repentance, faith, baptism, the laying on of hands, the resurrection, and eternal judgment. In short, these are basic doctrines (see Hebrews 6:1, 2). Once the foundation has been laid, the basic doctrines embraced and secured, you are to improve and progress forward, in your understanding and attitudes concerning spiritual things. Therefore, it is suggested that you choose to put away jealously and strife, and renounce, in the name of Jesus, anger, rage, fear, and insecurity, which are all demonically encouraged. Read, understand, and embrace 1 Peter 2:1-3. Then, through the eyes of faith, visualize yourself, demanding anger, rage, fear, and insecurity to leave you. See suggested course of action.

Middle or Junior High (6th – 9th grades): Something is required of you in order for you to go to the next level in your Christian walk, and become promoted or ordained, by God and man. First, it is necessary to say that it is only due to Christ's work on the cross that you are able to press on to maturity. Maturity is when your understanding of truth and your actions are one, and the same. God wants you to mature in Christ. Dreamer needs to do whatever it takes to experience, security, peace, and a sense of personal well-being (a contented state of being happy, healthy, and prosperous). For instance, what will it take for you to experience, a sense of security and peace? What will it take, for you to experience happiness, healthiness (e.g. by seeking medical attention or become more health conscious), or prosperity (e.g. good stewardship)? You will need to integrat e your faith and life choices as part of your religious life, seeing work, family, social relationships, and political choices as part of your religious life; that, your understanding of truth, and your actions are one. It is suggested that you seek spiritual growth through study, reflection, prayer, and discussion with others. Seek to be part of a community of believers who give witness to their faith and support and nourish one another. Hold life-affirming values, including commitment to racial and gender equality, and a personal sense of responsibility for the welfare of others. As well as, serve humanity, consistently and passionately, through acts of love and justice, and most important; trusts in God's redeeming features towards all mankind an d His divine providence; this is the level of maturity that God wants from you, and this is called a perfect faith. The only way to perfect your relationship with God and improve your walk in holiness is do it by faith and obedience to His word. "With the mind you need only to understand. With the heart, you need to obey". By this, progress, promotion, and exaltation, will manifest.

High School (10th – 12th grades): This dream has two meanings (one or both may apply). (1) The first step towards spiritual maturity is to be willing to ask the tough question of yourself: Am I spiritually mature? This first step indicates that you are willing to push through the process, and to become self-aware of where you are spiritually and of your life true circumstances. This step acknowledges that you are no longer willing to, easily dismiss things you do, and you are no longer willing to surrender to your bad habits. For example, when you lose your patience, your conscience tugs at you. This first step enables you to examine the situation so that you can get to the root of it and ultimately root it out of your life. This may prove to be a long process, but dreamer be willing, even eager, to embark on it. This process should begin to feel necessary to you. (2) You should first be partaker of your own ministry. Once you've completed your lessons, on maintaining peace within your life, not disturbing your own peace, nor the peace of others (e.g. via drama, trifling) this will lead to you being the first partaker of your own ministry. However, maintaining this kind of peace will prove to be a challenge for you. Therefore, understand, and respect, the value of who you are to God. With understanding and self-value, there, will be an inner clarity, healing, peace of mind, spiritual refreshment, tranquility, and rejuvenation. Your witness will also bring new depths to others emotional state, effecting spiritual refreshment, tranquility, peace of mind, inner clarity, rejuvenation, knowledge, and healing.

College, University (institutions of higher education): Dreamer you are entering into a season within your life that will prepare you spiritually for the visitation of the Lord in your individual life. During this time, you will experience His love and presence, as you've never known it before. For, He is saying to you, "I will teach you godly wisdom". You will receive direct insight of divine truth. You will come to know, without a doubt, that God is the true source of your strength and wisdom, an d He is your sufficiency. As a result, a greater love for self, family, and others will begin to manifest, affecting wholeness within your life. Be available to Him and seize the moments and opportunities as they are presented, especially an opportunity for you to advance your education, with a focus on teaching. In addition, independent and capable, you are becoming a celebrated and powerful man or woman of God. A leader and master teacher in your own right, you will become, if not already, a preeminent part of a ministry. Therefore, understand, and respect, your value to God and to His Kingdom. Moreover, use your strength exclusively for the Kingdom of God; to choose otherwise, at this point, will not be beneficial to you, it will devalue you.

Educator, facilitator, or student was in the, see one of the following.

Hallway: You are a teacher of God's word. Therefore, use your past to teach those whom God has purposed for you to reach, via mentoring, inspirational writing, acting, teaching, or preaching. Pray, "Father, your will be done in my life, as you've purposed it in heaven". Dreamer, your time to teach is upon you now.

Lunchroom: Dreamer, be whom God made you to be, use your God given talents, as best you can, to make the world a better place. Take your past and use it to teach those whom God has purposed you to reach. Additionally, no matter who you are and what the situation, the words of the Psalms will speak the words of your heart and those words will be heard on High. Thus, began singing a new song, see Psalm 96:1-13. Start listening to, and embracing, inspirational music, music that praises our Lord and Savior. After this, you will become productive and go forth, bearing spiritual fruit that you might be counted amongst those who are sagacious; whose character is faithful, law-abiding, moral, open, scrupulous, sincere, straightforward, trustworthy, upright, reasonable in many situations, and submissive to God.

Principal's Office: Listen to your Heavenly Father's instructions, pay attention, and gain understanding. Do not forsake God's teachings. Lay hold of God's Word with all your heart, keep His commands and you will live. Get wisdom, get understanding; do not forget God's Word or swerve from it. Do not forsake wisdom, and she will protect you; love her, and she will watch over you. Wisdom is supreme; therefore get wisdom. Though it cost all you have, get understanding. Esteem her, and she will exalt you; embrace her, and she will honor you. Listen, and, accept what it said to you, and the y ears of your life will be many. God's Word will guide you in the way of wisdom and lead you along straight paths. When you walk, your steps will not be hampered; when you run, you will not stumble. Hold on to instruction; do not let it go; guard it well, for it is your life. Do not set foot on the path of the wicked or do the same things as evil men. Avoid them, do not travel with them ; turn from them, and go on your way. For they cannot sleep until they do evil; until they make someone fall. They ea t the bread of wickedness and drink the wine of violence. However, the path of the righteous is like the first glow of the sun in the early morning, shining brighter until the full light of day. The way of the wicked is like deep darkness; they do not kn ow what makes them stumble. Dreamer, listen closely to God's Word. Keep it within your heart, for it will be health to your whole body. Above all else, guard your heart, for it is the wellspring of life. Put away perversity from your mouth; keep corrup t talk far from your lips. Let your eyes look straight-ahead, fix your gaze directly before you. Make level paths for your feet; and take ways, only, that are firm. Do not swerve to the right or the left; keep your foot from evil (Proverbs 4). See suggested course of action.

Reading Room, Reader: This dream has two meanings (choose one). (1) Your dream denotes one, namely the dreamer, who is faithfully performing your ministerial duties, and studying to show him or herself approved of God, a worker who will not be made ashamed, rightly dividing the word of truth (2 Timothy 2:15). (2) Illiterate or unable to read: Your dream denotes one who is spiritually blind, by choice, having carelessly risked your life and soul, pretending to be ignorant of the things of God, His creative works in, and around, you, and to His principles. Dreamer, God's love is calling you back to Him; forgiveness will cover all your mistakes from this day forward. Now give careful thought to this from this day on. From this d ay forward, God will bless you; therefore, perceive God's grace, and embrace the love that is calling you home. No longer, pretend that you do not sense His providence within your life. See suggested course of action.

Restroom: Dreamer, the following is necessary for you to hear, understand, and heed. If you want to approach and worship the Holy One by way of inspirational teaching, preaching, or some other form of inspirational uplifting of others, yo u should come before Him in a sense of appropriateness. Meaning you should aspire for some level of truthfulness, modesty, and reliability. No other is responsible for this in your life but you; therefore, deal with an existing situation that would hinder your approach to God with some level of purity (Leviticus 11:45, 1 Peter 1:13-2:3). See suggested course of action.

Teacher's Lounge, Breakroom: Dreamer, you are a teacher, especially of the Word of God. Are you teaching, in some manner or another? If you are not, your dream is to engender an awareness of your untapped potential and to encourage you to develop toward this purpose via studious research (e.g. school, a bible concordance, bible illustrated dictionary, encyclopedia, or internet). Make this happen, that you may be found a good and faithful servant on your day of the Lord (Matthew 25:14-30), the day of your reckoning. Christians praise the Lord, by reaching their potential, and by service. Therefore, be careful to adhere to God's expectations of you, especially, for you to be fearless. For, fear takes many forms, and often presents itself as self-sabotaging of one's success, addictions, slow suicide, via food, pills, sexual immorality, or some other unhealthy lifestyle choices, as well as, an unwillingness to control anger, lying, gossiping, backbiting, jealously, hating, denial. Moreover, if applicable, teach your children not to fear, as well. Adherence will cause many things to go well for you, and cause you to increase greatly, especially during this time of fulfillment of God's promises within your life. Be aware, you will shortly have to give an account of the fulfilling of your purpose for which you was design, as well as, of your philosophy and words.

Foodservice (Baker, Caterer, Chef, Cook, Restaurateur, any food service related job): All food service related persons, represents one who is a traditionalist, very important, influential, and powerful; as well as, one, namely the dreamer, who i s predestined to become born again within the Kingdom of God (see John 3:1-17). Couple this with one of the following.

Baker: This dream has three meanings (one, two may apply). Your dream was sent to warn and encourage the dreamer. (1) Dreamer, be very encouraged, for you are highly favored and blessed of God. To be blessed: Gifts of God's grace, anything God freely gives you, absolution, the Holy Spirit, salvation, regeneration, eternal life, health, children, love of family, longevity, necessities, prosperity, and dominion over all that is yours; and all are parts of the supply of grace, and all are sanctified by the Lord, and technically belongs to Him. The result of this supply in your life will be peace. As well, the dreamer is being deliv ered and made complete spiritually. You will be restored to your divine ordained place within a ministry. With your spirit of avariciousness under control, withhold not your hand in the day of your prosperity, but receive and keep all that God has ordained for you and your family (implying good stewardship). As well, you are a righteous person, with a strong desire to uplift humanity. You will now be led into situations where you can express your desire to serve others. You will show up wh en most needed, and then disappear without a thought of compensation. Many will be inspired by y our faith in Christ and humility. (2) Dreamer is warned to withdraw your hand and heart, mind, and soul, from avariciousness. (3) Jail: if dreamer was in Jail: See Genesis 40, Pharaoh's chief wine butler and baker. This is due to avariciousness. See suggested course of action.

Chef, caterer, or cook: Your dream denotes one, the dreamer, whose calling is to become an adjunct (e.g. associate, friend, personal assistant, secretary) to a very prominent Christian leader. An adjunct is one who escorts and protects the one they are divinely directed to protect. This person is under God's protection. For, he or she, who honors Jesus Christ, is u nder God's protection and has been made clean. This person is down-to-earth, fair, humble, just, unpretentious, not rude or obscene, and one whom a believer may interact with socially on very personal levels. Dreamer, you are God's chosen person, as well as one who is moderate in all things, just and fair, not rude or obscene. You are strong, emotionally and ph ysically, and you know how to follow, as well as lead. Be encourage, you always perform outstandingly well.

Restaurateur: God has sent an apprentice to you, to be taught by you the prophetic nature of God. This person will remain within your life for at least one year, not more than three. Train him or her well, for he or she is your replacement (1 Kings 19-21). Dreamer, you're not getting ready to die physically, God's plans for you are to prosper you financially and health wise, and to cause you to rest peacefully with everything you will need and desire. Only accept that it is your time to retire, therefore, retire gracefully, and give your best to the coming apprentice. Moreover, allow God to give you what He chooses to give you, and if He gives you more than you need, then be a good steward over that. The following is a suggested prayer to keep one balanced, "Jesus, I don't want any more than God wants me to have. Give me my portion, don't give me too much so that I worship my wealth instead of God, and become self-sufficient, and don't give me too little so that I'll steal and dishonor God's name" (Proverbs 30:8.9). Additionally, a nefarious leader, annoyed at you because of your spiritual purity and righteo us words, is seeking to harm you. When asked to come before this leader, and you will be asked to come, you are to relay God's message to this leader. The message: This leader will not recover from an illness that is upon him or her, because of their immorality. Allow your apprentice to accompany you for this word will come to past, and he or she will be your witness.

Going to work or leaving from work: This dream has three meanings (choose one). (1) If dreamer was going to work, the dreamer will get a job within a month or so. (2) If dreamer was leaving from work, the dreamer will be asked to leave a job, aka "get fired". If dreamer suspects that you are in jeopardy of losing your job, resign now that you may be able to ob tain gainful employment without the stain of having been fired. You simply need to say, I resigned. If necessary, see suggested course of action. (3) "Out to lunch": This choice has two parts (choose one). (a) Dreamer, God will teach you faith and perseverance, and this may take a while; therefore, be patience and persevere. (b) To dream you're out to lunch denotes one who is not paying attention and thus slow to react; overcome with astonishment or disbelief, you're in a state of mental numbness, stunned, or confused. Note; this state will cause you, the dreamer, to lose clear vision. See suggested course of action.

Judicial or Law Enforcement Officials (e.g. Judge, Advocacy, Attorney, Police Officer, Investigator, Detective, Spy, PI, or Operative; anyone connected to an establishment, facility, or place concerned with the law, courts, government): This is figurative of one, who will, or does, start churches, couple this with one of the following.

Judge, Advocacy, Attorney: Your dream is a guidance dream, and is meant to be a catalyst for change. Dreamer, your purpose is that of becoming a forerunner for change, freedom, progressive thought, and action. You are a great leader, with the capacity to lead many to Christ. Christian in belief, with a generous nature, you have the capacity to spearhead a fresh revival, leading a generation that will usher in a time of great spiritual revelation regarding the Truth of God, the Holy Sp irit, and God's Holy Word. The offspring of this revival will embrace the knowledge of a personal and saving relationship with Christ Jesus. You're heading towards your destiny. You are going in the right direction, doing good things, and your cause is noble. You are naturally endowed with the ability to perceive wisdom; and it is this, which guides you towards your intend ed destination. Every step you take is toward purpose. Unfortunately, as this present age will have it, your message on progressive thinking, with a primary focus on loyalty to God and holiness, will offend those who choose to forget Creator God. Politely disassociate yourself from those who do not respect or understand your cause, for they will hinder your purpose. Other than that, you will get to wherever it is you're destined to get. God has promised to make known to you His presence, His guidance, and protection. You will be strengthen and enlighten because of this revelation. Be encouraged.

Police Officer, Investigator, Detective: Dreamer, you are endowed with multiple talents that may be expressed through inspirational teaching, preaching, acting, or art, and you have access to prophetic wisdom, thus, you are required to be a transformational force in people's lives, via not neglecting the gift that is within you. Do not say what gift, for this is sin for you? As your dream supposes that, you are aware of, at least, one of your gifts (talent, skill). You will now be led into situations, where you will show up when most needed, and then disappear without a thought of compensation. You will be dispatched on missions, to help believers who are facing urgent needs during a crisis, and/or in an emergency, and to give instant help, as well as, to express God's loving kindness, His grace, mercy, and compassion. You are sent to protect and defend those who obediently love God, and who is loved by God. Some examples of altruistic service or "acts of kindness" to others are, provide a child with necessities, such as food, clothing, shelter, toys, medical equipment. Visit the sick, provide free medical services, and give charity to the poor, (see Ben Sira 29). Offer hospitality to strangers, help families bury their dead, via religious services, help with marriage ceremonies, and/or help a person make peace with his or her family member, fellow humankind, or their Maker. Provide free roadside assistance and emergency mechanical help, or freely help with structural problems in private homes. All of these, and more, are examples of service to the Kingdom of God. Often, an individual starts the initiative of service without leadership or community support. God will give you the necessary tools, courage, strength, and wherewithal, to do it. Dreamer, love God so completely that you will never forsake His service for any reason. Moreover, dreamer this kind of service to God and others will prove beneficial to you. Caution, although you have the power of free choice, you should not think that your accomplishments are purely of your own volition. Truthfully, it is God, who gives you the capability and strength to achieve success. This is especially true of your struggles with your sinful tendencies, whether they manifest as a lack of concern or interest in the things of God, a stubborn resistance to the will of God, or laziness. If it had not been for God's efforts on your behalf, you would not have been able to overcome any negative tendencies. He delivered you. Any achievements you will accomplish, or have accomplished, any good deeds you've done, any fulfillment of God's will, was, and still is, dependent upon divine aid and guidance. One merely places his or her hand under the weight carried exclusively by God. Moreover, avoid excess sleep, do not claim credit for your achievements, and respect cautionary advice about something imminent (especially imminent danger or other unpleasantness), remain thankful, and become aware and tap into the intuitive insight you are (or will be) receiving. An angel (perhaps disguised as human, or one, who is a true serva nt of God, with the Spirit of Truth within) will lead the way.

Spy, PI, or any Operative: Your dream denotes one who is, or will be, secretly introduced into a group to spy on others that you might know how to, strategically introduce the mentality of Christ into the situation. Do not reveal your religious beliefs at first. Begin noting all erroneous beliefs within this group. Any beliefs that contradict the inspired word of God, including His provision for humankind to be save namely belief and faith in Jesus Christ as Savior, God incarnate, and grace without works. Then wisely and cautiously begin pointing out the error in this group's belief system to certain others, as you are led to, by Holy Spirit. Do not be afraid of their status, words, or any other characteristic, that might be intimidating. Stay focus and remember your mission.

Manufacturing, Work Places (any place where work is done, e.g. Archaeological Sites, Architectural Work, Assembly Plant, Barber Shop, Beauty Salon, Brewery, Bricklayer, Cannery, Construction. Excavation, Fabrication, Factory, Foundry, Machine Shop, Mail, Mailbox, Mailperson, Manicurist, Masonry, Mill, Mining, Nail Technician, Painter, Plant, Postal Clerk, Post Office. Potter, Pottery, Refineries, Saw Mills, Steelworks, Sweatshop, Water Mill, and Windmill): Generally these types of dreams, suggests that the dreamer will be put into environments, where the dreamer will be responsible to, empathically usher God's presence into the mentality of those situations. Your responsibility is to usher God's Presence in and magnify the Lord. This you do, when you proclaim His goodness and His truth. You are a vessel of God's glory, and a possessor of the truth needed for the place and situation at hand, the greater the truth, the greater your authority, the greater your success. Moreover, know that there are angels about you to protect and uphold you in case that's needed, therefore, do not be afraid of their faces, their positions, titles, wealth, nor of the place or circumstances. You are equipped to handle your, and God's, business. Have faith in God. If relevant, couple this with one of the following.

Architectural Work or Bricklayer or Construction or Fabricator or Masonry (any work connected to the construction of buildings): Dreamer, you have the ability to inspire. Couple this with the following three (one or all may apply). (1) Your dream is an expression of the joy and happiness you have experienced serving the Lord. You are encompassed about with righteousness and purity. The intents and motives of your heart are pure and righteous. You are honorable in the eyes of God. Many will be inspired by your faith in Christ, your humility, and your unpretentiousness. Consequently, you are prepared for any spiritual conflict or evil activity that may come your way because of the pride, criticism, and littleness of mind of others. Do not allow others to dampen your joy. (2) This type of dream is to bring about an awareness of an appointed inheritance o f abundant peace, comforts, and sufficient wealth for the dreamer. At some point in the undisclosed future, honor and wealth will be bestowed upon the dreamer, if not already. You are becoming self-sufficient and unrelenting, capable of handling much responsibility, especially when required to make major decisions. Many will be inspired by your wisdom, co nfidence, and blameless actions. (3) You have learned the Christian values and principles that leads one to reach out and touch other s in a loving and graceful manner; ultimately finding yourself promoting the genuine cause of Christ and the good of others. You have an open connection to divine revelation, which will at times be used on a prophetic platform. Properly developed, your link to prophetic revelation can and should be used to help others. If not already, you will inspire others to dream and to make their dreams come true. Dreamer, you are gifted in many areas, and you have access to prophetic wisdom, thus, you are required to be a transformational force in people's lives, via not neglecting the gift that is within you. You will now be led into situations, where you will show up when most needed, and then disappear without a thought of compensation. You will be dispatched on missions, to help believers who are facing urgent needs during a crisis, and/ or in an emergency, and to give instant help, as well as, to express God's loving kindness, His grace, mercy, and compassion. You are sent to protect and defend those who obediently love God, and who is loved by God. An angel (perhaps disguised as human, or one, who is a true servant of God, with the Spirit of Truth within) will lead the way. Read, understand, and embrace Psalm 147:12-20. Altruistic, goodhearted, and generous service to God and others is beneficial at this time. Freely received, freely give. Dreamer, love God so completely that you will never forsake His service for any reason.

Bricks: This dream has two meanings (choose one). (1) If bricks were highlighted in any way in your dream, your dream was sent to encourage. Dreamer, because of the loving kindness of God, a spiritual reawakening is happening for you. Your spiritual life is being cleaned up; a personal revival is imminent, and you are being called upon to participate in that purification process. Dreamer, the Spirit of Truth is coming to you. That is to say, one who has the Spirit of Truth abiding within them is coming. He or she will testify of Jesus; a side of Him you do not know. This new truth will usher you into a spiritual and personal revival, affecting restoration of better and happier times (e.g. deliverance, restoration, peace, purity, righteousness, joy, maturity, integrity, dignity, cleanliness, awareness, and new beginnings) or a new birth experience for one needing to b e born again (see John 3:1-17). Do you trust that God can effect a revival within you? He can and will. Believe and you will receive, and you will be set free. At present, continue to allow the Paraclete to complete the work of purification and sanctification within you. For those who go forth in tears, shall return rejoicing (Psalm 126:5, 6). Be diligent and patient, everything will be done proper, and in its own time; you will be ordained within a ministry, and if deserved, honored in some respect in another area. Moreover, there will be a flash of insight, a sudden awareness, recognition, or realization of God's truth. (2) To the unmarried female: A potential spouse is looking carefully at you at present. Your faithfulness and unpretentiousness is beautiful in his sight. An introduction will present itself shortly. The question of the possibility of relocation may be asked.

Assembly or Factory Plant: This dream has two meanings (choose one). (1) Assembly: Your dream is figurative of a messenger angel and a demon is involved in a discussion or debate, about a group of people, regarding a religious matter that involves public, business, or political views. Dreamer; sit quietly, and remain very discerning as to what is being said, and what is being implied within the discussion. Learn to distinguish between condemnation and conviction, and between hatred, racism, partiality, or any other divisive rhetoric, for surely two voices are being presented. Then, side with righteousness, no matter the majority. See suggested course of action. (2) Factory: Your dream is figurative of a place, with a complex hierarchy of power, where power and greed are the principle things. Status is often achieved dishonestly. This mentality is concerned only with your personal comfort, material wealth, and status, at any expense. Dreamer, now, having in yourself nothing that you respect more than power and greed, you are willing to sacrifice all, God, principle, family, and friend, to the image or idol of vanity. Your new way is based on exploring alternatives to God's righteous principles, as well as, creating a sense of unity with the wickedness around you. This mentality sacrifices children, family, and morality, to the hollowness o f satisfying immoral desires and appetites. All carried out, with the hope of finding happiness by pacifying jealously and covetousness. Dreamer must choose this day whom you will serve, God, money, or power, and then commit to that, but you can't serve or worship both (Matthew 6:24). It's one or the other.

Beauty Salon or Barbershop (all the processes connected to a beauty salon, barbershop, e.g. Barber, Beautician, Manicurist, or Nail Technician): If hair was cut or someone shaved, see category, Cutting (Shave or Haircut). If hair was washed, see category, Body (Hair). Otherwise, this dream has two meanings (choose one). (1) Your dream pronounces that the understanding of the act of delivering from sin and saving from evil, done by Jesus on the cross, will become clearer to the dreamer. You will become aware of who you are in Christ Jesus and the spiritual state that you are in. The psychological result of reasoning, perception, and learning of this information will usher you into what is called, "ultimate peace" or "glory". Glory in this sense is a state of high honor, spiritual beauty, and great illumination. Moreover, the dreamer will return to a place or state of safety and plenty and will return to Christ and to His church. Accordingly, your soul and lifestyle will begin to b ear fruit of positive choices, resulting in spiritual strength and power within the dreamer's life; this is also "glory". (2) If you are an unbeliever (one who has no religious beliefs, a non-religious person, or one who has no religious faith or belief in Jesus Christ, or one who does not embrace a personal relationship with Jesus Christ, at present). Jesus loves you, thus, He is petitioning you to accept Him as your personal Savior, for you are valuable in His eyes. The first step in receiving Him as your personal Savior is repentance (see in the Holy Bible, Acts 2:37-41). Repentance is seeking pardon for having done something awry, and for having hurt someone, and expressing sincere feelings of regret and brokenness. To Jesus pray, Psalm 51:1-19. Moreover, if you will accept the Heavenly Father's Words, via the Bible, and store up His principles, and accept His ways and means, turning your ear to wisdom and applying your heart to understanding, calling out for insight and crying aloud for discernment, Jesus will meet you. This, coupled with a lifestyle of prayer and fasting, followed by appropriate application of wisdom, and you will know the Messiah, Jesus Christ, intimately, and find the knowledge of God you seek. For the Lord gives wisdom and from His mouth comes knowledge and understanding. Then you will understand what is right and just and fair–every good path. When wisdom enters your heart and knowledge becomes sweet to your soul, discretion will protect you, understanding will guard you, and His Truth will lead you. To deliver you from the ways of wickedness, and from demons whose words and ways are perverse, who causes you to walk in darkness gladly, whose paths are crooked and devious, causing you to leave straight paths (Proverbs 2:1-6, 9-15). This is one of God's covenant promises to you. Have faith in this. See suggested course of action.

Cannery: Your dream is figurative of a place of confinement. Dreamer will enter into, or re-locate to, a domain where there are strict restrictions and limitations. That you may abide there for a long time, and that things may go well with you, obey the rules, for they are not strenuous, but for the betterment of you. As well, your dream also denotes the deepest or innermost part of one's feelings and emotions will (or should) be dealt with during this time of confinement.

Foundry or Machine Shop: This is figurative of one who ushers idolatrous practices into the mentality of situations, for profit. If such practices are not halted, you will be considered as one of those referenced in Revelation 2:14-17, 20-23. See suggested course of action.

Mill (machinery that processes materials by grinding or crushing): Your dream denotes one who is quick-tempered and quick to fight. Dreamer, there is an old saying that goes; "if one gives oneself over to anger it is as if one worships idols". Anger insinuates complaining, deception, disobedience, disrespect, harsh treatment, jealousy, sexual violations and/or unrighteous dealings, and causes you to move about in a confused manner. When you realize that the rectification of another first depends upon the rectification of yourself, you will learn to be patient, especially with others. For patience is the antidote to anger. With regard to others and/or your spouse, you must strive for the godly attribute of patience. Patience is the wisdom, which nurtures one's ability to wait for conflict to resolve itself, to suspend judgment, to continuously check and control your innate tendency to relate to others impulsively. It is the key to avoiding the damage you can inflict upon others and upon yourself, when you are unable to control the responses of your first nature to life situations. Only toward your own evil inclinations, is your problem with anger, in order. As a wise person once said, "One should always stir up the anger of his or her good inclination against his or her evil inclination". Dreamer, consider Proverbs 12:16, 14:17, 1 Corinthians 13:4, Titus 1:7-9. See suggested course of action.

Mining or Archeological Site or Excavation or Mineshaft (the act of extracting ores, coal from the earth via mining, or to get from the earth by excavation or digging): This indicates a severe warning of divine discipline (the Lord's chastening - correction that leads to instruction and reformation). If not already, within two days, dreamer will be found "judging" someone or a situation, unrighteous, and will be strongly convicted of this within, and it will feel overpowering, do not ignore the strong alarm of the Holy Ghost. Examples of judging, have you thought or said, "They're life is not holy, or they're not Christian, because I know they behave this way, or do that", or thought to yourself, "They need to sit down with all the emotional or physical hardship they're going through; they're not a super person". "How can they witness about God one moment, and then beg for money the next?" Or, "They have mental health issues". Have you never been in a fallen state, or had a material need, at the same time, you were required to testify of the Kingdom of God, the world to come or, did you just disobey the commission because of a preconceived notion or pseudo-image? Have you not been under such pressure emotionally or physically that you could have experienced an emotional or mental breakdown, and yet you were still required to witness, or to preach, on behalf of the Kingdom of God? With that said, dreamer, now you're judged as an offender, in that you have violated your own standard, the one you've held up, so high, for others to follow, for he or she who knows to do right and do not, to him or her it is a sin. You should have done what you expected of others or at least remembered from where you've come. While Christ does not deny the necessity of exercising a certain degree of discernment, or of making valid judgments with respect to sin in others. Jesus condemns the habit of criticizing others, while ignoring your own faults. A believer must first submit him or herself to God's righteous standard before attempting to examine and influence the conduct of others, which is often done in an unjust or unloving manner if you haven't judged yourself first. Another cause includes condemning a wrongdoer without a genuine desire to see the offender return to God, but to be condemned to hell. Here again, discharging a preset law within this type of offense, which is to not see you, as an offender, return to God, but to be condemn to hell also. Dreamer, genuinely deal with why you are so judgmental or critical, and repent over judging others, th is will remove such severe and unsympathetic standards from over your own life, and your dreams will change. Also, by so doing, a more compassionate, understanding, empathic and loving spirit will begin to manifest within you. Other reasons for such a severe warning are an unforgiving attitude towards someone, or literally rejecting the teachings of Christ and His apostles (Hebrews 6:4-8). See suggested course of action.

Painter: If not already, you will become a very prosperous and influential leader, and will acquire the title of such. You will reach prosperity suddenly. Use your influence exclusively for the Kingdom of God. God has given you a great gift. It would be to your advantage to recognize your Creator and to serve and worship Him, who is Jesus Christ. Submitting to Him as your Lord and Savior, will help you subdue your dark side that you may walk into your purpose. With that said, see category, Colors, e.g. color of paint. This will reveal any issues, if any, within you spiritually, which will need to be handled or su bdued, before your exaltation from the Lord comes, nonetheless, it will reveal your spiritual level.

Postal Service (e.g. Mail, Mailbox, Mailperson, Postal Clerk, or Post Office): Your dream generally suggests that the dreamer will be put into environments, where you will be responsible to usher God's presence into the mentality of those situations. Promoting the fundamentals of the gospel (see Acts 2:37-41), and the wisdom of the Word of God. Questions to journal: to whom was the mail addressed? Where was the mail delivered? What kind of customer and what was his or her action towards you? The where, what, and/or who connected to the mail, suggests the situations dreamer will be sent to. Generally, those who you are sent to are people whose ideas, arguments, and/or beliefs are base. Their arguments, ideas, and beliefs are illogical, non-mainstream, and without favorable conclusions. Your responsibility is to usher God's Presence in and magnify the Lord. This you do, when you proclaim His goodness and His truth. You are a vessel of God's glory, and a possessor of the truth needed for the place and situation at hand, the greater the truth, the greater your authority, the greater your success. Moreover, know that there are angels about you to protect and uphold you in case that's needed, therefore, do not be afraid of people faces, their positions, titles, wealth, nor of the place or circumstances. You are equipped to handle yo ur, and God's, business. Have faith in this.

Potter, Pottery (including all that's connected to pottery): The dreamer has been continually changed, converted, improved, rehabilitated, renewed, and transformed. As well, the Lord has destroyed your enemies from before you, even unto this time. Yet, you continue to embrace excessive indulgences, a lack of self-control, lack of knowledge, and spiritual uncleanness. Your behavior insinuates anger, animosity, confusion, out of order, an unforgiving spirit, and/or a weakness, is present within your heart. Your dream was sent to warn a rebellious person, namely the dreamer, in the spirit of grace (the free and unmerited favor and beneficence of God) of your irresponsible behavior and the consequences of such actions. To see if you will yet be worked upon, and change your mindset, or else to leave you inexcusable, in your accusations against God, because of your ruin (e.g. continually plundered, seized, and disfavored, also see Jeremiah 9:7-9; Zechariah 13:9; Matthew 23:37-39; Revelation 3:15-21). The more God allows you to see your emptiness, it is suggested that you be more earnest to repent that you may find Him to be grace and healing, refreshment, and a refuge in the midst of your resultant troubles. If necessary, see suggested course of action.

Refineries: Dreamer, you are creating your own difficulty by confounding "heart" issues with "nature" issues; they are quite distinct. It is important to recognize this, for you are confused. The Scriptures make the distinction clear enough. The heart is the center of your responsibility, and to deny that you are to improve and keep it clean is to deny your accountability (Psalm 51:10, James 4:8). The devil has sought to persuade you that you are not responsible for the state of your heart and that you cannot change the emotional state of your heart; and dreamer, your flesh, "nature issues", finds this lie very agreeable to its case. Dreamer, we do not believe with our nature, for things of our nature are just that "nature", but we a re ask to believe with our hearts. God does not ask you to perfect your nature, but He does ask you to perfect your heart (Deuteronomy 10:16, 1 Kings 8:61, Joel 2:13, Romans 10:10, et al.). Dreamer, while you have this great task before you to make your heart what it ought to be, according to Holy Writ. You are encouraged to press, daily, to seek grace to fulfill your responsibility. Instead of being discouraged by the difficulty of the work required, cry the more fervently to the Paraclete for His enablement. The Christian who means business will labor to have a "willing" heart, which acts spontaneously and gladly, not of necessity; but of a sincere, genuine, and a tender heart, yielding and pliable (Exodus 35:5, 1 Chronicles 29:9, 2 Chronicles 34:27). Strive for a perfect and upright heart, which is a broken heart, sorrowing over all failure and sin; a united heart, with all your affections centered on God; delighting in every part of Christian service, in His Word, and loving all God's people; and a sound heart, right in doctrine and practice.

Saw Mills: This is figurative of a person, namely the dreamer, whose deeds, hard work, and perseverance is recognized by God. The dreamer cannot tolerate wicked men. You have tested those who claim to be apostles but are not, and have found them false. You have persevered and endured hardships in Jesus name, and have not grown weary. However, now, you are forsaking your first love. Therefore, remember how you started your Christian walk, loving God, and ask for a revival, a nd a restoration of your first love, and it will be given you.

Steelworks: This is figurative of one who empowers others, physically, emotionally, and/or spiritually. Dreamer, you are gifted with multiple talents that may be expressed through inspirational acting, preaching, teaching, or writing. Dreamer, do not bury your prophetic gifts (see Luke 19:12-26); for many will be drawn to God because of your loving disposition and positive attitude; others will be dramatically changed by your example. Do not say what gift, for this is sin for you? As your dream supposes that, you are aware of, at least, one of your gifts (talent, skill). Thus, this dream comes to encourage the dreamer, if not already, to get busy doing something for the Kingdom. The Holy Spirit will lead the way. See suggested course of action.

Sweatshop: Your dream comes to warn an immoral leader or one who is in line for some level of leadership. Your activities are illegal. You have deliberately chosen to become enslaved to that which is forbidden by the One True and Living God. Your choices are not only spiritually forbidden and unhealthy, but are illegal as well. You use witchcraft in some for m or another, for you compel individuals to follow other gods, and hard-press people to believe what you say. As a result you will now begin to experience serious mental health issues and will have to be restrained, against your will if needs be. Dreamer, if urged by God, declare a one, two, or three day fast for sanctification purposes; also, wash (bathe) and make yourself, clothing, and personal surroundings clean. If not a day fast, you will need to declare some kind of fast and comm it to it, for a period-of- time, to abate this coming influence. Refrain from wickedness and do no one harm, physically, sexually, emotionally, and/or spiritually, any longer. Start treating God's people, your family, and others, with respect. By this, God will pardon your injustices. See suggested course of action.

Water Mills: This is figurative of a very spiritual place, and kindness shown to the dreamer. The religious practice of the people in this place is reflected within your dream. If not, do the research of the primary kinds of worship of the people depicted. What were the people primarily doing? This reveals their manner of worship. Do not allow the kindness of people to cloud God's truth that Jesus is the Way, the Truth, and the Life (John 14:6). Remember, your responsibility is to usher G od's Presence into whatever situation, people, or place, no matter the kindness, and magnify the Lord. This you do, when you proclaim His goodness and His truth.

Windmills: Dreamer, any large-scale calamities, and/or annoying irritations that have angered you intensely, something you've experienced recently, was indeed sent by God but not without purpose. Your experiences have (or should have) produced within you, soundness, integrity, and an honesty that would be "hard-pressed" or nearly impossible, to become corrupted again. Dreamer, begin to thank God for His longsuffering and loving kindness shown you, for now all your troubles will cease, having learned your lesson. Take great delight in this message of encouragement.

Physician, Psychiatrist, Healer, or Health Aides (any health care provider): Your dream denotes that your voice will be used as an instrument of righteousness. The dreamer's spiritual strength, tenacity, and knowledge, will be used of God; penetrating the soul of those who listen, affecting conversion. Dreamer now you will begin to experience a miraculous increase in divine knowledge and wisdom. This knowledge and wisdom will be imparted to you to be used exclusively for interpreting the gospel of Jesus Christ to others, and for the edifying of the Body of Christ; the body of believers. For, you are one who is fitted to teach the things concerning God, and the duties of man, namely those things regarding repentance and baptism of sin, teaching men the way of salvation, very much like John the Baptist's ministry. Dreamer, you are greatly anointed, enable to teach with great power and to reach many, very large crowds. You are becoming a master teacher and champion of the Word of God. Therefore, from now on, conduct yourself as a teacher, meaning, develop habits to be always willing and ready to teach anywhere, delivering didactical discourses, and imparting instructions. By this, you will become a very prestigious and honored leader, overseeing churches.

Plumbers, Plumbing: This dream has six meanings (one, two, etc., or all may apply). (1) Dreamer, God is going to heal your broken heart. If necessary, see suggested course of action. (2) Dreamer, character traits from ancestors, namely genetic codes and traits, will often trouble and taunt the offspring of a given progenitor, especially generational issues (Exodus 20:5-7). The demons that have so plague your family line, are now visiting (re-visiting) you, namely voices that whisper, you are without value, insignificant, or pointless, and it is the embracing of those voices that will lead to other issues, such as sexual perversion (e.g. adultery, fornication, homosexuality, prostitution, or whorishness), and on to a bleak and desolate atmosphere. This will lead to much sadness, and feelings of being forsaken or abandoned. Favorably, generational curses and issues can stop with you (Jeremiah 31:29, 30; Ezekiel 18:2-14, 20-23). Hence, your Heavenly Father is requiring that you overcome and subdue negative and dark emotions, feelings, behaviors, and/or ideas that have come to influence you, before they overcome you; and leave you desolate. Dreamer, God is not asking you to do something you cannot do. For a surety, vanquishing of dark influences can be done. By faith, you will need to declare some kind of fast and commit to it, for a long period -of-time, to abate the demonically instigated circumstance, you find yourself in now, Matthew 6:16-18. Try abstaining from food and drink (midnight to 6 PM), twice a week, and refrain from words, attitudes, people, places, and things, including music, magazines, videos, TV, or any such things that fuel anger and discontent, and stir up lustful feelings. This is also known as, faith with works, read, understand, and embrace James 2:14-26. Nonetheless, earnestly pray, God will guide, enable, and answer you as to the type of fast. Additionally, if relevant, forgive your mother and/or father for the darkness (aka curse) they may have perpetuated, for they knew not what they done. Forgiveness is important to your success (Matthew 6:12-15, 8:21-35). See suggested course of action. (3) Dreamer, you are insincere in your dealings with people, especially by being outwardly friendly but secretly disloyal. All of these behaviors are a sign of a hardened heart or a heart becoming hardened and deep -seated anger. Your behavior opened the door for a demonic instigated situation or issue. Dreamer, your present situation, or issue, whatever "it" is, "it" was demonically instigated, and "it" is spiritually perverse. Dreamer, the Lord Jesus, is asking you to come to Him, come away privately, and ask Him to heal you, come, and ask Him to deliver you; and give Him authority over your life that you might be healed, delivered, and set free. Thus says the Lord, "I will sprinkle clean water on you, and you will be clean; I will cleanse you from all your impurities and from all your idols. I will give you a new heart and put a new spirit in you; I will remove from you your heart of stone and give you a heart of flesh (Ezekiel 36:25-27). Dreamer, God knows your thoughts afar off, so genuinely repent. Other than heartfelt repentance to Jesus, no other excuse or weak justification will be heard. See suggested course of action. (4) Your dream also represents some type of spiritual privileges and a purification process, dreamer God will now separate you from people, places, and circumstances that will hinder your growth. View this separation as a blessing from God and not as an evil thing has happen. Under all adversities retain a spirit of joy, and continue to ma ke progress in your spiritual life. Subsequently, dreamer, because of your humble and submissive faith in God's word, you will be declared as one who is a righteous minister, planted in the House of the Lord, and you will continue to prosper and mature. The same God, who plants you in your ministry, is the same God who will cause you to mature and prosper. Further, another benefit of allowing Jesus to have authority of your life; is that independent of outward circumstances, you will live and thr ive where most things perish, via divine grace. Dreamer, while your spiritual growth may not be so rapid, if you endure, you will become a beautiful picture of a godly man or woman, who in your uprightness, aims to glorify God. Accordingly, gladness, thanksgiving, singing, strength, intense energy, and fertility will be your recompense, and your praise will be a sweet aroma in the nostrils of the Lord. If applicable, this promise is also to your generations to come. Come what may, you shall make steady progress and flourish in a very impressive manner; bringing forth fruit, even in your old age. Dreamer, as you age, your anointing to minister, and divine revelations, will always be fresh and edifying. See Psalm 92:12-15. Therefore, put the spiritual work in and go through what you need to go through now. If necessary, see suggested course of action. (5) Male dreamer: An event or situation that will cause intense fear is coming to discourage and terrify you. This will be in the fo rm of an annoying, difficult, and unpleasant person. The trouble this person will cause will become so overwhelming, because they will expose a secret regarding you. This spiritual battle will be great, and will demand your full attention. Although you will walk through this alone, know that God will walk you through it. Dreamer, learn wisdom from the situation, for truth do set one free; and go on from there unashamed. Then, suddenly, unexpectedly, and without any warning, all the evil and wickedness that caused you to fear and be troubled, will disappear. It will be as though it was never there. At that point, you will express great joy, and feel extremely happy. Take courage and be strong, knowing that the Lord knows where you are, what's going on, and He cares. See suggested course of action. (6) Male dreamer (unmarried): Your dream denotes that a very attractive and sensual female; one whom the dreamer, may marry, especially before having sex, will enter your life. If necessary, see suggested course of action.

Volunteer (working without compensation): Your dream was sent to encourage the dreamer. Even now, when things appear at their worst, and it seems that your state of affairs, because of your own neglect or other misfortune, is worthy of harsh and cruel criticism, as well as, is unacceptable. This too shall pass. You will overcome your personal issues, and no longer give power to those who do not care about you, nor your situation; those who would be pleased to continue to see you in bondage, unstable, and dominated by them. You will receive an act of kindness from someone, because of your friendly attitude, with no strings attached. This is God's favor granted you. Dreamer, you will be comforted double to the sorrows you've experienced, and double blessings (see also Zechariah 9:12). God has saved the best for last. Continue to hope in God, and seriously no longer exalt others, image, or other fleeting vanities above your personal relationship with God.

Worker's Compensation (paid for injury at work): Your dream was sent to demonstrate grace, via a warning. Dreamer, due to your challenging life activities, personal illness, and/or the wearying of others, you have become very exhausted emotionally. Overcome by profound discouragement and a sense of being alone in your conflicts, coupled with exhaustion, an old familiar lifestyle has reared (or will rear) up its' ugly head to try to take advantage of your physical weakness. Dream er stand still, cease from your ministerial work and take a rest; know that God is God. He is able to care for you, to care for His ministry He has assigned to you, and He knows where you are. He alone will deliver you out of the snares of the enemy. Go take a long vacation. Schedule it within two months at the latest. If you do not take a sabbatical, you will be forced into one via a serious illness. This illness may be avoided if you will rest. During your rest, your Heavenly Father will heal your discouragement in a caring and understanding manner. He will allow you to sleep, and He will nourish and visit you with inspiring revelations of His Power and Presence and give additional revelation regarding direction for your life. The hope, labor, love, and struggle of your life's work are not in vain. You are not alone; neither should you feel that way.

Working Late, Double Shift, or Overtime: God is getting ready to restore you, and you will reap your due recompense, for God rewards those who diligently serve Him. You have been judged diligent in your efforts. Many will rejoice with you, they that are rich and powerful and those who are full of faith. You shall go out with joy and be led forth with peace.

Suggested Course of Action

Question to consider and journal, did your dream depict any symbols that alludes to, the dreamer will make the necessary changes, spiritually, emotionally, and/or physically to affect a more positive outcome? If changes are initiated, your dreams will change. Notwithstanding, in a state seemingly irrecoverable, is when Christ, great light will arise, and shine upon you; and communicate spiritual light, life, and purpose, to guide the work of your hands into the way of peace, His peace, via the blo od of His cross. He will lead you into the true way of enjoying the fruit of your labor, spiritual peace, and eternal peace hereafter, if you so choose His way. Dreamer, though there are difficulties on your way to heaven, yet the grace of God will carry you over them, and make even the laborious ways a way. Therefore, since you are being called, converted, and enlightened by Christ, go and show yourself amongst the people and children of God, in His house (aka a church), commit, and submit to the ordinances of that house, if it's a bible believing congregation. Once you're settled, be a light to others. Nonetheless, be encourage God will lead you.

Now, pray (See Prayer of Deliverance, pg. 897)

Specific Meaning

Unless otherwise noted elsewhere, if, in your everyday living, your awaked state, as part of your lifestyle, work, or ministerial activities, or a special event, you have a very real connection with any activity involving work of any kind, especially that listed. Dreams of this sort, for the most part, are ordinary dreams, resulting from your daily activities (see Chapter One, Chalom). These sorts of dreams are usually about your routine, mundane activities or anxieties that overwhelm your mind during the day. They are an inner release mechanism, which helps provide you with emotional balance and the maintaining of your sanity. These dreams are not significant, and do not warrant special attention.

Note: If, within your dream, your work, depicted accidents or any harmful incidents, this type of dream may be heeded as an alert or warning in the physical realm, to the dreamer. Do not assume that things are safe or ok, caution should be heeded. The dreamer may consider his or her dream as a clue given to assist in finding facts, needed to support a prevailing situation or investigation. The alarm, kept within context of the dream, should be relevant to your lifestyle and closely resemble your real-life situations. Meaning it can actually occur during your awaked state. Consider all the people, places, backgrounds, and activity highlighted within your dream. This will help you narrow down the specific area of concern. However, if your dream was inundated with symbols that are not specifically related to your job and/or responsibilities, then the spiritual implications should be heeded.

AGRICULTURE AND FORESTRY

And God said, Let the earth put forth grass, herbs yielding seed, and fruit-trees bearing fruit after their kind, wherein is the seed thereof, upon the earth: and it was so. And the earth brought forth grass, herbs yielding seed after their kind, and trees b earing fruit, wherein, is the seed thereof, after their kind: and God saw that it was good. And there was evening and there was morning, a third day. And God said, Behold, I have given you every herb yielding seed, which is upon the face of all the ear th, and every tree. In which is the fruit of a tree yielding seed; to you it shall be for food: and to every beast of the earth, and to every bird of the heavens, and to everything that creepiest upon the earth, wherein there is life, I have given every green h erb for food: and it was so. And God saw everything that he had made; and behold it was very good. And there was evening and there was morning, the sixth day. And out of the ground made Jehovah God to grow every tree that is pleasant to the sight, and goo d for food, the tree of life was in the midst of the garden, and the tree of the knowledge of good and evil. And Jehovah God commanded the man, saying, of every tree of the garden thou may freely eat: but of the tree of the knowledge of good and evil, thou shalt not eat of it: for in the day that thou eat thereof thou shalt surely die (Genesis 1:11-13, 29-31; 2:9, 16, 17 ASV).

{Then Jesus said,} "I am the true vine, and my Father takes care of the vineyard. He removes every one of my branches that doesn't produce fruit. He also prunes every branch that does produce fruit to make it produce more fruit. Live in me, and I will live in you. A branch cannot produce any fruit by itself. It has to stay attached to the vine. In the same way, you cannot produce fruit unless you live in me. "I am the vine. You are the branches. Those who live in me while I live in them will produce a lot of fruit. But you can't produce anything without me. (John 15:1, 2, 4, 5 GW)

Give ear, and hear my voice; give attention, and hear my speech. Does he who plows for sowing plow continually? Does he continually open and harrow his ground? When he has leveled its surface, does he not scatter dill, sow cumin, and put in whe at in rows and barley in its proper place, and emmer as the border? For he is rightly instructed, his God teaches him. Dill is not threshed with a threshing sledge, nor is a cart wheel rolled over cumin, but dill is beaten out with a stick, and cumin with a rod. Does one crush grain for bread? No, he does not thresh it forever, when he drives his cart wheel over it with his horses, he does not crush it. This also comes from the Lord of hosts; he is wonderful in counsel and excellent in wisdom. (Isaiah 28:23-29 ESV).

This category deals with farming, gardening, planting, burying, ground, soil, dirt, harvesting, crops, flowers, plants, and trees. Some short descriptions of types, phrases, and other processes and particulars, connected in some way to this category are, for example, barns, farmers, farming equipment, food, fruit, hedges, land, soil conditions, leaves, pruning, seeds, spices, water, weeds. Also, see category content list, or index.

All Symbols and Referents, Notes (1, 2, 3, etc.), Suggested Course of Action, and Specific Meaning offer guidance toward a more comprehensive interpretation.

Notes

1. Unless otherwise noted elsewhere, if, in your everyday living, your awaked state, as part of your lifestyle, work, or ministerial activities, or a special event, you have a very real connection with any agriculture or forestry activity. For example, arbor culturist, botanist, builder, seller of farm buildings or equipment, cultivator, Department of Forestry, farmer, farm worker, fieldworker, forester, gardener, harvester, horticulturist, landscaper, logger, lumberjack,

migrant or seasonal worker, nursery, restaurateur, tiller, tree farmer, USDA, vineyard, winery, your dream is not significant and does not warrant special attention.

Otherwise noted, per your lifestyle, if your dream closely resembled real life situations, meaning it can actually occur during your awaked state, this dream may be an Ordinary Dream, resulting from your daily activities (see Chapter One, Chalom). These sorts of dreams are usually about your routine, mundane activities or anxieties that overwhelm your mind during the day. They are an inner release mechanism, which helps provide you with emotional balance and the maintaining of your sanity. These dreams are not significant, and do not warrant special attention.

2. Probables: As agriculture and forestry are frequently demonstrated in many, and very personal ways; for example, was you raised in a farming community? Were your parents migrant workers? Were you married in a rose garden? Thus, could the agriculture or forestry depicted be a possible probable (see Chapter One, section entitled, Probables)? Hence, dreamer may also consider your own personal and special associations with agriculture and forestry, as long as the interpretation is kept within the principles of spiritual boundary markers, landmarks, and property lines, (see Chapter One, section entitled, Spiritualizing Boundary Markers, Landmarks, and Property Lines).

3. Determine who your dream is for you or another. Always, considering yourself first, reflecting on your present behaviors. Ask yourself, why am I dreaming about this now? What is this dream revealing about me? Have I taken on new attributes? Has anyone commented on my present behaviors as being untypical of me? Has my ministry changed for the better or for the worse? What about my beliefs, doctrine, or philosophy, are they still based on Holy Writ? Is there something I need to know about those I am ministering to or serving?"

Remember your actions and emotions within your dream. Did you do the, tilling, pruning, planting, growing, harvesting, eating, or cutting down? Did you try to separate weeds from crops (weeding), or use insecticides, in any way? Did you cook, eat, and/or serve anything? Did a tree fall down by itself? Unless otherwise noted elsewhere, an answer of yes, to one or more of these, or similar questions, is a good indicator that your dream is about you (the dreamer). Dreamer what symbolic "seeds" are you planting, growing, or reaping? This planting can be of a sacrosanct or sacrilegious doctrine or philosophy; thus, this dream. On another vein, could the results of good choices, or the consequences of bad choices, be growing, or producing good or bad "returns" during this season within your life? Are you in a process of renewal, sanctification, or transformation; hence a dream of tilling or cultivation of land, which is symbolic of your attitude, mind, mental health, understanding, perspective, and/or reasoning? Are you judgmental, self - righteous, or intolerant of others, thus, an attempt by the dreamer to separate, pull, or kill weeds? In light of your dream, via the relevant interpretation, do you believe that your behavior will enhance or endanger your well-being, safety, and/or happiness, if so, how and why? Do you believe that your belief system will strengthen or weaken you spiritually in any way, if so, how and why? Is spiritual or physical death a possibility (e.g. a falling tree), perhaps because of lifestyle choices? See following relevant subcategory, the interpretation is about and for you.

Did someone else prune, till, cut down, plant, grow, or gather crops? Did someone else prepare or cultivate land? Did someone else try to separate weeds from crops (weeding), or use insecticides, in any way? Did another cook, eat, and/or serve anything? Unless otherwise noted elsewhere, an answer of yes, to one or more of these, or similar questions, is a good indicator that your dream is about another and their role, and/or influential effects, within the life of the dreamer. Consider, is someone greatly influencing your physical, spiritual, or mental health, your understanding, perspective, and reasoning regarding spiritual issues? Are they enhancing your spiritual and/or literal prosperity, or are they responsible for the dwindling thereof? Could they be influencing your ministry, on some level? Do you know someone whose life activities or physical being is similar to that which stood out the most within your dream? Could it be that person? If you sense that your dream is for or about another, the question as to why you have been made privy to this information, and how do you factor into the equation, should be seriously considered along with necessary actions. Perhaps the dreamer is being made aware of the plight of someone, and you are to get involved (see Chapter One, Are You Ready to Hear the Messages in Your Dreams, section entitled, The 10% for others).

If your dream is for, or about another:

Dreams that reference others and the revelation within those dreams, is not given haphazardly to any individual, but only to those with the ability, and influence to do something with the information; this is also prophecy. With that, journal the following questions, and if unable to answer the questions now, this denotes that the person, represented within your dream, will enter your life shortly. Are you entering into a personal relationship with someone? Do you not know or understand what you're looking at, especially certain behaviors, when learning about this person? Has someone new entered your life or maybe you've just begun opening up to someone not so new, and have started listening to their advice, accepting their assistance, or are you enabling someone? Are you in denial regarding the toxicity of one of your present relationships, particularly a spouse, family member, or friend? Are you anxious, concerned, frightened, and/or troubled by recent changes in your behavior, especially because of someone's influence upon your life at present? Have you allowed someone to convince you to deceive another? Have you recently become aware of (or is being made aware of, via your dream) certain undesirable behaviors within you towards another? Are you trying to cut ties with one that is bad company? Have you just joined (or re-joined) a church, fellowship, or social group?

Note: If your dream has attributes that indicate that your dream is about you, and other attributes that indicate that your dream is about another, dreamer should consider that your dream is about you and another. For example, while you may have prepared the land, thus indicating that the dream is about the dreamer, someone else may have done the weeding, thus indicating that your dream is about another. Therefore, while your dream is about the dream er, the dreamer should expect the role and/or influential effects of another, also plays a part in your interpretation. For example, another may have cut down trees on the dreamer's property without permission. Now the dreamer is in a heated legal battle with someone, again, see relevant interpretation.

More questions to consider. Why has the person been allowed within your life, and/or how did they get there? Again, if unable to answer the questions now, this denotes that the person, represented within your dream, will enter your life shortly. If their activity, within your dream, has proven positive, via the interpretation, this someone will prove, unwittingly, to be a very strong ally, benefactor, defender, and supporter. God has sent this someone into your life to help you carry out your next endeavor by enlarging your spiritual capacity. Allow the strength of that person's character to guide, help, and support you. On the other hand, if his or her presence and/or activity, within your dream, proved negative, via the interpretation, for sure, this person will prove to be a very strong and formidable challenge for you, perhaps unto death. If negative, this dream is a dire warning. Take steps accordingly to struggle against, or to cut off, adverse and unfavorable relationships. Remember certain personalities are all encompassing, affecting everything, cataclysmic, contagious, deadly, harmful, infectious, predatory, and/or venomous. Symbolically meaning that if allowed to continue or prosper within your life, serious harm or devastation to the dreamer may result. Idolize no one, especially beyond the warning of the Lord, and we are definitely not to lay our lives down for no one. No longer, allow that particular person's influence within your life to continue or thrive. Then again, this person maybe allowed within your life, because of the dreamer's unwillingness to abstain from immorality after having been asked to abstain from such by

God, see 1 Corinthians 6:9-20, Galatians 5:19-21, or the dreamer's self-righteous behavior, or a lack of a balanced and honest view of your own personality. In this case, this person will affect self-awareness within the life of the dreamer, exposing the negative traits of your personality, especially those traits, which cause you to follow, or to be so easily misled, and/or your wrong beliefs; no matter, this type of mentality needs reckoning with. Graciously, all of this will restore the dreamer to his or her right place with God, opening your eyes to see how far you've strayed from God (1

Corinthians 5:4-7; James 5:20). The lesson is, no matter how personable, powerful, or difficult a person, or how uncertain or unpopular the choices and issues, always take the next biblical and ethical step, for obedience to God's principles will always prove safer and stronger foundationally. Although, you will need all kinds of outside support to recover from this person's domination, again, no longer, allow that particular person's influence within your life to continue or thrive, especially if negative, end it abruptly.

4.   Consider all the people, places, backgrounds, and activity highlighted within your dream.
Known (in your awaked life) person, animal, place, or organization within your dream:
Unless otherwise noted elsewhere, people, animals, places, backgrounds that are actually known by the dreamer in your awaked life, indicates a part of you that you recognize within yourself on some level or another. Question to journal, if dreamer seriously considers all the particulars, what stood out the most, what features, or character traits stood out the most. For example, age, color, height, size, happiness, considerate, loving, let you be yourself, peacefulness, encourager, irrational, leader, liar, mentor, passionate, personable, neglected, poor, run-down, sage, shyster, unwise, upscale, vengeful. Write down (journal) the particular highlighted within your dream. The attribute or activity highlighted is for a reason. Since the attribute written down is a part of you, namely the dreamer's nature, demeanor, and/or lifestyle, an honest and unbiased assessment is very important for truth sake. Happy note, considering that other people's attributes, within dreams, also represent attributes of your own personality, causes one to look at another in a better light. According to your capacity to embrace self-awareness and a rectification of mind, body, and spirit, God will begin to enhance, make better, more attractive, sanctify, diminish, and make pure and free from sin and guilt, this part of you.

Otherwise noted, if the person, animal, place, or background within your dream is actually known by the dreamer, in your awaked life, this person, animal, place, or background may represent him or herself, or itself.

Unknown in your awaked life or although known, was unseen, invisible, or only talked about - person, animal, place, or organization within your dream:
Unless otherwise noted elsewhere, if you did not recognize, the person, place, thing, they, or it, was not seen, invisible, or only talked about within your dream, this indicates an attribute or activity within your life that you are unfamiliar with, or are in denial about, or you refuse to acknowledge it, but it does exists. Question to journal: what character trait, feature, action, or activity, stood out the most? For example, age, color, height, size, happiness, considerate, loving, let you be yourself, peacefulness, encourager, irrational, leader, liar, mentor, passionate, personable, neglected, poor, run-down, sage, shyster, unwise, upscale, vengeful. Although, on some conscious level, you are aware of a certain behavior or attribute within you, you have chosen to filter out or simply ignore certain information about yourself that contradicts your view of yourself and/or your preconceived notions of others and of the world around you. Possibly protecting yourself, emotionally and psychologically, from a situation, which you are unable to cope with at this time, or you lack control over; then again, perhaps the dreamer has an exaggerated or unrealistic view of yourself. No matter the reason, right now a question is before you, via your dream. Do you want to know this part of yourself? According to your ability to handle self-awareness, God will begin to reveal this side of you to you. Why, He wants

to balance your understanding of things; thus, effecting wholeness within your life, so that the enemy will no longer be able to manipulate your emotions so easily. The Holy Spirit is with you to help you throughout th is entire process, listen to Him. Now, in your life, this activity or attribute needs reckoning with, somehow or some way.

Otherwise noted, (known or unknown), if the person, place or thing that initiated (or was a recipient of) the action or activity within your dream was not seen, invisible, or only talked about within your dream, this may indicate that the dreamer does not recognize the influential effects another has within your life, or upon your attitude.

If more than one person (known or unknown):

Consider what the group had in common. What behavior, character trait, feature, action, or activity, stood out the most? For example, were they argumentative, authoritative, beautiful, criminal minded, dancing, difficult, dressed unusual, enigmatic, fighting, focused, flirty, helpful, hurtful intentions, powerful, promiscuous, quiet, secretive, seemed unreal, unassuming? What about age, color, height, size, happiness, considerate, loving, let you be yourself, peacefulness, encourager, irrational, leader, liar, mentor, passionate, personable, neglected, poor, run-down, sage, shyster, unwise, upscale, vengeful, death. Was it a group of cucumber pickers, or was topography or weather primary? What condition was the ground, or state of the weather? Was there adverse conditions? The attribute, activity, or condition highlighted, its characteristic, property, or quality is for a reason. That which was highlighted and noted is what you need to focus on at present.

If the attribute or quality is a desirable or positive one, allow the strength of that attribute to help you overcome some manner of immorality or irreverence within your life and/or to help you to become better, productively, for the Kingdom of God in some manner. If the attribute is an undesirable or negative one, take steps accordingly to struggle against the growing desires of the carnal side of you. If applicable, get help and support via prayer, fasting, and a Christian based support group.

For dreams of the dead see following note.

Was someone buried in a field, who and why? While the dead has nothing to do with the living (Ecclesiastes 9:4-6), it may be considered what character trait did that person represent to the dreamer, while the person was actually alive, what character feature stood out the most. With that trait noted, dreamer may consider that the trait noted, is within the dreamer, and that trait is no longer useful or needed for the progression of your spiritual walk, on this side of heaven. Dreamer, it is suggested that you render that trait (good or bad) obsolete, and began anew attempting to move forward, using different tactics to overcome unproductive habitual life cycle choices, and for maneuvering through this thing we call life in a more, better way. See category, Death, and/or other relevant categories.

5. In addition to the following interpretations, see index or relevant categories for more information. For example, if money was involved in some way, see category, Currency; if weather was highlighted, see category, Weather. If buildings were involved in some way, see category, Buildings Kept within context of your dream and the interpretation, the additional symbols are perhaps relevant. It will be within the sum of all the symbols that you will find a more thorough interpretation.

6. Since the following list is not extensive, dreamer is encouraged to seek biblical guidelines and other relevant research to determine the metaphorical meaning of your particular agriculture or forestry activity, depicted within your dream, via a Bible concordance, Bible illustrated dictionary, encyclopedia, or internet. Having done your research you should be able to determine some basic behaviors or attributes your Lord and Savior wants you to focus on.

Symbols and Referents

In keeping with the fact that believers are, likened unto plants and trees, and their behaviors and consideration for others, to flowers and fruits, most dreams of agriculture and forestry activity (e.g. farming, flowers, gardening, and/or trees) generally imply a need to reflect on, your behavior, if it's correct or appropriate and on your spiritual health. As well as, a time to reflect on your ministry, does it properly consider others, and on your prosperity (or the dwindling thereof). It also implies a ti me to consider your physical health.

In addition to the varied meanings of agricultural and forestry activity, other common words, expressions, usages (e.g. slang or clichés), or a 'probable' that are metaphorically represented by the following are also considered (this section is an addendum at the end of the relevant subcategory). For example, do you have your and a special someone initials engraved onto a certain tree?

Category Content - if not listed, see index, perchance, for your specific type of agriculture type dream.

- Agricultural Structures (Barn or Granary or Root Cellar or Silo; Farmhouse or Shed or Storm cellar, or any shelter for farmers, farm workers, and their families; Greenhouse or Glasshouse (a building with glass walls and roof); Stable or Chicken Coop or Cowshed or Sty)
- Agricultural Vehicles (e.g. Farm Truck, Harvester, Mower, Plough, Tractor, see category Vehicles (Farming Vehicles)
- Crops (Orchards, Groves, Fields, Patch, or other crops, e.g. Apple Orchard, Orange Grove, Cucumber Field, Strawberry Patch, Plantations, refers to crops grown and/or harvested on a large scale)
- To work on a Plantation
- Cuttings or Grafting or Rooting (refers to a Bud, Leaf, or Root, removed from a plant to propagate a new plant through grafting or rooting)
- Farmer (Dairy Farmer, Grazer, Herder, Sharecropper, Shepherd, Sower, Truck Farmer)
- Farm Worker (Fieldworker, Harvester, Migrant or Seasonal Worker, doing farm work, does not own the farm)
- Food or Foodstuff (Bread or Yeast, Leaven (flat, unleavened bread); Bread, Cornbread, Muffins, see subcategory, Cereal Grasses, Grains; Butter; Cereal Grasses, Grains [e.g. Barley, Buckwheat, Cornbread, Flour, Indian Corn, Maize, Meal, Millet, Oats, Rice, Rye, Wheat, and any foodstuff prepared from Cereal Grasses, Grains, e.g. Bread, Breakfast Cereals, Crackers, Grits, Hominy, Muffins, Oatmeal, Pasta, Tortillas]; Eggs, see category, Animals, Note 5; Fruit [refers to the edible, or non-edible, fruit of a plant, e.g. Apples, Bananas, Grapes, Lemons, Oranges, Strawberries, or poisonous fruits, such as Daphne, European Spindle, Horse Chestnut, and Jerusalem Cherry Tree. This category also includes food or drink made primarily of fruit, e.g. Applesauce, Fruit Juice, Grape Juice, Lemonade, Pumpkin Pie, Apple Fritters, Fruit Salads, and other foods and drinks that are primarily made with fruit]; Figs: see subcategory, Fig Tree; Fruity; Herbs and Spices [e.g. Anise, Basil, Bay Leaf, Chives, Cinnamon, Cloves, Garlic, Mints, Mustard, Oregano, Pepper, Parsley, Salt, Spikenard, Thymes, to taste, see, or smell-appropriate smell, any of a variety of pungent aromatic spices used for flavoring food]; Salt (incl. Salt Mines); To not eat, want, dislike, or to reject any herbs or spices: See subcategory, Vegetables [to not eat, want, dislike, or to reject any vegetables, herbs, or spices]; Honey; Milk; Oil, Cooking with oil, or Drinking it [Canola, Olive, or Vegetable Oil]; Pastries or Cake or Candy; Salad Dressings or Sauces [savory dressings or sauces for salads and other foods, e.g. Balsamic, Blue Cheese, French, Italian, Ketchup, Ranch, Vinaigrette, Gravies]; Vegetables [any plants whose leaves, stems, or flowers are cooked and used for food, e.g. Bell or Red Peppers, Beets, Broccoli, Brussels Sprouts, Carrots, Corn, Cucumbers, Greens, Gourds, Squashes, Tomatoes]; Roots, Stems, Stalks, Tubers [the underground portion of a plant that supports a plant, e.g.

Bulbs, Corms, Potatoes, Rhizomes, Tubers, Tulips, Lilies, Daffodils, Beets, Carrots, Potatoes, Turnips, Yams; Vinegar, Cider

- Flowers (Annuals, Biennials, and Perennials, any parts of a plant that consists of Leaves, Petals, Sepals, surrounding Stamens and Pistils, they are colorful, sometimes scented, and cultivated for their blooms or blossoms, and known for their aesthetic values)
    - Annuals (any flower, plant, vegetable, or herb, completing their life cycle within the space of one year, they germinate, produce seeds, flower, and die all in one year); Biennials (any flower, plant, vegetable, or herb, completing their life cycle within the space of two years); Perennials (any flower, fruit, plant, vegetable, or herb, whose life cycle lasts three seasons or more, or lasting an indefinitely long time; recurring again and again); Face appears in the middle of a flower; Plastic Flowers (or if flowers were laminated or heat sealed in plastic); Potted Plants; Smelling Roses or Flowers, "stop and smell the roses" or "stop and smell the flowers"
- Garden or Gardening or Gardener or Nurseryman (a plot of ground where flowers, vegetables, fruits, or herbs are cultivated)
    - Garden of Eden; To lead or take somebody up or down a Garden Path
- Ground or Soil, Dirt (the earth, soil, or any other similar medium, in which agricultural growth and development takes place, or development ceases, because of adverse conditions)
    - Broken up ground (to break-up and turn over earth; ground separated into parts or pieces, usually with shovel, pick), see subcategory, Plowing. Cultivated and Good Ground, Soil, or Dirt (rich looking earth, cleared of debris, plowed, and fertilized); Uncultivated Ground (ground not tilled or land unusable for the growing of crops); Dry, Desert, or Infertile Ground, see category, Landforms (Desert, Sand); Thorns and Thistles; Track of land trodden down (e.g. Dirt Road); Rocky Ground; Weeds; Ground; Soil
- Harvesting or Reaping (the gathering or reaping of a crop during a particular season)
- Hedges (a row of shrubs, a close-set row of bushes, usually with their branches intermingled, forming a barrier or boundary in a garden, lawn, or field)
- Leaf, Leaves (the foliage of a plant or tree)
    - Autumn or Fall Foliage (bright multi-color leaves, especially orange, reds, and yellows); Dried-up or Withered Leaves; Falling Leaves; Summer, Spring Foliage (green leaves); Making use of Leaves for Arts and Crafts, Clothing, Eating, or Smoking; Take a Leaf out of somebody's book; Turning over a new Leaf (or a leaf in good condition)
- Plants, Planting, Sowing (Saplings, Seedlings, Plants; to put any number of plants or seeds into the ground to grow)
    - Blighted Plants (any plant disease that mars and/or prevents growth); Plant a Bush, Seedling, Shrub, Thicket, Tree, or Grain into the Ground; Plant any manner of Flowers, Shrubs, Trees, Vegetables, or Herbs, in or around a Church, Sanctuary, Synagogue, Temple, any consecrated place; Plant or bury a literal bug, listening, or explosive device (e.g. "bugging a room", planting a bomb, or to bury landmines); Plant or bury any type of building (e.g. to dream of planting or burying a church, house, or school); Plant or bury one who is a cleric or ministerial leader; Plant or bury evidence (to dream of planting or burying some kind of evidence, especially that which has to do with the legal system); Plant a literal foot (to dream of planting or burying something 12 inches "one foot" underground, or to Plant or bury a literal foot)
- Plowing (to break-up and turn over earth; usually with shovel, pick, or some type of plowing machine)
- Prune or Weeding (to cut back the growth of, trim, weed-out)
- Trees, Bushes, Forests, Shrubs, and Thickets
    - Condition of Trees, Kinds of Trees, Parts of Trees, and Activities connected to Trees (Barren, Dead, or Withered Tree, Bush, Forest, Shrub, or Thicket [does not include

deciduous trees, bushes, shrubs, and thickets in winter]; Beautiful Trees, Tree of Life [tree appeared beautiful]; Budding [to see a tree budding]; Tree[s] falling down; Trees going from bad to good; Trees going from good to bad; Tree with People, Animals, Clothing hanging from it, on it, or in it; Tree House, Tree Shaping, and Trees Growing Wildly; Large, enormous, big tree [or to watch a tree grow very large]; Trees beside a stream)

- Kinds of Trees (Algum Tree; Almond tree; Aromatic Trees, Bushes, Shrubs, or Thickets [that exudes a distinct odor that is specific to that species]; Jasmine Bush; Lilac Bush; Lemon Tree; Pine Tree; Spicebush]; Carob Tree; Cedar Tree; Cypress Tree; Evergreen Tree; Juniper Tree; Palm Tree; Palmetto Tree; Pine Tree; Chestnut Tree; Deciduous Trees, Bushes, Shrubs, and Thickets; Elm Tree; Ferns; Fig Tree; Fir Tree; Forests [aka Woods]; Oak Tree; Olive Tree; Terebinth Tree; Pomegranate Tree; Sapling, Seedling (a young plant or tree grown from a seed); Shade Trees; Weeping Willow
- Parts of Trees (Branches; Rod, Scepter, Staff, Wand, or Baton [a long thin implement usually made of wood or metal]; Stump; Wood or Bark [incl. gopher wood]; Cutting the Bark of a tree, see subcategory, Cut down or Burned branches
- Activities Connected to Trees (Climb a tree, up in a tree; Chased or Forced up a Tree; Cross, Crucifix [to see a cross or symbol of a cross, crucifix, or any symbol connected to the crucifixion of Jesus Christ]; Smelling a Branch, or putting a branch [or leaf] to, or on, your Nose)
- Vines and Vineyard (e.g. grapevines or where wine grapes are grown)

Agricultural Structures

Barn, Granary, Root Cellar, or Silo: Your dream denotes abundant provision. The dreamer is strongly encouraged to be careful to do all that the Lord has commanded you to do, up until this moment. Dreamer, if you diligently obey the voice of Jehovah God, the blessings of obedience will now begin to overtake you. The blessings of obedience include but are not limited to gifts of God's grace that will produce spiritual growth within you. Gifts of God's grace, anything God freely gives you, absolution, the Holy Spirit, salvation, regeneration, eternal life, health, children, love of family, longevity, necessities, prosperity, and dominion over all that is yours; and all are parts of the supply of grace, and all are sanctified by the Lord, and technically, belongs to Him. The result of this supply in your life will be peace. If you are not obedient and/or diligent, you should expect to receive the fruits of rebellion, leading to spiritual and/or physical devastation, also be aware of covetousness. See suggested course of action.

Farmhouse or Shed or Storm Cellar, or any shelter for farmers, farm workers, and their families): Your dream implies one who is a natural mediator; perhaps a judge, teacher, or an apologist (one who defends and justifies Christian ity), as you is genuine, tactful, and adaptable. Dreamer, you've experienced a great balancing of your theology, resulting in a belief that is complete, with solid attributes, and your inspirations will make for very good teaching. Moreover, your sensitivity and gentleness will be (is) a great healing force in the lives of others, bringing harmony and support to them, via defending them, by any right means necessary, against the deceit and trickery of the enemy, and by teaching them about simple faith. By this, you advance the cause of God, against the enemies of His Kingdom. Additionally, if applicable, your children will reap the fruits of the blessing of your giving. As you are now able to handle great responsibility and wealth, and are one who is tolerant, you will experience receiving an act of kindness, monetarily, from someone who is affluent. You must also become a fundraiser for, and giver of, charity.

Greenhouse or Glasshouse (a building with glass walls and roof): This word of the Lord has come to the dreamer twice. Your dream denotes a choice of life or devastation and has several parts. There is a need for sanctification within the life of the dreamer, for your dream was sent to expose human glory, celebrity, arrogance, shortness of life, and/or a serious extended illness. God, and God alone is to be worship", for God has said, "I will not give my glory to another" (Isaiah 42:8). For Jesus has been counted worthy of more glory, inasmuch as the builder of the house has more honor than the house; for, every house is built by someone, but the builder of all things is God" (Hebrews 3:2-4). Therefore, dreamer you are warned to be careful lest you become so prideful that there creeps into you the idea that you can be deified. Self-deification is of Satan. God can dwell in the human, via the Holy Spirit, but forever the human is the human, and Adonai Elohim is forever God. Graciously, and compassionately, God has you in a process of sanctification at present, recognize, and respect the process. Sanctification is a process by which one is made holy via fasting, prayer, and a genuine return to living life on God's terms and not yours. Your attitude, mind, mental health, understanding, perspective, and reasoning are being renewed and transformed. Additionally, your dream strongly emphasizes the need to guard your unique gift of words. For, through your words, you will receive healing or your healing will remain "unclaimed". You, and only you, are responsible for your words, for, as King Solom on says, the tongue has the power of life and death, (Proverbs 18:21). Moreover, it is written, blessed is the one who does not walk in step with the wicked or stand in the way that sinners take or sit in the company of mockers, (Psalm 1:1), you are also solely responsible for your actions, no other is at fault. Dreamer, negative speech is even worse than the illness itself. If no a ction is taken to set a guard over your mouth, emotions, and thinking, when the overwhelming scourge sweeps by, you will be beaten down by it, see Isaiah 28:18. Consequently, it will be necessary to say to you, the same God trustworthy in life, even when we are not, can be trusted at the ending of our life or during an extended or chronic illness. If you loved God and loved y our neighbor as you loved yourself, there is nothing in this world or the next to fear. Love is what you will take with you, and love is what will await you when you have finally arrived in eternity. On the other hand, if you genuinely choose life, on this side of eternity, choose forgiveness, and allow and embrace, the process of sanctification, you will now begin to experience good health, great happiness, satisfaction, and achievement. Be mindful to give all your praise, thanksgiving, and worship, to the Most High God that you may continue to prosper. For He who exalts, also makes low because of pride. Remember God. See suggested course of action.

In addition, the following is a common word, expression, or usage (e.g. slang or cliché), or a 'probable' that is metaphorically represented by glasshouse:

- **People who live in glass houses shouldn't throw stones (An actual glass house, with people in it, with perhaps rocks, should have been highlighted within your dream):** Your dream denotes that the dreamer has great weaknesses; therefore, you should not be pointing out or talking about the weaknesses of others. Thus, in judging others, you have set a precedent over your own life, discharging a universal law, with the same judgments you judge others, so will you be judged. See, understand, and embrace, Matthew 7:1-5.

Stable, Chicken Coop, Cowshed, or Sty: Your dream is to advise and encourage. Dreamer, a divine charge you have to keep, and a God to glorify. You are sent to a group or an entire nation of people for evangelistic purposes. Read Matthew 28:19, 20, this is your prime directive, to lead them to the King. Moreover, dreamer, the state of affairs in your life at p resent, may not be to your liking; but God allows them. God is using your situations to work things out for your good. Therefore, do not attribute (or call) that which is of God, unclean (e.g. confusion, erroneous, out of order, unlawful, weak, wicked, or an y other attributes of the unregenerate). No matter how difficult or how uncertain the issues always take the next biblical, ethical, and most informed step, for obedience is better than sacrifice. If necessary, see suggested course of action.

CROPS

Orchards, Groves, Fields, Patch, or other crops, e.g. Apple Orchard, Orange Grove, Cucumber Field, Strawberry Patch, Plantations, refers to crops grown and/or harvested on a large scale: Orchards, groves, fields, patch, or crops beginning to fructify or bloom: This dream has two meanings (choose one). (1) Dreamer, your words have pleased the Lord, for they are words of wisdom. Thus, He has done according to your words; go forward with purpose, expecting results. Additionally, you will become part of a group of believers, and you will be one whom believers will interact with socially on very personal levels (e.g. business partner, friendship, marriage, other mutual relationships). Moreover, God will grant you both riches and hono r, and if you continue to walk in His ways, diligently and obediently, you will have long life too. This is His promise to you, and He will do according to His promise. (2) To see orchards, groves, fields, patch, plantations, harvested or reaped: Your zeal for power and headship is premature, you're moving faster than is advisable. Dreamer, a high level of leadership demands great personal sacrifice of rights and freedoms and requires the subduing of your passions. "To whom much is given, much is required". Therefore, dreamer, flee immorality, as your dream implies some manner of decadence within you, and your dream comes to alert the dreamer of the approaching consequences of your choices. Dreamer, you must bring your appetites, lusts, and sensual desires under subjection, sacrificing fleshy satisfaction for the cause. You will have to practice restricting yourself in all things, this includes your diet, activities, associations, and friendships (see Psalm 119:9). Fate will put you in a position for some level of public exposure, either for honoring, because you sincerely chose to apply the truths of God's word to your life, or for open shame, due to a lack of self-restraint. Moreover, as you are a natural born leader, you have the power to lead others towards God, or away from the truth of His word, on to rebellion, and you will influence oth ers to do according to your choice. If you choose to live life on God's terms, embracing His principles, you will become a great leader, leading many to Christ, and the favor of the Lord will be upon your life to cause men to honor and respect you; the glory of the Lord will rise upon you (see Isaiah 60:1-22). Glory in this sense is a state of high honor, spiritual beauty, and great illumination. If you choose to serve your fleshly desires, worshipping at the altar of demons, desolation, and open shame i s the inheritance of those who worship there (also see Galatians 5:19-21). For honor or open shame, public exposure is imminent. See suggested course of action.

To work on a Plantation: Your dream denotes one who is in rebellion. You are influencing and/or controlling another in a very negative way; a way that will lead (or has led) to bondage, or dreamer is under one who is the influencer or controlle r. See suggested course of action.

Cuttings, Grafting, or Rooting (refers to a Bud, Leaf, or Root, removed from a plant to propagate a new plant through grafting or rooting): This dream has two meanings (choose one). (1) If dreamer cut, grafted, or rooted any part of a bud, flower, leaf, plant, or root, your dream denotes one, who is, or will be very soon, deemed a heretic. Dreamer, you believe in a god of your own making, coupled with outrageous claims you have wholeheartedly embraced from other erroneous guides. You say Adonai Elohim creates imperfect beings and then forces them to rise up to a level of perfection, which by design, they are unable to attain, by torturing them, causing millions to suffer in body and soul. You reason that this is God's only way, a path of pain, torture, and then death. You ask what human being aspires to evolve through this endless agony. You proclaim that God's promises are no more than vague words of doubtful happiness, and implacable laws that promise remote and unknowable joy, under the mask of love of humanity. You say His ways are nothing more than a profound i ndifference and a hardened selfishness. Further, you believe that God's intolerance of sin and the inherent results of sin, mainly separation from Him, as written within Holy Writ, and expressed in Christian dogma, are the picture of an angry god, conjured up by angry, unwise, and foolish men. You boast of philosophies, which appeal to the lustful desires of human nature, condoning rebelliou s, unhealthy, immodest, immoral, indecent, lewd, and lascivious, behavior. Desires that if not checked, can and oft en do lead to early death, as you have personally witnessed. This is what you call love. You exalt your wisdom above the Creator. While you discredit the Creator's wise and sensible guidelines for living life, on this side of eternity, as healthy, human ly, and sanely as possible; and in harmony with His provision for life on the other side of eternity, in heaven. You respect your truth, while never acknowledging, it is delivered without grace; thus, it is never enough to fill an emaciated soul. Read, understand, and embrace Galatians 5:13-25. See suggested course of action. (2) If another cut, grafted, or rooted any part of a bud, flower, leaf, plant, or root: There is someone within the life of the dreamer, who appears perfectly innocent and legiti mate. Yet, that someone saps you of your strength, and subsequently, negatively blurs and shifts your focus, especially concerning your spiritual and emotional health. You are deeply influenced by the thoughts and beliefs of another without realizing just how much you are affected. Fortunately, your dream insinuates that there will be a falling away, or a dropping off, of people, places, and things, to some extent, great or small, within the dreamer's life. Allow this season, for there is a need within the dreamer's life to let go of someone(s), places, and things, in order to further your growth. The purpose of that person(s) within your life is finished, and by letting go; the dreamer will gain the ability, to become a great teacher and writer. Additionally, since beginnings and endings, will become constant elements within the dreamer's life. It would be wise for you to allow each transitional experience, each life change, to teach you how to deal with life issues more successfully than you've done before, so that your strength may become strong, and that you may continue to grow and mature in your relationship with Christ. See suggested course of action.

Farmer

Dairy Farmer, Grazer, Herder, Sharecropper, Shepherd, Sower, or Truck Farmer : This dream has three meanings (choose one). (1) First, it must be said that your dream denotes one, the dreamer, whose calling is to give sermons, spread the gospel, and conduct religious services, a cleric of some kind (e.g. bishop, evangelist, minister, missionary, parson, pastor, preacher, priest, rabbi, or teacher). A large part of your mission should center on you raising the spirits of your fellow mankind, and establishing yourself as an inspirational person spreading hope. Your gift is to inspire and motivate. You will live and thrive where most things perish, independent of outward circumstances, via divine grace. (2) Unfortunately, although you are prosperous, and physically capable, you are not walking in your purpose. Thus, you are experiencing strong inner conflict.

This is your inner man struggling to fulfill purpose. Dreamer, a change of direction and attitude is highly recommended. Re- think your views and attitude, regarding the doctrine you are adhering to, and your philosophy, and/or your plans for establishing or joining an institution or organization. Why, because your interpretation of the Word of God has become unrecognizable to those you influence. When those who seek truth, ask Jesus why they do not recognize your teachings, the words spoken of you are that you are true to yourself. To be true to self or another, is to seek affirmation with respect to condoning your particular sin, while basing your ideas, arguments, and/or beliefs on something that is sacrilegious, profane, illogical, and non-mainstream doctrine or philosophy. Your ideology is without favorable conclusions, thus this dream. Dreamer, you are full of pride, and if you persist on perpetuating your self-serving ideology and calling it divinely ordained, you will be stripped and humiliated publicly, and replaced because of shameful acts. (3) Dreamer, decline the temporary relations of darkness that you might inherit an entrance into paradise having sincerely answered God's request upon your life, and seriously re-consider how you are being true to yourself. Remember how far you have fallen. Return to me and change the way you think and act, and do what you did at first (Revelation 2:5 GW). Further, for selfless altruism to be complete within your life, once you repent, you must be refined, polished, and educated in four areas. A change must occur in your human interaction with God, others, and if relevant, especially with respect to your marital relationship, it being the most person al and intense of human interactions, and with yourself. With respect to God, selflessness involves humble submission and obedience to His will. With respect to others, this involves the heart felt practice of regard for, and devotion to, the wel fare of others. With respect to marriage, this involves the heart felt practice of regard for, and devotion to your spouse, this means viewing and finding in your spouse, your spiritual helper. With respect to yourself, selflessness means refining your character, and finding within yourself contentment with God's affirmation of you. See suggested course of action.

Farm Worker (Fieldworker, Harvester, Migrant, or Seasonal Worker, doing farm work, does not own the farm): This dream has three meanings (choose one). (1) Unmarried male dreamer: Your dream denotes marriage. If you are unmarried, your wife is before you. With that said, God's love for you, and your love for someone, and your love for yourself, needs to be seriously reflected upon, with emphasis on a lifelong commitment to love and faithfulness. God will strengthen you, so that you and she will fulfill your God given responsibility within marriage, and both of you, will fulfill your covenant relationship with Jesus Christ. (2) Female dreamer: This choice has three parts (one or all may apply). (a) Unmarried dreamer: Your dream denotes a wedding and marriage. Dreamer, your potential husband is before you at present, or will be, very shortly. Handle the relationship, on God's terms, embracing His ethics, and not yours, as you've done before. (b) Your dream references a son, the birth of a son, or one who is already living (your eldest son). This son will carry out the official role of that o f a bishop, evangelist, pastor, or preacher, and he will be of good reputation, full of the Spirit, and wise. Lay hands on this child, and pronounce the blessings of the Lord upon him. (c) Those, who do not know the Heavenly Father, will oppress you, and attempt to slander your name. Dreamer, continue to speak God's word, for it is your sword against the enemy, and remain a good steward in that which God has given you to do, wavering in nothing. They will not prosper in the evil they have plotted against you (see Isaiah 54:17). You will see their downfall. (3) Your dream denotes possible idolatry. Idolatry is "foreign service", any act that expresses devotion or fanatical admiration to something or someone other than Adonai Elohim. Dreamer, your advisers, and friends are scoffers, in that they are contemptuous, cynical, distrustful, misanthropists, mocking, sarcastic, suspicious, and negative. They hate people in general, and dislike and distrust others. They are men and women, who will not make the leap of faith that changes the ordinary into the extraordinary. If you give their words power, you will be liken to those who worship idols, for you would have exalted their words, and them, above Christ. This will be your downfall. You, because of their words, if heeded, will become despairingly overwhelmed with anxiety; you will reach a point of losing hope, resulting in drastic and reckless choices. Extremely desperate, because of difficult times and great need, your wickedness will go beyond hope of recovery. Consequently, you will become very sick and frail, leading to an incu rable sickness. You are strongly advised to carefully consider, and heed the Word of God, as oppose to men's opinions. Pray Psalm 38:1-22. See suggested course of action.

Food Or Foodstuff: Your dream generally denotes God's will and Christ's strong doctrines, and each are elements of the Holy Bible and are characteristic of abundance, satisfaction, endurance, spiritual life, or the lack thereof. Couple this with one of the following.

Bread, Yeast, or Leaven (flat, unleavened bread): This dream has two meanings (choose one). (1) Flat, Unleavened Bread (e.g. matzah, any flat bread, or any substance, depicted as containing no leaven, yeast, or any substance that causes fermentation): Your dream denotes one who is mentally strong, firm, and courageous. Your spiritual journey has created a disposition, within you that is marked by meekness (knowing your need of God) and modesty, not arrogance. Now, your burdens, having been dealt with, freedom from your weaknesses is yours. You will be favored with complete healing, go and sin no more. For, if anyone knows the good they ought to do and doesn't do it, it is sin for them (see James 4:17). Therefo re, from this moment forward, choose good habits and deeds, e.g. good stewardship and commitment to ministry; speak to yourself what is true and good, see Philippians 4:8, and choose good nutritional habits that you might remain in good health. These choices will help you progress forward towards your transformation and freedom, and help guide you toward, and enable you to fulfill, your purpose. All these blessings are rain. Dreamer, as one perfects him or herself, God helps by sending 'rains of blessings', then situations prosper. The rain is coming! As well, there will be clarity and freedom in the way you communicate yourself to others, especially prophetically. Thus; from this time forward, so speak and act as those who are judged by the law of liberty; see James 2:12, 13. For example, remove condemnation from your message of grace and holiness, see John 3:17, Romans 8:1, 1 John 3:20, 21, for there is a difference between conviction and condemnation. Additionally, you are now entering into a season within your life that will prepare you spiritually for the visitation of the Lord in your individual life. During this time, you will experience His love and presence, as you've never known it before. Moreover, take note of this, you should be quick to listen, slow to speak, and slow to anger, see James 1:19 -25. The servant of God always experiences a gap between his or her thoughts and deeds. Meaning, before you literally act or speak, there is an instant of time for you to decide, to do, or say, what is wise and good or unwise and evil. Hence, your words should align with your moral stance, and with respect to the rest of the world. For example, you may not agree with another's lifestyle choices, but you do know, and should voice if necessary, that they do have a right to enter into the House of God to repent, pray, and praise Adonai, without being condemned by you or others, see John 3:17. With that said dreamer, the rains of blessings are coming, get ready! (2) Yeast, Leaven (any leavening agent containing yeast cells; used to raise the dough in making bread and for fermenting beer or whiskey): You have deliberately chosen to become enslaved to that which is forbidden by the One True and Living God. Your choices are spiritually forbidden. Dreamer, you believe in a god of your own making. You say Adonai Elohim creates imperfect beings and then forces them to rise up to a level of perfection, which by design, they are unable to attain, by torturing them, causing millions to suffer in body and soul. You reason that this is God's only way, a path of pa in, torture, and then death. You ask what human being aspires to evolve through this endless agony. You proclaim that God's promises are no more than vague words of doubtful happiness, and implacable laws that promise remote and unknowable joy, under the mask of love of humanity. You say His ways are nothing more than a profound indifference and a hardened selfishness. Further, you believe that God's intolerance of sin and the inherent results of sin, mainly separation from Him, as written within Holy Writ, and expressed in Christian dogma, are the picture of an angry god, conjured up by angry, unwise, and foolish men. You boast of philosophies, which appeal to the lustful desires of human nature, condoning rebellious, unhealthy, immodest, immoral, indecent, lewd, and lascivious, behavior. Desires that if not checked, can and often do lead to early death, as you have personally witnessed. This is what you call love. You exalt your wisdom above the Creator. While you discredit the Creator's wise and sensible guidelines for living life, on this side of eternity, as healthy, humanly, and sanely as possible; and in harmony with His provision for life on the other side of eternity, in heaven. You respect your truth, while never acknowledging, it is delivered without grace; thus, it is never enough to fill an emaciated soul. Read, understand, and embrace Galatians 5:13-25. Moreover, you compel individuals to follow other gods, and hard-press people to believe what you say. Dreamer, promoting and encouraging others to approach God the Father, without the essential provision He has provided for mankind to approach Him properly; that provision being Yeshua HaMashiach, is not safe and is deceptive. Some call God's provision Jesus, Wonderful Counselor, Mighty God, Everlasting Father, Prince of Peace, our atonement, advocate, liberator, propitiator, and our salvation. It is only through this channel that we may hope through faith to conciliate with our Creator, see John 3:16, Acts 2:37-42, 1 Timothy 2:4-7. Dreamer, reacting in such a "temper tantrum" and rebellious manner, as you do, because you disagree with certain spiritual principles, is not good. You may not like God's ways and means, but you do have to accept and surrender to them all. For, your human understanding of, and reaction to, spiritual realities is oftentimes crudely green. Dreamer, at this crossroad in your life, it is counseled that you do as the Apostle Paul, and count all that you know, all that has brought you to this point, to be worthless (Philippians 3:8). Your dream has come to let you know that there is still hope and time for you to recognize the wrong in what you're doing, feel the regret about your past actions, and change your ways and habits. Dreamer, seize this opportunity to sincerely repent, denounce the erroneous teachings you've embraced, and go on from here. Repentance is seeking pardon and expressing sincere feelings of regret and brokenness for having done something awry and/or for having hurt someone, see 2 Corinthians 7:10, 11. To Jesus pray, Psalm 51, this coupled with prayer and fasting, and followed by appropriate application of wisdom, can conceivably avert some of the repercussions of your choices. This is known as leaving a blessing behind. If you've led others away, humble yourself and apologize, and let them know you was wrong, and let them know, bottom line, their salvation is their own responsibility (Philippians 2:12, 13), to individuals, a phone call or a letter of apology is a good place to start. Dreamer, I encourage you to seek clarity and understanding from the Lord, regarding your decision making processes and identity issues, and apply His wisdom vigilantly.

Go and seek truth for yourself that not all may be eternally lost. If done, during this season within your life, there will be some very dark hours and major conflict (significant in scope, extent, or effect). Encouragingly, dark times can be replaced with a beauty or handsomeness that radiates brilliance and righteousness via diligent obedience to God through His Word and endurance. By this, grace and faith will once again be made manifest in your life. See suggested course of action.

Butter: This dream denotes one who is "doing" (or is not "doing") the will of God that has been purposed for your life. Thus, this dream has two meanings (choose one). (1) If dreamer is actually living out the will of God for your life, meaning fulfilling your purpose, via utilizing your spiritual gift(s) the ascended Christ has endowed you with; for example of the various spiritual gifts, see 1 Corinthians 12:7-11. Then your dream to you is sent as an encouragement. Dreamer, if you are exercising the measure of faith God has given you (Romans 12:3) that you operate successfully in your gifting(s). It will be by God's Power that a way out of no way will be made for you, and your state of affairs will be turned around and worked out. Jesus will come and see about you, keep your faith regarding what you've believed God for; He has promised never to leave you alone. You are not alone neither will you be made ashamed. (2) If dreamer is not living out, "doing" the will of God for your life, meaning fulfilling your purpose, via utilizing your spiritual gift(s) the ascended Christ has endowed you with; for example of the various spiritual gifts, see 1 Corinthians 12:7-11. Your dream was sent as a stern rebuke. Dreamer, you are not exercising the measure of faith God has given you (Romans 12:3) that you might operate successfully in your gifting(s). Your use of smooth words, have proven deceptive. You have opened the door for great trouble. Favorably, God will use your troubles to work things out for your good. Be grateful that the Lord Jesus, by giving you notice of trouble, designed to take off the terror of it, that it might not be a surprise to you. For by being forewarned, you may become forearmed. After troubled has done what it was sent to affect, Jesus will be waiting for you to come to Him in prayer. You can always pray, "Lord I don't know how I'm going to make it. I can't see my way, come, and see about me. Lord, I must confess, I'm weak now, I'm faltering, and I'm becoming discouraged". You can tell Him what you want Him to know. Somehow, God will make a way for you. For it will be by His Power that a way out of no way will be made for you, and your state of affairs turned around and worked out, only pray. Additionally, if relevant, teach wisdom and discipline to your children. Do not allow your children to practice abominations, weaknesses, or other practices that make for weak and unprofitable living (Proverbs 23:13-14). Tell them genuine truths of God, no matter the temporary pain or strain on relationships; allow them to "sit" with the knowledge of what makes for a better life. If not, they will count the cost and hold you in account. All these things consider well, lest you find yourself killing yourself spiritually, emotionally and physically (also see Proverbs 23:1-24:12).

Cereal Grasses, Grains (Barley, Buckwheat, Cornbread, Flour, Indian Corn, Maize, Meal, Millet, Oats, Rice, Rye, Wheat, and any foodstuff prepared from Cereal Grasses, Grains, e.g. Bread, Breakfast Cereals, Crackers, Grits, Hominy, Muffins, Oatmeal, Pasta, Tortillas): If sandwich or sub was made, which included meat, coupled with this interpretation, also see category, Animals (Sandwiches). With that, this dream has two meanings (choose one). (1) Your dream denotes that this is the season of the Lord's favor upon your life. However, as feelings go, because of your bad behavior and deeds, you are discouraged, and feel unfit and unworthy of God's favor and restoration. Nonetheless, promises of deliverance, restoration, and fruitfulness are before you, because of God's grace. God will by His grace prepare and qualify you for mercy and then bestow it on you. Not because of any good thing you've done, but because of His grace, mercy, and faithfulness. Dreamer, you will be delivered from your impurities (e.g. addictions, anger, animosity, cheating, confusion, exposing confidences to others, greedy, gossiping, immoral, impure, unchaste conduct, jealously, lying, out of order, stealing, an unforgiving heart, or any other sinful attribute), and God is taking away your disgrace. Instead of shame, you will receive double honor, instead of disgrace you will rejoice in an inheritance left for you long ago. When delivered from your uncleanness, from your sins, which kept good things from you,

you will once again enjoy the good of the Lord's favor (see Isaiah 54:4-17, 61:7, Ezekiel 36:30-32). Then you will know that God is God, and worship, obey, and serve Him as such. (2) To not, eat any kind of cereal grasses, grains: Your dream denotes that dreamer will forfeit the blessings of God fated you, see previous interpretation. There is either a refusal to repent, or a refusal to accept that you are forgiven, thus exalting your own knowledge above the Creator, who has deemed you justified by grace. Both will result in delay or perhaps denial in opportunities that come to prosper. Read, understand, and embrace Romans 5:1-11, you are not without hope. See suggested course of action.

Fruit (refers to the edible, or non-edible, fruit of a plant, e.g. Apples, Bananas, Grapes, Lemons, Oranges, Strawberries, or poisonous fruits, such as Daphne, European Spindle, Horse Chestnut, and Jerusalem Cherry Tree. This category also includes food or drink made primarily of fruit, e.g. Applesauce, Fruit Juice, Grape Juice, Lemonade, Pumpkin Pie, Apple Fritters, Fruit Salads, and other foods and drinks that are primarily made with fruit)

Note: Were the fruit annuals, biennials, or perennials? For example, watermelons are annuals. Biennial fruit occurs in fruit trees such as apple and pear trees. Perennial fruit are grapes, strawberries, raspberries, blackberries, and others. If fruit life cycle was, highlighted in any way, see category, Flowers (Annuals, Biennials, and Perennials). You may also reference resources available to determine if your fruit were annuals, biennials, or perennials (e.g. dictionary, encyclopedia, or the internet).

Note: Fruit, classified, characterized, and categorized in many ways, are biblically grouped into two categories, good and bad. Good fruit and fruit in good condition, within a dream are not harmful to human life. On the other hand, bad, decaying, or rotten fruit is poisonous or hazardous to human life. To determine if the fruit within your dream is good, poisonous, or hazardous to human life, see relevant resources (e.g. dictionary, encyclopedia, or internet). Having done your research you should be able to determine some basic behaviors or attributes your Lord and Savior wants you to focus on; for, by your fruit, you will be recognized (Matthew 7:16). If the believer is to bring forth good fruit, within your life, "in and out of season", you should ponder John 15:1-17, pray for direction and for the wisdom and fortitude to obediently, commit to those directions. Couple this with one of the following.

Bad Fruit (decayed, rotten, spoiled, poisonous fruit, or food or drink made primarily of fruit): Bad fruit is associated or connected to one of three character traits (choose one). (1) Bad fruit signifies the aftereffects of a sinful nature, sexual immorality, impurity, debauchery, idolatry (idolatry is "foreign service", any act that expresses devotion or fanatical admiration to something or someone other than Adonai Elohim), witchcraft, hatred, discord, jealousy, fits of rage, selfish ambition, dissensions, factions, envy, drunkenness, orgies, and the like (Galatians 5:19-21). Dreamer, you are disobedient, badly behaved, troublesome, wayward, mischievous, unmanageable, unruly, willful, rude, volatile, stubborn, unyielding, and a great pretender. A toxic person, out of the evilness of his or her heart, speaks and does that which is no xious (aka bad, poisonous, hazardous, decayed, or rotten fruit). Thus, you are known by the fruit you yield, engender, emanate, you present. Those possessing bad fruit are very much like those wicked servants in Matthew 25; those who live like them, will not inherit the Kingdom of God (also see Galatians 5:19-21). Dreamer, he or she, who do not respect the opportunities placed before them shall have the things that support their peace taken away. Choose this day whom you will serve, God, or yourself. G od is not condemning you, He's holding out His Hand of hope, giving you an opportunity to start anew. God wants to pardon (Isaiah 55:7-13, Matthew 7:17-23, Luke 6:43-45). Dreamer, if you are diligent in subduing your negative traits you can turn a bad situation into a good one overnight and begin doing mighty works and wonders for the Kingdom of God, like Apostle Paul. Prayer and repentance is the first step. Jesus will meet you wherever you are. Have faith in this. See suggested course of action. (2) This type of fruit (bad) is also, connected to a false prophet or shepherd, one who feeds only him or herself. If dreamer is, known as a prophet or shepherd, predatorily, you join in with others of like mind, to victimize and exploit peopl e. You rush for profit without the slightest qualm. Greedily destructive and ruthlessly aggressive, you are the cause of constant anxiety and grief in the lives of those who love or befriend you. You teach erroneous and compromising doctrine and speak abusively against whatever you do not understand. You also encourage others to do the same.

As well, you threaten those who genuinely care for God's people. In this mind-set, you're brutal, cruel, vicious, violent, and do not respect anyone, you are best avoided. See suggested course of action. (3) Bad, poisonous, hazardous, decayed, or rotten fruit is also associated with homosexuality and/or one who indulges in very dark and life threatening sexual habits. Because of your disgraceful behavior, a scandalous exposure of truth will occur, and you will reap the consequences of uncleanness, namely a life threatening disease and possible loss of heaven (see Galatians 5:19-21). Notwithstanding, you will be stripped of position, status, and/or finances, of all that 'covers' you. See suggested course of action.

Eating fruit that's good or bad (or food or drink made primarily of fruit): This dream has three meanings (choose one). (1) Your dream exposes the dreamer's character, good, or bad. The content of your character, also known as fruit, signifies one who gets satisfaction from embracing wise and good habits, this is depicted by dreamer eating or looking at good fruit. Or, it signifies one who gets satisfaction from embracing bad habits, this is depicted by dreamer eating or looking at bad fruit. Dreamer, you will reap the fruit of your doings (good or bad). For interpretation of good or bad fruit, see subcategory, good fruit, or bad fruit. (2) Your dream reveals a literal pregnancy or a spiritual pregnancy (choose one). The dreamer, or if male, your spouse, is either actually pregnant, will become pregnant very shortly, or you two are becoming grandparents. If not pregnant, and you desire children, continue to have faith and hope in God, He will have mercy on you, and grant you the desire of your heart, suddenly and very soon. Note, if pregnancy is a possibility, concern, or desire, the fruit of your womb (your child), will be known by the fruit represented within your dream, be it good or bad. Note, if bad fruit was depicted, this dream was sent to urge the dreamer to discipline your child (or grandchild) early and appropriately that foolishness may be driven far from their heart, that he or she may live a good life (Proverbs 20:11, 22:6, 22:15, 23:13, 29:15 - this is wisdom). (3) If a literal pregnancy is not an issue or desire, perhaps due to age, then your dream represents a spiritual pregnancy. A spiritual pregnancy, this choice has two parts (one or both may apply). (a) A spiritual pregnancy denotes the fruit of your natural talents, pursuits, and morality is coming into full fruition. Your conduct towards others (for benefit or harm) will be openly manifested before all. You will reap what you have sown. For interpretation of good or bad fruit, see subcategory, good fruit, or bad fruit. (b) A spiritual pregnancy denotes a ministry will be birth from within you, the dreamer. You are full of nurturing abilities; thus, you will become, responsible for a few young men and women being born again into the Kingdom of God (see John 3:1-17). You know how to nurture and accept anyone; therefore, many are intended to connect with you, including those, others label as indigents, via your ministry. If good fruit was depicted, within your dream, under yo ur tutelage, those newly born into the Body of Christ will become strong and active, for the cause of the Kingdom of God. They will become those who speak and does that which is good, counted amongst those who are faithful and submissive to God. If the f ruit depicted was bad, those young "born-again" Christians will need one who will consistently provide advice and much support, one who will watch over and foster their Christian progress, greatly encouraging them to embrace a very spiritually disciplin e life (e.g. consistent fasting, prayer, church attendance, bible study, and mentoring). This help will come via your ministry. Dreamer, the Holy Spirit has made you fruitful, by first forming Christ in you. Just as natural parents provide the genetic makeup of their child's body, and by this, the child grows into their likeness. In like manner, Heavenly Father has provided His incorruptible nature, via the Holy Spirit (see 1 John 3:9, 10), and by this, we are shaped into the likeness of His Son that we should show forth the praises of Him who has called us (see 1 Peter 2:9-12). Subsequently, because of His likeness, nature, knowledge, and wisdom, within you, you will take part in helping others to reach for a deeper, more spiritual and valuable thing in life, a born again experience. Thus, by this, you are responsible for one being born-again, and this is fruit. Dreamer, be willing, obedient, prepared, and in place (accountable to a specific house of worship, church), for the birthing of your ministry and for those who will become born again because of your ministry.

Eating stolen fruit or fruit that is not yours (or food or drink made primarily of fruit): This dream has two meanings (choose one). (1) The dreamer is absorbed in the pursuit of identity void of foundation (e.g. pretending to be someone you are not; and not knowing what it takes to be whom, or what, you're pretending to be). This type of identity pursuit will not withstand your storms of life. You will begin to crack in your personality, and your dream denotes that the "crack" is beginning to happen. The only foundation upon which humankind should wisely establish his or her identity, are the principles within the Word of God and the leading of the Holy Spirit. Additionally, fortunately, your dream also denotes that the dreamer is meek enough to change what has been exposed, especially if negative. If necessary, see suggested course of action. (2) Dreamer, you are embracing another word, one independent and separate from the teachings of Jesus Christ, an ideology not based on God's revealed word, via Holy Writ. Consequently, you will shortly be, or now is, introduced to secretive books containing incantations and other dark sinister knowledge. It is likely that you will embrace such teachings, for the enemy of your soul; has been allowed to deceive you, because you get satisfaction from embracing negative behavior. Evil is taking root because your focus is on your own desires rather than on God and His desires. You evaluate all your experiences only in terms of your own narrow-minded and bigoted sense of good. Please reconsider your stance, and repent. It's not too late to turnaround. One can, and many do, go from bad to good in one day. See suggested course of action.

Good Fruit (fresh, healthy, ripe fruit, or food or drink made primarily of fruit): Good fruit represents one whose character is faithful, law-abiding, moral, open, and submissive to God, scrupulous, sincere, straightforward, trustworthy, upright, and reasonable in particular situations. Good fruit is the result of sound living, living according to moral truth and upright character. A person that speaks and does that which is good (aka good fruit), is respected as a good and sagacious person. Many, touched by your wisdom, are inspired to make their dreams come true. You are amongst the righteous, demonstrating the results of good fruit, which is love, joy, peace, patience, kindness, goodness, faithfulness, gentleness, a nd self-control. Against such things, there is no law. Those who belong to Christ Jesus have crucified the sinful nature with its passions and desires, thus they are demonstrating good fruit (Galatians 5:22-24). God is favoring you now. Therefore, much blessings and prosperity will be yours. The benefits of good fruit will begin to manifest even more within your life starting now (Proverbs 12:14, 18:20). A benefit of good fruit is, but not limited to, the dreamer will be successful in your endeavors, especially after practical planning and effort. Dreamer, receive the affirmation, validation, and encouragement your dream is meant to impart.

Grapes (or food or drink made primarily of grapes): For grapevines, see subcategory, Vines and Vineyard. As grapes are also perennials, see section entitled, Annuals, Biennials, and Perennials. Additionally, depending on the condition of the fruit, see subcategory, Good or Bad fruit. Other than that, this dream has three meanings (choose one). (1) Your waiting has not been in vain, those within your family who are spiritually and emotionally dead, shall live, those whom you've been praying for, they will rise and increase in rank, status, and position in life, especially employment wise, and move on to a better qualit y of life. Expect this in a spirit of excited anticipation, sing for joy! For, Jesus loves you and you are valuable in His eyes. (2) Your dream was sent to encourage, especially a ministerial leader. Your dream denotes one who has the power and strength, via Jesus Christ, to accomplish what is before you. No matter the various circumstances of life, you must conclude that you can do all things through Christ who strengthens you (Philippians 4:13). You are counseled to begin to embrace this mindset, especially now, if not already, because of the great leader you are called to be (or is). Dreamer, you can bear any trial, perform any duty, subdue any evil propensity of your nature, and meet all the temptations consequence to any condition of prosperity or adversity. You need not sink under any trial, nor yield to temptation, nor be harassed, vexed, and tortured with improper thoughts and unholy desires, for there is one, Holy Spirit, who can strengthen you, make a way for your escape, and enable yo u to renounce unholy thoughts from your mind, and restore the right balance to the affections of your soul. Only, do not shrink from duty, but express confidently and firmly to yourself that nothing is required of you that you will be unable to perform. (3) Only, if such a situation is going on at present within the dreamer's life, regrettably, a close friend, one who gives you sound advice, has betrayed you before those who hate you. This friend is one who has been treated lovingly and trusted explicitly. This betrayal has grieved you very deeply. Moreover, you will experience embarrassment, shame, great fear, and internal stress because of vicious lies told against you. Although your anger is justifiable (righteous indignation), remain silent a nd watch things play out. Jehovah will cause a rift amongst the group, and stop their lies and other talking, via an ally of yours sent by God to join the group. This ally's mission is to confuse, divide, and separate, and he or she does that well. So kn ow that not everyone in the group is one with the group. Do not return evil for evil. Only, pray and cry aloud evening, morning, and at noon, and let your prayers come from a right heart that loves God, and not from angry vengeful motives. See your deliverance as a present fact, and know, without a doubt that God hears you, and will turn things around. Moreover, he or she will reap what they have sown.

Lemons: As lemons are also perennials, see section entitled, Annuals, Biennials, and Perennials. Additionally, depending on the condition of the fruit, couple the following interpretation, with the previous interpretation of good or bad fruit. Other than that, your dream denotes a need to ask forgiveness from someone the dreamer has offended due to your previous lifestyle, your past, behaviors, deeds, or actions. If dreamer does not know of such a person, (person is unknown), the dreamer does not care about the hurt or trail of hurts you've left behind; and you are in denial of you awful deeds and action. Notwithstanding, repentance and rectification are needed. Warning, if no seeking of forgiveness from individuals hurt by you is done, and no rectification of your behavior is heeded, the following will not be manifested within your life. You will have forfeited purpose, and blessings, for foolishness, denial, and pride. Graciously, however, if you genuinely return to God in love and surrender, your deliberate transgressions will become like actual merits (also see Luke 7:37-50). Because, the realization of your distance from God, resulting from your transgressions (Isaiah 59:2), becomes the motivating force to return to God with a passion even greater than that of someone who has never sinned in such a manner (Acts 9:1 -30). Love within this context is the practice of living life on God's terms for no other reason or benefit than to be close to God, this is called holiness. Then, God will raise you up and sit you amongst His people. You will receive the benefits of participating in a local church (community, support, proper ordination, burial, honor, respect, edification, accountability). Moreover, the dreamer should always maintain an attitude of love and service towards others; for all the law is fulfilled in you loving your fellow man as yourself. Love is the sum of the whole law and it is not arrogant or rude (see 1 Corinthians 13:1-13), as well, visit and fellowship with those who are glad and sincere of heart. Dreamer, you are well able to return in love and surrender, only se ize the miraculous moment of spiritual strength that is before, and within, you at present. Additionally, read, understand, and embrace 1 Corinthians 13, as well as, 1 John 2:15-17, 1 Timothy 6:10, and 2 Timothy 3:2-9. Allow these verses to lead and guide you. By applying wisdom, dreamer, you will begin to experience the promises the Lord God has in store for you, just as He promised you. Be careful to obey His directives over your individual life, as you've been taught these past years that yo u may increase greatly, and that it may go well with you as you walk into your prosperity. Love the Lord your God with all your heart, with all your soul, and with all your strength, and if relevant, studiously teach your children, to do so as well (Deuteronomy 6:3-7). With that said dreamer, be encouraged for love will be the banner over your life.

Looking at fruit going from good to bad or vice versa (or food or drink made primarily of fruit): You will very shortly begin to experience, if not already, a paradigm shift in your core beliefs and spirituality. If fruit went from bad to good, dreamer will approach new and deeper dimensions. This transition will affect within you a far-reaching hope, profoundly greater faith, and a more intense love for all things Jesus, including His people; allow it. This revival and renewal of strength is a process. If fruit went from good to bad, dreamer, your reality of God is based on emotions and personal preconceptions, due to observable phenomena. Unfortunately, while what you observe may be true, your paradigm is "gridded" through the emotions of fear and rejection. Paradigm shift, a deeper trust in God and Him alone outside of your emotions and personal biases, is needed that you might go on to spiritual maturity. Dreamer, at your very core, you want to know love and trust, b ut you cannot "touch it" or receive it, because you do not believe you are lovable. You are encouraged to think on things that are true, see Philippians 4:8. See suggested course of action.

No fruit (when fruit was anticipated): This dream has two meanings (choose one). (1) A lack of fruit is an indication that your repentance was not genuine. You are one who affiliates with Jesus and His people, and you put on a facade of faith in Him; however, your association is superficial. There is a need to re-consider your relationship with Christ, namely the lack thereof, and make the necessary changes to make it real, or you will be removed from the congregation of the righteous. Therefore, to Jesus pray, Psalm 51, this followed by appropriate application of wisdom, can conceivably avert some of the repercussions of your choices. If no abandonment of hypocrisy occurs, your choices will possibly lead you to be counted amongst those illustrated in Matthew 7:21-23. Dreamer, is it wise to forfeit the eternality of heaven, for that which is an illusion of piety, especially after having been warned? Receive God's message in simple childlike faith, trusting that by it you will be saved (Matthew 18:3-5, 7-9). In doing this, you will be justified solely based on grace (the free and unmerited favor and beneficence of God) and faith. Even more, having accepted Jesus, your desires will also change and be more satisfying. See suggested course of action. (2) Your dream denotes subtle craftiness, cunningness, false doctrine, godlessness, invoking of demonic presences, sneakiness, and worldly sensual wisdom. Dreamer, instigating evil, you have dishonored the Lord by your erroneous sensual beliefs, and the spreading of those false beliefs. Your attitude, ideas, and values create great distance between God and man. You have proven contrary, disobedient, and stubborn, having shut your eyes to righteousness. You will have to give an account of the fulfilling of your purpose, as well as, of your philosophy and words, very shortly. Consider your dream sufficient warning. If there is no genuine change, another will replace you, via someone taking over your ministry, your job, or a relationship of some kind. No one will respect your knowledge again. For even the fig tree, when found not fulfilling its purpose, Jesus cursed it, and it dried up from the root (Matthew 21:18, 19; Mark 11:12-14). Note; replacing anyone who does not honor His ways and respect their individual purpose is the Lord's prerogative. See suggested course of action

In addition, the following is a common word, expression, usage (e.g. slang or cliché) or a 'probable' that is metaphorically represented by fruit:

- **Fruity (to dream something is "fruity", in appearance, taste, or smell):** As this is an informal or slang term meaning insane, strange, eccentric or stupid, one should consider that mental health issues is a concern. Your dream also denotes a male who is excessively or inappropriately effeminate and/or one who is excessively sentimental in behavior content.

Herbs and Spices (e.g. Anise, Basil, Bay Leaf, Chives, Cinnamon, Cloves, Garlic, Mints, Mustard, Oregano, Pepper, Parsley, Salt, Spikenard, Thymes, to taste, see, or smell-appropriate smell, any of a variety of pungent aromatic spices used for flavoring food): Your dream warns that the words of another towards the dreamer are words of anger. Their words have breed contempt within the dreamer, as well as, emotional and/or physical suffering. Dreamer, in seeking the proper actions regarding an active struggle between you and another, between justice and injustice, always seek guidance through prayer and sagacious elders, and always desire peace and simplicity. We all take action in different ways, however, to forgive is God; and sometimes to just walk away is common sense and peace. Moreover, be very aware that your emotional and/or physical suffering has been allowed by God that you might be humbled; thus, made ready and prepared to render your gifts unto the Lord properly. God will use your sufferings to instill His principles into your mind, and make His ways penetrate your heart. He or she who has suffered in the flesh has ceased from sinning (1 Peter 4:1) that the sacrificial offerings of your worship, service, and financial support to the ministry, might be a sweet smell unto the Lord. Subsequently, you will become productive and go forth, bearing spiritual fruit that you might be counted amongst those who are sagacious; whose character is faithful, law-abiding, moral, open, scrupulous, sincere, straightforward, trustworthy, upright, reasonable in many situations, and submissive to God. Blessings, joy, protection, and prosperity will be yours.

Note: Were the herbs or spices annuals, biennials, or perennials? For example, anise and basil are annual herbs. Parsley is a biennial herb. Chives, fennel, garlic, ginger, mints, oregano, saffron, and thymes are perennial plants. If life cycle was highlighted in any way, see, in this category, section entitled, Annuals, Biennials, and Perennials. Do reference resources available to determine if your herbs or spices were annuals, biennials, or perennials (e.g. dictionary, encyclopedia, the internet). This may point to a timeframe in reference to the interpretation.

Fresh and good smelling herbs, spices, or foods: If herb or spice was fresh, and smelled good, this reflects your character and your dream comes as an encouragement. Good character reaps good benefits. Dreamer, you have been found faithful, law-abiding, moral, open, scrupulous, sincere, straightforward, trustworthy, upright, reasonable in many situations, and submissive to God. Therefore, you will become productive and go forth, bearing spiritual fruit that you might be counted amongst those who are sagacious. Moreover, blessings, joy, protection, and prosperity will be yours.

Bitter or foul smelling herbs, spices, or foods: See subcategory, Vegetables (To dream of eating or handling spoiled or rotten vegetables, bitter herbs, or foul smelling spices)

Garlic: As garlic is a perennial, also see, in this category, section entitled, Annuals, Biennials, and Perennials. Dreamer, God wants you to focus on your character. You are known, or will be known, by the content of your character, and will be judged by such? There is an old saying, "your gifting can take you, where your character can not keep you". That is to say, although you may be prospering now, due to natural endowment, unethicalness, dishonesty, hatefulness, bitterness, and an unforgiving and unloving attitude, will bring ruin and desolation upon your head. Therefore, ethicalness, honor, compassion, and empathy, are of upmost important, and will cause your prosperity to continue. See suggested course of action.

Salt (incl. salt mines): This dream has two meanings (choose one). (1) Dreamer, God is confirming His promises and pledges via your dream. He has promised to deliver you from the ways of wickedness and from demons whose words and ways are perverse, whose paths are crooked and devious. Thus, your dream denotes a literal separation and distance, a departing to another place, and the ending of a union, friendship, or another significant relationship, spiritually and emotionally (e.g. unhealthy "soul ties", negative co-dependent or abusive type relationship, or any negativity that is the antithesis of Christ). Dreamer, you are leaving a space, and will be letting go of someone(s) that you may go forward to a more harmonious state of being, and to a place where you will be used to minister to others. Moreover, dreamer you are entering into a season within your life that will prepare you spiritually for the visitation of the Lord in your individual life. During this time, you will experience His love and presence, as you've never known it before. For, He is saying to you, "I will teach you godly wisdom". You will receive direct insight of divine truth. You will come to know, without a doubt, that God is the tru e source of your strength and wisdom, and He is your sufficiency. As a result, a greater love for self will begin to manifest, affecting wholeness within your life. Be available to Him and seize the moments and opportunities as they are presented, especially an opportunity for you to advance your education. Additionally, and if relevant, meaning at present, there is a formal agreement between the dreamer and another. A formal agreement to perform or not perform some action is correct. Also, there will be additional proof that something that was believed (some fact, hypothesis, or theory) is valid, and this will be formally confirmed. (2) To eat salt: Dreamer is exhibiting wisdom and grace in your words and actions.

Honey: The dreamer is approaching a critical season in which the state of affairs within your life will become very difficult, painful, and uncertain. This turbulence is purposed to disturb and shake-up your foundation of pleasure, with an intense and life-changing upheaval, breaking up hardened ground that a new foundation may begin. This transition will also include transforming your spiritual concepts (beliefs, ideas, impressions, notions, perceptions, theories, thoughts, and views) into actions that will reunite you with God, for God desires to bring you back into a right relationship with Him. Also, the Spirit of Truth will begin challenging, checking, and threatening, the atypical, illicit, and/or unsafe "thrills" you are accustomed too. For, you have primarily focused your life upon a foundation of personal pleasure; thus, you have settled for a voluptuary typ e way of life. How can you say, "I have great desire, thus my physical enjoyment, luxury, and sensual gratifications are my primary concerns? This is a characterization of the ungodly or spiritually immature. Weigh: The child thinks that all that appears pleasant and tasty belongs to them and that he or she has the right to partake of any and everything. Consideration of others, and/or of the resulting outcome is unfamiliar to him or her. They will never consider the results of their behavior, nor how their behavior will affect others. This type of consideration is not within a child's mind-set, because he or she is a child. As the immature child takes what they want, when they want it, and believes that it's theirs, and that they do have a right t o whatever it is, so does the spiritually immature, do what they want, when they want, and believe that it's OK, using grace as a cover for sin. Unfortunately, spiritual change cannot begin with this kind of expectation and mind-set. Dreamer, rather say, "I have great desire, but what can I do, since my Father in Heaven forbids me from involving myself in such acts". Moreover, action must be taken on your part to avoid complete disaster or breakdown, e.g. acknowledgment of your denial of illicit sensuous relations, and repentance, or else, all the evils your desires attract will prove very detrimental to you and your family. Consider this warning dream as God's faithfulness, loving kindness, mercy, and grace towards you. See suggested course of action.

Milk: Your dream denotes spiritual infancy, and it is a warning against falling away from Christ (see Hebrews 5:11-6:20). Spiritual infancy is lack of spiritual growth after the new birth. The spiritual infant is concerned with self rather than service. The spiritual infant is concerned with argument rather than action. The spiritual infant looks to people rather than the Messiah. Thus, dreamer has not readied yourself for "solid" teaching of the Word of God. There is still jealously, strife, and insecurity within you. You are still carnal minded (see 1 Corinthians 3:1-3). Favorably, because of God's grace, you will be starting all over again, with some kind of learning experience, be it a life experience, person, people experience, or work experience; this experience is meant to affect a spiritual maturity within you, leading to a better walk with God. Yes, you've been through this lesson, experience before, hopefully; you will learn from this second time around, what you did not get the first time, and then progress forward, to the next level. Dreamer, God wants you to leave the elementary principles of Christ, (to leave, not abandon), for they are the foundational principles. However, He wants you to progress beyond them. What are the elementary principles? They are mentioned as repentance, faith in God, baptisms, the laying on of hands, the resurrection of the dead and eternal judgment (Hebrews 6:1, 2). In short, these are basic and foundational doctrines. Once the foundation has been laid, you are to improve not only in your understanding but also in your practice and attitudes concerning spiritual things. Therefore, it is suggested that you choose to put away jealously and strife, and renounce, in the name of Jesus, ang er, rage, fear, and insecurity, which are all demonically encouraged. Read, understand, and embrace 1 Peter 1:25-2:1-3. Then, through the eyes of faith, visualize yourself, demanding anger, rage, fear, and insecurity to leave you, and see yourself spiritually maturing. If necessary, see suggested course of action.

Oil, Cooking with oil, or Drinking it (Canola, Olive, or Vegetable Oil): This dream has two meanings (choose one). (1) If oil was fresh, encouragingly, you have tasted the Anointing of God, and you have risen (or will rise) to a level the Anointing of God and your acumen deem you should be. This spiritual level, which you have reached, demands great personal sacrifice of rights and freedoms, and require the subduing of your appetites and passions; for to whom much is given much is required, (see Luke 12:48). With that said, in your present business or personal dealings, you will be satisfied and take delight in your goals. If you are involved in any situation that is competitive, you will triumphant, God will lead the way. Ad ditionally, you have the miraculous power to change history on some level or another. For example, by introducing radically new insight into complex models or paradigms, far beyond the norm, or family generational curses can stop with you (Exodus 20:5, 7; Psalm 112:2). Whatever the miraculous historical change is, perhaps you becoming a great leader and orator, you are equipped to handle large-scale undertakings. Dreamer, a large part of your mission in life centers on raising the spirits of your fellow mankind; thus changing history in the lives of those, you touch. The driving force behind all this is your support of others. Your first step is to start by recognizing and thanking Jesus for the small blessings that are before you now and for the miracu lous endowment of history changing vision and courageous leadership. Do you want your miracle? Then prepare yourself mentally for it. (2) If oil was rancid, your dream warns of a weakness, within the dreamer that is demonically instigated. Scripture states that it is impossible for those who have once been enlightened, who have tasted the heavenly gift, who have shared in the Holy Spirit, who have tasted the goodness of the Word of God and the powers of the coming age, if they fall away, to be brought back to heartfelt repentance. Because, to their loss they are crucifying the Son of God all over again and subjecting Him to public disgrace (Hebrews 6:4-6). You have heard this word before, from God, and your spirit man is a witness to this. Thus, your dream is a last warning, for you also have free will. Dreamer, you believe that God's intolerance of sin and the inherent results of sin, mainly separation from Him, as written within Holy Writ, and expressed in Christian dogma, are the picture of an angry god, conjured up by angry, and unwise and foolish men. You boast of knowledge that appeals to the lustful desires of human nature, condoning rebellious, unhealthy, immodest, immoral, indecent, lewd, and lascivious, behavior. Desires that if not checked, can and often do lead to early death, as you have personally witnessed. This is what you call love. While you discredit the Creator's wise and sensible guidelines for living life, on this side of eternity, as healthy, humanly, and sanely as possible; and in harmony with His provision for life on the other side of eternity, in heaven. You exalt your wisdom above the Creator. Moreover, you use witchcraft in some form or another, for you compel individuals to follow other gods, and hard-press people to believe what you say. Dreamer, promoting and encouraging others to approach God the Father, without the essential provision He has provided for mankind to approach Him properly; that provision being Yeshua HaMashiach, is not safe and is deceptive. Some call God's provision Jesus, Wonderful Counselor, Mighty God, Everlasting Father, Prince of Peace, our atonement, advocate, liberator, propitiator, and our salvation. It is only through this channel that we may hope through faith to conciliate with our Creator, see John 3:16, Acts 2:37-42, 1 Timothy 2:4-7. Dreamer, reacting in such a "temper tantrum" and rebellious manner, as you do, because you disagree with certain spiritual principles, is not good. You may not like God's ways and means, but you do have to accept and surrender to them all. Favorably, there is still hope and time for you. Repent and renounce your wicked ideas, and warn others of the error you've perpetuated that you might find mercy in the Eyes of God, on your Day of the Lord, the day of your reckoning. See suggested course of action.

Pastries, Cake, or Candy: Your dream was sent to demonstrate grace, via a warning. Dreamer, consider carefully what is being offered or presented to you, at this moment, or in your very near future, by someone in an influential position. Although the offer is pleasing and very tempting, it is deceptive, because every step they make towards helping you, in any way, will cost you greatly, oftentimes, without you knowing that you owe. The consequences behind the temptation are stronger and more dangerous, to one, namely the dreamer, who is not use to such distractions, diversions, and pursuits that this person indulges in, and you will be required to engage also. Dreamer, you will regret entering into an agreement with this individual, as it is a snare to you. You are unable, emotionally, to pay the hidden costs, as you are not yet ready to deal with what is called "th e swelling (or thickets) of Jordan" (Jeremiah 12:5). It is counseled that you consider yourself in danger, be on your guard, and just say no, to the offer that is before you, for it is truly, "too good to be ethical, legal, and true". If necessary, see suggested course of action.

Salad Dressings or Sauces (savory dressings or sauces for salads and other foods, e.g. Balsamic, Blue Cheese, French, Italian, Ketchup, Ranch, Vinaigrette, or Gravies): The dream personifies someone who is an extraordinarily gifted minister, evangelist, teacher, or pastor. Commissioned by God, to guide and instruct the people of God in the things of God that they may be gathered unto God at the time appointed for that event. You are a natural born leader; you have the power to lead others towards God. You will become productive and go forth, bearing spiritual fruit that you might be counted amongst those who are sagacious, and submissive to God. God will raise you up and sit you amongst His people. You will receive the benefi ts of participating in a local church (community, support, proper ordination, burial, honor, respect, edification, accountability). Additionally, under your tutelage, young men will become extremely strong and active, particularly for the cause of the Kingdom of God. They will be persons who speak, and does, that which is good, and will become respected as good men. Counted amongst those who are wise; whose character is faithful, law-abiding, moral, open, and submissive to God, scrupulous, sincere, straightforward, trustworthy, upright, and reasonable in many situations. Moreover, the dreamer should always maintain an attitude of love and service towards others; for all the law is fulfilled in you loving your fellow man as yourself; this is easy for you because you are kindhearted and intuitively concerned for souls. Even more, dreamer, the place where God wants to take you, namely a higher level of leadership, demands great personal sacrifice of rights and freedoms and requires the subduing of your passions. Hence, if you choose to live life on God's terms, embracing His principles, you will become a great leader, leading many to Christ, and the favor of the Lord will be upon your life to cause men to honor and respect you; the glory of the Lord will rise upon you (see Isaiah 60:1-22). Glory in this sense is a state of high honor, spiritual beauty, and great illumination. Blessings, joy, protection, and prosperity will be yours. Unfortunately, on the other hand, if you choose to serve your fleshly desires, using your leadership to turn people away from God, instructing them in disobedience, then desolation, and open shame is the inheritance of those who follow this way.

Vegetables (any plants whose leaves, stems, or flowers are cooked and used for food, e.g. Bell or Red Peppers, Beets, Broccoli, Brussels Sprouts, Carrots, Corn, Cucumbers, Greens, Gourds, Squashes, Tomatoes): This dream has three meanings (choose one). (1) To dream of eating or handling any vegetables, denotes the birth of sons, literally and/or spiritually, who are extremely strong and active, physically and mentally. Thus, the dreamer, is either actually pregnant, or will become pregnant very shortly. If male, your spouse is pregnant or will become pregnant shortly. If not pregnant, and you desire children, continue to have faith in God, He will have mercy on you, and grant you the desire of your heart, namely to have children, suddenly and very soon. If pregnancy is not an issue or desire; then dreamer is, or will become, responsible for a few young men being born-again into the Kingdom of God, this is a spiritual birth. Whether, literal or spiritual birth, under your tutelage, young men will become extremely strong and active, particularly for the cause of the Kingdom of God. They will be persons who speak, and does, that which is good, and will become respected as good men. Counted amongst those who are sagacious; whose character is faithful, law-abiding, moral, open, and submissive to God, scrupulous, sincere, straightforward, trustworthy, upright, and reasonable in many situations. Blessings and prosperity will be yours, because of your guidance, and theirs, if they do not reject what's being given to them, namely your guidance. (2) Eating or handling spoiled or rotten vegetables, bitter herbs, or foul smelling spices: This choice has three parts (choose one). (a) There is an unclean spirit, sent to you, whose sole purpose is to convince you that he is God, and to deceive you because of your strong gift of intercession. He will come, sounding very much like God and will play on your bitterness and on your sinful thoughts and desires, for there is bitterness within you. He seeks to gain access to your heart and mind, to use your words to bring harm to the Body of Christ. One of its goals is to cause your mouth to come into agreement with the realms of darkness. Thus; from this time forward, so speak and act as those who are judged by the law of liberty; see James 2:12, 13. For example, remove condemnation from your message of grace and holiness, see John 3:17, Romans 8:1, 1 John 3:20, 21, for there is a difference between conviction and condemnation. Moreover, take note of this, you should be quick to listen, slow to speak, and slow to anger, see James 1:19-25. The servant of God always experiences a gap between his or her thoughts and deeds. Meaning, before you actually act or speak, there is an instant of time for you to decide, to do, or say, what is wise and good or unwise and evil. Hence, your words should align with your moral stance, and should be seasoned with empathy, compassion, and understanding. For example, you may not agree with another's lifestyle choices, but you do know, and should voice if necessary, that they do have a right to enter into the House of God to repent, pray, and praise Adonai, without being condemned by you (see John 3:17). See suggested course of action. (b) There is a need to remember your past. Become very aware that your emotional and/or physical suffering was allowed by God that you might be humbled; thus, made ready and prepared to render your gifts unto the Lord properly. God will use your sufferings to instill His principles into your mind, and make His ways penetrate your heart. He or she who has suffered in the flesh has ceased from sinning (1 Peter 4:1) that the sacrificial offerings of your worship, service, and financial support to the ministry, might be a sweet smell unto the Lord. Therefore, take your past and use it to teach those whom God has purposed you to reach. Dreamer, be who God made you to be, use your God given talents, as best you can, to make the world a better place. Additionally, no matter who you are and what the situation, the words of the Psalms will speak the words of your heart and those words will be heard on High. Thus, began singing a new song, see Psalm 96:1-13. Start listening to inspirational music, music that praises our Lord and Savior. After this, you will become productive and go forth, counted amongst those who are sagacious; whose character is faithful, law-abiding, moral, open, scrupulous, sincere, straightforward, trustworthy, upright, reasonable in many situations, and submissive to God. See suggested course of action. (c) Your dream denotes one who has a bad character and a disobedient spirit; thus, your dream comes as a warning. Dreamer, taking ownership of what your warning dream is revealing to you about you, and working from that point, via prayer, fasting, earnest and diligent self-examination. Also including, persistent practice of truthfulness, and in embracing the fruits of the spirit (see Galatians 5:22-26), and respecting candid support from family and friends, and Christian counseling, all this will help truth inwardly begin to emerge; at a pace, you'll be able to "wrap your mind around" comfortably. This followed by appropriate application of wisdom, can conceivably avert self-deception and denial, and the repercussions thereof. This is what is called leaving a blessing behind. See suggested course of action. (3) To not eat, want, dislike, or to reject any vegetables, herbs, or spices: Your dream denotes that dreamer is rejecting, or does not want, what that vegetable, herb, or spice represents symbolically; see relevant subcategory, it is a rejection or dismissal, of that.

In addition, the following is a common word, expression, or usage (e.g. slang or cliché), or a 'probable' that is metaphorically represented by vegetable (medical condition):

- This denotes a serious medical condition. There is a person whose body and/or brain has become damaged so that they cannot interact with the surrounding environment. God can create a miracle, and this person can be healed. If you lack faith, ask Jesus to heal your unbelief.

Roots, Stems, Stalks, or Tubers (the underground portion of a plant that supports a plant, e.g. Bulbs, Corms, Potatoes, Rhizomes, Tubers, Tulips, Lilies, Daffodils, Beets, Carrots, Turnips, Yams): Your dream speaks of one who has great capacity for growth. You can become firm in purpose and belief, and develop an unshakeable faith. On another vein, it alludes to one who needs to abstain from immorality, and other profane acts. It would be wise for you, at this time in your life, to embrace holiness, wholeheartedly, to prevent the practice of greater immoral acts; for such acts are grossly unclean and will defile you spiritually and physically completely. Further, all devotion to sin; reveals a total lack of respect towards God, and all that is sacred. Your acts of immorality, will unequivocally lead to you selling your "birthright", just to satisfy the growing lust in your flesh and heart (Genesis 25:29-34; Hebrews 12:14-17). The repercussions of such acts see Ezekiel 18:24-32, 33:10-13, Galatians 5:19-21. Dreamer, without holiness no one shall see the Lord. Therefore, look diligently within, and consider the state of great suffering and distress, you are experiencing. Dreamer, you are able to stand resolutely, against the enemy of your soul, especially your own fleshly desires. See suggested course of action.

Potatoes: Your dream denotes one who is loved of God greatly, celibacy, and marriage. Dreamer, God loves you; thus, you are encouraged to read and embrace the entire book, Song of Songs (aka the Song of Solomon). This is God's love song to you. On another vein, unfortunately, as another song goes, the dreamer has looked (will look) for love in all the wrong places and looked (will look) for love in too many faces. Consequently, there will be marriage(s), divorce(s), and remarriage(s); this all depends on how many potatoes, up to at least three marriages, and between each will be long seasons of celibacy. Your season of celibacy is meant to affect a wholeness within you that will eventually lead to a "wholesome" marriage. Favorably, because of God's grace and mercy, and after a long season of celibacy, things will finally culminate into a "righteous" marriage; so don't give-up and say your life is through because of your few bad choices. Be encourage, you will finally get it right. In between times, especially during periods of celibacy, allow God to love you intimately and to fill your soul with His tender warmth. For, according to your capacity to handle self-awareness and a rectification of mind, body, and spirit, God will begin to enhance, make more attractive, and sanctify parts of you, and He will diminish the effects of sin and guilt. Allowing this will result in a wholeness within that will guide you in choosing the "right" mate finally. If necessary, see suggested course of action.

Vinegar, Cider: Your dream denotes one who is embittered, due to overwhelming grief and resentfulness. Dreamer, although you are grieving deeply, you are able, at this point, to make some rational decisions regarding your spirituality an d livelihood, thus, the following is necessary to say. Definitely, you are in need of wisdom. At present, your behavior contradicts practicality, basic reality, and deviates from the morality of God. Yours is a life full of unnecessary words and activities, which have no basis in fact or reality, and they are not rooted in faith in God. Reality is understood to be what God says it to be via His Word. For example, we are saved by grace through faith, not by works (Ephesians 2:5-10). Hence, anyone who does not correspond with His truth, in a levelheaded and practical manner, is deceived and erroneous in your thoughts and ideas; thus, exposing your rejection of the certainty of God's word. Moreover, dreamer is becoming cruel, oppressive, and ruthless, due to deep-seated resentment. Dreamer, your part is to make a go of freeing yourself from the residuals of grief and embitterment, by freeing yourself from things that hinder clarity, and rid your atmosphere of things like shrines, mementoes, memorials tha t sorrowfully remind you of past events. Free yourself of all stuff, words, and talk that keeps you from enjoying the goodness of the Lords' favor today, allow this by faith and gratitude. Dreamer, the place where God wants to take you, namely a higher level of leadership, demands great personal sacrifice of rights and freedoms and requires the subduing of your passions. Moreover, as you are a natural born leader, you have the power to lead others towards God, or away from the truth of His word, on to rebellion, and you will influence others to do according to your choice. If you choose to live life on God's terms, embracing His principles, you will become a great leader, leading many to Christ, and the favor of the Lord will be upon your life to cause men to honor and respect you; the glory of the Lord will rise upon you (see Isaiah 60:1-22). Glory in this sense is a state of high honor, spiritual beauty, and great illumination. However, if you choose to serve your fleshly desires, worshipping at the altar of demons, desolation, and open shame is the inheritance of those who worship there. Taking ownership of what your warning dream is revealing to you about you, and working from that point, via prayer, fasting, diligent self-examination, persistent practice of truthfulness, candid support from family and friends, and/or Christian counseling, will help truth inwardly begin to emerge; at a pace, you'll be able to "wrap your mind around" comfortably. This followed by appropriate application of wisdom, can conceivably avert self-deception and the repercussions thereof. This is what is called leaving a blessing behind. See suggested course of action.

Flowers (Annuals, Biennials, and Perennials, any parts of a plant that consists of Leaves, Petals, Sepals, surrounding Stamens and Pistils, they are colorful, sometimes scented, and cultivated for their blooms or blossoms, and known for their aesthetic values):

Do reference resources available to determine if your flowers were Annuals, Biennials, or Perennials (e.g. dictionary, encyclopedia, the internet). See following subcategory (annuals, biennials, and perennials). This dream generally denotes human glory, celebrity, arrogance, shortness of life, and/or a serious and extended illness. With that this dream has seven meanings (choose one). (1) Flowers blooming: You will now begin to experience good health, great happiness, satisfaction, and achievement. Moreover, because of your accomplishments, you will encounter promotion, some level of fame, admiration, honor, and distinction. Dreamer, as all these things have a high potential to give rise to arrogance. Be mindful to give all your praise, thanksgiving, and worship, to the Most High God that you may continue to prosper. For He who exalts, also makes low because of pride. (2) Flowers withering or fading (to lose brightness, color, or freshness): Your dream denotes an extended illness. Dreamer, you are not in good health, and require medical attention. It is suggested that you seek medi cal attention as soon as possible, and call for the elders of your church, for it is through their prayers of faith and anointing of oil upon you that sin is forgiven and healing is bestowed[36]. Have faith in this, for this is a true saying (Matthew 9:29). Dreamer, it is time to have faith in Jesus and in God's Word. You pray, Psalm 38:1-22. See suggested course of action. (3) Flowers disappearing, falling, or blowing away: Your dream is a notice. Dreamer, for someone who has met God, we experience Him in our ordinary days and moments, in His grace afforded us, and in His miracles bestowed upon us. He is with us, leading us onward, even sharing our tears. This same God trustworthy in life, even when we are not, can be trusted at the ending of lif e and/or during an extended or chronic illness. If we love God and love our neighbor as we love ourselves, there is nothing in this world or the next to fear. Love is what we take with us, and love is what awaits us when we have finally arrived. With that, dreamer, get your house and papers in order (e.g. insurances, bequeaths, untold truths that need to be said). Gather your family together for prayer, support, wisdom, and truthfulness, and prepare to meet your Maker. Preparation, on this sid e of eternity, to meet your Creator, if you have not already, includes repentance, baptism, and a receiving of the gift of the Holy Spirit (see John 3:3-21, Acts 2:37-47). It is time to have faith in Jesus and in God's Word. You pray, Psalm 38:1-22. It is also suggested that you seek medical attention as soon as possible, and call for the elders of your church, for it is through their prayers of faith and anointing of oil upon you that sin is forgiven and healing is bestowed[36]. Have faith in this, for this is a true saying (Matthew 9:29). See suggested course of action. (4) Flowers swaying in the wind: Dreamer, you are (or will be) entering into a process of being humbled, by means of a sickness. Favorably, this sickness is not unto death. This sickness is upon you that you may learn humility, as well as, to teach you to identify with, and understand, other people feelings and difficulties, with compassion and empathy. Do not be afraid. The Lord has come to mature you, so that the fear of God will be instilled within you, to keep you from sinning (Exodus 20:20). Pray Psalm 38:1-22. Couple this with one of the following (choose one): (a) Male dreamer: Dreamer, many, who have faltered and were weak are healed, restored, and strengthened by the grace of God. Spiritual renewal is accessible to you now. Jesus is petitioning you, via your dream, to cleanse evil from your heart, allow the process. With that said, the following is necessary. Dreamer, endowed with a clever, quick mind, and with the ability, experience, and vision to accomplish a great deal in a short period-of-time; your talents lured you into a false sense of security. Erroneously assuming that nothing but good comes to you. Confessing that no one you know can compare with you, or even pretend to be your equal. You put confidence in your flesh, fearing no danger, living carelessly. Y ou harbor wicked thoughts, are ruthlessly aggressive, and greedily eager to steal from, or destroy others, for gain. Dreamer, what God has given you to serve His people, you have perverted, and profaned, making it the source of your lusts; swelling you up with extreme pride. The goodness which God has blessed you with all these years, was to glorify His Kingdom, instead you have used His blessings to glorify yourself. God humbles the haughty and causes all his joy and laughter to cease (see Zephaniah 2:15). If you are ready to acknowledge that you have faltered, and remain mindful of your weaknesses, especially pride, God will in an extraordinary way, increase your strength. The more God allows you to see your arrogance, and the horribleness of it all, be more earnest to repent that you may find Him to be grace and healing, refreshment, and a refuge. He is willing to help you, surrender to His process of help, with a humble dependence upon Him. Pray Psalm 51 and you will find that God will not fail you. You will receive help sufficient for renewal of spiritual strength. See suggested course of action. (b) Female dreamer: This choice has two parts (choose one). (i) Dreamer, Jesus loves you, and you are valuable to Him and to His Kingdom. Unfortunately, you are unclean, at this moment. Within the life of a believer, this denotes anger, animosity, and an unforgiving heart are present within you, and excessiveness regarding immoral impurities (e.g. addictions, cheating, covetousness, exposing confidences to others, greedy, gossiping, jealously, lying, extreme arrogance, stealing, unchaste conduct, see 1 Corinthians 6:9-20, Ephesians 5). This causes one's anointing to fade and spiritual authority to wane. See suggested course of action. (ii)

Your dream denotes that you hold to views and practices that are erroneous, unlawful, toxic, and spiritually and/or physically deadly. Dreamer, Jesus loves you; thus, He is petitioning you to accept Him as your personal Savior, for you are valuable in His eyes. If you are an unbeliever (one who has no religious beliefs, a non-religious person, or one who has no religious faith or belief in Jesus Christ, or one who does not embrace a personal relationship with Jesus Christ, at present). The first step in receiving Him as your personal Savior is repentance (see in the Holy Bible, Acts 2:37-41). Repentance is seeking pardon for having done something awry, and for having hurt someone, and expressing sincere feelings of regret and brokenness. To Jesus pray, Psalm 51:1-19. To individuals, a phone call or a letter of apology is a good place to start, if appropriate. Moreover, if you will accept the Heavenly Father's Words, via the Bible, and store up His principles, and His w ays and means within you, turning your ear to wisdom and applying your heart to understanding, calling out for insight and crying aloud for discernment, Jesus will meet you. This, coupled with a lifestyle of prayer and fasting, followed by appropriate application of wisdom, and you will know the Messiah, Jesus Christ, intimately, and find the knowledge of God you seek. For the Lord gives wisdom and from His mouth comes knowledge and understanding. Then you will understand what is right and just and fair, every good path. When wisdom enters your heart and knowledge becomes sweet to your soul, discretion will protect you, understanding will guard you, and His Truth will lead you. To deliver you from the ways of wickedness, and from demons whose words and ways are perverse, who causes you to walk in darkness gladly, whose paths are crooked and devious, causing you to leave straight paths (Proverbs 2:1-6, 9-15). This is one of God's covenant promises to you. Have faith in this. See suggested course of action. (5) Long stem flowers (no matter the lifecycle): Denotes that dreamer is in line for a celebrity type status position, on some level (small or high profile), exercise your office with humility, love, faith, compa ssion, and empathy. Moreover, your dream reveals that the dreamer may be unaware of the deepest innermost part of your feelings and emotions, which is often provoked by the actions of others. For example, your feelings of rejection, will often stir -up your "fight nature", or deepen, perhaps, more "reclusive" behaviors. No matter the feelings, your feelings run deep, and dreamer needs to become more self-aware of your defense mechanisms. For example, you may feel like time is running out for you to mate, so you stop caring for yourself; you are less health conscious, image conscious, and become more reclusive. Dreamer, you can choose to live life, because as mentioned earlier, you are in line for promotion to a high level within your sphere. This promotion will bring a revival within the soul, if you choose to persevere. If necessary, see suggested course of action. If color of flower was highlighted, may also see category, Colors. (6) Plastic flowers (or if flowers were laminated or heat-sealed in plastic): Dreamer, don't justify your wrong words said and wrong actions taken recently. There is a need to repent to Jesus for using your gift of words, negatively, during a fit of anger. For, you dreamer, was given a time between how you felt and wha t you wanted to say. Dreamer, God has given you the unique gifts of speech, writing, and teaching. Your dream strongly emphasizes the need to guard your unique gift of words. For, through your words, you can build individuals, with praise and encouragement. By making others feel important, you build them up, as if to say, "Your existence is necessary". This is life giving and life affirming. Dreamer, you are able to restore one back to God by simply caring enough to say, "Good morning".

On the other hand, by your unique attribute of speech you can also destroy. Words like, "you're worthless", or "you are not holy" may wipe out a person's self-esteem. Statements such as, "you can judge all Christians by my actions if you want too, and not accept Christ as your personal Savior, good luck with that on judgment day, when you're facing the Savior". This does not express the love and sensitivity of Jesus Christ; nor does it present the Good News wisely. Hence, as a Christian, you a re responsible for your actions and words. For it is written, blessed is the one who does not walk in step with the wicked or stand in the way that sinners take or sit in the company of mockers, (Psalm 1:1). Moreover, as King Solomon says, the tongue has the power of life and death, (Proverbs 18:21). Negative speech is even worse than a sword, since it kills many people, even at great distances. Further, just as the Word of God advises against speaking negative speech, we are also counseled from even listening to it; by listening to negative talk, we fuel the viciousness, and become desensitized to its effect on others. Negative talk, gossip, and unwise words, "kills" three people, the one who is spoken about, because his or her reputation is ruined. The one who speaks negatively, because he or she transgresses and lowers him or herself spiritually, and the one who listens to the negativity, because he or she is providing the speaker with the opportunity to transgress, and also his or her opinion of the one who was spoken about is ruined. If you do hear words spoken negatively of another, do not believe that it's true, unless you have proof, in the mouth of two other witnesses (Deuteronomy 19:15, Matthew 18:16, 2 Corinthians 13:1, 1 Timothy 5:19).

You can be suspicious and check it out, but may not accept it as fact. See also, Psalm 26:4, 73:8, and Proverbs 21:24. If no action is taken to set a guard over your mouth, when the overwhelming scourge sweeps by, you will be beaten down by it, see Isaiah 28:18. See suggested course of action. (7) Potted plants: This choice has two parts (choose one). (a) There is a need for sanctification within the life of the dreamer. Sanctification is a process by which one is, made holy via fasting, prayer, and a genuine return to living life on God's terms and not yours. Further, dreamer has been hesitant to perform God's will, which is to prophesy to someone or many. This word of the Lord has come to the dreamer twice, also read Jonah 3:1-10. (b) Your dream is to one who is a head of state, country, or nation. Your dream warns of impending national destruct ion, merciless punishment, and war (e.g. implosion of a government, country, state, an act of terrorism, kidnapping of a country's citizens by another country, killing of one who is a national threat, civil or national war). The dreamer, chosen by God, to warn the public of this, need not been hesitant to perform God's will. Dreamer, you have the wherewithal to do something with this information and to stop impending destruction. Read Jonah 1-4. If necessary, see suggested course of action.

Note: If the color of flowers were primary within your dream, what color were they? Along with the applicable interpretation, see category, Colors.

Note: Were the flowers, within your dream, annuals, biennials, or perennials? For example, did you dream of pink tulips (perennials): Annuals, Biennials, and Perennials (the life cycle of any flower, plant, vegetable, or herb): The life cycle of a flower, plant, vegetable, or herb, denote the duration of a particular situation or issue, within dreams. Thus, the categorization of a particular type of flower, plant, vegetable, or herb, if highlighted within your dream, whether annual, biennial, or perennial, is alluding to time. An indefinite period, the continuum of experience in which events pass from the future through the present to the past, an instance or single occasion for some event, the speed, duration, and manifestation of an event or action. For example, a dream of annuals swaying in the wind may imply that the duration of an illness is approximately on e year. Within the year, the dreamer will recover. If flowers were biennials, this may imply some sort of relapse, or perhaps the remission and recurrence of an illness, within a two-year period. If flowers were perennials, this dream, hints at something happening again, and again, on a continuing basis, year after year, perhaps a chronic illness or something lasting indefinitely.

Annuals (any flower, plant, vegetable, or herb, completing their life cycle within the space of one year, they germinate, produce seeds, flower, and die all in one year): Your dream insinuates that a person, place, or organization - who or whatever it is, will diminish, end, or go away, in some manner, in one year. For example, celebrity status will abate, a death, illness, scandal, or any concern, issue, situation, illness, will end in one year. On another vein, your dream may spotlight something happening once a year (e.g. an affair, some sort of relapse, a positive or unwise life cycle, or any annual event, such as an appreciation or awards ceremony, family reunion, festival, graduation). One year's time is the primary focus here. If a positive or unwise life cycle, after one year, consideration of the cycle needs to happen, especially if negative. If necessary, see suggested course of action.

Biennials (any flower, plant, vegetable, or herb, completing their life cycle within the space of two years): Your dream implies an illness, addiction, situation, or issue may become inactive, or go into remission, but is capable of recurring or becoming active again within two years, with the possibility of all or some of the symptoms or concerns returning. Thus, your dream points to some sort of relapse. Dreamer, take great care and heed God's warnings. Go and sin no more, lest a worse thing come upon you (see John 5:1-14). If relapsing is a real issue within your life, consider this, you will very quickly lose everything, family, home, and freedom. It will be as though you never stopped using; you will pick up where you left off. Dreamer, as a believer, you are to exhibit faith by steadfast obedience, determination, confidence, fortitude, thanks, and lo ve. The genuineness of your faith expresses itself by your response to hardships and opposition engendered by your inner temptations to sin, and/or by your identification with Christ. We must exhibit courage under trials, and not take lightly God' s presence, divine support, and/or His wise instructions. If urged by God, declare a one, two, or three day fast to start things off. Dreamer, a lifestyle of fasting (declaring to fast perhaps twice a week until), daily prayer, and a renewal of your mindset b y reading, understanding, and mastering Philippians 4:8, 9, are imperative, as well as, resolutely separating yourself from people, places, and circumstances that hinders clarity and keeps you from enjoying the goodness of the Lords' favor. See suggested course of action.

Perennials (any flower, fruit, plant, vegetable, or herb, whose life cycle lasts three seasons or more, or lasting an indefinitely long time; recurring again and again): A dream with emphasis on the perennial nature of plants intimates something happening again, and again, on a continuing basis, recurring repeatedly, year after year, indefinitely. Further, your dream signals a renewal of some sort, perhaps going from bad to good in a day, and remaining good indefinitely; e.g. "perennial happiness". Thus, your dream points to a person, place, or organization that will not die soon, nor abate or diminish, but will continue for a long time. On the other hand, depending on the condition of the plant (e.g. bad, barren, fruitful, good, lifeless, or withered), your dream may imply, unfortunately, an illness. Perhaps an ongoing chronic illness (e.g. diabetes, heart disease, HIV) which will continue for a long time, or an illness that will recur, repeatedly; if, the appropriate health initiatives, or lifestyle changes, are not, taken. Pray Psalm 38:1-22. If necessary, see suggested course of action.

In addition, the following is a common word, expression, usage (e.g. slang or cliché) or a 'probable' that is metaphorically represented by flowers:

- **Smelling roses or flowers, "stop and smell the roses" or "stop and smell the flowers":** Your dream denotes one, namely the dreamer, who needs to relax, to take time out of your busy schedule to enjoy and appreciate the beauty of life around you.

GARDEN OR GARDENING OR GARDENER OR NURSERYMAN (a plot of ground where flowers, vegetables, fruits, or herbs are cultivated):

This type of dream usually alludes to human interaction, with respect to God, to others (especially one's marital relationship, it being the most personal and intense form of human interaction), and with respect to yourself. With that, this dream has three meanings (choose one). (1) Gardening, Gardener, nurseryman (or woman), taking care of a garden, or employed to work in a garden: This choice has two parts (choose one). (a) Male dreamer: Your dream refers to one's offensively abnormal and aggressive interest or desire in sexual activity, sexual involvement, sexual appeal, sexual potency, love affair, fantasy role-play, pornography, and/or voyeurism. Dreamer, if your true intent is on doing God's will, reaping prosperity, experiencing genuine joy, and most importantly inheriting eternal life, you will need to lay aside every obstacle that hinders you and causes you to forfeit God's principles, including abstaining from sexual immorality. See Galatians 5:19-21. You must bring your overtly lustful appetites and addictions under subjection, sacrificing fleshly desires that you might reach the point where you are capable of accomplishing your mission. This type of discipline will also help you see yourself and your issues more clearly. It will be up to you. You are free to do as you please; you still have personal liberty. However, you can no longer pretend to have a spiritually pure and steadfast quality; you must actually possess it within, in order to complete yo ur purpose and to prosper. Prayer and fasting are the first steps in this process towards clarity, as well as, acknowledging yourself just as you are, your weaknesses and flaws and your strengths. Afterward, develop specific and reachable goals and objective s, and some manner of accountability that will help you develop a disciplined and determined spirit (see Psalm 51:10), focusing your mind on spiritual matters, such as achieving a closer unity with God, and on spiritual maturity for ministry. See suggested course of action. (b) Female dreamer: You live in excess, mischievousness, and unruliness, to the point of recklessness, while blaming your lack of anointing, faithfulness, commitment, and stewardship on others. Not only this, but you trample those yo u consider less than yourself, harmful to those about you; taking advantage of their spiritual and natural poverty, necessity, and inability to help themselves, making them poorer and needier than they were, before meeting you. While, you give nothing in return, especially in the form of service and care, exposing your selfish concern for your own interests and welfare, you lack any kind of altruism. See suggested course of action. (2) Enclosed Garden (to be in one): Your dream is figurative of the Shekinah. The Creator, in His mercy, is expressing His nearness to the dreamer, to make known His thoughts and feelings regarding you. Dreamer, God's opinion of, and high regard for you, is as if there is no fault. His love towards you, and delight in you, is no small matter. "For I know the plans I have for you," declares the Lord, "plans to prosper you and not to harm you, plans to give you hope and a future" (Jeremiah 29:11 NIV). Dreamer, you have reached the end of a refining process, see Proverbs 17:3, 27:21. The prosperity of your soul, your lifestyle, and choice of friends, God takes great delight in. So impressive are you, you will be honored, notable, and weighted with goods, property, and money, as well as given some level of authority (if not already). In all this, glorify God's loving Hand upon your life, which is worthy of praise, and continue giving Him the honor. Moreover, give a "thank offering" to the ministry you're a part of. (3) Fragrant garden (to smell the plants within a garden, good or bad, foul smell): This choice has three parts (choose one). (a) Unmarried dreamer, see 1 Corinthians 7:8, 9, couple this with one of the following. (b) Good smelling garden: To smell the plants within a garden, and the smell was a good smell to the dreamer. This refers to two things: the dreamer's lifestyle and place of worship are acceptable unto the Lord. Thus, continue basing your life on hard work, wisdom, common sense, and remain where you are, the church you are now attending. Your dream also refers to intimate human love between a husband and wife. Your spouse is beckoning you to come to him or her. Absence of intimacy and sexual love makes will power weak and temptation strong. See also 1 Corinthians 7:3-5, 33, 34. Additionally, heeding your spouse's gestures of love will cause your marriage to merit children, if none, born of you and your spouse strength, adventure, excitement, passion, romance, and other aspects of human love. (c) Bad or foul smelling garden: To smell the plants within a garden, and the smell was a bad or foul smell to the dreamer. Your manner of Christian duty, sacrifice, and worship is of the kind that grieves the presence of a Holy God. Then, you try to ju stify your actions in front of people, see Luke 16:15. God knows what's in your heart. You are lacking holiness and purity. Heartfelt repentance to Jesus is needed now. True repentance of sin is indeed a sweet aroma of holiness to God. To Jesus pray, Psalm 51, this followed by appropriate application of wisdom, can conceivably avert some of the repercussions of your choices. This is known as leaving a blessing behind. When a man/woman genuinely return to God in love and surrender, your deliberate transgressions become like actual merits (also see Luke 7:37-50). Because, the realization of your distance from God, resulting from your transgressions (Isaiah 59:2), becomes the motivating force to return to God with a passion even greater than that o f someone who has never sinned in such a manner. See suggested course of action.

Garden of Eden: To dream of entering the Garden of Eden, denotes that the dreamer is (or will shortly be) faced with the choice of presenting, to a person or group, God's truth, or being politically correct. By openly expressing tolerance for sin, even that which is considered an abomination per the Written Record dictated by God. Dreamer, always choose to speak and practice God's unadulterated truth, without second guessing it, or double mindedness, lest you endanger yourself of sin which causes separation, for it is written, no one who speaks falsely will stand in My Presence (Psalm 101:7, Matthew 5:19, 20). Dreamer, although you are precious in the sight of God, for you to deny His truth, second-guess His Word per Holy Writ, or exalt ancient or contemporary philosophies over God's truth, will result in physical and spiritual devastation for you, possible loss of sanity, or you becoming a heretic. Thus, you are strongly encouraged to speak God's truth, as handed down to us via Holy Writ, that you may have peace (Luke 12:1-12). Don't say, "I don't know His truth", simply open your bible and study what's before your eyes. Focusing on one verse per day, this is a start. Further, in the genuineness of your heart, set Chr ist as Lord. Further, always be prepared to give an answer to everyone who asks you to give the reason for the hope and faith that you have, and do this with gentleness and respect (1 Peter 3:15). Dreamer, there are those amongst you, who are in a very low state, who are destined to receive God's truth from you. They really need to hear godly truth and wisdom, because they've heard lies, half-truths, and tricks far too long. Your loyalty and studiousness to God and His Word will cause the Light of God to shine forth in the lives of those needing to hear His truth, and envelope them. See suggested course of action.

In addition, the following is a common word, expression, usage (e.g. slang or cliché) or a 'probable' that is metaphorically represented by a garden:

To lead or take somebody up or down a garden path: This denotes one who is deceiving or misleading somebody, or one who is being deceived or misled, often gradually, and over a period of time. Additionally, see category: Walking (To walk down the primrose path). See suggested course of action.

Ground Or Soil, Dirt (the earth, soil, or any other similar medium, in which agricultural growth and development takes place, or development ceases, because of adverse conditions):

Your dream refers to issues of the mind, your mental and emotional health, with emphasis primarily on confusion of the mind, as well as your spiritual condition. Your attitude, understanding, perspective, and/or reasoning, will play (or have played) major parts as to the level of confusion you are experiencing or will experience. In addition, your dream points to self- esteem concerns, your penchant, a strong liking, taste, or tendency for something, as well as, your ethics, environment, morals, and upbringing.

Note: To plant anything in any type of ground, also see subcategory, Plants, Planting, and Sowing.

Journal the following questions: In what condition was the ground, soil, dirt? Were there efforts to improve or develop the ground? What was the activity surrounding the land? Was the soil broke up with the help of an animal, machine, or other farming implements? Did someone else work and prepare the ground for crops? If someone else worked the ground, see Note 3 at the beginning of this category. Kept within context of your dream and the interpretation, your answers to one or more of these questions, maybe an area (or situation) of relevance. Dreamer, the condition of the ground, and what was done regarding the condition, figuratively exposes your emotional and spiritual state, and your attitude and what possibly needs to happen to affect a healthier you. See one of the following.

Conditions and Types of ground, soil, dirt: Condition of ground, soil, dirt should be highlighted within your dream.

Cultivated and Good Ground, Soil, or Dirt (rich looking earth cleared of debris, plowed, and fertilized): This dream has three meanings (one, two, or all may apply). (1) To dream of cultivated, good, healthy, rich earth, or to plant or scatter seeds into cultivated ground, your dream refers to the concentration of the mind on spiritual matters and the beginning of a ministry. Dreamer, you've been blessed with a heart that understands knowledge, thus, you aspire to achieve a closer unity with God. Desiring this closer relationship has elevated you to a level of maturity that merits the granting of divine authority to minister. It will be in you ministering faithfully and obediently, ushering the mentality of God into circumstances and situations that you will begin to experience God's faithfulness, His grace abounding, fullness, full measure, full recompense, full reward, holiness, and deliverance. You will experience all this fullness, according to your capacity to handle fullness (Mark 4:20), no more, no less. Therefore, be encouraged, and stay in the process you're experiencing. You will begin to see the fruit of your labor, if you faint not. Moreover, your bad life cycles and those negative habits and ways of doing things, have been broken because of th e Word of God. (2) Unmarried dreamer: Your dream is also a sign or indication of an engagement and wedding. This covenant relationship is honored by God. (3) Your dream also points to the birth of a child, especially if so desired. A pregnancy is about to happen.

Uncultivated Ground (ground not tilled or land unusable for the growing of crops): To dream of uncultivated ground or to plant or scatter seeds on uncultivated ground, this denotes a prodigal heart. Dreamer, you are one who have become hardened, bitter, and depressed, waiting for someone to save you from yourself. No one can save you from you, except God, and that can't happen without repentance. Heartfelt repentance is seeking pardon and expressing sincere feelings of regret and brokenness for having done something awry and/or for having hurt someone, see 2 Corinthians 7:10, 11. A simple prayer of repentance, "Jesus, I beg your forgiveness. I know I've broken your heart, I never meant to treat you this way. Heavenly Father, I'll do whatever it takes to never hurt you again, and I'll love you for the rest of my life". See also Psalm 51. See suggested course of action.

Thorns and Thistles: If thorns or thistles pricked the body in any way, see category, The Body (Thorns). Other than that, to dream of ground, or an area, covered with thorns and thistles, or to plant or scatter seeds amongst thorns and thistles, denotes spiritual poverty. Dreamer, your work is in vain. You are investing in things that perish. Dreamer, there is a need to renounce religious beliefs that are based on faithless ritualistic practices, customs, and traditions, as well as pride. Your dream is a second witness and warning. God has sent someone to you, calling for you to repent, in preparation for an unadulterated personal relationship with Christ. Heartfelt repentance to Jesus is required of the dreamer at this time. Repentance is seeking pardon and expressing sincere feelings of regret and brokenness for having done something awry and/or for having hurt someone. To Jesus pray, Psalm 51, this followed by appropriate application of wisdom, can conceivably avert some of the repercussions of your choices. If no abandonment of such practices occurs, as well as pride, your choices will possibly lead you to be counted amongst those illustrated in Matthew 7:21-23. Dreamer, is it wise to forfeit the eternality of heaven, for that which gratifies only a short time, especially after having been warned? Receive God's message in simple childlike faith, trusting that by it you will be saved (Matthew 18:3-5, 7-9). In doing this, you will be justified solely based on grace (the free and unmerited favor and beneficence of God) and faith. Even more, having accepted Jesus, your desires will also change and be more satisfying. See suggested course of action.

Track of land trodden down (e.g. Dirt Road): To dream of a trodden path, dirt road, or to plant or scatter seeds onto a dirt road suggests a rectification of chaos and waywardness within the life of the dreamer, and it denotes a lack of understanding of the Word of God. Dreamer, where there is a lack of trust in the integrity of God and in His goodwill towards humankind, and a lack of understanding His Nature, His Word, and His intentions; genuine godly truth can be, and often is, twisted. With that said, two things, both apply. (1) Dreamer, you are one who moves from place to place, church to church, ministry to ministry, without a known destination, without commitment, and without purpose. You are one who strays from the course, a wanderer. As a result of wandering, you've lost (or is losing) your spiritual identity, and/or the willingness and ability to listen, think, concentrate, speak, and/or write on the truths, principles, and precepts of Jesus, in a coherent ma nner. (2) You've allowed others to trample upon the truths of the Gospel taught you, to appear tolerant. So much so, that this has caused a confusion of mind. Your attitude of tolerance has now put you in the hands of cruel and wicked leaders, and amongst the nefarious rich. Those who are hostile towards the truth of God's Word, who spread beliefs based on the premise that sensual desires are our primary concern. Their beliefs and doctrine are snares, hastening judgment and a shameful death. Favorably, the Lord can deliver you from bondage, if you would but, with bold faith, seek Him while He may be found, and call upon Him while He is near. Recognize and respect your time of visitation from the Lord, for it is upon you. Attend a church that adheres to The Record (Holy Scriptures), appreciate that place of worship, and don't leave until seven cycles of something have passed over you (e.g. months, years, anniversaries, seven winter, spring, summer, or fall seasons). You declare the seven cycles, and God will meet you there. In doing this, your soul will be made quiet and the chaos will subside long enough for you to make an intelligent decision to start again embracing the simplicity of God's truths and His peace. Allow God's love to surround your weariness. See suggested course of action.

Rocky Ground: To dream of very rocky ground or areas, or to plant or scatter seeds amongst rocks denotes three concerns (one or all may apply). (1) Jesus Christ, our Lord and Savior, is in your midst; and it is for a purpose, thus recognize and respect your time of visitation. (2) Your dream also denotes a superficial approach to a spiritual life due to obstacles, namely people, places, or things that hinder clarity. Dreamer, although you present as one who has a determined and steadfast quality, and wants to be respected as such, in reality, you are not. You handle your duties and responsibilities carelessly, you give-up too easily, and quit too soon. You can no longer pretend to have a determined and steadfast quality; you must actually possess it within, in order to complete your purpose and to prosper. Moreover, you are one who "bumps- up" against the Word of God, especially His principles. You hear the truth of God's Word, you like what you hear, and you sa y, "That changed my life", "That was deep", "I never knew that", "I never looked at it like that before". However, when changes are needed to transition, you, having no personal experience with Jesus, via the Holy Spirit, and no deeply rooted spiritual foundation. A foundation that is, biblical established, firmly held, and time-honored, you can't, as it were, "take the heat".

Lacking a moral compass, you become intolerant of God's principles, bumping-up against those things you do not understand, and stumbling over those things you consider too challenging. Hence, you begin demeaning His ways as methods that stand in the way of achieving personal goals. Alleged difficulties and hindrances to your spiritual development and limits on your freewheeling, has given rise to grumbling, complaining, whining, frustration, and resentfulness. Instead of allowing the Word of God to instruct you on the choices that are needed to prosper you spiritually, emotionally, and financially, you go back t o that familiar and comfortable place; unwilling to make a leap of faith. This mind-set has become a cycle within your life, and you have justified this cycle far too long. Dreamer, the excuse of good intentions is often used to support your bad actions. Your complaints and objections, display of disagreement, and refusal to submit to righteous principles are all bad actions. The first steps towards turning things around are fervent prayer and consistent fasting, coupled with repentance. A simple praye r of repentance, "Jesus, I beg your forgiveness. I know I've broken your heart, I never meant to treat you this way. Heavenly Father, I'll do whatever it takes, to never hurt you again, and I'll love you for the rest of my life". This process will begin to help you see yourself and your issues more realistically. Afterward, develop specific and reachable objectives, and some manner of accountability that will help lead you to your desired goals, and help you develop a disciplined and determined spirit. Set "time frames" for major choices. For example, do not move from your present place of worship for at least seven years, and make it happen. Dreamer, by genuinely applying these disciplines to your life, you will, soon be respected as one who is purposeful and persevering. (3) The dreamer has begun to embrace the teachings of one, whose beliefs are illogical, extremely superficial, one-dimensional, bigoted, and without foundation. This person believes that those who do not believe as they do; should be treated rudely, by deliberately ignoring them and by treating them as one who is unimportant. To think of anyone as unimportant, epitomizes contempt. See suggested course of action.

Weeds: To dream of ground that is full of weeds, or to plant or scatter seeds amongst weeds, denotes one who has heard the truth of God's Word, and it didn't lend support to, or was not actively in favor of, your lifestyle choices, so you became angry. You speak angrily and threateningly against God and against those who have embraced a Kingdom of God mind-set. So powerfully convincing the stranglehold of deception within your life, it has convinced you out of believing, thinking, feeling, or doing anything connected to Jesus Christ and His Kingdom. You are involved in so many conflicting priorities and distractions that you're in a state of confusion from which there is no easy exit. Moreover, this confusion has caused a division within you, a serious mental health issue, as well as robbed you of physical strength. Dreamer, while God is absolute ruler, over His Theocratic Kingdom, and total obedience, by His people, to His Word, is preferable; He is not tyrannical, brutal, cruel, oppressive, or suppressive; nor, is serving Him, according to His principles a "poverty trap". On the contrary, following God's principles actually empowers, encourages embracing ethical and moral principles, and fosters discipline, prudence, and prosperity, spiritually, physically, and literally, and all this done without strain, even when the pressures of life feel like they're chocking you. Allow God's love to separate you from worthless and vain thoughts, teachings, and words. He can, and is willing, to restore things to a good state for you. If weeding was done, may also see category, Plowing (Weeding). See suggested course of action.

In addition, the following are common words, expressions, usages, (e.g. slang or clichés), or a 'probable' that are metaphorically represented by weeds:

- A person who is physically weak and ineffectual; A black garment (dress) worn by a widow as a sign of mourning; A black band worn by a man (on the arm or hat) as a sign of mourning; A street name for marijuana

In addition, the following are common words, expressions, usages (e.g. slang or cliché), or a 'probable' that are metaphorically represented by ground, soil:

- **Ground:** To teach somebody the basics about something, or to base ideas, arguments, or beliefs on something, unfortunately your ideas or arguments are illogical, non-mainstream, and without favorable conclusions. See suggested course of action.
- **Soil:** Some manner of physical uncleanness or unclean acts; moral corruption; immoral behavior; lack of moral standards; to bring dishonor on, to damage somebody's reputation, character, or good name, or to wallow is present within the life of the dreamer. See suggested course of action.

HARVESTING OR REAPING (gathering or reaping of a crop during a particular season):

Your dream hints at the aftereffects of previous activities, choices, and/or behavior. It can be good consequences, marked by pleasurable, amusing, and lovely moments, or bad consequences, with unpleasant and difficult results. Things sown, promises made or broken, are coming into full fruition. You will reap the consequences of your past deeds; see Galatians 6:7. The Lord your God will now bless (or judge) you in all the work (or slackness) of your hands (Ezekiel 33:13, 14-20). See suggested course of action.

In addition, the following is a common word, expression, usage (e.g. slang or cliché) or a 'probable' that is metapho rically represented by harvesting:

- This denotes some type of removal of bodily organs, fluids, or tissue for, transplantation, testing, or research.

HEDGES (break through a hedge, hedge made of thorns, a row of shrubs, a close-set row of bushes, usually with their branches intermingled, forming a barrier or boundary in a garden, lawn, or field):

This dream has three meanings (choose one). (1) Your dream strongly urges the dreamer to adhere to God's instructions, and principles that guide actions and moral behavior. Dreamer, it is imperative that you subdue and govern your desires and passions with wisdom. You have a journey to go on, spiritual warfare to fight, and a great work to do. God's guiding princi ples, as outlined in the Bible, are hedges that protect. Following godliness is, aimed at making you not only wiser, but also better. God wants to purify you that you might fulfill the righteous purpose for which you were designed. Dreamer, you must learn to discipline your mind, inner man, and affections, to restrain from extravagances. Pray Psalm 51:10. Let your strength and quickness of mind be used, fulfilling your obligations to God and His cause. Be temperate and modest in apparel, business, drinking, eating, recreation, and in all your behavior, demonstrating humility in your opinions and in practice. The decision to allow the wisdom of God to direct your life will never be forced upon you. You must choose. Moreover, choose to not, say, "I have great desire, thus my physical enjoyment, luxury, and sensual gratifications are my primary concerns". This is a characterization of the ungodly or spiritually immature. Weigh: The child thinks that all that appears pleasant and tasty belongs to them and that he or she has the right to partake of any and everything. Consideration of others, and/or of the resulting outcome is unfamiliar to him or her. They will never consider the results of their behavior, nor how their behavior will affect others. This type of consideration is not within a child's mind-set, because he or she is a child. As the immature child takes what they want, when they want it, and believes that it's theirs, and that they do have a right to it, so does th e spiritually immature, do what they want, when they want, and believe that it's OK, using grace as a cover for sin. Spiritual change cannot begin with this kind of expectation and mind-set. Rather say, "I have great desire but what can I do, since my Father in Heaven forbids me from involving myself in such acts?" Whenever you partake of anything you are required to pause and ask yourself if that particular activity is permitted or not; and even if it is permitted, you must inquire whether you should participate or involve yourself in it at that moment. This will help train you to pause briefly between the moment that your desire demands to be satisfied and the moment that you actually satisfy it or not. For you already know that desire causes you to act compulsively even when you know you will regret your actions later. Thus, that pause is the decisive moment. It will transform your tendency, your desire, into an act of will. The will is what leads to action after your desire passes through the filter of your thought. All this may be accomplished within your life, by prudently embracing the principles and precepts of Jesus Christ, the one who has made you holy, via His blood sacrifice. Additionally, very shortly, you will have to give an a ccount of the fulfilling of your purpose for which you was design, as well as, of your philosophy and words. Consider your dream as sufficient warning. See suggested course of action. (2) Break through a hedge (to make an opening or gap in a hedge by, e.g. sticking your arm through it, running through it, or by cutting an opening through the hedge): Your dream denotes that the dreamer actions are in total disregard of God's principles, precepts, and ways. Your behavior hinders the sanctification process, thus, reckoning you as a rebellious child of God. You disagree with the Word of God, and are in violation of it. This type of attitude will prevent you from achieving your goals, having forfeited purpose for foolishness. There is a need for repentance. Dreamer, a character, and lifestyle change can occur through prayer and heartfelt repentance to Jesus. To Jesus pray, Psalm 51, this coupled with prayer, fasting, and follow-thru with appropriate application of wisdom, can conceivably avert some of the repercussions of your choices. This is known as leaving a blessing behind. When a man or woman genuinely return to God in love and surrender, your deliberate transgressions become like actual merits (also see Luke 7:37 -50). Because, the realization of your distance from God, resulting from your transgressions (Isaiah 59:2), becomes the motivating force to return to God with a passion even greater than that of someone who has never sinned in such a manner (or never left his Father's house, Acts 9:1-30). However, until you own up to your rebellious behavior, repent, and become submissive, obedient, and useful within God's Kingdom again, you will begin to decrease, and become weaken in spirit and body. In addition, your actions and behavior, that which is secret, and previously known only to a few, will become public informat ion. See suggested course of action. (3) Hedge made of thorns: Dreamer is slothful; lazy, disliking work or any form of physical exertion. This behavior is going to lead you to poverty. See Proverbs 6:6-11, 24:30-34. Adhere to wisdom. See suggested course of action.

In addition, the following are common words, expressions, usages (e.g. slang or cliché), or a 'probable' that are metaphorically represented by hedge:

- Someone has made an ambiguous, evasive, or guarded, statement.
- Someone has restricted the scope or applicability of something by means of something else (e.g. a set of regulations, conditions, or qualifications).
- Someone has taken measures to offset any possible loss on a financial transaction, especially by investing in counterbalancing securities as a guard against price fluctuations.

LEAF, LEAVES (the foliage of a plant or tree):

Leaves symbolically alludes to doing good deeds, and your ability to think, reason, and remember, especially later in life (old age), with primary emphasis on the ability or skill you was born with, or have learned. Your dream also denotes sexual intercourse.

Autumn or Fall Foliage (bright multi-color leaves, especially orange, reds, and yellows): Your dream denotes that, any ability or skill you were born with, or have learned, it is now time, to master that gifting and diligently make use of it, or it will begin to decline. Dreamer, it would be wise for you to, carefully manage your innate resources. Use them or lose them. If losing them is your choice, you will be ashamed because of your attitude, an attitude, which you delight in; or you will be disgraced because of your choices. Dreamer, desire not to be counted amongst those who buried their talents, wicked servants who buried their unique expression of God to the world, blaming their lack of faithfulness, commitment, and stewardship on God or others. When in reality, you are actually choosing to remain spiritually immature. Upon facing your Maker, there will be none to blame but you. You will have to give an account of the use of your talent. Consider your dream as sufficient warning. Moreover, dreamer needs to adapt more easily to change, and embrace learning new things and enjoy going to new places. See suggested course of action.

Dried-up or Withered leaves: Your dream denotes one who darkens God's counsel with words without knowledge (Job 38:2). You cause others to become unhappy, less hopeful, and/or angry because of your words, and those words are spoken, without careful consideration. Words based on ignorance and presumption. Additionally, couple this with one of the following (choose one). (1) The dreamer has made someone feel confused, embarrassed, foolish, incapable, and/or unsettled. You are aware of who this person is, and how this person feels about what you've said. You have openly insinuated that they lack the ability, character, and/or strength, required to do something, or that they're not good enough to function or perform adequately. You have made them an object of scorn and contempt, and have caused them to lose confidence in the face of others. Consequently, you will begin to experience a noticeable deterioration of your intellectual functions, marked by mental deterioration, memory loss, and/or disorientation, until you genuinely respect and acknowledge the feelings and struggle of another. At which point, you will be restored to health. However, until you empathize with that person's feelings and difficulties, you will progressively become weaker, to the point of decline. See suggested course of action. (2) Your dream denotes one, namely the dreamer, found not fulfilling the purpose for which you were designed. You are contrary, disobedient, and stubborn, having shut your eyes to righteousness, instigating evil, and settling for a voluptuary type philosophy. You say, "I have great desire, thus my physical enjoyment, luxury, and sensual gratifications are my primary concerns", and you desire to propagate your beliefs. Spiritual change cannot begin with this kind of expectation and mind-set. Rather say, "I have great desire but what can I do, since my Father in Heaven forbids me from involving myself in such acts?" Dreamer, you will have to give an account of the fulfilling of your purpose, as well as, of your philosophy and words, very shortly. Consider your dream a sufficient warning. For even the fig tree, when found not fulfilling the purpose for its existence was, cursed, dried up from the root (Matthew 21:18, 19, Mark 11:12-14). See suggested course of action.

Falling Leaves: Dreamer, you insult God, when you insult the sacredness of religion. You treat God's sacred ordinances disrespectfully through your words and actions (e.g. when one Christian goes to law against another, backbiting, thievery, greed, slander, sexual immorality, or any other attribute of those who practices sin, see 1 Corinthians 6:6-20, Ephesians 5). You blaspheme matters you do not understand, driven by your brutish nature. You are not even subject to self-restraint. You are a rebellious person, whose anointing and spiritual authority will now begin to abate, if no change occurs, within and without, you. Moreover, you will begin to experience a noticeable deterioration of intellectual functions, marked by mental deterioration, memory loss, and/or disorientation, if no change occurs. Fortunately, if change does occur, you will have merited God's mercy, allowing you to continue living with keen mental ability and health. See suggested course of action.

Summer, Spring Foliage (green leaves): Your keen mental abilities, ministry, and any talent or skill you were born with or learned, will continue at a high functioning level into your old age. Keep a flexible attitude, coupled with physical activi ty, exercise, and a diet that helps lower cholesterol levels and blood pressure. Moreover, your sensitivity and gentleness are a great healing force to others. You will always have a powerful effect on anyone who enters your life. Your dream was sent to encourage the dreamer to keep progressing forward, and don't worry about age, nor about any limitations that come with aging, you will be strengthen, only stay active and healthy as best you can.

Making use of Leaves for Arts and Crafts, Clothing, Eating, or Smoking: This dream has four meanings (choose one). (1) Your dream denotes one who has been filled with the Holy Spirit, and with ability, knowledge, and skill. Any talents or skills you were born with or learned, use them, if not already, to inspire others to embrace Christ Jesus. For, artistic expression, in some form or another, is the gift you bring to the world for the cause of God's Kingdom. This talent or gifting will continu e at a high functioning level into your old age. In addition, it is suggested that you "take-up" or maintain, any activities that stimulate your mind (e.g. keeping a flexible attitude, crossword puzzles, reading, writing, and learning new things). Moreover, reaching out and touching the people around you and within your community, perhaps via volunteerism, this will play a big part in helping you stay mentally and physically fit. (2) Clothing: To dream of using leaves as clothing denotes shame due to unrighteous behavior. Dreamer, rather than repent and turn from unrighteousness, you are attempting to cover your sinful behavior that the shame of your disobedience might not be openly, manifested. The effort you've put into covering your behavior, has caused you to neglect your ministerial duties. So preoccupied with ducking, dodging, and hiding, you've irreverently neglected serving others. You give very little, and demand and expect a lot. By this, you have caused God's governance via His church and sacred ordinances to be insulted. Dreamer, allow Christ to clothe you with His righteousness and grace. That the shame of your nakedness might be properly covered, and the glory of the Lord and the beauty of His holiness be revealed. Repentance, coming clean about your unholy and bad activities, and allowing the means of God, and the strength within you, to help you overcome your sinful ways, and what has been declared can be halted (Ezekiel 33:12-19). If, no repentance and change; your lack of commitment, stewardship, and faithfulness to God's word will be exposed. For condition and type of leaves; also see relevant subcategories, this will allude to whether dreamer will repent or not. See suggested course of action. (3) Eating leaves: Your dream denotes emotional, mental, physical, and spiritual healing. Dreamer, because you have chosen to take the Word of God to heart, and applied it to your life, it will yield the healing force and spiritual medicine needed to make you healthy. Good health includes physical, mental, emotional, and spiritual well- being; a healthy mind contributes to a healthy body. Once healed and restored to health, it is suggested that eating nutritiously, namely a diet that helps lower cholesterol levels and blood pressure, seeking medical treatment when necessary, physical activity, and limiting alcohol consumption, will help maintain a healthy mind, body, and spirit, and improve your mental abilities and energy levels. Dreamer, also stay connected with family and friends. These preventive measures will help you be happy, enjoy life and pursue new dreams and endeavors as you age, and prevent or alleviate depression. These are also good steps towards maintaining your healing and for healthy aging. (4) Smoking leaves: see category Cigarettes.

In addition, the following are common words, expressions, usages (e.g. slang or cliché), or a 'probable' that are metaphorically represented by foliage:

- Take a leaf out of somebody's book: Your dream denotes one who is under good mentorship, and one who is a good example.
- Turning over a new leaf (or a leaf in good condition): Your dream denotes an improvement (or a need of improvement) in the dreamer's behavior. Reformation and a new beginning are before you. Start, if not already, choosing better habits, by developing habits of holiness, and choose

to behave in a better and different way. Behave in a more acceptable way in the eyesight of God and society. There are many things which one can learn in theory, but which are only, really learned, in practice. The Lord Jesus Christ knew all things by omniscience; nevertheless, He had to learn obedience by actual experience, while human. Everyone who wants to make a success out of his or her life has to remain teachable. See suggested course of action.

PLANTS, PLANTING, SOWING (saplings, seedlings, plants; or to put any number of plants or seeds into the ground to grow):

Your dream generally refers to one who will become pregnant, as well as, great blessings after great physical or mental distress (Proverbs 18:12, also see Job's story). See one of the following.

Blighted Plants (any plant disease that mars and/or prevents growth): Dreamer, any large-scale calamities, or annoying irritations that have angered you intensely, especially something you've experienced recently, was indeed sent by God but not without purpose. Your experiences have produced within you soundness, integrity, and an honesty that would be "hard - pressed" or nearly impossible, to become corrupted again. Dreamer, begin to thank God for His longsuffering and loving kindness shown you, for now all your troubles will cease, you having learned your lesson. Take great delight in this message of encouragement.

Plant a Bush, Seedling, Shrub, Thicket, Tree, or Grain into the Ground: Dreamer, it is your role in life to inspire and motivate others, you are, purposed to raise the spirits of your fellow mankind. That they might be known as trees of righteousness, the planting of Jehovah, that He may be glorified. Your dream is one of encouragement, and validation. You will now, be led into situations where you will be the agent who ushers God's Presence into the mentality of the situation. You will show up when most needed, and then disappear without a thought of compensation, having faith that Jehovah Jireh, will provide for you (Genesis 22:13-14). Many will be inspired by your humility, wisdom, blameless actions, confidence, and by your faith in Christ Jesus. All of this implies that the dreamer has a balance of love and respect for the Lord and toward others. With that said, dreamer, you must develop your abilities to communicate more effectively in order to motivate others, and you will inspire others to dream and to make their dreams come true. Your words of inspiration will set people free (John 8:32, 36). Moreover, capable and unrelenting, you will handle much responsibility, and will be required to make major decisions. At some point in the undisclosed future, honor and wealth will be bestowed upon the dreamer, if not already. You will be as a tree planted by streams of water, which yields its fruit in season and who leaf does not wither, whatever you do will prosper.

Plant any manner of Flowers, Shrubs, Trees, Vegetables, or Herbs, in or around a Church, Sanctuary, Synagogue, Temple, any consecrated place: Dreamer, you shall flourish in your endeavors; and have the health, strength, and capacity of mind to accomplish all. You will not be beholden (be under a moral or financial obligation) to others for necessary food, clothing, and shelter, because of a lack of provision. God's blessings will make a little go a very long way. This promise of provision is firm and dependable, subject to very little fluctuation. Dreamer, if you fear God and walk in His ways, take comfort in this promise, and expect the benefit of it, as if it were directed to you by name. Moreover, your family shall enjoy what they have reaped; and others will not come and take the provision of the Lord from them. Dreamer, do not look around with fret; God's promises will surely happen. The enemy, that robber, stealer, and destroyer, or those who would attempt to deceive or oppress you, will be unable to take from you. It shall be well with you; whatever happens to you and your family, good will come out of it, from now on, while you live, and better, when you meet Jesus, because of eternal life that awaits you.

In addition, the following are common words, expressions, usages (e.g. slang or cliché), or a 'probable' that are metaphorically represented by planting:

- **Plant or bury a literal bug, listening, or explosive device, (e.g. "bugging a room", planting a bomb, or to bury landmines):** Dreamer (or another, if someone else did the planting) has placed something in a concealed position or place, where others will not easily find it. The planter's motive is to destroy someone, or to expose and ruin a plan or situation. Your criminal clandestine deeds will publicly be exposed. This exposure will prove explosive or volatile in nature, likely to end, in an angry disagreement or violence. Dreamer, go and undo what you've done. Notwithstanding, what has been done in the dark, will be shouted from the rooftops. This truth will set one free. Additionally, if dreamer dreamt of a literal bug, also see category, Animals (Insects). See suggested course of action.

- **Plant or bury any type of building (e.g. to dream of planting or burying a church, house, or school):** Dreamer, you are a builder of the world. Yours is the path of great men and women, who leave their marks on history. You will found or establish a church, colony, school, or settlement, or send people to a place as missionaries, colonists, or settlers, (if someone else did the planting or burying, then it will be another, one closely connected to you. You will play a major role in their endeavor). Your good deeds will be made known to others.
- **Plant or bury one who is a cleric or ministerial leader:** Your dream denotes that you will start churches, if not already. If dreamer is not a cleric, you will become one soon. Additionally, your dream denotes one, perhaps the dreamer, who will secretly be introduced into a group to spy on others that you might learn how to, strategically introduce the mentality of Jesus Christ into the situation. Do not be afraid of their status, words, or any other characteristic, that might be intimidating. Stay focus and remember your mission.
- **Plant or bury evidence (to dream of planting or burying some kind of evidence, especially that which has to do with the legal system):** Dreamer (or another if someone else did the planting) has secretly place something somewhere, where others will easily discover it later. You did this to incriminate someone who is guilty, and this person really is guilty. You will victor, and someone's clandestine or monstrous deeds will be exposed publicly. Favorably, the person, subsequently, will become spiritually free. For, truth sets one free.
- **Plant a literal foot (to dream of planting or burying something 12 inches "one foot" underground, or to Plant or bury a literal foot):** This dream has two meanings (choose one). (1) Dreamer has formally taken possession of some property, or has purposed to do so, or (2) Dreamer, you have taken a position firmly and decisively, for, or against, someone or something. Your actions, be it #1 or 2, will be revealed publicly. Therefore, make your choices compassionately, empathically, ethically, wise, and legal. No matter how difficult or how uncertain the issues; always take the next biblical, ethical, and most informed step, full of sensitivity. If necessary, see suggested course of action.

Plowing (to break-up and turn over earth; usually with shovel, pick, or some type of plowing machine): This dream has dual meanings and it addresses two groups within Christendom; laity (a member within a religious community that is not an ordained cleric), and an ordained cleric (e.g. bishop, elder, minister, pastor, pope, priest, or a religious teacher or guide). Question: Dreamer, are you laity or an ordained cleric? Choose one of the following. (1) To laity, while your dream alludes to your aspirations to improve, develop, or embrace something on a more spiritual level, such as achieving closer unity with God, and maturity for ministry. It also exposes the exploitation of the dreamer. Dreamer, you are misled, taken advantage of, treated badly, and perhaps abused, by an ordained cleric, one who is considered a leader within your faith based community. Do not allow this victimization to continue any longer. Accept the interpretation of your dream, as sufficient warning. If you continue to remain victimized, God's correction will follow, that you will once again trust and depend on the Lord, exclusively, and not fear anybody, nor exalt anyone above God. Dreamer, if you continue to allow the victimization, God will lift up His rod and His staff against you that you may learn obedience by things you will suffer (Psalm 23:4, Proverbs 23:13, 14; 29:15). Fortunately, after a short while, your suffering will cease, as will God's displeasure. All this can be avoided, if you will heed your dream's warning, and just say "enough is enough", I need to be respected, as an adult, and as a child of God. It is you r choice;

only know that suffering is not for Christ's sake, but for discipline only. (2) To an ordained cleric, if you are an ordained cleric, to you your dream is an announcement of judgment. You are guilty of treating those whom the Lord has given you to guide and watch over, so badly that your actions are comparable to one who, single handedly, destroys his or her own home and family, and tramples others. You covet the property of others, defraud people, rob them of their wealth and your words can be bought. Corruption and greed, combined with a false confidence that the Lord condones your actions, has blinded you to the truth of your actions. So serious and deep-rooted is your greed, corruption, and oppressive spirit that God can only move in judgment. Therefore, the Lord is planning disaster against you, from which you cannot save yourself. Even now, deemed a false guide, a leader who has misled the people, you will be disgraced, exposed, put to shame, and people will ridicule you, until you no longer walk proudly. In your time of trouble the Lord will withdraw; that is, God will abandon you to your fate and refuse to answer your prayers, you will be in the dark without vision and without answers. Although, this is a stern rebuke, a hard word to believe, because of the judgment and correction; if you go on sinning willingly, after receiving this truth, there no longer remains a sacrifice for sins, but a fearful expectation of judgment. This censure must not be undermined by notions that presuppose, the warning is real, but the possibility of an actual loss of a God-given ministry, your prosperity, or even life itself is not. If you want to come back to the Lord, you must genuinely come back to Him, in words and deeds, and not wander away from Him anymore. Then you can speak words like, "As God lives", and have them mean something true, just, and right. You are advised to passionately embrace an attitude of, you simply do not want to hurt Jesus (or grieve the Holy Spirit) anymore, because of unrighteous choices. God will not immediately cut you off but will wait to see if you will yet be worked upon, and change your mindset, or else to leave you inexcusable, in your accusations against God, because of your ruin (also see Jeremiah 9:7-9; Zechariah 13:9; Malachi 3:3; Matthew 23:37-39; Revelation 3:15-21). See suggested course of action.

PRUNE OR WEEDING (cut back the growth of, trim, weed-out):

There is someone within the life of the dreamer, who appears perfectly innocent and legitimate. Yet, that someone saps you of your strength, and subsequently, negatively blurs or shifts your focus, especially concerning your spiritual and emotional health. You are deeply influenced by the thoughts of others without realizing just how much you are affected. Fortunately, your dream insinuates that there will be a falling away, or a dropping off, of people, places, and/or things, to some (great or small) extent, within the dreamer's life. Allow this season, for there is a need within your life to let go of people, places, and/or things in order to further your growth. The purpose of that person(s) within your life is finished, and by letting go; the dreamer will gain the ability, to become a great teacher and writer. Additionally, dreamer beginnings and endings, growth and variety will become constant elements in your life. It would be wise for you to allow each transitional experience, each life change, to teach you how to deal with life issues more successfully than you've done before, so that your strength may become strong, and that you may continue to grow and mature in your relationship with Christ. See suggested course of action.

TREES, BUSHES, FORESTS, SHRUBS, AND THICKETS:

This category refers to tall and low perennial woody plants having a main trunk, branches, and/or several major stems, as well as, saplings and seedlings. This category also includes trees, shrubs, and bushes in large densely wooded areas or wilderness (e.g. forests). Trees, bushes, forests, shrubs, or thickets primarily represent the tenor of a person's lifestyle, his or her predisposition to think, act, behave, or proceed in a particular way; your more frequent acts, especially those that appear to be free, and least under the influence of external motives and inducements, those acts and behaviors most your own. Additionally, believers are likened unto good trees, and unbelievers to bad trees

(Matthew 7:17-20). Thus, you generally may identify righteousness, evil, or devastation (physically or spiritually) within you, based on the kind of tree depicted withi n your dream.

Trees, Bushes, Forests, Shrubs, and Thickets: Trees, bushes, forests, shrubs, and/or thickets are classified, characterized, and categorized in many ways; however, within the Bible they are figuratively grouped into three categories, good and healthy or bad, poisonous, unhealthy, corrupt or lifeless. A good and healthy tree produces good fruit. A good tree can't produce bad, rotten, or poisonous fruit (Matthew 7:17, 18). A bad, unhealthy, corrupt tree produces bad, poisonous, or evil fruit, hazardous to human life. A bad tree can't produce good fruit. A lifeless tree is no longer good or bad, no longer having force or relevance. If needed, to help determine if the tree within your dream is good, healthy, bad, poisonous, unhealthy, corrupt, or lifeless, see relevant resources (e.g. dictionary, encyclopedia, internet). Having done your research you should be able to determine some basic behaviors or attributes your Lord and Savior wants you to focus on.

Note: If the color of the trees, bushes, shrubs, and/or thickets were primary within your dream, what color were they?

For example, did you dream of a beautiful "pink" wooded area, an autumn forest, full of fall colors, or perhaps a multi -colored tree with circles? Along with the applicable interpretation, see category, Colors.

Note: While all trees, bushes, shrubs, and thickets are perennials some are, categorized as deciduous and others as evergreens. Perennial, deciduous, and evergreens, are generally the life cycles of trees, bushes, shrubs, and thickets. Example, Christmas trees, blue spruce, firs, hemlock, and white pine are all evergreens. These trees have leaves that persist and remain green throughout the year. Oak, maple, and elm are examples of deciduous trees. They lose their foliage in the fall, and grow new leaves in the spring. Before they lose their leaves, the foliage turns into several bright colors, before shedding. Deciduous trees are generally bare during the cold of winter, appearing lifeless. Thus, this kind of dream, when emphasis is on the tree's life cycle, alludes to time (the speed, duration, and manifestation of an event or action), particular the duration of a situation or issue, within the life of the dreamer at present, coupled with one of the following interpretations of conditions, kinds, and parts of trees. If life cycle is highlighted, may also see subcategory, Flowers (Perennials).

Question to journal, dreamer what type of tree, bush, forest, shrub, or thicket was depicted within your dream, and what was the condition of the tree, bush, forest, shrub, or thicket, within your dream (e.g. were they bad, barren, fruitful, good, lifeless, or withered)? If you know what type of tree, bush, forest, shrub, or thicket it was, and/or its condition, you may learn what behaviors are basic parts of your character and/or your physical condition, as well as, what the Lord wants you focus on.

You can realize more fully the symbolic nature of some trees, bushes, forests, shrubs, or thickets, as the following gives an interpretation of them.

Condition of Trees, Kinds of Trees, Parts of Trees, and Activities connected to Trees:

Barren, Dead, or Withered Tree, Bush, Forest, Shrub, or Thicket (does not include deciduous trees, bushes, shrubs, and thickets in winter): This dream has three meanings (choose one). (1) As barrenness within a dream denotes an inability to bear offspring (female or male), if this is your state, seriously consider the following. Although dreamer is unable to bear children, and is perhaps crushed by grief as a result, and always wanting or lacking, dreamer, you are powerful and strong and are well able to do mighty works for the Kingdom of God. God has given you a rare sense of purpose from birth. Ultimately, that purpose is seriously tied to the Word of God. For you, a purposeless existence will cause only frustration and despair. Therefore, you must choose a lifelong commitment to sowing "seeds" that will ultimately uproot and replace the wicked seeds planted by demonic forces some time ago, at an earlier age, perhaps the reason for your inability to bear young. Your seeds should be intentional development of habits of holiness, prayer, fasting, theological study, abstinence, sobriety, and separa tion from people, places, and circumstances that are contrary to your development of holiness, clarity, and stability. Dreamer, wise choices will bring you authentic joy, happiness, divine purpose, and miraculous knowledge and power, in due time. Dreamer, you are under the special protection of the Lord. Have faith in God, and not in state of affairs. God is promising that no longer will hurt be done you, if you respect His principles and precepts, and most importantly reverence Him. Moreover, God has persuaded others to be very compassionate, sensitive, and to take care, when dealing or speaking with you. Additionally, dreamer, know that a person, even you, can go from bad to good in one day. That place or thing previously unusable or unprofitable can become suitable for good and/or profitable in some way, or that which is, emptied can be refilled again. Indeed one or all of these situations maybe rectified, if dreamer adheres to wisdom; put works with your faith, see James 2:14-26. For example, proper nutrition, exercise, and rest, can stabilized or cease, some diseases; prudence with finances, can stop constant foreclosure notices, end a cycle of poverty, or any kind of money shortages; and prayer and fasting can push any kin d of darkness or demonic force far away from you. (2) If you are a preacher, educator, prophet, praise leader, your dream denotes that God will deal with the dreamer; He will mark you with a sign of His displeasure, by way of a trial. He will also strip you of your anointing, and you will no longer inspire. Your works and words have testified against you, for you have proven proud, covetous, false, and oppressive. Dreamer, if you pretend to be a spiritual leader of some sort, and are immoral, your immorality exposes your pretensions for what they are, false. See Philippians 3:1-21. One should regard your dream, with sincere alarm. This warning must not be undermined by notions that presuppose, the warning is real, but the possibility of a n actual loss of a God-given ministry, your prosperity, or even life itself is not. Favorably, grace will be shown you via a probationary period. This probationary period decreed might be a proving by trial (e.g. a wilderness experience); by humiliation and servitude (Judges 13:1; Acts 13:21, 22); or by waiting (Acts 7:23-30). This probationary season points to grace, leads to repentance, and ends in revival and renewal. During this season, you are counseled to begin implementing godly principles that will move you toward discipline and humility, while embracing faith and love of God. Thank God for His patience, long-suffering, and grace (the free and unmerited favor and beneficence of God), while you get things decent and in order. Therefore, be earnest to repent, and God will deliver you from death and your feet from stumbling, that you may again walk before God in the light of life (Psalm 56:13). See suggested course of action. (3) If dreamer has a chronic illness at present, your dream implies an illness, perhaps a chronic (ongoing) illness, (e.g. cancer, diabetes, heart disease, HIV), will continue for a little while longer, or an illness that will recur, again, and again; if, the appropriate health initiatives, or lifestyle changes, are not, taken. Proper nutrition, exercise, healthy lifestyle choices, and rest, can stabilized or cease, some dise ases. Dreamer, your malady may lead to early death if the appropriate lifestyle changes are not heeded. This warning must not be undermined by notions that presuppose, the warning is real, but the possibility of an actual loss of life itself, is not. Wi th that said, if you haven't already, dreamer is encouraged to seek medical attention as soon as possible, and call for the elders of your church, for it is through their prayers of faith and anointing of oil upon you that sin is forgiven and healing bestowed[36]. This is a true saying, thus it is time to have faith in God. Moreover, dreamer it is always a good time to get your house and papers in order (e.g. insurances, bequeaths, untold truths that need to be said), and always a good time to gather family together for prayer, support, wisdom, and truthfulness (Ecclesiastes 12:6). Additionally, dreamer although you may be currently suffering or soon will enter a season of suffering, suffering has a purifying effect in one's life so that after you have suffered you will cease (stop, restrain, refrain, quit, desist) from sin, especially the sin that chronically assails you. This should be your attitude toward sin and it should be so intense that even in your suffering, your determination remains, I'm done with sin! See 1 Peter 4:1-3. Dreamer, know that a person, can go from bad to good in one day, if wisdom is adhered to. For example, faith, prayer, and fasting do affect deliverance and healing, spiritually and physically, especially when traditional medicine has reached its end. Moreover, proper diet, water, vitamins, prescription medication, exercise, and rest, can stabilized or cease some symptoms, or restore health. The key here is to stop sinning via a complete change of lifestyle choices. See suggested course of action.

    Beautiful Trees, Tree of Life (tree appeared beautiful): It is necessary to say first, dreamer you are Christian, and filled with the Holy Spirit, thus, God will not take His Spirit away from you, nor blot your name out of the Book of Life. However, your dream does speak of one who is angry, dishonest, frustrated, resentful, self-centered, and imprisoned to your own ego, with no sincere intent or desire to change. You have severe mood changes, and are greatly immoral, especially sexually. You also have a tendency to blame others for your personal misfortune. Drunk with power, material possessions, and pride, you put everything before God, worshipping anything but God (spiritual adultery). Your actions have provoked divine punishment. Before reaching this point, you were clearly warned, and reproved; yet, you have not taken care. There will be a decrease in help from the only real true God, including any Word from the Lord regarding you and His hedge will be removed. Your finances will dwindle greatly; you will have to downsize. Your family, friends, mentors, and teachers will leave from before your face. This "famine" will leave only anxiety, fear, and despair as your food. On another vein, since your frustration with Christianity, God, His principles, and standards was demonically influenced this famine will not be completely devastating, according to God's tender mercies and grace (the free and unmerited favor and beneficence of God). All this will create within you a clean heart and restore an upright spirit within you. Pray Psalm 51. See suggested course of action.

Budding (to see a tree budding): It is your season to begin choosing purposeful choices. You are responsible for your unique purpose in life, and all that is involve in fulfilling that purpose. You are responsible for planning your actions and your life, around your purpose. You must make calculated decisions as to how you will live your life, and who and what you will allow in your life; and relying on emotions alone is a dangerous, an unreliable route to follow. It will not lead to purpose. Dreamer, do not allow your life to be weighed down with indulgence in sensual relations, useless or profitless activity, licentiousness, wastefulness, drunkenness and the anxieties of life. Be always vigilant and careful, attentively observing negative "triggers" in your life. Questions to journal: who do you want to be and how do you want to live, if not for Jesus, promoting the Kingdom of God? Make an earnest effort to find out, learn, and determine, with certainty, how to live your life on God's terms, according to His purpose for you; and what actually is required. This usually begins with prayer, joining, attending, and committing to a church, bible study, Sunday school. Also pray that you might be able to escape all that is about to happen, and that you may be able to stand before Adonai Elohim, knowing that the end of days is near.

Tree(s) falling down: Your dream is a notice (or message). Your dream symbolizes shortness of life. Your dream is one of God's ways of breaking it to you gently, preparing you for one of life's common denominators, and if heeded, can prevent you from being emotionally blindsided by loss. For someone who has met Jesus, we experience Him in the little graces, the big miracles, the ordinary days, and the curious moments. He is with us, leading us onward, even sharing our tears. This same Jesus trustworthy in life, even when we are not, can be trusted at the ending of life, for He is the resurrection (John 11:25, 26). If we love Jesus and love our neighbor as we love ourselves, there is nothing in this world or the next to fear. Love is what we take with us, and love is what awaits us when we have finally arrived. Nonetheless, dreamer seek medical attention as soon as possible, and call for the elders of your church, for it is through their prayers of faith and anointing of oil upon you that sin is forgiven and "spiritual" healing bestowed, and perhaps physical healing.[36] This is a true saying, thus it is time to have faith in God. Additionally, it is always a good time to get your house and papers in order (e.g. insurances, bequeaths, untold truths that need to be said), and always a good time to gather family together for prayer, support, wisdom, an d truthfulness (Ecclesiastes 12:6). Additionally, if relevant, more than one tree will symbolize just as many deaths at once or back-to-back.

Trees going from bad to good: Tree, bush, forest, shrub, or thicket going from bad to good implies that the dreamer will go from bad to good, be it spiritual and/or physical, in one day or suddenly. Having previously, been deemed bad, untrustworthy, or wicked in some manner; or ill, you will now become able and good, spiritually and physically, and will be profitable in some way or another.

Trees going from good to bad: Tree, bush, forest, shrub, or thicket going from good to bad, dreamer, read and clearly understand Ezekiel 33:12, 13; this is to you. As your dream implies that, the dreamer will go from good to bad, in one day or suddenly. Having previously, been deemed righteous and trustworthy in some manner, you will be deemed bad, untrustworthy, and/or wicked. See suggested course of action.

Tree with People, Animals, Clothing hanging from it, on it, or in it: Dreamer, you are gagging on pieces of sin, because of heartaches, emotional and psychological pains, anxieties, worries, and concerns. Gagging on pieces of sin points to three issues (choose one). (1) Dreamer needs to understand the cost of your salvation, and to learn to not be carried away by all kinds of strange teachings, or easily removed from the Gospel of Jesus Christ. We are not serving an angry God who cannot be embraced or pleased, or a God that needs to be appeased via a set of regimented and legalistic rules to prove our dedication to Him, and to prove our holiness and righteousness, all of which are of no value to those who practice such. It is good for our hearts to be strengthened by God's love, via His grace. For, God's primary identity is love (John 3:16, 1 John 4:7, 16). By His word, God first loved us while we remained in sin, not thinking about Himself; nor desiring to appease Himself, yet He became our propitiation. Therefore, our service should not come from a mind-set of appeasing God, but from a space of gratefulness and love, declaring His worthiness of our praise. Dreamer, we were made alive with Christ even when we were dead in transgressions, it is by grace you have been saved through faith, and this not from yourself, it is the gift of God (Romans 4:16; Ephesians 2:1-10; Hebrews 13:9). With that said, dreamer, God will now separate you from your surroundings that hinder spiritual clarity, and draw you away from any trust in yourself that you might seek your life in Him alone, and confidently entrust yourself to His care. View this separation as a blessing from God and not as an evil thing has happen. The Holy Spirit will lead and guide you to discipline your will, strength, efforts, and pleasures, so that the whole energy of your being will be free, and open to receive the Holy Spirit inwardly. This promise comes by grace; and if applicable, is guaranteed to your offspring. Also, the refining and purifying work of the Paraclete, and a greater service to others, will cause the emergence of a divine led wisdom. Moreover, you must not allow yourself to be annoyed with acts of devotion, for example, family bible study and other quality times, fellowshipping with other believers, church attendance, acknowledging God's goodness to you, to others, and the like. See suggested course of action. (2) Dreamer, you carry out plans that are not of the Lord, form alliances that you were not led to form, heaping sin upon sin. You have proven yourself rebellious, deceitful, and unwilling to listen to the Lord's instructions. You no longer want to hear what is right and just; only what is pleasing and satisfying to the flesh. You are majoring in illusions. Because you have rejected His message, and relied on oppression and depended on deceit, you will begin to experience very humiliating and disastrous circumstances. Yet, while this will be allowed, the experiences are designed to bring you to a state of prayer and heartfelt repentance to Jesus and to individuals affected by your actions, in the form of an apology (if possible). Repentance is seeking pardon and expressing sincere feelings of regret and brokenness for having done something awry and/or for having hurt someone, see 2 Corinthians 7:10, 11. To individuals, a phone call or a letter of apology is a good place to start. To Jesus pray, Psalm 51, this coupled with prayer and fasting, and followed by appropriate application of wisdom, can conceivably avert some of the repercussions of your choices. Moreover, as soon as Jesus hears your voice of repentance, He will answer you, for the Lord, yet longs to be gracious to you. Thus, He will show you compassion during this time of discipline. For the Lord is a God of justice. Blessed are all who wait for Him. Dreamer, although the Lord gives you the bread of adversity and the water of affliction, your ears will hear a voice behind you, saying, "This is the way; walk in it". At that time, you will no longer refuse the process of renewal and transformation; thus, affecting a better you. See suggested course of action. (3) Dreamer, your lack of Christian service comes down to indifference. The level of indifference you have for the commands of God, and for the destiny of the lost, has caused many to perish, spiritually and/or physically. Even more, the risks you take in disappointing the One who shed His blood for you is unwise. Those that follow the choices of their own hearts, feelings, emotions, rather than the dictates of the divine will, oftentimes, find themselves far from peaceful shores. Stop yourself from walking down the path of reaction. Be willing to release those things that are in conflict with, or hinder, what God has called you to do. Brining to the forefront of your mission statement that, while God is absolute ruler, over His Theocratic Kingdom, and total obedience, by His people, to His Word, is preferable; He is not tyrannical, brutal, cruel, oppressive, or suppressive; nor, is serving Him, according to His principles a "poverty trap". Your carnal mind may fight you on it, but your heart and mouth can still agree and defeat any thought of doubt or unbelief, or fear. When working to eliminate negative thoughts and feelings, pray, and think before you act! When you practice this, you will see that God will meet all your needs and you will be better able, emotionally and spiritually, to meet the needs of those God has sent you to (see also Ezekiel 37:7). See suggested course of action.

Tree House, Tree Shaping, and Trees Growing Wildly: Your dream denotes your spiritual condition. Dreamer, for three years, Jesus has come to you, via His servants, with His message, performing miracles, expounding on the Scriptures, and offering ample evidence of His claim to be the Messiah. Yet, despite three years of testimony, the dreamer still refuses to believe in the One and only true God, embracing unnecessary cynicism. You believe in a god of your own making, coupled with outrageous claims you have wholeheartedly embraced from other erroneous guides. You say Adonai Elohim creates imperfect beings and then forces them to rise up to a level of perfection, which by design, they are unable to attain, by torturing the m, causing millions to suffer in body and soul. You reason that this is God's only way, a path of pain, torture, and then death. You ask what human being aspires to evolve through this endless agony. You proclaim that God's promises are no more than vague words of doubtful happiness, and implacable laws that promise remote and unknowable joy, under th e mask of love of humanity. You say His ways are nothing more than a profound indifference and a hardened selfishness. Further, you believe that God's intolerance of sin and the inherent results of sin, mainly separation from Him, as written within Holy Writ, and expressed in Christian dogma, are the picture of an angry god, conjured up by angry, unwise, and foolish men. You boast of philosophies, which appeal to the lustful desires of human nature, condoning rebellious, unhealthy, immodest, immoral, indecent, lewd, and lascivious, behavior. Desires that if not checked, can and often do lead to early death, as you have personally witnessed. This is what you call love. You exalt your wisdom above the Creator. While you discredit the Creator's wise and sensible guidelines for living life, on this side of eternity, as healthy, humanly, and sanely as possible; and in harmony with His provision for life on the other side of eternity, in heaven. You respect your truth, while never acknowledging, it is delivered without grace; thus, it is never enough to fill an emaciated soul. Read, understand, and embrace Galatians 5:13-25. Dreamer, reacting in such a "temper tantrum" and rebellious manner, as you have done, because you disagree with certain spiritual principles, is not good. You may not like God's ways and means, but you do have to accept and surrender to them all. Dreamer, promoting and encouraging others to approach God the Father, without the essential provision He has provided for mankind to approach Him properly; that provision being Yeshua HaMashiach, is not safe. Some call God's provision Jesus, Wonderful Counselor, Mighty God, Everlasting Father, Prince of Peace, our atonement, advocate, liberator, propitiator, and our salvation. It is only through this channel that we may hope through faith to conciliate with our Creator, see John 3:16, Acts 2:37-42, 1 Timothy 2:4-7. Dreamer, at this crossroad in your life, it is counseled that you do as the apostle, and count all that you know, all that has brought you to this point, to be worthless (Philippians 3:8). Your dream has come to let you know that there is still hope and time for you to recognize the wrong in what you're doing, feel the regret about your past actions, an d change your ways and habits. There is still hope and time. You will be given one more year, with special attention on submitting to the teachings of Jesus. Dreamer, seize this opportunity to sincerely repent, denounce the erroneous teachings you've embraced, and go on from here. If you've led others astray, apologize, let them know you was wrong, and let them know, bottom line, their salvation is their own responsibility (Philippians 2:12, 13). Go and seek truth for yourself that n ot all may be eternally lost. Unfortunately, if you still fail to understand, and submit, you will be cut down (destroyed). See suggested course of action.

Large, enormous, big tree (or to watch a tree grow very large): You are destined to become a great leader, and as a natural born leader, you have a flair for taking charge of any situation. Unfortunately, you are failing as a follower. Dreamer, you will have to learn to follow for a while before allowed to

319

lead. This may prove to be a very difficult time for you, depending on your attitude. You will likely be very dissatisfied with your circumstances. However, if you start expressing yourself very negatively, this will result in you not being fully developed into the leader you are purposed to be. Your attitude, if no change, will cause you to become self-centered, always demanding to have your way in many circumstances; too self-serving, selfish, and egotistical. Dreamer, avoid being too bossy and demanding. Advancement for you, now, is the development of the imagination. Imagination brings out ideas and skills needed for starting something for the first time, introducing something new, and in being quick-witted. You have a good mind and the ability to use it for your advancement. You have great potential for achievement and financial rewards; only keep God on top. If necessary, see suggested course of action.

Trees beside a stream: see Psalm 1:1-3.

Kinds of Trees:

Almond tree: As your dream alludes to wisdom and old age, dreamer you have made (or will make) a very wise decision, because you are wise. Further, you will live to reach a good old age, in good health.

Aromatic Trees, Bushes, Shrubs, or Thickets (that exudes a distinct odor that is specific to that species, e.g. Jasmine, Lilac Bushes, Lemon Tree, Pine Tree, or Spicebush): If there was a pleasant smell, from a tree, bush, forest, shrub, or thicket, your dream comes to calm the mind, to instill tranquility, and to bring peace and inner stillness. Dreamer, you are where you are supposed to be, namely a divine ordained place (e.g. church, neighborhood, family). No one can change that. Even more, God will cause you to grow spiritually, emotionally, and financially, and help you bear fruit that you may bless others. However, in this process of growth, He cultivates and develops. Hence, the transition, oftentimes, does not feel comfortable or seem peaceful. Favorably, if you allow and abide in, the process, you will be called the planting of the Lord, and righteous that the Lord might be glorified.

Carob Tree: Dreamer, those who love the Lord God is primarily responsible for the religious education of their children (also see, Deuteronomy 6:7). You are to encourage them to participate and get involved in activities that will draw them near to Christ Jesus, His cause, and His Kingdom, that your Christian legacy might continue on to your generations (also see Proverbs 13:22; Ecclesiastes 7:11). Dreamer that which is so graciously given unto us we must pass on to those that comes after us. Frequently and repeatedly, tell and teach God's principles, precepts, and statues to your children, and not your children only, but their friends, and all those that are in anyway under your care, mentorship, and/or teaching. God's word and ways are so very easy and straightforward that anyone can instruct children in it. Try all ways of instilling His principles into their minds, and making His ways penetrate their hearts. God will enlighten you in your endeavors to perpetuate your Christian heritage.

Cedar, Cypress, Evergreen, Juniper, Palm, Palmetto, Pine, Algum trees: This dream has three meanings (one, two or all may apply). (1) Your dream was sent to encourage. Dreamer, because of your humble and submissive faith in God's word, and not your works alone, you are declared as one who is a righteous minister. Planted in the House of the Lord, you will continue to prosper and mature. The same God, who planted you in your ministry, is the same God who will cause you to mature and prosper. Independent of outward circumstances, you will live and thrive where most things perish, via divine grace. With that said, dreamer, while your spiritual growth may not be so rapid, if you endure, you will become a beautiful picture of a godly man or woman, who in your uprightness, aims to glorify God. Your dream also represents some type of spiritual privileges and a purification process, dreamer God will separate you from people, places, and circumstances that will hinder your growth. View this separation as a blessing from God and not as an evil thing has happen. Under all adversities retain a spirit of joy, and continue to make progress in your spiritual life. Accordingly, gladness, thanksgiving, singing, strength, intense energy, and fertility will be your recompense, and your praise will be a sweet aroma in the nostrils of the Lord. If applicable, this promise is to your generations to come. Come what may, you shall make steady progress and flourish in a ver y impressive manner; bringing forth fruit, even in your old age. Dreamer, as you age, your anointing to minister, and divine revelations, will always be fresh and edifying. See Psalm 92:12-15. (2) Male dreamer: In addition to the previous interpretation, an event or situation that will cause intense fear is coming to discourage and terrify you. This will be in the form of an annoying, difficult, and unpleasant person. The trouble this person will cause will become so overwhelming, because they will expose a secret regarding you. This spiritual battle will be great, and will demand your full attention. Although you will walk through this alone, know that God will walk you through it. Dreamer, learn wisdom from the situation, for truth do set one free; and go on from there unashamed. Then, suddenly, unexpectedly, and without any warning, all the evil and wickedness that caused you to fear and be troubled, will disappear. It will be as though it was never there. At th at point, you will express great joy, and feel extremely happy. Take courage and be strong, knowing that the Lord knows where you are, what's going on, and He cares. (3) Unmarried male dreamer: A palm tree also symbolizes a very attractive, sensual, and sexy female; one whom the dreamer, if male, may marry, especially before having sex.

Chestnut Tree: This dream is for a male. Your dream is to warn a male dreamer. If dreamer is a female, your dream is for a significant male in your life, especially if he is Christian (e.g. husband, son, brother, boyfriend, or friend), make known the message within this interpretation to him. Male person, beware and be sensible. You are counseled to become very shrewd and prudent, but subtle in your dealings with another at present. Become very difficult to detect or analyze. One who is very crafty and cunning is before you now. If necessary, see suggested course of action.

Deciduous Trees, Bushes, Shrubs, and Thickets: There is someone within the life of the dreamer, which appears perfectly innocent and legitimate. Yet, that someone robs you of your strength, and negatively blurs or shifts your focus, spiritually and emotionally. You are deeply influenced by the thoughts of this person without realizing just how much you ar e affected. Fortunately, your dream insinuates that there will be a falling away, or a dropping off, of people, places, and things, to some (great or small) extent, within the dreamer's life. Allow this season, without murmuring or complaint, for there is a need within the dreamer's life to let go of someone in order to further your growth. That someone has had their place within your life; and their purpose within your life is completed. Dreamer by letting go; you will gain the ability, to become a gr eat teacher and writer. Additionally, since beginnings and endings, growth and variety will become constant elements in the dreamer's life. It would be wise for you to allow each transitional experience, each life change, to teach you how to deal with life issues more successfully than you've done before that your strength may become strong, and that you may continue to grow and mature in your relationship with Christ.

Elm Tree: Your dream denotes one who tries to bear all their own burdens, only to be broken in the process. Dreamer, you are counseled to break your heartaches, pains, anxieties, worries, and concerns in half and give some to Jehovah-Rapha (Psalm 147:3), and to share with another, for you cannot bear them alone; lest you find yourself gagging and choking on pieces of your sin, forfeiting the peace that comes with humbly asking for help from God and others. Dreamer, you are encouraged, in every trial to call upon the Lord, and He will save you. He will hear you, and not blame you for coming too often, the more often you come the more you're welcome. Give all your worries and cares to God, for He cares about you, the Lord will take care of you. He will not permit the godly to slip and fall. See Psalm 55:22, 1 Peter 5:7. Therefore, humble yourself under the mighty hand of God, that He may exalt you at the proper time. Dreamer, humility preserves peace and order; pride disturbs them. God will give you grace to be humble, and He will give you wisdom and faith. Dreamer, to be humble, and to lean on God, will bring greater comfort to the soul than the gratification of pride. Therefore, cast all your cares; personal cares, family cares, cares for the present, cares for the future, cares for yourself, for others, for the church, cast all your cares on God, and in God's due time; not in your time, will your burdens be lighten.

Ferns: Jesus wants you to abide in Him, which means to dwell or stay put, especially within the ministry you are vested in right now. Don't run off and try to do your own thing in your own strength and carnal knowledge. Jesus wants to continue Hi s ministry through you, healing the sick, delivering the oppressed, fulfilling His ministry to His people, first, within the ministry you are now a member of at present. Questions to journal: who do you want to be and how do you want to live, if not for Jesus, promoting the Kingdom of God? For truly you are a healer to many, if you choose to humbly submit to leadership, order, and biblical teachings, that you might fulfill your mission. If you choose rightly, you will be spiritually fulfilled. See suggested course of action.

Fig Tree: This dream has two meanings (choose one). (1) If fig tree had fruit, if dreamer picked figs, or dreamer ate figs, or handled figs in any way: Dreamer, never allow the world to shape you, be who God purposed you to be. Take your past and use it to teach those whom God has purposed you to reach. Even more, the dreamer must offer God a first-fruit offering of your time, and not only your time, but, also your finances. Additionally, you must also give an offering of acknowledgment (financial) to the senior priest of your church. This is symbolically acknowledging that you support your spiritual leaders, and are available for service, with your whole life, in any way to the Body of Christ, the Kingdom of God, to the church, to a ministry, and to the community. This good deed also acknowledges your appreciation to God for your daily bread. This offering will open streams of income for you personally that you may again prosper, as well; it will cause the blessings of t he Lord to rest upon your house (Ezekiel 44:30). God's blessings: Gifts of God's grace, anything God freely gives you, absolution, the Holy Spirit, salvation, regeneration, eternal life, health, children, love of family, longevity, necessities, prosperity, and dominion over all that is yours; and all are parts of the supply of grace, and all are sanctified by the Lord, and technically belongs to Him. The result of this supply in your life will be peace. (2) Fig tree had no figs: This choice has two parts (choose one). (a) A change of direction and attitude is highly recommended. You are encouraged to re-think your views and attitude, regarding the doctrine you are adhering to, and your philosophy, and/or your plans for establishing or joining an institution or organization. Why, because your interpretation of the Word of God has become unrecognizable to those you influence. When those who seek truth, ask Jesus why they do not recognize your teachings, the words spoken of you are that you are true to yourself. To be true to self or another, is to seek affirmation with respect to condoning your particular sin, while basing your ideas, arguments, and/or beliefs on something that is sacrilegious, profane, illogical, and non-mainstream doctrine or philosophy. Your ideology is without favorable conclusions, thus this dream. You are full of pride. Moreover, believing and encouraging others to approach God the Father, without the essential provision He has provided for humanity, to approach Him properly; that provision being Yeshua HaMashiach, is not safe. Some call God's provision Jesus, Wonderful Counselor, Mighty God, Everlasting Father, Prince of Peace, our atonement, advocate, liberator, propitiator, and our salvation. Dreamer, you are counseled to decline the temporary relations of darkness; that you might inherit an entrance into paradise having answered God's call upon your life and turned to His Word and His intents. If you persist on perpetuating your self -serving ideology and calling it divinely ordained, you will be stripped and humiliated publicly, and replaced because of shameful acts. Therefore, repent and encourage others you've influenced to repent, by this you "rectify" and elevate yourself and ministry. Dreamer set your heart towards understanding godly knowledge. See suggested course of action. (b) Your behavior is haphazard and/or reckless, specifically in the area of handling God's word and ministering it to His people. Having attained some level of importance, your prideful ingratitude of God's generosity has escalated. You have openly insulted God, have broken covenant with Him, and have proven unthankful of His benefits. You have attributed your prosperity to the power of demons. Thus, you give to those whom the Lord disapproves. You have chosen to commit to philosophies that does not honor Jesus Christ as Lord and Savior, your choices do not concur with His principles morally. You have forsaken godliness, and now believe in something akin to Spiritism. You worship with spiritists and witches. Yet, you still expect God to continue to walk with you, take your part, act for you, and reassure you of His presence, though you care not to repent nor agree with His way s and means. You should not expect a close relationship with the Lord unless you first make peace with Him. You are forfeiting the privileges that come with His Kingdom, even eternal life. Dreamer, turn back to the Lord seeking forgiveness. Choosing to, once again, agree with His Word. In doing this, you may again prosper spiritually and be blessed. See Proverbs 16:18. See suggested course of action.

Fir Tree: This tree is associated with one, who has wisely and prudently, denounced false and idolatrous worship. You are now, producing fruit, good enough for repentance and which leads to praise, worship, and sanctification of the One True Living God. Additionally, a high-ranking leadership position that you are destined for, and was prophesied to you long ago. If you have not obtained this status as of your dream, you will shortly. You are blessed, because you come in the name of the Lord.

Forests (aka Woods): The dreamer is part of a group of people banded together into a social group, a "clique" sort to say (e.g. family, friends, or a fellowship). Your group will desire to confront a diabolical leader. This leader will feign hospitality and peace, but the group's downfall is his/her ultimate plan. Warning: Do not go before this person. Although this leader is responsible for a tragic event, the Lord knows how to reserve the unjust and wicked unto the Day of Judgment. You and your group will not be able to overcome this leader. He (or she) will assassinate the reputations of 90% of those within your gro up, by exposing their character, thus destroying their life as they enjoy it now. For they too have done forbidden things, and have not judged themselves appropriately. Additionally, couple this with one of the following (choose one). The distinct attributes associated with the group you are a part of implies one of two meanings, depending on the type of trees, the condition of the trees, and/ or what activity was connected to the forest. For example, did dreamer hunt for animals in woods full of barren trees? Also, see other relevant subcategories. Questions to journal; why was the dreamer in the woods? What type of trees, and what was the condition of the trees in the forest? (1) If trees were healthy, fruitful, pleasantly aromatic, or good in any way, this denotes that the dreamer is part of a group of people who are sagacious believers, living out and perpetuating the will of God as best they know how. The dreamer needs to remain with the group, as they will prove very wise in spiritual matters. For, where no advice is, the people fall; but in the multitude of counsellors there is safety (Proverbs 11:14). Additionally, the dreamer will be remembered as one who cared enough to stand on the side of godly justice and righteousness. (2) On the other hand, if trees were unhealthy, barren, withered, unfruitful, foul smelling, or bad in any way, the dreamer has allied with a group of people, who are likened unto unbelievers (Matthew 7:17-20). This group is a rebellious sort; who are obstinate. You are not to be in awe of them. Questions to consider; dreamer, do you see a godly oriented focus; a focus on integrity, character, right, and wrong, or an emphasis on living your life today in light of eternity, within this group? Do they care? You need to ask yourself before God, "Am I living in the world or is the world living in me?" Deal with your issues via prayer and fasting, with emphasis on a greater commitment to God, and consider the company you are keeping. Be not deceived, evil companionships corrupt good morals (1 Corinthians 15:33). See suggested course of action.

Oak, Terebinth Trees: This dream has four meaning (choose one). (1) To the married couple without children and you desire children: Read Isaiah 54:1-10, Psalm 113:9, it is the meaning of your dream. Husband pray on behalf of your wife, as Isaac did on behalf of his wife, and the Lord will answer your prayer, and your wife will become pregnant (Genesis 25:21). (2) Married couple with children: If you have not, "bullied or harassed in any manner" the married couple without children. The ordeal you think will destroy you, it will not. The current darkness and gloom that surrounds you at present, is intended to elevate you; causing you to stand up and become an anointed and powerful force within the Kingdom of God. Dreamer, your adversity is affecting a dependable, faithful, loyal, reliable, responsible, resourceful, upright, and upstanding spirit within both of you. Do not be confused or dismayed, you will not be made ashamed. It is understood on high that at present you don't feel elevated while going through your making season. Yet, this is when you can expect God to come and show Himself strong on your behalf. Dreamer, even in your dilemma, you are to elevate and promote the righteousness of Christ to those around you. You are endowed with the power of God, to cause some to become alive again, from a depressed, inactive, or unused state, those who are broken, and who sit in darkness. In you, they will find refuge, because your source is preeminent in Go d's Will. Someone, a prayer warrior, will come to pray for you. This person is someone you least expect to be so powerful in the realm of prayer; more than likely it will be a male who is very humble and unassuming. During the prayer, you will see yourself, spiritually, getting up from a sitting or prostrate position. Let your dream, and the vision during prayer, be your comfort for the endurance. (3) To the married with children, and if you have "bullied or harassed in any way or manner" the married couple without children, your dream implies that you will begin to lose vigor, health, and strength because of grief. Moreover, you are contemptuous in your dealings with others. See suggested course of action. (4) To the unmarried, the year of the Lord's favor is upon you. Immediately you will find favor before God, and He will withhold from you anything causing misery or death, and/or severe affliction. He will provide for you, bestow a crown of beauty instead of ashes, you shall rec eive the oil of gladness instead of mourning, and a garment of praise instead of a spirit of despair. You will be known as righteous.

Olive Tree: Encouragingly, you have tasted the Anointing of God, and you have risen (or will rise) to a level the Anointing of God and your acumen deem you should be. With that said, in your present business or personal dealings, you will be satisfied and take delight in your goals. If you are involved in any situation that is competitive, you will triumphant, God will lead the way. Additionally, you have the miraculous power to change history on some level or another. For example, by introducing radically new insight into complex models or paradigms, far beyond the norm, or family generational curses can stop with you (Exodus 20:5, 7; Psalm 112:2). Whatever the miraculous historical change is, perhaps you becoming a great leader and orator, you are equipped to handle large-scale undertakings. Dreamer, a large part of your mission in life centers on raising the spirits of your fellow mankind; thus changing history in the lives of those, you touch. The driving force behind all this is your support of others. Your first step is to start by recognizing and thanking Jesus for the small blessings that a re before you now and for the miraculous endowment of history changing vision and courageous leadership. Do you want your miracle? Then prepare yourself mentally for it.

Pomegranate Tree: Your dream exposes one, namely the dreamer, who has; conflicting attributes within, and is empty spiritually, yet, at the same time is full of good deeds. Dreamer, your good deeds, have little or no effect on your character and nature, and most importantly good deeds does not, effect a deep intimacy with Christ. Dreamer, demonic oppression has you acting "good" in public, and "foolish" in private. Thus, your dream addresses hypocrisy, in that the dreamer persists on "acting" better and godlier than you really are, while you refuse to reconcile yourself to your spiritual and moral responsibilities. Dreamer although you have the capacity to overreach yourself and to do and achieve things that are utterly incompatible with who and what you are at present, your true nature, your contradictory internal spiritual state, won't allow you to remain in those "truly good" places. You are the epitome of the cliché, "your gifts can take you where your character can't keep you". That is to say, although you may be prospering now, your dishonesty, hatefulness, bitterness, and an unforgiving and unloving attitude, will eventually bring ruin and desolation upon your head. A reconciling of yourself to your spiritual and moral duties is required of you at this time (Luke 17:10), for the Lord your God has brought you into a good land. If no change, the land the Lord your God has brought you too will be in jeopardy of lost or ruin. See suggested course of action.

Sapling, Seedling (a young plant or tree grown from a seed): Dreamer, it is important to expose your child, and each and every child in your care, in one manner or another, to the teachings of Christ, at an early age, during their formative years, up to age 17, for they are, chosen. This exposure includes, but is not limited to, His salvation, grace, principles, be it with inspirational pictures, songs, or stories, and discipline (Proverbs 13:24, 22:15); thus your dream. Moreover, you must be very careful when educating children. Handle with care, and encourage them, while leading and guiding them into the person and minister they will eventually become. God will let you know who they are in Him and their purpose. This is your job, to tend to the precious seeds that have been, placed in your care. A job well done will lead to spiritual blessings, financial prosperity, and a joyful heart.

Shade Trees: This dream has two meanings (choose one). (1) To see shade trees, your dream comes to guide. Dreamer, as trite and commonplace as this may sound, it is necessary to say, "life is very short, yet it is eternal"; therefore, recognizing the transitory and eternal nature of it all, be a genuinely heartfelt source of comfort for others and provide resources for those in need, as though you are doing it unto Adonai (Matthew 25:31-46). Although you may stand alone and be misunderstood, in doing this, meaning loving your neighbor, especially against all odds, providing physical and spiritual shelter to many, you are fulfilling your God ordained purpose, and you will prosper greatly in whatever your hands do. Dreamer, if you love your neighbor, as you love yourself, and love God, there is nothing in this world or the next to fear. Love is what we take with us, and love is what awaits us when we have finally arrived. (2) To be under shade trees: Dreamer you will receive help from the Lord, He will keep you (psalm 121:5).

Weeping Willow: God is good to those who trust in Him and seek Him out. One must never give up hope and should always wait for God's salvation for it will come. God's kindness and mercy never ends. With that said, dreamer, false prophets lulled you into a false sense of security; subsequently, you hold in contempt and despised other righteous prophets for rebuking you about your deeds. Dreamer, you did not contemplate the results of your decadence, because you believed the negative consequences of your behavior, could not happen to you. You have disregarded the Almighty, and forgotten your destiny; thus, you will begin to experience, if not already, a sudden decline in strength, and a failure that will result in a loss of position and reputation. The windows of Heaven are closed to your prayers, until you, from the depth of your pain, turn to the Almighty in prayer, crying, "Remember me and all of my suffering!" Suffering brings us to the realization that we have free will and we should cry over our mistakes and misdeeds, the cause of our sufferings. When you make a personal introspection of your deeds and fully return to God, admitting your indulgence in sensual relations, excessive and immoral activities, your disregard for others, and pride. Then God will hear your prayers. Suddenly, there will be comfort, and inspiration. See suggested course of action.

Parts of Trees:

Branches: This dream has eight meanings (choose one). (1) Branches with leaves only: Your dream is to warn the dreamer. Although, you have a reputation of being alive, you are spiritually lifeless. God knows your deeds and the foolishness of your heart. You do not realize the great danger you are in spiritually. Wake up! Strengthen that which rema ins and is about to die, for your deeds and words have been found incomplete in the sight of God. Read and hear Revelation 3:1-6. Examine yourself to see whether you are in the faith; test yourself. Do you not realize that Christ Jesus is in you, unl ess, of course, you fail the test? Remember, therefore, what you have received and heard, from before, in time past, repent, and obey it. If no genuine change, Jesus will suddenly come, and you will be caught off guard. At that time, your personal day of reckoning would have come. See suggested course of action. (2) Broken Branch: As your dream symbolizes shortness of life, specifically, the life of one very close to the dreamer (e.g. a spouse, significant other, child, sibling, parent, very close friend), it is sent as a notice. This type of dream is one of God's ways of breaking it to you gently, preparing you for one of life's common denominators, and if heeded, can prevent you from being emotionally blindsided by loss. They, one very close to the dreamer, will not recover from their illness, but will go on to be with Jesus in heaven. Dreamer, for someone who has met God, we experience Him in the little graces, the big miracles, the ordinary days, and the curious moments. He is with us, leading us onward, even sharing our tears. This same God trustworthy in life, even when we are not, can be trusted at the ending of life, especially the life of a loved one. If your love one, loves God and loves his or her neighbor as they love them self, there is nothing in this world or the next to fear. Love is what we take with us, and love is what awaits us when we have finally arrived. With that said, encourage your love one to seek medical attention as soon as possible, and call for the elders of your church, for it is through their prayers of faith and anointing of oil upon you that sin is forgiven and, albeit "spiritual" healing bestowed[36]. This is a true saying, thus it is time to have faith in God. Moreover, dreamer it is always a good time to get your house and papers in order (e.g. insurances, bequeaths, untold truths that need to be said), and always a good time to gather family together for prayer, support, wisdom, and truthfulness (Ecclesiastes 12:6). (3) Broken branch seen at a distant (far away from the dreamer): This indicates a serious illness, even unto death, in the distant future, within the life of the dreamer. Therefore, it is suggested that the dreamer call for the elders of your church, for it is through their prayers of faith and anointing of oil upon you that sin is forgiven and, healing bestowed[36]. After this, dreamer should expect a miraculous healing. If you are not part of a faith-based community, it is time to joined one, for you will need that community of elders in the future. See suggested course of action. (4) Cut down or burned branches, or someone yelling, "Timber": Your dream is a stern warning to check your own spiritual life and make sure your salvation is real. For, a part of your temper, conduct, philosophy, beliefs, and doctrines are contrary to Holy Writ, thus, contrary to the mind of Christ. Moreover, you are propagating such beliefs, as if from God, but they are actually your own opinions. See suggested course of action. (5) If someone else was cutting or burning branches: Dreamer, embracing or adopting the sensual, soothing, flattering philosophies, beliefs, and doctrines, of those who oppose divine truth, will prevent you from becoming a true follower of Christ. Their "opinions" come not from God, and do lead to sin. The impious person(s) will be known by the effects of their doctrines. For example, 80-90% of their group dies from the same thing. That's called an epidemic. The epidemic hints at the terrible fate of those who only appear to be a part of, or connected to, God's people. They don't really abide in Him, and possibly, they were never a part of those of The Way. Christ warns plainly against embracing and/or spreading heretical doctrines, teachings tha t oppose Holy Writ (see Romans 11:20-24). Those branches were cut off (or taken away) because of unbelief. See suggested course of action. (6) Tree with lots of branches: Your dream comes as a rebuke and a correction. The rebuke: Dreamer, adversity will come to anyone who trusts in "flesh". Threaten with divine punishment is the person who trusts in people and makes mortals their strength, and turn their heart away from God. The correction: Don't be wise in your own eyes, fear God, and depart from evil (Proverbs 3:7). Get rid of all moral filth and the evil that is so prevalent within your life, and humbly accept the word planted in you, which can save you. Do not merely listen to the word, and so deceive yourself. Self -deceit will be found the worst deceit at last. Do what the word says, that you may practice what you hear (James 1:20-22). Moreover, be quick to listen, slow to speak, and slow to become angry, for anger does not bring about the righteous life that God desires from us. Dreamer, there must be an inward practice of prayer, and an outward practice of true obedience. See suggested course of action. (7) Tree with few branches: Since your deeds exceed your wisdom, because you actually practice what you preach, God will favor you with the wisdom, knowledge, and wherewithal, you will need to lead a people, and no one will be able to stand up against you from this day forward. Only, be studious to "take-in" and learn what the Lord is revealing to you, and teaching you, plus be careful to obey what He has required of you, that you may be successful wherever you go. God is going to give you, figuratively, every place you set your foot and you will be prosperous and successful. Be strong and courageous. Do not be terrified; do not be discouraged, for the Lord your God will be with you wherever you go, for blessed is the person who trust in God and in God they place their trust (Joshua 1:3-9). (8) Tree with no branches: Many scriptures make it very clear that true saving faith will result in a transformed life, which is demonstrated by the service we do. Moreover, how we live reveals what we believe and whether the faith we profess to have is a living faith. Dreamer, you are spiritually weak, because you lack the faith and knowledge that leads to power, strength, and eternal life. You have chosen rituals and regimented rules, supposing you are, worshipping and serving God. Your ways and means do not promote confidence and security in salvation, only condemnation. You have made your own way hard, believing God to be a hard taskmaster. This attitude reveals an unchanged life or a spiritually dead heart. There is a need to renounce religious beliefs that are, based on faithless ritualistic practices, customs, and traditions. Make it your habit to speak and act like those who shall be judged by the law of liberty, see James 2:12, 13. Honesty with yourself and God, realistically admitting your limitations, trusting in Christ's redemptive work, and accepting that His grace (the free and unmerited favor and beneficence of God), alone, is sufficient; can change things around for the best. Choose to live for Him, and not die. Choose the path of truth and liberty. If no abandonment of present religious practices occurs, your choices will lead you to be counted amongst those illustrated in Matthew 7:21-23. See suggested course of action.

Rod, Scepter, Staff, Wand, or Baton (a long thin implement usually made of wood or metal): This dream has three meanings (choose one). What was the baton, rod, scepter, staff, or wand used as? (1) If used to symbolize imperial auth ority (e.g. a king's scepter extended to you). Your dream denotes that the dreamer needs to know, without a doubt, that you, just as you are, may come to the Throne of God boldly. Dreamer, Christ is our High Priest, so then, since we have a great High Priest who has entered heaven, Jesus the Son of God, let us hold firmly to what we believe. This High Priest of ours understands our weaknesses, for he faced all of the same testings' we do, yet he did not sin. So, let us come boldly to the throne of our gracious God. There we will receive his mercy, and we will find grace to help us when we need it most (Hebrews 4:14-16 NLT). Here, before the Throne of God, nothing is to be feared, provided the heart is right with God, truly sincere, and trusting alone in the sacrificial blood. For, as Jesus Christ tasted death for every man, so every man may go to that propitiatory, and take the mercy that is suited to his or her degree of guilt. Mercy refers to the pardon of sin, and being brought into the favor of God. Grace is that by which the soul is supported after it has received this mercy, and by which it is purified from all unrighteousness, and upheld in all trials and difficulties, and enabled to prove faithful unto death (Adam Clarke's Commentary). (2) If used for corrective purposes (e.g. a rod of discipline, a police baton). See Proverbs 3:11, 12, Hebrews 12:5-29. Dreamer, despise not the correction of Jehovah, neither be weary of His discipline, for whom He loves, He admonishes. You are also to respect any other godly and/or wise authority figure in your life, in like manner, when admonished. If necessary, see suggested course of action. (3) If used for magic or divination purposes (e.g. a wand used by a magician, or to conjure, or water diviner); this denotes one, namely the dreamer, who claims to have discovered hidden knowledge with the aid of supernatural powers. You have gained a dark and erroneous knowledge, the devil's so-called deep secrets (Revelation 2:20, 24). Your knowledge gained has primarily been demonically communicated. Hence, your form of worship, your devotion and service, is to the prince of darkness and his demons. This is what you have conjured. The knowledge gained will lead you to that dark ominous place on the other side, emotionally, spiritually, and if not aborted, eternally. See suggested course of action.

Stump: Your dream warns of heavy judgment and unusual loss or reduction. Your imperious attitude is leading to a mental and spiritual breakdown, opening the door for demons to run havoc within your life and to bring you down to desolation. Weakened by frequent panic attacks, you will begin to crack in your personality. Your dream is warning you to act, to commit to some type of positive and righteous change so calamity will not befall you. First repenting to Jesus can diminish a tragic outcome. A genuine, "I'm sorry", and a changing of one's ways towards righteousness and a refraining from nefarious actions in the future will often suffice, "go, and sin no more". If your change is sincere, fruits of said change will begin to manifest, via actions and good deeds. If you do not respond, the tragedy will come. See suggested course of action.

Wood or Bark (incl. gopher wood): Your dream was sent to encourage. Dreamer, because of your humble and submissive faith in God's word, and not your works alone, you are declared as one who is a righteous minister. Planted in the House of the Lord, you will continue to prosper and mature. The same God, who planted you in your ministry, is the same God who will cause you to mature and prosper. Independent of outward circumstances, you will live and thrive where most things perish, via divine grace. With that said, dreamer, while your spiritual growth may not be so rapid, if you endure, you will become a beautiful picture of a godly man or woman, who in your uprightness, aims to glorify God. Your dream also represents some type of spiritual privileges and a purification process, dreamer God will separate you from people, p laces, and circumstances that will hinder your growth. View this separation as a blessing from God and not as an evil thing has happen. Under all adversities retain a spirit of joy, and continue to make progress in your spiritual life. Accordingly, glad ness, thanksgiving, singing, strength, intense energy, and fertility will be your recompense, and your praise will be a sweet aroma in the nostrils of the Lord. If applicable, this promise is to your generations to come. Come what may, you shall make ste ady progress and flourish in a very impressive manner; bringing forth fruit, even in your old age. Dreamer, as you age, your anointing to minister, and divine revelations, will always be fresh and edifying. See Psalm 92:12-15. With that said, the following is necessary. In addition to the previous interpretation, an event or situation that will cause intense fear is coming to discourage and terrify you. This will be in the form of an annoying, difficult, and unpleasant person. The trouble this per son will cause will become so overwhelming, because they will expose a secret regarding you. This spiritual battle will be great, and will demand your full attention. Although you will walk through this alone, know that God will walk you through it. Dreamer, learn wisdom from the situation, for truth do set one free; and go on from there unashamed. Then, suddenly, unexpectedly, and without any warning, all the evil and wickedness that caused you to fear and be troubled, will disappear. It will be as though it was never there. At that point, you will express great joy, and feel extremely happy. Take courage and be strong, knowing that the Lord knows where you are, what's going on, and He cares.

Activities connected to Trees: Climb a tree, up in a tree, chased or forced up a tree:

Climbing a tree or up in a tree: This dream has two meanings (choose one). (1) Dreamer you are deeply, vested in an intimate relationship. You spend money, time, and energy on the relationship. For you, your dream is encouragement or a warning. Questions to journal: What type of tree was depicted within your dream and what condition was the tree? For example, was it a very big tree with lots of branches? Depending on the type of tree, and the condition of the tree, this will denote the type of person (their beliefs, character, or health) you are investing your time in. This suggests if it would be wise for dreamer to continue or withdraw from the relationship. It will always be your choice. See relevant subcategories. If necessary, see suggested course of action. (2) Your dream announces that the dreamer will be clothed formally in ecclesiastical garments, ordained as a clergy. Therefore, from this moment forward, if not already, become seriously vested in your set place of worship, submissive to the head leadership (e.g. pastor, bishop, elder). In addition, read, Ecclesiastes 10:4, and remember the verse.

Chased or Forced up a tree: Your dream was sent to warn the dreamer. Dreamer you will begin to experience a very difficult situation and you will be at a great disadvantage, regarding the best way to achieve something. All of this is a result of dreamer having behaved irrationally. Actions and choices not consistent with good reasoning, and that are not based on the wisdom of the Word of God are irrational, and are carried in out fear. This is not of the Lord. Fear is a spirit and it is, sent from the devil. From now on, choose wisely, especially regarding your present dealings with others. See suggested course of action.

Cross, Crucifix (to see a cross or symbol of a cross, crucifix, or any symbol connected to the crucifixion of Jesus Christ): Dreamer needs to understand the cost of your salvation, and to learn to not be carried away by all kinds of strange teachings, or easily removed from the Gospel of Jesus Christ. We are not serving an angry God who cannot be embraced or pleased, nor a God that needs to be appeased via a set of regimented and legalistic rules to prove our dedication to Him, and to prove our holiness and righteousness, all of which are of no value to those who practice such. It is good for our hearts to be strengthened by God's love, via His grace. For, God's primary identity is love (John 3:16, 1 John 4:7, 16). By His word, God first loved us while we remained in sin, not thinking about Himself, nor desiring to appease Himself, yet He became our propitiation. Therefore, our service should not come from a mind-set of appeasing God, but from a space of gratefulness and love, declaring His worthiness of our praise. We were made alive with Christ even when we were dead in transgressions, it is by grace you have been saved through faith, and this not from yourself, it is the gift of God (Romans 4:16; Ephesians 2:1 -10; Hebrews 13:9). With that said, dreamer, God will now separate you from your surroundings that hinder spiritual clarity, and draw you away from any trust in yourself that you might seek your life in Him alone, and confidently entrust yourself to His care. The Holy Spirit will lead and guide you to discipline your will, strength, efforts, and relations, so that the whole energy of your being will be free, and open to receive the Holy Spirit inwardly. This promise comes by grace; and if applicable, is guaranteed to your offspring. Also, the refining and purifying work of the Paraclete, and a greater service to others, will cause the emergence of a divine led wisdom. Moreover, you must not allow yourself to be annoyed with acts of devotion, for example, family bible study and other quality times, fellowshipping with other believers, church attendance, acknowledging God's goodness to you, to others, and the like. See suggested course of action.

Smelling a Branch, or putting a branch (or leaf) to, or on, your Nose: Your dream is a stern rebuke. It alludes to a deliberate offensive act, an act of great disrespect, the giving of a very great affront and provocation to God. Dreamer, you have insulted God and one of His servants. Even more, you perpetuate violence and continually provoke God to anger. You are an abusive person. Are you not afraid to speak against God, and His servants? How dare you abuse any servant of God, especially one who is a friend, a confidant, and excellent steward of the House of God? Dreamer, is nothing sacred? Do you think the detestable things you are doing are small, are of little consequence, and are of little importance to God, His ways, His Kingdom, His people (the Body of Christ)? Did you not expect that God would resent it, and take it as an affront to Himself personally? You take great risk, when you have no fear of saying or doing anything against God, and against the servants of the Lord; you put yourself in harm's way, for Jesus will plead their case, and consider those who touch them as touching Him likewise. It is a dangerous thing to offend Christ and His servants. You show yourself presumptuous, when you do not fear t o speak evil of the Lord or His servants. Your character is one of extreme haughtiness, presumptuousness, pride, and self- assuredness in the very negative sense of the word. All are signs that your heart is hardened. If this disposition is not let go, it will lead to a great fall (Proverbs 11:2; 16:18, 19; 29:23). Turn from your wicked ways. Ask Jesus for wisdom, and for the courage to apply it. Notwithstanding, the harshness of the Lord is, kindled against you. Therefore, now, He will deal with you harshly. You will begin to experience a change in your anointing, authority, and favor given from the Lord. Moreover, as He knows your thoughts afar off, don't "play", but repent. Take words to Jesus, "'I have sinned, and I have done wrong and acte d wickedly". Other than prayer and heartfelt repentance to Jesus and to individuals affected by your actions, in the form of an apology (if possible), no other excuse or weak justification will be heard. Repentance is seeking pardon and expressing sincere feelings of regret and brokenness for having done something awry and/or for having hurt someone, see 2 Corinthians 7:10, 11. To individuals, a phone call or a letter of apology is a good place to start. To Jesus pray, Psalm 51, this followed by appr opriate application of wisdom, can conceivably avert some of the repercussions of your choices. See suggested course of action.

Vines And Vineyard (e.g. vineyard of grape or other vines):

This dream has two meanings (choose one). (1) Vines: This choice has four parts (choose one). (a) Vines had fruit or indication of fruit: Your dream denotes a literal or spiritual pregnancy, the dreamer, or if male, your spouse, is either actually pregnant, will become pregnant very shortly, or you two are becoming grandparents. If not pregnant, and you desire children, continue to have faith and hope in God, He will have mercy on you, and grant you the desire of your heart, to have bear children, suddenly and very soon. Note, if pregnancy is a possibility, or desire, the fruit of your womb will be known by the fruit represented in your dream, be it good or bad. (b) If pregnancy is not an issue or desire, perhaps due to age, then your dream represents a spiritual pregnancy. A spiritual pregnancy denotes a ministry will be birth from within you, the dreamer. You are full of nurturing abilities; thus, you will become, responsible for a few young men and women being born again into the Kingdom of God (see John 3:1-17). You know how to nurture and accept anyone; therefore, many will be drawn to you, including those, others call "ne'er-do-wells", via your ministry. Under your tutelage, those newly born into the Body of Christ will become strong and active, for the cause of the Kingdom of God. They will be known as persons who speak and does that which is good, counted amongst those who are faithful and submissive to God. Dreamer, be willing, obedient, prepared, and in place (accountable to a specific house of worship, church), for the birthing of your ministry and for those who will become born again because of your ministry. (c) Vines had no fruit or fruit was dried up and fallen to the ground. If dreamer (or spouse) is actually pregnant, there is the possibility of a miscarriage. It is suggested that you seek medical attention, or husband should encourage wife to seek medical attention, as soon as possible. (d) Vines had no fruit or fruit was dried up and fallen to the ground and pregnancy is not an issue, your dream denotes approaching judgment from God upon the dreamer is near, because of disobedience. See suggested course of action. (2) Vineyard: This choice has two parts (choose one). (a) Vineyard was cultivated, plowed, fertilized, developed, and/or well cared for: Dreamer, the Lord, and Savior, Jesus Christ, has not cast you away. You are His servant, chosen, and not rejected. You are His according to the election of grace, and a distinguished friend and minister. Here is an account of the mercy God has in store for you. All who fight and rage against you will surely be dishonored and embarrassed; their plots will not prosper, and this is happening now. So d o not fear, for He is with you; do not be disappointed for He is your God. Your Heavenly Father is making a way for you, creating paths of peace, causing you to go forth in serenity. (b) Vineyard was, all grown over with thorns, was not cultivated, plowed, or developed, basically, not well cared for: Your dream denotes one who has the potential to be a leader, but is unwilling to embrace your purpose. Dreamer, you are lazy, you dislike work or any kind of physical exertion, you are prideful, and live unwise and foolishly, because you have been taught desolation. Without purpose, and remaining detached from the Body of Christ, you will physically die before your time, or poverty and lack will suddenly overtake you. Dreamer; pray for truth and wisdom inwardly and for the courage to apply them within your life. Ask, and it shall be given you. One may suffer needlessly, becau se he or she will not ask Jesus for wisdom. Ask Jesus as often as you need to, regarding all of your emotional concerns, considering how personal His promises are, He will meet you in your need. See suggested course of action.

Suggested Course of Action

Question to consider and journal, did your dream depict any symbols that alludes to, the dreamer will make the necessary changes, spiritually, emotionally, and/or physically to affect a more positive outcome? If changes are initiated, your dreams will change. Nevertheless, in keeping with the fact that believers are likened unto plants and trees and their behaviors and consideration for others, to flowers and fruits, most dreams of agriculture activity (e.g. farming, flowers, gardening, and/or trees) generally imply a need to seriously, reflect on your behavior. If you are here, your behavior is not correct or appropriate. This inappropriateness also includes your spiritual health.

In view of your dream's context, what does the primary symbol reveal about you, your ethics, or mental state? You will need to earnestly look within and consider that your answers are a reflection of where you are emotionally, physically, and spiritually, presently, and possibly who you are becoming. What was your reaction to the activity? Were you angry, concerned, confused, defensive, fearful, happy, helpful, pleased, shocked, or unconcerned? Your reaction to the activity, or the circumstance, reveals your attitude regarding this information about yourself.

Dreamer, consider seriously your observations. If what was revealed prevail, will it sabotage any good that's happening at present within your life? Will it build or destroy, strengthen or weaken, enlighten or blind? If you lack wisdom, ask Jesus for wisdom. He gives wisdom to all, generously, no matter who you are and what you've done; wisdom is available (see James 1:5-8, Proverbs 2:1-6, 10). Hence, if, by just asking, you may get wisdom, one may suffer needlessly, because you will not ask Jesus for wisdom.

Now, pray (See Prayer of Deliverance, pg. 897)

Specific Meaning

If you have a very real connection with any agriculture activity, these sorts of dreams are usually about your routine, mundane activities or anxieties that overwhelm your mind during the day. They are an inner release mechanism, which helps provide you with emotional balance and the maintaining of your sanity. These dreams are not significant, and do not warrant special attention.

Note: The dreamer may consider his or her dream as a clue given to assist in finding facts, needed to support a prevailing theory or thought. Example, grafting may produce a new plant or hybrid that may prove beneficial to mankind. Dreamer, consider it not strange for someone, such as an agriculturalist, to receive inspirations regarding husbandry via their dreams. The details, kept within context of your dream, should be relevant to your life, and closely resemble your real-life situations. Meaning it can actually occur during your awaked state. This will help you narrow down the specifics needed to support your theories, findings, data. It is suggested that you seize the opportunity your dream is presenting to fulfill the purpose for which it was sent. However, if your dream was inundated with symbols not easily linked to your life activities, then you should heed the spiritual implications (the interpretation).

ANGELS AND DEMONS

*He saw a stairway resting on the earth, with its top reaching to heaven, and the angels
of God were ascending and descending on it. (Jacob's dream, Genesis 28:12 NIV)*

*"I looked, and there before me was a messenger, a holy one, coming down
from heaven". (Nebuchadnezzar's dream, Daniel 4:13 NIV)*

*Don't let anyone condemn you by insisting the worship of angels
(Colossians 2:18 NLT)*

*And I fell at his feet to worship him. But he said to me, "See that you do not do that! I
am your fellow servant, a nd of your brethren who have the testimony of Jesus. Worship
God! For the testimony of Jesus is the spirit of prophecy" (Revelation 19:10 NKJV)*

This category deals with a few of the common names of angels. Some short descriptions of types, phrases, and other processes and particulars, connected in some way to this category. For example, Archangel, Cherubim, cherubs, couriers or messengers, burning ones, demons, dominions, envoy, fallen, guardian, holy living ones, messengers, Nephilim, the principalities, protector, rulers, Seraphim, Seraph, sons of God, the thrones, the virtues, watchers, wheels, and winged creatures of heaven.

All Symbols and Referents, Notes (1, 2, 3, etc.), Suggested Course of Action, and Specific Meaning offer guidance toward a more comprehensive interpretation

Notes

1. Unless otherwise noted elsewhere, if, in your everyday living, your awaked state, as part of your lifestyle, work, or ministerial activities, or a special event, you have a very real connection with any angelic activity. For example, an artisan or author whose primary interests are in angels, or some theological study of angels, your dream is not significant and does not warrant special attention.

2. Probables: As angels are frequently demonstrated in many, and very personal ways; for example, does a particular angel remind you of a particular moment in time? Thus, could the angel depicted be a possible probable (see Chapter One, section entitled, Probables)? Hence, dreamer may also consider your own personal and special associations with various actions or activities connected to angels, as long as dreamer considers that demons are also angels, and as long as the interpretation is kept within the principles of spiritual boundary markers, landmarks, and property lines, (see Chapter One, section entitled, Spiritualizing Boundary Markers, Landmarks, and Property Lines).

3. Determine who your dream is for you or another. Did the angel actually say your dream was for another? If not, dreamer should presume your dream is for you.

    If your dream is for, or about another:

    Dreams that reference others and the revelation within those dreams, is not given haphazardly to any individual, but only to those with the ability, and influence to do something with the information; this is also prophecy. With that, did the angel give you a message for another or for a group of people? If person(s) is unknown, the person(s) will be introduced to dreamer shortly. Allow the strength of the message, to guide, help, and support you. Do not allow no particular person's influence within your life to thrive. Do not be afraid because of them ; idolize no one. Read, understand, and embrace, Jeremiah 1:7, 8, and Ezekiel 2:6, 7. The lesson is, no matter how personable, powerful, or difficult a person, or how uncertain or unpopular the choices and issues, always take the next biblical and ethical step, for obedience to God's Word and to His principles will always prove safer and stronger foundationally.

If angel says, dream message is for another, and person(s) is actually known by the dreamer, in your awaked life, the person(s) represents him or herself.

4. In addition to the following interpretations, see index or relevant categories for more information. For example, if a musical instrument was involved in some way, see category, Music; if colors was highlighted, see category, Colors. If a statuette was involved, see category, Cutting. Kept within context of your dream and the interpretation, the additional symbols are perhaps relevant. It will be within the sum of all the symbols that you will find a more thorough interpretation.

5. Since the following list is not extensive, dreamer is encouraged to seek biblical guidelines and other relevant research to determine the metaphorical meaning of your particular angel and/or angel activity, depicted within your dream, via a Bible concordance, Bible illustrated dictionary, encyclopedia, or internet. Having done your research you should be able to determine some basic behaviors or attributes your Lord and Savior wants you to focus on.

Symbols and Referents

Angels come to serve, via some manner of guidance and/or protection. Are not all angels ministering spirits sent to serve those who will inherit salvation? (Hebrews 1:14) Thus, angels depicted within our dreams denotes an attending to (or an answer to) an urgent need or desire of the dreamer. Moreover, every angel is "coded" with divine instructions to perform certain tasks; hence, the names of the angels are in accordance with their mission. The behavior of the angels is prophetic, usually beneficent, and sometimes punitive, depending on the nature of their mission.

Warning: No angel, who is upright (not fallen) never ever accepts worship from mankind, even if they are mistaken to be worthy of such worship. See, Colossians 2:18, Revelation 19:10.

Warning: As, you have been truly visited, albeit within your dream, by a genuine angel, beware of the angel, be on your guard before him, pay attention, take heed, and listen to what the angel says. Do not rebel against or provoke him; the angel will not forgive your rebellion, since My Name is in him (Exodus 23:20-23), or encoded within him.

My Name is in him (Exodus 23:21). God's name stands in for His purpose and His characteristics. His Name is linked to the specific circumstances of how He reveals His Power and glory to humankind. Thus, every angel is "coded" with divine instructions to perform certain tasks. For instance, if you need healing, His Name, "coded" within His servant (the angel) is Jehovah-Rapha; the Lord God heals (Psalm 147:3). Therefore, perhaps the archangel Raphael, whose name means, God heals, will appear within your dream. Other names of God, Jehovah-Maccaddeshem, the Lord your sanctifier (Exodus 31:13), Jehovah-Jireh, the Lord will provide (Genesis 22:13-14), or Jehovah-Shalom, the Lord is peace (Judges 6:24). Each angel has a unique form of divine service; therefore, angels will appear, within a dream, with God's purpose, according to the name of God within him. The names of the angels will sometimes change in accordance with their mission, and their mission will never contradict the Word of God, unless the angel is one of the "fallen". Other than that, the requisite attached to the promise of guidance and protection is that you be obedient to the messenger, and the message.

In addition to the varied meanings of angel activity, other common words, expressions, usages (e.g. slang or clichés), or a 'probable' that are metaphorically represented by the following are also considered (this section is an addendum at the end of the category).

Category Content: if not listed, see index, perchance, for your specific type of angel dream.

Most of the angels listed are actually archangels, employing countless "underling" angels that assist them in fulfilling their duties.

- Angels (ascending and descending)
- Angels flying (to see angels flying overhead in the air)
- Ariel

- Azrael (aka the Death Angel, Grim Reaper, or The Destroyer)
- Barachiel
- Gabriel (incl. Cherub/Cherubim)
- Haniel
- Jeremiel
- Khamael (leader of the Powers, one of the Dominions)
- Lucifer or Demons (aka Beelzebub; Satan; the devil; prince of darkness; prince of the air; Azazel, leader of demons; fallen, Nephilim, imps, tempter of mankind, or any names demons are traditionally known by)
- Michael (Seraph/Seraphim)
- Metatron (Seraph/Seraphim)
- Raphael (leader of the Virtues)
- Raziel
- Samael
- Sandalphon
- Selaphiel
- Tzadkiel
- Tzaphkiel (leader of the Thrones)
- Uriel
- Angels watching over you or guarding you

Angels (ascending and descending): Your prayers and concerns have reached God and appointed messengers have been dispatch on your behalf. God will bless you, including favoring you with the land you desire. To be blessed: Gifts of God's grace, anything God freely gives you, absolution, the Holy Spirit, salvation, regeneration, eternal life, health, children, love of family, longevity, necessities, prosperity, and dominion over all that is yours; and all are parts of the supply of grace, an d all are sanctified by the Lord, and technically belongs to Him. The result of this supply in your life will be peace.

Angels flying (to see angels flying overhead in the air): It's imperative that you subdue feeding your fleshly desires. See Galatians 5:13-21. Dreamer, you must govern your desires, lusts, and passions with wisdom. You have a journey to go on, a walk-to-walk, spiritual warfare to fight, and a great work to do. God wants to purify you that you may fulfill the righteous purpose, for which, you are designed. For even the fig tree, when found not fulfilling the purpose for its existence was, cursed, thus, dried up from the root (Matthew 21:18, 19, Mark 11:12-14). You have settled for a voluptuary type philosophy and desire to propagate your beliefs. You say, "I have great desire, thus my physical enjoyment, luxury, and sensual gratifications are my primary concerns". This is a characterization of the ungodly or spiritually immature. Weigh: The child thinks that all that appears pleasant and tasty belongs to him or her and that they have the right to partake of everything. Consideration of others, and/or of the resulting outcome is unfamiliar to him or her. They will never consider the results of their behavior, nor how their behavior will affect others. This type of consideration is not within a child's mind-set, because he or she is a child. As the immature child takes what they want, when they want it, and believes that it's theirs, and that they do have a right t o whatever it is, so does the spiritually immature, do what they want, when they want, and believe that it's OK, using grace as a cover for sin. Unfortunately, spiritual change cannot begin with this kind of expectation and mind-set. Rather say, "I have great desire but what can I do, since my Father in Heaven forbids me from involving myself in such acts?" Whenever you partake of anything you are required to pause and ask yourself if that particular activity is permitted or not; and even if it is permitted, you must inquire whether you should participate or involve yourself in it at that moment. This will help train you to pause briefly between the moment that your desire demands to be satisfied and the moment that you actually satisfy it or not. For you already know that desire causes you to act compulsively even when you know you will regret your actions later. Thus, that pause is the decisive moment. It will transform your tendency, your desire, into an act of will. The will is what lead s to action after your desire passes through the filter of your thought. By prudently embracing the principles and precepts of Jesus Christ, the One who has made you holy, via His blood sacrifice, all may be accomplished. Additionally, very shortly, you will have to give an account of the fulfilling of your purpose for which you was design, as well as, of your philosophy and words. Consider your dream as sufficient warning. See suggested course of action.

Ariel: This archangel denotes protection and deliverance from woes. This angel will appear within your dream, when the dreamer is suffering from intense affliction, serious mental and/or physical pain, because of negative path's you've taken in life. Thus, the dreamer is greatly troubled by pain or loss, very unhappy, full of misery. As well, you've had to put up with somebody, or something, very unpleasant. Nonetheless, all of your "woes" are a result of sin within your life. Dreamer, what God has given you to serve His people, you have perverted and abused, making it the source of your lusts; swelling y ou up with extreme pride. The goodness which God has blessed you with all these years, was meant to glorify His Kingdom, instead you have used His blessings to glorify yourself. Your pride has lured you into a false sense of security. Erroneously assumi ng that nothing but good comes to you. Confessing that no one you know can compare with you, or even pretend to be your equal. You have put confidence in your flesh, fearing no danger, living carelessly. You harbor wicked thoughts, are ruthlessly aggressive, and greedily eager to steal from, and destroy others, for gain. God humbles the haughty and causes all his or her joy and laughter to cease. Graciously, spiritual renewal is accessible to you now. Jesus is petitioning you, via your dream, to cleanse evil from your heart, allow the process. Dreamer, many, who have faltered and were weak, are healed, restored, and strengthened by the grace of God. If you are ready to acknowledge that you have faltered, and remain mindful of your weaknesses, especially pride, God will suddenly, and in an extraordinary way, increase your strength and protect you from further hurt or harm. The more God allows you to see your arrogance, and the horribleness of it all, be more earnest to repent that you may find Him to be grace and healing, refreshment, and a refuge. He is willing to help you, surrender to His process of help, with a humble dependence upon Him. You will find that God will not fail you, and you will have grace sufficient for renewal of spiritual strength. An angel (perhaps disguised as a human) or one, a human, who is a true servant of God, with the Spirit of Truth within, will lead the way. See suggested course of action.

Azrael (aka the Death Angel, Grim Reaper, or The Destroyer): Your dream is a notice. This archangel symbolizes shortness of life. Your dream is one of God's ways of breaking it to you gently, preparing you for one of life's common denominators, and if heeded, can prevent you from being emotionally blindsided by loss. For someone who has met Jesus, we experience Him in the little graces, the big miracles, the ordinary days, and the curious moments. He is with us, leading us onward, even sharing our tears. This same Jesus trustworthy in life, even when we are not, can be trusted at the ending of life, for He is the resurrection (John 11:25, 26). If we love Jesus and love our neighbor as we love ourselves, there is nothing i n this world or the next to fear. Love is what we take with us, and love is what awaits us when we have finally arrived. Nonetheless, dreamer seek medical attention as soon as possible, and call for the elders of your church, for it is through their prayers o f faith and anointing of oil upon you that sin is forgiven and "spiritual" healing bestowed, and perhaps physical healing.[36] This is a true saying, thus it is time to have faith in God. Additionally, it is always a good time to get your house and papers in or der (e.g. insurances, bequeaths, untold truths that need to be said), and always a good time to gath er family together for prayer, support, wisdom, and truthfulness (Ecclesiastes 12:6). An angel (perhaps disguised as human, or one, who is a true servant o f God, with the Spirit of Truth within) will lead the way to your deliverance. See suggested course of action.

Barachiel: This archangel denotes protection, and the blessings of children to the childless. This angel comes with the message that if children are a desire, you will be granted the strength, support, and physician to help you bear children of your own body. Moreover, this angel comes with the message that God's blessings will be manifested in your (the dreamer's) earthly lifetime. These blessings are gifts of God's grace, anything God freely gives you, absolution, the Holy Spirit, salvation, regeneration, eternal life, health, children, love of family, longevity, necessities, prosperity, and dominion over all that is yours; and all are parts of the supply of grace, and all are sanctified by the Lord, and technically belongs to Him. The result of this supply in your life will be peace. An angel (perhaps disguised as human, or one, who is a true servant of God, with the Spir it of Truth within) will lead the way.

Gabriel (incl. Cherub/Cherubim): This archangel brings a significant message to the dreamer, regarding guidance for the future. There is an old saying, "When the student is ready, the teacher will appear". Dreamer, you are the student, another is your teacher, and you are ready. Although, you may be very accomplished, prosperou s, and/or wise, you have need of a teacher at present. God is sending someone into your life to help you carry out your next undertaking, by enlarging your spiritual capacity. This person is modest and unassuming in attitude, behavior, and dress. Notwithstanding, great respect towards them is appropriate and required, as well as some form of compensation. You will need to be honest, open, and transparent, to get what you need from him or her. Your undivided attention is required, thus you may need to t ake a vacation from your normal business and/or ministerial activities. Your dream is to bring about an awareness of this person's coming, and to prepare you to meet them sagaciously. Additionally, they will not feed your vanity; therefore, do not be, conceited in your attitude. An angel (perhaps disguised as human, or one, who is a true servant of God, with the Spirit of Truth within) will lead the way.

Haniel: This archangel denotes needed direction, and the grace of God. God's wisdom, care, and guidance, coupled with His divine intervention, has kept you, and will, again, cause your mouth to be filled with laughter, and your tongue with sin ging. When God reverse your tragedy, you will testify that the Lord has done great things for you, and you will be glad. Your situation will change and He will give you a new song in your heart. You will sing a new song. An angel (perhaps disguised as human, or one, who is a true servant of God, with the Spirit of Truth within) will lead the way to your deliverance.

Jeremiel: This archangel's mission is two-fold. He denotes God's mercy is present, and he serves as an angel of death. His message is one of hope and guidance to the dreamer. He has come to tell you your prayers have been heard by the Most High. God will give you new insight, a truthful vision, and it shall "come to pass". Dreamer, although you are discouraged or troubled, do not allow the spirit of fear to intimidate you, only be strong and courageous. Read and understand Romans 8:15, 2 Timothy 1:7. You've gotten to the point where you're spiritually weak and feel discouraged, feeling that your faith has been in vain. Dreamer, by God's power, a way out of no way will be made for you, and your state of affairs turned around. Somehow, God will make a way for you. He has promised never to leave you alone. You will experience a miracle. Additionally, you are encouraged to re-evaluate your life and figure out, what God would like you to change in order to better fulfill His purpose within your life. Learn from your mistakes, find new direction in solving problems, pursue healing, and seek out encouragement. Joy shall then be revealed, rest shall appear, and then healing shall descend, disease shall withdraw, anxiety, anguish, and crying shall pass from you; gladness will happen. Only, abstain from a judgmental attitude, abusive talking, contentions, revenge, envy, and hatred. Moreover, as this angel also serves as an angel of death, take heed and abstain from all that you are asked to abstain from, lest you die an early death (Ecclesiastes 7:17). As well, read and understand Galatians 5:19-21, for this speaks of spiritual death. An angel (perhaps disguised as human, or one, who is a true servant of God, with the Spirit of Truth within) will lead the way. See suggested course of action.

Khamael (leader of the Powers, one of the Dominions): This archangel has come for one of three reasons. (1) This angel comes in peace, and in response to the dreamer's seeking understanding of something and the truth of the matter. Dreamer, at present, your understanding of something, and the truth of that something, needs to be more reasoned out. You are not asking the important, nor the right, questions. Deliberate, discuss, and debate with colleagues, experts, and other Christians, for there is wisdom in the counsel of many. See Proverbs 11:14, 15:22, 23. Listen attentively, become moderate in your business affairs, and allow humility, joy, and purity to be that, which intercedes on your behalf. It is known that you love God, and Jesus loves you, so continue with your learning. An angel (perhaps disguised as human, or one, who is a true servant of God, with the Spirit of Truth within) will lead the way. (2) This angel is here to purify the words of a prophet or prophetess. Dreamer, you have prophetic capacity, and you possess the necessary endowments to carry out the task of a prophet or prophetess. Although, many words have been spoken, regarding your ability, scholarly and intellectually, you have not become conceited in your learning, thus, celestial fire from the Altar on High will come to purify the prophet's lips, to purify your words that you may continue towards your purpose. An angel (perhaps disguised as human, or one, who is a true servant of God, with the Spirit of Truth within) will lead the way. (3) This angel has come to mete out punishment because of continued evildoing (Daniel 4:5-18). If you've found yourself practicing evildoing, consider your dream a warning. You are warned to restrain from wickedness, lest judgment (divine reprimand for folly and sin) will be meted out. Your dream is warning the dreamer to act, to commit to some type of positive and righteous change so calamity will not befall you. First repenting to Jesus can diminish a tragic outcome. A genuine, "I'm sorry", and a changing of one's ways towards righteousness and a refraining from nefarious actions in the future will often suffice. As a result, fruits of said change will begin to manifest, via actions and good deeds. If you do not respond appropriately, the tragedy will come. An angel (perhaps disguised as human, or one, who is a true servant of God, with the Spirit of Truth within) will lead the way. See suggested course of action.

Lucifer or Demons (aka Beelzebub; Satan; the devil; prince of darkness; prince of the air; Azazel, leader of demons; fallen, Nephilim, imps, tempter of mankind, or any names demons are traditionally known by): Lucifer, demons, the fallen, are all adversarial to the Word of God. With that said, this evil has come for one of three reasons. (1) This fallen one has come to oppose spiritual intimacy with Christ, via fear and phobias. Dreamer you are allowing, the spirit of fear to terrorize you, it has become your own personal terrorist. Read and understand Romans 8:15, 2 Timothy 1:7. No, you do not have mental health issues, you are not crazy, nor are you having a nervous breakdown. This wicked one has come to terrorize you in your thoughts, e.g. when you are paranoid, sleeping with a knife or gun under your pillow. When you are afraid, insecure, impatient, confused, filled with worry, uneasy and unsure, when you hesitate, is full of apprehension, when your thoughts forecast only doom and gloom, when panic and stress comes, and despair and depression find you, when you are restless, frightful, full of dread, anxious, nervous. When your fears are extreme and irrational, especially regarding simple things or social situations and/or when you feel hopeless. You will find this diabolical entity in every phobia. Question to journal: What would it feel like if all of your fears were suddenly released from you at one time? Pause and feel that. Bible story, there was that herd of pigs that Legion was cast into, and these pigs found their thoughts to be so unbearable that they all ran off a cliff to commit suicide, because they could not bear what had been unleashed upon them (Matthew 8:28 -34, Mark 5:1-20, Luke 8:26-39). On the other hand, the man whom, the devils were suddenly released from, was found sitting, clothed, healed, and in his right mind. Therefore, dreamer, earnestly oppose the subtle voice of the devil. Dreamer, think on things that are true, whatever is noble, whatever is right, whatever is pure, whatever is lovely, whatever is admirable, if anything is excellent or praiseworthy, think about those things, see Philippians 4:8. For, if you truly can believe God's word, it will change all the rules that darkness will attempt to establish in your heart and mind. Now I say to you that before you can move forward, fear must be cast out, and renounced. If you will daily come away and pray, then God will heal you of all things, only come with much prayer and spiritual fasting. Spiritual fasting is a time of waiting when you are praying and asking the Lord to come and perform that which only He can perform. Similar to a literal fast, during this time you must abstain. But this fast you must refrain from any counsel or thoughts that tempt you, to put your hand on the matter, or to turn you away from waiting on the Lord. During this time of waiting, you simply need to continue in prayer and be still. Then the Lord will say, "My love is able to break this curse of darkness from over your mind, body, and spirit". Warning, it will be during your spiritual fast that weaknesses, such as unbelief, doubt, fear, pride, arrogance, will come forth to tempt you to eat the counsel of this angel of lies, rather than to wait for the Lord to come to deliver, heal, help, save, reveal, and/or guide. If urged by God, declare a one, two, or three day fast without food. Wait on the Lord, for He is faithful to come, and again I say wait on the Lord. An angel (perhaps disguised as human, or one, who is a true servant of God, with the Spirit of Truth within) will come, to protect and guide. They will lead the way. Take heed to this angel of light. See suggested course of action. (2) Dreamer, because of your frailties and unwise and foolish passions, the sharp reproofs of the Word, and the severe censures of men, you are allowing a weakening of your core beliefs, namely a rejection of all or some of the original foundational teachings of Christ and His apostles to take root within you spiritually. For, the depiction of demons denotes one who has chosen low or base standards, morals, ethics, ideas, principles, tenets, or beliefs. Further, you may even now, deny the existence or power of God, and of evil spirits. Now the Holy Spirit speaks expressly, that in the latter times some shall depart from the faith, which is in Jesus Christ, giving heed to seducing spirits, and doctrines of devils (1 Timothy 4:1-5). Instead of moving towards, and thus fulfilling, your divine purpose, and reaching a pinnacle in your life, thereby with, you will prosper, you have begun to listen to, and be fooled by, demons. Having listened, you have begun to decrease and fall, eventually running amok your life. Your attitude is leadi ng to a mental and spiritual breakdown, opening the door for demons to run havoc within your life and to bring you down to desolation. Your kind of choices leads to prostitution, poverty, homelessness, begging, imprisonment, and/or early death. You are forfeiting purpose for foolishness and ruin. Demonic influences will swarm around you, ready to help you in your wicked, evil, despicable, immoral, reprehensible, disreputable, degenerate, infamous, or perverse choices. Your lifestyle choices ar e, or will become, offensive and repulsive (abominable) in the sight of God and humankind. Dreamer, devils have had thousands of years to master human weaknesses and can rival men and women of God if we are not careful. Compassionately, because of grace and the many mercies of God extended to you, your dream is only a warning and not an official declaration. Favorably, utilizing the powerful resources of prayer and heartfelt repentance to Jesus and to individuals affected by your actions, coupled with, fasting, a changed mindset, serious re-consideration of God's ways and means, and an honest acknowledgement of God's hand within your life. Then the severe impact of your choices and actions, upon your life, can be reversed and damages repaired (see Ezekiel 33:12-19). Repentance is seeking pardon and expressing sincere feelings of regret and brokenness for having done something awry and/or for having hurt someone, see 2 Corinthians 7:10, 11. To individuals, a phone call or a letter of apology is a good place to start. To Jesus pray, Psalm 51, this, followed by appropriate applicati on of wisdom, can conceivably avert some of the repercussions of your choices. This is what is called leaving a blessing behind. Dreamer is counseled to seek all kinds of spiritual support now, to possibly avert or turn things around, and perhaps move away from your present environment, definitely walk away from all negativity abruptly. If you do not genuinely seek help and change, for sure ruin will be your destiny. An angel (perhaps disguised as human, or one, who is a true servant of God, with the Spirit of Truth within) will lead the way. See suggested course of action. (3) Dreamer, if you are an unbeliever (one who has no religious beliefs, a non-religious person, or one who has no religious faith or belief in Jesus Christ, or one who does not embrace a personal relationship with Jesus Christ, at present). Jesus loves you, thus, He is petitioning you to accept Him as your personal Savior, for you are valuable in His eyes. The first step in receiving Him as your personal Savior is repentance (see in the Holy Bible, Acts 2:37-41). Repentance is seeking pardon for having done something awry, and for having hurt someone, and expressing sincere feelings of regret and brokenness. To Jesus pray, Psalm 51:1-19. To individuals, a phone call or a letter of apology is a good place to start, if appropriate. Moreover, if you will accept the Heavenly Father's Words, via the Bible, and store up His principles, and His ways and means within you, turning your ear to wisdom and applying your heart to understanding, calling out for insight and crying aloud for discernment, Jesus will meet you. This, coupled with a lifestyle of prayer and fasting, followed by appropriate application of wisdom, and you will know the Messiah, Jesus Christ, intimately, and find the knowledge of God you seek. For the Lord gives wisdom and from His mouth comes knowledge and understanding. Then you will understand what is right and just and fair, every good path. When wisdom enters your heart and knowledge becomes sweet to your soul, discretion will protect you, understanding will guard you, and His Truth will lead you. To deliver you from the ways of wickedness, and from demons whose words and ways are perverse, who causes you to walk in darkness gladly, whose paths are crooked and devious, causing you to leave straight paths (Proverbs 2:1-6, 9-15). This is one of God's covenant promises to you. Have faith in this. An angel (perhaps disguised as human, or one, who is a true servant of God, with the Spirit of Truth within) will lead the way. See suggested course of action.

Michael (Seraph/Seraphim): This dream has two meanings (both may apply). (1) This archangel brings awareness of a pregnancy. (2) This archangel is concerned primarily with protection, truth, integrity, courage, and strength. He comes to protect and defend those who obediently love God, and who is loved by God. He is dispatched on missions, to help believers who are facing urgent needs during a crisis, in an emergency, and to give instant help, as well as, to encourage the dreamer to express God's loving kindness, His grace, mercy, and compassion, to others. Altruistic, goodhearted, and generous service to God and others is beneficial at this time. Dreamer, love God so completely that you will never forsake His s ervice for any reason. Often, an individual starts the initiative of service without leadership or community support. Some examples of altruistic service or "acts of kindness" to others are, provide a child with necessities, such as food, clothing, shelter, toys, medical equipment. Visit the sick, provide free medical services, and give charity to the poor, (see Ben Sira 29). Offer hospitality to strangers, help families bury their dead, via religious services, help with marriage ceremonies, and/or help a person make peace with his or her family member, fellow humankind, or their Maker. Provide free roadside assistance and emergency mechanical help, or freely help with structural problems in private homes. All of these, and more, are examples of service to the Kingdom of God. God will give you the necessary tools, courage, strength, and wherewithal, to do it. Caution, although you have the power of free choice, you should not think that your accomplishments are purely of your own volition. Truthfully, it is God, who gives you the capability and strength to achieve success. This is especially true of your struggles with your sinful tendencies, whether they manifest as a lack of concern or interest in the things of God, a stubborn resistance to the will of God, or laziness. If it had not been for God's efforts on your behalf, you would not have been able to overcome any negative tendencies. He delivered you. Any achievements you will accomplish, or have accomplished, any good deeds you've done, any fulfillment of God's will, was, and still is, dependent upon divine aid and guidance. One merely places his or her hand under the weight carried exclusively by God. Moreover, avoid excess sleep, do not claim credit for your achievements, and respect cautionary advice about something imminent (especially imminent danger or other unpleasantness), remain thankful, and become aware and tap into the intuitive insight you are (or will be) receiving. An angel (perhaps disguised as human, or one, who is a true servant of God, with the Spirit of Truth within) will lead the way. See suggested course of action.

Metatron (Seraph/Seraphim): This archangel's mission is two-fold. (1) Dreamer, you are entering a time of great inner change, and is on the verge of spiritual transformation; thus, this angel has come to help you discover your personal spiritual power and to help you learn how to use it to bring glory to God and to make the world a better place. (2) Moreover, as this archangel is also known as God's scribe, writing down our deeds, and words spoken by us, whether, idle, encouraging, or edifying (Malachi 3:16, Matthew 12:36, 37). Your dream was sent to encourage the dreamer to be wise, careful, and aware of your deeds and words. Dreamer, by your words you will be acquitted, and by your words, you will be condemned (Matthew 12:37). Moreover, the positive progression of your spiritual transformation is predicated upon your deeds and words. Warning, anyone who speaks against the Holy Spirit will not be forgiven, either in this age or in the age to come (Matthew 12:32). God judges those who utter hurtful or hateful words, or words that cause injury to others. When we speak to others, without seasoning our words with grace to honor the Lord, we have wasted those words. Lifetime friendships have been created and destroyed by words. Dreamer, words are very powerful, suggested reading, The Law of Confession, Bill Winston. Dreamer, embrace this visitation; make it the catalyst that ends your moments of doubt, fear, and uncertainty. An angel (perhaps disguised as human, or one, who is a true servant of God, with the Spirit of Truth within) will lead the way. See suggested course of action.

Raphael (leader of the Virtues): This archangel's primary responsibility is to heal; thus, he denotes healing to one who is suffering spiritually, physically, emotionally, and mentally, or even healing for your land. He will often appear within you r dream with the notice, "God has healed". Therefore, dreamer, you are made whole, now, for God has healed you. Hence, stop sinning so that something worse doesn't happen to you (John 5:14). An angel (perhaps disguised as human, or one, who is a true servant of God, with the Spirit of Truth within) will lead the way. See suggested course of action.

Raziel: This archangel brings words of wisdom. As you are now ready to receive the deepest measure of understanding, it must be said that wisdom and folly, advertise similar want ads. Both broadcast that they are multifaceted, mysterious, meaningful, fun, and boundless. However, wisdom (godly, spiritual wisdom) exalts God and leads to maturity and genuine joy, while folly (sensual wisdom) devalues and runs down life, bringing upon the head God's asperity and early death (also see Ecclesiastes 2:13). One, calls for open commitment, the other offers secret, illicit relations and a sensual, secular wisdom. Listen to your Heavenly Father's instructions, pay attention, and gain understanding. Do not forsake God's teaching. Lay hold of God's Word with all your heart, keep His commands and you will live. Get wisdom, get understanding; do not forget God's Word or swerve from it. Do not forsake wisdom, and she will protect you; love her, and she will watch over you. Wisdom is supreme; therefore get wisdom. Though it cost all you have, get understanding. Esteem her, and she will exalt you; embrace her, and she will honor you. Listen, and, accept what it said to you, and the years of your life will be many. God's Word w ill guide you in the way of wisdom and lead you along straight paths. When you walk, your steps will not be hampered; when you run, you will not stumble. Hold on to instruction; do not let it go; guard it well, for it is your life. Do not set foot on the path of the wicked or do the same things as evil men. Avoid them, do not travel with them; turn from them, and go on your way. For they cannot sleep until they do evil; until they make someone fall. They eat the bread of wickedness and drink the wine of violence. The way of the wicked is like deep darkness; they do not know what makes them stumble. However, the path of the righteous is like the first glow of the sun in the early morning, shining brighter until the full light of day. Dreamer, listen closely to God's Word. Keep it within your heart, for it will be health to your whole body. Above all else, guard your heart, for it is the wellspring of life. Put away perversity from your mouth; keep corrupt talk far from your lips. Let your eyes look straight - ahead, fix your gaze directly before you. Make level paths for your feet; and take ways, only, that are firm. Do not swerve t o the right or the left; keep your foot from evil (Proverbs 4). Additionally, dreamer, you will experience a very distinct moment of divine guidance, a "flash" of inspiration. An idea will pop into your head, apparently out of nowhere. It is an idea wai ting to be developed. The prophetic wisdom, via inspired intellect, will allow you to create something, seemingly out of nothing. However, the process of investigating and understanding the implications of this "flash of inspiration", the idea, is on you exclusively. This process is known as, "faith with works" (James 2:17-26). Dreamer, by examining the length and breadth of the inspired idea (aka doing the research), and establishing a thorough understanding of the concept, conclusions can be reached. Conclusions such as, is there a market for your idea? Where is the market located? How should I market my idea? Do I need further education to learn about my idea? Are there investment resources, and so on? When your process is finally complete, an idea will be born and should be ready for market. This idea will prosper you greatly, and it should benefit peo ple, greatly transforming lives. Seize the moment, and capitalize on it, while you have an open link to divine inspiration. Moreover, selflessness will serve as the vessel that contains all the insight you'll be receiving. An angel (perhaps disguised as huma n, or one, who is a true servant of God, with the Spirit of Truth within) will help lead the way.

Samael: This archangel is sent to one whose life is filled with hypocrisy (pretending). Dreamer, you believe in a god of your own making, coupled with outrageous claims you have wholeheartedly embraced from other erroneous guides. You say Adonai Elohim creates imperfect beings and then forces them to rise up to a level of perfection, which by design, they are unable to attain, by torturing them, causing millions to suffer in body and soul. You reason that this is God's only way, a path of pain, torture, and then death. You ask what human being aspires to evolve through this endless agony. You proclaim that God's promises are no more than vague words of doubtful happiness, and implacable laws that promise remote and unknowable joy, under the mask of love of humanity. You say His ways are nothing more than a profound indifference and a hardened selfishness. Further, you believe that God's intolerance of sin and the inherent results of sin, mainly separation from Him, as written within Holy Writ, and expressed in Christian dogma, are the picture of an angry god, conjured up by angry, unwise, and foolish men. You boast of philosophies, which appeal to the lustful desires o f human nature, condoning rebellious, unhealthy, immodest, immoral, indecent, lewd, and lascivious, behavior. Desires that if not checked, can and often do lead t o early death, as you have personally witnessed. This is what you call love. You exalt your wisdom above the Creator. While you discredit the Creator's wise and sensible guidelines for living life, on this side of eternity, as healthy, humanly, and sanely as possible; and in harmony with His provision for life on the other side of eternity, in heaven. You respect your truth, while never acknowledging, it is delivered without grace; thus, it is never enough to fill an emaciated soul. Read, understand, and embrace Galatians 5:13-25. Dreamer, promoting and encouraging others to approach God the Father, without the essential provision He has provided for humankind to approach Him properly; that provision being Yeshua HaMashiach, is not safe. Some call God's provision Jesus, Wonderful Counselor, Mighty God, Everlasting Father, Prince of Peace, our atonement, advocate, liberator, propitiator, and our salvation. It is only through this channel that we may hope through faith to conciliate with our Creator, see John 3:16, Acts 2:37-42, 1 Timothy 2:4-7. You may not like God's ways and means, but you do have to accept and surrender to them all. For, your human understanding of, and reaction to, spiritual realities is oftentimes crudely green. Dreamer, at this crossroad in your life, it is counseled that you do as the apostle Paul, and count all that y ou know, all that has brought you to this point, to be worthless (Philippians 3:8). Your dream has come to let you know that there is still hope and time for you to recognize the wrong in what you're doing, feel the regret about your past actions, and cha nge your ways and habits. Although, scripture states that it is impossible for those who have once been enlightened, who have tasted the heavenly gift, who have shared in the Holy Spirit, who have tasted the goodness of the Word of God and the powers of t he coming age, if they fall away, to be brought back to heartfelt repentance. Because, to their loss they are crucifying the So n of God all over again and subjecting Him to public disgrace (Hebrews 6:4-6). Fortunately, there is still hope and time for you. Dreamer, seize this opportunity to sincerely repent, denounce the erroneous teachings you've embraced, and go on from here. If you've led others away, humble yourself and apologize, and let them know you was wrong, and let them know, bottom line, their salvation is their own responsibility (Philippians 2:12, 13). Repentance is seeking pardon and expressing sincere feelings of regret and brokenness for having done something awry and/or for having hurt someone, see 2 Corinthians 7:10, 11. To individuals, a phone call or a letter of apology is a good place to start. To Jesus pray, Psalm 51, this coupled with prayer and fasting, and followed by appropriate application of wisdom, can conceivably avert some of the repercussions of your choices. This is known as leaving a blessing behind. Go and seek truth for yourself that not all may be eternally lost. An angel (perhaps disguised as human, or one, who is a true servant of God, with the Spirit of Truth within) will lead the way. Take heed, as this angel is also considered an angel of death, see subcategory, Azrael. See suggested course of action.

Sandalphon: This archangel brings notice that someone is praying on the dreamer's behalf, interceding to the Ruler of rulers. They are reminding Him of your courageous good works towards them on behalf of the Kingdom of God. Moreover, dreamer your prayers are especially effective now, what you decree, God will fulfill. Only remember to s eek first the Kingdom of God, via His Son. Yeshua is the key to activate all that comes with seeking the Kingdom of God. For, He is our righteousness required to access the Kingdom blessings, then will God give you the keys of the Kingdom of Heaven; whatever you bind on earth will be bound in heaven, and whatever you loose on earth will be loosed in heaven (ref Matthew 16:19). Dreamer, be who God made you to be, use your God given talents, as best you can, to make the world a better place. Take your past and use it to teach those whom God has purposed you to reach. Additionally, no matter who you are and what the situation, the words of the Psalms will speak the words of your heart and those words will be heard on High. Thus, began singing a new song, see Psalm 96:1-13. Start listening to inspirational music, music that praises our Lord and Savior. An angel (perhaps disguised as human, or one, who is a true servant of God, with the Spirit of Truth within) will lead the way.

Selaphiel: This archangel brings notice. The dreamer needs to, humbly, re-connect with God through prayer. Dreamer, there is a need to, wholeheartedly, block out distractions and concentrate on praying. You are encouraged to focus on expressing your deepest thoughts and feelings to God in prayer, and to listen carefully for God's response. While anticipating God's response there may be a time of waiting, especially when you are praying and asking the Lord to come and perform that which only He can perform. During this time, you must deny any counsel or thoughts that tempt you to turn away from waiting on the Lord. During this time of waiting, you simply need to continue in prayer and be still. Warning, it will be during your waiting that weaknesses, such as unbelief, doubt, fear, pride, arrogance, will come forth to distract you, or tempt you to embrace lies, rather than to wait for the Lord to come to comfort, guide, heal, help, protect you and your family, save, reveal, and/or deliver, especially from addictions. Wait on the Lord, for He is faithful to come. Then you will hear and know that only God's love is able to break the curse of darkness from over your mind, body, and spirit, and rescue you from the devil's deceptions. Additionally, start listening to inspirational music, music that praises our Lord and Savior (see Psalm 96:1-13). An angel (perhaps disguised as human, or one, who is a true servant of God, with the Spirit of Truth within) will lead the way. See suggested course of action.

Tzadkiel: This archangel brings awareness to the dreamer that a dispensing of justice, swiftly and without prejudice or bias, is coming. Seeing this angel within your dream is often a call to expose the practice of being unjust and/or unfair to wards others, or to expose an injustice being done to you (the dreamer). Dreamer, God is merciful, but only to those asking for His mercy, while forsaking any practice of injustice towards others. For if injustice continues, even after asking for mercy, yo u will reap what you sow. If the dreamer does not expose and forsake any practice of injustice, your dream is a severe warning of divine discipline coming your way. If, on the other hand, an injustice is being done to dreamer, you will see the guaranteed justice of the wicked, and an outcome they're not expecting. However, your boundaries are to obey God's standards for you exclusively. Namely, disrespect, on any level, towards those in authority over you is forbidden. Disrespect on any level towards any of God's children, especially the least of them, as well as prejudice and hatred is forbidden. Your expressed disapproval of justice handed down by God will not be tolerated. Since you will see justice handed down, do not say, "God is not fair by allowing this or that to happen". Letting go of negativity, and the people, places, and/or things that fuel i t, and appreciating the justice and grace (the free and unmerited favor and beneficence of God) afforded you, will bring sweetness t o your soul. An angel (perhaps disguised as human, or one, who is a true servant of God, with the Spirit of Truth within) w ill lead the way. See suggested course of action.

Tzaphkiel (leader of the Thrones): This archangel's mission is tri-fold. (1) This archangel is sent to one, the dreamer, who needs help learning how to love others with the unconditional love (aka Agape) God has for you. Dreamer, use your conflicts to motivate you to develop a compassion to serve others in need. Especially, boldly deliver God's love to people i n all situations closely tied to moments of death and destruction. (2) Additionally, to see this angel within your dream denotes forgiveness and a resolving of conflicts, by crushing an unwanted situation, and ending a long-term pain. (3) Moreover, as this angel also serves as an angel of death, take heed and abstain from all that you are asked to abstain from, lest you die an early death. An angel (perhaps disguised as human, or one, who is a true servant of God, with the Spirit of Truth within) will lea d the way. See suggested course of action.

Uriel: This archangel comes to interject the light of God's truth into the darkness of your confusion of mind. God's truth is that God has chosen you, He has filled you with His Spirit; and with skill, ability, knowledge, and understanding, to do whatever it is He has purposed for you to do, via service to your local church. It is suggested that you, dreamer, come up with fresh creative ideas, learn new information, solve problems, resolve conflicts. If you find yourself lacking in education, seek a learning institution (e.g. college, trade school, GED), go talk to a professor. Whatever you do, study in order to teach those God has purposed you to reach. Further, always seek Jesus's will before making decisions, let go of destructive emotions such as fear, anxiety, and anger, which can prevent you from discerning wisdom, and recognizing dangerous situations. Moreover, it is not wise to use up positive energy on negative actions, activities, and thoughts. Therefore, dreamer began embracing moderation in pleasure. Develop a good attitude, settle yourself in patience, without complaining, limiting your words. Know your place, and be content with your lot in life. Trust those wiser than you, and be of service to your fellow human being, sharing burdens. An angel (perhaps disguised as human, or one, who is a true servant of God, with the Spirit of Truth within) will lead the way. See suggested course of action.

In addition, the following is a common word, expression, or usage (e.g. slang or cliché), or a 'probable' that is metaphorically represented by angels

- Angels watching over you or guarding you: see Psalm 91:9-14; Luke 4

Suggested Course of Action

Question to consider and journal, did your dream depict any symbols that alludes to, the dreamer will make the necessary changes, spiritually, emotionally, and/or physically to affect a more positive outcome? If changes are initiated, your dreams will change.

Always, considering your self-first, reflecting on present situations, ask yourself, why am I dreaming about this now? What was your reaction to the angel? Were you angry, concerned, confused, defensive, fearful, happy, helpful, pleased, shocked, or unconcerned? Your reaction to the angel reveals your attitude regarding this information about yourself. Am I in a crisis of my faith? If relevant, also take time to consider your physical health. You will need to earnestly look within and consider that your answers are a reflection of where you are emotionally, physically, and spiritually, presently, and possibly who you are becoming. Nevertheless, dreamer, consider seriously your observations. If what was revealed prevail, will it build or destroy, strengthen or weaken, enlighten or blind? If you lack wisdom, ask Jesus for wisdom. He gives wisdom to all, generously, no matter who you are and what you've done; wisdom is available (see James 1:5-8, Proverbs 2:1-6, 10). Hence, if, by just asking, you may get wisdom, one may suffer needlessly, because you will not ask Jesus for wisdom.

Now, pray (See Prayer of Deliverance, pg. 897)

Specific Meaning

Unless otherwise noted elsewhere, if, in your everyday living, your awaked state, as part of your lifestyle, work, or ministerial activities, or a special event, you have a very real connection with any angelic activity. For example, an artisan or author whose primary interests are in angels, or some theological study of angels, dreams of this sort, for the most part, are ordinary dreams, resulting from your daily activities (see Chapter One, Chalom). These sorts of dreams are usually about your routine, mundane activities or anxieties that overwhelm your mind during the day. They are an inner release mechanism, which helps provide you with emotional balance and the maintaining of your sanity. These dreams are not significant, and do not warrant special attention.

Note: Dreamer may consider his or her (specific) dream as a clue given to assist in finding facts, needed to support a prevailing theory or thought, or to prevent a disaster. Example, an angel has been sent to help develop a new medicine, or is sent to prevent dreamer from murder. Dreamer, the details, kept within context of your dream, should be relevant to your life, and closely resemble your real-life situations. Meaning it can actually occur during your awaked state. This will help you narrow down the specifics needed to support you or to steer you clear of possible erroneous information. However, if your dream was inundated with symbols not easily linked to your life activities, then you should heed the spiritual implications (the interpretation).

ANIMALS

She came to him, bowed down, and said, "Lord, help me!" Jesus replied, "It's not right to take the children's food and throw it to the dogs." She said, "You're right, Lord. But even the dogs eat scraps that fall from their masters' tables." Then Jesus answered her, "Woman, you have strong faith! What you wanted will be done for you." At that moment her daughter was cured. (Matthew 15:25-28 GW)

And God said, Let the waters swarm with swarms of living creatures, and let birds fly above the earth in the open firmament of heaven. And God created the great sea-monsters, and every living creature that moves, wherewith the waters swarmed, after their kind, and every winged bird after its kind: and God saw that it was good. And God blessed them, saying, be fruitful, and multiply, and fill the waters in the seas, and let birds multiply on the earth. And there was evening and there was morning, a fifth day. And God said, let the earth bring forth living creatures after their kind, cattle, and creeping things, and beasts of the earth after their kind: and it was so. And God made the beasts of the earth after their kind and the cattle af ter their kind and everything that creepiest upon the ground after its kind: and God saw that it was good. And God said, Let us make man in our image, after our likeness: and let them have dominion over the fish of the sea and over the birds of the heavens, and over the cattle, and over all the earth, and over every creeping thing that creepiest upon the earth (Genesis 1:20-26 ASV).

The wolf also shall dwell with the lamb, the leopard shall lie down with the young goat, the calf, the young lion, and the fatling together; and a little child shall lead them. The cow and the bear shall graze; their young ones shall lie down together; and the lion shall eat straw like the ox. The nursing child shall play by the cobra's hole, and the weaned child shall put h is hand in the viper's den. They shall not hurt nor destroy in all My holy mountain, for the earth shall be full of the knowledge of the Lord as the waters cover the sea (Isaiah 11:6-9 NKJV)

Jesus said, "Blessed is the lion which becomes man when consumed by man; and cursed is the man whom the lion consumes, and the lion becomes man" Gospel of Thomas, Logion

This category deals with the kingdom Animalia. Some short descriptions of types, phrases, and other processes and particulars, connected in some way to this category are, for example, mammals and reptiles, cold or warm blooded, domesticated or wild, animals. Also, see category content list, or index.

All Symbols and Referents, Notes (1, 2, 3, etc.), Suggested Course of Action, and Specific Meaning offer guidance toward a more comprehensive interpretation.

Notes

1. Unless otherwise noted elsewhere, if, in your everyday living, your awaked state, as part of your lifestyle, work, or ministerial activities, or a special event, you have a very real connection with animals. For example, an animal activist, owner, taxidermy, trainer, veterinarian, zoologist, keeper of unwanted animals, or any activity connected to animals, your dream is not significant and does not warrant special attention.

   Otherwise noted, this dream may be a Prophetically Simple Dream (see Chapter One: The 60th Part of Prophecy). Whereas, the dreamer is warned to stop any illegal or illicit activity going on within your life that involves animals, e.g. poacher, abuser of animals, bestiality, or any other criminal minded, under-handed, or perverse activity that primarily involves animals. You should surrender to the appropriate authorities, especially if this is an issue within the dreamer's life, or submit or yield to other relevant persons. If any of the preceding is happening, this dream is a first step intervention and an alarm. Skip interpretation and re-consider your activity as harmful, hurtful, illegal, or life threatening, at present. Handle the situation appropriately by surrendering, first to God, for Adonai Elohim knows all, and then to appropriate authorities or relevant others. Animals are also a valuable part of the Creator's creation, and they are not without purpose. Also, see Specific Meaning at the end of this category, section entitled, Note (Specific Meaning).

Otherwise noted, per your lifestyle, if your dream closely resembled real life situations, meaning it can actually occur (or has occurred) during your awaked state; this dream may be an Ordinary Dream, resulting from your daily activities (see Chapter One, Chalom). These sorts of dreams are usually about your routine, mundane activities or anxieties that overwhelm your mind during the day. They are an inner release mechanism, which helps provide you with emotional balance and the maintaining of your sanity. These dreams are not significant, and do not warrant special attention.

2. Probables: As animals are frequently demonstrated in many, and very personal ways; for example, does a particular animal remind you of a particular moment in time? Thus, could the animal depicted be a possible probable (see Chapter One, section entitled, Probables)? Hence, dreamer may also consider your own personal and special associations with various actions or activities connected to animals. As long as the interpretation is kept within the principles of spiritual boundary markers, landmarks, and property lines, (see Chapter One, section entitled, Spiritualizing Boundary Markers, Landmarks, and Property Lines).

3. Determine who your dream is for you or another. Always considering yourself first, reflect on your present behaviors. Ask yourself, why am I dreaming about this now? What is this dream revealing about me? Have I taken on new attributes? Has anyone commented on my present behaviors as being untypical of me? Has my ministry changed for the better or for the worse? What about my beliefs, doctrine, or philosophy, are they still based on Holy Writ? Is there something I need to know about those I am ministering to or serving?

Remember your actions and emotions within your dream. Was the animal your pet? Did you change into an animal? Did you eat the animal (cooked or raw)? Did you pat or stroke the animal? Did dreamer just stand still and watch, or stare at, the animal? Was the animal on you in any way? Did you have sex with the animal? Did you clean or wash the animal, or clean or wash the place or surface the animal was on/in? Did you try to save the animal or set it free? Was the animal invisible? Was the animal in your house? Unless otherwise noted elsewhere, an answer of yes, to one or more of these, or similar questions, is a good indicator that your dream is about you (the dreamer), your behaviors, and/or character. Could you be stroking or embracing the characteristics ascribe to that particular animal (good and bad)? Are you in a process of renewal, sanctification, or transformation, thus a cleaning, conquering over, or setting free, of the animal in some way? Are you in denial, or running away, from certain character attributes within yourself, anxious, frightened, or troubled, by recent changes in your behavior or character; thus, running and/or hiding? If dreamer was afraid or fearful, could a 'spirit of fear' be assailing the dreamer? Read and understand Romans 8:15, 2 Timothy 1:7. Are you changing or pretending to change your ways in order to mislead another? Are you attempting to deceive now? See following relevant subcategory, the interpretation is about and for you.

Was the animal connected in any way to another? For example, was the animal on the person, or did the person change into an animal? Did animal just stand still and watch, or stare at, the dreamer? Was the animal a "help animal", e.g. a Seeing Eye dog? Was the animal an unwelcome pest? Did someone serve you the animal to eat (cooked or raw)? Did someone give you the animal or was responsible for bringing the animal into your life, living space, or environment? Did you try, or want to, get rid of the animal in some way? Did you run or hide from the animal? Were you afraid of the animal? Was the animal a possible source of danger, a nuisance, wild, life threatening, or excited in some way? Was the animal docile, domesticated, or non-aggressive? Did you talk to the animal, or did the animal talk to you, and if so, what was said? Was there a message? Did someone have sex with the animal? Unless otherwise noted elsewhere, an answer of yes, to one or more of these, or similar questions, is a good indicator that your dream is about another, their character traits and behaviors, and their role and influential effects within the life of the dreamer. Influencing your attitude, your physical, spiritual, and/or mental health, your understanding, perspective, and reasoning regarding spiritual issues, your ministry, and/or prosperity or the dwindling thereof. Do you know someone whose life activities or physical being is similar to that which stood out the most within your dream? Could it be that person? If you sense that your dream is for or about another, the question as to why you have been made privy to this information, and how do you factor into the equation, should be seriously considered along with necessary actions. Perhaps the dreamer is being made aware of the plight of someone, and you are to get involved (see Chapter One, Are You Ready to Hear the Messages in Your Dreams, section entitled, The 10% for others).

If your dream is for, or about another:

Dreams that reference others and the revelation within those dreams, is not given haphazardly to any individual, but only to those with the ability, and influence to do something with the information; this is also prophecy. With that, journal the following questions, and if unable to answer the questions now, this denotes that the person, represented within your dream, will enter your life shortly. Are you entering into a personal relationship with someone? Do you not know or understand what you're looking at, especially certain behaviors, when learning about this person? Has someone new entered your life or maybe you've just begun opening up to someone not so new, and have started listening to their advice, accepting their assistance, or are you supporting or enabling someone? Are you in denial regarding the toxicity of one of your present relationships, particularly a spouse, family member, or friend? Are you anxious, concerned, frightened, and/or troubled by recent changes in your behavior, especially because of someone's influence upon your life at present? Have you allowed someone to convince you to deceive another? Have you recently become aware of (or is being made aware of, via your dream) certain undesirable behaviors within you towards another? Are you trying to cut ties with one that is bad company?

Note: If your dream has attributes that indicate that your dream is about you, and other attributes that indicate that your dream is about another, dreamer should consider that your dream is about you and another. For example, while the animal was in your home; thus indicating that the dream is about the dreamer; the animal was an unwelcomed pest, thus indicating that your dream is about another. Therefore, while your dream is about the dreamer, the dreamer should expect the role and/or influential effects of another, also plays a part in your interpretation. Another example, dreamer may be an animal activist, and is now being called upon to help with the investigation of a potential abuser of animals. The potential abuser, due to a friendship with the dreamer, expects unusual favors, which the dreamer is unable to fulfil, again, see relevant interpretation.

More questions to consider. Why has the person been allowed within your life, and/or how did they get there? Again, if unable to answer the questions now, this denotes that the person, represented within your dream, wi ll enter your life shortly. If their activity, within your dream, has proven positive, via the interpretation, this someone will prove, unwittingly, to be a very strong ally, benefactor, defender, and supporter. God has sent this someone into your life to help you carry out your next endeavor by enlarging your spiritual capacity. Allow the strength of that person's character to guide, help, and support you. On the other hand, if his or her presence and/or activity, within your dream, proved negative, via the interpretation, for sure, this person will prove to be a very strong and formidable challenge for you, perhaps unto death. If negative, this dream is a dire warning. Take steps accordingly to struggle against, or to cut off, adverse and unfavorable relationships. Remember certain personalities are all encompassing, affecting everything, cataclysmic, contagious, deadly, harmful, infectious, predatory, and/or venomous. Symbolically meaning that if allowed to continue or prosper within your life, serious harm or death to the dreamer may result. Idolize no one, especially beyond the warning of the Lord, and we are definitely not to lay our lives down for no one. No longer, allow that particular person's influence within your life to continue or thrive. Then again, this person maybe allowed within your life, because of the dreamer's unwillingness to abstain from immorality after having been asked to abstain from such by God, see 1 Corinthians 6:9-20, Galatians 5:19-21, or the dreamer's self-righteous behavior, or a lack of a balanced and honest view of your own personality. In this case, this person will affect self-awareness within the life of the dreamer, exposing the negative traits of your personality, especially those traits, which cause you to follow, or to be so easily misled, and/or your wrong beliefs; no matter, this type of mentality needs reckoning with. Graciously, all of this will restore the dreamer to his or her right place with God, opening your eyes to see how far you've strayed from God (1 Corinthians 5:4-7; James 5:20). The lesson is, no matter how personable, powerful, or difficult a person, or how uncertain or unpopular the choices and issues, always take the next biblical and ethical step, for obedience to God's principles will always prove safer and stronger foundationally. Although, you will need all kinds of outside support to recover from this person's domination, again, no longer, allow that particular person's influence within your life to continue or thrive, especially if negative, end it abruptly.

4. Consider all the people, places, backgrounds, and activity highlighted within your dream.

Known (in your awaked life) person, animal, place, or organization within your dream:

Unless otherwise noted elsewhere, people, animals, places, backgrounds that are actually known by the dreamer in your awaked life, indicates a part of you that you recognize within yourself on some level or another. Question to journal, if dreamer seriously considers the person, animal, place, or background attributes, what character traits stood out the most, or what features stood out the most. For example, age, color, height, size, happiness, considerate, loving, let you be yourself, peacefulness, encourager, irrational, leader, liar, mentor, passionate, personable, neglected, poor, run-down, sage, shyster, unwise, upscale, vengeful. Write down (journal) the particular highlighted within your dream. The attribute or activity highlighted is for a reason. Since the attribute written down is a part of you, namely the dreamer's nature, demeanor, and/or lifestyle, an honest and unbiased assessment is very important for truth sake. Happy note, considering that other people's attributes, within dreams, also represent attributes of your own personality, causes one to look at another in a better light. According to your capacity to embrace self-awareness and a rectification of mind, body, and spirit, God will begin to enhance, make better, more attractive, sanctify, diminish, and make pure and free from sin and guilt, this part of you.

Otherwise noted, if the person, animal, place, or background within your dream is actually known by the dreamer, in your awaked life, this person, animal, place, or background may represent him or herself, or itself.

Unknown in your awaked life or although known, was unseen, invisible, or only talked about - person, animal, place, or organization within your dream:

Unless otherwise noted elsewhere, if you did not recognize, the person, place, thing, they, or it, was not seen, invisible, or only talked about within your dream, this indicates an attribute or activity within your life that you are unfamiliar with, or are in denial about, or you refuse to acknowledge it, but it does exists. Question to journal: what character trait, feature, action, or activity, stood out the most? For example, age, color, height, size, happiness, considerate, loving, let you be yourself, peacefulness, encourager, irrational, leader, liar, mentor, passionate, personable, neglected, poor, run-down, sage, shyster, unwise, upscale, vengeful. Although, on some conscious level, you are aware of a certain behavior or attribute within you, you have chosen to filter out or simply ignore certain information about yourself that contradicts your view of yourself and/or your preconceived notions of others and of the world around you. Possibly protecting yourself, emotionally and psychologically, from a situation, which you are unable to cope with at this time, or you lack control over; then again, perhaps the dreamer has an exaggerated or unrealistic view of yourself. No matter the reason, right now a question is before you, via your dream. Do you want to know this part of yourself? According to your ability to handle self-awareness, God will begin to reveal this side of you to you. Why, He wants to balance your understanding of things; thus, effecting wholeness within your life, so that the enemy will no longer be able to manipulate your emotions so easily. The Holy Spirit is with you to help you throughout this entire process, listen to Him. Now, in your life, this activity or attribute needs reckoning with, somehow or someway. Again, what actions or behaviors of the unknown person, animal, place, or organization, stood out the most?

Otherwise noted, (known or unknown), if the person, place or thing that initiated (or was a recipient of) the action or activity within your dream was not seen, invisible, or only talked about within your dream, this may indicate that the dreamer does not recognize the influential effects another has within your life, or upon your attitude.

If more than one person (known or unknown):

Consider what the group had in common. What behavior, character trait, feature, action, or activity, stood out the most? For example, were they argumentative, authoritative, beautiful, criminal minded, dancing, difficult, dressed unusual, enigmatic, fighting, focused, flirty, helpful, hurtful intentions, powerful, promiscuous, quiet, secretive, seemed unreal, unassuming? What about age, color, height, size, happiness, considerate, loving, let you be yourself, peacefulness, encourager, irrational, leader, liar, mentor, passionate, personable, neglected, poor, run-down, sage, shyster, unwise, upscale, vengeful, death. That which was highlighted and noted is what you need to focus on at present.

If the attribute or quality is a desirable or positive one, allow the strength of that attribute to help you overcome some manner of immorality or irreverence within your life and/or to help you to become better, productively, for the Kingdom of God in some manner. If the attribute is an undesirable or negative one, take steps accordingly to struggle against the growing desires of the carnal side of you. If applicable, get help and support via prayer, fasting, and a Christian based support group.

For dreams of the dead see following note.

Did a zoo animal kill someone? While the dead has nothing to do with the living (Ecclesiastes 9:4-6), it may be considered what character trait did that person represent to the dreamer, while the person was actually alive, what character feature stood out the most. With that trait noted, dreamer may consider that the trait noted, is within the dreamer, and that trait is no longer useful or needed for the progression of your spiritual walk, on this side of heaven. Dreamer, it is suggested that you render that trait (good or bad) obsolete, and began anew attempting to move forward, using different tactics to overcome unproductive habitual life cycle choices, and for maneuvering through this thing we call life in a more, better way. See category, Death, and/or other relevant categories.

5. **Larvae, Eggs, Embryotic or Baby stage of animals:** This dream represents the beginning stages of your particular larvae, egg, embryo, or baby stage of their adult counterpart. You are embracing behaviors that will result in you developing the attributes representative of the particular larvae, egg or embryo adult counterpart. For example: eggs turn into chickens, turkeys, ducks, other birds, caterpillars turn into butterflies and moths; grubs turn into beetles, bees, wasps; maggots turn into flies; wrigglers turn into mosquitoes; tadpoles or polliwogs turn into frogs, amphibians. Kittens and puppies grow into adult cats and dogs. Although you do not exhibit the attributes of the adult counterpart of your larvae, egg, embryo, or baby stage of your particular animal, yet, the beginning stages of the

characteristics represented by the animal are present within you now, and those traits will suddenly begin to manifest, for good or bad. See adult counterpart of this animal.

6. Was the meat being cleaned and prepared for cooking? Was the animal or meat, processed for human consumption? Was the meat cooked, eaten? Was meat or animal processed for animal consumption? Was the animal crushed, hurt, or killed, dead, or rigidified (hardened in some way)? Did the animal disappear, was it unseen, or did you get away from the animal somehow? See following interpretations.

    Meat cleaned, prepared, and cooked for human consumption see subcategory, Meat cleaned, prepared, and/or processed for cooking and human consumption "eating".

    Animal Food (food processed for animal consumption): If you dreamt of animal food, refer to the animal that the food was prepared for. Examples of animal food: cat food, dog food, or rat food. Kept within the literal context of the purpose of the food, that animal characteristic, within you is, either killed or being fed. For example, rat food kills rats or mice; other food feeds an animal.

    Did an animal eat another animal? This denotes one who is embracing the attributes of the animal eaten, but without changing your basic character (the animal doing the eating). The characteristics of both animals are now, combined in one person. You have changed; you now have two faces but present one. This dream is an alarm and warning or encouragement, depending upon the animals. An alarm and warning about possible pretense and diabolical influences if animal is unclean or primarily negative. Enlightenment, if animal is clean or has positive traits. For clean or unclean animal, see Note 7: Clean and Unclean Animals.

    If animal was crushed, hurt, killed or Taxidermy (e.g., head cut off, roadkill, hunted, shot), dead, rigidified or, if the animal disappeared, was unseen or you escaped or got away from the animal somehow: Unless otherwise noted elsewhere. This would imply that only the negative activities, attributes, behaviors, or character traits associated with that animal have changed. Those negative traits, within you, are mortified, lifeless, or gone, and you are now opposite of what they were. The old negative attributes are no longer alive within the dreamer, nor are they appropriate, important, relevant, or useful, to the dreamer. Moreover, no longer does another's influence hold sway over you. You are free. Abstinence from pleasure, self-imposed discipline, for religious purposes, or some level of hardship, within the life of the dreamer, has put an end to the negative desires, passions, and foolishness associated with the animal. The dreamer will need to identify only the antonyms of the negative attributes that are associated with the animal within your dream. For example, faithlessness has been replaced with faithfulness; humility is the antonym of arrogance. Thus, faithfulness and humility are now the new attributes within the dreamer's life; having replaced the old attributes. This change has been, will be, or is being, effected within the dreamer's life.

7. Categorized, and characterized, in many ways, yet biblically, animals, are clean or unclean. God gave His laws, and those laws included which animals are clean or unclean that it might be well with you. Since the following list is not extensive, dreamer is encouraged to seek biblical guidelines for recognizing animals that are clean and unclean in Leviticus 11, or Deuteronomy 14:3-21. See also, other relevant research to determine the primary characteristics of your particular animal within your dream, via a Bible concordance, Bible illustrated dictionary, encyclopedia, or internet.

    Clean and Unclean Animals (symbolically speaking):

    Symbolically, clean animals personify those whom God foreknew and predestined to be conformed to the likeness of His Son, His according to the election of grace (the free and unmerited favor and beneficence of God). The called, justified, and glorified, according to His plan which works out everything in conformity with the purpose of His will (see Romans 8:29, 30; Ephesians 1:5, 11). You are clean according to the new covenant established through Jesus Christ; as well as moderate in all things, just and fair, not rude or obscene, and one whom a believer may interact with socially on very personal levels (e.g. business partner, friendship, marriage, other mutual relationships).

Symbolically, unclean animals personify one of two states regarding human behavior. (1) Within the life of a believer, it denotes anger, animosity, confusion, out of order, self-condemnation, sexual impropriety, an unforgiving spirit, as well as, other weaknesses, of the heart, e.g. immoral, impure, and unchaste conduct. For example, addictions, cheating, exposing confidences to others, greedy, gossiping, jealously, lying, stealing, or any other sinful attribute (see 1 Corinthians 6:9-20, Ephesians 5). This behavior causes one's anointing to fade and spiritual authority to wane. Favorably, you are now one, whom the body of believers should, and will, help restore back to God, in the spirit of empathy, mercy, leniency, and kindness, allow this. (2) An unclean animal also personifies one who is not re-born spiritually nor repentant, a non- believer (one who has no religious beliefs, a non-religious person, or one who has no religious faith or belief in Jesus Christ, or one who does not embrace a personal relationship with Jesus Christ, at present). You may also hold to views and practices that are erroneous, unlawful, toxic, and spiritually and/or physically deadly. The purpose of this dream is t o encourage the dreamer. God will save you from all your uncleanness that you might know God is God, and honor and glorify Him whose power is the power, and whose rule will endure eternally, and that you might know your God ordained destiny. Dreamer, He does as He pleases; and choose whom He please, with the powers of heaven and the peoples of the earth. Once you recognize your true destiny, and that being in Christ Jesus, your outlook on life will change. Then use your abilities and talents exclusively for the Kingdom of God. If you are careful to submit to His ordinances, you will be His people, and He will be your God and you will be made clean.

8. In addition to the following interpretations, see index or relevant categories for more information. For example, if chasing was involved, see category, Chasing and relevant category. If a color was highlighted, e.g., a white lion, see category, Color. Kept within context of your dream and the interpretation, the additional symbols are perhaps relevant. It will be within the sum of all the symbols that you will find a more thorough interpretation.

9. Since the following list is not extensive, dreamer is encouraged to seek other relevant research, via an encyclopedia, internet, or bible concordance, bible illustrated dictionary, to determine if your animal is venomous, poisonous, lethal, harmful, or non-venomous or of little effect to humans. As all animals symbolically represent personality, again certain personalities are all encompassing, affecting everything, venomous, deadly, harmful, infectious, predatory, cataclysmic, or contagious. Symbolically meaning that if allowed to continue or prosper within your life, serious harm or devastation to the dreamer may result. Having done your research you should be able to determine some basic behaviors or attributes your Lord and Savior wants you to focus on.

Symbols and Referents

Animals, within our dreams, for the most part, are given human characteristics or personality traits, behavioral pattern s, basic nature, and endowments (2 Peter 2:12). This type of dream helps the dreamer to know what your divine Counselor wants you to focus on; namely, your particular behaviors or attributes, or the primary role or function someone else's behaviors or desires have in your life and the subsequent effects. These dreams are largely warnings and/or messages of grace extended to you, that you might embrace God's power to direct, control, and change the animal instinct within you, knowing that you are a new creature in Christ (2 Corinthians 5:17).

In addition to the varied meanings of animals, other common words, expressions, usages, (e.g. slang or clichés), or a 'probable' that are metaphorically represented by any of the following are also considered (this section is an addendum at the end of the relevant subcategory).

Category Content - If not listed see index, perchance, for your specific type of animal dream.

- Larvae, Eggs, Embryotic or Baby stage of animals, see Note 5
- Animal Food (food processed for animal consumption) see Note 6
- Animal ate another animal see Note 6
- Animal was crushed, hurt, or killed (e.g. head cut off, roadkill, hunted, shot), dead, rigidified (hardened in some way), taxidermy, or if the animal disappeared, was unseen, or you escaped or got away from the animal somehow see Note 6
- Eaten by an animal
- Bestiality, Zooerasty (sexual activity between a person and an animal)
- Apes, Monkeys (Baboon, Capuchin, Chimpanzee, Gibbons, Gorilla, Guenon, Macaque, Marmosets, Orangutan, and Tamarin)
- Bear
- Birds (Albatrosses, Bat, Bittern, Canary, Cardinal, Chicken, Cock, Cormorant, Crane, Dove, Duck, Eagle, Falcon, Finch, Hawk, Gannet, Goose, Grouse, Halcyon, Hen, Heron, Lark, Ostrich, Owl, Partridge, Peacock, Pelican, Penguin, Petrel, Phoenix, Pigeon, Quail, Raven, Redbird, Rooster, Seagull, Songbirds, Sparrow, Swallow, Stork, Swan, Thrush, Turkey, Vulture, Yellow Bird)
- Feathers, Plumage
- Camel (Alpaca, Dromedary, Llama, and Vicuna)
- Canines (Coyote, Dog, Fox, Hyena, Jackal, and Wolf)
- Black Shuck (aka, Devil Dog or Hellhound, with black shaggy hair and enormous fiery red eyes the size of saucers)
- Werewolf
- Cattle (Bison, Buffalo, Bull, Calf, Cow, Oxen)
- Golden Calf
- Red Cow
- Deer, Antelope (Caribou, Doe, Elk, Gazelle, Hart, Hind, Moose, Reindeer, and Roebuck)
- Elephant
- Felines: (Cat, Cheetah, Leopard, Lion, Mountain Lion, Cougar, Panther, and Tiger)
- Winged Lion, Griffin, Griffon, or Gryphon
- Fish or Marine Mammals or Crustacea or Seafood (e.g. Polar Bear, Sea Otter, Seal, Whale)
- Fishhook
- Big fish (to dream that fish are larger than normal)
- Red Herring
- Shark
- Frogs (Bullfrog, Toads)
- Giraffe
- Goat, Ibex, and Kid
- Scapegoat
- Hippopotamus, Rhinoceros
- Horse or Donkey or Mule or Pony or Zebra (equidae family)
- The Four Horses of the Apocalypse
- White Horse
- Red Horse
- Black Horse
- Pale Horse (very light colored; highly diluted with white, can also be brown or yellowish green)
- Insects (Ants, Bees, Beetles, Butterfly, Caterpillar, Cockroaches, Crickets, Flies, Gnats, Grasshoppers, Hornets, Ladybugs, Locusts, Maggots, Moths, Roaches, Termites, Wasps). For other bugs, Insects, Flies, Worms, see category, Parasites, Bloodsuckers

- Marsupials (Kangaroos, Koala Bear, Opossum, Possums, Tasmanian devil, Wallaby, and Wombats)
- Meat cleaned, prepared, and/or processed for cooking and human consumption eating
- Sandwiches, Appetizers, or Hors d'oeuvres
- Monsters, Mythological or Legendary Creatures, or other Abominable Creatures (Beasts, Bigfoot, Black Shuck, Centaur, Dragon, Fairies, Fallen Angels, Gargoyles, Halcyon, Hydra, Imps, Medusa, Gorgon, Mermaids, Minotaur, Ogres, Pegasus, Phoenix, Sasquatch, Sirens, Sphinx, Unicorn, Vampires, Werewolf)
- Parasites, Bloodsuckers (Bedbugs, Black Fly, Fleas, Gadfly, Head Louse, Horsefly, Itch Mite, Leeches, Louse, Midge, Mites, Mosquitoes, Punkie, Tapeworm, Ticks, Tsetse Fly, Pinworms, Roundworms). For other bugs, insects, flies, worms, see category, Insects
- Reptiles (Alligator, Asps, Chameleon, Crocodile, Dinosaurs, Gecko, Gila Monster, Iguana, Lizard, Cobras, Tortoise, Turtle, or Vipers)
- Snake Eggs
- Rodents, Burrowing Animals, and Weasels (Aardvark, Anteater, Armadillo, Badger, Chipmunk, Ferret, Gerbil, Guinea Pig, Groundhog, Hamster, Mice, Mink, Mole, Otter, Porcupine, Rabbit, Raccoon, Shrew, Skunk, Sloth, and Squirrel)
- Spiders (Black house Spider, Black widow Spider, Brown recluse Spider, Camel Spider, Daddy Longlegs Spider, Funnel-Web Spider, Grass Spider, Hobo Spider, Huntsman Spider, Mouse Spider, Red Back Spider, Saint Andrew's Cross Spider, Sand Spider, Scorpion, Tarantulas, Trapdoor Spider, Water Spider, Wolf Spider, or Yellow Sac Spider). For other Arachnids, e.g. Mites, see category, Parasites
- Spider Cobwebs
- Sheep (Ewe, Lamb, ram)
- Swine, Boar, Pig, or Pork
- Worms, Millipedes, and Centipedes (for other worms, e.g. Leeches, Tapeworm, see category, Parasites)

Eaten by an animal: To dream that you are eaten by an animal denotes that the dreamer is allowing negative attributes to predominate your character namely those characteristics attributed to that particular animal, see relevant animal. You are allowing the wild, negative, dark side of your nature to reign, due to confusion on some level (mentally, emotionally, or spiritually). As your dream marks a transition within the dreamer's life, dreamer, is counseled to know your dark side and reject embracing it; for, while you faithfully sustain the outward signs of appearing to be blessed and/or to "have it all together"; your spirit is outrageously out of control. This confliction within will begin to manifest, and it will lead to dishonor and will prove publicly embarrassing for you. Dreamer, earnestly and genuinely, submitting to Jesus as your Lord and Savior will help you subdue your dark side that you may walk into your purpose; then your life's circumstances will begin to change. With that said, the following is also necessary to say, although hurtful, it is needed and should be heeded. Dreamer, you believe in a god of your own making, coupled with outrageous claims you have wholeheartedly embraced from other erroneous guides. You respect your truth, while never acknowledging, it is delivered without grace; thus, it is never enough to fill an emaciated soul. Moreover, you have adopted a bourgeois mentality, believing yourself above God's word and above the law of the land. This mentality is concerned only with your personal comfort, material wealth, and status, at any expense.

Now, having in yourself nothing that you respect more than power and greed, you are willing to sacrifice all, God, principle, family, and friend, to the image or idol of vanity. Your new way is based on exploring alternatives to God's righteous principles, as well as, creating a sense of unity with the wickedness around you. This is what you call love. This mentality sacrifices children, family, and morality, to the hollowness of satisfying immoral desires and appetites. All carried out, with the hope of finding happiness by pacifying jealously and covetousness. The selling-out of yourself over to immorality, while closing your eyes to it all are all principles based on values that are not only vile, but also increasingly unstable. This way cries out against godly ethics, and its' end offends any sense of godliness. Dreamer, you obey no one, and accept no correction. You do not trust in the Lord, nor do you draw near to Him, although He has given you space to repent; instead, you allow yourself to be seduced. Thus, sin will very soon turn your paradise into chaos, and dishonor the beauty of your name. You are also at risk of falling into a state of serious health problems and possibly loss of life, especially eternal life. So severe are things that restoration can only be by returning to Christ Jesus wholeheartedly. Dreamer when God hides His face from someone celebrations are turned into moaning and groaning, and the party is exchanged for depression and solitude. Your recklessness can be remedied by prayer and heartfelt repentance to Jesus and to individuals affected by your actions, and by rebuking and renouncing the "spirit of jezebel", that has attached itself to you. See suggested course of action.

Bestiality, Zooerasty (sexual activity between a person and an animal): Your dream comes as a very harsh warning. This dream has two meanings (one or both apply). (1) If you are one considered a teacher in spiritual matters in your awaked life, your dream denotes one who is a false teacher. (2) The dreamer is embracing the very negative traits attributed to the particular animal depicted within your dream. This coupled with, a way of life that is full of depravity, totally contrary to God's call, spiritual backsliding, and major mental, emotional, and spiritual confusion, on so many levels (Exodus 22:19, Leviticus 18:23, 20:15). Dreamer, he or she who harbors perversion and maintains evil gives rise to disillusionment (Psalm 7:14). Dreamer, you are not in harmony with the will of God for your life, nor with the particular objectives that are intended to ensure the fulfillment of that will. Your behavior contradicts practicality, basic reality, and deviates from the morality of God. Dreamer, you have shown yourself presumptuous, when you do not fear to do evil before the Lord or His servants. Your character is one of extreme haughtiness, presumptuousness, pride, and self-assuredness in the very negative sense of the word. All are signs that your heart is hardened. Yours is a life full of unnecessary words and activities, which have no basis in fact or reality, and they are not rooted in faith in God. Reality is understood to be what God says it to be via His Word. For example, we are saved by grace through faith, not by works (Ephesians 2:5-10). Hence, anyone who does not correspond with His truth, in a levelheaded and practical manner, is deceived and erroneous in your thoughts and ideas; thus, exposing your rejection of the certainty of God's word. If this disposition is not let go, it will lead to a great fall (Proverbs 11:2; 16:18, 19; 29:23). For particular animal depicted within your dream, see relevant subcategory. See suggested course of action.

APES, MONKEYS (Baboon, Capuchin, Chimpanzee, Gibbons, Gorilla, Guenon, Macaque, Marmosets, Orangutan, and Tamarin):

First, these animals are unclean; see Note 7: Clean and Unclean Animals, at the beginning of this category. If animal was crushed, hurt, or killed, see Note 6. With that you can realize more fully the symbolic nature of apes and monkeys, see the following.

Apes (chimpanzee, gibbons, gorilla, and orangutan): The depiction of an ape personifies one who was/is a victim of a tragic violation (e.g. bullying, diabolical cult practices, exploitation on some level or another, emotional or physical abus e, molestation, murder, rape, or robbery). Dreamer, as painful as this may hurt two things must be said (choose one). (1) Dreamer, if you are a victim of a tragic violation at this very moment in your life, there is a need to take action. To help with the pain of it all, Jesus will strengthen you emotionally, psychologically, and physically to go get help via the police, judicially, a Christian based support group, counseling, healthcare, inpatient, that your problems may be address at the root. Dreamer, go get help, God is opening a door for you, moving people, places, and circumstances around and in place, restraining wickedness, that you might go and receive the help needed to free you from this violation. The "time line" is short for you to move beyond the challenges of your violation, so seize the opportunity that is before you now. Allow your deliverance and healing to begin. Further, God will, if allowed, take your tragedies, and turn them into a door of hope for you and a beacon of light for others via you. Additionally, your dream was sent to counsel you to forfeit those habits of doom you've grown so accustom too, and for you to let go of anyone or anything that will hinder you from surrendering your life to Christ wholeheartedly. In this, you will find the strength to move on from that dark place and to further your growth. Dreamer, stretch your hands to Jesus, and He will lead you through the darkness, allow Him to be your light. See suggested course of action. (2) As painful as this may hurt, this question is necessary. Dreamer, if the violation is over, and hopefully it really is and you've moved on with your life, how and when do the negative effects of your violation stop playing a significant role in your life? A few examples of how the negative effects may play a significant role in your life. The dreamer may perhaps embrace words, and/or habits that make you feel confused, embarrassed, foolish, incapable, and unsettled. You may privately insinuate to yourself that you lack the ability, character, and/or strength, required to do something, or that you're not good enough to function or perform adequately, none of which is true. Justifying to yourself that you are not the right person, or "they" just do not like you anyway. You may unconsciously make yourself an object of scorn and contempt, subsequently causing you to lose confidence in yourself. Dreamer, because of your issues with a tragic violation, and the resulting pains and defense mechanisms that followed, you are hindering yourself from becoming the man or woman God needs for you to be at this moment in time, to fulfill your primary purpose for His Kingdom. Dreamer, if you genuinely acknowledge, struggle with, and overcome, your feelings of low esteem, fear, and any other psychological and/or emotional traumas that have resulted from your victimization, you will be restored to health, and will become the strong person needed to handle the blessings intended for you. You are now being asked to devote yourself to embracing Jesus and His teachings that you may go on to spiritual maturity, and go on to perfection through faith in God, which is a resolute trust in the integrity of God and in His Word. For, your time of missions is upon you. You are sent to those who are spiritually dead, yet a spark of life is hidden within them (also see Matthew 28: 19, 20). Dreamer, God's grace, and His promises are abounding towards you; very great blessings are coming quickly and in full measure to you. If you submit to Jesus' ways and means, His teachings, you will become renowned for your expertise and passion, as you go forth using your past to teach those whom you are destined to reach. Dreamer, this is also necessary to state, it was necessary for you to experience what you experienced so that you could develop a skill to the point of perfection, or be brought to a point of perfection that you may empathically understand situations that violate others, and subsequently devote yourself to this type of ministry in a specialist type position. As well, when you understand and respect why God allowed you to go through certain situations, this releases you from the situation on that very day.

In addition, the following are common words; expressions or usages (e.g. slang or clichés) or a 'probable' that are metaphorically represented by one or more of these animals:

- **800-pound gorilla:** This denotes a person or organization so powerful that it acts without regard to the rights of others or the law
- Someone who is sociable and intelligent
- A brutal person, especially a hired thug

Monkeys (baboon, capuchin, guenon, macaque, marmosets, and tamarin): This dream has three meanings (choose one). (1) Dead monkey: The dream signifies that the dreamer is being delivered from the monkey characteristics within your life. (2) Feeding a monkey: This dream denotes that dreamer is deceitful; consequently, comforted with lies, you will be betrayed by a flatterer. (3) The depiction of a monkey personifies one who is vain; excessively prideful; especially in your appearance; futile; and one who embraces the false imitations of this world. Although, you are emotionally dependent, you have an addictive personality, with a strong tendency to draw others into your circle of deceit. You are one who causes seri ous trouble, damage, and hurt to others, oftentimes intentionally. Dishonesty, foolishness, mischief, and vengefulness are all attributes of your character. You believe that fundamental

Christianity devalues and distorts rational thinking behind the m ask of faith. Your point of view is that God and the Bible are myths; and you are highly vocal when expressing definite opinions about that fact. Dreamer, the Lord gives wisdom and from His mouth comes knowledge and understanding. When wisdom enters your heart and knowledge becomes sweet to your soul, discretion will protect you, understanding will guard you, and God's Truth will lead you. To deliver you from the ways of demons whose words and ways are perverse, who causes you to walk in darkness gladly, whose paths are crooked and devious, causing you to leave straight paths (Proverbs 2:1-6, 9-15). Dreamer, Jesus loves you; thus, He is petitioning you to accept Him as your personal Savior, for you are valuable in His eyes. If you will accept the Heavenly Father's Words, via the Bible, and store up His principles, and His ways and means within you, turning your ear to wisdom and applying your heart to understanding, calling out for insight and crying aloud for discernment, Jesus will meet you. The first step in receiving Him as your personal Savior is repentance (see in the Holy Bible, Acts 2:37 -41). Repentance is seeking pardon for having done something awry, and for having hurt someone, and expressing sincere feelings of regret and brokenness. To Jesus pray, Psalm 51:1-19. To individuals, a phone call or a letter of apology is a good place to start, if appropriate. Moreover, this, coupled with a lifestyle of prayer and fasting, followed by appropriate application of wisdom, and you will know the Messiah, Jesus Christ, intimately, and find the knowledge of God you seek. This is one of God' s covenant promises to you. Have faith in this. See suggested course of action.

In addition, the following are common words; expressions or usages (e.g. slang or clichés) or a 'probable' that are metaphorically represented by monkeys:

- Someone who is childish and mischievous
- Somebody who has been made to look foolish or ridiculous
- One who has an addiction to drugs
- Someone who has a serious problem or serious difficulties
- One who imitates others

BEAR:

This dream has two meanings (one or both may apply). The depiction of a bear personifies someone who is very intense and loyal, with the potential to become a great leader nationally. However, this person is deadly, especially if there is a loss of his or her position to anyone. Couple this with one of the following, to see more fully the meaning. (1) If the animal was threatening, or if dreamer was eaten by this animal within your dream this implies someone, namely the dreamer, who is aggressively violent, brutal, and offensive as a leader (in any capacity), a wicked and vindictive ruler over humble and underprivileged people. Taking advantage of their spiritual and natural poverty, necessity, and inability to help themselves, making them poorer and needier than they were before meeting you, while you give nothing in return (especially in the form of service). Your dream comes as a rebuke. You live in excess, mischievousness, and unruliness, to the point of recklessness; and not only so, but you trample those you consider less than yourself, you are harmful to those about you; blaming your lack of anointing, faithfulness, commitment, and stewardship on others. The judgement of the Lord is imminent. See suggested course of action. (2) If the bear was killed, disappeared, or your got away somehow, the dreamer will begin to embrace the positive sides of your nature. In this, you will show yourself to be loyal, a great leader, and one who is deeply profound, having great perception, understanding, knowledge, and charity. Moreover, the dreamer will overcome the cruel jealously of a repressive leader within your life. This animal is considered unclean; see Note 7: Clean and Unclean Animals at the beginning of this category. See suggested course of action.

In addition, the following are common words; expressions or usages (e.g. slang or clichés) or a 'probable' that are metaphorically represented by a bear:

- One who has a bad-tempered
- Something difficult to endure or experience
- Unfavorable business conditions

BIRDS (Albatrosses, Bat, Bittern, Canary, Cardinal, Chicken, Cock, Cormorant, Crane, Dove, Duck, Eagle, Falcon, Finch, Hawk, Gannet, Goose, Grouse, Halcyon, Hen, Heron, Lark, Ostrich, Owl, Partridge, Peacock, Pelican, Penguin, Petrel, Phoenix, Pigeon, Quail, Raven, Redbird, Rooster, Seagull, Songbirds, Sparrow, Swallow, Stork, Swan, Thrush, Turkey, Vulture, Yellow Bird):

As this category is extensive, most birds are not listed. See Note 7 at the beginning of this category, if needed, to help determine if your bird is clean or unclean. If animal was crushed, hurt, or killed, see Note 6. Otherwise, you can realize more fully the symbolic nature of some birds see the following.

Feathers, Plumage: The dreamer is under extreme duress because of your labor and sacrifices within Christendom. Very soon, your diligence will be recompensed according to your capacity to handle prosperity. You will be comforted and ministered to by others. Do continue to allow your Heavenly Father's will to be done in your life state of affairs. Further, the reproach of your past will be taken away, and if ill, you will be totally healed and made whole, physically, emotionally, and psychologically.

Birds (to see any kind of birds flying overhead in the air): The selfish accumulation of wealth is never a worthy goal for the servant of the Lord. As long as you fixate on money, on the things of this world, and on those who are rich, when in actuality, they have only the shadow and appearance of riches; genuine wealth will remain elusive to you (also see 1 Peter 1:7; Revelation 3:17-19). Will you make yourself blind to God's ways for money? The dreamer is counseled not to be like those who covet riches and will do anything to get those riches. For the love of money, people will deceive, defraud, and swindle, and they don't care who they hurt or beat. A man or woman will sell his or her body, a Christian his or her soul. This attitude will separate you from God (Mark 8:36-37). Dreamer, taking advantage of, lying, stealing from others, and/or building your empire on the backs of those you stand before, especially the poor, while boasting of your riches is disgraceful. When trouble and humiliation come because of your arrogance and deceitfulness, and there will be speed in execution of judgment (divine reprimand for folly and sin), the Lord will not cover your shameful nakedness, no, not this time. Consider your dream sufficient warning. If necessary, see suggested course of action. Other behaviors, within you, can be determined by the type of bird flying, see one of the following.

Bat: Two things (choose one). (1) If your dream is about another, first see Note 3 of this category, to determine if your dream is actually about another. If your dream is truly about another, then dreamer must choose to separate from the one who is deemed a bat, in order to further your growth. The correct choice will add, not just to your character, but will also enhance your relationship with Jesus. For it is only by shining the light of truth and knowledge on your dark places that yo u can be freed from its influence. (2) Otherwise, the depiction of a bat personifies one, namely the dreamer, who is resentful and vindictive. As well, you are secretly prone to ideas that fuel hatred and excuse violence, thereby, causing a serious threat to others, and you will attempt to convert others to your violent and profane beliefs. You will "cross the line" with others. Moreover, outwardly, you will change your behavior to suit the circumstances of a particular situation in order to gain an advantage over others. You easily and frequently change and/or alter your beliefs and views, superficially, according to the situation. Dreamer, as long as you seethe in resentment and vindictiveness, just know that God will not ignore those who are hurt by you. Word of Wisdom, there is only one force that can break the power of hatred and resentment, and that is the rule of the Holy Spirit within one's life. When you stand for what is just and right, God will stand with you. On another vein, if you've been so hurt by others, that now, you also uncontrollably hurt others, to the point that you feel you are a hopeless cause, even to the point of suicide. You will only take all of your hurt with you and descend into some place that is a thousand times worse than what's going on with you right now, and it is not wise to meet your Maker like that. Therefore, you must choose to overcome hurts that your soul might be saved, no longer allow violations to hold sway over your future and eternal destiny. Unfortunately, those who deny the opportunity to change their wicked ways and refuse to treat others with kindness and respect, should not expect kindness and respect from others. Dreamer, make the choice to serve in a cause larger than your wants, desires, pains, and larger than yourself. This bird is considered unclean; see Note 7: Clean and Unclean Animals at the beginning of this category. See suggested course of action.

In addition, the following is a common word, expression, or usage (e.g. slang or cliché), or a 'probable' that is metaphorically represented by this bird:

- One who is unconventional

Bittern, Raven, and Owl: The depiction of a bittern, cormorant, raven, or owl, personifies three personalities (choose one). (1) These birds personify a believer who is so strong that you've put confidence in your flesh, fearing no danger, living carelessly. Erroneously assuming that nothing but good comes to you. Confessing that no one you know can compare with you, or even pretend to be equal with you because of your extraordinary prophetic abilities. God humbles the haughty and causes all of his or her joy and laughter to cease (see Zephaniah 2:15). Dreamer, exaggerated and unrighteous pride always turns a good situation into chaos, and pollutes everyone involved or connected. Moreover, where there is confusion, a lack of sincerity, truthfulness, and vitality, will follow. See suggested course of action. (2) These birds personify a non-Christian, or an unbeliever (one who has no religious beliefs, a non-religious person, or one who has no religious faith or belief in Jesus Christ, or one who does not embrace a personal relationship with Jesus Christ, at present), this animal personifies an arrogant, cruel, hostile, intimidating, immoral, unfriendly, unpleasant, unwise, and foolish individual. With you comes confusion, because of immaturity and unfruitfulness. Justifiably, you are allowed to enter into the home of a believer, or into a congregation, to bring confusion, because of error within a congregation that is allowed to flourish, or because of unrepentant sin in the life of a believer (see #1); this believer is behaving in an unholy manner, and is ungrateful. Additionally, to the non-Christian, Jesus loves you, thus, He is petitioning you to accept Him as your personal Savior, for you are valuable in His eyes. The first step in receiving Him as your personal Savior is repentance (see in the Holy Bible, Acts 2:37-41). Repentance is seeking pardon for having done something awry, and for having hurt someone, and expressing sincere feelings of regret and brokenness. To Jesus pray, Psalm 51:1-19. To individuals, a phone call or a letter of apology is a good place to start, if appropriate. Moreover, if you will accept the Heavenly Father's Words, via the Bible, and store up His principles, and His ways and means within you, turning your ear to wisdom and applying your heart to understanding, calling out for insight and crying aloud for discernment, Jesus will meet you. This, coupled with a lifestyle of prayer and fasting, followed by appropriate application of wisdom, and you will know the Messiah, Jesus Christ, intimately, and find the knowledge of God you seek. For the Lord gives wisdom and from His mouth comes knowledge and understanding. Then you will understand what is right and just and fair, every good path. When wisdom enters your heart and knowledge becomes sweet to your soul, discretion will protect you, understanding will guard you, and His Truth will lead you. To deliver you from the ways of wickedness, and from demons whose words and ways are perverse, who causes you to walk in darkness gladly, whose paths are crooked and devious, causing you to leave straight paths (Proverbs 2:1-6, 9-15). This is one of God's covenant promises to you. Have faith in this. See suggested course of action. (3) On another vein, this bird, or whom the bird represents, Christian or non-Christian, maybe allowed within the life of the dreamer, to support you during a difficult or oppressive situation. Here it should be noted that if God; therefore, will deliver His people, He can choose anybody, and use any means necessary, per His choosing, in effecting their deliverance. In addition, the fact that God uses people who are out of His will does not mean that He approves of evil. These birds are unclean; see Note 7: Clean and Unclean Animals at the beginning of this category. See suggested course of action.

In addition, the following are common words, expressions, usages, (e.g. slang or clichés), or a 'probable' that are metaphorically represented by one or more of these birds:

- These types of birds are symbols of doom, suggesting disaster or failure
- Someone who is meditative, sober, and who can discern others
- One who is greedy and/or predatory

Crane, Dove, Pigeon, and Swallow: While your dream was sent as a message of grace, to encourage, it is also sent as a dire warning. Dreamer, be encouraged, you are surely one who is very loyal, graceful, and harmless. You are faithful to Christ, meek and of a quiet temperament. You have fixed your eyes upon the splendor of the King. As a peacemaker and mediator, you bring harmony to all whom your life touches. You have a beautiful spirit in the sight of God. Christ delights in you; therefore, you may find rest in Him. On the other hand, your dream is also sent as a dire warning. The dire warning, dreamer, because you have demonstrated a lack of sensible, practical, and sagacious reasoning, you have been easily deceived. As a result, you are experiencing unhappiness and a sense of hopelessness, and you are becoming heartless, having, or showing no pity or kindness towards other, although, your own choices have brought you to this point. Conscious of your behavior, out of fear and shame, you have drawn back from the Lord, and have begun acting impractical and juvenile, a type of foolish insecurity. You shun even coming into His presence via praise, worship, and prayer. Your prayers, regarding your torment, are sporadic, and oftentimes interrupted, with grievances, groans, and desperate mourning. With that said, dreamer, you are being (or will be) humbled, by means of a sickness. This sickness is allowed to teach you to be sensible, practical, and sagacious in your reasoning. Pray Psalm 38:1-22, coupled with an authentic change in reasoning and attitude. Dreamer, begin embracing and practicing practical and sound judgment, and become aware intuitively and empathetically of people, places, and situations, and your prayers will be heard and accepted by God and will be answered. Christ is calling you back unto Himself. He invites you to once again, enter into a spiritual union with Him. Dreamer, God will purge you from your insensible and bad thinking, only come boldly to the throne of grace. It is suggested that you make time to be private with the Lord. The presence of the Holy Spirit is with you during this hard time in your spiritual life, this crisis of your faith, and your voice of prayer will be acceptable and sweet to God, moreover, read Jeremiah 29:11-13. Additionally, if applicable, teach your children the benefits of wise and sensible thinking, and dedicate your children to the Lord. While the dedication is by faith, have a literal private and personal ceremony amongst your immediate family for this dedication, a "quasi" bar mitzvah (a bar mitzvah is a ritual ceremony that marks the 13th birthday of a Jewish boy, after which he takes full responsibility for his moral and spiritual conduct). This ceremony can be done for girls too; a 'quasi' debutante ball (a very formal event where a young lady makes her debut into society, after which she also takes full responsibility for her moral and spiritual conduct). Your children will sit, and be rulers, amongst the righteous. For they are chosen and part of a royal priesthood, a holy nation, a people for God's own possession that they and you may proclaim the excellencies of Him, who has called you. These birds are considered clean; see Note 7: Clean and Unclean Animals at the beginning of this category.

In addition, the following are common words; expressions or usages (e.g. slang or clichés) or a 'probable' that are metaphorically represented by one or more of these birds:

- A representation of the Holy Spirit, and one who is a supporter of peace
- Somebody who is easily swindled or deceived, gullible

Eagle, Falcon, Hawk: The depiction of an eagle, falcon, or hawk personifies someone who has a clever, quick mind, with the ability and vision to accomplish a great deal in a short period-of-time. Regrettably, this skill has lured you into a false sense of security. Erroneously assuming that nothing but good comes to you. Confessing that no one you know can compare with you, or even pretend to be equal with you. You've put confidence in your flesh, fearing no danger, living carelessly. You harbor wicked thoughts, is ruthlessly aggressive, determined, and persistent, as well as greedily eager to steal from, or destroy, others for gain. God humbles the haughty and causes all his or her joy and laughter to cease (see Zephaniah 2:15). Your own conduct and actions have brought (or will bring) this upon you in some form or another. Favorably, in spite of all this, spiritual renewal is accessible to you now. Jesus is petitioning you to cleanse the evil from your heart that you might be restored into a right relationship with Him. Dreamer, although you feign courage and confidence, you lack authentic courage, boldness, and enthusiasm. You are actually weak in spirit and unfit for service. Notwithstanding, you can be healed, restored, and strengthened by grace (the free and unmerited favor and beneficence of God). If you are ready to acknowledge that you are weak, and remain mindful of your weaknesses, God will in an extraordinary way, increase your strength. For when we are weak, then we are strong in the Lord. The Lord is willing to help you, if you are willing to be helped, and to do your best, with a humble dependence upon Him. You will find that God will not fail you, and you will have grace sufficient for renewal of strength and anointing. These birds are unclean; see Note 7: Clean and Unclean Animals at the beginning of this category. See suggested course of action.

In addition, the following are common words; expressions or usages (e.g. slang or clichés) or a 'probable' that are metaphorically represented by one or more of these birds:

- One who is a ruthless swindler or con, who preys on unsuspecting victims, also called a shark
- A symbol of military or political power
- "Eagle-eyed", to see or have eagle's eyes, denotes one who is great foresight

Fowls, Poultry (Chicken, Cock, Duck, Goose, Grouse, Hen, Rooster, Partridge, or Turkey): This dream has four meanings (one, two, or three may apply). (1) Hear a Cock, Rooster crow: Your dream denotes a denial of Christ. See Matthew 10:33. (2) Chicken Fight (if the fowl, poultry is fighting): Your dream personifies one, especially one who is an animal fight pro moter or enthusiasts, who embraces the exact opposite of the attributes of this animal. Instead of representing a vision of peace, you are the seat of hostility and confusion, a rebellious kind. Abuser and accuser; your hostility is great. You ill -treat and/or victimized the men and women of God. Favorably, because of God's great love and long-suffering towards you, your dream was sent to a rebellious person, in the spirit of grace (the free and unmerited favor and beneficence of God). To see if you will yet be worked upon, and change your mindset, or else to leave you inexcusable, in your accusations against God, because of your ruin (also see Jeremiah 9:7-9; Zechariah 13:9; Malachi 3:3; Matthew 23:37-39; Revelation 3:15-21). The more God allows you to see your emptiness it is, suggested that you be more earnest to repent that you may find H im to be grace and healing, refreshment, and a refuge. You are morally unclean. See Note 7: Clean and Unclean Animals at the beginning of this category. See suggested course of action. (3) The depiction of any type of fowl (cooked or not, and no matter the recipe, e.g. eggs), personifies someone who is an extraordinarily gifted minister, evangelist, teacher, or pastor. Commissioned by God, to guide and instruct the people of God in the things of God that they may be gathered unto God at the time appo inted for that event. You are kindhearted and intuitively concerned for souls. Unfortunately, you are mistreated by some, dodged, and victimized by others. Some hostility is so great, they consider you a fool, and your inspiration is considered the word s of a maniac. Although, your abusers and accusers suppose they're doing God's will by coming against you (and they will come against you, i f not already), they don't know Him, nor His will, regarding why they are coming against you, they are in error. But for you, this is necessary to say. Matthew Henry's Commentary: Our Lord Jesus by giving us notice of trouble, is designed to take off the terror of it, that it might not be a surprise to us. Of all the adversaries of our peace, in this world of troubles, none insult us more violently, nor put our troops more into disorder, than disappointment does; but we can easily welcome a guest we expect, and being fore-warned are fore-armed, Praemoniti, praemuniti. Therefore, the purpose of the dream, to your harm their behavior will or has caused a spirit of animosity within you, from which you need (or will need) restoration. How do y ou feel knowing that some feel this way about you? Are you offended? Are there feelings of weariness, discouragement, embarrassment, hostility, rage, resentment, and/or revenge? You may feel a bit discombobulated, or perhaps you may shrug your shoulders as to say, "it's neither here or there", then again, you may feel a need to dissimulate. Unfortunately, their feelings or thoughts will be directly expressed to you; therefore, being warned beforehand, is meant to take some of the sting out of their words. For you, dreamer, take the "fight", out of your feelings, as well as any other negativity within you. V isualize yourself presenting the negativity to the feet of God as an enemy of His Kingdom (Psalm 110:1, Matthew 22:44), as an enemy of your spiritual work, and of your purpose, via prayer. Dreamer, you have in Christ, grace, healing, refreshment, and a ref uge. Embrace the help your Heavenly Father is offering you, via a sabbatical, and the effects of their negativity will no longer hold sway over your heart. (4) If bird was prepared in some manner for cooking or eating, this personify someone who is entering into the process of spiritual and emotional cleansing or someone who has completed the process and is on their way to the next juncture. This choice has three parts (choose one). (a) If dreamer was eating or getting ready to eat poultry, no matter the recipe, (e.g. cooked eggs, fried chicken, baked hen, roast duck): You are entering into a process of being purified and purged, examined, proven and tested, spiritually and emotionally cleansed. Everything that's unusable within you will give way to that which is beneficial and profitable, and that which is dull, but desirable, will become brightly polished, and all according to God's good pleasure. Your pride will soon give way to humbleness, dignity, honor, and righteous self -esteem, your foolishness to peace and wisdom, and your fear to love. This process will also heal the animosity within you. Allow the process without complaining or murmuring for it is preparing you for a great journey. Be as one who gets satisfaction from embracing good habits. (b) If someone else was cooking, and/or serving poultry: There is an old saying, "When the student is ready, the teacher will appear". Dreamer, you are the student, another is your teacher, and you are ready. Although, you may be very accomplished, prosperous, and/or wise, you have need of a teacher at present. God is sending someone into your life to help you carry out your next undertaking, by enlarging your spiritual capacity. This person is modest and unassuming in attitude, behavior, and dress. Notwithstanding, great respect towards them is appropriate and required, as well as some form of compensation. You will need to be honest, open, and transparent, to get what you need from him or her. Your undivided attention is required, thus you may need to take a vacation from your normal business and/or ministerial activities. Your dream is to bring about an awareness of this person's coming, and to prepare you to meet them sagaciously. Additionally, they will not feed your vanity. (c) If dreamer was cooking and/or preparing to serve (or was serving) others, poultry, no matter the recipe: Dreamer, you have completed the process of spiritual and emotional cleansing. This process has healed your animosity and healed you physically. It has also instilled within you an appropriate and balanced confidence in your own merit as an extraordinarily gifted minister, evangelist, teacher, or pastor, a unique individual operating on a rather different waveleng th than most of your contemporaries. Your course, now, should be towards developing your mind at searching out truth; and becoming skilled at translating very old schools of religious thought into useful wisdom tools for today. This process has also prepared you to properly, provide one of God's wisest servants with the necessary knowledge to carry out something. Your wisdom will refresh this person spiritually. A cherished friendship will result. Note, compliments merely feed vanity, you are sent to provide spiritual nutrients that feed the soul, making way for this person to operate at a higher capacity. The following (8) considerations are for the dreamer to reflect upon and hold closely in your heart, perhaps journal, that you may be successful in your endeavors. (I) Hold back your enthusiasm. Dreamer, when you are too enthusiastically eager and moving too fast and powerful. What you do, namely your behaviors and words, are felt, done, and expressed too forcefully and intensely. In this heightened state, you become too overly bearing, overly sensitive, too easily provoked or aroused, and quick to anger; thus, not easily received by others. You also tend to keep changing your mind, enthusiastic about something then unenthusiastic about it. (II) As a teacher, do not present as vain, and absolutely do not become sexually attracted to, involved with, or excited by any student, whether consenting adult or not, no matter whom the student. (III) Do not present, as one having some type of esoteric knowledge that no one knows about, or as overly wise. (IV) Know that what you are teaching may not be new, fresh, exciting, or popular. (V) Do not present as controversial, provoking opposition over principles, sparking disagreements and uncomfortable and unpleasant discussions. (VI) Do not follow too closely your student; being overly particular about things, requiring immediate attention to concepts or ideas. (VII) Keep away from absurd or obscene humor; that which lacks any meaning that would give purpose to the subject or topic at hand. (VIII) Reveal the source of your knowledge, Jesus Christ being the core source and other resources.

In addition, the following are common words; expressions or usages (e.g. slang or clichés) or a 'probable' that are metaphorically represented by one or more of these birds:

- A cowardly or timid person
- A situation in which it is impossible to know which of two related circumstances occurred first and caused the other
- To organized your life or a specific task so that it runs smoothly
- To have a natural talent for something
- Spur somebody to action
- To destroy something that is or has been a regular, dependable source of profit or benefit
- To complain in a grumbling, often self-serving way
- An arrogant, cocky or vain man
- Something that fails or flops, especially a bad performance
- An offensive term that deliberately insults somebody regarded as unintelligent, incompetent, or socially inept
- Deliberately insult a woman's personality, activity, and age
- A person lacking seriousness; given to too much frivolity and foolishness
- To talk honestly and bluntly
- "Talk turkey" (a turkey was highlighted in some way, e.g. mimic gobbling), see category, Talking

Ostrich: The depiction of an ostrich personifies an unconcerned parent, pastor, or anyone that keeps an eye on, or is responsible for, someone(s) in one way or another; as well as cruelty and desolation. This person, male or female, is a careless and unfeeling parent, pastor, ministry leader, supervisor, or anyone that keeps an eye on, or is responsible for, someone(s) in one way or another (e.g. baby sitter, bishop, CEO, day care provider, elder care provider, mentor, mother, nanny, pastor, special education provider, social worker, supervisor, teacher, youth service provider). You treat those you are responsible for, including your own family, as though you do not know them at all. To you, emotionally, they're strangers; thus, what concern are they to you. You exhibit sociopath tendencies. Not mindful of the atrocities that happens in both, the secular and spiritual arenas, you put those you should be caring for in harm's way; sacrificing them to systems, situations, or persons such as adoption agencies, foster care, abandonment, or leaving them with known abusers of children, child molesters, or any money making schemes. To leaders and supervisors, you cause those under you, such hardships that they leave their place in search of another, exposing them self to the wiles of the devil, and/or you force unemployment on others (e.g. termination of someone's employment), because of your antisocial personality, jealously, or some other abusive intent, while you continue to thrive. You are concerned only with your continued existence, at any expense. Devaluing those you should be protecting and nurturing, and allowing wickedness to prevail, while closing your eyes to it all, are all principles based on values that are not only increasingly unstable, but also vile. Further, know that while you treat God's child badly, God will remove your authority from over them, and restore them to better and easier times. To whom the dream represents, without a spiritual conversion, you will find it almost impossible to rise above your lack of natural affection and wisdom. Moreover, dreamer, be not deceived, God is not mocked; you will reap what you've sown (see Nehemiah 5:9, Galatians 6:7, 8). This bird is considered unclean; see Note 7: Clean and Unclean Animals at the beginning of this category. See suggested course of action.

In addition, the following is a common word, expression, or usage (e.g. slang or cliché), or a 'probable' that is metaphorically represented by this bird:

- Someone who tries to avoid unpleasant situations by refusing to acknowledge that they exist (e.g. serious denial)

Peacock or Penguin: The depiction of a peacock or penguin personifies someone, especially a male, who has recently adopted a bourgeois mentality. This bourgeois mentality is concerned only with your personal comfort, material wealth, and status, at any expense. Now, having in yourself nothing that you respect more than power and greed, you are willing to sacrifice all, God, principle, family, and friend, to the image or idol of vanity. Your new way is based on exploring alternatives to God's righteous principles, as well as, creating a sense of unity with the wickedness around you. This mentality sacrifices children, family, and morality, to the hollowness of satisfying immoral desires and appetites. All carried out, with the hop e of finding happiness by pacifying jealously and covetousness. Dreamer, the selling-out of self over to immorality, allowing wickedness to prevail in your life and in your home, devaluing those you should be protecting and nurturing, while closing your eyes to it all, are all principles based on values that are not only vile, but also increasingly unstable. This way cries out against godly ethics, and its' end offends any sense of godliness. Your recklessness can be remedied by prayer and heartfelt repentance to Jesus and to individuals affected by your actions, in the form of an apology (if possible). Repentance is seeking pardon and expressing sincere feelings of regret and brokenness for having done something awry and/or for having hurt someone, see 2 Corinthians 7:10, 11, also see Deuteronomy 6:10-15; 11:10-28. To individuals, a phone call or a letter of apology is a good place to start. To Jesus pray, Psalm 51, this coupled with prayer and fasting, and followed by appropriate application of wisdom, can conceivably avert some of the repercussions of your choices. This is known as leaving a blessing behind. This bird is considered unclean; see Note 7: Clean and Unclean Animals at the beginning of this category. See suggested course of action.

In addition, the following is a common word, expression, or usage (e.g. slang or cliché), or a 'probable' that is metaphorically represented by this bird:

- Someone who is very arrogant and vain, and who shows this especially in the way he or she behaves and dresses

Pelican, Seagull, Albatrosses, Cormorant, Gannet, and Petrels: The depiction of a pelican personifies someone who believes that they are so strong that they fear no evil. Confident that nothing but good will follow them; they live careles sly and disregard danger. Dreamer, you obey no one, and accept no correction. You do not trust in the Lord, nor do you draw near to Him. Sin will very soon turn your paradise into chaos, and dishonor the beauty of your name. You have chosen to liv e in a place, situation, or amongst people or things that causes you to be confused, desolate, a nd overwhelmed. Where there is confusion, there will soon be emptiness. Your choices, internal conflicts, and living conditions are causing a complete mora l, social, and economic collapse within your life. You are at risk of falling into a state of serious problems and possibly loss of life. So severe are things that restoration can only be by returning to Christ Jesus wholeheartedly. When God hides His face from someone, celebrations are turned into moaning and groaning, and the party is exchanged for depression and solitude. This is the time for you to sit alone to consider your ways. Do not sit alone to indulge in excessive grief, but to repent and retur n or convert to Jesus Christ. Pray: Hear my prayer, O Lord. Let my cry for help come to you. Do not hide your face from me when I am in distress. Turn your ear to me; when I call, answer me quickly. For my days, vanish like smoke, my bones burn like glowing embers.

My heart blighted and withered like grass, I forget to eat my food. Because of my loud groaning, I am, reduced to skin and bones. I am like a pelican of the wilderness (Psalm 102:1-6 NIV). This, coupled with prayer and fasting, and followed by appropriate application of wisdom, can conceivably avert some of the repercussions of your choices. This is known as leaving a blessing behind. This bird is considered unclean; see Note 7: Clean and Unclean Animals at the beginning of this category. See suggested course of action.

In addition, the following is a common word, expression, or usage (e.g. slang or cliché), or a 'probable' that is metaphorically represented by one or more of these birds:

- A person who is gullible and easy to take advantage, or dupe

Phoenix, Halcyon (mythical birds), see category, Monsters.

Quail: The depiction of a quail personifies someone whom the Lord has chosen to be a spiritual watchman or woman. A watchman's religious duties are to pronounce future events, which you will see in prophetic visions, give timely warnings of danger to God's people, especially where none is suspected, warn the wicked to turn from their way, from danger, that they may live. You are to warn of the enemies' approach, strategies, and to comfort, and sympathize with those who need comforting. As you receive the Word of the Lord, you are to present it faithfully and truthfully to His people, and to watch over or see that it is accepted, observed, and obeyed, as much as is possible. You are to keep your finger on the pulse of the peopl e. To see, who makes excuses for sin, who flatter sinners, and who encourages wrongdoers to believe they shall have peace, though the misery of their soul is neigh. If souls perish through the neglect of your duties, you will bring guilt upon yourself. If you warn the wicked, you are not chargeable with their ruin. There will be those, not most, who are offended at ministers who obey their Master's command, and give faithful warnings. They are those who would rather perish, listening to smooth things. Whosoever hears you hear God, and whosoever despises you despises Him who sent you. Dreamer, be encourage, the God who sends you, does have the power to keep and protect you; fear no man (see Psalm 118). You have the capacity to be inspirational, with a primary focus on a personal and saving relationship with Christ Jesus, as well as, the ability to lead merely by your own example. An inborn inner strength and awareness makes you an excellent advisor, philosopher, and teacher. Only do not be habitually careless, irresponsible, or guilty of, failing to properly prepare for your charge. Do not be negligent now, for your slackness will cause those you are purposely sent to, to become unproductive or unprofitable. See Ezekiel 3:18-21; 33:6-20, this scripture is for you. This bird is considered clean, see Note 7: Clean and Unclean Animals at the beginning of this category; however, this bird can become unclean, if disobedience is found within the life of the dreamer. See suggested course of action.

In addition, the following is a common word, expression, or usage (e.g. slang or cliché), or a 'probable' that is metaphorically represented by this bird:

- One that trembles or draws-back with fear or apprehension

Songbirds (Canary, Cardinal or Redbird, Finch, Lark, Sparrow, Thrush): Dreamer, you are facing (or will be facing) a situation or season in which things are becoming very uncertain, difficult, and painful. Dreamer, you're facing a critical moment in your life; something very important to your future will happen and it will change your religious beliefs. This will present a crisis of faith for the dreamer. You may feel as though the Father has turned His face away, and mocked at your dread, and laughed at your calamity. Devastation, feelings of abandonment and betrayal are common. You will begin to shed tears. Your dream is to bring about an awareness; the enemy of your soul has whispered in your ear, where is your God in all of this? Why has He forsaken you in your darkest hour? He, the enemy, has tried to convince you that God has led you into darkness, and not into light. That God has set you in dark places, and when you cry and ask Him why, He has shut out your prayers. These words are not true. Given, while those words may seem to reflect your reality and what you may be feeling o n the inside now, they are not God's reality. Dreamer, know that you are not forgotten, God knows His business, and you are Hi s business. God has not changed His mind about you. Nothing has happen to you that God did not allow, and for good reason. Your own choices have filled you with bitterness, and have caused you shame, disgrace, and contempt. God is simply correcting your unwise, foolish, and shameless brazenness. God's wisdom, care, and guidance, coupled with His divine intervention, has kept you, and will, again, cause your mouth to be filled with laughter, and your tongue with singing. When God reverse this tragedy, you will testify that the Lord has done great things for you, and you will be glad. Your situation will change and He will give you a new song in your heart. You will sing a new song. You wanna hear it, here it goes, when your heart is painfully torn apart, broken, and troubled, and darkness has come and covered all, God can take those disappointments, those trials, and tragedies, that experience, and make them a door of hope for you. These birds are considered clean; see Note 7: Clean and Unclean Animals at the beginning of this category.

In addition, the following are common words; expressions sin or usages (e.g. slang or clichés) or a 'probable' that are metaphorically represented by one or more of these birds:

- **Yellow Bird:** Denotes a person's true love; the one person you are externally and internally, consciously and subconsciously, attached to with the realization that those feelings will never die; the one person that you know you can't live without.
- **Yellow Bird:** Denotes a signal or warning. Miners used bring yellow birds (canaries) in the mines with them to detect poisonous gases. The birds have more delicate systems than the miners do so when the birds got sick or died the miners knew there were poisonous gasses and they had to get out of there.

Stork, Heron: The depiction of a stork personifies one, namely the dreamer, who is unhappy and feels hopeless. Because of your discontent and miserableness, you have become heartless, having or showing no pity or kindness towards others. You have begun acting impractical and juvenile. You shun even coming into God's presence via praise, worship, or prayer. Dreamer, Christ is calling you out of darkness, and out of ritualistic religion, unto Himself. He invites you to enter into an intimate spiritual union with Him. Pray Psalm 38:1-22. He will purge you from your evil thinking, only come boldly to the throne of grace (the free and unmerited favor and beneficence of God). Consequently, you are being (or will be) made humbled, by means of a sickness. This sickness is allowed to teach you empathy. Dreamer, come to know empathy and humility within your heart, then will your prayers be heard and accepted by God and answered. This bird is considered unclean; see Note 7: Clean and Unclean Animals at the beginning of this category. See suggested course of action.

Swan: The depiction of a swan personifies someone who is spiritually responsible for the death of others, due to your erroneous teachings and beliefs, especially regarding forbidden sexual behavior, e.g. adultery, fornication, polygamy, ritual harlotry, "swinging", same sex attraction, and other harmful sexual behaviors. Dreamer, you believe in a god of your own making, coupled with outrageous claims you have wholeheartedly embraced from other erroneous guides. You say Adonai Elohim creates imperfect beings and then forces them to rise up to a level of perfection, which by design, they are unable to attain, by torturing them, causing millions to suffer in body and soul. You reason that this is God's only way, a path of pa in, torture, and then death. You ask what human being aspires to evolve through this endless agony. You proclaim that God's promises are no more than vague words of doubtful happiness, and implacable laws that promise remote and unknowable joy, under the mask of love of humanity. You say His ways are nothing more than a profound indifference and a ha rdened selfishness. Further, you believe that God's intolerance of sin and the inherent results of sin, mainly separation from Him, as written within Holy Writ, and expressed in Christian dogma, are the picture of an angry god, conjured up by angry, unwis e, and foolish men. You boast of philosophies, which appeal to the lustful desires of human nature, condoning rebellious, unhealthy, immodest, immoral, indecent, lewd, and lascivious, behavior. Desires that if not checked, can and often do lead to early death, as you have personally witnessed. This is what you call love. You exalt your wisdom above the Creator. While you discredit the Creator's wise and sensible guidelines for living life, on this side of eternity, as healthy, humanly, and sanely as po ssible; and in harmony with His provision for life on the other side of eternity, in heaven. You respect your truth, while never acknowledging, it is delivered without grace; thus, it is never enough to fill an emaciated soul. Read, understand, and embrace Galatians 5:13-25. Dreamer, promoting and encouraging others to approach God the Father, without the essential provision He has provided for mankind to approach Him properly; that provision being Yeshua HaMashiach, is not safe and is deceptive. Some call God's provision Jesus, Wonderful Counselor, Mighty God, Everlasting Father, Prince of Peace, our atonement, advocate, liberator, propitiator, and our salvation. It is only through this channel that we may hope through faith to conciliate with our Creator, see John 3:16, Acts 2:37-42, 1 Timothy 2:4-7. Dreamer, reacting in such a "temper tantrum" and rebellious manner, as you have done, because you disagree with certain spiritual principles, is not good. You may not like God's ways and means, but you do have to accept and surrender to them all. For, your human understanding of, and reaction to, spiritual realities is oftentimes crudely green. Dreamer, at this crossroad in your life, it is counseled that you do as the apostle Paul, and count all that you know, all that has brought you to this point, to be worthless (Philippians 3:8). Your dream has come to let you know that there is still hope and time for you to recognize the wrong in what you're doing, feel the regret about your pa st actions, and change your ways and habits. Scripture states that it is impossible for those who have once been enlightened, who have tasted the heavenly gift, who have shared in the Holy Spirit, who have tasted the goodness of the Word of God and the powers of the coming age, if they fall away, to be brought back to heartfelt repentance. Because, to their loss they are crucifying the Son of God all over again and subjecting Him to public disgrace (Hebrews 6:4-6). Favorably, there is still hope and time for you. Dreamer, seize this opportunity to sincerely repent, denounce the erroneous teachings you've embraced, and go on from here. Repentance is seeking pardon and expressing sincere feelings of regret and brokenness for having done something awry and/or for having hurt someone, see 2 Corinthians 7:10, 11. To Jesus pray, Psalm 51, this coupled with prayer and fasting, and followed by appropriate application of wisdom, can conceivably avert some of the repercussions of your choices. This is known as leaving a blessing behind. If you've led others away, humble yourself and apologize, and let them know you was wrong, and let them know, bottom line, their salvation is their own responsibility (Philippians 2:12, 13), moreover, to individuals, a phone call or a letter of apology is a good place to start. Dreamer, I encourage you to seek clarity and understanding from the Lord, regarding your decision making processes and identity issues, and apply His wisdom vigilantly. Go and seek truth for yourself that not all may be eternally lost. If done, during this season within your life, there will be some very dark hours and major conflict (significant in scope, extent, or effect). Encouragingly, this can be replac ed with a beauty or handsomeness that radiates brilliance and righteousness via diligent obedience to God through His Word and endurance. By this, grace (the free and unmerited favor and beneficence of God) and faith will once again be made manifest i n your life. This bird is considered unclean; see Note 7: Clean and Unclean Animals at the beginning of this category. See suggested course of action.

In addition, the following are common words; expressions or usages (e.g. slang or clichés) or a 'probable' that are metaphorically represented by a swan:

- One's final public act, a final appearance, performance, or work, as a farewell to a career or profession
- To wander about idly, especially one regarded as irresponsible and/or selfish

Vulture: This bird is considered unclean; see Note 7: Clean and Unclean Animals at the beginning of this category. This dream has two meanings (one or both may apply). (1) The depiction of a vulture symbolizes one who is a false prophet, used by demonic spirits to carry out evil purposes that you might draw people away from God's truth. Moreover, having forsaken the teachings of Christ, you now believe that the spirits of dead people should, and do; communicate with the living, especially through mediums. Dreamer, Holy Writ does not encourage us to seek those in the domain of the dead, regarding our living here on earth. Wayne Jackson, the Christian Courier, put it this way, "It is not that they are unconscious in their current spirit state; rather, they are estranged from the experiences of this environment". The dead know not anything under the sun (also see Deuteronomy 18:10-12; Ecclesiastes 9:5-6; Isaiah 8:19, 20; Luke 16:27-31). God has given us strong warnings in the Bible on the topic of whether or not we should attempt to contact the dead or other spirits (e.g. angels, saints, deceased family members, or friends). Dreamer, seize this opportunity to repent and denounce the demonic and/or syncretistic teachings and rituals you've embraced, and go on from here. If you've led others away, humble yourself and apologize, and let them know you was wrong, and let them know, bottom line, their salvation is their own responsibility (Philippians 2:12, 13). Unfortunately, at present, dreamer, you are like those in Matthew 25, the unprofitable servants, who are cast into the outer darkness, where there shall be the weeping, and the gnashing of teeth. See suggested course of action. (2) To the dreamer of vultures (with children): Because of your beliefs, your children (ages 13+), in whom you glory in, now worship with spiritists and witches. Even more, your children have attributed their prosperity to the power of demons. Thus, they give to those whom the Lord hates. The prosperity God has provided you and them will begin to abate and your rebellion will be exposed. Your dream warns of great weeping, mourning, and bitter anguish of heart because of your children. Your children practices will eventually lead (or has led) to demonic possession or some other form of spiritual bondage, and may lead to jail time. Your children are not capable of handling the resulting effects of their choices and practices and are not likely to recover from them. Favorably, your situation is not without remedy; but man cannot help you, only God. However, you must help yourself via prayer and heartfelt repentance to Jesus and to individuals affected by your actions, in the form of an apology (if possible). Without repentance, and a renouncing of your thinking and beliefs, your situation will prove impossible to change.

Repentance is seeking pardon and expressing sincere feelings of regret and brokenness for having done something awry and/or for having hurt someone, see 2 Corinthians 7:10, 11. To individuals, a phone call or a letter of apology is a good place to start. To Jesus pray, Psalm 51, this coupled with prayer and fasting, and followed by appropriate application of wisdom, can conceivably avert some of the repercussions of your choices. This is known as leaving a blessing behind. Dreamer, there is indeed help, but you must apply yourself to God's ways and means, and denounce the erroneous teachings you've embraced and passed on to your children, resulting in their separation from the one true God. Turn back to Jesus, seek forgiveness, a nd tangibly, if applicable, participate in the "turning back" of your children to Jesus. See suggested course of action.

In addition, the following is a common word, expression, or usage (e.g. slang or cliché), or a 'probable' that is metaphorically represented by this bird:

- Someone who is a predator (e.g. abuser, molester, murderer, rapist, thief, criminal minded). He or she wait or look eagerly for opportunities to take advantage of others, especially someone weak or helpless. See suggested course of action.

CAMEL (Alpaca, Dromedary, Llama, and Vicuna):

These animals are considered unclean; see Note 7: Clean and Unclean Animals at the beginning of this category. If animal wa s crushed, hurt, or killed, see Note 6. This dream has three meanings (choose one). (1) The depiction of camel, alpaca, dromedary, llama, and vicuna personifies someone who is able to handle great responsibility and wealth, and one who is tolerant. (2) The depiction of camel, alpaca, dromedary, llama, and vicuna also refers to one who is unhappy, disliked, devoid of genuine spirituality, unable to discern between truth and error, and you do not realize that you are these things. You say, "I have need of nothing." Yet, you are excessive regarding immoral impurities (e.g. addictions, cheating, greedy, lying, stealing, unchaste conduct, see 1 Corinthians 6:9-20, Ephesians 5); which cause one's anointing to fade. Hypocrisy is a heavy and unnecessary burden that you bear. Today you possess the ability to choose between good and evil. Therefore, according to your choices, you will define the reward or punishment of your eternity. See suggested course of action. (3) The camel also symbolizes the angel of death, see category, Angels (Death Angel).

Canines (Coyote, Dog, Fox, Hyena, Jackal, and Wolf):

Puppy, see Note 5. The depictions of canines generally personify someone who primarily embraces negative characteristics and behaviors; especially those ascribed to the particular animal. All of these animals in their infant state represent behaviors (associated with that animal) in an early stage of development. Behaviors that if caught early, can be checked and controlled, with prayer, fasting, and disciplined. A non-aggressive action of any canine denotes that the person it represents is being used to help a believer in some way. Nonetheless, all these animals are deadly, and all are unclean; see Note 7: Clean and Unclean Animals at the beginning of this category. If animal was crushed, hurt, or killed, see Note 6. If necessary, see suggested course of action. You will realize more fully the symbolic nature of some canines see the following.

Dog: This dream has seven meanings (choose one). (1) Feeding a dog: See, 2 Corinthians 6:14–2 Corinthians 7:1. Dreamer is embracing a relationship with an unbeliever (one who has no religious beliefs, a non-religious person, or one who has no religious faith or belief in Jesus Christ, or one who does not embrace a personal relationship with Jesus Christ, at present), attempting to share biblical tenets with one who is not interested in your beliefs or your God. Do not give dogs what is sacred (spiritual food). If you do, they will trample it under their feet, and then turn and tear you to pieces (Matthew 7:6). See suggested course of action. (2) Dog was fearful of you, or non-aggressive, or if you overpowered or killed the animal: This implies that the dreamer desires to embrace God wholly and to subdue your carnal nature, putting an end to (or controlling) negative desires and passions, for religious purposes. It is counseled that you use (if not already doing) the principles of discipline and abstinence, via fasting, prayer, and reading and meditating on the Holy Bible in solitude, daily for about 3 hours. Not for study only, or to fill your head with trivia, but that you might as a believer and a spiritual leader, observe to do according to what is written therein; and that you might understand the Word and have it in you when occasion calls for you to know the Word. Moreover, discipline and abstinence helps to control and put an end to ungodly desires and passions. He or she, who will humble them self shall be exalted. If necessary, see suggested course of action. (3) Dog was barking only, no physical attack: Dreamer, someone around you hates you and doesn't agree with your actions, or they hate someone you're close to, possibly the person whom the dog was barking at, if not you. This someone wants to disturb or destroy the ministry you are doing in the name of the Lord (see John 16:2-4) possibly one within your church. They tell you off unfairly. They blame, criticize, or punish you. Insulting, slurring, and disrespecting your zeal for the Lord, they are quick to add insult to injury. Dreamer, some of the criticism is true and some is not. A humble and wise spirit can turn what someone means for harm, into constructive criticism; and so benefit from it spiritually, and be even wiser, instead of being provoked. Also, know the special protection you are under, namely angels, who are ready to protect you, because you are a genuine child of God. As well, it will be revealed clearly and openly, the difference between you and them. For you are great in the Lord, and they will be exposed for the hypocrite they are in the sight of many. (4) Dog tries to (or does) harm the dreamer, is chasing, or following the dreamer, or is threatening and/or wild in any way: This choice has three parts (choose one). (a) The character traits personified by this animal are overtaking the dreamer's life. Your choice of lifestyle will not withstand your storms of life. Your conscience will haunt you. Weakened by frequent panic attacks, brought on by your own guilt and the fear of God's retribution, you will begin to crack in your personality. He, who carries his or her own accuser, and their own tormentor, always in their bosom, cannot but be afraid on every side (Matthew Henry's Commentary on Job 18:11-21). The only foundation upon which one should wisely establish his or her identity is the principles within the Word of God. S ee suggested course of action. (b) An attitude of whining and complaining and/or flirtatious behaviors, have opened a door for the enemy to attempt to do some serious damage. Someone, being used by the enemy, represented by the dog, is sent to mar or tear down the dreamer's relationship with Christ. For example, if you are an unmarried male or female's life, in your weakness, a threatening dog will often represent an ungodly male or female, newly entered into your life, sent to open the door to sexual immorality. If you are involved in a potentially serious relationship with someone, do not be deceived, you are sexually in a weaken state. This relationship (you and the person represented by the dog) is a ploy from the enemy to cause an offense within you against your God, thus God against you. (c) If you are married, your flirtatious behaviors have open doors that welcome situations that often lead to adultery. Dreamer, abstain from sexual immorality; in addition to other morally wrong issues (also see Acts 15:29; 1 Peter 2:11). See suggested course of action. (5) Dead dog: Someone within your life; although powerful and capable of doing much harm; they will no longer do you harm. Consider it a waste of time to pursue or fight back at this point, forgive and progress forward. If a cleric of some kind, the fruit of your behavior is akin to false teachers or deceivers. Dreamer, you have shown yourself presumptuous, when you do not fear to do evil before the Lord or His servants. Your character is one of extreme haughtiness, presumptuousness, pride, and self-assuredness in the very negative sense of the word. All are signs that your heart is hardened. If this disposition is not let go, it will lead to a great fall (Proverbs 11:2 ; 16:18, 19; 29:23). Dreamer, God knows your thoughts afar off, so genuinely repent. Other than heartfelt repentance to Jesus and to individuals affected by your actions, in the form of an apology (if possible), no other excuse or weak justification will be heard. See suggested course of action. (6) A dog also personifies one who is insincere in his or her dealings with people, especially by being outwardly friendly but secretly disloyal. This person will prove deceitful, unstable, phony, and treacherous, as well as one, who will willingly set aside principles and personal integrity in order to obtain something, usually for selfish motives. Of these kinds, we are warned to watch out for (Philippians 3:2). The cost of such behaviors will often lead to one becoming sexually indiscriminate and basely immoral (e.g. prostitute, whoremonger, or one who is sodomitic), as this animal also symbolizes a male prostitute. See suggested course of action. (7) A dog also symbolizes a non-believer (one who has no religious beliefs, a non-religious person, or one who has no religious faith or belief in Jesus Christ, or one who does not embrace a personal relationship with Jesus Christ, at present). See suggested course of action

Black Shuck (aka, devil dog or hellhound, with black shaggy hair and enormous fiery red eyes the size of saucers): Your dream denotes great desolation. According to folklore, it is said that this dog seeks lost souls, and is an indication of doom. Desolation is the inheritance of those who worshipped it. As your dream presents an animal of folklore or myth, it is unclean; see Note 7: Clean and Unclean Animals at the beginning of this category. See suggested course of action. See also Monsters, Mythological or Legendary Creatures, or other Abominable Creatures.

In addition, the following are common words; expressions or usages (e.g. slang or clichés) or a 'probable' that are metaphorically represented by a dog:

- Someone who is a contemptible person and ruthlessly competitive, if they cannot have, or do not want, something, they will try to prevent somebody else from having or doing it also
- To live a wretched existence
- One, who displays wealth or knowledge ostentatiously or pretentiously
- Someone, who will take no action, in a potentially troublesome situation, when they should
- To be followed or troubled persistently by someone

Fox: The depiction of a fox personifies someone who is a professional, or at least a whiz, in the area of theology. However, you are a false prophet and an enemy to believers. You are one who loves to live off others blessings of good stewardship and prudence. Moreover, you are crafty, deceitful, and destructive. It is forbidden for a believer to associate with such a person on any level. See suggested course of action.

In addition, the following is a common word, expression, or usage (e.g. slang or cliché), or a 'probable' that is metaphorically represented by a fox:

- Someone who is charming and good looking, but sly and cunning, this person also brings confusion into situations.

Hyena: The depiction of a hyena personifies someone who disregards caution, diplomacy, discretion, good judgment, good insight, maturity, prudence, responsibility, wisdom. This is a non-spiritual person, dull minded to spiritual things, self-indulgent, hypocritical, and phony. This animal is also biblical associated with unwise and foolish women, false teachers and legalistic Christians, who love to revel in self-righteousness. Dreamer, you have shown yourself presumptuous, when you do not fear to do evil before the Lord or His servants. Your character is one of extreme haughtiness, presumptuousness, pride, and self-assuredness in the very negative sense of the word. All are signs that your heart is hardened. If this disposition is not let go, it will lead to a great fall (Proverbs 11:2; 16:18, 19; 29:23). The harshness of the Lord is kindled against you; you will begin to experience a change in your authority, and favor given from the Lord. Moreover, as He knows your thoughts afar off, repent. Other than heartfelt repentance to Jesus and to individuals affected by your actions, in the form of an apology (if possible), no other excuse or weak justification will be heard. It is forbidden for a believer to associate with such a person on any level. See suggested course of action.

In addition, the following is a common word, expression, or usage (e.g. slang or cliché), or a 'probable' that is metaphorically represented by a hyena:

- One who behaves in a coarse or rude manner

Jackal: The depiction of a jackal personifies someone who is arrogant, deceitful, treacherous, and a swindler. Nocturnal by nature, this person operates under the cover of darkness; coming around primarily at nighttime. He or she is not a believer. However, this person will be allowed to enter into the personal life of a believer, and to stay awhile, in order to separate the believer from someone who is cruel, domineering, and harsh. This is their mission at this time; thus, your dream. Your dream was sent to support and comfort the person of God, namely the dreamer. Dreamer, the one who has been a source of worry, stress, and trouble to you, their time has come. God will put an end to their troubling, using one with the attributes and spirit of a jackal. He or she, the person with the attributes and spirit of a jackal, is just as overbearing, as your oppressor, very capable of matching wit for wit, a formidable opponent for your oppressor. Dreamer, although you are grievously oppressed, sitting down in tears, because of someone's cruelty and haughtiness, God has not forsaken you. Your deliverance will soon follow your dream; your oppressor's day to cease from troubling is here. You need only to be still quietly and see the salvation of the Lord. Even more, your days of prosperity will be restored, because God has mercy in store for you, He has not forsaken nor forgotten you. The injuries done you and the tears you've shed because of another will be reckoned for and revenge will be in the Hands of the Lord. In one hour, things will begin to change. Allow the one with the spirit of the jackal to stay awhile; be aware, it could be one, perhaps kin, who might need a place to stay temporarily. Don't worry this person will be on his o r her best behavior towards you, but will become a source of agitation to your oppressor.

In addition, the following is a common word, expression, or usage (e.g. slang or cliché), or a 'probable' that is metaphorically represented by a jackal:

- One who works with others to deceive people, especially to swindle them out of money

Wolf, Coyote: This dream has a three meaning (choose one). (1) The depiction of a wolf or coyote personifies someone who has a dual nature. You can be on the side of good or evil. You start-off good and turn bad, or you start-off bad and turn good. You are fiery and inflexible, as well as soft and pliable.

369

On the one hand, you're very volatile, stubborn, unyieldin g, and fierce, but not always discerning. Predatorily, you join in with others of like mind, to victimize and exploit people (see Proverbs 1:10-16, 18, 19). You rush for profit without the slightest qualm. Greedily destructive and ruthlessly aggressive, you are the cause of constant anxiety and grief in the lives of those who love or befriend you. You speak abusively against whatever you do not understand and threaten those who genuinely care for God's people. This animal is also connected with a false prophet or shepherd, who feeds only him or herself. You are a great pretender. In this frame of mind, you're brutal, cruel, vicious, violent, without respect of person, and is best avoided. On the other hand, you can be very soft and gentle, long-suffering and meek. Brave and loyal, you are willing to make any sacrifice for your family; and you're true to your friends. Dreamer, your dream comes as counsel and extends grace (the free and unmerited favor and beneficence of God) to you. If you are diligent in bringing into balance your dual nature, subduing your negative traits and double mindedness for the good, you can turn a bad situation into a good one overnight and begin doing mighty works and wonders for the Kingdom of God, like Apostle Paul. Prayer and heartfelt repentance to Jesus and to individuals affected by your actions, in the form of an apology (if possible), are the first steps. Repentance is seeking pardon and expressing sincere feelings of regret and brokenness for having done something awry and/or for having hurt someone, see 2 Corinthians 7:10, 11. To individuals, a phone call or a letter of apology is a good place to start. To Jesus pray, Psalm 51, this coupled with prayer and fasting, and followed by appropriate applica tion of wisdom; and Jesus will meet you on your way back. Have faith in this. As well, you are truly endowed with prophetic insight, akin to that of Jeremiah. See suggested course of action. (2) These animals (wolf and coyote) are also associated with homosexuality and/or one who indulges in very dark and life threatening sexual habits, especially male dreamer. Dreamer, if you are promiscuous, sexually indiscriminate, you may have contracted a very serious sexually transmitted disease, e.g. gonorrhea, HIV, it is suggested that you go and be medically checked, immediately for your health's sake. See suggested course of action. (3) Female dreamer: Your actions are that of a woman desirous of changing sexes. The Lord your God forbids the confusing of the relationships of the sexes, men must not be effeminate or figuratively emasculated by a female, nor must women be virile, masculine, or very domineering, as to usurp authority over a male who has authority over you (e.g. husband, father, pastor, or male supervisor). As disobedience in small matters shows great contempt of God's principles, so obedience in small matters shows a very great regard for them. If dreamer is married, daughter, obey him that has rule over you, especially your husband. Like Sarah, who obeyed Abraham and called him her master, you are her daughter if you do what is right and do not give way to fear (1 Peter 3:6). Notwithstanding, female dreamer, if you do not gain control over your antagonistic and domineering attitude, standing before the Lord improperly, you will begin to experience a loss of glory. Glory in this sense is divine admiration, praise, prosperity, success, triumph, and/or respect of your husband and of others, within your life. See suggested course of action.

In addition, the following are common words; expressions or usages (e.g. slang or clichés) or a 'probable' that are metaphorically represented by a wolf or coyote:

- Someone who is greedy, cruel, and cowardly
- A sexually aggressive or predatory man (e.g. molester, rapist, stalker)
- Someone who brings illegal immigrants into the United States

To cry wolf (depicted by a wolf crying or one shouting the words "wolf" while crying): Your dream denotes one who has given a false alarm or cry for help too many times, so that when help is really needed, no one will believe you or give you h elp. See suggested course of action.

A wolf in sheep's clothing (depicted by a wolf appearing as a sheep, or with wool on its body in some fashion): This denotes somebody who looks harmless or pleasant, but is in fact very dangerous and unpleasant. See suggested course of action.

Keep the wolf from the door (a door and wolf should be highlighted in some way): Your dream denotes the dreamer has enough resources available to you to prevent hunger or homelessness, use the resources that are readily available to you (e.g. social service programs, family, emergency shelters). For these services have their place, at needful times. See suggested course of action.

Throw somebody to the wolves (depicted by one being thrown to wolves): Your dream denotes one who abandoned another, to be destroyed by enemies, in order to save yourself. See suggested course of action.

Werewolf: Your dream denotes masculinity - relating to, or having, the characteristics of an adult male, able to carry out the male sexual function, as well as one who is too strong and forceful. As your dream presents an animal of folklore or myth, it is unclean; see Note 7: Clean and Unclean Animals at the beginning of this category. See suggested course of action.

CATTLE (Bison, Buffalo, Bull, Calf, Cow, Oxen):

If animal was crushed, hurt, or killed, see Note 6. Other than that, generally, the image of cattle personifies someone who is extremely intense, aggressive, physically powerful, robust, sturdy, healthy, thriving, and emotionally resilient. This perso n is also very convincing, knowledgeable, influential, and effective. Couple this with one of the following (choose one). (1) If the animal was docile, domesticated, and/or non-threatening, this represents one who primarily embraces the positive side of the characteristics this animal represents. You are one who has the capacity to exemplify empathy, forgiveness, and understanding. People are drawn to you for absolution, and you are important to the well-being of others, and important as a leader within a ministry. You must always work in the service of God philanthropically, for this is your life's purpose. You are powerfully anointed for this. (2) If the animal was threatening in any way, or if the dreamer was riding the animal wildly, this represents someone in your life who embraces the negative aspects of his or her personality, and will prove to be a very strong adversary and a fiendish person. This person embodies mischievousness and has become an enemy of God's people; using them (the dreamer) for wicked gain. Having proved them self, many times, morally unclean for God's purposes; they will die before their time that their soul might be saved. These animals are considered clean, yet can be made unclean. See Note 7: Clean and Unclean Animals at the beginning of this category. If necessary, see suggested course of action. You will realize more fully the symbolic nature of some cattle as the following gives an interpretation of them.

Bison, Buffalo: The depiction of bison or buffalo personifies one who is very proud, strong, and fierce. This animal is a picture of great and mighty men or women; high rulers (e.g. leading activists, Christian dignitaries, senior clerics, church heads, presidents, prime ministers, heads of state, political rulers, the very affluent). Couple this with one of the following (choose one). (1) If the animal was docile, domesticated, or non-aggressive, this represents one who primarily embraces the positive side of the characteristics this animal represents. To you, your dream is encouragement. You are one who has a proper amount of self-respect. Your behavior is exemplary, living a life of integrity, and can be trusted. You are anointed, charismatic, and have a following to prove it. You also try to live out what you preach; having the necessary emotional qualities to virtuously deal with stress, grief, loss, risk, and other difficulties, authoritatively, knowledgeable, and skillfully. You' re deeply profound and fiercely loyal to God, His people, and to family. (2) If the animal was threatening in any kind of way, or if the dreamer was riding the animal wildly, this represents someone who embraces the negative aspects of his or her personality. To you, your dream is a stern rebuke. You have an exaggerated opinion of your personal worth and abilities and show a lack of humility. You're conceited, egotistical, vain, and possibly sexually immoral (e.g. adultery or fornication). You use your influence to force others to do what you say; this is akin to witchcraft (aka rebellion). You are aggressive, intense, and violent. You are morally unclean. See Note 7: Clean and Unclean Animals at the beginning of this category. See suggested course of action.

In addition, the following are common words; expressions or usages (e.g. slang or clichés) or a 'probable' that are metaphorically represented by a bison or buffalo:

- Someone who aggressively intimidates others
- One who throws others into a state of confusion; thus, he or she brings, initiates the confusion

Bull: The depiction of a bull personifies someone whose beliefs have been found lacking. Your understanding of, and reaction to, the foundational teachings of Christ Jesus is immature. While you promote John's baptism and his being that of repentance. You fail to wholly promote that which comes after the process of repentance, namely baptisms by water and the Holy Spirit, including the verification that one, beyond doubt, has received the Holy Spirit (see within the Holy Bible, Acts 10:44-48, 19:3-7). You have become obstinate; refusing to believe and/or publicly aligned yourself with "The Way" (Acts 9:2). You exalt your wisdom above the Creator's, when Jesus has openly expressed, it is proper to experience it all that you may fulfill all righteousness (see Matthew 3:15-17), especially if one live long enough, after receiving Christ as their Savior to experience it all. In addition, you boast of knowledge that appeals to the lustful desires of human nature, condoning rebellious, unhealthy, immodest, immoral, indecent, lewd, and lascivious, behavior. Desires that if not checked, can and often do lead to early death (as you have already seen). All of these choices expose, and say something about, your lack of love for God, and the things of God. You diligently study the Scriptures because you think that by them you possess eternal life. Yet, while they testify of Jesus as the door to eternal life, you refuse to come to Him, to have that life. You do not have the l ove of God in your heart, for you do not accept all of Him (see John 5:39-47). Dreamer, he that kills with the sword (the Word) will be killed by the sword, for the Lord is righteous. Favorably, the Creator has granted you a year's reprieve or pardon to set things in order. Now I will show you the excellent way, begin unconditionally to love God and others. For without love, especially for God, you have nothing (see 1 Corinthians 13:1-12). However, at present, you are morally unclean. See Note 7: Clean and Unclean Animals at the beginning of this category. See suggested course of action.

In addition, the following are common words; expressions or usages (e.g. slang or clichés) or a 'probable' that are metaphorically represented by a bull:

- One who talks a lot about nothing
- Someone who deals with difficult situations forcefully and decisively
- An investor who buys stocks, in anticipation of rising prices, with the intention to resell them soon, for profit; additionally, an attempt, by someone, to raise prices in a particular commodity or market by buying large quantities, reducing availability and increasing demand

Calf (including Golden Calf): This dream has two meanings (choose one). (1) The depiction of a calf personifies someone who is patience, humorous, playful, optimistic, and one who is a worshiper of God. However, your sins have been your downfall! Your dream has come to let you know that prayer and heartfelt repentance to Jesus; will bring God's blessings once again. Repentance is seeking pardon and expressing sincere feelings of regret and brokenness for having done something awry and/or for having hurt someone, see 2 Corinthians 7:10, 11. To Jesus pray, Psalm 51, this followed by appropriate application of wisdom, can conceivably avert some of the repercussions of your choices. Dreamer, return to the Lord. Take words with you and return to the Lord. Say to Him, "Forgive all my sins, and receive me graciously that I may, once again, genuinely, and freely, offer the fruit of my lips to you. Set yourself apart that you may be sanctified unto the Lord. For, if you reverence His name, behaving according to His morality, you will be made free. Then, healing, justice, and honesty regarding you will happen. Moreover, you will overcome those who have treated you badly; they will be as nothing on the day when the Lord restores justice and honesty over your life. This is known as leaving a blessing behind. To be blessed: Gifts of God's grace, anything God freely gives you, absolution, the Holy Spirit, salvation, regeneration, eternal life, health, children, love of family, longevity, necessities, prosperity, and dominion over all that is yours; and all are parts of the supply of grace, an d all are sanctified by the Lord, and technically belongs to Him. The result of this supply in your life will be peace. All of this will also be confirmed by one of the Lord's prophets, expect him or her. However, now, you are morally unclean. See Note 7: Clean and Unclean Animals at the beginning of this category. See suggested course of action. (2) Golden Calf: Your dream reveals severe sin in the life of the dreamer, and there is a great concern regarding the severing of your saving relationship with Christ, by a rejection of all or some of the original foundational teachings of Christ and His apostles. You resist truth; have resorted to deception; and have relapsed back into immorality. This type of attitude is spiritually poisonous to a believer. Not only have you brought guilt and ill repute upon your own head, but upon those within your family, and a ministry. Additionally, this animal (golden calf) is also a symbol of idolatry. Idolatry is "foreign service", any act that expresses devotion or fanatical admiration to something or someone other than Adonai Elohim), or any traits of these sorts (see 1 Corinthians 6:8-11). Which means the dreamer is fanatically or obsessively adoring (or devoted) to self, someone, or something. With that said, there i s a great need for repentance, and of seeking forgiveness from others. Oftentimes, a simple, "I'm sorry, please forgive me" will suffice. At other times, a peace offering of some kind or reimbursement is needed. They will let you know. All who touch you reassuringly in any way (handshake, hug, pat on the back), has forgiven you. God is also a forgiving God; therefore, grace (the free and unmerited favor and beneficence of God) is extended and repentance is still possible at this moment. With persistent hard work and effort in correcting your dangerous mindset and lifestyle, you can again remember Jesus, and once more respect His principles. Seek counsel from godly individuals, you will find wisdom with them. Dreamer, without repentance and change, your mindset will cause you, eventually, to forget God; and you will forget, only to remember Him again, with regret, on your "death bed". See suggested course of action.

In addition, the following is a common word, expression, or usage (e.g. slang or cliché), or a 'probable' that is metaphorically represented by a golden calf:

- One who has materialistic goals; who esteems unworthy objects as something, "a materialistic mentality". This is a form of idolatry (idolatry is "foreign service", any act that expresses devotion or fanatical admiration to something or someone other than Adonai Elohim). See suggested course of action.

Cow: The depiction of a cow personifies someone who was born to be a teacher and a nurturer. You should be teaching the elementary truths of God's word to your own children, and/or to those not familiar with the t eachings of righteousness, mainly new converts, and infants in Christ. Your diligent teaching will prepare others to spread the gospel of Jesus Christ; thus, reproducing your teaching ministry and abundantly blessing you. Moreover, you should be receiving wages for your diligence, if indeed you are earnestly diligent, from those you work for (e.g. the ministry you're working for). On the other hand, if you are not teaching those you are purposed to reach, your dream comes as a rebuke. You live in excess, mischievousness, and unruliness, to the point of recklessness; and not only so, but you trample those you consider less than yourself, you are harmful to those about you. Taking advantage of their spiritual and natural poverty, necessity, and inability to help themselves, making them poorer and needier than they were before meeting you, while you give nothing in return (especially in the form of service); all the while blaming your lack of anointing, faithfulness, commitment, and stewardship on others. Dreamer, like those you should be teaching, crave pure spiritual milk (the direct Word of God imparted to us through the words of others, such as a preacher in a worship service, a Sunday school teacher, and other bible studies), so that by it yo u may grow up in your salvation. Nevertheless, to not teach; the dreamer is morally unclean. See Note 7: Clean and Unclean Animals at the beginning of this category. See suggested course of action.

In addition, the following are common words; expressions or usages (e.g. slang or clichés) or a 'probable' that are metaphorically represented by a cow:

- Someone who is quick to anger or agitate

373

Wait until the cows come home (to wait for cows to come to your home should be highlighted): To wait until an extremely long time has elapsed.

Red Cow: This dream has two meanings (one or both may apply). (1) Thus says the Lord, "I will sprinkle clean water on you, and you will be clean; I will cleanse you from all your impurities and from all your idols. I will give you a new heart and put a new spirit in you; I will remove from you your heart of stone and give you a heart of flesh. Moreover, I will put my Spiri t in you and move you to follow my decrees and be careful to keep my laws. You will live in the land I gave your ancestors; you will be my people, and I will be your God. I will save you from all your uncleanness. I will call for the grain and make it plen tiful and will not bring famine upon you. I will increase the fruit of the trees and the crops of the field, so that you will no longer suffer disgrace among the nations because of famine. Then you will remember your evil ways and wicked deeds, and you will loathe yourself for your sins and detestable practices. I want you to know that I am not doing this for your sake, declares the Sovereign LORD. Be ashamed and disgraced for your conduct", (Ezekiel 36:25-33 NKJV). (2) Additionally, the depiction of a red cow also implies pregnancy or a mother cleaning up the mess of her children. Thus, this choice has two parts (choose one). (a) This cow denotes a literal or spiritual pregnancy. The dreamer, or if male, your spouse, is either actually pregnant, or will become pregnant very shortly. If not pregnant, and you desire children, continue to have faith in God, which is a resolute trust in the integrity of God and in His Word, He will have mercy on you, and grant you the desire of your heart, namely to birth children, suddenly and very soon. If pregnancy is not an issue or desire, perhaps due to age, then your dream represents a spiritual pregnancy. A spiritual pregnancy denotes a ministry will be birth from within you, the dreamer. You are full of nurturing abilities; thus, you will become, responsible for a few young men and women being born again into the Kingdom of God (see John 3:1-17). You know how to nurture and accept anyone; therefore, many will be drawn to you, including those, others call "ne'er-do-wells", via your ministry. Under your tutelage, those newly born into the Body of Christ will become strong and active, for the cause of the Kingdom of God. They will be known as persons who speak and does that which is good, counted amongst those who are faithful and submissive to God. Dreamer, be willing, obedient, prepared, and in place (accountable to a specific house of worship, church), for the birthing of your ministry and for those who will become born again because of your ministry. (b) Your dream, of a red cow, may imply a literal mother cleaning up the mess left behind by her child. The mess is a result of the child's sins and impurities. Mother, you have raised him or her up in the way they should go. Do not be worried, no matter their state, they will be purified (freed from sin, guilt, and uncleanness) and made complete. A rectification of sin and impurity will be achieved. As well, there is a need for amends and maturity between a mother and her child. If necessary, see suggested course of action. Dreamer may also see also category, Colors (Red). This animal is considered clean. See Note 7: Clean and Unclean Animals at the beginning of this category.

Ox: This dream has four meanings (choose one). (1) This choice has two parts (both apply). (a) An ox personifies someone who is energetic, witty, playful, harmonious, hardworking, and optimistic, especially within ministry. You are a person of great strength, emotionally, physically, and spiritually. It is important to you that your work assists and/or encourages others in some way. Your natural abilities are given you for the preaching of the gospel and ministerial support of your leaders. You are (or is becoming) a celebrated and powerful man or woman of God, a leader in your own right. Understand, and respect, the value of who you are to God. Moreover, your strength must be used exclusively for the Kingdom of God; to choose otherwise, at this point, will not be beneficial to you, and will devalue you. (b) With that said, dreamer, you have unintentionally wounded someone spiritually, with harsh and uncalled for words, causing mental anguish, heartache, and spiritual pain. The one effected, has drawn back from, or left, the ministry because of you. This incident could have happened as far back as three years ago. The moment is right for you to go and make amends and take some kind of apology and peace offering (e.g. money, gift card, fruit), as this is God's will that you do so. This person was a minister of helps in some manner within the ministry. For you to say you do not know who it is, reveals many have been w ounded spiritually by you, as well as a heart, hardened and self-righteous. If you do not know, the many will be revealed to you publicly. Moreover, you are asked to humble yourself, and go to the many you've hurt with peace offerings and amends. Until apologies are made and peace offerings are presented, you are morally unclean. See Note 7: Clean and Unclean Animals at the beginning of this category. See suggested course of action. (2) Kill an ox: Your dream warns of spiritual murder. Spiritual murder is a premeditated attempt to; cruelly destroy someone's reputation or an attempt to destroy someone's personal relationship with Christ, because of jealously. You are a very difficult person; it takes great effort and hardship, emotionally and spiritually, for others to get alone with you, including your leaders, superiors (anyone who has some authority over you). You are unpleasant, intolerant of others, demeaning and very sarcastic in your expression; imposing stress on your relationship with the Lord, as well as, with others. You have chosen your own ways and your soul delights in hatred. Even your small efforts are blighted because of your attitude. You have killed spiritually, causing mental anguish, heartache, and spiritual pain in lives of others. Those affected, have drawn back from, or left, the ministry because of you. Your actions were deliberate, and not in self- defense, nor because of any other extenuating circumstances, except cruelty. Your disposition has taken on a murderous demeanor. Why do you conspire and plot, against God's people? Your schemes are surely in vain. No further, will you be allowed to hurt His people. You will be found out, exposed, and judged harshly. The person killing the ox, you are morally unclean. See Note 7: Clean and Unclean Animals at the beginning of this category. See suggested course of action. (3) Oxen yoked (or bound) together: This choice has two parts (one or both may apply). (a) Your dream denotes that the dreamer is called to be a prophet; sent to the rebellious people of God. (b) Your dream also denotes that you are "equally yoked" with someone (e.g. spouse, ministry, business associate, friendship). To be equally yoked is to agree with one another; having th e same interests, desires, long term goals, and outlook. The person you're yoked with is clean also. See Note 7: Clean and Unclean Animals at the beginning of this category. (4) Ox was yoked (or bound) with another kind of animal: The dreamer is "unequally yoked" with someone. It is unwise for good people to join in association with the wicked and profane, you will jerk, pull, tug, or yank different ways, and that will become very irritating and bad for you. A wise saying, there is more danger that the bad will damage the good than hope that the good will benefit the bad. Let that relationship go. The person you're entering into a relationship with is morally unclean. See Note 7: Clean and Unclean Animals at the beginning of this category. See suggested course of action.

In addition, the following is a common word, expression, or usage (e.g. slang or cliché), or a 'probable' that is metaphorically represented by an ox:

- Someone who is slighted and judged wrongly as unintelligent and clumsy because of their large physical build

Deer, Antelope (Caribou, Doe, Elk, Gazelle, Hart, Hind, Moose, Reindeer, and Roebuck):

These animals are considered clean; see Note 7: Clean and Unclean Animals at the beginning of this category. If animal was crushed, hurt, or killed, see Note 6.

Deer (caribou, doe, elk, hart, hind, moose, reindeer, or roebuck): The depiction of a deer personifies someone who is courteous, polite, thoughtful, sure-footed, skilled, and confident in progressive change, and whose thirst for God and hunger for holiness will lead you to great places and before powerful rulers. Those rulers will respect you because of your dedicat ion to, and zeal for, your God. On another vein, if the animal was threatening in any, this denotes one who embraces the negative traits represented by this animal. You are conceited and self-satisfied, an overall smugness type of attitude, arrogant, complacent, and haughty (see Proverbs 16:18). In this, you are morally unclean. See Note 7: Clean and Unclean Animals at the beginning of this category. See suggested course of action.

Antelope, Gazelle: This dream has two meanings (choose one). (1) The depiction of an antelope or gazelle personifies someone who is charitable, courteous, graceful, good-natured, likeable, polite, physically and emotionally strong, steadfast, thoughtful, but one who is too easily ensnared or hoodwinked. To whom the dream represents, your tenacious zeal to help others is without knowledge, thus your dream. It is a warning against folly and a message of grace (the free and unmerited favor and beneficence of God). For, while charity is a noble trait and cause, your level of generosity is to a fault. Your behaviors will (or have already) opened a door for the enemy to cause an offense within you against God, and especially against God's people, and so God against you. You should adopt a way of helping people that is more God principled, practica l, and down-to-earth. See Proverbs 6:1-5; and read what care God has taken, in His Word, to make men and women good stewards over their assets and to teach them prudence in the managing of those assets. Charity has principles as well as promises, relating to life on this side of eternity, in the land of the living. It is every person's wisdom to keep out o f debt (literal and emotional) as much as possible, for debt is a burden upon people. Ensnaring them; putting them in danger of doing or suffering wrong. Your generosity needs discretion, prudence, and wisdom during these times. Do not co-sign or be a surety in any way for family members, friends, especially those who are ne'er-do-wells, and never for strangers or people you barely know. Malicious and mischievous persons are before you and their desire is to rob, steal, and destroy. Their desires have the capacity to bring poverty and ruin to you, if you allow yourself to become ensnared by their lure. If you have rashly entere d into such an agreement, through either hook or crook, know that you are snared by the words of your mouth. Humble yourself and faithfully pray to be discharged from the debt. Favorably, Adonai will no longer allow you to be trodden underfoot, but will raise you up, but you must learn the valuable lesson of your dream. For charity first begins at home. See suggested course of action. (2) To focus on the hoofs (feet) of a deer or antelope, or to see a human with the feet of a deer or antelope: Dreamer, look back, with thankfulness, on the great things God has done for you and the great distance he has brought you. For, when you stop and think about, what the Lord has already done for you, and how far He's brought you; think about His goodness. Think about His hedge of protection around you; the provisions and ways He's made for you, the doors He's open for you. Think about you're in your right mind, and how the Lord is blessing you right now. Reflect upon the process of endurance by which you have risen (or will rise) to your prosperity and the many other things that has contributed to your advancement. He has delivered you from most of your personal issues, made you to succeed over those who had targeted you for harm, and instilled a spirit of perseverance within you. God has given you skill and understanding in affai rs, which you had no knowledge of, nor was you designed for. He has given you bodily strength to go through the everyday businesses of life and the fortitude to endure the fatigue of conflict. He has made you very bold and daring for His cause, and given you spirit proportional to your strength. Gratefulness is the spirit you should be embracing. By divine assistance, if someone stands in your way, go pass them; if a wall blocks you, leap over it, for God has made your feet like hinds' feet on high places that you may not slip. Always acknowledge the Hand of God in all that you do, and do allow fear to overwhelm you, and you will continue to prosper and go far above your expectations. See also Psalm 18:30-36.

ELEPHANT:

This animal is considered unclean; see Note 7: Clean and Unclean Animals at the beginning of this category. If animal was crushed, hurt, or killed, see Note 6. This dream has three meanings (choose one). (1) Male dreamer, the depiction of an elephant personifies a male figure that is, for the most part, peaceful and quiet. People a re attracted to your harmonious demeanor. It literally feels good being around you. Sir, you are equipped to handle large-scale undertakings in the material world. If not already, you will become a very prosperous and influential leader, and will acquire the title of such. You will reach prosperity suddenly. Use your influence exclusively for the Kingdom of God. God has given you a great gift. It would be to your advantage to recognize your Creator and to serve and worship Him, via Jesus Christ. Sub mitting to Him as your Lord and Savior, will help you subdue your dark side that you may walk into your purpose. With that said, your dream comes as a warning and as a message of grace to the dreamer. Know your dark side and reject embracing it, for this animal is also considered unclean.

For, when in a rut, you are abusive, enraged, and out of control. You then become unpleasant, intolerant of others, demeaning and very sarcastic in your expression; imposing stress on your relationship with the Lord, as well as, with others. Avoid becoming too dogmatic, fixed in your opinions, greedy, rigid, self-righteous, and stubborn. This is wisdom: Listen, my son, be wise, and keep your heart on the right path. Do not join those who drink too much wine or gorge themselves on meat, for drunkards and gluttons become poor, and drowsiness clothes them in rags. Listen to your father [spiritual and/ or natural] who gave you, life and do not despise your mother when she is old. Buy the truth and do not sell it; get wisdom, discipline, and understanding. The father of a righteous man has great joy; he who has a wise son delights in him. May your father and mother be glad; may she who gave you birth rejoice! (Proverbs 23:19-25 NIV). See suggested course of action. (2) Female dreamer, the depiction of an elephant personifies a female who is endowed with the gift of discernment. Dreamer, an important decision is being considered and you will notice if "something just isn't right" about the options. Be confident in your intuition, and don't hold back counsel that more time should be taken to investigate if you sense this. As well, your natural inner strength and awareness; your ability to discern between positive and negative environments, truth an d lies, makes you an excellent advocate for the protection of children against predators of all kinds; and if not an advocate, definitely a counselor, social worker or teacher of young children, teens, and/or young adults. Additionally, your gift of discernment, has given you prophetic abilities that should be used exclusively for the Kingdom of God. You will find purpose in this. With all of that, dreamer, know that God has given you a great gift. It would be to your advantage to recognize your Creator and to serve and worship Him, via Jesus Christ. Dreamer, submitting to Jesus, as your Lord and Savior will help you master your gift of prophecy, as well as maintain loving relationships across the generations, using your experience and wisdom to assist the younger ones with the problems of life. You will demonstrate how close supportive relationships can be maintained between the generations. (3) White Elephant: To see or ride a white elephant denotes one who is embracing a false religion, because of your spiritual conflict with the will of God and that of men. This elephant also denotes a visitation of the Lord. Presently, you are attempting spiritual perfection via human means, which has led (will lead) to deception and oppression, and has open the door for heavy demonic activity. Favorably, you will experience God and come to know Jesus as your personal Savior, however, only if you accept Him as such, therefore, recognize and respect your time of visitation from the Lord, when it is upon you, and it is upon you now.

In addition, the following are common words; expressions or usages (e.g. slang or clichés) or a 'probable' that are metaphorically represented by an elephant:

- Someone who is extremely large or much larger than average
- One who is a member of the Republican Party

FELINES: (Cat, Cheetah, Leopard, Lion, Mountain Lion, Cougar, Panther, and Tiger):

While the depiction of felines personifies someone who is fierce, intelligent, intense, strong, unstoppable, and has a degree of prominence; your dream denotes one who is dealing with a present issue from an emotional standpoint, based on feelings of being overwhelmed, fear, or hopelessness. It is suggested that you regroup, and deal with your issue from a calm and rationa l manner. In addition, if the cat was domesticated or non-aggressive, this implies someone who is disciplined, educated, refined, and sophisticated. You embrace the positive attributes of this animal. Moreover, a domesticated or non-aggressive feline is a sign of wisdom and healing; perhaps the dreamer is in need of healing or is a healer. On the other hand, if the cat is wild, life threatening, excited, stalking, or frightening in some way, this implies someone who is disorderly, unwise, foolish, tempestuous, and violent (see 1 Peter 7:8, 9). This person primarily embraces the negative characteristics and behaviors ascribed to this animal, in addition to other issues. These animals are considered unclean; see Note 7: Clean and Unclean Animals at the beginning of this category. If kitten, see Note 5. If animal was crushed, hurt, or killed, see Note 6. You will realize more clearly the nature of some felines see the following.

Cat: First, if cat was non-threatening, refer to the preceding reference of domesticated, non-aggressive felines. If cat was threatening or wild in any way, this personifies someone who sins have separated you from God and from close fellowship with believers. You worshipped money and image, in all of its forms. Your dream was sent to encourage remembrance. Journal: Dreamer, God wants you to consider, and remember from this day forward, as a preservative against future idolatry, the following. Of all the things you've done to acquire wealth, and to remain youthful, did any of it, bring you freedom or exemption from accusations, blame, harm, reproach, or unpleasant consequences? Omitting God and His ways from your life is to omit true happiness, health, joy, and peace. Now, having gone through the fire and experienced the repercussions of covetousness, greed, vanity, and the worship of materialism, your mind set has changed. Beware therefore, that you no longer imitate the doings of others, and do not fear them. Lest the fear of them be allowed to seize you, but when you see them lifted-up and praised by others, say in your heart, only the Lord should be adored, and remember God is watching you and only He can demand an account of your soul.

In addition, the following are common words; expressions or usages (e.g. slang or clichés) or a 'probable' that are metaphorically represented by cat:

- Someone who is spiteful and malicious
- A woman who wanders around looking for a sexual partner
- An informal term for a youth or man

Leopard: This dream has two meanings (choose one). (1) The depiction of a leopard personifies someone who is ferociously fierce, intense, and intelligent. You have (or will have) a degree of prominence amongst well-known leaders. You are warned to not, create a sense of unity with the wickedness that will surround you, namely those of prominence who are pseudo-Christian, untruthful, and is the antithesis of Christ. For they respect their own truth, while never acknowledging, their truth is delivered without grace; thus, it is never enough to fill an emaciated soul. Moreover, do not adopt a bourgeois mentality. This mentality is concerned only with your personal comfort, material wealth, and status, at any expense. The lesson is, no matter how personable, powerful, or difficult a person, or how uncertain or unpopular the choices and issues, always take the next biblical and ethical step, for obedience to God's principles will always prove safer and stronger foundationally. (2) Additionally, this animal is also deadly. Question, was the animal a possible source of danger, a nuisance, or life threatening in any way to the dreamer? If so, your dream is a warning. A new person, represented by the leopard, is allowed within your life as a rod of correction because of your failure to change, when transformation was needed. Choosing to remain powerless, in spite of spiritual help, makes it easier for the unclean to subjugate. Evil spirits always lie-in-wait for those who are willing to be in denial or even slightly deceived. See suggested course of action.

Lion, Mountain Lion, Cougar, or Panther: This dream has three meanings (choose one). (1) The depiction of a lion, mountain lion, cougar, or panther personifies one of two contrasting personalities, antagonists. Both personalities have great power and influence; are great leaders, ferociously bold, impressive, successful, prosperous, and well versed in various religions. Yours is the path of great leaders who has the power to change history. You are powerful and strong, and know what to do with your authority. You see yourself a match for all you meet. Moreover, both personalities are going through a transformation process. As these felines are deadly, both personalities are deadly. In that, both have an intense desire fo r the defeat or downfall of its antagonist. However, one personality honors Jesus Christ and His cause (a holy lion), and the other is the antithesis of Christ. Questions to journal, was the lion, mountain lion, cougar, or panther non-aggressive, quiet, easy to control, unlikely to cause trouble? Did you pat or stroke the feline? Did the feline talk? If you answered yes, to any one of these questions, this implies two things within the life of the dreamer (both apply). (a) A new person, or old acquaintance, is allowed within the dreamer's life as a helper and protector (a holy lion). This person is represented by the lion, mountain lion, or panther, and they possess the positive characteristics represented by this animal. Allow the person into your life (e.g. adjunct, associate, friend, personal assistant, secretary, possible spouse). This person is under God's protection. For, he or she, who honors Jesus Christ, is under God's protection and has been made clean. (b) The dreamer is also a holy lion. Additionally, you, the dreamer, have all the rights of an apostle (1 Corinthians 9:1-27); thus, be encouraged, God's rule reigns over your life and you are made clean. (2) If the lion, mountain lion, cougar, or panther was a nuisance, a possible source of danger, harmful, stalking, wild, life threatening, or frightening, in any way, this implies three things (choose one). (a) If lion was threatening, or frightening in any way, See 1 Peter 5:8-11. (b) If animal was threatening, or frightening in any way, a new person, or old acquaintance, represented by the lion, mountain lion, or panther is allowed within the dreamer's life as a rod of discipline, and they do possess the negative characteristics represented by this animal. This is allowed, because of the believer's extreme admiration or fanatical devotion to somebody or something other than God (e.g. desiring to be someone you're not, or worship of materialistic things, personalities, self, vanity, or a literal image, or some form of idolatry). One lion is set over against the other to kill ego. The lesson is, no matter how personable, powerful, or difficult a person, or how uncertain or unpopular the choices and issues, always take the next biblical and ethical step, for obedience to God's principles will always prove safer and stronger foundationally. Although, you will need all kinds of outside support to recover from this person's domination, now, no longer, allow that particular person's influence within your life to continue or thrive. Dreame r, have no other gods before God. See suggested course of action. (c) The dreamer primarily embraces the negative characteristics and behaviors ascribed to this animal, namely beliefs, behaviors, and choices that do not honor God. You are a pseudo-Christian, untruthful, the antithesis of Christ. You boldly express anti-Christ behavior. You claim to represent the gospel and teachings of Jesus Christ, but you do not (also see Matthew 7:16-23, 2 Peter 2:1-21). You respect your truth, while never acknowledging, your truth is delivered without grace; thus, it is never enough to fill an emaciated soul. Fully aware of the implications of your choices, you choose to fabricate the Word of God, introducing destructive heresies, using empty, boastful words, appealing to the lustful desires of human nature, and denying the sovereign Lord. You teach others to do and act as you do, and many follow your shameful ways, perverting the way of truth, bringing it into disrepute; thus, bringing wr ath upon their heads. Moreover, all those who disagree with you, you oppose violently. You are considered greedily destructive, ruthlessly aggressive, proudly oppressive, and you survive by preying on others. You transform your persona as circumstances call for that by all possible means, you might over power and/ or influence many. You are one who provokes reverence, and people are not at ease around you. See suggested course of action. (3) Killed or eaten by a lion: Your dream denotes judgment (divine reprimand for folly and sin) is upon the dreamer, in the form of an enemy overpowering you, because of excessive immorality. See suggested course of action.

Winged lion, griffin, griffon, or gryphon: This dream has three meanings (choose one). (1) Dreamer, you are above average in intelligence, and are one who has the courage to stand up for what you believe in, especially those things regarding your spirituality. You sincerely believe that what you believe is truth. However, your truth is insufficient; thus, you are spiritually impoverished (Revelation 3:17-22). For, you are one who does not follow mainstream Christianity. Your religious practices are questionable, and are of no eternal value. Your beliefs are related to polytheistic or pantheistic religions. Question to journal, are your beliefs in harmony with God's provision for life on the other side of eternity, in heaven? Dreamer, I invite you to consider the following. Believing and/or encouraging others to approach God the Father, without the essential provision He has provided for humankind to approach Him properly; that provision being Yeshua HaMashiach, is not safe, and causes one to remain spiritually impoverish. Some call God's provision Jesus, Wonderful Counselor, Mighty God, Everlasting Father, Prince of Peace, our atonement, advocate, liberator, propitiator, and our salvation. It is only through this channel that we may hope through faith to conciliate with our Creator, see John 3:16, Acts 2:37-42, 1 Timothy 2:4-7. Your dream comes as a message of grace (the free and unmerited favor and beneficence of God). God wants to balance your understanding of His ways and means, for you are surely being called. Adonai Elohim has need of you in His Kingdom. At present, you are morally unclean. See Note 7: Clean and Unclean Animals at the beginning of this category. See suggested course of action. (2) Dreamer, prideful and powerful, you lack Christ-like humility, and is becoming a cruel and insensitive leader. Moreover, at present, concerned with your own interest, you are driven by, and occupied with, sensual app etites, rather than spiritual needs. Your desires, appetites, and attitude are leading to a chaotic and empty life. A life figurati vely similar to the condition of earth in Genesis 1:2, wasteful, empty, and dark. This type of carnal strain and toil lead s to sorrow and spiritual darkness. There is a need to re-connect with God. Favorably, there is a ray of light, sent by God, purposed to break through the darkness of your state of affairs. This ray of light is a person, anointed and sent, especially to you. Their words and inspiration will be to you, like Genesis 1:3-5 is to Genesis 1:2. Illuminatingly wise, this person will powerfully affect your life, externally and internally. Their inspiration, coupled with you earnestly embracing change, humility, contentedness, integrity, ethicalness, and a renewed faith in God's word and His process, will strengthen you to return in complete heartfelt repentance to Jesus, from a heart of love. By this, the severity of your transgressions becomes partially sweetened; for, when a man or woman genuinely return to God, in complete surrender and humility, your deliberate transgressions become like actual merits, aka "the sweetening" (Luke 7:37-50). Because, the realization of your distance from God, due to your transgressions (Isaiah 59:2-21; Luke 15:11-24), becomes the motivating force to return to God with a passion even greater than that of someone who has never sinned in such a manner, or never left the Father's house, completely converting your present to good (Acts 9:1-30). This is the secret of repentance and returning to God. Go; therefore now, and seek the Lord Jesus, repent and place your hope in Him. Hope, placed in Him, will not deceive. See suggested course of action. At present, you are morally unclean. See Note 7: Clean and Unclean Animals at the beginning of this category. See suggested course of action. (3) Dreamer, you will be cleared of blame, guilt, suspicion, and/or doubt. God has heard your plea, He will defend you, and justice will prevail, via divine power. Therefore, go on and fight for, and excel, in your "calling". You are a natural mediator, perhaps a judge, teacher, or an apologist (one who defends and justifies Christianity), as you are genuine, tactful, and adaptable. Your sensitivity and gentleness will be a great healing force in the lives of others, bringing harmony and support to them, via defending them, by any right means necessary, against the deceit and trickery of the enemy, and by teaching them about simple faith. A simple faith which is in Jesus Christ (a resolute trust in the integrity of God and in His Word), and in His absolute omnipresence, in this, you advance the cause of God, especially concerning restoration, transformation, and miraculous healings and strengthening, both physically and emotionally. Further, allow these to be the primary focus of you ministry. Additionally, dreamer, be aware, concerning the expectancy of something great, become aware of opportunities, and expect spiritual maturity. See Note 7: Clean and Unclean Animals at the beginning of this category. See suggested course of action.

In addition, the following are common words; expressions or usages (e.g. slang or clichés) or a 'probable' that are metaphorically represented by a lion, mountain lion, cougar, or panther:

- Someone who is celebrated
- A woman who wanders around looking for sexual partners younger than her self (aka a cougar)

Tiger: This dream has two meanings (choose one). (1) Few possess the charisma, elegance, intelligence, and power of you. However, you are also self-conceited, delusional, spiritually lifeless, deadly, and you are a false teacher. You have perverted the gospel of Jesus Christ and have caused great division and confusion. While promoting love, togetherness, and preparation for Armageddon (doomsday), if you are heeded, you will lead others to their downfall, perhaps death (e.g. Jim Jones and the Jonestown-Guyana tragedy, David Koresh and the Waco, Texas tragedy, Heaven's Gate tragedy). Yes, you have the potential to form a cult following. You will sacrifice your own family to your delusions. The self-indulgent, dull minded to spiritual things, phony, and hypocritical persons; those who disregard caution, discretion, good judgment, good insight, maturity, prudence, responsibility, and wisdom, are your major supporters. Unwise and foolish women, false teachers, legalistic and non-mainstream pseudo-Christians, who love to revel in self-righteousness, are also amongst your followers. Dreamer, you may not like God's ways and means, but you do have to follow them. We all have to accept and surrender to His wisdom, for it is greater than ours is. Your human understanding of, and reaction to, spiritual realities is oftentimes crudely green. Dreamer, it is counseled that you do as the apostle, and count all that has brought you to this point, to be worthless (Philippians 3:8). Your dream comes as a message of warning and one of grace (the free and unmerited favor and beneficence of God). There is hope for you, because you are still alive, there is no more hope in death. If professors of religion ruin themselves, their ruin will be the most reproachful of any; and they in a special manner will raise at the last day to everla sting shame and contempt (Matthew Henry's Bible Commentary). There is still time for you to recognize the wrong in what you're doing, feel the regret about your past actions, and change your ways and habits. Dreamer, seize this opportunity to repent, denounce the erroneous teachings you've embraced, and go on from here. Let it go (your erroneous beliefs and teachings) and do it quickly without reservation! If you've led others away, humble yourself and apologize, and let them know you was wrong, and let them know, bottom line, their salvation is their own responsibility (Philippians 2:12, 13). Go and seek truth for yourself that not all might be eternally lost. Otherwise, you and your major supporters will be counted amongst those illustrated in Matthew 7:21-23, to say the least, and counted amongst those who are considered murderers. You will lose your life too. We are not asked or required to do what we cannot do; therefore, you are able to reject this wickedness and live. (2) If the tiger was a nuisance, or a possible source of danger, harmful, stalking, wild, life threatening in any way, or attacked the dreamer. Your dream comes as a severe warning and as a message of grace to the dreamer. Dreamer, you are sternly warned that you are a major supporter and/or amongst the followers of a charismatic and powerful leader, who is a false teacher (see #1, regarding characteristics of major supporters and followers of such a leader). You are following a person and a group that will lead to your ultimate ruin, and possibly death. You are counseled to leave this fellowship immediately, without reservation, and go and establish a genuine personal and intimate relationship with Jesus Christ. He will save you via the born again experience (see in the Holy Bible John 3:1-17, Acts 2:37-40). So that, having been justified by grace (the free and unmerited favor and beneficence of God), you will have hope for eternal life. Then join a mainstream church, a faith based bible-believing community church and commit to that ministry. No matter, forsake not the gathering of yourself together with other mainstream Christians. Avoid isolated groups that teach something different from the gospel of Jesus Christ. Jesus di ed for the world, and not exclusively for any one sect or western denomination. Dreamer, exalt no one, or your public image of well-being, above God, especially to the point of death, even devastation emotionally or spiritually. To lie down your life for someone, something, or image, especially as a ritual offering, is idolatry (idolatry is "foreign service", any act that expresses devotion or fanatical admiration to something or someone other than Adonai Elohim). This is not humbleness. Why die needlessly (Ecclesiastes 7:17). Favorably, one, who does understand your situation, is near you. Seek them out. Dreamer, in spite of what we do not know about the many mysteries of God and life, one thing remains eternally true: God is our loving Father. He does not desire that any one perish; great effort is exercised to save us, even to the moment of our death. Therefore, cast your burdens upon the Lord, for He genuinely cares for you. Again, run with endurance the race set before you. This is a trustworthy saying. Please ponder on these words that you may be made clean and know truth, and then help others with the same truth. Question to journal, did you kill the animal or get away? This is one confirmation that you did (or will do) the right thing in leaving that cult and you should tell and/or help others to leave. See suggested course of action.

In addition, the following is a common word, expression, or usage (e.g. slang or cliché), or a 'probable' that is metaphorically represented by a tiger:

- One who is brave, strong, or fierce

Fish Or Marine Mammals Or Crustacea Or Seafood (e.g. Polar Bear, Sea Otter, Seal, Whale):

Fish, marine mammals, Crustacea, categorized, and characterized, in many ways, within the Bible, symbolically represent the diversity of peoples in the sea of life. As well, fish, seafood, as with all animals, are figuratively, grouped into two categories, clean and unclean. See Note 7: Clean and Unclean Animals at the beginning of this category. Additionally, all fish, marine mammals, or Crustacea, clean and unclean, represent those predestined to be, "born again" within the Kingdom of God (see in the Holy bible, John 3:1-17). You will realize more clearly the nature of clean and unclean fish see the following.

To dream of seeing, eating, handling, or walking in water amongst clean fish. Fish with fins and scales (e.g. anchovy, barracuda, bass, bluefish, carp, cod, crappie, drum fish, flounder, grouper, haddock, halibut, herring, kingfish, mackerel, minnow, mullet, perch, pike, rockfish, salmon, sardine, smelt, snapper, sole, steelhead, sucker, sunfish, tarpon, trout, tuna, whiting). This type of dream denotes two things (one or both may apply). (1) Symbolically clean fish refers to God's faithfulness, and great humility on the part of the dreamer. Dreamer, you are one who has re-directed your negative impulses, your natural inclinations to sin, especially your sexual desires, towards righteous activities (e.g. humanitarian efforts), and have desired to make God's will your own will, having your mind and thoughts clinging faithfully to the greatness of God. Accordingly, you are now decreed as one who is genuinely righteous, meaning you are one who is considered undefiled according to biblical standards (e.g. of a pure heart, with correct motives), down-to-earth, fair, humble, just, unpretentious, not rude or obscene, one who knows that God's grace is sufficient. This type of spiritual worthiness, after receiving the Lord as your Savior, is by grace, faith, and practicing good deeds, in your case, the re-directing of your sinful inclinations, with the help of the Paraclete. Now, you will begin to walk and grow into a mature spiritual being, enabled to see into the spiritual realm more clearly, going on towards perfection. No matter your hardships, you will never again look back. You have genuinely in words and deeds put away childish things. Dreamer, the Lord your God has chosen you, out of all the peoples on the face of the earth to be His people, as His treasured possession. The Lord did not set His affection on you and choose you because you were better than other peoples, but it was because the Lord loved you and kept the oath He swore to your forefathers (Deuteronomy 7:1-8). Moreover, as you were already predestined to be a miracle worker, you have now achieved a level of spiritual balance and purity necessary to successfully, fulfill the duties of this office. Your prayers are especially effective now, what you decree, God will fulfill. Additionally, you are one whom other believers may interact with socially on very personal levels, e.g. business associate, friendship, ministry, or spouse. (2) Your dream denotes that you are one who has been spiritually concealed, hidden, or kept secret by God, aka a hidden righteous (see Romans 11:3-5), appearing only to do God's will and then fading back into obscurity. You appear when needed, and then disappear without thought of anything in return. Now, you are moving from a state of obscurity to being prominent, widely known, and eminent; thus, there is a need for a solemn consecration, be it private and personal, or public.³⁵ Therefore, dreamer, choose this day, this moment, whom you will serve. God has set before you this day, this moment, life and good, and death and evil. Thus, you are beckoned this day to love the Lord your God, to walk in His ways, to embrace His commandments, statutes, and judgments, that you may live and multiply properly; and the Lord your God will bless you in your land. If you need only to believe that the Lord truly loves you, you will begin to walk in His ways and into His purpose for you. You will usher others into a totally new and higher level of spiritual awareness (see John 21:3-17). Those, whom you will reach for Christ, will stand before you as their teacher, connecting their thoughts with your thoughts, with love from their hearts. By fulfilling your mission and remaining humble, you will be worthy of your wage. Moreover, as already promised, you will eat and do very well, on this side of eternity, and inherit eternal life. Note; humility is a keyword for you. Know the full meaning of the word and define your life by it.

To dream of seeing, eating, handling, or walking amongst unclean fish, seafood. Fish, seafood

without fins or scale, soft body, and all marine mammals and Crustacea, are unclean (e.g. abalone, catfish, clam, conch, crab, crayfish, cuttlefish, dolphin, eel, jellyfish, lobster, marlin, mollusks, mussel, octopus, oyster, paddlefish, porpoise, scallop, shark, shrimp, squid, sturgeon, includes most caviar, swordfish, whale). Symbolically unclean fish, seafood refers to one who is predestined to become born again within the Kingdom of God; the receiving of the Holy Ghost, and/or understanding (see John 3:1-17). This type of fish (unclean) also personifies two states regarding human behavior (choose one). (1) To the believer, your dream denotes one who has committed an error in judgment or conduct, as well as one who is quarrelsome. You've reached a turning point within your life, from where you misstep or got lost. Dreamer, you will have to choose to let go of the negativity and to, again, embrace obedience to God's divine will, by this, there will be restoration of things within your life. Additionally, your turning point is hooked to an unbeliever (one who has no religious beliefs, a non-religious person, or one who has no religious faith or belief in Jesus Christ, or one who does not embrace a personal relationship with Jesus Christ, at present); because you also need to learn empathy by walking in another's steps. Therefore, the two personalities, yours and another, who is an unbeliever, will naturally attract and connect; moreover, this is why you are also unclean. See Note 7: Clean and Unclean Animals at the beginning of this category. Nonetheless, because of the connection, the two personalities will clash, conflicts and struggles will ensue, to the point of battle; with each one killing the ego of the other; thereafter blending i n true union, together. See suggested course of action. (2) You are one who is quarrelsome, and is unaware of spiritual knowledge that leads to a saving relationship with Jesus Christ. If you are an unbeliever (one who has no religious beliefs, a non-religious person, or one who has no religious faith or belief in Jesus Christ, or one who does not embrace a p ersonal relationship with Jesus Christ, at present). You are about to experience a paradigm shift, a spiritual turning point, and it is hooked to a believer, namely one personified by the preceding, see (#1). Moreover, to the unbeliever, Jesus loves you, thus, He is petitioning you to accept Him as your personal Savior, for you are valuable in His eyes. The first step in receiving Him as your personal Savior is repentance (see in the Holy Bible, Acts 2:37-41). Repentance is seeking pardon for having done something awry, and for having hurt someone, and expressing sincere feelings of regret and brokenness. To Jesus pray, Psalm 51:1-19. To individuals, a phone call or a letter of apology is a good place to start, if appropriate. Moreover, if you will accept the Heavenly Father's Words, via the Bible, and store up His principles, and His ways and means within you, turning your ear to wisdom and applying your heart to understanding, calling out for insight and crying aloud for discernment, Jesus will meet you. This, coupled with a lifestyle of prayer and fasting, followed by appropriate application of wisdom, and you will know the Messiah, Jesus Christ, intimately, and find the knowledge of God you seek. For the Lord gives wisdom and from His mouth comes knowledge and understanding. Then you will understand what is right and just and fair, every good path. When wisdom enters your heart and knowledge becomes sweet to your soul, discretion will protect you, understanding will guard you, and His Truth will lead you. To deliver you from the ways of wickedness, and from demons whose words and ways are perverse, who causes you to walk in darkness gladly, whose paths are crooked and devious, causing you to leave straight paths (Proverbs 2:1-6, 9-15). This is one of God's covenant promises to you. Have faith in this. See suggested course of action.

Dead fish, marine mammal, or Crustacea: Your dream is a dire warning and comes to rectify behavior, and/or to possibly, change the dreamer's direction of ministry. With that said, couple this with one of the following (choose one). (1) If you are a bishop, pastor, wife of a pastor, elder, or any kind of upper leadership within a ministry. Depending upon how man y fish dreamer observed, your dream denotes that you are causing great offenses within the lives of those you are called to lead; you have become a stumbling block to one or many (Leviticus 19:11-15, Ezekiel 3:20). Dreamer, all you need to do is go back, look back, consider who this person(s) might be, and rectify or mend the hurt. If you do not know of anyone, then many will be revealed to you publicly. Moreover, you are asked to humble yourself, and go to the many you've hurt with peace offerings and amends. Until apologies are made and peace offerings are presented, you are morally unclean. See Note 7: Clean and Unclean Animals at the beginning of this category. See suggested course of action. (2) Although dreamer is participating in some kind of ministry, it is not the primary ministry of service God has ordained for you to do. Dreamer, while many people are multi-talented, God has one primary ministry for all, while not neglecting other gifting's or ministries. Nevertheless, for one reason or another, you have chosen to believe that you may select what kind of service you want to do, how you want to do it, and who you want to be of service to, especially regarding unbelievers and/or the indigent. Dreamer, since all fish represent those predestined to be born again within the Kingdom of God, and since, God uses people, to get the good news out (Matthew 29:18, 20, see John 3:1-17). It is a Christian's duty to warn the wicked to turn from their way, that they may become born again, live, and prosper, even as their soul prospers (3 John 1:2). Unfortunately, if souls perish, symbolically represented by dead fish, because of your neglect of duty, you bring guilt upon yourself, (Ezekiel 33:1-9, Acts 18:5, 6). That is to be responsible, spiritually, for someone's death (or many deaths). With that said, dreamer, your lack of Christian service comes down to indifference. The level of indifference you have for the commands of God, and for the destiny of the lost, has caused many to perish, spiritually and/or physically. Even more, the risks you take in disappointing or disobeying the One who shed His blood for you is unwise. Those that follow the choices of their own hearts, feelings, emotions, rather than the dictates of the divine will, oftentimes, find themselves far from peaceful shores. Stop yourself from walking down the path of reaction. Be willing to release those things that are in conflict with, or hinder, what God has called you to do. Your carnal mind may fight you on it, but your heart and mouth can still agree and defeat any thought of doubt or unbelief, or fear. When working to eliminate negative thoughts and feelings, pray, and think before you act! When you practice this, you will see that God will meet all your needs and you will be better able, emotionally and spiritually, to meet the needs of those God has sent you to (see also Ezekiel 37:7). See suggested course of action.

In addition, the following is a common word, expression, usage, (e.g. slang or clichés), or a 'probable' that is metaphorically represented by dead fish

- Dead fish, marine mammal, or Crustacea may also represent, as a probable, a miscarriage, still born baby, or an abortion has (or may) happened.

Eating fish, marine mammal, or Crustacea: Your dream probably denotes someone is pregnant, or is becoming a grandparent, adoptive parent, or foster care parent (see Chapter One, Are the Dreams in the Bible Models for our Dreams Today, section entitled — Probables).

Eaten by a fish, marine mammal, or Crustacea: Dreamer, God will not afflict forever, He will only contend until we submit and turn from our sins. Read and embrace the story of Jonah. This is to you.

Fishhook: This dream has two meanings (choose one). (1) Your dream is one confirmation. To dream of being caught or hooked on a fishhook, you will accept (or has accepted) Christ as your personal Savior, thus, you "born again" (see John 3:1-17). On another vein, if you embrace another religion, another belief system, or is an atheist, your dream was sent to make you aware that you will shortly have a miraculous and life changing experience. This experience will convince you, unequivocally, that Jesus of Nazareth, who died on a cross approximately 2000 years ago. Who has been preached about through the years, and others martyred because of their belief in Him, this same Jesus, is the way, the truth, and the life, and that no one has approached (or may approach) the Creator God, except through Jesus (see John 14:6). If necessary, see suggested course of action. (2) To get loose and get away (off fishhook): You have been very obstinate. You carry out plans that are not of the Lord, form alliances that you were not led to form, heaping sin upon sin. You have proven yourself rebellious, deceitful, and unwilling to listen to the Lord's instructions. You no longer want to hear what is right and just; only what is pleasing and satisfying to the flesh. You major in illusions. Because you have rejected His message, and relied on oppression and depended on deceit, you will begin to experience very humiliating and disastrous circumstances. Yet, while this will be allowed, it is designed to bring you to a state of prayer and heartfelt repentance to Jesus. Repentance is seeking pardon and expressing sincere feelings of regret and brokenness for having done something awry and/or for having hurt someone, see 2 Corinthians 7:10, 11. To Jesus pray, Psalm 51, this coupled with prayer and fasting, and followed by appropriate application of wisdom, can conceivably avert some of the repercussions of your choices. As soon as He hears your voice of repentance, He will answer you, for the Lord, yet longs to be gracious to you. See Joel 2:12-19, this is to you. For the Lord is a God of justice. Blessed are all who wait for Him. Dreamer, although the Lord gives you the bread of adversity and the water of affliction, your ears will hear a voice behind you, saying, "This is the way; walk in it". At that time, you will n o longer refuse the process of renewal and transformation; thus, affecting a better you. By this, He is showing you grace and mercy. See suggested course of action.

In addition, the following are common words, expressions, usages, (e.g. slang or clichés), or a 'probable' that are metaphorically represented by fish:

- **Big fish (to dream that fish are larger than normal):** Your dream denotes that dreamer will connect with someone who is very important and influential. This person is very accomplished and knows where they're going, and what they want in life. They also associate with a very private and small group of friends. Note, if clean fish (to determine if your big fish was clean or unclean, see listing of some clean or unclean fish at the beginning of this subcategory, if not listed, see other research material). Nonetheless, if clean fish, this person is sent to help you do better in life and to push you towards your God ordained destiny. Moreover, this person, after judging your character, will financially contribute to your large benevolent aims; thus, manifesting your importance and influence, and possibly include you into their small circle of friends. If unclean fish, this is someone who is very important and influential, and will use you, and is already using their influence, to turn people, away from the truth of, and obedience to, Jesus Christ. Fortunately, as you are realistic and practical in your approach to establishing relationships with others, exercise sound judgment before connecting with this person in any undertaking, for their generosity does come with a very high price, namely you, and you causing others, to reject Christ Jesus as Lord and Savior, and His teachings. Much of your success will come due to your ability to judge character.
- **Red Herring:** Two things (choose one). (1) Your dream denotes that dreamer is creating a diversion intended to distract attention from the main issue, with the intention to deceive. See suggested course of action. (2) This phrase also denotes that the first draft of a prospectus; must be clearly marked to indicate that parts may be changed in the final prospectus.
- **Shark:** Your dream denotes one who is especially talented, yet greedy and unscrupulous. You make a living as a cheater or fraud, going after whatever you want, illegally or unethically, and with no regards to the well-being of others. See suggested course of action.
- **Loan shark (to dream of a shark connected to money in some way):** Your dream denotes one who lends money at excessively high rates of interest. See suggested course of action.

FROGS (Bullfrog, Toads):

This dream has two meanings (choose one). (1) Frogs in someone's mouth: Your dream denotes demon possession. See suggested course of action. (2) Your dream comes as a warning, hopefully to make way for grace and mercy. The Warning: The depiction of frogs personifies someone who works counterfeit miracles, via evil spirits, wicked signs, and lying wonders that very much amuse and deceive those who would be deceived (2nd Thessalonians 2:9-12, Revelation 16:13, 14). You are a leader of people, more than likely, a congregation. Unfortunately, you are, at present, deemed a false leader or prophet. Using the ecclesiastical authority granted you, legalism, religious falsehoods, and worldly tactics; you have turned many awa y from the true teachings of Christ, Jesus. Self-righteous, you reject the doctrine of grace (the free and unmerited favor and beneficence of God). You have replaced God's truth with cultic and diabolical teachings, beliefs, and practices; all are consequent of rebellion. You are one who takes upon him or herself undue praise, smug at the accolades of people, stuck on your own shadow. You do not give praise to God, but secretly commend yourself as one who should be adored and have divine honors paid to you. You love to give alms, pray, and appear righteous, publicly, but inwardly you are lifeless, and lawlessness prevails. Your spirituality is one of outward show and hypocrisy. Moreover, y our lack of genuine love towards others has contributed to your lack of, understanding and embracing of grace. Presently, you have a painful condition or disease that will not be healed, but will take you to your grave. Grace and mercy: Nonetheless, there is hope for you, because you are still alive, this is God's grace. There is still time for you to recognize the wrong in what you're doing, feel the regret about your past actions, and change your ways and habits. Dreamer, seize this opportunity to humbly repent, denounce the legalistic and erroneous teachings you've embraced, and go on from here. God will save you via an authentic born again experience (see John 3:1-17, Acts 2:37-40). If you've led others away, humble yourself and apologize, and let them know you was wrong, and let them know, bottom line, their salvation is their own responsibility (Philippians 2:12, 13). Go and seek truth for yourself that not all may be eternally lost, and you will be healed also in the process, this is called leaving a blessing behind. Other than repentance and a turning to Christ Jesus via grace and faith, and not works that you boast about, you will be counted amongst those illustrated in Matthew 7:21-23, to say the least, and/or counted amongst those who are considered murderers. You will lose your life too; there is no more hope beyond the grave. Dreamer, we are not asked or required to do what we cannot do; therefore, you are able to count all that has brought you here, to this point, as worthless (Philippians 3:8), and renounce a religious spirit, and live. This animal is considered unclean. See Note 7: Clean and Unclean Animals at the beginning of this category. If animal was crushed, hurt, or killed, see Note 6. See suggested course of action.

In addition, the following is a common word, expression, or usage (e.g. slang or cliché), or a 'probable' that is metaphorically represented by a frog:

- Someone who is unable to speak openly and plainly, see suggested course of action.

Giraffe:

This dream has two meanings (choose one). (1) The depiction of a giraffe personifies someone who is calm and reserved, a philosopher by nature. Your depth of understanding makes you an extraordinarily gifted teacher. Dreamer, you have been in a process of being made whole, emotionally, psychologically, and spiritually. Now, you will shortly experience a miraculous increase in knowledge and wisdom, regarding spiritual truths and concepts. You are chosen and endowed with an ability to handle this type of divine impartation. You are counseled to temper great wisdom and authority with humility and simplicity. Nonetheless, your access to prophetic wisdom, which has enabled you to discern truth from false, will prove to be a transformational influence in the lives of many. You will skillfully help develop minds at searching out truth, train discip les, refresh many spiritually, and encourage others to faithfully join religious organizations (e.g. churches, Christian colleges, Christian based support groups) for mutual help and support in building close relationships with other brothers and sisters i n Christ and with close significant others as well. You are a gift to the Body of Christ. If applicable, your first-born child will be well known or famous, especially for a skill or expertise, and he or she will be called blessed and redeemed of the Lord. None of your children will suffer lack. This animal is considered clean; see Note 7: Clean and Unclean Animals at the beginning of this category. If animal was killed, see Note 6. (2) Giraffe neck was broken (no matter how or who broke it): This personifies one who primarily embraces the negative attributes of this animal. You trivialize the honor your ancestors obtained by worshipping and honoring Jesus, and His righteousness, and have made yourself a renowned name by that which perpetually ruins good names. Born a natural philosopher, your understanding of deep things has led you to a dark foreboding place. You've gained dark and erroneous knowledge (the devil's so-called deep secrets, see Revelation 2:20, 24), through personal experience and through a supernatural imparting, which was demonically communicated. The knowledge gained will not allow you to praise the Lord, only to exalt one's self. This counterfeit image of godliness is excessively concern with outward forms and appearances, especially in religious matters. You boldly insult the rights of all those around you and trampled upon all that is just and sacred. (Matthew Henry's Commentary), "Those that have so much power over others as to be able to oppress them have seldom so much power over themselves as not to oppress; great might is a very great snare to many. So has it been to you. God has not immediately cut you off but has waited to see if you will yet be worked upon, and change your mindset, or else to leave you inexcusable, in your accusations against God, because of your ruin (also see Jeremiah 9:7-9; Zechariah 13:9; Malachi 3:3; Matthew 23:37-39; Revelation 3:15-21). You are morally unclean. See Note 7: Clean and Unclean Animals at the beginning of this category. See suggested course of action.

Goat, Ibex, And Kid:

The depiction of a goat, ibex, kid personifies someone who is independent, strong, curious, and a great leader. Question, was the animal docile, non-aggressive or wild, threatening, or frightening? Two things (choose one). (1) If animal was docile, non- aggressive, this denotes that yours, the dreamer, is the path of great leaders who has the power to change history. You are powerful and strong, and know what to do with your authority. You see yourself a match for all you meet. Dreamer, this is your season, your time of influence. In six years, if you seize the moment now to prepare, you will become a great leader. Your witness of Christ's death, burial, and resurrection is sustenance to many and your service is a covering for others. As well, your artistic abilities give us all a glimpse of heaven. (2) If goat was wild, threatening, or frightening, dreamer, you present as a terrorists; using violence or the threat of violence, to intimidate others, to gain control over them. You will also betray family and friends for money. To, you are especially against all that is sacred. You have abused your power and authority, and because none opposed you, you withheld not yourself from doing wrong and evil. You power and authority will be taken from you and given to another. Although you will fight them greatly; nonetheless, you will not be able to overwhelm this person. In this state, you are morally unclean. Nevertheless, this animal is considered clean. See Note 7: Clean and Unclean Animals at the beginning of this category. See suggested course of action. If animal was crushed, hurt, or killed, see Note 6.

In addition, the following are common words, expressions, usages, (e.g. slang or clichés), or a 'probable' that are metaphorically represented by a goat:

- **Scapegoat:** Someone who is made to take the blame for others One, perhaps someone who is very young, who is lewd, indecent, not educated, ignorant, crude, vulgar, and vile

Hippopotamus, Rhinoceros:

The depiction of a hippopotamus or rhinoceros personifies someone who is passionate by nature. Yet, you've chosen to embrace the dark side of this attribute; thus, you are angry, fierce, furious, quick-tempered, revengeful, and uncontrollable. Wherever you go, you profane God's holy name. You use your authority to do wrong to others, using God's ways and means to justify your negativity. To your own detriment, you take counsel from no one. Especially from those more experience, older, and/or wiser than you are. Dreamer, choosing to react in such an unwise, foolish, and rebellious manner, as you have done, governed by dark passions rather than by prudence; will shortly cause a separation between you, your family, and many others. You will become isolated, and judged according to your conduct and actions. God will allow this for the sake of His holy name, which you have profaned, and that others may know that no one is above God's justice. Fortunately, during this isolation, God will sprinkle clean water on you, and you will be made clean; He will cleanse you from your impurities, give you a new heart, and put a new Spirit in you. If you repent and turn from your wickedness, and are careful to observe His ordinances, you will be His people, and He will be your God. He will remove from you your heart of stone and give you a heart of flesh, and will put His Spirit in you and move you to follow His decrees. Moreover, you will again be physically reunited with your family and others, and He will not bring want upon you. He will save you from all your uncleanness that you might know your god ordained destiny, only repent. To Jesus pray Psalm 51. These animals are unclean; see Note 7: Clean and Unclean Animals at the beginning of this category. If animal was crushed, hurt, or killed, see Note 6. See suggested course of action.

In addition, the following is a common word, expression, or usage (e.g. slang or cliché), or a 'probable' that is metaphorically represented by hippopotamus or rhinoceros:

- Someone or something that is enormously big or powerful

Horse, Donkey, Mule, Pony, Or Zebra (equidae family):

This animal denotes someone who is passionate, powerful, prudent, and stubborn. Embracing the negative attributes of these animals is one who goes ahead of the Lord's timing. You have a tendency to act rashly or impulsive; spur of the moment with little or no consideration, especially when it comes to violating God's particular rulings over your life; consequently, affecting divine reprimand. Dreamer is counseled to balance your decisions with practical wisdom. Further, the depiction of any animal of the horse family generally denotes transition, a changing or progressing from the way something is, as well as, a state of agitation or depression. These animals are unclean; see Note 7: Clean and Unclean Animals at the beginning of this category. If animal was crushed, hurt, or killed, see Note 6. See suggested course of action. You will realize more clearly the nature of equines see the following.

Horse, Pony: The depiction of a horse or pony, personifies someone who is affectionate, focused, loving, enthusiastic, passionate, powerful, prudent, and romantic. Couple this with one of the following (choose one). (1) If the animal was domesticated or non-aggressive, the dreamer will experience spiritual progression and growth suddenly. If you are an unbeliever (one who has no religious beliefs, a non-religious person, or one who has no religious faith or belief in Jesus Christ, or one who does not embrace a personal relationship with Jesus Christ, at present), God will save you via the born again experience (see John 3:1-17, Acts 2:37-40) and you will be made clean. So that, having been justified by grace (unmerited favor and beneficence of God), you will have hope for eternal life. See suggested course of action. (2) On the other hand, if the animal was a possible source of danger, a nuisance, wild, life threatening, or excited in some way, this denotes the dreamer is embracing the negative characteristics attributed to this animal. You have no sincere acknowledgement of; nor faith in, God's omnipotence, only pretense. You say you have faith in God, which is a resolute trust in the integrity of God and in His Word, but with your heart you only trust in others or things that can be used as a source of help or information, for example, a reserve supply of money, your own ability to find solutions to your problems. While these attributes are certainly commendable, and have worked for you in the past, they are purely secondary causes and should be recognized as such. The following is a very basic explanation of first and secondary causes. The first cause is that which receives neither its power nor the exercise of its power from another; God alone is first cause. A second cause receives both its power and the use of it from the first cause; all creatures [and resources] are secondary causes (Christian Philosophy, Louis de Poissy). God is the first (or primary) cause of everything. He miraculously created, "creatio ex nihilo" (creation out of nothing), John 1:3. From this act of God comes secondary causes and their purposes, "creatio ex materia" (creation out of some pre-existent matter), Genesis 1:2-2, 2 Peter 3:5. With this very basic explanation stated, the following is made easier to present. This is for you, the dreamer. You are trusting only in secondary causes. Examples, you need healing. You may testify with words that God heals and can heal miraculously (first cause). But with your heart you believe your healing can only come through a doctor's medicine (secondary cause); except now your illness is incurable and you need a miracle (a miraculous act of God, something out of nothing, per se). Another example, perhaps, you stand before a judge, desiring a certain outcome. While you confess that God has said the charges will be dropped; and you say God controls men, and answers prayer, inwardly you fear an undesirable outcome, so you do that which you know; you take the plea (secondary cause). This is where you truly put your faith, in secondary causes. Subconsciously (your mental activity just below the level of awareness) you are giving up on God's love, His grace, and His mercy; believing no help can, or will, come from Him regarding you, because of your personal shortcomings, e.g. you've not obeyed completely, an order from the Lord, or that minor flaw in your character. Your present state is a result of an overall feeling of worthlessness, due to your own personal weaknesses. Dreamer, while your weaknesses maybe legitimate, do not deny the truth of God's report, "Therefore, there is now no condemnation for those who are in Christ Jesus"; as well, "Hi s grace is sufficient". Romans 8:1, 2 Corinthians 12:9, upon these two scriptures and similar others, base your ideas of God's mercy regarding personal weaknesses. Moreover, there is a difference between conviction and condemnation. All insinuations that God does not care, one way or the other, about your everyday living (bills, clothing, emotional well-being, family, finances, food, health care, political situations, safety, shelter, transportation, violence, war) are thoughts and beliefs conceived without grace. Dreamer, "dethroning" God from His providential sovereignty (the wisdom, care, and guidance provided by God) over your life, within your heart, coupled with your hasty and inconsiderate verdicts on His divine procedures, denies His Power. Thus, your love for Jesus is dwindling, and this gradual loss of love for Christ is festering within you like a cancer. You have stopped asking why, or for what reason this or that happened, but you need to go further and ask the deeper questions, seeking to understand why God allowed this or that, and what is the lesson to be learned, w hat is He revealing to you in His providential dealings with you. Dreamer, question not, His absolute goodness in His dealings with yo u, but ask, what are you to glean from it. See the Lord's providence behind all the events in your life, and change your paradigm. For, though apparently absent, He really is present, He has promised never to leave you. Nonetheless, the dreamer will experience spiritual progression and growth suddenly. See suggested course of action.

In addition, the following are common words; expressions or usages (e.g. slang or clichés) or a 'probable' that are metaphorically represented by equine:

- Someone who has adopted an arrogant attitude
- Someone who has pursued a topic or course of action that is likely to be unproductive
- To receive information from a well-informed and reliable source
- To criticized something that was given you
- Someone who is using the drug heroin

The Four Horses of the Apocalypse: The horses color (white, red, black, and pale) takes on unique symbolic meanings. They expose the insidious nature of sin, and the terrible consequences of such, namely that which works against the peace and abundance God has in mind for you. In addition to the following, see also Revelation 6:2-8. With that, you will realize more clearly the nature of each horse see the following.

White Horse: This horse is a representation of a syncretistic type belief system; see Syncretism[28], as well, this horse is associated with military conquests. With that, this horse personifies one, namely the dreamer, who is a pseudo-Christian, untruthful, the antithesis of Christ. You claim to represent the gospel and teachings of Jesus Christ, but you do not (also see Matthew 7:16-23, 2 Peter 2:1-21). You have replaced God's truth with cultic and diabolical teachings, beliefs, and practices; all are consequent of rebellion. Self-righteous, you reject the doctrine of grace (the free and unmerited favor and beneficence of God). Fully aware of the implications of your choices, and using the ecclesiastical authority granted you, you choose to fabricate the Word of God, introducing destructive heresies, using empty, boastful words, religious falsehoods, and worldly tactics, appealing to the lustful desires of human nature, and denying the sovereign Lord. You are one who takes upon him or herself undue praise, smug at the accolades of people, stuck on your own shadow. You do not give praise to God, but secretly commend yourself as one who should be adored and have divine honors paid to you. Many follow your shameful ways, perverting the way of truth, bringing it into disrepute; thus, bringing wrath upon their heads, you have turned many away from the true teachings of Christ, Jesus. Further, all those who disagree with you, you oppose violently. You are a wicked and vindictive ruler. Your vices will expose you; bringing grief into your life. Dreamer, this rebuke is only a precursor to ev en worse judgments that will come later, if you do not abandoned, and totally change, your ways. See suggested course of action.

Red Horse: The depiction of a red horse personifies one who is bitter, brutal, unforgiving, and clandestinely a murderer of righteous people, emotionally, spiritually, and perhaps physically. You sneakily create confusion and havoc wherever you go. With you come conflict, confrontation, hostilities, and division. You do not know the way of peace; there is no justice in your tracks. You have created crooked paths. The guilt of many righteous persons injured or brutally killed (spiritually) by you, requires justice, thus your dream. It denotes the beginning of divine judgment (divine reprimand for folly and sin). That your soul might be saved, peace will be taken from you, you will lose your place, your assignment, dwelling, job, locality, opportunity, position, rank, responsibility, seat, and status, and men will be allowed to destroy your reputation and to create havoc within your life. Conflicts, confrontations, and hostilities will be constant elements in your life. Dreamer, it is c ounseled that you take each change, turnaround, and up and down, as a stern rebuke that you might be made wise and made clean (also see Proverbs 9:8-12). This rebuke is only a precursor of even worse judgments that will come later, if you do not abandoned and change your way. See suggested course of action.

Black Horse: The depiction of a black horse denotes one who is prideful, greedy, and has feelings of spiritual superiority. Narcissistically drunk with power, material possessions, and pride, you put everything before God, worshipping anything but God (aka spiritual adultery). Moreover, you are angry, dishonest, frustrated, and resentful, with no sincere intent or desir e to change. Your actions have provoked divine punishment. Before reaching this point, you were clearly warned, and reproved; yet, you have not taken care. Instead, you use your influence as an occasion to behave toward others as though they are less important or intelligent than you are; arrogantly inciting arguments, controversies, or strife, especially amongst Christians, who may be of a different mind than you. Dreamer your boasting, in your own self-perceived strength, which, in reality, is non- existent, and your arrogance, self-reliance, poisoning of any sense of justice, exchanging righteousness for bitterness, and rejoicing in this, has reached a pinnacle. You will now begin to experience need and want. There will be a decrease in help from the only real true God, including any Word from the Lord regarding you and His hedge will be removed. There will be a loss of faith. Your family, friends, mentors, and teachers will leave from before your face. Your finances will dwindle greatly; poverty and lack will suddenly overtake you, and you will have to downsize. This "famine" will leave only anxiety, fear, despair, and devastation, as your food, exposing fake pride, foolishness, pompousness, pretentiousness, and other shallow characteristics. Your confidence will be shattered because it is groundless, via trouble, distress, worry, and/or health problems. You will blame others for your personal misfortune; but truthfully, this is due to you own irrational beliefs in y our own abilities and attractiveness in the eyes of others, and you having been taught desolation. Your dream is a final warning of the futility of self-confidence that God may withdraw you from your purpose and hide pride from you. Dreamer, respect and heed this warning from the Lord (also see Psalm 119:67, 68; Proverbs 3:11-18). Turn back to Jesus, seek forgiveness, and tangibly, if applicable, participate in the turning back of your children to Jesus that He may leave a blessing. See suggest ed course of action.

Pale Horse (very light colored; highly diluted with white, can also be brown or yellowish green): This dream has two meanings (choose one). (1) Your dream denotes a dealer in astrology, a false prophet, one who is participating in some type of demonic, antichrist activity, and the rise of a cult leader. Dreamer, although you are surrounded by many, and there is no doubt that you have charisma, and a following to prove it, you are spiritually empty, void of the Spirit of God. You have a form of godliness, but are not godly. Highly resourceful, adaptable, and very fierce, you worship money and image, in all of its forms (e.g. worship of materialistic things, personalities, self, vanity, and/or a literal statue). You respect your truth, while never acknowledging, your truth is delivered without grace; thus, it is never enough to fill an emaciated soul. You discredit the Creator's wise and sensible guidelines for living life, on this side of eternity, as healthy, humanly, and sanely as possible ; and in harmony with His provision for life on the other side of eternity, in heaven. Dreamer, you believe in a god of your own making, coupled with outrageous claims you have wholeheartedly embraced from other erroneous guides. You exalt your wisdom above the Creator. You even attribute your prosperity to the power of demons. You demand loyalty, and force o thers to view the world according to your truths. You describe yourself as Christ, and often claim that you are God. Death, devastation, and serious problems are in your tracks, because you are mentally disturbed and unstable. Even more, to avenge, comfort, and ease yourself, you take matters into your own hands, relying on your own strength and carnal knowledge, and is willing to tak e others down that road of desolation also. You excess on so many levels. Quickly, you become infatuated with power, but drugs, power, and paranoia will be your downfall, you will be bought down low, even unto death. You are counseled to fast and pray, for God's mercy to be upon you; afterwards, go and offer a peace offering to a mainstream Christian ministry (e.g. invest your time, money, and/or talent). If you've led others away, humble yourself and apologize, and let them know you was wrong, and let them know, bottom line, their salvation is their own responsibility (Philippians 2:12, 13), to individuals, a phone call or a letter of apology is a good place to start. As God knows your thoughts afar off, don't "play", but genuinely repent. Take words to Jesus, "'I have sinned, and I have done wrong and acted wickedly". Other than prayer and heartfelt repentance to Jesus and to individuals affected by your actions, in the form of an apology (if possible), no other excuse or weak justification will be heard. Dreamer, I encourage you to seek clarity and understanding from the Lord, regarding your decision making processes and identity issues, and apply His wisdom vigilantly. Go and seek truth for yourself that not all may be eternally lost. If urged by God, declare a one, two, or three day fast without food. See suggested course of action. (2) Female dreamer: You have a male relative following such a leader, as the one previously mentioned. Dreamer, as you've been endowed with a mind skilled at searching out the truth. It is time to use that gift to analyze, judge and discriminate the situation your male significant other (husband, son, father, brother, or friend) is involved in, and to earnestly pursue information needed to turn things around for that person, for their life is at stake. Dreamer, although, you have a bit of a problem coping emotionally with issues, you are very logical, and usually employ a quite rational approach to most things you do. Dreamer, you entered this life with a gift for investigation, analysis, and keen observation. You are a thinker of the first order. You evaluate situations very quickly, and with amazing accuracy; therefore, you are the one to "pull" your significant male from the very pits of hell. See suggested course of action.

Donkey: The depiction of a donkey personifies someone who has a dual nature, with a proclivity to lean heavily toward one side or the other. While you are a free spirit, enthusiastic, eager, humble, unconventional, and a person of peace, when you're good, you're very good, and when you're bad, you're very bad. Thus, this dream has two meanings (choose one). (1) If the donkey was domesticated, non-aggressive, and/or dreamer was riding on the donkey at ease, this personifies one who has been graced with the tools and sensibility to embrace the positive aspects of your character. Earnestly utilizing th ose tools, you will rise as a humble and outstandingly successful and prominent religious ruler, if not already. You desire to build yo ur home and ministry on a solid foundation based on hard work and common sense. You are loyal and it is important that your work provide security for others, be encouraged, you will continue to rise and prosper. As well, this animal, when acting in such a manner, also reveals a wise prophet or prophetess. Additionally, this donkey represents the fulfillment of prophecy given the dreamer some time ago. Your high leadership was prophesied to you long before you reached the status. If you have not obtained this status as of your dream, you will shortly. You are blessed, because you come in the name of the Lord. It is counseled that you work only five days a week maximum. Your nature requires that you rest fully from all labor, at least eight hours of rest per day, lest you become unpleasant, intolerant of others, demeaning and very sarcastic in your expressio n; imposing stress on your relationship with the Lord, as well as, on your personal and professional relationships. Rest is your key to successful relationships. (2) If the donkey was alarming, foreboding, frightening, intimidating, scary, threatening, wild, acting strangely in any way, this suggest that you are investing too much time and energy embracing the very bad and negative attributes this animal represents. Namely, you are inclined to flaunt your disregard for Christ Jesus, common decency, and societal rules. You are promiscuous, and stubborn. Your thought processes are based on extreme irrational thinking. For example, you desire to meet and mix with people of refinement and culture; however, you're too vulgar for most. This animal, when acting in such a manner, also reveals an unwise and foolish prophet or prophetess. Your words of prophecy are based purely on your own emotions, and are not words from the Lord. The purpose of your dream is to advise the dreamer that you will need to declare some kind of fast and commit to it, to control, defeat, and/or subdue the immorality within your life; that growing carnal side of you. If urged by God, declare a one, two, or three day fast without food. See suggested course of action.

In addition, the following is a common word, expression, or usage (e.g. slang or cliché), or a 'probable' that is metaphorically represented by a donkey:

- One who is thought of as lacking wisdom

Mule: This dream has two meanings (choose one). (1) The depiction of a mule personifies someone who is a ruler, and one who is highly regarded, especially within your field of achievement. You're extremely nice, considerate, courteous, generous, and reliable. Unfortunately, you do not have a distinct proclivity towards your Benefactor, Jehovah God; or of His ways or belief system. Dreamer, Jesus loves you; thus, He is petitioning you to accept Him as your personal Savior, for you are valuable in His eyes. One simple decision of accepting Jesus Christ as your Savior, on His terms and not yours (see Acts 2:37-42), is before you, now. Repentance is seeking pardon for having done something awry, and for having hurt someone, and expressing sincere feelings of regret and brokenness. To Jesus pray, Psalm 51:1-19. Additionally, this animal also represents someone who does not have the capacity to give of them self in any real meaningful way. See suggested course of action. (2) If dreamer is a believer, you are involved in a relationship that is forbidden for one reason or another (e.g. adulterous, destructive, illegal, or immoral). This association will not produce anything of spiritual value. Pray Psalm 51. See suggested course of action.

In addition, the following are common words; expressions or usages (e.g. slang or clichés) or a 'probable' that are metaphorically represented by a mule:

- One who is very stubborn
- Someone who is an illegal drug courier and/or dealer

Zebra: This dream has two meanings (choose one). (1) If the animal was domesticated or non-aggressive, the depiction of a zebra, personifies someone is very loving, friendly, and appreciative of others, and deeply involved in domestic activities. As well as, one who has a depth of understanding that makes you helpful, conscientious, and capable of rectifying and balancing any sort of inharmonious state of affairs. Thus your dream, it comes to encourage. Dreamer, you are encouraged to devote yourself to a ministry that expresses concern for the betterment of the home and of the community at large. If not at present, it is suggested that you become a person very much inclined to give help and comfort to those in need, particularly, as a resource person. Dreamer, you are destined to leave lifelong imprints on the minds and hearts of those you touch. The Lord will uphold you. (2) On the other hand, if the animal was confrontational, threatening, unrestricted, and wild, this personifies someone who is fierce, and so self-confident and tenacious that you sniff at trouble, do not heed, but laugh at, warnings, and rejoice in your strength. Bold to meet armed men and women (law or criminal), without the thought of turning back from danger, you are counseled to be wiser in your decisions and actions, and to view your mortality from a more practical and realistic point of view (see Ecclesiastes

7:17-19), you only die once and there is no return. The person who fears God will avoid extremes. See suggested course of action.

INSECTS (Ants, Bees, Beetles, Butterfly, Caterpillar, Cockroaches, Crickets, Flies, Gnats, Grasshoppers, Hornets, Ladybugs, Locusts, Maggots, Moths, Roaches, Termites, Wasps).

As this category is extensive, most insects are not included. If your particular insect is not included, see Note 9 at the beginning of this category. For other bugs, insects, flies, worms, see subcategory, Parasites, Bloodsuckers, or Worms, Millipedes and Centipedes. All insects are unclean, except crickets, grasshoppers, and locust. They are clean. See Note 7: Clean and Unclean Animals at the beginning of this category. If animal was crushed, hurt, or killed, see Note 6. Otherwise, you can realize more fully the symbolic nature of some insects see the following.

"Nothing is too small to master man when God commands it to assail him." James G. Murphy—*The Treasury of David*

Grasshoppers, crickets, and locusts: This dream has two meanings (choose one). (1) The depictions of these insects personify someone who will develop slowly into a person with extraordinary vision, focus, and authority. However, you are, i n many ways, dependent on others, functioning better in partnerships or groups. It is counseled that you become more independent, and take responsibility for your own choices, even within partnerships. Notwithstanding, you will be blessed and will not be given over to the desires of your foes. The Lord will protect and preserve your life. You shall be called blessed upon the earth. This animal is considered clean. (2) Swarming grasshoppers, crickets, or locusts: If this jumping insect is swarming all over and/or is devouring everything in sight, this implies someone who primarily embraces the negative characteristics and behaviors ascribed to this animal. Persistent and troubling, you can be sharply critical, caustic, and belittling of others, all over the place with criticism. You come to take status and possessions away from others, attempting to break them down. You hurl injurious remarks, knowing, full well, they are not true. All this, because of the littleness, you feel inside before God and before worthy opponents. Dreamer, in this state, you are morally unclean. See Note 7: Clean and Unclean Animals at the beginning of this category. See suggested course of action.

Ants (army ant, leafcutter ant, Pharaoh ant, red ant, slave ant, slave-making ant, termite, white ant): The depiction of ants personifies someone who is practical and well organized. You desire to build your home, your family, and your livelihoo d on a solid foundation based on hard work and common sense. Some will be transformed by your prudence. However, you adhere to a carnal wisdom in preparing for your future. Your concern with material wealth and possessions, are at the expens e of pertinent spiritual values, materialism at its best, and possibly greed. While you are prudent regarding material things, you are guilty of being slothful in your personal and quiet devotions to God, e.g. personal time set aside for prayers and quiet listening to God's still small voice, as well as, your ministerial duties. As a result, you've experienced God's reprimand via a betrayal, loss, rejection, or some manner of setbacks. Favorably, now, the Lord is calling you, to renew your enthusiasm towards Him. Moreover, in the midst of your service to God, you should always keep in mind that God desires integrity and diligence regarding your service to Him and to His Kingdom. Thus, in accomplishing the task that He has called you for, name ly the continuance of your spiritual transformation, and naturally, the upgrading and/or upkeep of your persona l place of worship, the church where you are a member, via donations of your time and finances (e.g. deacon or deaconess). You should be eager in spirit to be of service to God, to His Kingdom, and to His people. This is what you should be focused on, to be ready for a future that we will all encounter. It is counseled that you rest from your toil for seven days, to pause and consider just how real heaven and hell are, the reality of an afterlife, and, that God's Kingdom is the exact opposite of darkness, and what does it all mean to you? Give careful thought to this from this day forward, again via a sabbatical rest for seven days. Subsequently, God's blessings will flow abundantly, producing spiritual growth within you. God's blessings: Gifts of God's grace, anything God freely gives you, absolution, the Holy Spirit, salvation, regeneration, eternal life, health, children, love of family, longevity, necessities, prosperity, and dominion over all that is yours; and all are parts of the supply of grace, and all are sanctified by the Lord, and technically belongs to Him. The result of this supply in your life will be peace. Be encourage and be about your Heavenly Father's business, for God has chosen you and will make you clean. See suggested course of action.

In addition, the following are common words, expressions, usages, (e.g. slang or clichés), or a 'probable' that are metaphorically represented by ants:

- Someone who is impatience about something
- Someone who is completely dominated by another and forced to work for that person for no payment, and under very harsh and unfair condition
- One who lures and then enslaves others

Bees, Wasps (bumblebee, hornet, yellow jacket): The depiction of bees, wasps personifies someone who is confident, persistent, and energetic; couple this with one of the following (choose one). (1) If the bees or wasps were non-aggressive, this denotes a Christian who is walking within purpose because of your diligence, wisdom, and great usefulness to the public. As well, your kindness to your friends and sharpness to your enemies makes you a great sage. You have, or will have, plenty, if not prosperous already. (2) If the bees were threatening in any kind of way, this denotes the dreamer is an enemy to God's people. Through harassment, pestering, hostility, and singling out of clergy and laity alike, you have set out to do harm to God's people. You will not succeed. God will drive the enemies of His people far away from them. Come back to the Lord, and be made clean. If you repent and return, something beneficial will come out of the situation. See suggested course of action. You are morally unclean. See Note 7: Clean and Unclean Animals at the beginning of this category.

In addition, the following are common words, expressions, usages, (e.g. slang or clichés), or a 'probable' that are metaphorically represented by one or more of these animals:

- Someone who is an elitist
- There will be a gathering of some sort for activity, socializing, and/or networking. Could be an opportunity or place of interest to the dreamer

Butterfly, Moth: First determine who this dream is referencing, either the dreamer or another; thus, this dream has two meanings (choose one). To determine whom your dream is referencing see Note 3 of this category at the beginning of this category. (1) If your dream is referencing the dreamer, your dream should be considered an epiphany. The depiction of a butterfly personifies someone who is a great leader, powerfully convincing, and perhaps even historical. Dreamer, you are heading towards your destiny. You are, naturally endowed with a "homing device" to guide you towards your intended destination. Every step you take is toward purpose. You may not know where you're headed, at this very moment, or may not know your purpose, perhaps due to a young age or other factors. Nonetheless, you will get to wherever it is you're destined to get. With that said, dreamer, you are one who is powerfully convincing; you are a great leader, perhaps even histo rical. However, even if it seems like you are going in the right direction, doing only good, and your cause appears noble, for your purpose is that of becoming a forerunner for change, freedom, progressive thought, and action. Unfortunately, because of your growing disregard of God's ways and means, you are headed towards becoming gnostic in belief, in other words, the "end result" of your efforts is some manner of Gnosticism at best and humanism at worst. Further, as you have the capacity to spearhead a new dawn, giving birth to a generation that will usher in an age of philosophical and intellectual enlightenment, this new dawn will not usher in the Truth of God that comes via the Holy Spirit and Holy Writ. Regrettably, the offspring of this new dawn will lack the knowledge of a personal and saving relationship with Christ Jesus. For, not only is your way, delivered without grace, it will never be enough to fill an empty soul, for it approaches the spiritual realm without the provision tha t God has provided for man to approach, and reach, true spiritual perfection, and that provision being Jesus the Christ. While every step you take appears to take you toward purpose; your focus on enlightenment and progressive thinking is without holiness and will only placate those who choose to forget their God. You do have the ability to talk others out of believing, thinking, feeling, or doing anything connected to Jesus Christ, and you will attempt to do just that; which will result in great spirit ual famine in the lives of those you convince. Dreamer, like Saul, you are headed down a road, towards destiny and purpose, but for the wrong reasons and with the wrong information, favorably, and if allowed, your dream can be your "Damascus road" epiphany (Acts 22:5, 6). Allow this moment to be your epiphany. Dreamer, your human understanding of, and reaction to, spiritual realities is crudely green. Your best knowledge and greatest abilities are, at present, like your spiritual condition, narrow and temporary. This type of simplicity is compared to "springs without water or mists driven by a storm" (2 Peter 2:17). You mouth empty and boastful words that appeal only to the lustful desires of human nature, very much like Saul's mentality, prior to his name change to Paul. The spiritual truths you think you know, and what is being revealed to you, now, namely how blind you really are, via your dream and other means, if embraced, should lead you to acknowledge that your understanding of spiritual realities was childish at best, and perilously dangerous to others to say the worst. Read and deeply understand Galatians 1:12-24. At this crossroads in your life, you are counseled to count all that you know to be worthless (Philippians 3:3-9). Then, and only then, will you, as Paul, begin to walk and grow into a mature spiritual being, going on towards perfection, enabled to see into the spiritual realm more clearly. No matter the hardships, and they may be many, you will never again look back, but genuinely, in words and deeds, renounce erroneous teachings; subsequent, your capacity for greater illumination, intellectually and spiritually, will become enlarged, giving you access to more than a few of the gates of wisdom (2 Corinthians 12:2-7). When you mature enough to handle all of God's benefits and can prove trustworthy in all of His wisdom, without becoming conceited, prideful, self-aggrandizing, running amok, or trying to kill somebody because of differences (1 Corinthians 12:7). At that time, that which is imperfect shall make way for that which is perfect (teleios, finished, describing that which has achieved or reached its goal, objective, purpose, limit, end, completion, mature, or full - grown). Therefore, dreamer, accept your dream as a message of grace, giving you time to repent. Moreover, share this with others who may have already been influenced by you. See suggested course of action. At this moment, dreamer, you are morally unclean. See Note 7: Clean and Unclean Animals at the beginning of this category. (2) If your dream is referring to another, your dream is a sober warning to the dreamer. The previously described person, (#1), has entered into the life of the dreamer, and is attempting to lead the dreamer, and others, away from the One True Living God. This person is charismatic and a powerful and convincing leader. Dreamer, please share this warning with the powerful leader, the "butterfly", in your life; if him or her are truly leading others astray, as well as, with others who may be influence by this person. Do not be afraid, to warn this person, they will not be able to overcome you in any way.

In addition, the following is a common word, expression, or usage (e.g. slang or cliché), or a 'probable' that is metaphorically represented by a butterfly:

- Somebody who is unable to concentrate on any one activity or occupation for very long

Moth: The depiction of a moth personifies someone who is insecure and paranoid, because you are dishonorable within. You operate in darkness. Worldly-minded and hypocritical, you covet wealth, and the praise of men, under the cover of a publicly passable profession of religion; maximizing upon men and women weaknesses, especially those who judge by sight. Dreamer, that image and those possessions you have set your heart on, are weak when compared to God's rewards to them who diligently seek Him. Thus, your dream is a sober warning and a message of grace. Your pseudo glory is fading and God's judgment (divine reprimand for folly and sin) is upon you. Matthew

Henry's Commentary: If religious conviction is not real, it is the vilest imposture, and we should be earnest against it. However, if religion is worth anything, it is worth every thin g; thus, indifference is inexcusable. Dreamer, why awkwardly move between two opinions? If God is God, follow Him; if He is not, then you need to make a decision. There is no room for neutrality. Christ expects that men and women should declare themselves either for Him or against Him. Choose this day. See suggested course of action. At this moment, dreamer, you are morally unclean. See Note 7: Clean and Unclean Animals at the beginning of this category.

Caterpillar (Butterfly and Moth Larva): The depiction of a caterpillar personifies someone who is destined to become a great leader. Unfortunately, although you are endowed with many talents, you suffer from a lack of direction, and there is confusion surrounding you. Restless, discontent, and impulsive, there tends to be a quick turn over in your relationships, jobs, and other interests, without much accomplishment; you never finish what you start. Additionally, as you have a limited degree of trust in people, you are self-serving, selfish, egotistical, stubborn, self-righteous, and dominating. Position and means are important to you, thus, in order to create the impression of affluence; you will spend what you do not have, and/or steal what is not yours, be it position or money. Even more, you are one who causes division amongst the fellowship. Your end is to do a great deal of damage between Christians and their relationship with one another. If associated with, you will cause a slow a nd subtle corruption of another's attitude towards certain members of their own family and of the church; resulting in an impatience and intolerant attitude, within that person, towards others. Dreamer, it is hard to keep one's integrity in the midst of general corruption, thus, a sanctifying process is needed, and should be allowed, aright early. Dreamer, without repentance and change, your mindset will cause you, eventually, to forget God, only to remember Him again, with regret, on your deathbed. To Jesus pray Psalm 51, and be grateful for the ability and chance to repent and come to Christ. See suggested course of action. At this moment, dreamer, you are morally unclean. See Note 7: Clean and Unclean Animals at the beginning of this category.

Flies, Gnats, Maggots (bluebottle, crane fly, deer fly, fruit fly, gnat, horsefly, housefly):

Flies: This dream has two meanings (choose one). (1) The depiction of flies personifies one who is superstitious, treacherous, and very ambitious, and one who worships idols and false gods. You are conceited, self-satisfied, arrogant, complacent, and haughty, with an overall smugness type of attitude. Although you present as courteous, polite, thoughtful, sure-footed, skilled, and confident, you are not. You attempt to gain other's trust under false pretenses, using any one, or all, of the character traits attributed to flies. You also lack the capacity to feel normal and passionate human feelings, and to respond emotionally. Toxic, because of the evilness within your heart, you speak and do that which is noxious (aka bad, poisonous, or hazardous). Dreamer, you are not giving rise to appropriate and good choices; thus, you are becoming unprofitable to yourself, to others, and most importantly to the cause of Christ, nor do you seek your divine purpose. You a re not helpful or useful regarding the furtherance of the gospel of Jesus Christ, the Kingdom of God, nor the church. Dreamer, without repentance and change, your mindset will cause you, eventually, to forget God, only to remember Him again, with regret, on your deathbed. To Jesus pray Psalm 51, and be grateful for the ability and chance to repent and come to Christ. See suggested course of action. At this moment, dreamer, you are morally unclean. See Note 7: Clean and Unclean Animals at the beginning of this category. (2) Dead flies: Dreamer, although you cry out for true wisdom and honor, you are embracing thoughtless and reckless acts, behavior, and/or ideas that ruin reputations, and are hurtful to a good name. Your reasoning is irrational, and contrary to logic; thus, you have been easily deceived. This is perhaps due to some psychological or medical reason; nonetheless, you are unable to think clearly. You are encouraged to refrain from your present reckless behavior, and/or to give up your ideas, until your mental issues are dealt with, spiritually and/or professionally, go get help. Dreamer, continuing in your behavior, or with your idea, will prove excessively costly, and will lead to financial loss; as well, you have a great deal of reputation to lose. Moreover, it is wise, for you to walk circumspectly before the Lord, abstaining from all appearances of evil, because many eyes are upon you. See suggested course of action. At this moment, dreamer, you are morally unclean. See Note 7: Clean and Unclean Animals at the beginning of this category.

In addition, the following are common words, expressions, usages, (e.g. slang or clichés), or a 'probable' that are metaphorically represented by flies:

- A fly in the ointment (to see a fly in some ointment): This denotes a problem or situation that will ruin your reputation, as well as, spoil a good situation.

Gnats: The depiction of gnats personifies one who is disobedient, badly behaved, troublesome, wayward, mischievous, unmanageable, unruly, willful, rude, volatile, stubborn, unyielding, and a great pretender. Therefore, as you have demonstrated a lack of sensible reasoning and personal discipline, a door has opened for you to be easily deceived by demons. Dreamer, prayer, and heartfelt repentance to Jesus and to individuals affected by your actions, i n the form of an apology (if possible), are the first steps towards restoration. Repentance is seeking pardon and expressing sincere feelings of regret and brokenness for having done something awry and/or for having hurt someone, see 2 Corinthians 7:10, 11. To individuals, a phone call or a letter of apology is a good place to start. To Jesus pray, Psalm 51. Repentance, coupled with prayer and fasting, and followed by appropriate application of wisdom, can conceivably avert some of the repercussions of your choices. This is known as leaving a blessing behind. Jesus will meet you wherever you are. Moreover, see Ecclesiastes 10:1. A suggested course of action is that you walk very circumspectly, because many eyes are upon you, to see if you've chosen C hrist Jesus as your savior, wholly, living life on God's terms. At this moment, dreamer, you are morally unclean. See Note 7: Clean and Unclean Animals at the beginning of this category.

Maggots (fly larva): This dream has three meanings (choose one). (1) If maggots were on your children, two things, choose one. (a) There has been a sacrificing of your children to the prevailing wickedness of today. Dreamer, instead of you teaching your children the benefits of wise and sensible thinking, and the pure ways of Jesus, thus, dedicating your children to the Lord, you teach your children desolation. Favorably, no sin is beyond His ability to forgive (Romans 5:20). Jesus came to cleanse all sin: "Truly I tell you, people can be forgiven all their sins" (Mark 3:28 NIV). When you recognize your sin, and then deeply cry out to God for deliverance, with much fasting and prayer, He will hear you, forgive you, and sanctify you. Dreamer, you are ask to start over again, and begin loving the Lord your God with all your heart, with all your soul, and with all your strength, and to studiously teach your children, to do so as well (Deuteronomy 6:3-7). If you lack wisdom, ask Jesus for wisdom. He gives wisdom to all men generously, no matter who you are and what you've done; wisdom will be given you (James 1:5-8). Additionally, it is suggested that you dedicate your children back to the Lord, via a literal private and personal ceremony amongst your immediate family, a "quasi" bar mitzvah. A "quasi" bar mitzvah (a bar mitzvah is a ritual ceremony that marks the 13th birthday of a Jewish boy, after which he takes full responsibility for his moral and spiritual conduct). This ceremony can be done for girls too; a 'quasi' debutante ball (a very formal event where a young lady makes her debut into society, after which she also takes full responsibility for her moral and spiritual conduct). While the dedication is primarily symbolic, by faith, you are promising God to dedicate your children to Him, via studiously teaching your children in the ways of Jesus. If you teach them in the way they should go, namely the way of Jesus, it is promised that your children will sit, and be rulers, amongst the righteous, known as a people that proclaim the goodness of Him, who has called you out of darkness. Nevertheless, whether choice (a) or (b), at this moment, dreamer, you are morally unclean. See Note 7: Clean and Unclean Animals at the beginning of this category. (b) The parent, namely the dreamer, is allowing unpleasant, unfortunate, and nasty violations to be committed against your children by others. Dreamer, if you were abused as a child, and now, you have placed your child in harm's way, oftentimes the identical situation; feigning denial, go talk to God, and ask Him to help you emotionally and psychologically, to do what it takes to keep your child safe, from the same violation. Allow the darkness of the violation to stop with you, and it can with the help of the Holy Spirit. Moreover, if you suspect that your abuser is still harming others, please report it. You may also check with your local department of human services for reporting procedures. Medical, legal, and psychological intervention, are likely necessary. Children should never be left in abusive situations. Abuse of, or sex with, a child, teen, or incapacitated adult, is never justifiable; it is always wrong. Jesus says, it's better for you to sink to the bottom of the sea, tied to cement (Mark 9:42-48), than for anyone to perpetrate such acts against others. Abuse, molestation, rape, and any unwanted sexual activity or attention forced upon a child or teen is a sad reality, but it is not beyond God's ability to overcome. Often, abusers have been abused themselves. God can redeem and restore. We praise Him "who is able to do immeasurably more than all we ask or imagine, according to His power that is at work within us" (Ephesians 3:20 NIV). The "more than we can imagine" includes forgiveness and healing. You, the dreamer, may also ask, "Can I be forgiven if I knowingly allowed my child to be sexually abused, or if I actually did the abuse myself?" [34] Yes, God is gracious and merciful. No sin is beyond His ability to forgive (Romans 5:20). Jesus came to cleanse all sin (Mark 3:28). When you recognize your sin, and then deeply cry out to God for deliverance, He will hear you, forgive you, and sanctify you. In addition to God's forgiveness, the child and/or the parent may require professional help, and some manner of accountability, for stopping negative behaviors, healing from past wounds, and for seeking forgiveness from those, you may have injured. If you lack wisdom, ask Jesus for wisdom. He gives wisdom to all men generously, no matter who you are and what you've done; wisdom will be given you (James 1:5-8). See suggested course of action. (2) If maggots were on the dreamer, your dream is a first step intervention and a serious alarm. Your dream personifies one who is affected by the decaying, foul, and rotten smell of extremely unpleasant, unfortunate, and nasty violations committed against you by others (emotionally and spiritually), leaving you a victim of unwise and foolish thinking. Although, physically beautiful or handsome, your way of thinking has caused you to live well below acceptable standards of sagacious living (emotionally, physically, and spiritually), you are devoid of understanding anything of authentic value. You allow yourself to be the fall guy, prostitute, stooge, or culprit; often exploited on some level by others. This is actually worship of others (aka idolatry). Dreamer, your behavior is causing you to forget your God, coupled with your unwillingness to accept His ways and principles. Always afraid of being the one left behind, many nights you've tossed and turned, having carelessly risked your life and soul, pretending to be blind to the things of God. Dreamer, as painful as this may hurt the question needs to be asked and seriously considered. How and when do you stop allowing the effects of your past violations to stop playing a significant part in your life? You're running away from a world (Christianity) because of embarrassment, a world, which you will always long for. Dreamer, it's natural to yearn for God. God is love and love is real, and dreamer, God loves you. His love can empower you to walk uprightly, full of integrity and wisdom, and enable you to walk through, and on away, from your present darkness. God's love will also comfort you when you're alone; enabling you to see and embrace that you are not alone, neither should you feel that you are alone. Jesus can give you a new beginning. Dreamer, you are encouraged to seek God. You desperately need Him now, and He's making you aware of that via your dream. His presence is available to you, right now. Jesus loves you, and He will be what you need Him to be when you need Him to be it. Dreamer, you knew God once, know Him again. Nonetheless, if you continue the way you're going, you will end up being left behind, from an eternal perspective. To continue following your lifestyle and keeping the same attitude, for a surety, death will follow; therefore, all your very negative life cycles needs to be broken; this can be done via Jesus and the Holy Spirit (Acts 2:37, 38). Get to, personally know the God of the Bible and what He stands for, or one can be easily deceived, for only God's plan for salvation will work. In addition, significant persons in your life have possibly been taught desolation and they are stronger than you are; a needed change regarding those relationships should happen, separation is wisdom. Thus, it is suggested that the dreamer get rid of (tear down) everything within your life that exalts itself above God. Dreamer, immerse yourself into the cleansing Word of God and abide there, via prayer and fasting, for a long time. Coupled with spirituality, you will need Christian support, professional help, and other supports, to affect a personal revival within you. Jesus will strengthen you emotionally, psychologically, and physically, to go get help for your issues. See suggested course of action. Since, maggots are unclean; you are at this moment, morally unclean. See Note 7: Clean and Unclean Animals at the beginning of this category. (3) Maggots were on someone else, other than dreamer, known or unknown. If dreamer knew the person within your dream, this person represents him or herself. If person is unknown, then how that person was depicted within your dream, namely their behavior, actions, words, or certain characteristics, this will point to someone within the life of the dreamer, with those same characteristics represented by the unknown person. Some examples of unknown persons, behaviors, actions, words, or characteristics; are a famous actor may represent a well-known person, within your life who is hypocritical. A police officer may represent someone who is a minister of God's word, or perhaps a literal police officer. A person's head will represent headship within the life of the dreamer or someone intellectually inclined. Nevertheless, known or unknown, dreamer be warned, this person, this someone, will bring (or has brought) dishonor to you, and your home, and possibly a disease, a physical rottenness in the flesh (e.g. STD, HIV, AIDS). Therefore, a needed change regarding a relationship should happen, separation is wisdom. It is suggested that the dreamer get rid of (tear down) everyone within your life that exalts itself above God. Moreover, dreamer needs to, also go get yourself medically checked. Maggots are unclean. See Note 7: Clean and Unclean Animals at the beginning of this category.

In addition, the following are common words, expressions, usages, (e.g. slang or clichés), or a 'probable' that are metaphorically represented by maggots:

- A fanciful idea
- Someone who is despicable and despise

Ladybugs, Ladybirds, Lady Beetles (for other beetles, see category, roaches): Your purpose is to eagerly, and enthusiastically acquire wealth, to promote the interests of those seeking reasonable and fair resources for home and/or land ownership, especially those who are low to moderate in income. Dreamer, God will equip you to be one of those resources. You have within you the ability to change or create major laws, significant in scope, extent, or effect, regarding predatory activities, especially the lending practices of some. You are to be an advocate for victims of those who use their positions to fleece unsuspecting investors, those who are frauds, targeting the elderly, poor, and the uneducated. Dreamer, using your resources, and organizing ability, you can lead the fight, exposing the demoralizing and devastating effects of predatory actions, thereby empowering those who are negatively affected by it. You are enabled to give people and communities the resources they need to improve their futures. You can become a formidable advocate, as you fight aggressively for those who are unable and/or improperly equipped to fight. Hence, your spiritual journey has endowed you with a multi-dimensionality that enables you to understand, appreciate, and greatly benefit the lives of many kinds of people; and to endear you to such as well. Do your research extensively before publicly exposing those who practice such practices. If relevant, it is recommended that you seek a higher education, acquiring a degree in economics or some degree dealing with finances. On another vein, as, bugs are unclean; you are at this moment, morally unclean. See Note 7: Clean and Unclean Animals at the beginning of this category. Nonetheless, dreamer, seeking God will make you clean. Heartfelt repentance to Jesus and to individuals affected by your actions, in the form of an apology (if possible), are the first steps towards spiritual cleanliness. Repentance is seeking pardon and expressing sincere feelings of regret and brokenness for having done something awry and/or for having hurt someone, see 2 Corinthians 7:10, 11. To individuals, a phone call or a letter of apology is a good place to start. To Jesus pray, Psalm 51. Note, although, it will seem as if you're growing worse spiritually and/or physically, you are healed, physically and spiritually, because of your faith and repentance; you are truly getting better, believe this word. For though the outward man perishes, the inward man is renewed daily; seek God's strength through His Christ, for encouragement. See suggested course of action.

Roaches, Beetles (for ladybugs, lady beetles, see subcategory, ladybugs): The depiction of roaches or beetles, personifies someone who is rebellious, stubborn, and uncontrollable. Do you know where you are going spiritually? You follow the wrongful desires of your heart, refusing to submit your conduct to reason and divine revelation. You walk contrar y to God's righteous precepts, for darkness has blinded you to truth. A bold and daring seducer, you mouth empty, boastful words; propagating erroneous teachings, appealing to the lustful desires of sinful human nature. You also entice others to d o wrong; talking about freedom, while you yourself is a slave to uncleanness, for a man or woman is a slave to whatever it is that is master over him or her. You not only take pleasure in the contempt within your heart, but you boast malicious and judgmental words against those whom God has set in authority over you. Dreamer, having escaped the corruption of darkness by knowing the Lord and Savior Jesus Christ, if indeed you have, and to again become entangled in it, and overcome by it, viz. the darkness, you are worse off now than you were before accepting Christ as Savior. For it is better to, not know the way of righteousness, than to know it and then turn your back on Him who called you out of darkness into His wonderful light (2 Peter 2:20-22). You do not belong to the night nor to the darkness. Have nothing to do with the vain deeds of darkness, but rather expose them and repent. For He who has rescued us from the dominion of darkness and brought us into the Kingdom of the Son, loves you. So, put aside the deeds of darkness and He will again bring light to your heart and mind, and sanctify your hidden motives. You, especially, have much more to gain than to lose by choosing Christ. Read fully, understand, and apply Ephesians 4:17-5:21. See suggested course of action. At this moment, dreamer, you are morally unclean. See Note 7: Clean and Unclean Animals at the beginning of this category.

Marsupials (Kangaroos, Koala Bear, Opossum, Possums, Tasmanian devil, Wallaby, and Wombats):

Your dream personifies one who outwardly appears righteous before people, but you are neither righteous, nor sober minded; you are really, what you are inwardly. Moreover, although you sometimes suppose, if you had lived when Christ was upon the earth, that you would not have despised and rejected Him, as people did then, yet Christ, via His Holy Spirit, His word, and His ministers, you treat no better than those of long ago who despised and rejected Jesus. You are actually an enemy of the gospel of Christ, due to legalism, which is strict conformity to the letter of the law rather than its spirit. Dreamer, it is a bad way to keep away from Christ, and, it is even worse to keep others from Him also, and you are very earnest in your endeavors to turn souls away from Christ that you might make disciples of them, according to the doctrines you adhere to, making them twice as bad as you are. Dreamer, via your dream, the Lord is declaring the miseries you are about to bring upon yourself. Read and understand Matthew 23:13-33, for this is to you. Yet, even now, if you will allow your heart and spirit to be made anew, there will be a newness of life awaiting you. For, this is a gift of the Savior's tender love to all, who trust in Him and in His faithful care of them. Dreamer, Jesus is calling you to take refuge under His loving protection that He might keep you safe, and sustain you appropriately for eternal life. Nonetheless, it is just of God to give you up to your own hearts' desires and lusts, if you obstinately persist in gratifying fleshly desires (see Galatians 5:13-26). For, vengeance will fall on every one who is Christian in name only. In the meantime, the Savior stands ready to receive all who come to Him. There is nothing between sinners and eternal happiness, but their proud and unbelieving unwillingness. See suggested course of action.

Meat cleaned, prepared, and/or processed for cooking and human consumption eating, (including sandwiches, appetizers, and hors d'oeuvres):

This dream has six meanings (one, two, or three may apply). (1) Sandwiches, Appetizers, or Hors d'oeuvres: Blessed, are all who wait on Adonai. Your dream denotes that this is the season of the Lord's favor upon your life, and you are now ready to receive the deepest measures of understanding, so that the enemy will no longer be able to manipulate your emotions so easily. Dreamer, although the Lord has given you the bread of adversity and the water of affliction, you waited on the Lord, and you have completed the process of spiritual and emotional cleansing. This process has healed your animosity and healed you emotionally and physically. However, as feelings go, because of your questionable behavior and deeds, you are discouraged, and feel unfit and unworthy of God's favor and restoration. Nonetheless, promises of deliverance, restoration, and fruitfulness are before you, because of God's grace. God has by His grace, prepared and qualified you for mercy and then bestowed it on you. Your process and waiting, has also instilled within you an appropriate and balanced confidence in your own merit as an extraordinarily gifted prophet, minister, evangelist, teacher, or pastor. Your path, now, should be towards developing your mind at searching out the deeper truths of the Word of God; and at becoming a skilled "wa tchman or watchwoman", on guard always, keeping watch, and keeping to heart the word of the Lord. Now your ears will hear a voice behind you, saying, "This is the way; walk in it", obey the voice, for it is of God. (2) If you dreamt of meat that was cleaned, prepared, processed, and/or cooked for human consumption, dreamer, freed from the negative traits associated with that animal, you have completed the process of spiritual and emotional cleansing. You should begin a ministry, if not already. To know traits, refer to the animal from which the food comes. For example, eggs come primarily from birds, lamb chops from sheep or lamb, beef products, such as hamburgers, pepperoni, ox tails, steak, come from cows; poultry, such as fried chicken, turkey, come from fowl, poultry; and pork products, such as bacon, chitterlings, ham, ribs, come from swine, boar, pig. (3) Unmarried dreamer: Your dream denotes a marriage. The dreamer has been made "whole" from past negative experiences within relationships. Thus, your emotional and spiritual self has been made new. Favorably, there will be a literal wedding and it will be honored by the Lord. If engaged, go and prepare for your wedding in peace. If not, get ready to meet your spouse. (4) If dreamer is actually ill, although you are experiencing one of life's storms or "midnights", you have proven yourself truthful, sincere, wise, calm, and devoted to the Lord. This type of clarity of mind has opened the door for a miraculous physical healing. Dreamer, optimistically expect your miraculous healing. Moreover, once healed, go forth using your unique gifting of "instinctively knowing" about people, places, and things, to empathically teach and serve others, while recognizin g and acknowledging that God is the true source of your health, knowledge, and wisdom. (5) Your dream refers to one who has a passionate thirst to connect with God. Dreamer, you are leaving a space, or letting go of someone or something that you may progress forward to a place where you will be used to minister to others. You are entering into a season within your life that will prepare you spiritually for the visitation of the Lord in your individual life. A servant of the Lord will visit you, and instruct you on how to get out of your present negative situation. Dreamer, recognize and respect your time of visitation and respect the servant of the Lord. During this time, you will experience God's love and presence, as you've never known it before. For, He is saying to you, "I will teach you godly wisdom". You will receive direct insight of divine truth that you might go on and began to operate more fully in your unique spiritual gifting. You will come to know, without a doubt, that God is the true source of your strength and wisdom, and He is your sufficiency. As a result, a greater love for self, family, and others will begin to manifest, affecting wholeness within your life. Be available to Him and seize the moments and opportunities as they are presented, especially an opportunity for you to advance your education, with a focus on teaching. (6) Your dream denotes that this is the season of the Lord's favor upon your life. However, as feelings go, because of your bad behavior and deeds, you are discouraged, and feel unfit and unworthy of God's favor and restoration. Nonetheless, promises of deliverance, restoration, and fruitfulness are before you, because of God's grace. God will by His grace prepare and qualify you for mercy and then bestow it on you. Not because of any good thing you've done, but because of His grace, mercy, and faithfulness. Dreamer, you have been delivered from your impurities and God has taken away your disgrace. Instead of shame, you will receive double honor, instead of disgrace you will rejoice in an inheritance left for you long ago.

MONSTERS, MYTHOLOGICAL OR LEGENDARY CREATURES, OR OTHER ABOMINABLE CREATURES (Beasts, Bigfoot, Black Shuck, Centaur, Dragon, Fairies, Fallen Angels, Gargoyles, Halcyon, Hydra, Imps, Medusa, Gorgon, Mermaids, Minotaur, Ogres, Pegasus, Phoenix, Sasquatch, Sirens, Sphinx, Unicorn, Vampires, or Werewolf):

Your dream was sent to demonstrate grace, via a warning, regarding one's emotional, physical, and/or spiritual health. The depiction of these type creatures generally personify one who is predominantly a pretender, self-seeking, and/or materialistic, as well as one who is in denial about their spiritual condition. Dreamer, the more callous, deceptive, or secretive a person bears-out to be, the more likely, his or her dreams will present imagery that is monstrous, mythological, or even cartoonish. This sort of dream also speaks of the aftermath of such behavior; namely great desolation, emotionally, physically, and/or spiritually. Emotionally the symbol speaks of broken heartedness, deep loneliness, great unhappiness, or a sense of being inferior. Physically, it denotes the ruin of physical assets or the loss of physical ability or agility. Spiritually it refers to a rebellion that causes one to be trampled underfoot by demons and their enemies, and to be morally unclean. Given, the symbols themselves represent an attitude of denial of truth within the heart of the dreamer, as well as other things, the message they reveal is truth. Thus, the truth is revealed, to you beforehand, via your dream. Therefore, this type of dream, should be considered a forewarning, giving the dreamer an ample amount of time (a grace period), to change his or her mind and ways. How does a man or woman uncover truth inwardly, when they don't want to know the truth? Taking ownership of what your warning dream is revealing to you about you, and working from that point, via prayer, diligent self-examination, Christian counseling, and/or candid advice from family and friends, will bring about truth inwardly, and at a pace, you'll be able to "wrap your mind around" comfortably. This followed by appropriate application of wisdom, can conceivably avert the deception and the repercussions thereof. This is what is called leaving a blessing behind. See suggested course of action. Additionally, as all the following creatures are mythical, and demons are fallen angels, I consider them all unclean (to be considered debased and adulterated) see Note 7: Clean and Unclean Animals at the beginning of this category. If animal was crushed, hurt, or killed, see Note 6. Other than that, you can realize more fully the symbolic nature of Monsters, Mythological, or Legendary Creatures, or other Abominable Creatures see the following.

Monsters (Beasts, Black Shuck, Ogres, or other monstrous or abominable creatures): This dream has two meanings (choose one). (1) If dreamer was not scared of the monster, this denotes that the dreamer is the monster. Your behavior is cruel, wicked, and unpleasant, to the extent that it is morally unacceptable and shocking. You are in denial about your spiritual desolation. The dreamer is counseled to consider the consequences of such behavior. Moreover, if dreamer is a spiritual leader in your awaked life, the depiction of monsters personifies one who is a cruel, ruthless, and insensitive leader. You are only concerned with your interest. You are driven by, and occupied with, physical appetites, rather than spiritual needs (see Galatians 5:13-26). See suggested course of action. (2) If the monster was acting alarming, attacking, frightening, intimidating, or life threatening in any way, your dream is about another's influence within the life of the dreamer. The person (the influencer, the monster) is demonically possessed and is diametrically opposed to God's rule, and all things God. Dreamer is allowing yourself to be demonically influenced or led by this person, because, you are in denial about your emotional desolation. Dreamer be warned, this person, this someone, will bring (or has brought) dishonor to your life, your family, your home. Therefore, a needed change regarding a relationship should happen, separation is wisdom. It is suggested that the dreamer get rid of (tear down) everyone within your life that exalts itself above God. It is recommended that the dreamer consider the results, and the aftermath, of such behavior, if this person is allowed to continue. See suggested course of action.

In addition, the following are common words; expressions or usages (e.g. slang or clichés) or a 'probable' that are metaphorically represented by one or more of these monsters:

- One who is acting very irrational and brutal
- One who is experiencing a situation that is unpleasant
- Someone who is, for the most part, alarming, fear-provoking, unpleasant, and worrisome

Mythological and Legendary Creatures (Bigfoot, Centaur, Dragon, Fairies, Gargoyles, Halcyon, Hydra, Medusa, Mermaids, Minotaur, Pegasus, Phoenix, Sasquatch, Sirens, Sphinx, Unicorn, Vampires, or Werewolf): This dream has three meanings (choose one). (1) The depiction of a mythological or legendary creature personifies someone who is inclined to selfish behavior, imprisoned by their own ego, and have no sincere intent or desire to change or experience spiritual growth. There is a defection from the faith, which is in Jesus Christ, and subsequent worship of false gods. You are in denial of yo ur emotional, physical, and spiritual desolation. In addition, as you have chosen to operate within confusion an d lies wherever you go, you have drawn to yourself the imminent arrival of a lying spirit that comes to draw men and women away from genuine truth and possibly from God. Dreamer, the beginning, development, arrival, or manifestation of something large (significant in scope, extent, or effect) is about to happen within your life, in a threatening way. The dreamer is advised to consider the aftermath of such behavior if continued, without change. See suggested course of action. (2) Halcyon (mythical bird): The depiction of a halcyon personifies one, who often heralds peace, tranquility, and prosperity when there is none, pointing people down a road of possible catastrophe. You hard-press people, including your family, to believe what you say and compel individuals to follow false gods. You do not pursue by faith, the righteousness that only comes from the Lord, and is unable to acknowledge God's providence on any level. A change has come. The prosperity God has provided you will begin to abate and your anarchy will be exposed. Turn back to God, seek forgiveness, and tangibly, if applicable, participate in the turning back of your children to God that He may leave a blessing. One thing is for sure; you can no longer pursue perverseness, and continue as before. Dreamer, resist unruliness within your nature, and it will flee. See suggested course of action. (3) Phoenix (mythical bird): The depiction of a phoenix personifies one not yet re-born spiritually. This person holds to beliefs, views, and practices that are erroneous, unlawful, toxic, and spiritually and/or physically deadly. To whom the dream represents, you are running away from, or abandoning, the faith, and is now worshipping false gods and images, and adhering to lies. Moreover, while this mythical bird is known for its beauty and immortality, the phoenix is strongly associated with suicide and darkness. No creature symbolizes eternal life more than the phoenix. However, this eternal life is referencing eternal separation from God, eternally in darkness. Another myth of the phoenix is that only one can exist at a time. When it senses that, its' life is ending, about once every millennia, the phoenix builds itself a pile of burning material, particularly a pile of wood, cinnamon, or other aromatic material, and allows itself to be consumed by the flames (thus a strong reference to suicide and darkness). As the old phoenix is reduced to ashes, a new one rises to begin its life on earth. See suggested course of action.

In addition, the following are common words; expressions or usages (e.g. slang or clichés) or a 'probable' that are metaphorically represented by one or more of these mythical or legendary creatures:

- Dragon denotes a heroin user
- A woman who is regarded as fierce and formidable
- Fairies represents someone who is kindly malicious.
- Fairies also refers to homosexuality
- Medusa, gorgon represents a woman regarded as very frightening because of her anger and hostility, she's threatening
- and violent, generally too unpleasant to be around; thus, unattractive.
- Sirens represents a desirable, but dangerous, women
- Sphinx denotes a mysterious and unreadable person

PARASITES, BLOODSUCKERS (Bedbugs, Black Fly, Fleas, Gadfly, Head Louse, Horsefly, Itch Mite, Leeches, Louse, Midge, Mites, Mosquitoes, Punkie, Tapeworm, Ticks, Tsetse Fly, Pinworms, Roundworms):

This dream has two meanings (choose one). (1) If worms left your body or were killed in some way, dreamer, there is a restoration work happening within you that only God can do for you, and there is effort, which you must do for yourself (faith without works is dead, James 2:17). Human agency is always included in God's process. Nothing will ever take the place of personal effort and accountability. Dreamer, as God imparts a new power within you. Power that will enable you to work within His Kingdom, and/or within the general labor force, and power that encourages morality and holiness. You are encouraged to respect, as an act of kindness, the salvation He has bestowed upon you, and the restoration He is doing within your life. Consider not His generous work as a light thing, but with fear and trembling, continue to work out your salvation, with serious watchfulness. This watchfulness is a sensitive conscience; it is vigilance against temptation, it is taking heed lest you fall; it is a constant apprehension of the deceitfulness of the heart, and of the insidiousness of power corrupted. It is the caution and circumspection that draws back from whatever would offend and dishonor Jesus, our Lord, and Savior. (2) Dreamer, if worms were on you or in you. This season of rest and recovery, provided you by God, is never intended as an OK to embrace a lack of concern, a lack of interest, or indifference, towards your relationship with God and His purposes, or a lack of interest toward the state of affairs within your household, or to cast aside all restraint. That sort of attitude is immoral, and leads to a parasitic spirituality and mind-set. This is one where anger, animosity, confusion, and weakness are present within your heart, as well as, morally wrong, impure, and unchaste thoughts and conduct. For example, addictions, cheating, exposing confidences to others, greedy, gossiping, jealously, lying, stealing, using others for personal advantage, or any other sinful attribute (see 1 Corinthians 6:9-20, Ephesians 5). As well, this mindset, speaks of one living off the generosity of others without doing anything in return. This behavior causes one's anointing to fade and spiritual authority to wane and can assumed the form of a disease. These attributes are the enfeebling, disheartening, and distressing influences, which torment ; these are the parasites, the bloodsuckers. See suggested course of action. As all parasites, and bloodsuckers are unclean, you are at this moment, considered unclean, see Note 7: Clean and Unclean Animals at the beginning of this category. For other bugs, insects, flies, worms, see category, Insects.

REPTILES (Alligator, Asps, Chameleon, Crocodile, Dinosaurs, Gecko, Gila Monster, Iguana, Lizard, Cobras, Tortoise, Turtle, or Vipers):

The depiction of reptiles generally personifies subtle craftiness, cunningness, false doctrine, godlessness, invoking of demo nic presences, sneakiness, and worldly sensual wisdom; as well as, the spirit of prophecy (e.g. the spirit of Python). If animal was crushed, hurt, or killed, see Note 6. Unless otherwise noted elsewhere, these animals are unclean, see Note 7: Clean and Unclean Animals at the beginning of this category. As this category is extensive, most reptiles are not listed, see Note 9 at the beginning of this category. Otherwise, you can realize more fully the symbolic nature of some reptiles see the following.

Alligator or Crocodile: The depiction of an alligator or crocodile, personifies one who is focused, highly creative, reserved, serious, strongly independent, studious, with a quiet temperament, yet presence. As well, you have the passion and determination to accomplish the extraordinary, and you are very difficult to defeat. You have charisma, and a following to prove it; you are well known. On the other hand, you are cunning, rebellious, demonically lead, one who teaches false doctrine, and you are godless. You are considered, a "hireling". Couple this with one of the following (choose one). (1) If the alligator or crocodile was threatening in any kind of way, this implies someone who primarily embraces the negative characteristics and behaviors ascribed to this animal. You are insincere in your dealings with people, outwardly friendly but secretly cunning, disloyal, and unfair.

You have a natural instinct for putting people at ease, while keeping up a bunch of background mess. Your dream is to warn a rebellious person, in the spirit of grace (the free and unmerited favor and beneficence of God). The Creator has granted you a reprieve or pardon to set things in order. This is one of God's ways of calling you back unto Him that you might be saved, and to see if you will yet be worked upon, and change your mindset; or else to leave you inexcusable, in your accusations against God, because of your ruin. Thus, it is recommended that the dreamer seriously consider the results of your behavior. See suggested course of action. You are morally unclean. See Note 7: Clean and Unclean Animals at the beginning of this category. (2) If alligator or crocodile was non-aggressive, the dreamer has been crying false tears, and/or expressing a false sadness, an insincere show of grief. You are crying, complaining, or whining, expressing insincere remorse, either your sadness is not genuine or you are simply using tears to gain pity or sympathy where none is needed. For example, a father or mother feeling or expressing grief and powerlessness over the actions of their underage children, while he or she neglects to initiate and carry out any corrective measures or speak righteous truth to them for wisdom sake. Another example is someone who is unwilling to confront a destructive, painful, and troubling part of their character, or life; but is willing to moan and shed tears over it. Your dream assumes that the dreamer, after having read this interpretation, knows what the situation is and what really needs to be done, other than crying, complaining, or whining, for it has already been revealed to you by God and by His ministers previously. Your dream is a second or third witness. Dreamer, no matter how difficult or how uncertain the issues, always take the next biblical, ethical, and most informed step, for obedience is better than sacrifice. See suggested course of action.

In addition, the following are common words; expressions or usages (e.g. slang or clichés) or a 'probable' that are metaphorically represented by an alligator or crocodile:

- Someone who deliberately insults others
- One whose behavior or character is regarded as suspicious, untrustworthy, or sickeningly ingratiating

Dinosaurs (any of numerous extinct reptiles): Your dream alludes to a way of life that is going contrary to God's call; thus, a spiritual backsliding within the life of the dreamer. Dreamer, you are not in harmony with the will of God for your life, nor with the particular objectives that are intended to ensure the fulfillment of that will. Your behavior deviates from the morality of God. Your dream comes to help you understand what God wants you to focus on, namely your conduct. Two things; both apply. (1) Prideful and powerful, you, the dreamer, lack Christ-like humility, and is becoming cruel and insensitive. (2) The dreamer's philosophy, wisdom, and/or gift of healing, as well as, any manner of authentic spirituality, is in the pr ocess of passing from life to becoming dormant, to permanently inactive, spiritually. Concerned with your own interest, t he dreamer is driven by, and occupied with, sensual appetites, rather than spiritual needs; your type of carnality will lead to sorrow and spiritual darkness. Moreover, your desires, appetites, and attitude are the cause of your now chaotic and empty life, a life figuratively similar to the condition of earth in Genesis 1:2, wasteful, empty, and dark. There is a need to re-connect with God. Dreamer your attitudes, thoughts, and behaviors that are not useful or needed for the progression of your spiritual walk, on this side of heaven, needs to be reckon with. Favorably, via your dream, Jesus Christ is demonstrating grace (the free and unmerited favor and beneficence of God) by offering you a resurrection from dead works, people, places, and things. Consi der your dream an intervention. Jesus will strengthen you emotionally, psychologically, and physically, to go get help for your backsliding, via a Christian faith-based support group, Christian counseling, healthcare, or inpatient. Dreamer, have faith in this, followed with works (James 2:17). It is suggested that you render negative behaviors obsolete, and began anew attempting to move forward, using different tactics to overcome unproductive habitual life style choices, and for maneuvering through this thing we call life in a more, better way. See suggested course of action.

In addition, the following is a common word, expression, or usage (e.g. slang or cliché), or a 'probable' that is metaphorically represented by a dinosaur:

- An old-fashioned person, organization, or thing, not willing or able to change and adapt

Lizards (chameleon, Gila monster, gecko, iguana): This dream has two meanings (choose one). (1) If the lizard was acting alarming, attacking, frightening, intimidating, or life threatening in any way, this denotes one, namely the dreamer, who is embracing the negative aspects of lizards. You are subject to impulsiveness and unpredictability, suddenly. These action s communicate instability. As well, you show a total lack of kindness, sympathy, and care for one who is suffering. This person is close to you, perhaps a family member. Dreamer, God's grace is being extended to you a second time. You are asked to empathically, help that person who is suffering, showing kindness and compassion. This person is before you now, and you are well aware of their situation. He or she needs your help. As well, you need God's help, now more than ever; thus, your dream. He is revealing to you if you be willing to help another, He will be what you need Him to be at this time, for you to be clean. Through this, there is hope for spiritual growth for you. See suggested course of action. As these animals are unclean, you are at this moment considered morally unclean. See Note 7: Clean and Unclean Animals at the beginning of this category. (2) If lizard was non-aggressive, this personifies one, namely the dreamer, who is wise, versatile, and multidimensional. You've worked through, and rectified, the negative aspects of your personality, and are now able to move easily from one skill, subject, or task to another, focused and stable. Your dream was sent to encourage and guide the dreamer. In time, dreamer, you will experience the Shekinah, a glow of the Light of God's goodness, if you remain diligent and don't give up on your spiritual journey. Additionally, dreamer, you have a direct link to inspiration, which you can develop and use to help others; a gift or talent to do creative works; creating things that spiritually inspires others. You also have the capacity to be a sagacious spiritual counselor, empathically understanding the vicissitudes of life, and you are able to articulate those changes in life, in a way that can be easily understood and received by another. This is your gift to the world, your purpose. It is time that you begin using your inspirations to help encourage others, through their spiritual journey. In addition, the following is a common word, expression, or usage (e.g. slang or cliché), or a 'probable' that is metaphorically represented by one or more of these lizards:

- Somebody who easily and frequently changes personality or appearance

Snakes, serpents (asps, cobras, vipers): As the essence of the snake or serpent is that of chief headship, aggressiveness, astuteness, authoritative, healer, influencer, razor sharpness, and resourceful, this animal personifies one who is some kind of top leader or in some headship position (e.g. ecclesiastical or temporal, husband, pastor, father, chief government official or some other spiritual or temporal authority). You are charismatic, and have a following to prove it. Additionally, this animal is also associated with the prophetic, especially one who is a healer. This type of symbol helps you to comprehend what God wants you to focus on, namely your conduct, especially if you are a leader of some sort (ecclesiastical or secular). Couple this with one of the following (choose one). First, determine if your snake was venomous or non-venomous, see Note 9 and if snake bit the dreamer, or was acting alarming, attacking, frightening, intimidating, or threatening in any way, or if snake didn't acknowledge or respond to your presence. This dream has seven meanings (choose one). (1) If your snake or serpent was venomous (e.g. asps, cobras, vipers), this personifies one who is the antithesis of Christ. You respect your own truth, while never acknowledging, your truth is delivered without grace; thus, it is never enough to fill an emaciated soul. Further, especially to a spiritual leader, like that old serpent, the devil, your intentions are to get others to question the validity of God's power, God's word, and the genuineness of true Christians; subsequently, tricking them into sinning against God, because of doubt. Just as the serpent, the dreamer uses the weaknesses of the flesh, pride, spirituality, religion appealing to lustful desires, and all things appealing to flesh, to lure people into doubting God, and to draw them into lasciviousness. Dreamer, you are also a slave to all these things, having yourself been tricked, and deceived by that ancient serpent, the devil. You are embracing and fulfilling the desire of the evil one, which is to exalt himself as king over your life and over the lives of those connected to you. Dreamer, the enemy of your soul; has you in a state where you are at a loss of what to do. That old serpent, the devil, wants you to be perplexed, to be without resources, to be in straits, to be left wanting, to be embarrass ed, to be in doubt, not to know which way to turn, to be at a loss with one's self, not to know how to decide or what to do, to fear even insanity. Dreamer, your allowing the demonic to reign, is leading (or has led) you to a place of desolation, and all th is because of a spirit of fear that has possessed or oppressed you a long time. Dreamer, although you are confused, no longer allow the devil, to rule over you. If you will allow these words, "Fear Not" (Psalm 23:4), to be a banner sort to say over your life, starting from this moment forward, then the following will be before you, encouraging you, on your journey out of darkness. God's Spirit will give you the strength you need, to raise you up and to succeed, and for vision thru the night, H e gives you these words of light. "Fear not My child, for I am with you always, and I feel all of your pain, and I see all of your tears, fear not My child, for I'm gonna be with you always, and I know how to care of what belongs to Me" (Helen Baylor). Therefore, earnestly oppose the subtle, yet bold, voices of the demonic, and be strong and courageous. Dreamer, if you can once again believe that the Bible is the only word of God and the tenets of the Christian faith is the only true measure of relationship with the Heavenly Father. Then there is no fear, for the Lord will guard you from all evil, preserving your life (Psalm 121); God will not allow your foot to slip, pray (Psalm 123). See suggested course of action. Nonetheless, you are morally unclean at this moment. See Note 7: Clean and Unclean Animals at the beginning of this category. (2) If venomous snake bit the dreamer, or was acting alarming, attacking, frightening, intimidating, or threatening in any way, this indicate s that the dreamer primarily embraces the negative behaviors and characteristics ascribed to this animal. These behaviors include extreme bitterness towards the ways and means of God; intoxication (literal, emotional, and/or spiritual); cruelly demanding exclusive loyalty and compliance to you and to your demands; egotism; malice, treachery, and/or envious of your spouse or of another's, advantages, possessions, or favor. Even more, you have adopted a bourgeois mentality; having created a sense of unity with the wickedness that surrounds you. This mentality is concerned only with your personal comfort, material wealth, and status, at any expense. Additionally, you possibly use your inborn prophetic gifting for occult practices (e.g. astrolog y, necromancy, psychic, sorcery, spiritists, witchery, or wizardry; this is the spirit known as python, see Acts 16:16). Whichever practice, your manner of service is the use of witchcraft in some form or another, for you command people to believe and do what you say, and/or press individuals to follow other gods. Additionally, as venomous snakes, preferring to strike you at your weakest point, during your weakest moments, attack from behind attempting to catch you off guard; dreamer, this is your mindset, a primary part of your character; this is how you treat others, and this is how you are viewed by others. The Lord wants you to focus on, and rectify, this part of your character. In the life of a believer, repentance and a renunciation of your spiritually poisonous ways is the antivenin that counteracts the effects of venom from the bite of that serpent, the devil; that you may be made clean again. Alternatively, a genuine born again experience can make one clean and non-venomous (see John 3:1-17, Acts 2:37-40). See suggested course of action. Nonetheless, you are morally unclean at this moment. See Note 7: Clean and Unclean Animals at the beginning of this category. (3) If venomous snake didn't acknowledge or respond to your presence or didn't see you, your dream was sent to demonstrate grace, via a warning. Dreamer, because of your very negative morality issues, someone deceitful and treacherous has entered (or will enter) your life, within two years. How many snakes were there? This denotes how many people will enter your life, one after another, and they will all prov e deceitful and treacherous. This person(s) has all the negative characteristics of a serpent (see #1 and #2 for summary of negative traits). Therefore dreamer, be aware, the person(s) represented by the venomous snake(s), is someone with whom you will h ave a friendship or personal relationship with, as like kind attracts like kind. Nevertheless, this someone(s) will exploit your weaknesses, instigating indulging in fleshly relations, namely all those things that excite and inflame the vilest of relations and affections; attempting to cause a complete schism between the dreamer and Almighty God. The demonic intention is, when you have reaped what you've sown, including the desolations that come with base choices, you will find fault with God's ways and means, and become extremely bitter and turn completely away from Christ, reprobate in spirit. Dreamer, you can overcome your issues, and remove this demonic force from before you by heartfelt repentance. To Jesus pray Psalm 51, and be grateful for the ability and chance to repent and come back to Christ. For, followers of Christ Jesus are sanctioned to put a stop to the enemy's antics by any right means necessary (see Luke 10:19). Dreamer, you are morally unclean at this moment. See Note 7: Clean and Unclean Animals at the beginning of this category. See suggested course of action. (4) A non-venomous snake speaks of one demonstrating the positive traits of this symbol. You are authoritative, influential, knowledgeable, and wise. You are razor-sharp, resourceful, and one who is a genuine healer. Moreover, your dream is additional proof of something that you have believed God for is correct, and that there will be a rectification of any hindra nces to your spiritual clarity. Dreamer, you are prepared and set aside for the priesthood, to carry out the official role, position, or office of a priest (e.g. prophet, pastor, minister, or some type of a very visible cleric). Chosen, you are to show forth th e praises of Him who has called you out of darkness into His marvelous light (also see 1 Peter 2:9, 10). Further, there will be a flash of insight, a sudden awareness, recognition, or realization of your calling. You will also experience a spiritual and personal revival. This personal revival will connect and unify, again, your intellect to your spirituality, as well as revive and restore faith and prayer within your life. Instead of worshiping God from the perspective of your head (intellect), you will again worship Him with your whole heart, mind, body, and soul. (5) A non-venomous snake was acting alarming, attacking, frightening, intimidating, or life threatening in any way, this indicates that something is going on within the dreamer's life that is cau sing your anointing to fade and spiritual authority to wane. Something is blocking or hindering spiritual clarity within your life. Although you present as all is well, and nothing has changed, something has changed within you, and your dream assumes you know the issue. Dreamer, consider the following: Your Christian duty does not require perfection, but it does require [moral] diligence (Keith McMullin). It is not simply what is legal; but it is what is virtuous. Repentance to God and man (a godly sorrow for hurting God and others, see 2 Corinthians 7:10, 11) and positive changes regarding contrary behaviors can affect a spiritual renewal in your life and restore God's anointing upon your life. See suggested course of action. Dreamer, you are morally unclean at this moment. See Note 7: Clean and Unclean Animals at the beginning of this category. (6) If the snake or serpent (venomous or not) ate or completely wrapped itself around a person, place or thing, that which was overwhelmed by the snake will be lost. Meaning, no longer in your possession or control, unable to be found or recovered. For example, if a snake ate or completely wrapped itself around your car, dreamer will lose his or her automobile, perhaps through repossession, and/or you will be unable to maintain your lifestyle, as you known it now, as a car figuratively represent one's lifestyle. If snake ate or completely wrapped itself around your home, dreamer will lose his or her home, perhaps through foreclosure. If snake ate or completely wrapped itself around you or another, then you physical life is susceptible to harm or injury. See index or relevant category for particular that the serpent ate or completely wrapped itself around, within your dream. Kept within context of your dream and the interpretation, this may be an area (or situation) of relevance. It is suggested that dreamer make sure all your bills are paid and are up to date, or that you have a medical check-up. Nevertheless, whatever it was that was overwhelm by the snake, needs serious consideration to, perhaps, prevent loss, via earnest prayer. Go handle your business in a prudent manner. (7) If dreamer crushed, killed, or prevailed over the snake or serpent (venomous or not) this implies one whose ministry is within the realm of miraculous phenomena. Demons will submit to you in Jesus' name. For you have been anointed, and given high authority, to overcome all the power of the enemy, nothing will harm you. Dreamer, you are anointed to become a healer, and will begin to sense the healing power of God within your hands. You will begin to sense a feeling of "fire" or heat within your hands, and have probably been told this once or twice before, when you've prayed for another. With that said, dreamer your ministry of healing is being taken to another level. Additionally, like an exorcist, you are also purposed to cast out demons. If demonic possession is the case, it should be noted, exorcism (commanding demons and all unclean spirits to leave a person in the name of Jesus the Christ) was practiced by the disciples as part of Christ's instructions, see Matthew 10, Mark 9:38, Luke 11:18, 19, Acts 16, 19:11-16. Dreamer, you will need to "exorcise" the demon out of others and pray for them to be filled with the Holy Spirit, thus preventing the demon from re-entering them later (Matthew 12:43-45). However, do not rejoice that demonic spirits submit to you, but rejoice that your name is written in heaven. Even more, those who will listen to you will also listen to Jesus; those who reject you will also reject Jesus. Nonetheless, you have authority in Jesus name, your heavenly Father watches over you, and you have His ear. He has not forgotten His promises to you.

Snake Eggs: This dream has two meanings (choose one). (1) If dreamer ate the snake eggs, this signifies you are satisfied with embracing negative habits, behaviors that leads to an early death physically and spiritual death. Read and understand Ecclesiastes 7:17. As well, read and understand Galatians 5:19-21, for this speaks of spiritual death. (2) If you crushed an egg and a snake breaks forth, the lies you've told will be exposed.

In addition, the following is a common word, expression, or usage (e.g. slang or cliché), or a 'probable' that is metaphorically represented by a snake or serpent:

- Someone who deliberately insults somebody's reliability and honesty, especially in personal dealings

Turtle, Tortoise: The depiction of a turtle or tortoise personifies someone who is contemplative, gentle, peaceful, with great patience, and slow to react. You will live a long life. You attain your goals through hard work, amazing courage, and untiring determination. Regrettably, there were (are) those who attacked you, causing awful emotional and/or physical pain. Now, you hide behind reclusive behaviors to protect yourself from hurt, and have incidentally withdrawn from God. Thus, you are morally unclean at this moment. See Note 7: Clean and Unclean Animals at the beginning of this category. Dreamer, by embracing God's strength and compassion, you can put an end to the significant impact the enemy's foolishness has had upon you. The first step to putting an end to the emotional and/or physical pain that has held sway over you, is to consider that a t one time, you too were unwise, foolish, disobedient, deceived, and enslaved by all kinds of passions and other harmful sexual behaviors, living in malice and envy, being hated, and hating others. Now, the kindness and love of Jesus the Savior has come to you, via your dream. Jesus has come to heal, or to save, you, not because of righteous things you've done, or how good you are, but because of His mercy. He will heal you of you emotional scars, if allowed, or He will save you via the born again experience (see John 3:1-17, Acts 2:37-40). So that, having been justified by grace (the free and unmerited favor and beneficence of God), you will have hope for eternal life. This is a trustworthy saying. Please ponder on these words that y ou may be made clean.

In addition, the following are common words, expressions, usages, (e.g. slang or clichés), or a 'probable' that are metaphorically represented by a turtle or tortoise:

- Someone who moves very slowly
- One who has been figuratively turned upside down

RODENTS, BURROWING ANIMALS, AND WEASELS (Aardvark, Anteater, Armadillo, Badger, Chipmunk, Ferret, Gerbil, Guinea Pig, Groundhog, Hamster, Mice, Mink, Mole, Otter, Porcupine, Rabbit, Raccoon, Shrew, Skunk, Sloth, and Squirrel):

As this category is extensive, most animals are not listed; see Note 9 at the beginning of this category. All these animals are unclean; see Note 7: Clean and Unclean Animals at the beginning of this category. If animal was crushed, hurt, or killed, see Note 6. Otherwise, you can realize more fully the symbolic nature of some rodents, burrowing animals, and weasels, as the following gives an interpretation of the three categories.

Rodents (chipmunk, gerbil, guinea pig, groundhog, hamster, mice, porcupine, raccoon, rat, and squirrel): This dream has four meanings (choose one). (1) If your dream is about another, first see Note 3 of this category, to determine if your dream is actually about another. If your dream is truly about another, your dream is an alert to the dreamer. There are those who eagerly want to instigate anarchy or chaotic situations within your spiritual life, those who would have you to live in a confused, disorderly, and messy manner, in which there is a total lack of order or control. The result of their presence in your life has already caused negative fruit within your life. They object to spiritual leadership, and protest, that in this present day, bishops, pastors, elders, or any priestly type leadership, does not agree with, or is not in harmony with, the teachings of Jesus Christ, which, by the way, is erroneous. Dreamer, the proof against their arguments and claims that any type of spiritual leadership is not biblical, is as such. King David acknowledges kings and rulers of the earth and their authority (Psalm 2:10, 11, 8:16), and the prophet Isaiah (Isaiah 49:23). The apostle Paul encouraged Timothy to pray for leaders (1 Timothy 2:1-3). Most importantly, the apostles were chosen and appointed by Jesus Himself to be leaders and fathers, within Christendom. There are many other passages within scripture that reflect these sentiments as well (e.g. Exodus 18:25, Numbers 33:1, John 12:42; Acts 15:22, Romans 12:8, Hebrews 13:24). All authority is given by God. Therefore, earnestly rid your mind of any thought o r idea that compromises the word and divine order of God and do not be rattled by this insurgent. Moreover, while they are claiming holiness for themselves, their prideful deeds exposes them as reprehensibly profane. Do not be dissuaded by their actions or protests; for, their ignorance and pride are being exposed. You will hear of and/or see them in action, and you will be shown a way around their influence and away from them. Pray and believe that God will remove them from your life. See suggested course of action. (2) The purpose of your dream is to inform and warn you. You've reached a turning point within your life, from where you misstep or got lost. God is giving you the opportunity to freely choose to turn things around spiritually, emotionally, and if applicable, literally. Acknowledge, understand, and sincerely receive by faith, the reparation for your sins, accomplished by Jesus on the cross. You can really do this now. You are entering into a process of being purified and purged, examined, proven and tested, spiritually and emotionally cleansed. Everything that's undesirable and unusable within you will become brightly polished, according to God's good pleasure. Your pride will soon give way to humbleness, dignity, honor, and righteous self-esteem, your foolishness to peace and wisdom. This process will also heal the animosity within you. Allow the process without complaining or murmuring for it is preparing you for a great journey. Additionally, choose to embrace authentic love (also see 1 Corinthians 12:31-13:1-13), and obedience to God's divine word, all of these things will enable you to let go of the negativity. By this, you will be restored. Couple this with one of the following three concerns; thus, this choice has three parts (choose one). (a) In judging others as wrongdoers (e.g. condemnatory, critical, derogatory, disapproving, harsh, negative, scornful, or uncomplimentary in your thoughts or speaking aloud), you have set a precedent over your own life, discharging a universal law. The Universal Law: With the same judgments, you judge others, so will you be judged (see Matthew 7:1-5). Example, have you thought or said, "They're life is not holy, because I know they behave this way, or do that", or thought to yourself, "They need to sit down with all the emotional or physical hardship they're going through; they're not a super person". Have you never been in a fallen state, or had a material need, at the same time, you were required to testify of the Kingdom of God or, did you just disobey the commission because of a preconceived notion or pseudo-image? Now you're judged as an offender, in that you have violated your own standard, the one you've held up for others to follow, for he or she who knows to do right and do not, to him or her it is a sin. While Christ does not deny the necessity of exercising a certain degree of discernment, or of making valid judgments with respect to sin in others. Jesus condemns the habit of criticizing others, while ignoring your own faults. You should have done what you expected of others. Dreamer, genuinely deal with why you are so judgmental or critical, and repent over judging others, this will remove such severe and unsympathetic standards from over your own life, and your dreams will change. By so doing, a more compassionate, understanding, empathic, and loving spirit will begin to manifest within you. See suggested course of action. (b) An unforgiving spirit and animosity are present within your heart. The fruits thereof are feelings of doubt, guilt, and unworthiness, questioning whether God or anybody really cares. Ask yourself why an unforgiving spirit and animosity, or why the feelings of doubt, guilt, and unworthiness, are present within me? Dreamer, it's time to own up to, and deal with, your issues and their resulting fruit. The fruits of doubt, guilt, and unworthiness, are betrayal, deceitfulness, spitefulness, faithlessness, irrational beliefs, and eventual rebelliousness. If not dealt with now, you will soon reap the consequences o f said fruit and are possibly feeling some of the effects at present (e.g. inability to sleep, unrest, no quietness within, and/or anointing and spiritual authority are abating). Further, there is great potential for you becoming one who has an image of godliness, but denies the power of God. Dreamer, mend your broken heart and/or offended feelings, via genuine forgiveness that the forgiveness offered you by Jesus, will stand (also see Matthew 18:21-35), have faith in this, without faith, it is impossible to please God. See suggested course of action. (c) There is an excessiveness regarding immoral impurities, especially lust and/or adultery. (1 Corinthians 6:9-20, Ephesians 5); causing one's anointing to fade and spiritual authority to wane. Dreamer, God will save you from all your uncleanness that you might know God is God, and honor and glorify Him whose power is the power, whose rule will endure eternally, and that you might know your God ordained destiny. Dreamer, God does as He pleases; and choose whom He please, with the powers of heaven and the peoples of the earth. Once you recognize your true destiny, and that being in Christ Jesus, your outlook on life will change. Then use your abilities and t alents exclusively for the Kingdom of God. If you are careful to submit to His ordinances, you will be His people, and He will be your God. You will be made clean. See suggested course of action. (3) Married female: Your dream signifies that you are angry, antagonistic, and domineering. You have aligned yourself with your husband and other with male superiors. You have thrown off submission. You take on authority, which God has bestowed on men; and display mannerisms customarily appropriate for men only. Your actions are that of a woman desirous of changing sexes. The Lord your God forbids the confusing of the relationships of the sexes, men must not be effeminate nor figuratively emasculated by a female, nor must women be virile, masculine, or domineering. As disobedience in small matters shows great contempt of God's principles, so obedience in small matters shows a very great regard for them. Daughter, obey "him" that has rule over you, especially your husband, and other male superiors. See suggested course of action. (4) To a non-believer (one who has no religious beliefs, a non-religious person, or one who has no religious faith or belief in Jesus Christ, or one who does not embrace a personal relationship with Jesus Christ at present). Your dream personifies someone, namely the dreamer, who is an extremely annoying, envious, and troublesome person, you are one who is very negative in your thinking, and is secretly superstitious. As well, you, ignorant ly, stand out openly against God, attracting physical and spiritual harm to yourself. Additionally, you practice infidelity (unfaithfulness, faithlessness, disloyalty, or betrayal) on a couple of levels. First level, this infidelity is spiritual, d ue to a non- existence relationship with Christ. Second level, this infidelity is literal, per your personal relationships with your spouse, significant others, family members, and/or friends. With that said, favorably, because you are unaware of the spiritual knowledge that leads to an amicable relationship with Jesus Christ and others, He has sent your dream to you as a message of grace (the free and unmerited favor and beneficence of God). The kindness and love of our Lord and Savior is coming to you, and not because of who you are or what you've done, but because of His compassionate mercy. So that you, having been justified by grace, will have hope for eternal life; saved from eternal separation from God. See Acts 2:37-40, and go and sin no more, lest physical and spiritual harm come and overtake you at a time you least expect. See suggested course of action

In addition, the following are common words; expressions or usages (e.g. slang or clichés) or a 'probable' that are metaphorically represented by one or more of these rodents:

- Someone or something used as the subject of an experiment, for any kind of test or trial
- One who has very wide interests and will read, study, and generally absorb anything that is available
- A long time
- A racist and taboo term for a black person
- Buildings specially constructed to hold slaves for sale
- Somebody untrustworthy; a mean, sneaky, deceitful, person, especially somebody who betrays friends or confidences
- A person who is a criminal or who is suspected of having committed a crime
- Somebody who hoards things
- To be suspicious that something is not right
- One who needs to speak up now, for your rights, especially one who, is thought to be timid and cowardly

Burrowing Animals (aardvark, anteater, armadillo, mole, rabbit, shrew, and sloth): Two things (choose one). (1) If your dream is about another, first see Note 3 of this category, to determine if your dream is actually about another. If your dream is truly about another, your dream is an alert to the dreamer. Someone's presence, within your life is affecting your life very negatively. You have become weaken physically, spiritually, and emotionally, and your anointing has abated. Fortunately, you will see (or have already seen) them in action. Their ignorance and pride are being exposed. You will be shown a way around their influence and away from them. Pray and believe that God will remove them from your life. (2) Otherwise, your dream comes as a warning and as a message of grace, to the dreamer, for you are surely being called by God; He has need of you. The warning: Dreamer, you sincerely believe that what you believe is truth. However, your knowledge is lacking the more important parts; parts that lead to eternal life. Endeavoring to approach God or to know mysteries that are high above, without the essential provision Heavenly Father has provided; that provision being Yeshua HaMashiach is not safe. Some call God's provision Jesus, Wonderful Counselor, Mighty God, Everlasting Father, Prince of Peace, our Atonement, Advocate, Liberator, Propitiator, and our Salvation. It is only through this channel that we may hope to gain eternal life, as well as, acquire accurate knowledge of higher things (see Acts 2:37-42; 1 Timothy 2:4-7). Dreamer, if you accept your Heavenly Father's Words and store up His commands within you, turning your ear to wisdom and applying y our heart to understanding. Calling out for insight and crying aloud for discernment, looking for it as for silver and searching for it as for hidden tre asure, then you will know the love and fear of the Lord and find the knowledge you seek. With this knowledge, you will take part in teaching and helping others to reach for deeper, more spiritual and valuable things in life; improving their existence and inspiring them to make their dreams come true. Dreamer, will you be made clean? See suggested course of action. As these animals are considered unclean, you are morally unclean at this moment. See Note 7: Clean and Unclean Animals at the beginning of this category.

In addition, the following are common words; expressions or usages (e.g. slang or clichés) or a 'probable' that are metaphorically represented by one or more of these burrowing animals:

- Someone who is employed by a group or organization, such as a government ministry, who discloses sensitive information while keeping his or her own identity secret
- A long-distance runner who sets a fast pace for a stronger teammate in the early part of a race

- Someone who is sexually and morally confused
- A woman who is quarrelsome, nagging, and/or ill-tempered
- Someone who is lazy, they dislike work or any kind of physical exertion

Weasels (badger, ferret, mink, otter, and skunk):

Two things (choose one). (1) If your dream is about another, first see Note 3 of this category, to determine if your dream is actually about another. If your dream is truly about another, your dream is an alert to the dreamer. Someone's presence, within your life is affecting your life very negatively. You have become weaken physically, spiritually and emotionally, and your anointing has abated. Fortunately, you will see (or have already seen) them in action. Their ignorance and pride are being exposed. You will be shown a way around their influence and away from them. Pray and believe that God will remove them from your life. (2) Otherwise, the depiction of a weasel personifies one, namely the dreamer, who is hypocritical, is becoming egotistical, and one who is developing a lustful, self-centered approach to life. You are overly aggressive; and take much more than you could ever need. At this point you are hard to live with, imposing unnecessary stress upon your personal and professional relationships; no one wants to deal with you. Nevertheless, your dream comes as a message of grace and to counsel. Dreamer, you do not have to dominate and destroy in order to lead and manage. You do not have to be antagonistic or hardline to fulfill your destiny. Always afraid of being the one left behind, you've sacrificed much, even that which has eternal value; leaving you a victim of unwise and foolish thinking, wise up. You knew God once; know Him again. You desperately need Him now, and He's making you aware of that via your dream. His presence is available to you, right now. He will be what you need Him to be when you need Him to be it. Otherwise, the path you're on, will lead to desolation, for you will reap what sow. See suggested course of action. As these animals are considered unclean, you are morally unclean at this moment. See Note 7: Clean and Unclean Animals at the beginning of this category.

In addition, the following are common words; expressions or usages (e.g. slang or clichés) or a 'probable' that are metaphorically represented by one or more of these weasels:

- Someone who pesters or annoys others continually
- Someone who is regarded as sly or underhanded
- One who is evasive or tries to mislead others
- Somebody who is despised by others

SPIDERS (Black house Spider, Black widow Spider, Brown recluse Spider, Camel Spider, Daddy Longlegs Spider, Funnel-Web Spider, Grass Spider, Hobo Spider, Huntsman Spider, Mouse Spider, Red Back Spider, Saint Andrew's Cross Spider, Sand Spider, Scorpion, Tarantulas, Trapdoor Spider, Water Spider, Wolf Spider, or Yellow Sac Spider)

As this category is extensive, most arachnids are not listed; see Note 9 at the beginning of this category. All arachnids (8- legged creatures) are unclean; see Note 7: Clean and Unclean Animals at the beginning of this category. If animal was crushed, hurt, or killed, see Note 6. First, determine if your spider was non-venomous or low risk, non-toxic to humans, or non-aggressive, or venomous, poisonous, or aggressive, see Note 9. With that, this dream has two meanings (choose one). (1) Spiders: This choice has three parts (choose one). (a) Nonvenomous spiders or low risk, non-toxic to humans, or non- aggressive (e.g. camel spider, huntsman spider, Saint Andrew's cross spider, trapdoor spider, water spider): Dreamer, all support, financially, emotionally, or physically, will be cut. You are looking and hoping for family support, but there w ill be none. This is the consequent of you not keeping God in the forefront of your life choices, for not trusting Him, and for not considering His ways, but you trusted in vanity and lies. You have conceived mischief and have brought forth iniquity within your own life, it is your sins that have separated you from your God, causing Him to hide His Face from you, for you would not hear Him, nor hearken to His words sent you on countless occasions. Additionally, figuratively, "blood is on your hands" (Ezekiel 3:18). Dreamer, utilizing the powerful resources of prayer and heartfelt repentance to Jesus is needed. Repentance is seeking pardon and expressing sincere feelings of regret and brokenness for having done something awry and/or for having hurt someone. To Jesus pray, Psalm 51, this followed by appropriate application of wisdom, can conceivably avert the repercussions of your choices. If you lack wisdom ask God for wisdom; and He will give you wisdom. This, repentance and pray, coupled with fasting, a changed mindset, serious re-consideration of God's ways and means, and an honest acknowledgement of God's hand within your life, can halt the severe impact of your choices, upon your life, and damages can be restored (also see Ezekiel 33:12-19). This is what is called leaving a blessing behind. See suggested course of action. You are morally unclean. See Note 7: Clean and Unclean Animals at the beginning of this category. (b) Venomous, poisonous, or aggressive (e.g. black house spider, black widow spider, brown recluse spider, daddy longlegs spider, funnel-web spider, grass spider, hobo spider, mouse spider, red back spider, sand spider, scorpion, tarantulas, wolf spider, yellow sac spider): This toxic spider personifies one, namely the dreamer, who is a specialist in theology, although, gnostic in belief. You are disapproving of all things Jesus, especially what He represents. In addition to godlessness, you exhibit a depraved nature, deviating from what is considered moral, right, proper, or good; you are insecure, quick tempered, destructive, and very violent, even to the point of bloodshed of innocent people. You tend to choose your social contacts from people who live affluently, especially those who can benefit you, without regards for friendly relationships. Your thoughts are wicked, continually, and you do not know the way of peace and justice. See suggested course of action. You are morally unclean. See Note 7: Clean and Unclean Animals at the beginning of this category. (c) If your dream is about another, first see Note 3 of this category, to determine if your dream is actually about another. If your dream is truly about another, your dream is an alert to the dreamer. Question to journal: Was the spider in your home, if so where was it in the home? The area within the home, determines how close a certain person, represented by the spider, is to you. For example, the bedroom represents someone intimately close to the dreamer. Nevertheless, if in your home, someone has recently entered your life with the attributes of a venomous spider, disassociate from this person quickly. The result of this relationship will prove disastrous, especially if you're a believer. If outside the home, a new acquaintance will be introduced to you shortly, with the attributes of a venomous spider, do not allow this person in your life, especially within your inner circle of friends or associates. You have been warned. If necessary, see suggested course of action. (2) Spider cobwebs: This choice has two parts (choose one). (a) If spider's cobwebs were highlighted within your dream, this is indicative of a person who is committed to vain works, and thus ensnared by the consequences of such choices. You have forgotten God, turned to crookedness, and walk with them who know not peace, nor justice. Moreover, you are superficial and shallow, and it shows. What you cling to, and trust in, are weak and hopeless, and do not lead to eternal life in the world to come, the Kingdom of God. Dreamer, your beliefs will give way and prove calamitous. Such is the destiny of all who forget God; so perishes the hope of the godless. Dreamer, remember your God and come to Him that you may inherit life in the Kingdom of God. See suggested course of action. You are morally unclean. See Note 7: Clean and Unclean Animals at the beginning of this category. (b) To see (observe) a spider spinning a cobweb: This is a warning to the dreamer, of a snare or entrapment, devised against you. Your actions, choices, and behaviors, especially now, should be full of wisdom, integrity, and above aboard in all dealings. You have been warned. See suggested course of action.

SCORPION:

The scorpion is associated in Scripture with demons and the spirit of the antichrist and their effects are diabolic. Couple this with one of the following (choose one). (1) A scorpion personifies one, namely the dreamer, who is deceptive, malicious, self- indulgent, spiteful, vicious, and heavy burdened. You are the scorpion and you are controlled, or possessed, by an evil spirit. Dreamer, your dream comes as a warning and as a message of grace. The warning: Dreamer, your venomous ways have been directed towards a believer who is going through harshly severe times, or what is referre d to as a "wilderness experience", at this moment, and you've made this person's struggle more arduous. Consequently, you will shortly experience the same harsh and severe times, and one will come and treat you as you've treated one of God's children. You will reap what you've sown. Fortunately, it is written, in Matthew 11:28 NIV "Come to Me (Jesus Christ), all you who are weary and burdened, and I will give you rest. Dreamer, because of God's grace, the Lord wants to make you clean, and be with you through your hard times; therefore, it would be wise to, come to Jesus and be made clean, that you might find rest. See suggested course of action. At this moment, you are morally unclean. See Note 7: Clean and Unclean Animals at the beginning of this category. (2) If your dream is about another, first see Note 3 of this category, to determine if your dream is actually about another. If your dream is truly about another, your dream is an alert to the dreamer. Your dream indicates that someone, who works upon the dreamer's weaknesses, to instigate indulging in fleshly relations, all those things that excite and inflame our vilest affections, this person has entered your life, and for the sole purpose of causing a schism between the dreamer and Almighty God. They were allowed entrance into your circle of acquaintances, because of your own immorality or uncleanness. Dreamer, you need the help, prayers, and wisdom of local believers to help free you from this person. For, when, or if, their suggestive actions are rejected, especially when confronted, they will become covertly harmful, threatening, and unpleasant. One way they will try to hurt you is to steal from you that which they consider valuable to you (e.g. instigate an adulterous affair with your spouse, contribute to your children using drugs, or literally steal from you). This person's way is the path to destruction and ruin. Therefore, with the help of other believers, you are sanctioned to eradicate or put a stop to this person's antics by any right means necessary (see Luke 10:19). See suggested course of action.

Sheep (Ewe, Lamb, Ram):

All sheep represent one who is predestined to become born again within the Kingdom of God (see John 3:1-17), as well as, one who is a traditionalist, very important, influential, and powerful. Dreamer, you are God's chosen person, a Christian, clean according to the new covenant established through Jesus Christ; as well as moderate in all things, just and fair, not rude or obscene. You are strong, emotionally and physically, and you know how to follow, as well as lead. Be encourage, you always perform outstandingly well. If animal was killed, see Note 6. Additionally, you will realize more fully the symbolic nature of sheep see the following.

Sheep: If sheep appearance was abnormally marred or distorted in some way, this is indicative of one embracing the negative attributes of sheep. Although, strong emotionally and physically, you have perhaps become a member of a large group of people, blindly following one another on a course of action that will lead to destruction for all of you. As well, you are a "yes" man or woman. On another vein, you will take somebody's place or position by secret plotting, indicating an "underhandedness" type of character also. You are morally unclean. See Note 7: Clean and Unclean Animals at the beginning of this category. See suggested course of action.

Ewe (adult female sheep): The depiction of a ewe personifies one who is gentle and cares deeply for others. This animal also signifies one of two states regarding human behavior (choose one). (1) Within the life of a believer, it denotes one who has committed an error in judgment or conduct. There has been excessiveness regarding immoral impurities (e.g. addictions, cheating, greedy, lying, stealing, unchaste conduct, see 1 Corinthians 6:9-20, Ephesians 5); causing your anointing to fade and spiritual authority to wane. Dreamer, choose to let go of the negativity, via fasting from the "excessiveness" at least 21 days. For example, if pornography, you shall fast 21 days from pornography, if fornication, fast 21 days from fornication or adultery, if lying, fast 21 days from lying, whatever your "excessiveness" is. It is suggested that you fast 21 days, and your dream assumes that you know what the issue is. If your dreams do not change after the 21 day fast, then you shall fast a second ti me for 21 days. Afterward, you shall be cleaned; and you will be restored, and a great anointing will be poured upon your life that you might be about your Heavenly Father's business, and again begin to embrace obedience to God's divine will. See suggested course of action. (2) The dream signifies one who is unaware of spiritual knowledge that leads to a saving relationship with Jesus Christ. You are called; so, respect your time of visitation by God, for it is upon you now. He will save you via the born again experience (see John 3:1-17, Acts 2:37-40). So that, having been justified by grace (the free and unmerited favor and beneficence of God), you will have hope for eternal life in the world to come, the Kingdom of God. Moreover, with this revolutionary, life changing, knowledge, you will begin to take part in teaching and helping others to reach for a deeper spiritual relationship with Christ Jesus and to reach for more, genuinely valuable things in life, improving their existence and inspiring them to make their dreams come true. Dreamer, be clean (see also Leviticus 11:44 -47, 1 Peter 1:14- 16). See suggested course of action.

In addition, the following are common words; expressions or usages (e.g. slang or clichés) or a 'probable' that are metaphorically represented by a ewe:

- One, who is timid, submits readily to others and/or is easily, led. See suggested course of action.

Lamb (baby sheep): The depiction of a lamb personifies a new believer in Christ. You are still considered an infant spiritually, not fully acquainted with the teachings about righteousness. You are spiritually and emotionally weak, because you need to submit to the teachings of the basic truths of God's word. Dreamer, crave pure spiritual teachings, via the direct words of God imparted to us through the words of others, such as a preacher in a worship service, a Sunday school teacher, and o ther holy bible studies. It is through these avenues, the Christian experiences, and God's direct leading, that His deeper mysteries, which are more valuable than any knowledge gotten on one's own, are imparted. Your dream is a message of grace that you may be clean, for you are surely, called to be one of God's ministers. Respect your present place of worship and the appointed leaders of that place. Do not leave to, aimlessly, wander from place to place, and never allow anyone to deter you from learning God's word via pastors, preachers, and teachers; for faith comes by hearing, see Romans 10:17, and by studiously reading your Bible and other biblical resources. Further, it is not wise to take counsel from within your own head. Always seek counsel from your spiritual leaders and other believers. Deliberate, discuss, and debate with colleagues, experts, and other Christians, for there is wisdom in the counsel of many. See Proverbs 11:14, 15:22, 23. Dreamer, you are encouraged to continue your spiritual journey towards Jesus, and turn not back, for continuing on, Christianity promises a better you, and furthermore, you have too much to lose looking back. If necessary, see suggested course of action.

In addition, the following are common words; expressions or usages (e.g. slang or clichés) or a 'probable' that are metaphorically represented by a lamb:

- Someone who is going to face something unpleasant, difficult, or dangerous and they will face it calmly and without resistance

Ram (adult male sheep): Your dream comes as a message of affirmation and warning. Affirmation: The depiction of a ram personifies one who is a highly esteemed ruler. Chosen from birth, you have (or should have) stepped into your destiny. Your spiritual strength, tenacity, knowledge, and voice will be used as instruments of God; penetrating the soul of those who listen, affecting conversion. You will appoint times for rejoicing, and declare sacred assemblies, asserting that no one wor k, and these days will be a memorial before God. You will appoint fellowship offerings. You will also oversee great ceremonies for great men of God. Additionally, your voice will be used as an instrument of righteousness; coming against those who would attempt to oppress you and others. Your words will cause the enemy to turn on themselves. By all this, you will be remembered by the Lord your God and rescued from your enemies. Dreamer, you are called to a high calling; withdraw not your hand when that day is officially upon you. Warning, if you "morph" into something wicked, your headship will be taken violently away from you, and given to another, one more powerful than yourself (1 Samuel 15:22-16:1).

In addition, the following are common words; expressions or usages (e.g. slang or clichés) or a 'probable' that are metaphorically represented by a ram:

- A device designed to batter, crush, press, or push something
- To hit or collide with something, or make something hit something else, with great force or violence
- To force the passage of a bill or acceptance of a suggestion, usually despite strong objection

Swine, Boar, Pig, Or Pork:

If prepared for eating see, subcategory, Meat cleaned, prepared, and/or processed for cooking and human consumption "eating". This dream has three meanings (choose one). (1) This animal is biblically associated with unwise and foolish women, false teachers, and legalistic Christians, who love to revel in self-righteousness. This animal also alludes to one who exhibits at least two of the following characteristics (never all the characteristics). You disregard caution, diplomacy, discretion, good judgment, good insight, maturity, prudence, responsibility, and/or wisdom. Your character is one of extreme haughtiness, presumptuousness, pride, and self-assuredness in the very negative sense of the word. You are a fleshly person, self-indulgent, dull minded to spiritual things, phony, and/or hypocritical. All are signs that your heart is hardened. Dreamer, you have shown yourself presumptuous, when you do not fear to do evil before the Lord or His servants. If this disposition is not let go, it will lead to a great fall (Proverbs 11:2; 16:18, 19; 29:23). Fortunately, you too can be made clean and, what God cleans is clean, and no one can call it unclean. If you are a believer, a decision to repent, return, and reject the attitude of foolishness, hypocrisy, selfishness, and lack of commitment and stewardship to the ministry of the Kingdom of Jesus Christ, is before you now. If Christ, and His ways and means, is your choice, where there would be chaos, genuine peace will abide within your life. Further, where there is a lack of prudence, wisdom will rule. If no change, the harshness of the Lord will kindle against you; and you will begin to experience a change in your authority, and favor given from the Lord. Moreover, as He knows your thoughts afar off, repent. Other than heartfelt repentance to Jesus and to individuals affected by your actions, in the form of an apology (if possible), no other excuse or weak justification will be heard. See suggested course of action. You are morally unclean. See Note 7: Clean and Unclean Animals at the beginning of this category. See suggested course of action. (2) If you are an unbeliever (one who has no religious beliefs, a non-religious person, or one who has no religious faith or belief in Jesus Christ, or one who does not embrace a personal relationship with Jesus Christ, at present). Jesus loves you, thus, He is petitioning you to accept Him as your personal Savior, for you are valuable in His eyes. One simple decision of accepting Jesus Christ as your Savior, on His terms and not yours (see Acts 2:37-42), is before you, now. The first step in receiving Him as your personal Savior is repentance (see in the Holy Bible, Acts 2:37-41). Repentance is seeking pardon for having done something awry, and for having hurt someone, and expressing sincere feelings of regret and brokenness. To Jesus pray, Psalm 51:1-19.

To individuals, a phone call or a letter of apology is a good place to start, if appropriate. Moreover, if you will accept the Heavenly Father's Words, via the Bible, and store up His principles, and His ways and means within you, turning your ear to wisdom and applying your heart to understanding, calling out for insight and crying aloud for discernment, Jesus will meet you. This, coupled with a lifestyle of prayer and fasting, followed by appropriate application of wisdom, and you will know the Messiah, Jesus Christ, intimately, and find the knowledge of God you seek. For the Lord gives wisdom and from His mouth comes knowledge and understanding. Then you will understand what is right and just and fair, every good path. When wisdom enters your heart and knowledge becomes sweet to your soul, discretion will protect you, understanding will guard you, and His Truth will lead you. To deliver you from the ways of wickedness, and from demons whose words and ways are perverse, who causes you to walk in darkness gladly, whose paths are crooked and devious, causing you to leave straight paths (Proverbs 2:1-6, 9-15). This is one of God's covenant promises to you. Have faith in this. This animal is considered unclean; see Note 7: Clean and Unclean Animals at the beginning of this category. See suggested course of action. (3) Feeding swine: To dream of feeding swine, see: 2 Corinthians 6:14–7:1. Dreamer is embracing a relationship with an unbeliever (one who has no religious beliefs, a non-religious person, or one who has no religious faith or belief in Jesus Christ, or one who does not embrace a personal relationship with Jesus Christ, at present); attempting to share biblical tenets with one who is not interested in your God, or your beliefs. Do not give swine what is sacred (spiritual food). If you d o, they will trample the wisdom under their feet, and then turn and tear you to pieces (Matthew 7:6). See suggested course of action.

In addition, the following are common words; expressions or usages (e.g. slang or clichés) or a 'probable' that are metaphorically represented by swine:

- Someone who deliberately insults somebody's manners, behavior, or morality; behaving in a coarse, discourteous, and brutal manner (e.g. bully), see suggested course of action.
- This animal also signifies a greedy, gluttonous, sloppy, and careless person, see suggested course of action.

WORMS, MILLIPEDES, AND CENTIPEDES (for other worms, e.g. leech, tapeworm, see category, Parasites).

Three things (choose one). (1) The depiction of worms, millipedes, and centipedes personifies someone, who has a nasty, disrespectful, and unethical character, one who is undeserving of respect, because you give no respect. You are predatory, in that you are given to victimizing, plundering, and destroying others, for your own gain. You live to destroy and victimize others. You are hazardous to believers of Christ Jesus, and anyone else you meet. See suggested course of action. You are morally unclean. See Note 7: Clean and Unclean Animals at the beginning of this category. (2) If worms, millipedes, and centipedes were on any part of your body, this denotes an unforgiving spirit. An unforgiving heart is present within the heart of the dreamer, due to the offenses of others, and is causing your anointing to fade and spiritual authority to wane. Dreamer, ask yourself am I able to forgive? Yes, you are able, and God is willing to help, if allowed. Nonetheless, until the issue is cleaned up or rendered dead, avoid dwelling on trivial matters, especially gossip. See suggested course of action. You are morally unclean. See Note 7: Clean and Unclean Animals at the beginning of this category. (3) If your dream is about another, first see Note 3 of this category, to determine if your dream is actually about another. If your dream is truly about another, your dream is an alert to the dreamer. Dreamer you are a potential victim. Dreamer, while your words have inspired many, they have threatened others; thus, at a very low point in your life, you are made subject to hearing the critical words of someone(s). You are detested by those who would criticize you, those who are threatened. Your accuser(s), those who are threatened by your inspirational gifting, and by your significance and value as an individual and to the Kingdom of God, it i s those who have brought (or will bring) negativity within your sphere, and disturbed your rest spiritually. Their words have disturbed you emotionally and spiritually, more than you realized. You have tried to dismiss their words and the negativity brought to you, but it seems you can't rid your mind of them. Give heed no longer to their words, for they are ordinary people who have failed to make that leap of faith that changes the ordinary into the extraordinary. Be encouraged, and remain humble, for you are one who is anointed to preach the gospel and to inspire others. Your words will bring peace and unity to God's people. It is your role in life to inspire and motivate. A leader in your own right, you are a forerunner for change. A large part of your mission centers on raising the spirits of your fellow mankind; thus, your gifting inclines you to several streams of communication that may include writing, speaking, singing, acting, or teaching. You must continue to develop your ability to communicate effectively in order to inspire others. Never, do you ever, allow anyone or anything to hinder your growth and spiritual journey. Unfortunately, you are amongst those who have assembled against you, because of your message. Consequently, those who fight against you, particularly those who are within the fellowship you are connected to and/or within your family, God will now fight against them, and they will suffer a physical outbreak, some sort of sickness, affliction, and/or other troubles. As worms, millipedes and centipedes are also reminders of the brevity of life, forgive, and prayerfully intercede for them that their outbreak be stopped suddenly or perhaps prevented. In doing so, the Lord will sustain them upon their sickbed; and restore health back unto them.

In addition, the following are common words; expressions or usages (e.g. slang or clichés) or a 'probable' that are metaphorically represented by worms, millipedes, or centipedes:

- Someone who lacks character, and who behaves in a groveling manner, showing exaggerated and false respect out of fear, or in order to please somebody
- To crawl or lie face down on the ground in humility or out of fear
- Someone who indulges in things unworthy
- Something that torments, undermines, or corrupts a person from within
- A person who has a nasty and unethical character undeserving of respect
- One who is given to victimizing, plundering, or destroying others for their own gain

Suggested Course of Action

Question, did your dream depict any symbols that alludes to, the dreamer will make the necessary changes, spiritually, emotionally, and/or physically to affect a more positive outcome? If changes are initiated, your dreams will change.

If you are here, your behavior will endanger your well-being, safety, and/or happiness, weakening you spiritually in some way. Fortunately, dreams pertaining to the unclean or negative aspects of animals are warnings or precautionary dreams, and are not final declarations. People and situations can, and often do, change. If you heed warnings, a bad situation can turn good overnight, so don't faint. Read and embrace 2 Corinthians 4:2-16, Galatians 6:9. With that said, dreamer, you need help from your spiritual leader(s). To help you sincerely amend and clarify the true intents and purposes of your behaviors, and to bring to an end that which keeps you from being clean. Perchance, because of emotional scarring and/or insecurities resulting from past difficult situations, you may not have the ability to work through challenging circumstances at this time and to make the best decisions. Regrettably, this in turn can, and often do, result in emotional emptiness, and you rejecting the love, authority, and/or instructions of the Lord. A spirit of apathy towards your personal relationship with Christ is a bad frame of mind. In time, your carnal nature will begin to reign over your spiritual side. Carnality also opens the door for persons, under the influence of evil, to run amok your life, both physically and spiritually until you are unable to recover. Therefore, dreamer, consider seriously your observations. If what was revealed prevail, will it sabotage any good that's happening at present wi thin your life? Will it build or destroy, strengthen or weaken, enlighten or blind? If you lack wisdom, ask Jesus for wisdom. He gives wisdom to all, generously, no matter who you are and what you've done; wisdom is available (see James 1:5 -8, Proverbs 2:1-6, 10). Hence, if, by just asking, you may get wisdom, one may suffer needlessly, because you will not ask Jesus for wisdom, as well, seek counsel from your spiritual leaders, for there is wisdom in the counsel of many. See Proverbs 11:14, 15:22, 23.

Nonetheless, you are still expected to respect God, and His ways and means. His principles are not there to be obstacles to your progress, or to be a bore to you, but to keep you out of harm's way and to assure eternal life in the world to come, the Kingdom of God. Compassionately, grace (the free and unmerited favor and beneficence of God) is extended that you may change your heart. God is giving you the opportunity to turn things around spiritually and emotionally, and He will turn thi ngs around literally; however, you will have to choose to allow the opportunity, for you still have free will; thus, the choice is yours. Free will is the expression of you choosing to participate in the divine acts of God; albeit, you are only merely placing your hand under the weight carried exclusively by God. Thus, you are not being asked to do something you cannot do, or to do it alone. Dreamer is strongly urged to return to ideals that are holy, wise, well judged; ways that are in keeping with the nature of t he Bible, ways pertaining to, contained within, and are in accordance with the Bible; ways that are scriptural.

Consider and journal the following questions. The questions will help you determine; the issue at hand, how you feel about it, and what may have instigated it. What kind of animal was it? Was it clean or unclean? See Note 7: Clean and Unclean Animals at the beginning of this category. Was it deadly, frightening, threatening, wild, domesticated, calm, non- aggressive, safe, or growing? Certain animals are deadly or harmful, meaning that if the behaviors attributed to the animal are allowed to continue or prosper within your life, serious harm or death may result. Did anyone get hurt emotionally, physical ly, or was disturbed in any way? Were others involved? If yes, who and in what manner were they involved; keeping in mind that the others represent a quality of you. How did you feel, and what did you do, because, of your feelings, regarding the animal and/or how things ended up or was going? Was it agitating, confusing, dangerous, disturbing, frustrating, peace with the situation, happy, joyful, life threatening, safe, scary, or unsure? Your answers, coupled with the interpretation, plus any additional information, should begin to unfold the subject matter and issue at hand, if not now, mull over things a few days.

For more information, see index or relevant category and subcategory for specific action, activity, person, place, or organization primary within your dream. Dreamer; personally respond, by repenting, and genuinely committing to a righteous change, to have life; with primary emphasis on life after this present life. However, the issue of eternal life will not be forced upon anyone who desires to remain in sin.

Now, pray (See Prayer of Deliverance, pg. 897)

Specific Meaning

If, in your everyday living (your waking state), as part of your lifestyle or work related activities, you have a very special relationship with animals (e.g. an animal activist, husbandry, owner, trainer, veterinarian, zoologist, exterminator). Dream s of this sort, for the most part, are ordinary dreams, resulting from your daily activities (see Chapter One, Chalom). These sorts of dreams are usually about your routine, mundane activities or anxieties that overwhelm your mind during the day. They are an inner release mechanism, which helps provide you with emotional balance and the maintaining of your sanity. These dreams are not significant, and do not warrant special attention.

Note: To an animal activist, owner, trainer, veterinarian, if the animal was abused or traumatized in anyway within the dream, this may be heeded as an alert or warning in the physical realm, to prevent serious harm to the animal in question. D o not assume that the animal is safe or ok, caution should be heeded. The dreamer may consider his or h er dream as a clue given to assist in finding facts, needed to support a prevailing situation or investigation. For example, an animal caretaker might consider an animal head being crushed as possible abuse or human exploitation of an animal by someone. Possibly, the person in the dream who did the harm or who and/or what they represent to the dreamer. The trauma, kept within context of the dream, should be relevant to your lifestyle and closely resemble your real-life situations. Meaning it can actually occur during your awaked state. This will help you narrow down the specific area of concern. However, if your dream was inundated with symbols that are not specifically related to your job and/or responsibilities, then the spiritual implications should be heeded.

THE BODY

And God created man in his own image, in the image of God created he him, male and female
created he them. And God blessed them: and God said unto them, be fruitful, and multiply,
and replenish the earth, and subdue it. And Jeho vah God formed man of the dust of the
ground, and breathed into his nostrils the breath of life; and man became a living soul
(Genesis 1:27-28; 2:7 AMS)

"Now a word was secretly brought to me, and my ear received a whisper of it. In disquieting thoughts
from the visions of the night, when deep sleep falls on men, Fear came upon me, and trembling,
which made all my bones shake. Then a spirit passed before my face; the hair on my body stood up.
It stood still, but I could not discern its appearance. A f orm was before my eyes; there was silence;
then I heard a voice saying: 'Can a mortal be more righteous than God? Can a man be more pure than
his Maker? If He puts no trust in His servants, If He charges His angels with error, How much more
those who dwell in houses of clay, whose foundation is in the dust, who are crushed before a moth?
They are broken in pieces from morning till evening; they perish forever, with no one regarding.
Does not their own excellence go away? They die, even without wisdom' (Job 4:12-21 NKJV)

For the body is not one member, but many. If the foot shall say, because I am not the hand, I am not of
the body; it is not therefore not of the body? If the ear shall say, because I am not the eye, I am not of the
body; it is not therefore not of the body? If the whole body were an eye, where would be the hearing?
If the whole were hearing, where would be the smelling? God has set the members, each one of them,
in the body, even as it pleased him. The eye cannot say to the hand, I have no need of thee: or again the
head to the feet, I have no need of you. Moreover, those members of the body, which seem to be the
least or les s honorable, are necessary, upon these we bestow more abundant honor. Therefore, our
uncomely parts have abundant comeliness. Whereas our comely parts have no need: but God tempered
the body together, giving more abundant honor to that part which lacked (1 Corinthians 12:14-27 KJV)

…it is sown a natural body; it is raised a spiritual body. If there is a natural body, there is also a spiritual body
(1 Corinthians 15:44 KJV)

This category deals with the structure of the human body, the abdomen, arms, chest, feet, hands,
head, legs, neck. Some short descriptions of types, phrases, and other processes and particulars,
connected in some way to this category are, for example, anatomy, female, male, body and soul, head
to toe, disabled, bodily waste. Also, see category content list, or index.

All Symbols and Referents, Notes (1, 2, 3, etc.), Suggested Course of Action, and Specific Meaning
offer guidance toward a more comprehensive interpretation.

Notes

1. Unless otherwise noted elsewhere, if, in your everyday living, your awaked state, as part of
    your lifestyle, work, or ministerial activities, or a special event, you have a very real connection
    with any activity involving the human body. For example, athletics, weight training, bodily
    injury, disability, or handicapped of some type, medical practitioner, physical therapist,
    trainer, weight, or eating concerns, your dream is not significant and does not warrant special
    attention.

    Otherwise noted, this dream may be a Prophetically Simple Dream (see Chapter One: The
    60th Part of Prophecy). Whereas, the dreamer is warned to stop any unhealthy, foolish, illegal,
    or illicit activity going on within your life that involves your body, e.g. any form of physical

addiction, any daredevil activity, human trafficking, prostitution, or any other criminal minded, under-handed or perverse activity that primarily involves putting the physical body in harm's way. You should cease any reckless or impetuous activity, or surrender to the appropriate authorities, especially if this is an issue within the dreamer's life, or submit or yield to other relevant persons. If any of the preceding is happening, this dream is a first step intervention and an alarm. Skip interpretation and re-consider your activity as harmful, hurtful, illegal, or life threatening, at present. Handle the situation appropriately by surrendering, first to God, for Adonai Elohim knows all, and then to appropriate relevant others. Also, see Specific Meaning at the end of this category, section entitled, Note (Specific Meaning).

Otherwise noted, per your lifestyle, if your dream closely resembled real life situations, meaning it can actually occur during your awaked state, this dream may be an Ordinary Dream, resulting from your daily activities (see Chapter One, Chalom). These sorts of dreams are usually about your routine, mundane activities or anxieties that overwhelm your mind during the day. They are an inner release mechanism, which helps provide you with emotional balance and the maintaining of your sanity. These dreams are not significant, and do not warrant special attention.

2. Probables: As the body is very personal, dreamer may also consider your own personal and special associations with the body. For example, genetic and cultural differences between human beings, as well as, the effects upon the body due to the various norms of people groups and communities. Are you prejudice against, or just don't like, certain people groups? Do certain people remind you of a particular person, place, thing, environment, or event? Thus, could the body (or body part) depicted within your dream be a possible probable (see Chapter One, section entitled, Probables)? May consider probables, as long as the interpretation is kept within the principles of spiritual boundary markers, landmarks, and property lines, (see Chapter One, section entitled, Spiritualizing Boundary Markers, Landmarks, and Property Lines).

3. Determine who your dream is for you or another. Always, considering yourself first, reflecting on your present behaviors. Ask yourself, why am I dreaming about this now? What is this dream revealing about me? Have I taken on new attributes? Has anyone commented on my present behaviors as being untypical of me? Has my ministry changed for the better or for the worse? What about my beliefs, doctrine, or philosophy, are they still based on Holy Writ? I s there something I need to know about those I am ministering to or serving?

Remember your actions and emotions within your dream. Was it your body part depicted? Were you sick? Were you disabled in any way? Did you go blind? Were you naked? Were your body genitalia the opposite of your literally body (e.g. if female dreamer, did you have a penis)? Were you in a grave or dead? Did you turn your back on someone? Unless otherwise noted elsewhere, an answer of yes, to one or more of these, or similar questions, is a good indicator that your dream is about you (the dreamer). What happened to you in your dream? Dreamer, could the results of good choices, or the consequences of bad choices, be affecting your physical body, literally? Are you in a process of renewal or transformation; hence a dream of your body changing from one state to another, for example, a bad, sickly state to a good, healthy one? In light of your dream, via the relevant interpretation, do you believe that your behavior or choic es will enhance or endanger your well-being, safety, and/or happiness, if so, how and why? Is spiritual or physical death a possibility (e.g. due to age, or perhaps physical death because of lifestyle, or your spiritual ministerial work is done, hence your Heavenly Father is calling you home, welcoming you with a "well done good and faithful servant")? See following relevant subcategory, the interpretation is about and for you.

Was someone else body part depicted? What activity stood out the most, in your dream, regarding the person? For example, what was going on with their body or what body part was highlighted? Did someone else turn his or her back on you or another? Was someone else in the grave? Was someone else genitalia depicted opposite of who they are literally? Did someone else go blind? Did someone else transform before you, in any way? Unless otherwise noted elsewhere, an answer of yes, to one or more of these, or similar questions, is a good indicator that your dream is about another and/or their role, and influential effects, within the life of the dreamer or vice versa. Consider, is someone greatly influencing your physical, spiritual, or mental health, or are you influencing another? Are they enhancing your life or are they responsible for the dwindling thereof or vice versa? Is illness a possibility, perhaps because of another's lifestyle (e.g. spouse, significant other, friend, neighbor, or foe, is infected with a contagion; any infectious disease easily transmitted by contact)? Do you know someone whose life activities or physical being is similar to that which stood out the most within your dream? Could it be that person? If so, this dream is meant to alarm. If you sense that your dream is for or about another, the question as to why you have been made privy to this information, and how do you factor into the equation, should be seriously considered along with necessary actions. Perhaps the dreamer is being made aware of the plight of someone, and you are to get involved (see Chapter One, Are You Ready to Hear the Messages in Your Dreams, section entitled, The 10% for others).

If your dream is for, or about another:

Dreams that reference others and the revelation within those dreams, is not given haphazardly to any individual, but only to those with the ability, and influence to do something with the information; this is also prophecy. With that, journal the following questions, and if unable to answer the questions now, this denotes that the person, represented within your dream, will enter your life shortly. Are you entering into a personal relationship with someone? Do you not know or understand what you're looking at, especially certain behaviors, when learning about this person? Has someone new entered your life or maybe you've just begun opening up to someone not so new, and have started listening to their advice, accepting their assistance, or are you supporting or enabling someone? Are you in denial regarding the toxicity of one of your present relationships, particularly a spouse, family member, or friend? Are you anxious, concerned, frightened, and/or troubled by recent changes in your behavior, especially because of someone's influence upon your life at present? Have you allowed someone to convince you to deceive another? Have you recently become aware of (or is being made aware of, via your dream) certain undesirable behaviors within you towards another? Are you trying to cut ties with one that is bad company? Have you just joined (or re-joined) a church, fellowship, or social group?

Note: If your dream has attributes that indicate that your dream is about you, and other attributes that indicate that your dream is about another, dreamer should consider that your dream is about you and another. For example, were you (the dreamer) naked, thus indicating that the dream is about the dreamer, did someone else turn his or her back on you, thus indicating that your dream is about another. Therefore, while your dream is about the dreamer, the dreamer should expect the role and/or influential effects of another, also plays a part in your interpretation. For example, dreamer may have been responsible for the loss of another's limb; thus, some manner of restitution is needed. However, there was a degree of negligence on the part of victim, again, see relevant interpretation.

More questions to consider. Why has the person been allowed within your life, and/or how did they get there? Again, if unable to answer the questions now, this denotes that the person, represented within your dream, will enter your life shortly. If their activity, within your dream, has proven positive, via the interpretation, this someone will prove, unwittingly, to be a very strong ally, benefactor, defender, and supporter. God has sent this someone into your life to help you carry out your next endeavor by enlarging your spiritual capacity. Allow the strength of that person's character to guide, help, and support you. On the other hand, if his or her presence and/or activity, within your dream, proved negative, via the interpretation, for sure, this person will prove to be a very strong and formidable challenge for you, perhaps unto death. If negative, this dream is a dire warning. Take steps accordingly to struggle against, or to cu t off, adverse and unfavorable relationships. Remember certain personalities are all encompassing, affecting everything, cataclysmic, contagious, deadly, harmful, infectious, predatory, and/or venomous. Symbolically meaning that if allowed to continue or prosper within your life, serious harm or death to the dreamer may result. Idolize no one, especially beyond the warning of the Lord, and we are definitely not to lay our lives down for no one. No longer, allow that particular person's influence within your life to continue or thrive. Then again, this person maybe allowed within your life, because of the dreamer's unwillingness to abstain from immorality after having been asked to abstain from such by God, see 1 Corinthians 6:9-20, Galatians 5:19-21, or the dreamer's self-righteous behavior, or a lack of a balanced and honest view of your own personality. In this case, this person will affect self-awareness within the life of the dreamer, exposing the negative traits of your personality, especially those traits, which cause you to follow, or to be so easily misled, and/or your wrong beliefs; no matter, this type of mentality needs reckoning with. Graciously, all of this will restore the dreamer to his or her right place with God, opening your eyes to see how far you've strayed from God (1 Corinthians 5:4-7; James 5:20). The lesson is, no matter how personable, powerful, or difficult a person, or how uncertain or unpopular the choices and issues, always take the next biblical and ethical step, for obedience to God's principles will always prove safer and stronger foundationally. Although, you will need all kinds of outside support to recover from this person's domination, again, no longer, allow that particular person's influence within your life to continue or thrive, especially if negative, end it abruptly.

4. Consider all the people, places, backgrounds, and activity highlighted within your dream.

Known (in your awaked life) person, animal, place, or organization within your dream:

Unless otherwise noted elsewhere, people, animals, places, backgrounds that are actually known by the dreamer in your awaked life, indicates a part of you that you recognize within yourself on some level or another. Question to journal, if dreamer seriously considers all the particulars, what stood out the most, what features, or character traits stood out the most. For example, age, color, height, size, happiness, considerate, loving, let you be yourself, peacefulness, encourager, irrational, leader, liar, mentor, passionate, personable, neglected, poor, run-down, sage, shyster, unwise, upscale, vengeful. Write down (journal) the particular highlighted within your dream. The attribute or activity highlighted is for a reason. Since the attribute written down is a part of you, namely the dreamer's nature, demeanor, and/or lifestyle, an honest assessment is very important for truth sake. Happy note, considering that other people's attributes, within dreams, also represent attributes of your own personality, causes one to look at another in a better light. According to your capacity to embrace self-awareness and a rectification of mind, body, and spirit, God will begin to enhance, make better, more attractive, sanctify, diminish, and make pure and free from sin and guilt, this part of you.

Otherwise noted, if the person, animal, place, or background within your dream is actually known by the dreamer, in your awaked life, this person, animal, place, or background may represent him or herself, or itself.

Unknown in your awaked life or although known, was unseen, invisible, or only talked about - person, animal, place, or organization within your dream:

Unless otherwise noted elsewhere, if you did not recognize, the person, place, thing, they, or it, was not seen, invisible, or only talked about within your dream, this indicates an attribute or activity within your life that you are unfamiliar with, or are in denial about, or you refuse to acknowledge it, but it does exists. Question to journal: what character trait, feature, action, or activity, stood out the most? For example, age, color, height, size, happiness, considerate, loving, let you be yourself, peacefulness, encourager, irrational, leader, liar, mentor, passionate, personable, neglected, poor, run-down, sage, shyster, unwise, upscale, vengeful. Although, on some conscious level, you are aware of a certain behavior or attribute within you, you have chosen to filter out or simply ignore certain information about yourself that contradicts your view of yourself and/or your preconceived notions of others and of the world around you. Possibly protecting yourself, emotionally and psychologically, from a situation, which you are unable to cope with at this time, or you lack control over; then again, perhaps the dreamer has an exaggerated or unrealistic view of yourself. No matter the reason, right now a question is before you, via your dream. Do you want to know this part of yourself? According to your ability to handle self-awareness, God will begin to reveal this side of you to you. Why, He wants to balance your understanding of things; thus, effecting wholeness within your life, so that the enemy will no longer be able to manipulate your emotions so easily. The Holy Spirit is with you to help you throughout this ent ire process, listen to Him. Now, in your life, this activity or attribute needs reckoning with, somehow or some way.

Otherwise noted, (known or unknown), if the person, place or thing that initiated (or was a recipient of) the action or activity within your dream was not seen, invisible, or only talked about within your dream, this may indicate that the dreamer does not recognize the influential effects another has within your life, or upon your attitude.

If more than one person (known or unknown):

Consider what the group had in common. What behavior, character trait, feature, action, or activity, stood out the most? For example, were they argumentative, authoritative, beautiful, criminal minded, dancing, difficult, dressed unusual, enigmatic, fighting, focused, flirty, helpful, hurtful intentions, powerful, promiscuous, quiet, secretive, seemed unreal, unassuming? What about age, color, height, size, happiness, considerate, loving, let you be yourself, peacefulness, encourager, irrational, leader, liar, mentor, passionate, personable, neglected, poor, run-down, sage, shyster, unwise, upscale, vengeful, death. That which was highlighted and noted is what you need to focus on at present.

If the attribute or quality is a desirable or positive one, allow the strength of that attribute to help you overcome some manner of immorality or irreverence within your life and/or to help you to become better, productively, for the Kingdom of God in some manner. If the attribute is an undesirable or negative one, take steps accordingly to struggle against the growing desires of the carnal side of you. If applicable, get help and support via prayer, fasting, and a Christian based support group.

For dreams of the dead see following note.

Did you see a dead body? While the dead has nothing to do with the living (Ecclesiastes 9:4-6), it may be considered what character trait did that person represent to the dreamer, while the person was actually alive, what character feature stood out the most. With that trait noted, dreamer may consider that the trait noted, is within the dreamer, and that trait is no longer useful or needed for the progression of your spiritual walk, on this side of heaven. Dreamer, it is suggested that you render that trait (good or bad) obsolete, and began anew attempting to move forward, using different tactics to overcome unproductive habitual life cycle choices, and for maneuvering through this thing we call life in a more, better way. See category, Death.

5. In addition to the following interpretations, see index or relevant categories for more information. For example, if people were involved in some way, see category, People; if death was highlighted, see category, Buildings, Structures. Kept within context of your dream and the interpretation, the additional symbols are perhaps relevant. It will be within the sum of all the symbols that you will find a more thorough interpretation.

6. Since the following list is not extensive, dreamer is encouraged to seek biblical guidelines and other relevant research to determine the metaphorical meaning of your particular body part or activity, depicted within your dream, via a Bible concordance, Bible illustrated dictionary,

encyclopedia, or internet. Having done your research you should be able to determine some basic behaviors or attributes your Lord and Savior wants you to focus on.

Symbols and Referents

In keeping with the fact that parts of the human body, within dreams, refer to their spiritual roots, this type of dream is u sually about your spiritual health. Your dream about the body may also refer to your physical health as well.

In addition to the varied meanings of the body, other common words, expressions, usages, (e.g. slang or clichés), or a 'probable' that are metaphorically represented by any of the following are also considered (this section is an addendum at the end of the relevant subcategory).

Category Content: if not listed, see index, perchance, for your specific type of human body dream.

- Abdominal, Chest Cavity (unless listed separately, this category, aka Viscera, includes the soft internal organs of the body, specifically those within the abdomen and chest, e.g. the heart, lungs.
    - Belly (Stomach); Hernia; Heart (incl. heart attack, your heart was troubled, heart darkened)
- Agedness or Aging (looking or being older than you really are in your awaked life)
- Back (the posterior part of the body from the top of the spine to the end of the spine, bent over, e.g. Hunchback, Crookback, walking bent over, bent, bend over backwards, fall over backwards)
    - Behind someone's back, to be in the back of someone or to turn your back on someone; Back up against a wall; Stabbed someone in the back
- Blemish, Blisters, Piercings, Scabbed, Scarred, Sores, Tattoo, or Thorns (a flaw, mark, spot, disfigurement, or infection on the body)
    - Body Parts (chopped or hacked into pieces, cut, gash, nicked, stabbed, see category, Cutting [Chopped]); Body Piercings (e.g. tongue); Satanic symbol or mark (aka the mark of the beast) on your forehead or hands (or any satanic symbol or mark that was stated as representing Satanism, within your dream, e.g. 666, a pentagram); Scabbed or scarred (a scab or scar of some sort); Tattoo or Tattoo Artist (artistic drawings or writings on the skin); Thorns (small sharp-pointed tip resembling a spike on a stem or leaf, prickers, stickers, prickles)
- Bones
    - Skull and Crossbones
- Breasts or Chest (the front part of the thorax of woman, man, or animal)
    - Beating of Breasts or Chest (pounding one's chest or breasts area with your hands or fists); Breasts or Chest abnormalities (deformed, distorted, or maimed); Breast Fed or Breast Feeding (adult, animal, baby); Exposure of breast, see subcategory, Naked; Broad chest or large breasts (broader or larger than your normal chest or breasts in your awaked life); Embracing, hugging, or fondling of breasts or caressing of chest (by spouse; by someone who is married to another [e.g. illicit relation]; Family member or friends; Enemies)
- Excretory system (unless listed separately, this category includes the alimentary canal, bile, bladder, kidneys, intestine, liver, skin, urethra - this system deals with egestion, body waste, any discharges from the body. For example, fecal matter, urine, or any other kind of egestion; thus, this category also deals with droppings, dung, fecal matter, manure, stool, or urine)
    - Fecal matter (discharges such as feces or excretions such as kidney stones); Kidneys; Sweat, perspiration (see subcategory, Forehead, or category, Bleeding (Sweating blood, hematidrosis); Urine

- Giant, Dwarf (to appear gigantic or dwarfed, or to see one)
  - Dwarf, see category, Abating
- Hair (incl. hair washing, gray hair)
  - To cut hair, see category, Cutting (Shave); Beard (long beard [male/female]); Saliva on the beard; White (or gray) beard; To shave beard, see category, Cutting (Shave)
- Head, Neck, and Throat (this category includes the brain, cheeks, jaws, ears, eyes, face, forehead, head, mouth, teeth, tongue, neck, throat, and nose)
  - Brain; Cheeks, Jaws; Ears; Eyes, Eyeglasses, magnifying glass, see category, Buildings (Windows); Looking out a window, see category, Buildings (Windows); Black Eye or Full Black Iris; Blindness or Blindfolded; Blind Leading the Blind, see category, Walking (Blindly Walking); Cataracts, disfigured, defected, or dull looking eyes, or Scales falling from your eyes (thin flakes of dead epidermis); Eyebrows, Eyelids, Eyelashes; Watching or Staring or Gaze or Very Wide Opened Eyes (fixate your eyes on someone, or something, e.g. you staring at or watching something intensely, or someone staring at or watching you intensely, or "all eyes on you", or eyes wide open and fixed as in a deep stare); Face (Animal's face or reflection of an animal; Bright shining face, Face glowing [some manner of brightness in the face] or face had a comforting, encouraging, nurturing, and affectionate appearance; Color of face; Face of the Lord; Facial Expressions [To be angry, breathing hard, displeased, frightening, intimidating, menacing looking, or threatening and scary]; Dirty face or face was disfigured in some way; Sad, depressed, and/or crying, see category Emotions (Crying); Large face or "long face" (face appears larger or longer than normal); Large stone face, see category, Standing (Standing Stones); Mask, Masquerades (wearing one); Washing face, see category, Cleaning (Washing Face); Spit in your face, see category, Violence; Stand face to face (or have you face up against another), see category, Standing; Wine, or other alcoholic or fermented drinks thrown in your face, see category, Drinking; Forehead (Sweat, Perspiration on forehead, Wrinkled forehead); Head; Bald head; Bleeding from your head, or head was damage in some manner; Head cut off or floating away; Distorted, hit in the head, maimed, or smashed in the head; Hand extended to touch a head; Head bent over, see category, Bowing (To stoop over); Oil poured over your head; Small head; Big head (to see a head bigger than normal); Head on a platter or on something else or inside of something; Talking head (a head, without a body, is talking), see category, Talking; Mouth; Breath; Bad (foul) smelling; Good (fresh) smelling breath; Choking or Suffocating (struggle for breath; have; insufficient oxygen, breathe with great difficulty, caused by blocking the airways to the lungs); Happy mouth (e.g. smiling, laughing); Chewing food or gum; Kissing, see category, Emotions (Love); Tightly closed mouth or tight or pursed lips; Teeth; Bite (to grip, cut off, or tear, with the teeth); Cleaning Teeth, Brushing teeth, Flossing or at a Dentist; Dentures (artificial teeth); Good teeth or White Teeth (teeth in good condition); Teeth falling out of your mouth, or missing teeth, or teeth in bad condition; Sharp or Monstrous Teeth; Tongue; Biting your tongue or Tongue-Tied; Blemished, cancerous, canker sores, patches, or tongue was marred in some way or another; Cut out tongue or without a tongue; Hold your tongue (holding your tongue in some way or manner); Long tongue (abnormally long) or sticking tongue out; Normal tongue (healthy looking, unremarkable in appearance); Pierced tongue, see Body Piercings; Smooth tongued (an unusually smoothness of the tongue, or smooth to the touch); Thick tongue; Two tongues (two tongues in one mouth); Neck, Throat, Chin; Broken or wounded Neck or Chin; Long Neck or Chin; Yoked neck (put a yoke on or join with a yoke); Fat or distorted Neck or Chin; Nape or back of the neck; Cutthroat (throat is cut); Head-to-head, or neck-to-neck (to dream of two heads or necks, next to each other in some way, e.g. leaning next to, or touching, each other, or heads or necks; compared to each other); Nose; Broken or

Crooked nose or Nosebleed; Flat nose; Nostrils flared or large nose; Ring in the nose; Sniveling or runny nose, see Category, Crying; Your nose in the air or in the clouds

- Inoculation (e.g. flu shots, vaccine shots, any kind of shots)
- Limbs: This category includes the upper and lower limbs of the body, commonly called the arms and legs, and all the parts connected to the limbs, e.g. elbows, fingers, hands, wrists. The leg section includes ankle, buttock, calf, feet, knee, and thigh, toes
  - Limbs (upper and lower limbs of the body, healthy, six or more, sores); Healthy, strong, good looking limbs (elbows, fingers, toes, hands, shoulders, and wrists); Six or more Limbs (arms, legs, fingers, or toes); Skinny (unusually skinny upper and/or lower limbs), see category, Abating (To grow smaller);Sores on limbs; Arms (includes elbows, fingers/toes, hands, and wrists); Broken arm(s); Arm(s) cut off; Strong and/or well-defined arm(s); Elbow; Fingers or Toes; Fingerprints, Fingertips, or Toe Prints; Fingernails or Toenails (natural or synthetic); Hands; Broken hand or hand damaged, marred, mutilated in some way; Clapping hands, see category, Clapping; Holding hands; Palms; Palmistry (telling fortunes by lines on the palm of the hand); Right hand or healthy, beautiful, good looking or strong hands or a strong handshake; Blood on your hands; Praying hands; Hands tied, bound (e.g. tied or secured with a rope); Washing hands of something, see category, Cleaning (Washing hands); Writing instrument being removed from your fingers, hands; Wrist(broken or limp wrist); Legs (the lower portion of the body, from the hip to the toes, includes ankle, buttock, calf, feet, knee, thigh, toes); Ankles, Heel; ("Achilles" Heel); Buttocks or Hips (exposed or covered); Calf or Shank (the part of the human leg between the knee and the ankle); Feet, Foot; Barefoot, to be without shoes (barefoot), see category, Walking (Walking Barefoot) To admire feet; To sit at Christ's (or another's) feet, see category, Sitting; Feet of clay or stone or a statue's feet; Broken, disabled, or lame feet; To observe feet; One (or both) feet cut off; Put your foot in your mouth; Trodden underfoot, see category, Walking; Washing of someone one's feet. See category, Cleaning (Feet); Knees; Kneel down, see category, Bowing; Legs Crippled, Lame, or Unequal (including Prosthesis or Peg Leg); Break a leg; Pulling your leg; Thigh (femur, thighbone, the part of the leg between the hip and the knee); To hit or pat or inflict a heavy blow on a thigh with the hand or tool or weapon; Toes: See relevant subcategory, Limbs or Arms
- Naked (completely unclothed, au naturel, nude, "birthday suit")
- Swimming nude, see category, Swimming (Skinny-dipper); Naked and crying, see category, Emotions (Naked and crying)
- Pregnancy, see category, Pregnancy
- Reflections, Shadows, Shade or Pictures of People
  - Dancing before a mirror; Reflection in a mirror; Mirror, see category, Buildings (Windows); Picture of people, person; Sad, crying, or depressed reflection, see category Emotions (Crying); Shadows, Shade; To see God's shadow
- Sickness, Illness (cancer, leprosy, HIV, AIDS, STD, or any malignancy, or any chronic communicable disease or infection, or any wasting away of body parts or any serious illness)
  - Heart attack, see subcategory Heart; Lowered body temperature, see category Frozen
- Sexuality
  - Reproductive, Genital system; Castration or Circumcised, circumcision (removal of the foreskin, or to cut the skin over the clitoris); Penis (including woman with a penis); Vagina (including man with a vagina); Sexual Assault or Pedophile or Rapist or any sexual deviant (e.g. molestation, rape, sex slave, sexual abuse, sex crime, forcing another person to engage in any sexual act against their will, any act subjecting someone to unwanted or improper sexual advances or activity, especially children or women, by threat or force. Any statutory offense that provides that it is a crime to, knowingly cause another person

to engage in an unwanted sexual act by force); Sexual Relations or Sexual Orientation or Virginity (a person's tendency of sexual attraction; esp. whether heterosexual or homosexual or virginity); Sex with the dead; Heterosexual Relationship; Homosexuality, Homosexual Relationship, LBGT; Kissing, see category, Emotions (Love); Virginity, Virgin
- Soul or Out of Body Experience

ABDOMINAL, CHEST CAVITY (unless listed separately, this category, aka Viscera, includes the soft internal organs of the body, specifically those within the abdomen and chest, e.g. the heart, lungs. If needed, also see subcategory, excretory system):

This category has two meanings (choose one). (1) A dream of the abdominal and chest cavity denote one who has a tendency toward selfishness, and a predisposition to "take", except when it comes to giving up your own desires in order to advance your own cause, and at this point, you suppose, and boast, that you are doing a great service for others. When actually, you are only benefiting yourself and your cause, "only what you can get". You have distorted true religion, because of covetousness, greed, and selfishness. You have led people astray, causing the people of God to err in the things of God. Your cupidity will be uncovered, and evil will be brought upon you that will send you away from your place. Read, understand, and embrace, Psalm 51:6. See suggested course of action. (2) The viscera also expose your deepest and most genuine emotions or feelings about certain things, or "goings-on". Read, understand, and embrace, Psalm 51:6. Dreamer, Jesus wants you to abide in Him; this means to dwell or "stay put", and be patient. Don't run off and try to do your own thing in your own strength and carnal knowledge. He wants to continue His ministry through you, healing the sick, delivering the oppressed, fulfilling His ministry, via you, to His people and He wants you to give freely without thought of recompense. He will compensate you openly and generously. Your situation will change and He will give you a new song in your heart. You will sing a new song. Wait on the Lord, for He is faithful to come, and again I say wait on the Lord. See suggested course of action.

Belly (Stomach): Dreamer, having been in the process of rectification for a while, one's character trait is never to be jealous and/or contemptuous of others; and so, we are taught, "who is rich, he or she who is happy with their portion" (Ecclesiastes 2:24, 3:22, 5:18-20). Your jealous and contemptuous nature, if not replaced with contentment and gratitude, will lead to serious illnesses, diseases, addictions, and/or seriously broken relationships. Dreamer, stop and consider the bigger picture. For, when you stop and think about, what the Lord has already done for you, and how far He's brought you; think about His goodness. Think about His hedge of protection around you; the provisions and ways He's made for you, the doors He's open for you. Think about you're in your right mind, and how the Lord is blessing you right now. As well, you've been given the honor of knowing that you can boldly come before His Throne with prayer, and that He takes joy in you, let this be your contentment and gratitude; a sweet sound in your ear. Focus and think on these things, see Philippians 4:8, and put your trust in Him and in His provision, coupled with contentment with His provisions, and your peace will overflow. Pray for Jesus to heal your unbelief, refrain from jealously, and wait on the Lord, and again I say wait. See suggested course of action.

In addition, the following is a common word, expression, or usage (e.g. slang or cliché), or a 'probable' that is metaphorically represented by the stomach:

- **Her belly in between her teeth (e.g., a dream depicting biting a stomach, or someone putting their mouth on a stomach, or something along the line of teeth and stomach meeting):** Your dream denotes that a woman, perhaps the one doing the biting, or the dreamer if female, is in an advanced stage of pregnancy.

Hernia: Your dream denotes that the dreamer's negative traits, especially your jealous and/or contemptuous attitude towards others, has led (or will lead) to serious illnesses, diseases, addictions, and/or seriously broken relationships. Moreover, the reasons for your illnesses, namely your attitude, will be manifested publicly. Subsequently, your attitude, if lesson learned, will be replaced with a more contented and appreciative nature. See suggested course of action.

Heart: This dream has three meanings (choose one). (1) The promises made between you and God; you promised to worship and serve Jesus, and in return, Jesus promised you, life more abundantly on this side of eternity, and eternal life. If you have kept your promise to worship and serve, God's promise to you of abundance, on this side of eternity, will begin to manifest. Actually, the realization of those promises is happening now. Only, you are being asked to devote yourself to embracing God's divine order that you may mature. Dreamer; via divine order, go on to perfection through faith in God (a resolute trust in the integrity of God and in His Word). Moreover, you have been blessed with a great understanding of spiritual knowledge, and not without reason. Dreamer, one who is given the means to study and teach and has access to prophetic wisdom, is purposed to be a transformational force in people's lives. Per God's anointing, your power of speech and wisdom will convert souls to the Kingdom of God. The heart of your ministry should focus on teaching about the essence of God, the Blood of Christ, and divine order. Your time of missions is upon you. You are sent to those who are spiritually dead, yet a spark of life is hidden within them (also see Matthew 28:19, 20). Dreamer, it is necessary that you bring to remembrance your former state, when you were enslaved to sin. What benefits did you reap at that time from the things you now disdain, the filth, and foolishness of it all? Now that you have been set free from sin, you have become a servant of God. The benefits you reap are meant to lead to holiness and the end-result is eternal life (Romans 6:21, 22). To keep you humble, repentant, and watchful, you would do well to remember the time when you were a servant of sin, devoted to iniquity, embracing vanity, and reaping the same; and to remember the benefits of being a servant of God. (2) Heart attack or your heart was troubled: Dreamer, the manifestation of what you've been hoping for is postponed for a later time. An unfortunate situation happening within your life at present is hindering or impeding the manifestation of what you've been hoping for; moreover, your unfortunate issue or situation will prove very frustrating. Although you may question why this or that, is there a lesson to learn, and/or why is the pain so great? Dreamer, be encourage, and know that God knows where you are, He knows the hurt, frustration, and pain you bear, and He knows what you need. Note, it is written that hope deferred makes the heart sic k; but when the desire cometh, it is a tree of life (Proverbs 13:12). Know that what you are hoping for and desiring will happen or manifest. If necessary, see suggested course of action. (3) Heart darkened (to see an unusually dark colored heart): Dreamer, your thinking has become futile, perverse, distorted, and deviant. Dreamer you are allowing, the "spirit" (aka demon) of fear to terrorize you, it has become your own personal terrorist. This demon terrorizes you in your thoughts, when you are foc used on perverse, distorted, and deviant thoughts. When you are afraid, insecure, impatient, confused, filled with worry, uneasy and unsure, when you hesitate, is full of apprehension, when your thoughts forecast only doom and gloom, when panic and stress comes, and despair and depression find you, when you are restless, frightful, full of dread, anxious, nervous, and when you feel hopeless. You will find this demon in every phobia. Question to journal: What would it feel like if all of your fears were suddenly released from you at one time? Pause and feel that. Bible story, there was that herd of pigs that Legion was cast into, and these pigs found their thoughts to be so unbearable that they all ran off a cliff to commit suicide, because t hey could not bear what had been unleashed upon them (Matthew 8:28-34, Mark 5:1-20, Luke 8:26-39). On the other hand, the man whom the demons were suddenly released from, was found sitting, clothed, healed, and in his right mind. Therefore, dreamer, earnestly renounce the insidious voice of the devil. Dreamer think on things that are true, whatever is noble, whatever is right, whatever is pure, whatever is lovely, whatever is admirable, if anything is excellent or praiseworthy, thi nk about those things, see Philippians 4:8. Unfortunately, at present, your thoughts are adversarial to the Word of God that says all things will work together for good, to those who love God, and are called according to His purpose. For, if you truly ca n believe God's word, it will change all the rules that darkness has attempted to establish in your heart and mind. Now I say to you that before you can move forward, fear and doubt must be cast out, and renounced. If you will daily come away and pray, then God will heal you of all things, only come with much prayer and spiritual fasting. Spiritual fasting is a time of waiting when you are praying and asking the Lord to come and perform that which only He can perform. Similar to a literal fast, during this time you must abstain. But this fast you must refrain from any counsel that tempts you, to put your hand on the matter, or to turn you away from waiting on the Lord. During this time of waiting, you simply need to continue in prayer and be still. Then the Lord will say, "My love is able to break this curse of darkness from over your mind, body, and spirit". Warning, it will be during your spiritual fast that weaknesses, such as unbelief, doubt, fear, pride, arrogance, will come forth to tempt you to eat the counsel of lies, rather than to wait for the Lord to come to deliver, heal, help, save, reveal, and/or guide. Further, if urged by God, declare a one, two, or three day fast without food. Wait on the Lord, for He is faithful to come, and again I say wait on the Lord. See suggested course of action.

AGEDNESS OR AGING (looking or being older than you really are in your awaked life):

Dreamer is inefficiently, and inappropriately, wasting your life, natural gifting, talents, and prosperity. You spend your life thoughtlessly, and you spend extravagantly. You will begin to experience a decline in vitality, strength of body, and mind, resulting from a debilitating chronic disease, and you will experience grief. You will decline in physical and spiritual size, strength, power, and, if relevant, you will see a reduction in numbers of those who follow you. It will be as though God has shut out your prayers, blocked your ways, and hedged you in. You will become the ridicule of a few people. Yet, the very fa ct that you will live, and not die from your chronic disease, will be due to God's mercies and compassions, for even in your distress God will remember to be merciful. Therefore, you are counseled, to allow every day to be an opportunity for you to experience, anew, God's love. Having made it through the repercussions, and wages, of your inefficiency and wastefulness; in God's timing, things will get better, this too shall pass. Only, never again take your blessings from God for granted, and learn the meaning of godly stewardships. See suggested course of action.

BACK (the posterior part of the body from the top of the spine to the end of the spine):

This dream has three meanings (choose one). (1) To see your back or the back of another denotes that the dreamer will develop slowly into a person with extraordinary vision, focus, and authority. However, at present, a weakness is shown, because you are, in many ways, too dependent and focused on others. Consequently, hereafter, there is one, deemed wicked ethically, evil, disagreeable, unpleasant, and/or trifling, possibly a relative (e.g. sibling, aunt, uncle, cousin), who will attempt to cause you injury, misery, or some manner of distress or calamity. Be not dismayed, discouraged, nor frightened, you will not be given over to the desires of your foes, the Lord will protect and preserve your life. However, allow this drama to be a life lesson, and become again dependent upon the Lord and confident in His providential and miraculous care of you. Again, never do you ever, exalt, or fanatically focused upon, anyone, no matter his or her public persona, above God, His truths, and your relationship with Jesus. Moreover, see Luke 10:19, 20. If necessary, see suggested course of action. (2) Bent over (e.g. Hunchback, Crookback, walking bent over, bent, bend over backwards, fall over backwards): This dream denotes that physical and spiritual healing is available to the dreamer at this moment. Thus, this choice has three parts (one, two, or all may apply). (a) Your dream also denotes one who is trying very hard to please someone. Dreamer, consider why are you trying so hard to please another? While we are truly to love our neighbor as ourselves, as well as, empathically consider others, what is your motive behind "pleasing", to such an extent that your dream has come as an admonishment? See suggested course of action. (b) Your dream denotes a physical health issue or sickness, especially an illness that has drained the dreamer of stamina for quite some time now. If dreamer is physically ill, favorably, you will recover "overnight". (c) Dreamer is one who is spiritually impoverished. Note: If someone else was bent over, dreamer is unaware of (or does not acknowledge) the following behavior within yourself.

You lack the power to manifest that which is great and glorious, to restrain from corrupt desires, and to comply with the precepts and teachings of Jesus Christ; thus, there is a great need to understand the power and the purpose of the Holy Spirit within one's life. The Holy Spirit carries out the processes that transitions you from one state to another, obey His lead. With that said, unfortunately, many believers, including the dreamer, open their lives up to demonic involvement through the embracing of some sin or through cultic involvement (either knowingly or unknowingly). Examples may include immorality, drug, alcohol abuse that alters one's state of consciousness, rebellion, bitterness, and/or transcendental meditation (e.g. yoga). The book of Ephesians (2:2, 8-9, 4:17-24, 6:10-18) gives clear instructions on how we are able to have victory in our lives in the battle against the forces of evil. The first step is placing your faith in Christ, who breaks the rule of evil. Second, choose, again by God's grace, to put off ungodly habits and to put on godly habits by the renewing of your mind, and by resisting the devil, by not giving him room in your mind, your thought processes, your behaviors, and life, for there is truly a spiritual battle going on within the lives of all believers, including yours. Stand with truth, righteousness, the gospel, faith, salvation, the Word of God, and prayer; by this, you will recover all. With that said, the following are three possibilities as to why the spiritual impoverishment (choose one). (i) Dreamer is internally inconsistent and disordered, because of a violent violation in your past or recent present. The violation (e.g. abuse, assault, bullying, kidnapping, molestation, rape, stalked, or being held prisoner) has you spiritually "bent over". A diabolical entity, having possessed the person(s) who committed the literal act (the violator), was sent to rob, steal, and destroy a quality of life that has been destined you, to keep you from living that life abundantly, happily, and in peace. Favorably, the Lord is creating a miracle in your life. This miracle will stop the effects of your violation from playing a significant role in your life, enabling you to move forward with your life. However, the miracle's lasting success depends upon your willingness to be healed and set free; for one will always have the choice to say no, or perhaps sabotage their progress. Dreamer, recognize and respect your time of visitation from the Lord, for it is upon you, as well as the work of His Hand upon your life. Dreamer, hold on to your miraculous recovery "with your teeth", sort to say. See suggested course of action. (ii) Dreamer has chosen not to conform to mainstream Christianity (e.g. such as one looking to someone other than Jesus as Savior and Lord, one who is expecting another messiah, deliverer, unbelief in God and/or His Word, and/or one who is in disagreement with their church modes, such as attendance, practices, and/or rituals). Dreamer, your new way is based on exploring alternatives to God's righteous principles, as well as, creating a sense of unity with the wickedness around you. Therefore, servitude to the master of darkness is forced or imposed upon you, and you have conformed to his tenets. This recklessness can be remedied by repentance. Dreamer, take words to Jesus and pray, "'I have sinned, and I have done wrong and acted wickedly". Other than prayer and heartfelt repentance to Jesus and to individuals affected by your actions, in the form of an apology (if possible), no other excuse or weak justification will be heard. See suggested course of action. (iii) Dreamer, your mentality is concerned only with your personal comfort, material wealth, and status, at any expense. Now, having in yourself nothing that you respect more than power and greed, you are willing to sacrifice all, God, principle, family, and friend, to the image or idol of vanity. This mentality sacrifices children, family, and morality, to the hollowness of satisfying immoral desires and appetites. All carried out, with the hope of finding happiness by pacifying jealously and covetousness. The selling-out of yourself over to immorality, allowing wickedness to prevail in your home, devaluing those you should be protecting and nurturing, while closing your eyes to it all, are all principles based on values that are not only vile, but also increasingly unstable. This way cries out against godly ethics, and its' end offends any sense of God. Your recklessness can be remedied by prayer and heartfelt repentance to Jesus and to individuals affected by your actions, in the form of an apology (if possible). Repentance is seeking pardon and expressing sincere feelings of regret and brokenness for having done something awry and/or for having hurt someone, see 2 Corinthians 7:10, 11. To Jesus, pray Psalm 38:1-22. To individuals, a phone call or a letter of apology is a good place to start. This followed by appropriate application of wisdom, can conceivably avert some of the repercussions of your choices. This is what is called leaving a blessing behind. See suggested course of action.

In addition, the following are common words, expressions, usages, (e.g. slang or clichés), or a 'probable' that are metaphorically represented by the back:

- **Behind someone's back, to be in the back of someone or to turn your back on someone:** Your dream denotes help, support, and a miraculous strengthening is coming to aid the dreamer. Dreamer will also receive financial support, or backing from someone, perhaps anonymously. If dreamer was in the back of, or behind someone, your dream denotes that dreamer is helping to strengthen another. The reaping of your kind deeds sown will now begin to manifest.
- **Back up against a wall:** The dreamer is in a serious situation with few options to resolution. Dreamer, no matter how difficult or how uncertain the issues always take the next biblical, ethical, and most informed step, and consider obedience to God is always better than sacrifice, see 1 Samuel 15:22. See suggested course of action.
- **Stabbed someone in the back:** Your dream denotes betrayal on some level; and the betrayer is the one who was doing the stabbing, either the dreamer or another. Nonetheless, there is an attempt to deceive someone, thus, betraying a trust by means of deception. The dreamer has said or did one thing in someone's face, and then said or did the opposite without his o r her knowledge. Question to journal, who stabbed who, if known, the person(s) depicted may perhaps represent him or herself. If unknown, dreamer does not acknowledge this behavior within you. The reaping of your deceptive deeds will now begin to manifest, you will be expose as a great pretender. See suggested course of action.

BLEMISH, BLISTERS, PIERCINGS, SCABBED, SCARRED, SORES, TATTOO, OR THORNS (a flaw, mark, spot, disfigurement, or infection on the body):

This dream has two meanings (choose one). (1) To see a blemish, blisters, sores on your body, or to disfigure your body in anyway, this type of dream indicates sinful folly and some manner of impurity within the life of the dreamer, will lead to a serious disease, or illness within your body. Read and understand 2 Peter 2:13, this is to you. Dreamer, once the disease is manifested, your guilt will overwhelm you, you will be humiliated, bitterness will weigh heavy upon your heart, and this will be your focus constantly. Your companions, friends, associates, and neighbors, will avoid you, others will keep their distance, because of your illness, and you will be talked about. Dreamer, the consequences of your past choices and actions are upon you. Even more, you can no longer prosper under the anointing and authority of God, without prayer and heartfelt repentance to Jesus and to individuals affected by your actions, in the form of an apology (if possible). Please note that there is a difference in spiritual blessings and material prosperity. You cannot have spiritual blessings without material prosperity, but you can have the material without the spiritual. Favorably, Jesus Christ is demonstrating grace by offering you a resurrection from dead works, people, places, and things. There awaits you a spiritual resurrection, according to God's grace, and possib ly a miraculous healing, if you vow to live out genuinely and strongly, your personal relationship with Jesus Christ, committed to the cause of the Kingdom of God. However, before making such a vow to God, read Deuteronomy 23:21-23; nonetheless, the choice is yours. Consider your dream a first step intervention. Dreamer, utilizing the powerful resources of prayer and heartfelt repentance to Jesus and to individuals affected by your actions, in the form of an apology (if possible), is needed. Repentance is seeking pardon and expressing sincere feelings of regret and brokenness for having done something awry and/or for having hurt someone, see 2 Corinthians 7:10, 11. To Jesus, pray Psalm 38:1-22. To individuals, a phone call or a letter of apology is a good place to start. This followed by appropriate application of wisdom; and by the Spirit of God you will be revived to a new life and glory. Choose not to go out from the presence of the Lord, that is, to willingly renounce God, and to be content to forego the privileges He offers, namely eternal life, so that you might not be under His precepts; make things right. See suggested course of action. (2) See one of the following.

Body Piercings (e.g. tongue): This dream has three meanings (choose one). (1) Your dream of body piercing may be a Prophetically Simple Dream (see Chapter One: The 60ᵗʰ Part of Prophecy). Whereas, the dreamer is warned to seek medical attention due to a possible health issues related to piercing. Your dream is a first step intervention and an alarm. Skip interpretation and go get medical attention. (2) Dreamer, you have deliberately chosen to become enslaved to that which is forbidden by the one true and living God. Your choices are not only spiritually forbidden and unhealthy, but are illegal as well. Spiritual bondage, critical illness, and/or literal imprisonment are real fruits of your present activities, if you do not walk out of the situation that has enslaved you. Choose to be free within. For he or she who Christ sets free is truly free. However, freedom begins with a personal choice. Do you want to be free? See suggested course of action. (3) Pierced tongue: Dreamer, you follow the wrongful desires of your heart, refusing to submit your conduct to reason, and to divine revelation. You walk contrary to God's righteous precepts, for darkness has blinded you to truth. There is a need to consider, do you really know where you are going spiritually? A bold and daring seducer, you mouth empty, boastful words; propagating erroneous teachings, appealing to the lustful desires of sinful human nature. You also entice others to do wrong; talking about freedom, while you yourself is a slave to uncleanness, for a man or woman is a slave to whatever holds mastery over him or her. You n ot only take pleasure in the contempt within your heart, but you boast malicious and judgmental words against those whom God has set in authority over you. Dreamer, God is willing, and has already made a way for you to escape from, or leave, your pl ace of desolation. If you desire freedom, your desires will be granted you; and will result in your freedom, literally, emotionally, and spiritually. However, if, having escaped the corruption of darkness by knowing the Lord and Savior Jesus Christ, if indeed, you have, and again you become entangled in, and overcome by, the darkness, you will become worse off then, than you are right now (Matthew 12:43-45, Luke 11:24). For it is better to, not know the way of righteousness, than to know it and then turn your back on Him who called you out of darkness into His wonderful light (2 Peter 2:1). Dreamer, you do not belong to the night nor to the darkness. Have nothing to do with the vain deeds of darkness, but rather expose them and repent (see Psalm 51). For He who has rescued us from the dominion of darkness and brought us into the Kingdom of the Son, loves you. So put aside the deeds of darkness and He will again bring light to your heart and mind, and sanctify your hidden motives. Y ou, especially, have much more to gain than to lose by choosing Christ. Read fully, understand, and apply Ephesians 4:17-5:21. See suggested course of action.

Satanic symbol or mark (aka the mark of the beast) on your forehead or hands (or any satanic symbol or mark that was stated as representing Satanism, within your dream, e.g. 666, a pentagram): Dreamer, you are not in harmony with the will of God for your life. Nor, are you embracing the particular objectives that are intended to ensure the fulfillment of that will. Your behavior contradicts practicality, basic reality, and deviates from the morality of God. Yours is a life full of unnecessary words and activities, which have no basis in fact or reality, nor are your activities God sanctioned. With you, fantasy and reality oftentimes become intermingled, causing you to become very impractical. All this suggests a way of life that is going contrary to God's call. Dreamer, reality is understood to be what God says it to be via His Word. Hence, anyone who does not correspond with His truth, in a levelheaded and practical manner, is deceived and erroneous in your thoughts and ideas; thus, exposing your rejection of the certainty of God's word. See suggested course of action.

Scabbed or scarred (a scab or scar of some sort): Your dream denotes one who is reacting to a present situation too oversensitive, which is the root cause of your easy irritation and upset. Additionally, the dreamer often "crosses the line" with others, where you are not, necessarily, welcomed. Dreamer, if you genuinely want peace, within and without, seriously step back, and remove yourself from the present situation; by this, your irritation and upset will ease.

Tattoo or Tattoo Artist (artistic drawings or writings on the skin): This dream has two meanings (choose one). (1) Tattooing implies that the dreamer has embraced some form of veneration of the dead, such as ancestral worship, or worship of saints, and together with all that it implies, namely the dead possess the ability to influence the fortune of the living. The grassroots of the mysterious darker side of such practices are as such: among horticultural peoples with chiefdoms, the chief's ancestors, in time, became gods, and the rite of obligation, via worship or ceremony, was passed down from generation to generation, even unto the veneration of saints. Today, this type of ceremony looks like something else, e.g. psychic readings, fortune telling, tarot, Kwanzaa, Confucianism, Taoism, or the Catholic Church's veneration of dead saints, et.al. While all cultures attach ritual significance, to the passing of loved ones (e.g. funerals, memorial services, vigils); this is not equivalent to ancestral or saint veneration. You are a child of God; therefore, you shall not worship, nor establish annual rites of oblig ation for the dead. See Leviticus 19:28; Deuteronomy 14:1, 2; Job 14:21; Psalm 88:10-12; Ecclesiastes 1:11, 9:4, 5, 10; Isaiah 8:19, 20, 26:14; Matthew 8:22; Hebrews 9:27. These scriptures clearly state that the dead do not possess the ability to influence the living. Dreamer, the time to be about your heavenly Father's business is now, so let the dead "bury" (worship, venerate) the dead, and let the spiritually alive be concern with that which is living. Indecisiveness about this matter, will lead to you r spiritual and literal downfall. See suggested course of action. (2) Your dream of tattooing may be a Prophetically Simple Dream (see Chapter One: The 60th Part of Prophecy). Whereas, the dreamer is warned to seek medical attention due to possible health issues related to tattooing. This dream is a first step intervention and an alarm. Skip interpretation and go get medical attention.

Thorns (small sharp-pointed tip resembling a spike on a stem or leaf, prickles, stickers): If applicable, what part of the body was pricked? The particular body part pricked, is where, or how, the dreamer will experience mental, emotional, and/or physical anguish, discomforts, harassment, and trials, all instigated by a messenger of Satan, one who disguises him or herself as a believer, but is deceitful and false. A few examples of how some body parts are figuratively affected by thorns. Thorns piercing your heart may denote mental and/or physical anguish, discomforts, harassment, or trials affecting the promises made between you and God, and the manifestation of those promises, see subcategory, Abdominal, chest cavity (heart). Thorns piercing your stomach may denote mental and/ or physical anguish, discomforts, harassment, or trials affectin g your process of rectification. Thorns piercing your viscera may denote mental anguish, discomforts, or harassment affecting your deepest and most genuine emotions or feelings; see subcategory, abdominal, chest cavity. Thorns piercing your breasts or chest may denote mental anguish, or harassment, regarding the omnipotence of God, the security for the believer, and the comfort of God given His children, see subcategory Breasts, or chest. Thorns piercing your head, neck, or throat, may denote mental anguish, discomforts, or harassment, affecting the dreamer's inward thoughts and feelings, see subcategory, head and neck, throat. Prickling in your brain may denote mental and/or physical anguish, discomforts, harassment, or trials, regardi ng counsel and guidance the dreamer may be receiving, see subcategory, Head and Neck (brain). Pickers piercing your foot may denote mental anguish, discomforts, or harassment, regarding the mastering of something difficult, a change in you or in your surroundings, rejection, or something lost or destroyed, see subcategory, Legs (feet, foot). With that, this dream has two meanings (one or both may apply). (1) Favorably, and regardless of the anguish, discomforts, or harassment, which will pass, because of God's grace, His faithfulness, and His mercy towards you, dreamer, you will begin to experience a surge of positive feelings, due to restoration, transformation, and a miraculous healing and strengthening, both physically and emotionally. The emotional level is already happening within your inner most feelings and affections, for, God is first healing your broken heartedness. Now, your burdens, having been dealt with, freedom from your weaknesses is yours. Freedom from bondage, domination by evil, and hardship, is beginning for you. Dreamer, you are asked to give careful thought regarding your bondages and hardships, considering how things are, and have been for you, for your experiences have prepared you for ministry. From this day forward, God will bless you. You will be favored with complete healing, go and sin no more, but go and offer prayers, supplications, and thanksgiving before your Lord and Savior, Jesus Christ, for He is forgiving, compassionate, long-suffering, and full of loving-kindness, restoring more favorable conditions. In time, you may find yourself assistant to a high-ranking leader within a ministry, perhaps in the position of personal aide, leadership counselor, associate pastor, or CEO of your individual ministry. As well, there will be clarity and freedom in the way you communicate yourself to others, especially prophetically. Note, although your life is (or will become) very busy and full of concerns; it is advised that you do not forget your personal relationship with Christ, nor neglect the devotions that keep that personal relationship healthy. Nor must you allow yourself to be annoyed with other acts of devotion, e.g. family bible study and other quality times, fellowshipping with other believers, church attendance, acknowledging God's goodness to you, to others, and th e like. Further, during your discomforts and anguish, allow God's grace to be sufficient for you. For your temporary discomforts are allowed by God, primarily to keep you from becoming conceited because of the surpassing greatness of the revelations given you, (2 Corinthians 12:7). Fortunately, the person who is troubling you will bear his or her own judgment, (Galatians 5:10), and you will be victorious over their wickedness. Therefore, from this moment forward, choose good habits and deeds, e.g. good stewardship and commitment to ministry; speak to yourself what is true and good, embrace Philippians 4:8, and choose good nutritional habits that you might remain in good health. Also, these choices will greatly support you in your progress forwa rd towards your transformation and freedom, and help guide you toward, and enable you to fulfill, your purpose. All these blessings are rain. Dreamer, as one perfects him or herself, God helps by sending 'rains of blessings', then situations prosper. The rain is coming! (2) Unmarried Female dreamer: In addition to the previous interpretation, your dream also signifies a marriage. Dreamer, your husband is before you at present, or will be, very shortly. Handle the relationship, on God's terms, embracing His ethics, and not yours, as you've previously done. If necessary, see suggested course of action.

BONES:

The depiction of bones within a dream is multidimensional. Among the many aspects, bones denote a resurrection, resuscitation, renewal, revival, and/or your true nature or essence. Dreamer, there are two paths in this world. There is, in this world, a certain path illuminated with light, leading to a better you, and greater illumination, and there is a path that is dark, leading to hatred, blindness, a life of desolation, and extreme darkness. Dreamer, while both paths expose your true nature or essence, only one offers physical, emotional, and spiritual healing and wholeness, spiritual maturity, a world of h ope, and eternal life on the day of redemption. One of the following will help you determine what the Lord is prophesying over your bones. With that said, this dream has seven meanings (choose one). (1) Bones (joining limb to limb until they became skeletons): Dreamer, it must be said that you have experienced a spiritual death due to you embracing erroneous ideology and pride. Read and understand Galatians 5:19-21, for this speaks of spiritual death. Favorably, Jesus Christ is demonstrating grace by offering you a resurrection from dead works, people, places, and things. If you would give Jesus Christ authority of your life, submitting your will to Him and to His written Word (see Acts 2:37-39), there awaits you a spiritual resurrection, according to God's grace, because you are God's child. Consider your dream a first step intervention. Utilizing the powerful resources of prayer and heartfelt repentance to Jesus and to individuals affected by your actions, in the form of an apology (if possible), is needed. Repentance is seeking pardon and expressing sincere feelings of regret and brokenness for having done something awry and/or for having hurt someone, see 2 Corinthians 7:10, 11. To Jesus, pray Psalm 38:1-22. To individuals, a phone call or a letter of apology is a good place to start. This followed by appropriate application of wisdom; and by the Spirit of God you will be revived to a new life and glory. Glory in this sense is a state of high honor, spiritual beauty, and great illuminat ion. You will very shortly begin to experience, if not already, a paradigm shift in your core beliefs and spirituality. You will approach new and deeper dimensions. This transition will affect within you a far-reaching hope, profoundly greater faith, and a more intense love for all things Jesus, including His people; allow it. This revival and renewal of strength is a process. The process occurs with one bone, one sinew, one piece of flesh at a time, or one rectification of your ideology and pride issues at a time. This does not only mean fulfilling regular deeds (e.g. going to church, studying His word, developing a lifestyle of prayer, and fasting) but also it means trusting that God will do what is best for you. Dreamer; therefore, humble yourself before the True and Living God. Unfortunately, as "free-will" is, you can delay or sabotage your spiritual resurrection. If you deliberately choose to, again, embrace a belief that is not according to the teachings of Christ, His apostles, and mainstream Christianity, you will remain spiritually immature or dead, having chosen oppression rather than freedom, forfeiting purpose for foolishness. See suggested course of action. (2) Bones strewn all about: God is, if not already, bringing you to a place where you can no longer ignore His voice. You no longer have the luxury of "putting things off" until a later time. Dreamer, you have long-buried issues to address, and your present illness or the regretful condition of your present state is the wilderness, the place, from which you can no longer run away, and will be the stimulus to instigate change within your life. Those dry bones, strewn all over, are a lack of faith in the One True God, the hurts, resentments, an unforgiving heart, anger, disillusionments, and feelings of loss, long dormant. Dreamer although your emotional, and/or physical traumas were still close to the surface in your youth; quickly the pain came with such force that your only survival technique was to numb and deny it until, figuratively, the living flesh fell from your sinews, and the bones became desiccated parts of your life. Dreamer, this year is a critical time in your life; this is a season of renewal for you. This year, you must dig deeply in order to correct, rectify, and emotionally heal. It is important for you to reasonably deal with, and come to terms with, your pains and hurts of the past, "once and for all", despite psychological and emotional hindrances and/or difficulties. Dreamer, just as God told Ezekiel to "Prophesy over these bones, and say to them, 'O dry bones, hear the word of the Lord" (Ezekiel 37:1-14), you are counseled to allow God to revive you from your own valley of desiccated bones. First, you must make an effort to hear the word of the Lord (e.g. go to church, bible study, Sunday school, study His word, develop a lifestyle of prayer, and fasting). These steps will also encourage you to learn not to be afraid, but to be open to healing; God's Spirit will lead the way. (3) Bones with writing on them: Your bones symbolically can testify for or against you. Intentional, deliberate, and willful deeds, good or bad, are such that they come from the very core of one's personality, thus, your deeds are engraved on your bones (e.g. your marrow, bone, your very core, your true nature, your heart and soul, your essence). A righteous person has their noble deeds engraved on their bones, and so it is with a wicked person, his or her evil deeds are also engraved on their bones. Dreamer, per your dream, your bones are testifying for, or against you, now. Do you remember (or could you decipher) what was written on the bones? Was the writing, light or dark in color? If writing, on the bone(s), was written with some kind of light, was glowing, or was light in color: Unless otherwise written, dreamer, since your deeds and actions were connected with divine wisdom, there awaits you, a spiritual, physical, and emotional resurrection, resuscitation, renewal, and revival, according to God's grace. His grace is abounding towards you, and His promises will come quickly and in full measure. What are His promises to you? Dreamer, recall all His promises to you, journal them, and expect them all to manifest within you and within your life. Expect all of this (a resurrection, resuscitation, renewal, and revival, healing, grace abounding, and His promises to you, in full measure); therefore, wait on this. Spiritual wholeness is yours right now. This great favor is shown you because of God's great faithfulness towards you, (also see Psalm 35:10). Unless otherwise written, if writing, on the bone(s) was dark in hue: A destructive resurrection is occurring within the dreamer spiritually, a renewal of interest in something that was rendered spiritually dead long ago. This dark revival is due to some manner of licentiousness, to you embracing erroneous ideology, and to pride. One thing is for sure, your behavior, your new belief, and your pride has corrupted you, and if not checked can and oftentimes do lead to open shame and/or death. Favorably, via your dream, Jesus Christ is demonstrating grace by offering you a resurrection from dead works, people, places, and things. Consider your dream a first step intervention. Utilizing the powerful resources of prayer and heartfelt repentance to Jesus and to individuals affected by your actions, in the form of an apology (if possible), is needed. Repentance is seeking pardon and expressing sincere feelings of regret and brokenness for having done something awry and/or for having hurt someone, see 2 Corinthians 7:10, 11. To Jesus, pray Psalm 38:1-22. To individuals, a phone call or a letter of apology is a good place to start. This followed by appropriate application of wisdom, can conceivably avert some of the repercussions of your choices. You may also need professional help, will need spiritual counseling and support to affect a personal revival within you; coupled with fasting, a changed mindset, serious re- consideration of God's ways and means, and an honest acknowledgement of God's hand within your life. Jesus will strengthen you emotionally, psychologically, and physically, to go get help for your backsliding, via a Christian based support group, Christian counseling, healthcare, or inpatient. God is always ready to forgive the sinner who returns to Him in sincere repentance, for He says, "I delight not in the death of the wicked, but that he (or she) returns from their evil way and live" (Ezekiel 33:11-19). Dreamer, have faith in this, followed with works (James 2:17). In six years, if you seize this moment and genuinely seek help and change, you will become a great leader. You will be sent to leaders, who when they had power abused it, and because none opposed them, they withheld not themselves from doing wrong. Their power will be taken from them and given to you. Then you shall rejoice and your bones shall flourish like the grass. If you do not genuinely change, for sure ruin will be your destiny's declaration. (4) Broken bones: First, for broken arms, neck, see relevant subcategories, e.g. limbs, neck. Otherwise, your dream suggests that there is a fundamental weakness within the dreamer. Dreamer, your reality of God is based on emotion and personal bias, due to observable phenomena. Unfortunately, while what you observe may be true, your paradigm is "gridded" through the emotions of fear and rejection. Paradigm shift, a deeper trust in God and Him alone with your emotions is needed that you might go on to spiritual maturity. Dreamer, at your very core, you want to know love and trust, but you cannot "touch it" or receive it, because you do not believe you are lovable. The pain of rejection, abuse, and/or other emotional and physical violations, of your past, is the reason for your fears, and this same pain has become your "approach pattern" to all your relationships. You emotionally separate yourself from others, and from life. You've been hurt, so you hurt others. You despise yourself, so you hide yourself within yourself, and you do this well. Unfortunately, you've rendered yourself powerless to know love, to touch it, and to heal. You've been unable to fix your pain, thus, you've settled for a pseudo-fix. You want to appear independent of outward circumstances, definite in your ideas, self- governing, physically and mentally strong, and financially prosperous; yet, a fundamental weakness is shown, and your pain is incurable. Dreamer, by faith, began to embrace and trust your reasoning, thoughts, behaviors, and emotions to Jesus that a very personal relationship with Him may emerge. Go alone talk to Jesus, and ask the hard questions talk of your deep feelings. Why is my pain unending? Why is my wound grievous and incurable? Can you help me touch what I cannot feel? You are to me like a deceptive brook, like a spring that fails (see Jeremiah 15:18). He will answer you. Moreover, your dream has come to cause you to know that there is a fixed and definite time that God will heal that, which is incurable within you, and you wil l know His love, and know His love from an intimate and personal perspective. Develop a spirit of expectation, for your miracle is coming. If necessary, see suggested course of action. (5) Burn (or burnt) bones: Instead of a memorial that was intended as a remembrance of you, as a celebration of your life and work, there will be great dishonor to your memory, because of your heinous acts, which are great transgressions. Those without power or influence should have been able to trust and depend on you, instead you violated that trust, and justice was denied them. Moreover, because you are a greedy rich person, you've caused the lives of some to turn to poverty, oppression, and insecurity. Dreamer, you have violated your covenant relationsh ip with God. God is calling you to account for your violations, and He will not turn away His punishment. God shows the justice of His ways toward the penitent, and toward the rebellious. Read, understand, and heed Ezekiel 33:10 -20. See suggested course of action. (6) Prostrate (bones stretched out and lying at full length along the ground): Although you are depleted emotionally and physically, a spark of life remains hidden inside of you, and there awaits you a spiritual resurrection, acco rding to God's grace, because you are God's child. You will very shortly begin to experience, if not already, a paradigm shift in your core beliefs and spirituality. You are approaching new and deeper dimensions. This transition will affect within you a far - reaching hope, profoundly greater faith, and a more intense love for all things Jesus, including His people; allow it. Favorably, you are now one, whom the body of believers should, and will, help restore back to God's fold, in the spirit of empathy, mercy, leniency, and kindness. Therefore, humble yourself before the True and Living God and accept His blessings of healing, help, and restoration in a balanced manner. This great favor is shown you because of God's great faithfulness towards you and because of the prayers of others. No matter your emotional, physical, or spiritual state, remain where you are, your present place of worship, for this is your sat place for now. By remaining and continuing, deliverance will be affected within your life. You will be delivered from the overwhelming hurts and pains that have caused your negative attitude and state of affairs. If change and deliverance is welcomed by the dreamer, this transition will be full of exciting new subject matter and experiences. If change is arduous to the dreamer, the transformation will prove very demanding, difficult, and frustrating. The frustrations may cause you to feel resentful and even rebellious. You are counseled to keep an optimistic outlook and remain obedient to God's directives over your life. The change is needed. Note, you are, solely, responsible for your life and conduct, no other is to blame. Moreover, you have a responsibility towards the Body of Christ. A wise man or woman will multiply their gifts by teaching or passing them on to others; thus, prospering emotionally, financially, physically, and spiritually. The wicked will quit or bury their gift, blaming their hesitancy on God, circumstances, situations, or others, bringing great loss upon themselves (see Matthew 25:24-30). Thus, be very careful, then, how you live. Not unwise, but wise, making the most of every opportunity, because the days are evil. The secret of your redemption lay in absolute loyalty to God and His Word. See suggested course of action. (7) Skull: This choice has two parts (choose one). (a) Your dream comes to caution the dreamer. Although you have the power of free choice, you should not think that your accomplishments are purely of your own volition. Truthfully, it is God, who gives you the capability and strength to achieve success. This is especially true of your struggles with your sinful tendencies, whether they manifest as a lack of concern or interest in the things of God, a stubborn resistance to the will of God, or laziness. If it had not been for God's efforts on your behalf, you would not have been able to overcome any negative tendencies. He delivered you. Any achievements you will accomplish, or have accomplished, any good deeds you've done, any fulfillment of God's will, was, and still is, dependent upon divine aid and guidance. One merely places his or her hand under the weight carried exclusively by God. There is a need to acknowledge that the Lord is the source of your power and strength. Only through God's power of deliverance (Psalm 18:2), and His strength (Psalm 112:9) do we have the wherewithal to accomplish anything. See suggested course of action. (b) Broken skull: Your dream is a final warning of the futility of self-confidence that God may withdraw you from your purpose and hide pride from you. You boast of your own self- perceived strength, which, in reality, is non-existent. Your arrogance, self-reliance, exchanging righteousness for bitterness, poisoning all sense of justice, and rejoicing in all this, has reached a pinnacle. Demonically influenced, you now look to heretical ideology and fame to be your authority, strength, and satisfaction, rather than the Lord God. This is done, in spite of the fact that God has dealt with you according to His grace. You will be rejected and shown disapproval by the ones with whom you have committed spiritual fornication. Your confidence will be shattered because it is groundless, and your prominence will begin to abate, via trouble, distress, worry, and/or health problems. You will begin to experience need and want. Dreamer, respect and heed this warning from the Lord (also see Psalm 119:67, 68; Proverbs 3:11-18). Turn back to Jesus, seek forgiveness, and tangibly, if applicable, participate in the turning back of your children to Jesus that He may leave a blessing. See suggested course of action.

In addition, the following is a common word, expression, usage (e.g. slang or cliché) or a 'probable' that is metaphorically represented by skull:

- **Skull and Crossbones:** Your dream was sent to demonstrate grace, via a warning of serious danger that oftentimes leads to devastation and death, spiritually and physically. See suggested course of action.

BREASTS OR CHEST (the front part of the thorax of woman, man, or animal):

The depiction of breasts or chest within a dream is multidimensional. The various meanings regard the omnipotence of God, security for the believer, comfort of God given His children, God's provision, the double blessing of a child, a bond between a mother and her child, puberty, erotic love, and ruin. One of the following will help you determine what your dream is referencing regarding you. See one of the following:

Beating of Breasts or Chest (pounding one's chest or breasts area with your hands or fists):
Dreamer, in one year, you will become overwhelmed by the severe consequences of your bad choices.
There will be agony, mourning, and trouble, due to your carelessness, and your tears will be tears
of self-pity and of having been exposed, and not tears of repentance. There is a need for prayer and
heartfelt repentance to Jesus and man or woman. Dreamer, submit your ways unto God, and you will
again gain control over your life. Continue applying His principles no matter the "self" resistance. This
gaining control over your spirit is a process, it will not all happen in one day (or it miraculously could).
Until dreamer genuinely cries out, "Jesus, be thou merciful to me a sinner", your trouble will continue.
See suggested course of action.

Breasts or Chest abnormalities (deformed, distorted, or maimed): This dream has two meanings
(one or both may apply). (1) Dreamer, your great struggles, internally and externally, has accomplished
what they were meant to accomplish, emotionally and spiritually within you, despite all the setbacks.
Now, by grace, prayer, and change, your life will begin to transform and you will be restored to the
person you was intended to be. Therefore, go now and ask your Heavenly Father to forgive you of your
sins, as you forgive those who violated you, and forgive yourself, for all your sins will be pardoned.
Further, declare, "I will never hurt myself again". See suggested course of action. (2) Dreamer,
because of the way you were treated as a child, you began embracing behaviors that led to great
disillusionments, emotional breakdowns, and/or breaks with reality. Bad things do happen to innocent
people and a bad thing happened to you. You have been made aware of your unpredictable nature,
from a very young age. If this erratic part of your nature is allowed to continue to reign, and it can
reign under demonic influence, if not checked, you will become mentally unstable. Fortunately, you no
longer have to be the bad thing that happens to you and to others. Dreamer, Jesus loves you, and you
are valuable to Him and to His Kingdom; thus, He is calling you. If you will accept the Heavenly Father's
Words and store up His principles, and His ways and means within you, turning your ear to wisdom and
applying your heart to understanding, calling out for insight and crying aloud for discernment. Then
you will know the Messiah, Jesus Christ, intimately, and find the knowledge of God you seek, and no
longer will the bad thing hold sway over your entire life. For the Lord gives wisdom and from His mouth
comes knowledge and understanding. Then you will understand what is right and just and fair, every
good path. When wisdom enters your heart and knowledge becomes sweet to your soul, discretion
will protect you, understanding will guard you, and His Truth will lead you. To deliver you from the
ways of wickedness, and from people whose words are perverse, who leave the straight paths to walk
in darkness gladly, whose paths are crooked and who are devious in their ways (Proverbs 2:1-6, 9-15).
This is one of God's covenant promises to you, and the first step in receiving His promises is repentance
(see Acts 2:37-41). Therefore, go and ask your Heavenly Father to forgive you of your sins. To Jesus pray,
Psalm 51:1-19 (Mark 1:1-8, Luke 5:30-32, 24:46, 47). To individuals, a phone call or a letter of apology is a
good place to start, if appropriate. This coupled with prayer and fasting, and followed by appropriate
application of wisdom and Jesus will meet you. Have faith in this.

Breast Fed or Breast Feeding: This dream has four meanings (choose one). (1) Breast fed or breast-
feeding an Adult: This choice has two parts (choose one). (a) Male breast-feeding or being breast-fed,
there is a need to turn back to the one, true, and only living God, and there is a need to seek forgiveness
from someone. Moreover, you have forsaken godliness, and now believe in something akin to Spiritism.
You worship with spiritists and witches. Even more, you have attributed your prosperity to the power
of demons; thus, this dream also denotes the conjuring of evil upon the dreamer, utter obscenities,
profanities, ruin, and the excommunication from a church or religious community. You also give to
those whom the Lord disapproves of, and you teach your children desolation. The prosperity God has
provided you will begin to abate and your anarchy will be exposed. Dreamer, turn back to the one, true,
and only living God, and if applicable, participate in the turning back of your children to God that He
may leave a blessing. See suggested course of action. (b) Female dreamer (breast- feeding or being
breast feed): Dreamer, God's plans for you are spiritual growth and maturity. Therefore, you are able to
go on to maturity; and now is your time to grow up spiritually, leaving the elementary principles of

Christ, going on to perfection (Hebrews 6: 1, 2). How does one leave the elementary principles and go on to perfection? By asking Jesus to teach you, patience, kindness, maturity, and for a spirit to be more concerned for others than self, and by seekin g God's wisdom, these are the first steps. Further, by grace, prayer, and change, your life will begin to transform and you will be restored to the person you was intended to be. Unfortunately, if you stay a spiritual infant, you limit the good you can d o for the sake of Christ and His Kingdom. Some examples of spiritual infancy include, but are not limited to; one who has a tendency to be easily misled and easily fooled or naivety. One who is not able to tell right from wrong, either because of an inability to do so, or by deliberate choice, or one who sues others over relatively minor financial disputes, one caught up in coveting, swindling, viciousness, or one who is prone to violence. Selfishness, verbal aggression, adultery or fornication, drunkenn ess, condemning others, and one so committed to your own personal rights that you disdain the cause of Christ and the good of others. These are all indicators that you are still embracing your carnal side, living like a non-believer, motivated by their same values, and handling your problems in the same way they do; similarly, spiritual immaturity. Dreamer, choose not to remain immature and unskilled in the things that pertain to God and to living life ethically and strongly. Those who are mature have tr ained themselves to recognize the difference between right and wrong and then do what is right. See suggested course of action. (2) Animal (breast-feeding or being breast feed): The dreamer is embracing some very negative traits, namely those attributed to the particular animal depicted within your dream. Thus, your dream comes as a very harsh warning. This coupled with, a way of life that is contrary to God's call, spiritual backsliding, depravity, and confusion, on so many levels. Dreamer, he or she who nurses perversion and maintains evil gives rise to disillusionment (Psalm 7:14 NIV). You are embracing behaviors that lead to great disillusionments, emotional breakdowns, and/or breaks with reality. Dreamer, you are not in harmony with the will o f God for your life, nor with the particular objectives that are intended to ensure the fulfillment of that will. Your behavio r contradicts practicality, basic reality, and deviates from the morality of God. Yours is a life full of unnecessary words and activities, which have no basis in fact or reality, and they are not rooted in faith in God. Reality is understood to be what God says it to be via His Word. For example, we are saved by grace through faith, not by works (Ephesians 2:5-10). Hence, anyone who does not correspond with His truth, in a levelheaded and practical manner, is deceived and erroneous in your thoughts and ideas; thus, exposing your rejection of the certainty of God's word. See suggested course of action. (3) Breast-feeding a Baby: Your dream denotes that either, there is a very close bond between a mother and her child, or, there will be a blessing of a child to a marriage, or there will be an increase in your ministry. No matter which one, additionally, God will comfort and provide security for the dreamer. Further, couple this with one of the following four (choose one). (a) Unmarried female: You will very soon get married, if not already engaged. Do not be afraid; you will not suffer shame. Do not fear disgrace; you will not be humiliated. If germane, to this union there will be children born of your own body, and there will be a very close bond between mother and child. (b) Female, married female without children: Dreamer, God has granted you mercy. The reproach of your past will be put behind you. You will no longer feel ashamed because of something you've done wrong in your past (e.g. seriously bad behavior, unalterable life damaging actions, uninformed choices, and/or bad relationships). Additionally, you will very soon give birth to your own children. There will be a very close bond between mother and child. God will give you miraculous strength and knowledge, as well as, a door to the right physicians to help you bear and birth your children. Your husband will be a great support to you during this time. (c) This type of dream is to bring about an awareness of an appointed inheritance of abundant peace, comfort, and sufficient wealth for the dreamer's child or children, and greatness. At some point in your near future, wealth will be bestowed upon the dreamer's child or children, if not already. (d) Dreamer, the Paraclete has made you productive, by first forming Christ in you. Subsequently, because of His likeness, nature, knowledge, and wisdom, within you, you will take part in leading others into a born again experience (see John 3:1-17), and in helping others to reach for deeper, more spiritual and valuable things in life. Dreamer, you are full of nurturing abilities. You know how to nurture and accept anyone; therefore, many are intended to connect with you, via your ministry. Under your tutelage, those newly born into the Body of Christ will become strong and active, for the cause of the Kingdom of God. They will become those who speak and does that which is good, counted amongst those who are faithful and submissive to God. Dreamer, be willing, obedient, prepared, and in place (accountable to a specific house of worship, church), for the birthing of your ministry and for those who will become born again because of your ministry. (V) Refuse to breast-feed a baby: Your dream comes as a very harsh warning. This dream denotes one who is very cruel and cynical towards those you are sent to minister too, and/ or a mother who is very abusive toward her children. You will be exposed publicly. See suggested course of action. (4) Snatching a baby from the breast: The dreamer is self-righteous, and practices legalism. Thus, you have rejected the doctrine of grace (the free and unmerited favor and beneficence of God). Evil is always present in any form of spiritual legalism; thus, your dream comes as a very harsh warning. Your spirituality is one of outward show and hypocrisy. You love to give alms, pray, and appear righteous publicly, but inwardly you are lifeless, and lawlessness prevails. Your lack of love towards others has contributed to your lack of, understanding, receiving, and giving of genuine grace. Dreamer, allow the atonement of Jesus' sacrifice on the cross to become the fulfillment of the law in your life (Romans 13:8-10), repent, and ask Jesus to help you touch what you cannot feel. See suggested course of action.

Broad chest or large breasts (broader or larger than your normal chest or breasts in your awaked life): This dream has three meanings (choose one). (1) Dreamer, God's divine intervention has kept you; and will again, cause your mouth to be filled with laughter, and your tongue with singing. When God reverse your tragedy, you will testify that the Lord has done great things for you, and you will be glad. Your situation will change and He will give you a new song in your heart. You will sing a new song. You wanna hear it, here it goes, when your heart is painfully torn apart, broken, and troubled, and darkness has come and covered all, God can take those disappointments, those trials, and tragedies, that experience, and make them a door of hope for you, and for sure He will, via His provision, security, wisdom, care, and guidance. (2) Female dreamer (unmarried): You will very soon get married, if not already engaged. Do not be afraid; you will not suffer shame. Do not fear disgrace; you will not be humiliated. If germane, to this union there will be children born of your own body. There will be a very close bond between mother and child. (3) Female (married, without children): Dreamer, God has granted you mercy. The reproach of your past will be put behind you. You will no longer feel ashamed because of something you've done wrong in your past (e.g. seriously bad, unalterable, and life damaging actions, uninformed choices, and/or toxic relationships). Additionally, you will very soon give birth to your own children. There will be a very close bond between mother and child. God will give you miraculous strength and knowledge, as well as a door to the right physicians to help you bear and birth your children. Your husband will be a great support to you during this time.

Embracing, hugging, or fondling of breasts or caressing of chest: This dream has four meanings (choose one). (1) Embracing, hugging or fondling of breasts or caressing of chest of actual spouse God will comfort and provide security for the dreamer. As well, your dream denotes erotic love, the arousal and giving of sexual pleasure to one's spouse. There is a sexual need that needs to happen between husband and wife. See 1 Corinthians 7:3-5. If germane, to this union there will be children born of your own body. There will be a very close bond between parents and child. (2) Embracing, hugging or fondling of breasts or caressing of chest of someone who is married to another (e.g. illicit relation): This choice has two parts (choose one). (a) If dreamer is literally married: Dreams of embracing, hugging or fondling of breasts or caressing of chest of another, other than your spouse, denotes adultery, either literally or spiritually. Dreamer, if you found out that you were a victim of adultery, would you forgive your spouse? Imagine that the unfaithfulness was not a one-night stand, but a long affair. Imagine further that your spouse wasn't very repentant and was rather open about what he or she was doing. Would you still love your spouse? If that spouse left you, and then wanted to return, would you receive him or her back? Just as you have chased after other lovers, so have you chased after other gods, and dishonored the covenant between you and God and/or your spouse. In the same way you have sincerely answered the exploratory questions, from your heart, so it will, be done unt o you. Fortunately, people and state of affairs do change for the good, via prayer and heartfelt repentance to Jesus and to individuals affected by your actions, in the form of an apology (if possible). Repentance is seeking pardon and expressing sincere feelings of regret and brokenness for having done something awry and/or for having hurt someone, see 2 Corinthians 7:10, 11. To individuals, a phone call or a letter of apology is a good place to start. To Jesus pray, Psalm 51, this follo wed by appropriate application of wisdom, can conceivably avert some of the repercussions of your choices. This is what is called leaving a blessing behind. See suggested course of action. (b) If dreamer is unmarried: Dreams of embracing, hugging, or fondling of breasts or caressing of chest of another, who is married (married in the dream or is actually married in your awaked life), denotes one behaving in an obscene, indecent, and spiritually offensive manner, especially as you once behaved in your youth. Now that you are an adult literally and/ or spiritually, behavior indicative of one literally and/or spiritually mature is expected. If no genuine change, the Lord Jehovah will cause your lovers to be against you, and they will be against you on every side. As well, your joy, as you experience it now, will cease. See suggested course of action. (3) Embracing or hugging family member or friends: Dreamer, God will comfort and provide security for you. Dreamer, the Almighty God shall help you, and shall bless you with great blessings. The blessings of God are upon the dreamer. Gifts of God's blessings, anything God freely gives you, absolution, the Holy Spirit, salvation, regeneration, eternal life, health, children, love of family, longevity, necessities, prosperity, and dominion over all that is yours; and all are sanctified by the Lord, and technically belongs to Him. The result of this supply in your life will be peace. As well, if relevant, this type of dream is to bring about an awarenes s of an appointed inheritance of abundant peace, comfort, and sufficient wealth for the dreamer's child or children, and greatness. At some point in your near future, wealth will be bestowed upon the dreamer's child or children, if not already. (4) Embracing or hugging enemies: Dreamer, God will frustrate the plans of, and cause a great uproar (e.g. a recession, famine, or some great distress), within the life of one (or some) who has acted wickedly against the dreamer. As a result, the dreamer will inherit the wealth of one (or some) who has acted wickedly. Dreamer, the floodgates of heaven are open to you. Those floodgates are fullness in your spirituality, and the glory of God in the midst of your life. Glory in this sense is a state of high honor, spiritual beauty, and great illumination. God will comfort and provide security for the dreamer.

EXCRETORY SYSTEM (unless listed separately, this category includes the alimentary canal, bile, bladder, kidneys, intestine, liver, skin, urethra - this system deals with egestion, body waste, any discharges from the body. For example, fecal matter, urine, or any other kind of egestion; thus, this category also deals with droppings, dung, fecal matter, manure, stool, or urine):

Any parts of a person's excretory system, within a dream; says a lot about the dreamer's spiritual health. The excretory system is an essential function within the body, in that it exposes, within your dreams, something is wrong spiritually, and deals with serious spiritual conditions, which can become infectious. How often you go to the bathroom, how much waste you expelled, how much sweat poured off your brow or body, did you pass a kidney stone. All this indicates how much "waste" you have syncretized with healthy spiritual beliefs and concepts. Your dream is a critical alarm and a message of grace (the free and unmerited favor and beneficence of God). The critical alarm: the dreamer is morally unclean on some level or another, depending on what was excreted or expelled. See one of the following.

Fecal matter (discharges such as feces or excretions such as kidney stones): This dream has two meanings (choose one). (1) This type of dream denotes that the dreamer is embracing ideologies, practices, thoughts, beliefs, behaviors, and/or other choices that can, and will, taint your spiritual health. Dreamer you are slipping into darkness, due to a wisdom you've exalted above God's wisdom, hatred, prejudice, and/or an unforgiving spirit, hidden deep within your heart, even from yourself. Consequently, a severing of your personal relationship with Christ is probable (see Ezekiel

3:20, Matthew 6:14, 15). Dreamer, you are slowly abandoning all or some of the original foundational teachings of Christ and His apostles, especially the doctrine of grace, and on some level within your heart, there is a rejection or denial of God's Word and His truth (e.g. is belief and obedience to Jesus enough? Does God promises and then don't deliver? Does God still perform miracles?) It is these types of doubts; you have confused or blurred as legitimate interests and questions that have resulted in a corrupt, legalistic doctrine, and bondage (1 Timothy 4:1-16). Your ideas and arguments, regarding Christ, Christians, religion, and His church, are illogical, non-mainstream, and without favorable conclusions. Having lost your equilibrium within the sacred scheme of things, due to demonic influence, disillusionment, disappointment, and/or offenses, you have ceased to abide in Christ, and instead have become enslaved again to sin and immorality, trusting in your own righteousness. Low self-esteem and feelings of insignificance has also added to your corrupt behavior and beliefs. Your present difficult state of affairs bears witness of this. Not caring about your physical and spiritual well-being, will always leave you humiliated and in bondage. This is grace and mercy: Favorably, dreamer, the One True Living God can and will turn things around for you. God will help you overcome your issues, and rebuke the demonic force from before you. Dreamer, you will undergo a thorough purging from dead, obsolete, worthless, and weak religious dogma, erroneous ideas, and self-conceited talk against God. Whatever is currently going on in your life, anticipate a spiritual cleansing taking place, especially within those areas specific to this interpretation. This will produce a level of purity within your life that is requisite for ministry and will affect humility within you. Your emotions will become intense and situations perhaps more volatile, but you will be thoroughly purged. Take a seat and hold tight, it's going to get bumpy. Moreover, prayer and heartfelt repentance to Jesus and others, and a renunciation of your spiritually poisonous words and ways, is the antivenin to the venomous attack of that old serpent, the devil, upon your life. Repentance is seeking pardon for having done something awry, and for having hurt someone, and expressing sincere feelings of regret and brokenness. To Jesus pray, Psalm 51:1-19. To individuals, a phone call or a letter of apology is a good place to start, if appropriate. Further, if urged by God, declare a one, two, or three day fast (depending on the level of uncleanness, per what was excreted or expelled), coupled with studying the teachings of Jesus Christ, and you will again begin to experience God's truth, and see the demonic for what it is - a lie. If relevant, avoid personal isolation and isolated groups that teach something different from the gospel of Jesus Christ (e.g. condemnation, hate, any racist ideology, murder, murder, no one is "right" but our western sect, or any other oppressive or "hell bound" for everyone but me and/or our small group ideas). Jesus died for the world, and not exclusively for any one person, sect, or western denomination. Moreover, if not practiced regularly, go to church, join a church, a faith based bible-believing community, commit to that ministry, and don't leave, no matter what, for three years. Forsake not the gathering of yourself together with other mainstream Christians. A prophecy will be given you, via someone within that ministry, during this season, write it down for it will happen. Even mor e, entering the House of God should be done reverently rather than carelessly. Cease from many words (Ecclesiastes 5:1, 2) and rather humbly learn, and let your words be sprinkled with empathy. For, in spite of what we do not know about the many mysteries of God and life, one thing remains eternally true: God is our loving Father. He does not desire that any one perish; great effort is exercised to save us, even in the moment of our death. Hence, do not call anyone impure (e.g. unsaved, hypocrite, unregenerate, ignorant) that God alone has made clean (read Acts 10:15, Ephesians 4:17-5:21). See suggested course of action. (2) If dreamer saw animal's waste, coupled with the following interpretation, dreamer exhibits the negative characteristics of that animal. See category, animals, and relevant category.

Kidneys: This dream has three meanings (one, two, or all may apply). (1) Your dream denotes a literal physical condition, suggesting that the dreamer may need medical attention regarding kidneys function. (2) Other than that, dreamer, because of God's grace, His faithfulness, and His mercy towards you, you will begin to experience a surge of positive feelings, due to restoration, transformation, and a miraculous healing and strengthening, both physically and emotionally. The emotional level is already happening within your inner most feelings and affections, for, God is first healing your broken heartedness. Now, your burdens, having been dealt with, freedom from your weaknesses is yours. Freedom from bondage, domination by evil, and hardship, is beginning for you. Dreamer, you are asked to give careful thought regarding your bondages and hardships, considering how things are, and have been for you, for your experiences have prepared you for ministry. From this day forward, God will bless you. You will be favored with complete healing, go and sin no more, and go and offer prayers, supplications, and thanksgiving before your Lord and Savior, Jesus Christ, for He is forgiving, compassionate, long-suffering, and full of loving-kindness, restoring more favorable conditions. As well, there will be clarity and freedom in the way you communicate yourself to others, especially prophetically. In time, you may find yourself assistant to a high-ranking leader within a ministry, perhaps in the position of personal aide, leadership counselor, associate pastor, or CEO of your individual ministry. Note, although your life is (will become) very busy and full of concerns; it is advised that you do not forget your personal relationship with Christ, nor neglect the devotions that keep that personal relationship healthy. Nor must you allow yourself to be annoyed with other acts of devotion, e.g. family bible study and other quality times, fellowshipping with other believers, church attendance, acknowledging God's goodness to you, to others, and the like. Therefore, from this moment forward, choose good habits and deeds, e.g. good stewardship and commitment to ministry; speak to yourself what is true and good, embrace Philippians 4:8, and choose good nutritional habits that you might remain in good health. Also, these choices will greatly support you in your progress forward towards your transformation and freedom, and help guide you toward, and enable you to fulfill, your purpose. All these blessings are rain. Dreamer, as one perfects him or herself, God helps by sending 'rains of blessings', then situations prosper. The rain is coming! (3) Unmarried Female: Your dream signifies a wedding and marriage. Your potential husband is before you at present, or will be, very shortly. Handle the relationship, on God's terms, embracing His ethics, and not yours, as you've previously done.

Urine: Dreamer, because of bitter conflict, heated, often violent dissension, and a lack of agreement and harmony within your relationships, you are experiencing strong feelings of agitation and disturbance within, which has also stirred up deep feelings you are unaware of; the deepest innermost part of your feelings and emotions. Dreamer, you look too far back, revisiting many decisions, using them as a frame of reference for present day actions, disappointments, hurts, and pains, which, at present, the past has no relevancy anymore, especially today. All that to say, that your reaction to a volatile situation within your life at present is not based on rational conscious thought, nor are you being led by Holy Spirit who is within you, but is based upon your past. Dreamer, you are in a crisis of your faith and are under great stress. If the present and pressing situation or issues are not dealt with, rationally, truthfully, and with an awareness of the situation as it really is, relying on the present day facts and evidences, this will prove to your undoing spiritually; and will prove physically unhealthy for you, for your dream also symbolizes shortness of life. Dreamer, people, places, and situations are not the same; things have changed. If you look too far back, too long, and focus on your past losses, disappointments, hurts, and pains, you will fall. It is recommended that you call for the elders of your church, for it is through their prayers of faith and anointing of oil upon you that sin is forgiven and healing can be bestowed. See Endnotes, [36] The Prayer of Faith. This is a true saying. See suggested course of action.

GIANT (to appear gigantic or to see one):

This dream has three meanings (choose one). (1) If dreamer is seriously ill, your dream suggests that you will be healed by the miraculous power of God. You will be completely restored from your distresses. Your state of affairs is before God. Any condition that is upon you at present that seems hopeless and/ or extremely frustrating; you will overcome it. For instance, if you have been diagnosed with a serious or incurable illness, you will be healed and survive to declare the glories of the Lord. Go through your circumstances hopeful and optimistic (Psalm 27:5). Yes, you will experience loss materially and possibly physically, but all will be restored. Do not be dismayed, nor lose courage. Faith is a keyword for you at present. (2) Your dream counsels the dreamer to begin seriously contemplating your spiritual qualifications for an upper headship position within a ministry and/or your work environment. Dreamer, because of your faith, humility, strong leadership, and your courageous and optimistic spirit, you will be greatly honored. You will rise to a level the Anointing of God and your acumen deem you should be. Even more, in your present business or personal dealings, you will be satisfied and take delight in yo ur goals. If you are involved in any situation that is competitive, you will triumphant. With that, an upper level leadership position demands great personal sacrifice of rights and freedoms and requires the subduing of your appetites and passions. For, to whom much is given, much is required. At times, in order to fulfill your commission, you may need to forgo your dietary liberties and/or decline compensation (e.g. fulfill numerous fasts, eat what's put before you, only at the time it's put before you, and putting right back into a ministry your wage). God will lead the way. Even more, you have the miraculous power to change history on some level or another. For example, family generational curses can stop with you (Exodus 20:5, 7; Psalm 112:2), or by introducing radically new fundamental concepts, far beyond the norm (Acts 13:14-52). Whatever the miraculous history change is, perhaps you becoming a great leader and orator, you are equipped to handle large-scale undertakings. Dreamer, a large part of your mission in life centers on raising the spirits of your fellow mankind; thus changing history in the lives of those, you touch. The driving force behind all this is your support of others. Your first step is to start by recognizing and thanking Jesus for the small blessings that are before you now and for the miraculous endowment of history changing vision and courageous leadership. Do you want your miracle? Then prepare yourself mentally for it. See suggested course of action. (3) Your dream warns of a weakness, within the dreamer. The dreamer has embraced some form of veneration of the dead, such as ancestral worship, or worship of saints, and together with all that it implies, namely the de ad possess the ability to influence the fortune of the living. The grassroots of the mysterious darker side of such practices are as such: among horticultural peoples with chiefdoms, the chief's ancestors, in time, became gods, and the rite of obligation, via worship or ceremony, was passed down from generation to generation, even unto the veneration of saints. Today, this type of ceremony looks like something else, e.g. channeling, Kwanzaa, Confucianism, Taoism, or the Catholic Church's veneration of dead saints, et.al. While all cultures attach ritual significance, to the passing of loved ones (e.g. funerals, memorial services, vigils); this is not equivalent to ancestral worship or saint veneration. Dreamer, you are a child of God; therefore, you shall not worship, nor establish annual rites of obligation for the dead. See Leviticus 19:28; Deuteronomy 14:1, 2; Job 14:21; Psalm 88:10-12; Ecclesiastes 1:11, 9:4, 5, 10; Isaiah 8:19, 20, 26:14; Matthew 8:22; Hebrews 9:27. These scriptures clearly state that the dead do not possess the ability to influence the living. Dreamer, the time to be about your heavenly Father's business is now, so let the dead "bury" (worship, venerate) the dead, and let the spiritually alive be concern with that which is living. Indecisiveness about this matter, will lead to your spiritual and literal downfall. See suggested course of action.

HAIR:

This dream is concerned primarily with truth, integrity, courage, and strength. This dream has four meanings (choose one). (1) Your dream denotes that the understanding of the act of delivering from sin and saving from evil, done by Jesus on the Cross will become clearer to the dreamer. You will become aware of who you are in Christ Jesus and the spiritual state that you ar e in. The psychological result of reasoning, perception, and learning of this information will usher you into what is called, "ultimate peace" or "glory". Glory in this sense is a state of high honor, spiritual beauty, and great illumination. Moreover, the dreamer will return to a place or state of safety and plenty and will return to Christ and to His church. Accordingly, your soul and lifestyle will begin to bear fruit of positive choices, resulting in spiritual strength and power within the dreamer's li fe; this is also "glory". (2) Hair (washing): Your dream marks a transition within the dreamer's life. Although, at present, you faithfully sustain the outward appearances of being blessed and sanctified, your spirit is outrageously out of control; thus, the need for washing of the hair. You have allowed your sensual desires to run rampant. As a result, Christ will now begin to deal with your unruly and egotistical tendencies, the actual washing of the hair. Do not spurn the rectifying of you by the Lord. He is getting you in order, resulting in a greater commitment to your family, ministry, and to Christ, and for you to be highly blessed. This refinement process will create a righteous glory within your life. As well, you are going from a worn-out, tattered, and torn condition, emotionally, physically, and/or spiritually, to a better quality of being. After this, your life's circumstances will begin to change; state of affairs will spiritually be in favor of the dreamer. Some type of spiritual and/or physical enhancement and sophistication within the life of the dreamer will also happen. The Holy Spirit will carry out the process that will transition you from one state to another, obey His lead. Question to journal: What was the primary reason the dreamer's hair was being washed within the dream? Example, was you dyeing your hair? If so, what color? Was the dreamer washing bugs, ticks out of your hair, if so, what kind? What condition was your hair? Was it smelly? See index or relevant category for other particu lars within your dream. For example, if hair was dyed, see category, Color. If bugs or ticks were highlighted, see category, Animals. Was hair smelly? See category, Odors. This area needs to be cleaned-up or rectified in order for the refinement process to be complete. See suggested course of action. (3) White (or gray) hair: Dreamer is using wisdom regarding a present situation. Dreamer, be encourage for you do understand what is right and just and fair, every good path. Wisdom has entered your heart and knowledge has become sweet to your soul; therefore, discretion will protect you, understanding will guard you, and His Truth will lead you. Listen to that still small voice that is speaking to you at present; He speaks of peace. He will guide you, for He is of God. For the Lord gives wisdom and from His mouth comes knowledge and understanding. You will be delivered from the ways of wickedness, from demons whose words and ways are perverse, from those who have attempted to cause you to walk in darkness, those whose paths are crooked and devious. This is one of God's covenant promises to you. Have faith in this. (4) If you are an unbeliever (one who has no religious beliefs, a non-religious person, or one who has no religious faith or belief in Jesus Christ, or one who does not embrace a personal relationship with Jesus Christ, at present). Jesus loves you, thus, He is petitioning you to accept Him as your personal Savior, for you are valuable in His eyes. The first step in receiving H im as your personal Savior is repentance (see in the Holy Bible, Acts 2:37-41). Repentance is seeking pardon for having done something awry, and for having hurt someone, and expressing sincere feelings of regret and brokenness. To Jesus pray, Psalm 51:1-19. To individuals, a phone call or a letter of apology is a good place to start, if appropriate. Moreover, if you will accept the Heavenly Father's Words, via the Bible, and store up His principles, and His ways and means within you, turning your ear to wisdom and applying your heart to understanding, calling out for insight and crying aloud for discernment, Jesus will meet you. This, coupled with a lifestyle of prayer and fasting, followed by appropriate application of wisdom, and you will know the Messiah, Jesus Christ, intimately, and find the knowledge of God you seek. For the Lord gives wisdom and from His mouth comes knowledge and understanding. Then you will understand what is right and just and fair, every good path. When wisdom enters your heart and knowledge becomes sweet to your soul, discretion will protect you, understanding will guard you, and His Truth will lead you. To deliver you from the ways of wickedness, and from demons whose words and ways are perverse, who causes you to walk in darkness gladly, whose paths are crooked and devious, causing you to leave straight paths (Proverbs 2:1-6, 9-15). This is one of God's covenant promises to you. Have faith in this. See suggested course of action.

BEARD:

This dream has four meanings (choose one). (1) Long beard (male): Dreamer is a God ordained leader. Dreamer, because of your faith, humility, strong leadership, and your courageous and optimistic spirit, you will be greatly honored. You will ri se to a level the Anointing of God and your acumen deem you should be. Even more, in your present business or personal dealings, you will be satisfied and take delight in your goals. If you are involved in any situation that is competitive, you will tri umphant. (2)

Long beard (female): If female saw herself with a beard, you boast of your own wisdom, which, in reality, is non-existent or twisted. Your behavior contradicts practicality, basic reality, and deviates from the morality of God. Pray for divine trut h, for one should never exalt their thoughts, ideas, feelings, above God's truth, for, every house is built by someone, but the builder of all things is God" (Hebrews 3:2-4). Godly wisdom and obedience is your best bet. See suggested course of action. (3) Saliva on the beard: First determine who this dream is referencing, either the dreamer or another. For example, was saliva on someone else's beard? Was another responsible for the saliva on the beard (e.g. did someone spit on another or the dreamer's beard)? If yes to one or both questions, your dream is referencing another, and their possible effects within the dreamer's life, other than yes to the previous questions, your dream is referencing the dreamer. With that, your dream denotes foolish and senseless behavior, or one who is mentally healthy. See suggested course of action. (4) White or grayish beard: This choice has three parts (choose one). (a) Dreamer had white beard: Dreamer is using wisdom regarding a present situation. Dreamer, be encourage for you do understand what is right and just and fair, every good path. Wisdom has entered your heart and knowledge has become sweet to your soul; therefore, discretion will protect you, understanding will guard you, and His Truth will lead you. Listen to that still small voice that is speaking to you at present; He speaks of peace. He will guide you, for He is of God. For the Lord gives wisdom and from His mouth comes knowledge and understanding. You will be delivered from the ways of wickedness, from demons whose words and ways are perverse, from those who have attempted to cause you to walk in darkness, those whose paths are crooked and devious. This is one of God's covenant promises to you. Have faith in this. (b) To have seen another with a white beard denotes someone is before you at present, who is a spiritual guide or teacher. You should heed their wisdom.

HEAD, NECK, AND THROAT (this category includes the brain, cheeks, jaws, ears, eyes, face, forehead, head, mouth, teeth, tongue, neck, throat, and nose):

This type of dream generally sheds light on the dreamer's inward thoughts and feelings; regarding your spiritual, psychological, and literal health, outward circumstances and conditions, as well as, the dreamer's attitude towards others. See one of the following.

Brain:

This dream has two meanings (both may apply). (1) Dreamer, as you are super-sensitive and intuitive, you feel and sense much that you do not fully understand; consequently, you are deeply influenced by the thoughts of others without realizing just how much you are being affected. Because of this influence, you over-analyze, second-guess, and scrutinize your faith and/or you respond to life challenges with too much openness, not utilizing practical judgment. Dreamer, Jesus is reaching out to you. You are counseled to learn the voice of the Lord, and to separate truth from influence. One suggested course of action is for the dreamer to focus your thoughts on whatsoever things are true, whatsoever things are honest, whatsoever things are just, whatsoever things are pure, whatsoever things are lovely, whatsoever things are of good report; if there be any virtue, and if there be any praise, think on these things, see Philippians 4:8. Take this verse very seriously; it will support you on your next endeavor. (2) Dreamer, you are gifted with prophetic insight that may be expressed through inspirational preaching, teaching, and/or acting. Earnest and conscientious Christian efforts and endeavors will enhance your prophetic gifting. Allow the Lord's will to be done in you, via faithfully serving Him.

Cheeks, Jaws:

This dream has two meanings (choose one). (1) Cheeks that were normal (unmutilated, unmarred): Your dream denotes that the selfless good deeds, done by the dreamer, for others, will be repaid, you will reap, if you faint not (Galatians 6:9). As well, your dream denotes a short-term loss in return for greater power. The dreamer and, if applicable, your children will reap the fruits of the blessing of your giving. Moreover, as you are able to handle great responsibility and wealth, and are one who is tolerant, you will experience receiving an act of kindness, monetarily, from someone who is affluent. (2) Cheeks that were mutilated, marred, or swollen in some way: This choice has two parts (choose one). (a) Your dream was sent as a stern rebuke. It alludes to a deliberate offensive act, an act of great disrespect, the giving of a very great affront and provoca tion to God and/or others. Dreamer, is nothing sacred? You have greatly insulted God and one of His servants. Even more, you perpetuate violence and continually provoke God to anger. You are an abusive person. Your character is one of extreme haughtiness, presumptuousness, pride, and self-assuredness in the very negative sense of the word. All are signs that your heart is hardened. If this disposition is not let go, it will lead to a great fall (Proverbs 11:2; 16:18, 19; 29:23). Dreamer, turn from your wicked ways. Ask Jesus for wisdom and for the courage to apply it. Dreamer, God knows your thoughts afar off, so genuinely repent. Take words to Jesus, "'I have sinned, and I have done wrong and acted wickedly". Other than prayer and heartfelt repentance to Jesus and to individuals affected by your actions, in the form of an apology (if possible), no other excuse or weak justification will be heard. See suggested course of action. (b) Dreamer, if you are an unbeliever (one who has no religious beliefs, a non-religious person, or no religious faith or belief in Jesus Christ, or one who does not embrace a personal relationship with Jesus Christ); Jesus loves you, thus, He is petitioning you to accept Him as your personal Savior, for you are valuable in His eyes. The first step in receiving Him as your personal Savior is repentance (see in the Holy Bible, Acts 2:37-41). Repentance is seeking pardon for having done something awry, and for having hurt someone, and expressing sincere feelings of regret and brokenness. To Jesus pray, Psalm 51:1-19. To individuals, a phone call or a letter of apology is a good place to start, if appropriate. Moreover, if you will accept the Heavenly Father's Words, via the Bible, and store up His principles, and His ways and means within you, turning your ear to wisdom and applying your heart to unde rstanding, calling out for insight and crying aloud for discernment, Jesus will meet you. This, coupled with a lifestyle of prayer and fasting, followed by appropriate application of wisdom, and you will know the Messiah, Jesus Christ, intimately, and find the knowledge of God you seek. For the Lord gives wisdom and from His mouth comes knowledge and understanding. Then you will understand what is right and just and fair, every good path. When wisdom enters your heart and knowledge becomes sweet to your soul, discretion will protect you, understanding will guard you, and His Truth will lead you. To deliver you from the ways of wickedness, and from demons whose words and ways are perverse, who causes you to walk in darkness gladly, whose paths are crooked and devious, causing you to leave straight paths (Proverbs 2:1-6, 9-15). This is one of God's covenant promises to you. Have faith in this.

Ears:

Your dream denotes that this is the season of the Lord's favor upon your life. By His grace, God has prepared and qualified you for mercy and then bestowed it upon you. However, as feelings go, because of your bad behavior and deeds, you are discouraged, and feel unfit and unworthy of God's favor and restoration. Nonetheless, because of God's grace an d His great faithfulness, the promise of deliverance, restoration, and fruitfulness are before you. Dreamer, you have been in a process of being made whole, emotionally, psychologically, and spiritually. Now, you will shortly experience a miraculous increase in knowledge and wisdom, regarding spiritual truths and concepts. You are chosen and endowed with an ability to handle this type of divine impartation. Your access to prophetic wisdom will enable you to discern truth from false; and you will prove to be a transformational influence in the lives of many. You will skillfully help develop minds at searching out truth, train disciples, refresh many spiritually, and encourage others to faithfully join religious organizations (e.g. churches, Christian colleges, Christian based support groups) for help and support in building close relationships with other brothers and sisters i n Christ and with close significant others as well. You are a gift to the Body of Christ. One thing, you are counseled to temper great wisdom and authority with humility and simplicity. God wants to continue His ministry through you, which also includes healing the sick, and delivering the oppressed, thus, fulfilling His ministry to His people via you. So, you are advised to stay put in whatever church or faith based community you are a part of, don't run off and try to do your own thing in your own strength and carnal knowledge. If necessary, see suggested course of action.

Eyes:

This dream has seven meanings (one, two, or three may apply). (1) Eyes are symbolic windows into the soul and are clues to the state of the dreamer's spiritual and/or physical health. Bright eyes suggest an uprightness of spirit and soul, a clear conscience, and a healthy manner of life, as well as, one who is very generous. For dull eyes, see following subcategory, cataracts, disfigured, defected, or dull looking eyes. (2) This dream is also a guidance dream, and is meant to be a catalyst for change. Dreamer, your purpose is that of becoming a forerunner for change, freedom, progressive thought, and action. You are a great leader, with the capacity to lead many to Christ. Christian in belief, with a generous nature, you have the capa city to spearhead a fresh revival, leading a generation that will usher in a time of great spiritual revelation regarding the Truth of God, the Holy Spirit, and God's Holy Word. The offspring of this revival will embrace the knowledge of a personal and saving relationship with Jesus Christ. You're heading towards your destiny. You are going in the right direction, doing good things, and your cause is noble. You are naturally endowed with the ability to perceive wisdom; and it is this, which guides you towards your intended destination. Every step you take is toward purpose. Unfortunately, as this present age will have it, your message on progressive thinking, with a primary focus on loyalty to God and holiness, will offend those who choose to forget God. Politely disassociate yourself from those who do not respect or understand your cause, for they will hinder your purpose. Nonetheless, you will get to wherever it is you're destined to get. God has promised to make known to you His presence, His guidance, and protection. You will be strengthen and enlighten. (3) Black Eye or Full Black Iris: Your dream denotes that the dreamer is under heavy demonic influence, or demonic possession. The Bible gives some examples of people possessed by, or under the influence of, demons (read Matthew 9:32, 33, 12:22; 17:18; Mark 5:1-20, 7:26-30; Luke 4:33-36, 22:3; Acts 16:16-18). From these examples, you will find some symptoms of demonic influence and gain insight as to how a demon possesses or influences someone. While it is believed that a believer can be influenced by the devil, see Matthew 16:23, there is no example in Scripture of a Spirit-filled believer in Christ being possessed by a demon. Thus, it is believed that a Christian cannot be possessed because he or she has the Holy Spirit abiding within them and the Spirit of God will not share residence with a demon (Matthew 12:29; Mark 3:27; Luke 11:21, 22). With that said, unfortunately, many believers, can and do, open their lives up to demonic influence; thus, demonic oppression, either through the embracing of some manner of evil or through cultic involvement, on some level or another (either knowingly or unknowingly). Examples may include sexual immorality, drug and alcohol abuse, or anything that alters one's state of consciousness, transcendental meditation, rebellion, and/or bitterness. The book of Ephesians (2:2, 8-9, 4:17-24, 6:10-18) gives instructions on how we are able to have victory in our lives in the battle against the forces of evil. The first step is placing your faith in Christ, who breaks the rule of evil. Second, choose, again by God's grace and enablement, to put off ungodly habits and to put on godly habits. By the renewing of your mind, and by resisting the devil, by not giving him room in your mind, in your thought processes, your behaviors, and life, for there is truly a spiritual battle going on within the lives of all believers, including yours. Dreamer, it is suggested that you sagaciously stand with truth, righteousness, the gospel, faith, salvation, the Word of God, and prayer. See suggested course of action. (4) Blindness or

Blindfolded: This dream denotes one who is spiritually blind, no spiritual vision, by choice, having carelessly risked your life and soul, pretending to be blind to, and ignorant of, the things of God, to His principles, and to His creative works in and around you; all, done in hopes to satisfy fleshly desires. Dreamer, God's love is calling you back to Him; forgiveness will cover all your mistakes, and you must forgive yourself and others. Now give careful thought to this, from this day on. From this day forward, no longer, pretend that you do not sense God's providence within your life, and God will bless you; therefore, perceive God's grace, and embrace the love that is calling you home. See suggested course of action. (5) Cataracts, disfigured, defected, or dull looking eyes, or Scales falling from your eyes (thin flakes of dead epidermis): Dreamer, the spiritual truths you think you know, and what will eventually be revealed to you (namely, how b lind you really are) will lead you to your own personal enlightenment. There will be a prophecy, a revelation, prophesied to you that will lead you to acknowledge that your understanding of spiritual realities is childish at best, and perilously dangerous to others to say the worst. Favorably, you will be given a grace period, to go away to "de-program" and reprogram yourself (Galatians 1:12-24). Afterwards, began to walk and grow into a mature, spiritual being, going on towards perfection, enabled to se e into the spiritual realm more clearly, and to see Jesus, as Lord and Savior. No matter your hardships and they will be grievously many, never again look back, but genuinely, in words and deeds, continue to progress forward. As a result, your capacity for greater illumination, intellectually and spiritually, will be enlarged giving you access to a fountain of wisdom and great revelation. See suggested course of action. (6) Eyebrows, Eyelids, or Eyelashes: This choice has two parts (choose one). (a) Your dream denotes a transition within the life of the dreamer, and good health and strength to make the changeover. This transition will affect within you a far-reaching hope, profoundly greater faith, and a more intense love for all things Jesus, including His people; allow it. Dreamer, as you have done well serving your present place of worship, the leadership, and members, especially by making them better and greater qualitatively. By this you have open the door for you to become a leader, namel y a CEO of your own ministry. God will send someone to help you along the way. He or she will lead and guide you to where you need to be. This relationship will be an "equal partner" or "friendship" type relationship, in other words they will not be head over you. You will always be respected as a lead person. Moreover, dreamer you have been blessed with a great understanding of spiritual knowledge, and not without reason. One who is given the means to study and teach and has access to prophetic wisdom, is purposed to be a transformational force in people's lives. Your power of speech and wisdom will convert souls to the Kingdom of God. Your time of missions is upon you. You are sent to those who are spiritually "asleep". You are counseled to focus your ministry on God's providence over life. Primarily, the wisdom, care, and guidance He has provided His people, for He always guards over His chosen; thus, He watches over His people. You must continue to encourage others, and encourage yourself too, that the feeling of rest and serenity that comes with trust in God's divine providence is available right now, and that it would be wise of them to put their trust in God now. This, coupled with, contentment, and theirs, and your, peace will overflow. Those who will listen and adhere will begin to experience the blessings spoken of in Leviticus 26:4-13, tell them this. In particular, (verse 6 GW), "I will bring peace to your land. You will lie down with no one to scare you". Moreover, you (the dreamer) will be leaving your present church, and you will experience a mega-ministry. You will become friends with major leaders, but not covenant partners with them. You will (or should) remain attached to your present church and come back to rest there. Shortly thereafter, because of your diligence and honorable service, you will be given the opportunity to take a sabbatical rest, covered by the Lord's grace. (b) Dreamer, there is one who is attempting to slander your name and reputation. It is the one with whom you are in a conflict of opinions, actions, or character, with at present, and you have had a personal relationship with this person on some level in the past. Note, slander, defamation, any false accusation or a malicious misrepresentation of someone's words or actions, or an abusive attack on a person's character or good name, always precede and accompany persecution, because malice itself cannot excite people against a good man or woman. As such, to do this, he or she must first be represented as a bad man or woman. What can be said of those who are busied in this manner, but that they are a "generation of vipers", the brood of the old serpent, that grand accuser and calumniator of the believers, having under their tongues a bag of poison, conveying instant death to the reputation on which they fasten. Thus, David was hunted as a rebel, Christ was crucified as a blasphemer, and Christians of long ago were tortured as guilty of incest and murder George Horne. Dreamer, you will be persecuted for righteousness sake; subsequently you will be promoted to a position of power. Thus, what the enemy will mean for harm, God will use to prepare you to handle power that does not corrupt. Therefore, now, resolve to forgive those who would be used by the enemy to come against you. To be forewarned is to prepare you emotionally for the experience. Our Lord Jesus by giving us notice of trouble, is designed to take off the terror of it, that it might not be a surprise to us. (7) Watching or Staring or Gaze or Very Wide Opened Eyes (fixate your eyes on someone, or something, e.g. you staring at or watching something intensely, or someone staring at you, or "all eyes on you", or eyes wide open and fixed as in a deep stare): This choice has four parts (choose one). (a) If dreamer was staring at any manner of immorality, dreamer is counseled to, no longer consider the immorality of your past. Do not limit God in this, namely whatever you was staring at; no longer limit God, by your thoughts of what was, nor, what might happen, for old things have passed away, and you have truly become new (2 Corinthians 5:17). Therefore, focus your heart, mind, and soul, your full understanding, on new principles, new rules, and new company. For you are truly created anew, a new heart has been given you. Therefore, let this be your focus, fixate your eyes upon these things. See suggested course of action. (b) If dreamer was staring at any manner of godliness, or any manner of beauty, your dream was sent as an encouragement. Dreamer, your necessity of regeneration and reconciliation with God through Christ is done; therefore, begin to prepare to be consecrated[35]. (c) Eyes watching or staring at you (or "all eyes on you"): Your dream comes to advise the dreamer regarding celebrity; you will obtain some level of being well known and much spoken about. Dreamer, one person, or many people, are watching and paying attention to you, or will be within one year. You are also being looked at thoughtfully; and observed by one or two persons, regarding your loyalty, diligence, and your reputation. (d) Very Wide Opened Eyes and fixated: Your dream denotes demonic possession or demonic oppression. Dreamer, you have opened a door for serious demonic activity. Demonic oppression, demons running havoc within your life, or demonic possession, is at hand. Along with prayer and fasting, you will now need to seek professional help from a Christian counselor, a faith based support group, and there is a need to set up an accountability system, and earnestly commit to that help. If you do not seek help, within one year, God's covering will be removed from over you. As a result you will begin to experience serious mental health issues and will have to be restrained, against your will, if needs be. Dreamer is counseled to steal away to a quiet and private place and talk to Jesus. Dreamer, if urged by God, declare a one, two, or three day fast for sanctification purposes; also, wash (bathe) and make yourself, clothi ng, and personal surroundings clean. Nonetheless, you will need to declare some kind of fast and commit to it, for a period-of- time, to defeat the demonic influence within your life. Moreover, refrain from wickedness and do no one harm, physically, sexually, emotionally, and/or spiritually, any longer. Start treating God's people, your family, and others, with respect. By this, God will pardon your injustices. See suggested course of action.

Face: *See one of the following*

Animal's face or reflection of an animal: Animals, within our dreams, for the most part "give a human face" to your character or personality traits, behavioral patterns, basic nature, and endowments (e.g. to see a scorpion on your face, poin ts towards the dreamer inward thoughts and feelings, and some outward circumstances and conditions). This, coupled with the interpretation of the particular animal depicted within your dream, should unveil the meaning of your dream. See category, Animals.

Bright shining face, Face glowing (some manner of brightness in the face) or face had a comforting, encouraging, nurturing, and affectionate appearance: This dream has two meanings (choose one). (1) Your dream represents someone, namely the dreamer, who will be sent to expose a crime, indiscretion, wrongdoing, or misbehavior, within the life of another, especially one who intends to harm the dreamer in some way. (2) If another's face was bright, there is one, who will be sent to the dreamer to expose a crime, indiscretion, wrongdoing, or misbehavior within the dreamer's life. Dreamer, if one is sent to you, be eager to repent, for in doing so, this can conceivably avert some of the repercussions of your choices. See suggested course of action.

Color of face: Your dream denotes dreamer's temperament, your attitude of mind, or your very public, excessive emotionalism, irritability, or excitability. See category, Color, for other specifics.

Face of the Lord: Dreamer, because of God's grace (the free and unmerited favor and beneficence of God); He desires to bring you back into a right relationship with Him. Thus, your dream's primary focus is about self-awareness. Dreamer, your best knowledge, and your greatest abilities are, at present, like your spiritual condition, narrow and temporary. Your human understanding of, and reaction to, spiritual realities is oftentimes crudely green. This type of simplicity is compared to "springs without water or mists driven by a storm" (2 Peter 2:17). You mouth empty and boastful words that appeal only to the lustful desires of your own carnal nature. Favorably, at this crossroads in your life, you will come to know Jesus as the Word made Flesh and as Messiah. As your dream also denotes that, there will be a personal enlightenment within the life of the dreamer. You will experience a miraculous revelation of who God truly is, and this will change your life dramatically, similarly to Isaiah's dramatic experience, which changed his life (see Isaiah 6). God will give you some quiet time to go deprogram and reprogram your belief system, counting all that you know to be obsolete or useless (Galatians 1:12-24). This experience will cause you to acknowledge that your understanding of spiritual realities is childish at best, and perilously dangerous to others to say the worst. Consequently, you will begin to walk and grow into a mature spiritual being, going on towards perfection, enabled to see into the spiritual realm more clearly. Note, utilizing the powerful resources of prayer and heartfelt repentance to Jesus and to individuals affected by your actions, in the form of an apology (if possible), is needed. Repentance is seeking pardon and expressing sincere feelings of regret and brokenness for having done something awry and/or for having hurt someone, see 2 Corinthians 7:10, 11. To Jesus, pray Psalm 38:1-22. To individuals, a phone call or a letter of apology is a good place to start. This followed by appropriate application of wisdom, can conceivably avert some of the repercussions of your choices. See suggested course of action.

Facial Expressions: This dream has three meanings (choose one). (1) To be angry, breathing hard, displeased, frightening, intimidating, menacing looking, or threatening and scary: This choice has two parts (choose one). (a) If dreamer saw his or her face looking this way, angry, breathing hard, displeased, frightening, intimidating, menacing looking, or threatening and scary, your dream indicates evil intent within the heart of the dreamer toward another that will result in tragic developments for the dreamer. See suggested course of action. (b) If another was looking at dreamer in an angry, breathing hard, displeased, frightening, intimidating, menacing looking, or threatening and scary way, there is one, who has evil intentions towards the dreamer, but they will not prevail. (2) Dirty face or face was disfigured in some way: This choice has two parts (choose one). (a) Dreamer, you take pleasure in falsely slandering, demeaning, and spiritually murdering others. Spiritual murder is a premeditated attempt to; cruelly destroy someone's reputation or an attempt to destroy someone's personal relationship with Christ, because of jealously. Therefore, slander and discredit of your reputation will be allowed; and the hearsay will be true, per the very public manifestation of your negative and demeaning attitudes and behaviors, all of this because of your very bad thought life. Regrettably, this is what it takes for you because you have not heeded other warnings. You have only feigned changed. See also Philippians 4:8, Romans 12:2. See suggested course of action. (b) Your dream is an alert to the dreamer. There are those who eagerly want to instigate chaotic situations, within your spiritual life, those who would have you to live in a confused, disorderly, and messy manner. You will hear of, and/or see them in action, soon. The result of their presence in your life will cause a negative mind-set within you. Dreamer, do not be dissuaded by their actions or protests; for, their ignorance and pride will be exposed. Therefore, earnestly rid your mind of any thought or ideas that compromises the word and divine order of God and do not be rattled by these insurgents, nor seek revenge. You will be shown a way around their influence and away from them. Pray and believe that Jesus will remove them from your life. (3) To a non-believer (one who has no religious beliefs, a non-religious person, or one who has no religious faith or belief in Jesus Christ, or one who does not embrace a personal relationship with Jesus Christ at present), your dream personifies someone, namely the dreamer, who practices infidelity (unfaithfulness, faithlessness, disloyalty, or betrayal) on several levels. Thi s infidelity is spiritual, due to a non-existence personal relationship with Christ, and a non-existence personal relationship with your spouse, significant other, family member, or friend. Further, dreamer, you are an extremely annoying, envious, and troublesome person, one who is very negative in their thinking, and is secretly superstitious. As well, you stand out openly against God (spiritual infidelity), attracting physical and spiritual harm to yourself. Fortunately, because you are unaware of spiritual knowledge that leads to an amicable relationship with Jesus Christ and others, He has sent your dream to you as a message of grace (the free and unmerited favor and beneficence of God). The kindness and love of our Lord and Savior has come to you, and not because of who you are or what you've done, but because of His compassionate mercy. So that you, having been justified by grace, will have hope for eternal life; saved from eternal separation from God. See Acts 2:37-40; therefore, go and sin no more, lest physical and spiritual harm come and overtake you at a time you least expect. See suggested course of action.

Large face or "long face" (face appears larger or longer than normal): Dreamer, your sin of hypocrisy must be acknowledged and forsaken, also see Psalm 50:16-23. See suggested course of action.

Mask, Masquerades (wearing one): This dream comes to alert the dreamer of the approaching consequences of your choices, and it has three meanings (choose one). (1) Your dream points towards fake pride, foolishness, pompousness, pretension, and other superficial characteristics. You use your influence as an occasion to behave toward others as though they are less important or intelligent than you are; arrogantly inciting arguments, controversies, or strife, especially amon gst Christians, who may be of a different mind than you. You are counseled to not allow yourself to act arrogantly, nor to provoke or envy others (Galatians 5:26). The dreamer should always maintain an attitude of love and service towards others; for all the law is fulfilled in you loving your fellow human as yourself. Love is the sum of the whole law and it is not arrogant or rude (see 1 Corinthians 13:1-13). See suggested course of action. (2) In judging others, you have set a precedent over your own life, discharging a universal law. The Universal Law: With the same judgments, you judge others, so will you be judged (see Matthew 7:1-5). Examples of judging, have you thought or said, "They're life is not holy, or they're not Christian, because I know they behave this way, or do that", or thought to yourself, "They need to sit down with all the emotional or physical hardship they're going through; they're not a super person". Or, "They have mental health issues". Have you never been in a fallen state, while at the same time, you were required to testify on behalf of the Kingdom of God, or did you just disobey the commission because of a preconceived notion or pseudo-image, ergo the mask? Have you not been under such pressure emotionally or physically that you could have experienced an emotional or mental breakdown, and yet you were still required to witness, or to preach? Nonetheless, now you're judged as an offender, in that, you have violated your own standard, the one you've held up for others to follow. While Christ does not deny the necessity of exercising a certain degree of discernment, or of making valid judgments with respect to sin in others. Jesus condemns the habit of criticizing others, while ignoring your own faults. You should have done what you expected of others. A believer must first submit him or herself to God's righteous standard before attempting to examine and influence the conduct of others, which is often done in an unjust or unloving manner if you haven't judged yourself first. This also includes condemning a wrongdoer without a genuine desire to see the offender return to God, but to be condemned to hell. Here again, discharging a preset law within this type of offense, which is to not see you, as an offender, return to God, but to be condemn to hell also. Dreamer, genuinely deal with why you are so judgmental or critical, and repent over judging others, this will remove such severe and unsympathetic standards from over your own life, and your dreams will change. Also, by so doing, a more compassionate, understanding, empathic and loving spirit will begin to manifest within you. See suggested course of action. (3) Your dream denotes one who presents as something that you're not. Masquerading as something before others, transforming yourself outwardly, but no change inwardly, for such are false clerics, and other false ministerial persons, deceiving and being deceived. Dreamer, the more you pretend, the harder it will be to change internally, when it's time to present your true self to Christ, and you will have to give an account to the King of kings. While it is still within your power to change, it is suggested that you take steps to do so. The first step is repentance (see in the Holy Bible, Acts 2:37-41). Pray to God Psalm 51. Then you will know the Messiah, Jesus Christ, intimately. For the Lord gives wisdom and from His mouth comes knowledge and understanding. Then you will understand what is right and just and fair, every good path. When wisdom enters your heart and knowledge becomes sweet to your soul, discretion will protect you, understanding will guard you, and His Truth will lead you. To deliver you from the ways of wickedness, and from demons whose words and ways are perverse, who causes you to walk in darkness gladly, whose paths are crooked and devious, causing you to leave straight paths (Proverbs 2:1-6, 9-15). This is one of God's covenant promises to you. Have faith in this. If you do not genuinely seek help and change, for sure ruin will be your destiny's declaration. See suggested course of action.

Forehead:

This dream has two meanings (choose one). (1) Sweat, Perspiration on Forehead: Dreamer, greatness is upon you, but you will only succeed via untiring determination, perseverance, and consistency. If you quit you will not attain your goals; unfortunately, nothing comes easy to you, only through hard work, but you will win, if you faint not. See also Philippians 4 :8, Romans 12:2. See suggested course of action. (2) Wrinkled Forehead: This choice has two parts (choose one). (a) Your dream is a stern warning and a harsh rebuke, alerting the dreamer of the need to commit to a serious and authentic change in your thought life immediately, aka repentance with fruits. Dreamer, repeated offensive and sinful thinking, will manifest openly in your attitude and behavior, for as one thinks in his or heart, so is he or she (Proverbs 23:7). Dreamer, you take pleasure in your thoughts of someone being falsely slandered, demeaned, and spiritually murdered. Spiritual murder is a premeditated attempt to; cruelly destroy someone's reputation or an attempt to destroy someone's personal relationship with Christ, because of jealously. Therefore, slander and discredit of your reputation will be allowed; and the hearsay will be true, per the very public manifestation of your negative and demeaning attitudes and behaviors, all of this because of your very ba d thought life. Regrettably, this is what it takes for you because you have not heeded other warnings. You have only feigned changed. See also Philippians 4:8, Romans 12:2. See suggested course of action. (b) Dreamer, you are allowing the results of a vicious and demonic instigated violation from your past, to hold sway over your entire life. Dreamer, y our vile violations, hurts, and rejections were demonically influenced, in an attempt to "bend" your personality, as early as possible, towards a certain direction, towards a way that is desolate. For it is Satan's scheme to kill and make desolate; thus, to keep you from fully experiencing a life fated you by God, a life of freedom and abundance, and to prevent you from rising up and leading your generation to Christ (see the birth of Moses, Exodus 1:15-2:10). Thus, dreamer, your life's violations have open a door for demonic possession or heavy demonic oppression. Subsequently, demonic forces are leading (or have led) you into becoming known as one who indulges in sexual perversion on so many levels, perhaps even homosexuality. For your dream also denotes homosexuality (male or female). Dreamer, your soul is buried underneath the pain of violations, and this has distorted your reasoning. The pain of rejection, abuse, and/or other emotional and physical violations, of your past, has affected your "approach pattern" to all your relationships. Dreamer, it is time, for you to ask God for healing and freedom from past traumas that have hindered your spiritual, emotional, and psychological maturity. Dreamer, Jesus wants to heal you. He wants you to live in the secret place of the Most High, abiding under the shadow of the Almighty; it's a warm and tender place there. Read and embrace Psalm 91, this is to you. Dreamer, the Most High has not forgotten you. God knows you've been living in your fortress, protecting yourself from further hurt. He sees you when you're restless, rolling on the floor, in pain, misery, and suffering. Jesus knows that you truly love Him and others, but you are still frightened by your fears. Dreamer, compassionately, the Lord is creating a miracle in your life. See suggested course of action.

Head:

As the head is the seat of the faculty of reason, your dream deals with the mental, spiritual, and physical aspects of ones psyche. It denotes one's mental health, divine revelation, and possibly head sicknesses. With that, see one of the following.

Bald head: This dream has two meanings (choose one). (1) Male dreamer: Dreamer, the beginning, development, arrival, or manifestation, of something large (significant in scope, extent, or effect) is about to happen within your life, in a threatening way. Because of this, you will now begin to experience a loss of glory (glory in this sense is divine admiration, praise, prosperity, success, triumph, and/or respect from others) within your life. Dreamer, gather your family together for support. See suggested course of action. (2) Female or male dreamer: Your dream warns of great weeping, mourning, and bitter anguish of heart because of someone within your family. That someone is in bondage, which may lead to jail time or death. There has been a lack of discipline and/or leadership by the dreamer, concerning your family, particularly this family member. Open your eyes to the reality of your family's social and emotional problems and seek professional support, if necessary, as well as pray and fast. See suggested course of action. Bleeding from your head, beaten on the head, or head was damage in some manner: Your dream denotes judgment (divine reprimand for folly and sin) and/ or physical death, is upon you; as to why, see category, Bleeding (Blood on, bubbling, gushing, oozing, running down, spurting, or heavily flowing from any part of the body). See suggested course of action.

Head cut off or floating away: This dream has three meanings (choose one). (1) Married female: This dream is about the approaching death of your husband, possibly within two or three years. The dreamer should pass on this information to her husband, while aggressively encouraging him to seek medical attention, averting a serious illness, having been caught in time, may perhaps save a life. Nevertheless, it is stressed that your spouse seek medical attention as soon as possible, and call for the elders of your church, for it is through their prayers of faith and anointing of oil that sin is forgiven and "spiritual" healing bestowed, and perhaps physical healing.[36] This is a true saying, thus it is time to have faith in God. Additionally, it is always a good time to get your house and papers in order (e.g. insurances, bequeaths, untold truths that need to be said), and always a good time to gather family together for prayer, support, wisdom, and truthfulness (Ecclesiastes 12:6). See suggested course of action. (2) Married male: Perhaps you're not a man given to sickness, except the common cold, thus, you rarely seek medical advice for problems, and have taken your health for granted. You are encourage to seek medical attention now, and call for the elders of your church. For it is through their prayers of faith and anointing of oil upon you that sin is forgiven and "spiritual" healing bestowed and perhaps physical healing[36]. If, due to denial, the message within your dream is not heeded with a sense of urgency, you will find yourself quickly needing to prepare for life on the other side of eternity, for example, getting your relationship with Jesus Christ in order, as well as, your house and business in order. See suggested course of action. (3) To the unmarried female and male: One, who has some level of authority, headship, or control over your life, will be removed from that leadership or controlling position, status (e.g. captor, parent, pastor, supervisor), especially from over your life, their authority will be removed.

Distorted, hit in the head, maimed, or smashed in the head: One who has violated you, or one, who has some level of control over your life, will be removed from that controlling position, status (e.g. abuser, captor, spiritual leader).

Hand extended to touch a head: The dreamer trusts in secondary causes. The following is a very basic explanation of first and secondary causes. The first cause is that which receives neither its power nor the exercise of its power from another; God alone is first cause. A second cause receives both its power and the use of it from the first cause; all creatures [and resources] are secondary causes Christian Philosophy, Louis de Poissy. God is the first (or primary) cause of everything. He miraculously created, "creatio ex nihilo" (creation out of nothing), John 1:3. From this act of God comes secondary causes and their purposes, "creatio ex materia" (creation out of some pre-existent matter), Genesis 1:2-2, 2 Peter 3:5. With this very basic explanation stated, the following is made easier to present. This is for you, the dreamer. You are trusting only in secondary causes. Examples, you need healing. You may testify with words that God heals and can heal miraculously (first cause). But with your heart you believe your healing can only come through a doctor's medicine (secondary cause); except now your illness is incurable and you need a miracle (a miraculous act of God, something out of nothing, per se). Another example, perhaps, you stand before a judge, desiring a certain outcome. While you confess that God has said the charges will be dropped; and you say God controls men, and answers prayer, inwardly you fear an undesirable outcome, so you do that which you know; you take the plea (secondary cause). This is where you truly put your faith, in secondary causes. You say you have faith in God, which is a resolute trust in the integrity of God and in His Word, but with your heart you only trust in others or things that can be used as a source of help or information, for example, a reserve supply of money, your own ability to find solutions to your problems. While these attributes are certainly commendable, and have worked for you in the past, they are purely secondary causes and should be recognized as such. Be it physical, emotional, or physical, dreamer, you need a miracle that only God can create, hence, put your faith in God, and Him alone. Dreamer, subconsciously (your mental activity just below the level of awareness) you are giving up on God's love, His grace, and His mercy; believing no help can, or will, come from Him regarding you, because of your personal shortcomings, e.g. you've not obeyed completely, an order from the Lord, or that minor flaw in your character. Thus, your present state is a result of an overall feeling of worthlessness, due to your own personal weaknesses. Dreamer, while your weaknesses maybe legitimate, do not deny the truth of God's report, "Therefore, there is now no condemnation for those who are in Christ Jesus"; as well, "His grace is sufficient". Romans 8:1, 2 Corinthians 12:9, upon these two scriptures and similar others, base your ideas of God's mercy regarding personal weaknesses. There is a difference between conviction and condemnation. All insinuations that God does not care, one way or the other, about your everyday living (bills, clothing, emotional well-being, family, finances, food, health care, political situations, safety, shelter, transportation, violence, war) are conceived without grace. Moreover, "dethroning" God from His providential sovereignty (the wisdom, care, and guidance provided by God) over your life, within your heart, coupled with your hasty and inconsiderate verdicts on His divine procedures, denies His Power. Thus, your love for Jesus is dwindling, and this gradual loss of love for Christ is festering within you like a cancer. You have stopped asking why, or for what reason this or that happened, but you need to go further and ask the deeper questions, seeking to understand why God allowed this or that, and what is the lesson to be learned, what is He revealing to you in His providential dealings with you. Dreamer, question not, His absolute goodness in His dealings with you, but ask, what are you to glean from it. See the Lord's providence behind all the events in your life, and change your paradigm. For, though apparently absent, He really is present, and He has promised never to leave you. Additionally, the dreamer will experience spiritual progression and growth suddenly. See suggested course of action.

Oil poured over your head: Your dream denotes one who is devoted in their service to God; as a result, you will experience spiritual growth, divine illumination, and some type of promotion, or exaltation on a prophetic level. Now, God will exalt you to a leadership position within your ministry and/or place of employment. Note, your height of spiritual progress and promotion will be according to your faith and obedience to God's will over your life personally.

Small head: Dreamer, low self-esteem and feelings of insignificance has caused you to act very corruptly. Your present difficult state of affairs bears witness of this. Not caring about your physical and spiritual well -being, coupled with your suggestive behavior will always leave you humiliated and in bondage. Unfortunately, you will be held accountable for all your actions, before God and man.

It is suggested that you go to a quiet place and study your bible. Go to church and forsake not the gathering of yourself together with other mainstream Christians. Avoid persons, places, or things that do not promote moral living, self-esteem, and emotional clarity. Dreamer, you personally, must learn to choose the good over the bad. See suggested course of action.

In addition, the following are common words, expressions, usages, (e.g. slang or clichés), or a 'probable' that are metaphorically represented by the hands:

- **Big head (to see a head bigger than normal):** Your dream denotes one who is conceited, and thinks that other people should admire them, and one who believes that they are very clever or very good at an activity. See suggested course of action.
- **Head on a platter or on something else or inside of something:** Your dream denotes one who is very angry with someone and wants them to be punished severely, thus asking for the head of your enemy. If dreamer's head is on the platter, then one wants you punished severely and is very angry with you. See suggested course of action.

Mouth, Teeth, Tongue:

As King Solomon says, "Life and death are in the power of the tongue" (Proverbs 18:21); thus, the mouth generally reveals your inner most thoughts, the articulation of those thoughts, and the manifestation of your thought life. One must be careful of the meditations of your heart and the words of your mouth, for what they manifest has eternal implications; what comes out of your mouth reveal what is in our heart. With that, see one of the following.

Mouth: See one of the following.

Breath (taking in and expelling air during breathing): The breath of a man or woman denotes their character; namely your attributes that determines your moral and ethical actions and reactions. Your character is who you truly are (read Matthew 12:33). Question to journal, was the breath good (fresh) or bad (foul) smelling? Was dreamer gasping for breath? This dream has three meanings (choose one). (1) Bad (foul) smelling: If breath was bad, foul smelling, this reflects bad character; hence, your dream comes as a warning. Dreamer, God wants you to focus on your character, namely your foolish behavior, choices, and immoral and unethical actions and reactions. Dreamer, you are known, and will be known, by the content of your character, and you will be judged by such, as one reaps what he or she sows. Moreover, there is an old saying, "your gifting can take you, where your character can not keep you". That is to say, although you may be prospering now, due to natural endowment, dishonesty, hatefulness, bitterness, an unforgiving and unloving attitude, will eventually bring ruin and desolation upon your head. Dreamer, ethicalness, honor, compassion, and empathy, is of upmost important, and if wholly embraced by you, will cause your prosperity to continue. Nonetheless, dreamer, taking ownership of what your warning dream is revealing to you about you, namely your character that is marked by dishonesty, hatefulness, bitterness, and/or an unforgiving and unloving attitude. Taking ownership and working from that point, via prayer, fasting, diligent self-examination, persistent practice of truthfulness, candid support from family and friends, and/or Christian counseling, will help truth inwardly begin to emerge; at a pace, you'll be able to "wrap your mind around" comfortably. This followed by appro priate application of wisdom, can conceivably avert self-deception and the repercussions thereof. This is what is called leaving a blessing behind. See suggested course of action. (2) Good (fresh) smelling breath: If breath was clean, fresh, overall good smelling, this reflects your character and this dream comes as an encouragement, with that, this choice has two parts (choose one). (a) Good character, sagacious behavior and choices, reaps good benefits. Dreamer, a spark of life remains hidden inside of you, and there awaits you a spiritual resurrection, according to God's grace. Thus, you will very shortly begin to experience, if not already, a paradigm shift in your core beliefs and spirituality. You are approaching new and deeper dimensions. Once you're restored to spiritual life, you will understand more clearly the nature of your covenant God, the eternally existing One, all - powerful, ever faithful, and lovingly concerned for His called people, even in their hopeless state. Moreover, see Isai ah 42:6, 48:1, 1 Corinthians 1:26, 27. (b) If you are an unbeliever (one who has no religious beliefs, a non-religious person, or one who has no religious faith or belief in Jesus Christ, or one who does not embrace a personal relationship with Jesus Christ, at present), dreamer, Jesus loves you; thus, He is petitioning you to accept Him, for you are valuable in His eyes. The first step in accepting Him as your personal Savior is repentance (see in the Holy Bible, Acts 2:37-41). Repentance is seeking pardon for having done something awry, and for having hurt someone, and expressing sincere feelings of regret and brokenness. To Jesus pray, Psalm 51:1-19. Moreover, your purpose, your mission, is to be sent to those who are spiritually dead, yet a spark o f life is hidden within them (also see Matthew 28:19, 20). See suggested course of action. (3) Choking or Suffocating (struggle for breath; have insufficient oxygen, breathe with great difficulty, caused by blocking the airways to the lungs): This choice has two parts (choose one). (a) Dreamer, you are counseled to break your heartaches, pains, anxieties, worries, and concerns in half and give some to Jehovah-Rapha (Psalm 147:3), and share them with another. For you cannot bear them alone; lest you find yourself gagging and choking on pieces of your sin, forfeiting the peace that comes with humbly asking for help from God and others. This breaking in half of your pains, coupled with the refining and purifying work of the Paraclete, and a greate r service to others, will cause the emergence of a greater divine led wisdom. In addition, dreamer is in need of endurance and patience, lest you received too much too soon and began figuratively choking on your own physical and spiritual prosperity. (b) If another was choking, dreamer is reminded to be of a greater service to others, via ministry. Your ministry is to those who believe that fundamental Christianity devalues and distorts rational thinking. Their take is that Christianity is cruel, brutal, despotic, exploitive, oppressive, strict, suppressive, a "poverty trap" and it demands obedience. Reality, they've heard the truth of God's Word, and it didn't lend support to, or was not actively in favor of, their lifestyle choices, so they became angry. They speak angrily and threateningly against God and against those who have embraced a Kingdom of God mind -set. So powerfully convincing the stranglehold of deception within their life, it has convinced them out of believing, thinking, feel ing, or doing anything connected to Jesus Christ and His Kingdom. They are involved in so many conflicting priorities and distractions that they're in a state of confusion from which there is no easy exit. Moreover, this confusion has caused a division within them, a serious mental health issue, as well as robbed them of physical strength. So, dreamer, your mission, should you accept, is to win souls wisely, and you will go in the spirt of the prophet Isiah (see Isaiah 6:9 -13). Brining to the forefront of your mission statement that, while God is absolute ruler, over His Theocratic Kingdom, and total obedience, by His people, to His Word, is preferable; He is not tyrannical, brutal, cruel, oppressive, or suppressive; nor, is serving Him, acc ording to His principles a "poverty trap". We are not serving an angry God, who needs to be appeased. The following words are what they will need to hear. Following God's principles actually empowers, encourages embracing ethical and moral principles, and fosters discipline, prudence, and prosperity, spiritually, physically, and literally, and all this is done without strain, even when the pressures of life feel like they're chocking you, for His yoke is easy, and His burdens are light (Matthew 11:30). Allow God's love to separate you from worthless and vain thoughts, teachings, and words. He can, and is willing, to restore things to a good state for you, and count this moment within your life as down time. Preach and teach these words. If necessary, see suggested course of action.

Happy mouth (e.g. smiling, laughing): Your dream refers to a promise made you by God, and the fulfillment of that promise made to you. The promise was made when you first invited Christ into your life. It will, very shortly happen. Moreover, God will reverse your tragedy, and you will testify that the Lord has done great things for you, and you will be glad. Dreamer, God's wisdom, care, and guidance, coupled with His divine intervention, has kept you, and will, again, cause your mouth to be filled with laughter, and your tongue with singing. Your situation will change and He will give you a new song in your heart. You will sing a new song. In addition, your dream points to one who was born to be a teacher and a nurturer. You should be teaching the elementary truths of God's word to your own children and to those not familiar with the teachings of righteousness, mainly new converts, and infants in Christ. Your diligent teaching will prepare others to spread the gospel o f Jesus Christ; thus, reproducing your teaching ministry and abundantly blessing you. You will receive wages for your diligence, if indeed you are diligent (Luke 10:2-7, 1 Timothy 5:18).

Chewing Food or Gum: This dream has four meanings (choose one). (1) To one approaching spiritual maturity, namely a believer, dreamer, you are undefiled according to biblical standards, down-to-earth, fair, humble, just, unpretentious, not rude, or obscene, and one whom a believer may interact with socially on very personal levels (e.g. business associate, friendship, ministry, and spouse). Therefore, take care to do your rightful duties (obligation to God, family, and if applicable, to country), offering mature service and exercising mature judgment. Moreover, the floodgates of heaven are open to you. Those floodgates are fullness in your spirituality, the glory of God in the midst of your life, and blessings of God. Gifts of God's grace, anything God freely gives you, absolution, the Holy Spirit, salvation, regeneration, eternal life, health, children, love of family, longevity, necessities, prosperity, and dominion over all that is yours; and all are parts of the supply of grace, an d all are sanctified by the Lord, and technically belongs to Him. The result of this supply in your life will be peace. (2) Dreamer, if you are an unbeliever (one who has no religious beliefs, a non-religious person, or no religious faith or belief in Jesus Christ, or one who does not embrace a personal relationship with Jesus Christ). Jesus loves you; thus, He is petitioning you to accept Him as your personal Savior, for you are valuable in His eyes. The first step in receiving Him as your personal Savior is repentance (see in the Holy Bible, John 3:1-17; Acts 2:37-41). Repentance is seeking pardon for having done something awry, and for having hurt someone, and expressing sincere feelings of regret and brokenness. To Jesus pray, Psalm 51:1-19. To individuals, a phone call or a letter of apology is a good place to start, if appropriate. Moreover, if you will accept the Heavenly Father's Words, via the Bible, and store up His principles, and His ways and means within you, turning your ear to wisdom and applying your heart to understanding, calling out for insight and crying aloud for discernment, Jesus will meet you. This, coupled with a lifestyle of prayer and fasting, followed by appropriate application of wisdom, and you will know the Messiah, Jesus Christ, intimately, and find the knowledge of God you seek. For the Lord gives wisdom and from His mouth comes knowledge and understanding. Then you will understand what is right and just and fair, every good path. When wisdom enters your heart and knowledge becomes sweet to your soul, discretion will protect you, understanding will guard you, and His Truth will lead you. To deliver you from the ways of wickedness, and from demons whose words and ways are perverse, who causes you to walk in darkness gladly, whose paths are crooked and devious, causing you to leave straight paths (Proverbs 2:1-6, 9-15). This is one of God's covenant promises to you. Have faith in this. See suggested course of action. (3) Chewing food gluttonously, ravenously, or exaggeratedly: Dreamer your time of action on behalf of the Kingdom of God is quickly approaching. However, you have need of harsh discipline, as your dream implies some manner of decadence within you; namely, immorality on various levels, and a lack of commitment, dependability, determination, and drive. Thus, your dream comes to alert the dreamer of the approaching consequences of your choices, and to caution the dreamer, to flee immorality. Dreamer, at present, concerned with your own interest, you are driven by, and occupied with, sensual appetites, rather than spiritual needs. The dreamer embraces a licentious liberty; you pursue your desires aggressively and egoistically, unchecked by morality. Your desires, appetites, and attitude are leading to a chaotic and empty life. A life figuratively similar to the condition of earth in Genesis 1:2, wasteful, empty, and dark. This type of carnal strain and toil leads to sorrow and spiritual darkness. Dreamer, you must bring your appetites, lusts, and sensual desires under subjection, sacrificing fleshy satisfaction for the cause of Christ, engaging all your power, with the help of the Paraclete, to do God's will. You will have to practice restricting yourself in all things; this includes your diet, activities, associations, and friendships as well (see Psalm 119:9). Dreamer, the place where God wants to take you, namely a high level of leadership, demands great personal sacrifice of rights and freedoms and requires the subduing of your passions. "To whom much is given, much is required". That being said, fate will put you in a position for some level of public exposure, either for honoring, because you sincerely choose to apply the truths of God's word to your life, or for open shame, due to a lack of self-restraint. On another vein, as you are a natural born leader, you have the power to lead others towards God, or away from the truth of His word, on to rebellion, and you will influence others to do according to your choice. If you choose to live life on God's terms, embracing His principles, you will become a great leader, leading many to Christ, and the favor of the Lord will be upon your life to cause men to honor and respect you; the glory of the Lord will rise upon you (see Isaiah 60:1-22). Glory in this sense is a state of high honor, spiritual beauty, and great illumination. If you choose to serve yo ur fleshly desires, worshipping at the altar of demons, desolation, and open shame is the inheritance of those who worship there. Nonetheless, for honor or open shame, public exposure is imminent. See suggested course of action. (4) Chewing Gum: Your dream is an alarm to the dreamer, for it denotes one committing loathsome sins, highly offensive, arousing aversion, and disgust. Dreamer, your physical life is something that should be valued, as well as, your spiritual life. For, even a good reputation and great wisdom can be easily lost and counted foul. One bad act or choice is hurtful to a good name; not only spoiling the goodness of it, but making it now, a name of ill-repute; base, disgraceful, low, scandalous, wicked (Ecclesiastes 10:1). Dreamer, your behavior and choices will bring great dishonor to you, and your home, if not already, and possibly disease, a physical rottenness in the flesh. There are many bitter and poisonous consequences of sexual immorality. Dreamer, your behavior is irresponsible, and if not diligently avoided, will usher you into the path of darkness, and your attitude and unwise choices will prove to your disadvantage, even to the point of being exposed openly. Therefore, flee sexual immorality, for this principle is a hedge of protection to the dreamer, against STDs, HIV, and another four-letter word that can take you to your final resting place, AIDS. With that said, dreamer you are warned to restrain and get your flesh under control. Your dream is one of God's ways of calling you back unto Him that you might be saved, and to see if you will yet be worked upon, and change your mindset; or else to leave you inexcusable, in your accusations against God, because of your ruin. Dreamer, of your own free will, you made a public profession of following Christ Jesus; thus, you need to walk according to that commitment, cautiously, refraining from all forms of evil, and approaches towards it, because many eyes are upon you. They watch your character, for error, faltering, stumbling; for any type of dishonor or violation, and surely, you have a great deal to lose. Before you are the possible loss of distinction, honor, reputation, and life. Thus, neglect not the purity of your covenant relationship with Christ, for God desires to bring you back into a right relationship with Him. Return to ideals that are holy, wise, well judged, and disciplined. This will lead you back to Christ. See suggested course of action.

Tightly closed mouth or tight or pursed lips: Your dream comes as a stern rebuke. Although you (the dreamer) is intended to be one who has the capacity to exemplify empathy, forgiveness, and understanding; one whom people will be drawn to for absolution, as well, one who will be important to the well-being of others, and important as a leader, promoting in every way the welfare of others, and powerfully anointed for this. Instead, you live in excess, mischievousness, arrogance, and unruliness, to the point of recklessness; and not only so, but you trample those you consider less than yourself, harmful to those about you, and have become an enemy of God's people; using them for wicked gain. Taking advantage of their spiritual and natural poverty, necessity, and inability to help themselves, making them poorer and needier than they were, while you give nothing in return (especially in the form of service); all the while blaming your lack of anointing, faithfulness, commitment, and stewardship on others. Your way of behaving causes one to become ineffective. Dreamer, you are by nature convincing, knowledgeable, influential, aggressive, physically powerful, of great strength, robust, sturdy, healthy, hardworking, optimis tic, thriving, and emotionally resilient. Thus, you must always consider your work as a service in t he Kingdom of God, for this is your life's purpose. It is important that your life's work assists and/or encourages others in many ways. Dreamer, take your

461

past and use it to teach those whom God has purposed you to reach. However, in order to fulfill your commission, to reach many, you will need to, seriously begin reflecting upon your moral weaknesses. How you might bring them under subjection to biblical principles, and how you might aspire for a certain level of purity. You are advised to discipline your body and your sensual desires and to bring them under control. Temperance in all things is your key word. Adopt a determined resolve, to go no further with an attitude of uncertainty about God, His Word, and Christianity. Rather, become intense a nd convicted when it comes to defending your beliefs. As well, steel your emotions and thoughts against all that will come against God's will for your life and you being able to fulfil that will in a sanctified way. God will lead the way. Nonetheless, if your negative behavior is not brought under subjection, you will become an object of scorn, derision, laughter, a joke to all who encounters you. Moreover, having proved yourself, many times, morally unclean for God's purposes, you will die before your time, in order for your soul to be saved. See suggested course of action.

Teeth: See one of the following.

Bite (to grip, cut off, or tear, with the teeth): Question, what kind of bite was it. Was it a defensive bite, or an act of aggression? Thus, this dream has two meanings (choose one). (1) Defensive bite: Dreamer, whatever is trying to raise-up and come against you; attempting to upset your spiritual rest and cause a spirit of fear within you. Read and understand Romans 8:15, 2 Timothy 1:7. Be encouraged, you are fighting against and strongly resisting "it", you will not let "it" reign again, within your mind, body, and spirit. You are holding on to your peace, "with your teeth". You will overcome. Moreover, dreamer, although, your previous lifestyle, your past, was overshadowed by negative experiences, and deferred hopes, God's righteousness dwells with and in you. God will raise you up and sit you amongst His people for the benefit of all within you r sphere, help God's people by doing good deeds. You will be considered, and now is, a righteous person (see Romans 8:1), for there is a difference between conviction and condemnation. Dreamer, if you will trust the empowering work of the Holy Spirit, which is beginning to manifest within your life on a conscious level; thus your dream, your emotional and spiritual well-being will be made whole (meditate upon and pray Psalm 51). Further, a conscientious and diligent effort on the part of the dreamer to, deeply reflect on your emotional fears and scars is needed; perhaps some type of Christian counseling may help as well. This coupled with, the refining and purifying work of the Paraclete will cause the emergence of a more divine led wisdom. It will also be through these pains that the wisdom of harmonizing, fear and love of the Lord within your life, will be imparted to you. Additionally, what did dreamer bite, why did you bite, and what emotions, feelings, was associated with the biting? Dreamer, the sum of all the symbols, will point you toward what is trying to raise-up or come against you, spiritually, emotionally, and/or physically. For example, a dead spouse, will point to issues, with your current leadership or any author ity over you, which was rendered dead, is now attempting to rise up again, but you will overcome. See suggested course of action. (2) Aggressive bite: This choice has two parts (choose one). (a) Dreamer, promotion of all kinds of indecent practices, sexual perversions and other odious traditions, under the guise of Christianity, dishonors God, His truth, and His church. Those who truly love Him, regards certain actions, characteristics, and behaviors as destructive to the church, family, and society. Consequently, the dreamer will begin to experience a loss of divine favor. Moreover, a third of the people that adhere to such practices as you do, will all die of the same illness, a third will fall away (becoming apostates) because of a lack of saving knowledge, and a third will "pull up stakes" with a stigma attached to their name. The dreamer will find him or herself within one of these three categories. When these things begin to happen, if not already, you will know that the Lord has spoken. Dreamer, dump your darken ideology, and enlighten and encourage others to do so as well that you, and they, might live. See suggested course of action. (b) To you who have not promoted any kinds of indecent practices, sexual acts of perversions or other horrible traditions. Your dream was sent to demonstrate grace, via a warning of a dark generational issue, hereditary within your family line (e.g. maternal and/or paternal, grandparents, siblings, aunts, uncles, cousins). Dreamer, character traits from ancestors, namely genetic codes and traits, will often trouble and taunt the offspring of a given progenitor, especially generational issues (Exodus 20:5-7). The demons that have so plague your family line, are now visiting (re-visiting) you. Your issue is demonically instigated and it is spiritually perverse, perhaps sexually perverse as well (e.g. adultery, fornication, homosexuality, prostitution, whorishness). These spirits attempt to "bend" the personality, as early as possible with regard s to age, towards a certain direction, oftentimes towards a way that is desolate and wicked, for it is Satan's scheme to kill and make desolate all; thus, to keep some from rising up and leading their generation to Christ (see the birth of Moses, Exodus 1:15- 2:10). Favorably, generational curses and issues can stop with you (Jeremiah 31:29, 30; Ezekiel 18:2-14, 20-23). Thus, your Heavenly Father is requiring that you overcome and subdue negative and dark emotions, feelings, behaviors, or ideas that would influence you, before they overcome you. Dreamer, God is not asking you to do something you cannot do. For a surety, vanquishing of the coming influence can be done. By faith, you will need to declare some kind of fast and commit to it, for a long period-of-time, to abate the demonically instigated circumstance, you find yourself in now, Matthew 6:16-18. Try abstaining from food and drink (midnight to 6 PM), twice a week, and refrain from words, attitudes, people, places, and thing s, including music, magazines, videos, TV, or any such things that fuel anger and discontent, and stir up lustful feelings. This is also known as, faith with works, read, understand, and embrace James 2:14-26. Nonetheless, earnestly pray, God will guide, enable, and answer you as to the type of fast. See suggested course of action.

Cleaning Teeth, Brushing Teeth, Flossing, or at a Dentist: Dreamer, God does not condone your transgressions (evildoings, or any violation of God's moral principles). You have gone beyond and overstepped God's boundaries and limits. Your way, your choices are morally unacceptable. Your dream has come to warn the dreamer of looming dangers and/or difficulties; you are approaching a time of great difficulty. Dreamer, somehow or another you have taken God out of the equation of your spiritual and temporal life, and have gotten His guiding principles, boundaries, and order of things twisted. In addition, you've been unresponsive to God's rebukes and reproofs. If you had responded to His rebuke, He would have poured out His heart to you and made His thoughts known to you. However, since you rejected Him when He called, and you did not give heed when He stretched out His hand to you. Since you hated knowledge and did not choose to fear the Lord, and you would not accept His advice, but spurned His rebuke, and ignored all His advice. You will eat the fruit of your ways, and be filled with the fruit of your schemes, (Proverbs 1:22-33). One thing is for sure, you will suffer some kind of great loss, and there will be a famine in your life. A very small thing will overwhelm you, so much so, that it will take you to the very edge of your mind. Wisdom, in turn will laugh at your disaster and mock, when calamity overtakes you like a storm, when disaster sweeps over you like a whirlwind, when distress and trouble overwhelm you. Notwithstanding, whatever trouble you may experience, God's grace (the free and unmerited favor and beneficence of God) is sufficient. You are exhorted to embrace wisdom, to be aware of enticements, and to, no longer take delight in foolishness and the hating of knowledge. Be on the alert; be watchful, and ready to deal with whatever happens. See suggested course of action.

Dentures (artificial teeth): This dream has two meanings (choose one). (1) Dreamer, while you are aware of your issues of covetousness, and jealousy, because of the prosperity of others, as well as, your grudging admiration, contempt, resentment, spite, even ridicule at seeing the success of others, you have only superficially dealt with your own issues. Mu ch that has taken place, within your heart spiritually is an artificial revival. You are "pumped up" artificially. You have chosen to "appear" strong in your faith and mature spiritually, but it is not so, this is only false pride. Dreamer there is still opp ortunity to affect a deep knowingness of yourself, especially regarding covetousness. Nonetheless, your ability (or inability) to change will have a direct effect on the quality and healthiness of your personal relationship with Christ Jesus. See suggested course of action. (2) Dreamer, if you are an unbeliever (one who has no religious beliefs, a non-religious person, or no religious faith or belief in Jesus Christ, or one who does not embrace a personal relationship with Jesus Christ); Jesus loves you, thus, He is petitioning you to accept Him as your personal Savior, for you are valuable in His eyes. The first step in receiving Him as your personal Savior is repentance (see in the Holy Bible, Acts 2:37-41). Repentance is seeking pardon for having done something awry, and for having hurt someone, and expressing sincere feelings of regret and brokenness. To Jesus pray, Psalm 51:1-19. To individuals, a phone call or a letter of apology is a good place to start, if appropriate. Moreover, if you will accept t he Heavenly Father's Words, via the Bible, and store up His principles, and His ways and means within you, turning your ear to wisdom and applying your heart to understanding, calling out for insight and crying aloud for discernment, Jesus will meet yo u. This, coupled with a lifestyle of prayer and fasting, followed by appropriate application of wisdom, and you will know the Messiah, Jesus Christ, intimately, and find the knowledge of God you seek. For the Lord gives wisdom and from His mouth comes knowledge and understanding. Then you will understand what is right and just and fair, every good path. When wisdom enters your heart and knowledge becomes sweet to your soul, discretion will protect you, understanding will guard you, and His Truth will lead you. To deliver you from the ways of wickedness, and from demons whose words and ways are perverse, who causes you to walk in darkness gladly, whose paths are crooked and devious, causing you to leave straight paths (Proverbs 2:1-6, 9-15). This is one of God's covenant promises to you. Have faith in this.

Good teeth or White Teeth (teeth in good condition): Dreamer, you are going through a maturing season, so between the mundane and the sacred, beginnings and endings will be constant elements in your life at this time. Not all the changes will be equal in significance, therefore, the diverse kinds of issues and situations, calls for regard in differing degrees, thus your dream. Within one year, dreamer will re-locate to another place. Finances will fluctuate, because of your issue with avarice and covetousness; as well, you will waver between conflicting positions or courses of action. No matter the issues, dreamer is encouraged to remain strong in your faith, and not be swayed by the circumstances of your life. Dreamer, allow the difficulties, changes, and turnarounds to affect a deep knowingness of yourself, especially regarding covetousness. Nonetheless, your ability (or inability) to change will have a direct connection to the quality and healthiness of your transformation.

Teeth falling out of your mouth, missing teeth, or teeth in bad condition: Your dream denotes extreme avarice, covetousness, and jealousness, because of the prosperity of others. Your grudging admiration, contempt, resentment, spite, criticism, even ridicule at seeing the success of others, spiritually, emotionally, materially, and/or physically, is unproductive false pride, an exaggerated sense of self-importance, with no useful purpose, and is sinful. Dreamer, resentfulness, unhappy feelings, and/or wanting somebody else's success, qualities, or possessions, any manner of avariciousness, will cause you to make mistakes that will lead to the mishandling of those you aid, comfort, encourage, guide, help, minister to, nurt ure, support, teach, or tend to, and it will to failure. Dreamer if you, in anything, set a bad example (e.g. arrogance, envious, greed, liar, maliciousness, rapacity, shyster, thievery), you do not know the great deal of harm you will do (or are doing) by your acts and choices, particularly to your family; and for sure, to those to whom you minister. Hence, there is a need to return to the path of righteousness and to God's great mercies. Dreamer, within your life, God has been compassionate towards you, while you were sinning, and He is compassionate towards you after your sinning is exposed. He will yet give you according to your needs, demonstrating mercy towards you, so that you do not become too overly distressed because of your sin. However, because of your extreme avariciousness, beginning from this moment, within one year, as a means of divine discipline, you will begin to experience the burning pain of correction and a reaping what you've sown. Fortunately this too will pass, once its mission is complete. Get up, dry your weeping eyes, and repent. See suggested course of action.

Sharp or Monstrous Teeth: This dream has two meanings (choose one). (1) Dreamer has sharp teeth: Dreamer, now, having in yourself nothing that you respect more than power and greed, you are willing to sacrifice all, God, principle, family, and friend, to the image or idol of vanity. Your new way is based on exploring alternatives to God's righteous principles, as well as, creating a sense of unity with the wickedness around you, which in turn is corrupting (altering, damaging, distorting, harming) your attitude towards Jesus. This mentality sacrifices children, family, friend, and morality to the hollowness of satisfying immoral desires and appetites. All carried out, with the hope of finding happiness by pacifying jealously and covetousness. Dreamer, the selling-out of yourself over to immorality, allowing wickedness to prevail in your home, devaluing those you should be protecting and nurturing, while closing your eyes to it all, are all principles based on values that are not only vile, but also increasingly unstable. This way cries out against godly ethics, and its' end offends any sense of godliness. Your recklessness can be remedied by prayer and heartfelt repentance to Jesus (seeking pardon and expressing sincere feelings of regret and brokenness for having done something awry, see Psalm 51, 2 Corinthians 7:10, 11, also see Deuteronomy 6:10-15; 11:10-28). Moreover, your dream cautions the dreamer that with persistent hard work and effort in correcting your dangerous mindset and lifestyle, you can again, remember Jesus, and once more respect His principles. Seek counsel from godly individuals, you will find wisdom with them. Dreamer, without repentance and change, your mindset will cause you, eventually, to forget God, only to remember Him again, with regret, on your deathbed. God wants you to consider, answer, and remember from this day forward, as a preservative against future idolatry, the following. Of all the things you've done to acquire wealth, and/or to remain youthful or popular, did any of it, bring you genuine freedom, authentic happiness, exemption from accusations, blame, harm, reproach, unpleasant consequences, confusion, or disorder? Having gone through, and experienced, the repercussions of covetousness, greed, vanity, and the worship of materialism, your mindset should have changed. Omitting God and His ways from your life is to omit genuine happiness, health, joy, and peace. See suggested course of action. (2) Dreamer was surrounded by those with sharp teeth: Dreamer, you will soon find yourself in the midst or presence of those who have a form of godliness, but are not godly. While they present as though they believe in a single supreme god who created and ruled the universe, survival after death, the practice of charity, and other beliefs similar to believers, their practices are a syncretic[29] fusion of demonology, necromancy, Spiritism, Satanism, witchcraft, and other heresies that leads to a path of descent. They will force you to view the world according to their truths. What they truly believe is that Elohim creates imperfect beings and then forces them to rise up to a level of perfection, which they are unable to reach, by torturing them, causing millions to suffer in body and soul, because of their natural instincts, which they were designed with, until they reach a so-called desired light or face karma. They reason that this is the only way, a path of pain, torture, and then death. They ask what human being aspires to evolve through this endless agony. They proclaim that God's promises, via Jesus' teachings, are no more than vague words of doubtful happiness, implacable laws that promise remote and unknowable joy, under the mask of love of humanity. They say His ways are nothing more than a profound indifference and a hardened selfishness. They respect their truth, but it is delivered without grace; thus, it is never enough to fill an emaciated soul. Although, these persons are highly resourceful, adaptable, and very fierce, they worship money and image, in all of its forms (e.g. worship of materialistic things, personalities, self, vanity, and/or a literal statue). They even attribute thei r prosperity to the power of demons. With that said, do not imitate their doings, deceived by their image of prosperity (Revelation 3:14-22), and do not fear them, lest the fear of them be allowed to seize you. When you see them lifted-up and praised by others, say in your heart, only the Lord should be adored, and remember God is watching you and only He can demand an account of your soul. Dreamer, have no other gods before God (see Matthew 22:37-40).

Tongue:

The symbol tongue is used throughout scripture, and is often referenced as the spoken word. For examples of scriptures that reference the tongue, see Psalm 34:13, Proverbs 15:4, 18:21, James 3:5, and other scriptures. The tongue is a small part of the body, yet it is written that the tongue has the power of life and death within it (Proverbs 18:21). This refers to emotional, physical, and spiritual, life or death. Thus, your dream denotes that the words, thoughts, and beliefs that the dreamer acknowledges, confesses, or professes, are truly from the core of your emotions, "your heart". And, as it is also true, that as one thinks so is he (or she), Proverbs 23:7, it would seem that you have attracted the situations, circumstances, and people, that are before you at present, albeit positive or negative. Hence, dreamer, you must be careful of the meditations of your heart and the words of your mouth, for what they manifest has eternal implications; words reveal what is in our heart. Thus, by your words you will be designated, and/or made free or condemned emotionally, physically, and/or spiritually (see Matthew 12:37). Your dream also refers to the dreamer's behavior, and your manner of living. See suggested course of action. Also, see one of the following.

Biting your tongue or Tongue-Tied: Dreamer, we are commanded to speak up and witness for the Lord Jesus Christ (Acts 1:8). We, as Christians, have an obligation to tell others about the redeeming grace of Jesus. To be silent about Christ is to deny Jesus (Mark 8:38). Dreamer, God puts His servants in situations where they are responsible to usher His Presence into the mentality of the situation. You usher His Presence in, and magnify the Lord, when you proclaim His goodness, His truth, harmonize with His word, and exalt His Mighty Name. Adoration of God, in all of its many forms, causes you to become more aware of His awesome power and authority. This enables you to handle the situation at hand by faith. The dreamer is one such servant and you have been put in a situation, as that mentioned, and God has told you your duty and what is required of you. Unfortunately, there remains, at present, a serious disregard of God's business within you. You have not been a witnes s, on any level, for the cause of Christ for some time now; nor are you producing anything of eternal value within the lives of those you are purposed to usher into the Kingdom of God. Your purpose has returned unto you void. Dreamer, you are a vessel of God's glory, and a possessor of the truth needed for the situation at hand, the greater the truth, the greater your authority, the greater your success. You are equipped to handle God's business. If you continue to disregard your duties, t he achievement, admiration, distinction, and/or honor given you in the past, because of praising God, will now begin to abate, as it is done with all who will not hearken to Him (Ezekiel 33:12, 13). If you do not want to be ashamed when the Lord returns, then don't be ashamed of Jesus today. Pray for opportunities to speak up for your Savior. See suggested course of action.

Blemished, cancerous, canker sores, patches, or tongue was marred in some way or another: This dream has three meanings (choose one). (1) To a ministerial leader: Dreamer, prideful and powerful, you lack Christ-like humility, and is becoming a cruel and insensitive leader. Moreover, at present, concerned with your own interest, you are driven by, and occupied with, sensual appetites, rather than spiritual needs. Your desires, appetites, and attitude are leading to a chaoti c and empty life. A life figuratively similar to the condition of earth in Genesis 1:2, wasteful, empty, and dark. This type of carna l strain and toil leads to sorrow and spiritual darkness. There is a need to re-connect with God. Favorably, there is a ray of light, sent by God, purposed to break through the darkness of your state of affairs. This ray of light is a person, anointed and se nt, especially to you. Their words and inspiration will be to you, like Genesis 1:3-5 is to Genesis 1:2. Illuminatingly wise, this person will powerfully affect your life, externally and internally. Their inspiration, coupled with you earnestly embracing change, humility, contentedness, integrity, ethicalness, and a renewed faith in God's word and His process. This, will strengthen you to return in complete heartfelt repentance to Jesus and man or woman, seeking pardon and expressing sincere feelings of regret and brokenness for having done something awry and/or for having hurt someone, see 2 Corinthians 7:10, 11, from a heart of love. By this, the severity of your transgressions becomes partially sweetened; for, when a man or woman genuinely return to God, in complete surrender and humility, your deliberate transgressions become like actual merits, aka "the sweetening" (Luke 7:37-50). Because, the realization of your distance from God, due to your transgressions (Isaiah 59:2-21; Luke 15:11-24), becomes the motivating force to return to God with a passion even greater than that of someone who has never sinned in such a manner, or never left the Father's house, completely converting your present to good (Acts 9:1-30). This is the secret of repentance and returning to God. Go; therefore now, and seek the Lord Jesus, repent and place your hope in Him. Hope, placed in Him, will not deceive. See suggested course of action. (2) Your dream references a season of change, confliction, noticeable loss of spiritual identity, a mind closed to spiritual realities, and the power of your words. As we ll, this type of dream refers to the old adage, "No lie can endure forever". Dreamer, noticeably conflicted, you no longer know who and what you truly believe in. God has not changed, you have. You have lost your spiritual identity, and have closed your m ind to spiritual realities that bring healing, genuine calmness, composure, contentment, mellowness, peacefulness, and tranquility. Unconsciously, you are against anything that will help you develop a closer friendship with Christ Jesus, to the point of rui n. Moreover, you will not allow yourself to get close enough to share love, trust, and intimacy qualitatively with others. You are ensnared by your own words, having trusted in oppression. Dreamer, no longer utter baseless words, and this action will be a s an offering unto the Lord. First step, pray Psalm 51. See suggested course of action. (3) Dreamer, your soul is buried underneath the pain of violations, contempt, and lustful malice. A malicious and contemptuous person disguises him or herself with their tongue (words), but in their heart, they harbor deceit; your malice is concealed by deception. Though your speech is charming, abominations fill your heart (Proverbs 26:24-28). As a result, your attitude and behavior, at present, are so negative that they are making you desolate, emotionally, physically, and spiritually. Thus, your dream was sent, in the spirit of grace (the free and unmerited favor and beneficence of God), to see if you will yet be worked upon, and change your mindset, or else to leave you inexcusable, in your accusations against God, because of your ruin (also see Jeremiah 9:7-9; Matthew 23:37-39; Revelation 3:15-21). Dreamer, repentantly pray Psalm 38:1-22, looking reflectively within, as to why you do what you do, and then seek available resources for help, support, and accountability. Know yourself; and resist those detrimental urges via a serious commitment to a lifestyle of prayer and fasting; humbly submitting your negative inclinations to Christ and to His principles. Dreamer, the strength and resistance you draw upon to resist those dark urges when you're before people, use that same level of resistance and control when no one is looking or suspects you, and your urges will eventually abate. Further, when a man or woman genuinely return to God, in complete surrender and humility, your deliberate transgressions become like actual merits (Luke 7:37-50). Because, the realization of your distance from God, due to your transgressions (Isaiah 59:2), becomes the motivating force to return to God with a passion even greater than that of someone who has never sinned in such a manner (or never left the Father's house, Acts 9:1-30). Completely converting your present to good, effecting restoration, transformation and a miraculous healing, this is the secret of repentance, returning to God, and serenity. Go; therefore now, and seek the Lord Jesus, taking words of repentance (see Psalm 38:1-22, 51) and place your hope in Him that you might find grace in the eyes of God, and grace in the eyes of others. Hope, placed in Him, will not deceive. When you have been restored completely, reach back and teach your experience that others might be saved and/ or spared the trouble. If no change, you will experience a physical illness due to an abomination within your life, as your sin is one that leads to early death. See suggested course of action.

Cut out tongue or without a tongue: Dreamer, you are allowing another to enslave you by bringing you down to their level, which happens to be a manner of living life that is evil. Runaway from this person, and the lifestyle that comes with them; their level or manner of living life is below your normal or "bottom"; thus, you are demeaned within yourself, emotionally, physically, and spiritually. You are to that person, considered worthless, viewed how those of long ago considered slaves, a human being who has no value, as well, you are viewed as such by those connected to that wicked lifestyle; you are allowing yourself to become accustomed to. Question to consider; dreamer, if God would give you the strength, courage, and wherewithal to "runaway" from the wickedness that surrounds you, at present, would you seize the opportunity? If yes, first, repent, pray Psalm 51, read fully, understand, and apply. Moreover, pray that you might be able to escape all that is about to happen, and that you may be able to stand before Adonai Elohim, considering that your Day of the Lord is near (Zephaniah 1:13-18), the day of your reckoning. Dreamer, God is willing, and has already made a way for you to escape from, or leave, your place of desolation. If you desire freedom, your desires will be granted you; and will result in your freedom, literally, emotionally, and spiritually. However, if, having escaped the corruption of darkness by knowing the Lord and Savior Jesus Christ, if indeed, you have, and again you become entangled in, and overcome by, the darkness, you will become worse off then, than you are right now

(Matthew 12:43-45, Luke 11:24). For it is better to, not know the way of righteousness, than to know it and then turn your back on Him who called you out of darkness into His wonderful light (2 Peter 2:1). Dreamer, you do not belong to the night nor to the darkness. Have nothing to do with the vain deeds of darkness, but rather expose them and repent. For He who will rescue you from the dominion of darkness and bring you into the Kingdom of the Son, loves you. So put aside the deeds of darkness and He will again bring light to your heart and mind, and sanctify yo ur hidden motives. You, especially, have much more to gain than to lose by choosing Christ. Read fully, understand, and apply Ephesians 4:17-5:21. See suggested course of action.

Hold your tongue (holding your tongue in some way or manner): Dreamer, you are urged to revere God, and to consider your actions, words, and thoughts, especially when you go to the House of God. Go to listen and learn rather than t o act as those, who do not know that they do wrong, pretending to be blind. Do not be quick with your mouth; do not be hasty in your heart to utter anything before God. God is in heaven and you are on earth, so let your words be few. As a dream comes when there are many cares, so the speech of a fool when there are many words. Do not let your mouth lead you in to sin (Ecclesiastes 5:1-3, 6). Hasty words, coupled with hasty and inconsiderate verdicts on God's divine procedures, denies His Power. Thus, your dream suggests that the dreamer should keep silent, especially regarding a present situation, and refrain from making rash judgments, because you truly lack knowledge and wisdom in your present situation. Moreover, see Proverbs 18:13 and James 1:19, read fully, understand, and apply. See suggested course of action.

Long tongue (abnormally long) or sticking tongue out: Dreamer, one of the things that can destroy home, family, friendships, church, ministry, and/or personal life is gossip. The dreamer has attempted to get others to believe or behave as you do; and, since that plot failed, you are now attempting to, cruelly destroy someone's spiritual reputation, especially one who has helped you and/or your family. This is spiritual murder. Spiritual murder is a premeditated attempt to; cruelly destroy someone's reputation or an attempt to destroy someone's personal relationship with Christ, because of jealously. You are tearing down and wounding others to hide your own unfaithfulness to the true and living God. You take pleasure in your thoughts of someone being falsely slandered and spiritually murdered. The evil you do to others will come back to haunt you. You will be ensnared by your own evil. You will be given over to mayhem in the form of slander and discredit of reputation, because of your very bad thought life. This will pursue you. On the other hand, this type of chastisement will cause you to know the Lord and affect a deep genuine love for others within your heart. Regrettably, this is what it takes for you because you have not heeded other warnings. You have only feigned changed. Dreamer, do not attempt to contaminate or taint others with your new thoughts or prideful behavior; or to ruin somebody's reputation by linking him or her with something reprehensible, simply because they will not follow you and your new ideas, you will not victor over them. If you insist on going this way, go alone, that the blood of others may not call out against you; adding extra to your coming desolation. See also, James 3:8, read fully, understand, and apply. See suggested course of action.

Normal tongue (healthy looking, unremarkable in appearance): Your dream comes to stir the dreamer to action, marking the right moment, which is now, to seize opportunities. Dreamer, you are blessed with a heart that understands knowledge, and not without reason. You are purposed to be a transformational force in other people's lives. You are one, who is given divine means to study and teach, and you have access to prophetic wisdom; this gives you the capacity to discern tru th from false. For you is truly a prophet, prophetess. Nurture your gift of discernment; seize the present time, via higher education institutions, bible school, or if you're a quick study, self-teach via studious study and research, utilizing the many biblical resources available, to develop your gift that others may spiritually benefit from your words of wisdom. Dreamer, you will plant seeds of wisdom, aspiring those under your tutelage to have faith in God, and to understand His wisdom. For sure, your efforts will be a revolutionary force in other people's lives, and truly devoted pupils will learn from your mouth, as you are a gifted teacher. Do not suppress the prophetic nature of your gifting out of fear or laziness; this will be detrimental to your spiritual and financial life. For your dream also denotes high honor and abundance. Moreover, you will be delivered from your present predicament. Someone has been sent by God to help you; therefore, receive, and allow their help; they are qualified. By helping you get free, they will be helping you go towards your divine destiny. Remember them in the day of your prosperity.

Smooth tongued (an unusually smoothness of the tongue, or smooth to the touch): This dream has two meanings (choose one). (1) This type of dream is sent to bring about an awareness of an appointed inheritance. At some point in the undisclosed future, honor and wealth will be bestowed upon the dreamer, if not already. (2) Your dream also denotes one, namely the dreamer, who has powerful and effective language skills. Artfully persuasive, you have a smooth ingratiating manner. Dreamer, while some people might fall for the flattery and give you what you want, most will see through it and deny you. Flattery is also a sin of the tongue. The Bible speaks of flattery as a characteristic of the wicked, not the righteous: "For there is no faithfulness in their mouth; their inward part is very wickedness; their throat is an open sepulcher; they flatte r with their tongue" (Psalm 5:9). Other scriptures on flattery, are Job 32:21, 22; Psalm 5:9, 12:3; Proverbs 27:6, 28:23, 29:5; Romans 16:18; 1 Thessalonians 2:1-20, read fully, understand, and apply. Flattery is just a form of lying, and it has no place in the life of a Christian. Imagine the improvements, which could be made in your emotional and spiritual life, if your words were based on straightforwardness, rather than on flattery. See suggested course of action.

Thick tongue: This dream addresses two types of Christians, a "long-time" Christian and one recently born again; thus, this dream has two meanings (choose one). (1) If you are a one who professed to be Christian, and have professed this for quite some time, your dream implies that you are slow to learn. Please see: Hebrews 5:11-14. Dreamer, it is a sin for a Christian that is mature in age spiritually, "long-time" Christian, to be a spiritual child and babe in understanding. Dreamer, it is not good to continue in a spiritual childish state; you should endeavor to pass the infant state. No one, being stil l a spiritual infant, is acquainted with the teachings about righteousness. You boast of knowledge that appeals to the lustful desires of human nature, condoning rebellious, unhealthy, immodest, immoral, indecent, lewd, and lascivious, behavior. Desires that if not checked, can and often do lead to early death (as you have already seen). All of these choices expose, and say something about, your lack of love for God, and the things of God. You diligently study the Scriptures because you think that by th em you possess eternal life. Yet, while they testify of Jesus, the door to eternal life, you refuse to come to Him, to have that li fe. You do not have the love of God in your heart, for you do not accept all of Him (see John 5:39-47). Further, you are forfeiting purpose for foolishness, blaming your slackness on God and on others, believing that others are standing in your way. This is not true; no one is standing in your way or hindering you, but you. Those who do not respect the opportunities placed before them shall have the things that support their peace taken away. Therefore, repent, and God will deliver you from that which is wicked, that you may walk before God in the light of life (Psalm 56:13). Favorably, the Creator has granted you a year's reprieve or pardon to set things in order. See suggested course of action. (2) If you are a recently born again Christian (see John 3:1-17); moreover, your dream refers to one, namely the dreamer, whose beliefs have been found lacking. A spirit of anger, bitterness, and resentment, is affecting your understanding of, and reaction to, the foundational teachings of Christ Jesus. Your understanding is spiritually immature. While you promote John's baptism, and his, being that of repentance. Yo u fail to wholly promote that which comes after the process of repentance, namely baptisms by water and the Holy Spirit, including the verification that one, beyond doubt, has received the Holy Spirit (see Acts 10:44 -48, 19:3-7). You have become obstinate; refusing to believe and publicly aligned yourself with "The Way" (Acts 9:2). You exalt your wisdom above the Creator's, when Jesus has openly expressed, it is proper to experience all that salvation has to offer, that you may fulfill all righteousness (see Matthew 3:15-17), especially if one lives long enough, after receiving Christ as their Savior to experience it all. Dreamer, do not forfeit purpose for foolishness; now I will show you the excellent way, begin unconditionally to love God and others. For without love, especially for God, you have nothing (see 1 Corinthians 13:1-12). See suggested course of action.

Two tongues (two tongues in one mouth): Your dream denotes one, namely the dreamer, who is hypocritical, insincere, and "two-faced". You profess a belief that you do not actually have. Read and wholly understand Matthew 7:21-27 and Matthew 25. Dreamer, allow the necessary rectifications within your soul, via the Paraclete. It is stressed that you must have a personal and intimate relationship with Jesus Christ. See suggested course of action.

Neck, Throat, Chin: See one of the following.

Broken or wounded Neck or Chin: This dream has two meanings (choose one). (1) Dreamer, you are overwhelmed by the severe consequences of your choices, your tears are tears of self-pity; there is a need for prayer and heartfelt repentance to Jesus and man or woman. Favorably, grace is available to the humble. Dreamer, if you will humble yourself and submit your ways unto God, and continue applying His principles no matter the "self" resistance, you will again gain control over your life again. This gaining control over your spirit is a process, it will not all happen in one day (or it miraculously could). Accordingly, your soul and lifestyle will begin to bear fruit of positive choices, resulting in spiritual strength and power within the dreamer's life. Pray Psalm 51; also see 2 Corinthians 7:10, 11. See suggested course of action. (2) Amongst all those who say that they love you, most have dealt very treacherously with you, and are as foes; fortunately, the enemy has not prevailed. You will now begin to see the manifestation of divine vengeance against those who trouble you. You will get relief from those who oppress you, and if pertinent, you or a loved one will get release from imprisonment. Nonetheless, be encourage, the wicked will cease from troubling, God will validate you and, if applicable, your children, and you will return to a place or state of safety and plenty. On another vein, all this will follow the downfall of a ministry you're connected too. This ministry is syncretistic, and it does not include the atonement work of Christ. Fortunately, the dreamer and/or a close family member will return to Christ and to a bible believing, faith based church. See suggested course of action.

Long Neck or Chin: This refers to one, who has great power and influence, one who is ferociously bold, impressive, successful, prosperous, well versed in various religions, and one who is deadly to others. In that, you have an intense desire for the defeat or downfall of anyone who offers opposition to you. You boldly express behaviors that are the antithesis of Christ. You are greedily destructive, ruthlessly aggressive, proudly oppressive, and you survive by preying on others. You transform your persona as circumstances call for, that by all possible means, you might over power and/or influence many. You also teach others to do and act as you do. You are one who provokes reverence, and people are not at ease around you. Unfortunately, you will now begin to experience divine punishment. A new person, or old acquaintance, will be allowed within the dreamer's life as a rod of discipline. You two, will be set over against the other to kill the ego of the dreamer. This person is under God's protection. For, he or she, who honors Jesus Christ, is under God's protection and has been made clean. Nevertheless, this person will be allowed, because of the believer's extreme pride and your admiration or fanatical devotion to somebody or something other than God (e.g. desiring to be someone you're not, or worship of materialistic things, personalities, self, vanity; literal image worship or idolatry). Dreamer, have no other gods before God. See suggested course of action.

Yoked neck (put a yoke on or join with a yoke): This dream has two meanings (choose one). (1) Dreamer, there is a need to humbly acknowledge the living and eternal King Jesus, via prayer, for having mercifully restored your soul (Psalm 23), and for His faithfulness towards you. Afterward, ask Jesus to reveal His new will for your life. Much love will be revealed to you that you might respond in acceptance of the yoke of God (Matthew 11:29, 30). Having accepted His yoke, your capacity to relate to God, to be faithful despite dark clouds, and to subdue your evil inclinations, will increase. Moreover, the desires of your heart, those that are expedient, will begin to manifest. For this dream also hints at the hidden power within you to manifest the desires of your heart, and God's will, for your life. The awareness of the presence of the Hand of God over your life, especially now, will become the banner, so to say, over your head. Additionally, you will be given authority to preside over a group of people. If necessary, see suggested course of action. (2) Break a yoke off your neck: Your dream denotes hopelessness within the heart of the dreamer. Dreamer, because you have demonstrated a lack of sensible reasoning, you have been easily deceived. As a result, you are experiencing unhappiness and a sense of hopelessness. You are also becoming heartless, having, or showing no pity or kindness towards others. Conscious of your behavior, out of fear and shame, you have drawn back from the Lord, and have begun acting impractical and juvenile, a type of foolish insecurity. You shun even coming into His presence via praise, worship, and prayer. Your prayers, regarding your torment, are sporadic, and are oftentimes interrupted, with grievances, groans, and desperate mourning. Dreamer, you are being (or will be) humbled, by means of a sickness, afterwards, you will recover. Once recovered, obedience to the unadulterated word of God, as well as, sagaciousness, is the key to your hope, joy, and to remaining free. See suggested course of action.

Fat or distorted Neck or Chin: Your dream refers to the power of speech. Dreamer, you have listened to wicked words, from one who is wicked. This person's words have impaired your health, and have caused you to function abnormally. With that said, dreamer, the recuperating of your health will be in the power of the Word of God and its truths. Therefore, no longer listen to your false prophets, namely those who tell you words and beliefs contrary to the Word of God, and words that led you away from serving Jesus, but speak God's truth over your health, and your abnormal condition. That you may love the Lord your God, that you may obey His voice, and that you may cling to Him, for He is your life and the length of your days (see Deuteronomy 30:20, Psalms 103: 1-5; 107: 19-20, Proverbs 4:20-23). Then your light will break forth like the dawn, and your healing will quickly appear; then your righteousness will go before you, and the glory of the Lord will be your rear guard (see Isaiah 58:8). See suggested course of action.

Nape or back of the neck: This dream has two meanings (choose one): (1) Dreamer, you are above average in intelligence, and are one who has the courage to stand up for what you believe in, especially those things regarding your spirituality. You sincerely believe that what you believe is truth. However, your truth is insufficient; thus, you are spiritually in bondage. Question to consider, are your beliefs in harmony with God's provision for life on the other side of eternity, in heaven? Dreamer, I invite you to consider the following. Believing and/or encouraging others to approach God the Father, without the essential provision He has provided for humankind to approach Him properly; that provision being Yeshua HaMashiach, is not safe, and causes one to remain spiritually in bondage. Some call God's provision Jesus, Wonderful Counselor, Mighty God, Everlasting Father, Prince of Peace, our atonement, advocate, liberator, propitiator, and our salvation. It is only through this channel that we may hope through faith to conciliate with our Creator, see John 3:16, Acts 2:37-42, 1 Timothy 2:4-7. This dream comes as a message of grace. God wants to balance your understanding of His ways and means, for you are surely being called. Adonai Elohim has need of you in His Kingdom. See suggested course of action. (2) The dreamer is warned that you must depart from iniquity. Do you not know that the body exists not for immorality, but for the Lord, and the Lord for the body? Read and fully understand 1 Corinthians 6:9-14. Do not be deceived. You are free, do not allow yourself to become enslaved to, nor practice, the things of the flesh again. Resist your carnal, sensual desires, lest you find yourself, once again enslaved, shunning even coming into God's presence via praise, worship, and prayer because of sin. Compassionately, God is giving you the knowledge and wherewithal that removes obstacles to, understanding and clarity. Once free, obedience is the key to remaining free. See suggested course of action.

In addition, the following are common words, expressions, usages, (e.g. slang or clichés), or a 'probable' that are metaphorically represented by the head and neck

- **Cutthroat (throat is cut):** Your dream denotes one who is ruthless in competition, as well as, who is agitated to the point of being violently extreme, causing much turbulence. Your violent attitude will land you in jail, if not subdued. See suggested course of action.
- **Head-to-head, or neck-to-neck (to dream of two heads or necks, next to each other in some way, e.g. leaning next to, or touching, each other, or heads or necks compared to each other):**

Your dream denotes a very intimate and private situation between two persons. As well, a matter or situation is inconclusive as to outcome, or is even or close in a competition or comparison.

Nose: See one of the following.

Broken or Crooked Nose or Nosebleed: Your dream was sent to demonstrate grace, via a stern rebuke. It alludes to a deliberate offensive act, an act of great disrespect, the giving of a very great affront and provocation to God and another. Dreamer, you have insulted God and His servant. You show yourself presumptuous, when you do not fear to speak evil of the Lord or His servants. Moreover, you perpetuate violence and continually provoke God to anger. Your character is one of extreme haughtiness, presumptuousness, pride, and self-assuredness in the very negative sense of the word; as well, you are abusive. All are signs that your heart is hardened. Do you think the detestable things you are doing are small, are of little consequence, and are of little importance to God, His ways, His Kingdom, His people? Did you not expect tha t God would resent it, and take it as an affront to Himself personally? You take great risk, when you have no fear of saying or doing anything against God, and against the servants of the Lord; you put yourself in harm's way, for Jesus will plead their case, and consider those who touch them as touching Him likewise. It is a dangerous thing to offend Christ. Thus, the harshness of the Lord is, kindled against you. Therefore, now, He will deal with you harshly. You will begin to experience a change in your authority, and favor given from the Lord. Dreamer, as He knows your thoughts afar off, repent. Take words to Jesus, "'I have sinned, and I have done wrong and acted wickedly". Other than prayer and heartfelt repentance to Jesus and to individuals affected by your actions, in the form of an apology (if possible), no other excuse or weak justification will be heard. Repentance is seeking pardon and expressing sincere feelings of regret and brokenness for having done something awry and/or for having hurt someone, see 2 Corinthians 7:10, 11. To individuals, a phone call or a letter of apology is a good place to start. To Jesus pray, Psalm 51, this followed by appropriate application of wisdom, can conceivably avert some of the repercussions of your choices. If your disposition is not let go, it will lead to a great fall (Proverbs 11:2; 16:18, 19; 29:23). Turn from your wicked ways. Ask Jesus for wisdom, and for the courage to apply it. See suggested course of action.

Flat Nose: Your dream denotes one who is lacking discernment, wisdom, and is incapable of distinguishing, good from evil. You need to remove the belief, from your mind, that another is the source of your understanding of the divine. Understanding is a gift from God. It is not something that we conjure within ourselves. The willing spirit is a spirit that understands, and an understanding spirit is steadfast, especially as it applies wisdom. Understanding strengthens our love for the Lord and gives us the peace we need as we journey through this life. Dreamer, we are told that if one lacks understanding and wisdom you should ask for it via prayer, for God is the source of our understanding and wisdom. He gives wisdom to all, generously, no matter who you are and what you've done; wisdom is available (see James 1:5-8, Proverbs 2:1-6, 10). Hence, if, by just asking, you may get wisdom, one may suffer needlessly, because you will not ask Jesus for wisdom. Thus, the primary key to acquiring spiritual understanding and wisdom is asking God for it, also see 1 Kings 3:9, Psalm 119:33-35, 73. See suggested course of action.

Nostrils flared or large nose: Your dream denotes anger. The dreamer is devious and guilty of cruelly destroying someone spiritually, because of your uncontrolled anger. Acknowledging that anger is a part of your character, and seeking help, via prayer, fasting, and an anger management program, will help determine the root cause of your anger. If you are unwilling to acknowledge, challenge, and/ or change you, you will be pursued by one with an unrelenting vendetta against you, and yes, it will be allowed. Your dream is challenging you to confront your dysfunction, one way, or another. One primary sign that anger is manifesting within us is a continual unforgiving heart towards another or a group of persons, a place, or a thing. An unforgiving heart is a most subtle thing that steals its way into your heart almost unknown, but in the sight of God, it is the greatest hindrance to your spiritual fellowship and communion with a Holy God who answers prayer. This is the one thing, spoken of in the Word that if found in the heart of a believer it will hinder answered prayer and it opens the door to all ki nds of sicknesses, even premature death. Dreamer, deliberately develop habits of holiness, prayer, fasting, theological study, abstinence, sobriety, and separation from people, places, and circumstances that are contrary to your development of clarity, cleanness, and stability. You will be healed emotionally, physically, and spiritually. See suggested course of action.

Ring in the nose: Your dream denotes slavery and bondage, mentally, emotionally and spiritually. Slavery and bondage is the state of being under the control of another person, place, or thing. The dreamer is under the control or influence of another person, place, or thing, especially one, who is influencing and/or controlling you, in a very negative way, a way that will lead (or has led) to bondage and slavery. This influence is very negative and leads to slavery. Moreover, see Galatians 5:1-11. See suggested course of action.

In addition, the following is a common word, expression, or usage (e.g. slang or cliché), or a 'probable' that is metaphorically represented by the nose:

- **Your nose in the air or in the clouds:** Denotes one who is haughty and/or disdainful. One behaving as if you think you are better than others, and do not want to speak to them. See suggested course of action.

INOCULATION (e.g. flu shots, vaccine shots, any kind of shots):

The dreamer is aware, although in denial, of the influential affects another or perhaps a formal association of people with similar interests, are having upon your belief system; as well, there is also a spiritual blindness regarding an existing situation. Dreamer, you are allowing other persons, particular, teachers, or places, environments, or systems to introduce ideas, attitudes, and beliefs, to you, that their dogmas, tenets, practices, rituals, and certain beliefs might be propagated. These beliefs will render you immune to God's truths. Questions to journal, has someone(s) new entered your life or maybe you've just begun opening up to someone not so new, and have started listening to their advice, their teachings, their beliefs, and accepting their assistance? Have you just joined (or re-joined) a church, fellowship, or social group? Have you allowed someone to deceive you, under the guise of denial? Have you recently become aware of (or is being made aware of, via your dream) certain undesirable behaviors within you regarding the behavior of another towards you? Are you anxious, concerned, frightened, and/or troubled by recent changes in your behavior, especially because of someone's influence upon your life at present? Are you trying to cut ties with one that is bad company? Are you in denial regarding the toxicity of one of your present relationships, particularly a spouse, family member, or friend? After your considerations, it is suggested, dreamer, that you take the time to become self-aware. Especially, you are counseled to learn from the relationships your dream is referencing, and from your experiences, and why have you, willingly, allowed others to deceive you. Learning from your experiences is imperative to your personal relationship with Jesus Christ and to your spiritual success spiritually. Therefore, dreamer, do not be afraid, to open up to the process, for the spirit of fear is not from God. Read and understand Romans 8:15, 2 Timothy 1:7. In addition, and favorably, your dream also denotes that you will succeed in your spiritual endeavors, because of your faith, humility, strong leadership, and your courageous and optimistic spirit. Your success will lead to you being greatly honored. You will also rise to a level the Anointing of God and your acumen deem you should be; and you will be strengthen and established in the Body of Christ, Jesus. Further, some type of promotion or confirmation on a prophetic level is ahead for you. Thus, be encouraged for Emmanuel knows your name.

LIMBS:

This category includes the upper and lower limbs of the body, commonly called the arms and legs, and all the parts connected to the limbs, e.g. elbows, fingers, hands, wrists. The leg section includes ankle, buttock, calf, feet, knee, and thigh, toes. See one of the following.

Limbs (upper and lower limbs of the body, healthy, six or more, sores): See one of one following.

Healthy, strong, good looking limbs (elbows, fingers, toes, hands, shoulders, and wrists): Unless otherwise noted elsewhere (e.g. arms), this dream has four meanings (choose one). (1) Your dream generally denote that God will strengthen you to be able to commit to, and/or embrace, His purposes for you, despite your emotional, physical, or spiritual condition. Dreamer, know that justice is being rendered, and God will remove an abominable offense from before you. God can, and will, check the violence of those who injure His people. As a result, you will find the peace and rest needed, physically, emotion ally, and spiritually; you will be comforted and healed. Further, you will no longer feel ashamed because of something you've done wrong in your past (e.g. seriously bad, unalterable, and life damaging actions, uninformed choices, and/or toxic relationship s). The reproach of your past will be put behind you. Do not be afraid; you will not suffer shame. Do not fear disgrace; you wil l not be humiliated. With that said, you are (or should be) intentionally developing habits of holiness, via prayer, fasting, theological study, abstinence, sobriety, and separation from people, places, and circumstances that are contrary to your development of holiness, clarity, and stability. This wise choice will in due course, bring you authentic joy, happiness, di vine purpose, and miraculous knowledge and power. Dreamer, desiring a closer relationship with God will elevate you to a level of maturity that merits the granting of divine authority to minister in defense of the gospel. It will be in your ministering f aithfully and obediently, ushering the mentality of God, into circumstances and situations that you will begin to experience God's faithfulness, His grace abounding, fullness, full measure, full recompense, full reward, holiness, and deliverance. You will experience all this fullness, according to your capacity to handle fullness (Mark 4:20), no more, no less. Therefore, embrace your process of renewal, sanctification, and transformation, allowing the process to affect your attitude, mind, mental healt h, understanding, perspective, and reasoning, with a concentration of the mind on spiritual matters and the beginning of a ministry. This will enlarge your capacity to handle more, reasonably. (2) The Lord your God will bless you in all the works of your hands. To be blessed: Gifts of God's grace, anything God freely gives you, absolution, the Holy Spirit, salvation, regeneration, eternal life, peace, health, children, love of family, longevity, necessities, prosperity, and dominion over al l that is yours; and all are parts of the supply of grace, and all are sanctified by the Lord, and technically belongs to Him. The result of this supply in your life will be peace. Your joy will be complete, be encouraged. (3) Married dreamer, without children: Dreamer, God has granted mercy to you. If so desired, you, if male, your spouse, will very soon give birth to your own children. To the female, God will give you miraculous strength and knowledge, as well as a door to the right physicians to help you bea r and birth your children. Your husband will be a great support to you during this time. Parents, it is important to expose your child and/or each and every child in your care, in one manner or another, to the teachings of Christ, at an early age, during their formative years, up to age 17, for they are chosen. This exposure includes, but is not limited to, His salvation, grace, principles, be it with inspirational pictures, songs, or stories. Moreover, you must be very careful when educating children. Handle with care, and encourage them, while leading and guiding them into the person and minister they will eventually become. God will let you know who they are in Him and their purpose. This is one of your jobs, to tend to the precious children that have been, placed in your care. A job well done will lead to spiritual blessings and financial prosperity, as well. (4) Unmarried dreamer, you will very soon get married, if not already engaged. If germane, to this union there will be children born of your own body or seed.

Six or more Limbs (arms, legs, fingers, or toes): Dreamer, this dream speaks of one, namely the dreamer, who practices syncretism[28], or one who is insensitive in your way of handling influence and authority. Thus, the dream has two meanings (choose one). (1) Dreamer you've met one who appears spiritual, yet he or she rejects authentic worship of Yeshua. He or she participates in a simulated worship of humanistic and superstitious ideas, which are in direct conflict with the inspired written Word of God. He or she praise and give thanks to a false god. Having rejected Christianity's core system of beliefs and practices (see John 3:16-21; 1 Corinthians 10:1-23; Hebrews 12:14; Revelation 20:1-15), he or she has encountered something that is not God's Shekinah (a glow of the Light of God's Goodness). Their wisdom only leads to shadows and desolation. Dreamer, choose this moment, to go no further with this hypocrisy. Do not participate in the unfruitful deeds of darkness, d o not share in the sins of others, keep yourself pure. For if you "welcome" or support on any level, those who practices such deeds, you become partaker of their evil deeds (Deuteronomy 13:1-3, 1 Timothy 5:22, 2 John 1:10, 11). See suggested course of actions. (2) Dreamer, the merciful God is giving you a chance for repentance. Repentance is seeking pardon and expressing sincere feelings of regret and brokenness for having done something awry and/or for having hurt someone. To Jesus pray, Psalm 51. This, followed by appropriate application of wisdom, and Jesus will meet you. Jehovah-Mekaddishkem, via the Paraclete will cleanse you from corruption, and purify you from sin, resulting in a detachment of your affections from the wo rld and its defilements. However if no immediate actions are taken to subdue your insensitive way of handling influence and authority, as well as, your subtle greed for power, formidable adversaries will rise up against you, and it will allowed. Dr eamer, you will not be able to withstand them. Therefore, halt what you're doing, and pray, and listen for God's agenda. Only within His will for your life, will you attain genuine power, security, and promotion. See suggested course of actions.

Sores on limbs: The dreamer has, with much thought and inner turmoil, chosen to commit to a lifestyle that serves the kingdom of darkness, and to worship at the altar of demons. You have forfeited the privileges that come with serving God's kingdom that you might not be under His precepts, because your lifestyle and choices do not concur with His principles morally. Even now, you're still unable to control the foulness you find within yourself. You have been led astray from those of The Way (Acts 9:2). You are counseled to declare a seven days fast, a fast of purification from things unclean (e.g. addictions, cussing, hatred, an unforgiving spirit, or any unrestrained lustful indulgences). Afterwards, go and present yourself to you r spiritual leader. Remain within that faith-based community and remain innocent and free from things that defile. If you sense within your spirit, no change has occurred within you, you shall fast another seven days, one meal a day or fast 3 days with no food, nor water. By this, you will be made clean and restored. Dreamer, if you make no attempt to change or make no effort to heed your dream's warning, get ready for open shame, for your particular habits, especially the lewd and lasciviousness, leads to desolation and ruin, and you will be exposed. For, this is the reward for serving the kingdom of darkness. See suggested course of action.

Arms (includes elbows, fingers/toes, hands, and wrists): See one of one following.

Broken arm(s): While the symbol of an arm denotes strength and one who has a clever, quick mind, with the ability, and vision, to accomplish a great deal in a short period-of-time. Regrettably, you have lured yourself into a false sense of security; therefore weakening yourself spiritually, physically, and emotionally. You erroneously assume that nothing b ut good come to you. Confessing that no one you know can compare with you, or even pretend to be equal with you. You've put confidence in your flesh, fearing no danger, living carelessly. You harbor wicked thoughts, is ruthlessly aggressive, determined, and persistent, as well as greedily eager to steal from or destroy others for gain. God humbles the haughty and causes all his o r her joy and laughter to cease (see Zephaniah 2:15). Your own conduct and actions have brought (or will bring) this upon you in some form or another. In spite of everything, spiritual renewal is accessible to you now. Jesus is petitioning you to, cleanse the evil from your heart and be saved. Dreamer, many lacking courage, boldness, or enthusiasm, weak in spirit and unfit fo r service, are healed, restored, and strengthened by the grace (the free and unmerited favor and beneficence of God). If you a re ready to acknowledge that you are weak, and remain mindful of your weaknesses, God will in an extraordinary way, increase your strength. For when we are weak, then we are strong in the Lord. The Lord is willing to help you, if you are willing to be helped, and to do your best, with a humble dependence upon Him. You will find that God wlll not fail you, and you will have grace sufficient for renewal of strength and anointing. Moreover, see subcategory, broken bones. See suggested course of action.

Arm(s) cut off: Dreamer, you have become obstinate, refusing to believe and/or publicly aligned yourself with "The Way" (Acts 9:2). You exalt your wisdom above the Creator's wise counsel. You have forfeit, or are forfeiting, purpose for foolishness. You lack judgment, and are a careless, neglectful, and unwise person, so given to pleasures that you are unwill ing to apply yourself to anything significant. You have, in full knowledge, laid aside excellence, purpose, usefulness, and a valuing of yourself, and have intentionally chosen to speak and act unwise and foolishly. Your behavior does not promote mental, emotional, and spiritual stability. Your behavior is dangerous and it will lead to extreme poverty. It is readily seen that you do not know or understand what you're doing. Dreamer, it is excellence, good words, purpose, usefulness, and a valuing of yourself that will raise you up. It is counseled that you learn, understand, and submit your will, to the book of proverbs for attaining wisdom and discipline, for understanding words of insight, for acquiring a disciplined and prudent life, and for practicing what is right and just and fair. Let the wise listen and add to their learning, and let the discerning get guidance (Proverbs 1:1-5), or else, foolishness will take you down. Unfortunately, if no change, now, your dream denotes that your, physical, emotional, and spiritual strength will be cut off. Moreover, you will not experience, nor inherit the blessings that would have been granted you, because of the righteousness of your ancestors, due to your dishonorable behavior. You have sinned against yourself, and against the Lord. Therefore, no one will be urged, from this time forward, to intercede for you. You will no longer receive the blessings of the Lord upon your life, but will reap the consequences of your choices, namely, desolations. You will not live to be old. Thus, dreamer is urged to make some changes. See suggested course of action.

Strong and/or well-defined arm(s): Your dream denotes physical, emotional, and spiritual strength, as well as, one, namely the dreamer, who has a clever, quick mind, with the ability, and vision, to accomplish a great deal in a short period-of- time. Moreover, dreamer because of your studiousness, you will be (or already has been) appointed to take charge of meetings or formal gatherings, and you will hold a top position in a company or organization, e.g. the head of an educational or governmental establishment, or the head of a club, organization, or society. Subsequent, you will become a member of a church's governing board, and on to becoming a pastor, a first lady, head elder, minister, teacher, or deacon. According to divine order, as God blesses and prospers you, give Him a tenth of service. One example, tithing God 10% of your day, via 2 hours and 40 minutes of deeply private and personal pray, praise, and meditation on His Word (Joshua 1:8, 9). If applicable, schedule consistent family bible study (e.g. twice weekly at 7:00 pm); thus giving Him your family. In addition, give Him, via your church, a tenth (tithe) of your harvest (revenues), while not forgetting to give offerings and benevolent donations that you may continue to prosper, lacking nothing. If living, bless your parents first, with your time and finances (e.g. date ni ght twice weekly). Second, bless your assigned house of worship, as well as others (Ecclesiastes 11:1-6). This is God's order, His government, and His ways and means. By this, you will become one who can handle much.

Elbow: If an elbow was highlighted in any way, the dreamer will be provided the opportunity to increase in wisdom and knowledge, regarding a spiritual truth or concept you may be wrestling with now. This increase will happen through personal experience and a miraculous impartation. You will be blessed because of the emotional, psychological, and spiritual clarity this increase of wisdom will bring. Your quest for truth has brought you here. If necessary, see suggested course of action.

Fingers or Toes: First, dreamer, God cares for you, thus your dream. Dreamer, you are a vested leader within a God led ministerial team within a church or a faith based community. You are caution to lead by wisdom, or you will shipwreck. Note, wisdom and folly, advertise similar want ads. Both broadcast they are deeply mysterious, meaningful, and fun. However, wisdom exalts God and leads to spiritual maturity and genuine joy, while folly cheapens and runs down life, bringing upon the head God's asperity and early death (also see Ecclesiastes 2:13, 1 Corinthians 6:12). The one, calls for open commitment, the other offers secret illicit relations and/or a sensual, secular knowledge. Depending on your choice, wisdom or folly, the Lord or the angel of death, soon will visit you. Therefore, be observant and pray, thus, found by God, mindful of Him. Further, you have the ability "gifting" to produce something original. A truly gifted person, you possess the most exceptional awe-inspiring skills, especially within the verbal expression arena, such as speaking, acting, writing, or similar endeavors. People are inspired and see beauty, harmony, and pleasure, in your words. Embracing and harnessing your "creative-self" is your purpose. You will find your life lived to the fullest by sharing your talents with the world. Moreover, according to divine order, as God blesses and prospers you, give Him a tenth of service. One example, tithing God 10% of your day, via 2 hours and 40 minutes of deeply private and personal pray, praise, and meditation on His Word (Joshua 1:8, 9). See one of the following.

Fingerprints, Fingertips, or Toe Prints: This dream has two meanings (choose one). (1) Your dream addresses the dreamer's unique "spiritual" identity. Dreamer, you are uniquely different, endowed differently, and you live life differently. God has deemed it so, because you are purposed to operate on a rather different and highly unusual spiritual level than many of your cohorts; only those that are similarly gifted will understand and respect your uniqueness, which is within the prophetic realm. Therefore, do not "take to heart" the validation, or non-validation, from others. You are counseled to resolutely, with firm determination and purpose, settle within yourself, and know, who you are within the spiritual scheme of life, especially regarding the fulfilling of your specific purpose; thus, your dream. Dreamer, you are a part of something important, and much larger that you are. Many are awaiting your particular ministry, your unique way of presenting the gospel, which is from a prophetic platform, that they may be elevated spiritually and raised up. You will now, begin to noticeably experience the miraculous wonders of divine providence, the wisdom, care, and guidance provided by God that you might fulfill your mission, your purpose. Dreamer, wisely establish your identity upon the principles within the Word of God. Remember your identity in Christ and shape your life consistent with it. For, how you view yourself, is what you will focus upon. For example, if you view yourself as a child of God, one who is secure in Christ, strong, whom God promises to care for in this life, and in the life to come, as one who is called to the high honor of representing God in this world, then you will value God, family, and others, and so on. If you view yourself as a financial survivor, you will value material gain. If you view yourself as a victim, or one who needs pity or sympathy, you will value, victimization on many levels. If you view yourself primarily as a sexual object, you will value sexual immorality. Therefore, your responsibility is to make an earnest effort to become self-aware, and to understand and embrace your unique identity is very important at this time. See suggested course of action. (2) Fingerprints, fingertips, or toes bitten off, or burned off, or cut off, or distorted, or flatten, or plastic surgery to alter prints, removed, skin grafted, surgically misshapen, or torn or worn off: Your dream denotes an identity crisis, mentally, emotionally, and/or spiritually. Dreamer, you do not know who you are on some level or another. One of the most serious causes of identity crisis within one's life is insecurity, which is the erosion of the self-value and self-esteem of a human being. For example, perhaps you was/ is a victim of a tragic violation (e.g. diabolical cult practices, molestation, murder, rape, robbery, or some other great distress), and the pain of it all has been buried deep within yourself. Consequently, you now allow yourself to be the fall guy, stooge, or culprit; often exploited on some level by others. In addition, you are allowing the "spirit" of fear to rob you, even more, of your identity (the individual characteristics by which the dreamer is known or is recognized by), and to terrorize you. This spirit of fear has become your own personal terrorist. This demon terrorizes you in your thoughts, when you are paranoid, when you are afraid, when you hesitate, when you are insecure, when you are impatient, when you are confused, when panic comes, when your thoughts are filled with worry, when you are uneasy and unsure, when despair and depression find you, when stress comes, when you are full of apprehension, when your thoughts forecast only doom and gloom, when you are restless, when you are frightful, when you are full of dread, when are anxious, when you are nervous, and when you feel hopeless. You will find this demon in every phobia. Questions to consider and journal: How do you view yourself? Do you know that you have issues with your identity? Have you forgotten your identity within the spiritual scheme of life? Why has this identity crisis happened to you, and why now? Dreamer, how can the effects of your identity crisis stop playing a significant role in your life? What would it feel like if all of your fears were suddenly released from you at one time? Pause and feel that. Bible story, there was that herd of pigs that Legion was cast into, and these pigs found their thoughts to be so unbearable that they all ran off a cliff to commit suicide, because they could not bear what had been unleashe d upon them (Matthew 8:28-34, Mark 5:1-20, Luke 8:26-39). On the other hand, the man whom, the devils were suddenly released from, was found sitting, clothed, healed, and in his right mind. Now I say to you that before you can move forward, fear must be cast out and renounced. Dreamer, if you will daily come away and pray, then God will heal you of all things, only come with much prayer and spiritual fasting. Spiritual fasting is that time of waiting when you are praying and asking the Lord to come and perform that which only He can perform. Very much like a literal fast, (meaning abstinence from food), during this time you must deny any counsel or thoughts that tempt you to put your hand on the matter, or to turn you away from waiting on the Lord. During this time of waiting, you simply need to continue in prayer. Seek clarity and understanding from the Lord, regarding your decision-making processes and/ or identity issues, and apply His wisdom vigilantly. Further, if urged by God, declare a one, two, or three day fast (abstinence from food). Nonetheless, during this season within your life, there will be some very dark hours and major conflict (significant in scope, extent, or effect). Warning, it will be during your spiritual fast that weaknesses, such as unbelief, doubt, fear, pride, arrogance, will come forth to tempt you to eat the counsel of their lies, rather than to wait for the Lord to come to deliver, heal, help, save, reveal, and/or guide. Encouragingly, this can be replaced with a beauty or handsomeness that radiates brilliance and righteousness via diligent obedience to God through His Word and endurance. Then the Lord will say; only "My" love is able to break this curse of darkness from over your mind, body, and spirit. Grace and faith will guide you, and once again be made manifest in your life. Wait on the Lord, for He is faithful to come. Moreover, you are in line to be prosperous.

Fingernails or Toenails: While your dream denotes strength and endurance, the condition and type of nails will determine the manner of strength and endurance. This dream has two meanings (choose one). (1) Natural Fingernails or Toenails (not manufactured in any way, not "man-made"), this choice has two parts (choose one). (a) Broken or chipped nails, not manicured, pedicured, unpolished, generally was in bad condition: The natural process of aging, the changes, and challenges endured has begun to make you feel as though life is passing you by, and has robbed you of strength. You feel a need to take a more pro-active and forceful role in your life; yet you have little strength. As a result, you feel angry, a silent frustration, and have become hasty with your words, as well, you have begun to embrace your carnal side, those dark habits, and ways, you were familiar with when you was in darkness. Dreamer, seek God's strength through His Christ for encouragement and/or salvation. Moreover, the strength and resistance you draw upon to resist your "dark" ways when you're before people, use that same level of resistance and control when no one is looking or suspects you. Be patient in doing well, coupled with faith in God (a resolute trust in the integrity of God and in His Word), and you will overcome! See suggested course of action. (b) Manicured, pedicured, trimmed neatly, polished, generally was in good condition: Dreamer, you are passionate and protective when it comes to standing up for your beliefs. You never doubt your "God given" inner strength and ability to handle any challenge. Many will be inspired by your confidence; while others will feel threaten by it. Do not allow those intimidated by you, to weary you, in your well doing. They will attempt, if not already. Further, dreamer, have faith in God, which is a resolute trust in the integrity of God and in His Word, for He has promised good things to you, His servant. Now, He is pleased to bless your house that it may continue in His sight, and it will be blessed. From this day forward, God's blessings will flow abundantly, producing spiritual growth within you. God's blessings: Gifts of God's grace, anything God freely gives you, absolution, the Holy Spirit, salvation, regeneration, eternal life, health, children, love of family, longe vity, necessities, prosperity, and dominion over all that is yours; and all are parts of the supply of grace and all are sanctified by the Lord, and technically belongs to Him. The result of this supply in your life will be peace. (2) Synthetic Fingernails or Toenails (no matter the condition of the fingernails or toenails): This choice has two parts (choose one). (a) Your dream is a final warning of the futility of self-confidence that God may withdraw you from your purpose and hide pride from you. You boast in your own self-perceived strength, which, in reality, is non-existent. Arrogance, self-reliance, poisoning of any sense of justice, exchanging righteousness for bitterness, and rejoicing in this, has reached a pinnacle in your life. Demonically influenced, you now look to heretical ideology and fame to be your strength and satisfaction, rather than the Lord God. This is done, in spite of the fact that God has dealt with you according to His grace (the free and unmerited favor and beneficence of God). He chose you and covered you with His protection and riches. Now, your confidence will be shattered because it is groundless, via trouble, distress, worry, and/or health problems. You will begin to experience need and want. Respect and heed this warning from the Lord (see Psalm 119:67, 68; Proverbs 3:11-18). Righteous humility will cause you to eat again in prosperity. See suggested course of action. (b) Pregnant female dreamer: Something negative you are doing, or taking (e.g. stress, physical and mental health issues, pharmaceutical, drugs and/or alcohol use or abuse, medications prescribed), will cause harm to your unborn infant. Dreamer, get a second opinion on the medication, drugs, on how to handle stress, or perhaps on a contemplation of abortion. This child is dedicated to the Lord from the womb, destined to communicate instructions from God, and to make known intended destiny and purpose of others. See Judges 13:4-14. See suggested course of action.

Hands:

Your dream comes as a word to propel one upward, spiritually, emotionally, and physically. Dreamer you are well able, capable, and naturally endowed to prosper in a technical field and in some kind of inspirational arena, especially within an endeavor which is before you now, or is coming. Yes, you are strong and capable enough to handle the responsibility. If health issues are a problem, believe and have faith that you are more than able to take your health back, especially by following go od nutritional habits. You can become healthy. Our health and our habits reveal what we believe about ourselves, what we believe about God, and whether the faith we profess to have is a living faith. Faith without works is dead faith because the lack of works reveals an unchanged mind, life, and/or a spiritually dead heart. See James 2:14-26. See suggested course of action. See one of the following.

Broken hand or hand damaged, marred, mutilated in some way: Your dream refers to one who is spiritually impoverished, and who lacks the power to grasp truth, especially regarding the precepts and teachings of Jesus Christ. See suggested course of action.

Holding hands: Your dream indicates a potentially strong, and possibly legal, commitment to an agreement, covenant, philosophy, or lifestyle; thus, the dreamer is encouraged, or forewarned, about a decision you have made (or is making) regarding a particular commitment, possibly a long-term commitment. Whose hand were you holding? This is a good indicator that the dreamer has with much thought and inner turmoil chosen to commit to a certain lifestyle. Either you have chosen to honor Jesus Christ as Lord and Savior, or you have forfeited the privileges that comes with serving His Kingdom that you might not be under His precepts, because your lifestyle and choices do not concur with His principles morally. See suggested course of action.

Palms: This dream has two meanings (one or both may apply). (1) Your dream intimates the hidden power within you to manifest the desires of your heart and to fulfill God's will, for your life. However, first there is a need to humbly acknowledge the living and eternal King Jesus, via prayer, for having mercifully restored your soul (Psalm 23), and for His faithfulness towards you, and ask Jesus to reveal His new will for your life. Subsequent, the awareness of the presence of the Hand of God over your life, during this season, will become the banner, so to say, over your head. Much love will be revealed to you tha t you might respond in acceptance of the yoke of God (Matthew 11:29, 30) and mature spiritually. Having accepted His yoke, your capacity to relate to God, to be faithful despite dark clouds, and to subdue your evil inclinations, will increase. In addition, you will also, be given authority to preside over a group of people. Even more, your dream is also meant to bring about an awareness of an appointed inheritance of abundant peace, comforts, and sufficient wealth for the dreamer. At some point in the undisclosed future, honor and wealth will be bestowed upon the dreamer, if not already. The desires of your heart, those that are expedient, will begin to manifest, expect something great! You are becoming self-sufficient and unrelenting, capable of handling much responsibility, especially when required to make major decisions. Many will be inspired by your wisdom, confidence, and blameless actions, while others will feel threaten by it. Those who plot evil against you (family, friend, o r foe) will not prevail, but will yield willingly to your authority. (2) Unmarried male or female: Your dream also implies that God has appointed a spouse for you, a religious or civil leader (e.g. politician, representative, or an official of some kind), and t hat person is very near you at present. As they are sensitive to God's leading right now, so should you be sensitive to God's leading. Moreover, seek out the true and practical meaning of unequally yoked, and you will better understand relationships. If you seek truth, truth will come, by this God is showing His loving kindness towards you.

Palmistry (telling fortunes by lines on the palm of the hand): This dream has two meanings (choose one). (1) If dreamer was reading palms, your dream denotes one, who is the antithesis of Christ; in that you pretend to be a god or you naively embrace a mélange of ancient religions and syncretistic practices, which leads to demonic possession. Your lack of an objective critical analysis of a belief system's infrastructure, namely its foundation, existence, deity, nature of worship, sacred text, values, attitudes, earthly and eternal benefits and recompense; and whether its tenets and beliefs are worthy of consideration or not, has led you towards dark and erroneous knowledge, the devil's so -called deep secrets. As a result, you are now an advocate of a type of worship that is in direct conflict with the inspired written Word. You view spirituality from a secular, dark perspective; the source of your knowledge is limited to tools instigated by devils. You have forsaken godliness, and now believe in something akin to Spiritism. You worship with spiritists and witches, and have attributed your prosperity to the power of demons. Further, your manner of service is to exert control and power over others, via deceptive means, primarily for your advantage. You often herald peace when there is none, pointing people down a road of possible catastrophe. You hard-press people, including your family, to believe what you say and compel individuals to follow false gods. You do not pursue by faith, the righteousness that only comes from the Lord, and is unable to acknowledge God's providence on any level. A change has come. The prosperity God has provided you will begin to abate and your anarchy will be exposed. Dreamer; you are counseled to turn back to God, seek forgiveness, and, if applicable, tangibly participate in the turning back of your children to God that He may leave a blessing. One thing is for sure; you can no longer pursue perverseness, and continu e as before. Dreamer, resist unruliness within your nature, and it will flee. See suggested course of action. (2) If someone else was reading palms, your dream exposes a need of refinement of character, within the life of the dreamer, namely, in the area dealing with the deeds of the flesh. Such as, dishonesty, adultery, sensuality, hostility, feuding, vendettas, grudges, unfriendliness, strife, jealousy, outbursts of anger, disputes, dissensions, discord, factions, cliques, envying, drunkenness, carousing, or idolatry (idolatry is "foreign service", any act that expresses devotion or fanatical admiration to something or someone other than Adonai Elohim), or any traits of these sorts (see 1 Corinthians 6:8-11). This also includes a possible belief in, and/or practice of, necromancy. You (the dreamer) also give to those whom the Lord disapproves. You do not pursue by faith, the righteousness that only comes from the Lord. A change has come. This transition can be an easy one, if obedience to God is adhered to, or it can get rough and rugged, if there is open defiance. One thing is for sure, you can no longer pursue waywardness nor allow it to pursue you, and continue as before. Dreamer, resist unruliness within your nature, and it will f lee. See suggested course of action.

Right hand or healthy, beautiful, good looking or strong hands or a strong Handshake: The Lord, your God, has bestowed some level of authority upon you. Moreover, He will bless you in all the works of your hands. To be blessed: Gift s of God's grace, anything God freely gives you, absolution, the Holy Spirit, salvation, regeneration, eternal life, peace, health, children, love of family, longevity, necessities, prosperity, and dominion over all that is yours; and all are parts of the s upply of grace, and all are sanctified by the Lord, and technically belongs to Him. The result of this supply in your life will be peace. Your joy will be complete, be encouraged.

In addition, the following are common words, expressions, usages, (e.g. slang or clichés), or a 'probable' that are metaphorically represented by the hands:

- **Blood on your hands:** Your dream denotes one who is responsible for someone's death, either physically or spiritually. Spiritual murder is a premeditated attempt to; cruelly destroy someone's reputation or an attempt to destroy someone's personal relationship with Christ, because of jealously. Therefore, slander and discredit of your reputation will be allowed; and the hearsay will be true, per the very public manifestation of your negative and demeaning attitu des and behaviors, all of this because of your very bad thought life. Regrettably, this is what it takes for you because you have not heeded other warnings. You have only feigned changed. See also Philippians 4:8, Romans 12:2. See suggested course of action. You are guilty of causing someone's death, or are responsible for violent injuries. See also Ezekiel 3:18 -21, Isaiah 59:1-4. See suggested of action.
- **Praying hands:** Dreamer, because of your humble submission to the will of Jesus Christ, the spiritual truths you think you know, and what will be revealed to you, will lead to a paradigm shift and personal enlightenment within your spirituality. This fresh revelation will cause you to acknowledge that your understanding of spiritual realities was immature (Philippians 3:3- 9). Dreamer will declare that the spiritual knowledge you've learned in the past is disordered, and does not lead to life. In addition, by humbling yourself, you are entering into a state of supplication and prayer to the King of kings that you might find God's will for your life. Now you will begin to walk and grow into a mature spiritual being, going on towards perfection, enabled to see into the spiritual realm more clearly, never to look back again.
- **Hands tied, bound (e.g. tied or secured with a rope):** This is figurative of someone who is unable to help or intervene. You are not free to behave, nor act, in the way that you would like). See suggested of action.
- **Writing instrument being removed from your fingers, hands:** You are counseled to think twice before you write that book, document, letter, because your words and influence will plant the seed of either success or failure in the mind of another; state your words carefully. Moreover, that book, document, or letter, is not inspired by God. See suggested of action.

Wrist:

This dream speaks of two issues; it brings insight to an urgent need or desire of the dreamer, and it speaks of sanctificatio n. (1) Dreamer, at present, your understanding of something, and the truth about that something needs to be more reasoned out, especially concerning an urgent need or desire. You are not asking the important questions. Deliberate, discuss, and/or debate with friends, colleagues, experts, and other believers, for there is wisdom in the counsel of many. See Proverbs 11:14, 15:22, 23. Moreover, consider your surroundings and determine what you will include in your life and what you won't, set godly standards, and then stand by them. Listen attentively, become moderate in your business affairs, and allow humility, joy, and purity to be that, which intercedes on your behalf. (2) The process of sanctification must be allowed to continue withi n your life, for this is the will of God. Dreamer, you are set apart, sanctified, and not without divine purpose. His purpose is to sanctify you; therefore, you are to remain holy unto the Lord, set apart from the wicked games people play. Dreamer, you are to bear fruit that defines how different you are from those who are of the kingdom of darkness; a distinction demonstrated, within your life, is expected; for, there is a difference between the sacred and the profane. Jehovah -Mekaddishkem, via the Paraclete will cleanse you from corruption, and purify you from sin, resulting in a detachment of your affections from the world and its defilements. This process will effect sanctification and holiness within you. Further, there is a need to set aside a day, as sacred, dedicated wholly unto the Lord (also see Romans 14:4-6). If you do so, you will know the Lord in His process of sanctification for you. For it is not His will that you should perish; but that you would come to heartfelt repentance to Je sus and man or woman. If needful, see suggested of action.

In addition, the following are common word, expression, usage, (e.g. slang or clichés), or a 'probable' that is metaphorically represented by wrists:

- **Broken or limp wrist**: This symbol denotes a man that is known to be gay

Legs (the lower portion of the body, from the hip to the toes, includes ankle, buttock, calf, feet, knee, thigh, toes):

Generally, your dream denotes that the dreamer has, with much thought and inner turmoil, chosen to commit to a certain lifestyle. Either you have chosen to honor Jesus Christ as your Lord and Savior, or you have forfeited the privileges that come with serving His Kingdom that you might not be under His precepts, because your lifestyle and choices do not concur with His principles morally. In addition, as you are a natural born leader, you have the power to lead others towards God, or away from the truth of His word, and you will influence others to do according to your choice. Hence, your dream comes to alert the dreamer of the approaching consequences of your choices. Fate will put you in a position for some level of public exposure, either for honoring, because you have chosen to support the truths of God's word, or for open shame. Dreamer, no matter your circumstances the Kingdom of Light always guarantees a better you, and a promise of eternal life in heaven. On the hand, service in the kingdom of darkness, will always lead to desolation and emptiness, and subsequently, eternal damnation (aka a burning place of pain, eternal separation from God). If you choose to follow God, you will become a great leader, leading many to Christ, and the favor of the Lord will be upon your life to cause men to honor and respect you; the glory of the Lord will rise upon you (see Isaiah 60:1-22). Glory in this sense is a state of high honor, spiritual beauty, and great illumination. This is your time for the Lord's favor to be upon your life. This is the benefit of having served God. If needful, see suggested of action. See one of the following.

Ankles, Heel: Your dream denotes some manner of treachery. Someone is adversarial and contentious towards the dreamer. He or she will attempt to get you to believe something that is not true, and/or to defeat you through some fraudulent scheme or manner of trickery or deceit. This person engages in deceitful behavior, practices trickery, and fraud. Thus, your dream comes to forewarn the dreamer of one who would dare come against you, to cheat you, in some manner. Dreamer, evil has come against you, although you have behaved wisely. Favorably, the Lord has not, and will not, forsake you. You will see the guaranteed reward of the wicked. An expectation they're not expecting. However, if dreamer has schemed to deceive another; acting in a fraudulent, deceitful, and crooked manner, with the intentions to hold back and/or defraud another; or have acted in a vengeful or vindictive manner, then another will see the just reward of your wicked behavior. See suggested of action.

In addition, the following is a common word, expression, or usage (e.g. slang or cliché), or a 'probable' that is metaphorically represented by ankles, heel:

- **"Achilles' Heel"**: Your dream denotes a weakness, seemingly small, but is actually a mortal weakness that can kill you spiritually. See suggested of action.

Buttocks or Hips (exposed or covered): This dream has two meanings (choose one). (1) Dreamer you and a male member of your family, is stepping into a situation that will lead to ruin and desolation, you will crash and burn. At present, you have not heeded the Word of God, and you have hindered your son, grandson, or a male member of your family, from heeding God's word also. You've been warned of the dangers of your interests, but you have not regarded God's words, nor the counsel of His servants sent to you. All that has been presented to you, as from the Lord Himself, has been regarded by you as fairy-tales, rumors, or gossip. Further, you have not allowed the discipline from the Lord, you've received thus far, to calm, controlled, and bring order to your life and your male member of your family. You have been presumptuous in committing shameful offenses, and downright maliciousness. How can those who will not hearken to the Word of God, but do wickedly? Dreamer, God has told you your duty and what is required of you; yet, there remains, at present, a serious disregard of God's business within you. You have secretly, and maliciously, carried rumors from house to house; telling stories not fit to be told. Although, the stories had some truth in them, you twisted and misrepresented the truth. All this was done with the motive to damage people's reputation, to break-up friendships, and to cause division and trouble amongst family members and friends, especially regarding a male member of your family, setting each one against the other. Dreamer, according to Proverbs 29:23, pride brings a person low, but the lowly in spirit gain honor. Therefore, humble yourself under God's mighty hand, that He may lift you up in due time (Luke 18:14, James 4:6, 1 Peter 5:6). See suggested course of action. (2) To put your hands on yours (or another's) hips or buttocks: Dreamer, you have insulted one of God's servants. Consider who it is you've insulted. Were you not afraid to speak against God's servant? How dare you abuse any servant of God, especially one that is a friend, a confidant, and excellent steward of the House of God! Did you not expect that God would resent it, and take it as an affront to Himself personally? Your dream is to warn you. You take great risk, when you have no fear of saying or doing anything against the servants of the Lord; you put yourself in harm's way, for Jesus will plead their case, and consider those who touch them as touching Him likewise. It is a dangerous thing to offend Christ's servants. You show yourself presumptuous, when you do not fear to speak evil of the Lord or His servants. Dreamer, your character is one of extreme haughtiness, presumptuousness, pride, and self-assuredness in the very negative sense of the word. All are signs that your heart is hardened. If this disposition is not let go, it will lead to a great fall (Proverbs 11:2; 16:18, 19; 29:23). Dreamer is counseled to ask Jesus for wisdom, and for the courage to apply it. Notwithstanding, the harshness of the Lord is kindled against you; you will begin to experience a change in your anointing, authority, and favor given from the Lord. Moreover, as He knows your thoughts afar off, repent. Other than prayer and heartfelt repentance to Jesus and to individuals affected by your actions, in the form of an apology (if possible), no other excuse or weak justification will be heard. Repentance is seeking pardon and expressing sincere feelings of regret and brokenness for having done something awry and/or for having hurt someone, see 2 Corinthians 7:10, 11. To individuals, a phone call or a letter of apology is a good place to start. To Jesus pray, Psalm 51, this followed by appropriate application of wisdom, can conceivably avert some of the repercussions of your choices. This is what is called leaving a blessing behind. See suggested course of action.

Calf or Shank (the part of the human leg between the knee and the ankle): Dreamer, have faith in God, which is a resolute trust in the integrity of God and in His Word, for He has promised good things to you, His servant. Now, He is pleased to bless your house that it may continue in His sight, and it will be blessed, for this is your season. You will prosper abu ndantly wherever you go. Moreover, you will overcome those who have treated you badly; they will be as nothing, all wicked deeds done to you will be forgotten by you, on the day when the Lord restores justice and honesty over your life. This will also be confirmed by one of the Lord's prophets, expect him or her. God will cause you to forget the hurt, harm, and pains of yesterday. From this day forward, God's blessings will flow abundantly, producing spiritual growth within you. God's blessings: Gifts of God's grace, anything God freely gives you, absolution, the Holy Spirit, salvation, regeneration, eternal life, health, children, love of family, longevity, necessities, prosperity, and dominion over all that is yours, are all parts of t he supply of grace, and it all belongs to the Lord and is sanctified by Him. The result of this supply in your life is to be peace.

Knees: This dream has two meanings (choose one). (1) Your dream denotes one who is weak from fear. Dreamer you are allowing, the "spirit" (aka demon) of fear to terrorize you, it has become your own personal terrorist. Read and understand Romans 8:15, 2 Timothy 1:7. This demon terrorizes you in your thoughts, when you are paranoid. When you are afraid, insecure, impatient, confused, filled with worry, uneasy and unsure, when you hesitate, is full of apprehension, when your thoughts forecast only doom and gloom, when panic and stress comes, and despair and depression find you, when you are restless, frightful, full of dread, anxious, nervous, and when you feel hopeless. You will find this demon in every phobia. Question to journal: What would it feel like if all of your fears were suddenly released from you at one time? Pause and fe el that. Bible story, there was that herd of pigs that Legion was cast into, and these pigs found their thoughts to be so unbearable that they all ran off a cliff to commit suicide, because they could not bear what had been unleashed upon them (Matthew 8:28-34, Mark 5:1-20, Luke 8:26-39). On the other hand, the man whom the demons were suddenly released from, was found sitting, clothed, healed, and in his right mind. Dreamer, if you continue listening to, and embracing the words of that demo n, namely that spirit of fear, your fate will be like that of the pigs. Therefore, earnestly renounce the subtle voices of demo ns; resisting the devil and he will flee from before you (James 4:7). Dreamer, although you are discouraged or troubled, and hav e gotten to the point where you're spiritually weak, feeling that your faith has been in vain; via God's power, a way out of no way will be made for you, and your state of affairs will turn around. Somehow, the Lord will make a way for you. Therefore, do not allow the spirit of fear to intimidate you any longer; only be strong and courageous. Jesus will come and see about you; so, keep your faith, regarding what you've believed God for, because He has promised never to leave you alone. Fear not, for He knows how to take care of you. He will mend you shattered courage, don't worry about nothing, no need to look about you, dreamer, you will experience a miracle. With that said, you are encouraged to re-evaluate your life and figure out what Adonai would like for you to change, in order to better fulfill His purpose within your life. Hence, learn from your mistakes, find new direction in solving problems, pursue healing, and seek out encouragement. Further, dreamer think on things that are true, whatever is noble, whatever is right, whatever is pure, whatever is lovely, whatever is admirable, if anything is excellent o r praiseworthy, think about those things, see Philippians 4:8. (2) Dandled on the knees: Who was dandled on the knee, the dreamer, or another? Thus, this choice has two parts (choose one). (a) If dreamer was dandled on the knee, your dream denotes that the dreamer will learn of Elohim, from one of His chosen teachers. There is an old saying, "When the student is ready, the teacher will appear". Dreamer, you are the student, another is your teacher, and you are ready. Although, you ma y be very accomplished, prosperous, and wise, you have need of a teacher at present. God is sending someone into your life to help you carry out your next undertaking, by enlarging your spiritual capacity. This person is modest and unassuming in attitude, behavior, and dress. Notwithstanding, great respect towards him or her is appropriate and required, as well as some manner of compensation. The honorarium should be agreed upon, between you and the teacher, at the onset of the relationship. Dreamer, to learn and get what you need from this chosen teacher, you will need to be honest, open, and transparent. Your undivided attention is requisite, thus you may need to take a vacation from your normal business and/or ministerial activities. Your dream is to bring about an awareness of this person's coming, and to prepare you to meet him or her sagaciously. Additionally, they will not feed your vanity, for they do not worship nor bow down to mankind. (b) If ano ther was dandled on the knee, then the dreamer is the teacher, and you are one of God's chosen teachers, sent to help another carry out their next undertaking, by enlarging their spiritual capacity.

Legs Crippled, Lame, or Unequal (including Prosthesis or Peg Leg): This dream has two meanings (choose one). (1) Dreamer, for a man (or woman) to talk devoutly, but their lifestyle is a constant contradiction to his or her talk; this makes him or her, a liar. Dreamer, your good words have raised you up, but your bad character and lifestyle will take you down, and so your legs, figuratively, are not equal. You are proving to be hypocritical, and are becoming egotistical, developing a lustful, self-centered approach to life. At this point you are hard to live with, imposing unnecessary stress upon your personal and professional relationships; none wants to deal with you. Your dream was sent to counsel, and is a message of grace (the free and unmerited favor and beneficence of God). Dreamer is counseled, you do not have to dominate and/or destroy in order to lead and manage. You do not have to be antagonistic or "hard line" to fulfill your destiny. Always afraid of being the one left behind, you've sacrificed much, even that which has eternal value; leaving you a victim of unwise and foolish thinking, wise up. You knew God once; know Him again. You desperately need Him now, and He's making you aware of that via your dream. His presence is available to you, right now. He will be what you need Him to be when you need Him to be it. Be available to Him and seize the moments and opportunities as they are presented. See suggested course of action. (2) Legs Cut off, Prosthesis, or Peg Leg: Your dream comes as constructive criticism. Dreamer, a business venture is supposed to be coming your way. However, you are not ready to take over any important undertakings, and/or are not fit to represent any serious venture; as you are unable to handle any matter of serious weight. You lack judgment, and are a careless, neglectful, and unwise person, so given to pleasures that you are unwilling to apply yourself to anything significant. Most all put in your hands is half forgotten, and the rest unprofessionally delivered, with many mistakes, mix-ups, and slip-ups. It is readily seen that you do not know or understand what you're doing. It will be to someone's discredit to make use of your service. You have, in full knowledge, laid aside excellence, purpose, usefulness, and a valuing of yourself, and have intentionally chosen to speak and act unwise and foolishly. Your behavior does not promote mental, emotional, and spiritual stability. Your behavior is dangerous and it will lead to extreme poverty. Dreamer, it is excellence, good words, purpose, usefulness, and a valuing of yourself that will raise you up. You are counseled to learn, understand, and submit your will, to the book of proverbs for attaining wisdom and discipline, for understanding words of insight, for acquiring a disciplined and prudent life, doing what is right and just and fair. Let the wise listen and add to their learning, and let the discerning get guidance (Proverbs 1:1-5), or else, foolishness will take you down. See suggested course of action.

In addition, the following are common words, expressions, usages, (e.g. slang or clichés), or a 'probable' that are metaphorically represented by legs:

- **Break a leg:** To dream of a broken leg denotes that you will have a favorable outcome on your endeavor.
- **Pulling your leg:** To dream of someone or something pulling a leg, denotes two things (choose one). (1) Your dream means that the dreamer is being misled, deceived, teased, or is having a joke played on you, in a mild, benign, humorous, or playful way. (2) Your dream means that someone has "tripped" the dreamer up, that he or she might use your disorientation as an opportunity to take something away from you by force or without your consent, namely they have "ripped you off", e.g. by asking an unreasonable price. Therefore, if relevant, be wary, or suspicious of something being offered now (e.g. life insurance policies with too much advertisement, especially upgrades, deals too good to be true, telemarketers, you have not solicited, especially any one asking for your private and confidential information, credit card information, date of birth, s ocial security number. Dreamer, if it's too good to be true, it is untrue and/or illegal. See suggested course of action.

Thigh (femur, thighbone, the part of the leg between the hip and the knee): This dream has five meanings (choose one). (1) Dreamer your day, your time, your moment, has come. Your season of reaping is upon you. If you have sown good things, have been altruistic, goodhearted, and generous in service to God and others, have not lived by the sword, but by the principles of Christ, within a 24-hour period you will be "set-up" for prosperity, financially, emotionally, and spiritually. (2) On the other hand, if you have lived contrariwise, the time has come for you to abstain from indulgence, vice, and/

or crime. Yo u are being "set-up", entrapped, or framed, and you will not be able to overcome your enemies. You will be in the wrong place at the wrong time, and suffer badly. Dreamer, you are in an evil state of affairs; thus, that which will affect humility and a level of purity within you has come. If married, there may be a separation between you and your spouse, resulting also in a decrease in income, or your work may get harder, while remaining at the same rate of pay. Whatever "will be, will be"; things will get worse. See suggested course of action. (3) Dreamer, your spiritual immaturity, sin, and other fleshliness, are hindering what God has purposed for you (your individual, personal ministry). Your carnality is such that others are unable to speak to you, or of you, as a spiritual person. At this stage in your spiritual development, your attitude is embarrassing. Dreamer, you are counseled to repent and to love God so completely that you will never forsake His service for any reason, ever again. See suggested course of action. (4) If you are an unbeliever (one who has no religious beliefs, a non-religious person, or no religious faith or belief in Jesus Christ), Jesus loves you, thus, He is petitioning you to accept Him as your personal Savior, for you are valuable in His eyes. The first step in receiving Him as your personal Savior is repentance (see in the Holy Bible, Acts 2:37-41). Repentance is seeking pardon for having done something awry, and for having hurt someone, and expressing sincere feelings of regret and brokenness. To Jesus pray, Psalm 51:1-19. To individuals, a phone call or a letter of apology is a good place to start, if appropriate. Moreover, if you will accept the Heavenly Father's Words, via the Bible, a nd store up His principles, and His ways and means within you, turning your ear to wisdom and applying your heart to understanding, calling out for insight and crying aloud for discernment, Jesus will meet you. This, coupled with a lifestyle of prayer and fasting, followed by appropriate application of wisdom, and you will know the Messiah, Jesus Christ, intimately, and find the knowledge of God you seek. For the Lord gives wisdom and from His mouth comes knowledge and understanding. Then you will understand what is right and just and fair, every good path. When wisdom enters your heart and knowledge becomes sweet to your soul, discretion will protect you, understanding will guard you, and His Truth will lead you. To deliver you from the ways of wickedness, and from demons whose words and ways are perverse, who causes you to walk in darkness gladly, whose paths are crooked and devious, causing you to leave straight paths (Proverbs 2:1-6, 9-15). Have faith in this. See suggested course of action. (5) To hit or pat or inflict a heavy blow on a thigh with the hand or tool or weapon: You, and your son, or grandson, or a male child, or male member of your family; namely, one you are praying for. He will return to the place you desire and will; according to the greatness of God's power, be preserve from death. Further, within a 24-hour period, you, and your son, or grandson, or a male child, or male member of your family will be set free from associating with those who are doomed to death. However, you, and your son, or grandson, or a male child, or male member of your family, will unfortunately, return to that desired place with some type of stigma attached to your or their name, due to past behaviors. Dreamer, be advised, that because of rejection by some, the probability of bitterness setting in, within your heart, is high. You are counseled to toss love and understanding at anger, bitterness, hate, and ignorance (see 1 Corinthians 13:4-13; Philippians 4:4-8). This will accelerate the process of you becoming spiritually mature, strong, and powerful within Christ Jesus. See suggested course of action.

Toes: See relevant subcategory, Limbs or Arms

Feet, Foot:

A dream of feet, foot generally indicates one of two issues (choose one): (1) Dreamer, its ok to walk through your trouble, as long as you know you're free. Moreover, have faith in the following - that which has been lost or destroyed will be restored double unto you (see Zechariah 9:12). (2) Dreamer, because of an earnest and urgent request and much prayer (e.g. petitioning, adoration, and thanksgiving) made from a heart of humility there will be a success in mastering something difficult, and a change in you and in your surroundings. Unfortunately, you will be rejected by some because of the change. Nonetheless, continue on, in Christ, bearing the "Good News" of Jesus Christ death, burial, and resurrection to those who will hear, for you will be recompensed for your diligence, in this life and in the life after this. See one of the following.

To admire feet: This dream has two meanings (choose one). (1) To the unmarried: You will very soon get married, if not already engaged. Do not be afraid; you will not suffer shame. Do not fear disgrace; you will not be humiliated. If germane, to this union there will be children born of your own body. (2) To the married: Your dream denotes erotic love, the arousal and giving of sexual pleasure to one's spouse. There is a sexual need that needs to happen between husband and wife. See 1 Corinthians 7:3-5. If germane, to this union there will be children born of your own body.

Feet of clay or stone or a statue's feet: Your dream implies character attributes that are unethical, dishonorable, and corrupt. A soul that is not upright due to greed, false impressions, or some form of character exaggeration. Dreamer, the Lord does not approve of your actions. Repentance is the first step in returning to the Lord. To Jesus pray, Psalm 51:1-19. See suggested course of action.

Broken, disabled, or lame feet: This dream has two meanings (choose one). (1) Dreamer, because of your noncompliance, stubbornness, and pride, God is becoming adversarial towards you. You will begin to implode, and you will be unable to recover on your own; that is, not without the help of God. Moreover, you are being watched, and you will be found out and appropriate actions will be taken. Your community, be it your family, friends, co-workers, and/or some faith based community you're involved with, will expose you. You have not fooled God. Repentance is the first step in returning to the Lord. To Jesus pray, Psalm 51:1-19. See suggested course of action. Moreover, see subcategory, broken bones. (2) Dreamer has been recently hurt by another, and this has caused an offense within you. There is a need of forgiveness, r egardless if you receive an apology from that person or not. See suggested course of action.

To observe feet: There will be an acknowledgement of you winning something, because of the rectification of your soul, and the conquering of sin, within your life. In addition, read Psalm 91:7-16, for God is declaring this word over your life from this moment forward.

One (or both) feet cut off: There will be a proclamation made regarding the existence and reality of an extreme state of confusion and disorder within your mind. See suggested course of action.

In addition, the following is a common word, expression, or usage (e.g. slang or cliché), or a 'probable' that is metaphorically represented by foot:

- **Put your foot in your mouth:** Your dream denotes one who has said or did something inappropriate that has offended, upset, wronged, or embarrassed someone. You have shown yourself insensitive and tactless. The thing you said (or did) has gotten you into trouble; you will experience embarrassment and regret. See suggested course of action.

NAKED (unclothed, nude, "birthday suit"):

Your dream denotes an exposure of truth will occur within the dreamer's life, be it clandestine conduct marked by hidden aims or methods, or some shameful secret, particularly, something wicked covered by the dreamer. The truth of your diabolical motives or secret will be exposed. This reveal is due to some manner of spiritual adultery within the life of the dreamer. Spiritual adultery, at its core, and in its various forms, is unfaithfulness to God, which leads to one becoming antagonistic against God. Consequently, spiritual adultery includes any form of idolatry; any act that expresses devotion or fanatical admiration to something or someone other than Adonai Elohim, or any particulars of these sorts. Moreover, fear is akin to idolatry; for one may exalt the spirit of fear, above God's promised word of protection from all hurt, harm, and danger. Serious fear issues, makes one spiritually irrational and demonically influenced. Therefore, dreamer is advised to exalt no one, nor your public image of well-being, nor fear or worry, above God, especially to the point of death, even death emotionally or spiritually. Why die needlessly (Ecclesiastes 7:17). Other forms of spiritual adultery include anger problems. One primary sign that anger maybe manifesting within you is a continual unforgiving heart towards another or a group of persons, a place, or a thing. An unforgiving heart is a most subtle thing that steals its way into your heart almost unknown, but in the sight of God, it is the greatest hindrance to your spiritual fellowship and communion with a Holy God who answers prayer. This is the one thing, spoken of in the Word that if found in the heart of a believer it will hinder answered prayer and it opens the door to all kinds of sicknesses, even premature death. Spiritual adultery, then, is the forsaking of God's love and the embracing of the world's values and desires. Your dream is challenging you, the dreamer, to confront your dysfunction, one way, or another; and your dream exposes a need of refinement of character, namely in the area dealing with the deeds of the flesh. For example, dishonesty, adultery, sensuality, hostility, feuding, vendettas, grudges, unfriendliness, strife, jealousy, outbursts of anger, disputes, dissensions, discord, factions, cliques, envying, drunkenness, carousing (see 1 Corinthians 6:8-11). Dreamer, a decision to repent, and return, and reject the attitude of foolishness, hypocrisy, and selfishness; and where there would be chaos, genuine peace will abide. Where there is a lack of prudence, wisdom will rule. A simple prayer of repentance is in order. "Jesus, I beg your forgiveness. I know I've broken your heart, I never meant to treat you this way. Heavenly Father, I'll do whatever it takes, to never hurt you again, and I'll love you for the rest of my life". Further, take steps now to avert feeding the growing desires of your carnal nature. Deliberately develop habits of holiness, prayer, fasting, theological study, abstinence, sobriety, and separation from people, places, and circumstances that are contrary to your development of clarity, cleanness, and stability. Dreamer, by acknowledging that spiritual adultery, at its core, is part of your character, and by seeking help, via prayer, fasting, and/or an anger management program, this will help determine the root cause of your idolatry, anger, and your fears. With all that said, dreamer, one, who does understand your situation, is near you. Seek them out, for when at least two agree; that which needs "binding or loosening", will give, and heaven will hear and honor the agreement (Matthew 18:19-20). The Lord is awaiting your agreement with Him (Matthew 9:20-21, Luke 6:19). Dreamer, look to Jesus. Love and forgiveness can and will embrace and restore you, wait for it. For God knows what you need, the burdens you bear, and the pain you feel, dreamer, He knows. You can be healed emotionally, physically, and spiritually. On another vein, he or she, who do not respect the opportunities placed before them shall have the things that support their peace taken away. Thus, if you are unwilling to acknowledge, challenge yourself, and change, you will be stripped of position, status, and finances, namely of all that 'covers' you, and yes, it will be allowed. See suggested course of action.

REFLECTIONS, SHADOWS, SHADE OR PICTURES OF PEOPLE:

Dancing before a mirror: This dream has two meanings (choose one). (1) Your dream was sent to bring an awareness to the dreamer. Dreamer, you have been given insight into prophetic wisdom and by this, you are now able to discern truth from false. Even more, you are gifted with multiple talents that may be expressed through inspirational acting, preaching, teaching, or writing. Hence, dreamer you are warned, to not bury your prophetic gifting (see Luke 19:12 -26); for many will be drawn to God because of your loving disposition and positive attitude; others will be dramatically changed by your example. On the other hand, dreamer, fully trust God in whatever situation you find yourself in at present, and never, do you ever, exalt the "troublesomeness" of any situation above God's ability to handle it, and to handle it for your good. In addition, and favorably, you will no longer feel ashamed because of something you've done wrong in your past (e.g. seriously bad behavior, unalterable, and life damaging actions, uninformed choices, and/or negative relationships). The reproach of your past will be put behind you. Do not be afraid; you will not suffer shame; do not fear disgrace; you will not be humiliated, God has grant ed mercy to you. (2) To the unmarried: You will very soon get married, if not already engaged. Do not be afraid; you will no t suffer shame. Do not fear disgrace; you will not be humiliated. If germane, to this union there will be children born of you r own body or seed.

Reflection in a mirror: Your dream denotes a need to face reality regarding your inward thoughts, and your feelings on your outward, external circumstances, and regarding your spiritual condition, and treatment of others. With that, this choice has two parts (choose one). (a) Happy and beautiful reflection: Dreamer, because of your adoration, dependence, and submission to Christ, God will abundantly bless you. Dreamer, from this day forward God's blessings will flow abundantly, producing spiritual growth within you. God's blessings: Gifts of God's grace, anything God freely gives you, absolution, th e Holy Spirit, salvation, regeneration, eternal life, peace, health, children, love of family, longevity, necessities, prosperity, and dominion over all that is yours; and all are parts of the supply of grace, and all are sanctified by the Lord, and technically belongs to Him. The result of this supply in your life will be peace. Additionally, you will experience a divine visitation, sent from the Lord that will deliver you from the evil and wickedness that has surrounded you. (b) Seeing someone else's reflection or a strange reflection: Your dream represents an identity crisis, be it mentally, emotionally, or spiritually. Dreamer, you do not know who you are on some level or another. Question to journal: Why has this identity crisis happened to you, and why now? Perhaps you was/is a victim of a tragic violation (e.g. diabolical cult practices, molestation, murder, rape, robbery, or some other great distress), and the pain of it all has been buried deep within yourself. Subsequently, you now allow yoursel f to be the fall guy, stooge, or culprit; often exploited on some level by others. Another question, how can, and when will, the effects of what's causing your identify crisis stop playing a significant role in your life? Dreamer, if embraced, Jesus can and will strengthen you emotionally and/or psychologically, to go get help via a Christian based support group, counseling, healthcare, or inpatient; nevertheless, dreamer, you need to go get help. See suggested course of action.

Picture of people, person: Dreamer, from this day forward God's blessings will flow abundantly, producing spiritual growth within you. God's blessings: Gifts of God's grace, anything God freely gives you, absolution, the Holy Spirit, salva tion, regeneration, eternal life, peace, health, children, love of family, longevity, necessities, prosperity, and dominion over all that is yours; and all are parts of the supply of grace, and all are sanctified by the Lord, and technically belongs to Him. The result of this supply in your life will be peace. As well, you will experience a divine visitation, sent from the Lord that will deliver you from the evil and wickedness that has surrounded you.

Shadows, Shade: This dream has five meanings (choose one). (1) If dreamer's shadow was highlighted, your dream concerns social and emotional problems, which are enhanced by demonic activity, within the life of the dreamer. Dreamer, it is your behavior that is affecting the quality and level of peace within your life, and your behavior opened th e door for demons to run amok. There is much drama and confliction within you. Your spirit is adversarial to the Word of God that says all th ings will work together for good, to those who love God, and are called according to His purpose. Dreamer is encouraged to open your eyes to the reality, and root cause, of your social and emotional problems, namely demons. Now I say to you that before you can move forward, this spirit must be renounced or cast out. If you will daily come away and pray, then God w ill heal you of all things, only come with much prayer and spiritual fasting. The spiritual fast is that time of waiting when you are pra ying and asking the Lord to come and perform that which only He can perform. Similar to a literal fast, during this time you must abstain, but from any counsel or thoughts that tempt you to put your hand on the matter, or to turn you away from waiting on the Lord. During this time of waiting, you simply need to continue in prayer and be still. Then you will hear and kn ow that only God's love is able to break the curse of darkness from over your mind, body, and spirit. Warning, it will be during your spi ritual fast that weaknesses, such as unbelief, doubt, fear, pride, arrogance, will come forth to tempt you to eat the counsel of their lies, rather than to wait for the Lord to come to deliver, heal, help, save, reveal, and/or guide. Wait on the Lord, for He is faithful to come. Further, if urged by God, declare a one, two, or three day fast without food (Matthew 17:19 -21; Mark 9:27- 29). If you truly can believe this word of God, it will change all the rules that darkness has established, or is attempting to establish, within your heart and mind. See suggested course of action. (2) As this symbol denotes physical dea th is imminent and perhaps even spiritual death. Read and understand Galatians 5:19-21, for this speaks of spiritual death. Your dream has come to set life and death soberly before you, the dreamer, and if you will not choose behaviors, actions, thoughts, and choices that promote life, you will physically die, and perhaps spiritually also. To the dreamer it is said, for you to reme mber your Creator, before your days of trouble come and time has caught up with you (Ecclesiastes 12:1 -7). Further, no dead philosophy, or any other lifeless "ism" will come to life to tell you truth, nor will a dead person come to life to tell you of what he or she has seen. For, if the "ism" did contain a spark of life, or if the dead did come back to tell you of what he or she is experiencing, you would not believe the teaching, nor would you believe the dead. For, relationship with Christ, appeals to people not by half-truths or lies, or ghosts or frightful apparitions; it appeals to your reason, your conscience, and your hopes. God's Holy Spirit leads to genuine truth. Further, dreamer death is not only physical, but death also denotes a spiritual separation from God, a place of torment, aka "Tartarus", which is also death. Dreamer, if you will not hear the Son of God a nd the warnings of the Scriptures, there is nothing, which you will, or can, hear; you will never be persuaded, and one can neve r escape the place of torment. See suggested course of action. (3) If another's shadow was highlighted, a familiar or kindr ed "spirit", has come, in the form of a person, to awaken a contentious nature, within the dreamer, which earlier had been laid dormant (inactive but capable of becoming active). This person's behaviors will affect, or is affecting, the quality of peac e within the life of the dreamer. Dreamer, are you in denial regarding the toxicity of one of your present relationships, particularly an ex or present spouse, family member, or friend? This person is extremely annoying, envious, and/or troublesome, one who is very negative in their thinking, and is secretly superstitious. As well, they stand out openly against God (spiritual infidelity); attracting physical and spiritual harm to them self. This malicious and mischievous person is before you and their desire is to rob, steal, and destroy a positive quality of life that is fated you. Their desires have the capacity to bring poverty and ruin to you, if you allow yourself to become ensnared by their lure of drama, or allow them to reign in som e level or another within your life. Therefore, deal with the source of the "familiar spirit", via remove that person or situation from your domain, and repent for damage done. If this person is allowed to continue, to reside, within your domain, you will also personally experience the physical and spiritual harm they are attracting. (4) To see dark shadows or shadows of monsters or demons, dreamer is embracing great and deep anger. There is a need to deal with your rage. Moreover, the enemy of your soul is using your deep-rooted bitterness that led to your anger, to cause you to forfeit purpose for foolishness. If dreamer overcame the shadow somehow, this denotes that you will deal with and overcome your extreme anger. See suggested course of action. (5) To see God's shadow or be under the shadow of God: Read, understand, and embrace Psalm 91, for this is God's word to you during this stage in your life, from this moment on until. If necessary, see suggested course of action.

SICKNESS, ILLNESS (cancer, leprosy, HIV, AIDS, STD, or any Malignancy, or any Chronic Communicable Disease or Infection, or any wasting away of body parts or any serious illness:

Your dream refers to one who is going through a refining process (see Proverbs 17:3, 27:21). The refinement process that you are going through (or will go through shortly) is meant to bring honor and glory to the One who died to redeem you. Dreamer, you're under new management, you have been redeemed. As you have been saved from the power of sin, you will now be refined in the "crucible" of suffering and adversity. Dreamer, be very aware that your emotional and physical suffering has been allowed by God that you might be humbled and made ready and prepared to render your gifts unto the Lord properly. God will use your sufferings to instill His principles into your mind, and make His ways penetrate your heart. He or she who has suffered in the flesh has ceased from sinning (1 Peter 4:1) that the sacrificial offerings of your worship, service, and financial support to the ministry, might be a sweet smell unto the Lord. Quoting (Matthew Henry Concise Commentary), "Temptations could not prevail, were it not for man's own corruption; but true Christians make the will of God, not their own lust or desi res, the rule of their lives and actions. And true conversion makes a marvelous change in the heart and life. It alters the mind, judgment, affections, and conversation. When a man is truly converted, it grieves him to think how the time past of his life has been spent (Matthew Henry Concise Commentary). After this, you will become productive and go forth, bearing spiritual fruit that you might be counted amongst those who are sagacious; whose character is faithful, law-abiding, moral, open, scrupulous, sincere, straightforward, trustworthy, upright, reasonable in many situations, and submissive to God. Blessings, joy, protection, and prosperity will be yours. See suggested course of action.

SEXUALITY:

Reproductive, Genital system:

Dreamer, having been in the process of rectification for a while, one's character trait is never to be jealous and/or contemptuous of others; and so, we are taught, "who is rich, he or she who is happy with their portion" (Ecclesiastes 2:24, 3:22, 5:18-20). Your jealous and contemptuous nature, if not replaced with contentment and gratitude, will lead to serious illnesses, diseases, addictions, and/ or seriously broken relationships. Dreamer, consider the bigger picture. For, when you stop and think about, what the Lord has already done for you, and how far He's brought you; think about His goodness. Think about His hedge of protection around you; the provisions and ways He's made for you, the doors He's open for you. Think about you're in your right mind, and how the Lord is blessing you right now. As well, you've been given the honor of knowing that you can boldly come before His Throne with prayer, and that He takes joy in you, let this be your contentment and gratitude; a sweet sound in your ear. Focus and think on these things, see Philippians 4:8, and put your trust in Him and in His provision, coupled with contentment with His provisions, and your peace will overflow. Pray for Jesus to heal your unbelief, refrain from jealously, and wait on the Lord, and again I say wait. See suggested course of action.

Castration or Circumcised, circumcision (removal of the foreskin, or to cut the skin over the clitoris): This dream has three meanings (choose one). (1) Castrated male: this choice has two parts (choose one). (a) Female castrates a male: see subcategory, Woman with a penis. (b) Your dream is figurative of an effeminate male. The Lord your God forbids the confusing of the relationships of the sexes, men must not be effeminate. Deal with this issue, which is betwe en you and your God, and respect your time of deliverance and healing which is upon you. As well, dreamer is encouraged to pray and fast. If urged by God, declare a one, two, or three day fast without food. See suggested course of action. (2) Your dream warns of great weeping, mourning, and bitter anguish of heart because of someone within your family. That someone is in bondage, which may lead to jail time or death. There has been a lack of discipline and/or leadership by the dreamer, concerning you r family, particularly this family member. Dreamer, open your eyes to the reality of your family's social and emotional problems and seek professional support, if necessary. As well, pray and fast. If urged by God, declare a one, two, or three day fast without food. For your family member needs mercy, and not justice; for justice will lead your family member to jail, mercy will set them free. See suggested course of action. (3) Circumcised, circumcision (removal of the foreskin, or to cut the skin over the clitoris): Dreamer, see Romans 2:25-29; 3:1-4:16; 1 Corinthians 7:19; Galatians 2:12-6:15; Ephesians 2:11-22; Philippians 3:3-11; and Titus 1:10, couple these scriptures with one of the following. With that, this choice has four parts (choose one). (a) See Colossians 2:6-23. This Word of God is for you, right now. It speaks of your freedom from human traditions and regulations, because of your life with Christ. You are free to separate from those who would have you bound to legalistic ceremonies, regulations, and traditions. Make it your habit to speak and act like those who shall be judged by the law of liberty, see James 2:12, 13. (b) Dreamer you have been unable to hear and receive the prophetic messages of God to you personally, because of an impediment, obstacle, namely, some kind of habit that has made your progress difficult. Favorably, in eight days, you will be delivered from your impurities (e.g. addictions, anger, animosity, cheating, confusion, exposing confidences to others, greedy, gossiping, immoral, impure, unchaste conduct, jealously, lying, out of order, stealing, an unforgiving heart, or some other sinful attribute), and God is taking away your disgrace. Instead of shame, you will receive double honor, instead of disgrace you will rejoice in an inheritance left for you long ago. Take note, this is not because of any good thing you've done, but because of God's grace, mercy, and great faithfulness. Further consideration, when delivered from your uncleanness, from your sins, which kept good things from you. Your role is to resolutely separate yourself from people, places, and circumstances that hinders clarity and keeps you from enjoying the goodness of the Lords' favor. Dreamer Christ has truly made you free, therefore, keep your free condition, your spiritual freedom, and let no man, nor you, put a yoke on you again. No one can make you feel free inside, or set you free, except Jesus. Read, understand, respect, and embrace Galatians 5:1-11. Additionally, embracing a lifestyle of daily prayer, a renewal of your mindset by reading, understanding, and mastering Philippians 4:8, 9, is imperative. Further, if urged by God, declare a one, two, or three day fast; and adopting a lifestyle of fasting (perhaps declaring to fast twice a week until), is also spiritually healthy. Further, an attitude of gratefulness and humility is of utmost importance, if you are to successfully participate in and enjoy God's covenant blessings over your life. Dreamer, you are well able to do what is necessary to, once again, enjoy the good of the Lord's favor. Then you will know that God is God, and that God is good, and that you should worship, obey, and serve Him as such. See suggested course of action. (c) Married male or female dreamer without children: You will very soon give birth to your own children. To the female, God will give you miraculous strength and knowledge, as well as a door to the right physicians to help you bear and birth your children. Your husband will be a great support to you during this time. Husband pray on behalf of your wife, as Isaac did on behalf of his wife and the Lord will answer your prayer and your wife will become pregnant. (d) Dreamer or another performed a circumcision: The dreamer is depending on good works for entrance into heaven, to achieve spiritual worthiness, and to validate your righteousness. Dreamer, your beliefs are in stark contrast to grace (the free and unmerited favor and beneficence of God) and faith (also see Romans 4:16; 11:6; Ephesians 2:5, 8; Hebrews 13:9). If this attitude is embraced any longer, your beliefs, will affect a loss of the advantages of grace provided by Jesus Christ. Therefore, your dream advises the dreamer to stand fast in the liberty wherewith Christ has made you free. Within the gospel we are set free and are brought into, a state of liberty; we are freed from ceremonial traditions and laws, and from the curse of the law, which curses every one that does not continue to do all things written therein. We owe this liberty to Jesus Christ. For, it is He, who has made us free. By His merits, He has satisfied the demands of the broken law. His atonement and authority has discharged us from the obligation of those decrees, laws, and regulations. It is therefore our duty to stand fast in this liberty, and to faithfully, adhere to the gospel and to the liberty within it. Do not allow yourself, upon any consideration, to be persuaded to embrace legali sm. See suggested course of action.

Penis: This dream has two meanings (choose one). (1) To talk about, see, or touch, a penis, male, or female, your dream denotes a rectifying process and it marks a transition, within the dreamer's life. At present, while you, the dreamer, faithfully sustain the outward signs of appearing to be blessed and sanctified, your spirit is outrageously out of control. As a result, Christ will now begin to deal with your unruly and narcissistic tendencies; this can be a very short process, depending upon your willingness to allow God to work and to, quickly renounce the wickedness within. Subsequently, your life's circumstances will begin to change; state of affairs will spiritually, and financially, be in favor of the dreamer in a very short while, particularly after the rectifying process. Therefore, do not spurn the rectifying of you by the Lord. Additionally, do not call your peace boring. His principles are not there to be obstacles to your progress, or to be a bore to you, but to keep you out of harm's way and to assure eternal life in the world to come, the Kingdom of God. God is giving you the opportunity to turn things around emotionally, and He will turn things around literally. Dreamer, God is getting you in order, resulting in a greater commitment to Christ, ministry, family, and for you to be highly blessed. To be blessed: Gifts of God's grace, anything God freely gives you, absolution, the Holy Spirit, salvation, regeneration, eternal life, health, children, love of family, longevity, necessities, prosperity, and dominion over all that is yours; and all are parts of the supply of grace, and all are sanctified by the Lord, and technically belongs to Him. The result of this supply in your life will be peace. See suggested course of action. (2) Woman with a penis: This choice has three parts (choose one). (a) Male dreamer: To see a woman with a penis, speaks of a significant female (e.g. wife, daughter, sister, friend) within your life. Your prayers, wise counsel, empathy, support, and other resources, are necessary tools to be used to minister to her, at present. Is this significant female unmarried or married? See one of the following for guidance, as to your approach to her situation. (b) Married female dreamer: Your dream signifies that you are angry, antagonistic, and domineering. You have aligned yourself, with your male superiors, especially your husband, and have thrown off submission. You take on authority, which God has bestowed on men; and display mannerisms customarily appropriate for men only. Your actions are that of a woman desirous of changing sexes. The Lord your God forbids the confusing of the relationships of the sexes, men must not be effeminate or figuratively emasculated by a female, nor must women be virile, masculine, or domineering. As disobedience in small matters shows great contempt of God's principles, so obedience in small matters shows a very great regard for them. Daughter, obey him that has rule over you, especially your husband. Like Sarah, who obeyed Abraham and called him her master. You are her daughters if you do what is right and do not give way to fear 1 Peter 3:6 NIV. If you do not gain control over your antagonistic and domineering attitude, standing before the Lord improperly, you will begin to experience a loss of glory (glory in this sense is divine admiration, praise, prosperity, success, triumph, and/or respect of your husband and of others) within your life. See suggested course of action. (c) To the unmarried female dreamer: Dreamer, you are internally inconsistent and disordered, because of a violent violation in your past or recent present; examples of the violation are abuse, assault, bullying, kidnapping, molestation, rape, stalke d, or being held prisoner. The diabolical entity, having possessed the person(s) who committed the literal act, was sent to rob, steal, and destroy a quality of life that has been intended you, to keep you from living that life abundantly, happily, and in peace. The demon's mission is to get you to entertain, embrace, and live out the negative results of your particular violation, with a hope to oppress, persecute, and bring you into bondage of an ungodly and unprofitable lifestyle. Desiring that the unfavorable consequences of that ungodly and unprofitable lifestyle; will cost you your emotional sanity, possibly your life, and ultimately your soul. Thus, instead of you moving towards, and thus fulfilling, your divine purpose, and reaching a pinnacle in your life, thereby with, you will prosper, you have begun to listen to, and be fooled by, demons. Having listened and embraced their lies, you have begun to decrease and fall, eventually running amok your life, literally digressing, when you should be clear and focused mentally, emotionally, and spiritually. Dreamer; oftentimes, bad things happen to innocent and good people. A bad thing happened to you, and you are good and innocent. Compassionately, the Lord is creating a miracle in your life. This miracle will stop the effects of your violation from playing a significant role in your life, enabling you to move forward with your life. However, the miracle's success depends upon your willingness to be healed and set free; for one will always have the choice to say no, or perhaps sabotage their progress. First, recognize and respect your time of visitation from the Lord, for it is upon you, as well as the work of His Hand upon your life. If you lack wisdom ask God for wisdom; and He will give you wisdom. For the Lord gives wisdom and from His mouth comes knowledge and understanding. Then you will understand what is right and just and fair, every good path. When wisdom enters your heart and knowledge becomes sweet to your soul, discretion will protect you, understanding will guard you, and His Truth will lead you. To deliver you from the ways of wickedness, and from demons whose words and ways are perverse, who causes you to walk in darkness gladly, whose paths are crooked and devious, causing you to leave straight paths (Proverbs 2:1-6, 9-15). This is one of God's covenant promises to you. Have faith in this. Further, with fortitude choose not to be a victim or to perpetuate the desolation. Stop what you're doing; go, and separate from anyone and anything that hinders your clarity and emotional stability. Again, if you are in a negative place, move away from your present environment, definitely, you should run away from all negativity abruptly, God will provide, trust Him. Additionally, and if applicable, go, and continue your education, the Lord will help you in your endeavor. Dreamer, if you do not respect the work of the Lord within your life, and the opportunities He is offering you, to be set free, spiritually, emotionally and physically. You will have nothing to work with, but your body, namely deviant sexual promiscuousness, and all that comes with it, including physical death; having forfeited purpose, reasonable resources, and wise counsel that has surrounded you. For, your kind of choices, at present, leads to begging, early death, homelessness, homosexuality, imprisonment, poverty, and/or prostitution. Working with and using your intellect (mind) and/or strength, and good ethics, for your livelihood, will always out last the use of your body immorally for sustenance, and these choices makes life easier. Dreamer is counseled to seek all kinds of spiritual support now, to possibly avert or turn things around. If you do not genuinely seek help and change, for sure ruin will be your destiny. Utilizing the powerful resources of prayer and heartfelt repentanc e to Jesus is needed. Repentance is seeking pardon and expressing sincere feelings of regret and brokenness for having done something awry and/or for having hurt someone. To Jesus pray, Psalm 51, this followed by appropriate application of wisdom, can conceivably avert some of the repercussions of your choices. Again, if you lack wisdom ask God for wisdom; and He will give you wisdom. This, coupled with a lifestyle of fasting, a changed mindset, serious re-consideration of God's ways and means, and an honest acknowledgement of God's hand within your life, then the severe impact of your choices and actions upon your life, can be reversed and damages repaired (also see Ezekiel 33:12-19). This is what is called leaving a blessing behind.

Vagina: This dream has two meanings (choose one). (1) To see or touch a vagina (male or female), your dream denotes one who needs to demonstrate compassion, mercy, empathy, and pity. Dreamer, you need to express deeply, non-sexual, tender affection to a significant other (e.g. wife, husband, child, family member, friend, widow, victim of violence, or some other who is experiencing broken pieces of life, or one who is in need at the moment). Couple your affection with an expression of love (e.g. gifts, cards, flowers, or some other expression of love). See suggested course of action. (2) Man with a vagina: Dreamer, you are internally inconsistent and disordered, because of a violent violation in your past or recent present; examples of the violation are abuse, assault, bullying, kidnapping, molestation, rape, stalked, or being held prisoner. The diabolical entity, having possessed the person(s) who committed the literal act, was sent to rob, steal, and destroy a quality of life that has been intended you, to keep you from living that life abundantly, happily, and in peace. The demon's mission is to get you to entertain, embrace, and live out the negative results of your particular violation, with a hope to oppress, persecute, and bring you into bondage of an ungodly and unprofitable lifestyle. Desiring that the unfavorable consequences of that ungodly and unprofitable lifestyle; will cost you your emotional sanity, possibly your life, and ultimately your soul. Thus, instead of you moving towards, and thus fulfilling, your divine purpose, and reaching a pinnacle in your life, thereby with, you will prosper, you have begun to listen to, and be fooled by, demons. Having listened and embraced their lies, you have begun to decrease and fall, eventually running amok your life, literally digressing, when you should be clear and focused mentally, emotionally, and spiritually. Dreamer; oftentimes, bad things happen to innocent and good people. A bad thing happened to you, and you are good and innocent. Compassionately, the Lord is creating a miracle in your life. This miracle will stop the effects of your violation from playing a significant role in your life, enabling you to move forward with your life. However, the miracle's success depends upon your willingness to be healed and set free; for one will always have the choice to say no, or perhaps sabotage their progress. First, recognize and respect your time of visitation from the Lord, for it is upon you, as well as the work of His Hand upon your life. If you lack wisdom ask God for wisdom; and He will give you wisdom. For the Lord gives wisdom and from His mouth comes knowledge and understanding. Then you will understand what is right and just and fair, every good path. When wisdom enters your heart and knowledge becomes sweet to your soul, discretion will protect you, understanding will guard you, and His Truth will lead you. To deliver you from the ways of wickedness, and from demons whose words and ways are perverse, who causes you to walk in darkness gladly, whose paths are crooked and devious, causing you to leave straight paths (Proverbs 2:1-6, 9-15). This is one of God's covenant promises to you. Have faith in this. Further, with fortitude choose not to be a victim nor to perpetuate the desolation. Stop what you're doing; go, and separate from anyone and anything that hinders your clarity and emotional stability. Again, if you are in a negative place, move away from your present environment, definitely, you should run away from all negativity abruptly, God will provide, trust Him. Additionally, and if applicable, go, and continue your education, the Lord will help you in your endeavor. Dreamer, if you do not respect the work of the Lord within your life, and the opportunities He is offering you, to be set free, spiritually, emotionally and physically. You will have nothing to work with, but your body, namely deviant sexual promiscuousness, and all that comes with it, including physical death; having forfeited purpose, reasonable resources, and wise counsel that has surrounded you. For, your kind of choices, at present, leads to begging, early death, homelessness, homosexuality, imprisonment, poverty, and/or prostitution. Working with and using your intellect (mind) and/or strength, and good ethics, for your livelihood, will always out last the use of your body immorally for sustenance, and these choices makes life easier. Dreamer is counseled to seek all kinds of spiritual support now, to possibly avert or turn things around. If you do not genuinely seek help and change, for sure ruin will be your destiny. Utilizing the powerful resources of prayer and heartfelt repentance to Jesus is needed. Repentance is seeking pardon and expressing sincere feelings of regret and brokenness for having done something awry and/or for having hurt someone. To Jesus pray, Psalm 51, this followed by appropriate application of wisdom, can conceivably avert some of the repercussions of your choices. Again, if you lack wisdom ask God for wisdom; and He will give you wisdom. This, coupled with a lifestyle of fasting, a changed mindset, serious re-consideration of God's ways and means, and an honest acknowledgement of God's hand within your life, then the severe impact of your choices and actions upon your life, can be reversed and damages repaired (also see Ezekiel 33:12-19). This is what is called leaving a blessing behind. See suggested course of action.

Sexual Assault or Pedophile or Rapist or any sexual deviant (e.g. molestation, rape, sex slave, sexual abuse, sex crime, forcing another person to engage in any sexual act against their will, any act subjecting someone to unwanted or improper sexual advances or activity, especially children or women, by threat or force. Any statutory offense that provides that it is a crime to, knowingly cause another person to engage in an unwanted sexual act by force):

Sex with a child, teen, or incapacitated adult is never justifiable; it is always wrong, it is an abomination. With that sai d, this dream has three meanings (choose one). (1) If dreamer was a victim or if victim depicted was unknown, your dream is for, and about, the dreamer. This choice has two parts (choose one). (a) If you are experiencing, at present, being molested, or sexually violated or abused in any way, you must contact the appropriate authorities. Do not be afraid, God is with you. Remove yourself, runaway, from the unsafe environment and contact the proper authorities immediately (e.g. police, child, and/or adult protective services). Dreamer, if the perpetrator has not respected you enough not to violate you, do not respect or fear him or her, but expose their abomination, their criminal act against you. Jesus says, it's better for you to sink to the bottom of the sea, tied to cement (Mark 9:42-48), than for anyone to perpetrate such acts against others. Molestation, rape, or any unwanted sexual activity or attention forced upon a child, teen, or incapacitated adult (consensual or not) is a sad reality, but it is not beyond God's ability to overcome. Dreamer; oftentimes, bad things happen to innocent and good people. A bad thing is happening to you, and you are good and innocent. Dreamer, your welfare is Christ's concern, for God's eyes ar e upon you now. Therefore, allow no threats of any kind to keep you from going to seek help. The perpetrator will not be allowed to carry out any threats against you, or anyone else. Go get help immediately. (b) If dreamer has in the past been sexually violated your dream comes to bring about an awareness that emotional, psychological, and physical healing is needed, and to hopefully give rise to healing. Dreamer, your violations, hurts, and rejections were demonically influenced, in an attempt to "bend" your personality, as early as possible, towards a certain direction, towards a way that is desolate and wicked. For it is Satan's scheme to kill and make desolate; thus, to keep you from fully experiencing a life fated you by God, a life of freedom and abundance, and to prevent you from rising up and leading your generation to Christ (see the birth of Moses, Exodus 1:15-2:10). Dreamer, your soul is buried underneath the pain of violations, and this has distorted your reasoning. The pain of rejection, abuse, and other emotional and physical violations, of your past, has affected your "approach pattern" to all your relationships, even your personal relationship with the Lord. Dreamer, it is time, for you to ask God for healing and freedom from past traumas that have hindered your spiritual, emotional, and psychological maturity. Dreamer, Jesus wants to heal you. He wants you to live in the secret place of the Most High, abiding under the shadow of the Almighty ; it's a warm and tender place there. Read and embrace Psalm 91, this is to you. The Most High knows you've been living in your fortress, protecting yourself from further hurt. He sees you when you're restless, rolling on the floor, in pain, misery, and suffering. Jesus knows that you truly love Him and others, but you are still frightened by your fears. Compassionately, the Lord is creating a miracle in your life. This miracle will stop the effects of your violation from playing a significant role in your life, enabling you to move forward with your life. God will redeem and restore. Jesus will hold you warmly, and He will tenderly anoint your life that you might see your way, and allow healing to begin. Moreover, dreamer, as painful as this may hurt the question needs to be asked. How and when do you stop allowing the effects of your past violations to stop playing a significant part in your life today? For, if one is not careful, hurt and pain in your heart oftentimes makes you blind to the real thing once it comes along. Dreamer, Jesus is the real thing. Accordingly, by faith, dreamer began to entrust your reasoning, thoughts, and emotions to Jesus, so that a very personal relationship with Him may emerge and healing and wholeness may begin. Consider your dream as God's faithfulness, loving kindness, tender mercy, and grace (the free and unmerited favor and beneficence of God) towards you. Note, authentic freedom, and wholeness, come with responsibility. Your responsibility is to make an earnest effort to become self-aware, and to understand your "defense mechanism", as well as, to forgive those who violated, hurt, and/or rejected you. Dreamer, deliberately develop habits of holiness, prayer, fasting, theological study, abstinence, sobriety, and separation from people, places, and circumstances that are contrary to your development of clarit y, cleanness, and stability. Then you will begin to appreciate healing, emotionally, physically, and spiritually. See suggested course of action. (2) Pedophile or Rapist or Deviant: If you dreamt that you committed any sexual criminal act within your dream, e.g. pedophile, rapist, any sexual behavior, or act that is done in secret or hidden, not openly practiced or engaged in, covert, your dream is a severe warning. This dream denotes physical death is imminent and perhaps even spiritual death. Read and understand Galatians 5:19-21, for this speaks of spiritual death. Your dream has come to set life and death soberly before you, the dreamer, and if you will not choose behaviors, actions, thoughts, and choices that promote a life; and that can be live d openly, ethically, and honorable, you will die an ignoble death. For, it is expressed within Holy Writ, it is better for you to sink to the bottom of the sea, tied to cement than for anyone to cause another to walk before his or her God unsteadily or degenerately (Mark 9:42). Recognizing that oftentimes, abusers have been abused themselves, God's grace is extended to you; however, it is up to you to accept God's grace, and on His terms and not yours. God's terms, your abominations will now be exposed, and the darkness within you, will abate long enough, for you to seize the moment to make an intelligent decision to repent, and turn from your wickedness and walk with good character and conscience. Therefore, depending on your choice, repentance or not, the Lord or the angel of death, soon will visit you. You, the dreamer, may ask, "Can I be forgiven if I knowingly sexually violated a child, teen, or incapacitated adult?" [34] Yes, God is gracious and merciful. No sin is beyond His ability to forgive (Romans 5:20). Jesus came to cleanse all sin: "Truly I tell you, people can be forgiven all their sins" (Mark 3:28). When you recognize your sin, acknowledge that it is evil, and then genuinely and deeply cry out to God for deliveranc e, with much fasting and prayer, He will hear you, forgive you, and sanctify you. If no genuine change is earnestly sought after, you will physically die. With that said, unfortunately, whether you repent or not, you will always have some type of stigma attached to your name, due to your past behaviors. Therefore, be advised, that because of rejection and/or ridicule by some, the probability of bitterness setting in, within your heart, is high. This is understanding, dreamer, as a perpetrator, you have not respected others enough not to violate them; hence, neither will you be respected. You are counseled to toss understanding at anger, bitterness, and hate; and it will come.

Understanding will accelerate the process of you becoming spiritually clean within Christ Jesus. In addition to God's forgiveness, you may also require professional help and accountability support for, stopping certain behaviors, healing from past wounds, and seeking forgiveness from those, you have injured. See suggested course of action. (3) If your dream is about another, first see Note 3 of this category, to determine if your dream is actually about another. If your dream is truly about another, your dream is an alert to the dreamer, and your dream is a first step intervention. On occasion, one may have an Oneirovatic or "OV" dream (see Chapter One: The 60th part of prophecy, other prophetic dreams). An "OV" dream may reveal molestation, rape, or any unwanted sexual activity or attention, forced or threatened, upon a child, teen, or a psychological, physically weaker, incapacitated adult (consensual or not). If the dreamer saw or sensed within his or her dream, a child, even if it is your child, teen, or adult, being sexually assaulted, e.g. molested, raped, any sexual crime, first, the victim within your dream, should realistically be, or have been, in a situation where the criminal act could happen (e.g. Adult care facility, class room, day care, hospital, neighborhood playground, nursery room, nursing home, at home, outside play area at home, school, summer camp, Sunday school class, in the care of foster parents, or in your own home, by a natural or step parent or sibling). Do you actually know the victim? Is (was) child abuse, molestation, or rape actually suspected? As well, the victim should (or will) actually show signs of a violation, no matter how subtle. If you sense that your dream is for or about another, possibly a child, sibling, parent, friend, or significant other, the question as to why you have been made aware of this information, and how do you factor into the equation, should be seriously considered, along with necessary actions. If you suspect abuse, even within your own home, dreamer, you are sent to get involved. If possible, how can you stop the violation? Have authorities been notified? Establishing a safe environment, alerting the law and other pertinent individuals is strongly recommended. If sexual abuse is (was) in your home, dreamer, remove yourself, your children, or loved one, from the unsafe environment and contact the proper authorities immediately (e.g. police, child, and/or adult protective services). On a more serious note, dreamer, if you were abused as a child, or teen, or raped, and no w, you have placed your child or loved one in harm's way, often the identical situation; feigning denial. Go talk to God, and ask Him to help you emotionally and mentally, to do what it takes to keep your child or loved one safe, from the same violation. Allow the darkness of the violation, this abomination, to stop with you. Moreover, if you suspect that your abuser is still harming others, please report it. You may also check with your local department of human services for reporting procedures. Medical, legal, and psychological intervention, are likely necessary. Children, teens, or a psychological, physically weaker adult, or any significant other, should never be left in abusive situations. Molestation, rape, or any unwanted sexual activity or attention forced upon a child, teen, or incapacitated adult (consensual or not) is a sad reality, but it is not beyond God's ability to overcome. God can redeem and restore. We praise Him "who is able to do immeasurably more than all we ask or imagine, according to His power that is at work within us" (Ephesians 3:20). The "more than we can imagine" includes forgiveness and healing. See suggested course of action.

Sexual Relations or Sexual Orientation or Virginity (person's tendency of sexual attraction, esp. whether heterosexual or homosexual or virginity): See one of one following.

Sex with the dead: Dreamer read, understand, and weigh, and apply, Isaiah 28:15-22. This is for you. See suggested course of action.

Heterosexual Relationship: This dream has two meanings (choose one). (1) Married dreamer: To dream of having experienced a heterosexual relationship, or sexual activity with your spouse, you will very shortly begin to experience, if n ot already, a paradigm shift in your core beliefs and spirituality. Dreamer will approach new and deeper dimensions. This transition will affect within you a far-reaching hope, profoundly greater faith, and a more intense love for all things Jesus, including His people; allow it. This revival and renewal of strength is a process. With that said, dreamer should con sider the following question; does dreamer feel that you are a part of something that's important, something bigger than you are? Your paradigm shift should include this consideration. Additional, if sexual activity between dreamer and your spouse was go ing on, your dream, may also be an ordinary dream, see

Chapter One, Ordinary Dreams. (2) Unmarried dreamer: To dream of having experienced a heterosexual relationship, or sexual activity with the opposite sex dreamer, not your spouse, see category, Buildings (Bedroom). See suggested course of action.

Homosexuality, Homosexual Relationship, LBGT: To dream of having experienced a homosexual relationship, this dream has two meanings (choose one). (1) Dreamer, your reality of God is based on emotions and personal preconceptions, due to observable phenomena. Unfortunately, while what you observe may be true, your paradigm is "gridded" through the emotions of fear and rejection. Paradigm shift, a deeper trust in God and Him alone, coupled with an honest and sensible rendering of the Holy Bible, outside of your emotions and personal biases, is needed that you might go on to spiritual maturity. Dreamer, at your very core, you want to know love and trust, but you cannot "touch it" or receive it, because you do not believe you are lovable or trustworthy. See suggested course of action. (2) Dreamer, the pain of rejection, abuse, and/or other emotional and physical violations, of your past or recent present, has affected your "approach pattern" to all your relationships. Examples of the violation are abuse, assault, bullying, kidnapping, molestation, rape, stalked, or being held prisoner. This has left you internally inconsistent and disordered. The diabolical entity, having possessed the person(s) who committed the literal act, was sent to rob, steal, and destroy a quality of life that has been destined you, to keep you from living that life abundantly, happily, and in peace. The demon's mission is to get you to entertain, embrace, and live out th e negative results of your particular violation, with a hope to oppress, persecute, and bring you into bondage of an ungodly and unprofitable lifestyle. Desiring that the unfavorable consequences of that ungodly and unprofitable lifestyle; will cost you your emotional sanity, possibly your life, and ultimately your soul. Dreamer; oftentimes, bad things happen to innocent and good people. A bad thing happened to you, and you are good and innocent. Compassionately, the Lord is creating a miracle in your life. This miracle will stop the effects of your violation from playing a significant role in your life, enabling you to move forward with your life and to make good decisions. However, the miracle's success depends upon your willingness to be healed and set free; for one will always have the choice to say no, or perhaps sabotage their progress. First, recognize and respect your time of visitation from the Lord, for it is upon you, as well as the work of His Hand upon your life. If you lack wisdom ask God for wisdom; and He will give you wisdom. For the Lord gives wisdom and from His mouth comes knowledge and understanding. Then you will understand what is right and just and fair, every good path. When wisdom enters your heart and knowledge becomes sweet to your soul, discretion will protect you, understanding will guard you, and His Truth will lead you. To deliver you from the ways of wickedness, and from demons whose words and ways are perverse, who causes you to walk in darkness gladly, whose paths are crooked and devious, causing you to leave straight paths (Proverbs 2:1-6, 9-15). This is one of God's covenant promises to you. Have faith in this. Further, with much fortitude choose not to perpetuate the desolation. Dreame r, go and separate yourself from anyone and anything that hinders your clarity and emotional stability. Moreover, if relevant, go, and continue your education, the Lord will help you in your endeavors. Dreamer, if you do not respect the work of the Lord within your life, and the opportunities He is offering you, to be set free, spiritually, emotionally and physically. You will have nothing to work with, but your body, namely, deviant sexual promiscuousness, and all that comes with that manner of behavior. See suggested course of action.

Virginity, Virgin: This dream has three meanings (choose one). (1) Male dreamer: Dreamer, at present, your dream denotes that the wherewithal needed by you, to create, nourish, and enhance all facets of your life, is available to you. Al l that you need, to take something from the state of potential, develop it, and bring it to actualization through creative abilities, and to accomplish your goals, is within your reach, especially working within a team that you can lead. Note, dreamer, all the blessings you can receive are connected to the worth of your choices; for, there is no genuine blessings within life without honor. When you express yourself from a place of honor, you are handling your primary responsibility of maintaining peace, spiritually and naturally. Additionally, the worth of a man is largely dependent on how he treats his family, not just in public but also behind closed doors. This is honorable in the eyes of God. Then blessings come. Hence, the benefits of honor with in your life will begin to manifest even more within your life starting now (Proverbs 12:14, 18:20). Dreamer, the benefits of honorable choices are, but not limited to, the dreamer will be successful in your endeavors, especially after practical plann ing and effort. Dreamer, receive the affirmation, validation, and encouragement your dream is meant to impart. (2) Your dream was sent to engender an awareness of God's wisdom, healing, and faithfulness that are before the dreamer, at present, and to engender an awareness of some kind of ministry that may be initiated now. Additionally, dreamer, you will increase in wisdom and knowledge, regarding godly spiritual truths or concepts you may be wrestling with, now. (3) Your dream represents a cleric of some kind (e.g. bishop, evangelist, minister, missionary, parson, pastor, preacher, priest, rabbi, or teacher). Thus, your dream denotes one whose calling is to give sermons, spread the gospel, and conduct religious services. If this represents the dreamer, a large part of your mission should center on, you raising the spirits of your fellow mankind, and establishing yourself as an inspirational person spreading hope. Your gift is to inspire and motivate.

SOUL OR OUT OF BODY EXPERIENCE:

This dream has two meanings (choose one). (1) The promises made between you and God; you promised to worship and serve Jesus, and in return, you are promised life more abundantly on this side of eternity, and eternal life. If you have kept your promise to worship and serve, God's promise to you of abundance, on this side of eternity, will begin to manifest. The realization of those promises is happening. Moreover, you have been blessed with a great understanding of spiritual knowledge, and not without reason. One who is given the means to study and teach and has access to prophetic wisdom, is purposed to be a transformational force in people's lives. Your power of speech and wisdom will convert souls to the Kingdom of God. The heart of your ministry should focus on teaching about the essence of God, the Blood of Christ, and divine order. Your time of missions is upon you. You are now being asked to devote yourself to embracing God's divine order that you may mature. You are sent to those who are spiritually dead, yet a spark of life is hidden within them (also see Matthew 28:19, 20). Dreamer; via divine order, go on to perfection through faith in God (a resolute trust in the integrity of God and in His Word). Dreamer, it is necessary that you bring to remembrance your former state, when you were

> *It is made clear to the soul that it is embarking on a perilous journey full of distractions and enticement. The soul is made to take an oath that she will remain righteous, and even if persuaded by those around her that she is perfect, she should always deem herself in need of improvement.*
> *-Nissan Dovid Dubov*

enslaved to sin. What benefits did you reap at that time from the things you now disdain, the filth, and foolishness of it all? Now that you have been set free from sin, you have become a servant of God. The benefits you will reap will lead to holiness, a "better you", and the end-result is eternal life (Romans 6:21, 22). To keep you humble, repentant, and watchful, you would do well to remember the time when you were a servant of sin, devoted to iniquity, embracing vanity, and reaping the same; and to remember the benefits of being a servant of God. (2) Your dream denotes a serious illness that is life threatening. Dreamer needs to first, call for the elders of a church. For it is through their prayers of faith and anointing of oil upon you that your sins will be forgiven, and that spiritual and physical healing might occur[36]. Dreamer there is a great need for repentance, for your sickness is primarily due to unhealthy lifestyle choices, unwillingness to forgive or show mercy, and sinful and wicked behaviors and evil practices, thus a change in thoughts, actions, deeds, and beliefs is needed, with a sense of urgency. Second, seek medical attention as soon as possible, and perhaps physical healing, might be bestowed. This is a true saying, thus it is time to have faith in God. Additionally, it is always a good time to get your house and papers in order (e.g. insurances, bequeaths, untold truths that need to be said), an d always a good time to gather family together for prayer, support, wisdom, and truthfulness. See suggested Course of action.

Suggested Course of Action

Question to consider and journal, did your dream depict any symbols that alludes to, the dreamer will make the necessary changes, spiritually, emotionally, and/or physically to affect a more positive outcome? If changes are initiated, your dreams will change.

In view of your dream's context, and the primary symbols, what does your dream reveal about you, your ethics, intents, mental state, and motives? You will need to earnestly look within and consider that the sum of your answers is a reflection of where you are emotionally, physically, and spiritually, and a reflection of who you are becoming. What was your reaction to the situation? Were you angry, concerned, confused, defensive, fearful, happy, helpful, pleased, shocked, unconcerned, or ready to get out of someone's presence? Your reaction to the person, the activity, or the circumstances, and their reaction to you, reveals your attitude regarding this information about yourself.

Dreamer, consider seriously your observations. If what was revealed prevail, will it sabotage any good that's happening at present within your life? Will it build or destroy, strengthen or weaken, enlighten or blind? If you lack wisdom, ask Jesus for wisdom. He gives wisdom to all, generously, no matter who you are and what you've done; wisdom is available (see James 1:5-8, Proverbs 2:1-6, 10). Hence, if, by just asking, you may get wisdom, one may suffer needlessly, because you will not ask Jesus for wisdom.

Nevertheless, Jesus said that "the good man brings good things out of the good stored up in him, and the evil man brings evil things out of the evil stored up in him" (Matthew 12:35 NIV). That being said, dreamer, if your true intent is on glorifying God, doing His will, reaping prosperity, experiencing genuine joy, and most importantly inheriting eternal life, you will have to practice restricting yourself in all things (weaning yourself from sensual appetites). Dreamer, in the rectification of your character traits, in order to reach your level of proficiency in ministry, you must bring your appetites and sensual desires under subjection, sacrificing fleshy satisfaction, during your days of preparation and grounding. This includes your diet, activities, relationships, associations, friendships, partying, and your lack of Christian fellowship. You will need to lay aside every obstacle that hinders you and causes you to forfeit God's principles, including laziness; that you might reach the point where you are capable of accomplishing your mission, and learn contentment.

Dreamer is strongly urged to return to ideals that are holy, wise, well judged; ways that are in keeping with the nature of the Bible, ways pertaining to, contained within, and are in accordance with the Bible; ways that are scriptural. Dreamer, when a person begins to pursue an issue, in a manner consistent with their purpose, with a vital drive toward the fulfillment of t heir goals, sacrificing many sensual urges for the Kingdom's sake, mindful to observe rules, while accomplishing their pursuit. You will begin to experience confidence, sincerity, truthfulness, a willingness to serve God, and an active trust that God will give you the power to accomplish your objectives in life, also see Luke 3:4-6, 10-14. Now, pray (See Prayer of Deliverance, pg. 897)

Specific Meaning

If, in your everyday living (your waking state), as part of your lifestyle or work related activities, you have a very real connection with any activity involving the human body. For example, athletics, body builder, weight training, bodily injury, disability, or handicapped of some type, medical practitioner, physical therapist, trainer, weight, or eating concerns. Dreams of this sort, for the most part, are ordinary dreams, resulting from your daily activities (see Chapter One, Chalom). These sorts of dreams ar e usually about your routine, mundane activities or anxieties that overwhelm your mind during the day. They are an inner release mechanism, which helps provide you with emotional balance and the maintaining of your sanity. These dreams are not significant, and do not warrant special attention.

Note: It has been recorded that some within the medical field, have received diagnosis, treatments, and discoveries that have benefited mankind, within their dreams. The dreamer may or should consider his or her dream as an answer or clue given to assist in finding facts, needed to support a prevailing situation or theory. Further, if any part of the body was abused or traumatized in anyway within the dream, or an interpretation alludes to physical illness, this may be heeded as an alert o r warning in the physical realm, to prevent a serious physical condition. Do not assume that you are safe or ok, caution should be heeded. However, if your dream was inundated with symbols that are not specifically related to your job and/or responsibilities, then the spiritual implications should be heeded.

BUILDINGS AND STRUCTURES

Every man (they say) has two houses, first, our "earthly" house, not the house of brick and mortar,
but the house of the body, the house that serves us as the home of our souls on earth. It is said to
be an "earthly" house, because it is from th e earth; is supported by earthly things; has its present
abode on the earth, and will quickly return to it. Second, the house of the soul, because the soul is
"more excellent" than the body, is independent of it, and capable of a separate existence from it: it
is said to be an "everlasting habitation", a house not made with hands, eternal in the heavens. The
one is the outward, the other the inward house, (Job 4:19-21, 2 Corinthians 5:1, 2 Peter 1:13, 14).

For we know that if the earthly tent which is our house is torn down, we have a building
from God. For, in our Father's house, there are many mansions, whose Builder and Maker
is God, which God has prepared for those that love him: everlasting habitations, not like
the earthly tabernacle (John 14:2, Hebrews 11:10) Loosely based on Gill's Exposition

For every house is built by someone, but He who built all things is God.... but Christ
as a Son over His own house, whose house we are if we hold fast the confidence
and the rejoicing of the hope firm to the end. (Hebrews 3:4, 6 NKJV)

Do you not see that you are God's holy house, and that the Spirit of God has his place
in you? If anyone makes the house of God unclean, God will put an end to him; for
the house of God is holy, and you are his house. (1 Corinthians 3:16, 17 BBE)

This category deals with structures that have a roof and walls and stands more or less permanently in one place, the act of constructing structures, activity involved in repairing or constructing structures, and activity within buildings. Some short descriptions of types, phrases, and other processes and particulars, connected in some way to this category are, for example, houses, churches, buildings, towers, masonry, bridges, hospitals, plumb line, landlord, surveyor. Also, see category content list, or index.

All Symbols and Referents, Notes (1, 2, 3, etc.), Suggested Course of Action, and Specific Meaning offer guidance toward a more comprehensive interpretation.

Notes

1. Unless otherwise noted elsewhere, if, in your everyday living, your awaked state, as part of your lifestyle, work, or ministerial activities, or a special event, you have a very real connection with any activity involving buildings, structures. For example, architectural work, carpentry, construction, masonry, bricklayer, bridge builder, surveyor, landlord, real estate developer, or any other activity involved in the selling, repairing, or constructing of buildings or structures, your dream is not significant and does not warrant special attention.

    Otherwise noted, this dream may be a Prophetically Simple Dream, (see Chapter One: The 60th Part of Prophecy). Whereas, the dreamer is warned to stop any illegal or illicit activity connected to a building, e.g. a brothel, drug house, or illegal storage of goods, illegal foreclosures or evictions, slum landlord, or any other criminal minded, ill-repute, under- handed activity that primarily involves structures. If any of the preceding is happening, this dream is a first step intervention and an alarm. Skip interpretation and re-consider your activity as diabolical, distasteful, harmful, hurtful, illegal, life threatening, and wicked at present. Handle the situation appropriately by surrendering, first to God, for Adonai Elohim knows all, and then to appropriate authorities. Dreamer, you should surrender to the appropriate authorities, especially if this is an issue within the dreamer's life, and submit or yield to other relevant persons. Also, see Specific Meaning at the end of this category, section entitled, Note (Specific Meaning).

   Otherwise noted, per your lifestyle, if your dream closely resembled real life situations, meaning it can actually occur during your awaked state, this dream may be an Ordinary Dream, resulting from your daily activities (see Chapter One, Chalom). These sorts of dreams are usually about your routine, mundane activities or anxieties that overwhelm your mind during the day. They are an inner release mechanism, which helps provide you with emotional balance and the maintaining of your sanity. These dreams are not significant, and do not warrant special attention.

2.   Probables: As buildings can be very personal, for example, the home you was raised in, your first apartment, your college dorm, the place where you retired from, or your church. Thus, could the building depicted within your dream be a possible probable (see Chapter One, section entitled, Probables)? Hence, dreamer may also consider your own personal and special associations with various buildings, as long as the interpretation is kept within the principles of spiritual boundary markers, landmarks, and property lines, (see Chapter One, section entitled, Spiritualizing Boundary Markers, Landmarks, and Property Lines).

3.   Determine who your dream is for you or another. Always, considering yourself first, reflecting on your present behaviors. Ask yourself, why am I dreaming about this now? What is this dream revealing about me? Have I taken on new attributes? Has anyone commented on my present behaviors as being untypical of me? Has my ministry changed for the better or for the worse? What about my beliefs, doctrine, or philosophy, are they still based on Holy Writ? Is there something I need to know about those I am ministering to or serving?

   Remember your actions and emotions within your dream. Was it your church, home, educational facility, place of employment depicted? Was a structure depicted as your residence within your dream, although you do not live in such a home in your awaked life? Were you architectonically designing the building? Were you building a school? Were you an employee at a facility? Was the church depicted the one you attend at present? Unless otherwise noted elsewhere, an answer of yes, to one or more of these, or similar questions, is a good indicator that your dream is about you (the dreamer). What were you doing in your dream? What happened to you in your dream? Are you in a process of spiritual renewal or transformation; hence a dream of your church appearing different or in another location. Perhaps your job was relocated, or your primary health care facility changed from a beautiful facility to a bad one? In light of your dream, via the relevant interpretation, do you believe that your choices will enhance or endanger your well-being, safety, and/or happiness, if so, how and why? Is spiritual or physical death a possibility (e.g. a dream of a burning house)? Perhaps the building was old and run-down, due to age or it not being properly maintained or cared for, unkempt. What was the condition of the lawn? See following relevant subcategory, the interpretation is about and for you.

   Was someone else's church, educational facility, place of employment, or home depicted? Did another build the structure? Was someone other than the dreamer the supervisor or overseer of the facility? Was the church depicted not one you've attended before? Unless otherwise noted elsewhere, an answer of yes, to one or more of these, or similar questions, is a good indicator that your dream is about another and/or their role, and influential effects, within the life of the dreamer. Is someone enhancing or mentoring you, thus a dream of another doing the building or, is him or her, responsible for the dwindling thereof; thus a tearing down of a structure or building within your dream? If you sense that your dream is for or about another, the question as to why you have been made privy to this information, and how do you factor into the equation, should be seriously considered along with necessary actions. Perhaps the dreamer is being made aware of the plight of someone, and you are to get involved (see Chapter One, Are You Ready to Hear the Messages in Your Dreams, section entitled, The 10% for others).

If your dream is for, or about another: Dreams that reference others and the revelation within those dreams, is not given haphazardly to any individual, but only to those with the ability, and influence to do something with the information; this is also prophecy. With that, journal the following questions, and if unable to answer the questions now, this denotes that the person, represented within your dream, will enter your life shortly. Are you entering into a personal relationship with someone? Do you not know or understand what you're looking at, especially certain behaviors, when learning about this person? Has someone new entered your life or maybe you've just begun opening up to someone not so new, and have started listening to their advice, accepting their assistance, or are you supporting or enabling someone? Are you in denial regarding the toxicity of one of your present relationships, particularly a spouse, family member, or friend? Are you anxious, concerned, frightened, and/or troubled by recent changes in your behavior, especially because of someone's influence upon your life at present? Have you allowed someone to convince you to deceive another? Have you recently become aware of (or is being made aware of, via your dream) certain undesirable behaviors within you towards another? Are you trying to cut ties with one that is bad company? Have you just joined (or re-joined) a church, fellowship, or social group?

Note: If your dream has attributes that indicate that your dream is about you, and other attributes that indicate that your dream is about another, dreamer should consider that your dream is about you and another. For example, were you building for another, or re-modeling someone else's home? Was another in your house? This, indicating that the dream is about the dreamer, because dreamer was working for another or it was your house; and, also dream was about another, because building was for another, or another was in your house. Therefore, while your dream is about the dreamer, the dreamer should expect the role and/or influential effects of another, also plays a part in your interpretation. Perhaps, dreamer is apprehensive or fearful regarding another coming into your domain; thus, you have begun embracing a spirit of fear, from which now the dreamer needs deliverance. For God has said, do not be afraid, read and understand Romans 8:15, 2 Timothy 1:7. Did another burned down the dreamer's home, and someone close to the dreamer died in the fire. Now, dreamer is emotionally wounded, violated, hurt, by this act, and now that hurt has bred bitterness and an unforgiving spirit within the dreamer. From which now the dreamer needs deliverance, again, see relevant interpretation.

More questions to consider. Why has the person been allowed within your life, and/or how did they get there? If their activity, within your dream, has proven positive, via the interpretation, this someone will prove, unwittingly, to be a very strong ally, benefactor, defender, and supporter. God has sent this someone into your life to help you carry out your next endeavor by enlarging your spiritual capacity. Allow the strength of that person's character to guide, help, and support you. On the other hand, if his or her presence and/or activity, within your dream, proved negative, via the interpretation, for sure, this person will prove to be a very strong and formidable challenge for you, perhaps unto death. If negative, this dream is a dire warning. Take steps accordingly to struggle against, or to cut off, adverse and unfavorable relationships. Remember certain personalities are all encompassing, affecting everything, cataclysmic, contagious, deadly, harmful, infectious, predatory, and/or venomous. Symbolically meaning that if allowed to continue or prosper within your life, serious harm or death to the dreamer may result. Idolize no one, especially beyond the warning of the Lord, and we are definitely not to lay our lives down for no one. No longer, allow that particular person's influence within your life to continue or thrive. Then again, this person maybe allowed within your life, because of the dreamer's unwillingness to abstain from immorality after having been asked to abstain from such by God, see 1 Corinthians 6:9-20, Galatians 5:19-21, or the dreamer's self-righteous behavior, or a lack of a balanced and honest view of your own personality. In this case, this person will affect self-awareness within the life of the dreamer, exposing the negative traits of your personality, especially those traits, which cause you to follow, or to be so easily misled, and/or your wrong beliefs; no matter, this type of mentality needs reckoning with. Graciously, all of this will restore the dreamer to his or her right place with God, opening your eyes to see how far you've strayed from God (1 Corinthians 5:4-7; James 5:20). The lesson is, no matter how personable, powerful, or difficult a person, or how uncertain or unpopular the choices and issues, always take the next biblical and ethical step, for obedience to God's principles will always prove safer and stronger foundationally. Although, you will need all kinds of outside support to recover from this person's domination, again, no longer, allow that particular person's influence within your life to continue or thrive, especially if negative, end it abruptly.

4. Consider all the people, places, backgrounds, and activity highlighted within your dream. Known (in your awaked life) person, animal, place, or organization within your dream:

If the building within your dream; is actually known by the dreamer, in your awaked life, this building may perhaps represent a specific location or activity connected to that particular place. For example, did a hostage situation take place within the particular building? Was the building a childhood kindergarten? Additionally, unless otherwise noted, people, animals, places, backgrounds that are actually known by the dreamer in your awaked life, indicates a part of you that you recognize within yourself on some level or another. Question to journal, if dreamer seriously considers all the particulars, what features stood out the most. For example, age, color, height, size, neglected, poor, run-down, or upscale. Write down (journal) the particular highlighted within your dream. The attribute or activity highlighted is for a reason. Since the attribute written down is a part of you, namely the dreamer's nature, demeanor, and/ or lifestyle, an honest and unbiased assessment is very important for truth sake. Happy note, considering that other people's attributes, within dreams, also represent attributes of your own personality, causes one to look at another in a better light. According to your capacity to embrace self-awareness and a rectification of mind, body, and spirit, God will begin to enhance, make better, more attractive, sanctify, diminish, and make pure and free from sin and guilt, this part of you.

Otherwise noted, if the person, animal, place, or background within your dream is actually known by the dreamer, in your awaked life, this person, animal, place, or background may represent him or herself, or itself.

Dreams of graveyards or any realms of the dead, see following note.

While the dead, graveyards or any realms of the dead, has nothing to do with the living (Ecclesiastes 9:4-6), it may be considered what features does the place or person represent to the dreamer, or what particular stood out the most. With that noted, dreamer must consider that the attribute noted, is within the dreamer, and that trait is no longer useful or needed for the progression of your spiritual walk, on this side of heaven. Dreamer, it is suggested that you render that attribute (good or bad) obsolete, and began anew attempting to move forward, using different tactics to overcome unproductive habitual life cycle choices, and for maneuvering through this thing we call spiritual life in a more, better way. See category, Death, Dying, and the Dead, Heaven and Hell (Grave, Graveyard, or Realms of the Dead.

Unknown in your awaked life or although known, was unseen, invisible, or only talked about - place, organization, or people within your dream:

Unless otherwise noted elsewhere, if you did not recognize, the building or structure, or it, was not seen, invisible, or only talked about within your dream, this indicates an attribute or activity within your life that you are unfamiliar with, or are in denial about, or you refuse to acknowledge it, but it does exists. Question to journal, what activity stood out the most, in your dream, regarding the building? For example, what was going on within the church, home,

505

educational facility, or place of employment? What feature, action, or activity, stood out the most? For example, topography, weather, was the building being constructed, remodeled, or neglected, poor, run-down. Is this dream meant to alarm? Although, on some conscious level, you are aware of a certain behavior or attribute within you, you have chosen to filter out or simply ignore certain information about yourself that contradicts your view of yourself and/ or you r preconceived notions of others and of the world around you. Possibly protecting yourself, emotionally and psychologically, from a situation, which you are unable to cope with at this time, or you lack control over; then again, perhaps the dreamer has an exaggerated or unrealistic view of yourself. No matter the reason, right now a question is before you, via your dream. Do you want to know this part of yourself? According to your ability to handle self-awareness, God will begin to reveal this side of you to you. Why, He wants to balance your understanding of things; thus, effecting wholeness within your life, so that the enemy will no longer be able to manipulate your emotions so easily. The Holy Spirit is with you to help you throughout this entire process, listen to Him. Now, in your life, this activity or attribute needs reckoning with, somehow or some way. Again, what actions or behaviors of the unknown place, organization, or structure stood out the most?

Otherwise noted, (known or unknown), if the building, or structure and the activity within, was not seen, invisible, or only talked about within your dream, this may indicate that the dreamer does not recognize the influential effects another has within your life, or upon your attitude.

If more than one building (known or unknown):

Consider what the complex has in common. For example, was it a complex of shopping malls, houses, and roads in a new town? That which was highlighted and noted is what you need to focus on at present, see relevant interpretation.

5. Buildings and Structures in good condition, beautifully adorned: Unless otherwise noted elsewhere, any building, structure, or any part of a building, within your dream that was in good condition, beautifully adorned, or was in the process of being repaired, remodeled, or under construction (e.g. a hard-hat area). This dream denotes a transition within the life of the dreamer, and good health and strength to make the changeover. This transition will affect within you a far - reaching hope, profoundly greater faith, and a more intense love for all things Jesus, including His people; allow it. Further, dreamer you have been blessed with a great understanding of spiritual knowledge, and not without reason. One who is given the means to study and teach and has access to prophetic wisdom, is purposed to be a transformational force in people's lives. Your power of speech and wisdom will convert souls to the Kingdom of God. Dreamer, your time of missions is upon you. You are sent to those who are spiritually "asleep". You are counseled to focus your ministry on God's providence over life. Primarily, the wisdom, care, and guidance He has provided His people, for He always guards over His chosen; thus, He watches over His people. You must encourage others that the feeling of rest and serenity that comes with trust in God's divine providence is available to them, right now, as well as, the ability to release stress by putting confidence in God's support; and that it would be wise of them to put their trust in Him at present. This, coupled with, contentment, and their peace will overflow. Those who will listen and adhere will begin to experience the blessings spoken of in Leviticus 26:4-13, prophesy this also. In particular, (verse 6 GW), "I will bring peace to your land. You will lie down with no one to scare you". Additionally, God will send someone to help you along the way. He or she will lead and guide you to where you need to be. This relationship will be a type of "equal partner" or "friendship" type relationship, in other words they will not be head over you. You will always be respected as the lead person. Moreover, you (the dreamer) will be leaving your present church, and you will experience a mega-ministry. You will become friends with major leaders, but not covenant partners with them. You will (or should) remain attached to your present church and come back to rest there. After this,

because of your diligence and honorable service, you will be given the opportunity to take a sabbatical rest or retire, and you will be covered by the Lord's grace.

In a dilapidated condition, displeasingly adorned: Unless otherwise noted elsewhere, any building, structure, or any part of a building, within your dream that was damaged beyond use or repair, reduced to ruins, was in the process of becoming dilapidated, in any irrecoverable state of devastation or destruction, or displeasingly adorned, this dream denotes a serious illness that is life threatening. Dreamer needs to first, call for the elders of a church, for it is through their prayers of faith and anointing of oil upon you that your sins will be forgiven and that spiritual and physical healing might occur[36]. Dreamer, there is a great need for repentance, for your sickness is primarily due to unhealthy lifestyle choices, unwillingness to forgive or show mercy, and sinful and wicked behaviors and evil practices, thus a change in thoughts, actions, deeds, and beliefs is needed, with a sense of urgency. Second, seek medical attention as soon as possible, that physical healing might be bestowed. This is a true saying, thus it is time to have faith in God. Additionally, it is always a good time to get your house and papers in order (e.g. insurances, bequeaths, untold truths that n eed to be said), and always a good time to gather family together for prayer, support, wisdom, and truthfulness (Ecclesiastes 12:6).

6. In addition to the following interpretations, see index or relevant categories for more information. For example, if fire was involved in some way, see category, Explosion or Fire. If land was highlighted, see category, Landforms. If cleaning was highlighted, see category, Cleaning. Kept within context of your dream and the interpretation, the additional symbols are perhaps relevant. It will be within the sum of all the symbols that you will find a more thorough interpretation.

7. Since the following list is not extensive, dreamer is encouraged to seek biblical guidelines and other relevant research to determine the metaphorical meaning of your particular building or parts of buildings, depicted within your dream, via a Bible concordance, Bible illustrated dictionary, encyclopedia, or internet. Having done your research you should be able to determine some basic behaviors or attributes your Lord and Savior wants you to focus on.

8. Most building, structures subcategories deal only with the structure, for activities within buildings, see relevant category for activity or index.

Symbols and Referents

Generally all buildings, structures, and all parts of a building, reveal the varied conditions, status, and well-being of your physical health, and the emotional state of your inner person, and if appropriate, what possibly needs to happen to affect a healthier you. The direction of spiritual and emotional growth for the dreamer will be in embracing the positive attributes that may be ascribed to the building, structure, or the particular room you were in, with emphasis on an earnest resolve towards betterment.

In addition to the varied meanings of buildings, structures, other common words, expressions, usages, (e.g. slang or clichés), or a 'probable' that are metaphorically represented by any of the following are also considered (this section is an addendum at the end of the relevant subcategory).

Category Content: if not listed, see index, perchance, for your specific type of buildings, structures dream.

- Agricultural Buildings, Structures (e.g. barn, farmhouse, greenhouse, stable, granary, root cellar, and silo shed, chicken coop, cow shed, or sty), see category Agriculture and Forestry (Agricultural Structures)
- Arts and Entertainment Facilities (Amphitheater, Art Gallery, Concert Hall, Film Studio, Movies, Museum, or Opera House, including Concerts, Plays, Stage, or Red Carpet)

- Athletic, Sport Facilities or Fields (Athletic, Sport Facilities or Fields, Arenas, Dugouts, Gyms, Stadiums, any place where athletic activities may occur), see category Games (Sports)
- Buildings Flying Away (to see buildings flying overhead in the air), see category, Flying
- Attic or Loft
- Bathroom or Lavatory or Restroom or Toilet
    - Bathtub or Shower ; To clean one or take a bath or shower, wash hands, or feet, see category, Cleaning; Cleaning bathroom or any parts, see category, Cleaning (Bathroom); Sink or Basin or Washbasin; Brushing teeth, see category The Body (Teeth)
- Bedroom or Bed or Sleeping Quarters
    - Asleep in bed, see category, Sleeping; Bed Coverings (e.g. Blankets, Duvet Covers, Linen, Pillows, or Sheets); On the Bed or Underneath the Bed (someone or something)
- Bridges and bridge like structures (Aqueducts, Overpasses, Trestles)
- Ceilings (the overhead upper surface of a covered space)
- Community Hall or Convention Center or Forum (any public facility to meet for open discussion or programs)
- Jail or Prison or Fortress or Barriers or Incarceration (any places of confinement, includes Prison camp)
- Eatery (Bakery, Deli, Fast Food Place, Lounge, Night Club, Pizzeria, Pub, Restaurant, Sports Bar, any building where people go to eat and drink)
    - Bakery; Deli or Fast Food Place or Pizzeria; Nightclub or Lounge or Pub or Sports Bar; Restaurant (a place where you sit down and are served, non-fast food service)
- Educational Facilities, see category, Working (Educator)
- Entryways or Enclosures (Doors, Entrances, Fences, Gates, Palisades, Porch, Portal, Stoop, or Veranda, or any entrance attached to the exterior of a building or structure)
    - Doors (incl. doorbell); Fences or Palisades (any barrier that serves to enclose an area); Gates or Prison Bars; Hallway or Corridor or Portal; Porch or Stoop or Veranda
- Health Care Facility (e.g. Asylum, Clinic, Hospice, Hospital, Nursing Home, Psychiatric Hospital, Rehab, Sanatorium, Veterinary Office, any facility where patients receive some manner of medical treatment)
    - Physician or Psychiatrist or Healer or Health Aides (any health care provider), see category Working (Physician)
- Hotel or Inn (any establishment where transients or travelers pay for lodging, meals, or other services, includes Bed and Breakfast, Boarding House, Brothel, Love Hotel, Casino Hotel, Dormitory, Guest House, Inn, Hotel, Motel, any Resort)
    - Brothel or Love Hotel; Casino or Resort; Hotel or Motel or Inn or Bed and Breakfast or Boarding House or Dormitory or Guesthouse
- Kitchen or Annex or Dining Area
    - Cabinets, Cupboards; Pots and Pans; Refrigerator, see category, Frozen, Frost, Refrigeration, Snow, Cold (Refrigeration, Refrigerator); Stove; Table (includes Coffee Table, Counter Tops, Dinettes, or Kitchen-Island)
- Living Room or Family Room or Sitting Room or Lounge Room (e.g. Employee's Lounge, Breakroom, TV Room, Recreation Room, a relaxation room in a private residence, business, or institution)
- Market Facilities or Employment Facilities (Department Store, Farmer's Market, Kiosks, Mall, Mini Market, Office Buildings, Supermarket, any mercantile establishment for the retail sale of goods or services)
- Military Buildings (Barracks, Blockhouse, Bunker, Citadel, Dugout, any facility, residence, or structure connected to the armed forces, or any fortification or defensive stronghold structure, and any military structure where arms, ammunition, and other military equipment are stored, and any type of stronghold into which people could go for shelter during a battle)

- Religious Buildings (Basilica, Cathedral, Chapel, Church, Meeting House, Mosque, Monastery, Shrine, Synagogue, Temple, or any place of worship). For Religious Residences, see subcategory Residential Buildings
- Residential Buildings (Apartment, Bungalow, Castle, Cloister, Cottage, Condominium, Consulate, Duplex, Embassy, Emergency Shelter, House, Hut, Log Cabin, Mansion, Monastery, Orphanage, Palace, Parsonage, Public Housing, Rectory, Retirement Complex, Row House, Tent, Townhouse, Vicarage, Villa, or White House. Any private, religious or government residences)
    - Apartment or Condominium or Duplex or Row House or Townhouse or Public Housing; Bungalow or Cottage or Villa; Emergency Shelter or Temporary Shelter; House or Mansion or Palace or Castle; Hut or Tent ; Log Cabin; Orphanage; Religious or Government Residences (e.g. Parsonage, Monastery, Rectory, Vicarage, Cloister, or any religious residence or government residence, e.g. Consulate, Embassy, White house, or any government residence); Retirement or Senior Citizen Living Complex
- Roof
- Storage Facilities or Parking Structures (Airport terminal, Aviation Control towers, Automobile repair shop, Boathouse, Boat lift, Building Canopies, Car dealership, Carport, Carwash, Dock, Garage, Gas station, Hangar, Marina, Metro Station, Parking Garage, Piers, Snow Shed, Stall, Warehouse, or any Depository for goods. Any place relating to any mode of transportation)
- Vestibule or Concourse or Foyer or Lobby (any large interior entrance, reception room, or waiting area)
- Walls
- Windows (includes any type of glass, be it, a looking glass, such as a Mirror, Optical Instruments, such as Eyeglasses, Transparent Drinking Glass, Bottles, or any transparent openings that allow you to see through it)
    - "Walking on Broken Glass"; Dancing before a mirror, see category, The Body (Face); Greenhouse, Glasshouse (a building with glass walls and roof), see category, Agriculture (Agricultural structures); Reflection in a mirror, see category, The Body (Face, Reflections, Shadows)
- Waste Yard or Garbage Dump or Dumpster or Dumpsite (or any container that holds rubbish, garbage can, trash can, ash tray)

ARTS AND ENTERTAINMENT FACILITIES (Amphitheater, Art Gallery, Concert Hall, Film Studio, Movies, Museum, or Opera House, including Concerts, Plays, Stage, or Red Carpet):

This dream has three meanings (one, two, or all may apply). (1) Dreamer, you are gifted with prophetic insight that may be expressed through inspirational preaching, teaching, and/or acting. Earnest and conscientious Christian efforts and endeavors will enhance your prophetic gifting. Moreover, allow the Lord's will to be done in you, via faithfully serving Him. (2) If dreamer was in the audience or working in some manner behind the scenes, your dream denotes one who is initiative and get s things done. Opportunities to pursue your goals are just ahead; wait for them, for they are worth waiting for. (3) If you were on:

Stage: Dreamer, your door, your opportunity to become who God has ordained for you to become is worth waiting for. Your unique style of artistic expression, and in presenting the gospel of Jesus Christ, is the gift you bring to the world; thus be who you "uniquely" are, and let none, not even you, "morph" you into someone you are not, for this type of identity is void, without foundation, and will lead to a crack in your personality. If not already, you will, bring joy and inspiration to many by your positive mindset and creative talents, via writing, drama, music, speaking, or teaching. Therefore, you must not get ti red of doing "good", for you will reap at the proper time if you don't give up. Dreamer, don't allow yourself to get tired of li ving the right way - living life on God's terms, and in pursuing your gifting. For sure, you will receive your due just on this side of heaven at the proper time, if you don't give up, and everlasting life. Moreover, while you have the opportunity, do good to all people, and especially to those who are of the household of faith (Galatians 6:8-10).

Red carpet: Upon stepping into your destiny, which is before you now, remember you have been wounded emotionally and/or physically by an abuser, one sent by the enemy of your soul to sabotage your eternal destiny. The violation has left you seriously wounded and caused you to act out sacrilegiously, irreverently, and disrespectfully towards God and those of the household of faith in the past. If not dealt with holistically, via prayer, fasting, Christian counseling, or support, the a cting out you did because of your wounds, will come back to haunt you "hard", and you will embarrass yourself publicly. See suggested course of action.

Attic Or Loft:

This dream has three meanings (choose one). (1) To be up in an attic, or loft denotes one, namely the dreamer, who will shortly begin to experience, if not already, a paradigm shift in your core beliefs and spirituality. You are approaching new and deeper dimensions. This transition will affect within you a far-reaching hope, profoundly greater faith, and a more intense love for all things Jesus, including His people; allow it. Moreover, you have been blessed with a great understanding of spiritual knowledge, and not without reason. One who is given the means to study and teach and has access to prophetic wisdom, is purposed to be a transformational force in people's lives. Your power of speech and wisdom will convert souls to the Kingdom of God. Your time of missions is upon you. You are sent to those who are spiritually dead, and to those who have multiple belief systems, yet a spark of life is hidden within them (also see Matthew 28:19, 20). Moreover, you will become renowned for your expertise and passion, as you go forth using your past to teach those whom you are destined to reach. (2) Dreamer is reminded that a level of purity is required of those chosen for the task of promoting the Kingdom of God. Since, it is the soul that connects us to God we must honor and keep our souls pure by embracing the morals and ethics of the Bible. Jesus said, "The spirit is willing, but the flesh is weak" (Matthew 26:41). However, true believers who are "born again" (see John 3:1-17), and endowed with the Holy Spirit, are able to battle against the still-corrupt parts of themselves; thus rectifying their soul. Dreamer; while it is acknowledged, and readily known, that the body is still under the bondage of sin and is therefore imperfect, and that it will be rectified on Judgement Day. Believers are still counseled to, earnestly take pains to lay aside every sin and bondage that hinders a dedicated and devoted life to the Kingdom of God, for judgement day will happen. You are counseled to subdue those sins of impurity within your life. See suggested course of action. (3) Physically, an attic, or loft may also point to literal health issues within the head, indicating possible issues with the brain, cheeks, jaws, ears, eyes, face, forehead, brow, mouth, teeth, or tongue. Seek medical attention.

Bathroom, Lavatory, Restroom, Or Toilet:

A bathroom generally symbolizes the need for cleansing, purging, and/or elimination of something or someone in your life that is considered wasteful, isn't quite working, or has served its purpose. Now it's time to eliminate that and move on. This dream has four meanings (choose one). (1) Opening the door to a bathroom: This dream reveals the past spiritual condition of the dreamer, and it reveals the present spiritual condition of another or possibly a ministry. See Note 4. Dreamer, use your past to, empathically reach another, or others, whose spiritual condition is similarly akin to the spiritual condition you once found yourself. What and whom you saw, and where you were, may perhaps point you in the direction of the person or ministry that may be in trouble spiritually at present. Nonetheless, reach out and touch them using the wisdom of experience, remembering from where you were lifted. If unknown, they will be introduced to you soon. Dreamer may also see subcategory, Doors. If necessary, see suggested course of action. (2) If normal activities connected to bathrooms were going on within your dream, e.g. some manner of cleaning or elimination. Your dream was sent to encourage the dreamer. It implies you are taking responsibility for your physical health and/or you are purifying yourself morally, by dealing with the sin issues in your life, no matter how seemingly insignificant. You have begun, again, to listen to the Paraclete within you, instead of relying on your emotions and opinions. This is good. Dreamer, the state of affairs in your life at present, may not be to your liking; but God allows them. God is using your situations to work things out for your good, namely to mature you spiritually, and to make you stronger emotionally and mentally. Therefore, do not attribute (or call) that which is of God, unclean (e.g. confusion, erroneous, out of order, unlawful, weak, wicked, or any other negative attribute). No matter how difficult or how uncertain the issues always take the next biblical, ethical, and most informed step, for obedience is better than sacrifice. (3) Smaller (bathroom smaller than normal or too small): Dreamer, you're capacity to handle certain issues, emotionally, physically, and mentally has enlarged. Now, a spirit of gratitude for the emotional, physical, and psychological work done within you, via the help of the Paraclete should be hardily embraced, coupled with an honest acknowledgement of spiritual growth within you to you, that you may go on to maturity, able to handle much more than you were able to previously. See suggested course of action. (4) If unusual activities, actions not usually connected to bathrooms were going on within your dream, your dream implies dreamer is not taking responsibility for your physical health and/or you are not purifying yourself morally, by dealing with the sin issues in your life. Your behavior will cause your anointing to fade and spiritual authority to wane. Thus, your dream is to warn a rebellious person, in the spirit of grace (the free and unmerited favor and beneficence of God). To see if you will yet be worked upon, and change your mindset, or else to leave you inexcusable, in your accusations against God, because of your ruin (e.g. continually plundered, seized, and disfavored, also see Jeremiah 9:7-9; Zechariah 13:9; Matthew 23:37-39; Revelation 3:15-21). See suggested course of action. See one of the following.

Bathtub or Shower: Be encouraged, you will be healed emotionally, physically, and spiritually. Trust and obey God's guidance. Further, begin deliberately developing habits of holiness, prayer, fasting, theological study, abstinence, sobriety, and separation from people, places, and circumstances that are contrary to your development of clarity, cleanness, and stability. See suggested course of action.

Sink, Basin, or Washbasin (any activity occurring in, around, or on, a sink, basin, or washbasin): Dreamer, it is necessary that you bring to remembrance your former state, when you were enslaved to sin. What benefits did you reap at that time from the things you now disdain, the filth, and foolishness of it all? Now that you have been set free from sin, you have become a servant of God. To keep you humble, repentant, and watchful, you would do well to remember the time when you were a servant of sin, devoted to iniquity, embracing vanity, and reaping the same; and to remember the benefits of being a servant of God. With that, also deeply focus on the benefits you are reaping now. Moreover, serving God has led to holiness and the end-result is eternal life (Romans 6:21, 22). Couple this with one of the following three (choose one). (1) Someone will be allowed to enter into the life of the dreamer, to support you during a difficult or oppressive situation. Your situation and difficulties were sent to purge you from sin; prayerfully you've learned lessons. Here it should be noted that if God; therefore, will deliver His people, He can choose anybody, and use any means necessary, per His choosing, in effecting their deliverance. The fact that God uses persons, who are out of His will, perhaps it is that someone allowed within your life, does not mean that He approves of evil. See suggested course of action. (2) To dream of a sink also denotes that one, namely the dreamer, who is so strong that you've put confidence in your flesh, fearing no danger, living carelessly. Erroneously assuming that nothing but good comes to you. Confessing that no one you know can compare with you, or even pretend to be equal with you because of your extraordinary prophetic abilities. God humbles the haughty and causes all of his or her joy and laughter to cease (see Zephaniah 2:15). Dreamer, exaggerated and unrighteous pride always turns a good situation into chaos, and pollutes everyone involved or connected. Moreover, where there is confusion, a lack of sincerity, truthfulness, and vitality, will follow. A purging from over confidence in your own flesh will now begin. See suggested course of action. (3) Physically, a sink or washbasin may also point to literal health issues within the upper respiratory tract, indicating possible issues with the neck or nose. If relevant, it is suggested that you contact your primary physician, especially if you are experiencing any health issues.

BEDROOM, BED, OR SLEEPING QUARTERS:

Spiritually, a bedroom denotes, rest, the private side of one's life, sexual activity or a bedroom may also point to literal health issues within your reproductive, genital system. If there has been a health concern in this area, it is sugg ested that you consult your GYN or urologist, as soon as possible; see, Note 6. With that, this dream has four meanings (choose one). (1) Awake in bedroom, bed, sleeping quarters: Your dream denotes dreamer will be granted a time of rest, via a sabbatical, or is in desperate need of rest, thus you will experience a serious weakening and loss of energy, a "total exhaustion" type medical emergency; hence, forcing you to rest. If necessary, see suggested course of action. (2) Entering into, getting into, your bedroom, bed, sleeping quarters: Dreamer needs to become (or is becoming) more self-aware; particularly, aware of your private self as a spiritual individual, who you are to God, who you are to yourself, and aware of why you behave as you do. See suggested course of action. (3) People in bedroom, bed, sleeping quarters: This choice has two parts (choose one). (a) I t reveals the past spiritual condition of the dreamer, and it reveals the present spiritual condition of another, or possibly a ministry. What did the people have in common? Were the people known or unknown by the dreamer? See Note 3 of this category. (b) Your dream was sent as a warning. Dreamer, do not set foot on the path of the wicked or do the same things a s evil men and women. Avoid them, do not travel with them; turn from them, and go on your way. For they cannot sleep until they do evil; until they make someone fall. They eat the bread of wickedness and drink the wine of violence. The way of the wicked is like deep darkness; they do not know what makes them stumble. However, the path of the righteous is like the first glow of the sun in the early morning, shining brighter until the full light of day. Dreamer, listen closely to God's Word. Keep it within your heart, for it will be health to your whole body. Above all else, guard your heart, for it is the wellspring of life.

Make level paths for your feet; and take ways, only, that are firm, (Proverbs 4). See suggested course of action. (4) Sexual activity in bedroom, bed, sleeping quarters: This choice has two parts (choose one). (a) Married dreamer: If sexual activity between dreamer and your spouse was going on, your dream, maybe an ordinary dream, see Chapter One, Ordinary Dreams. (b) Illicit sexual activity (adultery or fornication acts): Your dream denotes spiritual adultery. Spiritual adultery, at its core, and in its various forms, is unfaithfulness to God, which leads to one becoming antagonistic against God. Hence, spiritual adult ery includes any form of idolatry; any act that expresses devotion or fanatical admiration to something or someone other than Adonai Elohim. Moreover, fear is akin to idolatry; for one may exalt the spirit of fear, above God's promised word of protection from all hurt, harm, and danger. Serious fear issues, makes one spiritually irrational and demonically influenced. Therefore, dreamer is advised to exalt no one, nor your public image of well-being, nor fear or worry, above God, especially to the point of death, even death emotionally or spiritually. Other forms of spiritual adultery include anger problems. One primary sign that anger maybe manifesting within you is a continual unforgiving heart towards another or a group of persons, a place, or a thing. An unforgiving heart is a most subtle thing that steals its way into your heart almost unknown, but in the sight of God, it is the greatest hindrance to your spiritual fellowship and communion with a Holy God who answers prayer. Th is is the one thing, spoken of in the Word that if found in the heart of a believer it will hinder answered prayer and it opens the door to all kinds of sicknesses, even premature death. Your dream is challenging you, the dreamer, to confront your dysfunction, one way, or another; and your dream exposes a need of refinement of character, namely in the area dealing with the deeds of the flesh, see 1 Corinthians 6:8-11. Dreamer, a decision to repent, and return, and reject the attitude of foolishness, hypocrisy, and selfishness; and where there would be chaos, genuine peace will abide. Where there is a lack of prudence, wisdom will rule. With all that said, dreamer, one, who does understand your situation, is near you. Seek them ou t, for when at least two agree; that which needs "binding or loosening", will give, and heaven will hear and honor the agreement (Matthew 18:19-20). The Lord is awaiting your agreement with Him (Matthew 9:20-21, Luke 6:19). Dreamer, look to Jesus. Love and forgiveness can and will embrace and restore you, wait for it. For God knows what you need, the burdens you bear, and the pain you feel, dreamer, He knows. You can be healed emotionally, physically, and spiritually. On another vein, he o r she, who do not respect the opportunities placed before them shall have the things that support their peace taken away. Thus, if you are unwilling to acknowledge, challenge yourself, and change, you will be stripped of position, status, and finances, namely of all that 'covers' you, and yes, it will be allowed. See suggested course of action.

Bed Coverings (e.g. Blankets, Duvet Covers, Linen, Pillows, or Sheets): This dream has two meanings (choose one). (1) Bed coverings within a dream denotes one who is in the process of being made whole, emotionally, psychologically, p hysically, and financially, because of your reverence for God. You are entering into a process of being purified and purged, examined, proven and tested, spiritually and emotionally cleansed. Everything that's unusable within you will give way to that wh ich is beneficial and profitable, and that which is undesirable will become brightly polished, according to God's good pleasure. Yo ur pride will soon give way to humbleness, dignity, honor, and righteous self-esteem, your foolishness to peace and wisdom. This process will also heal the animosity within you resulting in a physical healing you've believed God for, for some time now. Allow the process without complaining or murmuring for it is preparing you for a great journey. Be as one who gets satisfaction from embracing good habits. (2) If dreamer is already seriously ill, or facing a life threatening event, your dream is one of God's ways of breaking it to you gently, preparing you for one of life's common denominators, and if heeded, can prevent you from being emotionally blindsided by loss, as your dream is a notice; it symbolizes shortness of life. For someone who has met Jesus, we experience Him in the little graces, the big miracles, the ordinary days, and the curious moments. He is with us, leading us onward, even sharing our tears. This same Jesus trustworthy in life, even when we are not, can be trusted at the ending of life, for He is the resurrection (John 11:25, 26). If we love Jesus and love our neighbor as we love oursel ves, there is nothing in this world or the next to fear. Love is what we take with us, and love is what awaits us when we have finally arrived. Nonetheless, dreamer seek medical attention as soon as possible, and call for the elders of your church, for it is through their prayers of faith and anointing of oil upon you that sin is forgiven and "spiritual" healing bestowed, and perhaps physical healing.[36] This is a true saying, thus it is time to have faith in God. Additionally, it is always a good time to get your house and papers in order (e.g. insurances, bequeaths, untold truths that need to be said), and always a good time to gather family together for prayer, support, wisdom, and truthfulness (Ecclesiastes 12:6). See suggested course of action.

On the Bed or Underneath the Bed (someone or something): Dreamer, although God has given you much rest from emotional turbulence and outward distractions and drama, and you are no longer fearful, privately, in a secret place, a place hidden from most. You are quietly without hope, because there seems to be no possibility of comfort or success for your inner most desires. Your secret place, although quiet, is bleak and desolate, with much sadness, resulting primarily from you feel ings of being forsaken or abandoned, and feelings of solitariness, fractured in your very soul. Dreamer, the King of kings is summoning you. Do not be afraid, the thing that will bring you out of hiding is grace, and it will not harm you. Compassionately, instead of no hope and insufficiency, you will receive a new life, in a way that you have not known since before your hopelessness, and loneliness. No more should you embrace bleakness, sadness, solitariness, for God has not forsaken you. Read Isaiah 54:8-17, for this is God promise to you. At last, you will be able to enjoy the benefits of being an heir to a King in a spirit of wholeness. God will even restore to you the land that belonged to your family. Dreamer, what Christ is doing for you, if you will simply come to Him as He summons you out of your depression, is a beautiful picture of grace. Will you allow Jesus to heal your fragmented soul, and your unbelief? Will you forgive God of desires not fulfilled; and release your anger towards Him, for the Lord gives and the Lord takes away (Job 1:21, 22, Luke 17:1-10)? Will you allow His will to be done as He has declared via your dream? Further, what was on or underneath the bed? How did it get there? It will be within that interpretation that you will find what the Lord will do in place of your bleakness. He will exchange the bleakness and barrenness of "that" for His favor upon your life. For example, instead of death, there will be health, instead of lonel iness, there will be a relationship, or instead of harshness, there will be forgiveness. See relevant categories, and journal the particulars highlighted. It will be within those interpretations that you will find what God's primary focus will be in rest oring you to wholeness within. Be encouraged, and again, do not be afraid, for no more will you have to live beneath the promises of the Lord for your life, they will begin to manifest now. Do you see it? If not, God will also heal you unbelief. See su ggested course of action.

BRIDGES AND BRIDGE LIKE STRUCTURES (Aqueducts, Overpasses, or Trestles):

Dreamer, your "woe" has passed. You are encouraged to begin rebuilding, using your best skills to recover. This time, make sure your choices and activities are ethical, morally allowable, innocent, moderate, modest, and sober. Moreover, your increase shall be devoted to God, to His honor, and used for His service. If necessary, see suggested course of action.

CEILINGS:

This dream has three meanings (choose one). (1) Your dream is symbolic of your subconscious mind, your mental activity just below the level of awareness. Your dream was sent to bring awareness to the dreamer of your prophetic ability, which you are unaware. Dreamer, your thoughts, considerations, perceptions, learning, and/or reasoning have given you pro phetic abilities. Your prophetic gifting is beginning to awaken. Now, you may begin to use your prophetic abilities, confidently, to help others. As you are naturally endowed with this ability, freely help others, without thought of recompense. Additio nally, make sure your reasoning are founded on the certainty of the Word of God, in other words, keep a level head, remain practical, stay within biblical guidelines, and you will fare well. (2) Ceiling crumbling, falling down, or leaking: This choice has three parts (choose one). (a) Dreamer, the main deliberations you are thinking about and considering carefully, including your personal beliefs and judgments, these weighing's are not sound, nor are they spiritually edifying or fulfilling, nor can they ever be. This is why you are beginning to question the reality of God, and your own personal belief system. In reality, your dark practices have depleted you spiritually, emotionally, and physically, and have blocked and impaired you from perceiving truth. The dark prince of this world has a demonically blinding influence over your soul, to keep you from seeing the light of the gospel of Jesus, the Messiah. Favorably, a spark of life remains hidden inside of you, and there awaits you a spiritual resurrection, according to God's grace. You will very shortly begin to experience, if not already, a paradigm shift in your core beliefs a nd spirituality. You are approaching new and deeper dimensions. Dreamer is counseled to trust in Jesus, the risen Messiah, and the gift of divine sight will provide an inner radiance within you that comes from Elohim alone. Dreamer, Jesus loves you; thus, He is petitioning you to accept Him, for you are valuable in His eyes. See suggested course of action. (b) Dreamer is unaware that you are allowing the "spirit of fear" to cause you to lose your identity (the individual characteristics by which the dreamer is known or is recognized by), and to terrorize you. It has become your own personal terrorist. Read and understand Romans 8:15, 2 Timothy 1:7. No, you do not have mental health issues, you are not crazy, nor are you having a nervous breakdown. This demon, this spirit of fear, has come to terrorize you in your thoughts, e.g., when you are paranoid, sleeping with a knife or gun under your pillow, when you are afraid, when you hesitate, when you are insecure, when you are impatient, when you are confused, when panic comes, when your thoughts are filled with worry, when you are uneasy and unsure, when despair and depression find you, when stress comes, when you are full of apprehension, when your thoughts forecast only doom and gloom, when you are restless, when you are frightful, when you are full of dread, when are anxious, when you are nervous, and when you feel hopeless. You will find this demon in every phobia. Question to journal: What would it feel like if all of your fears were suddenly released from you at one time? Pause and feel that. Bible story, there was that herd of pigs that Legion was cast into, and these pigs found their thoughts to be so unbearable that they all ran off a cliff to commit suicide, because they could not bear what had been unleashed upon them (Matthew 8:28-34, Mark 5:1-20, Luke 8:26-39). This is what the spirit of fear oftentimes leads to, if embraced wholly. On the other hand, the man whom, the devils were suddenly released from was found sitting, clothed, healed, and in his right mind. Now I say to you, that before you can move forward, fear must be cast out and renounced. Therefore, dreamer, earnestly renounce the insidious voice of the devil. The spirit of fear is adversarial to the Word of God that says all things will work together for good, to those who love God, and are called accord ing to His purpose. For, if you truly can believe the Word of God, it will change all the rules that darkness has established in your heart and mind. If you will daily come away and pray, then God will heal you of all things, only come with much prayer and spiritual fasting. The spiritual fast is that time of waiting when you are praying and asking the Lord to come and perform that which only He can perform. Similar to a literal fast, during this time you must abstain, but from any counsel or thoughts that tempt you to put your hand on the matter, or to turn you away from waiting on the Lord. During this time of waiting, you simply need to continue in prayer and be still. Then you will hear and know that only God's love is able to break the curse of darkness from over your mind, body, and spirit. Warning, it will be during your spiritual fast that weaknesses, such as unbelief, doubt, fear, pride, arrogance, will come forth to tempt you to eat the counsel of their lies, rather than to wait for the Lord to come to deliver, heal, help, save, reveal, and/ or guide. Wait on the Lord, for He is faithful to come, and again I say wait. If urged by God, declare a one, two, or three day fast without food. See suggested course of action. (c) If you are an unbeliever (one who has no religious beliefs, a non-religious person, or one who has no religious faith or belief in Jesus Christ, or one who does not embrace a personal relationship with Jesus Christ, at present). Jesus loves you, thus, He is petitioning you to acc ept Him as your personal Savior, for you are valuable in His eyes. The first step in receiving Him as your personal Savior is repentance (see in the Holy Bible, Acts 2:37-41). Repentance is seeking pardon for having done something awry, and for having hurt someone, and expressing sincere feelings of regret and brokenness. To Jesus pray, Psalm 51:1-19. Moreover, if you will accept the Heavenly Father's Words, via the Bible, and store up His principles, and accept His ways and means, turni ng your ear to wisdom and applying your heart to understanding, calling out for insight and crying aloud for discernment, Jesus will meet you. This, coupled with a lifestyle of prayer and fasting, followed by appropriate application of wisdom, and you will know the Messiah, Jesus Christ, intimately, and find the knowledge of God you seek. For the Lord gives wisdom and from His mouth comes knowledge and understanding. Then you will understand what is right and just and fair –every good path. When wisdom enters your heart and knowledge becomes sweet to your soul, discretion will protect you, understanding will guard you, and His Truth will lead you. To deliver you from the ways of wickedness, and from demons whose words and ways are perverse, who causes you to walk in darkness gladly, whose paths are crooked and devious, causing you to leave straight paths (Proverbs 2:1-6, 9-15). This is one of God's covenant promises to you. Have faith in this. See suggested course of action.

COMMUNITY HALL, CONVENTION CENTER, OR FORUM (any public facility to meet for open discussion or programs):

Your dream exposes one, namely the dreamer, who has; conflicting attributes within, and is empty spiritually, yet, at the same time is full of good deeds. Dreamer, your good deeds, have little or no effect on your character and nature, and most importantly good deeds does not, effect a deep intimacy with Christ. Dreamer, demonic oppression has you acting "good" in public, and "foolish" in private. Thus, your dream addresses hypocrisy, in that the dreamer persists on "acting" better and godlier than you really are, while you refuse to reconcile yourself to your spiritual and moral responsibilities. Dreamer although you have the capacity to overreach yourself and to do and achieve things that are utterly incompatible with who and what you are at present, your true nature, your contradictory internal spiritual state, won't allow you to remain in those "truly good" places. You are the epitome of the cliché, "your gifts can take you where your character can't keep you". That is to say, although you may be prospering now, your dishonesty, hatefulness, bitterness, and an unforgiving and unloving attitude, will eventually bring ruin and desolation upon your head. A reconciling of yourself to your spiritual and moral duties is required of you at this time (Luke 17:10), for the Lord your God has brought you into a good land. If no change, the land the Lord your God has brought you too will be in jeopardy of lost or ruin. See suggested course of action.

JAIL, PRISON, FORTRESS, BARRIERS, OR INCARCERATION (any places of confinement, includes Prison camp):

This dream has three meanings (choose one). (1) First question, is dreamer actually in any kind of illegal trouble? Your dream may be a Prophetically Simple Dream (see Chapter One: The 60th Part of Prophecy). Whereas, the dreamer is warned to cease any illegal or illicit activity that you may be involved with (e.g. any activity prohibited by law, such as illegal handling of drugs, money, or weapons, prostitution, embezzlement, thievery on any level, stalking, or any other criminal minded, under-handed activity). Handle the situation appropriately by surrendering, first to God and then to others, if necessary. You are advised to yield to relevant persons or surrender to the appropriate authorities, especially if any illegal activity is an issue within the dreamer's life. For God will not deliver you from that which you refuse to acknowledge as wicked. Moreover, in your situation, especially if you are truly guilty, prayer requests for "mercy", instead of "justice", is appropriate. For justice will convict you to a long-term sentence, whereas, mercy will set you free, or at least reduce a sentence. Nonetheless, if any of the preceding is happening, your dream is a first step intervention and an alarm. Re-consider your activity as harmful, hurtful, illegal, and life threatening, at present. See suggested course of action. (2) Your dream denotes a leader, possibly the dreamer, who sabotages positive ministry opportunities presented by others, because of your covetousness, ignorance, jealously, and/or spite. Those whom God has placed under you are there to support the ministry God has purposed for you. Unfortunately, because of your own shortsightedness, and extreme jealously of those who perform in an excellent way, with their hearts on enhancing "your" ministry. You deliberately undermine their efforts, with the intent on hindering, disrupting, and damaging their efforts. This is akin to one, male or female, who tears down their own home foolishly, destructively, and without cause (loosely based on Proverbs 14:1). Dreamer, do not be negligent to repent and learn to "know yourself", for your slackness will cause those, you are purposely sent to, within your ministry, to become non-productive, and this will prove very unprofitable for you, first relationally with Christ Jesus, spiritually, financially, and physically. See suggested course of action. (3) Release or Escape from any place of confinement: Your dream denotes some level of freedom, or a conditional release from some type of confinement, condition, or unwanted control, is available to the dreamer, now. If the dreamer chooses to, seriously commit to a lifestyle of right living, based upon God's revealed precepts of morality and righteousness, freedom from bondage will be yours, and should be expected. For he or she who Christ sets free is truly free. Particularly, you are free to separate from those who would have you bound to legalistic ceremonies, regulations, traditions, or relationships, or from anyone who hinders spiritual and emotional clarity. Additionally, dreamer make it your habit to speak and act like those who shall be judged by the law of liberty, see James 2:12, 13. Moreover, if we live in the Spirit, let us also walk by the Spirit. Let us not become conceited, provoking one another, envying one another (Galatians 5:25). See suggested course of action.

EATERY (Bakery, Deli, Fast Food Place, Lounge, Night Club, Pizzeria, Pub, Restaurant, Sports Bar, any building where people go to eat and drink):

Question, where was the dreamer, what type of eatery? See one of the following.

Bakery: Dreamer you are in the presence of one, considered a great leader and one who is considered financially rich. Although he or she presents as benevolent, philanthropic, and good-hearted, this person is nefarious. Thus, your dream comes to forewarn, and to caution the dreamer, that this person's behavior will cause a spirit of animosity within you, from which you will need spiritual and emotional restoration. Therefore, regard carefully all "gifts" received from him or her, for there are many "strings attached" to his or her giving. Dreamer, within the spiritual realms, the lender, or "giver", is always in a higher place than the borrower or receiver. Thus, because of the person's villainous "ego", he or she will make you feel confused, embarrassed, foolish, incapable, and/or unsettled. For this person will openly insinuate that you lack the ability, character, and/or strength, required to do something or that you're not good enough to function or perform adequately. At their worst, they will make you an object of scorn and contempt in front of others, and cause them to lose confidence in you. Consequently, you will begin to experience a strong feeling of ill will, which will lead to active hostility, and a noticeable deterioration of your intellectual functions, marked by mental disorientation. It would be wise, especially at present, to reject the gift and learn a lesson. See Proverbs 23:1-8. See suggested course of action.

Deli or Fast Food Place or Pizzeria: Dreamer, your wisdom at this moment in your life is temporal. It is worldly and is of no eternal value. Dreamer is counseled to take inventory of what you believe, and why, and to become clear about your beliefs. You cannot worship man and God; this is a conflict of interest. You are advised to use biblical and godly wisdom to take inventory, regularly, of your sense of right and wrong, and religious principles and beliefs, to make sure that they are based on the infallible Word of God and not on sensual desires. See suggested course of action.

Nightclub, Lounge, Pub, or Sports Bar: Dreamer, you are not free from the consequences of your choices. If your true intent is on doing God's will, reaping prosperity, experiencing genuine joy, and most importantly inheriting eternal life, yo u will have to practice restricting yourself in all things (weaning yourself from sensual appetites). This includes your diet, activities, relationships, associations, friendships, partying, and your lack of Christian fellowship. Dreamer, in order to reach any level of proficiency within ministry, and within a career, you must bring your appetites and sensual desires under subjection, sacrificing fleshy satisfaction, during your days of preparation and grounding. You will need to lay aside every obstacle that hinders y ou and causes you to forfeit God's principles, including laziness, that you might reach the point where you are capable of accomplishing your mission and that you might live sagaciously and properly. See suggested course of action.

Restaurant (a place where you sit down and are served, non-fast food service): Dreamer you are entering into a season within your life that will prepare you spiritually for the visitation of the Lord in your individual life. During this time, you will experience His love and presence, as you've never known it before. For, He is saying to you, "I will teach you godly wisdom". You will receive direct insight of divine truth. You will come to know, without a doubt, that God is the true source of your strength and wisdom, and He is your sufficiency. As a result, a greater love for self, family, and others will begin to manifest, affecting wholeness within your life. Be available to Him and seize the moments and opportunities as they are presented, especially an opportunity for you to advance your education, with a focus on teaching.

ENTRYWAYS OR ENCLOSURES (Doors, Entrances, Fences, Gates, Palisades, Porch, Portal, Stoop, or Veranda, or any entrance attached to the exterior of a building or structure):

Generally, entryway attached to the exterior of a building or structure denotes a belief system, and its creed, is being contemplated or embraced by the dreamer, as a possible way of living. Your dream is also sent to engender an awareness of God's wisdom, healing, and faithfulness that are before the dreamer, at present, and/or to engender an awareness o f some kind of ministry that may be initiated now. In addition, was the entryway or enclosure beautiful, broken down, rusted, narrow, or wide? What kind of entryway or enclosure was it? See one of the following.

Doors (incl. doorbell): This dream has six meanings (choose one). (1) Closed Door or Locked Out or Door closed in your face (unable to enter a building for any reason): The dreamer is refusing to pay attention to the alarms, danger signs, and warning bells you have been receiving, forewarning of imminent danger, physically and spiritually. You have previously been extensively warned, and now warned via your dream. Thus, your dream was sent as a stern rebuke and serious warning. It exposes one, the dreamer, who is regarded as an arrogant person. Dreamer, it is written within Holy Writ; the arrogant have no place before the Lord (Psalm 5:5). Even more, dreamer, you lack the knowledge that prevents one from perishing; you have been very unwise in your words and deeds. You have not "invested" in that which illuminates the mind, body, and soul, spiritually and physically, but you have despised the Word of God, and have trusted in oppression and perversity. Rebellious ly, you are unwilling to hear the instructions of the Lord. You tell those who speak truth to you, do not speak truth, but tell me smooth things, and teach me lies and illusions. I don't want to hear no more about the Holy One of Israel (Isaiah 30:9-13). Consequently, danger is approaching, even near your doors. The beginning, development, arrival, or manifestation of something large (significant in scope, extent, or effect) is about to happen within your life, in a threatening way. This re buke is only a precursor of even worse judgments that will come later, if you do not abandoned and change your ways. God is not condemning you, He's holding out His Hand of Hope, giving you an opportunity to start anew. Let the wicked forsake his way, God wants to pardon (Isaiah 55:7-13, Matthew 7:17-23, Luke 6:43-45). Your dream is to warn a rebellious person, in the spirit of grace, to see if you will yet be worked upon, and change your mindset, or else to leave you inexcusable, in your accusatio ns against God, because of your ruin (e.g. continually plundered, seized, and disfavored, also see Jeremiah 9:7-9; Zechariah 13:9; Matthew 23:37-39; Revelation 3:15-21). Dreamer, if you earnestly change your ways, you will be healed from your present condition and pardoned from the guilt previously mentioned. Dreamer, humbly seek to restore your relationship with God. For the Door of God allows for only the humble of spirit to enter. Prayer and repentance is the first step. See suggested course of action. (2) Narrow and Wide Door or Gate (if width, not height, of door or gate was highlighted within your dream): See Matthew 7:12-14. (3) Opened door: Dreamer will be presented with the opportunity, and the wherewithal, to do, and complete, what you need to finish, that you may progress upward, spiritually and naturally. Note, and consider very carefully the following. Dreamer, it is up to you to be ready to seize the opportunities God is putting before you to advance you in s ome manner. The spiritual conditions, which must be complied with, in order to receive from the Kingdom of God, are that you must have faith, be perceptive, be prepared, and remain humble. Dreamer, you will begin to experience His benevolence speedily, via His servants. One other thing; remember your reputation and life was given back to you because of His grace, mercy, kindness, and love for you. It is absolutely nothing you have done. Give God all the glory, and glorify not yourself thi s time. See suggested course of action. (4) Walk In through a door: To walk in through any door denotes that the dreamer has submissively, and wisely, allowed him or herself to be broken to the point that you now embrace humility and contriteness. You will soon have a visitation from the Lord. Anticipate this with great gladness, and if you have never received the Holy Spirit within, you will, and with the initial evidence of having received the Holy Spirit (Acts 2:4). (5) Walk Out a door: Your dream denotes the dreamer will be leaving a space, or letting go of someone or something that you may go forward to a place where you will be used to minister to others. Dreamer you are entering into a season within your life that will prepare you spiritually, for a very personal visitation of the Lord. During this time, you will experience His love and presence, as you've never known it before. For, He is saying to you, "I will teach you godly wisdom". You will receive direct insight of divine truth. You will come to know, without a doubt, that God is the true source of your knowledge, strength, and wisdom, and He is your sufficienc y. As a result, a greater love for self, family, and others will begin to manifest, affecting wholeness within your life. Be avail able to Him and seize the moments and opportunities as they are presented, especially an opportunity for you to advance your education, with a focus on teaching. (6) Doorbell, Doorknocker (ring a doorbell or knock on a door): First, see Matthew 7:7-11. Then, couple this with one of the following, considering what was on the other side of the door (choose one). (a) If there was a welcoming, peaceful, and beautiful atmosphere on the other side of the door, your dream denotes that the dreamer will receive what you are expecting from God, and you will be goodly recompensed. As well, an invitation to a place of importance will be attached to this recompense. For example, if you have an invitation, bid, or contract before you, you will be invited to receive your reward, contract, or bid, or if you have legal papers before you, you will receive what you're expecting. Keep the faith, for this too will "come to pass". (b) If there was a dark, foreboding, and ominous atmosphere on the other side of the door, your dream denotes that the dreamer will not receive what you are expecting from God, and you will become disappointed at an unexpected outcome. See James 1:5-8, this is your state of mind, now. See suggested course of action.

Fences or Palisades (any barrier that serves to enclose an area): If any type of fence or palisade is highlighted within your dream, your dream denotes a necessity to deal with the moral impurities, the uncleanness, the evil deed, and/or the guilt, within your life. Dreamer is urged, and with a sense of urgency, to purify your character, namely in the area dealing with the deeds of the flesh - dishonesty, adultery, sexuality, hostility, feuding, vendettas, grudges, unfriendliness, strife, jealousy, outbursts of anger, disputes, dissensions, discord, drunkenness, carousing, or traits of these sorts (Galatians 5:19 -21). It is essential that you purify yourself by rejecting the sin, the influence that so easily overwhelms you. There is a need to be clean morally, and of a clear conscience. Read and understand, Ezekiel 33:12-16, and then repent. If your character and choices remains unchanged, the door will be left wide-open for even more chaos and negativity to manifest in your life. See suggested course of action.

Gates or Prison Bars: Generally, gates denote that knowledge is, or will be, imparted to the dreamer miraculously. Per the context of your dream, either that knowledge is godly imparted or demonic departed. With that, this dream has three meanings (choose one). (1) Beautiful Gate or Portal (walking, entering through a beautiful gate or portal) or If there is a beautiful, lighted, and welcoming atmosphere on the other side of that gate or portal: This choice has two parts (choose one). (a) Dreamer, you will increase in wisdom and knowledge, regarding godly spiritual truths or concepts you may be wrestling with, now. This increase will happen through personal experience and through a miraculous impartation that will be communicated via the Holy Spirit. Dreamer, because you are God's child according to grace, He wants to balance your understanding of things; effecting wholeness within your life. For you are now ready to receive the deepest measures of understanding, so that the enemy will no longer be able to manipulate your emotions so easily. The Paraclete is with you to help you throughout this entire process. Moreover, you will be used, if not already, to usher others into a totally new and higher level of spiritual awareness. Even amongst the "broken", a spark of life remains hidden, awaiting your particular ministry, your unique way of presenting the gospel. You will appear when needed, and then disappear without thought of anything in return. Dreamer, by fulfilling your part and remaining humble, you will be worthy of your wage. You will eat an d do very well, on this side of eternity, and inherit eternal life. Humility is the key to your success (requisite). Know the full meaning of the word and define your life by it. Additionally, this is your year of restoration, restitution, freedom, and fu llness of life. (b) If dreamer is seriously ill, meaning you have been declared by professional doctors as incurable, or if you are very advanced in years and your strength is failing, your dream is one of God's ways of breaking something to you gently, your dream is a notice; it symbolizes shortness of life. Dreamer, for someone who has met Jesus, we experience Him in the little graces, the big miracles, the ordinary days, and the curious moments. He is with us, leading us onward, even sharing our tears. This same God trustworthy in life, even when we are not, can be trusted at the ending of life. See suggested course of action. (2) Broken-down, Rusted Gate, Portal, or Prison Bars (walking, entering through a broken down, rusted, gate, portal, or prison bars) or If there was a dark foreboding ominous place on the other side of that gate or portal or prison bars: This choice has two parts (choose one).

(a) Dark and erroneous knowledge, the devil's so-called deep secrets (Revelation 2:20, 24), will be imparted into the dreamer. You will gain this knowledge through a supernatural imparting, demonically communicated. The knowledge gained will lead you to that dark ominous place on the other side of the gate, emotionally, spiritually, and if not aborted, eternally. See suggested course of action.
(b) If dreamer is seriously ill, meaning you have been declared by professional doctors as incurable. Dreamer, there is a great need for repentance, for your sickness is primarily due to sinful and wicked behaviors and evil practices, thus a change in thoughts, actions, deeds, and beliefs is needed, and with a sense of urgency. Even if dreamer is very advanced in years and your strength is failing, in either situation, dreamer needs to first, call for the elders of a church, for it is through their prayers of faith and anointing of oil upon you that your sins will be forgiven and that spiritual and physical healing might occur[36]. Again, seek medical attention as soon as possible, that perhaps physical healing might be bestowed. This is a true saying, thus it is time to have faith in God. Additionally, it is always a good time to get your house and papers in order (e.g. insurances, bequeaths, untold truths that need to be said), and always a good time t o gather family together for prayer, support, wisdom, and truthfulness (Ecclesiastes 12:6). See suggested course of action.

Hallway, Corridor, or Portal: This dream has two meanings (choose one). (1) To dream of walking down, or just being in, a hallway or corridor denotes transition, and it symbolizes the dreamer's walk of righteousness and obedience to God. Dreamer, you've come through great trials and tribulations, and God has bottled up every one of your tears. Favorably, you will now be recompensed accordingly, for your endurance and diligence, regarding God and His Kingdom. Dreamer, your life's storms are over, you can now begin to rebuild. Your life as you know it, will begin to transition, and situations will becom e easier and better. (2) If hallway or corridor was in bad condition, in need of repair, dark, foreboding, ominous, this denotes health issues, for females, within your pelvic cavity, fallopian tubes, or uterus, or for males, within your prostate or abdo men area. Seek medical attention, now, so that any serious health condition might be diagnosis early, treated, and healed

Porch, Stoop, or Veranda: This dream is to engender an awareness of God's wisdom, healing, and faithfulness that are before you at present. Two things: (1) recognize your time of visitation of the Lord, be watchful and prayerful, (2) and once healed, go, and sin no more, lest a worse thing come upon you (see John 5:1-14). Don't know what the sin factor is that has effected such great affliction, difficulty, or distress within your life? Consider all the people, places, backgrounds, and activity highlighted within your dream. For example, what activity was highlighted? Was anyone sitting on the porch/stoop with you? Was dreamer mopping, or sweeping the porch? Kept within context of your dream, those other references highlighted may also be points of relevance. It will be within the totality of those symbols that you will find your answer. See index or relevant category for more information. See suggested course of action.

In addition, the following is a common word, expression, or usage (e.g. slang or cliché), or a 'probable' that is metaphorically represented by an entrance, porch, or veranda:

- This symbolizes one who is undecided, contemplative, uncommitted, or withdrawn. See suggested course of action.

HEALTH CARE FACILITY (e.g. Asylum, Clinic, Hospice, Hospital, Nursing Home, Psychiatric Hospital, Rehab, Sanatorium, Veterinary Office, any facility where patients receive some manner of medical treatment):

This dream has three meanings (one or all may apply). (1) If dreamer was a patient in a health care facility, or if illness is a concern within your life at present, dreamer, you will recover from this, and live. Moreover, dreamer has a sense of duty an d respect to others. You are one who voluntarily offers help or sympathy in times of trouble, one who demonstrates mercy, and truly loves his or her neighbor. You are the proverbial "Good Samaritan" (Luke 10:25-37). You have learned to handle much; therefore, much will be given you. His grace is abounding towards you, and His promises will come quickly and in full measure. What are His promises to you? Dreamer, recall His promises to you. Expect all of this (spiritual resurrection, grace abound ing, His promises to you, full measure); therefore, wait on it. Warning, these great blessings, can result in an excessive concern for your image, the false imitations of this world, pride, and vanity. These attributes will keep you from being in the right pl ace, at the right moment, to hear God through the ears of faith. Therefore, humble yourself before the True and Living God and accept His blessings of healing, help, and restoration in a balanced manner. This great favor is shown you because of God's great faithfulness towards you. You will live to testify of God's great love, everlasting kindness, and of His great faithfulness. (2) Dreamer, do not entangle yourself with affairs, concerns, or situations, so much so that you become hindered, diverted, or drawn away, from your relationship with Jesus, and from the responsibilities of your Christian duties "your calling", because of them. As a Christian, you are a soldier of Jesus Christ; thus, you fight for His cause, and against His enemies, including y our own lustful flesh. As a soldier in the army of God, you must be faithful to Him, and persevere in His cause and in your calling. So, avoid worldly entanglements, pray, consult God, and your spiritual leaders, deny self, endure hardness, be self-controlled, and be alert. Read, understand, and embrace, Ephesians 6:10-18, for this is to you now. Moreover, bring every thought, the intents of your mind and will, into obedience of Christ. Your pace of spiritual progress and promotion will be according to your faith and obedience to God's will over your life personally. Additionally, dreamer, love God so completely that you will never forsake His service for any reason. (3) Dreamer, there are those amongst you, close significant others, who are diametrically opposed to holiness and have essentially separated themselves from God. It is said of them that their feet descend into death, and they are ultimately responsible for bringing death into their own life's situations. This is also said of you, by some, not most. Favorably, as your dream also references election according to grace, expectancy, God's faithfulness, grace abounding, fullness, full measure, full recompense, full reward, holiness, and redemption of those who have fallen away, a spark of life remains hidden inside of you, and in them, because both, you and they are God's children. There awaits you, and them, a spiritual resurrection, according to God's grace, expect it, and wait on it. If necessary, see suggested course of action.

HOTEL OR INN (any establishment where transients or travelers pay for lodging, meals, or other services, includes Bed and Breakfast, Boarding House, Brothel, Love Hotel, Casino Hotel, Dormitory, Guest House, Inn, Hotel, Motel, any Resort).

To dream of being in any establishment where transients or travelers pay for lodging, meals, or other services, includes bed and breakfast, boarding house, brothel, love hotel, or any building of ill repute, casino hotel, dormitory, guest house, inn, hotel, motel, any resort, see one of the following.

Brothel or Love Hotel: Your dream exposes the dreamer's actions, which are in total disregard of God's principles, precepts, and ways. Your behavior hinders the sanctification process, thus, reckoning you as a rebellious child of God, aka a "backslider". You disagree with the Word of God, and your great grumbling, complaining, and murmuring, are clear indicators of your backslidden state. Dreamer, your attitude will prevent you from achieving your goals, having forfeited purpose for foolishness. There is a need for repentance. Repentance is seeking pardon and expressing sincere feelings of regret and brokenness for having done something awry and/or for having hurt someone, see 2 Corinthians 7:10, 11. To individuals, a phone call or a letter of apology is a good place to start. To Jesus pray, Psalm 51, this coupled with prayer, fasting, and follow- thru with appropriate application of wisdom, can conceivably avert some of the repercussions of your choices. When a man or woman genuinely return to God in love and surrender, your deliberate transgressions become like actual merits (also see Luke 7:37-50). Because, the realization of your distance from God, resulting from your transgressions (Isaiah 59:2), becomes the motivating force to return to God with a passion even greater than that of someone who has never sinned in such a manner (or never left his Father's house, Acts 9:1-30). However, until you own up to your rebellious behavior, repent, stop the grumbling, complaining, and murmuring and become submissive, obedient, and useful within God's Kingdom again, you will continue to decrease, and become weaken in spirit and body. In addition, your actions and behavior, that which is secret, and previously known only to a few, will become public information. See suggested course of action.

Casino or Resort: This dream has two meanings (choose one). (1) Dreamer, noticeably conflicted, you no longer know who, nor what you truly believe in. God has not changed, you have. You have lost your spiritual identity, and have closed your mind to spiritual realities that bring genuine truth, calmness, composure, contentment, mellowness, peacefulness, and tranquility. A great change is necessary, for the sake of ministry, for the sake of your prosperity, for the sake of your natural and spiritual life. Dreamer, God's Word, has two sides, a "Light" side, which is a manifestation of God's providential care towards His people, namely believers, who believe and heed His Word (Psalm 36:9), and another side, which is put to use, against sin, and the evildoer, or unrepentant (1 Corinthians 1:18). The side that is revealed to you is your choice. Thus, this warning must not be undermined by notions that presuppose, the possibility of an actual loss of a God-given ministry, your prosperity, or even life itself is not. Favorably, thank God for His patience, long-suffering, and grace (the free and unmerited favor and beneficence of God), while you get things decent and in order. Dreamer, grace is before you once more. See suggested course of action. (2) Dreamer, you are entering into a year that is meant to prepare you spiritually for the visitation of the Lord in your individual life. Beginnings and endings, diversity, and growth, will be constant elements in your life. You will learn to let go of anything or anyone in order to further your spiritual growth. Moreover, uncover, practice, and become skilled in the talents you were born with, lest you be found fruitless in the Kingdom of God, and be cast aside or replaced. Neither of which will be profitable for you. No longer, take chances with your spiritual life, do not deceive yourself; if you think that you are wise, become a fool that you might become wise. For the wisdom of this world is folly with God. For it is written, "He catches the wise in their craftiness", and again, "The Lord knows the thoughts of the wise, that they are futile." So let no one boast in his or her ability (1 Corinthians 3:18-21). Dreamer, God has set before you today life and good, death and evil. If you obey the commandments of the Lord your God that He commands you today; particularly, by loving the Lord your God, by walking in His ways, by embracing His commandments, His statutes, and His rules; according to Holy Writ. Then you shall live and multiply, and the Lord your God will bless you in the land that the Lord has allotted you as an inheritance, which you will soon take possession. However, if your heart turns away, and you will not hear, but are drawn away to worship other gods and serve them, I declare to you today, that you shall surely perish. You shall not live long in the land that you are going over to enter and possess. Moreover, heaven and earth are called to witness against you today that God has set before you, life, and death, blessing and a curse. Therefore, choose life that you and your offspring may live, loving the Lord your God, obeying His voice and holding fast to Him, for He is your life and length of days that you may dwell in the land that the Lord has allotted you as an inheritance. Dreamer, what is required of you today is not too hard for you, nor does it include unreachable objectives (Deuteronomy 30:11-20). If this message is heeded, within one year, you will experience God's love and presence, as you've never known it before. See suggested course of action.

Hotel or Motel or Inn or Bed and Breakfast or Boarding House or Dormitory or Guesthouse:
Dreamer, no one will ever love God and his or her neighbor with any measure of pure, spiritual love, who is not a partaker of grace. Christ gave an instance of a poor man in distress, relieved by a "good" neighbor, (Luke 10:32-37, parable of the Good Samaritan). This poor man fell among thieves, who left him about to die of his wounds. He was slighted by those who should have been his friends, and was cared for by a stranger, a person, who himself was despised and detested. Dreamer, this person is you, and this is how you've been treated by some, although not all. The enemy has robbed you, stole from you, and destroyed (damaged you, cast you down, and wounded or violated you emotionally, spiritually, and physically), via some people, perhaps even family members, and some Christians. In spite of, Jesus had compassion on you during your trials and tribulations. For, when you stop and think about, what the Lord has already done for you, and how far He's brought you; think about His goodness. Think about His hedge of protection around you; the provisions and ways He's made for you, the doors He's

open for you. Think about you're in your right mind, and how the Lord is blessing you right now. As well, you've been given the honor of knowing that you can boldly come before His Throne with prayer, and that He takes joy in you, let this be your contentment; a sweet sound in your ear. Moreover, from this moment on, the Lord has someone, a wonderful person, and a "good Samaritan". This person is sent especially to you for support. This person will even more, demonstrate the kindness and love of our Savior toward you, via genuine friendship. On another vein, dreamer, the Lord is asking something of you. The Lord is now asking you to use what the enemy has done, as a tool, as a testimony, to reach those whom you are purposed to reach. It is your duty, in your places, and according to your ability, to help those in difficult situations, and to relieve those in distress and in need. For, the true Christian has the law of love written in his or her heart; therefore, serve, support, and help others fr om a place of empathy and unconditional love, especially without regard to whether one is grateful of your kindness, or is able to repay the kindness (Matthew 5:46-48).

KITCHEN, ANNEX, OR DINING AREA:

This dream has three meanings (choose one). (1) If dining area was clean, your dream denotes healing to one who has been suffering emotionally, especially with heart issues (physical or emotional). With that, dreamer, there is a struggle within you, between your old nature and your new nature, the leftovers of sin and the beginnings of grace. The carnal part of you is struggling against the spiritually renewed you. Your old nature is resisting everything that is spiritual and is opposing all the suggestions of the Holy Spirit and the ethical urgings of your conscience. This is spiritual circumcision of the heart. Fortunately, you are choosing to side with godly principles and to stand on your convictions. Now, the old has gone, and the new has come (2 Corinthians 5:17). Dreamer, you will have success overcoming old things; and there will be joy about your success, especially publicly. Additionally, due to the intensity of your struggle, one of God's messengers is sent to give you the support needed at this time. Be aware that the new person within your midst may be that messenger. (2) I f dining area was not clean, unfortunately, dreamer is choosing to side with ungodly principles, resisting the suggestions of the Holy Spirit and the ethical urgings of your conscience. With that said, this is necessary to say, dreamer, you're well, now; therefore, stop sinning so that something worse doesn't happen to you (John 5:14, James 4:17). Additionally, there is a need to give or supply what is desired or needed, via support, food, or sustenance to yourself, to your family, and to your ministry. By this, yo u aid your own body, mind, and soul. See suggested course of action. (3) Physically kitchens, annex, or any dining areas may point to a literal health issue within the heart or lungs, or the digestive tract, or some serious mental or emotional health problems. It is suggested that dreamer seek professional medical attention as soon as possible. If area was clean, also, see choice #1. Nonetheless, dreamer seek medical attention as soon as possible, and call for the elders of your church, for it is thro ugh their prayers of faith and anointing of oil upon you that sin is forgiven and "spiritual" healing bestowed, and perhaps physical healing.[36] This is a true saying, thus it is time to have faith in God. See the following.

Cabinets, Cupboards: Dreamer needs to read, fully understand, and embrace Philippians 4:11-13(NIV): I am not saying this because I am in need, for I have learned to be content whatever the circumstances. I know what it is to be in need, and I know what it is to have plenty. I have learned the secret of being content in any and every situation, whether well fed or hungry, whether living in plenty or in want. I can do all this through him who gives me strength.

Pots and Pans: Even now, there will be a real and noticeable difference between your present low and afflicted state and your succeeding prosperity. There will be a beautiful state of quiet and peace for you, and a level of holiness (spiritual richness) in your life, per God's declaration over you. Your low and afflicted state has highlighted the difference between the light and dark parts of your life, effecting humility, and a more sympathetic, tolerant, broad -minded, and compassionate spirit within you (Proverbs 15:33; 22:4). Dreamer, it is your role in life to inspire and motivate. Your sympathetic, tolerant, broad- minded, and compassionate point of view, has given you the potential to inspire others, and you are capable of much human understanding. You have a lot to give to others; so, you must work well with people. By working well with others, you will become greatly respected, even by those who have judged you poorly; and there are those who consider you of low social position, perhaps poor, at present. Nonetheless, people will take refuge in your wisdom (Proverbs 21:2). Stay focus on positive projects, those that lift one up to God, edify the Body of Believers, and withhold not your hand in the day of your prosperity.

Stove: A stove represents a spiritual heart issue that needs attention; couple this with one of the following (both may apply). (1) Dreamer, you are on the brink of success, happiness, and prosperity, and your "sensing" or "knowing" that you are becoming a celebrated man or woman of God has triggered your "self-sabotaging" behavior, which has also open the door for a spirit of fear to gain power over your emotions. You will find this demon (the spirit of fear) in every phobia, and in every "self-sabotaging" behavior. Read and understand Romans 8:15, 2 Timothy 1:7. Additionally, go and make an offering of $20.00 to your church, and consider this money an offering unto the Lord. (2) A stove also denotes the screams of an unhealed heart's cry for inner healing. The thoughts that overwhelm your mind, do reveal (or prophesy) a debilitating physic al or spiritual condition. You are so often, focused on your outer world that often times the outer does not match the inner. The Holy Spirit, by way of your dream, has placed into the forefront that which you've been avoiding and is revealing the truth of your heart. Thus, your dream is sent to convict you of your current path, to give you a peek at some hidden motives you have, and provide you with new direction, if you would but heed the warnings. Dreamer, when you genuinely attempt to understand why God has allowed certain situations to happen to you, and you own up to your own turbulent and highly emotional issues, you will be release from those situations, and healing and deliverance will commence that very same day. Dreamer, go and pray, seeking help regarding your heart issues, you need healing, especially spiritually. See suggested course of action.

Table (includes Coffee Table, Counter Tops, Dinettes, or Kitchen-Island): This dream has four meanings (choose one). (1) Unmarried female: Dreamer, patience is still needed, for a little while longer, for the "right" mate to appear, be still he will come. Unfortunately, and the reason for your dream, namely to bring awareness that the dreamer's deep longings and yearnings, for an intimate relationship, has open the door, for someone who is insincere in his dealings with people, especially by being outwardly friendly but secretly disloyal, to attempt to approach your life; he is demonically led. Dreamer, if anyo ne comes to you denying Jesus is the Christ, do not take him into your home, or give him words of love, for if you do, you also take in his evil works. Note; there are a number of false teachers who have gone out into the world, who do not give witness that Jesus Christ came in the flesh; therefore, keep watch over yourself, lest you be overtaken with his foolish talk and teachings, by whom, others have been completely overturned. While this person is a legalist, he is not ruled by the law of God, and he tak es money for teaching things, which are not right (Titus 1:10-13, 2 Peter 2:1-3, 2 John 1:7-13). Dreamer, although this person will appear charming, he will take you for your money, simply because he does not like to work, he is jealous and he is violent. His character is one of extreme haughtiness, presumptuousness, pride, and self-assuredness in the very negative sense of the word. All are signs that his heart is hardened. If this person is a cleric of some kind, specially a Christian deacon, past or, teacher, or some other kind of minister, seriously and sensibly, in a reasonable and intelligent manner, consider his behavior, past and present, and the fruit thereof. Is his behavior akin to false teachers or deceivers? Does his behavior mirror that of the referenced scriptures? Nevertheless, no matter his cleric title, do not accept this male in your life, as he is more violent than the one before him that was in your life. See suggested course of action. (2) Your dream denotes God's provision, as well; it encourages the dreamer to strive for a more intimate fellowship with your Savior, your family, and with other believers. Dreamer, God is completely restoring things materially and spiritually within your life and in the lives of those immediately connected to you. Because of your brokenness over your past sins, you have opened the door to contriteness and humility. It is through this door that an act of kindness will come very soon. With that said, dreamer there is a need to understand the unadulterated and full meaning of divine providence, get a bible dictionary, and respect the meaning. For, there is also a need to recognize, acknowledge, and respect divine providence, God's absolute control over the affairs of humankind, and to renounce the belief that humans are in complete control (see Job 9:12, Isaiah 14:27; 43:13). There is a difference between divine providence and the will of humankind. Although you have the power of free choice, you should not think that your accomplishments are purely of your own volition. It is God, who gives you the capability and strength to achieve success. This is especially true of your struggles with your sinful tendencies, whether they manifest as a lack of concern or interest in t he things of God, a stubborn resistance to the will of God, or laziness. If it had not been for God's efforts on your behalf, you would not have been able to overcome any negative tendencies. He delivered you. Any achievements you've accomplished, any good deeds you've done, any fulfillment of God's will, was, and still is, dependent upon divine aid and guidance. One merely places his or her hand under the weight carried exclusively by God. Just say and truly believe, "I will exalt you, Go d, for you have lifted me up", and strive for a more intimate fellowship with your Savior. See suggested course of action. (3) Dreamer, in practicing Christian liberties, you are cautioned to beware of temptation and unbelief, and to be conscious of affiliation with demons, actually you are sitting and eating at the tables of demons. You cannot have part in both the Lord's Table and the table of demons. Dreamer, if anyone advocates the belief that all beings will be reconciled to God, including the devil and the fallen angels, they are mistaken (Matthew 25:41). As well as those who hold to the belief that Jesus, as one's Lord and Savior, has little or no impact on your personal lifestyle and values; that God has little interest in the way we live our lives. They are rejecting Christianity's core system of beliefs and practices (see John 3:16-21; 1 Corinthians 10:1-23; Hebrews 12:14; Revelation 20:1-15). Dreamer, if anyone denies Jesus is the Christ, do not take them into your home or give them words of acceptance, for if you do, you also take in their evil works (Titus 1:10-13, 2 Peter 2:1-3, 2 John 1:7-13). Note; Solomon's extraordinary gift of wisdom did not preserve him from falling into grievous and fatal errors; for he allowed his wives to practice their superstitions, worshipping images of wood or stone in sight of the very temple which, in early life, he had erected to the true God. He also allowed these foreign ideas to spread throughout the country (1 Kings 11:1-11); thus, partaking in their idolatry, aka sitting and eating at the tables of demons. It is also written within Holy Writ, "Do not those who eat the sacrifices participate in the altar? Am I implying then that a sacrifice offered to an idol is anything, or that an idol is anything? No, but the sacrifices of pagans (the spiritually unenlightened), are offered to demons, not to God, and I do not want you to be participants with demons. You cannot drink the cup of the Lord and the cup of demons too; you cannot have a part in both the Lord's Table and the table of demons. Are we trying to arouse the Lord's jealousy? Are we stronger than He is? (Ref. 1 Corinthians 10:18-22). Dreamer, if those that are in reputation for wisdom, honor, and for perpetuating the teachings of Christ, in anything set a bad example, they know not what great deal of harm they may do by it, particularly to those you minister too. One bad choice of a good person, may be more damaging to others than, twenty of a wicked man or woman. As well, one bad choice is hurtful to a good name; not only spoiling the goodness of it, but making it now, a name of ill-repute; base, disgraceful, low, scandalous, and wicked (see Ecclesiastes 10:1). See suggested course of action. (4) Dreamer, there is a need to check your theology. There is something missing in your belief system that has affected someone who is very close to you. It has caused them to seek God in other teachers, in other faces, and most are evil. Fortunately, that l ove one lead astray, because of you, will come home, embracing Jesus. Moreover, altruistic, goodhearted, and generous service to God and others is beneficial at this time. See suggested course of action.

LIVING ROOM, FAMILY ROOM, SITTING ROOM, LOUNGE ROOM (e.g. Employee's Lounge, Breakroom, TV Room, or Recreation Room, a relaxation room in a private residence, business, or institution):

Your dream symbolizes your interactions with others, namely family, friends, and close associates; also, other people will appear in these types of rooms within your dream. Persons depicted in the rooms of this category primarily represent aspects of the dreamer's character, and not necessarily, the person(s) depicted. This is also the way the dreamer appears to God, and some others. At times, and depending on the context of the dream, others may perhaps represent them sel f, see Note 3 or Note 4 of this category. Context will also point to other issues that may need consideration. Question to journal, who was in the living room or lounge area? Consideration to journal, describe one word that would describe that person or the common thread between persons within your dream. This is possibly a character trait, within the dreamer, that needs to be focus on. What were their actions, behaviors? For instance, if person(s) was argumentative, this may indicate the dreamer anger issue needs rectifying. If people were relaxed and "laid back", dreamer may, perhaps, need to spend quality time relaxing with family and friends. Another example, if, when dreamer walked into the area, and no one acknowledge your presence, perhaps dreamer is losing the respect of close significant others, here the question is why. Another example, if area needed cleaning and no cleaning was done, perhaps dreamer needs to "clean up" relevant relationships for the sake of the Kingdom, this coupled with interpretation within category, Cleaning (To do no cleaning). In addition, dreamer may consider category Working, Work Places, e.g. butler, housemaid, educator. See suggested course of action.

MARKET FACILITIES OR EMPLOYMENT FACILITIES (Department Store, Farmer's Market, Kiosks, Mall, Mini Market, Office Buildings, Supermarket, any mercantile establishment for the retail sale of goods or services):

Within the varied meanings of market, this category generally symbolize a transferring from one circumstance, situation, position, state, place, person, thing, to another, a type of "passing over", a transitioning. Additionally, the dreamer will also, need to consider one of the following six that is pertinent to your circumstance, situation, position, or state, at present. (1) Your dream denotes a pregnancy. (2) Dreamer, read, understand, and believe 1 John 4:1-6, this is wisdom for you to embrace, especially now, or in the very near future. For, there is one who is before you now, or who will be soon, whom you will need to discern wisely and separate truth from error. Establishing a new relationship with anyone at this point in your life will ne ed to be based upon, you and the new person, having the same or very similar beliefs in God that the relation ship might be edifying for all involved. Additionally, listen to your Heavenly Father's instructions, pay attention, and gain understanding. Do no t forsake God's teaching. Lay hold of God's Word with all your heart, keep His commands and you will live. Get wisdom, get understanding; do not forget God's Word or swerve from it. Do not forsake wisdom, and she will protect you; love her, and she will watch over you. Wisdom is supreme; therefore get wisdom. Though it cost all you have, get understanding. Esteem her, and she will exalt you; embrace her, and she will honor you. Listen, and, accept what is said to you now, and the years of your life will be many. God's Word will guide you in the way of wisdom and lead you along straight paths. See suggested course of action. (3) Dreamer, if co-signing for something is a situation that is before you now, dreamer, is counseled to consider the wisdom of Proverbs 11:15 and 17:18. See suggested course of action. (4) Dreamer is strongly counseled, to do not take a pledge in exchange for your property, e.g. reverse mortgage, and do not use your property for collateral, bail, simply, do not "put your property up" for nothing. If you do, you will lose your property, home, inheritance, and assets, and end up with nothing. See suggested course of action. (5) Dreamer is one, who is a seller of inferior products at highly inflated prices. This topic is one that God takes very seriously. Dreamer, you embrace the world's economic advice, as to how to succeed and profit financially while rejecting God's perspective, namely what should be avoided in order to be financially successful, both spiritually and naturally, and what is necessary. First lesson begins with how not to conduct your business, administratively, in an unjust and greedy manner. You are advised to balance expense and profit that you be not found charging exorbitant prices, especially for inferior products, to unwitting customers. This is thievery. See suggested course of action. (6) Your dream denotes the dreamer is being cleansed from sin. Moreover, seeing "the Blood", the angel of death will pass over you. So, consider it pure joy, whenever you face trials of many kinds, knowing that the testing of your faith deve lops perseverance, therefore, do not view them as an opportunity to run amok. Perseverance must finish its work that you may be mature and complete, lacking nothing. An honest acknowledgement of God's part in your circumstances will bring clarity, wholeness, strength of purpose, and closure to your present predicament. See suggested course of action.

MILITARY BUILDINGS (Barracks, Blockhouse, Bunker, Citadel, Dugout, any facility, residence, or structure connected to the armed forces, or any fortification or defensive stronghold structure, and any military structure where arms, ammunition, and other military equipment are stored, and any type of stronghold into which people could go for shelter during a battle):

This dream has two meanings (choose one). (1) Dreamer, there is a struggle within you, between your old nature and your new nature, the leftovers of sin and the beginnings of grace. The carnal part of you is struggling against the spiritually renewed you. Your carnal nature is resisting everything that is spiritual and is opposing all the suggestions of the Holy Spirit and the ethical urgings of your conscience. Fortunately, you are choosing to side with godly principles and your convictions. Thus, your dream was sent to encourage the dreamer. Dreamer, God's providential blessing is upon you to increase. Be mindful of your words and do not boast of your increase. Furthermore, due to the intensity of your struggle, one of God's messengers is sent to give you the support needed at this time. Be aware that the new person within your midst may be that messenger. Dreamer, all things will be made beautiful in their own time. Don't ever give up. (2) Your dream denotes one, namely the dreamer, who has a clever, quick mind, with the ability and vision to accomplish a great deal in a short period-of-time. Regrettably, this skill has lured you into a false sense of security. Erroneously assuming that nothing but good comes to yo u. Confessing that no one you know can compare with you, or even pretend to be equal with y ou. You've put confidence in your flesh, fearing no danger, living carelessly. You harbor wicked thoughts, is ruthlessly aggressive, determined, and persisten t, as well as greedily eager to steal from or destroy others for gain. God humbles the haughty and causes all his or her joy and laughter to cease (see Zephaniah 2:15). Your own conduct and actions have brought (or will bring) this upon you in some form or another. Favorably, in spite of all this, spiritual renewal is accessible to you now. Jesus is petitioning you to, cleanse the evil from your heart, humble yourself, and be saved. Dreamer, many lacking wisdom, courage, boldness, enthusiasm, weak in spirit and unfit for service, are healed, restored, and strengthened by grace (the free and unmerited favor and beneficence of God). If you are ready to acknowledge that, you are weak, and remain mindful of your weaknesses, and earnestly humble yourself, God will in an extraordinary way, increase your strength. For when we are weak, then we are strong in the Lord. The Lord is willing to help you, if you are willing to be helped, and to do your best, with a humble dependence upon Him. Rethink your attitude of pride and arrogance, and you will find that God will not fail you, and you will have grace sufficient for renewal of strength and anointing. See suggested course of action.

RELIGIOUS BUILDINGS (Basilica, Cathedral, Chapel, Church, Meeting House, Mosque, Monastery, Shrine, Synagogue, Temple, or any place of worship).

For Religious Residences, see subcategory Residential Buildings. Amongst the varied meanings of the many kinds of places of worship, any place acting as a place of worship, within your dreams, generally they symbolize your current spiritual health, and other spiritual affairs. Questions to journal: What condition was the building? For example, clean and beautifully adorned, well kept, or was it, deteriorated, in ruins, leveled to the ground, burned down, being reconstructed or remodeled? Was dreamer inside or outside of the building? With that, this dream has three meanings (choose one). (1) Your dream is a confirmation of two issues: (a) There will be presented to the dreamer, additional information, or proof that confirms or verifies that some pressing situation, before you now, is valid. (b) Favorably, the dreamer will experience some kind of promotion, and/or a cleric ordination, on some level. If a promotion or cleric ordination is expected, your dream denotes th at there will be an open acknowledgement, in the near future, that you, the dreamer, is successfully completing (or has successfully completed), a course, which God has you on. Moreover, divinely set aside for the priesthood, you are being prepared to carry out the official role, position, or office of a priest (e.g. prophet, pastor, minister, or some type of a very visible cleric). With this office comes spiritual growth and divine illumination, dreamer, if you have genuinely sought after truth, truth will continue to be revealed to you and lead and guide you. At present, continue to allow the Paraclete to complete the work of purification and sanctification within you. For those who go forth in tears, shall return rejoicing (Psalm 126:5, 6). Be diligent and patient, everything will be done proper, and in its own time; you will be ordained to a priestly office, and if relevant, your request in another area of your life will be granted. With that said, the following is necessary to say. Your promotion is predicated upon your understanding of, and continued obedience to, God's directives over your life. Second, pray to God for divine truth, for one should never exalt their thoughts, ideas, feelings, emotions, above God's truth, for, e very house is built by someone, but the builder of all things is God (Hebrews 3:2-4). Further, chosen, you are to show forth the praises of Him who has called you out of darkness into His marvelous light (also see 1 Peter 2:9, 10). Again, your height of spiritual progress and promotion will be according to your faith and obedience to God's will over your life personally. See suggested course of action. (2) If building depicted within your dream, was not in accordance with, or commonly used, in yo ur awaked life, for religious purposes, your dream implies one who is being true to him or herself, or to another, but is not true to God's Word. To be true to self or another, is to seek affirmation with respect to condoning your particular sin, while basin g your ideas, arguments, and/or beliefs on something that is sacrilegious, profane, illogical, and non-mainstream doctrine or philosophy. Your ideology is without favorable conclusions, thus this dream. You are full of pride. Moreover, dreamer, you r interpretation of the Word of God has become unrecognizable to those you influence. When those who seek truth, ask Jesus why they do not recognize your teachings or reflections, the words spoken of you are that you are true to yourself. Actually, you have settled for a voluptuary type philosophy and desire to propagate your beliefs. How can you say, "I have great desire, thus my physical enjoyment, luxury, and sensual gratifications are my primary concerns? This is a characterization of the ungodly or spiritually immature. Weigh: The child thinks that all that appears pleasant and tasty belongs to them and that he or she has the right to partake of any and everything. Consideration of others, and/or of the resulting outcome is unfamilia r to him or her. They will never consider the results of their behavior, nor how their behavior will affect others. This type of consideration is not within a child's mind-set, because he or she is a child. As the immature child takes what they want, when they want it, and believes that it's theirs, and that they do have a right to whatever it is, so does the spiritually immature, do what they will, when they want, and believe that it's OK, using grace as a cover for sin. Unfortunately, spiritual change ca nnot begin with this kind of expectation and mind-set. Dreamer, I invite you to consider the following. Accepting Jesus Christ as your Savior, on His terms and not yours, and where there would be chaos emotionally and spiritually, genuine peace will abide. Choose not to go out from the presence of the Lord, that is, to willingly renounce God, and to be content to forego the privileges He offers, that you might not be under His precepts, make things right. Moreover, believing and encouraging other s to approach God the Father, without the essential provision He has provided for humanity, to approach Him properly; that provision being Yeshua HaMashiach, is not safe. Some call God's provision Jesus, Wonderful Counselor, Mighty God, Everlasting Father, Prince of Peace, our atonement, advocate, liberator, propitiator, and our salvation. Dreamer, re-think your attitude and views regarding your beliefs and philosophy, and you are strongly counseled to decline the temporary relations o f darkness; that you might inherit an entrance into paradise having answered God's call upon your life and turned to His Word and His tenets. Dreamer set your heart towards understanding and embracing godly knowledge. See suggested course of action. (3) What condition was the building? For example, clean and beautifully adorned, well kept, or was it, deteriorated, in ruins, leveled to the ground, burned down, being reconstructed or remodeled or distorted in some manner? Thus, this choice has two parts (choose one). (a) If building was clean, beautifully adorned, and well kept, or was being reconstructed or remodeled, your dream denotes one who has purified (or is purifying) him or herself in preparation for ministry. Now that you have purified (or is purifying) yourself by obeying the leading of the Holy Ghost, and by obeying the truth of God's word, so that you have sincere love for other Christians, dreamer, love deeply from your heart (see 1 Peter 1:22-24). Your height of spiritual progress and promotion will be according to your faith and obedience to God's will over your life personally. (b) If religious building depicted within your dream, was burned down, deteriorated, in ruins, or leveled to the ground, or distorted in some manner, your dream comes as a stern rebuke and as a message of grace. Dreamer, there are many bitter and poisonous consequences of your irresponsible behavior. Your ways are perverse and wicked, paths that are devious. Ways that have caused you to walk in darkness gladly. While in defiance against God and the teachings of Christ, you exalt your wisdom above the Creator. A bold and daring seducer, you mouth empty, boastful words; discrediting the Creator's wise and sensible guidelines for living life, on this side of eternity, as humanly and sanely as possible; and in harmony with His pro vision for life on the other side of eternity, in heaven. You have become contrary to God's righteous precepts, for darkness has blinded you to truth. Dreamer, after all this time, still you hesitate to give God you heart, mind, and soul. If you love, and need Him then why won't you give Him you? Yes, He understands and can handle all your doubts and fears. When wisdom enters your heart and knowledge and truth becomes sweet to your soul, discretion will protect you, and understanding will guard you. Favorably, although you walk in darkness, the Lord will be your Light. Will you allow Him to be? Dreamer, own up to your wrongdoings to God and others, and make amends to those you've hurt and offended. As God has delivered you in the past because of His faithfulness, so He will deliver you now, only repent and allow His Word to be a light unto your path that the work of purification and sanctification may be complete within you. Prayer and repentance is the first step. Repentance is seeking pardon and expressing sincere feelings of regret and brokenness for having done something awry and/or for having hurt someone. To Jesus pray, Psalm 51. To individuals, a phone call or a letter of apology is a good place to start, if appropriate. This coupled with prayer and fasting, and followed by appropriate application of wisdom and Jesus will meet you. Have faith in this. Otherwise, unfit for Kingdom business, you will become disqualified for the prize (Matthew 22.1-14, 1 Corinthians 9:27). See suggested course of action. (4) Was dreamer inside or outside of a religious building? This choice has three parts (choose one). (a) If dreamer entered into, was walking around, or standing, inside a religious building, see interpretation #1. (b) If dreamer remained outside of a religious building, specifically one in accordance with, or commonly used, for religious purposes, the following is necessary for you to hear, understand, and heed. If you want to approach and worship the Holy One by way of inspirational music, praise and worship, teaching, or preaching, you should come before Him in a sense of appropriateness. Meaning you should aspire for some level of truthfulness, modesty, and reliability. No other is responsible for this in your life but you; therefore, deal with an existing situation that hinders your approach to God with some level of purity (Leviticus 11:45, 1 Peter 1:13-2:3). Moreover, to remain outside of the church standing, walking around, or just remaining outside, denotes one who, rather than choosing to approach, and embrace (enter into) God's righteousness, is opting to refrain from ministering. Dreamer this choice will surely be unprofitable for you. Therefore, rid yourself of all malice and all deceit, hypocrisy, envy, and slander of every kind, and crave that which will help you mature spiritually in the Lord (see 1 Peter 1:24-2:3). See suggested course of action. (c) If dreamer remained outside of a religious building, specifically one not in accordance with, or commonly used, for religious purposes, dreamer has purified (or is purifying) him or herself in preparation for ministry. Now that you have purified (or is purifying) yourself, by obeying the leading of the Holy Ghost, a nd by obeying the truth of God's word, so that you have sincere love for other Christians, love deeply from your heart (see 1 Peter 1:22-24). Additionally, for dreamer, to have remained outside of the religious building that was not in accordance with, or commonly used, for religious purposes, denotes one, possibly the dreamer, who is, or will be, introduced secretly into a pseudo religious group, deep undercover. The purpose for this mission undercover, is for dreamer to stealthily learn the mentality, and mechanics, of the group beliefs, that you, might know how to, strategically introduce the menta lity of Christ within the group, with hopes of saving some of its members from eternal damnation.

Note, do not reveal your religious beliefs. Begin noting all erroneous beliefs within this group. Any beliefs that contradict the inspired word of God, inc luding His provision for humankind to be save; namely belief and faith in Jesus Christ as Savior, God incarnate, and their beliefs on gr ace without works. Then, after a long while, wisely and cautiously begin pointing out the errors of the group's belief system to certain others you are led to, by Holy Spirit. Do not be afraid of their status, words, or any other characteristic, that mi ght be intimidating. Stay focus and remember your mission.

RESIDENTIAL BUILDINGS (Apartment, Bungalow, Castle, Cloister, Cottage, Condominium, Consulate, Duplex, Embassy, Emergency Shelter, House, Hut, Log Cabin, Mansion, Monastery, Orphanage, Palace, Parsonage, Public Housing, Rectory, Retirement Complex, Row House, Tent, Townhouse, Vicarage, Villa, or White House. Any private, religious, or government residences):

Amongst the varied meanings of the many kinds of residential buildings, permanent or temporary, within your dreams, generally they symbolize your spiritual state of affairs and/or physical condition. Questions to journal: Where were you located within the building? What kind of residential building was depicted? Is this type of building commonly used as a place where you live, permanent or temporary? What condition was the building in, e.g. clean and beautifully adorned, well kept, burned down, deteriorated, in ruins, leveled to the ground, or was under construction or being remodeled? See the following.

Apartment, Condominium, Duplex, Row house, Townhouse, or Public housing: This dream has two meanings (both may apply). (1) Dreamer you will be asked to act on behalf of another. You, as a third party, will be given permission or authorized to act on behalf of another, to assist someone; you will be authorized to help another with financial matters, legal issues, or to act as a proxy, regarding another's health directives, because they are unable to act for them self. A properly written authorization letter will be presented to you, sometime in the near future, with the authorization to act. Be that "good Samaritan". (2) Dreamer, your unique style of artistic expression, especially in presenting the gospel of Jesus Christ, is the gift you bring to the world. If not already, you will bring joy and inspiration to many by your positive mindset and creative talent, via writing, drama, music, speaking, or teaching. Therefore, dreamer, do not get tired of doing "good" for you will reap at the proper time if you don't give up. Dreamer, don't allow yourself to get tired of living the right way, living life on God's terms and in pursuing your gifting. For sure, you will receive your just due, on this side of heaven, at the proper time, and everlasting life, if you don't give up. Moreover, while you have the opportunity, do good to all people, and especially to those who are of the household of faith (Galatians 6:8-10). By this, you will continue to experience "rains of blessings".

Bungalow, Cottage, or Villa: Dreamer, do your rightful religious duties, professionally minded and complete, without murmurings. Do them all, and do not find fault with doing. For the enemy of your soul is devising and plotting evil against you, to create an offense within you against God and His cause, thus an offense against you by God. Therefore, min d your ministerial duties, and do not quarrel about them. God's expectations were given to be obeyed, not to be disputed. As well, dedication to His cause, without complaining, testifies to the world that you serve a good Lord. The service you do, in Jesus name, leads to freedom, and the work for His cause, has its own great rewards. A cheerful and willing spirit to do God's service, also greatly adorns. Moreover, learn to not injure anyone, in word or deed, and give no occasion for offense that you may be counted as blameless and harmless, a child of God, without need of rebuke. See suggested course of action. Emergency Shelter or Temporary Shelter: The dreamer has been wounded or crushed by the words of someone considered spiritual. Dreamer, a "righter of wrongs" will handled them. Therefore, take the "fight" out of your feelings, as well as any other negativity within you, for you have no need to fight this battle (2 Chronicles 20:17). Visualize yourself presenting the negativity of the "wrong" to the feet of God, via prayer, as an enemy of His Kingdom (Psalm 110:1, Matthew 22:44), as an enemy of your spiritual work, and of your purpose. Seek refuge in the House of God, around His people, and you will be covered. Dreamer, you have in

Christ, grace and healing, refreshment, and a refuge. Don't forfeit these graces. Embrace the help your Heavenly Father is offering you, via a sabbatical, and the effects of their negativity will no longer hold sway ove r your heart.

House, Mansion, Palace, or Castle: This dream has three meanings (choose one). (1) Married male dreamer: Read and understand 1 Peter 3:7. There is a need to honor your wife. The question is how do you properly minister to, and support, your wife, per this scripture, and as the priest of the house? Dreamer, dwell with your wife according to understanding. See suggested course of action. (2) Dreamer you have the wherewithal within to become a primary catalysts that keeps family and friends coming together (e.g. some kind of regular reunions), and to become one who is good at resolving conflict, bringing peace, hope, and joy to many. You will be considered, and now is, a righteous person (see Romans 8:1). Moreover, d reamer, God will raise you up and sit you amongst His people for the benefit of all within your sphere, help God's people by doing good deeds, e.g. some large-scale humanitarian effort. Suggestions, perhaps dreamer may consider a humanitarian effort along the line of, for example, build rent-free or mortgage-free housing for God's people, or use your organizing ability, to become a child advocate, on behalf of abused, abandoned, neglected, and at-risk children, or becoming a foster care parent, or support the agencies and individuals who work on these children behalf. Notwithstanding, initiate some effort that promotes human welfare and/or social reforms, with a primary focus on God's love and His kindness towards His people. (3) Dreamer, there will be quick turnovers in your interests and relationships, and perhaps jobs; these changes will give you a multi-dimensionality that will befriend you to people of every "walk of life". Fortunately along with these changes will come, business, power, and money, people will elect you to lead. With that said, dreamer that you might go forth spiritually and emotionally clear, and only if necessary, one of the following three issues will be dealt with (a, b, or c). (a) Unfortunately, because you learn so quickly you have little patience with those whose mental processes are somewhat slower; thus, you could become supercilious or somewhat a "know it all" in your attitude, becoming intolerant and critical of others, quick to argue and to dominate situations. This characteristic is called pride. After being puffed up with pride and arrogance, you could experience falling flat on your face. In other words too much arrogance and self-pride are sure to bring bad and disappointing results. However, dreamer, if you are diligent in subduing your negative traits you can turn bad situations into a good overnight; people can and do change, and sometimes overnight, e.g. Apostle Paul. Thus, dreamer you are urged to heed this warning. See Proverbs 16:18. See suggested course of action. (b) Flee sexual immorality. Every other sin that a man or woman commits is outside the body, but the immoral man or woman sins against his or her own body. Do you not know that your body is a temple of the Holy Spirit who is in you, whom you have from God, and that you are not your own? For you have been bought with a price: therefore glorify God in your body (see 1 Corinthians 6:18-20). See suggested course of action. (c) To you who have not promoted any kinds of indecent practices, sexual acts of perversions or other horrible traditions. Your dream was sent to demonstrate grace, via a warning of a dark generational issue, hereditary within your family line (e.g. maternal and/or paternal, grandparents, siblings, aunts, uncles, cousins). Dreamer, character traits from ancestors, namely genetic codes and traits, will often trouble and taunt the offspring of a given progenitor, especially generational issues (Exodus 20:5-7). The demons that have so plague your family line, are now visiting (re-visiting) you. Your issue is demonically instigated and it is spiritually perverse, perhaps sexually perverse as well (e.g. adultery, fornication, homosexuality, prostitution, whorishness). These spirits attempt to "bend" the personality, as early as possible with regards to age, towards a certain direction, oftentimes towards a way that is desolate and wicked, for it is Satan's scheme to kill and make desolate all; thus, to keep some from rising up and leading their generation to Christ (see the birth of Moses, Exodus 1:15-2:10). Favorably, generational curses and issues can stop with you (Jeremiah 31:29, 30; Ezekiel 18:2-14, 20-23). Thus, your Heavenly Father is requiring that you overcome and subdue negative and dark emotions, feelings, behaviors, or ideas that would influence you, before they overcome you. Dreamer, God is not asking you to do something you cannot do. For a surety, vanquishing of the coming influence can be done. By faith, you will need to declare some kind of fast and commit to it, for a long period-of-time, to abate the demonically instigated circumstance, you find yourself in now, Matthew 6:16-18. Try abstaining from food and drink (midnight to 6 PM), twice a week, and refrain from words, attitudes, people, places, and things, including music, magazines, videos, TV, or any such things that fuel anger and discontent, and stir up lustful feelings. This is also known as, faith with works, read, understand, and embrace James 2:14-26. Nonetheless, earnestly pray, God will guide, enable, and answer you as to the type of fast. Additionally, if relevant, forgive your mother and/or father for the darkness (aka curse) they may have perpetuated, for they knew not what they done. Forgiveness is important to your success (Matthew 6:12-15, 8:21-35). See suggested course of action.

Hut or Tent: There is something the Lord wants the dreamer to learn, a lesson. Sincerely acknowledge that God is in complete control of your state of affairs, and earnestly wait for Him to work it out for your good and for His glory. Harmon ize your life with His agenda and you will learn this lesson well. Sacrifice your flesh for your soul's sake, and your pride will soon give way to humbleness, dignity, honor, and righteous self-esteem, your foolishness to peace and wisdom. This process will also heal the animosity within you. Allow the process without complaining or murmuring for it is preparing you for a great journey. Moreover, be as one who gets satisfaction from embracing good habits. See Psalms 55 and 56; use these Psalms as a form of supplication, as a venue to express your regret for sin, to vent your frustration because of your enemies, and to offer praise and thanksgiving to God. See suggested course of action.

Log Cabin: The dreamer has been continually changed, converted, improved, rehabilitated, renewed, and transformed. As well, the Lord has destroyed your enemies from before you, even unto this time. Yet, you continue to embrace excessive indulgences, a lack of self-control, lack of knowledge, and spiritual uncleanness. Symbolically, spiritual uncleanness, within the life of a believer, denotes anger, animosity, confusion, out of order, self-condemnation, sexual impropriety, an unforgiving spirit, and/or other weaknesses, see (1 Corinthians 6:9-20, Ephesians 5). This behavior causes one's anointing to fade and spiritual authority to wane. Your dream is to warn a rebellious person, in the spirit of grace. To see if you will yet be worked upon, and change your mindset, or else to leave you inexcusable, in your accusations against God, because of your ruin (e.g. continually plundered, seized, and disfavored, also see Jeremiah 9:7-9; Zechariah 13:9; Matthew 23:37-39; Revelation 3:15-21). Favorably, you are now one, whom the body of believers will help restore back to God, in the spirit of empathy, mercy, leniency, and kindness, until the issue is cleaned up or rendered dead, allow this. The more God allows you to see your emptiness, it is suggested that you be more earnest to repent that you may find Him to be grace and healing, refreshment, and a refuge. See suggested course of action.

Orphanage: Your dream suggests that the dreamer will be delivered from a life-threatening phobia, subsequently, you will develop an ability to help others grow and go forward spiritually in Christ, you will be a great mentor. Moreover, dreamer, you will be able to enjoy the fellowship of family and friends openly, without fear or pretense, and there will be a time and place of laughter, the charm of celebrations will return. You will grow to a good old age; in perfect peace and safety, and will be blessed of God. To be blessed: Gifts of God's grace, anything God freely gives you, absolution, the Holy Spirit, salvation, regeneration, eternal life, health, children, love of family, longevity, necessities, prosperity, and dominion over all that is yours; and all are parts of the supply of grace, and all are sanctified by the Lord, and technically belongs to Him. The result of this supply in your life will be peace.

Religious or Government Residences (e.g. Parsonage, Monastery, Rectory, Vicarage, Cloister, or any religious residence or government residence, e.g. Consulate, Embassy, White house, or any government residence): Your dream speaks of your mission, and your purpose. As well as, why certain things have been allowed within your life, or have been done to you. Dreamer, you will be used, if not already, to usher others into a totally new and higher level of spiritual awareness, also see Matthew 28:19, 20. Even amongst the "broken", a spark of life remains hidden, awaiting your particular ministry, your unique way of presenting the gospel that they may be elevated and raised up. It is for this reason, you will now, begin to noticeably experience the miraculous wonders of divine providence; particularly, the wisdom, care, and guidance provided by God that you might fulfill your mission, your purpose. Moreover, your past experiences and lessons learned, will be used to strengthe n your witness. Take care that you become sensitive to, and respect, the continuous acts of God's providential care. For, there is a promise that you will eat and do very well, on this side of eternity, and inherit eternal life. As well, the feeling of re st and serenity that comes with trust in God's divine providence is available to you right now. In addition, note, it is wise to stay within mainstream Judeo-Christianity. Privately study your bible and publicly express your understanding of it to others. Believe nothing you cannot express, in its' entirety, openly and sensibly to the whole world. Do not lie, nor hide your beliefs or the beliefs and/or actions of others. Reject any form of isolated groups or beliefs that put forth, "we are the only ones". Jesus died for the world, for all who will believe, and not exclusively for any one sect or western denomination. Most importantly, do not die, emotionally, spiritually and/or physically, for any person, group, or unconventional cause. For example, any "heaven's gate" type cults, suicide bombers, kamikaze, ISIS, Aryan Alliance, any and all hate, anti-Christian, anti-Semitic groups. Remember to go to church and forsake not the gathering of yourself together with other mainstream Christians. For this is a strong part of God's government.

Retirement or Senior Citizen Living Complex: Your dream was sent to encourage the dreamer to keep progressing forward, and don't worry about age, nor about any limitations that come with aging, you will be strengthen, and there will be a time and place of laughter, the charm of celebrations will return. Dreamer, God will renew your life and sustain you in your old age, because of your loyalty (allegiance, commitment, dedication, trueness) to His Kingdom and to His cause. Your sensitivity and gentleness has been, and will continue to be, a great healing force to others. Moreover, your keen mental abilities, ministry, and any talent or skill you were born with or learned, will continue at a high functioning level into your old age. You will always have a powerful effect on anyone who enters your life. Are you ready for another measure, another level, of God's love? Are you ready for a better you? Humility is the key for sustainment; pride is a robber and destroyer. Dreamer is counseled to keep a flexible attitude, coupled with physical activity and a diet that helps lower cholesterol levels and blood pressure, and from time to time reflectively check your pride level.

ROOF:

This dream has two meanings (choose one). (1) To be up on a roof, dreamer, now, you will begin to experience a miraculous increase in divine knowledge, and wisdom, as your dream denotes one who is spiritually prepared for spiritual growth, divine illumination, and some type of promotion or confirmation. This knowledge and wisdom will be imparted to you to be used exclusively for interpreting the gospel of Jesus Christ to others, and for the edifying of the Body of Christ; the body of believers; as your dream, also, points to one who was born to be a teacher and a nurturer. Therefore, prepare your mind for action; be self-controlled; set your hope fully on the grace to be given you when Jesus Christ is revealed, and no longer conform to your carnal desires (see 1 Peter 1:13-16). Your dream also confirms that you're in order for heaven. Moreover, your dream is additional proof of something you have believed God for is correct (e.g. for a spouse, rectification of an attitude of anger, frustration, discontent, or for a healing of unbelief, or a healing of your faith level, or a healing of physical health, or for any hindrances to your spiritual clarity that you have recognized). (2) To fall off a roof denotes that instead of you, the dreamer, moving towards, and thus fulfilling, your divine purpose, and reaching a pinnacle in your life, thereby with, you will prospe r, you have begun to listen to, and be fooled by, demons, and have begun sacrificing to your flesh, instead of getting your soul right. Having listened and embraced the lies, you have begun to decrease and fall, eventually running amok your life, litera lly crashing, when you should be clear and focused mentally, emotionally, and spiritually. Compassionately, the Lord is creating a miracle in your life, enabling you to move forward with your life and to make good decisions. However, the miracle's success depends upon your willingness to be delivered and set free; for one will always have the choice to say no, or perhaps sabotage their progress. If you lack wisdom ask God for wisdom; and He will give you wisdom. For the Lord gives wisdom and from His mouth comes knowledge and understanding. Then you will understand what is right and just and fair, every good path. When wisdom enters your heart and knowledge becomes sweet to your soul, discretion will protect you, understanding will guard you, and His Truth will lead you. To deliver you from the ways of wickedness, and from demons whose words and ways are perverse, who causes you to walk in darkness gladly, whose paths are crooked and devious, causing you to leave straight paths (Proverbs 2:1-6, 9-15). This is one of God's covenant promises to you. Have faith in this. Further, dreamer, go and separate yourself from anyone and anything that hinders your clarity and emotional stability; literally stop what you're saying, feeli ng, or doing. See suggested course of action.

STORAGE FACILITIES OR PARKING STRUCTURES (Airport terminal, Aviation Control Towers, Automobile Repair Shop, Boathouse, Boat Lift, Building Canopies, Car Dealership, Carport, Carwash, Dock, Garage, Gas station, Hangar, Marina, Metro Station, Parking Garage, Piers, Snow Shed, Stall, Warehouse, or any Depository for goods. Any place relating to any mode of transportation):

Give contributions, according as you've prospered. Give, especially to those who live uprightly, and do not resent the givin g of the gift when you make it. Moreover, do not turn your face away from the poor, and the face of God will not be turned away from you. Help a poor man for the commandment's sake, and because of his need do not send him away empty; (see Ben Sira 29). Dreamer, no one can serve two masters, for either he (or she) will hate the one and love the other, or they will be devoted to the one and despise the other, see Matthew 6:24, Luke 16:13. You cannot serve God and mammon (at its most basic level, the word mammon means riches or wealth, but it implies an idea of personified wealth gained with avarice, often taking on a deified nature). This warning, challenges the dreamer to appropriate wealth according to the commandments of the Most High, for this is an example of the principle, reaping what you sow or "measure for measure". Allow this attitude to become part of your conduct, your "MO" sort to say, that your character might become full of love and generosity. In the words of Jesus, "Stop storing up treasures for yourselves on earth, where moths and rust destroy and where thieves break in and steal. But keep on storing up treasures for yourselves in heaven, where moths and rust do not destroy and where thieves do not break in and steal, because where your treasure is, there your heart will be also" (Matthew 6:19-21 ISV). Moreover, "Bring the entire tithe into the storehouse that there may be food in my house. So, put me to the test in this right now", s ays the Lord of the Heavenly Armies, "and see if I won't throw open the windows of heaven for you and pour out on you blessing without measure. In addition, I'll prevent the devourer from harming you, so that he does not destroy the crops of your land. Nor will the vines in your fields drop their fruit", says the Lord of the Heavenly Armies. "Then all the nations will call you blessed, for you will be a land of delight," says the Lord of the Heavenly Armies" (Malachi 3:10-12 ISV).

VESTIBULE, CONCOURSE, FOYER, OR LOBBY (any large interior entrance, reception room, or waiting area):

Dreamer, your dream denotes that there are some issues within yourself, which must be dealt with, in order for you to be received into the Kingdom of God; namely, your issues of an unforgiving heart. Dreamer, forgiveness and a letting go, needs to happen, in order for you to go forward properly and for you to enter into heaven. Read, understand, and embrace Matthew 6:12-15, 18:21-35. An unforgiving heart is the single most popular poison the enemy of our soul uses against God's people, and it is the deadliest poison a person can take spiritually. Dreamer, while it is easier said than done, it is necessary to say; one cannot grow or go forward stuck in the past. Do not lose today holding on to yesterday; let it go. It is imperative that you seize this opportunity to repent and forgive. Seek help, if necessary, on how to forgive, suggested recommended reading, "Deliverance in Forgiveness, through obedience to the Holy Spirit, A. M. Perry". Nonetheless and unfortunately, without forgiveness, there can be no forgiveness of your trespasses and indiscretions; and no progressing forward in the Lord and on towards your divine purpose. Dreamer, you are purposed to inspire others to become steadfast in their personal relationship with Christ, especially those who are showing fear, hesitancy, or discouragement. Moreover, dreamer, you are a Christian minister sent to those who are babes in Christ. See suggested course of action.

WALLS:

This dream has three meanings (choose one). (1) Your dream refers to a promise made to you by God, and the fulfillment of that promise made to you, the dreamer. The promise was made when you first invited Christ into your life. It will, very sho rtly happen. Dreamer, God's wisdom, care, and guidance, coupled with His divine intervention, has kept you, and will, again, cause your mouth to be filled with laughter, and your tongue with singing. When God reverse your tragedy, you will testify that th e Lord has done great things for you, and you will be glad. Your situations will change and He will give you a new song in your heart. You will sing a new song. Additionally, your dream points to one, the dreamer, who was born to be a teacher and a nurturer. You should be teaching the elementary truths of God's word to those not familiar with the teachings of righteousness, mainly new converts, and infants in Christ, and if relevant, to your own children and their friends. Your diligent teaching will prepare others to spread the gospel of Jesus Christ; thus, reproducing your teaching ministry and abundantly blessing you even more. You will receive wages for your diligence, if indeed you are diligent (Luke 10:2-7, 1 Timothy 5:18). (2) Building without walls (any building without walls, to appear to be in a building, but outside, e.g. house without walls, school without walls, or church without walls): Your dream comes as a warning and stern rebuke. Your dream denotes one who is so undisciplined that your spirit is without restraint (Proverbs 25:28). Although the dreamer is intended to be one who has the capacity to exemplify empathy, forgiveness, and understanding; one whom people are drawn to for absolution, as well as, one who is important to the well-being of others, and important as a leader, promoting in every way the welfare of others, and is powerfully anointed for this. Instead, you live in excess, mischievousness, arrogance, and unruliness, to the point of recklessness; and not only so, but trample those you consider less than yourself, harmful to those about you. Dreamer, in order to fulfill your commission, to reach many, you will need to, seriously begin reflecting upon your moral weaknesses, especially your lack of self-restraint and arrogance. How you might bring them under subjection to biblical principles, and how you might aspire for a certain level of spiritual purity. Sidebar, regarding your condescendingly arrogant attitude towards others, this is why you are uncontrollably spending money wastefully, as well, this is why no healing has manifested in an area you so desire healed. Dreamer, you are advised to discipline your body and your sensual desires and to bring them under control. Temperance in all things is your key word. Moreover, earnestly adopt a determined resolve to go no further with an attitude of uncertainty about God, His Word, and Christianity. Rather, become intense and convicted when it comes to defending your beliefs. As well, steel your emotions and thoughts against all that will come against your God. God will lead the way. If not brought under subjection, you will become an object of scorn, derision, laughter, a joke to all who encounters you. Moreover, having proved yourself, many times, morally unclean for God's purposes, you will die before your time, that your soul to might be saved. Dreamer, utilizing the powerful resources of prayer and heartfelt repentance to Jesus is needed. To Jesus pray, Psalm 51, this followed by appropriate application of wisdom, can conceivably avert some of the repercussi ons of your choices. This coupled with fasting, a changed mindset, serious re-consideration of God's ways and means, and an honest acknowledgement of God's hand within your life, then the severe impact of your choices and actions, upon your life, can be lessen. This is what is called leaving a blessing behind. Further, questions to journal: What kind of building or structure was depicted? Why were there no walls? Your answers, along with this interpretation, and the additional references highlighted (kind of building); see relevant categories, should, point you towards the area within your life that needs primary focus. See suggested course of action. (3) Walls falling, tumbling, or crumbling, down or in ruin: Dreamer, your life is before God, and mayhem is your modus operandi "MO" (mode or state of operating, living, or lifestyle). The matter at hand that you desire God to make happen on your behalf will not happen. The big event you are expecting to happen will not. Illustrations: If you are lead to believe that a specific person will marry you, you are deceived; he or she will not, if you expecting a cash settlement that might result because of some questionable behavior on your part, you will not receive the settlement. Dreamer, thank God for His patience, long-suffering, and grace (the free and unmerited favor and beneficence of God), while you get things decent and in order. Utilizing the powerful resources of prayer and heartfelt repentance to Jesus is needed. To Jesus pray, Psalm 51, this followed by appropriate application of wisdom, can conceivably avert some of the repercussions of your choices. This coupled with fasting, a changed mindset, serious re-consideration of God's ways and means, and an honest acknowledgement of God's hand within your life, then the severe impact of your choices and actions, upon your life, can be lessen. This is what is called leaving a blessing behind. See suggested course of action.

WINDOWS (includes any type of glass, be it, a looking glass, such as a Mirror, Optical Instruments, such as Eyeglasses, Transparent Drinking Glass, Bottles, or any transparent openings that allow you to see through it):

This dream has three meanings (choose one). (1) As your dream reveals your past and present emotional and spiritual condition, the following is necessary for you to weigh. Dreamer, due to your present yearnings that you might not attract to yourself, past "fleshly" desires, it is now needful that you bring to remembrance your former state, when you were enslaved to sin; what benefits did you reap at that time from the things you now disdain, the foolishness of it all. Now that you have been set free from sin, you have become a servant of God. The benefits you reap are meant to lead to holiness and the en d-result is eternal life (Romans 6:21, 22). To keep you humble, repentant, and watchful, you would do well to remember the time when you were a servant of sin, devoted to iniquity, embracing vanity, and reaping the same; and to remember the benefits of be ing a servant of God. If necessary, see suggested course of action. (2) The condition of the windows denotes how you, the dreamer, personally view yourself, and your spiritual condition. Questions to journal: What condition was the glass? This choice has three parts (choose one). (a) Broken window, mirror, eyeglasses, transparent drinking glass, bottles, or any transparent openings that allow you to see through it: This type of dream helps the dreamer to know what your Divine Counselor wants you to focus on, particularly, your thought life. The image the dreamer presents publicly, oftentimes contradict what's within, namely your inner spiritual person. The dreamer is absorbed in the pursuit of identity void of foundation (e.g. pretending to be someone you are not; and not knowing what it takes to be whom, or what, you're pretending to be). This type of identity pursuit will not withstand your storms of life. You will begin to crack in your personality, and your dream denotes that the "crack" is beginning to happen. The only foundation upon which humankind should wisely establish his or her identity, are the principles within the Word of God and the leading of the Holy Spirit. Fortunately, your dream a lso denotes that the dreamer is meek enough to change what has been exposed, especially if negative. See suggested course of action. (b) Clean, clear, transparent, and/or brightly polished window, mirror, eyeglasses, transparent drinking glass, bot tles, or any transparent openings that allow you to see through it: This choice has two parts (choose one). (i) The Creator, in His mercy, will show you some of the Light of His Glory, by way of a prophecy; receive it; thus, your dream is your first witness that a prophecy is coming. Dreamer, something is happening within your life that is large in scope, and life changing. A prophecy, reiterating this message in some similar manner, and clearly defining the specifics, will be your second witness (2 Corinthians 13:1); therefore, heed the prophecy when it is given. (ii) Dreamer, use your past to, empathically reach another, namely one, who is before you at present, whose spiritual condition is similarly akin to the spiritual condition you once found yourself. Considering the images that were reflected within your dream, particularly, whom and/or what you saw, and where you were. This may perhaps point you in the direction of the person or ministry that is in need of you, and your unique way of ministering. Dreamer, reach out and touch them using the wisdom of experience, remembering from where you were lifted. If person, situation, or ministry, is unknown, they, or it, will be introduced to you soon. (c) Dirty, cloudy, foggy, murky, shadowy, or not so clear or opaque window, mirror, eyeglasses, transparent drinking glass, bottles, or any transparent openings that allow you to see through it: Your dream denotes that the dreamer does not have a clear or correct understanding of spiritual truths and spiritual realities. Especially of those truths and realities, that articulates the true nature of God and leads to everlasting life. Your manner of reasoning is weak and inconclusive; and your thoughts, plans, and arguments are shortsighted and puerile. Dreamer is advised that for the next seven days to use this time to re-think your views and attitude, regarding the doctrine you are adhering to, and your philosophy, and opinions on joining a church. Why, because your interpretation of the Word of God has become unrecognizable to those you influence. When those who seek truth, ask Jesus why they do not recognize your teachings, the words spoken of you are that you are true to yourself. To be true to self or another, is to se ek affirmation with respect to condoning your particular sin, while basing your ideas, arguments, and/or beliefs on something that is sacrilegious, profane, illogical, and non-mainstream doctrine or philosophy. Your ideology is without favorable conclusions. You are full of pride. Dreamer the counsel here; is that you begin to practice to speak and reason more sagaciously, resisting your habits and manners of foolish and double talking, that you might go on to a spiritual immaturity that is useful to yours elf and to others. Moreover, read, understand, and embrace, 1 Corinthians 13:9-13. The wisdom to be glean from the scripture is, that the knowledge you've acquired through the years, is now deemed as unworthy of your attention, those imperfect views, lay them aside. Count them worthless to your spiritual progression. Dreamer; fix your attention on things that are truly eternal, are of spiritual value, and are spiritually wise, via faith, hope, and love for God and His ways and means. See suggested course of action. (3) What was reflected or depicted on the other side of the glass, mirror, optical instrument, or window? Dreamer, the reflection(s) depicted, and/or what you were looking at, references three matters (one, two or all may apply). (a) The reflection depicted, and/or what you were looking at, is a reflection of who you were, and who you are, emotionally and spiritually; that is to say, your past and present emotional and spiritual condition. If necessary, see suggested course of action. (b) Your dream exposes who or what you've been hankering for recently. If necessary, see suggested course of action. (c) If dreamer is actually considered a religious leader, e.g. bishop, deacon, deaconess, elder, evangelist, minister, overseer, pastor, pope, preacher, priest, rabbi, superintendent, teacher, or any cleric or ecclesiastical leader type role. Your dream exposes the emotional and spiritual condition of your personal ministry, specifically those that are closely connected to your ministry. For oftentimes, a ministry will take on the persona of its leaders. Thus, your dream comes to caution the dreamer that there is a need to remember from where the Lord has brought you from, and to, closely consider the spiritual condition of your ministry and to act on those observations. If necessary, see suggested course of action.

In addition, amid the following are common words, expressions, usages, (e.g. slang or clichés), or a 'probable' that are metaphorically represented by glass:

- **"Walking on Broken Glass"**: Your dream exposes two issues within the life of the dreamer (both apply). (1) Your dream exposes that your fears and limitations are self-imposed. (2) Your dream also reveals that the dreamer is being divinely discipline for something you've done. Dreamer your dream was sent to encourage you and to bring about an awareness that your particular form of divine discipline is a tool meant to impart skills and knowledge to the dreamer, in hopes, that you might change, grow, and overcome your fears and limited beliefs, in order to do things you previously thought impossible. Dreamer, you can change the cycle of self-limiting beliefs, and those other thoughts and beliefs that are holding you back from your true potential. See suggested course of action.

WASTE YARD OR GARBAGE DUMP OR DUMPSTER OR DUMPSITE (or any container that holds rubbish, garbage can, trashcan, or ashtray):

This dream has two meanings (one or both may apply). (1) Your dream denotes one has spoken viciously against one of God's children, one whom He cherishes. It is said of you, may you be ashamed and dismayed. Dreamer, your dream is to warn a rebellious person, in the spirit of grace, to see if you will yet be worked upon, and change your mindset, or else to leave y ou inexcusable, in your accusations against God, because of your ruin (also see Jeremiah 9:7-9; Matthew 23:37-39). Jesus is petitioning you to cleanse the evil from your heart. If you are ready to acknowledge that you have spoken wrongly against someone, and remain mindful of your weaknesses, God is willing to help you, if you are willing to be helped. The more God allows you to see your "garbage", it is suggested that you be more earnest to repent that you may find Him to be grace and healing, and a refuge. See suggested course of action. (2) Dreamer, you have made your paths crooked because of bitterness and an unforgiving spirit. Your thoughts are thoughts of iniquity, you do not know the way of peace, and there is no justice in your tracks. With you come conflict, confrontation, drama, and hostilities. You create confusion and havoc wherever you go. You are bitter, brutal, and unforgiving. You will now begin to experience divine discipline (the Lord's chastening, correction that leads to instruction and reformation). That your soul might be saved, peace will be taken from you, and people will be allowed to destroy your reputation and to create havoc within your life. Conflicts, confrontations, difficulties, and hostil ities will become constant elements in your life. Dreamer, it is counseled that you take each change, turnaround, and up and down, as a stern rebuke of you by God, that you might become wiser and made clean (also see Proverbs 9:8 -12). This rebuke is only a precursor of even worse judgments that will come later, if you do not abandoned and change your ways. God is not condemning you, He's holding out His Hand of Hope, giving you an opportunity to start anew. Let the wicked forsake his way, God wants to pardon (Isaiah 55:7-13, Matthew 7:17-23, Luke 6:43-45). Dreamer, if you earnestly change your ways, you will be healed from your present condition and pardoned from the guilt previously mentioned. Prayer and repentance is the first step. To Jesus pray, Psalm 51. This, followed by appropriate application of wisdom and Jesus will meet you. Have faith in this. See suggested course of action.

Suggested Course of Action

Question to consider and journal, did your dream depict any symbols that alludes to, the dreamer will make the necessary changes, spiritually, emotionally, and/or physically to affect a more positive outcome? If changes are initiated, your dreams will change.

Nevertheless, in view of your dream's context, and the primary symbols, what does your dream reveal about you, your ethics, intents, mental state, and motives? Using a one-word answer, answer the following questions. What condition was the building, structure in (e.g. beautiful, broken, clean, dirty, hollowed, run-down, unsafe)? What did the building, structure mean to you, within your dream (e.g. dangerous, family, the past, safety, violations), or what does the building, structure mean to you in your awaked life? What was your reaction to the building, structure? Were you angry, concerned, confused, defensive, fearful, happy, helpful, pleased, shocked, unconcerned, or ready to get out of someone's presence? Did anyone get hurt emotionally, physically, or was disturbed in any way? Were others involved? If yes, who and in what manner were they involved, keeping in mind that the others represent a quality of you. Your answers, coupled with the interpretation, plus any additional information, should begin to unfold the subject matter and issue at hand, if not now, mull over things a few days. Nonetheless, your answers are indicative of your present spiritual state; thus, honesty with yourself is essential. You will need to earnestly look within and consider that the sum of your answers are a reflection of where you are emotionally, physically, and spiritually, and a reflection of who you are becoming. Additionally, your reactions to the building, structure, the people, the activity, the circumstances, and/or situation, reveals your attitude regarding this information about yourself.

Dreamer, consider seriously your observations. If what was revealed prevail, will it sabotage any good that's happening at present within your life? Will it build or destroy, strengthen or weaken, enlighten or blind? Dreamer, if the behaviors, per the interpretation, attributed to the building, structure is allowed to continue or prosper within y our life, serious harm or death may result. If the attribute is an undesirable or negative one, take steps accordingly to struggle against the growing desires of the carnal side of you.

Here, it must be acknowledge that because of emotional scarring and insecurities resulting from past difficult situations, unfortunately, dreamer, you may not have the ability to work through challenging circumstances at this time and to make the best decisions. Dreamer is therefore counseled to seek help from your spiritual leader(s). To help you sincerely clarify and amend the true intents and purposes of your actions, and to bring to an end that which keeps you from being, emotionally and spiritually, built up on a strong foundation. For, you are still expected to respect God, and His ways and means. His principles are not there to be obstacles to your progress, or to be a bore to you, but to keep you out of harm's way and to assure etern al life in the world to come, the Kingdom of God. God is giving you the opportunity to turn things around emotionally and spiritually, and He will turn things around literally; however, you will have to choose to allow the opportunity, for you still have free will; thus, the choice is yours. Free will is the expression of you choosing to participate in the divine acts of God; albeit, you are only merely placing your hand under the weight carried exclusively by God. Thus, you are not being asked to do something you cannot do, or to do it alone. Dreamer is also counseled that, if you lack wisdom, ask Jesus for wisdom. He gives wisdom to all, generously, no matter who you are and what you've done; wisdom is available (see James 1:5-8, Proverbs 2:1-6, 10). Hence, if, by just asking, you may get wisdom, one may suffer needlessly, because you will not ask Jesus for wisdom.

Warning, if you do not allow the grace of God extended to you, and the wise counsel of your leadership to prevail, regrettably, this in turn can, and often do, result in emotional emptiness, and you rejecting the love, authority, and instructions of God. A spirit of apathy towards your personal relationship with Christ is a bad frame of mind. In time, your carnal nature will dominantly reign over your spiritual side. Carnality always opens the door for someone, under the influence of evil, to run amok your life, both physically and spiritually until you are unable to recover. Therefore dreamer; personally respond, by repenting, and genuinely committing to a righteous change, with primary emphasis on life after this present life. However, the issue of eternal life will not be forced upon anyone who desires to remain in sin.

Now, pray (See Prayer of Deliverance, pg. 897)

Specific Meaning

Unless otherwise noted elsewhere, if, in your everyday living, your awaked state, as part of your lifestyle, work, or ministerial activities, or a special event, you have a very real connection with any activity involving buildings or structures. For exa mple, architectural work, construction, masonry, bricklayer, bridge builder, surveyor, or landlord, real estate developer, or any other activity involved in the selling, repairing, or constructing of buildings or structures. Dreams of this sort, for the most part, are ordinary dreams, resulting from your daily activities (see Chapter One, Chalom). These sorts of dreams are usually about your routine, mundane activities or anxieties that overwhelm your mind during the day. They are an inner release mechanism, which helps provide you with emotional balance and the maintaining of your sanity. These dreams are not significant, and do not warrant special attention.

Note: If the building, structure was condemned, destroyed, demolished, fined, or ruined in anyway within the dream, this may be heeded as an alert or warning in the physical realm, to the dreamer.

Do not assume that the building is safe or ok, caution should be heeded. The dreamer may consider his or her dream as a clue given to assist in finding facts, needed to support a prevailing situation or investigation. For example, was the building collapsing, crushing someone, or damaging something, the dreamer might consider a building collapsing as a possible danger to someone. The potential danger, kept within context of the dream, should be relevant to your lifestyle and closely resemble your real-life situations. Meaning it can actually occur during your awaked state. This will help you narrow down the specific area of concern. However, if your dream was inundated with symbols that are not specifically related to your job and responsibilities, then the spiritual implications should be heeded.

CARDINAL DIRECTIONS, THE MOON, AND STARS

The gatekeepers were on the four sides: east, west, north, and south (1 Chronicles 9:24)

There were three gates on the east, three on the north, three on the south, and three on the west (Revelation 21:13)

In addition, after these things I saw four angels standing on the four corners of the earth, holding the four winds of the earth, that the wind should not blow on the earth, nor on the sea, nor on any tree. John The whole compound was surrounded by a high fence with only one entrance. A person could not simply come from any direction into the tabernacle as he pleased — he had to enter through the one gate, which was always located to the east (so that people were facing west when they entered the tabernacle) The Tabernacle Place "Where is He who has been born King of the Jews? For we have seen His star in the East and have come to worship Him" (Matthew 2:2 NKJV)

This category deals with the four chief directions of the compass, the north, south, east, and west points and stars. Some short descriptions of types, phrases, and/or other processes and particulars, connected in some way to this category are, for example, the four winds, four corners of the earth, compass points, stars. Also, see category content list, or index.

All Symbols and Referents, Notes (1, 2, 3, etc.), Suggested Course of Action, and Specific Meaning offer guidance toward a more comprehensive interpretation.

Notes

1. Unless otherwise noted elsewhere, if, in your everyday living, your awaked state, as part of your lifestyle, work, or ministerial activities, or a special event, you have a very real connection with any activity involving the cardinal points or stars. For example, astronomy, work with compass or any navigational instruments, any geographical type activity, map making, meteorology, or any navigational type jobs, satellite-based global position systems (GPS), or any activity or science dealing with the phenomena of the cardinal points or stars, your dream is not significant and does not warrant special attention.

    Otherwise noted, on occasion, one may experience an Oneirovatic or "OV" dream (see Chapter One, "The 60th Part of Prophecy", section entitled – Other Prophetic Dreams). This type of dream should be regarded a vision and received as a precautionary warning. For example, to dream you are warned, within your dream, to go in flight so that you may be safe. Waiting no longer, for you are warned that harm, destruction, or misfortune will come from the north (Jeremiah 4:6); or, to dream of hearing a news report that goes as such, "Behold, waters rise up out of the north, and shall be an overflowing flood, and shall overflow the land (the Apocalypse). Or, to dream that any crucial earth event will be located at, or is headed towards a particular geographic coordinate, all these types of dreams should be heeded as a warning. This type of dream bares insight into the life of those who may seriously be affected by the coming event. The dreamer is urged to strongly advise, insist upon, or warn others, due to possible disastrous issues related to, perhaps violent weather conditions, especially if this is a common issue within that area. The dreamer is also being warned to be extra cautio us regarding the location "pin-pointed", because of a high chance for personal harm, as well. Especially if dreamer lives within or near the location depicted. Your dream should closely resemble real life situations, with the dream events actually being capable of happening. If you sense that your dream is a prophetic dream, the question as to why you have been made aware of this information, and how do you factor into the equation, should be seriously considered, along with necessary actions. Dreamer, you are meant to get involved. If possible, how can you ease the situation, especially for yourself and others? Dreams that reference others and the revelation within those dreams, is not given haphazardly to any individual, but only to those with the ability, and influence to do something with the information; this is also prophecy. Skip interpretation, Jesus will strengthen you emotionally, psychologically, and physically to seek help and support in your endeavors.

Otherwise noted, per your lifestyle, if your dream closely resembled real life situations, meaning it can actually occur during your awaked state, this dream may be an Ordinary Dream, resulting from daily activities (see Chapter One, Chalom). These sorts of dreams are usually about your routine, mundane activities or anxieties that overwhelm your mind during the day. They are an inner release mechanism, which helps provide you with emotional balance and the maintaining of your sanity. These dreams are not significant, and do not warrant special attention.

2. Probables: As cardinal points and stars are frequently demonstrated in many, and very personal ways; for example, does the Star of David symbolize Judaism to you? Were you raised in the south? Are you from the east? Thus, could the cardinal point or star depicted be a possible probable (see Chapter One, section entitled, Probables)? Hence, dreamer may also consider your own personal and special associations with various cardinal points or stars, as long as the interpretation is kept within the principles of spiritual boundary markers, landmarks, and property lines, (see Chapter One, section entitled, Spiritualizing Boundary Markers, Landmarks, and Property Lines).

3. Determine who your dream is for you or another. Always, considering yourself first, reflecting on your present behaviors. Ask yourself, why am I dreaming about this now? What is this dream revealing about me? Have I taken on new attributes? Has anyone commented on my present behaviors as being untypical of me? Has my ministry changed for the better or for the worse? What about my beliefs, doctrine, or philosophy, are they still based on Holy Writ? Is there something I need to know about those I am ministering to or serving?

Remember your actions and emotions within your dream. For example, did you leave the north and go towards the south? Did you see a storm heading in your direction? Did someone or a sign, point you towards a certain direction? Did you lose your way while driving? Were you flying on Northeastern, Northwestern, or Eastern Airlines? Was a strong westerly wind blowing making you unsteady? Did you visit a relative down south, out west, up north, in the east? Did dreamer see a star in the sky towards the east (Matthew 2:2)? Unless otherwise noted elsewhere, an answer of yes, to one or more of these, or similar questions, is a good indicator that your dream is about you (the dreamer). In light of your dream, via the relevant interpretation, do you believe that your behavior will enhance or endanger your well-being, safety, and/or happiness, if so, how and why? Do you believe that your belief system will strengthen or weaken you spiritually in any way, if so, how and why? See following relevant subcategory, the interpretation is about and for you.

Did dreamer sense, within your dream that a crucial earth event is headed toward a particular geographic coordinate? Was the wind blowing towards the direction of another or causing another to become unsteady? Was another flying on Northeastern, Northwestern, or Eastern Airlines? Who was the pilot? Did dreamer point someone towards a cardinal direction? Was someone driving or walking in the wrong direction? Did someone give the dreamer wrong directions? Unless otherwise noted elsewhere, an answer of yes, to one or more of these, or similar questions, is a good indicator that your dream is about another and their role, and/ or influential effects, within the life of the dreamer. Consider, is someone greatly influencing your physical, spiritual, or mental health, your understanding, perspective, and reasoning regarding spiritual issues? Are they enhancing your spiritual and/or literal prosperity, or are they responsible for the dwindling thereof? Could they be influencing your ministry, on some level? Do you know someone whose life activities or physical being is similar to that which stood out the most within your dream? Could it be that person? If you sense that your dream is for or about another, the question as to why you have been made privy to this information, and how do you factor into the equation, should be seriously considered along with necessary actions. Perhaps the dreamer is being made aware of the plight of someone, and you are to get involved (see Chapter One, Are You Ready to Hear the Messages in Your Dreams, section entitled, The 10% for others).

If your dream is for, or about another:

Dreams that reference others and the revelation within those dreams, is not given haphazardly to any individual, but only to those with the ability, and influence to do something with the information; this is also prophecy. With that, journal the following questions, and if unable to answer the questions now, this denotes that the person, represented within your dream, will enter your life shortly. Are you entering into a personal relationship with someone? Do you not know or understand what you're looking at, especially certain behaviors, when learning about this person? Has someone new entered your life or maybe you've just begun opening up to someone not so new, and have started listening to their advice, accepting their assistance, or are you enabling someone? Are you in denial regarding the toxicity of one of your present relationships, particularly a spouse, family member, or friend? Are you anxious, concerned, frightened, and/or troubled by recent changes in your behavior, especially because of someone's influence upon your life at present? Have you allowed someone to convince you to deceive another? Have you recently become aware of (or is being made aware of, via your dream) certain undesirable behaviors within you towards another? Are you trying to cut ties with one that is bad company? Have you just joined (or re-joined) a church, fellowship, or social group?

Note: If your dream has attributes that indicate that your dream is about you, and other attributes that indicate that your dream is about another, dreamer should consider that your dream is about you and another. For example, while you may have lost your way while driving, thus indicating that the dream is about the dreamer, someone else may have pointed you in the right direction, thus indicating that your dream is about another. Therefore, while your dream is about the dreamer, the dreamer should expect the role and/or influential effects of another, also plays a part in your interpretation. For example, dreamer may have been physically wounded in a bad accident, and due to a lawsuit, dreamer is now being treated badly by the parties responsible and the party insurance company; and because the lawsuit is costly and laborious, this is causing the dreamer to become bitter, again, see relevant interpretation.

More questions to consider. Why has the person been allowed within your life, and/or how did they get there? Again, if unable to answer the questions now, this denotes that the person, represented within your dream, will enter your life shortly. If their activity, within your dream, has proven positive, via the interpretation, this someone will prove, unwittingly, to be a very strong ally, benefactor, defender, and supporter. God has sent this someone into your life to help you carry out your next endeavor by enlarging your spiritual capacity. Allow the strength of that person's character to guide, help, and support you. On the other hand, if his or her presence and/or activity, within your dream, proved negative, via the interpretation, for sure, this person will prove to be a very strong and formidable challenge for you, perhaps unto death. If negative, this dream is a dire warning. Take steps accordingly to struggle against, or to cut off, adverse and unfavorable relationships. Remember certain personalities are all encompassing, affecting everything, cataclysmic, contagious, deadly, harmful, infectious, predatory, and/or venomous. Symbolically meaning that if allowed to continue or prosper within your life, serious harm or death to the dreamer may result. Idolize no one, especially beyond the warning of the Lord, and we are definitely not to lay our lives down for no one.

No longer, allow that particular person's influence within your life to continue or thrive. Then again, this person maybe allowed within your life, because of the dreamer's unwillingness to abstain from immorality after having been asked to abstain from such by God, see 1 Corinthians 6:9-20, Galatians 5:19-21, or the dreamer's self-righteous behavior, or a lack of a balanced and honest view of your own personality. In this case, this person will affect self-awareness within the life of the dreamer, exposing the negative traits of your personality, especially those traits, which cause you to follow, or to be so easily misled, and/or your wrong beliefs; no matter, this type of mentality needs reckoning with. Graciously, all of this will restore the dreamer to his or her right place with God, opening your eyes to see how far you've strayed from God (1 Corinthians 5:4-7; James 5:20). The lesson is, no matter how personable, powerful, or difficult a person, or how uncertain or unpopular the choices and issues, always take the next biblical and ethical step, for obedience to God's principles will always prove safer and stronger foundationally. Although, you will need all kinds of outside support to recover from this person's domination, again, no longer, allow that particular person's influence within your life to continue or thrive, especially if negative, end it abruptly.

4. Consider all the people, places, backgrounds, and activity highlighted within your dream.

Known (in your awaked life) person, animal, place, or organization within your dream:

Unless otherwise noted elsewhere, people, animals, places, backgrounds that are actually known by the dreamer in your awaked life, indicates a part of you that you recognize within yourself on some level or another. Question to journal, if dreamer seriously considers all the particulars, what stood out the most, what features, or character traits stood out the most. Write down (journal) the particular highlighted within your dream. The attribute or activity highlighted is for a reason. Since the attribute written down is a part of you, namely the dreamer's nature, demeanor, and/or lifestyle, an honest and unbiased assessment is very important for truth sake. Happy note, considering that other people's attributes, within dreams, also represent attributes of your own personality, causes one to look at another in a better light. According to your capacity to embrace self-awareness and a rectification of mind, body, and spirit, God will begin to enhance, make better, more attractive, sanctify, diminish, and make pure and free from sin and guilt, this part of you.

Otherwise noted, if the person, animal, place, or background within your dream is actually known by the dreamer, in your awaked life, this person, animal, place, or background may represent him or herself, or itself.

Unknown in your awaked life or although known, was unseen, invisible, or only talked about - person, animal, place, or organization within your dream:

Unless otherwise noted elsewhere, if you did not recognize, the person, place, thing, they, or it, was not seen, invisible, or only talked about within your dream, this indicates an attribute or activity within your life that you are unfamiliar with, or are in denial about, or you refuse to acknowledge it, but it does exists. Question to journal: what character trait, feature, action, or activity, stood out the most? For example, age, color, height, size, happiness, loving, peacefulness, irrational, leader, liar, mentor, passionate, neglected, poor, sage, shyster, unwise, upscale, vengeful. Although, on some conscious level, you are aware of a certain behavior or attribute within you, you have chosen to filter out or simply ignore certain information about yourself that contradicts your view of yourself and/or your preconceived notions of others and of the world around you. Possibly protecting yourself, emotionally and psychologically, from a situation, which you are unable to cope with at this time, or you lack control over; then again, perhaps the dreamer has an exaggerated or unrealistic view of yourself. No matter the reason, right now a question is before you, via your dream. Do you want to know this part of yourself? According to your ability to handle self-awareness, God will begin to reveal this side of you to you. Why, He wants to balance your understanding of things; thus, effecting wholeness within your life, so that the enemy will no longer be able to manipulate your emotions so easily. The

Paraclete is with you to help you throughout this entire process, listen to Him. Now, in your life, this activity or attribute needs reckoning with, somehow or someway.

Otherwise noted, (known or unknown)**,** if the person, place or thing that initiated (or was a recipient of) the action or activity within your dream was not seen, invisible, or only talked about within your dream, this may indicate that the dreamer does not recognize the influential effects another has within your life, or upon your attitude.

If more than one person (known or unknown):

Consider what the group had in common. What behavior, character trait, feature, action, or activity, stood out the most? For example, were they argumentative, authoritative, beautiful, criminal minded, dancing, difficult, dressed unusual, enigmatic, fighting, focused, flirty, helpful, hurtful intentions, powerful, promiscuous, quiet, secretive, seemed unreal, unassuming? What about age, color, height, size, happiness, considerate, loving, let you be yourself, peacefulness, encourager, irrational, leader, liar, mentor, passionate, personable, neglected, poor, run-down, sage, shyster, unwise, upscale, vengeful, death. That which was highlighted and noted is what you need to focus on at present.

If the attribute or quality is a desirable or positive one, allow the strength of that attribute to help you overcome some manner of immorality or irreverence within your life and/or to help you to become better, productively, for the Kingdom of God in some manner. If the attribute is an undesirable or negative one, take steps accordingly to struggle against the growing desires of the carnal side of you. If applicable, get help and support via prayer, fasting, and a Christian based support group.

For dreams of the dead see following note.

Were many people dead in a particular region? While the dead has nothing to do with the living (Ecclesiastes 9:4-6), it may be considered what character trait did that person represent to the dreamer, while the person was actually alive, what character feature stood out the most. With that trait noted, dreamer may consider that the trait noted, is within the dreamer, and that trait is no longer useful or needed for the progression of your spiritual walk, on this side of heaven. Dreamer, it is suggested that you render that trait (good or bad) obsolete, and began anew attempting to move forward, using different tactics to overcome unproductive habitual life cycle choices, and for maneuvering through this thing we call life in a more, better way. See category, Death, and/or other relevant categories.

5. In addition to the following interpretations, see index or relevant categories for more information. For example, if weather conditions were involved in some way, see category, Weather; if a roof was highlighted, see category, Buildings, Structures. If mode of travel was highlighted, see category, Vehicles. Kept within context of your dream and the interpretation, the additional symbols are perhaps relevant. It will be within the sum of all the symbols that you will find a more thorough interpretation.

6. Since the following list is not extensive, dreamer is encouraged to seek biblical guidelines and other relevant research to determine the metaphorical meaning of your particular cardinal point or star, depicted within your dream, via a Bible concordance, Bible illustrated dictionary, encyclopedia, or internet. Having done your research you should be able to determine some basic behaviors or attributes your Lord and Savior wants you to focus on.

7. If cardinal direction is somewhere between the chief points, dreamer should consider point that is most highlighted (e.g. NNW, interpretation for north should be considered, ENE, interpretation for east should considered, and so forth.

Symbols and Referents

This dream generally deals with the directions, and repercussions or consequences, your attitude and behaviors, are leading too.

In addition to the varied meanings of cardinal directions, points, other common words, expressions, usages, (e.g. slang or clichés), or a 'probable' that are metaphorically represented by any of the following are also considered (this section is an addendum at the end of the relevant subcategory).

Category Content - If not listed see index, perchance, for your specific type of cardinal point and stars dream.

- East, East Wind, Eastward
  - East and West (mid-point); East to West (westward)
- Moon
- North, North Wind, or Northward
  - North to South
- South, South Wind, or Southward
- Stars
  - Sun; Star of David (a six-pointed star formed from two equilateral triangles; an emblem symbolizing Judaism); Astrology, astrological signs, horoscope (star divination); Pentagram (a five-pointed star, usually with two points upward, associated with Satanism, occultism, secret societies, e.g. Eastern Star); Stars turn dark (to see stars stop shining, similarly to lights going out)
- West, West Wind, or Westward

EAST, EAST WIND, OR EASTWARD:

Dreamer, you are one who is powerfully convincing; you are a great leader, perhaps even historical. However, even if it seems like you are going in the right direction, doing only good, and your cause appears noble, for your purpose is that of becomin g a forerunner for change, freedom, progressive thought, and action. Unfortunately, because of your growing disregard of God's ways and means, you are headed towards becoming gnostic in belief, in other words, namely, possessing intellectual or esoteric knowledge of spiritual things. The "end result" of your efforts is some manner of Gnosticism at best and humanism at worst, namely a doctrine that emphasis a person's capacity for self-realization through reason; and one that rejects religion and the miraculous. Further, as you have the capacity to spearhead a new dawn, giving birth to a generation that will usher in an age of philosophical and intellectual enlightenment, this new dawn will not usher in the Truth of God that comes via the Holy Spirit and Holy Writ. Regrettably, the offspring of this new dawn will lack the knowledge of a personal and saving relationship with Christ Jesus. For, not only is your way, delivered without grace, it will never be enough to fill an empty soul, for it approaches the spiritual realm without the provision that God has provided for man to approach, and reach, true spiri tual perfection, and that provision being Jesus the Christ. While every step you take appears to take you toward purpose; your focus on enlightenment and progressive thinking is without holiness and will only placate those who choose to forget their God. As you do have the ability to talk others out of believing, thinking, feeling, or doing anything connected to Jesus Christ, and you will attempt to do just that; which will result in great spiritual famine in the lives of those you convince. Hence, your dream is a sober warning. Dreamer, your behavior hinders the sanctification process, thus, reckoning you as one who is leaving God, a rebellious child of God (Luke 9:62), or as one known as a "backslider". Even more your grumbling, complaining, and murmuring are clear indicators of your backslidden state. Your attitude will mar spiritual growth and prosperity within your life; preventing you from achieving your goals, having forfeited purpose for foolishness. Dreamer you are soberly warned to disassociate yourself from this heresy, and there is a need for repentance. Repentance is seeking pardon and expressing sincere feelings of regret and brokenness for having done something awry and/or for having hurt someone, see 2 Corinthians 7:10, 11. To Jesus pray, Psalm 51, this coupled with prayer, fasting, and follow-thru with appropriate application of wisdom, can conceivably avert some of the repercussions of your choices. When a man or woman genuinely return to God in love and surrender, your deliberate transgressions become like actual merits (also see Luke 7:37-50). Because, the realization of your distance from God, resulting from your transgressions (Isaiah 59:2), becomes the motivating force to return to God with a passion even greater than that of someone who has never sinned in such a manner (or never left his Father's house, Acts 9:1-30). However, until you own up to your rebellious behavior, repent, stop the grumbling, complaining, and murmuring, and become submissive, obedient, and useful within God's Kingdom again, you will begin to decrease, and become weaken in spirit and body. In addition, your actions and behavior, that which is secret, and previously known only to a few, will become publ ic information. See suggested course of action.

East and West (mid-point): To be between east and west (mid-point), dreamer in time, you will experience the Shekinah, a glow of the Light of God's Goodness, if you remain diligent and don't give up on your spiritual journey, and again, never do you ever give up. See suggested course of action.

East to West (westward): To go from east to west, namely traveling westward, your dream refers to instantaneous knowledge. Dreamer will be miraculously endowed with spiritual knowledge. Remember, Jesus is the source of that knowledge, and just like the Lord gives, He can take away, due to disobedience, and none of your righteousness will be remembered no more (Ezekiel 33:12). Stay humble and balanced.

MOON:

Dreamer is not properly acknowledging your mother on some level of another.

NORTH, NORTH WIND, OR NORTHWARD:

Your dream was sent as a stern and severe rebuke. Dreamer, you are conceited, egotistical, vain, and possibly sexually immoral (e.g. adultery or fornication). You have an exaggerated opinion of your personal worth and abilities, and you lack humility. You are aggressive, intense, and violent. With you comes a state of confusion; and you aggressively intimidate others, using your influence to force others to do what you say, this is also known as witchcraft and rebellion (1 Samuel 15:23). Dreamer, your attitude is leading to a mental and spiritual breakdown and corruption, opening the door for demons to run havoc within your life. Demonic influences will swarm around you, ready to help you in your wicked, evil, despicable, immoral, reprehensible, disreputable, degenerate, infamous, and/or perverse choices. Your lifestyle choices will become offensive and repulsive (abominable) in the sight of God and humanity. Moreover, your attitude, if con tinued, will open a portal, through which you will gain dark and erroneous knowledge, through personal experience and through a supernatural imparting, which is demonically communicated. The knowledge gained will not allow you to praise the Lord, only to exalt yourself. Dreamer, demons have had thousands of years to master human weaknesses and can rival men and women of God if we are not careful. If no change in your attitude, you will be defeated spiritually (Ezekiel 18:24). Favorably, because of grace (the free and unmerited favor and beneficence of God) and the many mercies of God extended to you, your dream is only a stern and severe rebuke and not an official declaration. Understanding that your choices may be evil is not enough; you have an obligation to fight to overcome the evil. Dreamer is counseled to endure divine discipline and divine reprimand for folly and sin, which is the Lord's chastening and correction that leads to reformation. Dreamer it is also suggested, to possibly avert or turn some things around, that you definitely walk away from all that feeds pride and vanity abruptly and from all that hinders spiritual clarity. If relevant, also flee fornication. Begin loving the Lord, with all your strength and might, via obedience to His Holy Word.

Utilizing the powerful resources of prayer and heartfelt repentance to Jesus and to individuals affected by your actions, in the form of an apology (if possible), is needed. Repentance is seeking pardon and expressing sincere feelings of regret and brokenness for having done something awry and/ or for having hurt someone, see 2 Corinthians 7:10, 11. To individuals, a phone call or a letter of apology is a good place to start. To Jesus pray, Psalm 51, this followed by appropriate applicatio n of wisdom, can conceivably avert the repercussions of your choices. This coupled with fasting, a changed mindset, serious re - consideration of God's ways and means, and an honest acknowledgement of God's hand within your life, then the severe impact of your choices and actions upon your life, can be lessen. This is what is called leaving a blessing behind. If you do not genuinely seek help and change, for sure ruin will be your destiny's declaration. If you are careful to submit to His ordina nces, you will be His people, and He will be your God and you will be clean. See suggested course of action.

North to South: To leave the north and go towards the south, your dream denotes that dreamer will earnestly put forth efforts to become spiritually clear. Consequently, you will eventually reach your ultimate goals; those that you are working towards, and you will fulfill your purpose, reaching your destiny, embracing peace, love, and happiness.

SOUTH, SOUTH WIND, OR SOUTHWARD:

Dreamer, your words have pleased the Lord, for they are words of wisdom. Thus, He has done according to your words; go forward with purpose, looking for results. No longer will you be on the outside of things, looking in, and no longer will you be charge falsely, especially with malicious intent. If not already, you will become part of a group of believers, and you will be one whom believers will interact with socially on very personal levels (e.g. business partner, friendship, marriage, other mutual relationships). Moreover, God will grant you both riches and honor, and "if" ("if" is conditional) you continue to walk in His ways, diligently and obediently, you will have long life too. This is His promise to you, and He will do according to His pr omise. Further, use your creative passion to inspire others, via inspirational preaching, teaching, acting, or some other medium of expression. For you are gifted in many areas. Additionally, "it" (whatever "it" is to you personally and presently) will happen, and you will be blessed. To be blessed of God: gifts of God's grace that will produce spiritual growth within you. Absolution, children, eternal life, health, the Holy Spirit, longevity, love of family, necessities, peace, prosperity, regeneration, sa lvation, and dominion over all that is yours; and all are parts of the supply of grace, and all are sanctified by the Lord, and technically belongs to Him. The result of this supply in your life will be peace. All of these promises will begin now.

STARS:

Great caution is necessary in the interpretation of this symbol. The dream's context will play a major part in its meaning. With that said, this dream has five meanings (choose one). (1) Sun: Dreamer is not properly acknowledging your father on some level of another. (2) Star of David (a six-pointed star formed from two equilateral triangles; an emblem symbolizing Judaism). This choice has two parts (one or both may apply). (a) This dream is referencing the dreamer's literal siblings. Dreamer will become eminent amongst your siblings, for you are above average in wisdom, and formidable in strength and power. On the other hand, and unfortunately, your unrighteous pride, and unnatural sexual attractions and desires, will be dealt with first. Thus, you will now begin to experience a "humbling". This "humbling", aka your journey, particularly towards eminency, will be fraught with jealously, betrayal, and deceit. All these troubles and "twists and turns" will be by the schemes of your li teral siblings, as well as others, as you are guided on your way, and the troubles will be allowed that you might be made complete, lacking nothing. See suggested course of action. (b) See Romans 4:1-25, Galatians 3:6-25. Dreamer is already a spiritual descendant of Abraham and needs to be reminded and encouraged of that fact, or dreamer needs to embrace that Jesus loves you, thus, He is petitioning you to accept Him as your personal Savior, for you are valuable in His eyes. This act of receiving Christ as your personal Savior will lead to you becoming a spiritual descendant of Abraham. The first step in receiving Him as your personal Savior is repentance (see in the Holy Bible, Acts 2:37-41). Repentance is seeking pardon for having done something awry, and for having hurt someone, and expressing sincere feelings of regret and brokenness. To Jesus pray, Psalm 51:1-19. (3) Astrology, astrological signs, horoscope (star divination): Your dream denotes that the dreamer is a false prophet, one who is participating in some type of demonic, antichrist activity, and the rise of a cult leader. You will be exposed as such. See suggested course of action. (4) Pentagram (a five-pointed star, usually with two points upward, associated with Satanism, occultism, secret societies, e.g. Eastern Star). This star denotes a dealer in astrology, a false prophet, or one who is participating in some type of occult activity. Often a pentagram, or some star type image, used for worship, or some type of occult practices, will be depicted. This practice is the root of idolatry, and witchcraft, and is the antithesis of Christ. You respect your truth, while never acknowledging, your truth is delivered without grace; thus, it is never enough to fill an emaciated soul. You discredit the Creator's wise and sensible guidelines for living life, on this side of eternity, as healthy, humanly, and sanely as possible; and in harmony with His provision for life on the other side of eternity, in heaven. You ex alt your wisdom above the Creator. Favorably, your dream is only a warning and is sent in the spirit of grace. If your thoughts, feelings, and beliefs are not rectified, you will open the door of your spirit to abominations of various types, to "stir up" feelings of disgust and abhorrence towards Jesus and His ways and means, even more. Your behaviors will become so vicious and vile; your actions will arouse distaste and/or hate of you by others, and you will feel the brunt of those feelings of ot hers towards you. There will be no response of love, sympathy, or tenderness toward you. Moreover, you will expose your physical body to illnesses, from which you will be unable to recover without divine help, via Jesus. Repentance to Jesus, coupled wit h a renunciation of your spiritually poisonous words and ways are the antivenin to the venomous attack of that old serpent, the devil, upon your life. Further, if urged by God, declare a one, two, or three-day fast, no food or water, coupled with studying the teachings of Jesus Christ. By this, you will again begin to experience God's truth, and see the demonic for what it is - a lie. If relevant, avoid personal isolation and isolated groups that teach something different from the gospel of Jesus Christ (e.g. condemnation, hate, any racist ideology, murder, no one is "right" but our western sect, or any other oppressive or "hell bound" for everyone but me and/or our small group ideas). Moreover, if not practiced regularly, go to church, join a church, a faith based bible-believing community, commit to that ministry, and don't leave, no matter what, for three years. Forsake not the gathering of yourself together with other mainstream Christians. A prophecy will be given you, via someone within that ministry, during this season, write it down for it will happen. Even more, entering the House of God should be done reverently rather than carelessly. Cease from many words but rather humbly learn, and let your words be sprinkled with empathy, humility, and understanding. For, in spite of what we do not know about the many mysteries of God and life; one thing remains eternally true God is our loving Father. He does not desire that any one perish; thus, great effort is exercised to save us, even in the moment of our death. See suggested course of action. (5) Stars turn dark (to see stars stop shining, similarly to lights going out): As this symbol denotes physical death is imminent and perhaps even spiritual death. Read and understand Galatians 5:19-21, for this speaks of spiritual death. Your dream has come to set life and death soberly before you, the dreamer, and if you will not choose behaviors, actions, thoughts, and choices that promote life, you will die, especially physically. To the dreamer it is said, for you to remember your Creator, before your days of trouble come and time has caught up with you (Ecclesiastes 12:1-7). Dreamer take heed, no dead philosophy, or any other lifeless "ism" will come to life to tell you truth, nor will a dead person, come to life, to tell you of what he or she has seen. For, if the "ism" did contain a spark of life, or if the dead did come back to tell you of what he or she experienced or saw, you would not believe the teaching, nor would you believe the dead (Luke 16:27-31). Dreamer, relationship with Christ, appeals to people not by half-truths or lies, or ghosts or frightful apparitions; it appeals to your reason, your conscience, and your hopes. Additionally, about your dream, dreamer death is not only physical, but also it denotes a spiritual separation from God, a place of torment, aka "Tartarus", which is also death. Dreamer, accepting Jesus as your Lord and Savior, and the guiding of His Holy Spirit, leads to truth and eternal life. Nevertheless, if you will not hear the Son of God, follow the leading of His Holy Spirit, and heed the warnings of Holy Writ; there is nothing, which you will or can hear, you will never be persuaded, and will never escape the place of torment. See suggested course of action.

WEST OR WEST WIND OR WESTWARD:

Your dream denotes a "coming to God". The following is paraphrased and is meant to convey a brief meaning of coming to God. Jesus says, come to Him, all who are tired from carrying heavy loads and He will give you rest. Place God's yoke over your shoulders, and learn from Him, because He is gentle and humble. Then you will find rest for yourself because God's yoke is easy and His burden is light. All that the Father gives Jesus will come to Jesus, and the one who comes to Jesus, He will by no means cast out. No one can come to Jesus unless the Father who sent Jesus draws him; and Jesus will raise him up at the last day. Therefore, everyone who has heard and learned from the Father comes to Jesus. It is written in the prophets, "In addition, they shall all be taught by God". The LORD says, I will instruct you. I will teach you the way that you should go. God will advise you as His eyes watch over you. If anyone thirsts, let him come to Jesus and drink. He who believes in Jesus, a s the Scripture has said, out of his heart will flow, rivers of living water. Jesus was speaking concerning the Holy Spirit, whom those believing in Him would receive. Therefore, repent, and be baptized in the name of Jesus Christ for the remission of your sin s, and you shall receive the gift of the Holy Spirit; for the promise is unto you, and to your children, and to all that are afar off, even as many as the Lord our God shall call. This is what coming to God is. Reference Psalm 32:8; Joel 2:12-13, Matthew 11:28-30; John 6:37, 6:44-45, 7:37-39, Acts 2:38, 39. With all of that, the purpose of your dream is to encourage the dreamer. Dreamer, God will save you from all your uncleanness that you might know God is God, and honor and glorify Him whose power is the power, and whose rule will endure eternally, and that you might know your God ordained destiny. Dreamer, God does as He pleases; and chooses whom He pleases, with the powers of heaven and the peoples of the earth, and He has chosen you. Once you recognize your true destiny, and that destiny is being in Christ Jesus, your outlook on life will begin to change. Therefore the Lord says, turn now, unto Him, with all your heart, and with fasting, weeping, and with mourning, and rend your heart, not your garments, and turn unto the Lord your God. Repentance is an inward change that will produce outward changes. Afterwards, if relevant, join a church. Moreover, you will gain knowledge on how to be moderate in all things, just and fair, and you will become one whom other believers will interact with socially on very personal levels, and will, help restore you back to God, in the spirit of empathy, mercy, leniency, and kindness, allow this. See suggested course of action.

Suggested Course of Action

Question to consider and journal, did your dream depict any symbols that alludes to, the dreamer will make the necessary changes, spiritually, emotionally, and/or physically to affect a more positive outcome? If changes are initiated, your dreams will change.

Did anyone get hurt emotionally, physically, or was disturbed in any way? Were others involved? If yes, who and in what manner were they involved; keeping in mind that the others represent a quality of you. How did you feel, and what did you do, because, of your feelings, regarding the direction and/ or how things was going, or things ended up? Was it agitating, confusing, dangerous, disturbing, frustrating, peace with the situation, happy, joyful, life threatening, safe, scary, or uns ure? Your answers, coupled with the interpretation, plus any additional information, should begin to unfold the subject matter and issue at hand, if not now, mull over things a few days.

Nevertheless, in view of your dream's context, and the primary symbols, what does your dream reveal about you, your ethics, intents, mental state, and motives? You will need to earnestly look within and consider that the sum of your answers is a reflection of where you are emotionally, physically, and/ or spiritually, and a reflection of who you are becoming. What was your reaction to the situation? Were you angry, concerned, confused, defensive, fearful, happy, helpful, pleased, shocked, unconcerned, or ready to get out of someone's presence? Your reaction to the activity, or the circumstance, reveals your attitude regarding this information about yourself. Nonetheless, if the behaviors, per the interpretation, are allowed to continue or prosper within your life, serious harm may result.

Dreamer, consider seriously your observations. If what was revealed prevail, will it sabotage any good that's happening at present within your life? Will it build or destroy, strengthen or weaken, enlighten or blind? If you lack wisdom, ask Je sus for wisdom. He gives wisdom to all, generously, no matter who you are and what you've done; wisdom is available (see James 1:5-8, Proverbs 2:1-6, 10). Hence, if, by just asking, you may get wisdom, one may suffer needlessly, because you will not ask Jesus for wisdom.

Moreover, because of emotional scarring and/or insecurities resulting from past difficult situations, you may not have the ability to work through challenging circumstances at this time and to make the best decisions. Regrettably, this in turn can, and often do, result in emotional emptiness, and you rejecting the love, authority, and instructions of God. A spirit of apathy towards your personal relationship with Christ is a bad frame of mind. In time, your carnal nature will dominantly reign ove r your spiritual side. Carnality always opens the door for someone, under the influence of evil, to run amok your life, both physically and spiritually until you are unable to recover. Dreamer, you need help from your spiritual leader(s). To help y ou sincerely clarify and amend the true intents and purposes of your actions, and to bring to an end that which keeps you from being built up on a strong foundation. For, you are still expected to respect God, and His ways and means. His principles a re not there to be obstacles to your progress, or to be a bore to you, but to keep you out of harm's way and to assure eternal life in the world to come, the Kingdom of God. Compassionately, grace is extended, giving you time to change your heart. God is giving you the opportunity to turn things around spiritually and emotionally, and He will turn things around literally; however, you will have to choose to allow the opportunity, for you still have free will; thus, the choice is yours. Free will is the expression of you choosing to participate in the divine acts of God; albeit, you are only merely placing your hand under the weight carried exclusively by God. Thus, you are not being asked to do something you cannot do, or to do it alone. Dreamer; personally respond, repent, and genuinely commit to a righteous change to have life; with primary emphasis on life after this present life. However, the issue of eternal life will not be forced upon anyone who desires to remain in sin. For more information, see index or relevant category and subcategory for specific action, activity, person, place, or organization primary within your dream.

Now, pray (See Prayer of Deliverance, pg. 897)

Specific Meaning

Unless otherwise noted elsewhere, if, in your everyday living, your awaked state, as part of your lifestyle, work, or ministerial activities, or a special event, you have a very real connection with any activity involving the cardinal points or stars. For example, astronomy, work with compass or any navigational instruments, any geographical type activity, map making, meteorology, or any navigational type jobs, satellite-based global position systems (GPS), or any activity or science dealing with phenomena of the cardinal points or stars. Dreams of this sort, for the most part, are ordinary dreams, resulting from your daily activities (see Chapter One, Chalom). These sorts of dreams are usually about your routine, mundane activities or anxieties that overwhelm your mind during the day. They are an inner release mechanism, which helps provide you with emotional balance and the maintaining of your sanity. These dreams are not significant, and do not warrant special attention.

Note: If your work within astronomy, any geographical type activity, meteorology, or any navigational type jobs, satellite- based global position systems (GPS), or any activity or science dealing with phenomena of the cardinal points or stars, depict any abnormal or unusual anomalies, then something need to be done, reported, or heeded. This type of dream may be heeded as an alert or warning in the physical realm, to the dreamer. Do not assume that things are safe, ok, or not important, caution, or at least inquiry, should be heeded. The dreamer may consider his or her dream as a clue given to assist in finding facts, needed to support a prevailing situation or investigation. The alarm, kept within context of the dream, should be relevant to your lifestyle and closely resemble your real-life situations. Meaning it can actually occur during your awaked state. Consider all the people, places, backgrounds, and activity highlighted within your dream. This will help you narrow down the specific area of concern. However, if your dream was inundated with symbols that are not specifically related to your job and/or responsibilities, then the spiritual implications should be heeded.

CELEBRATIONS AND EVENTS

"For everything there is a season, and a time for every purpose under heaven. A time to be born, and a time to die; a time to plant, and a time to pluck up that, which is planted, a time to kill, and a time to heal; a time to break down, and a time to build up; a time to weep, and a time to laugh. A time to mourn and a time to dance; a time to cast away stones, and a time to gather stones together; A time to embrace, and a time to refrain from embracing; a time to seek, and a time to lose; a time to keep. In addition, a time to cast away; a time to rend, and a time to sew; a time to keep silence, and a time to speak; A time to love, and a time to hate, a time for war, and a time for peace" (The words of the Preacher, the son of David, king in Jerusalem)

This category deals with celebrations and events, the public observances and performances of a formal event performed on special occasions, be it, a joyful occasion for special festivities to mark some happy event, or a sad occasion to mark a solemn event. Some short descriptions of types, phrases, and other processes and particulars, connected in some way to this category are, for example, birthdays, festivals, funerals, parades, protests, showers, weddings. Also, see category content list, or index.

All Symbols and Referents, Notes (1, 2, 3, etc.), Suggested Course of Action, and Specific Meaning offer guidance toward a more comprehensive interpretation.

Notes

1. Unless otherwise noted elsewhere, if, in your everyday living, your awaked state, as part of your lifestyle, work, or ministerial activities, or a special event, you have a very real connection with any activity involving celebrations or event s. For example, event organizer, celebration planner, celebration or event sponsor or host, or any other activity involved in the observance and/or performance of any public celebration or event, your dream is not significant and does not warrant special attention.

    Otherwise noted, per your lifestyle, if your dream closely resembled real life situations, meaning it can actually occur during your awaked state, this dream may be an Ordinary Dream, resulting from your daily activities (see Chapter One, Chalom). These sorts of dreams are usually about your routine, mundane activities or anxieties that overwhelm your mind during the day. They are an inner release mechanism, which helps provide you with emotional balance and the maintaining of your sanity. These dreams are not significant, and do not warrant special attention.

2. Probables: As celebrations and events are frequently demonstrated in many, and very personal ways; for example, do you celebrate Anniversaries, Christmas, Easter, Hanukah, national holidays or attend community vigils? Does the day of your wedding bring beautiful memories? Thus, could the celebration or event depicted be a possible probable (see Chapter One, section entitled, Probables)? Hence, dreamer may also consider your own personal and special associations with various mediums of exchange, as long as the interpretation is kept within the principles of spiritual boundary markers, landmarks, and property lines, (see Chapter One, section entitled, Spiritualizing Boundary Markers, Landmarks, and Property Lines).

3. Determine who your dream is for you or another. Always, considering yourself first, reflecting on your present behaviors. Ask yourself, why am I dreaming about this now? What is this dream revealing about me? Have I taken on new attributes? Has anyone commented on my present behaviors as being untypical of me? Has my ministry changed for the better or for the worse? What about my beliefs, doctrine, or philosophy, are they still based on Holy Writ? Is there something I need to know about those I am ministering to or serving?

    Remember your actions and emotions within your dream. Was the dreamer the event organizer, celebration planner, or a primary participant in any of the activities involved in the observance and/or performance of the celebration or event? Was the dreamer the celebration or event sponsor? Did the dreamer host the event? Unless otherwise noted elsewhere, an answer of yes, to one or more of these, or similar questions, is a good indicator that your dream is about you (the dreamer). What happened to you in your dream? How did the celebration or event end? Are you retiring or is in a position of being freed from activity such as work, strain or responsibility; hence a dream of a celebration? Are you in a backslidden state, hence a dream of your funeral? Are you caught up in serious spiritual warfare right now, hence a dream of war? In light of your dream, via the relevant interpretation, do you believe that your choices will enhance or endanger your well-being, safety, and/or happiness, if so, how and why? Is spiritual or physical death a possibility? See following relevant subcategory, the interpretation is about and for you.

Was someone else the event organizer, planner, or a primary participant in any of the activities involved in the observance and/or performance of the celebration or event? Was someone else the celebration or event sponsor? Did someone else host the event? Unless otherwise noted elsewhere, an answer of yes, to one or more of these, or similar questions, is a good indicator that your dream is about another and/or their role, and influential effects, within the life of the dreamer. Does someone find fault with your beliefs, God's truth, His church, and/or His people, thus you were the subject of a protest event? Are you sharing the "Good News" with someone, and encouraging him or her to accept Christ as his or her Savior, thus you attending someone else wedding? Are you dealing with someone, who truly believes in their heart that they will not have to give an account of their service to Heavenly Father? If you sense that your dream is for or about another, the question as to why you have been made privy to this information, and how do you factor into the equation, should be seriously considered along with necessary actions. Perhaps the dreamer is being made aware of the plight of someone, and you are to get involved (see Chapter One, Are You Ready to Hear the Messages in Your Dreams, section entitled, The 10% for others).

If your dream is for, or about another:

Dreams that reference others and the revelation within those dreams, is not given haphazardly to any individual, but only to those with the ability, and influence to do something with the information; this is also prophecy. With that, journal the following questions, and if unable to answer the questions now, this denotes that the person, represented within your dream, will enter your life shortly. Are you entering into a personal relationship with someone? Do you not know or understand what you're looking at, especially certain behaviors, when learning about this person? Has someone new entered your life or maybe you've just begun opening up to someone not so new, and have started listening to their advice, accepting their assistance, or are you supporting or enabling someone? Are you in denial regarding the toxicity of one of your present relationships, particularly a spouse, family member, or friend? Are you anxious, concerned, frightened, and/or troubled by recent changes in your behavior, especially because of someone's influence upon your life at present? Have you allowed someone to convince you to deceive another? Have you recently become aware of (or is being made aware of, via your dream) certain undesirable behaviors within you towards another? Are you trying to cut ties with one that is bad company? Have you just joined (or re-joined) a church, fellowship, or social group?

Note: If your dream has attributes that indicate that your dream is about you, and other attributes that indicate that your dream is about another, dreamer should consider that your dream is about you and another. For example, while you (the dreamer) sponsored the event, thus indicating that the dream is about the dreamer, another was the honoree, thus indicating that your dream is about another. Therefore, while your dream is about the dreamer, the dreamer should expect the role and/or influential effects of another, also plays a part in your interpretation. For example, dreamer may feel a need to be honored by someone, so much so that you have begun to despised that person, to your own peril (the story of Haman and Mordecai, the book of Esther, the Old Testament), again, see relevant interpretation.

More questions to consider. Why has the person been allowed within your life, and/or how did they get there? Again, if unable to answer the questions now, this denotes that the person, represented within your dream, will enter your life shortly. If their activity, within your dream, has proven positive, via the interpretation, this someone will prove, unwittingly, to be a very strong ally, benefactor, defender, and supporter. God has sent this someone into your life to help you carry out your next endeavor by enlarging your spiritual capacity. Allow the strength of that person's character to guide, help, and support you. On the other hand, if his or her presence and/or activity, within your dream, proved negative, via the interpretation, for sure, this person will prove to be a very strong and formidable challenge for you, perhaps unto death. If negative, this dream is a dire warning. Take steps accordingly to struggle against, or to cut off, adverse and unfavorable relationships. Remember certain personalities are all encompassing, affecting everything, cataclysmic, contagious, deadly, harmful, infectious, predatory, and/or venomous. Symbolically meaning that if allowed to continue or prosper within your life, serious harm or death to the dreamer may result. Idolize no one, especially beyond the warning of the Lord, and we are definitely not to lay our lives down for no one. Then again, this person maybe allowed within your life, because of the dreamer's unwillingness to abstain from immorality after having been asked to abstain from such by God, see 1 Corinthians 6:9-20, Galatians 5:19-21, or the dreamer's self-righteous behavior, or a lack of a balanced and honest view of your own personality. In this case, this person will affect self-awareness within the life of the dreamer, exposing the negative traits of your personality, especially those traits, which cause you to follow, or to be so easily misled, and/or your wrong beliefs; no matter, this type of mentality needs reckoning with. Graciously, all of this will restore the dreamer to his or her right place with God, opening your eyes to see how far you've strayed from God (1 Corinthians 5:4-7; James 5:20). The lesson is, no matter how personable, powerful, or difficult a person, or how uncertain or unpopular the choices and issues, always take the next biblical and ethical step, for obedience to God's principles will always prove safer and stronger foundationally. Although, you will need all kinds of outside support to recover from this person's domination, no longer, allow that particular person's influence within your life to continue or thrive, especially if negative, end it abruptly.

4. Consider all the people, places, backgrounds, and activity highlighted within your dream.

Known (in your awaked life) person, animal, place, or organization within your dream:

Unless otherwise noted elsewhere, people, animals, places, backgrounds that are actually known by the dreamer in your awaked life, indicates a part of you that you recognize within yourself on some level or another. Question to journal, if dreamer seriously considers all the particulars, what stood out the most, what features, or character traits stood out the most? For example, age, color, height, size, happiness, considerate, loving, let you be yourself, peacefulness, encourager, irrational, leader, liar, mentor, passionate, personable, neglected, poor, run-down, sage, shyster, unwise, upscale, vengeful. Write down (journal) the particular highlighted within your dream. The attribute or activity highlighted is for a reason. Since the attribute written down is a part of you, namely the dreamer's nature, demeanor, and/or lifestyle, an honest and unbiased assessment is very important for truth sake. Happy note, considering that other people's attributes, within dreams, also represent attributes of your own personality, causes one to look at another in a better light. According to your capacity to embrace self-awareness and a rectification of mind, body, and spirit, God will begin to enhance, make better, more attractive, sanctify, diminish, and make pure and free from sin and guilt, this part of you.

Otherwise noted, if the person, animal, place, or background within your dream is actually known by the dreamer, in your awaked life, this person, animal, place, or background may represent him or herself, or itself.

Unknown in your awaked life or although known, was unseen, invisible, or only talked about - person, animal, place, or organization within your dream:

Unless otherwise noted elsewhere, if you did not recognize, the person, place, thing, they, or it, was not seen, invisible, or only talked about within your dream, this indicates an attribute or activity within your life that you are unfamiliar with, or are in denial about, or you refuse to acknowledge it, but it does exists. Question to journal: what character trait, feature, action, or activity, stood out the most, for example, age, color, height, size, loving, peacefulness, encourager, irrational, leader, liar, mentor, passionate, poor, sage, shyster, unwise, upscale, vengeful. Although, on some conscious level, you are aware of a certain behavior or attribute within you, you have chosen to filter out or simply ignore certain information about yourself that contradicts your view of yourself and/or your preconceived notions of others and of the world around you. Possibly protecting yourself, emotionally and psychologically, from a situation, which you are unable to cope with at this time, or you lack control over; then again, perhaps the dreamer has an exaggerated or unrealistic view of yourself. No matter the reason, right now a question is before you, via your dream. Do you want to know this part of yourself? According to your ability to handle self-awareness, God will begin to reveal this side of you to you. Why, He wants to balance your understanding of things; thus, effecting wholeness within your life, so that the enemy will no longer be able to manipulate your emotions so easily. The Paraclete is with you to help you throughout this entire process, listen to Him. Now, in your life, this activity or attribute needs reckoning with, somehow or someway.

Otherwise noted, (known or unknown), if the person, place or thing that initiated (or was a recipient of) the action or activity within your dream was not seen, invisible, or only talked about within your dream, this may indicate that the dreamer does not recognize the influential effects another has within your life, or upon your attitude.

If more than one person (known or unknown):

Consider what the group had in common. What behavior, character trait, feature, action, or activity, stood out the most? For example, were they argumentative, authoritative, beautiful, criminal minded, dancing, difficult, dressed unusual, enigmatic, fighting, focused, flirty, helpful, hurtful intentions, powerful, promiscuous, quiet, secretive, seemed unreal, unassuming? What about age, color, height, size, happiness, considerate, loving, let you be yourself, peacefulness, encourager, irrational, leader, liar, mentor, passionate, personable, neglected, poor, run-down, sage, shyster, unwise, upscale, vengeful, death. That which was highlighted and noted is what you need to focus on at present.

If the attribute or quality is a desirable or positive one, allow the strength of that attribute to help you overcome some manner of immorality or irreverence within your life and/or to help you to become better, productively, for the Kingdom of God in some manner. If the attribute is an undesirable or negative one, take steps accordingly to struggle against the growing desires of the carnal side of you. If applicable, get help and support via prayer, fasting, and a Christian based support group.

For dreams of the dead see following note.

Was someone life ritually sacrificed? While the dead has nothing to do with the living (Ecclesiastes 9:4-6), it may be considered what character trait did that person represent to the dreamer, while the person was actually alive, what character feature stood out the most? With that trait noted, dreamer may consider that the trait noted, is within the dreamer, and that trait is no longer useful or needed for the progression of your spiritual walk, on this side of heaven. Dreamer, it is suggested that you render that trait (good or bad) obsolete, and began anew attempting to move forward, using different tactics to overcome unproductive habitual life cycle choices, and for maneuvering through this thing we call life in a more, better way. See category, Death, and/or other relevant categories.

5. Categorized, and characterized, in many ways, most celebrations and events fall into two general categories: those, which are celebrated festively, and those, which are solemn.

6. In addition to the following interpretations, see index or relevant categories for more information. For example, if a tree was involved in some way, see category, Agriculture; if music was highlighted, see category, Music. If costumes were highlighted, see category, Clothing. What other activity was involved, may also see category, Actions and Activities. Kept within context of your dream and the interpretation, the additional symbols are perhaps relevant. It will be within the sum of all the symbols that you will find a more thorough interpretation.

7. Since the following list is not extensive, dreamer is encouraged to seek biblical guidelines and other relevant research to determine the metaphorical meaning of your particular celebration or event, depicted within your dream, via a Bible concordance, Bible illustrated dictionary, encyclopedia, or internet. Having done your research you should be able to determine some basic behaviors or attributes your Lord and Savior wants you to focus on.

Symbols and Referents

Most dreams of celebrations and events generally imply, coupled with the relevant interpretation, the status of your spiritual life, as well as the intents and purposes of your heart regarding your spiritual life.

In addition to the varied meanings of celebrations or events, other common words, expressions, usages, (e.g. slang or clichés), or a 'probable' that are metaphorically represented by any of the following are also considered (this section is an addendum at the end of the relevant subcategory).

Category Content - If not listed see index, perchance, for your specific type of celebration or event dream.

- Birthday
- Birth or Pregnancy, see category, Pregnancy
- Dance, see category Dance
- Divorce, see category Divorce
- Funeral, see category, Death
- Major Festivals of the Old Testament (Passover, The Feast of Unleavened Bread, First Fruits, The Feast of Weeks, Pentecost, The Feast of Trumpets, The Day of Atonement, and The Feast of Booths, Tabernacles or Ingathering)
    - Passover; The Feast of Unleavened Bread; First Fruits; The Feast of Weeks or Pentecost; The Feast of Trumpets; The Day of Atonement; The Feast of Booths, Tabernacles, or Ingathering
- Parents Day (Father's Day, Mother's Day, Grandparent's Day)
- Party
- War, see category, Fighting (War), or Parades (Military)
- Wedding or Marriage or Bridegroom or Bride or Engagement or Marriage proposal (includes customary clothing and jewelry)
    - Bridegroom or Bride or Marriage proposal; "Same Sex" Wedding or Marriage, see category, The Body (Homosexual Relationship); Guest or Invitee of a Wedding
- For the following celebrations, events, see category Parades:
    - Christmas, Cinco de Mayo; Easter; Festivals, Flag Day; Good Friday; Halloween; Independence Day; Labor Day; Mardi Gras Carnival, Martin Luther King's Day; Memorial Day, Military Victory, New Year's Day; Patriot's Day, President's Day, Pride Festival,

Protest Event; Sport's Event (high school, youth, Olympics, World Olympics, any professional games, usually with a sport activity theme); St Patrick's Day; Thanksgiving Day; Valentine's Day, Veterans Day

BIRTHDAY (a birthday celebration, a birthday feast):

If age was highlighted, also see category, Numbers. This dream has four meanings (choose one). (1) Your dream was sent to encourage, and it denotes one, having escaped your dark side, by accepting Christ as your Savior and Lord, you are now declared a "born again" (see John 3:1-17), behold all things have become new, and old things have passed away (2 Corinthians 5:17). Dreamer, always attribute your deliverance to the amazing grace of God and the efficacy of the redeeming Blood of Christ, who, has given you beauty for ashes, the oil of joy for mourning, and the garment of praise for the spirit of heaviness (Isaiah 61:3). So thorough is the work of deliverance within you that your old habits and inclinations have been completely taken away. Your change, like Apostle Paul's, is startling, to most, to say the least. Notwithstanding, go forth in your newness, like that apostle, for you will no longer have the slightest desire to return to your former ways, all longings for the thing s, which once delighted you, are gone. Therefore, dreamer, wholeheartedly declare that God has made you a new creation in Christ, Jesus, and old things are passed away, and all things have become new. (2) Your state of affairs is before God. If dreamer is seriously ill, your dream suggests that you will be healed by the miraculous power of God. For instance, if you have been diagnosed with a serious or incurable illness, you will be healed and survive to declare the glories of the Lord. You will be completely restored from your distresses. Any condition that is upon you at present that seems hopeless and/or extremely frustrating; you will overcome it. Go through your circumstances hopeful and optimistic (Psalm 27:5). Yes, you will experience minor losses materially and possibly physically, but all will be restored. Do not be dismayed, nor lose courage. Faith is a keyword for you at present. (3) For dreamers 15 years of age to 29, your dream is a warning of a dark generational issue, hereditary within your family line (e.g. maternal and/ or paternal, grandparents, siblings, aunts, uncles, cousins). Dreamer, character traits from ancestors, namely genetic codes and traits, will often trouble and taunt the offspring of a given progenitor, especially generational issues (Exodus 20:5-7). The demons that have so plague your family line, are now visiting (re-visiting) you. Your issue is demonically instigated and it is spiritually perverse, perhaps sexually perverse as well (e.g. adultery, fornication, homosexuality, prostitution, whorishness). These spirits attempt to "bend" the personality, as early as possible with regards to age, towards a certain direction, oftentimes towards a way that is desolate and wicked, for it is Sa tan's scheme to kill and make desolate all; thus, to keep some from rising up and leading their generation to Christ (see the birth of Moses, Exodus 1:15-2:10). Favorably, generational curses and issues can stop with you (Jeremiah 31:29, 30; Ezekiel 18:2-14, 20-23). Thus, your Heavenly Father is requiring that you overcome and subdue negative and dark emotions, feelings, behaviors, and/or ideas that would influence you, before they overcome you. Dreamer, God is not asking you to do something you cannot do. For a surety, vanquishing of the coming influence can be done. By faith, you will need to declare some kind of fast and commit to it, for a long period-of-time, to abate the demonically instigated circumstance, you find yourself in now, Matthew 6:16-18. Try abstaining from food and drink (midnight to 6 PM), twice a week, and refrain from words, attitudes, people, places, and things, including music, magazines, videos, TV, or any such things that fuel anger and discontent, and st ir up lustful feelings. This is also known as, faith with works, read, understand, and embrace James 2:14-26. Nonetheless, earnestly pray, God will guide, enable, and answer you as to the type of fast. See suggested course of action. (4) On a darker note, your dream warns of a weakness, within the dreamer. The dreamer has embraced some form of veneration of the dead, such as ancestral worship, or worship of saints, and together with all that it implies; namely, a belief that the dead possess the ability to influence the fortune of the living. The grassroots of the mysterious darker side of such practices are as such: among horticultural peoples with chiefdoms, the chief's ancestors, in time, became gods, and the rite of obligation, via worship or ceremony, was passed down from generation to generation, even unto the veneration of saints. Today, this type of ceremony looks like something else, e.g. psychic readings, fortune telling, tarot, Kwanzaa, Confucianism, Taoism, or the Catholic Church's veneration of dead saints, et.al. While all cultures attach ritual significance, to the passing of loved ones (e.g. funerals, memorial services, vigils); this is not equivalent to ancestral or saint veneration. Dreamer, you are a child of God; therefore, you shall not worship, nor establish annual rites of obligation for the dead. See Leviticus 19:28; Deuteronomy 14:1, 2; Job 14:21; Psalm 88:10-12; Ecclesiastes 1:11, 9:4, 5, 10; Isaiah 8:19, 20, 26:14; Matthew 8:22; Hebrews 9:27. These scriptures clearly state that the dead do not possess the ability to influence the living. Dreamer, the time to be about your heavenly Father's business is now, so let the dead "bury" (worship, venerate) the dead, and let the spiritually alive be concern with that which is living. Indecisiveness about this matter, will lead to your spiritual and literal downfall. See suggested course of action.

MAJOR FESTIVALS OF THE OLD TESTAMENT:

Generally, the major festivals of the Old Testament are sent, within our dreams, to impart knowledge, and to give instructions or direction. They impart knowledge on the reality of slavery and darkness, the reality of sin, judgment, atonement, forgiveness, the importance of trusting and knowing God, the need for thanksgiving and praise, to God, and on the need for deliverance, within the dreamer's life. Moreover, the symbolism within the festivals and events denotes a need to remember God's deliverance and redemption, which is fulfilled in Yeshua HaMashiach[20]. Since the following are very short synopsis of the symbolic meaning of some of the major festivals, dreamer is encouraged to seek biblical guidelines for recognizing the greater metaphorical meanings of the festivals, celebrations, and events of the Hebrew people. See also, other relevant research to determine the metaphorical meaning of the particular observances and performances of the occasions; depicted within your dream, via a Bible concordance, Bible illustrated dictionary, encyclopedia, or internet. Having done your research you should be able to determine some basic behaviors or attributes your Lord and Savior wants you to focus on. With that, see one of the following.

Passover: Passover festival denotes a time of great deliverance within the life of the dreamer. Recognize your time of visitation when it is upon you and seize the moment.

The Feast of Unleavened Bread: Jesus is petitioning you, via your dream, to cleanse evil from your heart, allow the process. Dreamer, many, who have faltered and were weak are healed, restored, and strengthened by the grace of God. If you are ready to acknowledge that you have faltered, and remain mindful of your weaknesses, especially pride, God will suddenly, and in an extraordinary way, increase your strength. The more God allows you to see your arrogance, and the horribleness of it all, be more earnest to repent that you may find Him to be grace and healing, refreshment, and a refuge. He is willing to help you, only surrender to His process of help, with a humble dependence upon Him. You will find that God will not fail you, and you will have grace sufficient for renewal of spiritual strength. An angel (perhaps disguised as a human) or one, a human, who is a true servant of God, with the Spirit of Truth within, will lead the way. See suggested course of action.

First Fruits: Your dream signifies the dreamer's need to express your gratitude to, and dependence on, God; further, learned not to hoard but to trust God for provision. Give a "first fruit" offering to God, via your place of worship. It is suggested, if needed, that you discover, via personal research and study, what "first fruit" is, that you might offer it to God, via your church. See suggested course of action.

The Feast of Weeks or Pentecost: Your dream denotes that there is a need to remember God's deliverance and redemption, of you, the dreamer, which was fulfilled in Yeshua HaMashiach. Also, see category, Numbers (50).

The Feast of Trumpets: This feast denotes judgments occurring, or coming. See suggested course of action.

The Day of Atonement: Jesus is petitioning you, the dreamer, to slip away and fast and pray. You will need to fast and pray for 24 hours, abstaining from many forms of pleasure. This fast and prayer is for the remission of sins, therefore, wor ds of repentance should be considered. See suggested course of action.

The Feast of Booths, Tabernacles, or Ingathering: Your dream denotes that there is a need to remember from where the Lord has brought you, the dreamer. For the next seven days, respect and use this time as a time of renewed fellowship with Yeshua, remembering His sheltering provision and care for you, particularly as you travelled through your dry places. Your dream also symbolizes a need to acknowledge to yourself, your dependence upon God's care and sustenance. See suggested course of action.

PARENTS DAY (FATHER'S DAY, MOTHER'S DAY, AND GRANDPARENT'S DAY):

This dream has three meanings (choose one). (1) Father's Day: This choice has four parts (choose one). (a) If male dreamer, you are possibly becoming a father. (b) To dream of celebrating Father's day, dreamer is counseled to heed the instructions of your earthly father, regarding a pressing situation at present. Further, dreamer is counseled to heed your heavenly Father's instructions, daily, via the Holy Bible. Especially the instructions that the Lord has before you at present, and by your obedience, the Lord will keep and bear you up. To do otherwise, particularly to embrace unwise choices, will bring shame upon your life, possibly bringing you to the brink of illness. See suggested course of action. (c) Dreamer is counseled to confess and forsake sin that you might receive mercy from the Lord, for he or she who covers their sins shall not prosper, but whoso confesses and forsakes sin, shall have mercy. See suggested course of action. (d) If dreamer is using his or her father (or mother) for profit, gain, or is behaving toward them, in any inappropriate manner (words or deeds), or is threatening or planning to kill your father or mother, you will no longer be able to proceed with your atrocious behavior. Although you think and say, you have done no evil or wrong to them, demons are guiding you, and are leading you in the path of darkness and death. In your darkness, death is upon you, even nearer and suddenly than you think. If you do not genuinely seek help and change, for sure ruin will be your destiny. Utilizing the powerful resources of prayer and heartfelt repentance to Jesus is needed. Repentance is seeking pardon and expressing sincere feelings of regret and brokenness for having done something awry and/or for having hurt someone. To Jesus pray, Psalm 51, this followed by appropriate application of wisdom, can conceivably avert some of the repercussions of your choices. If you lack wisdom ask God for wisdom; and He will give you wisdom. This coupled with fasting, a changed mindset, serious re-consideration of God's ways and means, and an honest acknowledgement of God's hand within your life, then the severe impact of your choices and actions upon your life, can be reversed and damages repaired (also see Ezekiel 33:12-19). This is what is called leaving a blessing behind. Moreover, dreamer, Jesus loves you, thus, He is petitioning you to accept Him as your personal Savior, for you are valuable in His eyes. The first step in receiving Him as your personal Savior is repentance (see in the Holy Bible, Acts 2:37-41). Then you will know the Messiah, Jesus Christ, intimately, and find the knowledge of God you seek. For the Lord gives wisdom and from His mouth comes knowledge and understanding. Then you will understand what is right and just and fair, every good path. When wisdom enters your heart and knowledge becomes sweet to your soul, discretion will protect you, understanding will guard you, and His Truth will lead you. To deliver you from the ways of wickedness, and from demons whose words and ways are perverse, who causes you to walk in darkness gladly, whose paths are crooked and devious, causing you to leave straight paths (Proverbs 2:1-6, 9-15). This is one of God's covenant promises to you. Have faith in this. If you do not genuinely seek help and change, immediately, for sure ruin and death will be your destiny's declaration. See suggested course of action. (2) Mother's Day: This choice has four parts (choose one). (a) If female dreamer, you are possibly becoming a mother. (b) To dream of celebrating mother's day, dreamer is counseled to heed the instructions of your earthly mother, if mother is living, regarding a pressing situation at present. (c) Your dream denotes that dreamer is one who is intolerant and critical of others, quick to argue and to dominate situations; therefore, you are counseled to know yourself, become more self-aware, thereby averting a division, or parting of paths, between you and your mother. If there has been any division or parting of ways, the issue was demonically instigated, and dreamer needs to make things right. Utilizing the powerful resources of prayer and heartfelt repentance to Jesus is needed. Repentance is seeking pardon and expressing sincere feelings of regret and brokenness for having done something awry and/or for having hurt someone. To Jesus pray, Psalm 51, this followed by appropriate application of wisdom, can conceivably avert some of the repercussions of your choices. If you lack wisdom ask God for wisdom; and He will give you wisdom. See suggested course of action. (d) Dreamer, is counseled to take control of your strong appetites, if not, you appetites will find an outlet through excessive eating, causing overweight and resultant problems, and other health weaknesses centered on female functions, or skin conditions, or through emotional experiences, which could create unsettled conditions in your personal life. Dreamer there is a need to re-focus your strong appetites, towards urges of inspiration to bring hope, joy, and beauty to others. See suggested course of action. (3) Grandparent's Day: This choice has four parts (choose one). (a) Dreamer, you are possibly becoming a grandparent. (b) Your dream was sent to encourage the dreamer. The dreamer has a genuine unconditional love for the Lord and for His people. You have a deepness that is the source of much generosity, kindness, and understanding. Thus, dreamer is encouraged to employ your innate benevolent qualities, making them a focal point of your personal ministry. Some examples of "acts of kindness" to others are, a ministry geared towards working with the elderly, the young, the sick, or the underprivileged. One may provide the elderly with necessities, such as food, clothing, shelter, medical equipment. Visit the sick, provide free medical services, and give cha rity to the poor, (see Ben Sira 29). Offer hospitality to strangers, help families bury their dead, via religious services, help with marriage ceremonies, and/or help a person make peace with his or her family member, fellow humankind, or their Maker. Provide free roadside assistance and emergency mechanical help, or freely help with structural problems in private hom es. All of these, and more, are examples of benevolent service. Moreover, often an individual starts the initiative of service witho ut leadership or community support. Thus, God will give you the necessary tools, courage, strength, and wherewithal, to d o it. Dreamer, love God so completely that you will never forsake His service for any reason. If your ministry is already established, and focuses on different initiatives, dreamer will need to, also, consider incorporating your natural qualities of gene rosity, kindness, and understanding into your ministry, with a focus on the elderly. (c) A diagnosis of a serious illness of a family member, possibly a grandparent, resulting in you becoming primary caretaker, is approaching, and this will change your everyday living and life drastically, especially, because of your family member or grandparent, needing to come live with you. This will require major adjustments within your home (significant in scope, extent, and effect). Dreamer, a painful and unsettling situation, can be diminished by first praying to Jesus for the strength and courage to endure this "ministry" to your family member. Taking ownership of what your dream is revealing to you about an upcoming situation, and working from that point, via diligent self-examination and preparation will bring divine support. Our Lord Jesus by giving us notice of major adjustments, is designed to take off the terror of it, that it might not be a surprise to us. Of all the adversaries of our peace, in this world of troubles, none insult us more violently, nor put us more into disorder, than life changes, ups and down, and turn arounds does; but we can easily welcome a guest we expect, and being fore-warned, we are thus well prepared. In addition, dreamer, resolve to vigorously and quickly release hurts, pains, disappointments, disillusionments, and a reluctance to change. Quickly forgive and move on to prevent being stuck in a negative and self-sabotaging mind-set for many years. See suggested course of action. (d) Your dream suggests that the dreamer set aside ten days, and those ten days are to be to you a time of sacrifice. A time of sacrificial fasting, giving of you, and offering. Concerning, sacrificial fasting, do not eat any breads, pasta, or potatoes for ten days. Regarding, giving of you, visit family members, especially grandparents, if living, and the elderly, sick, and widows, a total of ten days. About, offering, you are to give a part of your increase to the support of an elderly person, especially a grandparent, as a sacrificial offering unto the Lord, within ten days. By these, after completion, within ten days you will be freed from a specific bondage within your life. Specifically that which has attacked, harassed, or troubled you for a very long time. Not only freed, but able to embrace your new freedom with a humbled heart, and a fresh perspective.

PARTY:

This dream has two meanings (choose one). (1) Your dream was sent to encourage the dreamer that it is time for you to celebrate, during this season of your life. Read Psalm 126:1-3, this word is for you. Dreamer it would be beneficial to your emotional well-being for you to participate in the various upcoming social celebrations that you may be invited to, as well as, to vacation more. Moreover, visit and fellowship with those who are glad and sincere of heart. Additionally, dreamer is encouraged to laugh more and to embrace a more "lighter" demeanor, for a cheerful heart is good medicine (Proverbs 17:22). (2) If dreamer was crying at a party, dreamer, when God hides His face from someone, celebrations, are turned into moaning and groaning, and the party is exchanged for solitude. This is your time, your season in life, to sit alone to consider your ways, and how might your ways reflect the teachings of Christ Jesus that a better you might result. Do not sit alone to indulge in excessive grief, but to repent and return or convert to Jesus Christ. See suggested course of action.

WEDDING, MARRIAGE, BRIDEGROOM, BRIDE, ENGAGEMENT, OR MARRIAGE PROPOSAL (includes customary clothing and jewelry):

This dream has four meanings (choose one). (1) Your dream denotes that there will be a literal wedding, and it is honored by the Lord. Therefore, go and prepare for your wedding in peace. (2) Your dream denotes salvation. Someone, namely one of the wedding participants, has received the Lord, Jesus Christ as his or her Savior (Revelations 19:7-9). (3) If dreamer was not a wedding participant, but only an observer, or dreamer heard, or knew, of a wedding, from afar. One of the wedding participants received the Lord as their Savior because of the dreamer's witness. Dreamer, while your influence upon their decision to commit to the Lord Jesus may never be made known to you personally, or be made known publicly, it is being made known to you, via your dream. Consequently, that there will be a wonderful miracle performed in the dreamer's life. (4) To the married, if you are involved in an illicit relationship, or there is infidelity in some manner, your dream was sent as a stark warning and rebuke to the dreamer; you will be caught in adultery, and is already caught by God, read Hebrews 13:4. See suggested course of action. See one of the following.

Bridegroom or Bride or Marriage proposal: Your dream denotes dreamer will become a public figure. It is your season to come upon the stage of ministry, and to begin publicly proclaiming the word of the Lord, and miracles will be performed and attributed to your ministry. God will raise you up and sit you amongst His people. You will receive the benefits of participating in a local church (community, support, proper ordination, burial, honor, respect, edification, accountability). Moreover, vi sit and fellowship with those who are glad and sincere of heart. Additionally, your dream is symbolic of love of the Lord. Love within this context is the practice of living life on God's terms for no other reason or benefit than to be close to God, thi s is called holiness. Dreamer, go forth, with the confidence that God supports you. May, the words of your mouth and the meditations of your heart always be acceptable in the sight of the Lord. Read Psalm 19:14 and allow this to be your anthem.

Guest or Invitee of a Wedding: This dream has two meanings (choose one). (1) Dressed (dressing) properly for a wedding (e.g. clean, and appropriate formal attire for a wedding): Dreamer, because of your faith, humility, strong leadership, and your courageous and optimistic spirit, you will be greatly honored. You will rise to a level the Anointing of God and your acumen deem you should be. Even more, in your present business or personal dealings, you will be satisfied and take delight in your goals. If you are involved in any situation that is competitive, you will triumphant. This new truth, if embraced, should usher you into a personal revival, affecting restoration of better and happier times (e.g. improved health, economic security, improved family relations) or a new birth experience for one needing to be born again (see John 3:1-17). Believe and you will receive the promise of eternal life, and you will be set free. See suggested course of action. (2) Dressed (dressing) improperly for a wedding (e.g. dirty or inappropriate, informal clothing for a wedding): Dreamer although severe, the following is necessary. Without the proper wedding apparel of righteousness, which is found in Christ Jesus, and His grace, we have no right to sit at the wedding banquet of God. Without uprightness of walk, we should not hope to enter the wedding banquet above. Read, understand, and embrace Matthew 22:11-14, for this is your spiritual state at present. Dreamer, members of the visible church, here on earth, which is God's tabernacle of worship, should diligently see to it, that they have the preparation of heart, which fits them to be participants of the wedding banquet of God, which is above. Dreamer, he or she, who do not respect the opportunities placed before them shall have the things that support their peace taken away. Choose this day whom you will serve, God, or yourself. God is not condemning you, He's holding out His Hand of hope, giving you an opportunity to start anew. Let the wicked forsake his way, God wants to pardon (Isaiah 55:7-13, Matthew 7:17-23, Luke 6:43-45). Dreamer, if you want to follow Jesus you will need to fully understand that discipleship requires total commitment (Matthew 8:19-22). Therefore, now, begin to choose good deeds and habits that will lead to the fulfilment of your God given purpose, and strengthen your resolve. Your boundaries are to obey God's standards for you exclusively. Especially, your expressed disapproval of justice handed down by God, this attitude will not be tolerated. Since you will see justice handed down, do not say, "God is not fair by allowing this or that to happen". Dreamer, resolve to vigorously and quickly release hurts, pains, disappointments, disillusionments, and a reluctance to change. Quickly forgive and move on to prevent being stuck in a negative and self-sabotaging mind-set for many years. While it is easier said than done, one cannot grow or go forward stuck in the past. Do not lose today holding on to yesterday; let it go. Moreover, disrespect, on any level, towards those in authority over you is forbidden. Disrespect on any level towards any of God's children, especially the least of them, as well as prejudice and hatred is forbidden. Dreamer, you are endowed with the power of God, to cause some to become alive again, to restore others from a depressed, inactive, and unused state, and others to return from the dead (spiritually). Therefore, elevate and promote the righteousness of Christ to those around you. Lead people to pray to Jesus personally, to embrace God, and come to know and love God from whatever situation they find them self. Choose not to go out from the presence of the Lord, that is to, willingly renounce God, and to be content to forego the privileges He offers, that you might not be under His precepts, make things right. If no change, your place in heaven is in jeopardy. Dreamer if you are diligent in subduing your inappropriate beliefs and character traits, you can turn a bad situation into a good one overnight and begin doing mighty works and wonders for the Kingdom of God. Prayer and repentance is the first step. Jesus will meet you wherever you are. Have faith in this. See suggested course of action.

Suggested Course of Action

Question to consider and journal, did your dream depict any symbols that alludes to, the dreamer will make the necessary changes, spiritually, emotionally, and/or physically to affect a more positive outcome? If changes are initiated, your dreams will change. If no change, your place in heaven is in jeopardy. Moreover, see Matthew 22:11-14.

Nevertheless, in view of your dream's context, and the primary symbols, what does your dream reveal about you, your ethics, intents, mental state, and motives? You will need to earnestly look within and consider that the sum of your answers is a reflection of where you are emotionally, physically, and/or spiritually, and a reflection of who you are becoming. What was your reaction to the situation? Were you angry, concerned, confused, defensive, fearful, happy, helpful, pleased, shocked, unconcerned, or ready to get out of someone's presence? Your reaction to the activity, or the circumstance, reveals your attitude regarding this information about yourself.

Dreamer, consider seriously your observations. If what was revealed prevail, will it sabotage any good that's happening at present within your life? Will it build or destroy, strengthen or weaken, enlighten or blind? If you lack wisdom, ask Je sus for wisdom. He gives wisdom to all, generously, no matter who you are and what you've done; wisdom is available (see James 1:5-8, Proverbs 2:1-6, 10). Hence, if, by just asking, you may get wisdom, one may suffer needlessly, because you will not ask Jesus for wisdom.

Dreamer, God's Word, has two sides, a "Light" side, which is a manifestation of God's providential care towards His people, namely believers, who believe and heed His Word (Psalm 36:9), and another side, which is put to use, against sin, and the evildoer, or unrepentant (1 Corinthians 1:18). The side that is revealed to you is your choice. However, consider the following before choosing. Dreamer, everyone experiences life events, eventually; for, there is a time and season for every event. Unfortunately, because of some seasons, at times, we suffer bitter anguish, disillusionment, depression, isolation, loneliness, heartbreak, loss, bereavement, and/or pain. Times and seasons may come dramatically, or unexpectedly, and oftentimes we are powerless over those moments. Such events as aging, broken romance, children making bad choices, debilitating disease, death, depression that won't go away, divorce, singleness, aloneness, and the list can go on. Unfortunately, whatever your experience is, or was, it has inevitably led you, the dreamer, into darkness. D reamer, things are as they are, the charm of celebrations is gone, and absolutely nothing can change the past. Therefore, now, you must make a choice to go on from this place, into the Light of God's Word that you might live emotionally, spiritually, and physically.

Dreamer, to use a cliché, your time of "break down" is over, and now you need to "break through". One breaks through the darkness of "broken-down" by turning to Jesus and offering praise. However, this kind of praise, this kind of "hallelujah", is not the result of a happy feeling, or is not necessarily from one who has seen the light. It is offered through the teeth of pain, it is broken, and it is offered in spite of emotional numbness. This kind of praise is offered to Jesus as a pure act of obedience, and as a naked act of the will. It comes from a place deep down, within the heart, beneath the changes and turnarounds of feelings, and the vicissitudes of life. Such acts of praise are acts of defiance, through which we defy the darkness, and confess our faith in Jesus who lives above tears, and who calls us to Himself, the One and only Light of the world, and He is the only rescuer for those in the darkness of pain and despair. When one, namely the dreamer, is able to praise Jesus in such circumstances, you are acknowledging that you are not the center of the universe, and that your pain and loss, though personally difficult, has not changed the faithfulness of God. Like Job looking to God, who appeared to him out of the whirlwind, dreamer, lift up your eyes from yourself to behold the Lord, and find a whole new perspective and peace. It is time, and you are able.

Now, pray (See Prayer of Deliverance, pg. 897)

Specific Meaning

Unless otherwise noted elsewhere, if, in your everyday living, your awaked state, as part of your lifestyle, work, or ministerial activities, or a special event, you have a very real connection with any activity involving celebrations or events. Dreams o f this sort, for the most part, are ordinary dreams, resulting from your daily activities (see Chapter One, Chalom). These sorts of dreams are usually about your routine, mundane activities or anxieties that overwhelm your mind during the day. They are an inner release mechanism, which helps provide you with emotional balance and the maintaining of your sanity. These dreams are not significant, and do not warrant special attention.

Note: If, within your dream, your celebration, festival, or event, depicted accidents or any harmful incidents, this type of dream may be heeded as an alarm in the physical realm. Do not assume that things are safe or ok, caution should be heeded. The dreamer may consider his or her dream as a clue given to assist in finding facts, needed to support a prevailing situation or investigation. The alarm, kept within context of the dream, should be relevant to your lifestyle and closely resemble your real-life situations. Meaning it can actually occur during your awaked state. Consider all the people, places, backgrounds, and activity highlighted within your dream. This will help you narrow down the specific area of concern. However, if your dream was inundated with symbols that are not specifically related to your job and/or responsibilities, then the spiritual implications should be heeded.

CLOTHING, JEWELRY, AND SHOES

Man, who stood all but naked in the Garden of Eden, was clothed by God in an act of compassion, his embarrassment covered (Genesis 3:7, 21) Rabbi Ari Kahn

I counsel you to buy from Me gold refined in the fire, that you may be rich; and white garments, that you may be clothed, that the shame of your nakedness may not be revealed. (Revelation 3:18 NKJV)

How beautiful are thy feet with shoes, O prince's daughter! The joints of thy thighs are like jewels, the work of the hands of a cunning workman. (Song of Solomon 7:1 KJV)

God so amply provide for the necessaries of life, that we are never obliged to wear tattered garments, nor our feet injured for lack of shoes or sandals. (Deuteronomy 8:4)

Humans are called upon to thank God for clothing, to use cotton, flax, wool, animal fur and skin, and shoes or sandals to protect ourselves from evil. (Based on Calvin Seerveld - The Complete Book of Everyday Christianity)

This category deals with coverings, jewelry, and footwear designed to be worn on a person's body. Some short descriptions of types, phrases, and/or other processes and particulars, connected in some way to this category is, for example, adornment, attire, apparel, bracelets, earrings, footwear, garments, necklace, rings, sandals, shoes, gems, metals, stones, or vestiary. Also, see category content list, or index.

All Symbols and Referents, Notes (1, 2, 3, etc.), Suggested Course of Action, and Specific Meaning offer guidance toward a more comprehensive interpretation.

Notes

1. Unless otherwise noted elsewhere, if, in your everyday living, your awaked state, as part of your lifestyle, work, or ministerial activities, or a special event, you have a very real connection with any activity involving clothing, jewelry, or shoes. For example, cobbler, dressmaker, entrepreneur, fashion design, hats, jewelry making, modeling, milliner (hat maker), seamstress, shoemaking, suit maker, tailor, vendor, or any activity dealing with the buying, merchandising, or marketing of clothing, jewelry, or shoes, your dream is not significant and does not warrant special attention.

    Otherwise noted, this dream of clothing, jewelry, and shoes may be a Prophetically Simple Dream (see Chapter One: The 60th Part of Prophecy). Whereas, the dreamer is encouraged, for example, if a new fashion, jewelry, or shoe design was introduced to you within your dream, adopt the design as your own signature brand. Did you invent something? Skip interpretation, go, and start designing, brand-mark, and marketing your divine sent invention.

    Otherwise noted, per your lifestyle, if your dream closely resembled real life situations, meaning it can actually occur during your awaked state, this dream may be an Ordinary Dream, resulting from daily activities (see Chapter One, Chalom). These sorts of dreams are usually about your routine, mundane activities or anxieties that overwhelm your mind during the day. They are an inner release mechanism, which helps provide you with emotional balance and the maintaining of your sanity. These dreams are not significant, and do not warrant special attention.

2. Probables: As clothing, jewelry, and shoes are very personal, for example, a class ring, your mother's wedding rings, a wedding dress, a graduation cap, a locket handed down from your

grandmother, bronzed baby shoes. Also, generational and cultural differences, as well as, the norms for various people groups and communities, e.g. kilts, a knee-length pleated skirt worn by Scotsmen as part of a traditional dress. Moreover, does dreamer has an affinity towards certain clothing, jewelry, and shoes. Are you required to wear specific clothing, jewelry, and shoes? Thus, could the clothing, jewelry, and shoes depicted within your dream be a possible probable (see Chapter One, section entitled, Probables)? Hence, dreamer may also consider your own personal and special associations with various clothing, jewelry, and shoes, as long as the interpretation is kept within the principles of spiritual boundary markers, landmarks, and property lines, (see Chapter One, section entitled, Spiritualizing Boundary Markers, Landmarks, and Property Lines).

3. Determine who your dream is for you or another. Always, considering yourself first, reflecting on your present behaviors. Ask yourself, why am I dreaming about this now? What is this dream revealing about me? Have I taken on new attributes? Has anyone commented on my present behaviors as being untypical of me? Has my ministry changed for the better or for the worse? What about my beliefs, doctrine, or philosophy, are they still based on Holy Writ? Is there something I need to know about those I am ministering to or serving?

    Remember your actions and emotions within your dream. Were you naked? Were you appropriately dressed for the occasion? What kinds of clothes where you wearing, for example a wedding gown, tuxedo, work clothes, casual, or mix matched clothing? Did you have shoes on your feet? What kind of jewelry were you donning? What happened to you in your dream? How did things end? If dreamer was the focal point meaning the dreamer, and what you were wearing was primarily the highlight. This is a good indicator that your dream is about you (the dreamer). In light of your dream, via the relevant interpretation, do you believe that your behavior will enhance or endanger your well-being, safety, and/or happiness, if so, how and why? Do you believe that your belief system will strengthen or weaken you spiritually in any way, if so, how and why? See following relevant subcategory, the interpretation is about and for you.

    Did dreamer focus on someone else garments? Was someone else naked or inappropriately dressed? Were the paparazzi around another? Unless otherwise noted elsewhere, an answer of yes, to one or more of these, or similar questions, is a good indicator that your dream is about another and their role, and/or influential effects, within the life of the dreamer. If someone else was the focal point and/or what he or she was wearing, was primarily the highlight of your dream. Consider, is someone greatly influencing your physical, spiritual, or mental health, your understanding, perspective, and reasoning regarding spiritual issues? Are they enhancing your spiritual and/or literal prosperity, or are they responsible for the dwindling thereof? Could they be influencing your ministry, on some level? Do you know someone whose life activities or physical being is similar to that which stood out the most within your dream? Could it be that person? If you sense that your dream is for or about another, the question as to why you have been made privy to this information, and how do you factor into the equation, should be seriously considered along with necessary actions. Perhaps the dreamer is being made aware of the plight of someone, and you are to get involved (see Chapter One, Are You Ready to Hear the Messages in Your Dreams, section entitled, The 10% for others).

    If your dream is for, or about another:

    Dreams that reference others and the revelation within those dreams, is not given haphazardly to any individual, but only to those with the ability, and influence to do something with the information; this is also prophecy. With that, journal the following questions, and if unable to answer the questions now, this denotes that the person, represented within your dream, will enter your life shortly. Are you entering into a personal relationship with someone? Do you not know or understand what you're looking at, especially certain behaviors, when learning about this person? Has someone new entered your life or maybe you've just begun opening up to someone not so new, and have started listening to their advice, accepting their assistance, or are you supporting or enabling someone? Are you in denial regarding the toxicity of one of your present relationships, particularly a spouse, family member, or friend? Are you anxious, concerned, frightened, and/or troubled by recent changes in your behavior, especially because of someone's influence upon your life at present? Have you allowed someone to convince you to deceive another? Have you recently become aware of (or is being made aware of, via your dream) certain undesirable behaviors within you towards another? Are you trying to cut ties with one that is bad company? Have you just joined (or re-joined) a church, fellowship, or social group?

Note: If your dream has attributes that indicate that your dream is about you, and other attributes that indicate that your dream is about another, dreamer should consider that your dream is about you and another. For example, both you and another were inappropriately dressed, or a jewel thief stole your jewelry, thus indicating that the dream is about the dreamer, and about another. Were both of you wearing the same outfits? Therefore, while your dream is about the dreamer, the dreamer should expect the role and/or influential effects of another, also plays a part in your interpretation. For example, dreamer may perhaps be attempting to mimic another's lifestyle, pretending to be someone you are not; and not knowing what it takes, or the costs, to be that which you are pretending, or desiring, to be, again, see relevant interpretation.

More questions to consider. Why has the person been allowed within your life, and/or how did they get there? Again, if unable to answer the questions now, this denotes that the person, represented within your dream, will enter your life shortly. If their activity, within your dream, has proven positive, via the interpretation, this someone will prove, unwittingly, to be a very strong ally, benefactor, defender, and supporter. God has sent this someone into your life to help you carry out your next endeavor by enlarging your spiritual capacity. Allow the strength of that person's character to guide, help, and support you. On the other hand, if his or her presence and/or activity, within your dream, proved negative, via the interpretation, for sure, this person will prove to be a very strong and formidable challenge for you, perhaps unto death. If negative, this dream is a dire warning. Take steps accordingly to struggle against, or to cut off, adverse and unfavorable relationships. Remember certain personalities are all encompassing, affecting everything, cataclysmic, contagious, deadly, harmful, infectious, predatory, and/or venomous. Symbolically meaning that if allowed to continue or prosper within your life, serious harm or death to the dreamer may result. Idolize no one, especially beyond the warning of the Lord, and we are definitely not to lay our lives down for no one. Then again, this person maybe allowed within your life, because of the dreamer's unwillingness to abstain from immorality after having been asked to abstain from such by God, see 1 Corinthians 6:9-20, Galatians 5:19-21, or the dreamer's self-righteous behavior, or a lack of a balanced and honest view of your own personality. In this case, this person will affect self-awareness within the life of the dreamer, exposing the negative traits of your personality, especially those traits, which cause you to follow, or to be so easily misled, and/or your wrong beliefs; no matter, this type of mentality needs reckoning with. Graciously, all of this will restore the dreamer to his or her right place with God, opening your eyes to see how far you've strayed from God (1 Corinthians 5:4-7; James 5:20). The lesson is, no matter how personable, powerful, or difficult a person, or how uncertain or unpopular the choices and issues, always take the next biblical and ethical step, for obedience to God's principles will always prove safer and stronger foundationally. Although, you will need all kinds of outside support to recover from this person's domination, no longer, allow that particular person's influence within your life to continue or thrive, especially if negative, end it abruptly.

4.   Consider all the people, places, backgrounds, and activity highlighted within your dream.

Known (in your awaked life) person, animal, place, or organization within your dream:

Unless otherwise noted elsewhere, people, animals, places, backgrounds that are actually known by the dreamer in your awaked life, indicates a part of you that you recognize within yourself on some level or another. Question to journal, if dreamer seriously considers all the particulars, what stood out the most, what features, or character traits stood out the most. For example, age, color, height, size, happiness, considerate, loving, let you be yourself, peacefulness, encourager, irrational, leader, liar, mentor, passionate, personable, neglected, poor, run-down, sage, shyster, unwise, upscale, vengeful. Write down (journal) the particular highlighted within your dream. The attribute or activity highlighted is for a reason. Since the attribute written down is a part of you, namely the dreamer's nature, demeanor, and/or lifestyle, an honest and unbiased assessment is very important for truth sake. Happy note, considering that other people's attributes, within dreams, also represent attributes of your own personality, causes one to look at another in a better light. According to your capacity to embrace self-awareness and a rectification of mind, body, and spirit, God will begin to enhance, make better, more attractive, sanctify, diminish, and make pure and free from sin and guilt, this part of you.

Otherwise noted, if the person, animal, place, or background within your dream is actually known by the dreamer, in your awaked life, this person, animal, place, or background may represent him or herself, or itself.

Unknown in your awaked life or although known, was unseen, invisible, or only talked about - person, animal, place, or organization within your dream.

Unless otherwise noted elsewhere, if you did not recognize, the person, place, thing, they, or it, was not seen, invisible, or only talked about within your dream, this indicates an attribute or activity within your life that you are unfamiliar with, or are in denial about, or you refuse to acknowledge it, but it does exists. Question to journal, what piece of clothing, jewelry, shoes, action, or activity, stood out the most. For example, color, size, condition, value. Although, on some conscious level, you are aware of a certain behavior or attribute within you, you have chosen to filter out or simply ignore certain information about yourself that contradicts your view of yourself and/or your preconceived notions of others and of the world around you. Possibly protecting yourself, emotionally and psychologically, from a situation, which you are unable to cope with at this time, or you lack control over; then again, perhaps the dreamer has an exaggerated or unrealistic view of yourself. No matter the reason, right now a question is before you, via your dream. Do you want to know this part of yourself? According to your ability to handle self-awareness, God will begin to reveal this side of you to you. Why, He wants to balance your understanding of things; thus, effecting wholeness within your life, so that the enemy will no longer be able to manipulate your emotions so easily. The Paraclete is with you to help you throughout this entire process, listen to Him. Now, in your life, this activity or attribute needs reckoning with, somehow or someway.

Otherwise noted, (known or unknown), if the person, place or thing that initiated (or was a recipient of) the action or activity within your dream was not seen, invisible, or only talked about within your dream, this may indicate that the dreamer does not recognize the influential effects another has within your life, or upon your attitude.

If more than one person (known or unknown):

Consider what the group had in common. What behavior, character trait, feature, action, or activity, stoo d out the most? For example, were they argumentative, authoritative, beautiful, criminal minded, dancing, difficult, dressed unusual, enigmatic, fighting, focused, flirty, helpful, hurtful intentions, powerful, promiscuous, quiet, secretive, seemed unreal, unassuming? That which was highlighted and noted is what you need to focus on at present.

If the attribute or quality is a desirable or positive one, allow the strength of that attribute to help you overcome some manner of immorality or irreverence within your life and/or to help you to become better, productively, for the Kingdom of God in some manner. If the attribute is an undesirable or negative one, take steps accordingly to struggle against the growing desires of the carnal side of you. If applicable, get help and support via prayer, fasting, and a Christian based support group.

For dreams of the dead see following note.

Did you see a corpse dressed up? While the dead has nothing to do with the living (Ecclesiastes 9:4-6), it may be considered what character trait did that person represent to the dreamer, while the person was actually alive, what character feature stood out the most. With that trait noted, dreamer may consider that the trait noted, is within the dreamer, and that trait is no longer useful or needed for the progression of your spiritual walk, on this side of heaven. Dreamer, it is suggested that you render that trait (good or bad) obsolete, and began anew attempting to move forward, using different tactics to overcome unproductive habitual life cycle choices, and for maneuvering through this thing we call life in a more, better way. See category, Death, and/or other relevant categories.

5. In addition to the following interpretations, see index or relevant categories for more information. For example, if a color was highlighted, see category, Colors. Kept within context of your dream and the interpretation, the additional symbols are perhaps relevant. It will be within the sum of all the symbols that you will find a more thorough interpretation.

6. Since the following list is not extensive, dreamer is encouraged to seek biblical guidelines and other relevant research to determine the metaphorical meaning of your particular clothing, jewelry, and/or shoes, depicted within your dream, via a Bible concordance, Bible illustrated dictionary, encyclopedia, or internet. Having done your research you should be able to determine some basic behaviors or attributes your Lord and Savior wants you to focus on.

Symbols and Referents

While clothing, jewelry, and shoes generally reveal the hidden man or woman, disclosing where their heart is, the thoughts and reflections of the heart, and exposure of truth, for both, the one who is dressed to kill and the one who rejects the God-given opportunity of adornment. As well as, point to promotion, or preparation for minister. Clothing, jewelry, and shoes also denote God's way of hiding our shame and embarrassment; thereby covering the individual, hiding the real person, namely our inward thoughts and reflections, from the world, similarly as our body is a covering to our soul. As, God, clothing of Adam and Eve was an emblem of the remission of sin (sin being the shame and embarrassment). Hence, figuratively clothing also denote the remittance of sins, so that God is no longer displeased with you, but is perfectly reconciled, via the acceptance and belief in His Son, Jesus Christ, the 2nd Adam, and the atoning work of the cross, and the clothing of the Holy Spirit (John 3:16, Acts 2:17, 18, 38, Romans 5:12-21). On the other side, the darker side, clothing given to cover shame can be perverted by our vanity, particularly speaking of those who reject the God-given opportunity of godly adornment. For example, the sexually enticing show of a leg, breast, or chest, the exposure of under clothes, or other private parts of your body meant to be only uncovered, at your wedding bed, is evil, especially if it supplants hope in the Lord's mercy or distracts us from righteous love for our neighbor. With that said, you can realize more fully the symbolic nature of some clothing, jewelry, and shoes as the following gives an interpretation of them.

In addition to the varied meanings of clothing, jewelry, and shoes, other common words, expressions, usages, (e.g. slang or clichés), or a 'probable' that are metaphorically represented by any of the following are also considered (this section is an addendum at the end of the relevant subcategory). For example, your mother's wedding dress, or an athletic jersey.

Category Content - If not listed see index, perchance, for your specific type of clothing, jewelry, shoes dream.

- Apron
- Black Clothing (dressed in all black)
- Bloody, Clothing soaked with blood, see category, Bleeding (Clothing soaked with blood)
- Clean or Cleaning or Washing Clothes, Jewelry, or Shoes or Dry Cleaner or Washing Machine and Dryer
- Coat or Jacket (an outer garment, usually worn outdoors to protect against the elements)
- Dirty or Wrinkled or Spot or Stained Clothes, Jewelry, or Shoes
- Ecclesiastical or Clergy Garments (e.g. collars, headwear, robes, sashes)
- Gray Clothing
- Hats (fashion hats, headgear used for protection e.g. rain hats, winter hats, sun hats, safety hats, e.g. hard-hats, helmets, chef hats, hairnets, any protective headgear or headwear for sanitary purposes, ceremonial hats, e.g. graduations headwear, cap, fitted hat, with or without a brim, hoodie, cloak)
  - Big hat, no cattle (to have a big hat, and notice there is a need of cattle); "At the drop of a hat" (to drop a hat in your dream); "Eat my Hat" (dream of eating a hat); Hang your Hat on something (to hang your hat up); Wear many Hats (to have on two or more hats at one time)
- Jewelry or Accessories
  - Belt or Suspenders (a band to tie or buckle around the body, or elastic straps that hold trousers); Earrings; Gloves; Mask (wearing one), see category, The Body (Mask); Necklace (jewelry consisting of a cord or chain worn about the neck as an ornament); Pearls; Rings (circlet jewelry usually worn on the finger); Engagement Ring or Wedding Ring or Friendship Ring, see category, Celebrations (Wedding); Gold or Silver Rings, see category, Colors
- Leaves as clothing, see category, Agriculture (Leaf)
- Men's Wear (casual, formal, informal, or immodest)
- Naked
  - Birthday Suit, see category, The Body (Naked); Caught with your Pants down; Give the shirt off your back (to take your shirt off and give to another); Ripping of Clothes (or tearing clothing); Stripper or Undress
- Pajamas or Nightclothes or Robe
- Seal (a stamp affixed to a document as to attest to its authenticity)
- Shoes (any manner of footwear, e.g. sandals, shoes, sneakers)
  - Barefoot (to be without shoes, see category, Walking; Big Shoes (shoes too big); Boots; "Church Shoes" or Dress Shoes or Good Fitting Shoes; Dead man shoes (to possess or put on shoes that belonged to a dead person); Give your shoe(s) to someone; To look for, or to need, shoes; To put on shoes; To take off shoes, see category, The Body (Feet); Dig your heels in (to dig you heels into something); Drag your heels (to drag your shoes by the heel); If the shoe fits, wear it (to try on a shoe to see if it fits); Walk in someone else's shoes or in their footsteps, see category, Walking; Walk one mile in someone shoes (the distance was highlighted), see category, Walking
- Uniforms see category, Working
- Wedding Clothing, see category, Celebrations, Events (Wedding)
- White Clothing (dressed in all white)
- Women's Wear (casual, formal, informal, or immodest)
- All dressed up and nowhere to go
- All talk and no trousers, see category, Talking
- Best Dressed or First Up (to be nominated best dressed)
- Big girl's blouse (a blouse too big for dreamer)
- Blue stockings (to have on, or to see, blue stockings)

- By the seat of your pants (the seat of your pants is highlighted in some way)
- Fly by the seat of one's pants (to move about in the air with your pants hooked to something)
- Cut from the same cloth (to cut two or more pieces from one cloth)
- Deep pockets (pockets that relatively large, in size)
- Dressed to the nines (to have clothing designed with the number nine on it, see category, Numbers (#9)
- Dyed in the wool (to dye wool)
- Hanging by a Thread (clothing, jewelry, or shoes hanging by a thread)
- Have a trick up your sleeve
- Hot under the collar (to be hot around the collar area of your clothing)

APRON:

This dream has two meanings (choose one). (1) Your dream denotes that the dreamer, or one connected to you, will experience a miraculous healing. (2) Apron Strings (to hold on to, or see apron strings): This choice has two parts (choose one). (a) Male dreamer, a man who is tied to a woman's apron strings is excessively dependent on her, especially when it is his mother or wife's apron strings. Dreamer, you are, in many ways, too dependent on others. It is counseled that you become more independent, and take responsibility for your own choices, especially within partnerships. By earnestly resolving to take responsibility for your choices, actions, and behaviors, and by acknowledging that your choices and behaviors are wrong, followed by repentance to Jesus, pray Psalm 51. You will be blessed and will not be given over to the desires of your foes. The Lord will protect and preserve your life. You will be called blessed upon the earth, and the Lord will protect and preserve your life. See suggested course of action. (b) Female dreamer, because of your issues with a tragic violation, and the resulting pains and defense mechanisms that followed; you are hindering yourself from becoming the woman God needs for you to be at this moment in time, to fulfill your primary purpose for His Kingdom. You are also, in many ways, hindering others, namely those closely connected to you, from becoming the man or woman God needs for them to be at this moment in time, to fulfill their primary purpose for His Kingdom. Dreamer, if you genuinely acknowledge, struggle with, and overcome, your feelings of low esteem, fear, and any other psychological and/or emotional traumas that have resulted from your victimization, you will be restored to health, and will become the strong person needed to handle the blessings intended for you. You will also become a key catalyst for change within the lives of those closely connected to you. Encouraging them back to Christ; thus, effecting happier times and healing, within their lives as well. See suggested course of action.

BLACK CLOTHING (DRESSED IN ALL BLACK):

This dream has two meanings (choose one). (1) To be dressed in black suggests that sophistication and formality is needed to be successful in your endeavor at hand, particularly when approaching another regarding promotion or sponsorship, as this color is often worn by royalty, clergy, judges, government officials; namely those in positions of authority. Therefore, you are advised to embrace certain rules governing socially acceptable behavior (etiquette) and dress codes. Dreamer, your inward glory should have a profound effect on your outward attitude and appearance, especially your public presentation. Inner glory is reflected in our display, in our natural clothing, in our emotions and behaviors, and in our spirituality. Yet many today hold the idea that the outward way of dressing and proper etiquette is a matter of little importance. This popular notion reveals a sad loss of understanding. If we care little about the way we present, then something is missing in our understanding. Our glory and dignity that is growing inwardly, needs to begin to show forth outwardly, thus you, the dreamer, is being asked to consider your outward presence. The clothes you wear, your behaviors, your attitude regarding socially acceptable behavior, have far more importance than you realize. For all this is a very personal expression of who you are. Dreamer, this is not about having an inordinate affection, or focus, on clothing or image; for the world's exaggerated obsession with image is a distorted counterfeit of what God intended to be honorable, dignified, and cleanliness. Instead, we are to have an understanding that the way we present in the natural realm, is related to our inner growth and understanding in the spiritual realm; and is related to what is required of you to reach those who you are purposed to reach. Moreover, life requires a dre ss code. See suggested course of action. (2) If dreamer, at present, is actually considering leaving your God assigned place of worship and/or ministry, then your dream comes as a warning. Dreamer, spiritual death, or mourning, will result if you fully embrace your present thinking, feelings, and/or ideas of leaving your place of worship and/or ministry. Read and understand Galatians 5:19-21, for this speaks of spiritual death. Dreamer, you are not rejecting people or places, your ministry, your church, or your leaders, you are rejecting God. You are actually walking away from God, for God is not leading you to leave. You may feel tired of your ministry, or feel that you no longer receive anything of spiritual value from your church or leade rs. There is nothing wrong with your church or ministry. There is a breech in your spirituality and the enemy of your soul is deliberately causing you to focus on negative and superficial feelings and issues; concerns that if embraced, will cause you to walk far away from God. Therefore, consider your focus on the negative, an illusion, sent from the devil to cause a breach within you, thus, allowing demons to run havoc within your life. Leaving you asking, "How did I get here, in this dark place?" Dreamer, talk to someone, for there is wisdom in the counsel of many (see Proverbs 11:14, 15:22, 23); talk to others with varying opinions about what you are feeling or going through. Only receive wisdom that will shake you up, stir up your thinking, and/or read a book about your issue, do something, other than taking counsel in your head, based on emotions rather than principles. Matthew Henry's Commentary, Proverbs 15:22: Of what ill consequence it is to be precipitate and rash, and to act without advice: Men's (and women) purposes are disappointed, their measures broken, and they come short of their point, gain not their end, because they would not ask counsel about the way. If men (and women) will not take time and pains to deliberate with themselves, or are so confident of their own judgment that they scorn to consult with oth ers, they are not likely to bring anything considerable to pass; circumstances defeat them, which, with a little consultation, might have b een foreseen and obviated. It is a good rule both; in public and domestic affairs, to do nothing rashly and of one's own head; plus "vident oculi quam oculus" - many eyes see more than one. That often proves best which was least our own doing. How much it will be for our advantage to ask the advice of our friends. In the multitude of counsellors (provided they be discreet and honest, and will not give counsel with a spirit of contradiction) purposes are established. Further, and most important, ask for prayer from truthful and sagacious friends, for there is deliverance in prayer. See suggested course of action.

CLEAN, CLEANING, WASHING CLOTHES, JEWELRY, OR SHOES, DRY CLEANER, OR WASHING MACHINE AND DRYER:

This dream has two meanings (choose one). (1) The dreamer will have an eye-opening revelation regarding the turmoil and confusion within your life. This havoc is due to the endeavors of unrighteous and wicked persons. From this day forward, they shall be no more. There shall be a recovery of your material possessions, and a restoration of your joy and strength. Cloth e yourself with this joy, for the joy of the Lord is your strength. Clothe yourself with His strength that you may be enabled to do all things through Christ Jesus who strengthens you. In addition, read and embrace Zechariah 3:4 for this is God's word to y ou from this moment forward. (2) Dry Cleaner, or used a Washing Machine and Dryer: This dream indicates a change for the better, a renewal, or restoration of your spirit is beginning to happen. However, there is a necessity, for a seven -day fast that you may be made clean. Appropriately, declare your own fast regarding the area that needs cleaning. For example, if pornography, you shall fast seven days from pornography, if fornication, fast seven days from fornication or adultery. If yo ur dreams do not change after the seven day fast, then you shall fast a second time for seven days.

Afterward, you shall be cleaned; a great anointing poured upon your life will follow this that you might be about your Heavenly Father's business.

COAT OR JACKET (an outer garment, usually worn outdoors to protect against the elements):

This dream has four meanings (choose one). (1) To dream of wearing a coat, denotes the dreamer will receive an inheritance from one within your family, and the dreamer will always walk in the blessings of your ancestors. (2) Colorful Coat: Dreamer, prepare for a great journey that will ultimately lead you to a very high status of importance. Your ascent to eminence will lead to you holding an official position, allowing you to exercise power and influence. Unfortunately, at present having been put in a precarious position, there (are) will be those who will snub and hurt you, and put you in harm's way. Consequently, due to feelings of rejection and hurt, bitterness will attempt to overcome dreamer. Moreover, there is an implication of arrogance within the dreamer, exposing an overbearing level of pride, as evidenced by your superior manner toward those you consider inferior to you. However, if dreamer can readily recognize the effects of evil, namely that which has caused harm, destruction or misfortune, within yourself, and from others, and allow the precariousness of your journey to effect holiness, humility, wisdom, and a sense of purpose, like nothing else could, within you. Your journey, which is oftentimes beset with difficulties; will be shorten and your ascent to eminence will manifest shortly. Also, see Genesis Chapters 37-45, the Story of Joseph, his coat of many colors, and his journey. Moreover, dreamer is a dream interpreter, thus, become skilled at interpretation, via study and practice. See suggested course of action. (3) Fur coat on with no underclothes (aka fur coat with no knickers): Your dream denotes one who is full of 'airs and graces', but no real class, nor good foundation. You are embracing beliefs, views, and practices that are erroneous, unlawful, toxic, and spiritually and/or physically deadly. Your choice of lifestyle will n ot withstand your storms of life. Your conscience will haunt you. Weakened by frequent panic attacks, brough t on by your own guilt and the fear of God's retribution, you will begin to crack in your personality. He, who carries his or her own accuser, and their own tormentor, always in their bosom, cannot but be afraid on every side (Matthew Henry's Commentary on Job 18:11-21). The only foundation upon which one should wisely establish his or her identity is the principles within the Word of God. Your attitude is leading to a mental and spiritual breakdown, opening the door for demons to run havoc within your l ife and to bring you down to desolation. You are forfeiting purpose for foolishness and ruin. Rebuild your "infrastructure". See suggested course of action. (4) Lose your coat (or to have coat taken or stolen): Dreamer, you will be persecuted for righteousness sake; subsequently you will be promoted to a position of power. Thus, what the enemy will mean for harm, God will use to prepare you to handle power that does not corrupt, for there is a need to deal with your narcissistic tendencies and pride. Therefore, now, resolve to forgive those who would be used by the enemy to come against you. To be forewarned is to prepare you emotionally for the experience. Our Lord Jesus by giving us notice of trouble, is designed to take off the terror of it, that it might not be a surprise to us. See suggested course of action.

DIRTY, WRINKLED, SPOT, OR STAINED CLOTHES, JEWELRY, OR SHOES:

This dream has three meanings (choose one). (1) Your dream is a very stern and harsh rebuke to the dreamer. Your dream reveals one, namely the dreamer, who has some serious faults. You count it a pleasure to indulge and revel, often noisily, i n drinking, and unrestrained licentiousness. As well, you openly engage in illegal and ill-repute enterprises, such as extortion, fraud, drug peddling, and/or prostitution, on some level, all for ungodly profit. You are loud and disturbing, lewd and lascivious. You are an immoral person attached to a godly community. Moreover, you have brought (or is bringing) shame and disgrace to Christ and His church, and have offended many with your actions, especially our Lord and Savior. You have made yourself useless or profitless in spiritual matters, having used, expended, and consumed, all manner of wickedness, thoughtlessly and carelessly. See 2 Peter 2:13.

(2) Wrinkled Clothing: Your dream is a critical alarm. Your dream refers to repeated cycles of hateful, wicked, insulting, and provoking behavior by the dreamer, towards others, possibly due to a hormonal imbalance. Further, due to hatred and an unforgiving spirit, deep within the heart of the dreamer, so as to hide it from yourself, a severing of your personal relationship with Christ is probable (see Matthew 6:14, 15). Dreamer, your unforgiving heart, resulting from you having held on to hatred too long; has caused you to be reckoned as unforgiven within the spiritual realm. Read, understand, and embrace, Matthew 6:14, 15 and 18:21-25, Galatians 5:13-26, 1 John 3:15, 4:20. Consequently, you have slowly abandoned all or some of the original foundational teachings of Christ and His apostles, especially the doctrine of grace (the free and unmerited favor and beneficence of God). This has resulted in a corrupt doctr ine and perverse bondage (1 Timothy 4:1-16). You have ceased to abide in Christ, and instead have become enslaved again to sin and immorality, trusting in your own righteousness. Evil and depravity is your guiding force, thus sin has separated you fro m God. You have been led astray from those of The Way (Acts 9:2). Dreamer, the beginning, development, arrival, or manifestation of something large (significant in scope, extent, or effect) is about to happen within your life, in a threaten ing way. Favorably, the One True Living God can change things. However, this may be your last alarm or warning regarding attitude and thought life. After a seven day fast of purification from things unclean (e.g. hatred, an unforgiving spirit, o r any unrestrained lustful indulgences), go and present yourself to your spiritual leader. Remain within that faith-based community and remain innocent and free from behaviors and choices that defile. By this, you will be made clean, and restored. Moreover, studying the teachings of Jesus Christ and His disciples, and God's relation to it, you will experience God's truth again, and see the demonic for what it is - a lie. See suggested course of action. (3) If you are one considered a teacher in spiritual matters in your awaked life, your dream denotes one who is a false teacher. Dreamer, you have shown yourself presumptuous, when you do not fear to do evil before the Lord or His servants. Your character is one of extreme haughtiness, presumptuousness, pride, and self-assuredness in the very negative sense of the word. All are signs that your heart is hardened. If this disposition is not let go, it will lead to a great fall (Proverbs 11:2; 16:18, 19; 29:23). The harshness of the Lord is kindled against you; you will begin to experience a change in your authority, and favor given from the Lord. Moreover, as He knows your thoughts afar off, repent. Other than heartfelt repentance to Jesus and to individuals affected by your actions, in the form of an apology (if possible), no other excuse or weak justification will be heard. See suggested course of action.

ECCLESIASTICAL OR CLERGY GARMENTS (e.g. collars, headwear, robes, or sashes):

This dream has three meanings (choose one). (1) Religious Headwear (any type of hats worn for religious purposes, such as religious rituals, events, or customs): Your dream denotes one who has a great reverence for God, and who honors the name of Elohim, not only in words, but also in deeds. Therefore, because you have set your heart on the Most High, He will deliver you from your troubles, temptations, and evils of every kind. God will place you out of reach of all your enemies, will honor and elevate you, because you rendered Him the worship due Him, and have known Him to be the God of mercy and love. See also Psalm 91, John 3:16. (2) To dream that you are wearing any article of ecclesiastical garments denotes that dreamer has been scrutinized by your superiors, and has been found to be a wise man or woman. You have proven fit to be officially ordained or promoted to a senior official appointment. Thus, your dream announces that the dreamer will be clothed formally in ecclesiastical garments, ordained as a clergy. You will be rendering conclusive decisions on dubious matters. Moreover, as you are genuine, tactful, and adaptable, your sensitivity and gentleness will be a great healing force, bringing harmony and support to many. The dreamer will begin to see the omnipotent Hand of God within your life's circumstances. Those that hindered you will now go from before you. You will gain the respect of a leader in upper management, because of your faith in God (a resolute trust in the integrity of God and in His Word). This person will cause benefits and favors to flow towards y ou, and he or she will acknowledge, and revere the power of your God within your life. Therefore, from this moment forward, if not already, become seriously vested in your set place of worship, submissive to the head leadership (e.g. pastor, bishop, elder). Nonetheless, one thing is for sure; you are highly favored and blessed of God. To be blessed: Gifts of God's grace, anything God freely gives you, absolution, the Holy Spirit, salvation, regeneration, eternal life, health, children, love of family, longevity, necessities, prosperity, and dominion over all that is yours; and all are parts of the supply of grace, and all are sanctified by the Lord, and technically belongs to Him. The result of this supply in your life will be peace. Moreover, you are expected to promote qualified friends to leadership positions at within ministry and at work also. Do not underestimate anyone. In this, you will show yourself faithful to God and man. (3) Stripped of Ecclesiastical Garments: To dream of being stripped of, or having your ecclesiastical garments, taken from you or removed from your body, this choice has two parts (choose one). (a) Your dream denotes that the dreamer will be removed from your position as a head cleric. You will lose position, title, influence, power, and benefits that came with your position; and other possessions will be taken away. Your extreme pride and refusal to repent has caused you to lose your God given ministry. Dreamer should regard the warning of your dream with sincere alarm. This warning must not be undermined by notions that presuppose the warning is real, but the possibility of an actual loss of a God-given ministry, your prosperity, or even life itself is not. Although you will experience great loss; favorably, grace will be shown you, via a probationary period. Thus, your dream also comes to alert the dreamer of a definite probationary period decreed within your life. This probationary period decreed might be a proving by trial (e.g. a wilderness experience); by humiliation and servitude (Judges 13:1; Acts 13:21, 22); or by waiting (Acts 7:23-30). This probationary season points to grace, leads to repentance, and ends in revival and renewal. During this season, you are counseled to begin implementing godly principles that will move you toward discipline and humility, while embracing faith and love of God. Thank God for His patience, long-suffering, and grace, while you get things decent and in order. See suggested course of action. (b) Your dream denotes the expiry of a cleric, be it the dreamer or another. Question, who was stripped of, or had their ecclesiastical garments taken from the, the dreamer or another? If dreamer's ecclesiastical garments was removed, dreamer, your dream is one of God's ways of breaking it to you gently, preparing you for one of life's common denominators, and if heeded, can prevent you from being emotionally blindsided by loss, as your dream is a notice; it symbolizes shortness of life. For someone who has met Jesus, we experience Him in the little graces, the big miracles, the ordinary days, and the curious moments. He is with us, leading us onward, even sharing our tears. This same Jesus trustworthy in life, even when we are not, can be trusted at the ending of life, for He is the resurrection (John 11:25, 26). If we love Jesus and love our neighbor as we love ourselves, there is nothing in this world or the next to fear. Love is what we take with us, and love is what awaits us when we have finally arrived. Nonetheless, dreamer seek medical attention as soon as possible, and call for the elders of your church, for it is through their prayers of faith and anointing of oil upon you that sin is forgiven and "spiritual" healing bestowed, and perhaps physical healing.[36] This is a true saying, thus it is time to have faith in God. Additionally, it is always a good time to get your house and papers in order (e.g. insurances, bequeaths, untold truths that need to be said), and always a good time to gather family together for prayer, support, wisdom, and truthfulness (Ecclesiastes 12:6). If you sense that your dream is for or about another, the question as to why you have been made privy to this information, and how do you factor into the equation, should be seriously considered along with necessary actions. Perhaps the dreamer is being made aware of the plight of someone, and you are to get involved (see Chapter One, Are You Ready to Hear the Messages in Your Dreams, section entitled, The 10% for others).

GRAY CLOTHING (dressed in all gray):

Your dream denotes one who has (or will have) a lot of power in business or politics. Moreover, although, dreamer is not well known or charismatic at present, you will become shortly. If needful, dreamer may see category, Color (Gray)

HATS (fashion hats, headgear used for protection e.g. rain hats, winter hats, sun hats, safety hats, e.g. hard-hats, helmets, chef hats, hairnets, any protective headgear or headwear for sanitary purposes, ceremonial hats, e.g. graduations headwear, cap, fitted hat, with or without a brim, hoodie, cloak):

Hats are worn for various reasons. For example, ceremonial purposes, as a fashion accessory, for protection against the elements, for safety purposes, for religious reasons. You will need to, first determine the reason or purpose of the type of hat within your dream. With that, this dream has six meanings (choose one). (1) Fashion Hats: Christ will now begin to deal with your unruliness and egotistical tendencies. Do not spurn the rectifying of you by the Lord. He is getting you in order, resulting in a greater commitment to your family, ministry, and to Christ, and for you to be highly blessed. To be blessed: Gifts of God's grace, anything God freely gives you, absolution, the Holy Spirit, salvation, regeneration, eternal life, health, children, l ove of family, longevity, necessities, prosperity, and dominion over all that is yours; and all are parts of the supply of grace, and all are sanctified by the Lord, and technically belongs to Him. The result of this supply in your life will be peace. See suggested course of action. (2) Hats, Headgear used for protection against the elements (e.g. rain hats, winter hats, sun hats): Dreamer, dethroning God's providential sovereignty (the wisdom, care, and guidance provided by God) from over your life, which has started within your thoughts, coupled with your hasty and inconsiderate verdicts on His divine procedures, denies His Power. You are beginning to hijack God's authority within your life, and are replacing faith in Him, with your own set of beliefs an d opinions, rendering your faith in God's omnipotence as pretense. It is by your own beliefs and opinions that you are shaping the way you think, understand, and believe God. Thus, you have an image of godliness, but deny its power; as well, your love for Jesus has dwindled to little or nothing. If not corrected, you will begin to experience a loss of glory (glory in this sense is divine admiration, praise, prosperity, success, triumph, and/or respect from others) within your life. Dreamer, ask God for wisdom, and rest assure that He has wisdom to give, and is generous and liberal enough to give to whomever ask, that includes you. He will not correct or criticize in a harsh manner, for He knows you are seeking wisdom. One may suffer needlessly, because he or she will not ask Jesus for wisdom. See suggested course of action. (3) Safety Hats (e.g. hard-hats, helmets, chef hats, hairnets, any protective headgear or headwear for sanitary purposes): Your dream denotes that you are a fighter and a quick-tempered person naturally, either by generational, family inheritance or because of the hardships of life over the years. Unfortunately, a familiar or kindred combative "spirit", has come, in the form of a person, to stir-up your contentious nature, which earlier has been laid dormant (inactive but capable of becoming active). Consequently, you are now inclined, again, to disagree and argue; you frequently engage in, and seem to enjoy, arguments and disputes. It does not matter to you if you ar e accurate, as long as you feel in control. Opposite of mediator and person of unity, you are likely to cause disagreements and disputes between people with differing views, provoking strong disagreements and disapproval of you, within others. Deal with the source of the "familiar spirit" by removing that person or situation from your domain, repent for damage done, and render again, dead, your "fighting" spirit. For, it is time to go on to perfection, within the spirit realm. Dreamer, read Matthew 5:3-12, with a focus on verse 9. Understand and embrace these scriptures. See suggested course of action. (4) Ceremonial Hats (e.g. graduations headwear, or any other non-ecclesiastical events): For religious or clergy hats, see subcategory, Ecclesiastical Garments. This choice has two parts (choose one). (a) Your dream warns of great weeping, mourning, and bitter anguish of heart because of someone within your family. That someone is in bondage, which may lead to jail time or death. There has been a lack of discipline and leadership by the dreamer, concerning your family, particularly this family member. Open your eyes to the reality of your family's social and emotional problems and seek professional support, if necessary. As well, pray and fast. If urged by God, declare a one, two, or three day fast without food, because this someone needs mercy, and not justice. For, justice will send them to jail for a long time, on the other hand, mercy will set them free. See sugg ested course of action. (b) Dreamer, there is a need to renounce religious beliefs that are based on faithless ritualistic practices, customs and traditions, as well as pride. Your dream is a second witness and warning. God has sent someone to you, calling for you to repent, in preparation for an unadulterated personal relationship with Christ. Dreamer, you are chosen; hesitate not to answer the call. If no abandonment of such practices occurs, as well as pride, your choices will lead you to great weepin g, mourning, and bitter anguish of heart, to say the least, and possibly lead to you being counted amongst those illustrated in Matthew 7:21-23. A change is needed; therefore, pray to Jesus Psalm 51, this followed by appropriate application of wisdom, can conceivably avert some of the repercussions of your choices. This is what is called leaving a blessing behind. See suggested course of action. (5) Cap (a close-fitting hat, with a peak, with or without a brim): This choice has three parts (choose one). (a) Cap in hand (to hold you cap, especially in your hand): Your dream denotes one who will, or has, humbly asked for something. You will receive what you are expecting. (b) Feather in your cap (to have or see a feather in your ha t): Your dream denotes one whose networking will prove successfully helpful to your achievements in your future. (c) Fitted Cap: Your dream denotes that the dreamer is being criticized. However, if the description is correct, and the words are describin g the truth, then, the words of another should be received as constructive. If dreamer is being critical of another, you are counseled to make sure your words are sprinkled with empathy, are correct, and are describing the truth of the matter. See suggested course of action. (6) Hoodie or Cloak: Dreamer, you will gain (are gaining) dark and erroneous knowledge, through personal experience and through a supernatural imparting, which is demonically communicated. The knowledge gained will not allow you to praise the Lord, only to exalt one's self. You are abandoning faith in Jesus Christ, and is now worshipping false gods and images, and adhering to lies. You hold to beliefs, views, and practices that are erroneous, unlawful, toxic, and spiritually and/or physically deadly. Your attitude is leading to a mental and spiritual breakdown and corruption, opening the door for demons to run havoc within your life and to bring you down to desolation. Your kind of choices leads to prostitutio n, poverty, homelessness, begging, imprisonment, and/or early death. You are forfeiting purpose for foolishness and ruin. Demonic influences will swarm around you, ready to help you in your wicked, evil, despicable, immoral, reprehensible, disreputable, degenerate, infamous, or perverse choices. Your lifestyle choices are, or will become, offensive and repulsive (abominable) in the sight of God and humanity. Dreamer, demons have had thousands of years to master human weaknesses and can rival men and women of God if we are not careful. Favorably, because of grace (the free and unmerited favor and beneficence of God) and the many mercies of God extended to you, your dream is only a warning and not an official declaration. Dreamer is counseled to seek all kinds of spiritual support now, to possibly avert or turn things around, and perhaps move away from your present environment, definitely walk away from all negativity abruptly. Utilizing the powerful resources of prayer and heartfelt repentance to Jesus and to individuals affected by your actions, in the form of an apology (if possible), is needed. Repentance is seeking pardon and expressing sincere feelings of regret and brokenness for having done something awry and/or for having hurt someone, see 2 Corinthians 7:10, 11. To individuals, a phone call or a letter of apology is a good place to start. To Jesus pray, Psalm 51, this followed by appropriate application of wisdom, can conceivably avert some of the repercussions of your choices. This coupled with fasting, a changed mindset, serious re-consideration of God's ways and means, and an honest acknowledgement of God's hand within your life, then the severe impact of your choices and actions upon your life, can be reversed and damages repaired (also see Ezekiel 33:12-19). This is what is called leaving a blessing behind. If you do not genuinely seek help and change, for sure ruin will be your destiny's declaration. See suggested course of action.

In addition, amid the following are common words, expressions, usages, (e.g. slang or clichés), or a 'probable' that are metaphorically represented by hats:

- **Big hat, no cattle (to have a big hat, and notice there is a need of cattle):** Your dream denotes one who talks big, but cannot back it up. See suggested course of action.
- **"At the Drop of a Hat" (to drop a hat in your dream):** Your dream denotes one who is doing something rashly, perhaps without thinking things through, nor considering the end results or the fruit of your choices. Dreamer needs to re- consider your thinking; and begin to count the costs of your choices. Dreamer, ask God for wisdom, and rest assure that He has wisdom to give, and is generous and liberal enough to give to whomever ask, that includes you. He will not correct or criticize in a harsh manner, for He knows you are seeking wisdom. One may suffer needlessly, because he or she will not ask Jesus for wisdom. See suggested course of action.
- **"Eat my Hat" (dream of eating a hat):** Your dream denotes one who does not believe that something is going to happen, and believes that they are absolutely right in their assumption, and are willing to let you know that there is no chance of them being wrong. Dreamer, your dream comes to bring awareness that you are wrong in your assumptions. Dreamer needs to re-consider your thinking. Dreamer, ask God for wisdom, and rest assure that He has wisdom to give, and is generous and liberal enough to give to whomever ask, that includes you. He will not correct or criticize in a harsh manner, for He knows you are seeking wisdom. One may suffer needlessly, because he or she will not ask Jesus for wisdom. See suggested course of action.
- **Hang your Hat on something (to hang your hat up):** Your dream denotes one who is depending on, and believing that something will happen shortly. Dreamer, make sure your hopes are scripturally based, or you will be greatly disappointed, even to the point of weeping, mourning, and bitter anguish of heart. Dreamer, ask God for wisdom, and rest assure that He has wisdom to give, and is generous and liberal enough to give to whomever ask, that includes you. He will not correct or criticize in a harsh manner, for He knows you are seeking wisdom. One may suffer needlessly, because he or she will not ask Jesus for wisdom. See suggested course of action.
- **Wear many Hats (to have on two or more hats at one time):** Your dream denotes one who performs many roles or tasks. Questions, are you performing your roles or tasks good, great, or poorly? Is it better to be good at many things or great at one thing? Dreamer, while, everyone has at least a few areas in which they could be good, with much effort, a spirit of excellence is what a believer should strive for, especially when operating within the ministry of God. Another consideration, it is better to do one thing well than ten things poorly (quote by Heather Hart).

JEWELRY OR ACCESSORIES:

Belt or Suspenders (a band to tie or buckle around the body, or elastic straps that hold trousers): A belt or suspenders, denotes divine truth. The truth of God is before the dreamer, via Holy Writ. Thus, dreamer is cautioned to take no risks, regarding a situation at hand, but to base your decisions only on verifiable truths, and on sound wisdom, found within the Word of God. The lesson is, no matter how personable, powerful, or difficult a person, or how uncertain or unpopular the choices and issues, always take the next biblical and ethical step, for obedience to God's principles, and His truths, per Holy Writ, will always prove safer and stronger foundationally. If necessary, see suggested course of action.

Earrings: Dreamer, freedom from bondage, domination by evil, and hardship, is beginning for you. Grace will be shown you, via a probationary period, and regard this period with sincere alarm. This probationary period decreed might be a proving by trial (e.g. a wilderness experience); by humiliation and servitude (Judges 13:1; Acts 13:21, 22); or by waiting (Acts 7:23-30). This probationary season points to grace, leads to repentance, and ends in revival and renewal. During this season, you are counseled to begin implementing godly principles that will move you toward discipline and humility, while embracing faith and love of God. Regularly thank God for His patience, long-suffering, and grace (the free and unmerited favor and beneficence of God), while you get things decent and in order. Moreover, you are to reject people, places, and circumstances that hinder spiritual clarity, growth, and stability. In addition, your Lord and Savior will contend with those who contend with you during your deliverance season. In time, through the workings of grace, there will be deliverance, freedom, and rest for you. It will be known that the Lord is your Savior and your Redeemer, the Mighty One of Jacob. In addition, if applicable, your children will be saved.

Gloves: This dream has four meanings (one, two may apply). (1) Put on gloves, your dream denotes that the dreamer has, or will, develop an extremely close relationship with another, particularly someone who has very recently entered (re- entered) your life. Question, what condition were the gloves? Couple this with one of the following two (choose one). (2) Took off gloves, to dream of taking gloves off, denotes that the dreamer, and another, will start to argue and fight in a more serious way. It is wiser, and better, to attempt resolution, instead of embracing opposition. Dreamer is counseled to re - evaluate your behavior, reasons, and choices, and to learn from your mistakes, find new directions in solving problems, and simply take the higher ground. See suggested course of action. (3) If gloves were in good condition, this relationship will prove to be a very strong ally and supporter. God has sent this someone into your life to help you carry out your next endeavor. Allow the strength of this person's character to help and support you. (4) If gloves were in bad condition, this relationship will prove negative. This person will prove to be a very strong and formidable challenge for you; thus, your dream is a warning. Dreamer, take steps accordingly to struggle against this unfavorable relationship. Remember certain personalities are all encompassing, affecting everything, cataclysmic, contagious, deadly, and harmful. Then again, this person maybe allowed within your life, because of the dreamer's unwillingness to abstain from immorality after having been asked to abstain from such by God, or because of the dreamer's self-righteous behavior and condescending attitude. See suggested course of action.

Necklace (jewelry consisting of a cord or chain usually worn about the neck): Dreamer, although you are physically very attractive, the depth of your beauty is only skin-deep. Hence, you are found to be incomplete or immature regarding spiritual order. Examples of spiritual order, per Holy Writ, seek first God's Kingdom and His righteousness, and all other things will be given you, to obey (God's word) is better than sacrifice. To do what is right and just, is more acceptable to the Lord than sacrifice (Matthew 6:33; 1 Samuel 15:22; Proverbs 21:3). In another place it is written, God is the head of Christ, Christ is the head of every man, and man is the head of woman (1 Corinthians 11:3- 12). God's spiritual order is intended to affect a deep abiding commitment and obedience to Christ. Submissiveness to His ways and means leads to an intensely deep, strong, and authentic beauty or handsomeness in God's sight. This beauty is so deep that it emanates outwardly, humbleness, prudence, tactfulness, and unpretentiousness; setting you up for victory in all your dealings, for a promotion, and for other blessings. Dreamer, while beauty or handsomeness attracts the eye, and worldly allures entice us, all is fading, but the soul lasts forever; an immortal soul cannot have contentment in anything that fades. Therefore, dreamer, you ought to have faith in God, which is a resolute trust in the integrity of God and in His Word for your earthly affairs, as well as, for your heavenly affairs, especially those principles that do not fade, particularly, sacrificing your fleshly desires that your soul might be saved. See suggested course of action.

Pearls: Your dream is the start of the fulfillment of a prophecy given the dreamer some time ago. Your high leadership and prophetic abilities was prophesied to you long before you reached this point. Now, you, the dreamer, will begin to experience a miraculous increase in knowledge and wisdom, regarding spiritual truths and concepts, enabling you to discern between verities and false. This gift of discernment will give you access to prophetic insight, and awaken within you prophetic abilities. You are chosen and will become endowed with an ability to handle this type of divine impartation. Dreamer, you will find purpose in this, and know that God has given you a great gift. Further, your prophetic gifting and discernment should be used exclusively for the Kingdom of God. Dreamer, submitting to

Jesus, as your Lord and Savior will help you master your gift of prophecy, as well as maintain loving relationships across generations, using your experience and wisdom to assist the younger ones with the problems of life. You will prove to be a transformational influence in the lives of many. It would be to your advantage to recognize your Creator and to serve and worship Him, via Jesus Christ, otherwise, your words of prophecy will be based purely on your own emotions, and not words from the Lord; thus, reckoning you an unwise and foolish prophet or prophetess. Moreover, if not practiced regularly, go to church, join a church, a faith based bible-believing community, commit to that ministry, and don't leave, no matter what, for three years. Forsake not the gathering of yourself together with other mainstream Christians. Another prophecy will be given you, via someone within that ministry, during this season, write it down for it will happen. See suggested course of action.

Ring (circlet jewelry usually worn on the finger): This dream has two meanings (choose one). (1) Your dream denotes promotion and authority in all areas of the dreamer's life. Be encouraged. (2) Lost a Ring: This choice has two parts (choose one). (a) If ring was lost and not found, dreamer, is forfeiting promotion and authority, and is embracing words of doubt, fear, and unbelief, words that are demonically instigated and are spiritually perverse. There is a story of David and Goliath in 1 Samuel 17. As Goliath targeted David's identity, to strike fear in David's heart, so has the devil targeted everything about you concerning Christ, to strike fear and instigate hopelessness within you, resulting in an offense within you against God. Demons targets your identity as a Christian, as a blood-bought Believer, a child of the King of kings, a son or daughter of Elohim. Dreamer, when you embrace God's word and live those words out in your natural life, this releases courage, faith, and life, and like David, victory over the giants that would dare to defy who you truly are in Christ Jesus. You literally become a better you. Question to journal, how has the enemy used his "weapons of words" to defeat you or how can he use this weapon to defeat you? Dreamer, ask Jesus to deliver you from the enemy within and without, and from the demonic voices that persecute you mentally. It is also suggested that you write down three tactics or strategies you can quickly initiate, to overcome the plots and schemes of the enemy concerning your identity in Christ. In order to win this spiritual warfare, you must have an offensive strategy. If you do not have a plan, you will not win, and will end up forfeiting opportunities for advancement. David was able to triumph against his enemy because he knew his God and he knew that his God would give him victory. Therefore, know that God will give you the victory! See suggested course of action. (b) If ring was lost and then found, this denotes a temporary setback, concerning promotion and authority, due to dreamer lack of vision regarding your primary purpose, and lack of knowing, who you are, and your value, to the Kingdom of God. Unfortunately, you allowed the tactics of the enemy, and spiritual warfare, to slow down your progress, thwart your vision, and to hinder and hold you back. Fortunately, you will regroup, get up, and continue moving forward, progressing towards your set place. You will get there, only later. Moreover, now, resolve to forgive those who would be used by the enemy to come against you that you might progress forward, faster. See suggested course of action.

MEN'S WEAR (casual, formal, informal, or immodest):

This dream has four meanings (choose one). (1) Male dreamer, there is a need for the dreamer to mentor and affirm young men of their manhood, via a young men's ministry or some kind of mentorship program; this is purpose. The type of clothing (e.g. casual clothing, work clothes, formal to semiformal type clothing, immodest), suggests a ministry's primary focus and t he mentality of the various young men sent to you. For example one dressed in work clothes, would suggests a primary focus on job responsibility, good work ethics, types of jobs, formal clothing might suggests characteristics of, or befitting a person, in authority, white and blue collar outfits, suggests white or blue collar jobs and responsibilities, immodest or sexual type clothing might suggest a ministry focused on sexual morality. Moreover, the type of background setting will give you a coloring of the type of mentality of the young men who will be under your tutelage. Dreamer, it is suggested that your ministry include, but not be limited to, classes, seminars, mentorships, and sponsorships, and all with a focus on how God views manhood, the responsibilities of manhood, work, becoming a father, sexuality, financial responsibility, and discipline. It is also suggested this ministry culminates into a formal dedication ceremony of some sort, dedicating young men to God and celebrating their entrance into manhood. While the dedication is by faith, have a literal ceremony amongst young men that come into your ministry, a 'quasi' bar mitzvah (the ritual ceremony that marks the 13ᵗʰ birthday of a Jewish boy, after which he takes responsibility for his moral and spiritual conduct). The young men, who will be sent, attracted, and connected to your ministry, guided there by God, will sit and be rulers amongst the righteous. For they are chosen and part of a royal priesthood, a holy nation, a people for God's own possession that they, and you, may proclaim the excellencies of Him, who has called you and them, out of darkness into His marvelous light (see 1 Peter 2:9, 10). Therefore, take care and handle the young men righteously and sagaciously. See suggested course of action. (2) Married female dreamer, if you were dressed in male clothing or supposing yourself to be a male and was dressed as one, your dream comes as a dire warning. Your dream signifies that you are angry, antagonistic, and domineering. You have aligned yourself, with your male superiors, especially your husband, and have thrown off submission. You take on authority, which God has bestowed on men; and display mannerisms customarily appropriate for men only. Your actions are that of a woman desirous of changing sexes. The Lord God forbids the confusing of the relationships of the sexes, men must not be effeminate or figuratively emasculated by a female, nor must women be virile, masculine, or domineering. As disobedience in small matters shows great contempt of God's principles, so obedience in small matters shows a very great regard for them. Daughter, obey him that has rule over you, especially your husband. Like Sarah, who obeyed Abraham and called him her master. You are her daughters if you do what is right and do not give way to fear (1 Peter 3:6 NIV). If you do not gain control over your antagonistic and domineering attitude, standing before the Lord improperly, you will begin to experience a loss of glory (glory in this sense is divine admiration, praise, prosperity, success, triumph, and/or respect of your husband and of others) within your life. Additionally, while the following is not about imminent death, as that is a long way off, dreamer is counseled to deeply, begin considering your life, after dea th, in eternity and the rewards (or loss of rewards) thereof, due to your choices at present. Moreover, consider Deuteronomy 22:5, and believe the Word of God. See suggested course of action. (3) Unmarried female dreamer, your dream denotes that the dreamer is internally inconsistent and disordered, because of a violent violation in your past or recent present; examples of the violation are abuse, assault, bullying, kidnapping, molestation, rape, stalked, being held prisoner. The diabolical enti ty, having possessed the person(s) who committed the literal act, was sent to rob, steal, and destroy a quality of life that has been destined you, to keep you from living that life abundantly, happily, and in peace. The demon's mission is to get you to entertain, embrace, and live out the negative results of your particular violation, with a hope to oppress, persecute, and bring you into bondage of an ungodly and unprofitable lifestyle. Desiring that the unfavorable consequences of that ungodly and unprofitable lifestyle; will cost you your emotional sanity, possibly your life, and ultimately your soul. Thus, instead of you moving towards, and thus fulfilling, your divine purpose, and reaching a pinnacle in your life, thereby with, you will prosper, you have begun to listen to, and be fooled by, demons. Having listened and embraced their lies, you have begun to decrease and fall, eventually running amok your life, literally crashing, when you should be clear and focused mentally, emotionally, and spiritually. Dreamer; oftentimes, bad things happen to innocent and good people. A bad thing happened to you, and you are good and innocent. Compassionately, the Lord is creating a miracle in your life. This miracle will stop the effects of your violation from playing a significant role in your life, enabling you to move forward with your life. However, the miracle's success depends upon your willingness to be healed and set free; for one will always have the choice to say no, or perhaps sabotage their progress. First, recognize and respect your time of visitation from the Lord, for it is upon you, as well as the work of

His Hand upon your life. If you lack wisdom ask God for wisdom; and He will give you wisdom. For the Lord gives wisdom and from His mouth comes knowledge and understanding. Then you will understand what is right and just and fair, every good path. When wisdom enters your heart and knowledge becomes sweet to your soul, discretion will protect you, understanding will guard you, and His Truth will lead you. To deliver you from the ways of wickedness, and from demons whose words and ways are perverse, who causes you to walk in darkness gladly, whose paths are crooked and devious, causing you to leave straight paths (Proverbs 2:1-6, 9-15). This is one of God's covenant promises to you. Have faith in this. Further, with fortitude choose not to be a victim or to perpetuate the desolation. Stop what you're doing; go, and separate from anyone and anything that hinders your clarity and emotional stability. Again, if you are in a negative place, move away from your present environment, definitely, you should run away from all negativity abruptly, God will provide, trust Him. Additionally, and if applicable, go, and continue your education, the Lord will help you in your endeavor. Dreamer, if you do not respect the work of the Lord within your life, and the opportunities He is offering you, to be set free, spiritually, emotionally and physically. You will have nothing to work with, but your body, namely deviant sexual promiscuousness, and all that comes with it, including physical death; having forfeited purpose, reasonable resources, and wise counsel that has surrounded you. For, your kind of choices, at present, leads to begging, early death, homelessness, homosexuality, imprisonment, poverty, and/or prostitution. Working with and using your intellect (mind) and/or strength, and good ethics, for your livelihood, will always out last the use of your body immorally for sustenance, and these choices make s life easier. Dreamer is counseled to seek all kinds of spiritual support now, to possibly avert or turn things around. Moreover, if you do not genuinely seek help and change, for sure ruin will be your destiny. Utilizing the powerful resources of pray er and heartfelt repentance to Jesus is needed. Repentance is seeking pardon and expressing sincere feelings of regret and brokenness for having done something awry and/or for having hurt someone. To Jesus pray, Psalm 51, this followed by appropriate application of wisdom, can conceivably avert some of the repercussions of your choices. This, coupled with a lifestyle of fasting, perhaps twice a week, a changed mindset, serious re-consideration of God's ways and means, and an honest acknowledgement of God's hand within your life, then the severe impact of your choices and actions upon your life, can be reversed and damages repaired (also see Ezekiel 33:12-19). This is what is called leaving a blessing behind. Moreover, consider Deuteronomy 22:5, and believe the Word of God. See suggested course of action. (4) If you are an unbeliever (one who has no religious beliefs, a non-religious person, or one who has no religious faith or belief in Jesus Christ, or one who does not embrace a personal relationship with Jesus Christ, at present). Jesus loves you, thus, He is petitioning you to accept Him as your personal Savior, for you are valuable in His eyes. The first step in receiving Him as your personal Savior is repentance (see in the Holy Bible, Acts 2:37-41). Repentance is seeking pardon for having done something awry, and for having hurt someone, and expressing sincere feelings of regret and brokenness. To Jesus pray, Psalm 51:1-19. Moreover, if you will accept the Heavenly Father's Words, via the Bible, and store up His principles, and accept His ways and means, turning your ear to wisdom and applying your heart to understanding, calling out for insight and crying aloud for discernment, Jesus will meet yo u. This, coupled with a lifestyle of prayer and fasting, followed by appropriate application of wisdom, and you will know the Messiah, Jesus Christ, intimately, and find the knowledge of God you seek. For the Lord gives wisdom and from His mouth comes knowledge and understanding. Then you will understand what is right and just and fair– every good path. When wisdom enters your heart and knowledge becomes sweet to your soul, discretion will protect you, understanding will guard you, and His Truth will lead you. To deliver you from the ways of wickedness, and from demons whose words and ways are perverse, who causes you to walk in darkness gladly, whose paths are crooked and devious, causing you to leave straight paths (Proverbs 2:1-6, 9-15). This is one of God's covenant promises to you. Have faith in this. See suggested course of action.

NAKED:

Caught with your Pants down: This type of dream, denote that dreamer will be exposed in an embarrassing situation, and that you are unprepared for the situation or an event. See suggested course of action.

Give the Shirt off your back (to take your shirt off and give to another): This type of dream, denote that the dreamer would do anything to help another, no matter what the personal sacrifice. Be encouraged, you will receive as you've given to others, and go on to prosper greatly.

Ripping of Clothes (or tearing clothing): This type of dream denotes that there will be an outward manifestation of the dreamer's inward frustration. Due to loss of assets, such as property, finances, loss of authority, dominion, divine appointment, special honor, special privilege, or God's blessings upon your specific ministry and/or loss of family. This loss is due largely to your negligence of a God given responsibility, or your allowance of negligence, by individuals connected with your ministry. Unfortunately, your part will be given to another. To prevent public embarrassment, via uncontrollable burst of anger, dreamer is counseled to speak your truth to God, laying your frustrations on Him, for only He can help you now. See suggested course of action.

Stripper or Undress: This type of dream, denote that the dreamer is seriously ill, possibly a life threatening illness. If dreamer is seriously ill, consult a physician immediately. With that noted, it is also suggested that you call for the elders of your church, for it is through their prayers of faith and anointing of oil upon you that your sins will be forgiven and that spiritual and physical healing might occur[36]. Dreamer there is a great need for repentance, for your sickness is primarily due to unhealthy lifestyle choices, unwillingness to forgive or show mercy, and sinful and wicked behaviors and evil practices, thus a change in thoughts, actions, deeds, and beliefs is needed, with a sense of urgency. Again, seek medical attention as soon as possible, that perhaps physical healing might be bestowed. This is a true saying, thus it is time to have faith in God. Additionally, it is always a good time to get your house and papers in order (e.g. insurances, bequeaths, untold truths that need to be said), and always a good time to gather family together for prayer, support, wisdom, and truthfulness. See suggested course of action.

PAJAMAS, NIGHTCLOTHES, OR ROBE:

This dream has two meanings (choose one). (1) This is a warning to the dreamer. Take heed of hypocrisy and pride. You pride yourself on your authority, influence, status, and titles, validating yourself by them, commanding respect, and demanding others to honor you before people, as Saul demanded of Samuel (1 Samuel 15:30). This is a fruit of pride. You pretend to appear very good, robing yourself with a pseudo-piety and long prayers. You are ambitious, greedy, and covet applause and VIP privileges, all this to satisfy your vanity. You build your wealth on the back of the poor, and other tricks, and then hide yourself from suspicion of dishonesty. By much bother, trouble, and upheaval you will be made aware of your faults and brought to a point of contriteness and sorrow. As well, your position and standing are threatened with being unseated. You must begin to humbly do an about-turn, get real with yourself and others, embrace contentment, and sincerely admit to Jesus that you have sinned. No one is to be worshipped but God alone. If no authentic change is effected, you will lose all, and you have much to lose, as did King Saul. See suggested course of action. (2) To see another walking around in pajamas: Dreamer, you are cautioned to take heed of allowing yourself to be imposed upon by a hypocritical and prideful leader, and of being infected with his or her pride and hypocrisy. Be on the alert and on your guard, that you do not absorb his or her ideas, nor their weird and outrageous claims and opinions. Neither, be swayed by the opinions of people concerning them. This leader appears very intimidating, twisting God's word to make others subservient to them, and to rob men and women of their honest wage. Don't believe the hype. He or she will be punished most severely. See also Mark 12:38-40. You will be spared the judgment (divine reprimand for folly and sin) coming upon those who allow such a leader to prosper, if you do an about - turn, get real with yourself, embrace God's truth, and sincerely admit to Jesus that you have sinned, by exalting another above His word, and just walk away. If necessary, see suggested course of action.

SEAL (a device incised to make an impression; to imprint a mark or design, usually used to authenticate document):

This type of dream is concerning a choice you've made, recently, regarding an issue, or situation. Your choice has been judged by the Divine Council. This judgment is irrevocably, incapable of being retracted or revoked. Example of such a degree, see Genesis 25:29-34. Favorably, although a weakness has been shown, failure has resulted, and a divine decision has been made regarding that failure, not all is lost. Like King David, when he committed adultery (see 2 Samuel 11, 12), or when Jonah rose up to flee unto Tarshish from the presence of Jehovah (see Jonah), or when Peter denied the Christ (see Matthew 26:69-:75). Utilizing the powerful resources of prayer and heartfelt repentance to Jesus and to individuals affected by your actions, in t he form of an apology (if possible), is needed. To Jesus pray, Psalm 51, this followed by appropriate application of wisdom, can conceivably avert some of the repercussions of your choices; this is what is called leaving a blessing. Without trust in God's mercy and grace, you will choose like Judas, suicide, albeit spiritual (Acts 1:18). Therefore, if your change of will, though produced by sorrow for sin, is one which does not lead to reformation, it is not repentance; for there was a change in the wi ll of Judas, produced by sorrow for sin, yet Judas did not repent (Matthew 27:3-5). The change in his case led to suicide, not to reformation (Acts of the Apostles). See suggested course of action.

SHOES (any manner of footwear, e.g. sandals, shoes, sneakers):

Shoes generally denote preparation for ministry; couple this with one of the following.

Big Shoes (shoes too big): Dreamer, God is asking you to set in motion, start, and prepare the way your ministry that may initially seem too big, too hard, or too overwhelming for you. Notwithstanding, if you accept what God is asking you to do, and submit to His request, and prepare yourself properly, via training, education, and research, you will prosper greatly. On th e contrary, if you deny God's request, allowing fear, insecurity, or any other excuse that you may adopt, to keep you from doing, e.g. "they" won't let me minister, another will take you place, and the prosperity attached to the ministry, will be given to that person, and your part will be jealously. Note, God will never ask you to do something you are genuinely unable to do. Therefore, you are personally responsible for the ministry God is asking of you now. If necessary, see suggested course of action.

Boots: This dream has two meanings (choose one). (1) This type of dream, denote that the dreamer is one who was in a position of weakness, but is now in a position of strength. Now, use your position to strengthen what remains and is about to die. If necessary, see suggested course of action. (2) To give someone a boot: This type of dream, denote that the dreamer will soon be dismissed from a job, or expel from an organization. If dreamer suspects that, you are in jeopardy of losing yo ur job, resign now that you may be able to obtain gainful employment without the stain of having been fired. You simply need to say, I resigned. If you reputation is in jeopardy, the reason being, you being expelled from an organization, repent, and mo ve on. See suggested course of action.

"Church Shoes" or Dress Shoes or Good Fitting Shoes: This dream has two meanings (both may apply). (1) Dreamer, you have access to prophetic wisdom because you have the capacity to discern truth from false. Nurture your gift of discernment; developing it, that others may spiritually grow by your words of wisdom. For you are, truly a prophet or prophetess. Do not suppress the prophetic nature of your gifting out of fear or laziness; this may prove detrimental to your spiritual and financial life. Your efforts will be a revolutionary force in other people's lives. For this reason, you will be delivered from your present predicament. Someone has been sent by God to help you. Receive, and allow their help; they are qualified. By helping you get free, they will be helping you go towards your divine destiny. Remember them in the day of your prosperity. Note; there will be those who will mock you as you learn and begin to operate within your prophetic ministry. J ust know, you do have prophetic authority in the spiritual realm, and as no prophet is acceptable in his or her own country, nor will you be accepted in certain places, unable to facilitate an atmosphere for miracles to manifest. Therefore, read and embrace Luke 4:23-30, Revelation 11:4-6, and take comfort that if it happened to Jesus, there's a good chance it will happened to you also, as with other believers. (2) Unmarried dreamer: Your dream denotes a marriage. The dreamer has been made "whole" from past negative experiences within relationships. Thus, your emotional and spiritual self has been made new. Favorably, there will be a literal wedding and it will be honored by the Lord. If engaged, go and prepare for your wedding in peace. If not, get ready to meet your future spouse. He or she is recognized as a priest on some level or another, e.g., pastor, elder, bishop, reverend, or some type of a very visible cleric. You will be a great asset to his or her ministry.

Dead man shoes (to possess or put on shoes that belonged to a dead person): This type of dream, denote that the dreamer is one who is trying to get rid of, or replace someone, in order to obtain a promotion. Your activities are unethica l. Remember, Elohim sees all. The same one you are trying to get rid of, or replace, you will have to, openly honor them, and to your embarrassment. Moreover, they will gain authority over you. See suggested course of action.

Give your shoe(s) to someone: This type of dream, denote that the dreamer is entering (or have entered) into a contract, an agreement, or a deal with someone, possibly, if actually known, the one you gave your shoe to in the dream. This pact is spiritually binding, and possibly legally binding (Deuteronomy 23:21-23; Ecclesiastes 5:2-5); know all the facts, and read the very fine print, before totally committing. If necessary, see suggested course of action.

To look for, or to need, shoes: This type of dream denote that at present, the dreamer lacks what it takes to successfully, succeed within the particular ministerial position you desire. Although you are naturally endowed with certain gifting's, your lack of discipline, studiousness, and experience, prevents you from being promoted. Moreover, your lack of depth of intellec t and knowledge, leaves you only concern with what is superficial. Consequently, the dreamer will not receive a confirmation regarding a promotion or ordination within a ministry at this time. It is suggested that you do not exalt yourself, nor speak with insolent pride, for exaltation comes from God (see Psalm 75:6, 7). Instead, dreamer is counseled to, no longer concern yourself with issues that are without depth, emotionally and intellectually, but only concern yourself sagaciously with dilig ent study, deeply embracing skills, and training that will increase wisdom, and raise your level of discipline, thereby improving self- control, and experience. See suggested course of action.

To put on shoes: This type of dream, denote that there will be an open acknowledgement that the dreamer is successfully completing a course, which God has you on. Moreover, set aside for the priesthood, you are being prepared to carry out the official role, position, or office of a priest (e.g. prophet, pastor, minister, or some type of a very visible cleric). With this office comes spiritual growth and divine illumination. Consequently, if dreamer has genuinely sought after truth, God's truth will continue to be revealed to you and it will continue to lead and guide you. Further, chosen, you are to high ly, give praise to Him who has called you out of darkness into His marvelous light (see 1 Peter 2:9, 10). At present, continue to allow the Paraclete to complete the work of purification and sanctification within you. For those who go forth in tears, sha ll return rejoicing (Psalm 126:5, 6). Be diligent and patient, everything will be done proper, and in its own time; you will be ordained to a priestly office, and if relevant, your request in another area of your life will be granted. Again, your heigh t of spiritual progress and promotion will be according to your faith and obedience to God's will over your life personally. If necessary, see suggested course of action.

In addition, amid the following are common words, expressions, usages, (e.g. slang or clichés), or a 'probable' that are metaphorically represented by hats:

- **Dig your heels in (to dig you heels into something):** This type of dream, denote that the dreamer is starting to resist something. Dreamer, your opposition is without your cause, not being well grounded in logic and truth. Your resistance is primarily likened to antipathy issues and faithlessness. The dreamer is encouraged to seek and understand the underlying causes of your hostility issues and why such a lack of faith in God. It is wiser, and better, to attemp t resolution, instead of embracing opposition. Therefore, accept God's long suffering towards you, giving you time to get the appropriate help to make things right within. If you lack wisdom, ask Jesus for wisdom. He gives wisdom to all, generously, no matter who you are and what you've done; wisdom is available (see James 1:5-8, Proverbs 2:1-6, 10). Hence, if, by just asking, you may get wisdom, one may suffer needlessly, because you will not ask Jesus for wisdom. Nonetheless, earnestly seek to once again, become faithful to God and His ways. See suggested course of action

- **Drag your heels (to drag your shoes by the heel):** This type of dream, denote that the dreamer is delaying something, because you don't want to do it. Dreamer is counseled to simply tell the truth, which is, you just don't want to do it, and accept the consequences, thus, no longer delaying a project. Dreamer, persistent practice of truthfulness, and in embracing the fruits of the spirit (see Galatians 5:22-26), all this will help truth inwardly begin to emerge; at a pace, you'll be able to "wrap your mind around" comfortably. See suggested course of action

- **If the shoe fits, wear it (to try on a shoe to see if it fits):** This type of dream, suggests that whatever, recently, has been said or exposed regarding the dreamer, is truthful, and does apply to the dreamer. Therefore, dreamer, question not, who said what and why, but ask God, what are you to glean from what has been exposed, and see the Lord's providence behind all the events in your life. See suggested course of action.

WHITE CLOTHING (dressed in all white):

This dream has two meanings (choose one). (1) Dreamer, you live a life pleasing to God in every way, worthy of the Lord acknowledgement; thus your dream. Elohim will fulfill every good purpose of your heart and every act prompted by your faith; therefore be encouraged. Moreover, God will very shortly restore you to a place of honor that you may serve Him as His spokesperson; He will divinely authorize you to speak on behalf of His cause and His Kingdom. Dreamer, worthy of respect, self-controlled, and sound in your faith, in love, and in endurance, you are counted worthy of this calling. Your strong unyielding will and courage to defend your convictions, makes you one who will stand firm in one spirit, contending for the faith of the gospel, bearing fruit in every good work, and growing in the knowledge of God. (2) As, this color also denotes death and mourning. If dreamer is actually ill at present, you are encouraged to seek medical attention as soon as possible; and call for the elders of your church, for it is through their prayers of faith and anointing of oil upon you that sin is fo rgiven and healing is bestowed[36]. Have faith in this, for it will be by your faith that you will be healed wholly. This is a true saying. God has appointed someone, to help you through this difficult time. See suggested course of action.

WOMEN'S WEAR (casual, formal, informal, or immodest):

This dream has four meanings (choose one). (1) Female dreamer, there is a need for the dreamer to mentor and affirm young women of their womanhood, via a young women's ministry or some kind of mentorship program; this is purpose. The type of clothing (e.g. casual clothing, work clothes, formal to semiformal type clothing, immodest or sexual), suggests a ministry's primary focus and the mentality of the various young women sent to you. For example one dressed in work clothes, would suggests a primary focus on job responsibility, good work ethics, types of jobs, formal clothing might suggests characteristics of, or befitting a person, in authority, casual clothing, suggests white or blue collar jobs and responsibilities, immodest o r sexual type clothing might suggest a ministry focused on sexual morality. Moreover, the type of background setting will give you a coloring of the type of mentality of the young women who will be under your tutelage. Dreamer, it is suggested that your ministry include, but not be limited to, classes, seminars, mentorships, and sponsorships, and all with a focus on how God views womanhood, the responsibilities of womanhood, work, becoming a mother, sexuality, financial responsibility, and discipline. It is also suggested this ministry culminates into a formal dedication ceremony of some sort, dedicating young women to God and celebrating their entrance into womanhood. While the dedication is by faith, have a literal ceremony amongst young women that come into your ministry, a 'quasi' debutante ball (a very formal event where a young lady makes her debut into society, after which she takes full responsibility for her moral and spiritual conduct). The young women, sen t, attracted, or connected, to your ministry by God, will sit and be, spiritual leaders amongst the righteous. For they are chosen, holy women of God, God's own possession, that they, and you, may proclaim the excellence of Him, who has called you and them, out of darkness into His marvelous light (see 1 Peter 2:9, 10). Therefore, take care and handle the young women righteously and sagaciously. See suggested course of action. (2) Married male dreamer, if you were dressed in female clothing or supposing yourself to be a female and was dressed as one, your dream comes as a dire warning. Dreamer, because you have demonstrated a lack of sensible reasoning, you have been easily deceived by demons. The dreamer is internally inconsistent and disordered, because of a violent violation in your past or recent present; examples of the violatio n are abuse, assault, bullying, kidnapping, molestation, rape, stalked, being held prisoner. The diabolical entity, having possessed the person(s) who committed the literal act, was sent to rob, steal, and destroy a quality of life that has been destined you, to keep you from living that life abundantly, happily, and in peace. The demon's mission is to get you to entertain, embrace, and li ve out the negative results of your particular violation, with a hope to oppress, persecute, and bring you into bondag e of an ungodly and unprofitable lifestyle. As a result, you are experiencing unhappiness and a sense of hopelessness. Moreover, you are also becoming heartless, having, or showing no pity or kindness towards others, especially toward your wife and family. Conscious of your behavior, out of fear and shame, you have drawn back from the Lord, and have begun acting impractical and juvenile, a type of foolish and unwise insecurity. You shun even coming into His presence via praise, worship, and prayer. Your prayers, regarding your torment, are sporadic, and oftentimes interrupted, with grievances, groans, and desperate mourning. Unfortunately, if your change of will, though produced by sorrow for sin, is one, which does not lead to reformation, it is n ot repentance. Example, for there was a change in the will of Judas, produced by sorrow for sin, yet Judas did not repent (Matthew 27:3-5). The change in his case led to suicide, not to reformation (Acts of the Apostles). Without trust in God's mercy and grace, you will choose like Judas, suicide, albeit spiritual (Acts 1:18). Dreamer, you are being (or will be) humbled, by means of a sickness. This sickness is allowed to teach you to be sensible in your reasoning. Pray Psalm 38:1 -22. If dreamer will to begin embrace reason and sound judgment, and become aware intuitively and empathetically of people, places, and situations, your prayers will be heard and accepted by God and will be answered. Dreamer, Christ is calling you back unto Himself. Jesus invites you to once again, enter into a spiritual union with Him. The presence of the Holy Spirit will be with you during this hard time in your spiritual life, this crisis of your faith. He will purge you from your insensible, bad, and unwise thinking, only come boldly to the throne of grace, with much prayer and repentance. Your voice of earnest prayer will be acceptable to God. Afterwards, continue to make time to be private with the Lord. Read Jeremiah 29:11-13. Additionally, if applicable, teach your children the benefits of wise and sensible thinking, and dedicate your children to the Lord. (3) Unmarried male dreamer, your dream is figurative of an effeminate male. Your dream denotes that the dreamer is internally inconsistent and disordered, because of a violent violation in your past or recent present; examples of the violation are abuse, assault, bullying, kidnapping, molestation, rape, stalked, being held prisoner. The diabolical entity, having possessed the person(s) who committed the literal act, was sent to rob, steal, and destroy a quality of life that has been destined you, to keep you from living that life abundantly, happily, and in peace. The demon's mission is to get you to entertain, embrace, and live out the negative results of your particular violation, with a hope to oppress, persecute, and bring you into bondage of an ungodly and unprofitable lifestyle. Desiring that the unfavorable consequences of that ungodly and unprofitable lifestyle; will cost you your emotional sanity, possibly your life, and ultimately your soul. Thus, instead of you moving towards, and thus fulfilling, your divine purpose, and reaching a pinnacle in your life, thereby with, you will prosper, you have begun to listen to, and be fooled by, demons. Having listened and embraced their lies, you have begun to decrease and fall, eventually running amok your life, literally crashing, when you should be clear and focused mentally, emotionally, and spiritually. Dreamer; oftentimes, bad things happen to innocent and good people. A bad thing happened to you, and you are good and innocent. Compassionately, the Lord is creating a miracle in your life. This miracle will stop the effects of your violation from playing a significant role in your life, enabling you to move forward with your life. However, the miracle's success depends upon your willingness to be healed and set free; for one will always have the choice to say no, or perhaps sabotage their progress. First, recognize and respect your time of visitation from the Lord, for it is upon you, as well as the work of His Hand upon your life. If you lack wisdom ask God for wisdom; and He will give you wisdom. For the Lord gives wisdom and from His mouth comes knowledge and understanding. Then you will understand what is right and just and fair, every good path. When wisdom enters your heart and knowledge becomes sweet to your soul, discretion will protect you, understanding will guard you, and His Truth will lead you. To deliver you from the ways of wickedness, and from demons whose words and ways are perverse, who causes you to walk in darkness gladly, whose paths are crooked and devious, causing you to leave straight paths (Proverbs 2:1-6, 9-15). This is one of God's covenant promises to you. Have faith in this. Further, with fortitude choose not to be a victim or to perpetuate the desolation. Stop what you're doing; go, and separate from anyone and anything that hinders your clarity and emotional stability. Again, if you are in a negative place, move away from your present environment, definitely, you should run away from all negativity abruptly, God will provide, trust Him. Additionally, and if applicable, go, and continue your education, the Lord will help you in your endeavor. Dreamer, if you do not respect the work of the Lord within your life, and the opportunities He is offering you, to be set free, spiritually, emotionally and physically. You will have nothing to work with, but your body, namely deviant sexual promiscuousness, and all that comes with it, including physical death; having forfeited purpose, reasonable resources, and wise counsel that has surrounded you. For, your kind of choices, at present, leads to begging, early death, homelessness, homosexuality, imprisonment, poverty, and/or prostitution. Working with and using your intellect (mind) and/or strength, and good ethics, for your livelihood, will always outlast the use of your body immorally for sustenance, and these choices makes life easier. Dreamer is counseled to seek all kinds of spiritual support now, to possibly avert or turn things around. Moreover, if you do not genuinely seek help and change, for sure ruin will be your destiny. Utilizing the powerful resources of prayer and heartfelt repentance to Jesus is needed. Repentance is seeking pardon and expressing sincere feelings of regret and brokenness for having done something awry and/or for having hurt someone. To Jesus pray, Psalm 51, this followed by appropriate application of wisdom, can conceivably avert some of the repercussions of your choices. This, coupled with a lifestyle of fasting, perhaps twice a week, a changed mindset, serious re-consideration of God's ways and means, and an honest acknowledgement of God's hand within your life, then the severe impact of your choices and actions upon your life, can be reversed and damages repaired (also see Ezekiel 33:12-19). This is what is called leaving a blessing behind. Moreover, consider Deuteronomy 22:5, and believe the Word of God. The Lord your God forbids the confusing of the relationships of the sexes, men must not be effeminate. Deal with this issue, which is between you and your God only, no one else is to be involved, nor blamed for anything. If you seek truth, you will find truth, but only in God. Therefore, take your issues to God; you can't handle it all, by yourself, lest you find yourself gagging on pieces of sin, delivered without grace, and never enough to fill an empty soul. Moreover, your time of healing is upon you, will you be made whole? If so, receive your healing, and go and sin no more, lest a worse thing come upon you (see John 5:1-14). If urged by God, declare a one, two, or three day fast without food. See suggested course of action. (4) If you are an unbeliever (one who has no religious beliefs, a non-religious person, or one who has no religious faith or belief in Jesus Christ, or one who does not embrace a personal relationship with Jesus Christ, at present). Jesus loves you, thus, He is petitioning you to accept Him a s your personal Savior, for you are valuable in His eyes. The first step in receiving Him as your personal Savior is repentance (see in the Holy Bible, Acts 2:37-41). Repentance is seeking pardon for having done something awry, and for having hurt someone, and expressing sincere feelings of regret and brokenness. To Jesus pray, Psalm 51:1-19. Moreover, if you will accept the Heavenly Father's Words, via the Bible, and store up His principles, and accept His ways and means, turning your ear to wisdom and applying your heart to understanding, calling out for insight and crying aloud for discernment, Jesus will meet you. This, coupled with a lifestyle of prayer and fasting, followed by appropriate application of wisdom, and you will know the Messiah, Jesus Christ, intimately, and find the knowledge of God you seek. For the Lord gives wisdom and from His mouth comes knowledge and understanding. Then you will understand what is right and just and fair–every good path. When wisdom enters your heart and knowledge becomes sweet to your soul, discretion will protect you, understanding will guard you, and His Truth will lead you. To deliver you from the ways of wickedness, and from demons whose words and ways are perverse, who causes you to walk in darkness gladly, whose paths are crooked and devious, causing you to leave straight paths (Proverbs 2:1-6, 9-15). This is one of God's covenant promises to you. Have faith in this.

Additionally, the following are more, common words, expressions, usages, (e.g. slang or clichés), or a 'probable' that are metaphorically represented by clothing, jewelry, or shoes:

- **All dressed up and nowhere to go:** This type of dream, denote that the dreamer has prepared for something that isn't going to happen. See suggested course of action.
- **Best Dressed or First Up (to be nominated best dressed):** This type of dream, denote that the dreamer has an advantage, and is ahead of, whatever situation is before you. You endeavor will proved successful.
- **Big girl's blouse (a blouse too big for dreamer):** This type of dream, denote that the dreamer is a person who is very weak and fussy. You put yourself in a situation that has proven too much for you. Read, understand, and embrace Romans 12:3. Embracing this scripture, should help you view yourself in a more balance and realistic way, resulting in less complaints, discontentment, displeasure, and unhappiness. See suggested course of action.
- **Blue stockings (to have on, or to see, blue stockings):** This type of dream denotes a woman who is very intellectual, rather than one who is emotional, instinctive or 'street wise'. Question to journal, do you need instinctive or "street-wise" knowledge to handle a situation at present? Do you need emotional reasoning, rather than trying to, logically reason out a situation, to be successful in your endeavor? Dreamer needs to use whatever reasoning will prove beneficial in making the outcome of your endeavor, or situation, be in your favor. See suggested course of action.
- **By the seat of your pants, (the seat of your pants is highlighted in some way):** This type of dream, denote that the dreamer is one who does things without advance preparation, and/or one who achieves, but only by a narrow margin. This type of attitude leads one to performing your roles or tasks poorly. Although you are naturally endowed with, certain gifting's, your lack of preparation, studiousness, and discipline will prevent you from being promoted. Studiousness to God and His Word will cause the Light of God to shine forth in your life and envelope you. Nevertheless, dreamer, while, everyone has at least a few areas in which they could be good, with much effort, a spirit of excellence is what a believer should strive for, especially when operating within the ministry of God. See suggested course of action.
- **Fly by the seat of one's pants (to move about in the air with your pants hooked to something):** This type of dream, denote that the dreamer is one who will take on a difficult challenge, even

though you don't have the experience or training required. Knowledge is wisdom, read the manual. See suggested course of action.

- **Cut from the same cloth (to cut two or more pieces from one cloth):** Your dream denotes that two or more people are very similar, to the dreamer, in terms of ideas, opinions, and beliefs.
- **Deep pockets (pockets that are relatively large):** If you dream that your pockets are deep, or large, the dreamer will become wealthy, if not already, both naturally and spiritually.
- **Dyed in the wool (to dye wool):** Your dream denotes that the dreamer is one who supports another without question, especially of a political party, dreamer your thinking is not wise. You are counseled to, always seek to understand fully who or what you're supporting, this is wisdom. Your lack of an objective critical analysis and judgment of a system's infrastructure, its foundation, nature, values, attitudes, and perhaps its earthly and eternal benefits and recompense, and whether its beliefs are worthy of consideration or not, may lead you towards a very inexpedient place. See suggested course of action.
- **Hanging by a Thread (clothing, jewelry, or shoes "hanging by a thread"):** Your dream denotes that there is a very small chance that the dreamer will survive or be successful in your endeavor at hand. Your lack of preparation, studiousness, and discipline will prevent you from being successful. With much effort, and a spirit of excellence, you will be able to increase your chance at becoming successful in whatever you are endeavoring to achieve. See suggested course of action.
- **Have a trick up your sleeve (or have something up your sleeve):** Your dream denotes the dreamer has a secret strategy, to use when the time is right. Continue to wait for the right moment, you strategy will prove advantageous and beneficial to your success.
- **Hot under the collar (to be hot around the collar area of your clothing):** Your dream denotes one who is angry or bothered by someone or something. Dreamer, when you speak in anger, you fail to show God's love, whether speaking to a family member or a stranger, your communication should always come forth in a loving and truthful manner (Colossians 3:8, 9, James 1:19). The best way to be sure what comes from your mouth is pure and truthful, is to be aware of what is in your heart. See suggested course of action.

Suggested Course of Action

Question to consider and journal, did your dream depict any symbols that alludes to, the dreamer will make the necessary changes, spiritually, emotionally, and/or physically to affect a more positive outcome? If changes are initiated, your dreams will change.

That stated, dreamer, if you are here, you are encourage to seek healing from God for your spiritual blindness, spiritual ambiguity, and from religion. No, your case is not hopeless, only pray that you might see, and be convinced of, your true spiritual state, for one must call their wicked doing, wrong, for deliverance to be effected. You must also acknowledge and respect where your help lies, and that is with Christ Jesus, that you might be made whole. Regard this rebuke as serious, and change the way you think and act. Dreamer, Christ corrects and disciplines those He loves, those that belong to Christ will be rebuked (Proverbs 3:11-12). Through His rebuke and correction, the Lord shapes His faithful into the people He desires them to become. Although, the correction of the Lord can often be severe, you are in need of much instruction, that your bleakness might be remedied. Jesus Christ wants to offer you the only remedy to your spiritual blindness, ambiguity, and religious spirit, via the enlightening influences of the Holy Spirit. Therefore, seek healing and deliverance through faith in Christ's anointing, utilizing the powerful resources of repentance, prayer, and fasting. It is available to you right now, come aside into a quiet and solitary place, and hear Jesus. Ask Jesus, what need does He have of you, and what does He want you to do with your life? Offer yourself unto Him as a living sacrifice, holy and acceptable unto Him; see Romans 12:1-21. Dreamer, recognize and respect your time of visitation from the Lord, for He is in your midst. Moreover, in the true and proper sense of the word, true religion, is embracing the favor and friendship of the Redeemer. Although, the lies of the world, has blinded many, Jesus promises that those who seek after Him will have their spiritual eyes opened, and His truths would be revealed to them. By this, you will have all that you really need, and will never be in want.

Dreamer, consider seriously your observations. If what was revealed prevail, will it sabotage any good that's happening at present within your life? Will it build or destroy, strengthen or weaken, enlighten or blind? If you lack wisdom, ask Je sus for wisdom. He gives wisdom to all, generously, no matter who you are and what you've done; wisdom is available (see James 1:5-8, Proverbs 2:1-6, 10). Hence, if, by just asking, you may get wisdom, one may suffer needlessly, because you will not ask Jesus for wisdom.

Now, pray (See Prayer of Deliverance, pg. 897)

Specific Meaning

Dreamer, consider this question; could you be receiving inspiration, via your dream, regarding a unique clothing, jewelry, or footwear design or idea? Especially, if you have a very real connection (or perhaps not) with any activity involving clothing, jewelry, or shoes, and your dream closely resembled real life situations. Meaning it can actually occur during your awaked state, this dream may very well be a divine inspiration. Per chapter one, sometimes the most meaningless dream will help change your life in ways you would have never thought, especially entrepreneurially and/or enterprisingly. Throughout history, humankind has received life changing insight and guidance from their dreams. Most of the time the information acquired within dreams exceeds that which we could obtain during our normal, analytical, waking state of mind.

COLORS

*There were hangings of white cloth, of green, and of blue, fastened with cords of fine
linen and purple to silver rings and pillars of marble: the couches were of gold and
silver, upon a pavement of red, and white, and yellow, and black marble.*
(Esther 1:6 ASV)

*God has created this world very colorful. They are the colors of our soul; they are the colors
of covenant, colors have spiritual and natural significance. From the prismatic rainbow,
reminding us that darkness shall not reign unchallenged forever, to the amber waves of grain,
that feed the black, brown, red, white, yellow, colors of humankind. Like the time of day,
when the orange sun settles down, and casts a golden glow all around, to the purple mountain
majesties, to the countless other colors which surround us at every step in our lives.*

This category deals with colors, described in terms of the perception of their hue, brightness, and
saturation. Some short descriptions of types, phrases, and/or other processes and particulars,
connected in some way to this category is, for example, color wheel, primary, secondary, tertiary
colors, chromatic, light, darkness, hues, tints, tones, shades, or vividness. Also, see category content
list, or index.

All Symbols and Referents, Notes (1, 2, 3, etc.), Suggested Course of Action, and Specific Meaning
offer guidance toward a more comprehensive interpretation.

Notes

1. Unless otherwise noted elsewhere, if, in your everyday living, your awaked state, as part of
   your lifestyle, work, or ministerial activities, or a special event, you have a very real connection
   with any activity involving colors. For example, artists, decorator, designer, painter, science,
   technical, or specialist that deals with colors or any activity dealing with the developing or
   marketing of colors, your dream is not significant and does not warrant special attention.

   Otherwise noted, this dream of colors may be a Prophetically Simple Dream (see Chapter
   One: The 60th Part of Prophecy). Whereas, the dreamer is encouraged, for example, if a new
   tint was introduced to you within your dream, to adopt the unique color as your own signature
   brand (e.g. a paint brand name), especially if you are part of the science, technical, or specialist
   areas of colors. Did you invent something? Skip interpretation, go, and start designing,
   creating, brand mark, and marketing your divine sent inspiration.

   Otherwise noted, per your lifestyle, if your dream closely resembled real life situations,
   meaning it can actually occur during your awaked state, this dream may be an Ordinary Dream,
   resulting from daily activities (see Chapter One, Chalom). These sorts of dreams are usually
   about your routine, mundane activities or anxieties that overwhelm your mind during the day.
   They are an inner release mechanism, which helps provide you with emotional balance and
   the maintaining of your sanity. These dreams are not significant, and do not warrant special
   attention.

2. Probables: As color is frequently demonstrated in many, and very personal ways; for example,
   do you have a favorite color, does a particular color remind you of a particular person, place,
   thing, or environment? Thus, could the color depicted be a possible probable (see Chapter One,
   section entitled, Probables)? Hence, dreamer may also consider your own personal and special
   associations with various colors, as long as the interpretation is kept within the principles of
   spiritual boundary markers, landmarks, and property lines, (see Chapter One, section entitled,
   Spiritualizing Boundary Markers, Landmarks, and Property Lines).

3. Determine who your dream is for you or another. Always, considering yourself first, reflecting on your present behaviors.

    Ask yourself, "Why am I dreaming about this now? What is this dream revealing about me? Have I taken on new attributes? Has anyone commented on my present behaviors as being untypical of me? Has my ministry changed for the better or for the worse? What about my beliefs, doctrine, or philosophy, are they still based on Holy Writ? Is there something I need to know about those I am ministering to or serving?

    Remember your actions and emotions within your dream. Were you wearing a certain color? Were you watching a beautiful sunset? Was there a rainbow? What colors where you focusing on? Did you mix any two or more colors together? Was dreamer coloring something? Was dreamer another color (race) other than what you are actually, in your awaked life? Was dreamer an unusual color (e.g. blue face)? Did dreamer see a white light emanating from you? Unless otherwise noted elsewhere, an answer of yes, to one or more of these, or similar questions, is a good indicator that your dream is about you (the dreamer). What happened to you in your dream? How did things end? In light of your dream, via the relevant interpretation, do you believe that your choices will enhance or endanger your well-being, safety, and/or happiness, if so, how and why? Do you believe that your belief system will strengthen or weaken you spiritually in any way, if so, how and why? Is spiritual or physical death a possibility? See following relevant subcategory, the interpretation is about and for you.

    Was someone else painting or coloring something? Did someone else mix colors together? Did someone else present a coloring wheel? If known, was someone else another color (race), other than what he or she is, actually, in your awaked life. Was another an unusual color (e.g. red body)? Did dreamer focus on the color of someone else garments? Did dreamer see a dark light encircling someone? Unless otherwise noted elsewhere, an answer of yes, to one or more of these, or similar questions, is a good indicator that your dream is about another and their role, and/or influential effects, within the life of the dreamer. If someone else was the focal point, meaning, another, was primarily the highlight of your dream. How was he or she connected to the colors? Consider, is someone greatly influencing your physical, spiritual, or mental health, your understanding, perspective, and reasoning regarding spiritual issues? Are they enhancing your spiritual and/or literal prosperity, or are they responsible for the dwindling thereof? Could they be influencing your ministry, on some level? Do you know someone whose life activities or physical being is similar to that which stood out the most within your dream? Could it be that person? If you sense that your dream is for or about another, the question as to why you have been made privy to this information, and how do you factor into the equation, should be seriously considered along with necessary actions. Perhaps the dreamer is being made aware of the plight of someone, and you are to get involved (see Chapter One, Are You Ready to Hear the Messages in Your Dreams, section entitled, The 10% for others).

    If your dream is for, or about another:

    Dreams that reference others and the revelation within those dreams, is not given haphazardly to any individual, but only to those with the ability, and influence to do something with the information; this is also prophecy. With that, journal the following questions, and if unable to answer the questions now, this denotes that the person, represented within your dream, will enter your life shortly. Are you entering into a personal relationship with someone? Do you not know or understand what you're looking at, especially certain behaviors, when learning about this person? Has someone new entered your life or maybe you've just begun opening up to someone not so new, and have started listening to their advice, accepting their assistance, or are you supporting or enabling someone? Are you in denial regarding the toxicity of one of your present relationships, particularly a spouse, family member, or friend? Are you anxious, concerned, frightened, and/or troubled by recent changes in your behavior, especially because of someone's influence upon your life at present? Have you allowed someone to convince you to deceive another? Have you recently become aware of (or is being made aware of, via your dream) certain undesirable behaviors within you towards another? Are you trying to cut ties with one that is bad company? Have you just joined (or re-joined) a church, fellowship, or social group?

Note: If your dream has attributes that indicate that your dream is about you, and other attributes that indicate that your dream is about another, dreamer should consider that your dream is about you and another. For example, did another point or motion for you to notice a rainbow? Did dreamer and another create a new tint? Did dreamer and another, paint or color a picture together. Did a circle of color surround you and another? Unless otherwise noted elsewhere, an answer of yes, to one or more of these, or similar questions, is a good indicator that the dream is about the dreamer, and about another. Therefore, while your dream is about the dreamer, the dreamer should expect the role and/or influential effects of another, also plays a part in your interpretation. For example, is plagiarizing an issue? Did another, paint the dreamer's picture, and sell it without dreamer's permission? Did dreamer help a child color a picture in a book, and the picture revealed a violent violation going on within the child's life? Again, see relevant interpretation.

More questions to consider. Why has the person been allowed within your life, and/or how did they get there? Again, if unable to answer the questions now, this denotes that the person, represented within your dream, will enter your life shortly. If their activity, within your dream, has proven positive, via the interpretation, this someone will prove, unwittingly, to be a very strong ally, benefactor, defender, and supporter. God has sent this someone into your life to help you carry out your next endeavor by enlarging your spiritual capacity. Allow the strength of that person's character to guide, help, and support you. On the other hand, if his or her presence and/or activity, within your dream, proved negative, via the interpretation, for sure, this person will prove to be a very strong and formidable challenge for you, perhaps unto death. If negative, this dream is a dire warning. Take steps accordingly to struggle against, or to cut off, adverse and unfavorable relationships. Remember certain personalities are all encompassing, affecting everything, cataclysmic, contagious, deadly, harmful, infectious, predatory, and/or venomous. Symbolically meaning that if allowed to continue or prosper within your life, serious harm or death to the dreamer may result. Idolize no one, especially beyond the warning of the Lord, and we are definitely not to lay our lives down for no one. Then again, this person maybe allowed within your life, because of the dreamer's unwillingness to abstain from immorality after having been asked to abstain from such by God, see 1 Corinthians 6:9-20, Galatians 5:19-21, or the dreamer's self-righteous behavior, or a lack of a balanced and honest view of your own personality. In this case, this person will affect self-awareness within the life of the dreamer, exposing the negative traits of your personality, especially those traits, which cause you to follow, or to be so easily misled, and/or your wrong beliefs; no matter, this type of mentality needs reckoning with. Graciously, all of this will restore the dreamer to his or her right place with God, opening your eyes to see how far you've strayed from God (1 Corinthians 5:4-7; James 5:20). The lesson is, no matter how personable, powerful, or difficult a person, or how uncertain or unpopular the choices and issues, always take the next biblical and ethical step, for obedience to God's principles will always prove safer and stronger foundationally. Although, you will need all kinds of outside support to recover from this person's domination, no longer, allow that particular person's influence within your life to continue or thrive, especially if negative, end it abruptly.

4. Consider all the people, places, backgrounds, and activity highlighted within your dream.

    Known (in your awaked life) person, animal, place, or organization within your dream:

    Unless otherwise noted elsewhere, people, animals, places, backgrounds that are actually known by the dreamer in your awaked life, indicates a part of you that you recognize within yourself on some level or another. Question to journal, if dreamer seriously considers all the particulars, what stood out the most, what features, or character traits stood out the most. For example, age, color, height, size, happiness, considerate, loving, let you be yourself, peacefulness, encourager, irrational, leader, liar, mentor, passionate, personable, neglected, poor, run-down, sage, shyster, unwise, upscale, vengeful. Write down (journal) the particular highlighted within your dream. The attribute or activity highlighted is for a reason. Since the attribute written down is a part of you, namely the dreamer's nature, demeanor, and/or lifestyle, an honest and unbiased assessment is very important for truth sake. Happy note, considering that other people's attributes, within dreams, also represent attributes of your own personality, causes one to look at another in a better light. According to your capacity to embrace self-awareness and a rectification of mind, body, and spirit, God will begin to enhance, make better, more attractive, sanctify, diminish, and make pure and free from sin and guilt, this part of you.

Otherwise noted, if the person, animal, place, or background within your dream is actually known by the dreamer, in your awaked life, this person, animal, place, or background may represent him or herself, or itself.

Unknown in your awaked life or although known, was unseen, invisible, or only talked about - person, animal, place, or organization within your dream:

Unless otherwise noted elsewhere, if you did not recognize, the person, place, thing, they, or it, was not seen, invisible, or only talked about within your dream, this indicates an attribute or activity within your life that you are unfamiliar with, or are in denial about, or you refuse to acknowledge it, but it does exists. Although, on some conscious level, you are aware of a certain behavior or attribute within you, you have chosen to filter out or simply ignore certain information about yourself that contradicts your view of yourself and/or your preconceived notions of others and of the world around you. Possibly protecting yourself, emotionally and psychologically, from a situation, which you are unable to cope with at this time, or you lack control over; then again, perhaps the dreamer has an exaggerated or unrealistic view of yourself. No matter the reason, right now a question is before you, via your dream. Do you want to know this part of yourself? According to your ability to handle self-awareness, God will begin to reveal this side of you to you. Why, He wants to balance your understanding of things; thus, effecting wholeness within your life, so that the enemy will no longer be able to manipulate your emotions so easily. The Paraclete is with you to help you throughout this entire process, listen to Him. Now, in your life, this activity or attribute needs reckoning with, somehow or someway.

Otherwise noted, (known or unknown), if the person, place or thing that initiated (or was a recipient of) the action or activity within your dream was not seen, invisible, or only talked about within your dream, this may indicate that the dreamer does not recognize the influential effects another has within your life, or upon your attitude.

If more than one person (known or unknown):

Consider what the group had in common. What behavior, character trait, feature, action, or activity, stood out the most? For example, were they argumentative, authoritative, beautiful, criminal minded, dancing, difficult, dressed unusual, enigmatic, fighting, focused, flirty, helpful, hurtful intentions, powerful, promiscuous, quiet, secretive, seemed unreal, unassuming? That which was highlighted and noted is what you need to focus on at present.

If the attribute or quality is a desirable or positive one, allow the strength of that attribute to help you overcome some manner of immorality or irreverence within your life and/or to help you to become better, productively, for the Kingdom of God in some manner. If the attribute is an undesirable or negative one, take steps accordingly to struggle against the growing desires of the carnal side of you. If applicable, get help and support via prayer, fasting, and a Christian based support group.

For dreams of the dead see following note.

Was a dead person covered with paint? While the dead has nothing to do with the living (Ecclesiastes 9:4-6), it may be considered what character trait did that person represent to the dreamer, while the person was actually alive, what character feature stood out the most. With that trait noted, dreamer may consider that the trait noted, is within the dreamer, and that trait is no longer useful or needed for the progression of your spiritual walk, on this side of heaven. Dreamer, it is suggested that you render that trait (good or bad) obsolete, and began anew attempting to move forward, using different tactics to overcome unproductive habitual life cycle choices, and for maneuvering through this thing we call life in a more, better way. See category, Death, and/or other relevant categories.

5. In addition to the following interpretations, see index or relevant categories for more information. For example, if clothing was involved in some way, see category, Clothing, if the body was highlighted, see category, the Body. Kept within context of your dream and the interpretation, the additional symbols are perhaps relevant. It will be within the sum of all the symbols that you will find a more thorough interpretation.

6. Since the following list is not extensive, dreamer is encouraged to seek biblical guidelines and other relevant research to determine the metaphorical meaning of your particular color, within your dream, via a Bible concordance, Bible illustrated dictionary, encyclopedia, or internet. Along with that, dreamer is encouraged to consider the mixture of certain colors, especially those not listed. For example, pink is a mixture of red and white, turquoise or teal are mixtures of blue and green, and maybe some white or black. Hence, the interpretations of the colors red and white, for pink, or blue, green, and black or white for turquoise or teal, are to be combined and considered. Having done your research you should be able to determine some basic behaviors or attributes your Lord and Savior wants you to focus on.

Symbols and Referents

Most dreams of color generally imply, coupled with the relevant interpretation, there is a spiritual presence in your mist, o r that there will be a visitation from the spirit realm to determine recompense of some kind, for either glory or dishonor. Additionally, color may perhaps represent a distinctive but intangible quality surrounding a person or thing.

In addition to the varied meanings of colors, other common words, expressions, usages, (e.g. slang or clichés), or a 'probable' that are metaphorically represented by any of the following are also considered (this section is an addendum at the end of the relevant subcategory).

Category Content: If not listed see index, perchance, for your specific type color dreams. Note, colors not listed, see Note 6 of this category.

- Black
  - Dressed in black, see category, Clothing
- Brown
- Darkness (absence of light or illumination)
- Gray
- Light (anything serving as a source of illumination, this includes lamps and all lighting fixtures)
  - Unable to illuminate a place (unable to use a light switch or light a candle)
- Painting or Coloring (apply paint to; creating a picture with paints, or coloring)
- Primary Colors
  - Blue; Red; Yellow or Gold
- Rainbow
- Secondary colors
  - Green; Orange; Purple or Violet
- Silver

- Silver Cord (to see a silver cord, rope, or string); Silver Lining (to see a lining that is silver in any garment or object); Silver Spoon (to see, have, own, or receive, a silver spoon); Silver Tongued (to see or have a silver tongue, or silver on the tongue in some way)
  - Tertiary Colors (mixture of primary and secondary, see interpretations for both colors, combining both interpretations, Note 6)
    - Blue-Green (see colors blue and green); Blue-Violet (see colors blue and purple); Red-Orange (see colors red and orange); Red-Violet (see colors red and purple); Yellow-Green (see colors yellow and green); Yellow-Orange (see colors yellow and orange); Other Colors: (since all other colors are a mixture of primary, secondary, and/or tertiary colors, see interpretations for all relevant colors, combining all interpretations, also Note 6
- White
  - Dressed in white, see category, Clothing

BLACK:

This color in a dream denotes one of two meanings (choose one). (1) Your dream denotes one who is wholly beautiful, meaning spiritually and physically. As well, your dream refers to one who is abiding in the presence and secret place of the Father. Read Psalm 91, this is God's word to you. Additionally, the dreamer will be healed and cleansed in your personal life and ministry. (2) Alternatively, because of violent sinfulness, within the life of the dreamer, without genuine repentance, there will be a spiritual and literal mourning, due to deep regret over the consequences of your actions and behaviors. If this type of violence is going within your life, expect to experience deep sorrowfulness through loss and deprivation very shortly. See suggested course of action.

BROWN:

This color in a dream denotes one, who has become lukewarm and judgmental, because of jealously and trivialness. Further, this color implies excessiveness on so many levels. Dreamer, you are very angry and unforgiving, with no sincere intent or desire to change. Even more, to avenge, comfort, and ease yourself, you have taken matters into your own hands, relying on your own strength and carnal knowledge, against those you supposed have slighted you, but who, have not. Your behavior and choices have depleted you emotionally and physically; consequently, rendering you as one who is spiritually dead, being without God's Spirit and guidance. Although you deeply yearn for a closer more intimate relationship with the Creator, your emotional and spiritual state has blocked and impaired you from perceiving truth, thus, the dark prince of this world has a blinding influence over your soul to keep you for seeing the light of the gospel and the glory of the Messiah. Favorably, a spark of life remains hidden inside of you, and there awaits you a spiritual resurrection, according to God's grace. Dreamer, approaching God the Father, without the essential provision He has provided for humankind, to approach Him properly; that provision being Yeshua HaMashiach, is not safe. Some call God's provision Jesus, Wonderful Counselor, Mighty God, Everlasting Father, Prince of Peace, our atonement, advocate, liberator, propitiator, and our salvation. It is only through this channel that we may hope through faith to conciliate with our Creator, see John 3:16, Acts 2:37-42, 1 Timothy 2:4-7. Dreamer, trust in the risen Messiah, and the gift of divine sight will provide an inner radiance that comes from God Himself. You will very shortly begin to experience, if not already, a paradigm shift in your core beliefs and spirituality, this is your second touch from God, beyond the initial touch and breath that gave rise to your physical life. Moreover, as this color is also symbolic of death, devastation, and other serious problems, you are urged to earnestly repent of your sinful ways and to, genuinely change, and do this without delay, otherwise, instead of a spiritual revival, you will experience ruin. Therefore, go and pray, for God's mercy to be upon you; afterwards, go and offer a peace offering to a ministry (e.g. invest your time, money, and/or talent within a church). If urged by God, declare a one, two, or three day fast without food. See suggested course of action.

DARKNESS (absence of light or illumination):

To dream of darkness denotes six issues. One or all of the following issues is going on within the dreamer's life; (1) adversity, (2) God's judgment, (3) death, (4) an absence of moral or spiritual values, (5) hatred, and/or (6) one who is spiritually famished. With that said, dreamer is one who lacks spiritual substance, because of a deceitful lifestyle and other sin issues. Deceitfulness and other sinful behaviors and choices are leading you towards an ominous and evil life. Your life is one bent on evil intent, especially against God. Your behavior and choices will lead to tragic developments, adversity, and God's judgment, and, if applicable, all this will carry over into your individual ministry. Dreamer it would be wise of you to heed this warning. You are urged to respect the cost that was paid for your salvation, and to become spiritually aware of the Holy Ghost, who abides within you, and to respect His presence (Ephesians 4:30). Grieve not the Holy Spirit of God, by giving way to any awry temper, unholy words, or unrighteous actions. Even those who have already a measure of the light and life of God, both of which are not only brought in by the Holy Spirit, but also maintained by His constant indwelling, may give way to sin, and so grieve the Holy Spirit that He shall withdraw both his light and presence. In proportion, as He withdraws, then hardness and darkness take place; and, what is still worse, a state of insensibility is the consequence; for the darkness prevents the fallen state from being seen, and the hardness prevents it from being felt (Adam Clarke's Commentary). Dreamer, your lifestyle choices are leading to much sadness, many troubles, and awful heartaches. Stop, reconsider your behavior, and repent that the repercussions of your actions might not be so severe. If no authentic change; unfortunately, you will now begin to experience the consequences of sowing to the flesh, which is a regression of the blessings bestowed upon you and other blessings, as promised by God. See suggested course of action.

GRAY:

God's power has made a way out of no way for you, and your state of affairs is turning around. Dreamer, there will be a relaxation or slackening of tension in your life, stop, and feel the tension leaving. Those who have charged you falsely, wi th malicious intent, attacking your good name and reputation will be far from you. Others will become less hostile, as will you. You will be more relaxed, easygoing, and genial. The necessity to be reconciled with others than to always be in opposition has been resolved. Dreamer, you have simply taken the higher ground. You have re-evaluated your life, learned from your mistakes, found new directions in solving problems, pursued healing, sought out encouragement, and figured out what God would like you to change in order to, better fulfill His purpose. You have learned the principles and Christian values that encourage one to reach out and touch others in a loving and graceful manner; ultimately finding yourself promoting the genuine cause of Christ and the good of others. Moreover, spiritually mature, you are a very peaceful and poised individual; now, prepared, you will be honored publicly. Caution, you should not think that your accomplishments are purely of your own volition. Truthfully, it is God, who gives you the capability and strength to achieve success. This is especially true of your struggles with your sinful tendencies, whether they manifest as a lack of concern or interest in the things of God, a stubbor n resistance to the will of God, or laziness. If it had not been for God's efforts on your behalf, you would not have been able to overcome any negative tendencies. He delivered you. Any achievements you will accomplish, or have accomplished, any good deeds you've done, any fulfillment of God's will, was, and still is, dependent upon divine aid and guidance. One merel y places his or her hand under the weight carried exclusively by God. Therefore, do not claim credit for your achievements. Nevertheless, your words have pleased the Lord, for they are words of wisdom. Thus, He has done according to your words; go forward with purpose, looking for results, for you are headed towards your chosen destiny. You will experience a miracle very soon, "it" will happen (whatever "it" is to you personally), and you will be blessed. All of these promises will begin now. Even now, Jesus is coming to see about you, keep your faith, regarding what you've believed God for, because He has promised an d He will fulfill His promise. God will grant you both riches and honor, "if" (if refers to "conditional") you continue to walk in His ways, diligently and obediently, you will have long life too. This is His promise to you, and He will do according to His pro mise.

Light (anything serving as a source of illumination, this includes lamps and all lighting fixtures): This dream has three meanings (one or both may apply). (1) Your dream denotes great illumination. Dreamer, you are spiritually prepared for spiritual growth, divine illumination, and some type of promotion or confirmation. Therefore, prepare your mind for action; be self-controlled; set your hope fully on the grace afforded you when Jesus Christ was revealed within your heart, and no longer conform to your carnal desires (see 1 Peter 1:13-16). Additionally, your dream is additional proof of something that you have believed God for, is correct (e.g. rectification of an attitude of anger, frustration, discontent, a physical healing, heighten faith level, deliverance or support for a spouse or other family member, financial help, wisdom regarding stewardship, or for removal of any hindrances to your spiritual clarity). (2) Dreamer, you are being prepared and set aside for the priesthood, to carry out the official role, position, or office of a priest (e.g. prophet, pastor, minister, or some type of a very visible cleric). Further, chosen, you are to show forth the praises of Him who has called you out of darkness into His marvelous light (also see 1 Peter 2:9, 10). There will be a flash of insight, a sudden awareness, recognition, or realization of your calling. You will also experience a spiritual and personal revival. This personal revival will connect and unify, again, your intellect to your spi rituality, as well as revive and restore faith and prayer within your life. Instead of worshiping God from the perspective of y our head (intellect), you will again worship Him with your whole heart, mind, body, and soul. (3) Unable to illuminate a place (unable to use a light switch or light a candle): This choice has two parts (choose one). (a) If light switch didn't work, dreamer, consider this, (Matthew Henry Concise): When we go from the plain "path of duty", everything draws us further aside, (e.g. loneliness, fearfulness, and any negative life cycle), and increases our perplexity and temptation[33]. See suggested course of action. (b)

Unable to light a candle, dreamer, seeking the Light of God, and His truths only, and His way, via prayer, fasting, reading, understanding, believing, and embracing what is written in the Holy Bible, and joining and becoming a vested member within a church, will illuminate your path, and dispel the darkness. Favorably, a spark of life remains hidden inside of you, and there awaits you a spiritual resurrection, according to God's grace. Dreamer, approaching God the Father, without the essential provision He has provided for humankind, to approach Him properly; that provision being Yeshua HaMashiach, is not safe. Some call God's provision Jesus, Wonderful Counselor, Mighty God, Everlasting Father, Prince of Peace, our atonement, advocate, liberator, propitiator, and our salvation. It is only through this channel that we may hope through faith to conciliate with our Creator, see John 3:16, Acts 2:37-42, 1 Timothy 2:4-7. Dreamer, trust in the risen Messiah, and the gift of divine sight will provide an inner radiance that comes from God Himself. You will very shortly begin to experience, if not already, a paradigm shift in your core beliefs and spirituality. Therefore, go and pray, for God's mercy to be upon you; afterwards, go and offer a peace offering to a ministry (e.g. invest your time, money, and/or talent within a church). If urged by God, declare a one, two, or three day fast without food. See suggested course of action.

PAINTING OR COLORING (creating a picture with paints or coloring):

Your dream marks the beginning of, and is one confirmation of, full spiritual maturity, God is calling you to a higher, and new spiritual level; therefore, draw closer to Him. The growing and stretching process and preparation that has led to a spiritual capacity that is now able to contain and handle the amazing and miraculous things that the Lord has prepared for you is done. Encouragingly, you have risen (or will rise) to a level the Anointing of God and your acumen deem you should be; you hav e tasted, and will continue to taste, the Anointing of God. You are spiritually ready to progress forward. You have learned t hat your union with Christ in death and in His resurrection is done; you have fully connected with Him in His death, burial, and resurrection. No longer are you conformed to the pattern of this world, but have been transformed by the renewing of your mind, able to test and approve what God's will is, His good, pleasing and perfect will (Romans 12:1, 2, 1 Peter 2:9, 10). With that process, now done, there is a need to, apprehend by faith, and to declare, that God accepts you, accepts your talents, accepts your efforts, and accepts the spirit for which they are presented, definitively. Therefore, resolve exactly what are your talents and efforts, e.g. preacher, teacher, healer, writer, singer, poet, whatever your endowments, see Matthew 25:14, parable of the talents), write them down, and present them to God, with a mindset that, as you've been diligent with what you've been given, He accepts, and is ok, with what you have presented. The fact that God receives what you present is proof that a sanctifying and purification process has happened, and a perfecting, via a consecration, is beginning. Moreover, fait h comes with a statement that says, "God has accepted what I have presented." This is faith with works, believing that He accepts. It is necessary that your faith is alive, for what will be the practical outcome of all your presenting, if you do not believe that God accepts what you give? Moreover, dreamer, you will have to, continually be intentional regarding embracing mental and emotional habits of holiness, for habits are formed by practice or neglect. You must by faith, deliberately, and purposefully, offer you, your mind, spirit, and body in a sober, firm, and dignified manner, as a living sacrifice, holy and pleasing to God, as this is a spiritual act of worship. With a confident and unquestionable belief in the validity of your salvation, and the atoning work of the cross, knowing that it is enough to justify righteousness within a believer's life. And the Lord your God is to be loved with all your heart, and with all your soul and with all your strength. On another note, in your present business or personal dealings, you will be satisfied and take delight in your goals. If you are involved in any situation that is competitive, you will triumphant, God will lead the way. Additionally, you have the miraculous power to change history on some level or another. For example, by introducing radically new insight into complex models or paradigms, far beyond the norm, or family generational curses can stop with you (Exodus 20:5, 7; Psalm 112:2). Whatever the miraculous historical change is, perhaps you becoming a great leader and orator, you are equipped to handle large-scale undertakings. Dreamer, a large part of your mission in life centers on raising the spirits of your fellow mankind; thus changing history in the lives of those, you touch. The driving force behind all this is your support of others. Your first step is to start by recognizing and thanking Jesus for the small blessings that are before you now and for the miraculous endowment of history changing vision and courageous leadership. Do you want your miracle? Then prepare yourself mentally for it.

PRIMARY COLORS:

To dream of any of the primary colors, generally denote that the dreamer is responsible for initiating, setting in motion, preparing the way, encouraging, and/or played a major role, regarding a very personal and present situation or issue. Additionally, dreamer what you have initiated or encouraged, will be perpetrated or imitated by others, on some level or another, for years to come. Couple this with one of the following.

Blue: This color in a dream has two meanings (one or both may apply). (1) Your dream refers to one who has a passionate thirst to connect with God. Dreamer, you are leaving a space, or letting go of someone or something that you may progress forward to a place where you will be used to minister to others. You are entering into a season within your life that will prepare you spiritually for the visitation of the Lord in your individual life. A servant of the Lord will visit you, and instruct you on how to get out of your negative situation. Dreamer recognize, and respect, your time of visitation from the Lord; and respect the servant of the Lord. During this time, you will experience God's love and presence, as you've never known it before. For, He is saying to you, "I will teach you godly wisdom". You will receive direct insight of divine truth that you might go on and began to operate more maturely and fully in your unique spiritual gifting. You will come to know, without a doubt, that God is the true source of your strength and wisdom, and He is your sufficiency. As a result, a greater love for self, family, and others will begin to manifest, affecting wholeness within your life. Be available to Him and seize the moments and opportunities as they are presented, especially an opportunity for you to advance your education, with a focus on teaching. (2) Although dreamer is experiencing one of life's storms or "midnights", you have proven yourself truthful, sincere, wise, calm, and devoted to the Lord. This type of clarity of mind has opened the door for a serious physical healing. Dreamer, optimistically expect your miraculous healing. Moreover, once healed, go forth using your unique gifting of "instinctively knowing" about people, places, and things, to empathically teach and serve others, while recognizing and acknowledging that God is the true source of your prophetic gifting, knowledge, and wisdom.

Red: First thing, this denotes atonement and an overcoming and being victorious in one's spiritual and temporal life. For, you are a Christian soldier, a battle-seasoned Christian, who knows quickly what to do because of your experience and familiarity with Scripture; therefore you are ready to fight. Hence, no matter the issue at present, this color indicates that you will triumph; there will be a successful ending of your struggles. With that said, this dream denotes one of two possible struggles within the life of the dreamer at present (choose one). (1) Your dream denotes spiritual warfare within the life of the dreamer. The reason for the warfare is the Lord is changing your heart. Dreamer has been hard-hearted, lacking empathy and compassion towards others. Thus, via your hard trials and tribulations, you are learning empathy and compassion; by a llowing the work of the Paraclete. He is taking away your stony hard heart and giving you a heart of flesh, to be complete. Endure, as a good solider, learning what needs to be learned. If necessary, see suggested course of action. (2) There is a conflict, which needs to be resolved, between the dreamer and another, be it a family member, or friend, or foe. There is a necessity to be reconciled with another, rather than to, always be in opposition and/or contrary. Dreamer, you simply need to take the higher ground. In this, you will learn principles and Christian values that will encourage you to reach out and touch others in a loving and graceful manner; ultimately finding yourself promoting the genuine cause of Christ and the good of others. A deeper understanding of the meaning of the shed Blood of Christ for the remission of your sins, aka atonement, is needed. Read, understand, and embrace, Matthew 6:12-15, 18:23-35. Recall your own sins and errors; look over your life, and see how often you've offended God; and remember that all has been forgiven you. Dreamer Jesus is petitioning you to slip away and fast and pray. Pray Psalm 51. You will need to fast and pray for 24 hours, abstaining from many forms of carnal pleasure. This fast and prayer is to help you overcome distrust and animosity. By this, you will be cleansed from sin, and the covenant between you and the Lord will be restored. Then, renewed, with this feeling, if needful, go to the one who has offended you, with forgiveness in your heart and words of forgiveness on your lips. See suggested course of action.

Yellow or Gold: This dream has two meanings (choose one). (1) These colors in a dream denotes one who is in the process of being made whole, emotionally, psychologically, physically, and financially, because of your reverence for God. You are entering into a process of being purified and purged, proven and tested, spiritually and emotionally cleansed. Everythin g that's unusable within you, will give way to that which is beneficial and profitable, and that which is undesirable will become brightly polished, according to God's good pleasure. Your pride will soon give way to humbleness, dignity, honor, and righteous self-esteem, your foolishness to peace and wisdom. This process will also heal the animosity within you resulting in a physical healing you've believed God for, for some time now. Allow the process without complaining or murmuring for it is preparing you for a great journey. Be as one who gets satisfaction from embracing good habits. (2) Read, understand, and embrace, Daniel 3:1-30, and have faith in God. See suggested course of action.

RAINBOW:

Your dream denotes that God has remembered His promises to you. The present chaos within your life is merely the storm before the calm. Dreamer, be encourage, your present darkness shall not reign unchallenged forever, but will eventually dissipate and fade from your memory. Moreover, after the chaos and darkness, there will be clarity of purpose and a great er love of God. Moreover, strive to reflect godliness in your life, via embracing God's principles, ways and means. If necessary, see suggested course of action.

SECONDARY COLORS:

To dream of any of the secondary colors generally denotes generational issues, namely genetic codes and traits, hereditary within your family line, is now visiting the dreamer. Dreamer, character traits from ancestors, particularly generational issues, will often trouble and taunt the offspring of a given progenitor (Exodus 20:5-7). These spirits attempt to "bend" the personality, as early as possible with regards to age, towards a certain direction, oftentimes towards a way that is desolate and wicked, for it is Satan's scheme to kill and make desolate all; thus, to keep some from rising up and leading their generation to Christ (see the birth of Moses, Exodus 1:15-2:10). Favorably, generational curses and issues can stop with you (Jeremiah 31:29, 30; Ezekiel 18:2-14, 20-23). Thus, your Heavenly Father is requiring that you overcome and subdue negative and dark emotions, feelings, behaviors, and/or ideas that would influence you, before they overcome you. Dreamer, God is not asking you to do something you cannot do. For a surety, vanquishing of the coming influence can b e done. By faith, you will need to declare some kind of fast and commit to it, for a long period-of-time, to abate the demonically instigated circumstance, you find yourself in now, Matthew 6:16-18. Try abstaining from food and drink (midnight to 6 PM), twice a week, and refrain from words, attitudes, people, places, and things, including music, magazines, videos, TV, or any such things that fuel anger and discontent, and stir up lustful feelings. This is also known as, faith with works, read, understand, and embrace James 2:14-26. Nonetheless, earnestly pray, God will guide, enable, and answer you as to the type of fast. Additionally, if relevant, forgive your mother and/or father for the darkness (aka curse) they may have perpetuated, for they knew not what they done. Forgiveness is important to your success (Matthew 6:12-15, 8:21-35). See suggested course of action. Couple this with one of the following.

    Green: This color in a dream, speaks of life that can be good or evil, you have free choice. See Deuteronomy 30:15-20. Dreamer, there are spiritual privileges awaiting you, but these privileges are conditional. There is before you, positive changes, such as spiritual growth, natural and spiritual rest in the Lord, hope, healing, good health, fertility, vigor, vitality, peace; prosperity, basically an overall renewal in one's life. See Psalm 37:9, Isaiah 40:31, this is to you, during this season in your life. However, you must abide in the Lord, Jesus Christ and in His grace and love. Dreamer, approaching God the Father, without the essential provision He has provided for humankind, to approach Him properly; that provision being Yeshua HaMashiach, is not safe. Some call God's provision Jesus, Wonderful Counselor, Mighty God, Everlasting Father, Prince of Peace, our atonement, advocate, liberator, propitiator, and our salvation. It is only through this channel that we may hope through fai th to conciliate with our Creator, see John 3:16, Acts 2:37-42, 1 Timothy 2:4-7. On the other side, if a weakness is shown within the heart of the dreamer, because of your choices, behaviors, and actions. Specifically, spiritual legalism, self-righteousness, jealousy, envious of others lifestyle, materialism, cheating, deceit, difficulties with sharing, or some manner of terrorism, life will prove not so good and the consequences of your negativity will produce all kinds of evils, which will begin to manifest shortly. Dreamer, any manner of spiritual immaturity, any rejection of the doctrine of grace, spiritual legalism, or living life according to your will and not God's, is not good. Your spirituality is one of outward show and hypocrisy. You love to give alms, pray, and appear righteous publicly, but inwardly you are lifeless, and lawlessness prevails. Your lack of love towards others has contributed to your lack of understanding, receiving, and giving genuine grace, consequently, your relationship wi th the Lord has begun wither. Choose not to go out from the presence of the Lord, that is to, willingly renounce God, and to be content to forego the privileges He offers, that you might not be under His precepts, make things right. See suggested course of action.

Orange: Your dream was sent to encourage. Although, this color in a dream denotes one who is in great jeopardy or danger, and an evil force is trying to destroy your spiritual and/or natural life. The situation, and the evil force, has co me up against one, the dreamer, who is spiritually and physically prepared, mentally alert, and ready to fight. Dreamer, you have the strength and endurance to overcome your situation. What evil has meant for harm, God is using to purify and perfect the dreamer. Dreamer, the fiery trail you're going through is a necessity. Therefore, as it is written, see 1 Peter 1:7-9, 4:12-19, so you must resolve to think it not strange concerning the fiery trial, which has come to prove your faith. Moreover, let them that suffer according to the will of God, commit their souls in well doing unto a faithful Creator, for God is faithful and just to recompense your diligence. By going through faithfully and tenaciously, dreamer will become more calm, hopeful, friendly, flexible, courtesy, lively, sociable, and outgoing. You will expand your horizons and look into new in terests. Dreamer, be encouraged, you will be purified, unhurt, and recompensed for your diligence. Additionally, God will send an angel to rescue you out of an extremely severe situation, because of your faith. Be aware that the stranger within your mid st may be that angel. He comes to lead the way. Further, because of your deliverance, your oppressor will bow to and respect your God, acknowledge His Power, and respect you.

Purple or Violet: This dream has two meanings (one or both may apply). (1) Your dream was sent to encourage the dreamer to become very deeply aware of God's caring, loving kindness, and compassion for you, and His closeness to you. Steal away, for a moment, to a quiet place, and feel and experience God's love for you. By this, you will find physical and spiritual healing. Additionally, your dream is to bring about an awareness of an appointed inheritance of abundant peace, comforts, and sufficient wealth for the dreamer. At some point in the undisclosed future, honor and wealt h will be bestowed upon the dreamer, if not already. You are becoming self-sufficient and unrelenting, capable of handling much responsibility, especially when required to make major decisions. You will be appointed to a very high-ranking position. Many will be inspired by your wisdom, confidence, and blameless actions, while others will feel threaten by it. Those who plot evil again st you (family, friend, or foe), via mockery of your riches, power, and authority, causing you much sorrow and suffering, will not prevail but will yield willingly to your authority. Caution, only use your God given blessings to help edify God's people, a nd not for selfish motives, otherwise, you will experience the consequences of sowing to the flesh, which is a regression of the blessings bestowed upon you or promised by God. (2) To the unmarried male or female dreamer, in addition to the preceding interpretation, this color within a dream also implies that God has appointed a spouse for you, a religious or civil leader, and that person is very near you at present. As they are sensitive to God's leading right now, so should you be sensitive to God's leading. Moreover, seek out the true and practical meaning of equally yoked and unequally yoked, and you will better understand relationships. If you seek truth, truth will come, by this God is showing His loving kindness towards you.

SILVER:

This dream is to open wide the eyes of, and disconcert, a secure and careless person, the dreamer, who proclaims peace to him or herself. With a calm resignation, you say you are godly and will inherit paradise, yet you have no genuine love for Christ Jesus, the Door into paradise (see John 5:39). The dreamer is on a path of declining from a higher standard of holiness to a lower state. Couple this with one of the following two (choose one). (1) Dreamer, your ideas and arguments, regarding Christ, Christians, religion, and His church, are illogical, non-mainstream, and without favorable conclusions. Having lost your equilibrium within the sacred scheme of things, due to demonic influence, disillusionment, disappointment, and/or offenses, you have ceased to abide in Christ, and instead have become enslaved again to sin and immorality, trusting in your own righteousness. Favorably, the One True Living God can and will turn things around for you. God will help you overcome your issues, and remove this demonic force from before you. Dreamer, you will undergo a thorough purging from dead, obsolete, worthless, and weak religious dogma, erroneous ideas, and self-conceited talk against God, basically, any ungodliness. Whatever is currently going on in your life, anticipate a spiritual cleansing taking place, especially within those areas specific to this interpretation. This will produce a level of purity within your life that is requisite for ministry and will affect humility within you. Your emotions will become intense and situations perhaps more volatile, but you will be thoroughly purged. Take a seat and hold tight, it's going to get bumpy. Moreover, prayer, heartfelt repentance to Jesus, and a renunciation of your spiritually poisonous words and ways, are needful at present. By this, you will again begin to experience God's truth, and see the demonic for what it is - a lie. If relevant, avoid personal isolation and isolated groups that teach something different from the gospel of Jesus Christ (e.g. condemnation, hate, any racist ideology, murder, no one is "right" but our western sect, or any other oppressive or "hell bound" for everyone but me and/or our small group ideas). Jesus died for the world, and not exclusively for any one person, sect, or western denomination. Moreover, if not practiced regularly, go to church, join a church, a faith based bible-believing community, commit to that ministry, and don't leave, no matter what, for three years. Forsake not the gathering of yourself together with other mainstream Christians. A prophecy will be given you, via someone within that ministry, during this season, write it down for it will happen. Additionally, entering the House of God should be done reverently rather than carelessly. Cease from many words but rather humbly learn, and let your words be sprinkled with empathy. For, in spite of what we do not know about the many mysteries of God and life, one thing remains eternally true; God is our loving Father. He does not desire that any one perish; great effort is exercised to save us, even in the moment o f our death. Hence, do not call anyone impure (e.g. unsaved, hypocrite, unregenerate, ignorant) that God alone has made clean (read Acts 10:15, Ephesians 4:17-5:21). See suggested course of action. (2) Dreamer, you have settled for a voluptuary type philosophy and desire to propagate your beliefs. How can you say, "I have great desire, thus my physical enjoyment, luxury, and sensual gratifications are my primary concerns? This is a characterization of the ungodly or spiritually immature. Weigh: The child thinks that all that appears pleasant and tasty belongs to them and that he or she has the right to partake of any and everything. Consideration of others, and/or of the resulting outcome is unfamiliar to him or her. They will never consider the results of their behavior, nor how their behavior will affect others. This type of consideration is not within a child's mind-set, because he or she is a child. As the immature child takes what they want, when they want it, and believes that it's theirs, and that they do have a right to whatever it is, so does the spiritually immature, do what they want, when they want, and believe that it's OK, using grace as a cover for sin. Unfortunately, spiritual change cannot begin with this kind of expectation and mind- set. Dreamer, I invite you to consider the following. Accepting Jesus Christ as your Savior, on His terms and not yours, and where there would be chaos emotionally and spiritually, genuine peace will abide. Moreover, believing and encouraging others to approach God the Father, without the essential provision He has provided for humankind, to approach Him properly; that provision being Yeshua HaMashiach, is not safe. Some call God's provision Jesus, Wonderful Counselor, Mighty God, Everlasting Father, Prince of Peace, our atonement, advocate, liberator, propitiator, and our salvation. It is only through this channel that we may hope through faith to conciliate with our Creator, see John 3:16, Acts 2:37-42, 1 Timothy 2:4-7. Choose not to go out from the presence of the Lord, that is to, willingly renounce God, and to be content to forego the privileges He offers, that you might not be under His precepts, make things right. You will shortly, have to give an account of the fulfilling of your purpose for which you was design, as well as, of your philosophy and words. Dreamer, no authority, bravery, greatness, riches, or strength will be able to support you when your earth is shaken, when your time of divine discipline (the Lord's chastening, correction that leads to instruction and reformation) is approaching. Consider your dream as sufficient warning. See suggested course of action.

In addition, the following are common words, expressions, usages, (e.g. slang or clichés), or a 'probable' that are metaphorically represented by silver:

- Silver Cord (to see a silver cord, rope, or string): This symbol is one of God's ways of breaking it to you gently, preparing you for one of life's common denominators, and if heeded, can prevent you from being emotionally blindsided by loss, as your dream is a notice; it symbolizes shortness of life. For someone who has met Jesus, we experience Him in the little graces, the big miracles, the ordinary days, and the curious moments. He is with us, leading us onward, even sharing our tears. This same Jesus trustworthy in life, even when we are not, can be trusted at the ending of life, for He is the resurrection (John 11:25, 26). If we love Jesus and love our neighbor as we love ourselves, there is nothing in this world or the next to fear. Love is what we take with us, and love is what awaits us when we have finally arrived. With that, dreamer is also advised to seek medical attention as soon as possible, and call for the elders of your church, for it is through their prayers of faith and anointing of oil upon you that sin is forgiven and spiritual healing bestowed, and perhaps physical healing[36]. This is a true saying, thus it is time to have faith in God. Additionally, it is always a good time to get your house and papers in order (e.g. insurances, bequeaths, untold truths that need to be said), and always a good time to gather family together for prayer, support, wisdom, and truthfulness (Ecclesiastes 12:6).
- Silver Lining (to see a lining, a piece of cloth used as the inside surface of a garment that is silver in any garment or object): Your dream denotes that dreamer will greatly benefit from your adversity. Your situation, although, adverse, offers hope and benefit to the dreamer. If applicable, dreamer is advised to make sure all information needed is in order, presented properly, in a timely manner, and to be patient.
- Silver Spoon (to see, have, own, or receive, a silver spoon): Your dream denotes that the dreamer will greatly prosper financially, and will reach a very high social status, if not already, via an inheritance.
- Silver Tongued (to see or have a silver tongue, or silver on the tongue in some way): Your dream denotes one who is very eloquent. You definitely have the gift of persuading or complimenting people with charm. You put things in a way that can be easily received, which makes for an excellent teacher and peacemaker. However, although charming, dreamer is counseled to always, speak God's truth and to speak truthfully. Utilizing this wisdom will allow you to prosper greatly and to, be in good reputation, and to, always remain eloquent, especially in the eyes of God.

WHITE:

This dream has four meanings (choose one). (1) This color denotes one, the dreamer, who is too relaxed spiritually, daydreaming, even to the point of indulging in fantasy, to quote a cliché, you're building a castle in the sky, and actually moving into it. This spiritual state of mind keeps you unaware of your surroundings, thus, making you an easy prey for the devil. Favorably, because of the loving kindness of God, a reawakening is happening for you. There will be a flash of insight, a sudden awareness, recognition, or realization of God's truth. Do not fear, your spiritual life is being cleaned up; a personal revival is happening within you and you are being called upon to participate in that purification process. The context of your dream, especially your attitude regarding the color, and what was highlighted, exposes your level of participation needed and your submissiveness to the leading and guiding of the Paraclete. See suggested course of action. (2) Dreamer, the Spirit of Truth is coming to you. That is to say, one who has the Spirit of Truth abiding within them is coming. He or she will testify of Jesus; a side of Him you don't know. This new truth will usher you into a spiritual and personal revival, affecting restoration of better and happier times (e.g. deliverance, restoration, peace, purity, righteousness, joy, maturity, integrity, dignity, cleanliness, awareness, and new beginnings) or a new birth experience for one needing to be born again (see John 3:1-17). Do you trust that God can effect a revival within you? He can and will. Believe and you will receive, and you will be set free. At present, continue to allow the Paraclete to complete the work of purification and sanctification within you. For those who go forth in tears, shall return rejoicing (Psalm 126:5, 6). Be diligent and patient, everything will be done proper, and in its own time. Additionally, you will be ordained within a ministry, and if earned, honored in some respect, in another area of your life. If necessary, see suggested course of action. (3) If you've been wrestling with believing God for healing, or wondering if God really delivers, He will and He does. Dreamer, mercy, and compassion have been extended to you. You will experience a state of high honor, spiritual beauty, physical healing, and great illumination, and you will travel. Expect your miracle. (4) Regarding your sexual life, while this color represents purity unto the Lord, it is necessary to remind the dreamer, that it is written, Do not stir up nor awaken love until it pleases (Song 2:7 NKJV). Be patient, your love is coming, for your dream also denotes marriage, a very loving spouse, and if relevant, children.

Suggested Course of Action

Question to consider and journal, did your dream depict any symbols that alludes to, the dreamer will make the necessary changes, spiritually, emotionally, and/or physically to affect a more positive outcome? If changes are initiated, your dreams will change.

Nevertheless, if you are here, your chance to make things right, and to make a good go of things is before you; therefore, seize the moment to turn things around. In view of your dream's context, and the primary symbols, what does your dream reveal about you, your ethics, intents, mental state, and motives? You will need to earnestly look within and consider that the sum of your answers is a reflection of where you are emotionally, physically, and/or spiritually, and a reflection of who you are becoming. What was your reaction to the color or situation? Were you angry, concerned, confused, defensive, fearful, happy, helpful, pleased, shocked, unconcerned, or ready to get out of someone's presence? Your reaction to the color, activity, or circumstance, reveals your attitude regarding this information about yourself.

Dreamer, consider seriously your observations. If what was revealed prevail, will it sabotage any good that's happening at present within your life? Will it build or destroy, strengthen or weaken, enlighten or blind? If you lack wisdom, ask Jesus for wisdom. He gives wisdom to all, generously, no matter who you are and what you've done; wisdom is available (see James 1:5-8, Proverbs 2:1-6, 10). Hence, if, by just asking, you may get wisdom, one may suffer needlessly, because you will not ask Jesus for wisdom.

This is necessary to say, although it may seem, despairing at first, maintaining faith and honest ways, especially in the face of a life having been filled with corruption. The tasks may prove daunting, to say the least, living out the truths that most everyone you know prefer to ignore or ridicule, but if you would endure and remain faithful, the promises of God will manifes t, endurance will solidify you. If you would but endure and remain faithful, fighting the good fight of faith.

Dreamer, God hears your pondering, and He gives you this, seven colors (principles) by which you can survive, thrive, and spiritually illuminate your life, and that you might positively color the lives of those in your immediate community, and then abroad. These seven or "rainbow" colors are principles that build solid spiritual and life foundations, and enhance your relationship with Christ, and with those connected to you in one way or another.

THE SEVEN COLORS (aka the Noahic Covenant):

1. Acknowledge that there is only one God, who is infinite and supreme above all things, do not replace that Supreme Being with finite idols, be it yourself, or other beings, or things, and establish a personal relationship with Him, via Jesus Christ. You may approach God the Father, with the essential provision He has provided for mankind to approach Him properly, that

provision being Yeshua HaMashiach. Some call God's provision Jesus, Wonderful Counselor, Mighty God, Everlasting Father, Prince of Peace, our atonement, advocate, liberator, propitiator, and our salvation. It is only through this channel that we may hope through faith to conciliate with our Creator, see John 3:16, Acts 2:37-42, 1 Timothy 2:4-7.

2. Respect and reverence your Creator. As frustrated and angry as you may be, or become, do not vent it by cursing your Maker.

3. Respect human life. Every human being is an entire world. To save a life is to save that entire world. To destroy a life is to destroy an entire world. To help others live is a corollary of this principle. Therefore, agape your neighbor, see Luke 10:29-37.

4. Respect the institution of marriage. Marriage is a most Divine act. The marriage of a man and a woman is a reflection of the oneness of God and His creation. Disloyalty in marriage is an assault on that oneness.

5. Respect the rights and property of others. Be honest in all your business dealings. By relying on God rather than on our own conniving, we express our trust in Him as the Provider of Life.

6. Respect God's creatures. At first, man was forbidden to consume meat. After the Great Flood, he was permitted - but with a warning: Do not cause unnecessary suffering to any creature.

7. Maintain justice. Justice is God's business, but we are given the charge to lay down necessary laws and enforce them whenever we can. When we right the wrongs of society, we are acting as partners in the act of sustaining the creation.

Listen, whenever your skies are darken because of your deeds done that were (are) contrary to your welfare. Whenever your collective performance, grow heavy from sinful pursuits. When you are in denial, embracing dishonesty, cruelty, and depravity, and the consequences of your behaviors began to tear your life apart, and your world implodes because of violence and injustice. When those you've oppressed (your victims), blood and tears, fall hopeless to the ground and disappear beneat h the sullenness of your conscience, there would yet appear a redeeming rainbow, there is still hope for you. Dreamer, yes, God is slow to anger, and the guilty are punished; however, because of His amazing grace, mercy, and compassion, there is still yet a blessing to be left for you. Embrace the rainbow, and lay hold of its principles.

Now, pray (See Prayer of Deliverance, pg. 897)

Specific Meaning

If, you have a very high chance of introducing a new tint, or color, it is suggested that you may perhaps adopt the unique co lor as your own signature brand (e.g. a paint brand name), especially if you are a part of the science, technical, or specialist areas of colors. If you sense that, your dream is some type of inspiration regarding invention, then go, and start designing, brand mark, and marketing your divine sent inspiration. For God does give invention, via dreams, and it is meant to prosper your life.

Otherwise noted, per your lifestyle, if your dream closely resembled real life situations, meaning it can actually occur during your awaked state, this dream may be an Ordinary Dream, resulting from daily activities (see Chapter One, Chalom). These sorts of dreams are usually about your routine, mundane activities or anxieties that overwhelm your mind during the day. They are an inner release mechanism, which helps provide you with emotional balance and the maintaining of your sanity. These dreams are not significant, and do not warrant special attention.

However, if your dream was inundated with symbols that are not easily linked to your life activities, then the spiritual implications (the interpretation) should be heeded.

COMMUNICATIONS AND COMMUNICATION DEVICES

Now the Lord had told Samuel in his ear the day before Saul came, saying, (1 Samuel 9:15(NKJV)

And they heard the voice of Jehovah God walking in the garden in the cool of the day: And Jehovah God called unto the man, and said unto him, "Where art thou?" And he said, I heard thy voice in the garden, and I was afraid, (Genesis 3:8-10 ASV)

God called unto him out of the midst of the bush, and said, Moses, Moses. And he said, "Here am I". (Exodus 3:4 ASV) And Moses went up unto God, and Jehovah called unto him out of the mountain, saying, (Exodus 19:3 ASV)

According to all that I show thee, the pattern of the tabernacle, and the pattern of all the furniture thereof, even so shall ye make it (Exodus 25:9 ASV)

There is an old joke in which a gentleman, who never had time for God, was having a heart attack. In the midst of his dilemma, he remembered the song, Jesus on the main line; you can call Him up and tell Him what you want. Oh, if you're sick and you want to get well, tell Him what you want. His line is never busy. So, the gentleman decides to call Him up. An angel answers the phone, "hello heaven". The guy shouts, "This is... I need to talk to Jesus right away, it's an emergency!" The angel responds, I'm sorry, I'm gonna have to put you hold.

This category primarily deals with communicative methods and devices. Some short descriptions of types, phrases, and other processes and particulars, connected in some way to this category are, for example, apple, boom box, CD, cell phones, computer, DVD, Flash drive, HP, internet, modem, lap top, radio, stereo systems, tablet, telephone booth, TV, wireless.

All Symbols and Referents, Notes (1, 2, 3, etc.), Suggested Course of Action, and Specific Meaning offer guidance toward a more comprehensive interpretation.

Notes

1. Unless otherwise noted elsewhere, if, in your everyday living, your awaked state, as part of your lifestyle, work, or ministerial activities, or a special event, you have a very real connection with any activity involving communication s and communication devices. For example, broadcasting, computers, desktop publications, telecommunications tele vision, telemarketing, or any branch of engineering concerned with the processing of information, or connected in anyway with the technology involved with communications and/or communicative devices; your dream is not significant and does not warrant special attention.

   Otherwise noted, this dream of communications and communication devices may be a Prophetically Simple Dream (see Chapter One: The 60th Part of Prophecy). Whereas, the dreamer is encouraged, for example, if a new technology was introduced to you within your dream, to adopt the unique technology as your own signature brand, especially if you are a part of the science, technical, or specialist areas of communications and communication devices. Did you invent something? Skip interpretation, go, and start designing, brand mark, and marketing your divine sent invention.

   Otherwise noted, this dream of communications and communication devices may be an Oneirovaticicritica or OVC dream, to decipher or interpret and prophesy by dreams (see Chapter One: The 60th Part of Prophecy, The Elevated Parts of Sleep). Did dreamer hear about a disastrous event over the radio, or while watching the news? Did dreamer broadcast something? If so, what was broadcasted? Was there a warning of some kind? For example, to dream that you, either, by TV, radio, phone, or internet, heard that a disastrous event is headed toward your location and that it may prove catastrophic, e.g. terrorist or sniper attack, hurricane, explosion. On some level, this type of dream will affect the dreamer's life, requiring action on the part of the hearer, and it bares insight into the life of those who may seriously be affected by the coming event. This type of dream should closely resemble real life situations, with the dream events actually being capable of happening. If you sense that your dream is a prophetic dream, the question as to why you have been made aware of this information, and how do you factor into the equation, should be seriously considered, along with necessary actions. Dreamer, you are meant to get involved. If possible, how can you alleviate the effects of the situation? Dreams that reference others and the revelation within those dreams, is not given haphazardly to any individual, but only to those with the ability, and influence to do something with the information; this is also prophecy. Skip interpretation, Jesus will strengthen you emotionally, psychologically, and physically to seek help and support in your endeavors, and possibly how to help others.

Otherwise noted, per your lifestyle, if your dream closely resembled real life situations, meaning it can actually occur during your awaked state, this dream may be an Ordinary Dream, resulting from daily activities (see Chapter One, Chalom). These sorts of dreams are usually about your routine, mundane activities or anxieties that overwhelm your mind during the day. They are an inner release mechanism, which helps provide you with emotional balance and the maintaining of your sanity. These dreams are not significant, and do not warrant special attention.

2. Probables: As communications and/or communicative devices are frequently used as referents in many, and very personal, aspects of our lives; hence, dreamer may also consider your own personal, special, or cultural associations with various communications. For examples, apps and/or other communicative devices, as long as the interpretation is kept within the principles of spiritual boundary markers, landmarks, and property lines, (see Chapter One, section entitled, Spiritualizing Boundary Markers, Landmarks, and Property Lines).

3. Determine who your dream is for you or another. Always, considering yourself first, reflecting on your present behaviors. Ask yourself, "Why am I dreaming about this now? What is this dream revealing about me? Have I taken on new attributes? Has anyone commented on my present behaviors as being untypical of me? Has my ministry changed for the better or for the worse? What about my beliefs, doctrine, or philosophy, are they still based on Holy Writ?

Remember your actions and emotions within your dream. Were you attempting to contact someone? Were you having difficulty hearing what was being said? Did you see yourself featured on TV or YouTube? Did you program a computer? Were you a DJ? Were you watching a beautiful sunset on your computer screen? Were you texting while driving? If dreamer was the focal point, meaning, you was primarily the highlight. Unless otherwise noted elsewhere, this is a good indicator that your dream is about you (the dreamer). In light of your dream, via the relevant interpretation, do you believe that your behavior will enhance or endanger your well-being, safety, and/or happiness, if so, how and why? Do you believe that your belief system will strengthen or weaken you spiritually in any way, if so, how and why? Is spiritual or physical death a possibility? See following relevant subcategory, the interpretation is about and for you.

Was someone featured on TV or YouTube? Did someone broadcast something? Was someone calling you? Was someone else a hacker, plagiarist, or stole your ideas? Did another cause an accident, due to texting while driving? Unless otherwise noted elsewhere, an answer of yes, to one or more of these, or similar questions, is a good indicator that your dream is about another and their role, and/or influential effects, within the life of the dreamer. If someone else was the focal point, meaning, another, was primarily the highlight of your dream. How was he or she connected to the communicative devices or involved in some way with communication? Consider, is someone greatly influencing your physical, spiritual, or mental health, your understanding, perspective, and reasoning regarding spiritual issues? Are they enhancing your spiritual and/or literal prosperity, or are they responsible for the dwindling thereof? Could they be influencing your ministry, on some level? Do you know someone whose life activities or physical being is similar to that which stood out the most within your dream? Could it be that person? If you sense that your dream is for or about another, the question as to why you have been made privy to this information, and how do you factor into the equation, should be seriously considered along with necessary actions. Perhaps the dreamer is being made aware of the plight of someone, and you are to get involved (see Chapter One, Are You Ready to Hear the Messages in Your Dreams, section entitled, The 10% for others).

If your dream is for, or about another:

Dreams that reference others and the revelation within those dreams, is not given haphazardly to any individual, but only to those with the ability, and influence to do something with the information; this is also prophecy. With that, journal the following questions, and if unable to answer the questions now, this denotes that the person, represented within your dream, will enter your life shortly. Are you entering into a personal relationship with someone? Do you not know or understand what you're looking at, especially certain behaviors, when learning about this person? Has someone new entered your life or maybe you've just begun opening up to someone not so new, and have started listening to their advice, accepting their assistance, or are you supporting or enabling someone? Are you in denial regarding the toxicity of one of your present relationships, particularly a spouse, family member, or friend? Are you anxious, concerned, frightened, and/or troubled by recent changes in your behavior, especially because of someone's influence upon your life at present? Have you allowed someone to convince you to deceive another? Have you recently become aware of (or is being made aware of, via your dream) certain undesirable behaviors within you towards another? Are you trying to cut ties with one that is bad company? Have you just joined (or re-joined) a church, fellowship, or social group?

Note: If your dream has attributes that indicate that your dream is about you, and other attributes that indicate that your dream is about another, dreamer should consider that your dream is about you and another. For example, was there some news broadcast about the dreamer and another? Was dreamer on a "two-way" or business call? Was dreamer a co-creator of a new device? Did another steal your idea? Did dreamer plagiarize someone else work? Unless otherwise noted elsewhere, an answer of yes, to one or more of these, or similar questions, is a good indicator that the dream is about the dreamer, and about another. Therefore, while your dream is about the dreamer, the dreamer should expect the role and/ or influential effects of another, also plays a part in your interpretation. For example, dreamer may have to; legally bear the repercussions of the theft of another's intellectual property. From which now the dreamer needs proper legal representation, again, see relevant interpretation.

More questions to consider. Why has the person been allowed within your life, and/or how did they get there? Again, if unable to answer the questions now, this denotes that the person, represented within your dream, will enter your life shortly. If their activity, within your dream, has proven positive, via the interpretation, this someone will prove, unwittingly, to be a very strong ally, benefactor, defender, and supporter. God has sent this someone into your life to help you carry out your next endeavor by enlarging your spiritual capacity. Allow the strength of that person's character to guide, help, and support you. On the other hand, if his or her presence and/or activity, within your dream, proved negative, via the interpretation, for sure, this person will prove to be a very strong and formidable challenge for you, perhaps unto death. If negative, this dream is a dire warning. Take steps accordingly to struggle against, or to cut off, adverse and unfavorable relationships. Remember certain personalities are all encompassing, affecting everything, cataclysmic, contagious, deadly, harmful, infectious, predatory, and/or venomous. Symbolically meaning that if allowed to continue or prosper within your life, serious harm or death to the dreamer may result. Idolize no one, especially beyond the warning of the Lord, and we are definitely not to lay our lives down for no one. Then again, this person maybe allowed within your life, because of the dreamer's unwillingness to abstain from immorality after having been asked to abstain from such by God, see 1 Corinthians 6:9-20, Galatians 5:19-21, or the dreamer's self-righteous behavior, or a lack of a balanced and honest view of your own personality. In this case, this person will affect self-awareness within the life of the dreamer, exposing the negative traits of your personality, especially those traits, which cause you to follow, or to be so easily misled, and/or your wrong beliefs; no matter, this type of mentality needs reckoning with. Graciously, all of this will restore the dreamer to his or her right place with God, opening your eyes to see how far you've strayed from God (1 Corinthians 5:4-7; James 5:20). The lesson is, no matter how personable, powerful, or difficult a person, or how uncertain or unpopular the choices and issues, always take the next biblical and ethical step, for obedience to God's principles will always prove safer and stronger foundationally. Although, you will need all kinds of outside support to recover from this person's domination, no longer, allow that particular person's influence within your life to continue or thrive, especially if negative, end it abruptly.

4. Consider all the people, places, backgrounds, and activity highlighted within your dream.

Known (in your awaked life) person, animal, place, or organization within your dream:

Unless otherwise noted elsewhere, people, animals, places, backgrounds that are actually known by the dreamer in your awaked life, indicates a part of you that you recognize within yourself on some level or another. Question to journal, if dreamer seriously considers all the particulars, what stood out the most, what features, or character traits stood out the most. For example, age, color, height, size, happiness, considerate, loving, let you be yourself, peacefulness, encourager, irrational, leader, liar, mentor, passionate, personable, neglected, poor, run-down, sage, shyster, unwise, upscale, vengeful. Write down (journal) the particular highlighted within your dream. The attribute or activity highlighted is for a reason. Since the attribute written down is a part of you, namely the dreamer's nature, demeanor, and/or lifestyle, an honest and unbiased assessment is very important for truth sake. Happy note, considering that other people's attributes, within dreams, also represent attributes of your own personality, causes one to look at another in a better light. According to your capacity to embrace self-awareness and a rectification of mind, body, and spirit, God will begin to enhance, make better, more attractive, sanctify, diminish, and make pure and free from sin and guilt, this part of you.

Otherwise noted, if the person, animal, place, or background within your dream is actually known by the dreamer, in your awaked life, this person, animal, place, or background may represent him or herself, or itself.

Unknown in your awaked life or although known, was unseen, invisible, or only talked about - person, animal, place, or organization within your dream:

Unless otherwise noted elsewhere, if you did not recognize, the person, place, thing, they, or it, was not seen, invisible, or only talked about within your dream, this indicates an attribute or activity within your life that you are unfamiliar with, or are in denial about, or you refuse to acknowledge it, but it does exists. Although, on some conscious level, you are aware of a certain behavior or attribute within you, you have chosen to filter out or simply ignore certain information about yourself that contradicts your view of yourself and/or your preconceived notions of others and of the world around you. Possibly protecting yourself, emotionally and psychologically, from a situation, which you are unable to cope with at this time, or you lack control over; then again, perhaps the dreamer has an exaggerated or unrealistic view of yourself. No matter the reason, right now a question is before you, via your dream. Do you want to know this part of yourself? According to your ability to handle self-awareness, God will begin to reveal this side of you to you. Why, He wants to balance your understanding of things; thus, effecting wholeness within your life, so that the enemy will no longer be able to manipulate your emotions so easily. The Paraclete is with you to help you throughout this entire process, listen to Him. Now, in your life, this activity or attribute needs reckoning with, somehow or someway.

Otherwise noted, (known or unknown), if the person, place or thing that initiated (or was a recipient of) the action or activity within your dream was not seen, invisible, or only talked about within your dream, this may indicate that the dreamer does not recognize the influential effects another has within your life, or upon your attitude.

If more than one person (known or unknown):

Consider what the group had in common. What behavior, character trait, feature, action, or activity, stood out the most? For example, were they argumentative, authoritative, beautiful, criminal minded, dancing, difficult, dressed unusual, enigmatic, fighting, focused, flirty, helpful, hurtful intentions, powerful, promiscuous, quiet, secretive, seemed unreal, unassuming? What about age, color, height, size, happiness, considerate, loving, let you be yourself, peacefulness, encourager, irrational, leader, liar, mentor, passionate, personable, neglected, poor, run-down, sage, shyster, unwise, upscale, vengeful, death. That which was highlighted and noted is what you need to focus on at present.

If the attribute or quality is a desirable or positive one, allow the strength of that attribute to help you overcome some manner of immorality or irreverence within your life and/or to help you to become better, productively, for the Kingdom of God in some manner. If the attribute is an undesirable or negative one, take steps accordingly to struggle against the growing desires of the carnal side of you. If applicable, get help and support via prayer, fasting, and a Christian based support group.

For dreams of the dead see following note.

Did you communicate with a dead person? While the dead has nothing to do with the living (Ecclesiastes 9:4-6), it may be considered what character trait did that person represent to the dreamer, while the person was actually alive, what character feature stood out the most. With that trait noted, dreamer may consider that the trait noted, is within the dreamer, and that trait is no longer useful or needed for the progression of your spiritual walk, on this side of heaven. Dreamer, it is suggested that you render that trait (good or bad) obsolete, and began anew attempting to move forward, using different tactics to overcome unproductive habitual life cycle choices, and for maneuvering through this thing we call life in a more, better way. See category, Death, and/or other relevant categories.

5. As some of the following are your basic communicative devices (earlier state or stages of development of your modern day devices); the dreamer should consider the basic device that is equivalent to your modern day device. For example, a telegraph, an apparatus used to communicate at a distance, is your modern day landline or iPhone, or an 8-trace, or 45 record, or CD is your modern day iTunes, and so on. Seek guidelines for modern day equivalents, via internet.

6. In addition to the following interpretations, see index or relevant categories for more information. For example, if a dead person was involved in some way, see category, Death; if a intoxication was highlighted, see category, Drinking. Kept within context of your dream and the interpretation, the additional symbols are perhaps relevant. It will be within the sum of all the symbols that you will find a more thorough interpretation.

7. Since the following list is not extensive, dreamer is encouraged to seek biblical guidelines and other relevant research to determine the metaphorical meaning of your particular communication and communicative device, depicted within your dream, via a Bible concordance, Bible illustrated dictionary, encyclopedia, or internet. Having done your research

you should be able to determine some basic behaviors or attributes your Lord and Savior wants you to focus on.

Symbols and Referents

Most dreams of communications and/or communicative devices generally imply; coupled with the relevant interpretation, that there is a need to be diligent in reading, studying, memorizing, and meditating on the Word of God that you might more fully understand what God is trying to communicate to you, and how He communicates with us. God speaks to all believers through the vehicle of the Bible, which is fundamentally all we need to equip us for the Christian life (2 Timothy 3:16, 17). Trying to shortcut this process by seeking other revelations that do not support meditating on the Word of God (Joshua 1:8), such as meditative disciplines that claim to train the consciousness for a state of perfect spiritual insight and tranquility, which they say is achieved through paths of actions, knowledge, and devotion. Not only is this course or discipline, delivered without grace, it will never be enough to fill an empty soul, nor does it prepare you for eternal life, for it approaches the spiritual realm without the provision that God has provided for man to approach, and reach, true spiritual perfection, and that provision being Jesus the Christ. Moreover, this way opens you up to be deceived regarding your own fallen nature or worse, and to the deception of demons, that are always looking for inroads into our minds, and it is unscriptural.

In addition to the varied meanings of communications and/or communicative devices, other common words, expressions, usages, (e.g. slang or clichés), or a 'probable' that are metaphorically represented by any of the following are also conside red (this section is an addendum at the end of the relevant subcategory).

Category Content: If not listed see index, perchance, for your specific type of communication dream.

- Bugging (secretly listen in on a communication channel), See category, Agriculture (Plant)
- Communication Breakdown (having difficulty hearing what was being said, device stop operating or functioning, or an obstacle of some sort resulted in a failure in communicating)
- Communications originating, located, or occurring outside of earth or its atmosphere, non-terrestrial, e.g. God, Jesus, angels, demons, alien life, or spirits
- Communications Towers or Radios (ROHN structures, e.g. antennas, small radio communication, ham radio, emergency communication, PCS, broadband, wireless)
- Computer or Books (any medium used for processing information or for searching the internet, e.g. e-books, tablets, laptop, mainframe, network, notebook, PC, Talking Book)
    - Talking Book
- Mail (any medium or system whereby messages are transmitted, e.g. correspondences, e-mails, fax machine, texting, telegraph, cable, wire, transmit, telex, or telegram, or any form of social media, e.g. Facebook, Google, Twitter)
- Telephone (any device used to transmit speech at a distance, e.g. cell or mobile phones, iPhone, Bluetooth device, smart phone, headset, earpiece, mouthpiece, walkie-talkie)
    - Bullhorn, Intercom Speaker, Loudspeaker, Squawk Box
- Talking, see category Talking
- Television, TV or Movie or Video or Camera (electronic device that has visual and/o audible components, receives signals, and displays them on a screen, any device used to broadcast visual images of moving or stationary objects, e.g. Instagram, video camera, YouTube)

COMMUNICATION BREAKDOWN (having difficulty hearing what was being said, device stop operating or functioning, or an obstacle of some sort resulted in a failure in communicating):

Dreamer, God speaks to all believers through the vehicle of the Bible, which is fundamentally all you need to equip you for the Christian life (2 Timothy 3:16, 17). Trying to shortcut this process by seeking other revelations that do not support meditating on the Word of God, such as meditative disciplines, has led to you gaining dark and erroneous knowledge, through personal experiences and through a supernatural imparting, which was demonically communicated. The knowledge you've gained does not allow you to praise the Lord, only to exalt one's self. You have abandoned the faith, and is now adhering to lies; thus a breakdown in communication, with the Heavenly Father, and with the Body of Christ, aka Christians. You are embracing beliefs, views, and practices that are erroneous, unlawful, toxic, and spiritually and/or physically deadly. Your choices will not withstand your storms of life. Your conscience will haunt you. Weakened by frequent panic attacks, brought on by your own guilt and the fear of God's retribution, you will begin to crack in your personality. He, who carries his or her own accuser, and their own tormentor, always in their bosom, cannot but be afraid on every side (Matthew Henry's Commentary on Job 18:11-21). The only foundation upon which one should wisely establish his or her identity is the principles within the Word of God. Your attitude is leading to a mental and spiritual breakdown, opening the door for demons to run havoc within your life and to bring you down to desolation. You are forfeiting purpose for foolishness and ruin. Demonic influences will swarm around you, ready to help you explore all manner of wickedness, and evil, despicable, immoral, reprehensible, disreputable, degenerate, infamous, and perverse choices. Your lifestyle choices will become offensive and repulsive (abominable) in the sight of God and humanity. Dreamer, demons have had thousands of years to master human weaknesses and can rival men and women of God if we are not careful. Favorably, while your dream is a seriously severe rebuke and warning, because of grace and the many mercies of God extended to you, it is not an official declaration. Dreamer is counseled to seek all kinds of spiritual support now, to possibly avert or turn things around, and perhaps move away from your present environment, definitely walk away from all negativity that is the antithesis of Christ, abruptly. Utilizing the powerful resources of prayer and heartfelt repentance to Jesus is a good place to start. To Jesus pray, Psalm 51, this followed by appropriate application of wisdom, can conceivably avert some of the repercussions of your choices. This coupled with fasting, a changed mindset, serious re-consideration of God's ways and means, and an honest acknowledgement of God's hand within your life, then the severe impact of your choices and actions upon your life, can be reversed and damages repaired (also see Ezekiel 33:12-19). This is what is called leaving a blessing behind. If you do not genuinely seek help and change, for sure ruin will be your destiny's declaration. See suggested course of action.

COMMUNICATIONS ORIGINATING, LOCATED, OR OCCURRING OUTSIDE OF EARTH OR ITS ATMOSPHERE, NON-TERRESTRIAL, E.G. GOD, JESUS, ANGELS, DEMONS, ALIEN LIFE, OR SPIRITS:

Communication from God, Jesus, or Holy Spirit: An old song goes something like this, "Jesus is on the main line, tell Him what you want. You can call Him up and tell Him what you want. Go on, call Him up, and tell Him what you want. If you're sick and you want to get well, tell Him what you want. Oh, if you're sick and you want to get well, tell Him what you want" (Author unknown). This song is for you; therefore ask Jesus, via prayer, and it shall be given you. Ask what I shall give thee, (2 Chronicles 1:7 ASV). Question, what would you have Jesus do for you? Dreamer, with great delight put your entire confidence in the protection and wisdom of the Lord, for He knows you, and He will give you the desires of your heart. And you are ready to receive those desires, for your dream also hints at the hidden power within you to manifest those desires of your heart, because you are embracing God's will for your life. The awareness of the presence of the Hand of God over your life, especially now, will become the banner, so to say, over your head, so tell Him what you want.

Communication from alien life, or spirits: Dreamer, your lifestyle choices are leading to much sadness, many troubles, and awful heartaches, and your practices and beliefs have led to you gaining dark and erroneous knowledge, through personal experiences and through a supernatural imparting, which was demonically communicated. The knowledge you've gained does not allow you to praise the Lord, only to exalt one's self. You have abandoned the faith, and are now adhering to lies. You are embracing beliefs, views, and practices that are erroneous, unlawful, toxic, and spiritually and/or physically deadly. Your choices will not withstand your storms of life. Your conscience will haunt you. Weakened by frequent panic attacks, brought on by your own guilt and the fear of God's retribution, you will begin to crack in your personality. He, who carries his or her own accuser, and their own tormentor, always in their bosom, cannot but be afraid on every side (Matthew Henry's Commentary on Job 18:11-21). The only foundation upon which one should wisely establish his or her identity is the principles within the Word of God. Your attitude is opening the door for demons to run havoc within your life and to bring you down to desolation. Demonic influences will swarm around you, ready to help you explore all manner of wickedness, and evil, despicable, immoral, reprehensible, disreputable, degenerate, infamous, and perverse choices. Your lifestyle choices will become offensive and repulsive (abominable) in the sight of God and humanity. Dreamer, demons have had thousands of years to master human weaknesses and can rival men and women of God if we are not careful. Fortunately, your dream is a seriously severe rebuke and warning, because of grace and the many mercies of God extended to you. Stop, reconsider your behavior, and repent that the repercussions of your actions might not be so severe. You are urged to become spiritually aware of the Holy Ghost, who abides within you, and respect His presence, and to respect the cost that was paid for your salvation. If no genuine change; unfortunately, you will, now, begin to experience the consequences of adhering to the practices of darkness, which is a regression of the blessings bestowed upon you or promised by God. See suggested course of action.

COMMUNICATIONS TOWERS OR RADIOS (ROHN structures, e.g. antennas, small radio communication, ham radio, emergency communication, PCS, broadband, wireless):

Your dream suggests that the dreamer's voice, will be used as an instrument of righteousness; coming against those who would attempt to oppress you and others. The dreamer's spiritual strength, tenacity, and knowledge, will be used of God; penetrating the soul of those who would listen, affecting conversion. By all this, you will be remembered by the Lord your God and rescued from your enemies. For, your words will cause your enemies to turn on themselves. Your dream comes as a message of affirmation. You have been called to a high calling; for you are a true defender and protector of the people; therefore, withdraw not your spirit when that day is officially upon you.

COMPUTER OR BOOKS (any medium used for processing information or for searching the internet, e.g. e-books, tablets, laptop, mainframe, network, notebook, PC):

Depending upon your emotions, within your dream, this dream has three meanings (choose one). (1) If dreamer was pleasantly entertained, laughing, or happy because of what you saw or sensed in your dream, dreamer, you have been given insight into prophetic wisdom, and by this, you are now able to discern truth from false. Trust God fully in whatever you are facing, and never, do you ever, exalt a situation above God's ability to handle it in your life, and to handle it for your good. Even more, you will no longer feel ashamed because of something you've done awry in your past (e.g. seriously bad, unalterable, and life damaging actions, uninformed choices, and/or toxic relationships). The reproach of your past will be put behind you. Do not be afraid; you will not suffer shame; do not fear disgrace; you will not be humiliated, God has granted mercy to you. In addition, you are gifted with multiple talents that may be expressed through inspirational acting, preaching, teaching, or writing. Dreamer, do not bury your prophetic gifts (see Luke 19:12-26); for many will be drawn to God because of your loving disposition and positive attitude; others will be dramatically changed by your example. From this day forward, God's blessings will flow abundantly, producing spiritual growth within you. God's blessings: Gifts of God's grace, anythin g God freely gives you, absolution, the Holy Spirit, salvation, regeneration, eternal life, peace, health, children, love of family, longevity, necessities, prosperity, and dominion over all that is yours; and all are parts of the supply of grace, and all ar e sanctified by the Lord, and technically belongs to Him. The result of this supply in your life will be peace. As well, you will experience a divine visitation, one sent from the Lord who will deliver you from the evil and wickedness that has surrounded you. (2) If dreamer was sad, crying, depressed or melancholy because of what you saw or sensed in your dream: Your dream comes to warn the dreamer of looming dangers and difficulties. You were sent this warning dream because you are a believer. Dreamer, you are approaching a time of great difficulty. So much so, that it will take you to the very edge of your mind. One thing is for sure, you will suffer some kind of great loss. Favorably, no matter the trouble you may experience, or is experiencing, God's grace (the free and unmerited favor and beneficence of God) is sufficient. Be on the alert, be watchful, and ready to deal with whatever happens, and most importantly, look to Jesus, who is the author and finisher of your faith.

Dreamer, the approaching situation can be dealt with sagaciously, if you do your research on what you're dealing with, and how to deal with it practically. For example, grief does not need medication, it's a natural process of a significant loss; therefore, it must be allowed to run its course, be it five days or five years. Allow the process naturally, and resist anyone who tries to coerce you, because of your weaken state, into taking mind or emotional altering drugs. For grief has its place and purpose, and as the word goes, "this too will end". Dreamer, whatever your difficulty, keep a rational mindset, don't fear, and know that you're not alone. You are also exhorted to be aware of enticements, and to embrace wisdom. See suggested course of action. (3) If dreamer felt confused, astonished, shocked, or frightened because of what you saw or sensed in y our dream, your dream represents an identity crisis, be it mentally, emotionally, or spiritually. Dreamer, you do not know who you are on some level or another. Question to consider: Why has this identity crisis happened to you, and why now? Perhaps yo u was or is a victim of a tragic violation (e.g. diabolical cult practices, molestation, murder, rape, robbery, or some other great stooge, or culprit; often exploited on some level by others. How can the effects of what's causing your identify crisis stop playing a significant role in your life? Dreamer; oftentimes, bad things happen to innocent and good people. A bad thing happened to you, and you are good and innocent. Compassionately, the Lord is creating a miracle in your life. This miracle will stop the effects of your violation from playing a significant role in your life, enabling you to move forward with your life and to make good decisions. However, the miracle's success depends upon your willingness to be healed and set free; for one will always have the choice to say no, or perhaps sabotage their progress. First, recognize and respect your time of visitation f rom the Lord, for it is upon you, as well as the work of His Hand upon your life. If you lack wisdom ask God for wisdom; and He will give you wisdom. For the Lord gives wisdom and from His mouth comes knowledge and understanding. Moreover, Jesus will strengthen you emotionally and/or psychologically, to go get help via a Christian based support group, counseling, healthcare, inpatient, dreamer, go get help. See suggested course of action.

Talking Book: Your dream denotes one who is spiritually blind, by choice, having carelessly risked your life and soul, pretending to be blind to, and ignorant of, the things of God, His principles, and His creative works in and around you, in h opes to satisfy fleshly desires. Dreamer, God's love is calling you back to Him; forgiveness will cover all your mistakes from this day forward. Now give careful thought to this from this day on. From this day forward, God will bless you; therefore, perceive God's grace, and embrace the love that is calling you home. No longer, pretend that you do not sense His providence within your life and, when applicable, let it be known publicly. See suggested course of action.

MAIL (any medium or system whereby messages are transmitted, e.g. correspondences, e-mails, fax machine, texting, telegraph, cable, wire, transmit, telex, or telegram, or any form of social media, e.g. Facebook, Google, Twitter):

Did dreamer excitedly receive or send a message or did dreamer reject a message. Thus dream has two meanings (choose one). (1) If dreamer received or sent a message, especially excitedly, dreamer you are commissioned to preach the gospel of Jesus Christ, through evangelism, outreach efforts, or a pastorate. You are sent to many, of every nation and tongue. You should already know by now who you are in Christ, an evangelist, outreach organizer, or pastor. Do you love Jesus? If so, then feed His flock (figuratively and literally). You love Him when you obey Him. Additionally, write your vision down, that you may articulate it to others properly, for the vision will happen, suddenly and quickly. Prepare a good proposal, name your ministry, and write down all the details and specifics. Give it your best that it may be acceptable to any reputable financial entity, benefactor, or merit a grant of some kind. Perhaps, hire a grant writer. That which you will need to fulfill your aims, surely, you will have. (2) If dreamer rejected a message, your dream is a severe rebuke. Dreamer, a wicked servant would bury his or her gift, blaming their lack of faithfulness, commitment, and stewardship on God or others. When in reality, you have literally chosen to remain spiritually immature. Upon facing your Maker, there will be no one else to blame but you. You will have to give an account of the fulfilling of your specific purpose. You can never claim you have not been sufficiently warned. Consider your dream as sufficient warning. See suggested course of action.

TELEPHONE (any device used to transmit speech at a distance, e.g. cell or mobile phones, iPhone, Bluetooth device, smart phone, headset, earpiece, mouthpiece, walkie-talkie):

No matter if dreamer called someone, or someone called the dreamer, your dream was sent to encourage and warn. Dreamer, those who plot evil against you (family, friend, or foe) will not prevail, but will yield willingly to your authority. The warning, dreamer, keep quiet and appear speechless or deaf, for the time being. Take on an unassuming disposition (also see Deuteronomy 8:6-20). On another vein, at some point in the undisclosed future, honor and wealth will be bestowed upon the dreamer, possibly you benefiting from another's inheritance, if not already. Nonetheless, you are becoming self-sufficient and unrelenting, capable of handling much responsibility, especially when required to make major decisions. Many will be inspired by your wisdom, confidence, and blameless actions, while others will feel threaten by it.

    Bullhorn, Intercom Speaker, Loudspeaker, Squawk Box: Your dream denotes that the dreamer is in some kind of distress. Dreamer, although enemies are about you, the storms of life are raging, and the winds are blowing, and you have cried out to God from a place of pain, don't let your faith be moved, for the Lord God has heard your cry. Suddenly, the Lord Jesus will rescue and vindicate you, and cause your fears to dispel. Lift your hands to Jesus, for the Lord will strengthen, renew, and rebuild and His Holy Spirit will lead and guide you.

TELEVISION, TV OR MOVIE OR VIDEO OR CAMERA (electronic device that has visual and/o audible components, receives signals, and displays them on a screen, any device used to broadcast visual images of moving or stationary objects, e.g. Instagram, video camera, YouTube):

Question, what was depicted on the TV? The images broadcasted, and the highlighted features, or what the person, place, or thing represented, is overtaking the dreamer's life. This type of dream helps the dreamer to know what your divine Counselor wants you to focus on; namely, your particular behaviors. Couple this with one of the following (choose one). (1) If, according to biblical standards, not the "secular world" standards, a godly, and very positive, and truthful, persona was presented. Then it is these standards, which the dreamer is absorbed in pursuing; these attributes are overtaking the dreamer's life. Thus, your Lord's sight. (2) Anything broadcasted, that was "secular", namely anything relating to, or that rejects, religious considerations, denotes, unfortunately, that the dreamer is absorbed in the pursuit of identity void of foundation (e.g. pretending to be someone you are not; and not knowing what it takes, or the costs, to be that which you are pretending, or desiring, to be). This type of identity pursuit will not withstand your storms of life. You will begin to crack in your per sonality. The only foundation upon which humankind should wisely establish his or her identity, are the principles within the Word of God. See suggested course of action.

Suggested Course of Action

Question to consider and journal, did your dream depict any symbols that allude to, the dreamer will make the necessary changes, spiritually, emotionally, and/or physically to affect a more positive outcome? If changes are initiated, your dreams will change.

Nevertheless, in view of your dream's context, what does the primary symbol reveal about you, your ethics, or mental state? You will need to earnestly look within and consider that your answers are a reflection of where you are emotionally, physically, and spiritually, presently, and perhaps who you are becoming. What was your reaction to the activity? Were you angry, concerned, confused, defensive, fearful, happy, helpful, pleased, shocked, or unconcerned? Your reaction to the activ ity or the circumstance reveals your attitude regarding this information about yourself. Thus, if you are here, drea mer you must re-examine how you communicate with others. It is understood that no filthy communication should escape from the lips of a Christian, whether said in jest or in earnest. Moreover, when you speak in anger, you fail to show God's love, whether speaking to a family member or a stranger, your communication should always come forth in a loving manner (Colossians 3:8, 9, James 1:19). The best way to be sure what comes from your mouth is pure, is to be aware of what is in your heart. With that, dreamer, you should constantly examine your mode of communication.

If the attribute or quality revealed within your dream is a desirable or positive one, allow the strength of that attribute t o help you overcome some manner of immorality or irreverence within your life and/or to help you to become better, productively, for the Kingdom of God in some manner. If the attribute is an undesirable or negative one, take steps accordin gly to struggle against the growing desires of the carnal side of you. If applicable, get help and support via prayer, fasting, and a Christian based support group.

Dreamer, consider seriously your observations. If what was revealed prevail, will it sabotage any good that's happening at present within your life? Will it build or destroy, strengthen or weaken, enlighten or blind? If you lack wisdom, ask Jesus for wisdom. He gives wisdom to all, generously, no matter who you are and what you've done; wisdom is available (see James 1:5-8, Proverbs 2:1-6, 10). Hence, if, by just asking, you may get wisdom, one may suffer needlessly, because you will not ask Jesus for wisdom.

Communicating with God, Communicating with our fellow man:

The two most important types of communication are between God and man and between human beings, for we need each other. Your primary mode of communication with God is prayer; dreamer, go to God in prayer for all your needs. In your communication with others, dreamer is advised to consider the "tone" of newer forms of communication such as email and text messaging. Never allow the safety of a phone or computer screen to lead you to harsh or ungodly words toward others, nor into lewd and lascivious communications. Additionally, consider your body language and facial expressions toward others as well. Simply withholding words is meaningless when your body language communicates disdain, anger, or hatred toward another. When engaged in conversation, as you prepare to speak, ask yourself these questions: it is true, is it kind, and is it necessary.

Now, pray (See Prayer of Deliverance, pg. 897)

Specific Meaning

If, you have a very high chance of introducing a new technology it is suggested that you may perhaps adopt the unique technology as your own signature brand, especially if you are a part of the science, technical, or specialist areas of communications and communication devices. If you sense that, your dream is some type of inspiration regarding invention, then go, and start designing, brand mark, and marketing your divine sent invention. For God does give invention, via dreams, and it is meant to prosper your life.

Note: If any illegal activity was depicted within your dream, or any manner of unauthorized access to a computer, network, or organization personal records, or anyone's concepts, ideas, e.g. hacking, copyright, plagiarism, or trademark infringements. This dream is a warning, especially if dreamer is actually involved in any illegal activity, to prevent serious legal ramifications, or perhaps harm to yourself, and/or others, due to violating the law or to disgruntle persons. There is a potential for incarceration, homicide, or some kind of incident. Dreamer, re-consider your activity as harmful, hurtful, illegal, and perhaps life threatening, at present. Handle your business by surrendering, first to Jesus, thanking Him for His grace, and then to appropriate authorities. The details, kept within context of your dream, should be relevant to your life, and closely resemble your real-life situations. Meaning it can actually occur during your awaked state. This will help you narrow down the specifics needed to support and steer you clear of possible mishaps.

If dreamer is involved in any illicit sexual activity, especially online, e.g. adult or child pornography, this dream is a warning to make you aware of the serious legal ramifications, due to violating the law and perhaps harm to yourself due to disgruntle persons.

Moreover, if, there is a very high propensity for accidents, due to, for example, texting while driving, or if circumstances may perhaps lead to an accident, for example, viewing a device, while driving or walking, dreamer is warned to heed cautionary advice, and don't text or view, while driving, or walking. Dreamer, pay close attention to your surroundings, the re may be potential for a serious accident. Do not assume that you're safe or it's ok, caution should be heeded at this time. T he accident, kept within context of the dream, should be relevant to your everyday working life and/or closely resemble real lif e situations. This will help you narrow down the specifics, and steer clear, of an accident.

Otherwise noted, per your lifestyle, if your dream closely resembled real life situations, meaning it can actually occur during your awaked state, this dream may be an Ordinary Dream, resulting from daily activities (see Chapter One, Chalom). These sorts of dreams are usually about your routine, mundane activities or anxieties that overwhelm your mind during the day. They are an inner release mechanism, which helps provide you with emotional balance and the maintaining of your sanity. These dreams are not significant, and do not warrant special attention.

However, if your dream was inundated with symbols that are not easily linked to your life activities, then the spiritual implications (the interpretation) should be heeded.

CURRENCY, MONEY, CONTRACTS

(a system of money or other items used as a medium of exchange
or an agreement between two people for services)

Buy the truth, and sell it not; Yea, wisdom, and instruction, and understanding (Proverbs 23:23 ASV)

*But the wise answered, saying, 'No, lest there should not be enough for us
and you; but go rather to those who sell, and buy for yourselves.' And while
they went to buy, the bridegroom came (Matthew 25:9-10 NKJV)*

*This is the message from the one who is the Amen the faithful and true witness,
the beginning of God's new creation: So I advise you to buy gold from me gold that
has been purified by fire. Then you will be rich. (Revelation 3:14, 18 NLT)*

*For the love of money is a source of all kinds of evil; and in their eager desire to be rich some have been
led astray from the faith, and have pierced themselves with many sorrows. (1 Timothy 6:10 MON)*

This category deals with the various mediums of exchange. Some short descriptions of types, phrases, and other processes and particulars, connected in some way to this category are, for example, coins of brass, bronze, copper, gold, iron, silver, credit cards, debit cards, gift cards, paper money, precious gems, anything received and sanctioned by law and usage as legal tender, money changer, banker, scales, balances, wages. Also, see category content list, or index.

All Symbols and Referents, Notes (1, 2, 3, etc.), Suggested Course of Action, and Specific Meaning offer guidance toward a more comprehensive interpretation.

Notes

1. Unless otherwise noted elsewhere, if, in your everyday living, your awaked state, as part of your lifestyle, work, or ministerial activities, or a special event, you have a very real connection with any activity involving money or other items used as mediums of exchange. For example, accounting, banking, bartering, benefactor, bookkeeper, broker, cashier, cash handler, CFO, economist, financial consultant, fiscal operations, lottery, money changer, pawn broker, precious gems dealer, tax preparer, stock market, Wall Street, or any activity or business involved in the handling or exchange of money or any mediums of exchange, skip interpretation and go to Specific Meaning: of this category.

    Otherwise noted, this dream may be a Prophetically Simple Dream (see Chapter One: The 60th Part of Prophecy). Whereas, the dreamer is warned to stop any illegal or illicit activity going on within your life that involves any mediums of exchange, e.g. illegal or illicit handling of art, diamonds or other precious gems, drugs, merchandise, weapons, or embezzlement, money laundering, kidnapping, prostitution, robberies, or any other criminal minded, under-handed activity that primarily involves currency. You should surrender to the appropriate authorities, especially if this is an issue within the dreamer's life, or submit or yield to other relevant persons. If any of the preceding is happening, this dream is a first step intervention and an alarm. Skip interpretation and re-consider your activity as harmful, hurtful, illegal, or life threatening, at present. Handle the situation appropriately by surrendering, first to God, for Adonai Elohim knows all, and then to appropriate authorities or relevant others. Also, see Specific Meaning at the end of this category, section entitled, Note (Specific Meaning).

    Otherwise noted, per your lifestyle, if your dream closely resembled real life situations, meaning it can actually occur during your awaked state, this dream may be an Ordinary Dream, resulting from your daily activities (see Chapter One, Chalom). These sorts of dreams are usually about your routine, mundane activities or anxieties that overwhelm your mind during the day. They are an inner release mechanism, which helps provide you with emotional balance and the maintaining of your sanity. These dreams are not significant, and do not warrant special attention.

2. Probables: As currency is frequently demonstrated in many, and very personal ways; for example, were you a victim of a Ponzi scheme? Do you have a lawsuit pending? Thus, could the medium of exchange depicted be a possible probable (see Chapter One, section entitled, Probables)? Hence, dreamer may also consider your own personal and special associations with various mediums of exchange, as long as the interpretation is kept within the principles of spiritual boundary markers, landmarks, and property lines, (see Chapter One, section entitled, Spiritualizing Boundary Marker s, Landmarks, and Property Lines).

3. Determine who your dream is for you or another. Always, considering yourself first, reflecting on your present behaviors. Ask yourself, why am I dreaming about this now? What is this dream revealing about me? Have I taken on new attributes? Has anyone commented on my present behaviors as being untypical of me? Has my ministry changed for the better or for the worse? What about my beliefs, doctrine, or philosophy, are they still based on Holy Writ? Is there something I need to know about those I am ministering to or serving?

   Remember your actions and emotions within your dream. Was the dreamer a banker, broker, dealer, or a money handler in any way? Did dreamer have an issue with the way the currency was handled? Was the dreamer in any way, a sponsor of a fundraiser or contributor to charity? Did dreamer need charity? Did dreamer receive a check or was given currency, diamonds, or any other costly item that had a value attached to it? Was dreamer a prostitute? Unless otherwise noted elsewhere, an answer of yes, to one or more of these, or similar questions, is a good indicator that your dream is about you (the dreamer). What happened to you in your dream? How did things end? In light of your dream, via the relevant interpretation, do you believe that your choices will enhance or endanger your well-being, safety, and/ or happiness, if so, how and why? Do you believe that your belief system will strengthen or weaken you spiritually in any way, if so, how and why? Is spiritual or physical death a possibility? For example, are you sharing the "Good News" for profit only? Are you perpetuating a "twisted" prosperity message that primarily feeds greed? Are you perhaps ministering to others at your own expense and is now beginning to feel "angry" at God about the expense? Are you drawing back on financially supporting the ministry? See following relevant subcategory, the interpretation is about and for you.

   Was someone else the banker, broker, dealer, or a money handler in any way? Was someone else a primary sponsor of an event? Did another donate a sizeable contribution to a college? Did another receive charity? Did another rob a bank? Was another a prostitute? Did someone steal from his or her mother? Unless otherwise noted elsewhere, an answer of yes, to one or more of these, or similar questions, is a good indicator that your dream is about another and their role, and/or influential effects, within the life of the dreamer. Does another find fault with your financial support of God's church, and/or His people? Are you dealing with someone, who truly believes in their heart that they will not have to give an account of their service to Heavenly Father? Are they enhancing your spiritual and/or literal prosperity, or are they responsible for the dwindling thereof? Do you know someone whose life activities or physical being is similar to that which stood out the most within your dream? Could it be that person? If you sense that your dream is for or about another, the question as to why you have been made privy to this information, and how do you factor into the equation, should be seriously considered along with necessary actions. Perhaps the dreamer is being made aware of the plight of someone, and you are to get involved (see Chapter One, Are You Ready to Hear the Messages in Your Dreams, section entitled, The 10% for others).

If your dream is for, or about another:

Dreams that reference others and the revelation within those dreams, is not given haphazardly to any individual, but only to those with the ability, and influence to do something with the information; this is also prophecy. With that, journal the following questions, and if unable to answer the questions now, this denotes that the person, represented within your dream, will enter your life shortly. Are you entering into a personal relationship with someone? Do you not know or understand what you're looking at, especially certain behaviors, when learning about this person? Has someone new entered your life or maybe you've just begun opening up to someone not so new, and have started listening to their advice, accepting their assistance, or are you supporting or enabling someone? Are you in denial regarding the toxicity of one of your present relationships, particularly a spouse, family member, or friend? Are you anxious, concerned, frightened, and/or troubled by recent changes in your behavior, especially because of someone's influence upon your life at present? Have you allowed someone to convince you to deceive another? Have you recently become aware of (or is being made aware of, via your dream) certain undesirable behaviors within you towards another? Are you trying to cut ties with one that is bad company? Have you just joined (or re-joined) a church, fellowship, or social group?

Note: If your dream has attributes that indicate that your dream is about you, and other attributes that indicate that your dream is about another, dreamer should consider that your dream is about you and another. For example, did dreamer meet and converse with a millionaire? Did another rob a bank, and held the dreamer hostage? Was the dreamer a participant in a money laundering scheme with others? Did another have an issue with the way the dreamer paid them their rightful wage? Did another donate a sizeable contribution to the dreamer's event? Did another receive charity from the dreamer? Did dreamer kidnap someone for ransom money? Thus indicating that your dream is about the dreamer, and another; therefore, while your dream is about the dreamer, the dreamer should expect the role and/or influential effects of another, also plays a part in your interpretation. For example, was dreamer part of a bank robbing gang? And now dreamer is facing jail time for his or her part, again, see relevant interpretation.

More questions to consider. Why has the person been allowed within your life, and/or how did they get there? Again, if unable to answer the questions now, this denotes that the person, represented within your dream, will enter your life shortly. If their activity, within your dream, has proven positive, via the interpretation, this someone will prove, unwittingly, to be a very strong ally, benefactor, defender, and supporter. God has sent this someone into your life to help you carry out your next endeavor by enlarging your spiritual capacity. Allow the strength of that person's character to guide, help, and support you. On the other hand, if his or her presence and/or activity, within your dream, proved negative, via the interpretation, for sure, this person will prove to be a very strong and formidable challenge for you, perhaps unto death. If negative, this dream is a dire warning. Take steps accordingly to struggle against, or to cut off, adverse and unfavorable relationships. Remember certain personalities are all encompassing, affecting everything, cataclysmic, contagious, deadly, harmful, infectious, predatory, and/or venomous. Symbolically meaning that if allowed to continue or prosper within your life, serious harm or death to the dreamer may result. Idolize no one, especially beyond the warning of the Lord, and we are definitely not to lay our lives down for no one. Then again, this person maybe allowed within your life, because of the dreamer's unwillingness to abstain from immorality after having been asked to abstain from such by God, see 1 Corinthians 6:9-20, Galatians 5:19-21, or the dreamer's self-righteous behavior, or a lack of a balanced and honest view of your own personality. In this case, this person will affect self-awareness within the life of the dreamer, exposing the negative traits of your personality, especially those traits, which cause you to follow, or to be so easily misled, and/or your wrong beliefs; no matter, this type of mentality needs reckoning with. Graciously, all of this will restore the dreamer to his or her right place with God, opening your eyes to see how far you've strayed from God (1 Corinthians 5:4-7; James 5:20). The lesson is, no matter how personable, powerful, or difficult a person, or how uncertain or unpopular the choices and issues, always take the next biblical and ethical step, for obedience to God's principles will always prove safer and stronger foundationally. Although, you will need all kinds of outside support to recover from this person's domination, no longer, allow that particular person's influence within your life to continue or thrive, especially if negative, end it abruptly.

4. Consider all the people, places, backgrounds, and activity highlighted within your dream.
   Known (in your awaked life) person, animal, place, or organization within your dream:
   Unless otherwise noted elsewhere, people, animals, places, backgrounds that are actually known by the dreamer in your awaked life, indicates a part of you that you recognize within yourself on some level or another. Question to journal, if dreamer seriously considers the person, animal, place, or background attributes, what character traits stood out the most, or what features stood out the most. For example, age, color, height, size, happiness, considerate, loving, let you be yourself, peacefulness, encourager, irrational, leader, liar, mentor, passionate, personable, neglected, poor, run-down, sage, shyster, unwise, upscale, vengeful. Write down (journal) the particular highlighted within your dream. The attribute or activity highlighted is for a reason. Since the attribute written down is a part of you, namely the dreamer's nature, demeanor, and/or lifestyle, an honest and unbiased assessment is very important for truth sake. Happy note, considering that other people's attributes, within dreams, also represent attributes of your own personality, causes one to look at another in a better light. According to your capacity to embrace self-awareness and a rectification of mind, body, and spirit, God will begin to enhance, make better, more attractive, sanctify, diminish, and make pure and free from sin and guilt, this part of you.
   Otherwise noted, if the person, animal, place, or background within your dream is actually known by the dreamer, in your awaked life, this person, animal, place, or background may represent him or herself, or itself.
   Unknown in your awaked life or although known, was unseen, invisible, or only talked about - person, animal, place, or organization within your dream:
   Unless otherwise noted elsewhere, if you did not recognize, the person, place, thing, they, or it, was not seen, invisible, or only talked about within your dream, this indicates an attribute or activity within your life that you are unfamiliar with, or are in denial about, or you refuse to acknowledge it, but it does exists. Question to journal: what character trait, feature, action, or activity, stood out the most? For example, age, color, height, size, happiness, considerate, loving, let you be yourself, peacefulness, encourager, irrational, leader, liar, mentor, passionate, personable, neglected, poor, run-down, sage, shyster, unwise, upscale, vengeful. Although, on some conscious level, you are aware of a certain behavior or attribute within you, you have chosen to filter out or simply ignore certain information about yourself that contradicts your view of yourself and/or your preconceived notions of others and of the world around you. Possibly protecting yourself, emotionally and psychologically, from a situation, which you are unable to cope with at this time, or you lack control over; then again, perhaps the dreamer has an exaggerated or unrealistic view of yourself. No matter the reason, right now a question is before you, via your dream. Do you want to know this part of yourself? According to your ability to handle self-awareness, God will begin to reveal this side of you to you. Why, He wants to balance your understanding of things; thus, effecting wholeness within your life, so that the enemy will no longer be able to manipulate your emotions so easily. The Paraclete is with you to help you throughout this entire process, listen to Him. Now, in your life, this activity or attribute needs reckoning with, somehow or someway.
   Otherwise noted, (known or unknown), if the person, place or thing that initiated (or was

a recipient of) the action or activity within your dream was not seen, invisible, or only talked about within your dream, this may indicate that the dreamer does not recognize the influential effects another has within your life, or upon your attitude.

If more than one person (known or unknown):

Consider what the group had in common. What behavior, character trait, feature, action, or activity, stood out the most? For example, were they argumentative, authoritative, beautiful, criminal minded, dancing, difficult, dressed unusual, enigmatic, fighting, focused, flirty, helpful, hurtful intentions, powerful, promiscuous, quiet, secretive, seemed unreal, unassuming? That which was highlighted and noted is what you need to focus on at present. If the attribute or quality is a desirable or positive one, allow the strength of that attribute to help you overcome some manner of immorality or irreverence within your life and/or to help you to become better, productively, for the Kingdom of God in some manner. If the attribute is an undesirable or negative one, take steps accordingly to struggle against the growing desires of the carnal side of you. If applicable, get help and support via prayer, fasting, and a Christian based support group.

For dreams of the dead see following note.

Did you have problems paying for a funeral? While the dead has nothing to do with the living (Ecclesiastes 9:4-6), it may be considered what character trait did that person represent to the dreamer, while the person was actually alive, what character feature stood out the most. With that trait noted, dreamer may consider that the trait noted, is within the dreamer, and that trait is no longer useful or needed for the progression of your spiritual walk, on this side of heaven. Dreamer, it is suggested that you render that trait (good or bad) obsolete, and began anew attempting to move forward, using different tactics to overcome unproductive habitual life cycle choices, and for maneuvering through this thing we call life in a more, better way. See category, Death, and/or other relevant categories.

5. In addition to the following interpretations, see index or relevant categories for more information. For example, if a discount in value or amount was involved in some way, see category, Abating, if embezzlement was highlighted, see category, Cheating. If counting was highlighted, see category, Numbers. Kept within context of your dream and the interpretation, the additional symbols are perhaps relevant. It will be within the sum of all the symbols that you will find a more thorough interpretation.

6. Since the following list is not extensive, dreamer is encouraged to seek biblical guidelines and other relevant research to determine the metaphorical meaning of your particular currency, depicted within your dream, via a Bible concordance, Bible illustrated dictionary, encyclopedia, or internet. Having done your research you should be able to determine some basic behaviors or attributes your Lord and Savior wants you to focus on.

Symbols and Referents

Most dreams of mediums of exchange generally imply, coupled with the relevant interpretation that conditionally, God is completely restoring things materially and spiritually within your life and in the lives of those immediately connected to yo u, per dreamer meeting the prerequisites. As well, these types of dreams touch on the status of your spiritual life, as well as the intents and purposes of your heart regarding your spiritual life.

In addition to the varied meanings of actions and activities, other common words, expressions, usages, (e.g. slang or clichés), or a 'probable' that are metaphorically represented by any of the following are also considered (this section is an addendum at the end of the category or subcategory).

Category Content - If not listed see index, perchance, for your specific type of currency dream.

- Accountant, Banker, Bookkeeper, Broker, Cashier, Cash Handler, CFO, Economist, Financial Consultant, Fiscal Operations, Moneychanger, Stock Market, Tax Preparer, Wall Street, or any business involved in the handling or exchange of money, currency, see subcategory Working, Work places (Accountant)
- Cheap, cheaply (cheapness is highlighted in some manner), see category, Abating
- Contracts (agreement between two people for services, legally binding)
- Counterfeit Currency
- Currency (e.g. credit cards, debit cards, gift cards, paper money)
- Embezzlement, burglary, larceny, robbery, stealing money, see subcategory, Cheating, Thievery
- Food Stamps or Social Service Benefits (e.g. welfare)
- Gift, Inheritance, or Endowment (something acquired without compensation)
- Merchant, Bargainer, Barterer, Dealer, Marketer, Trader, or Pawnbroker (anyone engaged in bartering, retail trade, marketing, merchandising, and/or in export and import of goods and services)
- Precious Metals and other coins (e.g. brass, bronze, copper, dimes, gold, nickels, pennies, quarters, silver, and other coins)
  - Gold and Silver, also see category, Colors (gold or silver)
- Savings, Trust, Settlement, or Bank (any depository financial institution or any property held by one party, the trustee, for the benefit of another, the beneficiary)
- Stones, Gems, or Prized Art (e.g. amethyst, diamonds, emeralds, opals, pearls, rubies, sapphires, topaz, turquoise, or prized art, e.g. Da Vinci, Michelangelo, Monet, Picasso, Rembrandt, Van Gogh)
- Wage (compensation paid for work, e.g. pay check)
  - Illegal Wages (e.g. drug money, gigolo, murder for hire, prostitution), see subcategory Working, Work places (Work illegally)

CONTRACTS (agreement between two people for services, legally binding):

This dream has three meanings (choose one). (1) If contract was annulled, broken, violated, or void, your dream is an alarm to the dreamer, for it denotes one committing loathsome, highly offensive sins. The dreamer has acted very treacherously, deceitfully, and faithlessly, offending many, as well as, God. You are an oppressor of God's people. You have lived in luxury and self-indulgence, using the money of those who do not dispute your words. Dreamer, your spiritual life is something that should be valued, as well as, your reputation. For, even a good reputation and great wisdom can be easily lost and counted foul. One bad act or choice is hurtful to a good name; not only spoiling the goodness of it, but making it now, a name of ill-repute; base, disgraceful, low, scandalous, wicked (Ecclesiastes 10:1). Dreamer, your desires, appetites, and attitude are leading to a chaotic and empty life. A life figuratively similar to the condition of earth in Genesis 1:2, wasteful, empty, and dark. This type of carnal strain and toil leads to sorrow and spiritual darkness. As well, the money of those you've used will testify against you. Your behavior and choices will bring great dishonor to you, and your home, if not already. Notwithstanding, dreamer, the cries of an innocent person against you, has reached the ears of the Lord Almighty. You will weep and wail because of the misery that is coming upon you. Dreamer, you are counseled to flee immorality, and you must bring your appetites, lusts, sensual desires, deceitfulness, and faithlessness under subjection, sacrificing fleshy satisfaction for the cause of Christ, engaging all your power, with the help of the Paraclete, to do God's will. You will have to practice restricting yourself in all things; this includes your activities, associations, and friendships as well (see Psalm 119:9). Dreamer, the place where God wants to take you, demands great personal sacrifice of rights and freedoms and requires the subduing of your passions. "To whom much is given, much is required". See suggested course of action. (2) If another breached the contract, in any way, this denotes that amongst all those who say that they love you, the dreamer, most have dealt very treacherously with you, and are as foes; fortunately, the enemy has not prevailed. You will now begin to see the manifestation of divine vengeance against those who trouble you. You will get relief from those who oppress you, and if pertinent, you or a loved one will get release from imprisonment. Nonetheless, be encourage, the wicked will cease from troubling, God will validate you and, if applicable, your children, and you will return to a place or state of safety and plenty. On another vei n, all this will follow the downfall of a ministry you're connected too. This ministry is syncretistic, and it does not include the atonement work of Christ. Fortunately, the dreamer and/or a close family member will return to Christ and to a bible believing, faith based church. (3) If no breach, in any way, this denotes that the dreamer is one who is approaching spiritual maturity. Dreamer, you are undefiled according to biblical standards, down-to-earth, fair, humble, just, unpretentious, not rude, or obscene, and one whom a believer may interact with socially on very personal levels (e.g. business associate, friendship, ministry, and spouse). Therefore, take care to do your rightful duties (obligation to God, family, and if applic able, to country), offering mature service and exercising mature judgment. Moreover, the floodgates of heaven are open to you. Those floodgates are fullness in your spirituality, the glory of God in the midst of your life, and blessings of God. Gifts of God's grace, anything God freely gives you, absolution, the Holy Spirit, salvation, regeneration, eternal life, health, children, love of family, longevity, necessities, prosperity, and dominion over all that is yours; and all are parts of the supply of grace, an d all are sanctified by the Lord, and technically belongs to Him. The result of this supply in your life will be peace.

COUNTERFEIT CURRENCY:

This type of dream, challenges the dreamer to appreciate wisdom. Wisdom and folly, advertise similar want ads. Both broadcast they are deeply mysterious, meaningful, and fun. Question, did dreamer determine the counterfeit? You will choose wisdom. Nevertheless, wisdom exalts God and leads to spiritual maturity and genuine joy, while folly cheapens and runs down life, bringing upon the head God's asperity and early death. The quality of being rash and foolish indicates a loss of self-respect, due to a cheapening of one's self-value and talents, as well as a loss of respect from others. Further, dreamer, just as you would grieve if your integrity, self-worth, and your dignity were cheapen or compromised, God Himself grieves, via Holy Spirit, when His integrity, His worth, His dignity are cheapen or compromised by us. When we do not have faith in God and in His covenant promises, principles, and comforts to humanity; His integrity, worth, and dignity are cheapened and diminished within us. To value or have faith in God, which is a resolute trust in the integrity of God and in His Word, is to please Hi m, for God's integrity, worth, and dignity, is His Word. Dreamer, you are becoming a Christian leader, so you are caution to lead by wisdom, or you will shipwreck. You must strive to have faith in your God, and confidence in His Word, especially if you are to influence the rest of the world to embrace His Word and His Way also. When you do this; then God will wipe away the tears from your face and eyes (Isaiah 25:8, Revelation 7:17). Therefore, be observant and pray, thus, found by God, mindful of Him. Moreover, read, Proverbs 26:1-28. Really, understand the differences between the two persons. Additionally, according to divine order, as God blesses and prospers you, give Him a tenth of service. One example, tithing God 10% of your day, via 2 hours and 40 minutes of deeply private and personal pray, praise, and meditation on His Word (Joshua 1:8, 9). See suggested course of action.

CURRENCY (e.g. credit cards, debit cards, gift cards, paper money):

This dream has two meanings (choose one). (1) Credit Cards or Credit: Dreamer, you have the passion and determination to accomplish the extraordinary and you are very difficult to defeat. You have charisma, and a following to prove it; you are well known. Moreover, you are focused, highly creative, reserved, serious, strongly independent, charming, and good looking. On the other hand, dreamer, although you have some very strong qualities, your dream denotes one who is sly and cunning, and who brings confusion into situations. You have a natural instinct for putting people at ease, while keeping up a bunch of background mess. You are insincere in your dealings with people, outwardly friendly but secretly cunning, disloyal, and unfair. Thus, your dream is to open wide the eyes of, and disconcert, a secure and careless person, the dreamer, who proclaims peace to yourself. With a calm resignation, you say you are godly and will inherit paradise, yet you have no genuine love for Christ Jesus, the Door into paradise (see John 5:39), nor His people. You are becoming godless, rebellious, demonically lead, and one who spreads a false doctrine. For example, you perpetuating a "twisted" prosperity message that primarily feeds greed, or sharing the "Good News" for profit only. In this, you are considered, a "hireling". Whatever the issue, the dreamer is on a path of declining from a higher standard of spiritual life and living to a lower state, so somethings need to be addressed. Dreamer, a person's character is hurt and gives off a foul odor, by sinful folly, especially in the life of one respected for honor (Ecc lesiastes 10:1). Your dream is to warn a rebellious person, in the spirit of grace (the free and unmerited favor and beneficence of God). The Creator has granted you a reprieve or pardon to set things in order. This is one of God's ways of calling you back unto Him that you might be saved, and to see if you will yet be worked upon, and change your mindset; or else to leave you inexcusable, in your accusations against God, because of your ruin. Thus, it is recommended that the dreamer seriously consider the resul ts of your behavior. See suggested course of action. (2) Debit Cards, Gift Card, or Paper Money: This choice has three parts (choose one). (a) Your dream denotes healing to one who has been suffering physically, mentally, or emotionally, especially with heart issues (physical or emotional). There is a struggle within you, between your old nature and your new nature, the leftovers of sin and the new beginnings of grace. Your old nature is resisting everything that is spiritual and is opposing all the suggestions of the Holy Spirit and the ethical urgings of your conscience. This is spiritual circumcision of the heart. Fortunately, you are choosing to side with godly principles and to stand on your convictions. Dreamer, you will have success overcoming old things; and there will be joy about your success, especially publicly. Now, the old has gone, and the new has come (2 Corinthians 5:17). Furthermore, due to the intensity of your struggle, one of God's messengers is sent to give you the support needed at this time. Be aware that the new person within your midst may be that messenger. With that said, this is necessary to say, read, understand, and embrace John 5:14. Dreamer, you are healed, now, stop sinning so that something worse doesn't happen to you. See suggested course of action. (b) Your dream symbolizes the union of a groom and bride, and if relevant a pregnancy. The dreamer will marry sooner than you think. Additionally, you, or if male, your spouse, is either pregnant, or will become pregnant very shortly. If not pregnant, and you desire children, continue to have faith in God, which is a resolute trust in the integrity of God and in His Word, He will have mercy on you, and grant you the desire of your hear t, namely to birth children, suddenly and very soon. (c) Your dream denotes the fruit of your natural talents, pursuits, and morality is coming into full fruition, as your dream denotes a ministry will be birth from within you, the dreamer. You are full of nurturing abilities; thus, you will become, responsible for a few young men and women being born again into the Kingdom of God (see John 3:1-17). You know how to nurture and accept anyone; therefore, many will be drawn to you, including those, others call "ne'er-do-wells", via your ministry. Under your tutelage, those newly born into the Body of Christ will become strong and active, for the cause of the Kingdom of God. They will be known as persons who speak and does that which is good, counted amongst those who are faithful and submissive to God. Dreamer, be willing, obedient, prepared, and in place (accountable to a specific house of worship, church), for the birthing of your ministry and for those who will become born again because of your ministry. God's providential blessing is upon you to increase. All things will be made beautiful in their own time. With that said, dreamer, do not boast of your increase, and be very mindful of your words, for the universal law, with the same judgments, you judge others, so will you be judged, is still applicable to you. For example, words used in a patronizing and condescending manner towards others and/or embracing a judgmental nature, especially after you've reached prosperity, your same words and behaviors, and in like manner, will confront you, when understanding is expected. Your conduct towards others (for benefit or harm) will be openly manifested before all. You will reap what you have sown. See suggested course of action.

In addition, the following are common words, expressions, usages, (e.g. slang or clichés), or a 'probable' that are metaphorically represented by money:

- For the love of money is a source of all kinds of evil; and in their eager desire to be rich some have been led astray from the faith, and have pierced themselves with many sorrows. (1 Timothy 6:10 MON)
- Money is also a symbol of commercialism or greed

FOOD STAMPS OR SOCIAL SERVICE BENEFITS (e.g. welfare):

This dream has two meanings (choose one). (1) Dreamer is actually in need of some manner of social service benefits, be it food stamps, emergency housing, or some other benefits. Dreamer, social service benefits has its place, especially in times of need or emergencies. Fortunately, dreamer, you have a natural ability to get what you need for your survival. Th erefore, humble yourself, and go and seek social service assistance at this time. Furthermore, this season too shall pass. (2) First, what your dream references, the dreamer has unequivocally heard before. What God has been speaking to you, and is requiring of you, has been clearly laid-out earlier, there is no doubt or misunderstanding; you know His will, and it leads to only one conclusion; what you have heard on other occasions, at other times, is true, and denial of that truth is unacceptable at this point. This is dream a third or fourth warning. Dreamer, you've been clearly told to come out from among unbelievers, and to separate yourself from them, says the Lord, for what company has righteousness with unrighteousness, or what sharing of personal thoughts and feelings has light with darkness. Have nothing to do with their sinful and wicked deeds, and I will welcome you, read, understand, and embrace 2 Corinthians 6:14-18. Unfortunately, dreamer, concerned with your own interest, you are driven by, and occupied with, sensual appetites, rather than spiritual needs. Your new way is based on exploring alternatives to God's righteous principles, as well as, creating a sense of unity with the wickedness around you. You have adopted a bourgeois mentality. This mentality is concerned only with your personal comfort, material wealth, and status, at any expense. You, now, having in yourself nothing that you respect more than power and greed, are willing to sacrifice all, God, principle, family, and friend, to the image or idol of vanity. This mentality sacrifices children, family, and morality to the hollowness of satisfying immoral desires and appetites. All carried out, with the hope of finding happiness by pacifying jealously and covetousness. Dreamer, the selling-out of yourself over to immorality, allowing wickedness to prevail in your home, devaluing those you should be protecting and nurturing, while closing your eyes to it all, are all principles based on values that are not only vile, but also increasingly unstable. This way cries out against godly ethics, and its' end offends any sense of godliness. Moreover, your desires, appetites, and attitude are leading to a chaotic and empty life. This type of c arnal strain and toil leads to sorrow and spiritual darkness. There is a need to re-connect with God. Favorably, because of God's love for you, His abounding grace, and His long-suffering, there is a ray of light, sent by God, purposed to break through the darkness of your state of affairs. This ray of light is a person, anointed and sent, especially to you. Their words and inspiration will be to you, like Genesis 1:3-5 is to Genesis 1:2. Illuminatingly wise, this person will powerfully affect your life, externally and internally. Their inspiration, coupled with you earnestly embracing change, humility, contentedness, integrity, ethicalness, and a renewed faith in God's word and His process, will strengthen you to return in complete heartfelt repentance to Jesus, from a heart of love. By this, the severity of your transgressions becomes partially sweetened; for, when a man or woman genuinely return to God, in complete surrender and humility, your deliberate transgressions become like actual merits, aka "the sweetening" (Luke 7:37-50). Because, the realization of your distance from God, due to your transgressions (Isaiah 59:2-21; Luke 15:11-24), becomes the motivating force to return to God with a passion even greater than that of someone who has never sinned in such a manner, or never left the Father's house, completely converting your present to good (Acts 9:1-30). This is the secret of repentance and returning to God. Go; therefore now, and seek the

Lord Jesus, repent and place your hope in Him. Hope, placed in Him, will not deceive. If, you turn and genuinely repent, you will be favored with complete healing, however, go and sin no more. For, if anyone knows the good they ought to do and doesn't do it, it is sin for them (see James 4:17). From this moment forward, choose good habits and deeds, e.g. good stewardship and commitment to ministry; speak to yourself what is true and good, embracing Philippians 4:8. Authentic repentance, will affect complete restoration of things, materially and spiritually within your life and in the lives of those immediately connected to you; allowing freedom from your weaknesses to be yours. See suggested course of action.

GIFT, INHERITANCE, OR ENDOWMENT (something acquired without compensation):

This dream has two meanings (choose one). (1) Dreamer grace is being extended to you, via a verifiable miracle within the area of your mind or head, and deliverance from the dangers of your fleshly passions. Moreover, there will be a divine work upon your emotions, and this will manifest within your life in the form of liberality in Christ Jesus, thankfulness, and joy. All this is preparation, that you may become qualified, proven worthy, spiritually, morally, and ethically, for a religious position within an ecclesiastical order. Additionally, there is a need to make a sacrificial offering, financially, to the ministry which, you are connected. Weigh, he, or she who sows sparingly shall reap sparingly; and he or she who sows bountifully shall reap bountifully. Let each man or woman do according as you have purposed in your heart, not grudgingly, or of necessity for God loves a cheerful giver. For, God is able to make all grace abound unto you; that you, having always all sufficiency in every thing, may abound unto every good work (2 Corinthians 9:6-8). If necessary, see suggested course of action. (2) Dreamer will be gratuitously presented with two favors from two very different and very strong allies, benefactors, defenders, or supporters, via an "in-kindness" gift or grant, or through a pardon or forgiveness of a very large debt (e.g. auto loan, bank loan, college, student loan, or mortgage). Warning, the following is cautionary advice, therefore, dreamer, give ear. Dreamer two "favors" will be presented to you, one sacred, one profane. The key to knowing which favor is sacred, and which is profane. The profane favor will ask you to compromise your beliefs, namely to "gray area" some of God's unequivocal positions on certain tenets. Dreamer, never do you ever compromise your beliefs in Jesus Christ, as the Word of God made flesh, nor do you distort the meanings of His Holy Word, for any manner of favor, for this is akin to spiritual prostitution, aka idolatry. For example, they will require you to, perhaps, violently condemn those who voice their beliefs against the present political situation, sexual perversions, or any ideologies that differ and/or threaten their agenda. Therefore, consider carefully what is being presented to you, who is presenting it, and what "conditions" might be attached to the gift. Additionally, there is a need to make a sacrificial offering, financially, to the ministry which, you are connected. Weigh, he, or she who sows sparingly shall reap sparingly; and he or she who sows bountifully shall reap bountifully. Let each man or woman do according as you have purposed in your heart, not grudgingly, or of necessity for God loves a cheerful giver. For, God is able to make all grace a bound unto you; that you, having always all sufficiency in everything, may abound unto every good work (2 Corinthians 9:6-8). If necessary, see suggested course of action.

MERCHANT, BARGAINER, BARTERER, DEALER, MARKETER, TRADER, OR PAWNBROKER (anyone engaged in bartering, retail trade, marketing, merchandising, and/or in export and import of goods and services):

Your dream denotes an unsteadiness within the dreamer's spirit. The cause of the unsteadiness, and restoration, will become clear, if dreamer would but hold on to Jesus. Couple this with one of the following three (choose one). (1) If unethical dealings were depicted in any form, within your dream, e.g. "bait and switch", selling or trading inferior products, selling products at exorbitant prices, or lying to a consumer, etc. Your dream denotes a spirit of covetousness. Your insatiable desire for wealth and extreme greed for material wealth is reprehensible. Dreamer, only when the sin of coveting is rectified, will you recover from its' disastrous and deadly effects. You will not be able to rise before your enemies until you remove covetousness from your heart. Overcoming covetousness must first be done through prayer and then worked out in practice (Philippians 4:12, 13). Moreover, it is counseled that dreamer deal with apprehension, discouragement, pride, little to no s elf- awareness, and a lack of direction and guidance. See suggested course of action. (2) Male dreamer, your dream comes as cautionary advice about something imminent, especially some manner of unpleasantness, and as encouragement to the dreamer. Dreamer, your spirit of haughtiness, inexperience, and feelings of rejection, has led (or is leading) you into a precarious position, a situation that exposes your arrogance, as well as, your unethical aspirations, possibly "I'll show you one day" attitude. Fortunately, the precarious position you find (or will find) yourself in, is allowed, to affect humility, wisdom, and sense of purpose, within you like nothing else could. Therefore, you must now not allow yourself to get tired of choosing to live the right way, that is living life on God's terms, nor get tired of choosing the good over the evil. Read and understand, Isaiah 7:15, Hebrews 5:8. Dreamer, hold on to Jesus, through the darkness of "broken-down" by turning to Jesus and offering praise. However, this kind of praise, this kind of "hallelujah", is not the result of a happy feeling, or is not necessarily from one who has seen the light. It is offered through the teeth of pain, it is broken, and it is offered in spite of emotional numbn ess. This kind of praise is offered to Jesus as a pure act of obedience, and as a naked act of the will. It comes from a place deep down, within the heart, beneath the changes and turnarounds of feelings, and the vicissitudes of life. Such acts of praise a re acts of defiance, through which we defy the darkness, and confess our faith in Jesus who lives above tears, and who calls us to Himself, the One and only Light of the world, and He is the only rescuer for those in the darkness of pain and despair. When one, namely the dreamer, is able to praise Jesus in such circumstances, you are acknowledging that you are not the center of the universe, and that your pain and loss, though personally difficult, has not changed the faithfulness of God. Like Job lo oking to God, who appeared to him out of the whirlwind, dreamer, lift up your eyes from yourself to behold the Lord, and find a whole new perspective and peace. Moreover, while you have the opportunity, do good to all people, and especially to those who are of the household of faith (Galatians 6:8-10). By this, you will experience favor that lifts one up from despair and promotes. Therefore, if not already, bring joy and inspiration to many by your creative talents, via writing, drama, music, speaking, or teaching. Dreamer, your unique style of artistic expression, especially in presenting the gospel of Jesus Christ, is the gift you bring to the world. In time, dreamer, you will experience the Shekinah, a glow of the Light of God's goodness, if you remain diligent and don't give up on your spiritual journey. For sure, you will receive your just due, on this side of heaven, at the proper time, and everlasting life, if you don't give up. (3) Female dreamer, God knows that you're tired and you're feeling alone. Dreamer, due to your challenging life activities, personal illness, and/ or the wearying of others, you have become very exhausted emotionally. Overcome by profound discouragement and a sense of being alone in your conflicts, coupled with exhaustion, an old familiar lifestyle has reared (or will rear) up its' ugly head to try to take advantage of your physical weakness. Dreamer, although you are in the midst of hard trails, and tribulations, you are being purified spiritual ly. Whatever is going on, wherever you are, God's presence is there with you. He alone will deliver you out of the snares of the enemy. Dreamer, you are not alone; neither should you feel that way. Only, do not falter, for God is with you at all times. He is able to care for you, to care for His ministry He has assigned to you, and He knows where you are. The hope, labor, love, and struggle of your life's work are not in vain. Learn from your experience and mature. There will come a season of time when God, in a dramatic way, will bring deliverance and restorations for you, for you have been deemed righteous. This deliverance speaks of hope, prosperity, and unprecedented blessings; there is a "breaking of day" for you and there will be joy. In time, dreamer, you will experience the Shekinah, a glow of the Light of God's goodness, if you remain diligent and don't give up on your spiritual journey. Additionally, dreamer, you have a direct link to inspiration, which you can develop and use to help others; a gift or talent to do creative works; creating things that spiritually inspires others. You also have the capacity to be a sagacious spiritual counselor, empathically understanding the vicissitudes of life, and you are able to articulate those changes in life, in a way that can be easily understood and received by others. This is your gift to the world, your purpose. By this, you will experience favor that lifts one up from despair and promotes. Therefore, if not already, it is time that you begin usin g your inspirations to help encourage others, through their spiritual journey.

PRECIOUS METALS AND OTHER COINS (e.g. brass, bronze, copper, dimes, gold, nickels, pennies, quarters, silver, and other coins):

This dream has three meanings (choose one). (1) There is a conflict, which needs to be resolved, between the dreamer and another, be it a family member, or friend, or foe. The core cause of the conflict is your own stubbornness and/or rebelliousness. There is a necessity to be reconciled with another, rather than to, always be in opposition and/or contrary. Dreamer, you simply need to take the higher ground. Dreamer, if you are truly unaware of the part you've played within the conflict, you are being made aware via your dream. However, deep within, you recognize your own stubbornness, but are unwilling to own up to it. Nonetheless, this conflict really needs to be resolved; you need to heal the wounds that you've made, the war within you and without has to cease. See suggested course of action. (2) This type of dream exposes a need of refinement of character, namely in the area dealing with the deeds of the flesh. For example, dishonesty, adultery, sensuali ty, hostility, unfriendliness, jealousy, discord, factions, cliques, drunkenness, or any traits of these sorts (see 1 Corinthians 6:8-11). Your dream comes to warn an immoral believer that your choices are spiritually forbidden, and/or your activities are illegal. You have deliberately chosen to become enslaved to that which is forbidden by the One True and Living God. Read, understand, and embrace, Daniel 3:1-30, and have faith in God. Dreamer, refrain from wickedness and do no one harm, physically, sexually, emotionally, and/ or spiritually, any longer. Start treating God's people, your family, and others, wit h respect, as well as yourself. By this, God will pardon your injustices. If urged by God, declare a one, two, or three day fast for sanctification purposes; also, wash (bathe) and make yourself, clothing, and personal surroundings clean. You will need to declare some kind of fast and commit to it, for a period-of-time. Your dream is to warn a rebellious person, in the spirit of grace, to see if you will yet be worked upon, and change your mindset. Or, else to leave you inexcusable, in your accusations against God, because of your ruin (e.g. continually plundered, seized, and disfavored, also see Jeremiah 9:7-9; Zechariah 13:9; Matthew 23:37-39; Revelation 3:15-21). See suggested course of action. (3) Dreamer is seeking other knowledge and revelations, disciplines that do not support intimacy with Jesus Christ, and do not support meditating on the Word of God (Joshua 1:8), such as meditative disciplines. Disciplines that claim to train the consciousness for a state of perfect spiritual insight and tranquility, which they say is achieved through paths of actions, knowledge, and devotion. Not only is this course or discipline, delivered without grace, it will never be enough to fill an empty soul, nor does it prepare you for eternal li fe, for it approaches the spiritual realm without the provision that God has provided for man to approach, and reach, true spiritual perfection, and that provision being Jesus the Christ. Moreover, this way opens you up to be deceived regarding your own fallen nature or worse, and to the deception of demons, that are always looking for inroads into our minds, and it is unscriptural. Thus, your seeking has led to you gaining dark and erroneous knowledge, through personal experiences and through a supernatural imparting, which was demonically communicated. The knowledge you've gained does not allow you to praise the Lord, only to exalt one's self. You have abandoned the faith, and are now adhering to lies. You are embracing beliefs, views, and practices that are erroneous, unlawful, toxic, and spiritually and/ or physically deadly. Your choices will not withstand your storms of life. Your conscience will haunt you. Weakened by frequent panic attacks, brought on by your own guilt and the fear of God's retribution, you will begin to crack in your personality. He, who carries his or her own accuser, and their own tormentor, always in their bosom, cannot but be afraid on every side (Matthew Henry's Commentary on Job 18:11-21). The only foundation upon which one should wisely establish his or her identity is the principles within the Word of God. Your attitude is leading to a mental and spiritual breakdown, opening the door for demons to run havoc within your life and to bring you down to desolation. You are forfeiting purpose for foolishness and ruin. Demonic influences will swarm around you, ready to help you explore all manner of wickedness, and evil, despicable, immoral, reprehensible, disreputable, degenerate, infamous, and perverse choices. Your lifestyle choices will become offensive and repulsive (abominable) in the sight of God and humanity. Dreamer, demons have had thousands of years to master human weaknesses and can rival men and women of God if we are not careful. Favorably, while your dream is a seriously severe rebuke and warning, because of grace and many mercies of God extended to you, it is not an official declaration. Dreamer is counseled to seek all kinds of spiritual support now, to possibly avert or turn things around, and perhaps move away from your present environment, definitely walk away from all negativity that is the antithesis of Christ, abruptly. Utilizing the powerful resources of prayer and heartfelt repentance to Jesus is a good place to start. To Jesus pray, Psalm 51, this followed by appropriate application of wisdom, can conceivably avert some of the repercussions of your choices. This coupled with fasting, a changed mindset, serious re -consideration of God's ways and means, and an honest acknowledgement of God's hand within your life, then the severe impact of your choices and actions upon your life, can be reversed and damages repaired (also see Ezekiel 33:12-19). This is what is called leaving a blessing behind. If you do not genuinely seek help and change, for sure ruin will be your destiny's declaration. See suggested course of action.

SAVINGS, TRUST, SETTLEMENT, OR BANK (any depository financial institution or any property held by one party, the trustee, for the benefit of another, the beneficiary):

Your dream is to open wide the eyes of, and disconcert, a secure and careless person (the dreamer) who proclaims peace to him or herself. Dreamer although you are gentle, polite, quiet, charitable, courteous, graceful, good-natured, and/or likeable, you lack practical wisdom and practical understanding. Thus, you are too easily deceived, ensnared, cheated, or hoodwinked, especially financially. Your zeal to help others is without knowledge, thus your dream. It is a warning against folly and a message of grace (the free and unmerited favor and beneficence of God). For, while good-naturedness and charity are noble traits, dreamer, your level of impracticalness will cause feelings of resentment and rejection within you, resulting in an offense that will be difficult to overcome. Leaving you thinking that God has forgotten you or does not care about your present state of affairs, and neither do others, especially those you've so generously been kind too. Your behaviors will (or have already) opened a door for the enemy to cause an offense within you against God, and especially against God's people, and so God against you. You should adopt a way of helping people that is more God principled, practical, and down-to-earth. See Proverbs 6:1-5; and read what care God has taken, in His Word, to make men and women good stewards over their assets and to teach them prudence in the managing of those assets. Charity has principles as well as promises, relating to life on this side of eternity, in the land of the living. It is every person's wisdom to keep out of debt (literal and emotional) as much as possible, for debt is a burden upon people. Ensnaring them; putting them in danger of doing or suffering wrong. Your generosity needs discretion, prudence, and wisdom during these times. For example, do not co-sign or be a surety in any way for family members, friends, especially those who are ne'er-do-wells, and never for strangers or people you barely know. Dreamer, malicious and mischievous persons are before you and their desire is to rob, steal, and destroy. Their desires have the capacity to bring poverty and ruin to you, if you allow yourself to become ensnared by their lure. If you have rashly entered into such an agreement, through either hook or crook, know that you are snared by the words of your mouth. Humble yourself and faithfully pray to be discharged from the debt. Favorably, Adonai will no longer allow you to be trodden underfoot, but will raise you up, but you must learn the valuable lesson of your situation, namely using practical wisdom and practical understanding in your giving, the counsel of your dream. See suggested course of action.

STONES, GEMS, OR PRIZED ART (e.g. amethyst, diamonds, emeralds, opals, pearls, rubies, sapphires, topaz, turquoise, or prized art, e.g. Da Vinci, Michelangelo, Monet, Picasso, Rembrandt, Van Gogh):

Your dream refers to one who is redeemed; however, you are going through a refining process, see Proverbs 17:3, 27:21; thus, your dream. Dreamer is strongly urged, at this point in your life, to adhere to God's instructions and principles that guide actions and moral behavior, via His principles, as outlined within Holy Writ. Following godliness is, aimed at making you not only wiser, but also better. Dreamer, it is imperative that you govern your desires, lusts, and passions with wisdom during your refining process. You have a journey to go on, spiritual warfare to fight, and a great work to do. God wants to purify you that you might fulfill the righteous purpose for which you were designed. With that said, as you have been saved from the power of sin, you will now be refined in the "crucible" of adversity. Dreamer, if you allow God's power to break the residuals of sin within you, you will experience a great deliverance from oppression. Be very aware that your emotional and/or physical adversities have been allowed by God that you might be humbled and made ready and prepared to render your gifts unto the Lord properly. God will use your sufferings to instill His principles into your mind, and make His ways penetrate your heart. He or she who has suffered in the flesh has ceased from sinning (1 Peter 4:1) that the sacrificial offerings of your worship, service, and financial support to the ministry, might be a sweet smell unto the Lord. Moreover, the refinement process that you are going through (or will go through shortly) is meant to bring honor and glory to the One who died to redeem you. True conversion makes a marvelous change in the heart and life. It alters the mind, judgment, affections, and conversation. When a man is truly converted, it grieves him to think how the time past of his life has been spent (Matthew Henry Concise Commentary). After this, you will become productive and go forth, bearing spiritual fruit, counted amongst those who are sagacious; whose character is faithful, law-abiding, moral, open, scrupulous, sincere, straightforward, trustworthy, upright, reasonable in many situations, and submissive to God. Blessings, joy, protection, and prosperity will be yours. See suggested course of action. If relevant, see category, Cutting (Cut and Set stones, gems)

WAGE (compensation paid for work, e.g. paycheck):

First, it must be noted, a worker is worthy of your wage. Hence, you will receive wages appropriate for your diligence, on this side of heaven, and in eternity, if indeed you are (have been) diligent (Matthew 6:1, 1 Corinthians 3:11-15, 1 Timothy 5:18). Question to consider, within your dream, was dreamer compensated properly for work done? Thus, this dream h as two meanings (choose one). (1) If dreamer was properly compensated or if dreamer, in your awaked life, is actually diligent in your service to the Kingdom of God, and to His people, the righteous desires of your heart will now begin to manifest within your life. You will receive double, and you will live your life more peaceful and abundant than before and to its fullest (financially, happiness, love, and respect). If illness is a concern at present, you will recover from this, and live; all this because of your sense of duty and respect to others. Additionally, you are one who voluntarily offers help or sympathy in times of trouble, one who demonstrates mercy, and truly loves his or her neighbor, you are the proverbial "Good Samaritan" (Luke 10:25-37). You have learned to handle much; therefore, much will be given you. You will live to testify of God's great love, everlasting kindness, and of His great faithfulness. (2) If dreamer was not properly compensated within your dream or if dreamer, in your awaked life, is not diligent in your service to the Kingdom of God, and to His people, your dream denotes that the dreamer has committed an error in judgment or conduct, as well as one who is quarrelsome. You've reached a turning point within your life, from where you misstep or got lost. Choose to let go of the negativity and to embrace obedience to avoided, will usher you into the path of darkness, and your attitude and unwise choices will prove to your disadvantage, even to the point of being exposed openly. Therefore, flee immorality, for God's principles are a hedge of protection to the dreamer. With that said, dreamer you are warned to restrain and get your flesh under control. Your dream is one of God's ways of calling you back unto Him that you might be saved, and to see if you will yet be worked upon, and change your mindset; or else to leave you inexcusable, in your accusations against God, because of your ruin. Dreamer, of your own free will, you made a public profession of following Christ Jesus; thus, you need to walk according to that commitment, cautiously, refraining from all forms of evil, and approaches towards it, because many eyes are upon you. They watch your character, for error, faltering, stumbling; for any type of dishonor or violation, and surely, you have a great deal to lose. Before you ar e the possible loss of distinction, honor, reputation, and life. Thus, neglect not the purity of your covenant relationship with Christ, for God desires to bring you back into a right relationship with Him. Return to ideals that are holy, wise, well judged, and disciplined. This will lead you back to Christ. See suggested course of action.

Suggested Course of Action

Question to consider and journal, did your dream depict any symbols that alludes to, the dreamer will make the necessary changes, spiritually, emotionally, and/or physically to affect a more positive outcome? If changes are initiated, your dreams will change. Nevertheless, if you are here, your chance to make things right, and to make a good go of things is before you; therefore, seize the moment to turn things around.

In view of your dream's context, and the primary symbols, what does your dream reveal about you, your ethics, intents, mental state, and motives? You will need to earnestly look within and consider that the sum of your answers is a reflection of where you are emotionally, physically, and/or spiritually, and a reflection of who you are becoming. What was your reaction to the situation? Were you angry, concerned, confused, defensive, fearful, happy, helpful, pleased, shocked, unconcerned, or ready to get out of someone's presence? Your reaction to the activity, or the circumstance, reveals your attitude regarding this information about yourself.

Dreamer, consider seriously your observations. If what was revealed prevail, will it sabotage any good that's happening at present within your life? Will it build or destroy, strengthen or weaken, enlighten or blind? If you lack wisdom, ask Jesus for wisdom. He gives wisdom to all, generously, no matter who you are and what you've done; wisdom is available (see James 1:5-8, Proverbs 2:1-6, 10). Hence, if, by just asking, you may get wisdom, one may suffer needlessly, because you will not ask Jesus for wisdom.

Moreover, there is a need to understand the unadulterated and full meaning of divine providence, get a bible dictionary, and respect the meaning. For, there is also a need to recognize, acknowledge, and respect divine providence, God's absolute control over the affairs of humankind, and to renounce the belief that humans are in complete control (see Job 9:12, Isaiah 14:27; 43:13). There is a difference between divine providence and the will of humankind. Although you have the power of free choice, you should not think that your accomplishments are purely of your own volition. It is God, who gives you the capability and strength to achieve success. This is especially true of your struggles with your sinful tendencies, whether they manifest as a lack of concern or interest in the things of God, a stubborn resistance to the will of God, or laziness. If it had not been for God's efforts on your behalf, you would not have been able to overcome any negative tendencies. He delivered you. Any achievements you've accomplished, any good deeds you've done, any fulfillment of God's will, was, and still is, dependent upon divine aid and guidance. One merely places his or her hand under the weight carried exclusively by God. Just say and truly believe, "I will exalt you, God, for you have lifted me up".

This is also necessary to say, although it may seem despairing at first, maintaining faith and honest ways, especially in the face of a life having been filled with corruption. The tasks may prove daunting, to say the least, living out the truths tha t most everyone you know prefer to ignore or ridicule, but if you would endure and remain faithful, the promises of God will manifest, endurance will solidify you. Altruistic, goodhearted, and generous service to God and others is beneficial at this time. Dreamer, God hears your pondering.

Now, pray (See Prayer of Deliverance, pg. 897)

Specific Meaning

If, you have a very high chance of, acquiring or handling, large sums of money, it is suggested that you may perhaps hire an accountant or bookkeeper, especially for tax purposes. Your dream should closely resemble real life situations. Meaning it can actually occur during your awaked state.

Note: If you sense that, your dream is some type of inspiration regarding currency, then go, and start doing business, perhaps designing, brand mark, and marketing a divine sent idea. For God does give invention, via dreams, and it is meant to prosper your life.

If criminal activity is a very real issue in your life, your time of reckoning and restitution is upon you. Repent, ethicall y and honestly admit your illegal activity, apologize to those affected by your actions, and then go and fast for three days, praying for will send you away a very long time. Ask God what kind of fast is needed, and He will direct you.

Otherwise noted, per your lifestyle, if your dream closely resembled real life situations, meaning it can actually occur during your awaked state, this dream may be an Ordinary Dream, resulting from daily activities (see Chapter One, Chalom). These sorts of dreams are usually about your routine, mundane activities or anxieties that overwhelm your mind during the day. They are an inner release mechanism, which helps provide you with emotional balance and the maintaining of your sanity. These dreams are not significant, and do not warrant special attention. However, if your dream was inundated with symbols that are not easily linked to your life activities, then the spiritual implications (the interpretation) should be heeded.

DEATH, DYING, THE DEAD, HEAVEN AND HELL

Murmur at it, dispute it, despise it, mock at it, put it aside, hate it, and hide from it, as men may, but here emperors, kin gs, statesmen, warriors, heroes, and butchers of all kinds, with peasants and beggars, meet. However various their routes, they terminate in the same point. Remember your Creator before the silver cord is snapped, the golden bowl is broken, the pitcher is smashed near the spring, and the water wheel is broken at the cistern. Then the dust {of mortals} goes back to the ground as it was before, and the breath of life goes back to God who gave it. (Ecclesiastes 12:6, 7 GW)

But Jesus told him, "Follow me, and let the dead bury their own dead". (Matthew 8:22 GW)

But when this corruptible shall have put on incorruption, and this mortal shall have put on immortality, then shall come to pass the saying that is written, Death is swallowed up in victory. O death, where is thy victory? O death, where is thy sting? The sting of death is sin; and the power of sin is the law: but thanks be to God, who giveth us the victory through our Lord Jesus Christ. (1 Corinthians 15:53-57 ASV)

God will give us nothing farther to warn us. No dead man will come to life to tell us of what he has seen. If he did, we would not believe him. Religion appeals to man not by ghosts and frightful apparitions; it appeals to their reason, their conscience, their hopes, their fears. It sets life and death soberly before men, and if they will not choose the former, they must die. If you will not hear the Son of God and the warnings of the Scriptures, there is nothing, which you will or can hear, y ou will never be persuaded, and will never escape the place of torment. (Barnes' Notes on the New Testament)

Thou shalt surely die—Hebrew "moth tamuth"; literally, a death thou shalt die, or, dying thou shalt die. Thou shalt not only die spiritually, by losing the life of God, but from that moment, thou shalt become mortal, and shalt continue in a dying state till thou die. This we find literally accomplished; every moment of man's life may be considered as an act of dying, t ill soul and body are separated. The truth is God considers all those who are dead to men, in a state of conscious existen ce in another world. Therefore He calls himself the God of Abraham, and of Isaac, and of Jacob; now God is not the God of the dead, but of the living; because all live to Him, whether dead to men or not. (Mark 12:24-27, Adam Clarke's Commentary)

This category primarily deals with death, dying, the dead, heaven and hell, and some of their corresponding symbols. Some short descriptions of types, phrases, and other processes and particulars, connected in some way to this category are, for example, asleep, eternal death, the grave, heaven, hell, living soul, passed away, physical death, Rephaims, RIP, shades, silent shadow, SIP, spiritual death, suicide, sunset

All Symbols and Referents, Notes (1, 2, 3, etc.), Suggested Course of Action, and Specific Meaning offer guidance toward a more comprehensive interpretation.

Notes

1. Unless otherwise noted elsewhere, if, in your everyday living, your awaked state, as part of your lifestyle, work, or ministerial activities, or a special event, you have a very real connection with any activity involving death, dying, or the dead. For example, autopsy, coroner, embalmer, eulogist, funeral director, gravedigger, medical examiner, mortician, undertaker, one whose business is the management of funerals, or whose place of work is a cemetery, crematory, graveyard, mortuary, morgue, necropolis, your dream is not significant and does not warrant special attention.

   Otherwise noted: This dream of death, dying, and the dead, heaven and hell, may be an Oneirovatic "OV" dream, or an Oneirovaticicritica "OVC" dream, to see and prophesy by dreams (see Chapter One: The 60th Part of Prophecy, The Elevated Parts of Sleep). One may plainly see homicides, or other assaults taking place in their neighborhood or town before or after they happen, and soon thereafter, notice the violation reported in the news. On some level, this type of dream will affect the dreamer's life, requiring action on the part of the seer. Most people, who experience "OV" or "OVC" dreams, are usually found consulting and/ or supporting local police crime units. This type of dream should closely resemble real life situations, with the dream events actually being capable of happening.

Otherwise noted, per your lifestyle, if your dream closely resembled real life situations, meaning it can actually occur during your awaked state, this dream may be an Ordinary Dream, resulting from daily activities (see Chapter One, Chalom). These sorts of dreams are usually about your routine, mundane activities or anxieties that overwhelm your mind during the day. They are an inner release mechanism, which helps provide you with emotional balance and the maintaining of your sanity. These dreams are not significant, and do not warrant special attention.

2. Probables: As death, dying, and the dead, heaven and hell symbols are frequently used as referents in many, and very personal, aspects of our lives, for example, a long dead mother may beckon her senior citizen daughter or son to come, or death may be represented by one being embrace by father Abraham "in Abraham's bosom". Hence, dreamer may also consider your own personal and special associations with various death, dying, and the dead, heaven and hell symbols, as long as the interpretation is kept within the principles of spiritual boundary markers, landmarks, and property lines, (see Chapter One, section entitled, Spiritualizing Boundary Markers, Landmarks, and Property Lines).

3. Determine who your dream is for you or another. Always, considering yourself first, reflecting on your present behaviors. Ask yourself, "Why am I dreaming about this now? What is this dream revealing about me? Have I taken on new attributes? Has anyone commented on my present behaviors as being untypical of me? Has my ministry changed for the better or for the worse? What about my beliefs, doctrine, or philosophy, are they still based on Holy Writ? Is there something I need to know about those I am ministering to or serving?

Remember your actions and emotions within your dream. Were you the one dead, or dying? Were you connected to a life support machine? Were you in heaven or hell? Were you the undertaker? Did you put make-up on a dead person? Were you attempting to contact someone dead? Did a dead person bring you a message? Did you see a dead person, meaning actually dead in your awake life, dying or come back to life, or living? Did a loved one (e.g. spouse, parent, or child) who has actually passed away come to you angry, happy, or with a message. Did an angel of death visit you? If dreamer was the focal point, meaning, you was primarily the highlight. This is a good indicator that your dream is about you (the dreamer). In light of your dream, via the relevant interpretation, do you believe that your behavior will enhance or endanger your well-being, safety, and/or happiness, if so, how and why? Do you believe that your belief system will strengthen or weaken you spiritually in any way, if so, how and why? Is spiritual or physical death a possibilit y? See following relevant subcategory, the interpretation is about and for you.

Did someone walk into a graveyard? Was someone else dying? Was another connected to a life support machine? Was someone else an undertaker? Did someone cause the death of another? Did dreamer see someone, who is actually living in your awake life, dying or dead? Was another in heaven or hell? Also, see Note 7 of this category. Unless otherwise noted elsewhere, an answer of yes, to one or more of these, or similar questions, is a good indicator that your dream is about another and their role, and/or influential effects, within the life of the dreamer. If someone else was the focal point, meaning, another, was primarily the highlight of your dream. How was he or she connected to death, dying, and the dead, heaven or hell? Consider, is someone greatly influencing your physical, spiritual, or mental health, your understanding, perspective, and reasoning regarding spiritual issues? Are they enhancing your spiritual and/or literal prosperity, or are they responsible for the dwindling thereof? Could they be influencing your ministry, on some level? Do you know someone whose life activities or physical being is similar to that which stood out the most within your dream? Could it be that person? If you sense that your dream is for or about another, the question as to why you have been made privy to this information, and how do you factor into the equation, should be seriously considered along with necessary actions. Perhaps the dreamer is being made aware of the plight of someone, and you are to get involved (see Chapter One, Are You Ready to Hear the Messages in Your Dreams, section entitled, The 10% for others).

If your dream is for, or about another:

Dreams that reference others and the revelation within those dreams, is not given haphazardly to any individual, but only to those with the ability, and influence to do something with the information; this is also prophecy. With that, journal the following questions, and if unable to answer the questions now, this denotes that the person, represented within your dream, will enter your life shortly. Are you entering into a personal relationship with someone? Do you not know or understand what you're looking at, especially certain behaviors, when learning about this person? Has someone new entered your life or maybe you've just begun opening up to someone not so new, and have started listening to their advice, accepting their assistance, or are you supporting or enabling someone? Are you in denial regarding the toxicity of one of your present relationships, particularly a spouse, family member, or friend? Are you anxious, concerned, frightened, and/or troubled by recent changes in your behavior, especially because of someone's influence upon your life at present? Have you allowed someone to convince you to deceive another? Have you recently become aware of (or is being made aware of, via your dream) certain undesirable behaviors within you towards another? Are you trying to cut ties with one that is bad company? Have you just joined (or re-joined) a church, fellowship, or social group?

Note: If your dream has attributes that indicate that your dream is about you, and other attributes that indicate that your dream is about another, dreamer should consider that your dream is about you and another. For example, did you see a living person (in your awake life) dead? Were you amongst dead people? Were you eulogizing another? Did you put make-up on a dead person? Did you visit a morgue to identify a body? Did you visit someone who was dying? Did you embalm someone? Did you cut or disconnect some from a golden cord? Unless otherwise noted elsewhere, an answer of yes, to one or more of these, or similar questions, is a good indicator that the dream is about the dreamer, and about another. Therefore, while your dream is about the dreamer, the dreamer should expect the role and/or influential effects of another, also plays a part in your interpretation. For example, did dreamer kill someone who had committed a very bad crime? Dreamer may have to pay for someone's funeral, again, see relevant interpretation.

More questions to consider. Why has the person been allowed within your life, and/or how did they get there? Again, if unable to answer the questions now, this denotes that the person, represented within your dream, will enter your life shortly. If their activity, within your dream, has proven positive, via the interpretation, this someone will prove, unwittingly, to be a very strong ally, benefactor, defender, and supporter. God has sent this someone into your life to help you carry out your next endeavor by enlarging your spiritual capacity. Allow the strength of that person's character to guide, help, and support you. On the other hand, if his or her presence and/or activity, within your dream, proved negative, via the interpretation, for sure, this person will prove to be a very strong and formidable challenge for you, perhaps unto death. If negative, this dream is a dire warning. Take steps accordingly to struggle against, or to cut off, adverse and unfavorable relationships. Remember certain personalities are all encompassing, affecting everything, cataclysmic, contagious, deadly, harmful, infectious, predatory, and/or venomous. Symbolically meaning that if allowed to continue or prosper within your life, serious harm or death to the dreamer may result. Idolize no one, especially beyond the warning of the Lord, and we are definitely not to lay our lives down for no one. Then again, this person maybe allowed within your life, because of the dreamer's unwillingness to abstain from immorality after having been asked to abstain from such by God, see 1 Corinthians 6:9-20, Galatians 5:19-21, or the dreamer's self-righteous behavior, or a lack of a balanced and honest view of your own personality. In this case, this person will affect self-awareness within the life of the dreamer, exposing the negative traits of your personality, especially those traits, which cause you to follow, o r to be so easily misled, and/or your wrong beliefs; no matter, this type of mentality needs reckoning with. Graciously, all of this will restore the dreamer to his or her right place with God, opening your eyes to see how far you've strayed from God (1 Corinthians 5:4-7; James 5:20). The lesson is, no matter how personable, powerful, or difficult a person, or how uncertain or unpopular the choices and issues, always take the next biblical and ethical step, for obedience to God's principles will always prove safer and stronger foundationally. Although, you will need all kinds of outside support to recover from this person's domination, no longer, allow that particular person's influence within your life to continue or thrive, especially if negative, end it abruptly.

4. Consider all the people, places, backgrounds, and activity highlighted within your dream.

    Known (in your awaked life) person, animal, place, or organization within your dream:

    Unless otherwise noted elsewhere, people, animals, places, backgrounds that are actually known by the dreamer in your awaked life, indicates a part of you that you recognize within yourself on some level or another. Question to journal, if dreamer seriously considers all the particulars, what stood out the most, what features, or character traits stood out the most. For example, age, color, heaven, height, hell, size, topography, weather, neglected, run-down. Write down (journal) the particular highlighted within your dream. The attribute or activity highlighted is for a reason. Since the attribute written down is a part of you, namely the dreamer's nature, demeanor, and/or lifestyle, an honest and unbiased assessment is very important for truth sake. Happy note, considering that other people's attributes, within dreams, also represent attributes of your own personality, causes one to look at another in a better light. According to your capacity to embrace self-awareness and a rectification of mind, body, and spirit, God will begin to enhance, make better, more attractive, sanctify, diminish, and make pure and free from sin and guilt, this part of you.

    Otherwise noted, if the person, animal, place, or background within your dream is actually known by the dreamer, in your awaked life, this person, animal, place, or background may represent him or herself, or itself.

    Unknown in your awaked life or although known, was unseen, invisible, or only talked about - person, animal, place, or organization within your dream:

    Unless otherwise noted elsewhere, if you did not recognize, the person, place, thing, they, or it, was not seen, invisible, or only talked about within your dream, this indicates an attribute or activity within your life that you are unfamiliar with, or are in denial about, or you refuse to acknowledge it, but it does exists. Although, on some conscious level, you are aware of a certain behavior or attribute within you, you have chosen to filter out or simply ignore certain information about yourself that contradicts your view of yourself and/or your preconceived notions of others and of the world around you. Possibly protecting yourself, emotionally and psychologically, from a situation, which you are unable to cope with at this time, or you lack control over; then again, perhaps the dreamer has an exaggerated or unrealistic view of yourself. No matter the reason, right now a question is before you, via your dream. Do you want to know this part of yourself? According to your ability to handle self-awareness, God will begin to reveal this side of you to you. Why, He wants to balance your understanding of things; thus, effecting wholeness within your life, so that the enemy will no longer be able to manipulate your emotions so easily. The Paraclete is with you to help you throughout this entire process, listen to Him. Now, in your life, this activity or attribute needs reckoning with, somehow or someway.

Otherwise noted, (known or unknown), if the person, place or thing that initiated (or was a recipient of) the action or activity within your dream was not seen, invisible, or only talked about within your dream, this may indicate that the dreamer does not recognize the influential effects another has within your life, or upon your attitude.

If more than one person (known or unknown):

Consider what the group had in common. What behavior, character trait, feature, action, or activity, stood out the most? For example, were they argumentative, authoritative, beautiful, criminal minded, dancing, difficult, dressed unusual, enigmatic, fighting, focused, flirty, helpful, hurtful intentions, powerful, promiscuous, quiet, secretive, seemed unreal, unassuming? That which was highlighted and noted is what you need to focus on at present.

If the attribute or quality is a desirable or positive one, allow the strength of that attribute to help you overcome some manner of immorality or irreverence within your life and/or to help you to become better, productively, for the Kingdom of God in some manner. If the attribute is an undesirable or negative one, take steps accordingly to struggle against the growing desires of the carnal side of you. If applicable, get help and support via prayer, fasting, and a Christ ian based support group.

5. In addition to the following interpretations, see index or relevant categories for more information. For example, if land was involved in some way, see category, Landforms; if a weather was highlighted, see category, Weather. If a particular person was depicted, see also category, People. Kept within context of your dream and the interpretation, the additional symbols are perhaps relevant. It will be within the sum of all the symbols that you will find a more thorough interpretation.

6. Since the following list is not extensive, dreamer is encouraged to seek biblical guidelines and other relevant research to determine the metaphorical meaning of your particular death, dying, and the dead, heaven and hell activity, depicted within your dream, via a Bible concordance, Bible illustrated dictionary, encyclopedia, or internet. Having done your research you should be able to determine some basic behaviors or attributes your Lord and Savior wants you to focus on.

7. If a person who is actually alive was depicted as dead, or depicted as crossing over to another side, be it a river, street, or floating away in a hot air balloon, or in heaven or hell. This type of dream denotes one who is, or should be rendered by spiritually dead. Therefore, considerations, such as intimate relationships, partnerships, their teachings or ministering; should be carefully, and sagaciously, thought out, before committing to any binding commitment with the person depicted as dead. For what has the dead to do with the living?

8. On the other hand, while the dead has nothing to do with the living (Ecclesiastes 9:4-6), there are exceptions regarding communications from the dead, prophetic communications. The following are exceptions, and not the rule. Note, in 1 Samuel 28:20-31, a witch was used to summon the prophet Samuel, after his death. Other examples of exceptions are a child, or anyone, showing the dreamer, who killed them and the location of the homicide. This information may possibly be used in "fact-finding" of a possible homicide, or the exposure of one, who the dreamer is in denial regarding the character of an assassin. Another exception is someone communicating something that is actually imperative to the dreamer's awaked life at present, pointing the dreamer towards a resolution to a problem or a possible fate. With th ese exceptions, I must express again, the Bible expressly states that the dead has no more work amongst the living (Ecclesiastes 9:4-6). Further, OV dreams; see Note 1 of this category. Most people, who experience OV dreams, are usually found consulting and/or supporting

local police crime units. One may plainly see homicides, larceny, or other assaults taking place in their neighborhood or town before or after they happen, and soon thereafter, notice the violation reported in the news.

Symbols and Referents

Generally, this type of dream rarely denotes, again, not too often, that physical death is imminent. However, if dreamer is seriously ill, consult a physician. With that noted, most dreams of death, dying, and the dead, heaven and hell generally imply that a certain character trait, behavior, or activity, linked to the dreamer is to be considered no longer useful, therefore is obsolete, within the life of the dreamer. Question, what character trait did the dead person represent to the dreamer, while the person was actually alive, what character feature stood out the most? With that trait noted, dreamer may consider that the trait noted, is within the dreamer, and that trait is no longer useful or needed for the progression of your spiritual walk, on this side of heaven. Dreamer, it is suggested that you render that trait (good or bad) obsolete, and began anew attempting to move forward, using different tactics to overcome unproductive habitual life cycle choices, and for maneuvering through this thing we call life in a more, better way.

While the following few symbols are oftentimes connected with approaching death, the dream's context will play a major part in its meaning. It will depend on the way the symbols are contextually put together, and the background of which they appear; that will help to explain your dream's meaning. Therefore, other references highlighted, may also be points of relevance; it will be the sum of all the surrounding conditions. Dreamer, keeping in mind that death symbols oftentimes do not denote a physical death, but depicts spiritual death, namely a death to your carnal side, or a spiritual separation from God, a place of torment, aka "Tartarus" or hell, which is also death.

Symbols of physical death are Broken Bowl, Tree Branch, or Vessel, Cut Grass or Flowers, Death Angel, Death Row, Fire or Explosion, Grave, Graveyard, Head Cut Off and/or Floating Away, Hot Air Balloon, Ice, Myrrh (an embalming oil), Scythe, Shadows, Silver Cord, Rope, or String, Sleeping, or Crossing a River, Crossing the other side of a street. Question, what was on the other side of the river or street, a better life or "death like" situations? That is what awaits the dreamer, if you cro ssed over.

In addition to the varied meanings of death, dying, and the dead, heaven and hell, other common words, expressions, usages, (e.g. slang or clichés), or a 'probable' that are metaphorically represented by any of the following are also conside red (this section is an addendum at the end of the relevant subcategory).

Category Content: If not listed see index, perchance, for your specific type of death, dying, and the dead, heaven and hell dream.

- Autopsy
- Coroner, Embalmer, Embalmment, Medical Examiner, or Mortician
- Bury or Burial (place in a grave or tomb)
    - Bury one who is a cleric or ministerial leader, see category, Agriculture; Bury one's face in the dust
- Corpse or Cadaver
- Dead (spouse, family member, friend, foe, or anyone who has already passed away in your awaked life)
- Deceased Parents, see category, People (Parents); Person who is actually alive was depicted as dead, or depicted as crossing over to another side, be it a river, street, etc., see Note 7 of this category; Dead person came back to life or "Appear" as alive and living (person can be actually dead or living in dreamer's awake life); Dead loved one was angry, happy, silent, or spurned or rejected you or your advances; Deceased person shifted their appearance or appearance was unusual or presented, showed or communicated something; Dreamer was dead; Sitting with

the dead, see category, Sitting (Dead people); Sex with the dead, see category, The Body (Sex with the dead)

- Dying (in the process of passing from life, one who is about to die)
- Funeral
- Grave, Graveyard, Morgue, or Realms of the Dead (e.g. Gehenna, Hades, Sheol, Tartarus)
- Heaven, see category, Ascending or Expanding (Body in Heaven)
- Hell, see category, Falling into or Sinking or Sliding Downward (Hell)
- Suicide
- Undertaker

AUTOPSY:

Dreamer, God will rescue, or has rescued, you from a powerful enemy, one who is/was too strong for you. One who is misleading, out of order, untrue, who secretly practice immoral, impure, and unchaste conduct. This person confronted you during a very hard time in your life, but the Lord was your support (2 Samuel 22: 17-25). Fortunately, this hard time will (or did), effect within you a great balancing of your theology, resulting in a belief that is complete, with solid attributes. N ow, you will begin to experience a miraculous increase in divine knowledge, and wisdom. This knowledge and wisdom will be imparted to you to be used exclusively for interpreting the gospel of Jesus Christ to others, and for the edifying of the Body of Christ. Your inspirations will make for very good teaching. Your sensitivity and gentleness will be a great healing force in the lives of others, bringing harmony and support to them, via defending them, by any right means necessary, against the deceit and trickery of the enemy, and by teaching them about simple faith. By this, you advance the cause of God, against the enemies of His Kingdom. You would make an excellent apologist (witness) for the Kingdom of God. Seriously consider this branch of Christian theology. Additionally, as you are now able to handle great responsibility and wealth, and are one who is tolerant, you will experience receiving an act of kindness, monetarily, from someone who is affluent. You must also become a fundraiser for, and giver of, charity.

CORONER, EMBALMER, EMBALMMENT, MEDICAL EXAMINER, OR MORTICIAN:

Your dream denotes healing to one, the dreamer, who is suffering spiritually, physically, emotionally, and mentally. The dreamer has been suffering from intense affliction, serious mental and/or physical pain, because of negative path's you've taken in life. Thus, the dreamer is greatly troubled by pain or loss, very unhappy, full of misery. As well, you've had to put up with somebody, or something, very unpleasant. Nonetheless, all of your "woes" are a result of sin within your life. The goodness which God has blessed you with all these years, was meant to glorify His Kingdom, instead you have used His blessings to glorify yourself. Your pride lured you into a false sense of security. Graciously, spiritual renewal is access ible to you now. Jesus is petitioning you, via your dream, to cleanse evil from your heart, and to allow His process. The more God allows you to see your arrogance, and the horribleness of it all, be more earnest to repent that you may find Him to be grace and healing, refreshment, and a refuge. He is willing to help you, surrender to His process of help, with a humble dependence upon Him. God will suddenly, and in an extraordinary way, increase your strength and protect you from further hurt or harm. You will find that God will not fail you, and you will have grace sufficient for renewal of spiritual strength. Dreamer, many, who have faltered and were weak, are healed, restored, and strengthened by the grace of God. Favorably, you are now being made whole; for God is healing you. God has healed; therefore, dreamer is counseled, to stop sinning so that something worse doesn't happen to you (John 5:14). See suggested course of action.

BURY OR BURIAL (PLACE IN A GRAVE OR TOMB):

Although, your dream is a grave rebuke and serious alarm to the dreamer, fortunately, there is a ray of light, sent by God, purposed to break through the darkness of your state of affairs. This ray of light is a person, anointed and sent, especiall y to you. Their words and inspiration will be to you, like Genesis 1:3-5 is to Genesis 1:2. Illuminatingly wise, this person will powerfully affect your life, externally and internally. Their inspiration, coupled with you earnestly embracing change, humi lity, contentedness, integrity, ethicalness, and a renewed faith in God's word and His process, will strengthen you to return in complete heartfelt repentance to Jesus, from a heart of love. By this, the severity of your transgressions becomes partially sweetened; for, when a man/woman genuinely return to God, in complete surrender and humility, your deliberate transgressions become like actual merits, aka "the sweetening" (Luke 7:37-50). Because, the realization of your distance from God, due to your transgressions (Isaiah 59:2-21; Luke 15:11-24), becomes the motivating force to return to God with a passion even greater than that of someone who has never sinned in such a manner, or never left the Father's house, completely converting your present to good (Acts 9:1-30). This is the secret of repentance and returning to God. Go; therefore now, and seek the Lord Jesus, repent and place your hope in Him. Hope, placed in Him, will not deceive. A change has to come, and it needs to start now. With that said, couple this with one of the following, namely the grave rebuke and serious alarm to the dreamer (choose one). (1) This type of dream reveals the loss of a ministry (or ministries) due to spiritual immaturity and serious neglect, as well as the loss of honor and respect. Dreamer, it is a wicked servant who would bury, discount, disregard, or spurn their talents, skills, and/or ministerial responsibilities, blaming their lack of, commitment, faithfulness, knowled ge, and stewardship on God, others, or transitory circumstances (Matthew 25:24-30). If no action, commitment, or obligation to ministry, is heeded at this time, you may find yourself similar to the servant spoken of in the parable who buried his gift (Matthew 25:15). If your designated service is given to another, so will the prosperity that is attached to that service, be given to that person also, and for you, jealously will be your reward. Dreamer needs to consider your own well-being, emotionally, mentally, and spiritually. Think about what personal life cycles, denials, fears, failures, experiences, hang-ups, hindrances, lies, and/or rejections, have prevented you from developing, growing, expanding, increasing, and becoming all that you can be. What is lifeless in your life? What exactly is holding you back? For sure, it is not a person or thing. You, personally, will have to give an account of your stewardship to Jesus Christ, and your life choices will testify against you. You have been appointed to do certain things within your present fellowship, this is a small thing; do what is expected of you. Refer back to beginning of this interpretation, and see suggested course of action. (2) Dreamer, prideful and powerful, you lack Christ-like humility, and is becoming cruel and insensitive. Moreover, at present, concerned with your own interest, you are driven by, and occupied with, sensual appetites, rather than spiritual needs. Your desires, appetites, and attitude are leading to a chaotic and emp ty life. A life figuratively similar to the condition of earth in Genesis 1:2, wasteful, empty, and dark. This type of carnal strain and toil leads to sorrow and spiritual darkness. There is a need to re-connect with God. Refer back to beginning of this interpretation, and see suggested course of action.

In addition, the following is a common word, expression, or usage (e.g. slang or cliché), or a 'probable' that is metaphorically represented by bury:

- **Bury one's face in the dust:** Your dream denotes that the dreamer should be silent, abstain from grumbling, complaining, and murmuring, and wait for God's help, especially concerning a difficult situation or circumstance you are facing at present. Allow patience to prevail within you, and continue to wait on the Lord for He is faithful and just, and again I say wait on the Lord. If necessary, see suggested course of action.

CORPSE OR CADAVER:

Your dream denotes a false messiah, deliverer, prophet, preacher, teacher, religion, and religious dogma. Your dream is a second witness and warning to the dreamer. Dreamer, you've encountered something that appears spiritual, yet the teacher and teachings, rejects authentic worship of Yeshua; thus, you are spiritually weak, because you lack knowledge that leads to power, strength, and eternal life. The teaching is a simulated worship of humanistic and superstitious ideas, in direct conflict with the inspired written Word of God, rejecting Christianity's core system of beliefs, knowledge, and revelations that do not support meditating on the Word of God. Disciplines that claim to train the consciousness for a state of perfect spiritual insight and tranquility, which they say is achieved through paths of actions, knowledge, and devotion. Not only is this teaching delivered without grace, it will never be enough to fill an empty soul, nor does it prepare you for eternal life, for it approaches the spiritual realm without the provision that God has provided for man to approach, and reach, true spiritual perfection, an d that provision being Jesus the Christ. Moreover, this way opens you up to be deceived regarding your own fallen nature or worse, and to the deception of demons, that are always looking for inroads into our minds, and it is unscriptural. Thus, your seeking has led to you gaining dark and erroneous knowledge, through personal experiences and through a supernatural imparting, which was demonically communicated. The knowledge you've gained does not allow you to praise the Lord, only to exalt one's self. You have abandoned the faith, and are now adhering to lies. You are embracing beliefs, vi ews, and practices that are erroneous, unlawful, toxic, and spiritually and/or physically deadly. Your choices will not withstand your storms o f life. Your conscience will haunt you. Weakened by frequent panic attacks, brought on by your own guilt and t he fear of God's retribution, you will begin to crack in your personality. He, who carries his or her own accuser, and their own tormentor, always in their bosom, cannot but be afraid on every side (Matthew Henry's Commentary on Job 18:11-21) The only foundation upon which one should wisely establish his or her identity is the principles within the Word of God. Your attitude is leading to a mental and spiritual breakdown, opening the door for demons to run havoc within your life and to bring you down to desolation. You are forfeiting purpose for foolishness and ruin. Demonic influences will swarm around you, ready to help you explore all manner of wickedness, and evil, despicable, immoral, reprehensible, disreputable, degenerate, infamous, and perverse choices. Your lifestyle choices will become offensive and repulsive (abominable) in the sight of God and humanity. Favorably, while your dream is a seriously severe rebuke and warning, because of grace and the many mercies of God extended to you, it is not an official declaration. Dreamer is counseled to choose not to go out from the presence of the Lord that is to willingly, renounce God, e.g. relegating Him to a lower position; reduced in rank, perhaps to some alien visitation, but not Creator God in all of His Power. Dreamer, choose this moment, to go no further with this dissidence. Do not be content to forego the privileges Elohim offers, that you might not be under His precepts; make things right, and perhaps move away from your present environment, definitely walk away from all beliefs that are the antithesis of Christ Jesus, abruptly. Utilizing the powerful resources of prayer and heartfelt repentance to Jesus is a good place to start. To Jesus pray, Psalm 51, this follo wed by appropriate application of wisdom, can conceivably avert some of the repercussions of your choices. This coupled with fasting, a changed mindset, serious re-consideration of God's ways and means, and an honest acknowledgement of God's hand within your life, then the severe impact of your choices and actions upon your life, can be reversed and damages repaired (also see Ezekiel 33:12-19). This is what is called leaving a blessing behind. If you do not genuinely seek help and change, for sure ruin will be your destiny's declaration. See suggested course of action.

DEAD (spouse, family member, friend, foe, or anyone who has already passed away in your awaked life):

This dream has three meanings (choose one). (1) If dreamer has recently lost a loved, especially within the last seven years or less, and is still grieving, your dream denotes one who is anguished and is becoming disheartened due to loss or deprivation (e.g. widowhood, loneliness, financial decrease, or some disadvantage that resulted from lost, in some form or another). Emotionally you are experiencing broken heartedness, deep loneliness, great unhappiness, and/or a sense of being inferior. Privately, in a secret place, a place hidden from most, you are quietly without hope because there seems to be no po ssibility of comfort and/or success for your inner most desires. Your secret place, although quiet, is, or is becoming, bleak and desolat e, with much sadness. Dreamer, although you feel as though you may never experience authentic happiness or deep joy a gain, or that your heart's desires or dreams will never manifest, or that you are no longer good enough, your dream has come to let you know that God has not forgotten you, nor has He forgotten His promises made to you long ago. Dreamer, your experiences of hurts, disappointments, and loneliness, most through no apparent cause of your own, are all ways that the Lord will use to mature you; your many challenges will make you strong mentally, emotionally, and most importantly spiritually. A s well, your experiences are meant to draw a "hallelujah" from deep within you, a shout, and a song of praise to God. However, this kind of praise, this kind of "hallelujah", is not the result of a happy feeling, or is not necessarily from one who has seen the light. It is offered through the teeth of pain, it is broken, and it is offered in spite of emotional numbness. This kind of praise is offered to Jesus as a pure act of obedience, and as a naked act of the will. It comes from a place deep down, within the hea rt, beneath the changes and turnarounds of feelings, and the vicissitudes of life. Such acts of praise are acts of defiance, thro ugh which we defy the darkness, and confess our faith in Jesus who lives above tears, and who calls us to Himself, the One and on ly Light of the world, and He is the only rescuer for those in the darkness of pain and despair. With that said, this season of life is ending. Fortunately, for you, a change from one place, state, subject, or stage to another is happening within your life. Although you may not realize it, or feel it now, dreamer, God has given you much rest from emotional turbulence and outward distractions and drama. Your part is to make an earnest go of freeing yourself from the residuals of grief, by freeing yours elf from thoughts, behaviors, words, talk, and places that hinder clarity, and that keeps you from enjoying the goodness of the Lords' favor today; dreamer, allow this by faith and gratitude. The dreamer is counseled to obey the lead of the Holy Spirit. Do not be afraid, the situations and experiences that are coming now will bring you out of your heartache, and should be considered God's grace. The experiences will not harm you. Compassionately, instead of no hope, desolation, and insufficiency, you will receive a new life, in a way that you have not known since before your desolation, hopelessness, and loneliness. At last, you will be able to enjoy the benefits of being an heir to a King of kings. No more should you embrace bleakness, sadness, solitariness, and feelings like you've been forsaken or abandoned, for God has not forsaken you. Read Isaiah 54:8-17, this is God's Word and His promise to you. Dreamer, what Christ is doing for you, if you will simply come to Him as He summons you out of your depression, is a beautiful picture of grace. Great blessings are before you. (2) If dreamer has long ago lost a loved, particularly eight years or more ago. This choice has two parts (both apply). (a) Dreamer, although your way may seem difficult, due to loneliness, you are able, at this point, to make some rational decisions regarding your livelihood and spirituality; thus, the following is necessary to say. At present, your words, and/or behavior, contradicts practicality, basic reality, and deviates from faith in God. Yours is a life full of unnecessary words and activities, which have no basis in fact or reality, and they are not rooted in faith in God. Reality is understood to be what God says it to be via His Word. For exam ple, we are saved by grace through faith, not by works (Ephesians 2:5-10). Hence, anyone who does not correspond with His truth, in a levelheaded and practical manner, is deceived and erroneous in your thoughts and ideas; thus, exposing your rejection of the certainty of God's word. (b) Additionally, dreamer, the place where God wants to take you, namely a higher level of leadership, demands great personal sacrifice of rights and freedoms and requires the subduing of your passions. As you are a natural born leader, you have the power to lead others towards God, or away from the truth of His word, on to rebellion, and you will influence others to do according to your choice. If you choose to live life on God's terms, embracing His principles, by faith, you will become a great leader, leading many to Christ, and the favor of the Lord will be upon your life to cause men to honor and respect you; the glory of the Lord will rise upon you (see Isaiah 60:1-22). Glory in this sense is a state of high honor, spiritual beauty, and great illumination. Will you be made whole; will you allow Jesus to heal? Nonetheless, if you choose to serve your fleshly desires, worshipping at the altar of demons, desolation, and open shame is the inheritance of those who worship there. See suggested course of action. (3) See one of the following.

Dead person came back to life or "Appear" as alive and living: Persons can be actually dead or living, in dreamer's awaked life. (1) Fortunately, your dream denotes that the dreamer will experience a personal revival with your soul. This revival, if embraced, and allowed to do what it is sent to do, will correct a rebellious child of God and restore your soul. Allow Psalm 23 to be your faith, hope, love, and your testimony. However, if no change in your heart; dreamer, your attitude will prevent you from achieving your goals, having forfeited purpose for foolishness. See suggested course of action.

Dead loved one was angry, happy, silent, or spurned or rejected you or your advances: This dream has three meanings (choose one). (1) If deceased was angry or appeared angry in any way, your dream counsels that while the dreamer is experiencing the "anger" stage of grieving, meaning you are angry that your loved one has truly gone away from you, and you are truly having a "trying time" with the experience. Under no circumstances, do you allow yourself to medicate (or be prescribed medication for) the pain of grief; it will only hinder the natural process of grieving, allow the process naturally. You have a right to cry very much, and your tears are appropriate, as is your grief. The Holy Spirit will carry you, helping you t o be able to go on, and leading the way. Second, this experience will prove useful. You will draw upon your experience and prese nt more empathically and compassionately when ministering to others who are experiencing grief and great pain. With that said, that you may progress forward in a healthy manner, dreamer, you are counseled to make every effort to choose to go on and experience the final stage of grieving, which is "releasing" the deceased loved one, emotionally, that you may begin again experiencing life on this side of eternity, more fully. Dreamer, you can enjoy life again, and begin again, and if relevant, with another, and it's ok. If necessary, see suggested course of action. (2) If deceased was happy or silent, dreamer has transitioned through the stages of grieving, and has made a choice to go on experiencing life on this side of eternity, more fully, enjoying life again, and if relevant, will begin again with another, and it's ok. (3) Dead loved one spurned or rejected your advances towards them in some manner (e.g. did not allow you to kiss them or take hold of their hand, or waved you away from them): Read, understand, and embrace Isaiah 28:15-19. See suggested course of action.

Deceased person shifted their appearance or appearance was unusual or presented, showed or communicated something: This dream has three meanings (choose one). (1) If deceased person shifted their appearance, or their appearance was unusual, dreamer, a generational issue is visiting you again, namely genetic codes and traits that plagues you and other members of your family (e.g. parents, maternal or paternal grandparents, siblings, aunts, uncles, or cousins), traits that oftentimes lead to hurtful and devastating consequences, or a great fall. Dreamer, God has dealt with you regarding thi s issue in past times, and it went dormant, only, now, to rear its iniquitous head again, via some small "crack" in your spiritual life. This spiritual crack, break, or opening, may manifest itself as a (e.g. growing disinterest in God and His will, your ministry, prevarications, disillusionment regarding the realities of life, or a refusal to accept life, as it is, in all of its ups and downs, changes and turn-arounds. As well as, grief, mental health issues, or any thought, imagination, and behavior that exalt itself above the Creator's wisdom, including the repercussive experiences of such thoughts, actions, and behaviors). It will be one or more of these issues, or one similar, that have created the "crack" in your spiritual life, consequently leading to a revisit of the generational issue. Questions to journal, who was the deceased person, and what was the person's relationship to the dreamer in your awaked life, e.g. was the person your deceased spouse, parent, child, pastor, friend, foe, unknown? See category, People. Moreover, what was expressed, presented, or showed? What was the "it"? For example, did your deceased spouse reveal hidden money to you, did your deceased mother push you away, did your deceased father give you away in marriage, did a deceased child show you something, or did a deceased friend tell you a secret? Whatever "it" was, God is dealing with you regarding the possible deadly aspects and repercussions of whatever was highlighted. Example, a deceased spouse showing you hidden money, will expose that your heart's main priority is greed and this greed is taking authority within your life. A deceased mother pushing you away, dreamer is using outdated or irrelevant wisdom for a contemporary issue. A deceased father giving you away in marriage, is perhaps revealing that a present or near future relationship may prove emotionally devastating, perhaps even deadly. A child showing the dreamer, who killed them, denotes that God wants to deal with your grief and the bitterness and anger that have taken root within your heart because of a very bad situation, possibly a homicide that has grown cold, and the unforgivability of it all. Then again, perhaps you are a minister who has so neglected your ministry that it has died, being that a child also represent a ministry. Therefore, it is suggested that the dreamer journal at least one character trait that you, your parents, and other family members, e.g. siblings, grandparents, aunts, uncles, cousins, may have in common, particularly one that the Lord has squarely dealt with you personally in the past (e.g. deceptio n, greed, pride, promiscuousness, vanity, or any trait that feeds the flesh). Also, see relevant categories for other particulars.

Your answers, coupled with the interpretation, plus any additional information, should begin to unfold the subject matter, namely the issue that created the "crack" and what could be done to heal the breach. Favorably, that generational issue can stop with you (Jeremiah 31:29, 30; Ezekiel 18:2-14, 20-23). Dreamer, your Heavenly Father is requiring that you, once again, overcome and subdue negative and dark emotions, feelings, or ideas that would influence you, before they overcome you. Dreamer, God is not asking you to do something you cannot do. For a surety, vanquishing of the coming influence can be done with the help of the Paraclete. God can and will heal your issue, and you will never have to deal with that issue again, it having been rendered dead, and only, if you choose to overcome. See suggested course of action. (2) If deceased person presented, showed, or communicated something, if they conveyed a message or communicated directions, or anything, in any way (usually brief, spoken, or signaled). Dreamer, while considering what was said, and if applicable, reference other relevant categories, also consider this, it is said that, "When we go from the plain path of duty, everything draws us further aside, [e.g. loneliness, fearfulness, any negative life cycle], and increases our perplexity and temptation"[33]. For, you must keep in mind that once a person dies, his or her ties with earthly environments are severed. He or she has no awareness of the happenings transpiring upon this planet. He or she has no further earthly rewards to be received, because he or she has been removed from this realm. Former earthly associations, good or bad, are interrupted by death. The dead know not anything, it is not that they are unconscious in their current spirit state; rather, they are estranged from the experiences of this environment. When life is gone, this entire world is gone with it; there is an end of all our acquaintance with it, and the things of it; the deceased is removed forever from activity "under the sun" (Ecclesiastes 9:5, 6, other scriptures for consideration: Leviticus 20:27, Deuteronomy 18:11, 1 Samuel 28, Luke 16:26). See suggested course of action. (3) On another vein, regarding communications from the dead, there are prophetic exceptions regarding communications from the dead. A child or anyone showing the dreamer who killed them may possibly be used in "fact-finding" of a possible homicide, or the exposure of one, who the dreamer is in denial regarding the character of an assassin. Someone communicating something that is actually imperative to the dreamer's awaked life at present may point the dreamer towards a resolution to a problem. Regarding prophetic communications from the dead see Note [8] at the beginning of this category.

Dreamer was dead: If funeral, see subcategory, Funeral. This dream has three meanings (choose one). (1) Read, understand, and embrace Romans 7 and 8. Dreamer, there is therefore now no condemnation for those who are in Christ Jesus. For the law of the Spirit of life has set you free in Christ Jesus from the law of sin and death (Romans 8:1-2 ESV). (2) Your dream implies a spiritual backsliding. If dreamer has secretly yearned and/or have attempted to coldheartedly destroy a particular individual's reputation without cause, you will now begin to implode. Dreamer, you have misled people (Christians, community leaders, judicial authorities, or others) about this individual's character flaws, via deliberate exaggerations, lies. You are being watched, as well, you have not fooled God. You will be found out and appropriate actions will be taken. Your community, be it your family, friends, co-workers, or some faith based community you're involved with, will expose you. Your life will implode and you will be unable to recover on your own; that is without the help of God. On another vein, your plan s have literally made a clear-cut path for that individual to succeed, and indeed, they will succeed. She or he has divine favor and protection. On your part, you will be exposed. Your dangerous and negative thoughts and actions toward this particular individual, primarily due to jealously, needs to end now, your thoughts are of your own imagination, and of your bitterness due to personal hurts, rejection, and/or an unforgiving spirit. Favorably, even in this, there is nothing too hard for God; grace (the free and unmerited favor and beneficence of God) is extended that you may change your heart and mind. Unless you end this, there can be no forgiveness of your sins, only judgment (divine reprimand for folly and sin. Read, understand, and embrace Matthew 6:12-15. See suggested course of action. (3) Your dream has come to set life and death soberly before you, the dreamer, and if you will not choose behaviors, actions, thoughts, and choices that promote life, you will die physically. Th is choice has two parts (both may apply). (a) To the dreamer it is said, for you to remember your Creator, before your days of trouble come and time has caught up with you (Ecclesiastes 12:1-7). With that said, if dreamer is even remotely ill, take things seriously, and seek medical attention as soon as possible, and call for the elders of your church, for it is through their prayers of faith and anointing of oil upon you that sin is forgiven and healing is bestowed[36]. Have faith in this, for it will be by your faith that you will be healed wholly. This is a true saying. God has appointed someone, to help you through this difficult time. (b) Additionally, about your dream, dreamer death is not only physical, but can also be spiritual, namely a separation from God, and a place of torment, aka "Tartarus", which is also death. Dreamer, no dead philosophy, or any other lifeless "ism" will come to life to tell you truth, nor will a dead person, come to life, to tell you of what he or she has seen. For, if the "ism", you are embracing, did contain a spark of life, or if the dead did come back to tell you of what he or she had witnessed you would not believe the teaching, nor would you believe the dead. Dreamer, relationship with Christ, appeals to people not by half -truths or lies, or ghosts or frightful apparitions; it appeals to your reason, your conscience, and your hopes. God's Holy Spirit leads to truth. Dreamer, if you will not hear the Son of God, the warnings of the Scriptures, the preacher man, the believing teacher, unfortunately, there is nothing, which you will or can hear, you will never be persuaded, and will not escape that place of torment. See suggested course of action.

DYING (in the process of passing from life, one who is about to die):

This dream has three meanings (choose one). (1) If another was dying, whether the person is living, or dead in your awaked life, question to journal. What prominent attribute, or aspect of the dying person's personality, lifestyle, or behavior, stands out the most, to the dreamer, if person is actually alive? Or, what attribute or "particular" stood-out the most, if person is actually dead or was unknown within your dream? Noted; it will be this particular characteristic that is in the process of passing from liveliness to becoming dormant, within the life of the dreamer. Dreamer, you are becoming the exact opposite of what the person represented to you. For example, if person was considered spiritually dead by the dreamer, then the dreamer is becoming spiritually alive. If the person was considered a good and devoted Christian, then the dreamer is becoming a bad and disloyal Christian, similar to an apostate. Nonetheless, the time has come for a lifestyle change and for certain behaviors to end. Also, see category People. See suggested course of action. (2) If dreamer was dying, dreamer, although, you are a good and great person, your spirit is ready to sink and fail, because of the storms of life you've encountered lately. Dream er, know that God takes care of His children when they are oppressed, and you are His child. Hold on, God will revive and comfort you, and make things less oppressive, and more cheerful. "Divine consolations have enough in them to revive us even when we walk in the midst of troubles and are ready to die away for fear" (Matthew Henry Commentary). Dreamer, better days are before you. Encourage yourself with this hope. (3) If married, your spouse is not in good health, and requires medical attention. Encourage your spouse to seek medical attention as soon as possible, and call for the elders of your church, for it is through their prayers of faith and anointing of oil that sin is forgiven and healing is bestowed[36]. Have faith in this, for it will be by faith that your spouse will be healed wholly. This is a true saying. Moreover, the dreamer will need to support your spouse in a very hand's on kind of way. Accordingly, your dream deals with your attitude in giving to others, especially your spouse. Charity begins at home. You should be very available, and your attitude should be one of caring, cheerfulness, generous, gentleness, and thoughtfulness. Moreover, God has appointed someone, to help you through this difficult time. See suggested course of action.

FUNERAL:

This dream has three meanings (choose one). (1) To the unmarried male or female: Only if desired, your dream denotes that after one month of solemn consecration, it will be granted you to get married[35]. (2) To be at someone else's funeral, your dream brings notice. This choice has three parts (choose one). (a) Did you know the individual within your dream and are they alive in your awaked life? If so, this person is getting ready to pass away, and dreamer will need to, from the onset, offer your services and other kindness to the family, especially ministerially. Nonetheless, you will have a part in the person's funeral arrangements and service; therefore, make yourself freely available when the time comes. Alternatively, if known, dreamer is being made aware of this person's backsliding. They have openly relapsed back into a shameful and embarrassing lifestyle; having sabotage their covering of grace given by God to hide their indiscretions and they have lost their faith in God, in His power of deliverance, and in miracles. Dreamer, you have the God given authority to pray for this person, coupled with a biblical based, no-nonsense, straight talking rebuke. Your rebuke may wake them up to their wrongdoings. You will be given the opportunity to privately, and seriously, talk with them. Your prayers and straight talk has the power to cause this person to return to a place of life, and be preserve from death, and they will according to the greatness of God's power, be set free from associating with those who are doomed to death. (b) If person was unknown, unseen, or only talked about, the person is the dreamer. Dreamer, you intentionally deny the grave condition your relationship with Christ is in, having chosen to close your eyes to your spiritual issues. See suggested course of action. (3) If dreamer attended your own funeral, meaning you witnessed your own funeral. This dream is a critical alarm, and this may be your last alarm or warning regarding the issue. The issue, dreamer, due to hatred and an unforgiving spirit, deep within the heart of the dreamer, so as to hide it from yourself, a severing of your personal relationship with Christ is probable (see Matthew 6:14, 15). Dreamer, your unforgiving heart, resulting from you having held on to hatred too long; has caused you to be reckoned as unforgiven within the spiritual realm. Read, understand, and embrace, Matthew 6:14, 15, 18:21-25, Galatians 5:13-26, 1 John 3:15, 4:20. Consequently, you have slowly abandoned all or some of the original foundational teachings of Christ and His apostles, especially the doctrine of grace (the free and unmerited favor and beneficence of God). This has resulted in a corrupt doctrine and perverse bondage (1 Timothy 4:1-16). You have ceased to abide in Christ, and instead have become enslaved again to sin and immorality, trusting in your own righteousness. Evil and depravity is your guiding force, thus sin has separated you from God. You have been led astray from those of The Way (Acts 9:2). Dreamer, the beginning, development, arrival, or manifestation of something large (significant in scope, extent, or effect) is about to happen within your life, in a threatening way. Favorably, the One True Living God can change things. However, this may be your last alarm or warning regarding attitude and thought life. After a seven day fast of purification from things unclean (e.g. hatred, an unforgiving spirit, or any unrestrained lustful indulgences), go an d present yourself to your spiritual leader. Remain within that faith-based community and remain innocent and free from behaviors and choices that defile. By this, you will be made clean, and restored. Moreover, studying the teachings of Jesus Christ and His disciples, and God's relation to it, you will experience God's truth again, and see the demonic for what it is - a lie. Dreamer, renounce corrupt teachings and accept all of God's truth and ways, including His truths you do not prefer, and His grace. See suggested course of action.

GRAVE, GRAVEYARD, MORGUE, OR REALMS OF THE DEAD (e.g. Gehenna, Hades, Sheol, Tartarus):

To see at a distance, enter into, or to be in a grave, graveyard, morgue, or the realm of the dead, this dream has three meanings (choose one). (1) Your dream comes as a serious alarm. Dreamer, God is bringing about His pre-arranged appointment with you, in spite of the fact that you have not yet believed on His Messiah. Will you meet Him? The following is necessary to say, dreamer, no dead philosophy, or any other lifeless "ism" will come to life to tell you truth, nor will a dead person, come to life, to tell you of what he or she has seen. For, if the "ism" did contain a spark of life, or if the dead did come back to tell you of what he or she experienced, you would not believe the teaching, nor would you believe the dead. For, relationship with Christ, appeals to people not by half-truths or lies, or ghosts or frightful apparitions; it appeals to your reason, your conscience, and your hopes. Dreamer, if you will not hear the Son of God and the warnings of the Scriptures, there is nothing, which you will or can hear, you will never be persuaded, thus, you will never escape the place of torment. Dreamer death is not only physical, but also it denotes a spiritual separation from God, a place of torment, aka "Tartaru s", which is also death. Dreamer, will you accept Jesus invitation for eternal life. The granting of eternal life to individuals, because of their acceptance of, and submission to, the Son of God, as Lord over their life, and His blood sacrifice, is a truth. Nonetheless, your appointment is neigh. If done properly, your comfort will be abundant in Christ. You will receive all the encouragement, help, and support, needed for your conversion to the faith, which is in Jesus Christ, via a Christian, who will be led by the Holy Spirit, and God's Holy Spirit leads to truth. Dreamer, if you will not hear the Son of God and the warnings of the Scriptures, there is nothing, which you will or can hear, you will never be persuaded, and will never escape the place of torment. Death is not only physical, but also it denotes a spiritual separation from God, a place of torment, aka "Tartarus", which is also death. See suggested course of action. (2) Did dreamer see another entering, or near a graveyard, or being lowered into a grave, or in or near a morgue or the realm of the Dead? Your dream denotes that a relative within your immediate family, perhaps the one depicted within your dream, is not in good health, and requires medical attention, as your dream denotes possible death. The dreamer will need to help in a very hand's on kind of way until. Accordingly, your dream deals with your attitude in giving to others, especially your family. Charity begins at home. You should be very available, and your attitude should be one of caring, cheerfulness, generous, gentleness, and thoughtfulness. Additionally, it is always a good time to get your house and papers in order (e.g. insurances, bequeaths, untold truths that need to be said), and always a good time to gathe r family together for prayer, support, wisdom, and truthfulness (Ecclesiastes 12:6). See suggested course of action. (3) For dreamer to be in, or near, a graveyard, or was lowered into a grave, or in or near a morgue or the realm of the Dead. Your dream is one of God's ways of breaking it to you gently, preparing you for one of life's common denominators, and if heeded, can prevent you from being emotionally blindsided by loss, as your dream is a notice; it symbolizes shortness of life. For someone who has met Jesus, we experience Him in the little graces, the big miracles, the ordinary days, and the curious moments. He is with us, leading us onward, even sharing our tears. This same Jesus trustworthy in life, even when we are not, can be trusted at t he ending of life, for He is the resurrection (John 11:25, 26). If we love Jesus and love our neighbor as we love ourselves, th ere is nothing in this world or the next to fear. Love is what we take with us, and love is what awaits us when we have finally arrived. Nonetheless, dreamer seek medical attention as soon as possible, and call for the elders of your church, for it is through th eir prayers of faith and anointing of oil upon you that sin is forgiven and "spiritual" healing bestowed, and perhaps physical healing[36]. This is a true saying, thus it is time to have faith in God. Further, to the dreamer it is said, for you to remember your Creator, before your days of trouble come and time has caught up with you (Ecclesiastes 12:1 -7). Additionally, it is always a good time to get your house and papers in order (e.g. insurances, bequeaths, untold truths that need to be said), and always a good time to gather family together for prayer, support, wisdom, and truthfulness (Ecclesiastes 12:6). See suggested course of action.

SUICIDE:

Dreamer give ear to this word for this dream is an alarm. This dream has three meanings (choose one). (1) Dreamer, let not your heart be trouble, you believe in Jesus; so once again, open your heart to Jesus, go to Adona i for help so that you may have life. Ask Jesus to deliver you from the enemy within, and from the demonic voices that persecute you mentally. Dreamer, you are part of a faith-based community, a Christian community that supports the building up of your spirit, and who shares the truth of God's word, authentic truth that leads to a soul entering heaven properly, in a good way. With that said, dreamer, do not hasten "your" day of the Lord. What is the day of the Lord to you, and/or to him or her who takes his or her own life? It is your time when you stand before Adonai Elohim; it is your day of reckoning. The Day of the Lord is sorrow to those who are hastily looking for their day of the Lord; it is dark and not light. It is as if a man, running away from a lion, came face to face with a bear; or went into the house and put his hand on the wall and got a bite from a snake. Will not the Day of the Lord be dark and not light, even very dark, with no light shining in it (Amos 5:18-20). Suicide, the taking of one's own life, is ungodly because it rejects God's gift of life. God is the giver of life. He gives, and He takes away (Job 1:21). No man or woman should presume to take God's authority upon themselves to end his or her own life. God is the only one who is to decide when and how a person should die, when your personal Day of the Lord will be. Rather, you should say as the psalmist, "My times are in your Hands" Psalm 31:15. Pray Psalm 31. See suggested course of action. (2) Although this revelation may prove a bit overwhelming, dreamer if you will heed what your dream is revealing about your character, and use what your dream is revealing about you, to repent and re-group emotionally and spiritually, you will go forth anew. Pray, Psalm 61:1-3. With that said if I might quote an old saying, "Adversity does not build character, it reveals it" (James Lane Allen). Your dream comes to reveal the truth of the dreamer's character, and your attitude regarding this self-awareness. Dreamer, while it is known that you are in a state of adversity, affliction, and misfortune, experiencing life's hardships, feeling deep despair in life. Yo u must also acknowledge that your pursuit of pleasure, as well as, your own bad choices and evil doing, has caused you to reach the point where you hate life. In all actuality, your adversity has revealed a character that is noted for wickedness, one who l ives in excess, mischievousness, and unruliness, to the point of recklessness, while blaming your lack of anointing, faithfulness, commitment, and stewardship on others. You are an angry disturbance and trouble to the upright. Not only this, but you trample those you consider less than yourself, harmful to those about you; taking advantage of their spiritual and natura l poverty, necessity, and inability to help themselves, making them poorer and needier than they were, before meeting you. While, you give nothing in return, especially in the form of service and care, exposing your selfish concern for your own interests and welfare, you lack any kind of agape, while looking for love in return. Unfortunately, not knowing you were being led by demons, spiritually deceived, and too prideful to acknowledge that you need some serious help, has left you feeling sad and all alone, and desiring to leave your life of sin. The enemy of your soul has you primarily focusing on issues that lack depth and negatively concentrating on emotions and other needs of the soul that only God can filled. Favorably, while all this is true today, God will grant you His grace and mercy, to start afresh. Therefore, make an earnest effort at repentance and change, and never, do you ever, again allow Satan to have you lower the beautifulness of a Christian life and Christian people to something that needs to be rebuff. See suggested course of action. (3) Dreamer, you are allowing the spirit of fear to cause you to lose your psychological and spiritual identity (the individual characteristics by which the dreamer is known or is recognized by), and to terrorize you. It, the spirit of fear, has become your own personal terrorist. Weakened by frequent panic attacks, brought on by your own guilt and the fear of God's retribution, you will begin to crack in your personality. He, who carries his or her own accuser, and their own tormentor, always in their bosom, cannot but be afraid on every side (Matthew Henry's Commentary on Job 18:11-21). The only foundation upon which one should wisely establish his or her identity is the principles within the Word of God. Read and understand Romans 8:15, 2 Timothy 1:7. This demon terrorizes you in your thoughts, when you are paranoid, when you are afraid, when you hesitate, when you are insecure, when you are impatient, when you are confused, when panic comes, when your thoughts are filled with worry, when you are uneasy and unsure, when despair and depression find you, when stress comes, when you are full of apprehension, when your thoughts forecast only doom and gloom, when you are restless, when you are frightful, when you are full of dread, when you are anxious, when you are nervous, and when you feel hopeless. You will find this demon in every phobia. Question to journal: What would it feel like if all of your fears were suddenly released from you at one time? Pause and feel that. Bible story, there was that herd of pigs that Legion was cast into, and these pigs found their thoughts to be so unbearable that they all ran of f a cliff to commit suicide, because they could not bear what had been unleashed upon them (Matthew 8:28-34, Mark 5:1-20, Luke 8:26-39). This is what the spirit of fear oftentimes leads to, if embraced wholly. On the other hand, the man whom, the devils were suddenly released from, was found sitting, clothed, healed, and in his right mind, and all this done without medication. The spirit of fear is adversarial to the Word of God that says all things will work together for good, to those who love God, and are called according to His purpose. For, if you truly can believe the Word of God, it will change all the rules that darkness has established in your heart and mind. Now I say to you that before you can move forward, fear must be cast out, and renounced, and not medicated. Therefore, dreamer, earnestly renounce the insidious voice of t he devil. If you will daily come away and pray, then God will heal you of all things, only come with much prayer and spiritual fasting. The spiritual fa st is that time of waiting when you are praying and asking the Lord to come and perform that which only He can perform. Similar to a literal fast, during this time you must abstain, but from any counsel or thoughts that tempt you to put your hand on the matter, or to turn you away from waiting on, and having faith in, the Lord. During this time of waiting, you simply need to continue in prayer and be still. Then you will know that only God's love is able to break the curse of darkness from over your mind, body, and spirit. Warning, it will be during your spiritual fast that weaknesses, such as unbelief, doubt, fear, pride, arrogance, will come forth to tempt you to eat the counsel of their lies, rather than to wait for the Lord to come to deliver, heal, help, save, reveal, and/or guide. Wait on the Lord, for He is faithful to come, and again I say wait on the Lord. Moreover, if urged by God, declare a one, two, or three day fast without food. See suggested course of action.

UNDERTAKER:

This dream has four meanings (choose one). (1) If dreamer is actually considered a spiritual or religious leader, e.g. bishop, deacon, deaconess, elder, evangelist, minister, overseer, pastor, pope, preacher, priest, rabbi, superintendent, teacher, or any cleric or ecclesiastical leader type role. Your dream denotes that the dreamer presents as a terrorists; using violence or the threat of violence, to intimidate others, to gain control over them. You will betray family and friends for money. You have abused your power and authority, and because none opposed you, you withheld not yourself from doing wrong and evi l. Like that old serpent, the devil, the dreamer uses the weaknesses of the flesh, pride, spirituality, religion appealing to lustful desires, and all things appealing to flesh, to lure people into following your words, and into doubting the true essence of God's Word, and to draw them into lasciviousness. Your intentions are to get others to question the validity of God's power, God's word, and the genuineness of true Christians; subsequently, tricking them into sinning against God, because of doubt. Dreamer, you are also a slave to all these things, having yourself been tricked, and deceived by that ancient serpent, the devi l. You power and authority will be taken from you and given to another. Although you will fight them greatly; nonetheless, you will not be able to overwhelm this person. Additionally, your dream denotes a "prayer less" ministry. Dreamer, without prayer, you will not learn the authentic truth of God's Word; and will never be able to teach that truth. The dreamer is counseled to learn well the lesson and power of prayer. See suggested course of action. (2) Dreamer, you use your inborn prophetic gifting for occult practices (e.g. astrology, necromancy, psychic, sorcery, spiritists, witchery, or wizardry). Whichever practice, your manner of service is the use of witchcraft in some form or another, for you command people to believe and do what you say, and/or press individuals to follow other gods. Additionally, like a venomous snake, preferring to strike you a t your weakest point, during your weakest moments, and one who attacks from behind attempting to catch you off guard; dreamer, this is your mindset, a primary part of your character; this is how you treat others, and this is how you are viewed by others. The Lord wants you to focus on, and rectify, this part of your character. Repentance and a renunciation of your spiritually poisonous ways, is advised that you may be delivered and restored to right relationship with Jesus Christ. See suggested course of action. (3) Dreamer, you are one who is the antithesis of Christ. You respect your own truth, while never acknowledging, your truth is delivered without grace; thus, it is never enough to fill an emaciated soul. You are embracing and fulfilling the desire of the evil one, which is to exalt himself as king over your life and over the lives of those connected to you. Dreamer, the enemy of your soul; has you in a state where you are at a loss of what to do. That old serpent, the devil, want s you to be perplexed, to be without resources, to be in straits, to be left wanting, to be embarrassed, to be in doubt, not to know which way to turn, to be at a loss with one's self, not to know how to decide or what to do, to fear even insanity. Dreamer, your allowing the demonic to reign, is leading (or has led) you to a place of desolation, and all this because of a spirit of fear that has possessed or oppressed you a long time. Dreamer, although you are confused, no longer allow the devil, to rule over you. If you will allow these words, "Fear Not" (Psalm 23:4), to be a banner sort to say over your life, starting from this moment forward, then the following words will be before you, encouraging you, on your journey out of darkness. God's Spirit will give you the strength you need, to raise you up and to succeed, and for vision thru the night, He gives you these words of light. Fear not My child, for I am with you always, and I feel all of your pain, and I see all of your tears, fear not My ch ild, for I'm will be with you always, and I know how to care of what belongs to Me (Helen Baylor). Therefore, earnestly oppose the subtle, yet bold and strong, voices of the demonic; therefore, you must also be strong, as well as, courageous. Dreamer, if you can once again believe that the Bible is the only word of God and the tenets of the Christian faith is the only true measure of relationship with the Heavenly Father. Then there is no fear, for the Lord will guard you from all evil, preserving your life (Psalm 121); God will not allow your foot to slip, pray: Psalm 123. See suggested course of action. (4) Dreamer, in your most, inner deepest feelings, there is deep and bitter anger and ill will towards a person, place, or organization that represented God to you. Unfortunately, due to a vicious violation inflicted upon you, you blame God, although that person has, or will, receive their just punishment, and you will see justice. You have never admitted to yourself that the violation prospered due to you r victim mindset, and your unwillingness to stand up for yourself, this needs to be acknowledge also. Notwithstanding, in blaming God for everything, you, now, mouth that Adonai Elohim creates imperfect beings and then forces them to rise up to a level of perfection, which by design, they are unable to attain, by torturing them, causing millions to suffer in body and soul. You reason that this is God's only way, a path of pain, torture, and then death. You ask what human being aspires to evolve through this endless agony. You proclaim that God's promises are no more than vague words of doubtful happiness, and implacable laws that promise remote and unknowable joy, under the mask of love of humanity. You say His ways are nothing more than a profound indifference and a hardened selfishness. Further, you believe that God's intolerance of sin and the inherent results of sin, mainly separation from Him, as written within Holy Writ, and expressed in Christian dogma, are the picture of an angry god, conjured up by angry, unwise, and foolish men. You boast of philosophies, which appeal to the lustful desires of human nature, condoning rebellious, unhealthy, immodest, immoral, indecent, lewd, and lascivious, behavior.

Desires that if not checked, can and often do lead to early death, as you have personally witnessed. This is what you call love. You exalt your wisdom above the Creator. While you discredit the Creator's wise and sensible guidelines for living life, on this side of eternity, as healthy, humanly, and sanely as possible; and in harmony with His provision for life on the other side of eternity, in heaven. You respect your truth, while never acknowledging, it is delivered without grace; thus, it is never eno ugh to fill an emaciated soul. Read, understand, and embrace Galatians 5:13-25. Favorably, your dream is only a warning and is sent in the spirit of grace. If your thoughts, feelings, and beliefs are not rectified, you will open the door of your spiri t to more abominations of various types, to "stir up" more feelings of disgust and abhorrence towards Jesus and His ways and means. If you continue on this path, your behaviors will become so vicious and vile; your actions will arouse distaste and/or hate of y ou by others, and you will feel the brunt of those feelings of others towards you. There will be no response of love, sympathy, or tenderness toward you. Moreover, you will expose your physical body to illnesses, especially within the excretory system, from which you will be unable to recover without divine help, via Jesus. Dreamer, forgiveness of that person, place, or organization that viciously violated you, and heartfelt repentance to Jesus, coupled with a renunciation of your spiritually poisonous words and ways are the antivenin to the venomous attack of that old serpent, the devil, upon your life. Further, if urged by God, declare a one, two, or three day fast, coupled with studying the teachings of Jesus Christ. You will again beg in to experience God's truth, and see the demonic for what it is - a lie. If relevant, avoid personal isolation and isolated groups that teach something different from the gospel of Jesus Christ. Examples of "something different" are, no one is "right" but our western sect, condemnation theologies, teachings of hate, any racist ideology, or murder for everyone but me and/ or our small group, or any other oppressive ideology. Jesus died for the world, and not exclusively for any one person, sect, or western denomination. Moreover, if not practiced regularly, go to church, join a church, a faith based bible-believing community, commit to that ministry, and don't leave, no matter what, for three years. Forsake not the gathering of yourself together wi th other mainstream Christians. A prophecy will be given you, via someone within that ministry, during this season, write it down for it will happen. Even more, entering the House of God should be done reverently rather than carelessly. Cease from many words but rather humbly learn, and let your words be sprinkled with empathy. For, in spite of what we do not know about the many mysteries of God and life, one thing remains eternally true: God is our loving Father. He does not desire that any one perish; great effort is exercised to save us, even in the moment of our death. Hence, do not call anyone impure (e.g. unsaved, hypocrite, unregenerate, ignorant) that God alone has made clean (read Acts 10:15, Ephesians 4:17-5:21).

Suggested Course of Action

Question to consider and journal, did your dream depict any symbols that alludes to, the dreamer will make the necessary changes, spiritually, emotionally, and/or physically to affect a more positive outcome? If changes are initiated, your dreams will change. Nevertheless, if you are here, dreamer this moment, God is placing before you, life and good, death and evil, and He is asking that you choose life (Deuteronomy 30:15-20).

Some may ask, what good is it to choose life if ultimately the choice proves empty in view of one's imminent death? What good is it whether one is righteous or wicked if both paths lead to the same end? Do we serve God simply for what we get out of it, so that God is merely a means to an end? The wise author writes in Ecclesiastes, all this I laid to heart, ex amining it all, how the righteous and the wise and their deeds are in the hand of God; whether it is love or hate one does not know.

Everything that confronts them is vanity, since the same fate comes to all, to the righteous and the wicked, to the good and the evil, to the clean and the unclean, to those who sacrifice and those who do not sacrifice. As are the good, so are the sinners; those who swear are like those who shun an oath. The same fate comes to everyone. If all roads lead to the same end, why be righteous? Why sacrifice for others, why not "live it up" while one is alive. It would seem that faithfulness is not nearly as important as one's own happiness, even if this happiness is only short-lived and, in the end, futile. The most obvious answer here is that eternal life is the greatest of all things, for it does not end. Thus, from an eternal perspective, you must take time and consider your final destiny, hopefully heaven, as well as, the destiny of the arrogant and wicked (see 1 Corinthians 6:9-20, Ephesians 5). It is within this context that we must understand the reality of life and death and of heaven and hell. For, there are three types of life, and three types of death, physical, spiritual, and eternal.

The fact is that physical death is a part of life; in this, the same fate comes to all. We are to expect it and there is no way out of it. That fact noted, it is important, that while we are here on this earth, we invest in that which will enable help us to make the journey towards heaven, investing in that which will lead us out of this literal and spiritual exile into the Promised Land. This is why be righteous, for the wicked will not be found there. Read, understand, and embrace Matthew 25:1-13, the Parable of the wise and foolish.

Dreamer, it is time for you to learn to love God and learn to, follow His plan for your life. If you can do this, you can live forever in His paradise (heaven). On the other hand, the second kind of death, spiritual death, this is not fated for all, but only for those who have chosen death and evil, over life and good. It is when we think that we do not need God. It is when you embrace and live out the ideology of, "what good is it whether one is righteous or wicked if both paths lead to the same end, or I will not be one who serves God simply for what I can get out of it, I won't serve Him at all". The important point is that spiritual death is when we refuse to seek out and have fellowship with the one true and living God. Spiritual death is a separation from Adonai Elohim. There is nothing emptier than the emptiness one feel inside, in their hour of darkness, in their hour of reckoning, when they realize that ultimately the paths of the righteous and wicked do not lead to the same end. Spiritual death is what can, and often does, lead to eternal death. If we physically die while we are separated from God, that condition will be permanent, it will last for all eternity. The truth is that if we do not want to live with, and in, God's presence while we are on this earth, God will not force us to live with Him forever, on the other side of eternity. Also, read and understand Galatians 5:19-21, for this speaks of spiritual death.

Dreamer, God created us as free creatures. You are free to determine your own destiny, thus the question, will you choose life or death. God will never take that freedom away from you, even if it means being separated from Him forever. This death is not common to all, but only to those who choose to, not live life on God's terms, but on their own terms. So, what happens if we are separated from God forever? Well, in the spiritual realm, there are only two places. One is where God is and the other is where God is not. He (Jesus) is asking that you choose life.

How do we defeat spiritual death, and thus, eternal death? While we cannot escape physical death, we can escape spiritual death. Dreamer, will you not repent and receive God's gift of eternal life, while grace is here? Dreamer, the issue of eternal life will not, be forced upon you. Favorably, even in this, there is nothing too hard for God; grace is still available that you may change your heart. However, you must personally respond, by repenting and genuinely committing to some type of righteous change, to have life; with primary emphasis on life after this present life (see Acts 2:37-42). Therefore, begin again to hope for eternal life in heaven. Your soul is at stake. Re-shift your paradigm. It is suggested that you weight your choices, the good versus the wicked, the sacred versus the profane, those that promote life, and those that bring about death. Dreamer, there are character traits within you that you need to render obsolete, and began anew attempting to move forward, using different tactics to overcome unproductive habitual life cycle choices, and for maneuvering through this thing, we call life in a more, better way.

Now, pray (See Prayer of Deliverance, pg. 897)

Specific Meaning

If you sense that your dream is some type of inspiration regarding, death, dying, and the dead, heaven or hell (e.g. consideration of a business, a song, a movie). Consider your dream, hold it in your heart, and ponder it until your inspiration becomes clearer, then begin writing and promoting, your sermon, song, spiritual teaching, or divine inspiration.

Note: If, there is a very high propensity for situations that may lead to devastation, perhaps even death, then this dream is a precautionary warning, to prevent serious harm to yourself, and/or others, due to possible abuse, violence, or negligenc e. If there, is a potential for incarceration, homicide, or some kind of death or dying experience. Dreamer, re-consider your activity as harmful, hurtful, illegal, and life threatening, at present. Handle your business by surrendering, first to Jesu s, and then to appropriate authorities. The details, kept within context of your dream, should be relevant to your life, and closely resemble your real-life situations. Meaning it can actually occur during your awaked state. This will help you narrow down the specifics needed to support and steer you clear of possible mishaps.

Otherwise noted, per your lifestyle, if your dream closely resembled real life situations, meaning it can actually occur during your awaked state, this dream may be an Ordinary Dream, resulting from daily activities (see Chapter One, Chalom). These sorts of dreams are usually about your routine, mundane activities or anxieties that overwhelm your mind during the day. They are an inner release mechanism, which helps provide you with emotional balance and the maintaining of your sanity. These dreams are not significant, and do not warrant special attention.

However, if your dream was inundated with symbols that are not easily linked to your life activities, then the spiritual implications (the interpretation) should be heeded.

EMOTIONS

(anger, awe, crying, fear, hatred, humiliation, joy, laughter, love, pain, sad, and tired)

....a time to weep, and a time to laugh; a time to mourn, and a time to dance ...a time to keep silent, and a time to spea k; a time to love, and a time to hate... The Preacher (ref, Ecclesiastes 3:4, 8) Jesus wept. (John 11:35)

Emotions operate on many levels; they have a physical aspect as well as a psychological aspect. Emotions bridge thoughts, feelings, and actions, they operate in every part of a person, they affect many aspects of a person, and the person affects many aspects of the emotions." (John D. [Jack] Mayer)

This category deals with human emotions, defined as any strong feeling. Some short descriptions of types, phrases, and/or other processes and particulars, connected in some way to this category is, for example, agitated, anger, awe, blue, dejected, delighted, emotionless, excited, hate, indignation, joyful, love, outraged, pleased, regret, sad, sorry, worked-up Also, see category content list, or index.

All Symbols and Referents, Notes (1, 2, 3, etc.), Suggested Course of Action, and Specific Meaning offer guidance toward a more comprehensive interpretation.

Notes

1. Unless otherwise noted elsewhere, if, in your everyday living, your awaked state, as part of your lifestyle, work, or ministerial activities, or a special event, you have a very real connection with any activity involving emotions. For example, any work that is a potential catalyst for the expressions of strong feelings, e.g. acting, advisor, advocacy, art, counseling, drama, mentoring, music, preaching, protest, social worker, or teacher of young children, teens, and/ or young adults. Perhaps you're a physician, or are involve in hospice or care for someone who is incapacitated by a chronic illness or injury. Have you recently experienced the death of a loved one, or are you a victim of abuse or some manner of violation, or possibly in a season of grieving? Skip interpretation and go to Specific Meaning at the end of this category.

    Otherwise noted, if your dream closely resembles real life situations, meaning whatever event, situation, or catalyst that aroused the emotion, can actually occur (or has occurred) during your awaked state. This dream may be an Ordinary Dream (see Chapter One, Chalom), resulting from your daily activities (e.g. if you were crying over someone or a situation, literally known to you and the situation is actually real, this is your literal grief over the issue). These sorts of dreams are usually about your routine, mundane activities or anxieties that overwhelm your mind during the day. They are an inner release mechanism, which helps provide you with emotional balance and the maintaining of your sanity. These dreams are not significant, and do not warrant special attention.

2. Probables: Emotions are frequently demonstrated in many, and very personal ways; for example, is crying and everyday event for you, or does anger remind you of a particular person, place, thing, or environment? Thus, could the emotion depicted be a possible probable (see Chapter One, section entitled, Probables)? Hence, dreamer may also consider your own personal and special associations with various emotions, as long as the interpretation is kept within the principles of spiritual boundary markers, landmarks, and property lines, (see Chapter One, section entitled, Spiritualizing Boundary Markers, Landmarks, and Property Lines).

3. Determine who your dream is for you or another. Always, considering yourself first, reflecting on your present behaviors. Ask yourself, "Why am I dreaming about this now? What is this dream revealing about me? Have I taken on new attributes? Has anyone commented on my present behaviors as being untypical of me? Has my ministry changed for the better or for the worse? What about my beliefs, doctrine, or philosophy, are they still based on Holy Writ? Is there something I need to know about those I am ministering to or serving?

Remember your emotions within your dream. Were you happy, relieved, encouraged, or bewildered? Were you disappointed and sad? Were you anxious, concerned, frightened, offended, or fearful? Were there feelings of weariness, discouragement, embarrassment, hostility, rage, resentment, and/or revenge? Were you content? If dreamer's emotions were a focal point, this is a good indicator that your dream is about you (the dreamer). In light of your dream, via the relevant interpretation, do you believe that your emotions will enhance or endanger your well-being, safety, and/or happiness, if so, how and why? Do you believe that your belief system will be strengthen or weaken in any way, due your emotions, if so, how and why? See following relevant subcategory, the interpretation is about and for you.

Was someone else angry, anxious, confused, content, depressed, fearful, joyful, loving, peaceful, or sad? An answer of yes is a good indicator that your dream is about another and their role, and/or influential eff ects, within the life of the dreamer. If someone else, emotions were the focal point. Consider, is someone greatly influencing your physical, spiritual, or mental health, your understanding, perspective, and reasoning regarding spiritual issues? Are they enhancing your spiritual and/or literal prosperity, or are they responsible for the dwindling thereof? Could they be influencing your ministry, on some level? Do you know someone whose life activities or physical being is similar to that which stood out the most within your dream? Could it be that person? If you sense that your dream is for or about another, the question as to why you have been made privy to this information, and how do you factor into the equation, should be seriously considered along with necessary actions. Perhaps the dreamer is being made aware of the plight of someone, and you are to get involved (see Chapter One, Are You Ready to Hear the Messages in Your Dreams, section entitled, The 10% for others).

If your dream is for, or about another:

Dreams that reference others and the revelation within those dreams, is not given haphazardly to any individual, but only to those with the ability, and influence to do something with the information; this is also prophecy. With that, journal the following questions, and if unable to answer the questions now, this denotes that the person, represented within your dream, will enter your life shortly. Are you entering into a personal relationship with someone? Do you not know or understand what you're looking at, especially certain behaviors, when learning about this person? Has someone new entered your life or maybe you've just begun opening up to someone not so new, and have started listening to their advice, accepting their assistance, or are you supporting or enabling someone? Are you in denial regarding the toxicity of one of your present relationships, particularly a spouse, family member, or friend? Are you anxious, concerned, frightened, and/or troubled by recent changes in your behavior, especially because of someone's influence upon your life at present? Have you recently become aware of (or is being made aware of, via your dream) certain undesirable behaviors within you towards another? Are you trying to cut ties with one that is bad company? Have you just joined (or re-joined) a church, fellowship, or social group?

Note: If your dream has attributes that indicate that your dream is about you, and other attributes that indicate that your dream is about another, dreamer should consider that your dream is about you and another. For example, were you crying with others? Were you and another angry at each other in a heated dispute? Were you and another amorous towards each other? Unless otherwise noted elsewhere, an answer of yes, to one or more of these, or similar questions, is a good indicator that the dream is about the dreamer, and about another.

Therefore, while your dream is about the dreamer, the dreamer should expect the role and/or influential effects of another, also plays a part in your interpretation. For example, dreamer may have been emotionally wounded, violated, hurt, by another, and now that hurt has bred bitterness and an unforgiving spirit within the dreamer. From which now the dreamer needs deliverance, again, see relevant interpretation.

More questions to consider. Why has the person been allowed within your life, and/or how did they get there? Again, if unable to answer the questions now, this denotes that the person, represented within your dream, will enter your life shortly. If their activity, within your dream, has proven positive, via the interpretation, this someone will prove, unwittingly, to be a very strong ally, benefactor, defender, and supporter. God has sent this someone into your life to help you carry out your next endeavor by enlarging your spiritual capacity. Allow the strength of that person's character to guide, help, and support you. On the other hand, if his or her presence and/or activity, within your dream, proved negative, via the interpretation, for sure, this person will prove to be a very strong and formidable challenge for you, perhaps unto death. If negative, this dream is a dire warning. Take steps accordingly to struggle against, or to cut off, adverse and unfavorable relationships. Remember certain personalities are all encompassing, affecting everything, cataclysmic, contagious, deadly, harmful, infectious, predatory, and/or venomous. Symbolically meaning that if allowed to continue or prosper within your life, serious harm or death to the dreamer may result. Idolize no one, especially beyond the warning of the Lord, and we are definitely not to lay our lives down for no one. Then again, this person maybe allowed within your life, because of the dreamer's unwillingness to abstain from immorality after having been asked to abstain from such by God, see 1 Corinthians 6:9-20, Galatians 5:19-21, or the dreamer's self-righteous behavior, or a lack of a balanced and honest view of your own personality. In this case, this person will affect self-awareness within the life of the dreamer, exposing the negative traits of your personality, especially those traits, which cause you to follow, or to be so easily misled, and/or your wrong beliefs; no matter, this type of mentality needs reckoning with. Graciously, all of this will restore the dreamer to his or her right place with God, opening your eyes to see how far you've strayed from God (1 Corinthians 5:4-7; James 5:20). The lesson is, no matter how personable, powerful, or difficult a person, or how uncertain or unpopular the choices and issues, always take the next biblical and ethical step, for obedience to God's principles will always prove safer and stronger foundationally. Although, you will need all kinds of outside support to recover from this person's domination, no longer, allow that particular person's influence within your life to continue or thrive, especially if negative, end it abruptly.

4. Consider all the people, places, backgrounds, and activity highlighted within your dream.

Known (in your awaked life) person, place, or organization within your dream:

Unless otherwise noted elsewhere, people, animals, places, backgrounds that are actually known by the dreamer in your awaked life, indicates a part of you that you recognize within yourself on some level or another. Question to journal, if dreamer seriously considers all the particulars, what stood out the most, what features, or character traits stood out the most. For example, age, color, height, size, happiness, considerate, loving, let you be yourself, peacefulness, encourager, irrational, leader, liar, mentor, passionate, personable, neglected, poor, run-down, sage, shyster, unwise, upscale, vengeful. Write down (journal) the particular highlighted within your dream. The attribute or activity highlighted is for a reason. Since the attribute written down is a part of you, namely the dreamer's nature, demeanor, and/or lifestyle, an honest and unbiased assessment is very important for truth sake. Happy note, considering that other people's attributes, within dreams, also represent attributes of your own personality, causes one to look at another in a better light. According to your capacity to embrace self-awareness and a rectification of mind, body, and spirit, God will begin to enhance, make better, more attractive, sanctify, diminish, and make pure and free from sin and guilt, this part of you.

Otherwise noted, if the person, animal, place, or background within your dream is actually known by the dreamer, in your awaked life, this person, animal, place, or background may represent him or herself, or itself.

Unknown in your awaked life or although known, was unseen, invisible, or only talked about person, place, or organization within your dream:

Unless otherwise noted elsewhere, if you did not recognize, the person, place, thing, they, or it, was not seen, invisible, or only talked about within your dream, this indicates an attribute or activity within your life that you are unfamiliar with, or are in denial about, or you refuse to acknowledge it, but it does exists. Question to journal, what emotion stood out the most. Although, on some conscious level, you are aware of a certain attitude within you, you have chosen to filter out or simply ignore certain information about yourself that contradicts your view of yourself and/or your preconceived notions of others and of the world around you. Possibly protecting yourself, emotionally and psychologically, from a situation, which you are unable to cope with at this time, or you lack control over; then again, perhaps the dreamer has an exaggerated or unrealistic view of yourself. No matter the reason, right now a question is before you, via your dream. Do you want to know this part of yourself? According to your ability to handle self-awareness, God will begin to reveal this side of you to you. Why, He wants to balance your understanding of things; thus, effecting wholeness within your life, so that the enemy will no longer be able to manipulate your emotions so easily. The Paraclete is with you to help you throughout this entire process, listen to Him. Now, in your life, this activity or attribute needs reckoning with, somehow or someway.

Otherwise noted, (known or unknown), if the person, place or thing that initiated (or was a recipient of) the emotion or activity within your dream was not seen, invisible, or only talked about within your dream, this may indicate that the dreamer does not recognize the influential effects another has within your life, or upon your attitude.

If more than one person (known or unknown):

Consider what the group had in common. What behavior, character trait, feature, action, or activity, stood out the most? For example, were they argumentative, authoritative, beautiful, criminal minded, dancing, difficult, dressed unusual, enigmatic, fighting, focused, flirty, helpful, hurtful intentions, powerful, promiscuous, quiet, secretive, seemed unreal, unassuming? That which was highlighted and noted is what you need to focus on at present.

If the emotion is a desirable or positive one, allow the strength of that attribute to help you overcome some manner of immorality or irreverence within your life and/or to help you to become better, productively, for the Kingdom of God in some manner. If the attribute is an undesirable or negative one, take steps accordingly to struggle against the growing desires of the carnal side of you.

For dreams of the dead see following note.

Were you mourning the death of someone? While the dead has nothing to do with the living (Ecclesiastes 9:4-6), it may be considered what emotion did that person depict within your dream, e.g. was the person angry, crying, happy? See category, Death, and/or other relevant categories.

5. In addition to the following interpretations, see index or relevant categories for more information. For example, if a celebration was highlighted, see category, Celebrations. Kept within context of your dream and the interpretation, the additional symbols are perhaps relevant. It will be within the sum of all the symbols that you will find a more thorough interpretation.

6. The table of human emotions is like a spectrum, they are broad in range and deep in variations. Conventional scientific wisdom recognizes six basic emotions, happy, surprised, afraid,

disgusted, angry, and sad, but new research suggests there may only be four, happy, sad, surprise/fear, and anger/disgust. The experiment suggests the differences between surprise and fear and between anger and disgust developed later, more for social reasons than survival[11]. Others interposes that they are only two emotions in the world, love and fear. While the extensiveness of emotions is great, this category will deal with anger, awe, crying, fear, hatred, humiliation, joy, laughter, love, pain, sad, and tired.

It is suggested that the dreamer see also, other relevant research, via a Bible concordance, Bible illustrated dictionary, encyclopedia, or internet, to seek biblical guidelines for metaphorical meanings of a particular emotion. Having done your research you should be able to determine some basic emotions and behaviors your Lord and Savior wants you to focus on.

Symbols and Referents

Emotions are generally portrayed within dreams for the purpose of revelation. Emotions within dreams figuratively reveal what's in your heart; especially that which has not yet been actually acknowledged, displayed, or expressed. Since thoughts and behaviors come from either a place of positive human emotions or negative human emotions, these types of dreams often expose your thoughts, feelings, and subsequent actions, especially those thoughts, feelings, and actions that effect certain aspects of your life connected to others.

In addition to the varied meanings of emotions, other common words, expressions, usages, (e.g. slang or clichés), or a 'probable' that are metaphorically represented by any of the following are also considered (this section is an addendum at the end of the relevant subcategory).

Category Content: If not listed see index, perchance, for your specific type of emotion dream. Note: This category will deal with anger, awe, crying, fear, hatred, humiliation, joy, laughter, love, pain, sad, and tired. The varying degrees of intensity of these basic emotions, some being mild, others moderate, and others strong in intensity, will be parenthesized alongside th e primary emotions listed.

- Anger (angry, annoyed, destructive, disgusted, enraged, frustrated, hostile, indignation, intimidated, jumpy, mad, outraged, revenge, upset)
  - Indignation, Outrage, "Righteous Indignation"
- Awe (adore, inspired, respect, reverence, religious zeal)
- Crying (to shed tears as an expression of emotion)
  - Altar (crying at or upon); Baby, Child Crying; Cry baby (to see a baby crying, not your child); Bawling (to cry out in a deep loud voice, during prayer); Bawling (to cry out making violent twisting and rolling movements with your body because of severe pain); Crying (to shed tears of humiliation, joy, sadness, or grief); Dirge or Requiem (to hear a song or a slow mournful piece of music, causing you to cry); Embrace and weep (to weep upon, on); Groaning (frowning while grunting because of distress, pain, or anger due to being treated badly or unfairly); Hollering (yell, shout, or rejoice while crying); Lament (to verbally express grief, sadness, regret, or disappointment about an issue while shedding tears); Naked (to be naked and crying); People crying together (3 or more); Poke in the Eye and cause tears; Sniveling (whining and complaining with a runny nose); Sobbing (to weep aloud with convulsive gasping- hyperventilate); To stop crying; To not cry, or be unable to cry, or refuse to cry, or to be forbidden to cry; Wailing (to grieve loudly with a mournful high-pitched sound); Weeping (shedding tears quietly or to shed a tear); Cry for help (depicted by an SOS signal)
- Fear (anxious, apprehensive, cautious, concerned, confused, doubtful, exasperated, frightened, hesitant, insanity, nervous, overwhelmed, panic, scared, shocked, stressed, surprised, suspicious, wary, or worry)

- Hatred (animosity, contempt, envy, greed, grudgingness, hateful, ignored, indifferent, jealousy, manipulative, obnoxious, rude, vengeful)
- Humiliation see subcategory, Crying (Humiliation)
- Joy or Laughter (enthusiastic, excited, happy, humorous, joyful, lively, or smiling)
- Love (agape, eros, philia, and storge)
  - Kissing (a way of expressing human love for another, includes family or sexual)
- Pain (disappointed, dissatisfied, distressed, guilt, harassed, hurt, lonely, or physical or mental pressure)
- Sad, see subcategory, Crying (Sad)
- Tired (burdened, drained, exhausted, weary), see category, Abating (To decrease in degree, force, intensity, or grow tired)

ANGER (angry, annoyed, destructive, disgusted, enraged, frustrated, hostile, indignation, intimidated, jumpy, mad, outraged, revenge, upset):

This dream has three meanings (choose one). (1) This type of dream denotes spiritual jealousy, brokenness, and spiritual murder. Dreamer, because of deep-seated anger within you, that has not been dealt with by you; you are attempting to, spiritually murder another. Spiritual murder is a premeditated attempt to; cruelly destroy someone's reputation or an attempt to destroy someone's personal relationship with Christ. First, it is important to understand that anger, be it silent rage, emotional outburst, or expressed physically on some level or another, is not part of God's plan for your life. Favorably, God can ultimately use your anger to bring about His will. The following few principles may be applied to deep-seated anger that deliverance from anger may begin to manifest within you. First, you are to earnestly, attempt to love others in a way that reflects the agape love of Christ, see 1 John 4:7, 8. Second, you are not to judge others, but to genuinely show kindness, treating people the way you want to be treated, see Ephesians 4:37-32, Luke 6:37-49. This will keep you from becoming enslaved again to sin and immorality (see Romans 3:21-4:16). Another cause, in judging others (e.g. condemnatory, critical, derogatory, disapproving, harsh, negative, scornful, or uncomplimentary in your thoughts or speaking aloud) you set a precedent over your own life, discharging a universal law. The Universal Law: With the same judgments, you judge others, so will you be judged (see Matthew 7:1-5). Thus, you should not only respond gracefully, perhaps in the face of accusations, but also go out of the way to, "take the higher ground", to serve others. For, Jesus likens a congenial relationship to the bond He shares with everyone who believes in Him. In fact, Jesus' bond with believers is even stronger, since it is not marred by jealousy, anger, frustration, or disagreements. Therefore, dreamer, you are instructed to live at peace with others, avoiding arguments and conflict, and you are encouraged to take the higher ground by playing the role of peacemaker when disagreements arise. See suggested course of action. (2) Your dream denotes one who is under heavy demonic influence, possibly demonic possession. The Bible gives some examples of people possessed or influenced by demons. See Matthew 9:32, 33, 12:22; 17:18; Mark 5:1-20, 7:26-30; Luke 4:33-36, 22:3; Acts 16:16-18. From these examples, you can find some symptoms of demonic influence and gain insight as to how a demon possesses or influences someone. While it is believed that a believer can be influenced by the devil, see Matthew 16:23, there is no example in Scripture of a Spirit-filled believer in Christ being possessed by a demon. It is highly believed that a Christian cannot be possessed because he or she has the Holy Spirit abiding within them and the Spirit of God will not share residence with a demon (Matthew 12:29; Mark 3:27; Luke 11:21, 22), that's if you have the Holy Spirit dwelling within. With that said, unfortunately, many believers open their lives up to demonic involvement through the embracing of some sin, within the context of your dream, that sin is extreme anger, perhaps due to rebellion, bitterness, drug, alcohol abuse that alters one's state of consciousness, or just a tantrum against the way God has orchestrated things in life generally. Dreamer, you may not like God's ways and means, but you do have to accept and surrender to them all. For, your human understanding of, and reaction to, spiritual realities is oftentimes crudely green. The book of Ephesians (2:2, 8-9, 4:17-24, 6:10-18) gives clear instructions on how we are able to have victory in our lives in the battle against the forces of evil. The first step is to once again, place your faith in Christ Jesus, who breaks the rule of evil. Second, choose, again by God's grace, to put off ungodly habits and to put on godly habits by the renewing of y our mind, and by resisting the devil, not giving him room in your mind, your thought processes, your behaviors, and life, for there is truly a spiritual battle going on within you. Dreamer, stand on the side of truth, righteousness, the gospel, faith, salvation, the Word of God, and prayer. If demonic possession is the case, exorcism (commanding demons and all unclean spirits to leave in the name of Jesus the Christ) was practiced by the disciples as part of Christ's instructions, see Matthew 10, Mark 9:38, Luke 11:18, 19, Acts 16, 19:11-16. You will need another to "exorcise" the demon out of you, and pray for you to be filled with the Holy Spirit, thus preventing the demon from re-entering you later, with seven more demons. Thus your end is worse than your beginning (Matthew 12:43-45). See suggested course of action. (3) Dreamer, you are one who is spiritually blind, with no spiritual vision, by choice, having carelessly risked your life and soul, embracing anger, and remaining ignorant of, the thi ngs of God, His creative works in and around you, and to His principles. Dreamer, God's love is calling you back to Him; forgiveness will cover all your mistakes, and you must forgive yourself and others. Now give careful thought to this, from this day on. From this day forward, God will bless you; therefore, perceive God's grace, and embrace the love that is calling you home. No longer, pretend that you do not sense His providence within your life. See suggested course of action.

Indignation, Outrage, "Righteous Indignation": Dreamer, hear this commentary on Job, for it is about you. Adam Clarke's Commentary on Job: Job certainly was not a grievous sinner, but a most, upright man. This point is sufficiently proved; but that he accuses himself of nothing wrong, of no inward evil, is certainly not correct. He thought too highly of himself; he presumed too much, on what was without; but when God shone upon his heart, he saw that he was vile, and therefore might most properly loathe himself. There are multitudes who, are decent and correct in their outward behavior, whose hearts may be deceitful and desperately wicked. Job was a righteous and upright man: but at the time in question, he was not cleansed from all inward sin. This removes all contradiction from what he asserts, and from what he concedes. When a man or woman sees them self in the light of God, he or she sees, by their own discernment, what wisdom, and reason, he, or she had never seen before. His or her mind might have been previously deeply imbued with the principles of justice, righteousness, and truth, and their whole conduct be regulated by them, and they be conscious to them self that they have not wickedly departed from the laws imposed on them by these principles. But when the light that exposes, shines through the innermost recesses of the heart, and vibrates through the soul, then spiritual wickedness becomes evident, and the deceitfulness of the heart is discovered. That light refers everything to the Divine standard, the holiness of God; and the man or woman's own righteousness in this comparison is found to be imperfection itself, and little short of impurity. Job appear s to have been in this state. Job thought himself, rich and increased in goods and to have need of nothing, but when God shone in upon his heart, he found himself to be wretched, and miserable, and poor, and blind, and naked. And he was now as ready to confess his great vileness, as he was before to assert and vindicate the unimpeachable righteousness of his conduct. Here was no contradiction. His friends attacked him on the ground of his being a bad and wicked man: this charge he repels with indignation, and dared them to the proof. They had nothing to allege but their system and their suspicions: but he who suffers must have sinned. Job, being conscious that this was false as applied to him, knowing his own innocence, boldly requires on their ground to know why God contended with him. God's answer, shines into his heart, and then he sees that he is vile, and this humbles the self-confident yet upright man. When a beam of the solar light is admitted into an apartment, we see ten thousand atoms or motes dancing in that beam. These are no particles of light, nor did the light bring them there; they were there before, but there was not light sufficient to make them manifest. Just so, when the light of God visits the soul of a sincere man or woman, who has been laboring in all their outward conduct to stand approved of God, he or she is astonished at their inward impurity, loathes him or herself,

663

and is ready to think that many devils have suddenly entered into them. No, all the evils you see, were there before, but you did not have light sufficient to make them manifest. Shall it be said afte r this, that the conduct of Divine Providence cannot be vindicated in suffering an upright man to become a butt for the malice of Satan for so long a time, and for no purpose? The greatest, the most important purposes were accomplished by this trial. Jo b became a much better man than he ever was before; the dispensations of God's providence were illustrated and justified; Satan's devices unmasked; patience crowned and recompensed; and the Church greatly enriched by having bequeathed to it the vast treasury of Divine truth which is found in the Book of Job.

AWE (adore, inspired, respect, reverence, religious zeal):

Question, dreamer to whom was your emotion of awe, adoration, or reverence directed, to God or man? See category, Bowing.

CRYING (to shed tears as an expression of emotion)

Altar (crying at, or upon): This dream has two meanings (choose one). (1) You are overwhelmed by the severe consequences of your choices; your tears are tears of self-pity. There is a need for prayer and heartfelt repentance to Jesus and to others. Favorably, grace is available to the humble; thus, pray Psalm 51. Dreamer, if you will humble yourself and submit your ways unto God, and continue applying His principles no matter the "self" resistance, you will again gain control over your life again. This gaining control over your spirit is a process, it will not all happen in one day (or it miraculou sly could). Accordingly, your soul and lifestyle will begin to bear fruit of positive choices, resulting in spiritual strength and power within the dreamer's life. See suggested course of action. (2) Married dreamer, if you are actually married in your awaked life, crying upon an altar indicates you are in contempt of your marriage vows. This type of contempt exposes two vital matters of your heart, cruel and inhumane treatment of your spouse, or an unsympathetic negligence, causing your spouse to cry out before God, when they should be serving Him joyfully. You have abused and put away your spouse, perhaps to make room for another. You will be exposed, for Adonai Elohim knows all. As well, this type of contempt exposes your ill treatment of your relationship with Christ, via hypocritical prayers and tears, pretending great humiliation, which is only surface emotions an d outward signs, but not of the heart. Dreamer, there is a need to examine your motives, and to consider the demonic influences, which tempt you to act so callous towards your spouse and towards God. Breaking of a solemn vow, can be harmful, and suggests a weakening of your core beliefs, namely a rejection of all or some of the original foundational teachings of Christ and His apostles. God rebukes the proud cries of the self-righteous and calls them to prayer and heartfelt repentance to Jesus and man or woman, seeking pardon and expressing sincere feelings of regret and brokenness for having done something awry and/ or for having hurt someone, see 2 Corinthians 7:10, 11, also see Malachi 2:13-16. See suggested course of action.

Baby, Child Crying: This dream has two meanings (choose one). (1) If child crying, is your literal child in your awaked life, and if parent sense, even slightly, that your child may be in danger, physically or emotionally, then your dream is an alarm to a parent that your child is actually in serious danger or trouble, and needs your help immediately. If you suspect molestation or abuse, you must contact the appropriate authorities. Remove your child from the unsafe environment and contact the proper authorities immediately (e.g. police, child, and/or adult protective services). If you were abused as a child and now, you have placed your child in harm's way, often the identical situation; feigning denial, go talk to God, and ask Him to help you emotionally and mentally, to do what it takes to keep your child safe, from the same violation. Allow the darkness of the violation to stop with you. Moreover, if you suspect that your abuser is still harming others, please report it. You may also check with your local department of human services for reporting procedures. Medical, legal, and psychological intervention, are likely necessary, for you and/or your child. Nonetheless, children should never be left in abusive situations. Abuse of, or sex with, a child, teen, or incapacitated adult, is never justifiable; it is always wrong. Jesus says, it's better for you to sink to the bottom of the sea, tied to cement (Mark 9:42-48), than for anyone to perpetrate such acts against others. See suggested course of action. Other than that, if the child crying is your literal child in your awaked life, and there is no slightest sense of danger to the child. Then the child crying within your dream will be safe and become a great leader and prophet or prophetess to God's people, affecting many lives. This child will be mentored by someone wealthy within government. (2) To a non- parent literally, your dream has come as a warning. The dreamer has neglected your personal ministry, so much so, that it now cries out against you before God. Your attitude of, "I don't care", "they're going to do what they want to do anyway, so why try", or "They don't support me", only exposes your lack of faithfulness, commitment, and stewardship to what God has committed unto you. You do what you want to do, and what you don't want to do, you find an excuse not to do. Those who are not committed, faithful, and ready to serve are the ones who do not truly believe in their hearts that they will have to give an account of their service to your Heavenly Father. Dreamer, you lack a reverent fear of God (if girl child was crying) or a love of God (if boy child was crying). You are similar to those in Matthew 25, the unprofitable servants, who are cast into the outer darkness, where there shall be the weeping, and the gnashing of teeth. Therefore, choose this day whom you will serve, God, or yourself. See suggested course of action.

In addition, the following is a common word, expression, or usage (e.g. slang or cliché), or a 'probable' that is metaphorically represented by a baby crying:

- **Crybaby**: If dreamer saw yourself as a baby crying, to saw a baby crying, not your child, your dream denotes one, namely the dreamer, who is easily made to cry and who complains frequently without cause. See suggested course of action.

Bawling (to cry out in a deep loud voice, during prayer): Your heart is tender and you humbled yourself before the Lord, and wept, when you heard of the devastation of another, you are now heard; that which you are seeking and desire at present, via prayer, will "come to pass". Bawling (to cry out making violent twisting and rolling movements with your body because of severe pain): Amongst all those who say that they love you, most have dealt very treacherously with you, and are as foes; fortunately, the enemy has not prevailed. You will now begin to see the manifestation of divine vengeance against those who trouble you. Be encourage, the wicked will cease from troubling. God will validate you and, if applicable, your children. You will get relief from those who oppress you, and if pertinent, you or a loved one will get release from imprisonment. All this will follow the implosion of a ministry you're connected too.

Crying (to shed tears of humiliation, joy, sadness, or grief): This dream has three meanings (choose one). (1) Humiliation or Crying tears of humiliation (disgrace, embarrassment, or shame): The dreamer will return to a place or state of safety and plenty, but with some type of stigma attached to your name, due to your past behaviors and unwise choices. Because of rejection by some, the probability of bitterness setting in is high. Dreamer; toss understanding at anger, bitterness, and hate from others (see 1 Corinthians 13:4-13; Philippians 4:4-8). This will accelerate your process of becoming spiritually mature, strong, and powerful within Christ Jesus. See suggested course of action. (2) Crying tears of joy: The dreamer or a close family member will return to a place or state of safety and plenty and will return to Christ and to His church. Accordingly, your soul and lifestyle will begin to bear fruit of positive choices, resulting in spiritual strength and power within the dr eamer's life. If needful, may also see subcategory, Joy and Laughter. (3) Sad or Crying Tears of Grief or Sadness (agony, depressed, grief, misery, regretful, remorseful): Your dream symbolizes potential restoration of the dreamer and of a very close family member (spouse, child, very close significant other). Dreamer when you genuinely return to God in love and surrender, your deliberate transgressions will become like actual merits (also see Luke 7:37-50). Because, the realization of your distance from God, resulting from your transgressions (Isaiah 59:2), becomes the motivating force to return to God with a passion even greater than that of someone who has never sinned in such a manner (or never left the Father's house, Acts 9:1 -30). Dreamer, you are well able to return in love and surrender, only seize the miraculous moment of spiritual strength that is before, and within, you at present. If dreamer recognizes and respect your time of visitation from the Lord, and seize the opportunity t o return to Christ, you, and a close family member, will return to a place or state of safety and plenty. See suggested course of action.

Dirge or Requiem (e.g. to hear a song or a slow mournful piece of music, causing you to cry): This dream brings notice. This dream has two meanings (choose one). (1) Dreamer, someone is praying on your behalf, interceding to the Ruler of rulers. They are reminding Him of your courageous good works towards them on behalf of the Kingdom of God. Further, dreamer your prayers are especially effective now, what you decree, God will fulfill. Only remember to seek first the Kingdom of God, via His Son. Jesus is the key to activate all that comes with seeking the Kingdom of God. For, He is our righteousness required to access the Kingdom blessings, then will God give you the keys of the Kingdom of Heaven; whatever you bind on earth will be bound in heaven, and whatever you loose on earth will be loosed in heaven (ref Matthew 16:19). Additionally, dreamer, be who God made you to be, use your God given talents, as best you can, to make the world a better place; take your past and use it to teach those whom God has purposed you to reach. Additionally, no matter who you are and what the situation, the words of the Psalms will speak the words of your heart and those words will be heard on High. Thus, began singing a new song, see Psalm 96:1-13. Start listening to inspirational music, music that praises our Lord and Savior. (2) To the unmarried male or female: Only if desired of dreamer, your dream denotes that after one month of solemn consecration, it will be granted you to get married[35].

Embrace and weep (to weep upon, on): The dreamer is crying "appropriate tears", contrary to anybody's opinions, and no matter the reason why. Note, with the moving or passing away of a committed friend, partner in a shared mission, ministry, or someone who meant a lot to you, possibly a spouse, child, or anyone you significantly cared for, the dreamer has a right to cry very much, and your tears are appropriate, as is your grief. However, do not medicate the natural process of grieving, and no matter the length of time, allow the process naturally. The Holy Spirit will carry you, helping you to be able to go on, and leading the way.

Groaning (frowning while grunting because of distress, pain, or anger due to being treated badly or unfairly): You have suffered much because of the Word of the Lord. Like prophets of old, you have said, in sum and substance, "Ah, woe is me!

For the Lord has added sorrow to my pain; I am weary with my groaning and have found no rest". Dreamer, God has made an ending to all your groans. Be at peace with yourself and take a sabbatical, the Lord has commanded someone to sustain you during your time of rest and another to watch over your ministry. These are trustworthy persons ; allow them to do as God has instructed them. They will not harm you, hurt your ministry, or instigate a coup. Have faith in God (a resolute trust in th e integrity of God and in His Word), for He can be trusted. Moreover, unless God watch the house, the watchman watches in vain. Read, understand, and embrace Psalm 127:1, 2. Therefore, go and rest, be encouraged, recoup, and strengthen yourself, your present ordeal is over.

Hollering (to yell, shout): This dream has two meanings (choose one). (1) Your dream denotes a pregnancy. Dreamer, you are pregnant, or if male, someone is pregnant with your child. Nonetheless, your child will be counseled and mentored regarding the things of God and the importance of obedience to His ordinances by a prophet or prophetess. Your chil d will be a great leader and strategist, leading many to Christ. Do not abort, or encourage abortion, if this is an issue. Moreover, dedicate this child to the Lord from birth. Meaning, escort your child to a church, a faith based community, enroll the child in a Christian educational institution, and encourage a personal relationship with Jesus Christ, early. As well, parent, if applicable, you establish a personal relationship with Jesus Christ too; that you might better able lead your child in all th ings Jesus. (2) Dreamer, if your child bearing years have ended; or for some other medical reason you are unable to bear children. Your dream denotes that somebody significant within your life is pregnant. The question is why are you being made privy to this information? Is it perhaps, to prevent the aborting of the child or to prevent the child's assimilation into a foster care system? Is it for you to encourage a more genuine Christian upbringing of the child? For sure, you can exercise some authority within the situation. Are you the child's grandparent, guardian, adoptive parent, or possible mentor? Are you the prophet or prophetess mentioned in (#1)? Seriously consider why God has revealed this information to you. Surely, it's not for you just to know, or to talk about to others, but for you to act.

Lament (to verbally express grief, sadness, regret, or disappointment about an issue while shedding tears): You, or someone you are praying for, will return to the place you desire, and will, according to the greatness of God's power, be preserve from death and set free from associating with those who are doomed to death. If necessary, see suggested course of action.

Naked (to be naked and crying): Because of your rebellious behavior, a shameful exposure of truth will occur. Consequently, you will be stripped of position, status, and/or finances, of all that 'covers' you. Dreamer, he or she, who d o not respect the opportunities placed before them shall have the things that support their peace taken away. A decision to repent, and return, and reject the attitude of foolishness, hypocrisy, and selfishness; and where there would be chaos, genuine peace will remain. Where there is a lack of prudence, wisdom will rule. A simple prayer of repentance is in order. "Jesus, I beg your forgiveness. I know I've broken your heart, I never meant to treat you this way. Heavenly Father, I'll do whatever it takes, to never hurt you again, and I'll love you for the rest of my life". Dreamer, look to Jesus. Love and forgiveness can and will embrace and restore you, wait for it. Further, take steps now to avert feeding into the growing desires of your carnal natur e. Notwithstanding, this "uncovering" process will affect humility and a more "genuine" you. See suggested course of action.

People crying together (3 or more): This dream has two meanings (choose one): (1) a group of people within your church has decided to cry out together for help because of the injustices done within the ministry, and th eir cry has risen up to God. They have cried out to the Lord, "We have sinned because we have forsaken the Lord and have exalted man above God; but now deliver us from the hands of our enemy, and we will serve "You". The dreamer needs to join this group in their cry out against injustices within the ministry. You will be remembered as one who cared enough to stand on the side of godly justice and righteousness. (2) A group of people crying can also denote the death of a leader. If so, it is suggested that you acknowledge to yourself and before others, how that leader's ministry honestly affected your life. If you mourn, mourn no longer than sixty days.

Poke in the Eye and cause tears: This dream has two meanings (choose one). (1) If dreamer poked someone in the eye, your dream is a severe warning to the dreamer. Dreamer has violated someone (or allowed the violation), due to demonic possession and to a deep hatred within you. The violation is molestation, rape, any unwanted sexual activity, or attention forced upon a child, teen, or a psychological, physically weaker, incapacitated adult, perhaps it is one familiarly close to you. You will be exposed, for Adonai Elohim knows all. Abuse of, or sex with, a child, teen, or non-consensual sex is never justifiable; it is always wrong. Jesus says, it's better for you to sink to the bottom of the sea, tied to cement (Mark 9:42 -48), than for anyone to perpetrate such acts against others. Nevertheless, you will be referred to, as one who is wickedly unrighteous, and one who should be shunned, ostracized from your community and other groups. As well, you will no longer prosper, no matter how hard you work, and you will become homeless and a wanderer. Can you be forgiven if you have sexually abused a child or if you knowingly allowed a child to be sexually abused[34]? Yes, God is gracious and merciful. No sin is beyond His ability to forgive (Romans 5:20). Jesus came to cleanse all sin: "Truly I tell you, people can be forgiven all their sins" (Mark 3:28). When you recognize your sin, acknowledge that it is evil, and then genuinely and deeply cry out to God for deliverance, with much fasting and prayer, He will hear you, forgive you, and sanctify you. Often, abusers have been abused themselves. In addition to God's forgiveness, you may require professional help and accountability support for, stopping certain behaviors, healing from past wounds, and seeking forgiveness from those, you have injured. See suggested course of action. (2) If dreamer was poked in the eye, unfortunately, molestation, rape, or any unwanted sexual activity or attention forced upon you was a sad reality, but it is not beyond God's ability to overcome. God can redeem and restore. Dreamer; oftentimes, bad things happen to innocent and good people. A bad thing happened to you, and you are good and innocent. Compassionately, the Lord is creating a miracle in your life. This miracle will stop the effects of your violation from playing a significant role in your life, enabling you to move forward with your life and to make good decisions. However, the miracle's success depends upon your willingness to be healed and set free; for one will always have the choice to say no, or perhaps sabotage their progress. First, recognize and respect your time of visitation from the Lord, for it is upon you, as well as the work of His Hand upon your life. If you lack wisdom ask God for wisdom; and He will give you wisdom. For the Lord gives wisdom and from His mouth comes knowledge and understanding. Then you will understand what is right and just and fair, every good path. When wisdom enters your heart and knowledge becomes sweet to your soul, discretion will protect you, understanding will guard you, and His Truth will lead you. To deliver you from the ways of wickedness, and from demons whose words and ways are perverse, who causes you to walk in darkness gladly, whose paths are crooked and devious, causing you to leave straight paths (Proverbs 2:1-6, 9-15). This is one of God's covenant promises to you. Have faith in this. Further, with much fortitude choose not to be a victim or to perpetuate the desolation. Praise Him "who is able to do immeasurably more than all we ask or imagine, according to His power that is at work within us" (Ephesians 3:20). The "more than we can imagine" includes forgiveness and healing.

Sniveling (whining and complaining with a runny nose): Your constant complaining has provoked God and angered your leaders, for in it, that is, in your complaining, is implications you have rejected the Lord, supposing you did better, before becoming a Christian, than how you are faring now. Dreamer, so many times the Lord has made a way for you. When you cried to God, again and again, He rescued you according to His compassion, and many times, you have heard from heaven; but as soon as you rested, you did evil again before God; therefore, He has left you in the hands of those you hate. Dreamer is counseled to be content, and cease from whining and complaining, no matter the state of affairs you find yourself in, and endure your time of troubling, knowing that you are actually in the state you're in in due to your own unwise choices. Therefore, learn from your situation, and favorably, yet again you will be rescued according to God's compassion. See suggested course of action.

Sobbing (to weep aloud with convulsive gasping- hyperventilate): Your dream comes to bring about awareness. Humility is being affected within your life; this is the reason for the many hardships you are experiencing. Think it not strange concerning the fiery trials, which are proving you, particularly effecting meekness, modesty; and removing arrogance, and pride. Therefore, do not accuse God wrongly during this time; remain faithful unto Him and to His ways. You will be restored to a place of prosperity, if you abide and in Christ and endure, also see Proverbs 15:33, 22:4. See suggested course of action.

To stop crying: Dreamer is willing to receive help for overcoming difficulties and shortcomings, within your life; be they, spiritual, intellectual, and/or physical. Moreover, the dreamer is ready, willing, and able to understand the deeper things of God, and for restoration. See suggested course of action.

To not cry, or be unable to cry, or refuse to cry, or to be forbidden: Your dream comes as a warning to the dreamer. You are about to lose a vital person within your life, either through divorce, legal separation, imprisonment, or death. Through this ordeal, your clarity of speech, clear and sensible thinking, judgment, and actions, all based on reason rather than emotion, will reveal your lack of love for this person and/or how you've taken them for granted. For, how can one be so clear, emotionally, in the immediate midst of loss of a vital person within their life? Did dreamer, have anything to do with the lost? Your indiscretions and/or involvement will be exposed, for Adonai Elohim knows all, and your indiscretions will be exposed as God's justice to the name of the one gone or leaving. See suggested course of action.

Wailing (to grieve loudly with a mournful high-pitched sound): Dreamer, you are going to hear some very bad news that will cause you to wail loudly and bitterly. There will be great mourning within the faith-based community of which you're connected. It is time for fasting, praying, and interceding on behalf of another, as well as, for your church. Dreamer, declare a sacrificial fast (e.g. abstain from food and water, social gatherings, or entertainment, such as TV, computer, movies, or leisurely activities). Fast no less than three days. God will lead and enable you. As cliché as this may sound, it is necessary to say, your mourning will be turned into joy; at the end of your fasting, in six days, what you have grieved will no longer depress you or the ministry. The evil scheme of the enemy will be thwarted. See suggested course of action.

Weeping (shedding tears quietly or to shed a tear): Your dream implies that there is miraculous aid available to help you overcome some intellectual difficulties and to understand deep truths. For, God has appointed you, a prophet or prophetess to His people, and your purpose must meet preparation; thus the miraculous aid. God will touch your mouth to give you divine messages for His people and for individuals. This will help you go forward, with faith, in the center of your love for God. Dreamer, to not, carry out your purpose within the mandates and confines of God's orders and principles, is to cause your gifting to destroy you. See suggested course of action.

Cry for help (depicted by an SOS signal): This dream has two meanings (choose one). (1) Your dream acknowledges the dreamer's prayer for help, your SOS, sort to say, due to your distress, and approaching danger or trouble. God has heard your plea and help is on the way, be encouraged. (2) Your dream is an alarm that a significant other is in serious danger or trouble, and needs your help immediately. Reach out to one who is in a crisis. By this, help will be available to you, when you are facing similar situations.

FEAR (anxious, apprehensive, cautious, concerned, confused, doubtful, exasperated, frightened, hesitant, insanity, nervous, overwhelmed, panic, scared, shocked, stressed, surprised, suspicious, wary, or worry):

Your dream denotes that there is, within the dreamer, an anticipation of some specific pain or danger, usually accompanied by a desire to flee or fight. You are apprehensive about a possible or probable situation or event. No matter of the event is real or imagined, dreamer, you are allowing the "spirit" of fear to cause you to lose your identity (the individual characteristics by which the dreamer is known or is recognized by), and to terrorize you, it has become your own personal terrorist. Read and understand Romans 8:15, 2 Timothy 1:7. This demon terrorizes you in your thoughts, when you are paranoid, sleeping with a knife or gun under your pillow, when you are afraid, when you hesitate, when you are insecure, when you are impatient, when you are confused, when panic comes, when your thoughts are filled with worry. When you are uneasy and unsure, when despair and depression find you, when stress comes, when you are full of apprehension, when your thoughts forecast o nly doom and gloom, when you are restless, when you are frightful, when you are full of dread, when are anxious, when you are nervous, and when you feel hopeless. You will find this demon in every phobia. Question to journal: What would it feel like if all of your fears were suddenly released from you at one time? Pause and feel that. Bible story, there was a herd of pigs that Legion was cast into, and these pigs found their thoughts to be so unbearable that they all ran off a cliff to commit suicide, because they could not bear what had been unleashed upon them (Matthew 8:28-34, Mark 5:1-20, Luke 8:26-39). This is what the spirit of fear oftentimes leads to, if embraced wholly. On the other hand, the man whom, the devils were suddenly released from, was found sitting, clothed, healed, and in his right mind. The spirit of fear is adversarial to the Word of God that says all things will work together for good, to those who love God, and are called according to His purpose. For, if you tru ly can believe God's word, it will change all the rules that darkness has established in your heart and mind. Now I say to you that before you can move forward, fear must be cast out, and renounced. Therefore, dreamer, earnestly renounce the insidious voice of the devil. If you will daily come away and pray, then God will heal you of all things, only come with much prayer and spiritual fasting. The spiritual fast is that time of waiting when you are praying and asking the Lord to come and perform that which only He can perform. Similar to a literal fast, during this time you must abstain. But this fast you must abstain from any counsel or thoughts that tempt you to put your hand on the matter, or to turn you away from waiting on the Lord. During this time of waiting, you simply need to continue in prayer and be still. Then you will hear and know that only God's love is able to break the curse of darkness from over your mind, body, and spirit. Warning, it will be during your spiritual fast that weaknesses, such as unbelief, doubt, fear, pride, arrogance, will come forth to tempt you to eat the counsel of their lies, rather than to wait for the Lord to come to deliver, heal, help, save, reveal, and guide. Wait on the Lord, for He is faithful to come. Moreover, if urged by God, declare a one, two, or three day fast without food.

HATRED (animosity, contempt, envy, greed, grudgingness, hatefulness, ignored, indifferent, jealousy, manipulative, obnoxious, rude, or vengeful):

Your dream is a critical alarm. Question to journal, dreamer if you began to, fully embrace this emotion, where will this lead you? Consideration, this emotion is the opposite of love. With that said, due to hatred and an unforgiving spirit, deep within the heart of the dreamer, so as to hide it from yourself, a severing of your personal relationship with Christ is probable (see Matthew 6:14, 15). Dreamer, your unforgiving heart, resulting from you having held on to hatred too long; has caused you to be reckoned as unforgiven within the spiritual realm (see Matthew 6:14, 15, 18:21-25). Consequently, you have slowly abandoned all or some of the original foundational teachings of Christ and His apostles; especially the teachings on love, forgiveness, and the doctrine of grace (the free and unmerited favor and beneficence of God). This has resulted in a corrupt doctrine and perverse bondage (1 Timothy 4:1-16). You have ceased to abide in Christ, and instead have become enslaved again to sin and immorality, trusting in your own righteousness. Evil and depravity is your guiding force, thus sin has separated you from God. You have been led astray from those of The Way (Acts 9:2). Dreamer, the beginning, development, arrival, or manifestation of something large (significant in scope, extent, or effect) is about to happen within your life, in a threatening way. Favorably, the One True Living God can change things. However, this may be your last alarm or warning regarding th e issue of hate. After a seven day fast of purification from things unclean (e.g. addictions, cussing, hatred, an unforgiving spirit, or any unrestrained lustful indulgences), go and present yourself to your spiritual leader. Remain within that faith -based community and remain innocent and free from things that defile. By this, you will be made clean, and restored. Moreover, studying the teachings of Jesus Christ and His disciples, and God's relation to it, you will experience God's truth again, and see the demonic for what it is - a lie. Renounce corrupt teachings and accept all of God's truth and ways, including grace, and His truths you do not prefer. Moreover, see, 1 John 3:15, 4:20. See suggested course of action.

JOY OR LAUGHTER (enthusiastic, excited, happy, humorous, joyful, lively, or smiling):

Your dream denotes one who is eager to be in the service of the Lord, to others, and to your own soul. Consequently, you will experience a closeness to God you've never experience before and will become one with His will for your life. Dreamer, you have drawn true joy into your life because of your humility and faithfulness. Stop and feel the peace, don't try to understand it, just embrace it. For true joy and its fruit of peace is beyond the intellect, it can only be lived out. Moreover, from this moment on, in the mental, emotional, and spiritual state, and place you are at now, divine wisdom will come, bringing increased insight into the deeper mysteries of God, His Word, and righteousness, and an increase in spiritual power to you.

LOVE (agape, eros, philia, or storge):

Dreamer when you genuinely return to God in love and surrender, your deliberate transgressions will become like actual merits (also see Luke 7:37-50). Because, the realization of your distance from God, resulting from your transgressions (Isaiah 59:2), becomes the motivating force to return to God with a passion even greater than that of someone who has never sinned in such a manner (or never left the Father's house, Acts 9:1-30). Dreamer, you are well able to return in love and surrender, only seize the miraculous moment of spiritual strength that is before, and within, you at present. Additionally, read, understand, and embrace 1 Corinthians 13, as well as, 1 John 2:15-17, 1 Timothy 6:10, and 2 Timothy 3:2-9. Allow these verses to lead and guide you. See suggested course of action.

KISSING (a way of expressing human love for another includes family or sexual):

Your dream denotes one who is set aside for the priesthood. Dreamer, you are being prepared to carry out the official role, position, or office of a priest (e.g. prophet, pastor, minister, or some type of a very visible cleric). With this office co mes spiritual growth and divine illumination, if you have genuinely sought after truth, truth will continue to be revealed to you and lead and guide you. With that said, the following is necessary to say. First, your promotion is predicated upon your understanding of, and continued obedience to, God's directives over your life. Second, pray to God for divine truth, for one should never exalt their thoughts, ideas, feelings, emotions, above God's truth, for, every house is built by someone, but the builder of all things is God (Hebrews 3:2-4). Further, chosen, you are to show forth the praises of Him who has called you out of darkness into His marvelous light (also see 1 Peter 2:9, 10). At present, continue to allow the Paraclete to complete the work of purification and sanctification within you. For those who go forth in tears, shall return rejoicing (Psalm 126:5, 6). Be diligent and patient, everything will be done proper, and in its own time; you will be ordained to a priestly office, and if relevant, your request in another area of your life will be granted. Again, your height of spiritual progress and promotion will be according to your faith and obedience to God's will over your life personally. See suggested course of action.

PAIN (disappointed, dissatisfied, distressed, guilt, harassed, hurt, lonely, physical, or mental pressure):

Warning, as you will be truly visited by a genuine servant of the Lord, one with the Spirit of Truth within, or an angel (perhaps disguised as human), beware of this person. Be on your guard before him or her; pay attention, take heed, and listen to what the messenger of the Lord has to say. Do not rebel against, or provoke him or her. This person is coming because the dreamer is suffering from intense affliction, serious mental and/or physical pain. The dreamer is, troubled by pain or loss, very un happy, full of misery. You've had to put up with something or somebody very unpleasant, as well. Unfortunately, all of your "woe" is a result of sin within your life. Dreamer, what God has given you to serve His people, you have perverted, and profaned, making it the source of your lusts; swelling you up with extreme pride. The goodness which God has blessed you with all these years, was to glorify His Kingdom, instead you have used His blessings to glorify yourself. Your pride has lured you into a false sense of security. Erroneously assuming that nothing but good comes to you. Confessing that no one you know can compare with you, or even pretend to be your equal. You put confidence in your flesh, fearing no danger, living carelessly. You har bor wicked thoughts, are ruthlessly aggressive, and greedily eager to steal from, or destroy others, for gain. God humbles the haughty and causes all his or her joy and laughter to cease. Notwithstanding, spiritual renewal is accessible to you now. Jesus is petitioning you, via your dream, to cleanse evil from your heart; therefore, allow the process. Dreamer, many, who have faltered and were weak are healed, restored, and strengthened by the grace of God. If you are ready to acknowledge that you have faltered, and remain mindful of your weaknesses, especially pride, God will suddenly, and in an extraordinary way, increase your strength. The more God allows you to see your arrogance, and the horribleness of it all, be more earnest to repent that you may find Him to be grace and healing, refreshment, and a refuge. He is willing to help you, only surrender to His process of help, with a humble dependence upon Him. You will find that God will not fail you, and you will have grace sufficient for renewal of spiritual strength. Again, one, who is a true servant of God, with the Spirit of Truth within will lead the way, thus take heed. See suggested course of action.

Suggested Course of Action

Question to consider and journal, did your dream depict any symbols that alludes to, the dreamer will make the necessary changes, spiritually, emotionally, and/or physically to affect a more positive outcome? If changes are initiated, your dreams will change.

Nevertheless, since you are here, it is assumed that your dream's context depicted primarily negative emotions. This type of dream, challenges the dreamer to appreciate that, just as you would grieve if your integrity, self-worth, and your dignity were cheapen or compromised, God Himself grieves, via Holy Spirit, when His integrity, His worth, His dignity are cheapen or compromised by us. When we do not have faith in God and in His covenant promises, principles, and comforts to humanity; His integrity, worth, and dignity are cheapened or diminished within us. To value or have faith in God, which is a resolute trust in the integrity of God and in His Word, is to please Him, for God's integrity, worth, and dignity, is His Word. You must st rive to have faith in your God, and confidence in His Word, especially if you are to influence the rest of the world to embrace His Word also. When you do this; then God will wipe away the tears from your face and eyes (Isaiah 25:8, Revelation 7:17).

Consider and journal the following questions. The questions will help you determine; the issue at hand, how you feel about it, and what may have instigated it. Could this dream be due to dreamer is experiencing a qualitative change, a transformation process of some kind? Unfortunately, instead of you being courageous and facing things head on, see Philippians 2:13-15, the dreamer is murmuring, complaining, whining, via anger, crying, or fearfulness. Is the process of living a Christian life, or going from bad to good or vice versa, unpleasant to the dreamer, if so why? Is the dreamer experiencing physical or emotional pain or sadness, or is dreamer physically tired? Were others involved? If yes, who and in what manner were they involved; keeping in mind that the others represent a quality of you? Did anyone get hurt emotionally, physically, or was disturbed in any way? How did you feel, and what did you do, because, of your feelings? Was it agitating, confusing, disturbing, frustrating, life threatening, safe, scary, or unsure, or was dreamer at peace with the situation, happy, and joyful? Were you coherent? Where were you? Was the place unfamiliar to you? For more information, see index or relevant category and subcategory for other particulars within your dream. Your answers, coupled with the interpretation, plus any additional information, should begin to unfold the subject matter and issue at hand, if not now, mull over things a few days.

The following will help you determine the approximate length of time you have thus far dealt with the matter, and perhaps how much longer you will have to deal with the issue. If the emotions portrayed started at the beginning of the dream, you are dealing with this issue right now. If somewhere in the middle onward, you will encounter the issue shortly. Did your emotions stop at some point (e.g. did you stop being angry, stop crying, being fearful, stop hating, was relieved from pain, sadness, or refreshed from tiredness?); this indicates that you are now able to embrace the process that will heal the issue your dream is referencing. If things continued, and did not stop, the matter at hand will not end soon, if you continue avoidance, complaining, faithlessness in God's Word, and murmuring. You are counseled to deal with the issue without evasion or compromise, in other words head-on. All of these questions should pull together for you your dream. They summarize the issue at hand and what changes need to be made within the dreamer's attitude or life.

Dreamer, consider seriously your observations. In view of your dream's context, and the primary symbols, what does your dream reveal about you, your ethics, intents, mental state, and motives? You will need to earnestly look within and consider that the sum of your answers is a reflection of where you are emotionally, and a reflection of who you are becoming emotionally. What was your reaction to the situation? Were you angry, concerned, confused, defensive, fearful, happy, helpful, pleased, shocked, unconcerned, or ready to get out of someone's presence? Your reaction to the activity, or the circumstance, reveals your attitude regarding this information about yourself. What choices are you making that may encourage a desertion of the faith, which is in Jesus Christ, or impair your spiritual growth, judgment, health? If you lack wisdom, ask Jesus for wisdom. He gives wisdom to all, generously, no matter who you are and what you've done; wisdom is available (see James 1:5-8, Proverbs 2:1-6, 10). Hence, if, by just asking, you may get wisdom, one may suffer needlessly, because you will not ask Jesus for wisdom.

Now, pray (See Prayer of Deliverance, pg. 897)

Specific Meaning

If, you have a very real connection with any type of grieving, pain, sadness, or any situation that is provoking you to anger ; dreams of this sort, for the most part, are ordinary dreams, resulting from your daily activities (see Chapter One, Chalom). These sorts of dreams are usually about your routine, mundane activities or anxieties that overwhelm your mind during the day. They are an inner release mechanism, which helps provide you with emotional balance and the maintaining of your sanity. These dreams are not significant, and do not warrant special attention.

Note: If bawling, any manner of crying, fear, hatred, pain, or sadness was highlighted with your dream, due to a criminal act; this is a warning. There may be potential for harm. The details, kept within context of your dream, should be relevant to your life, and closely resemble your real-life situations. Meaning it can actually occur during your awaked state. This will help you narrow down the specifics needed to support criminal findings or to support or steer you clear of possible mishaps. This dream may reveal molestation, rape, any sexual crime, or any other crime, forced, or threatened, upon someone. If the dreamer saw or sensed, within his or her dream any act that involved criminal activity. Perhaps the dreamer is being made aware of the plight of someone, and you are to get involved (see Chapter One, Are You Ready to Hear the Messages in Your Dreams, section entitled, The 10% for others). If dreamer is involved in any criminal activity, God can redeem and restore. We praise Him "who is able to do immeasurably more than all we ask or imagine, according to His power that is at work within us" (Ephesians 3:20). The "more than we can imagine" includes forgiveness and healing. You can I be forgiven if you have sexually abused a child or if I knowingly allowed a child to be sexually abused[34]? Yes, God is gracious and merciful. No sin is beyond His ability to forgive (Romans 5:20). Jesus came to cleanse all sin: "Truly I tell you, people can be forgiven all their sins" (Mark 3:28). When you recognize your sin, acknowledge that it is evil, and then genuinely and deeply cry out to God for deliverance, with much fasting and prayer, He will hear you, forgive you, and sanctify you. Often, abusers have been abused themselves. In addition to God's forgiveness, you may require professional help and accountability support for, stopping certain behaviors, healing from past wounds, and seeking forgiveness from those, you have injured. However, if your dream symbols are not easily, linked to your life activities, heed the spiritual implications (the interpretation).

LANDFORMS AND BODIES OF WATER

(any geological feature such as a mountain, valley, earth, rock, and any area where water
flows and/or gathers; the earth is a terraqueous globe, consisting of land and water)

And the earth was waste and void; and darkness was upon the face of the deep: and the Spirit of God
moved upon the face of the waters. And God said, "Let the waters under the heavens be gathered together
unto one place, and let the dry land appear", and it was so. And God called the dry land Earth; and the
gathering together of the waters He called Seas: and God saw that it was good (Genesis 1:2, 9, 10 KJV).

Therefore will we not fear, though the earth do change, and though
the mountains be shaken into the heart of the seas;
though the waters thereof roar and be troubled, though the mountains tremble with the swelling
thereof, Selah. There is a river, the streams whereof make glad the city of God, (Psalm 46:2-4 ASV)

I will make rivers flow on bare hilltops. I will make springs flow through valleys. I will
turn deserts into lakes. I will turn dry land into springs (Isaiah 41:18 GW)

Verily I say unto you, whosoever shall say unto this mountain, be thou taken up
and cast into the sea; and shall not doubt in his or her heart, but shall believe that
what he or she says will come to pass; they shall have it (Mark 11:23 ASV)

...in that day the heavens will be rolled up with a great noise, and the elements shall be dissolved with
fervent heat, and the earth and the works that are therein shall be burned up (2 Peter 3:10 BBE)

This category deals with landforms and bodies of water, defined as natural physical features of
the earth's surface, the earth's surface, its geology, topography, as well as, its waters. Some short
descriptions of types, phrases, and/or other processes and particulars, connected in some way to this
category is, for example, canyons, caves, continent, crevice, desert, earth, end of the world, flats,
glaciers, hills, island, mountains, plain, plateaus, beach, brook, cistern, coastline, creek, ditch, gulf, lake,
ocean, reservoir, river, sea, seashore, strait, stream, well. Also, see category content list, or index.

All Symbols and Referents, Notes (1, 2, 3, etc.), Suggested Course of Action, and Specific Meaning
offer guidance toward a more comprehensive interpretation.

Notes

1. Unless otherwise noted elsewhere, if, in your everyday living, your awaked state, as part of
    your lifestyle, work, or ministerial activities, or a special event, you have a very real connection
    with any activity involving landforms or bodies of water. For example, archeology, geology,
    geoscience, earth science, aquatics, fisherman, navy, sailor, navy, or any work involving the
    natural physical features of the earth's surface, its waters, or the investigation thereof, your
    dream is not significant and does not warrant special attention.

    Otherwise noted, this dream may be a Prophetically Simple Dream (see Chapter One:
    The 60th Part of Prophecy). Whereas, the dreamer is warned to stop any unwise, reckless, or
    dangerous behavior or actions involving landforms or bodies of water, you should cease any
    daredevil or impetuous activity, especially if this is a thing within the dreamer's life. If any
    of the preceding is happening, or was depicted within your dream, this dream is a first step
    intervention and an alarm. Skip interpretation and re-consider your activity as harmful, hurtful,
    or life threatening, at present. Handle the situation wisely, by first thanking God for the

warning, for Adonai Elohim knows all. Also, see Specific Meaning at the end of this category, section entitled, Note (Specific Meaning).

Otherwise noted, if your dream closely resembles real life situations, meaning the activity, event, or situation, can actually occur (or has occurred) during your awaked state. This dream may be an Ordinary Dream (see Chapter One, Chalom), resulting from your daily activities (e.g. rock or mountain climbing, aquatics, sailing, surfing, fishing). These sorts of dreams are usually about your routine, mundane activities or anxieties that overwhelm your mind during th e day. They are an inner release mechanism, which helps provide you with emotional balance and the maintaining of your sanity. These dreams are not significant, and do not warrant special attention.

2. Probables: Landforms and Bodies of Water are frequently demonstrated in many, and very personal ways, as they are linked, in one way or another, to people and particular places, and often influence stories. For example, do the banks of the St. John's River represent beautiful quality moments fishing with your father and mother? Was Daytona Beach, or New Smyrna Beach, the location of your first date? Were you baptized at Rock Springs or Wekiva Springs? Does the Big Tree Park bring to mind your Junior Girl Scout "Outdoor Cook" badge? Is walking on the pier at Charlotte Beach the ending of a beautiful date? Was the island of Key Largo your last vacation with your husband or wife? Mt. Rushmore, a mountain in the Black Hills of South Dakota, may represent home to you, or the likenesses of Washington, Jefferson, Lincoln, and Roosevelt may represent something presidential to a politician. Thus, could the landform or body of water depicted be a possible probable (see Chapter One, section entitled, Probables)? Hence, dreamer may also consider your own personal and special associations with various landforms and bodies of water, as long as the interpretation is kept within the principles of spiritual boundary markers, landmarks, and property lines, (see Chapter One, section entitled, Spiritualizing Boundary Markers, Landmarks, and Property Lines).

3. Determine who your dream is for you or another. Always, considering yourself first, reflecting on your present behaviors. Ask yourself, "Why am I dreaming about this now? What is this dream revealing about me? Have I taken on new attributes? Has anyone commented on my present behaviors as being untypical of me? Has my ministry changed for the better or for the worse? What about my beliefs, doctrine, or philosophy, are they still based on Holy Writ? Is t here something I need to know about those I am ministering to or serving?

Remember your type of landform or body of water within your dream. Was dreamer exiled on an island or adrift in the middle of an ocean? Did a hurricane devastate your home? Did dreamer climb a mountain, enter in a cave, cross a raging sea, dig a ditch, or build a dam? Unless otherwise noted elsewhere, an answer of yes, to one or more of these, or similar questions, is a good indicator that your dream is about you (the dreamer). Were there feelings of being overwhelmed, weariness, discouragement, rage, or resentment? Were you content? In light of your dream, via the relevant interpretation, do you believe that your actions or behavior will enhance or endanger your well -being, safety, and/or happiness, if so, how and why? Do you believe that your belief system will be strengthen or weaken in any way, due your actions or behavior, via your landform interpretation, if so, how and why? See following relevant subcategory, the interpretation is about and for you.

Was someone else exiled on an island? Did a tsunami kill someone? Was another's life devastated because of flooding? Was someone else property destroyed due to an earthquake? Did someone own an island? Was another overwhelm, weary, discouraged, or hostile, due to a landform or body of water? Unless otherwise noted elsewhere, an answer of yes, to one or more of these, or similar questions, is a good indicator that your dream is about another and their role, and/or influential effects, within the life of the dreamer. Are you dealing with someone, who truly believes in their heart that they will not have to give an account of their service to Heavenly Father? Are they enhancing your spiritual and/or literal prosperity, or are they responsible for the dwindling thereof? Do you know someone whose life activities or physical being is similar to that which stood out the most within your dream? Could it be that person? If you sense that your dream is for or about another, the question as to why you have been made privy to this information, and how do you factor into the equation, should be seriously considered along with necessary actions. Perhaps the dreamer is being made aware of the plight of someone, and you are to get involved (see Chapter One, Are You Ready to Hear the Messages in Your Dreams, section entitled, The 10% for others).

If your dream is for, or about another:

Dreams that reference others and the revelation within those dreams, is not given haphazardly to any individual, but only to those with the ability, and influence to do something with the information; this is also prophecy. With that, journal the following questions, and if unable to answer the questions now, this denotes that the person, represented within your dream, will enter your life shortly. Are you entering into a personal relationship with someone? Do you not know or understand what you're looking at, especially certain behaviors, when learning about this person? Has someon e new entered your life or maybe you've just begun opening up to someone not so new, and have started listening to their advice, accepting their assistance, or are you supporting or enabling someone? Are you in denial regarding the toxicity of one of your present relationships, particularly a spouse, family member, or friend? Are you anxious, concerned, frightened, and/or troubled by recent changes in your behavior, especially because of someone's influence upon your life at present? Have you allowed someone to convince you to deceive another? Have you recently become aware of (or is being made aware of, via your dream) certain undesirable behaviors within you towards another? Are you trying to cut ties with one that is bad company? Have you just joined (or re-joined) a church, fellowship, or social group?

Note: If your dream has attributes that indicate that your dream is about you, and other attributes that indicate that your dream is about another, dreamer should consider that your dream is about you and another. For example, was dreamer part of a mountain climbing expedition? Did dreamer cross a desert with another? Was dreamer and another stranded on an island? Did another caused you to fall into a valley, or pushed you off a mountain? Was d reamer and another engaged in a land dispute? Unless otherwise noted elsewhere, an answer of yes, to one or more of these, or similar questions, is a good indicator that the dream is about the dreamer, and about another. Therefore, while your dream is about the dreamer, the dreamer should expect the role and/or influential effects of another, also plays a part in your interpretation. For example, was dreamer the lone survivor of a mountain expedition? Again, see relevant interpretation.

More questions to consider. Why has the person been allowed within your life, and/or how did they get there? Again, if unable to answer the questions now, this denotes that the person, represented within your dream, will enter your life shortly. If their activity, within your dream, has proven positive, via the interpretation, this someone will prove, unwittingly, to be a very strong ally, benefactor, defender, and supporter. God has sent this someone into your life to help you carry out your next endeavor by enlarging your spiritual capacity. Allow the strength of that person's character to guide, help, and support you. On the other hand, if his or her presence and/or activity, within your dream, proved negative, via the interpretation, for sure, this person will prove to be a very strong and formidable challenge for you, perhaps unto death. If negative, this dream is a dire warning. Take steps accordingly to struggle against, or to cut off, adverse and unfavorable relationships. Remember certain personalities are all encompassing, affecting everything, cataclysmic, contagious, deadly, harmful, infectious, predatory, and/or venomous. Symbolically meaning that if allowed to continue or prosper within your life, serious harm or death to the dreamer may result. Idolize no one, especially beyond the warning of the Lord, and we are definitely not to lay our lives down for no one.

Then again, this person maybe allowed within your life, because of the dreamer's unwillingness to abstain from immorality after having been asked to abstain from such by God, see 1 Corinthians 6:9-20, Galatians 5:19-21, or the dreamer's self-righteous behavior, or a lack of a balanced and honest view of your own personality. In this case, this person will affect self-awareness within the life of the dreamer, exposing the negative traits of your personality, especially those traits, which cause you to follow, or to be so easily misled, and/or your wrong beliefs; no matter, this type of mentality needs reckoning with. Graciously, all of this will restore the dreamer to his or her right place with God, opening your eyes to see how far you've strayed from God (1 Corinthians 5:4-7; James 5:20). The lesson is, no matter how personable, powerful, or difficult a person, or how uncertain or unpopular the choices and issues, always take the next biblical and ethical step, for obedience to God's principles will always prove safer and stronger foundationally. Although, you will need all kinds of outside support to recover from this person's domination, no longer, allow that particular person's influence within your life to continue or thrive, especially if negative, end it abruptly.

4. Consider all the people, places, backgrounds, and activity highlighted within your dream.

Known (in your awaked life) person, place, or organization within your dream:

Unless otherwise noted elsewhere, people, animals, places, backgrounds that are actually known by the dreamer in your awaked life, indicates a part of you that you recognize within yourself on some level or another. Question to journal, if dreamer seriously considers all the particulars, what stood out the most, what features, or character traits stood out the most. Write down (journal) the particular highlighted within your dream. The attribute or activity highlighted is for a reason. Since the attribute written down is a part of you, namely the dreamer's nature, demeanor, and/or lifestyle, an honest and unbiased assessment is very important for truth sake. Happy note, considering that other people's attributes, within dreams, also represent attributes of your own personality, causes one to look at another in a better light. According to your capacity to embrace self-awareness and a rectification of mind, body, and spirit, God will begin to enhance, make better, more attractive, sanctify, diminish, and make pure and free from sin and guilt, this part of you.

Otherwise noted, if the person, animal, place, or background within your dream is actually known by the dreamer, in your awaked life, this person, animal, place, or background may represent him or herself, or itself.

Unknown in your awaked life or although known, was unseen, invisible, or only talked about person, place, or organization within your dream:

Unless otherwise noted elsewhere, if you did not recognize, the person, place, thing, they, or it, was not seen, invisible, or only talked about within your dream, this indicates an attribute or activity within your life that you are unfamiliar with, or are in denial about, or you refuse to acknowledge it, but it does exists. Question to journal, what activity, stood out the most. Although, on some conscious level, you are aware of a certain behavior or attribute within you, you have chosen to filter out or simply ignore certain information about yourself that contradicts your view of yourself and/or your preconceived notions of others and of the world around you. Possibly protecting yourself, emotionally and psychologically, from a situation, which you are unable to cope with at this time, or you lack control over; then again, perhaps the dreamer has an exaggerated or unrealistic view of yourself. No matter the reason, right now a question is before you, via your dream. Do you want to know this part of yourself? According to your ability to handle self-awareness, God will begin to reveal this side of you to you. Why, He wants to balance your understanding of things; thus, effecting wholeness within your life, so that the enemy will no longer be able to manipulate your emotions so easily. The Paraclete is with you to help you throughout this entire process, listen to Him. Now, in your life, this activity or attribute needs reckoning with, somehow or someway.

Otherwise noted, (known or unknown), if the person, place or thing that initiated (or was a recipient of) the action or activity within your dream was not seen, invisible, or only talked about within your dream, this may indicate that the dreamer does not recognize the influential effects another has within your life, or upon your attitude.

If more than one person (known or unknown):

Consider what the group had in common. What behavior, character trait, feature, action, or activity, stood out the most? For example, were they argumentative, authoritative, beautiful, criminal minded, dancing, difficult, dressed unusual, enigmatic, fighting, focused, flirty, helpful, hurtful intentions, powerful, promiscuous, quiet, secretive, seemed unreal, unassuming? That which was highlighted and noted is what you need to focus on at present.

If the attribute or quality is a desirable or positive one, allow the strength of that attribute to help you overcome some manner of immorality or irreverence within your life and/or to help you to become better, productively, for the Kingdom of God in some manner. If the attribute is an undesirable or negative one, take steps accordingly to struggle against the growing desires of the carnal side of you. If applicable, get help and support via prayer, fasting, and a Christian based support group.

For dreams of the dead see following note.

Did someone jump off a cliff and die? While the dead has nothing to do with the living (Ecclesiastes 9:4-6), it may be considered what character trait did that person represent to the dreamer, while the person was actually alive, what character feature stood out the most. With that trait noted, dreamer may consider that the trait noted, is within the dreamer, and that trait is no longer useful or needed for the progression of your spiritual walk, on this side of heaven. Dreamer, it is suggested that you render that trait (good or bad) obsolete, and began anew attempting to move forward, using different tactics to overcome unproductive habitual life cycle choices, and for maneuvering through this thing we call life in a more, better way. See category, Death, and/or other relevant categories.

5. In addition to the following interpretations, see index or relevant categories for more information. For example, if trees were involved in some way, see category, Agriculture; if weather was highlighted, see category, Weather. Kept within context of your dream and the interpretation, the additional symbols are perhaps relevant. It will be within the sum of all the symbols that you will find a more thorough interpretation.

6. Landforms and Bodies of Water are broad and great in extent and variations, from one surface or body of water, to another. Thus, it is suggested that the dreamer see also, other relevant research, via a Bible concordance, Bible illustrated dictionary, encyclopedia, or internet, to seek biblical guidelines for metaphorical meanings of a particular landform or body of water. Having done your research you should be able to determine some basic behaviors or attributes your Lord and Savior wants you to focus on.

Symbols and Referents

The earth's surface, its geology, topography, as well as, its waters, is infused with metaphors, imagery, and spiritual meani ng, for example the rise and fall of spiritual leadership, fortunes, and misfortunes. As well, landforms generally denote progenitors, truths and untruths, and God's mercy and compassion are available. Bodies of water generally denote the working of the Holy Spirit, a quenching of a spiritual thirst (Isaiah 44:3, John 4:13, 14; 7:37-39), or a cleansing agent (Titus 3:5), and God's never failing provision to satisfy our spiritual needs (Revelation 7:17; 21:6; 22:17).

In addition to the varied meanings of landforms and bodies of water, other common words, expressions, usages, (e.g. slang or clichés), or a 'probable' that are metaphorically represented by any of the following are also considered (this section is an addendum at the end of the relevant subcategory).

Category Content: If not listed see index, perchance, for your specific type of landforms and bodies of water dream.

- Landforms:
  - Cataclysmic or End of the World (or any sudden violent change in the earth's surface, catastrophe, calamity, or disaster)
  - Cave or Cove (formation consisting of an underground enclosure with access from the surface of the ground or from the sea)
  - Cleft, Crevice, or Fissure (a narrow planar hole in a rock or material, usually with flattish sides)
  - Coastline, Seashore, or Beach (shore of a sea or ocean)
  - Continent (one of seven large landmasses of the earth)
  - Desert or Sand (dry, infertile ground or arid land with little or no vegetation)
  - Earthquake, Avalanche, Landslide, or Volcano
  - Glaciers (a slowly moving mass of ice), see category, Frozen (Snow)
  - Hill or Mound (an elevation of land consisting of an artificial heap or bank usually of earth or stones)
  - Island, Peninsula, Isthmus, Headland, or Rock of Gibraltar (a land mass, smaller than a continent that is surrounded by water or extends into the sea)
  - Mountains (a land mass that projects well above its surroundings)
  - Plains, Plateaus, Field, or Flats (a level tract of land)
  - Rocks or Stones, see category, Standing Stones
  - Valley, Basin, Canyon, Furrow, Hollow, Ravine, or Wadi (a long depression in the surface of the land that usually contains water)
- • Bodies of Water:
  - For activities or other particulars involving water, e.g. bathing, baptism, cleaning, cruise any kind of watercraft, flooding, torrents, wading in water, swimming, see index or relevant category
  - Canal, Channel, Ditch, Gulley, or Trench (any small narrow body of water)
  - Condition of Water (Brook, Creek, Ditch, Gulf, Lake, Ocean, Reservoir, River, Sea, Strait, Stream)
  - Clean, clear water (pretty color)
  - Dirty or Muddy water (not clean or fresh, bitter waters, salt waters, including used bath water, dirty dish or mop water)
  - Dam, Cistern, Fountain, Reservoir, or Well (barrier constructed to contain the flow of water)
  - Lake, Bayou, or Pond (body of usually fresh water surrounded by land)
  - Ocean, Gulf, Sea, or Strait (a large body of water constituting a principal part of the earth's surface; salt or fresh water, that is surrounded by land and/or is attached to, or flows into, another body of water)
  - Coastline, Seashore, or Beach (shore of a sea or ocean)
  - Swimming pool, see category, Swimming
  - Puddle or Standing Water (standing water or other liquid)
  - River, Brook, Creek, Geyser, or Stream (natural stream of water)

LANDFORMS:

Cataclysmic or End of the World (or any sudden violent change in the earth's surface, catastrophe, calamity, or disaster): Read, understand, and 2 Peter 3:1-18, for this is to you. Couple this scripture with one of the following four (choose one). (1) While this type of dream acknowledges that the dreamer is in the midst of a personal crisis, it also forewarn s of a season of suffering and struggle for the dreamer. This season will be marked with many 'turn-arounds', 'changes', and ups and downs, a very tumultuous and troubling season; all this because, your soul is not upright within you. Suffering has a pu rifying effect within one's life so that after you have suffered you will cease (stop, restrain, refrain, quit, desist) from sin (1 Peter 4:1-9), especially the sin that chronically assails you. Dreamer, you have chosen low or base standards, morals, ethics, ideas, principles, tenets, and/or beliefs. Further, you may even now, deny the existence or power of God, and of evil spirits. Now the Holy Spirit speaks expressly, that in the latter times some shall depart from the faith, which is in Jesus Christ, giving heed to seducing spirits, and doctrines of devils (1 Timothy 4:1-5). Having listened, you have begun to decrease and fall, eventually running amok your life. Your attitude is leading to a mental and spiritual breakdown, opening the door for demons to run havoc within your life and to bring you down to desolation. Your kind of choices leads to prostitution, poverty, homelessnes s, begging, imprisonment, and/or early death. You are forfeiting purpose for foolishness and ruin. Demonic influences will swarm around you, ready to help you in your wicked, evil, despicable, immoral, reprehensible, disreputable, degenerate, infamous, or perverse choices. Your lifestyle choices are, or will become, offensive and repulsive (abominable) in the sight of God and humankind. Dreamer, devils have had thousands of years to master human weaknesses and can rival men and women of God if we are not careful. Compassionately, because of grace and the many mercies of God extended to you, your dream is only a warning and not an official declaration. Utilizing the powerful resources of prayer and heartfelt repentance to Jesus, a changed mindset, serious re-consideration of God's ways and means, and an honest acknowledgement of God's hand within your life, and then the severe impact of your choices and actions upon your life can be reversed and damages repaired (also see Ezekiel 33:12-19). Repentance is seeking pardon and expressing sincere feelings of regret and brokenness for having done something awry and/or for having hurt someone, see 2 Corinthians 7:10, 11. To Jesus pray, Psalm 51, this, coupled with prayer and fasting, followed by appropriate application of wisdom, can conceivably avert some of the repercussions of your choices. This is what is called leaving a blessing behind. Dreamer is also counseled to seek all kinds of spiritual support now, to possibly avert or turn things around, and definitely walk away from all negativity abruptly. If you do not genuinely seek he lp and change, for sure ruin will be your destiny. An angel (perhaps disguised as human, or one, who is a true servant of God, with the Spirit of Truth within) will lead the way. See suggested course of action. (2) Dreamer, because of your frailties and unwise and foolish passions, as well as, your manner of noncompliance, stubbornness, and pride, the sharp reproofs of the Word, and the severe censures of men, you are allowing a weakening of your core beliefs. This weakening is a rejection of al l or some of the original foundational teachings of Christ and His apostles, and this weakening has taken root within you spiritually. Instead of moving towards, and thus fulfilling, your divine purpose, and reaching a pinnacle in your life, ther eby with, you will prosper, you have begun to listen to, and be fooled by, demons. The fallen one has caused you to oppose spiritual intimacy with Christ, via fear and phobias. Dreamer you are allowing, the spirit of fear to terrorize you, it has become your own personal terrorist. Read and understand Romans 8:15, 2 Timothy 1:7. No, you do not have mental health issues, you are not crazy, nor are you having a nervous breakdown. This wicked one has come to terrorize you in your thoughts. When you are afraid, insecure, impatient, confused, filled with worry, uneasy and unsure, when you hesitate, is full of apprehension, when your thoughts forecast only doom and gloom, when panic and stress comes, and despair and depression find you, when you are restless, frightful, full of dread, anxious, nervous. When your fears are extreme and irrational, especially regarding simple things or social situations and/or when you feel hopeless. You will find this diabolical entity in every phobia. Fav orably, there is still hope and time for you. Question to journal: What would it feel like if all of your fears were suddenly released from you at one time? Pause and feel that. Bible story, there was that herd of pigs that Legion was cast into, and these pi gs found their thoughts to be so unbearable that they all ran off a cliff to commit suicide, because they could not bear what had been unleashed upon them (Matthew 8:28-34, Mark 5:1-20, Luke 8:26-39). This is what the spirit of fear oftentimes leads to, if embraced wholly. On the other hand, the man whom, the devils were suddenly released from, was found sitting, clothed, healed, and in his right mind, and all this done without medication. The spirit of fear is adversarial to the Word of God that says all things will work together for good, to those who love God, and are called according to His purpose. For, if you truly can believe the Word of God, it will change all the rules that darkness has established in your heart and mind. Now I say to you that before you can move forward, fear must be cast out, and renounced, and not medicated. Therefore, dreamer, earnestly renounce the insidious voice of the devil. If you will daily come away and pray, then God will heal you of all things, only come with much prayer and spiritual fasting. The spiritual fast is that time of waiting when you are praying and asking the Lord to come and perform that which only He can perform. See suggested course of action. (3) Dreamer, you often herald peace when there is none, pointing people down a road of possible catastrophe. You hard-press people, including your family, to believe what you say and compel individuals to follow false gods. You do not pursue by faith, the righteousness that only comes from the Lord, and is now unable to acknowledge God's providence on any level. A change has come. The prosperity God has provided you will begin to abate and your anarchy will be exposed. Dreamer; you are counseled to turn back to God, seek forgiveness, and, if applicable, tangibly participate in the turning back of your children to God that He may leave a blessing. One thing is for sure; you can no longer pursue perverseness, and continue as before. A disastrous event is heade d toward you and it will prove catastrophic. God is planning a disaster against you, a calamity. He will use someone that you will not be able to overcome, until you confess your sins of arrogance, pride, and self-righteousness to Him and admit it to yourself, and turn from the error of your ways completely. Fortunately, this disaster will effect within you humility th at you might be saved. On the other hand, if you recognized, now, your transgressions and repent, calamity can be averted. Question to consider. Dreamer, if God would give you the courage and wherewithal to "cease and desist" from the wickedness that is within you, at present, would you seize the opportunity? If yes, first, repent, pray Psalm 51, and warn others that you've h ard- press to believe what you say, of the error of your words. Moreover, read, understand, and believe: 1 Corinthians 3:13-15. If dreamer would only repent and renounce your wicked ideas, you've perpetuated that you might find mercy in the Eyes of God, on your Day of the Lord, the day of your reckoning. Further, pray that you might be able to escape all that is about to happen, and that you may be able to stand before Adonai Elohim, considering that your Day of the Lord is near (Zephaniah 1:13-18), your day of your reckoning. The choice is up to you, you can do it easy (choosing to repent and change now), or you can do i t hard (repentance and change being worked within you, at the cost of great loss and pain). Those who walk humbly and uprightly will enter into peace; they will find rest. Choosing how to walk is up to you. See suggested course of action. (4) Dreamer, your life is before God, and mayhem is your modus operandi "MO" (mode or state of operating, living, or lifestyle). Thus, a door has been opened for you to be deceived. Unfortunately, this lack of faith in God and His power has caused God to become adversarial towards you; thus, you are being judged by the divine council. This marks a critical season within your life. Dreamer, the matter at hand that you desire of God to make happen on your behalf will not happen. The big event you are expecting to happen will not. Illustration: If you are lead to believe that a specific person will marry you, you are deceived; they will not. If you are expecting to receive a lump sum settlement, you will not. Dreamer, thank God for His patience, lo ng- suffering, and grace (the free and unmerited favor and beneficence of God), while you get things decent and in order. See suggested course of action.

Cave or Cove (formation consisting of an underground enclosure with access from the surface of the ground or from the sea): This dream has three meanings (choose one). (1) Your dream signifies that the dreamer is called to be a prophet or prophetess. You have an open connection to divine revelation, and access to prophetic wisdom; thus, you will minister and inspire others from a prophetic platform. You are required to be a transformational force in people's lives, via not neglecting the prophetic gift that is within you. Properly developed, your link to prophetic revelation, can and will be used to help o thers. Freely as the Lord has given, feely give, as you will now be led into situations where you can express your desire to serve others. (2) Your dream refers to a rectification of chaos and a spiritual purification process happening within the life of the dreamer, as well as your entire household. This season of cleansing will draw you away from personal pursuits, and allow time for you to devote yourself, and all that you are, to God's glory (e.g. by perfecting your inborn talent in some way for the g lory of God, or by starting or enhancing a ministry). It will also perfect a quietness within your soul, and a more compassionate and obedient spirit, leaving you more open to divine influence. You will gain knowledge on how to be moderate in all things, jus t and fair. This will take some time, be patient, and allow the process. (3) Dreamer, you are a vessel of God's glory, and a possessor of the truth needed for the situation at hand, the greater the truth, the greater your authority, the greater your success. You are equipped to handle your, and God's, business. God puts His servants in situations where they are responsible to usher His Presence into the mentality of the situation. We usher His Presence in, and magnify the Lord, when we proclaim His goodness, His truth, harmonize with His word, and exalt His Mighty Name. Your adoration of God, in all of its many forms, has caused you to become more aware of His awesome power and authority. This has enabled you to handle the situation at hand by faith. This situation is before you at present. This is necessary to say, although you are held in high esteem by many, immediately let them know, "Don't worship me, I too am just a man or woman like yourself, God, and God alone is to be worship", for God has said, "I will not give my glory to another" (Isaiah 42:8). Therefore, dreamer you are warned to be careful lest you become so prideful that there creeps into you the idea that you can be deified. Self-deification is of Satan. God can dwell in the human, via the Holy Spirit, but forever the human is the human, and Adonai Elohim is forever God. See suggested course of action.

Cleft, Crevice, or Fissure (a narrow planar hole in a rock or material, usually with flattish sides): Your dream comes to warn the dreamer that you will experience some level of public exposure, for open shame shortly. Therefore, a change is vitally needed in the way you behave, as your dream alludes to one who needs to abstain from immorality, and other profane acts. You profane that which is holy, because you have been wounded by one considered pious, who is not. No, one person, people, or denomination, hypocrite or not, is the full representation of the Kingdom of God ; therefore, no longer allow the enemy to rob you of your intended destiny. It would be wise for you, at this time in your life, to embrace holiness, wholeheartedly, to prevent the practice of greater immoral acts; for such acts are grossly unclean and will defile you spiritually and physically completely. Your acts of immorality, will unequivocally lead to you selling your "birthright", just to satisfy the growing lust in your flesh and heart (Genesis 25:29-34; Hebrews 12:14-17). The repercussions of such acts see Ezekiel 18:24-32, 33:10-13. Dreamer, without holiness no one shall see the Lord. Therefore, look diligently within, and consider the state of great suffering and distress, you are experiencing, is a result of your own choices, and no other is to blame. See suggested course of action.

Coastline, Seashore, or Beach (shore of a sea or ocean): Dreamer, God is confirming His promises to you via your dream. He has promised to deliver you from the ways of wickedness and from demons whose words and ways are perverse, whose paths are crooked and devious. Thus, your dream denotes a literal separation and distance, a departing to another place, and the ending of a union, friendship, or another significant relationship, spiritually and emotionally, e.g. unhealthy "soul tie s", negative co-dependent or abusive type relationship, or any negativity that is the antithesis of Christ. Dreamer, you are leaving a space, and will be letting go of someone(s) that you may go forward to a more harmonious state of things, and to a place where you will be used to minister to others. Moreover, dreamer you are entering into a season within your life that will prepare you spiritually for the visitation of the Lord in your individual life. During this time, you will experience His love and presence, as you've never known it before. For, He is saying to you, "I will teach you godly wisdom". You will receive direct insight of divine truth. You will come to know, without a doubt, that God is the true source of your strength and wisdom, an d He is your sufficiency. As a result, a greater love for self will begin to manifest, affecting wholeness within your life. Be available to Him and seize the moments and opportunities as they are presented, especially an opportunity for you to advance your education. Further, there will be additional proof that something that you believed, some fact, hypothesis, or theory, is valid, and this will be formally confirmed. Additionally, and if relevant, a formal agreement between the dreamer and another, a formal agreement to perform or not perform some action, this agreement is correct.

Continent (one of seven large landmasses of the earth): Dreamer, you are counseled to live by God's principles, precepts, and statutes, for this is the Lord's will. His standards are meant to be a hedge of protection around you, to keep you from hurt, harm, and danger, and to support life and living. Obedience, at this time, is also preparing and maturing you to reach those who have fallen away from Christ; this is your mission. When you choose to do things His way, you g ive God pleasure, in that you perform His will. Unfortunately, your will, your "ways and means", will only attract spiritual bondage ; captivity, destruction, and judgment (divine reprimand for folly and sin); thus, this warning dream. Dreamer, prideful and powerful, you lack Christ-like humility, and is becoming a cruel and insensitive leader. Moreover, at present, concerned with your own interest, you are driven by, and occupied with, sensual appetites, rather than spiritual needs. Your desires, appetites, and attitude are leading to a chaotic and empty life. A life figuratively similar to the condition of earth in Genesis 1:2, wasteful, empty, and dark. Your type of carnal strain and toil has led to sorrow and spiritual darkness. Dreamer, although you suppose, you are powerful and have command over your life, liberty, and freedom; you are without self -control, intemperate, powerless, unable to refrain from desolate pursuits. Your force, strength, power, might is an illusion. Additionally, dreamer, you have been attempting to establish a relationship with the Father according to your will, and not His Will. There is a need to re-connect with God. However, approaching God the Father, without the essential provision He has provided for humankind to approach Him properly; that provision being Yeshua HaMashiach, is not safe. Some call God's provision Jesus, Wonderful Counselor, Mighty God, Everlasting Father, Prince of Peace, our atonement, advocate, liberator, propitiator, and our salvation. It is only through this channel that you may hope through faith to conciliate with your Creator (see Acts 2:37-42; 1 Timothy 2:4-7). Compassionately, there is a ray of light, sent by God, purposed to break through the darkness of your state of affairs. This ray of light is a person, anointed and sent, especially to you. Their words and inspiration will be to you, like Genesis 1:3-5 is to Genesis 1:2. Illuminatingly wise, this person will powerfully affect your life, externally and internally. Their inspiration, coupled with you earnestly embracing change, humility, contentedness, integrity, ethicalness, and a renewed faith in God's word and His process, will strengthen you to return in complete heartfelt repentance to Jesus, from a heart of love. See suggested course of action.

Desert or Sand (dry, infertile ground or arid land with little or no vegetation): This dream has two meanings (choose one). (1) It is time for the dreamer to earnestly thirst and long for, those things by which, the soul is genuinely refreshed, supported, and strengthened by. It is suggested that you go away, into a quiet place, away from all the distractions to seriously fast, and deprogram and re-program yourself (Galatians 1:12-24). At this crossroads in your life, you need to count all that you know, to be worthless (Philippians 3:3-9). It is promised that afterwards you will begin to walk and grow into a more mature spiritual being, going on towards perfection, enabled to see into the spiritual realm more clearly. Additionally, no matter the hardships and they may prove grievously; never again look back, but genuinely, in words and deeds, continue to progress forward. By this, your capacity for greater illumination, intellectually and spiritually, will become enlarged, giving you access to more than a few gates of wisdom (2 Corinthians 12:2-10). See suggested course of action. (2) Dreamer, look to Jesus. Love and forgiveness can and will embrace and restore you, wait for it. A simple prayer of repentance is in order. "Jesus, I beg your forgiveness. I know I've broken your heart, I never meant to treat you this way. Heavenly Father, whatever it takes, I'll d o, that I might not hurt you again, and I'll love you for the rest of my life". With that said, your dream is associated with false teachers, and/or legalistic Christians, who love to revel in self-righteousness. You disregard caution, diplomacy, discretion, good judgment, good insight, maturity, prudence, responsibility, and wisdom. You are a fleshly person, self -indulgent, dull minded to spiritual things, and hypocritical. Dreamer, one simple decision to repent, and reject the attitude of foolishness, hypocrisy, selfishness, and lack of commitment and stewardship to the ministry of the Kingdom of Jesus Christ; and where there would be chaos, genuine peace will abide. Where there is a lack of prudence, wisdom will rule. See suggested course of action.

   Earthquake, Avalanche, Landslide, or Volcano: This dream has five meanings (one, two, etc., or all may apply). (1) Dreamer, you are insincere in your dealings with people, especially by being outwardly friendly but secretly disloyal. All of these behaviors are a sign of a hardened heart or a heart becoming hardened and deep-seated anger. Thus says the Lord, "I will sprinkle clean water on you, and you will be clean; I will cleanse you from all your impurities and from all your idols. I will give you a new heart and put a new spirit in you; I will remove from you your heart of stone and give you a heart of flesh (Ezekiel 36:25-27). Dreamer, God knows your thoughts afar off, so genuinely repent. Other than heartfelt repentance to Jesus, no other excuse or weak justification will be heard. See suggested course of action. If necessary, see suggested course of action. (2) Male dreamer: An event or situation that will cause intense fear is coming to discourage and terrify you. This will be in the form of an annoying, difficult, and unpleasant person. The trouble this person will cause will become so overwhelming, because they will expose a secret regarding you. This spiritual battle will be great, and will demand your full attention. Although you will walk through this alone, know that God will walk you through it. Dreamer, learn wisdom from th e situation, for truth do set one free; and go on from there unashamed. Then, suddenly, unexpectedly, and without any warning, all the evil and wickedness that caused you to fear and be troubled, will disappear. It will be as though it was never there. At that point, you will express great joy, and feel extremely happy. Take courage and be strong, knowing that the Lord knows where you are, what's going on, and He cares. See suggested course of action. (3) Your dream also represents some type of spiritual privileges and a purification process, dreamer God will now separate you from people, places, and circumstances that will hinder your growth. View this separation as a blessing from God and not as an evil thing has happen. Under all adversities retain a spirit of joy, and continue to make progress in your spiritual life. Subsequently, dreamer, because of your humble and submissive faith in God's word, you will be declared as one who is a righteous minister. Planted in the House of the Lord, you will continue to prosper and mature. The same God, who plants you in your ministry, is the same God who will cause you to mature and prosper. Further, another benefit of allowing Jesus to have authority of your life; is that independent of outward circumstances, you will live and thrive where most things perish, via divine grace. Dreamer, while your spiritual growth may not be so rapid, if you endure, you will become a beautiful picture of a godly man or woman, who in your uprightness, aims to glorify God. Accordingly, gladness, thanksgiving, singing, strength, intense energy, and fertility will be your recompense, and your praise will be a sweet aroma in the nostrils of the Lord. This promise is also to your generations to come. Come what may, you shall make steady progress and flourish in a very impressive manner; bringing forth fruit, even in your old age. Dreamer, as you age, your anointing to minister, and divine revelations, will always be fresh and edifying. See Psalm 92:12-15. Therefore, put the spiritual work in and go through what you need to go through now. If necessary, see suggested course of action. (4) Dreamer, character traits from ancestors, namely genetic codes and traits, will often trouble and taunt the offspring of a given progenitor, especially generational issues (Exodus 20:5-7). The demons that have so plague your family line, are now visiting (re-visiting) you, namely voices that whisper, you are without value, insignificant, or pointless, and it is the embracing of those voices that will lead to other issues, such as sexual perversion (e.g. adultery, fornication, homosexuality, prostitution, or whorishness), and on to a bleak and desolate atmosphere. This will lead to much sadness, and feelings of being forsaken or abandoned. Favorably, generational curses and issues can stop with you (Jeremiah 31:29, 30; Ezekiel 18:2-14, 20-23). Hence, your Heavenly Father is requiring that you overcome and subdue negative and dark emotions, feelings, behaviors, and/or ideas that have come to influence you, before they overcome you; and leave you desolate. Dreamer, God is not asking you to do something you cannot do. For a surety, vanquishing of dark influences can be done. By faith, you will need to declare some kind of fast and commit to it, for a long period-of-time, to abate the demonically instigated circumstance, you find yourself in now, Matthew 6:16-18. Try abstaining from food and drink (midnight to 6 PM), twice a week, and refrain from words, attitudes, people, places, and things, including music, magazines, videos, TV, or any such things that fuel anger and discontent, and stir up lustful feelings. This is also known as, faith with works, read, understand, and embrace James 2:14-26. Nonetheless, earnestly pray, God will guide, enable, and answer you as to the type of fast. Additionally, if relevant, forgive your mother and/or father for the darkness (aka curse) they may have perpetuated, for they knew not what they done. Forgiveness is important to your success (Matthew 6:12-15, 8:21-35). See suggested course of action. (5) This type of dream is sent to warn an immoral believer, namely the dreamer, that there is a need of refinement of character, especially in the area dealing with the deeds of the flesh. Dreamer, you have not considered the reality of the repercussions of your unwise choices. You emanate anger and rage, perpetuate violence, and possibly promote all kinds of indecent practices, sexual perversions, and other odious traditions, under the guise of Christianity. You dishon or God, His truth, His Kingdom, His church, and continually provoke God to anger. Are you not afraid to speak against God, and His ways and means? Dreamer, is nothing sacred? Do you think the detestable things you are promoting and perpetuating are smal l, are of little consequence, and are of little importance to God, His ways, His Kingdom, His people (the Body of Christ)? You take great risk, when you have no fear of promoting and perpetuating ideology that is clearly "adversarial" to God, per Holy Wri t. For, all scripture is inspired by God and is useful to teach us what is true and to make us realize what is awry in our lives. It corrects us when we are wrong and teaches us to do what is right (2 Timothy 3:16). You show yourself presumptuous, when you do not fear to speak evil of the Lord. It is a dangerous thing to offend Christ. Did you not expect that God would resent it, and take it as an affront to Himself personally? Thus, the harshness of the Lord is, kindled against you. Therefore, now, He will deal with you harshly. The dreamer will begin to experience a loss of divine favor and authority. Additionally, a third of the people that adhere to such practices as you do, will all die of the same illness, a third will fall away (becoming apostates) because of a lack of saving knowledge, and a third will "pull up stakes" with a stigma attached to their name. The dreamer will find him or herself within one of these three categories. Another repercussion, you will also begin to experience serio us mental health issues and will have to be restrained, against your will if needs be. When these things begin to happen, if no t already, you will know that the Lord has spoken. Dreamer, turn from your wicked ways, and dump your darken ideology, and enlighten and encourage others to do so as well. Moreover, as He knows your thoughts afar off, repent. Take words to Jesus, "'I have sinned, and I have done wrong and acted wickedly". Other than heartfelt repentance to Jesus and a change in your beliefs, behavior, and choices, no other excuse or weak justification will be heard. Ask Jesus for wisdom, and for the courage to apply it that you, might live, albeit, with a stigma set upon you. See suggested course of action.

Hill or Mound (an elevation of land consisting of an artificial heap or bank usually of earth or stones): Your dream was sent to encourage the dreamer. Dreamer, continue on the path you're on, for you are truly heading toward purpose. You are passionate and protective when it comes to standing up for your beliefs. You never doubt your inner strength and ability to handle any challenge. Many will be inspired by your confidence; while others will feel threaten by it. Do not allow those intimidated by you, to weary you, in your well doing, and they will attempt to weary, if not already. Favorably, God will protect you from their stress, and He will hide you under the shadow of His wings. He will never leave you nor forsake you. He will walk and talk with you. He will lead you on. If needful, may also see categories, Ascending and Descending (Going up and down), or Descend (Falling), or Sitting (High place).

Island, Peninsula, Isthmus, Headland, or Rock of Gibraltar (a land mass, smaller than a continent that is surrounded by water or extends into the sea): This dream has three meanings (one or two may apply). (1) Your dream signifies that the dreamer is called to be a prophet; sent to the rebellious people of God. Moreover, stop complaining. Additionally, visit th e sick and elderly, especially family members. Your visit will remove some of the burden of their sickness, thus lightening their load, and perhaps leave a physical healing behind[36]. Have faith in this, for it will be by your prayers that one will be healed wholly. This is a true saying. (2) If married, your dream denotes that you are "equally yoked" with someone (e.g. spouse, ministry, business associate, friendship). To be equally yoked is to agree with one another; having the same interests, desires, long term goals, and outlook. Your marriage is not defiled and, the wife should not usurp authority over her husband, moreover, the husband must learn to dwell with his wife according to knowledge. (3) If not married, your dream denotes a unity of man and wife in the presence of God, get married. There will be a chance encounter.

In addition, the following is a common word, expression, or usage (e.g. slang or cliché), or a 'probable' that is metaphorically represented by an island:

- **No Man is an Island:** Dreamer, you are not alone; neither should you feel alone, isolation from others is a choice. Human beings do not thrive when isolated from others. Dreamer is advised to seek a faith-based community to connect with and join, and to allow them to become your family and friends.

Mountains (a land mass that projects well above its surroundings): This dream has two meanings (choose one). (1) Running to, towards, or into a Mountain: Read, Genesis 19:17 and Matthew 24:15, and seek biblical commentary for contemporary relevance, and understanding, and embrace, applying the warning for you personally. (2) Your dream was sent to encourage the dreamer. Dreamer you are a hard worker concerning your duties, missions, and responsibilities. You devote yourself to work, as well as, show concern for the betterment of your community at large; and with your organized, efficient approach, things are done resourcefully. You radiate security. You often forfeit your own desires for your family and anyone else you consider a responsibility, as well as, for any worthy cause. Consequently, you will now reap the rewards of such diligence, including rest and graceful surroundings, and, if not already, a promotion to a high leadership position. You will highly blossom in the Kingdom of God. Moreover, as you are able to handle great responsibility and wealth, and are one who is tolerant, you will experience receiving an act of kindness, monetarily, from someone who is affluent. Even more, you are entering into a season within your life that will prepare you spiritually for the visitation of the Lord in your individual life. During this time, you will experience His love and presence, as you've never known it before. For, He is saying to you, "I will teach you godly wisdom". You will receive direct insight of divine truth. You will come to know, without a doubt, that God is the true source of your strength and wisdom, and He is your sufficiency. As a result, a greater love for self, family, and others will begin to manifest, affecting wholeness within your life. Moreover, if applicable, your children will reap the fruits of the blessing of your giving. On the other hand, words of caution. Dreamer, as it takes an unrivaled level of confidence to successfully endure mountain top experiences, without imploding, as you are elevated, it will be wise, for you, to periodically take a reflective look within, to check the pride level, within your heart (also see Deuteronomy 6:10-18). It is counseled that you set up 'mile markers', a type of accountability system for yourself along the way. Do not be deceived, with affluence, power, and wealth, comes good and evil; thus, today, you will need to choose between good and evil; and set "checks and balances" within yourself, because you have innate tendencies to become extreme and will judge others according to your "extremisms". Embracing this side of yourself will cause you to be deemed inappropriate, and delayed at that moment, to be of further service to the Kingdom of God. Regrettably, this will lead to you being unhappy, and unable to discern between truth and error, without you realizing your shortsightedness. Therefore, the "checks and balances" are meant to rectify the soul to increase its capacity to receive the blessings of the Lord more fully. Blessings; in this sense, is a state of high honor, spiritual beauty, and great illumination. Henceforth, in accordance with your decision as to how you shall continue from this day forward, will define your level of esteem from the Lord, whether little esteem or greatly esteem, in your future and beyond. Further, if you choose to embrace the positive, this will lead to a great balancing of your theology, resulting in a belief that is complete, with solid attributes, and your inspiration will make for very good teaching. Additionally, you would make an excellent apologist (witness) for the Kingdom of God. Seriously consider this branch of Christian theology. If needful, may also see categories, Ascending and Descending, or Descend, or Sitting, and relevant subcategories.

Plains, Plateaus, Field, or Flats (a level tract of land): Even when the Lord knows the works of His people are done in love, faith, zeal, and patience, yet if His eyes observe them committing, or allowing, what is evil, He will rebuke or correct them. Thus, this dream is a rebuke to some, a dire warning to some, and encouragement to others. This dream has four meanings (choose one). (1) Married male dreamer: If you are a married, ecclesiastical leader, such as a bishop, elder, minister, pastor, priest, rabbi, or is acting in any ecclesiastical leadership type role. Your dream comes as a rebuke. You indicate your consent, even encourage, wicked seducers, including your wife, also known as a prophetess and/ or teacher. In allowing those who embrace corrupt doctrine, to perpetuate heresy, you are therefore the greater seducer. Thus, you are responsible for the spiritual disarray of some of God's faithful, due to erroneous teachings and beliefs. You have the power to restrain your wife, and the others; but you do not do it, thus, she and her cohorts have every opportunity of seducing even more of the faithful. This is what Christ has against you. Sin will very soon turn your paradise into chaos, and dishonor the beauty of your name. God will bring your deeds to the light; He will show you that He is, according to His title, The Son of God; and that He knows your heart. He will pry into your actions, and like a fire, He will search into everything, and burn up the chaff, which cannot stand His trial. So severe are things that restoration can only be by returning earnestly to Christ Jesus wholeheartedly. Your recklessness can be remedied by prayer and heartfelt repentance to Jesus and to individuals affected by your actions, and by rebuking, and putting a stop to the "spirit of jezebel" that has been allowed to reign within your minis try. See suggested course of action. (2) Married female dreamer: If you are a wife of a bishop, elder, minister, pastor, pope, priest, rabbi, or is acting in any ecclesiastical leadership type role. Your dream is a severe and dire warning of coming chastening. Dreamer, you are a woman of power and influence, possibly, also known as a prophetess and/or teacher, unfortunately pride has deceived you; and you have corrupted the one true religion, with syncretistic [28] ideas, and you harass the followers of God. Your dream pronounces a judgment against your impenitence. Dreamer, you believe in a god of your own making, coupled with outrageous claims you have wholeheartedly embraced from other erroneous guides. You respect your truth, while never acknowledging, it is delivered without grace; thus, it is never enough to fill an emaciated soul. Moreover, you have adopted a bourgeois mentality, believing yourself above God's word and above the law of the land. This mentality is concerned only with your personal comfort, material wealth, and status, at any expense. Now, having in yourself nothing that you respect more than power and greed, you are willing to sacrifice all, God, principle, family, and friend, to the image or idol of vanity. Your new way is based on exploring alternatives to God's righteous principles, as well as, creating a sense of unity with the wickedness around you. This is what you call love. This mentality sacrifices children, family, and morality, to the hollowness of satisfying immoral desires and appetites. All carried out, with the hope of finding happiness by pacifying jealously and covetousness. The selling-out of yourself over to immorality, devaluing those, you should be protecting and nurturing, especially the faithful, while closing your eyes to it all, are all principles based on values that are not only vile, but also increasingly unstable. This way cries out against godly ethics, and its' end offends any sense of godliness. Dreamer, you obey no one, and accept no correction. You do not trust in the Lord, nor, do you draw near to Him, although He has given you space to repent; instead, you seduced others to follow you, perpetuating your sins. Thus, sin will very soon turn your paradise into chaos, and dishonor the beauty of your name. You are also at risk of falling into a state of serious health problems and possibly loss of life. So severe are things that restoration can only be by returning to Christ Jesus wholeheartedly. Dreamer when God hides His face from someone celebrations are turned into moaning and groaning, and the party is exchanged for depression and solitude. Your recklessness can be remedied by prayer and heartfelt repentance to Jesus and to individuals affected by your actions, and by renouncing the "spirit of jezebel", that has attached itself to you. See suggested course of action. (3) Unmarried male or female: Your dream was sent as encouragement to those who have kept themselves pure and undefiled from the teachings of heresy that has surrounded you; even within the ministry, you are connected. Your dream denotes that the dreamer has grown wiser and better. Continue to earnestly, desire that your last works might be your best works. There is promise of ample recompense to the persevering, victorious believer; also, knowledge and wisdom will be given that you might continue in the power of God. For now, do not leave your place of worship, stay right where you are, things will pan out. If necessary, God will give you a door to leave, and lead you to a faith - based community. Moreover, after things have calmed down, God will be glorified. (4) Field (an extensive tract of level open land, an open field): This choice has six parts (choose one). (a) Unmarried male or female, and if marriage is desired, a potential spouse is looking carefully at you at present. Your faithfulness and unpretentiousness is beautiful in the ir sight. An introduction will present itself shortly. The question of the possibility of relocation may be asked. God will honor the un ion. Moreover, if relevant and desired, the union of the groom and bride will result in a literal pregnancy. Continue to have faith in God, He will have mercy on you, and grant you the desire of your heart, namely to birth children of your own body, suddenly and very soon. (b) If dreamer is actually expecting an inheritance of some kind, this type of dream is to bring about an awareness of an appointed inheritance of abundant peace, comforts, and sufficient wealth for the dreamer. At some point in the undisclosed future, honor and wealth will be bestowed upon the dreamer, if not already. You are becoming self -sufficient and unrelenting, capable of handling much responsibility, especially when required to make major decisions. Moreover, there will be success publicly, regarding some kind of enterprise, as your dream also denotes a company with special status that is given preferential treatment by the federal government because it is owned by socially and economically disadvantaged persons (e.g. small businesses); perhaps development of a market, or investment in, new wireless technology, is an option (e. g. li fi). (c) Dreamer, you have learned the Christian values and principles that leads one to reach out and touch others in a loving and graceful manner; ultimately finding yourself promoting the genuine cause of Christ and the good of others. You have an open connection to divine revelation, which will at times be used on a prophetic platform. Properly developed, your link to prophetic revelation can and should be used to help others. If not already, you will inspire others to dream and to make their dreams come true. Dreamer, you are gifted in many areas, and you have access to prophetic wisdom, thus, you are required to be a transformational force in people's lives, via not neglecting the gift that is within you. You will now be led into situations, where you will show up when most needed, and then disappear without a thought of compensation. You will be dispatched on missions, to help believers who are facing urgent needs during a crisis, and/or in an emergency, and to give instant help, as well as, to express God's loving kindness, His grace, mercy, and compassion. You are sent to protect and defend those who obediently love God, and who is loved by God. An angel (perhaps disguised as human, or one, who is a true servant of God, with the Spirit of Truth within) will lead the way. Read, understand, and embrace Psalm 147. Altruistic, goodhearted, and generous service to God and others is beneficial at this time. As you've freely received, freely give. (d) If dreamer is presently experiencing a spiritual struggle within, that is very intensive. Dreamer, the intensity of your struggle, because of your anger or rage issues or any other manner of darkness within, is actually an inner spiritual warfare, couple w ith the refining, and purifying work of the Paraclete. Therefore, persevere, for this struggle will cause the emergence of a more divine led wisdom within you. It will also be through these pains that the wisdom of harmonizing, fear and love of the Lord within your life, will be imparted to you. Favorably, due to the intensity of your struggle, one of God's messengers will be sent, to give you the support needed at this time. Be aware that the new person within your midst may be that messenger. With that said, dreamer, you are encompassed about with righteousness and purity. The intents and motives of your heart are pure and righteous. You are honorable in the eyes of God. Dreamer, you will have success overcoming old things; and there will b e joy spiritually, as your dream is also an expression of the joy and happiness you will experience serving the Lord. As well, you are prepared for any spiritual conflict or evil activity that may come your way. Dreamer, many will be inspired by your faith in Christ, your humility, and your unpretentiousness. See suggested course of action. (e) If dreamer is actually ill, your dream denotes a virus or inflammation of the liver, or some toxic disease affecting the liver, such as Jaundice or gallstones, or anemia. Seek medical attention as soon as possible, and call for the elders of your church, for it is through their prayers of faith and anointing of oil upon you that sin is forgiven and healing is bestowed[36]. Have faith in this, for it will be by your faith that you will be healed wholly. This is a true saying. (f) Wandering around in a Field: Your dream refers to one who has strayed from the path of reason, you do not know the real way that leads to the place you are destined to reach; now, you've come to a state where you think that you will never achieve the goals you should achieve. Dreamer, if you would but returned to Christ, the church, and again, restore fellowship with other Christians, those who genuinely love you with the love (agape) of Christ, you will once again find your way and become able to achieve your goals. However, this way is against your nature; especially because you've embraced those who do not love you genuinely, and who hates God. By being together with those who love Christ, you will be able find your way back to God, and experience restoration. This is also known as the "the path of bestowal".

Valley, Basin, Canyon, Furrow, Hollow, Ravine, or Wadi (a long depression in the surface of the land that usually contains water): This dream has four meanings (choose one). (1) Male dreamer: An event or situation that will cause intense fear is coming to discourage and terrify you. This will be in the form of an annoying, difficult, and unpleasant person. Th e trouble this person will cause will become so overwhelming, because they will expose a secret regarding you. This spiritual battle will be great, and will demand your full attention. Although you will walk through this alone, know that God will wal k you through it. Dreamer, learn wisdom from the situation, for truth do set one free; and go on from there unashamed. Then, suddenly, unexpectedly, and without any warning, all the evil and wickedness that caused you to fear and be troubled, will disappear. It will be as though it was never there. At that point, you will express great joy, and feel extremely happy. Take courage and be strong, knowing that the Lord knows where you are, what's going on, and He cares. See suggested course of action. (2) Unmarried male dreamer: A very attractive and sensual female, one whom the dreamer, may marry, especially before having sex, will enter your life. (3) Dreamer, character traits from ancestors, namely genetic codes and traits, will often trouble and taunt the offspring of a given progenitor, especially generational issues (Exodus 20:5-7). The demons that have so plague your family line, are now visiting (re-visiting) you, namely voices that whisper, you are without value, insignificant, or pointless, and it is the embracing of those voices that will lead to other issues, such as sexual perversion (e.g. adultery, fornication, homosexuality, prostitution, or whorishness), and on to a bleak and desolate atmosphere. This will lead to much sadness, and feelings of being forsaken or abandoned. All of this is a sign of a hardened heart or a heart becoming hardened. Dreamer, your present issue, whatever "it" is, "it" is demonically instigated and it is spiritually perverse. Favorably, generational curses and issues can stop with you (Jeremiah 31:29, 30; Ezekiel 18:2-14, 20-23). Hence, your Heavenly Father is requiring that you overcome and subdue negative and dark emotions, feelings, behaviors, and/or ideas that have come to influence you, before they overcome you; and leave you desolate. Dreamer, God is not asking you to do something you cannot do. Dreamer, the Lord Jesus, is asking you to come to Him, come away privately, and ask Him to heal you, come, and ask Him to deliver you; and give Him authority over your life that you might be healed, delivered, and set free. In addition, dreamer, by faith, you will need to declare some kind of fast and commit to it, for a long period-of-time, for this is faith with works, read James 2:14-26. To abate this coming influence (Matthew 6:16-18), try abstaining from food and drink (midnight to 6 PM), twice a week, and/or refraining from words, attitudes, people, places, and things, including music, magazines, videos, TV, or any such things that fuel anger and discontent, and stir up lustful feelings. Earnestly pray, God will guide, enable, and answer you as to the type of fast. Dreamer, God knows your thoughts afar off, so genuinely repent. Other than heartfelt repentance to Jesus, no other excuse or weak justification will be heard. Additionally, if relevant, forgive your mother and/or father for the darkness (aka curse) they may have perpetuated, for they knew not what they done. Forgiveness is important to your success (Matthew 6:12-15, 8:21-35). Your dream also represents some type of spiritual privileges and a purification process, dreamer God will separate you from people, places, and circumstances that will hinder your growth. View this separation as a blessing from God and

689

not as an evil thing has happen. Under all adversities retain a spirit of joy, and continue to make progress in your spiritual life. Subsequently, dreamer, because of your humble and submissive faith in God's word, you will be declared as one who is a righteous minister. Planted in the House of the Lord, you will continue to prosper and mature. The same God, who plants you in your ministry, is the same God who will cause you to mature and prosper. Further, another benefit of allowing Jesus to have authority of your life; is that independent of outward circumstances, you will live and thrive where m ost things perish, via divine grace. Dreamer, while your spiritual growth may not be so rapid, if you endure, you will become a beautiful picture of a godly man or woman, who in your uprightness, aims to glorify God. Accordingly, gladness, thanksgiving, singing, strength, intense energy, and fertility will be your recompense, and your praise will be a sweet aroma in the nostrils of the Lord. If applicable, this promise is also to your generations to come. Come what may, you shall make steady progress and flourish in a very impressive manner; bringing forth fruit, even in your old age. Dreamer, as you age, your anointing to minister, and divine revelations, will always be fresh and edifying. See Psalm 92:12-15. Therefore, put the spiritual work in and go through what you need to go through now. See suggested course of action. (4) Dreamer, having been in the process of rectification for a while, you suppose God has forgotten you or has dealt too bitterly with you. Not so, it is because of yo ur beliefs and practices; you are unable to overcome your present predicament, for your wisdom only leads to shadows and desolation. The dreamer does not have a clear or correct understanding of spiritual truths, especially those that articulate s the true nature of God. When tempted, no one should say, "God is tempting me". For God cannot be tempted by evil, nor does He tempt anyone; but each one is tempted when, by his or her own evil desire, he or she is dragged away and enticed. Then, after desire has conceived, it gives birth to sin; and sin, when it is full-grown, gives birth to death. Read James 1:12-27. Moreover, your dream denotes one who is quick-tempered and quick to fight. Dreamer, there is an old saying that goes; "if one gives oneself over to anger it is as if one worships idols". Anger insinuates complaining, deception, disobedience, disrespect, harsh treatment, jealousy, sexual violations and/or unrighteous dealings, and causes you to move about in a confused manner. When you realize that rectification depends upon you, you will learn to be patient, especially with others. For patience is the antidote to anger. Additionally, blessed is the man or woman who perseveres under trial, because when he or she has stood the test, he or she will receive the crown of life that God has promised to those who love Him. Hence, patience is the wisdom, which nurtures one's ability to wait for conflict to resolve itself, to suspend judgment, to continuo usly check and control your innate tendency to relate to others impulsively. It is the key to avoiding the damage you can inflict upon others and upon yourself, when you are unable to control the responses of your first nature to life situations. Only toward your own evil inclinations, is your problem with anger, in order. As a wise person once said, "One should always stir up the anger of his or her good inclination against his or her evil inclination". The Lord can deliver you, if you would but, with bold faith, seek Him while He may be found, and call upon Him while He is near. Recognize and respect your time of visitation from the Lord, for it is upon you. Attend a church that adheres to The Record (Holy Scriptures), appreciate that place of worship, and don't leave until seven cycles of something have passed over you (e.g. months, years, anniversaries, seven winter, spring, summer, or fall seasons). You declare the seven cycles, and God will meet you there. In doing this, your soul will be made quiet and the chaos will subside, long enough for you to make an intelligent decision to start again embracing the simplicity of God's truths and His peace. Allow God's love to surround your weariness. If necessary, see suggested course of action.

BODIES OF WATER:

Canal, Channel, Ditch, Gulley, or Trench (any small narrow body of water): This dream has four meanings (choose one). (1) Canal or Channel (a long and narrow strip of water made for boats or for irrigation): Questions, dreamer, shall Christians, who have the knowledge of the light of the gospel before them, be careless about their souls, and unmindful of eternal life? Moreover, if you believe that the eyes of God are always upon you, and that there is another world to prepare for, is that no t enough reason to watch and be sober, both spiritually and physically? The time has come for you to wake from sleep. For salvation is nearer now than when you first believed. The night is far-gone; the day is at hand. So then, cast off the works of darkness and put on the armor of light. Walk properly, as in the daytime, not in orgies and drunkenness, not in sexual immorality and sensuality, not in quarreling and jealousy, not in bad company, or any in any unclean behavior, but put on the Lord Jesus Christ, and do not give thought to the flesh, to gratify its desires (Romans 13:11-14). Dreamer, true and fervent love to God, and towards the things of God, will keep you watchful and sober. Moreover, if you earnestly have hope of salvation; then let go of anything that would shake your trust in the Lord. Additionally, it is suggested that you join in prayer and praise with other Christians, and begin to set a good example before others. Read, understand, and embrace, 1 Thessalonians 5:1-13. See suggested course of action. (2) If dreamer was in, or around, a canal, channel, ditch, gulley, or trench, dreamer, now, having in yourself nothing that you respect more than power and greed, you are willing to sacrifice all, God, principle, family, and friend, to the image or idol of vanity. Your new way is based on exploring alternatives to God's righteous principles, as well as, creating a sense of unity with the wickedness around you, which in turn is corrupting (altering, damaging, distorting, harming) your attitude towards Jesus. This mentality sacrifices children, family, and morality to the hollowness of satisfying immoral desires and appetites, a bourgeois mentality. All carried out with the hope of finding happiness by pacifying jealously and covetousness. The selling-out of yourself over to immorality, allowing wickedness to prevail in your home, devaluing those you should be protecting and nurturing, while closing your eyes to it all, are all principles based on values that are not on ly vile, but also increasingly unstable. This way cries out against godly ethics, and its' end offends any sense of godliness. Your recklessness can be remedied by prayer and heartfelt repentance to Jesus (seeking pardon and expressing sincere feelings of regret and brokenness for having done something awry, see Psalm 51, 2 Corinthians 7:10, 11, also see Deuteronomy 6:10-15; 11:10-28). Your dream also advises the dreamer that with persistent hard work and effort in correcting your dangerous mindset and lifestyle, you can again remember Jesus, and once more respect His principles. Seek counsel from godly individuals, you will find wisdom with them. Dreamer, without repentance and change, your mindset will cause you to eventually, forget God, only to remember Him again, with regret, on your deathbed. God wants you to consider, and remember from this day forward, as a preservative against future idolatry the following. Of all the things you've done to acquire wealth, and/or to remain youthful or popular, did any of it, bring you freedom or exemption from accusations, blame, harm, reproach, unpleasant consequences, chaos, or disorder? Having gone through, and experienced, the repercussions of covetousness, greed, vanity, and the worship of materialism, your mindset should have changed. Omitting God and His ways from your life is to omit genuine happiness, health, joy, and peace. See suggested course of action. (3) If someone else was in, or around, a canal, channel, ditch, gulley, or trench, dreamer, you will soon find yourself in the midst or presence of those who have a form of godliness, but are not godly. While they believe in a single supreme god who created and ruled the universe, survival after death, the practice of charity, and other beliefs similar to believers, their practices are a syncretic[29] fusion of demonology, necromancy, Spiritism, Satanism, witchcraft, and other heresies, a path of descent. They will force you to view the world according to their truths. They say Elohim creates imperfect beings and then forces them to rise up to a l evel of perfection, by torturing them, causing millions to suffer in body and soul, because of their natural instincts, which they were designed with, until they reach a desired light or face karma. They reason that this is the only way, a path of pain, torture, and then death. They ask what human being aspires to evolve through this endless agony. They proclaim that God's promises are no more than vague words of doubtful happiness, implacable laws that promise remote and unknowable joy, under the mask of love of humanity. They say His ways are nothing more than a profound indifference and a hardened selfishness. They respect their truth, but it is delivered without grace; thus, it is never enough to fill an emaciated soul. Although, these persons are highly resourceful, adaptable, and very fierce, they worship money and image, in all of its forms (e.g. worship of materialistic things, personalities, self, vanity, and/or a literal statue). They even attribute their prosperity to the pow er of demons. With that said, do not imitate their doings, deceived by their image of prosperity (Revelation 3:14-22), and do not fear them, lest the fear of them be allowed to seize you. When you see them lifted-up and praised by others, say in your heart, only the Lord should be adored, and remember God is watching you and only He can demand an account of your soul.

Dreamer, have no other gods before God (see Matthew 22:37-40). See suggested course of action. (4) Your dream comes to warn the dreamer, for it denotes that life and death are soberly set before you. Dreamer, you have begun to grow careless in your worship of the one true God, because of extreme pride. Thus, if you will not choose behaviors, actions, thoughts, and choices that promote life, especially spiritual life, you will begin to experience extreme poverty, at the very least, or you will die, spiritually and perhaps physically. See suggested course of action.

Condition of Water (Brook, Creek, Ditch, Gulf, Lake, Ocean, Reservoir, River, Sea, Strait, or Stream): This dream has two meanings (choose one). (1) Clean, clear water (pretty color): Your dream denotes blessing on many levels. Dreamer, be encourage, you will experience, if not already, the baptism of the Holy Spirit, spiritual cleansing and growth, ministerial ordination, peace, purification, regeneration, salvation, sanctification, and inherit eternal life. Moreover, if dreamer is a spiritual leader, if needful, God will cure a doubting leader. Additionally, and, if applicable, go forth with business plan s. (2) Dirty or Muddy water (not clean or fresh, bitter waters, salt waters, including used bath water, dirty dish or mop water): T his choice has three parts (choose one). (a) If someone else dirtied the water, your dream was sent to encourage the dreamer. Dreamer because you have chosen to defend your beliefs and convictions regarding righteousness, someone is threatened by your stance, thus, they have attempted to make your way hard. Dreamer, be encouraged and continue to stand up for righteousness. Know that the situation or issues that have made your way hard; are allowed by God, because God is using your troubles to work things out for your good, a far reaching prosperous good, have faith in this. In addition, God will de al with your unrestrained leader, even if God has to remove him or her from before you or you from before them. (b) Your dream denotes that the state of affairs within the dreamer's life, at present, is not to your liking. For example, issues ar e out- of-order; there is much confusion; and stress has caused a literal physical illness or weaknesses within your body. Dreamer, your present states of affairs are a result of you having chosen to not, defend your beliefs and convictions regarding righteousness, especially before others that you might have felt intimidated by. Thus, God has allowed your present state of affairs, your issues, your literal physical illness, or weakness within your body, your "situation", as disciplinary tools, t o affect holiness, loyalty, and some level of purity within the life of the dreamer. See suggested course of action. (c) Your dream denotes rebelliousness on many levels (e.g. adultery, afflictions, cowardice, persecution, and/or a spiritually blind person). Dreamer, you continue to embrace excessive indulgences, a lack of self-control, a lack of knowledge, and spiritual uncleanness. Spiritual uncleanness, within the life of a believer, denotes anger, animosity, confusion, out of order, self-condemnation, sexual impropriety, an unforgiving spirit, and/or other weaknesses, are present within your heart, as well as, immoral, impure, and unchaste conduct. For example, addictions, cheating, exposing confidences to others, greedy, gossiping, jealously, lying, stealing, or any other sinful attribute (see 1 Corinthians 6:9-20, Ephesians 5). This behavior causes one's anointing to fade and spiritual authority to wane. Your dream is to warn a rebellious person, in the spirit of grace (the free and unmerited favor and beneficence of God), to see if you will yet be worked upon, and change your mindset. Or, else to leave you inexcusable, in your accusations against God, because of your ruin (e.g. continually plundered, seized, and disfavored, also see Jeremiah 9:7 -9; Zechariah 13:9; Matthew 23:37-39; Revelation 3:15-21). Favorably, the dreamer is now one, whom the body of believers will help restore back to God, in the spirit of empathy, mercy, leniency, and kindness, until your issues are cleaned up or render ed dead, allow this. Further, the more God allows you to see your emptiness, it is suggested that you be more earnest to repent that you may find Him to be grace and healing, refreshment, and a refuge. See suggested course of action.

Dam, Cistern, Fountain, Reservoir, or Well (barrier constructed to contain the flow of water):

This dream has three meanings (choose one). (1) Your dream denotes one, namely the dreamer, who is confident, persistent, and energetic, as well as, a Christian who is walking within purpose because of your diligence, wisdom, and great usefulness to the public. Your kindness to your friends and sharpness to your enemies makes you a great sage. You have, or will have, plenty, and will be blessed richly, especially financially. (2) If dam, cistern, reservoir, or well was overflowing, this denotes the dreamer is an enemy to God's people. Through harassment, pestering, hostility, and singling out of clergy and laity alike, you have set ou t to do harm to God's people. You will not succeed. God will drive the enemies of His people far away from them. In addition, something beneficial, towards His people, will come out of the negative situation you've initiated. Dreamer, come back to the Lord. See suggested course of action. (3) Cistern, Fountain, or Well was dry or empty: To come to a well or cistern and find it dry or empty of water. Dreamer, although you are surrounded by many, and there is no doubt that you have charisma, and a following to prove it, you are spiritually empty. Dreamer, you believe in a god of your own making, coupled with outrageous claims you have wholeheartedly embraced from other erroneous guides. You respect your truth, while never acknowledging, it is delivered without grace; thus, it is never enough to fill an empty soul. Dreamer, you are a person of power and influence, possibly, also known as a prophet or prophetess and teacher. Pride has deceived you; and you have corrupted the one true religion, with syncretistic[28] ideas, and you harass the followers of God. Moreover, you have adopted a bourgeois mentality, believing yourself above God's word and above the law of the land. This mentality is concerned only with your personal comfort, material wealth, and status, at any expense. Now, having in yourself nothing that you respect more than p ower and greed, you are willing to sacrifice all, God, principle, family, and friend, to the image or idol of vanity. Your new way is based on exploring alternatives to God's righteous principles, as well as, creating a sense of unity with the wickedness around you. This is what you call love. This mentality sacrifices children, family, and morality, to the hollowness of satisfying immoral desires and appetites. All carried out, with the hope of finding happiness by pacifying jealously and covetousness. The selling- out of yourself over to immorality, devaluing those, you should be protecting and nurturing, especially the faithful, while closing your eyes to it all, are all principles based on values that are not only vile, but also increasingly unstable. This way cries out against godly ethics, and its' end offends any sense of godliness. Dreamer, you obey no one, and accept no correction. You do not trust in the Lord, nor, do you draw near to Him, although He has given you space to repent; instead, you seduced your children to follow you, perpetuating your sins. Thus, sin will very soon turn your paradise into chaos, and dishonor th e beauty of your name. You are also at risk of falling into a state of serious health problems and possibly loss of life. So severe are things that restoration can only be by returning to Christ Jesus wholeheartedly. Dreamer when God hides His face from someone celebrations are turned into moaning and groaning, and the party is exchanged for depression and solitude. Your recklessness can be remedied by prayer and heartfelt repentance to Jesus and to individuals affected by your actions, and by rebuking and renouncing the "spirit of jezebel", that has attached itself to you. See suggested course of action.

Lake, Bayou, or Pond (body of usually fresh water surrounded by land): Your dream was sent to encourage and is one confirmation. Dreamer, you have fulfilled all requirements for righteousness and you have a clear conscience. Consequently, you have access to prophetic insight; enabling you to discern between true and false. This wisdom will be a transformational force in many people's lives. The dreamer has been chosen by God, and, if not already, will be approved by man, to be set aside and ordained as a ministerial leader. You have been found of good reputation, full of the Spirit, and wise; thus, you will be officially ordained. You are to carry out the official role and position of that office (e.g. bishop, deacon, deaconess, elder, evangelist, pastor, preacher, superintendent, or teacher). Dreamer, the way the ordination will be carried out may not be to your liking; nonetheless, do not attribute (or call) that which is of God, unclean (e.g. confusion, erroneous, out of order, unlawful, weak, wicked, or any other attributes of the unregenerate). Do not consider your ordination as unofficial or a small thing, for it is of God and His kindness towards you. Therefore, carry out the role of that particular office in a spirit of excellence, for this is part of your duty towards the Kingdom of God, and you will thus be recompensed according to the quality of your service.

Ocean, Gulf, Sea, or Strait (a large body of water constituting a principal part of the earth's surface; salt or fresh water, that is surrounded by land and/or is attached to, or flows into, another body of water): This dream has three meanings (one, two or all may apply). (1) Gulf or Strait (a large area of a sea or ocean partly enclosed by land): Dreamer, today the Lord is giving you a choice between life and death, between blessings and disfavor. Enough has been revealed to you for you to make an intelligent decision to choose life that you might live. You have been taught, you have been given enough information, an d you have seen the work of the Lord in your life and in the lives of others. As well, you have personally experience deliverance, a pushing back of all things that hindered clarity, emotionally and spiritually. With that said, it is declared that if you choose the way that leads to death, surely you will perish. You will not prolong your days in the place of your prosperity, and you will go on towards a way that will ultimately lead to a weakening of your core beliefs, namely a rejection of all or some of the original foundational teachings of Christ and His apostles. If you choose the way that leads to life, and subsequently, eternal life, it is promised that the banner over your head will be that, you are a great, wise, prosperous, and understanding person. Nonetheless, heaven and earth are being called on to witness the choice you will make. Therefore, dreamer take to heart all the words with which your dream is warning you today, and carefully observe all that the Lord has asked of you, for this is not idle words, or a small ting, it is your life. See suggested course of action. (2) Male dreamer, be encouraged, for your dream denotes that you are a man of quality, a chosen instrument in God's Hands, and you will be used as such, and recompensed for your services. (3) Male or female, your dream refers to instantaneous knowledge. Dreamer will be miraculously endowed with spiritual knowledge. Remember, Jesus is the source of that knowledge, and just like the Lord gives, He can take away, due to disobedience, for example, if dreamer becomes an assistant in accomplishing an evil deed. If disobedience and/or rebelliousness are found within your heart, none of your righteousness will be remembered no more (Ezekiel 33:12). Due to disobedience and/or rebelliousness, dreamer, along with removal of genuine and unadulterated truth and knowledge from your thought processes, dreamer may begin to experience extreme poverty; therefore, it is suggested that you "trust and obey", for there is no other way, to be happy in Jesus, but to trust and obey. See suggested course of action.

Puddle or Standing Water (standing water or other liquid): This dream has two meanings (choose one). (1) Puddle: Your dream denotes one, namely the dreamer, who indulges in the relations of sin. Dreamer, you have become so addicted to a particular pleasure that it has replaced God in your heart; thus, it has become an idol. Dreamer, the person who seeks a life of pleasure over a life of service to the King, is not only misguided, but is on a road that leads to spiritual destruction. One should not seek out what pleasures the world can bring to you, but rather seek out what good can you do, in bringing the world to God. Therefore, dreamer you are advised, do not become foolishly involved in the relations of sin, or allow another to bring this kind of foolishness into your life, for a season of sin will bring sorrow, perhaps for eternity. Dreamer is advised to seriously, consider the following; it is expressed that in the last days some will be lovers of pleasure rather than lovers of God (Titus 3:4). It is also expressed, do you not know that to whom you present yourself slaves to obey, you are that one's slav e who you obey, whether of sin to death, or of obedience to righteousness (Romans 6:16)? See suggested course of action. (2) Standing Water: Your dream implies one, specifically a male, who will trouble the kingdom of darkness. This choice has two parts (choose one). (a) Male dreamer, you are definitely a force spiritually, not to be underestimated. Similar to Moses, you have the capacity to usher in a time of revival and deliverance for God's people, called for such times as these. You will c ause the dishonorable and non-believer (one who has no religious beliefs, a non-religious person, or one who has no religious faith or belief in Jesus Christ, or one who does not embrace a personal relationship with Jesus Christ, at present). To break thei r agreement with death and choose to live, and cause the believer to remember once again the blood sacrifice of Jesus. (b) Female dreamer, a very close significant male (e.g. husband, son, nephew, someone you're mentoring or teaching), will be that force, you are sent as encouragement and a voice of wisdom.

River, Brook, Creek, Geyser, or Stream (natural stream of water): To dream of one of these natural streams of running water denotes one, namely the dreamer, who will be called upon to act as a fiduciary for someone, as well, you will inherit land and other assets. Warning, dreamer, acting in a fiduciary capacity, you must be careful to allocate property and inheritance properly and ethically, for it is illegal for a fiduciary to misappropriate money for personal gain. Note, as yo u are also in line for an inheritance, God has deemed that your ethicalness will determine what you will receive; whether it is bounteousness, modest, or forfeited, it will be allowed, because of your own personal honorableness, or the lack thereof ; note, Adonai Elohim knows all. See suggested course of action.

Suggested Course of Action

Question to consider and journal, did your dream depict any symbols that alludes to, the dreamer will make the necessary changes, spiritually, emotionally, and/or physically to affect a more positive outcome? If changes are initiated, your dreams will change.

As these dreams deal with truth on some level of another, it is necessary to say that God responds to truth. You may have a different version of what is going on at present. However, you may need to consider that you are p rimarily responsible for situations that affect you personally. Therefore, this is the time for you to sit alone to consider your ways truthfully. Do not sit alone to indulge in excessive grief, but to repent and return or convert to Jesus Christ.

Nevertheless, in view of your dream's context, and the primary symbols, what does your dream reveal about you, your ethics, intents, mental state, and motives? You will need to earnestly look within and consider that the sum of your answers is a reflection of where you are emotionally, physically, and/or spiritually, and a reflection of who you are becoming. What was your reaction to the landform or body of water? Were you angry, concerned, confused, defensive, fearful, happy, helpful, pleased, shocked, unconcerned, or ready to get out of someone's presence? Your reaction to the circumstance reveals your attitude regarding this information about yourself.

Dreamer, consider seriously your observations. If what was revealed prevail, will it sabotage any good that's happening at present within your life? Will it build or destroy, strengthen or weaken, enlighten or blind? If you lack wisdom, ask Je sus for wisdom. He gives wisdom to all, generously, no matter who you are and what you've done; wisdom is available (see James 1:5-8, Proverbs 2:1-6, 10). Hence, if, by just asking, you may get wisdom, one may suffer needlessly, because you will not ask Jesus for wisdom.

Therefore, I say to you, whatever you make a request for in prayer, have faith that it has been given to you, and you will have it. And whenever you make a prayer, let there be forgiveness in your heart, if you have anything against anyone; so tha t you may have forgiveness for your sins from your Father who is in heaven, (Mark 11:24-25)

Now, pray (See Prayer of Deliverance, pg. 897)

Specific Meaning

If, you have a very high propensity for accidents, because of activities surrounding landforms and bodies of water, e.g. mountain climbing, skiing, sky diving, exploration of some kind, or some other form of accident-prone or dare devil activity. A dream of this sort should be received as a precautionary warning, to prevent serious harm to yourself, and/or others, due to an accident, especially if this was depicted within your dream. Be careful. Do not assume that you're safe or it's ok, caution should be heeded at this time. The accident, kept within context of the dream, should be relevant to your everyday working life and/or closely resemble real life situations. This will help you narrow down the specifics, and steer clear, of an accident.

Note: If your dream depicted a specific piece of land, dreamer may consider purchasing the land, and developing the land with the expectation of profit. For example, Walt Disney purchased swampland in Orlando, Florida, because swampland was cheap there, and built Walt Disney World. Dreamer, consider this question; could you be receiving inspiration, via your dream, regarding an idea, or possible creation of something, that would benefit the masses or enhance living others; especially, if you have a very real connection (or not) with any activity involving land or bodies of water. Kept within con text, your dream may very well be a divine inspiration. Per chapter one, sometimes the most meaningless dream will help change your life in ways you would have never thought, especially entrepreneurially and/or enterprisingly. Throughout history, humankind has received life changing insight and guidance from their dreams. Most of the time the information acquired within dreams exceeds that which we could obtain during our normal, analytical, waking state of mind. With that said, your dream should closely resemble real life situations. Meaning it can actually occur during your awaked state.

If another had the accident, perhaps you are being made aware of the plight of someone, the person highlighted within your dream, and you are to get involved (see Chapter One, Are You Ready to Hear the Messages in Your Dreams, section entitled, The 10% for others). There may be potential for a serious accident. Did you know the individual within your dream? If not, God will bring them to your attention. Where did the accident occur? What kind of accident was it? Dreamer, the details, kept within context of your dream, should be relevant to the person's life, and/or closely resemble real life situations. Meaning it can actually occur during your awaked state. If you sense your dream is for or about another, namely the person highlighted within the dream, the question as to why you have been made aware of this information, and how do you factor into the equation, should be seriously considered, along with necessary actions. Call the person, and warn them of your concerns. Your warnings will help them narrow down the specifics needed to steer them clear of possible trouble. However, if your dream was inundated with symbols that are not easily linked to your life activities, then the spiritual implications (the interpretation) should be heeded.

MUSIC AND MUSICAL INSTRUMENTS

*What is it about music, the words, and the tempo, which has touched
the heart, soul, and mind of all, from time immemorial?
...that thou shalt meet a band of prophets coming down from the high place with a psaltery, and a
timbrel, and a pipe, and a harp, before them; and they will be prophesying (1 Samuel 10:5ASV).*

*In addition, David and all the house of Israel played before Jehovah with all manner
of instruments made of fir-wood, and with harps, and with psalteries, and with
timbrels, and with castanets, and with cymbals (2 Samuel 6:5 ASV).*

I cannot be silent! For I have heard the sound of the trumpet (shofar); the alarm of war (Jeremiah 4:1 AMP).

*Now if ye be ready that at what time ye hear the sound of the cornet, flute,
harp, sackbut, psaltery, and dulcimer, and all kinds of music, ye fall down and
worship the image which I have made, well (Daniel 3:15 ASV).*

This category deals with four of the major categories of instruments of music, electronic instruments, percussion instruments, stringed instruments, and wind instruments. Some short descriptions of types, phrases, and other processes and particulars, connected in some way to this category are, for example, banjo, bass, bells, cello, clarinet, cymbals, drums, gong, guitar, h arp, lute, lyres, musician, piano, singer, rhythm machines, saxophone, synthesizers, trombone, trumpet, tuba, viola, violin, xylophone. Also, see category content list, or index.

All Symbols and Referents, Notes (1, 2, 3, etc.), Suggested Course of Action, and Specific Meaning offer guidance toward a more comprehensive interpretation.

Notes

1. Unless otherwise noted elsewhere, if, in your everyday living, your awaked state, as part of your lifestyle, work, or ministerial activities, or a special event, you have a very real connection with any activity involving Music, Musical Instruments. For example, band member, musician, music festival coordinator or sponsor, or a broker, renter, seller, of any kinds of music, musical Instruments, praise and worship leader, psalmist, singer, songwriter, or any activity or business involved in the handling of Music, Musical Instruments, your dream is not significant and does not warrant special attention.

    Otherwise noted, this dream of Music, Musical Instruments may be a Prophetically Simple Dream (see Chapter One: The 60th Part of Prophecy). Whereas, the dreamer is encouraged, for example, to learn a new instrument, or if a uniquely new instrument was introduced to you within your dream, to create or invent a new style of instrument, or to initiate a new way of playing an instrument, and adopt the new style as your own signature style (e.g. name the style after you). Did you write a song? Skip interpretation and go do or learn the instrument or write the song.

    Otherwise noted, per your lifestyle, if your dream closely resembled real life situations, meaning it can actually occur during your awaked state, this dream may be an Ordinary Dream, resulting from your daily activities (see Chapter One, Chalom). These sorts of dreams are usually about your routine, mundane activities or anxieties that overwhelm your mind during the day. They are an inner release mechanism, which helps provide you with emotional balance and the maintaining of your sanity. These dreams are not significant, and do not warrant special attention.

2. Probables: As music, musical instruments are frequently demonstrated in many, and very personal ways; for example, does a saxophone remind you of playing in your high school band? Does a particular song remind you of home, of family reunions, or a love one? Thus, could the instrument or music depicted be a possible probable (see Chapter One, section entitled, Probables)? Hence, dreamer may also consider your own personal and special associations with various, Music, Musical Instruments, as long as the interpretation is kept within the principles of spiritual boundary markers, landmarks, and property lines, (see Chapter One, section entitled, Spiritualizing Boundary Markers, Landmarks, and Property Lines).

3. Determine who your dream is for you or another. Always, considering yourself first, reflecting on your present behaviors. Ask yourself, why am I dreaming about this now? What is this dream revealing about me? Have I taken on new attributes? Has anyone commented on my present behaviors as being untypical of me? Has my ministry changed for the better or for the worse? What about my beliefs, doctrine, or philosophy, are they still based on Holy Writ? Is there something I need to know about those I am ministering to or serving?

Was dreamer writing a musical composition? Was dreamer a coordinator or sponsor of a music event? Did dreamer own a record shop? Was dreamer a drum major? Was dreamer a band member, or part of a philharmonic orchestra? Was dreamer the conductor of an orchestra or leader of the band? Unless otherwise noted elsewhere, an answer of yes, to one or more of these, or similar questions, is a good indicator that your dream is about you (the dreamer). See following relevant subcategory, the interpretation is about and for you.

Was someone else a seller of instruments? Did another have an issue with what instrument was played, or the way the band was handled? Was another the conductor of an orchestra or leader of the band? Was someone singing or in concert? Unless otherwise noted elsewhere, an answer of yes, to one or more of these, or similar questions, is a good indicator that your dream is about another and their role, and/or influential effects, within the life of the d reamer. Are you dealing with someone, who truly believes in their heart that they will not have to give an account of their service to Heavenly Father? Are they enhancing your spiritual and/or literal prosperity, or are they responsible for the dwindling thereof? Do you know someone whose life activities or physical being is similar to that which stood out the most within your dream? Could it be that person? If you sense that your dream is for or about another, the question as to why you have been made privy to this information, and how do you factor into the equation, should be seriously considered along with necessary actions. Perhaps the dreamer is being made aware of the plight of someone, and you are to get involved (see Chapter One, Are You Ready to Hear the Messages in Your Dreams, section entitled, The 10% for others).

If your dream is for, or about another:

Dreams that reference others and the revelation within those dreams, is not given haphazardly to any individual, but only to those with the ability, and influence to do something with the information; this is also prophecy. With that, journal the following questions, and if unable to answer the questions now, this denotes that the person, represented within your dream, will enter your life shortly. Are you entering into a personal relationship with someone? Do you not know or understand what you're looking at, especially certain behaviors, when learning about this person? Has someone new entered your life or maybe you've just begun opening up to someone not so new, and have started listening to their advice, accepting their assistance, or are you supporting or enabling someone? Are you in denial regarding the toxicity of one of your present relationships, particularly a spouse, family member, or friend? Are you anxious, concerned, frightened, and/or troubled by recent changes in your behavior, especially because of someone's influence upon your life at present? Have you allowed someone to convince you to deceive another? Have you recently become aware of (or is being made aware of, via your dream) certain undesirable behaviors within you towards another? Are you trying to cut ties with one that is bad company? Have you just joined (or re-joined) a church, fellowship, or social group?

Note: If your dream has attributes that indicate that your dream is about you, and other attributes that indicate that your dream is about another, dreamer should consider that your dream is about you and another. For example, did another write a song for the dreamer to sing? Was dreamer teaching another how to play an instrument? Was dreamer asking for help with an instrumental musical composition from a friend? Thus indicating that your dream is about the dreamer, and another; therefore, while your dream is about the dreamer, the dreamer should expect the role and/or influential effects of another, also plays a part in your interpretation. For example, was dreamer co-creator of a musical composition, from which now the dreamer needs to be rightly compensated? Again, see relevant interpretation.

More questions to consider. Why has the person been allowed within your life, and/or how did they get there? Again, if unable to answer the questions now, this denotes that the person, represented within your dream, will enter your life shortly. If their activity, within your dream, has proven positive, via the interpretation, this someone will prove, unwittingly, to be a very strong ally, benefactor, defender, and supporter. God has sent this someone into your life to help you carry out your next endeavor by enlarging your spiritual capacity. Allow the strength of that person's character to guide, help, and support you. On the other hand, if his or her presence and/or activity, within your dream, proved negative, via the interpretation, for sure, this person will prove to be a very strong and formidable challenge for you, perhaps unto death. If negative, this dream is a dire warning. Take steps accordingly to struggle against, or to cut off, adverse and unfavorable relationships. Remember certain personalities are all encompassing, affecting everything, cataclysmic, contagious, deadly, harmful, infectious, predatory, and/or venomous. Symbolically meaning that if allowed to continue or prosper within your life, serious harm or death to the dreamer may result. Idolize no one, especially beyond the warning of the Lord, and we are definitely not to lay our lives down for no one. Then again, this person maybe allowed within your life, because of the dreamer's unwillingness to abstain from immorality after having been asked to abstain from such by God, see 1 Corinthians 6:9-20, Galatians 5:19-21, or the dreamer's self-righteous behavior, or a lack of a balanced and honest view of your own personality. In this case, this person will affect self-awareness within the life of the dreamer, exposing the negative traits of your personality, especially those traits, which cause you to follow, or to be so easily misled, and/or your wrong beliefs; no matter, this type of mentality needs reckoning with. Graciously, all of this will restore the dreamer to his or her right place with God, opening your eyes to see how far you've strayed from God (1 Corinthians 5:4-7; James 5:20). The lesson is, no matter how personable, powerful, or difficult a person, or how uncertain or unpopular the choices and issues, always take the next biblical and ethical step, for obedience to God's principles will always prove safer and stronger foundationally. Although, you will need all kinds of outside support to recover from this person's domination, no longer, allow that particular person's influence within your life to continue or thrive, especially if negative, end it abruptly.

4. Consider all the people, places, backgrounds, and activity highlighted within your dream.
    Known (in your awaked life) person, animal, place, or organization within your dream:
    Unless otherwise noted elsewhere, people, animals, places, backgrounds that are actually known by the dreamer in your awaked life, indicates a part of you that you recognize within yourself on some level or another. Question to journal, if dreamer seriously considers the person, animal, place, or background attributes, what character traits stood out the most, or what features stood out the most. For example, age, color, height, size, happiness, considerate, loving, let you be yourself, peacefulness, encourager, irrational, leader, liar, mentor, passionate, personable, neglected, poor, run-down, sage, shyster, unwise, upscale, vengeful. Write down (journal) the particular highlighted within your dream. The attribute or

activity highlighted is for a reason. Since the attribute written down is a part of you, namely the dreamer's nature, demeanor, and/or lifestyle, an honest and unbiased assessment is very important for truth sake. Happy note, considering that other people's attributes, within dreams, also represent attributes of your own personality, causes one to look at another in a better light. According to your capacity to embrace self-awareness and a rectification of mind, body, and spirit, God will begin to enhance, make better, more attractive, sanctify, diminish, and make pure and free from sin and guilt, this part of you.

Otherwise noted, if the person, animal, place, or background within your dream is actually known by the dreamer, in your awaked life, this person, animal, place, or background may represent him or herself, or itself.

Unknown in your awaked life or although known, was unseen, invisible, or only talked about - person, animal, place, or organization within your dream:

Unless otherwise noted elsewhere, if you did not recognize, the person, place, thing, they, or it, was not seen, invisible, or only talked about within your dream, this indicates an attribute or activity within your life that you are unfamiliar with, or are in denial about, or you refuse to acknowledge it, but it does exists. Question to journal: what character trait, feature, action, or activity, stood out the most? For example, age, color, height, size, happiness, considerate, loving, let you be yourself, peacefulness, encourager, irrational, leader, liar, mentor, passionate, personable, neglected, poor, run-down, sage, shyster, unwise, upscale, vengeful. Although, on some conscious level, you are aware of a certain behavior or attribute within you, you have chosen to filter out or simply ignore certain information about yourself that contradicts your view of yourself and/or your preconceived notions of others and of the world around you. Possibly protecting yourself, emotionally and psychologically, from a situation, which you are unable to cope with at this time, or you lack control over; then again, perhaps the dreamer has an exaggerated or unrealistic view of yourself. No matter the reason, right now a question is before you, via your dream. Do you want to know this part of yourself? According to your ability to handle self-awareness, God will begin to reveal this side of you to you. Why, He wants to balance your understanding of things; thus, effecting wholeness within your life, so that the enemy will no longer be able to manipulate your emotions so easily. The Paraclete is with you to help you throughout this entire process, listen to Him. Now, in your life, this activity or attribute needs reckoning with, somehow or someway.

Otherwise noted, (known or unknown), if the person, place or thing that initiated (or was a recipient of) the action or activity within your dream was not seen, invisible, or only talked about within your dream, this may indicate that the dreamer does not recognize the influential effects another has within your life, or upon your attitude.

If more than one person (known or unknown):

Consider what the group had in common. What behavior, character trait, feature, action, or activity, stood out the most? For example, were they argumentative, authoritative, beautiful, criminal minded, dancing, difficult, dressed unusual, enigmatic, fighting, focused, flirty, helpful, hurtful intentions, powerful, promiscuous, quiet, secretive, seemed unreal, unassuming? What about age, color, height, size, happiness, considerate, loving, let you be yourself, peacefulness, encourager, irrational, leader, liar, mentor, passionate, personable, neglected, poor, run-down, sage, shyster, unwise, upscale, vengeful, death. That which was highlighted and noted is what you need to focus on at present.

If the attribute or quality is a desirable or positive one, allow the strength of that attribute to help you overcome some manner of immorality or irreverence within your life and/or to help you to become better, productively, for the Kingdom of God in some manner. If the attribute is an undesirable or negative one, take steps accordingly to struggle against the growing desires of the carnal side of you. If applicable, get help and support via prayer, fasting, and a Christian based support group.

For dreams of the dead see following note.

Did you play an organ at someone's funeral? While the dead has nothing to do with the living (Ecclesiastes 9:4-6), it may be considered what character trait did that person represent to the dreamer, while the person was actually alive, what character feature stood out the most. With that trait noted, dreamer may consider that the trait noted, is within the dreamer, and that trait is no longer useful or needed for the progression of your spiritual walk, on this side of heaven. Dreamer, it is suggested that you render that trait (good or bad) obsolete, and began anew attempting to move forward, using different tactics to overcome unproductive habitual life cycle choices, and for maneuvering through this thing we call life in a more, better way. See category, Death, and/or other relevant categories.

5. In addition to the following interpretations, see index or relevant categories for more information. For example, if singing was involved in some way, see category: Talking; if a TV was highlighted, see category, Communication. Kept within context of your dream and the interpretation, the additional symbols are perhaps relevant. It will be within the sum of all the symbols that you will find a more thorough interpretation.

6. Since the following list is not extensive, dreamer is encouraged to seek biblical guidelines and other relevant research to determine the metaphorical meaning of your particular music or musical instrument activity, depicted within your dream, via a Bible concordance, Bible illustrated dictionary, encyclopedia, or internet. Having done your research you should be able to determine some basic behaviors or attributes your Lord and Savior wants you to focus on.

Symbols and Referents

Most dreams of music or musical instruments generally imply, coupled with the relevant interpretation, some manner of worship to God, or to someone (or thing). As well, this dream may be sent as an alarm.

In addition to the varied meanings of music and musical instruments, other common words, expressions, usages, (e.g. slang or clichés), or a 'probable' that are metaphorically represented by any of the following are also considered (this section is an addendum at the end of the category or subcategory).

Category Content - If not listed see index, perchance, for your specific type of musical instrument dream.

* Electronic Instruments (any musical instrument that produces or modifies sounds by electric, and usually electronic, means, these instruments are produced using the latest technology, e.g. digital drum, digital keyboard, organ, rhythm machine, samplers, synthesizers)
* Percussion Instruments (instruments that require you to strike the surface of the instrument to generate vibrations to produce your desired note, e.g. anvil, bells, chimes, cymbals, drum, gong, rattle, tambourine, triangle, wind chimes, xylophone)
* Singing, Chorus, or To Hear Music
* Stereo System (or any device that plays music, e.g. boom box, cassette player, record player, CD player)
* Stringed Instruments (music instruments that produce sound by means of a stretched vibrating string played by bowing, or other instruments played by plucking, or by instruments that are struck, e.g. banjo, clavichord, dulcimer, fiddle, guitar, harp, lyres, lutes mandolin, piano, ukulele, viola, violin, zither)
* Wind Instruments (music instruments which produce sound by a vibrating mass of air, e.g. accordion, bagpipe, bassoon, clarinet, cornet, flute, harmonica, horn, oboe, piccolo, saxophone, shofar, trombone, trumpet, tuba, or whistle)
* Blowing your own Horn (any horn, including a car horn, and is highlighted as belonging to dreamer)

ELECTRONIC INSTRUMENTS (any musical instrument that produces or modifies sounds by electric, and usually electronic, means, these instruments are produced using the latest technology, e.g. digital drum, digital keyboard, organ, rhythm machine, samplers, synthesizers):

Your dream is an alarm to you. You have begun to think upon, imagine, and fantasize about lustful experiences (unhealthy, immodest, indecent desires, erotic, lewd, and lascivious, behavior, or voyeurism), perhaps past issues that you've been freed from. Dreamer, don't be deceived, when lust has conceived, it brings forth sin. Sin, allowed to excite desires in you, will soon develop those desires into consent; strengthened by frequent acts, turns into a habit, resulting in death (spiritual, literal, and possibly eternal). Although, at present, the sin is in your mind, when it has grown to its full size in the mind, it will ma nifest openly and in full operation. Bring to an end the beginnings of sin, within your mind now; or else, all the evils it produces will be exposed publicly, and will prove very detrimental to you, your reputation, and your home. Blessed is the man or woman who perseveres under trial, because when he or she has stood the test, he or she will receive the crown of life that God has promised to those who love Him. When tempted, no one should say, "God is tempting me". For God cannot be tempted by evil, nor does He tempt anyone; but each one is tempted when, by his or her own evil desire, he or she is dragg ed away and enticed. Every good and perfect gift is from above, coming down from the Father of the heavenly lights, who does not change like shifting shadows. He chose to give us birth through the Word of Truth that we might be a kind of first fruits of all He created (James 1:12-18); therefore, respect your benefits of having received as your Lord and Savior. Do not call your peace boring. His principles are not there to be obstacles to your progress, or to be a bore to you, but to keep you out of harm's way and to assure eternal life in the world to come, the Kingdom of God. God is giving you the opportunity to turn things around emotionally, and He will turn things around literally. See suggested course of action.

PERCUSSION INSTRUMENTS (instruments that require you to strike the surface of the instrument to generate vibrations to produce your desired note, e.g. anvil, bells, chimes, cymbals, drum, gong, rattle, tambourine, triangle, wind chimes, xylophone):

This dream has two meanings (choose one). (1) Your dream is an alarm, to get your attention, to exhort you, the dreamer, to assemble yourself to God at the door of the church. Dreamer, you need to go to church. Every Christian should be faithfully attending and supporting a fundamental Bible believing church. Hebrews 10:25, Revelation 2:1-18, and 3:1-14, lets us know that God has ordained churches. These scriptures also shed light on the reason for participation in the local church, namely friendship, accountability, instruction, and it is good that you are there. We, the Body of Christ, are functionally interdependent; thus, we, out of love (agape), minister to one another, provoke one another to good works, and exhort one another to live consistent lives worthy of God that we might be beneficial to each other, and inherit eternal life. This is best done within the context of a local church, so we, as believers, are commanded not to forsake the assembling of ourselves together. The ultimate reason that we should participate in a local church is that it is specifically commanded by God. See suggested course of action. (2) Your dream denotes a time of consecration is upon you[35]. Dreamer, it is time for you to make a solemn commitment of your life and time, to purpose (your rightful service to the Kingdom of God). This should be your goal, "at this juncture", in your life. You are encouraged to make an obligation of yourself, intellectually, emotionally, and physically to a course of action, that edifies the Kingdom of God, via your innate talents. It will be by this that you will prosper. If no action, commitment, or obligation to divine purpose, is heeded at this time, you may find yourself similar to a parable of a servant who buried his gift (see Matthew 25:24-30). If your designated service is given to another, so will the prosperity that is attached to that service, be given to that person also, and for you, jealously will be your recompense. See suggested course of action.

SINGING, CHORUS, OR TO HEAR MUSIC:

Read Psalm 96:1-13, coupled with the following. Dreamer, when your heart has been painfully torn apart, broken, and troubled, and darkness has come and covered all, God will take those disappointments, those trials, and tragedies that experience, and put a new song in your heart. God is giving you a new song. For, your dream implies that a bad situation, within the dreamer's life, will begin to change quickly, because, those who wanted to harm you, have been put to confusion and shame. Dreamer, when God reverses this tragedy, you will testify that the Lord has done great things for you, and you will be glad, joyful, and thankful, and you will praise Him for His faithfulness. Moreover, you are the object of God's care, gui dance, loving kindness, righteousness, strength, and wisdom. These graces coupled, with God's divine intervention, will comfort you, and will again, cause your mouth to be filled with laughter, and your tongue with singing. You will now, begin to noticeably experience the miraculous wonders of divine providence — the wisdom, care, and guidance provided by God that you might fulfill your mission, your purpose. Moreover, your past experiences and lessons learned, will be used to strengthen your witness. Take care that you become sensitive to, and respect, the continuous acts of God's providential care. For, there is a promise that you will eat and do very well, on this side of eternity, and inherit eternal life. As well, the feeling of rest and serenity that comes with trust in God's divine providence is available to you right now. Dreamer, embrace God's love towards you and His providential care over you.

STEREO SYSTEM (or any device that plays music, e.g. boom box, cassette player, record player, CD player):

Read Psalm 149:1-5, coupled with the following. Your dream brings notice that someone is praying on your behalf, (the dreamer), interceding to the Ruler of Rulers. They are reminding Him of your courageous good works towards them on behalf of the Kingdom of God. Consequently, dreamer your prayers are especially effective now, what you decree, God will fulfill. Only remember to seek first the Kingdom of God, via His Son. Jesus is the key to activate all that comes with seeking the Kingdom of God. For, He is our righteousness required to access the Kingdom blessings, then will God give you the keys of the Kingdom of Heaven; whatever you bind on earth will be bound in heaven, and whatever you loose on earth will be loosed in heaven (ref Matthew 16:19). You will now, begin to noticeably experience the miraculous wonders of divine providence - the wisdom, care, and guidance provided by God that you might fulfill your mission, your purpose. Moreover, your past experiences and lessons learned, will be used to strengthen your witness. Take care that you become sensitive to, and respect, the continuous acts of God's providential care. For, there is a promise that you will eat and do very well, on this side of eternity, and inherit eternal life. As well, the feeling of rest and serenity that comes with trust in God's divine providence is available to you right now.

STRINGED INSTRUMENTS: (music instruments that produce sound by means of a stretched vibrating string played by bowing, or other instruments played by plucking, or by instruments that are struck, e.g. banjo, clavichord, dulcimer, fiddle, guitar, harp, lyres, lutes mandolin, piano, ukulele, viola, violin, zither):

This dream has two meanings (choose one). (1) Your waiting has not been in vain, those within your family who are spiritually and emotionally dead shall live, those whom you've been praying for, they will rise and increase in rank, status, and positio n in life, especially employment wise, and move on to a better quality of life. Expect this in a spirit of excited anticipation, sing for joy! For, Jesus loves you and you are valuable in His eyes. The following is specifically for the dreamer. If you will acc ept the Heavenly Father's Words, via the Bible, and store up His principles, and His ways and means within you, turning your ear to wisdom and applying your heart to understanding, calling out for insight and crying aloud for discernment, Jesus will meet yo u, regardless of wherever you find yourself, emotionally, spiritually, and physically, at the moment. This, co upled with a lifestyle of prayer, followed by appropriate application of wisdom, and you will know the Messiah, Jesus Christ, intimately, and find the knowledge of God you seek. For the Lord gives wisdom and from His mouth comes knowledge and understanding. Then you will understand what is right and just and fair, every good path. When wisdom enters your heart and knowledge becomes sweet to your soul, discretion will protect you, understanding will guard you, and His Truth will lead you. To deliver you from the wickedness that is before you, from demons whose words and ways are perverse, (Proverbs 2:1 -6, 9-15). This is one of God's covenant promises to you. Have faith in this. (2) Regrettably, a close friend, one who gives you sound advice, will betray, or has betrayed, you before those who hate you. This friend is one who has been treated lovingly and trusted explicitly. This betrayal will grieve you very deeply. You will experience embarrassment, shame, great fear, and internal stress because of the vicious lies told against you. Although your anger is justifiable (righteous indignation), remain silent and watch things play out. Jehovah will cause a rift amongst the group, and stop their lies, via an ally of yours sent by God to join the group. This ally's mission is to diffuse the lies, confuse, divide, and separate the group. So know that not everyone in the group is one with the group. Do not return evil for evil. Pray and cry aloud evening, morning, and at noon. Only, let your prayers come from a right heart that loves God, and not from angry vengeful motives. See your deliverance as a present fact, and know, without a doubt that God hears you, you are not alone, and God will turn things around. They will reap what they have sown, and your name will be vindicated. If necessary, see suggested course of action.

WIND INSTRUMENTS (music instruments that produce sound by a vibrating mass of air, e.g. accordion, bagpipe, bassoon, clarinet, cornet, flute, harmonica, horn, oboe, piccolo, saxophone, shofar, trombone, trumpet, tuba, or whistle):

Your dream was sent to encourage, especially a ministerial leader. Your dream denotes one who has the power and strength, via Jesus Christ, to accomplish what is before you. No matter the various circumstances of life, you must conclude that you can do all things through Christ who strengthens you (Philippians 4:13). You are counseled to begin to embrace this mindset, especially now, if not already, because of the great leader you are called to be (or is). Dreamer, you can bear any trial, perform any duty, subdue any evil propensity of your nature, and meet all the temptations consequence to any condition of prosperity or adversity. You need not sink under any trial, nor yield to temptation, nor be harassed, vexed, and tortured with improper thoughts and unholy desires, for there is one, Jesus Christ, who can strengthen you, make a way for your escape, and enable you to renounce unholy thoughts from your mind, and restore the right balance to the a ffections of your soul. Only, do not shrink from duty, but express confidently and firmly to yourself that nothing is required of you that you will be unable to perform. See suggested course of action.

In addition, the following is a common word, expression, or usage (e.g. slang or cliché), or a 'probable' that is metaphorically represented by a wind Instrument.

- **Blowing your own Horn (any horn, including a car horn, and is highlighted as belonging to dreamer):** Your dream exposes a prideful, arrogant, and boastful mind-set regarding your own power, authority, or importance. Warning: when pride comes, then comes disgrace, and haughtiness draws destruction (Proverbs 16:18). Any achievements you will accomplish, or have accomplished, any good deeds you've done, any fulfillment of God's will, was, and still is, dependent upon divine aid and guidance. One merely places his or her hand under the weight carried exclusively by God. Therefore, do not claim credit for your achievements. See suggested course of action.

Suggested Course of Action

Question to consider and journal, did your dream depict any symbols that alludes to, the dreamer will make the necessary changes, spiritually, emotionally, and/or physically to affect a more positive outcome? If changes are initiated, your dreams will change.

Nevertheless, in view of your dream's context, and the primary symbols, what does your dream reveal about you, your ethics, intents, mental state, and motives? You will need to earnestly look within and consider that the sum of your answers is a reflection of where you are emotionally, physically, and/or spiritually, and a reflection of who you are becoming. What was your reaction to the music or musical instrument activity? Were you angry, concerned, confused, defensive, fearful, happy, helpful, pleased, shocked, unconcerned, or ready to get out of someone's presence? Your reaction to the activity, or circumstance, reveals your attitude regarding this information about yourself.

Dreamer, be who God made you to be. Use your God given talents, and you do have talents, as best you can, to make the world a better place. Take your past and use it to teach those whom God has purposed you to reach. Additionally, no matter who you are and what the situation, the words of the book of Psalms will speak the words of your heart and those words will be heard on High; thus, start reading the book of Psalms, and if relevant, perhaps putting them to song. Also, start listening to inspirational music, particularly music that praises our Lord and Savior. Dreamer, at every step of your life, Christ is able to strengthen you, and can bring you triumphantly through your dilemmas, via prayer and fasting. Dreamer, what a privilege it is, to be a Christian, and to feel, in the trials of your life, that you have a friend, unchanging and powerful, one who can always help you! Therefore, engage in your duties, happily, and meet the trials that are before you, leaning on the arm of your Almighty Redeemer.

Now, pray (See Prayer of Deliverance, pg. 897)

Specific Meaning

If, you have a very high chance of composing a new song, or introducing a new way of playing an instrument, or inventing a new instrument it is suggested that you may perhaps complete and promote your song, or your unique way of playing an instrument. If you sense that, your dream is some type of divine inspiration regarding invention, then go, and start designi ng, brand mark, and marketing your divine sent inspiration. For God does give invention, via dreams, and it is meant to prosper your life. It is advisable for you to; prayerfully determine the kind of music that you wish to produce to ensure that you learn playing the right instrument that fits you perfectly. This will allow you to become the kind of musician that you have always dreamed of, and the kind that God desires you to be.

Otherwise, dreams of this sort, for the most part, are ordinary dreams, resulting from your daily activities (see Chapter One, Chalom). These sorts of dreams are usually about your routine, mundane activities or anxieties that overwhelm your mind during the day. They are an inner release mechanism, which helps provide you with emotional balance and the maintaining of your sanity. These dreams are not significant, and do not warrant special attention.

NUMBERS

"You, however, ordered all things by measure, number, and weight". (Wisdom 11:20)

Here is wisdom, let him who has understanding calculate the number... (Revelation 13:18 NKJV)

Our Maker, Creator God, has communicated with us using numbers, denoting signs, or indications of people, places, or things, past, present, or future, from time immemorial, Genesis to Revelation. The Hebrews was enslaved 400 years, were 40 years in the wilderness, and received 10 commandments. The African American was enslaved 400 years. It is written, work six days, on the seventh day rest from work; therefore, the number seven is constant in its meaning of rest and completion. There are twelve tribes of Israel, twelve disciples, John says, "I heard how many were sealed: 144,000, of all the tribes of the children of Israel". We are told, to calculate the number of the beast, for it is the number of a man; his number is 666. Jesus said, "Destroy this temple, and in three days I will raise it up", and in another place, "For just as Jonah was three days and three nights in the sea - the monster's belly, so the Son of man will be three days and three nights in the heart of the earth". There is 70 prophetic weeks in the book of Daniel, and during a 7 year tribulation, after 3 ½ years, the antichrist will be revealed. There was 30 pieces of silver, a 153 fish in the net, and 50 days until Pentecost. Scripture says God has numbered our days, month s, steps, our wanderings, the stars, even our hairs! Are these just random numbers or do they have some deep significance? Biblical numbers are highly symbolic and are meant to serve as means for expressing a message, a sign, or an indication of someone or thing. We are often too limited in our understanding of the meaning of numbers. How often do you delve into the deeper meanings of numbers? There is a deeper meaning behind them.

This category deals with numbers, integers, or figures. Some short descriptions of types, phrases, and other processes and particulars, connected in some way to this category are, for example, fractions, imaginary numbers, irrational numbers, negative numbers, rational numbers, whole numbers, zero, or quotient. In addition to their use in counting and measuring, numbers are often used for addresses, or codes, e.g. ISBNs, serial numbers, statistics, telephone numbers). Some numbers also have words to express them. For example, pair, couple, dozen, baker's dozen, score, gross, great gross, or ream). Also, see category content list, or index.

All Symbols and Referents, Notes (1, 2, 3, etc.), Suggested Course of Action, and Specific Meaning offer guidance toward a more comprehensive interpretation.

Notes

1. Unless otherwise noted elsewhere, if, in your everyday living, your awaked state, as part of your lifestyle, work, or ministerial activities, or a special event, you have a very real connection with numbers. For example, accountant, actuary, banking, bookkeeping, computer codes, economist, fiscal operations, lottery, mathematician, statistician, tax preparer, stock market, teacher, or any other activity dealing with numbers, your dream is not significant and does not warrant special attention.

    Otherwise noted, this dream of numbers may be a Prophetically Simple Dream (see Chapter One: The 60th Part of Prophecy). Whereas, the dreamer is encouraged, for example, if a mathematical equation, mathematical solution to a problem, mathematical proof, a mathematical certainty, was introduced to you within your dream, to publish the proof as your own, using your own name to authenticate or identify, especially if you are a part of the science, technical, or specialist areas of numbers, e.g. mathematician. Skip interpretation, go, and start working on and publishing your divine sent inspiration.

Otherwise noted, this dream may be a Prophetically Simple Dream (see Chapter One: The 60th Part of Prophecy). Whereas, the dreamer is warned to stop any unwise, foolish, illegal, or illicit activity going on within your life that involves numbers, e.g. fake social security cards, changing numbers on documents, rigging an election, rigging prices, insider trading, illegal daily lottery, or any other criminal minded, under-handed or perverse activity that primarily involves numbers. You should cease any illegal activity, and/or surrender to the appropriate authorities, especially if this is an issue within the dreamer's life. If any of the preceding is happening, this dream is a first step intervention and an alarm. Skip interpretation and re-consider your activity as harmful, hurtful, illegal, or life threatening, at present. Handle the situation appropriately by surrendering, first to God, for Adonai Elohim knows all, and then to appropriate relevant others. Also, see Specific Meaning at the end of this category, section entitled, Note (Specific Meaning).

Otherwise noted, per your lifestyle, if your dream closely resembled real life situations, meaning it can actually occur (or has occurred) during your awaked state; this dream may be an Ordinary Dream, resulting from your daily activities (see Chapter One, Chalom). These sorts of dreams are usually about your routine, mundane activities or anxieties that overwhelm your mind during the day. They are an inner release mechanism, which helps provide you with emotional balance and the maintaining of your sanity. These dreams are not significant, and do not warrant special attention.

2.   Probables: As numbers are frequently demonstrated in many, and very personal ways; for example, does noontime mean lunchtime, or does 6 pm mean dinnertime, to you? Is 110 Avenue the address of your childhood home? Is #587 your first apartment? Does the number 155 remind you of a particular time in your life? Does the number 777 remind you of good? Thus, could the number depicted be a possible probable (see Chapter One, section entitled, Probables)? Hence, dreamer may also consider your own personal and special associations with various numbers, as long as the interpretation is kept within the principles of spiritual boundary markers, landmarks, and property lines, (see Chapter One, section entitled, Spiritualizing Boundary Markers, Landmarks, and Property Lines).

3.   Determine who your dream is for you or another. Always, considering yourself first, reflecting on your present behaviors. Ask yourself, why am I dreaming about this now? What is this dream revealing about me? Have I taken on new attributes? Has anyone commented on my present behaviors as being untypical of me? Has my ministry changed for the better or for the worse? What about my beliefs, doctrine, or philosophy, are they still based on Holy Writ? Is there something I need to know about those I am ministering to or serving?

Remember your actions within your dream. Were you the only participant within your dream? Did dreamer take statistics? Did dreamer play lottery numbers? Did you see a certain number highlighted? Did you take over the numbering activity in any way? Unless otherwise noted elsewhere, an answer of yes, to one or more of these, or similar questions, is a good indicator that your dream is about you (the dreamer). What happened to you in your dream? How did things end? In light of your dream, via the relevant interpretation, do you believe that your behavior will enhance or endanger your well-being, safety, and/or happiness, if so, how and why? Do you believe that your belief system will strengthen or weaken you spiritually in any way, if so, how and why? For example, are you sharing the "Good News" for profit only or perhaps at your own expense and is now beginning to feel "angry" at God about the expense? Are you perpetuating a "twisted" prosperity message that primarily feeds greed? Are you drawing back on financially supporting a ministry? See following relevant subcategory, the interpretation is about and for you.

Did another play a major role in the numbers activity? Did someone else initiate the counting activity? Did someone else try to encourage you to number something? Did someone steal a certain amount of money? Unless otherwise noted elsewhere, an answer of yes, to one or more of these, or similar questions, is a good indicator that your dream is about another and their role, and/or influential effects, within the life of the dreamer. Consider, is someone greatly influencing your physical, spiritual, or mental health, your understanding, perspective, and reasoning regarding spiritual issues? Are they enhancing your spiritual and/or literal prosperity, or are they responsible for the dwindling thereof? Could they be influencing your ministry, on some level? Do you know someone whose life activities or physical being is similar to that which stood out the most within your dream? Could it be that person? If you sense that your dream is for or about another, the question as to why you have been made privy to this information, and how do you factor into the equation, should be seriously considered along with necessary actions. Perhaps the dreamer is being made aware of the plight of someone, and you are to get involved (see Chapter One, Are You Ready to Hear the Messages in Your Dreams, section entitled, The 10% for others).

If your dream is for, or about another:

Dreams that reference others and the revelation within those dreams, is not given haphazardly to any individual, but only to those with the ability, and influence to do something with the information; this is also prophecy. With that, journal the following questions, and if unable to answer the questions now, this denotes that the person, represented within your dream, will enter your life shortly. Are you entering into a personal relationship with someone? Do you not know or understand what you're looking at, especially certain behaviors, when learning about this person? Has someone new entered your life or maybe you've just begun opening up to someone not so new, and have started listening to their advice, accepting their assistance, or are you supporting or enabling someone? Are you in denial regarding the toxicity of one of your present relationships, particularly a spouse, family member, or friend? Are you anxious, concerned, frightened, and/or troubled by recent changes in your behavior, especially because of someone's influence upon your life at present? Have you allowed someone to convince you to deceive another? Have you recently become aware of (or is being made aware of, via your dream) certain undesirable behaviors within you towards another? Are you trying to cut ties with one that is bad company? Have you just joined (or re-joined) a church, fellowship, or social group?

Note: If your dream has attributes that indicate that your dream is about you, and other attributes that indicate that your dream is about another, dreamer should consider that your dream is about you and another. For example, while dreamer may have walked one mile, thus indicating that the dream is about the dreamer, someone else may have left the dreamer, causing the need to walk, thus indicating that your dream is about another. Did dreamer receive a certain amount of money from a benefactor? Did dreamer discover a mathematical solution to a problem but another was credited with the solution? Hence, since the dreamer was not properly credited with the solution, the dreamer is emotionally hurt, and now that hurt has bred bitterness and an unforgiving spirit within the dreamer. From which now the dreamer needs deliverance. Nonetheless, while your dream is about the dreamer, the dreamer should expect the role and/or influential effects of another, also plays a part in your interpretation, again, see relevant interpretation.

More questions to consider. Why has the person been allowed within your life, and/or how did they get there? Again, if unable to answer the questions now, this denotes that the person, represented within your dream, will enter your life shortly. If their activity, within your dream, has proven positive, via the interpretation, this someone will prove, unwittingly, to be a very strong ally, benefactor, defender, and supporter. God has sent this someone into your life to help you carry out your next endeavor by enlarging your spiritual capacity. Allow the strength of that person's character to guide, help, and support you. On the other hand, if his or her presence and/or activity, within your dream, proved negative, via the interpretation, for sure, this person will prove to be a very strong and formidable challenge for you, perhaps unto death. If negative, this dream is a dire warning. Take steps accordingly to struggle against, or to cut off, adverse and unfavorable relationships. Remember certain personalities are all encompassing, affecting everything, cataclysmic, contagious, deadly, harmful, infectious, predatory, and/or venomous. Symbolically meaning that if allowed to continue or prosper within your life, serious harm or death to the dreamer may result. Idolize no one, especially beyond the warning of the Lord, and we are definitely not to lay our lives down for no one. Then again, this person maybe allowed within your life, because of the dreamer's unwillingness to abstain from immorality after having been asked to abstain from such by God, see 1 Corinthians 6:9-20, Galatians 5:19-21, or the dreamer's self-righteous behavior, or a lack of a balanced and honest view of your own personality. In this case, this person will affect self-awareness within the life of the dreamer, exposing the negative traits of your personality, especially those traits, which cause you to follow, or to be so easily misled, and/or your wrong beliefs; no matter, this type of mentality needs reckoning with. Graciously, all of this will restore the dreamer to his or her right place with God, opening your eyes to see how far you've strayed from God (1 Corinthians 5:4-7; James 5:20). The lesson is, no matter how personable, powerful, or difficult a person, or how uncertain or unpopular the choices and issues, always take the next biblical and ethical step, for obedience to God's principles will always prove safer and stronger foundationally. Although, you will need all kinds of outside support to recover from this person's domination, no longer, allow that particular person's influence within your life to continue or thrive, especially if negative, end it abruptly.

4. Consider all the people, places, backgrounds, and activity highlighted within your dream.

Known (in your awaked life) person, animal, place, or organization within your dream:

Unless otherwise noted elsewhere, people, animals, places, backgrounds that are actually known by the dreamer in your awaked life, indicates a part of you that you recognize within yourself on some level or another. Question to journal, if dreamer seriously considers the person, animal, place, or background attributes, what character traits stood out the most, or what features stood out the most. For example, age, color, height, size, happiness, considerate, loving, let you be yourself, peacefulness, encourager, irrational, leader, liar, mentor, passionate, personable, neglected, poor, run-down, sage, shyster, unwise, upscale, vengeful. Write down (journal) the particular highlighted within your dream. The attribute or activity highlighted is for a reason. Since the attribute written down is a part of you, namely the dreamer's nature, demeanor, and/or lifestyle, an honest and unbiased assessment is very important for truth sake. Happy note, considering that other people's attributes, within dreams, also represent attributes of your own personality, causes one to look at another in a better light. According to your capacity to embrace self-awareness and a rectification of mind, body, and spirit, God will begin to enhance, make better, more attractive, sanctify, diminish, and make pure and free from sin and guilt, this part of you.

Otherwise noted, if the person, animal, place, or background within your dream is actually known by the dreamer, in your awaked life, this person, animal, place, or background may represent him or herself, or itself.

Unknown in your awaked life or although known, was unseen, invisible, or only talked about - person, animal, place, or organization within your dream:

Unless otherwise noted elsewhere, if you did not recognize, the person, place, thing, they, or it, was not seen, invisible, or only talked about within your dream, this indicates an attribute or activity within your life that you are unfamiliar with, or are in denial about, or you refuse to acknowledge it, but it does exists. Question to journal: what character trait, feature, action, or activity, stood out the most? For example, age, color, height, size, happiness, considerate, loving, peacefulness, encourager, irrational, leader, liar, mentor, passionate, personable, neglected, poor, run-down, sage, shyster, unwise, upscale, vengeful. Although, on some conscious level, you are aware of a certain behavior or attribute within you, you have chosen to filter out or simply ignore certain information about yourself that contradicts your view of yourself and/or your preconceived notions of others and of the world around you. Possibly protecting yourself, emotionally and psychologically, from a situation, which you are unable to cope with at this time, or you lack control over; then again, perhaps the dreamer has an exaggerated or unrealistic view of yourself. No matter the reason, right now a question is before you, via your dream. Do you want to know this part of yourself? According to your ability to handle self-awareness, God will begin to reveal this side of you to you. Why, He wants to balance your understanding of things; thus, effecting wholeness within your life, so that the enemy will no longer be able to manipulate your emotions so easily. The Paraclete is with you to help you throughout this entire process, listen to Him. Now, in your life, this activity or attribute needs reckoning with, somehow or someway.

Otherwise noted, (known or unknown), if the person, place or thing that initiated (or was a recipient of) the action or activity within your dream was not seen, invisible, or only talked about within your dream, this may indicate that the dreamer does not recognize the influential effects another has within your life, or upon your attitude.

If more than one person (known or unknown):

Consider what the group had in common. What behavior, character trait, feature, action, or activity, stood out the most? For example, were they argumentative, authoritative, beautiful, criminal minded, dancing, difficult, dressed unusual, enigmatic, fighting, focused, flirty, helpful, hurtful intentions, powerful, promiscuous, quiet, secretive, seemed unreal, unassuming? What about age, color, height, size, happiness, considerate, loving, let you be yourself, peacefulness, encourager, irrational, leader, liar, mentor, passionate, personable, neglected, poor, run-down, sage, shyster, unwise, upscale, vengeful, death. That which was highlighted and noted is what you need to focus on at present.

If the attribute or quality is a desirable or positive one, allow the strength of that attribute to help you overcome some manner of immorality or irreverence within your life and/or to help you to become better, productively, for the Kingdom of God in some manner. If the attribute is an undesirable or negative one, take steps accordingly to struggle against the growing desires of the carnal side of you. If applicable, get help and support via prayer, fasting, and a Christian based support group.

For dreams of the dead see following note.

Did you count the number of dead people? While the dead has nothing to do with the living (Ecclesiastes 9:4-6), it may be considered what character trait did that person represent to the dreamer, while the person was actually alive, what character feature stood out the most. With that trait noted, dreamer may consider that the trait noted, is within the dreamer, and that trait is no longer useful or needed for the progression of your spiritual walk, on this side of heaven. Dreamer, it is suggested that you render that trait (good or bad) obsolete, and began anew attempting to move forward, using different tactics to overcome unproductive habitual life cycle choices, and for maneuvering through this thing we call life in a more, better way. See category, Death, and/or other relevant categories.

5. Numbers in dreams can represent literal numbers in your awaked life, while, at the same time, be linked to something that needs to be interpreted symbolically. For example, when Joseph dreamt of eleven stars, the number eleven was literal, for he did have eleven brothers, but the stars were symbolic, as they represent siblings. Joseph was dreaming about his eleven brothers (Genesis 37:1-11). Another example is Pharaoh's dream of seven cows and ears of grain. While number seven actually denoted a period or season of time, the cows and grain were symbolic of famine; thus, pharaoh's dream was about seven years of famine (Genesis 41:1-7).

6. If there were two or more numbers highlighted within your dream, or your number is not listed, there are three possible steps to take. (1) All the numbers, and their interpretations

merged together, may be considered as one interpretation. (2) Dreamer could consider the common denominator between all the numbers. It will be the similarity, namely the common denominator, which you should focus on. (3) Dreamer may consider the product of the number. Either one of these steps, will be the more appropriate meaning. Also, see the following.

Product: If your number is a product (e.g. 62 = 2 x 31), the dreamer may consider referencing and merging its multiples (e.g. consider the numbers two and thirty-one).

Product of many multiples: If your number is a product of many multiples (e.g. 120 = 2 x 60; 3 x 40; 5 x 24; 6 x 20; 8 x 15; 10 x 12). The dreamer may consider referencing and merging only one set of the multiples. For example, two and sixty or three and forty or four and thirty, and so forth, but do not consider all the multiples. Coupled with the interpretation, choose the one set of multiples that are best relevant to your life's situation, now.

Triple digit numbers and beyond: The dreamer may consider grouping multiples and the calculating their sum. For example, 881 = (100 x 8) + (9 x 9). Here, the dreamer may consider 100, 8, and 9^2. Also, see following not on square roots.

Square root: If listed, and only if necessary (necessary for relief or append), dreamer may also consider the square of a number, e.g. 9^2 = 81. Thus, the square of 81 is 9. Dreamer should consider the number 9. A square root is a more absolute, concentrated, ardent, doubled measured in strength, forceful, and insistent, expression of a number, and is prophetic in nature. The interpretation for the number nine, as it relates to this number squared (9^2). The interpretation of the number nine will be more intense in strength, and doubled spiritually, in application, and prophetic in nature. Hence, the number 81 is in part, a more absolute, concentrated, ardent, doubled measured in strength, forceful, and insistent, expression of the number nine, and possibly conditional viz. application and manifestation.

Numbers that repeat themselves (e.g. 55, 66, 77): If listed, and only if necessary (necessary for relief or append), dreamer may also consider the single digit of a repetitive number. Although not more absolute, concentrated, ardent, doubled measured in strength, intensity, or forcefulness, as a square root, an increase in the strength of its meaning still applies prophetically and in application. In addition, the force of intensity of the interpretation increases as the numbers increase in repetitiveness (e.g. 222, 333, 666, 2222, 3333), and possibly conditional per application and manifestation.

Fractions: For fractions and decimals, the dreamer may reference the denominator (e.g. ⅛, consider the number eight, .25, consider the number twenty-five). Moreover, consider the interpretation ⅛ or ¼ less in strength spiritually, and possibly conditional viz. application and manifestation, but relevant just the same.

7. Some numbers are represented by words and letters (roman numerals). For example, deuce, couple, pair, or II= 2; trio=3, tetrad, quarter=4, cinque, quintet= 5, half dozen=6, dozen = 12, baker's dozen = 13; score = 20; gross = 144; great gross = 1728; ream= 480 or 500, and so on.

    Roman Numerals (a symbol in the old Roman notation): I, V, X, L, C, D, M, represents 1,5,10,50,100,500,1000 respectively. Refer to the number represented by the words or letters.

8. In addition to the following interpretations, see index or relevant categories for more information. For example, if money was involved in some way, see category, Currency; if a birthday was highlighted, see category, Celebrations. Kept within context of your dream and the interpretation, the additional symbols are perhaps relevant. It will be within the sum of all the symbols that you will find a more thorough interpretation.

9. Since the following list is not extensive, dreamer is encouraged to seek biblical guidelines and other relevant research to determine the metaphorical meaning of your particular number activity, depicted within your dream, via a Bible concordance, Bible illustrated dictionary, encyclopedia, or internet. Having done your research you should be able to determine some basic behaviors or attributes your Lord and Savior wants you to focus on.

Symbols and Referents

Numbers within our dreams primarily denote that the dreamer will eat and do well, on this side of eternity, and inherit eternal life. However, humility will be the key to your success (requisite). Moreover, the dreamer will be used to usher others into a totally new and higher level of spiritual awareness and selflessness. Numbers also refer to your mental condition, state of mind, reasoning abilities, your understanding of something or acumen, and your ethics – conscience, beliefs, integrity, moral code, principles, and/or values.

In addition to the varied meanings of numbers, other common words, expressions, usages, (e.g. slang or clichés), or a 'probable' that are metaphorically represented by numbers are also considered (this section is an addendum at the end of the relevant subcategory). With the exception of the following:

- **Out or Down for the Count:** To dream that you are knocked out, and someone is counting over you, denotes one who is unconscious or asleep, spiritually, and unlikely to wake again for some time. Figuratively, an inability to stand up, after being knocked down; therefore, losing the spiritual battle. See suggested course of action.

Category Content - If not listed see index, perchance, for your specific type of numbers dream.

- Accounting, see category, Working (Accountant)
- Numbers represented by Words, see Note 7
- Roman Numerals, see Note 7
- Counting (the act of reciting numbers in ascending order, or to determine the amount of something by counting)
- Distance or Pace: distance and/or pace (e.g. running, walking, or already there)
- Subtraction, subtraction in any form, see category, Abating
- Time (a point in time as given by a clock)
  - Morning (the first light of day, aka the breaking of day, 6 am up until 12 Noon); Noon, mid-day (12:00 pm up until 6:00 pm); Twilight (morning twilight 5 am to 6 am, aka dawn, just at sunrise, or evening twilight, 6 pm to 7 pm, aka dusk, just at sunset); Dawn (sunrise, morning twilight 5 am to 6 am); Dusk (sunset, evening twilight, 6 pm to 7 pm); Night (7 pm, after sunset up until 12 midnight); Midnight (12 am to 4 am); Lateness (quality of coming late or later in time); Past (an earlier period in your life, earlier than the present time; no longer current)
- Zero thru Thousands

COUNTING (the act of reciting numbers in ascending order, or to determine the amount of something by counting):

This dream denotes one of two issues (choose one). (1) The dreamer needs to seriously, consider someone to be of importance and valuable to your process, project, or team, and you need to include him or her in the loop, in the process, on the project, and on the team. This person is before you now. (2) The dreamer is split internally. Your thoughts are ambiguous, and are primarily, discouraging, faithless, fatalistic, and troubling to yourself and others. Dreamer, such dubio us thinking will cause you to be fretful, irritable, and fearful of going to Jesus boldly, supposing you're forcing your presence or opinions on Him, or that you are unwelcome in Jesus' sight, all of which, are untrue. Dreamer, although your faults are befo re you, Jesus loves you. Dreamer, go to God, aware of your own inadequacies, to ask for wisdom, and rest assure that He has wisdom to give, and is generous and liberal enough to give to whomever ask, that includes you. He will not correct or critic ize in a harsh manner, for He knows you are seeking wisdom. One may suffer needlessly, because he or she will not ask Jesus for wisdom. Further, regarding God's most Holy Word, do not be hesitant, suspicious, or faithless, about His promises, especially to think that His promises and benefits are limited to a select few, and exclude others. God gives to all men and women; yes you too, and He gives unabatedly. Ask Jesus as often as you need to, regarding all of your emotional concerns, considering how personal His promises are, He will meet you in your needs. There is only one thing required of you, and that is, in your asking, you ask with a believing, steady mind, for it is written, let him (or her) ask in faith, nothing wavering, see James 1:6. See suggested course of action.

DISTANCE OR PACE:

Distance and/or pace (e.g. running, walking, or already there) will often refer to a "time frame", the length of time before manifestation. For example, one already at their destination refers to the present, or denotes that dreamer is already at a destined place, while running, or walking, both refer to a future time. Moreover, one running, will reach their destination in approximately one-fourth the time quicker than walking. Note: one city block will often refer to approximately six months to one year. Note: if the "mph" is highlighted within your dream, reference the numbers that correspond with the "mph" depicted. Moreover, if mode of travel was highlighted, see index for relevant category, e.g. Vehicles, Walking, or Running.

TIME (a point in time as given by a clock):

Your dream denotes a "time frame". A set time is quickly approaching for a particular event, perhaps within a year. Dreamer, for everything there is a fixed time, and a time for every business under the sun. A time for birth and a time for death; a time for planting and a time for uprooting; a time to put to death and a time to make well; a time for pulling down and a time for building up; a time for weeping and a time for laughing; a time for sorrow and a time for dancing. A time to take stones away and a time to get stones together; a time for kissing and a time to keep from kissing; A time for search and a time for loss; a time to keep and a time to give away. A time for undoing and a time for stitching; a time for keeping q uiet and a time for talk; A time for love and a time for hate; a time for war and a time for peace (Ecclesiastes 3:10 BBE). Dreamer, one of the specific "times", referenced within this verse, you are getting ready to experience, be it (e.g. a birth, death, sowing, reaping, healing, mourning, joy, building, love, or recovery). The specific experience will be alluded to, within the other particulars within your dream; couple this with one of the following subcategories, morning, noon, mid-day, twilight, dawn, dusk, night, or midnight. Dreamer may also reference the numbers that correspond with a time depicted. For example, 7:00, dreamer may consider the numbers 7 and/or 700, or if 8:45, dreamer may consider the numbers 8, 45, and 845. If military time, e.g. 0600, dreamer may consider 0, the number 6, and the number 600. Moreover, AM or PM, should be considered as an event happening sooner (am), usually happening or manifesting within seven months, or later (pm), usually happening or manifesting within on e year.

Morning (the first light of day, aka the breaking of day, 6 am up until 12 Noon): First, it is necessary to say that the path of the righteous is like the first glow of the sun in the early morning, shining brighter until the full light of day. Dreamer, although you've been experiencing major distress, and have been nearly overcome by your enemies, the Lord has heard your prayers and He feels your loss. There will be a lifting up of troubles off you, and you will be protected from the cruelty o f your adversaries, as well, anticipate a miracle. It will become clearer to you the miraculous acts of God within your life, and on your behalf, for God will uphold you. Therefore, look diligently and anticipate His favor. Moreover, you will be restore d to divine favor, filled with joy, and brought into great prosperity; only glory in God alone. Read and embrace Psalm 30:5.

Noon, mid-day (12:00 pm up until 6:00 pm): Dreamer, now, you will begin to experience a miraculous increase in divine knowledge, and wisdom, as your dream denotes one who is spiritually prepared for spiritual growth, divine illumination, and some type of promotion or confirmation. This knowledge and wisdom will be imparted to you to be used exclusively for interpreting the gospel of Jesus Christ to others, and for the edifying of the Body of Christ; the body of believers; as your dream, also, points to one who was born to be a teacher and a nurturer. Therefore, prepare your mind for action; be self - controlled; set your hope fully on the grace to be given you when Jesus Christ is revealed, and no longer conform to your carnal desires (see 1 Peter 1:13-16). Your dream also confirms that you're in order for heaven. Moreover, your dream is additional proof of something that you have believed God. Whatever that something is, it is correct (e.g. for a spouse, rectification of an attitude of anger, frustration, discontent, or for a healing of unbelief, or a healing of your faith level, or a healing of p hysical health, or for any hindrances to your spiritual clarity that you have recognized). You will receive "it".

Twilight (morning twilight 5 am to 6 am, aka dawn, just at sunrise, or evening twilight, 6 pm to 7 pm, aka dusk, just at sunset): Your dream speaks of "something" happening quickly. Something, significant in scope, is going to happen suddenly and quickly. Instantly and suddenly, that "something" can, and will, happen very soon. Question, was it morning or evening twilight? According to the twilight hour depicted within your dream, dawn or dusk that "something", will refer to one of the following. Choose one of the following.

Dawn (sunrise, morning twilight 5 am to 6 am): Your dream refers to instantaneous knowledge. Dreamer will be miraculously endowed with spiritual knowledge. Remember, Jesus is the source of that knowledge, and just like the Lord gives, He can take away, due to disobedience, and none of your righteousness will be remembered no more (Ezekiel 33:12). Couple this with one of the following (choose one). (1) Male dreamer: You are commissioned to preach the gospel of Jesus Christ, through evangelism, outreach efforts, or a pastorate. You are sent to many, of every nation and tongue. You should already know by now who you are in Christ, an evangelist, outreach organizer, or pastor. You are one who is powerfully convincing, definitely, a great leader, perhaps even historical. With that said, do you love Jesus? If so, then feed His flock (figurat ively and literally). You love Him when you obey Him and submit to His ways and means. Additionally, write your vision down, that you may articulate it to others properly, for the vision will happen, suddenly and quickly. Prepare a good proposal, name your ministry, and write down all the details and specifics. Give it your best that it may be acceptable to any reputable financial entity, benefactor, or merit a grant of some kind. Perhaps, hire a grant writer. That which you will need to fulfill your aims, surely, you will have. (2) Female dreamer: You are being attacked relentlessly, due to the schemes of wicked persons. There is no rest. God is getting ready to, suddenly and quickly, move you away from where you are currently residing, worshiping, or working. Have faith, God will lead the way. Because of your move, relief from the evil schemes and lies of the adversary in that particular place (e.g. home, church, or work) will end. Most importantly, because of your move, you will find the peace and rest needed physically, emotionally, and spiritually. This is not an encouragement to forfeit fellowship with church or family, or resign from your place of employment, nor is it meant to engender strife, for you do not know which way the Lord is moving. Simply put, you will be rescued from that which is potentially dangerous to your personal relationship with Christ and your health. Allow God, not you, to handle His business of keeping His promises to you, namely, "I will give you rest" and "My peace I leave with you". If necessary, see suggested course of action.

Dusk (sunset, evening twilight, 6 pm to 7 pm): Your dream denotes one who has the power and strength, via Jesus Christ, to accomplish what is before you. No matter the various circumstances of life, you must conclude that you ca n do all things through Christ who strengthens you (Philippians 4:13). You are counseled to begin to embrace this mindset, especially now, if not already, because of the great leader you are called to be. Dreamer, you can bear any trial, perform any duty, subdue any evil propensity of your nature, and meet all the temptations consequence to any condition of prosperity or adversity. You need not sink under any trial, nor yield to temptation, nor be harassed, vexed, and tortured with improper thoughts and unholy desires, for there is one who can strengthen you, make a way for your escape, and enable you to renounce unholy thoughts from your mind. Dreamer, you can rebuke all unclean spirits from within and without, your life, and command them to go into outer darkness in Jesus name. This will affect, and restore, the right balance to the affections of your soul. Only, do not shrink from duty, but express confidently and firmly to yourself that nothing is required of you tha t you are unable to perform. On the other side, a wicked servant would bury his or her gift, blaming their lack of faithfulness, commitment, and stewardship on God or others. When in reality, he or she has actually chosen to remain spiritually immature. Upon facing your Maker, there will be no one else to blame but you. No one can ever claim he or she has not been sufficiently warned. You will have to give an account of the fulfilling of your specific purpose. Consider your dream as sufficient warning. See suggested course of action.

Night (7 pm, after sunset up until 12 midnight): Dreamer, although the Lord has given you the bread of adversity and the water of affliction, wait on the Lord, for you are more than able to complete the process of spiritual and emotional cleansing. This process will heal your animosity, and heal you emotionally and physically, allow the agitation, which is a result of a dying to self. For he or she who endures the agitation will rule over all, especially self, for agitation do effect self-awareness. However, as feelings go, because of your questionable behavior and deeds, you are discouraged, and feel unfit and unworthy of God's favor and restoration. Nonetheless, promises of deliverance, restoration, and fruitfulness are promised you, because of God's amazing grace. God, by His grace will prepare and qualify you for mercy and then bestowed it on you. Your process and waiting, will also instilled within you an appropriate and balanced confidence in your own merit as an extraordinarily gifted prophet, minister, evangelist, teacher, or pastor. Notwithstanding, your path, now, should be towards developing your mind at searching out the deeper truths of the Word of God; and at becoming a skilled "watchman or watchwoman", on guard always, keeping watch, and keeping to heart the word of the Lord. Now your ears will hear a voice behind you, saying, "This is the way; walk in it", obey the voice, for it is of God. See suggested course of action.

Midnight (12 am to 4 am): Dreamer, there is a spiritual presence in your mist, or there will be a visitation from the spirit realm suddenly. This spirit has come to determine recompense of some kind, for either glory or dishonor. Thus, this dream has two meanings (choose one). (1) Dreamer, the spiritual presence in your mist has come to impart glory. Glory in this sense is divine admiration, praise, prosperity, success, triumph, and respect from others within your life. You have been found glorifying the Kingdom of God, via your ministry, and your lifestyle, having exchanged your will for God's will, having presented your body a living sacrifice to the Lord and Savior. Dreamer, it is suggested that you do, as Paul and Silas did, see Acts 1 6:25-34, and arise at midnight, to give thanks unto Jesus because of His righteous ordinances (Psalm 119:62). For, a thankful heart drives out fear and makes room for praise. Hence, your praise, songs, and prayers of thanksgiving will turn your midnight ni ght into day. After this, there will be joy, for God has promised to make known to you His presence, His guidance, and protection. Be encouraged your will triumph over your enemies. (2) Dreamer, the spiritual presence in your mist has come to decide dishonor. Dishonor in this sense is a loss of glory, a loss of divine admiration, praise, prosperity, success, triumph, and respect from others within your life. Dreamer, the report of your sinful and shameful deeds, moral stupidity, drunkenness, and the overall darkness within your life has reached heaven, and the time of manifestation of the consequences of such dark behaviors, and the recompense of such, is upon you. Dreamer, if your evil deeds are not dealt with, soon mourning and death will follow, thus, it is suggested that you remember your Creator, see Ecclesiastes 12:1-7 and repent. See suggested course of action.

Lateness (quality of coming late or later in time): This dream has five meanings (choose one). (1) The dreamer is actually late regarding a life endeavor. Questions, what activity was connected to the lateness? What hindrances are before you that you have used to justify not going forward with your purpose? The time to initiate your project, embark upon purpose, or establish your ministry is now. No longer delay, or you will be found unprepared when opportunity to progress is presented. (2) The dreamer needs to seriously, consider someone to be of importance and valuable to your process, project, or team, and you need to include him or her in the loop, in the process, on the project, and on the team. Especially, one you have neglected to acknowledge, with gratefulness, because of a good done you by that person. This person is before you now, perhaps the person(s) depicted within your dream, no matter how long ago, it's better late than never, to say thank you, and with some kind of recompense. If necessary, see suggested course of action. (3) Your dream implies that the dreamer has been living too long in excess, mischievousness, and unruliness, to the point of recklessness. As a result, you are now becoming increasingly bitter, irritated, and resentful; blaming your lack of faithfulness, commitment, and stewardship on others. Actually, you have given the enemy of your soul an advantage; seizing the moment to benefit from your spiritual poverty, making you poorer and needier. It is not too late to re-group and re-gather. See suggested course of action. (4) Dreamer, you should be teaching, at present. However, you are still considered an infant spiritually; not fully acquainted with the teachings about righteousness. You are spiritually, emotionally, and perhaps physically, weak, because you have not submitted to the teachings of the basic truths of God's word. Dreamer, like those you should be teaching, crave pure spiritual word; the direct words of God imparted to us through the words of others, such as a preacher in a worship service, a Sunday school teacher, and other bible studies, so that by it you may grow up in your salvation. Read, understand, and embrace Hebrews 5:12-14, 2 Timothy 2:15. See suggested course of action. (5) If not already, within two days, dreamer will be found "judging" someone, or a situation unrighteous. You will be strongly convicted of this within, and it will feel overpowering, do not ignore the strong alarm of the Holy Ghost and your conscience. Perhaps dreamer has contrarily judged another as neglectful, lazy, or as one who is dishonoring God. Dreamer, you do not personally know their situation, you are truly on the outside looking in, judging by sight. Your words are just opinions, which happened to be very judgmental. Dreamer, in judging others, via condemnatory, critical, derogatory, disapproving, harsh, negative, scornful, or uncomplimentary in your thoughts and/or speaking aloud, you have set a precedent over your own life, discharging a universal law. The Universal Law: With the same judgments, you judge others, so will you be judged (see Matthew 7:1-5). Question, dreamer, what have you thought, or said, regarding the actions of another recently? For example, have you thought or said, "They're life is not holy, or they are not Christian, because I know they behave this way, or do that", or "How can they witness about God one moment, and beg for money or food the next? Have you never been in a fallen state, or had a material need, at the same time, you were required to testify on behalf of the Kingdom of God or, did you just disobey the commission because of a preconceived notion or pseudo - image? Nonetheless, now you're judged as an offender, in that you have violated your own standard, the one you've held up, so high, for others to follow, for him or her who knows to do right and do not, to him or her it is a sin. While Christ does not deny the necessity of exercising a certain degree of discernment, or of making valid judgments with respect to sin in others. Jesus condemns the habit of criticizing others, while ignoring your own faults. You should have done what you expected of others. A believer must first submit him or herself to God's righteous standard before attempting to examine and influence the conduct of others, which is often done in an unjust or unloving manner if you haven't judged yourself first. This also includes condemning a wrongdoer without a genuine desire to see the offender return to God, but to be condemned to hell. Here again, discharging a preset law within this type of offense, which is to not see you, as an offender, return to God, but to be condemn to hell also. Dreamer, genuinely deal with why you are so judgmental or critical, and repent over judging others, this will remove such severe and unsympathetic standards from over your own life, and your dreams will change. Also, by so doing, a more compassionate, understanding, empathic and loving spirit will begin to manifest within you. Other reasons for such a severe warning are an unforgiving attitude towards someone, or literally rejecting the teachings of Christ and His apostles (Hebrews 6:4-8). See suggested course of action

Past (an earlier period in your life, earlier than the present time; no longer current): Your dream is a reflection of your inward thoughts and deliberations, and expresses recognition of where you are emotionally, physically, and spiritually, and who you are becoming. Dreamer, although, your previous lifestyle, your past, was overshadowed by negative experiences, and deferred hopes. Dreamer is counseled to no longer, meditate on the immorality of your past. Compassionately, God's power has made a way out of no way for you, and your state of affairs is turning around. Dreamer, some type of conquering and spiritual awakening is happening within your life, particularly a completely new awakening regarding your relationship with Christ, Jesus. You are opening your eyes to what it means to truly, be a new creation in Christ. The necessity to be reconciled with God, others, and with your past mistakes, has been resolved. You have re-evaluated your life, learned from your mistakes, found new directions in solving problems, pursued healing, sought out encouragement, and figured out what God would like you to change in order to, better fulfill His purpose. God's righteousness dwells with and in you. Therefore, dreamer, no longer limit God by your thoughts of what was, or what might have been, for old things have passed away, and you have truly become new (2 Corinthians 5:17). Focus your heart, mind, and soul, upon new principles, new rules, thereby, expecting new endings. For you are truly created anew, a new heart has been given you. Let this be your focus. Additionally, dreamer, there will be a relaxation or slackening of tension in your life. STOP, and feel the tension leaving! Those who ha ve charged you falsely, with malicious intent, attacking your good name and reputation will be far from you. Others will become less hostile, as will you. You will be more relaxed, easygoing, and kind.

ZERO THRU THOUSANDS

0: The numerical symbol 0 refers to a turning point within the life of the dreamer. With that, this dream has two meanings (one or both may apply). (1) Unmarried dreamer: An arousal of desires is beginning to stir; desires that are simple and complex; hidden and revealed; nothing and everything; real and illusion; desires that at one point in time opposed each another and at another point embraced each other. Dreamer, all these feelings are leading you into an intimate relationship, culminating into a wedding. The dreamer and someone of the opposite sex, will meet, very soon if not already, and you two will naturally attract, and connect. This attraction is for marriage purposes. However, the arousal and purpose of all your desires and the contradictory nature of those desires is (was) meant to bring about an authentic awareness of the dreamer's personality and that of your potential spouse. As a result, of you two connecting, personalities will clash, conflicts and struggles, to the point of battle, will ensue. With each, killing the ego of the other; thereafter, blending together in a t rue union; meaningful and valuable. Hold on tight, things will get bumpy, don't give up, nor walk away, the marriage will prove worthy of every moment in its beginning. See suggested course of action. (2) Your dream represents the initial stirrings of intents to be like God. Dreamer, while we do have an obligation to imitate God in our actions, we are not to impersonate or aspire to be Him. Your turning point will be favorable if your intentions are wise and emotionally and psychologically balanced. Therefore, the dreamer is counsel that we are to imitate God in loving His Son with all our heart and loving others as we love ourselves, as well as other ethical behaviors; and we are to allow God to be God. Again, dreamer you are warned to be careful lest you become so prideful that there creeps into you the idea that you can be deified. Self-deification is of Satan. God can dwell in the human, via the Holy Spirit, but forever the human is the human, and Adonai Elohim is forever God. See suggested course of action.

In addition, the following is a common word, expression, or usage (e.g. slang or cliché), or a 'probable' that is metaphorically represented by the number 0:

- One who is regarded as a complete failure

1: The number one refers to education, love, and a teacher. Dreamer you are entering into a season within your life that will prepare you spiritually for the visitation of the Lord in your individual life. During this time, you will experience His love and presence, as you've never known it before. For, He is saying to you, "I will teach you godly wisdom". You will receive direct insight of divine truth. You will come to know, without a doubt, that God is the true source of your strength and wisdom, and He is your sufficiency. As a result, a greater love for self, family, and others will begin to manifest, affecting wholeness within your life. Be available to Him and seize the moments and opportunities as they are presented, especially an opportunity for you to advance your education, with a focus on teaching. In addition, independent and capable, you are becoming a celebrated and powerful man or woman of God. A leader and master teacher in your own right, you will become, if not already, a preeminent part of a ministry. Therefore, understand, and respect, your value to God and to His Kingdom. Moreover, use your strength exclusively for the Kingdom of God; to choose otherwise, at this point, will not be beneficial to you, it will devalue you. See suggested course of action.

In addition, the following are common words; expressions or usages (e.g. slang or clichés) or a 'probable' that are metaphorically represented by this number:

- One who is unique and distinct from all others
- A musical notation
- Something done or occurring only once and unlikely to happen again

2: This dream has five meanings (choose one): (1) Dreamer has heard testimony, evidence, or proof of something, from two or three people, in your awaked life, and their message was similar, your dream is a witness that what you heard, is hearing, or will hear, is true. See Deuteronomy 19:15, Matthew 18:19-20. If necessary, see suggested course of action. (2) Dreamer, as painful as this may hurt it must be said, come out from among unbelievers, and to separate yourself from them, says the Lord, for what company has righteousness with unrighteousness, or what sharing of personal thoughts and feelings has light with darkness. Have nothing to do with their sinful and wicked deeds, and I will welcome you, read, understand, and embrace 2 Corinthians 6:14-18. See suggested course of action. (3) If applicable, flee sexual immorality. Every other sin that a man or woman commits is outside the body, but the immoral man or woman sins against his or her own body. Do you not know that your body is a temple of the Holy Spirit who is in you, whom you have from God, and that you are not your own? For you have been bought with a price: therefore glorify God in your body (see 1 Corinthians 6:18-20). See suggested course of action. (4) To you who have not promoted any kinds of indecent practices, sexual acts of perversions or other horrible traditions. Your dream was sent to demonstrate grace, via a warning of a dark generational issue, hereditary within your family line (e.g. maternal and/or paternal, grandparents, siblings, aunts, uncles, cousins). Dreamer, character traits from ancestors, namely genetic codes and traits, will often trouble and taunt the offspring of a given progenitor, especially generational issues (Exodus 20:5-7). The demons that have so plague your family line, are now visiting (re-visiting) you. Your issue is demonically instigated and it is spiritually perverse, perhaps sexually perverse as well (e.g. adultery, fornication, homosexuality, prostitution, whorishness). These spirits attempt to "bend" the personality, as early as possible with regards to age, towards a certain direction, oftentimes towards a way that is desolate and wicked, for it is Satan's scheme to kill and make desolate all; thus, to keep some from rising up and leading their generation to Christ (see the birth of Moses, Exodus 1:15-2:10). Favorably, generational curses and issues can stop with you (Jeremiah 31:29, 30; Ezekiel 18:2-14, 20-23). Thus, your Heavenly Father is requiring that you overcome and subdue negative and dark emotions, feelings, behaviors, or ideas that would influence you, before they overcome you. Dreamer, God is not asking you to do something you cannot do. For a surety, vanquishing of the coming influence can be done. By faith, you will need to declare some kind of fast and commit to it, for a long period-of-time, to abate the demonically instigated circumstance, you find yourself in now, Matthew 6:16 -18. Try abstaining from food and drink (midnight to 6 PM), twice a week, and refrain from words, attitudes, people, places, and things, including music, magazines, videos, TV, or any such things that fuel anger and discontent, and stir up lustful feelings. This is also known as, faith with works, read, understand, and embrace James 2:14-26. Nonetheless, earnestly pray, God will guide, enable, and answer you as to the type of fast. Additionally, if relevant, forgive your mother and/or father for the darkness (aka curse) they may have perpetuated, for they knew not what they done. Forgiveness is important to your success (Matthew 6:12-15, 8:21-35). See suggested course of action. (5) Dreamer, your experiences of aloneness, depression, rejection, and/or low self-esteem is influencing your present behavior, without you realizing it. You are not allowing yourself to get close enough to share love, trust, and intimacy qualitatively with no one. Most of the conflicts within your present relationships, including your spiritual one, are provoked because of this. Unconsciously, you are against anything that will help you develop closer friendships, including your relationship with Christ Jesus, to the point of dissolution, divorce, or ruin. As a resul t, your feelings, thoughts, and memories, together, have prevented you from developing a balanced, discriminating, and an overall lifestyle of wholeness. Fortunately, although, your previous lifestyle, your past, was overshadowed by negative experiences, and deferred hopes, God's righteousness dwells with and in you. God will raise you up and sit you amongst His people for the benefit of all within your sphere, help God's people by doing good deeds. You will be considered, and now is, a righteous person (see Romans 8:1), for there is a difference between conviction and condemnation. Dreamer, if you will trust the empowering work of the Holy Spirit, which is beginning to manifest within your life on a conscious level; thus your dream, your emotional and spiritual well-being will be made whole (meditate upon and pray Psalm 51). Moreover, a conscientious and diligent effort on the part of the dreamer, to deeply reflect, on your emotional fears and scars is needed; perhaps some type of Christian counseling may help as well. This coupled with, the refining and purifying work of the Paraclete will cause the emergence of a more divine led wisdom. It will also be through these pains that the wisdom of harmonizing, fear and love of the Lord within your life, will be imparted to you. Fear within this context is the practice of living life on God's terms, in order to receive recompense, meaning while hoping for some benefit from your efforts. You respect God but your love for Him is conditional. A tenacious faith in, and acceptance of, all of the Word of God, the good and the not so easily received, and prayer, will lead you into the Light of His Love. Love within this context, is the practice of living life on God's terms, f or no other reason or benefit, than to be close to God, and to bless His Holy name for allowing you the honor to know Him, th is is called holiness. See suggested course of action.

In addition, the following are common words; expressions or usages (e.g. slang or clichés) or a 'probable' that are metaphorically represented by this number:

- Two persons involved in an awkward or unpleasant situation, are responsible or to blame, not just one.
- To work something out from the available evidence
- To indicate agreement with something expressed, or acknowledgment of something shared

3: First, expect the number three to mean that exact number of something (e.g. 3 hours, days, 3 weeks, cycles, people, 3 fortnights=1 month). With that, this dream has three meanings (one, two, or all may apply). (1) Dreamer, those who love God, love His people also, and they keep His commandments, read, understand, and embrace 1 John 5:1-21. See suggested course of action. (2) Your dream implies that the dreamer and, if applicable, your children will reap the fruits of the blessing of your giving. Blessings; in this sense, is being elevated to a state of high honor, spiritual beauty, and great illumination. Moreover, as you are able to handle great responsibility and wealth, and are one who is tolerant, you will experience receivi ng an act of kindness, monetarily, from someone who is affluent. You must also become a fundraiser for, and giver of, charity. (3) From here forward, speaks of God's "weaning" of a righteous person, the dreamer. Dreamer, do not be deceived, with affluence, power, and wealth, comes good and evil, reward and punishment, life and expiry. While all three of these (good, evil; reward, punishment; life, expiry) have the same ultimate aim, namely, the rectification of the soul to increase its capacity to receive the blessings of the Lord more fully. One way is easier, less arduous, on the mind, body, and spirit, than the other (e.g. acting justly is always wiser than revenge, repaying kindness is better than ignoring good deeds done you, or prosperity is always better than a coming to an end of it). Today, you will need to choose between good and evil; thus, exercising your free will. Why, because you have innate tendencies to become excessive regarding spiritual impurities (e.g. addictions, cheating, greedy, lying, stealing, unchaste conduct, see 1 Corinthians 6:9-20, Ephesians 5). Embracing this side of yourself will cause you to be deemed inappropriate to be of service to the Kingdom of God, as well as, cause a delay of promises. Regrettably, this will lead to you being unhappy, and unable to discern between truth and error, without you realizing that you are in such a state. In this state, hypocrisy will be a heavy and unnecessary burden that you will bear. Henceforth, in accordance with your decision as to how you shall continue from this day forward, will define your recompense or the lack thereof, in your future and beyond. Note, if you choose to embrace the positive, this will lead to a great balancing of your theology, resulting in a belief that is complete, with solid attributes, and your inspiration will make for very good teaching. Additionally, you would make an excellent apologist (witness) for the Kingdom of God. Seriously consider this branch of Christian theology. See suggested course of action.

In addition, the following is a common word; expression or usage (e.g. slang or clichés) or a 'probable' that is metaphorically represented by this number:

- Something three-dimensional or a surprise

4: Dreamer, God is completely restoring things materially and spiritually within your life and in the lives of those immediately connected to you. Because of your brokenness over your past sins, you have opened the door to contriteness and humility. It is through this door that an act of kindness will come very soon. With that said, dreamer there is a need to understand the unadulterated and full meaning of divine providence, get a bible dictionary, and respect the meaning. Dreamer is counseled to also recognize, acknowledge, and respect divine providence, God's absolute control over the affairs of humankind, and to renounce the belief that humans are in complete control (see Job 9:12, Isaiah 14:27; 43:13). There is a difference between divine providence and the will of humankind. Although you have the power of free choice, you should not think that your accomplishments are purely of your own volition. It is God, who gives you the capability and strength to achieve success. This is especially true of your struggles with your sinful tendencies, whether they manifest as a lack of concern or interest in the things of God, a stubborn resistance to the will of God, or laziness. If it had not been for God's efforts on your behalf, you would not have been able to overcome any negative tendencies. He delivered you. Any achievements you've accomplished, any good deeds you've done, any fulfillment of God's will, was, and still is, dependent upon divine aid and guidance. One merely places his or her hand under the weight carried exclusively by God. Just say and truly believe, "I will exalt you, God, for you have lifted me up". In addition, there is a need to check your theology. There is something missing in your belief system that has affected someone who is very close to you. It has caused them to seek God i n other teachers, in other faces, and most are evil. Fortunately, that love one lead astray, because of you, will come home, embracing Jesus. Moreover, altruistic, goodhearted, and generous service to God and others is beneficial at this time. Just say and truly believe, "I will exalt you, God, for you have lifted me up" (Psalm 30:1). See suggested course of action. If listed, and only if necessary, may consider the interpretation for the number 2, as it relates to this number squared; see Note 6 at the beginning of this category.

5: This number refers to restoration, transformation, and a miraculous healing and strengthening, both physically and emotionally. This is because of God's grace, His faithfulness, and His mercy towards you. Now, your burdens, having been dealt with, freedom from your weaknesses is yours. You will be favored with complete healing, go and sin no more. For, if anyone knows the good they ought to do and doesn't do it, it is sin for them (see James 4:17). Therefore, from this moment forward, choose good habits and deeds, e.g. good stewardship and commitment to ministry; speak to you what is true and good, earnestly embracing Philippians 4:8, and choose good nutritional habits that you might remain in good health. These choices will help you progress forward towards your transformation and freedom, and help guide you toward, and enable you to fulfill, your purpose. All these blessings are rain. Dreamer, as one perfects him or herself, God helps by sending 'rains of blessings', then situations prosper. The rain is coming! As well, there will be clarity and freedom in the way you communicate yourself to others, especially prophetically. Moreover; from this time forward, so speak and act as those who are judged by the law of liberty; see James 2:12, 13. For example, remove condemnation from your message of grace and holiness, see John 3:17, Romans 8:1, 1 John 3:20, 21, for there is a difference between conviction and condemnation. Additionally, take note of this: you should be quick to listen, slow to speak, and slow to anger (James 1:19-25). The servant of God always experiences a gap between his or her thoughts and deeds. Meaning, before you actually act or speak, there is an instant of time for you to decide, to do, or say, what is wise and good or foolish and evil. Hence, your words should align with your moral stance, and should be seasoned with empathy, compassion, and understanding. For example, you may not agree with another's lifestyle choices, but you do know, and should voice if necessary, that they do have a right to enter into the House of God to repent, pray, and praise Adonai, without being condemned by you or others, see John 3:17. Dreamer, with that said the rains of blessings are coming, get ready! If necessary, see suggested course of action.

In addition, the following are common words; expressions or usages (e.g. slang or clichés) or a 'probable' that are metaphorically represented by this number:

- One who needs to take a short break from doing something
- The fifth position in ballet
- A diatonic scale, an interval stretching from one note to another five notes higher, or the sound made when both these notes are played simultaneously
- A fifth part of a gallon of alcoholic liquor

6: Dreamer, prideful and powerful, you lack Christ-like humility, and is becoming a cruel and insensitive leader. Moreover, at present, concerned with your own interest, you are driven by, and occupied with, sensual appetites, rather than spiritual needs. Your desires, appetites, and attitude are leading to a chaotic and empty life. A life figuratively similar to the condition of earth in Genesis 1:2, wasteful, empty, and dark. This type of carnal strain and toil leads to sorrow and spiritual darkness. There is a need to re-connect with God. Favorably, there is a ray of light, sent by God, purposed to break through the darkness of your state of affairs. This ray of light is a person, anointed and sent, especially to you. Their words and inspiration will be to you, like Genesis 1:3-5 is to Genesis 1:2. Illuminatingly wise, this person will powerfully affect your life, externally and internally. Their inspiration, coupled with you earnestly embracing change, humility, contentedness, integrity, ethicalness, and a renewed faith in God's word and His process, will strengthen you to return in complete heartfelt repentance to Jesus, from a heart of love. By this, the severity of your transgressions becomes partially sweetened; for, when a man or woman genuinely return to God, in complete surrender and humility, your deliberate transgressions become like actual merits, aka "the sweetening" (Luke 7:37-50). Because, the realization of your distance from God, due to your transgressions (Isaiah 59:2-21; Luke 15:11-24), becomes the motivating force to return to God with a passion even greater than that of someone who has never sinned in such a manner, or never left the Father's house, completely converting your present to good (Acts 9:1-30). This is the secret of repentance and returning to God. Go; therefore now, and seek the Lord Jesus, repent and place your hope in Him. Hope, placed in Him, will not deceive. See suggested course of action. If listed, and only if necessary, dreamer may also consider other multiples of this number. First, see Note 6 at the beginning of this category.

In addition, the following is a common word, expression, or usage (e.g. slang or cliché), or a 'probable' that is metaphorically represented by this number:

- "At sixes and sevens", meaning someone who is disorganized, in disarray, or in disagreement with something

7: First, expect the number to mean that exact number of something (e.g. 7 days, years, or cycles). With that said, your dream denotes that a spiritual purification, rectification of chaos, and a refinement process is happening (or will happen) within the life of the dreamer. That you may go on to perfection spiritually, being built up in your faith and complete, lac king nothing. This purification, rectification, and refinement process will take some time, be patient, and allow the process. It will perfect a quietness within your soul, and a more compassionate and obedient spirit, leaving you more open to divine influence. You will gain knowledge on how to be moderate in all things, just and fair, and you will become one whom other believers will interact with socially on very personal levels. During this season of rectification, the dreamer will be favored with a sabbatical, including pay. However, this sabbatical should be used exclusively for the purpose it was intended, purification, rectification, and refinement. To draw the dreamer away from, personal pursuits and to allow time for you to devote yourself, and all that you are, to God's glory (e.g. perfecting your inborn talent in some way for the glory of God, or writing a book, song, or screen play). See suggested course of action.

In addition, the following is a common word, expression, or usage (e.g. slang or cliché), or a 'probable' that is metaphorically represented by this number:

- "At sixes and sevens", meaning someone who is disorganized, in disarray, or in disagreement with something.

8: In addition to one of the following, and only if necessary, dreamer may also consider other multiples of this number. First, see Note 6 at the beginning of this category. With that, this dream has four meanings (one, two, or thee may apply). (1) This number denotes there is a "new beginning" starting for the dreamer. Favorably, because of God's grace, you will be starting all over again, with some kind of learning experience, be it a life experience, person, people experience, or work experience; this experience is meant to affect a spiritual maturity within you, leading to a better walk with God. You have a good mind and the ability to use it for your advancement. You have great potential for achievement and financial rewards; only keep God on top, starting from this moment forward, and you will be successful in your endeavors. (2) Dreamer, there is a struggle within you, between your old nature and your new nature; the leftovers of sin and the new beginnings of grace Your old nature is resisting everything that is spiritual and is opposing all the suggestions of the Holy Spirit and the ethical urgings of your conscience. This is spiritual circumcision of the heart. Fortunately, you are choosing to side with godly principles and to stand on your convictions. Dreamer, you will have success overcoming old things; there will be joy about your success, publicly. Now, the old has gone, and the new has come (2 Corinthians 5:17). God's providential blessing is upon you to increase. All things will be made beautiful in their own time. Do not boast of your increase, and be very mindful of your words. For example, words used in a patronizing and condescending manner, and of embracing a judgmental nature, for the universal law, with the same judgments, you judge others, so will you be judged, is still applicable to you. Furthermore, d ue to the intensity of your struggle, one of God's messengers is sent to give you the support needed at this time. Be aware that the new person within your midst may be that messenger. See suggested course of action. (3) This number denotes the union of a groom and bride resulting in a pregnancy. The dreamer, or if male, your spouse, is either actually pregnant, or will become pregnant very shortly. If not pregnant, and you desire children, continue to have faith in God, which is a resolute trust in the integrity of God and in His Word, He will have mercy on you, and grant you the desire of your heart, namely to birth children, suddenly and very soon. (4) If pregnancy is not an issue or desire, perhaps due to age, then your dream represents a spiritual pregnancy. A spiritual pregnancy denotes two states of affairs. A spiritual pregnancy denotes the fruit of your natural talents, pursuits, and morality is coming into full fruition. Your conduct towards others (for benefit or harm) will be openly manife sted before all. You will reap what you have sown. Further, regarding renewal and heartfelt repentance, dreamer by seeking pardon and expressing sincere feelings of regret and brokenness for having done something awry, or having made bad choices, and/or for having hurt someone. Will lift the heavy burdens you are carrying, because of you reaping what you've sowed, and release a spirit of renewal (a spiritual revival) within your life. See 2 Corinthians 7:10, 11. As well, a spiritual pregnancy denotes a ministry will be birth from within you, the dreamer. You are full of nurturing abilities; thus, you will become, responsible for a few young men and women being born again into the Kingdom of God (see John 3:1 -17). You know how to nurture and accept anyone; therefore, many will be drawn to you, including those, others call "ne'er-do-wells", via your ministry. Under your tutelage, those newly born into the Body of Christ will become strong and active, for the cause of the Kingdom of God. They will be known as persons who speak and does that which is good, counted amongst those who are faithful and submissive to God. Dreamer, be willing, obedient, prepared, and in place (accountable to a specific house of worship, church), for the birthing of your ministry and for those who will become born again because of your ministry. If necessary, see suggested course of action.

In addition, the following is a common word, expression, or usage (e.g. slang or cliché), or a 'probable' that is metaphorically represented by this number:

- An 8(a) firm, a company with special status that is given preferential treatment by the federal government because it is owned by socially and economically disadvantaged people (e.g. small businesses)

9: In addition to one of the following, and only if necessary, dreamer may also consider other multiples of this number. First, see Note 6 at the beginning of this category. With that, this dream has four meanings (one or all may apply). (1) Your dream is an expression of the joy and happiness you have experienced serving the Lord. You are encompassed about with righteousness and purity. The intents and motives of your heart are pure and righteous. You are honorable in the eyes of Go d. Many will be inspired by your faith in Christ, and by your humility, and unpretentiousness. Consequently, you are prepared for any spiritual conflict or evil activity that may come your way because of the pride, criticism, and littleness of mind of oth ers. Do not allow others to dampen your joy. (2) This type of dream is to bring about an awareness of an appointed inheritance of abundant peace, comforts, and sufficient wealth for the dreamer. At some point in the undisclosed future, honor and wealth will be bestowed upon the dreamer, if not already. You are becoming self-sufficient and unrelenting, capable of handling much responsibility, especially when required to make major decisions. Many will be inspired by your wisdom, confidence, and blameless actions. (3) You have learned the Christian values and principles that leads one to reach out and touch others in a loving and graceful manner; ultimately finding yourself promoting the genuine cause of Christ and the good of others. You have an open connection to divine revelation, which will at times be used on a prophetic platform. Properly developed, your link to prophetic revelation can and should be used to help others. If not already, you will inspire others to dream and to make their dreams come true. Dreamer, you are gifted in many areas, and you have access to prophetic wisdom, thus, you are required to be a transformational force in people's lives, via not neglecting the gift that is within you. You will now be led into situations, where you will show up when most needed, and then disappear without a thought of compensat ion. You will be dispatched on missions, to help believers who are facing urgent needs during a crisis, and/or in an emergency, and to give instant help, as well as, to express God's loving kindness, His grace, mercy, and compassion. You are sent to prot ect and defend those who obediently love God, and who is loved by God. An angel (perhaps disguised as human, or one, who is a true servant of God, with the Spirit of Truth within) will lead the way. Read, understand, and embrace Psalm 147. Altruistic, goodhearted, and generous service to God and others is beneficial at this time. Freely received, freely give. Dreamer, love God so completely that you will never forsake His service for any reason. If necessary, see suggested course of action. (4) To the unmarried: A potential spouse is looking carefully at you at present. Your faithfulness and unpretentiousness is beautiful in their sight. An introduction will present itself shortly. The question of the possibility of relocation may be asked.

In addition, the following is a common word, expression, or usage (e.g. slang or cliché), or a 'probable' that is metaphorically represented by this number:

- Somebody who, briefly arouses great interest or excitement but is soon forgotten again

10: This number refers to completeness, divine order, and God's provision, via His mercy, great love, goodwill, and favor shown you. This number also points to a visitation. Dreamer, God cares for you. You are a vested leader of a God led ministerial team within a church or a faith based community. You are to lead by wisdom, or you will shipwreck. Note, wisdom and folly, advertise similar want ads. Both broadcast they are deeply mysterious, meaningful, and fun. However, wisdom exalts God and leads to spiritual maturity and genuine joy, while folly cheapens and runs down life, bringing upon the head God's asperity and early death (also see Ecclesiastes 2:13, 1 Corinthians 6:12). The one, calls for open commitment, the other offers secret illicit relations and/or a sensual, secular knowledge. Depending on your choice, wisdom or folly, the Lord or the angel of death, soon will visit you. Therefore, be observant and pray, thus, found by God, mindful of Him. For the next ten days, start praying at least three time's daily, morning, afternoon, and evening. Petitioning God for the courage and sensibility to choose and apply His wisdom within your life, thereby averting God's asperity. If you lack wisdom, ask Jesus, who will give it to you generously without finding fault (James 1:2-5). By this, He will answer your most personal prayers, and cause others to fix, repair, and renew things around your living quarters. Moreover, seeing the blood, the angel of death will pass over you. So, consider it pure joy, whenever you face trials of many kinds, knowing that the testing of your faith develops perseverance, therefore, do not view your trials as an opportunity to run amok. Perseverance must finish its work that you may be mature and complete, lacking nothing. An honest acknowledgement of God's part in your circumstances will bring clarity, wholeness, strength of purpose, and closure to your present predicament. Moreover, according to divine order, as God blesses and prospers you, give Him a tenth of service. One example, tithing God 10% of your day, via 2 hours and 40 minutes of deeply private and personal pray, praise, and meditation on His Word (Joshua 1:8, 9). Moreover, if applicable, schedule consistent family bible study (e.g. twice weekly at 7:00 pm); thus giving Him your family. In addition, give Him, via your church, a tenth (tithe) of your harvest (revenues), while not forgetting to give offerings and benevolent donations that you may continue to prosper, lacking nothing. If living, bless your parents first, with your time and finances (e.g. date night twice weekly). Second, bless your assigned house of worship, as well as others (Ecclesiastes 11:1-6). This is God's order, His government, and His ways and means. By this, you will become one who can handle much. If necessary, see suggested course of action. If listed, and only if necessary, dreamer may also consider other multiples of this number. First, see Note 6 at the beginning of this category.

In addition, the following are common words; expressions or usages (e.g. slang or clichés) or a 'probable' that are metaphorically represented by this number:

- "Drop a dime" (to drop a dime in your dream), this denotes one should, has, or will inform the police, authorities that someone was, or is, involved in a crime
- To give someone a heads up
- The Decalogue
- Something successful, a great achievement, result, or action
- A company's annual audited financial report that must be sent to the Securities and Exchange Commission within 90 days of the end of the company's fiscal year (aka 10Q)

- A company's financial report, for a particular quarter, that must be sent to the Securities and Exchange Commission within 45 days of the end of the quarter (aka 10K)
- An X-ray safeguard; a rule for women of childbearing age that lower abdominal X-ray examination is allowed only during the ten days after the first day of the last menstrual period. This is to avoid radiation damage to an early embryo or fetus.

11: This number signifies a scheme of the devil (ref Luke 31, 32). He is using someone, to trick the dreamer into acting rebellious against God, via a spirit of confusion and disorder. It is only a test on your part, for you are incomplete; not yet finished or fully developed spiritually. You have emotional and/or psychological wounds that have not been healed from long ago, because of something, you did, or because of something, someone else did to you. As well, your deep-seated anger, challenges to forgive, your need for power, to be recognized, to excel, and pride, all contribute to a tendency within you to feed into confusion and disorder. All these issues are being challenged and checked within you by God. The person being used is one who defies and opposes God's moral codes, provoking divine judgment (divine reprimand for folly and sin). This person speaks abusively against whatever they do not understand, and is critical of those, who genuinely respect God's ways and means, especially the dreamer. This individual exalts sensual wisdom, intending to undermine divine order. They are forfeiting purpose for foolishness and ruin. Why have you been made privy to their secrets? This person is a snare to you. If tolerated, you will become entangled with their foolishness, feeding into their negativity. In the spirit of grace, your dream is to make known to the dreamer that emotional and psychological healing is available to you now, and what the enemy has meant for harm, God will use for your deliverance into wholeness, if you embrace His ways and means. First things first, there is a need for forgiveness and a "letting go" of the past, via prayer and heartfelt repentance to Jesus and man or woman. Repentance is seeking pardon for having done something awry, and for having hurt someone, and expressing sincere feelings of regret and brokenness. To Jesus pray, Psalm 51:1-19. To individuals, a phone call or a letter of apology is a good place to start, if appropriate. A conscientious and diligent effort on the part of the dreamer, to deeply reflect, on your emotional scars is also needed; perhaps some type of Christian counseling may help as well; nevertheless, there is a need to come to some kind of acceptance and closure. Again, be very aware that your emotional and physical suffering has been allowed by God that you might be humbled; thus, made ready and prepared to render your gifts unto the Lord properly. God will use your sufferings to instill His principles into your mind, and make His ways penetrate your heart. He or she who has suffered in the flesh has ceased from sinning (1 Peter 4:1) that the sacrificial offerings of your worship, service, and financial support to the ministry, might be a sweet smell unto the Lord. Moreover, the refinement process that you are going through, or will go through shortly, is meant to bring honor and glory to the One who died to redeem you. True conversion makes a marvelous change in the heart and life. It alters the mind, judgment, affections, and conversation. When a man is truly converted, it grieves him to think, how the time past of his life has been spent (Matthew Henry Concise Commentary). Subsequent, you will become productive and go forth, bearing spiritual fruit, counted amongst those who are sagacious; whose character is faithful, law-abiding, moral, open, scrupulous, sincere, straightforward, trustworthy, upright, reasonable in many situations, and submissive to God. Blessings, joy, protection, and prosperity will be yours. See suggested course of action. If listed, and only if necessary, may consider the interpretation for the number 1, as it relates to the repetitiveness of this number (11). Hence, the number 11; is a more intense expression of the number 1, in strength and forcefulness, spiritually, prophetically, and in application. First, see Note 6 at the beginning of this category.

In addition, the following is a common word, expression, or usage (e.g. slang or cliché), or a 'probable' that is metaphorically represented by this number:

- "The eleventh hour", last moment before something happens

12: This number refers to the management and control of something, the reality of God having chosen you for salvation, for special favor, and for a mission. This number also denotes God's government, His purpose, healing, and deliverance. Therefore, your dream speaks of why certain things have been allowed within your life or been done to you, your purpose, and your mission. Dreamer your past experiences and lessons learned will be used to strengthen your witness. Take care that you become sensitive to and respect the continuous acts of God's providential care. For, there is a promise that you will eat and do very well, on this side of eternity, and inherit eternal life. As well, the feeling of rest and serenity that comes with tru st in God's divine providence is available to you right now. Use your time to privately study your bible and publicly express your understanding to others. Believe nothing you cannot express, in its' entirety, openly and sensibly to the whole world. Do n ot lie, nor hide your beliefs or the beliefs and actions of others. Reject any form of isolated groups or beliefs that put forth, "we are the only ones". Jesus died for the world, for all who will believe, and not exclusively for any one sect or western denomination. Most importantly, do not die, emotionally, spiritually and/or physically, for any person, group, or unconventional cause, e.g., any "heaven's gate" or jihadist type cults, suicide bombers, kamikaze, ISIS, Aryan Alliance, any and all hate, anti-Christian, anti-Semitic groups. It is wise to stay within mainstream Judeo-Christianity. Remember to go to church and forsake not the gathering of yourself together with other mainstream Christians. For this is a strong part of God's government. You will be used, if not already, to usher others into a totally new and higher level of spiritual awareness (also see Matthew 28:19, 20). Even amongst the "broken", a spark of life remains hidden, awaiting your particular ministry, your unique way of presenting the gospel that they may be elevated. Dreamer, you will now, begin to noticeably experience the miraculous wonders of divine providence, the wisdom, care, and guidance provided by God that you might fulfill your mission, your purpose. See suggested course of action. If listed, and only if necessary, dreamer may also consider other multiples of this number. First, see Note 6 at the beginning of this category

In addition, the following are common words; expressions or usages (e.g. slang or clichés) or a 'probable' that are metaphorically represented by this number:

- Someone who is a disciple of Jesus Christ
- An addiction recovery program
- Using serial music techniques

13: Dreamer, because of your frailties and unwise and foolish passions, the sharp reproofs of the Word, and the severe censures of men, you are allowing a weakening of your core beliefs, namely a rejection of all or some of the original foundational teachings of Christ and His apostles to take root within you spiritually. Your attitude is leading to a mental and spiritual breakdown and corruption, opening the door for demons to run havoc within your life and to bring you down to desolation. You are forfeiting purpose for foolishness and ruin. Favorably, because of grace (the free and unmerited favor and beneficence of God) and the many mercies of God extended to you, your dream is only a warning and not an official declaration. Dreamer, utilizing the powerful resources of prayer and heartfelt repentance to Jesus and man or woman, via seeking pardon and expressing sincere feelings of regret and brokenness for having done something awry and/or for having hurt someone, see 2 Corinthians 7:10, 11. Coupled with fasting, a changed mindset, serious re-consideration of God's ways and means, and an honest acknowledgement of God's hand within your life, then then the severe impact of your choices and actions upon your life, can be reversed and damages repaired (also see Ezekiel 33:12-19). See suggested course of action.

In addition, the following is a common word; expression or usage (e.g. slang or clichés) or a 'probable' that is metaphorically represented by this number:

- **"13ᵗʰ birthday":** If applicable, dedicate your child to the Lord, and teach your children the benefits of wise and sensible thinking. While the dedication is by faith, have a literal private and personal ceremony amongst your immediate family for this dedication, a "quasi" bar mitzvah (a bar mitzvah is a ritual ceremony that marks the 13ᵗʰ birthday of a Jewish boy, after which he takes full responsibility for his moral and spiritual conduct). This ceremony can be done for girls too; a 'quasi' debutante ball (a very formal event where a young lady makes her debut into society, after which she takes full responsibility for her moral and spiritual conduct). Your children will sit, and be rulers, amongst the righteous. For they are chosen and part of a royal priesthood, a holy nation, a people for God's own possession that they and you may proclaim the excellencies of Him, who has called you and them.

- A complex musical chord that, in addition to a seventh, also contains the interval of a thirteenth

14: This number refers to deliverance, remembrance, restoration, and service. Dreamer, freedom from bondage, domination by evil, and hardship, is beginning for you. Dreamer, you are asked to give careful thought regarding your bondages and hardships, considering how things are, and have been for you, for your experiences have prepared you for ministry. From this day forward, God will bless you. Therefore, go and offer prayers, supplications, and thanksgiving before your Lord and Savior, Jesus Christ, for He is forgiving, compassionate, long-suffering, and full of loving-kindness, restoring more favorable conditions. Note, although your life is (or will become) very busy and full of concerns; it is advised that you do not forget your personal relationship with Christ, nor neglect the devotions that keep that personal relationship healthy. Nor must you allow yourself to be annoyed with other acts of devotion, e.g. family bible study and other quality times, fellowshipping with other believers, church attendance, acknowledging God's goodness to you, to others, and the like. Additionally, in time, you may find yourself assistant to a high-ranking leader within a ministry, perhaps in the position of personal aide, leadership counselor, associate pastor, or CEO of your individual ministry. If necessary, see suggested course of action. If listed, and only if necessary, dreamer may also consider other multiples of this number. First, see Note 6 at the beginning of this category.

15: This number refers to deliverance, freedom, grace (the free and unmerited favor and beneficence of God), rejection, rest, and retribution. Dreamer deliverance and freedom from bondage, domination by evil, and hardship, is beginning for you. Grace will be shown you, via a probationary period, however, regard this probationary period with sincere alarm. This probationary period decreed might be a proving by trial (e.g. a wilderness experience); by humiliation and servitude (Judges 13:1; Acts 13:21, 22); or by waiting (Acts 7:23-30). This probationary season points to grace, leads to repentance, and ends in revival and renewal. During this season, you are counseled to begin implementing godly principles that will move you toward discipline and humility, while embracing faith and love of God. Regularly, thank God for His patience, long-suffering, and grace, while you get things decent and in order. Moreover, you are to reject people, places, and circumstances that hinder spiritual clarity, growth, and stability. Additionally, your Lord and Savior will contend with those who contend with you during your deliverance season. In time, through the workings of grace, there will be deliverance, freedom, and rest for you. It will be known that the Lord is your Savior and your Redeemer, the Mighty One of Jacob. If necessary, see suggested course of action. Additionally, if applicable, your children will be saved. If listed, and only if necessary, dreamer may also consider other multiples of this number. First, see Note 6 at the beginning of this category.

16: This number refers to true devotion, love, freedom, and salvation. Dreamer, you are not under the law, because of love. Read, understand, and earnestly embrace John 3:16-18, Acts 15:11, Ephesians 2:4-10, Acts 15:11. Do not allow anyone to compel you to follow a set of regimented and legalistic rules to prove holiness and righteousness. Nor must you allow yourself to be annoyed with acts of devotion (e.g. family bible study and other quality times, fellowshipping with other believers, church attendance, acknowledging God's goodness to you, to others, and the like). You are free, saved, and declar ed righteous by grace (the free and unmerited favor and beneficence of God). Jesus loves you just the way you are. Literally, thank God for you and for who you are becoming. From this time forward, so speak and act as those who are going to be judged by the law of liberty, see James 2:12, 13. See suggested course of action. If listed, and only if necessary, may consider the interpretation for the number 4, as it relates to this number squared; see Note 6 at the beginning of this category.

In addition, the following are common words; expressions or usages (e.g. slang or clichés) or a 'probable' that are metaphorically represented by this number:

- One who is approaching their 16th birthday, aka "sweet sixteen"
- A note that has the time value of one-sixteenth of a whole note

17: This number refers to beauty, spiritual order, and victory. Dreamer, although you are physically very attractive, the depth of your beauty is primarily hidden deep within you. Given that, you are found to be incomplete or immature regarding spiritual order. Examples of spiritual order: God is the head of Christ, Christ is the head of every man, and man is the head of woman (1 Corinthians 11:3- 12). In other places it is written, seek first His Kingdom and His righteousness, and all these things will be given you; to obey (God's word) is better than sacrifice. To do what is right and just, is more acceptable to the Lord than sacrifice (Matthew 6:33; 1 Samuel 15:22; Proverbs 21:3). You ought to have faith in God, which is a resolute trust in the integrity of God and in His Word for your earthly relations as well as for your heavenly affairs, instead of being hasty, tru sting earthly sensual wisdom rather than the living God. God's spiritual order is intended to affect a deep abiding commitment and obedience to Christ. Submissiveness to His ways and means is beautiful in His sight. This beauty is so deep that it emanate s outwardly, humbleness, prudence, tactfulness, and unpretentiousness; setting you up for victory in all your dealings. If necessary, see suggested course of action.

18: This number refers to one who is counseled to live by God's principles, precepts, and statutes, for this is the Lord's will. His standards are meant to be a hedge of protection around you, to keep you from hurt, harm, and danger, and to support life and living. His principles are not there to be obstacles to your progress, or to be a bore to you. Obedience, at this time, is also preparing and maturing you to reach those who have fallen away from Christ; this is y our mission. When you choose to do things His way, you give God pleasure, in that you perform His will. Unfortunately, your will, your "ways and means", will only attract spiritual bondage; captivity, destruction, and judgment (divine reprimand for folly and sin); thus, this warning dream. Dreamer, you are attempting to establish a relationship with the Father according to your will. When a person accepts by faith God's grace, he or she gives God, as it were, pleasure, in that he or she has performed God's will, by respecting that the atoning work of Jesus on the Cross is enough to justify righteousness within a believer's life. And this, with a confident and unquestionable belief in the validity of your salvation, and the atoning work of the cross; and loving the Lord your God with all your heart, and with all your soul and with all your strength. Dreamer, an acceptance of God's grace and truly understanding what that means, positive change can come. See suggested course of action. If listed, and only if necessary, dreamer may also consider other multiples of this number. First, see Note 6 at the beginning of this category.

In addition, the following is a common word, expression, or usage (e.g. slang or cliché), or a 'probable' that is metaphorically represented by this number:

- A tractor-trailer rig

19: Dreamer, it is necessary that you bring to remembrance your former state, when you were enslaved to sin. Now that you have been set free from sin, you have become a servant of God. The benefits you reap, as a servant of Jesus, leads to holiness and the end-result is eternal life (Romans 6:21, 22). To keep you humble, repentant, and watchful, you would do well to remember the time when you were a servant of sin, devoted to iniquity, embracing vanity, and reaping the same. What benefit did you reap at that time from the things you now disdain, the filth, and foolishness of it all? Therefore, remember the benefits of being a servant of God. For this number also refers to one telling, declaring, and making known the Scriptures. Your time of missions is upon you. You are now being asked to devote yourself to embracing God's divine order that you may mature. You are sent to those who are spiritually dead, yet a spark of life is hidden within them (also see Matthew 28:19, 20). Dreamer; via divine order, go on to perfection through faith in God (a resolute trust in the integrity of God and in His Word). See suggested course of action.

In addition, the following is a common word, expression, or usage (e.g. slang or cliché), or a 'probable' that is metaphorically represented by this number:

- A drinking place for golfers, especially the bar of a clubhouse

20: This number refers to expectancy of something great, your spiritual maturity, and your potential. Your dream hints at the hidden power within you to manifest the desires of your heart, and God's will, for your life. First, there is a need to, humbly acknowledge the living and eternal King Jesus, via prayer, for having mercifully restored your soul (Psalm 23), and for His faithfulness towards you. Moreover, ask Jesus to reveal His new will for your life. The awareness of the presence of the Hand of God over your life, during this season, will become the banner, so to say, over your hea d. Much love will be revealed to you that you might respond in acceptance of the yoke of God, see Matthew 11:29, 30. Having accepted His yoke, your capacity to relate to God, to be faithful despite dark clouds, and to subdue your evil inclinations, will increase. You will also be given authority to preside over a group of people. Additionally, the desires of your heart, those that are expedient, will begin to manifest. If necessary, see suggested course of action. If listed, and only if necessary, dreamer may also consider other multiples of this number. First, see Note 6 at the beginning of this category.

In addition, the following is a common word, expression, or usage (e.g. slang or cliché), or a 'probable' that is metaphorically represented by this number:

- A twenty-dollar bill (perhaps this is an offering of some kind?)

21: In addition to one of the following, and only if necessary, dreamer may also consider other multiples of this number. First, see Note 6 at the beginning of this category. With that, this dream has two meanings (choose one). (1) The number twenty-one refers to promotion to a top leadership position. You are active, conscientious, diligent, productive, resourceful, and very hard working. You do what you do, to the best of your ability, and you take pleasure, in it. Therefore, you will be gradually advanced, until you are in a top leadership position. You will lead according to all that your soul desires. Drea mer, those who God does a great kindness to, and has a great kindness for, He makes helpful to His church, as well. Hence, your abilities, skills, and advancement are primarily purposed to be resources instrumental in delivering God's people out of oppressive situations. You are designed for this particular mission. Since you are the one destined for this service, you are predisposed to do His will. Those whom God commissions for any service, the Holy Spirit immeasurably qualify you for it. Yo u may speak boldly, and you will be heard and heeded. The actions, events, procedures, and dealings connected with this mission, have been determined and are unalterable. They have thus far led you to this point, this moment in time, and they will lead you on further. Please note, the fact that God uses people who are, perhaps, out of His will, maybe the dreamer, does not mean that He approves of evil. If God therefore will deliver or support His people, He can use anybody He chooses, and any means necessary, per His choosing, in effecting their deliverance and/or support. In this case, He has chosen you. Do not be overly sinful in your ways from this time forward. See suggested course of action. (2) Your dream denotes one, namely the dreamer, who is one of God's end-time prophets; thus, the troubling visions you've been experiencing, especially concerning God's people, the church, and others. It is suggested that you, the dreamer, go on a three-week period of fasting and prayer. Pray and God will direct you as to the kind of fast to commit too. Moreover, in response to your prayer and fasting, God will send one of His messengers to explain your visions. Note, be aware that the stranger within your midst may be that messenger. It may very well be the person, at present, you don't quite take a liking too. He or she comes to lead the way. The messenger will lead and guide you through your time of "affliction of the soul", make good use of this opportunity. Additionally, they will not feed your vanity; therefore, do not be, conceited in your attitude. Also, meditate upon Psalm 10 and other Psalms. Use the Psalms, to vent your frustration because of your enemies, as a form of supplication, as a venue to express your regret over sin, and to offer praise and thanksgiving to God. However, always be alert that you are in spiritual warfare and the enemy of your soul is real and present, for this number is also the number of unbelief, wickedness, and Satan, who is a tempter of humankind, this archangel, demon comes to oppose spiritual intimacy with Christ. During this time, also be mindful of your words and do not boast of your increase. See suggested course of action.

In addition, the following is a common word, expression, or usage (e.g. slang or cliché), or a 'probable' that is metaphorically represented by this number:

- A card game known as "21" or blackjack

22: This number refers to poor leadership, increased disorganization, wastefulness, and unpreparedness. Dreamer, you are found unprepared and thus lacking. Question, what choices are you making that have caused you to be unprepared for your encounter with the blessings and promises of God? Due to your insecurity, and unstableness, lack of ability, and/or skill, in one way or another, your efforts have proven ineffective. Perhaps sagacious delegation and a humble acceptance of advice will prove helpful. Dreamer, it is suggested that you render your leadership style, organizational style, "last minute" behavior, without care of quality attitude, and greediness, obsolete, and began anew attempting to move forward, using different tactics to overcome unproductive habitual lifestyle choices, and for maneuvering through this thing we call life in ministry, in a mo re, better way. Nonetheless, if no authentic and earnest change is adopted and that right now there will be a breakdown, collapse, or dissolution of your undertaking. See suggested course of action. If listed, and only if necessary, may consider the interpretation for the number 2, as it relates to the repetitiveness of this number (22). Hence, the number 22; is a more intense expression of the number 2, in strength and forcefulness, spiritually, prophetically, and in application. First, see Note 6 at the beginning of this category.

In addition, the following are common words; expressions or usages (e.g. slang or clichés) or a 'probable' that are metaphorically represented by this number:

- **"Catch-22"** — a situation in which whatever outcome somebody desires is impossible to attain because the rules work s against it.
- A small handgun with a .22 caliber

23: This number refers to expiry. Whether this is an emotional, physical, or a spiritual coming to an end, is dependent upon the goings-on in the life of the dreamer. With that, this dream has two meanings (choose one). (1) If dreamer is experiencing medical issues or concerns, be it emotional or physical, at the time of the dream; your dream is one of God's ways of breaking it to you gently, preparing you for one of life's common denominators, and if heeded, can prevent you from being emotionally blindsided by loss. As your dream is a notice, it symbolizes shortness of life. Dreamer is urged to seek medical attention as soon as possible. Dreamer, stop putting off getting medical attention, and go get yourself some help from a doctor or medical facility, and don't stop until you are correctly diagnosis and healed. Do not settle for, they can't find anything wrong. Something urgent is happening within your body, as your dream is an alarm. Moreover, call for the elders of your church, for it is through their prayers of faith and anointing of oil upon you that sin is forgiven and "spiritual" healing bestowed, and perhaps physical healing[36]. This is a true saying, thus it is time to have faith in God. Additionally, it is always a good time to get your house and papers in order (e.g. insurances, bequeaths, untold truths that need to be said), and always a good time to gather family together for prayer, support, wisdom, and truthfulness (Ecclesiastes 12:6). In addition, your entire dream, whether it leans towards emotional, physical, or spiritual trouble, suggests if you are willing to love yourself enough to live, meaning, if you are willing to rectify your ways to ward off the coming trouble, then you will live. This includes your diet, activities, relationships, associations, friendships, partying, and your lack of Christian fellowship. Nevertheless, dreamer, for someone who has met Jesus, we experience Him in the little graces, the big miracles, the ordinary days, and the curious moments. He is with us, leading us onward, even sharing our tears. This same Jesus trustworthy in life, even when we are not, can be trusted at the ending of life, for He is the resurrection (John 11:25, 26). If we love Jesus and love our neighbor as we love ourselves, there is nothing in this world or the next to fear. Love is what we take with us, and love is what awaits us when we have finally arrived. See suggested course of action. (2) If your dream was inundated with symbols that are not easily linked to your life activities, namely no medical concerns, then the following spiritual implication (spiritual expiry) may be heeded. Dreamer you are in a crisis of your faith, and your proverbial "oil" is low. Read, understand, and embrace Matthew 25:1-13; hence, there is an urgent need to, deeply invest in that, which causes one to be ready to meet the Savior sagaciously. Unfortunately, right now, your choices are proving to be like that of the foolish. As, your dream denotes one who is spiritually blind, by choice, having carelessly risked your life and soul, pretending to be blind to, and ignorant of, the things of God, His principles, and His creative works in and around you, in hopes to satisfy fleshly desires. Graciously, this type of dream comes that God may withdraw you from your purpose, and hide pride from you, for pride is a killer (Job 33:14-30). Therefore keep watch (pay attention to your whole self), because you do not know the day or the hour. God's love is calling you back to Him; forgiveness will cover all your mistakes from this day forward. In addition, your entire dream, whether it leans towards emotional, physical, or spiritual trouble, suggests if you are willing to love yourself enough to live, meaning, if you are willing to rectify your ways to ward off the coming trouble, then you will live. It is a wicked thing to choose death, when God is saying live. Now give careful thought to this from this day on. From this day forward, perceive God's grace, and embrace the lovethat is calling you home. No longer, pretend that you do not sense His providence within your life and, when applicable, let it be known publicly, and God will bless you. See suggested course of action

24: This number refers to a chosen high priest. Dreamer, you are chosen and destined to be consecrated as a high- ranking cleric[35]. Your family is a chosen people, a royal priesthood, a holy nation, a people belonging to God, that you all may worship and declare the praises of Him who called you out of darkness into His wonderful light. Once you were not a people, but now you are a people of God; once you had not received mercy, but now you have received mercy. Therefore, now, you are urged, to abstain from sinful desires, which war against your soul and to go on to spiritual maturity. Live such good lives among others that though they accuse you of doing wrong, they may see your good deeds and glorify God (1 Peter 2:9-12). If listed, and only if necessary, dreamer may also consider other multiples of this number. First, see Note 6 at the beginning of this category.

In addition, the following are common words; expressions or usages (e.g. slang or clichés) or a 'probable' that are metaphorically represented by this number:

- "Round-the-clock", "day-and-night" care (e.g. hospice, nursing)
- Something permanent, constant, or unceasing

25: In addition to one of the following, and only if necessary, dreamer may also consider the interpretation for the number 5, as it relates to this number squared. First, see Note 6 at the beginning of this category. With that, this dream has two meanings (choose one). (1) This number denotes some manner of spiritual, emotional, and intellectual elevation or exaltation within the life of the dreamer; couple this with the following. Dreamer you have been endowed with a heart that understands knowledge. Your heart aspirations are to understand knowledge, which leads to godly wisdom.

Favorably, your dream implies that you will be gifted with miraculous aid to help you overcome some intellectual difficulties; thus, elevating you above the barriers of mental and emotional limitations, and aid to help support you in your understanding of deep truths, that you might learn in order to teach, and learn in order to do. For, God has appointed you, a prophet or prophetess to His people, and your purpose must meet preparation; thus the miraculous aid. God will touch your mouth to give you divine messages for His people and for individuals. This will help you go forward, with faith, expressing your devotion to, and love for, Jesus, His teachings, and for other Believers. Dreamer, to not, carry out your purpose within the mandates and confines of God's orders and principles, is to cause your gifting to destroy you. Just say and truly believe, "I will exalt you, God, for you have lifted me up" (Psalm 30:1). (2) Is there a need to repent to God, or someone for something? If not, perhaps to forgive or to "take the higher ground", regarding a relationship issue with another. Nevertheless, the number twenty -five denotes an earnest need to repent to, Jesus and man or woman. Repentance is seeking pardon for having done something awry, and for having hurt someone, and expressing sincere feelings of regret and brokenness. To Jesus pray, Psalm 51:1-19. To individuals, a phone call or a letter of apology is a good place to start. See Romans 6:1-23, 2 Corinthians 7:10, 11. See suggested course of action.

26: In addition to one of the following, and only if necessary, dreamer may also consider other multiples of this number. First, see Note 6 at the beginning of this category. The number twenty-six refers to a personal transformation, and healing, a victim of circumstances, and a nefarious leader. With that, this dream has three meanings (choose one). (1) Dreamer, from this moment forward choose good habits and deeds, e.g. good stewardship and commitment to ministry; speak to yourself what is true and good, see Philippians 4:8, and choose good nutritional habits that you might remain in good health. These choices will help you progress forward towards your transformation, freedom, and healing, and help guide you toward, and enable you to fulfill, your purpose. All these blessings are rain. Dreamer, as one perfects him or herself, God helps by sending 'rains of blessings', then situations prosper. The rain is coming! As well, there will be clarity and freedom in the way you communicate yourself to others, especially prophetically. Thus; from this time forward, so speak and act as those who are judged by the law of liberty; see James 2:12, 13. (2) Dreamer, you have been, or is, under a nefarious leader or you are the wicked leader. If, dreamer is actually, in your awaked life, under bad religious leadership, you are considered a kind of "prisoner of war" (spiritually). Moreover, the spirit of the ruler has risen up against you, making your way hard to minister. Consequently, their actions and behaviors are causing a silent rage, animosity, perhaps rebellion within you against God and them. Dreamer, if, and when the spirit of the ruler rises up against you, leave not your place; for yielding pacifies great offences (Ecclesiastes 10:4), and it produces endurance. Nonetheless, favorably, God is fighting for you. He will contend w ith those who contend with you. He will be what you need Him to be during this season in your life, just call on Him. Therefore, don't give up. Everyone will know that God is your Savior, your Redeemer, your help in despairing times. His mercy has been extended so that you may draw in, the wisdom of His word, be transformed, and live and go forth spreading the gospel of Jesus Christ to others. You will be removed, and placed under new leadership, be patience, all good things will manifest in due ti me. If necessary, see suggested course of action. (3) If dreamer is actually considered religious leader of some kind, e.g. bishop, deacon, deaconess, elder, evangelist, minister, overseer, pastor, pope, preacher, priest, rabbi, superintendent, teacher, or any cleric or ecclesiastical leader type role, you are the bad leader, and your dream comes as serious rebuke and alarm. Dreamer, you've been slipping into darkness, mistreating God's people, harmful to those about you, and trampling on those you consider less than. Taking advantage of their spiritual and natural poverty, necessity, and inability to help themselves, making them poorer and needier than they were before connecting with you, while you give nothing in return (especially in the form of service). You are an enemy to God's people; therefore, God will become your enemy. God will now begin to fight against you that His people may be free. Although, you might deny these allegations or state that you not the one responsible for the dwindling down of your ministry, and thus, continue with the same attitude and behaviors; making no attempt at change, you will lose greatly. Essentially the battle is over, and you have lost. See suggested course of action.

27: This number refers to expectancy of getting divine approval and release. Dreamer you are one chosen and released now, to preach and/or teach the Gospel of Jesus Christ. Go forth in confidence that God has approved, ordained, and anointed you for your task ahead, for this is your purpose. If listed, and only if necessary, dreamer may also consider other multiples of this number. First, see Note 6 at the beginning of this category.

28: This number refers to the process of sanctification within the life of the dreamer, as well as, miraculous strength and courage. Dreamer, you will be imparted the strength and courage needed to endure your process of sanctification, which is preparing you for a great ministry. Graciously, and compassionately, God has you in a process of sanctification at present, recognize, and respect the process. Sanctification is a process by which one is made holy via fasting, prayer, and a genuine return to living life on God's terms and not yours. Your attitude, mind, mental health, understanding, perspective, and reasoning are being renewed and transformed. Moreover, your dream strongly emphasizes the need to guard your unique gift of words. Additionally, be encourage, you will inherit eternal life. If necessary, see suggested course of action. If listed, and only if necessary, dreamer may also consider other multiples of this number. First, see Note 6 at the beginning of this category.

29: This number refers to reaping and sowing. Dreamer, you are entering into a season within your life, where you can now expect to reap what you've sown thus far. Your natural talents, pursuits, and morality are coming into full fruition. This season will expose the dreamer's character, good or bad, as well; your conduct towards others (for benefit or harm) will be openly manifested before all. You will reap the fruit of your doings (good or bad). Thus, good or bad is hidden within this season for you. Things sown, promises made, and desires hoped for, are coming into full fruition. Additionally, that which you have begotten emotionally, mentally, and/or spiritually will also arise within your children and/or within those you aid, comfort, encourage, guide, help, minister to, nurture, support, teach, or tend to. Dreamer, it is not too late to always, look for ways to build up the people around you. You do, what you think others should be doing. For, when you sow grace and mercy, you will reap the same in return. As well, one whose speech is gracious will have the King for a friend (Proverbs 22:11). Nonetheless, dreamer you will reap what you have sown, and the words you've spoken, they will be presented, back to you, in the same manner you presented words to others (e.g. words spoken to others, without compassion, empathy, and/or understanding, will be spoken to you without compassion). As you have done unto others, under the same or similar circumstances, it will be done unto, for empathy and compassion begets empathy and compassion. You will reap accordingly (Ezekiel 33:13, 14-20). For the Lord your God will bless (or judge) you in all your harvest and in all the work of your hands. Moreover, this number hints to a move from one place to another, a departure of some sort.

30: Your dream comes to stir the dreamer to action, marking the right moment (the present). Dreamer, you are blessed with a heart that understands knowledge, and not without reason. You are one who is given the means and gifting to study and teach. As well, you have access to prophetic wisdom and is purposed to be a transformational force in other people's lives. The heart of your ministry should focus on teaching about the essence of God, the Blood of Christ, and divine order. If not already, you should initiate your ministry now. With that said, this number also refers to aspirations, concentration of the mind on spiritual matters, such as achieving a closer unity with God, the beginning of ministry, maturity for ministry, and divine authority to minister, all are aspects of the season of life the dreamer is entering. Just say and truly believe, "I will exalt you, God, for you have lifted me up" (Psalm 30:1). If necessary, see suggested course of action. If listed, and only if necessary, dreamer may also consider other multiples of this number. First, see Note 6 at the beginning of this category.

In addition, the following is a common word; expression or usage (e.g. slang or clichés) or a 'probable' that is metaphorically represented by this number:

Something happening "once-a-month", prearranged, recurrent, periodic cycle, frequent, a period or season, mid-term

31: The number thirty-one has two meanings (choose one). (1) Dreamer, the Lord has the power and authority to give you the land He has promised to give to you, for you, and for you to allocate land to His chosen people (e.g. 70 acres of lan d for 70 families, including you, at no cost to the families, a community). Your authority and power to acquire develop, and build homes on the land is an actual extension of God's outstretched hand of the gift of the land to you. Note, prudent stewardshi p and ethicalness is of upmost important, and if earnestly embraced, will lead to your continued prosperity. If necessary, see suggested course of action. (2) Your dream refers to reaping and sowing. You can now expect to reap the results of something sown, the fruit, consequence, and/or effect of what you've sown. Dreamer, you are entering into a season within your life, where you can now expect to reap what you've sown thus far. Your natural talents, pursuits, and morality are coming into full fruition. This season will expose the dreamer's character, good or bad, as well; your conduct towards others (for benefit or harm) will be openly manifested before all. You will reap the fruit of your doings (good or bad). Thus, good or bad is hidden within this season for you. Things sown, promises made, and desires hoped for, are coming into full fruition. Additionally, that which you have begotten emotionally, mentally, and/or spiritually will also arise within your children and /or within those you aid, comfort, encourage, guide, help, minister to, nurture, support, teach, or tend to. Dreamer, it is not too late to always, look for ways to build up the people around you. You do, what you think others should be doing. For, when you sow grace and mercy, you will reap the same in return. As well, one whose speech is gracious will have the King for a friend (Proverbs 22:11). Nonetheless, dreamer you will reap what you have sown, and the words you've spoken, they will be presented, back to you, in the same manner you presented words to others (e.g. words spoken to others, without compassion, empathy, and/or understanding, will be spoken to you without compassion). As you have done unto others, under the same or similar circumstances, it will be done unto, for empathy and compassion begets empathy and compassion. You will reap accordingly (Ezekiel 33:13, 14-20). For the Lord your God will bless (or judge) you in all your harvest and in all the work of your hands. If necessary, see suggested course of action.

32: The promises that were made between you and God; you promised to worship and serve Jesus, and in return God promised you, life more abundantly on this side of eternity, and eternal life. If you have kept your promise to worship and serve, God's promise to you of abundance, on this side of eternity, will manifest very shortly. Read, understand, and embrace Numbers 6:24-26. The realization of those promises is happening. Moreover, you have been blessed with the power of speech and wisdom that converts souls to the Kingdom of God. Your ministry is primarily that of winning unregenerate souls to Christ. If not already, you should initiate your ministry now. Seriously, be mindful of greed, under the pretense of prosperity teachings. If necessary, see suggested course of action. If listed, and only if necessary, dreamer may also consider other multiples of this number. First, see Note 6 at the beginning of this category.

33: This number refers to a promise made you by God, and the fulfillment of that promise made to you. The promise was made when you first invited Christ into your life. It will, very shortly manifest. If listed, and only if necessary, may consider the interpretation for the number 3, as it relates to the repetitiveness of this number (33). Hence, the number 33; is a more intense expression of the number 3, in strength and forcefulness, spiritually, prophetically, and in application. First, see Note 6 at the beginning of this category.

34: This dream denotes some manner of spiritual, emotional, and intellectual elevation or exaltation within the life of the dreamer; couple this with the following. Dreamer you have been endowed with a heart that understands knowledge. Your heart aspirations are to understand knowledge, which leads to godly wisdom. Favorably, your dream implies that you will be gifted with miraculous aid to help you overcome some intellectual difficulties; thus, elevating you above the barriers of men tal and emotional limitations, and aid to help support you in your understanding of deep truths, that you might learn in order to teach, and learn in order to do. For, God has appointed you, a prophet or prophetess to His people, and your purpose must meet preparation; thus the miraculous aid. God will touch your mouth to give you divine messages for His people and for individuals. This will help you go forward, with faith, expressing your devotion to, and love for, Jesus, His teachings, and for other Believers. Dreamer, to not, carry out your purpose within the mandates and confines of God's orders and principles, is to cause your gifting to destroy you. Just say and truly believe, "I will exalt you, God, for you have lifted me up" (Psalm 30:1). If listed, and only if necessary, dreamer may also consider other multiples of this number. First, see Note 6 at the beginning of this category.

35: This number refers to hope, trust, and confidence towards a person or situation. Dreamer, you can trust the person or situation that is before you, at present. If listed, and only if necessary, dreamer may also consider other multiples of this number. First, see Note 6 at the beginning of this category.

36: This number refers to a special righteous person, namely the dreamer, who is leading a holy and humble life. Dreamer, you will be used, if not already, to usher others, particularly those who are presently at odds with you and other Christians, into a totally new and higher level of spiritual awareness and selflessness. Dreamer, even amongst the broken, a spark of life remains hidden, awaiting your particular ministry, your unique way of presenting the gospel. You will appear when needed, and then disappear without thought of anything in return. By fulfilling your mission and remaining humble, you will be worthy of your wage. Moreover, it is promised that you will eat and do very well, on this side of eternity, and inherit eternal life. Note humility is the key to your success (requisite). Know the full meaning of the word and define your life by it, for you must be an exemplar of humility. Additionally, dreamer, you will find yourself supporting someone spiritually, emotionally, and financially; and if it were not for you, he or she would implode, or die literally. If listed, and only if necessary, dreamer may also consider other multiples of this number. First, see Note 6 at the beginning of this category.

37: This number refers to a prophecy or strong teaching given the dreamer. Dreamer, there has been a word from the Lord given you recently, by a God sent prophet or prophetess. However, because of the nature of the message, and the strength or force it was given, you may have not received it as a word that came from the Almighty God, but it did; thus, there is a need to heed the word of the Lord. See suggested course of action.

38: Your dream comes to warn the dreamer of the fatal consequences of unbelief and faint-heartedness, which are confusion, delay, slavery, and wandering. As well as, to warn you to take heed of sinning like those around you. Dreamer, if you would consider seriously, think carefully, what would be the end of your sin, you would be afraid of the beginnings of it. Dreamer, you have recently adopted a bourgeois mentality. This mentality is concerned only with your personal comfort, material wealth, and status, at any expense. You, now, having in yourself nothing that you respect more than power and greed, are willing to sacrifice all, God, principle, family, and friend, to the image or idol of vanity. Your new way is based on exploring alternatives to God's righteous principles, as well as, creating a sense of unity with the wickedness around you. This mentality sacrifices children, family, and morality to the hollowness of satisfying immoral desires and appetites. All carried out with the hope of finding happiness by pacifying jealously and covetousness. The selling-out of yourself over to immorality, allowing wickedness to prevail in your home, devaluing those you should be protecting and nurturing, while closing your eyes to it all, are all principles based on values that are not only vile, but also increasingly unstable. This way cries out against godly ethics, and its' end offends any sense of godliness. Your recklessness can be remedied by prayer and heartfelt repentance to Jesus and man or woman, seeking pardon and expressing sincere feelings of regret and brokenness for having done something awry and/or for having hurt someone, see 2 Corinthians 7:10, 11, also see Deuteronomy 6:10-15; 11:10-28, Jeremiah 14:10, James 5:19, 20. See suggested course of action. If listed, and only if necessary, dreamer may also consider other multiples of this number. First, see Note 6 at the beginning of this category.

In addition, the following is a common word, expression, or usage (e.g. slang or cliché), or a 'probable' that is metaphorically represented by this number:

- A handgun with a .38 caliber

39: In addition to one of the following, and only if necessary, dreamer may also consider other multiples of this number. First, see Note 6 at the beginning of this category. With that, this dream has two meanings (one or both may apply). (1) This number references or touches upon the dreamer's purpose. Dreamer, your purpose is one of becoming a forerunner for change, freedom, justice, and intellectual and spiritual illumination. You have the power to change history. Therefore, it is of upmost importance that you, energetically and boldly, began to elevate and promote the righteousness of Christ to those around you. You should take this path, now. If necessary, see suggested course of action. (2) This number refers to one experiencing a physical sickness or disease or a spiritual malady. If a physical sickness or disease is a concern, dreamer seek medical attention as soon as possible, and call for the elders of your church, for it is through their prayers of faith and anointing of oil upon you that sin is forgiven and healing is bestowed[36]. Pray Psalm 38:1-22. Have faith in this, for it will be by your faith that you will be healed wholly. This is a true saying. If a spiritual malady, dreamer, now, begin to choose good deeds and habits that will lead to the fulfillment of your God given purpose. For instance, seeking pardon and expressing sincere feelings of regret and brokenness for having done something awry and/or for having hurt someone, will lift heavy burdens you are carrying, because of you reaping what you've sown, this will release a spirit of renewal within your life, and will strengthen your resolve. See suggested course of action.

40: In addition to one of the following, and only if necessary, dreamer may also consider other multiples of this number. First, see Note 6 at the beginning of this category. The number forty refers to wisdom or folly, pregnancy, or a new mission. With that, this dream has three meanings (choose one). (1) As you are now ready to receive the deepest measure of understanding that you may ascend (or mature) from one level to the next higher one, it must be said that wisdom and folly, advertise similar want ads. Both broadcast that they are multifaceted, mysterious, meaningful, fun, and boundless. However, wisdom (godly, spiritual wisdom) exalts God and leads to maturity and genuine joy, while folly (sensual wisdom) devalues and runs down life, bringing upon the head God's asperity and early death (also see Ecclesiastes 2:13). The one, calls for open commitment, the other offers secret, illicit relations and a sensual, secular wisdom. When we do not have faith in God and in His covenant promises, principles, and comforts to humanity; His integrity, worth, and dignity are cheapened or diminished within us. To value or have faith in God, which is a resolute trust in the integrity of God and in His Word, is to please Hi m, for God's integrity, worth, and dignity, is His Word. Therefore, the attainment of a higher level can only come after you first have gleaned and put into practice the wisdom from the previous level; thus enlarging your capacity for the emergence of something higher and more mature, no longer "eating" vegetables. Petition God for the courage and sensibility to choose and apply His wisdom within your life. Then thank and praise Him, for His presence is in your midst. If necessary, see suggested course of action. (2) As this number also denotes a pregnancy, the dreamer, or if male, your spouse, is either actually pregnant, or will become pregnant very shortly. If literal, do take care, especially around the early and very important stages of pregnancy. God will give you the strength to carry the child. If not pregnant, and you desire children, continue to have faith in God, which is a resolute trust in the integrity of God and in His Word, He will have mercy on you, and grant you the desir e of your heart, namely to birth children, suddenly and very soon. (3) If pregnancy is not an issue or desire, perhaps due to age, then your dream represents a spiritual pregnancy. A spiritual pregnancy denotes one of two states of affairs. (a) A spiritual pregnancy denotes the fruit of your natural talents, pursuits, and morality is coming into full fruition. Your conduct towards others (for benefit or harm) will be openly manifested before all. You will reap what you have sown. The words you've spoken, they will be presented, back to you, in the same manner you presented words to others (e.g. words spoken to others, without compassion, empathy, and/or understanding, will be spoken to you without compassion). As you have done unto others, under the same or similar circumstances, it will be done unto, for empathy and compassion begets empathy and compassion. You will reap accordingly (Ezekiel

33:13, 14-20). For the Lord your God will bless (or judge) you in all your harvest and in all the work of your hands. Dreamer, it is not too late to always, look for ways to build up the people around you. You do, what you think others should be doing. For, when you sow grace and mercy, you will reap the same in return. As well, on e whose speech is gracious will have the King for a friend (Proverbs 22:11). Moreover, dreamer, by seeking pardon and expressing sincere feelings of regret and brokenness for having done something awry, or having made bad choices, and/or for having hurt someone, this will lift the heavy burdens you are carrying, because of you reaping what you've sowed, and release a spirit of renewal (a spiritual revival) within your life. See 2 Corinthians 7:10, 11. See suggested course of action. (b) A spiritual pregnancy also denotes a ministry will be birth from within you, the dreamer. You are full of nurturing abilities; thus, you will become, responsible for a few young men and women being born again into the Kingdom of God (see John 3:1-17). You know how to nurture and accept anyone; therefore, many will be drawn to you, including those, others call "ne'er-do-wells", via your ministry. Under your tutelage, those newly born into the Body of Christ will become strong and active, for the cause of the Kingdom of God. They will be known as persons who speak and does that which is good, counted amongst those who are faithful and submissive to God. Dreamer, be willing, obedient, prepared, and in place (accountable to a specific hou se of worship, church), for the birthing of your ministry and for those who will become born again because of your ministry.

In addition, the following is a common word, expression, or usage (e.g. slang or cliché), or a 'probable' that is metaphorically represented by this number:

- "40-winks" (the number 40 and winking is highlighted in some way). See category: Sleeping (Have forty winks)

41: Your dream was sent to encourage the dreamer. It implies that the dreamer is a hard worker concerning your duties, missions, and responsibilities. You devote yourself to work, as well as show concern for the betterment of your community at large; and with your organized, efficient approach, things are done resourcefully. You radiate security. You often forfeit your own desires for your family and anyone else you consider a responsibility, as well as, for any worthy cause. You will now reap the rewards of such diligence, including rest and graceful surroundings. If applicable, your children will reap the fruits of the blessing of your giving. Moreover, as you are able to handle great responsibility and wealth, and are one who is tolerant, you will experience receiving an act of kindness, monetarily, from someone who is affluent. Dreamer you are entering into a season within your life that will prepare you spiritually for the visitation of the Lord in your individual life. During this time, you will experience His love and presence, as you've never known it before. For, He is saying to you, "I will teach you godly wisdom". You will receive direct insight of divine truth. You will come to know, without a doubt, that God is the true source of your strength and wisdom, and He is your sufficiency. As a result, a greater love for self, family, and others will begin to manifest, affecting wholeness within your life. From here forward, speaks of God's "weaning" of a righteous person, the dreamer. Dreamer, do not be deceived, with affluence, power, and wealth, comes good and evil. Today, you will need to choose between good and evil; and set "checks and balances" within yourself, because you have innate tendencies to become extreme and will judge others according to your "extremisms". Embracing this side of yourself will cause you to be deemed inappropriate, and delayed at that moment, to be of service to the Kingdom of God. Regrettably, this will lead to you being unhappy, and unable to discern between truth and error, without you realizing your shortsightedness. Therefore, the "checks and balances" are meant to rectify the soul to increase its capacity to receive the blessings of the Lord more fully. Blessings; in this sense, is a state of high honor, spiritual beauty, and great illumination. Henceforth, in accordance with your decision as to how you shall continue from this day forward, will define your increase or the dwindling thereof, in your future and beyond. Note, if you choose to embrace the positive, this will lead to a great balancing of your theology, resulting in a belief that is complete, with solid attributes, and your inspiration will make for very good teaching. You would make an excellent apologist (witness) for the Kingdom of God. Seriously consider this branch of Christian theology. If necessary, see suggested course of action.

42: This number alludes to false religion, as well as, a visitation of the Lord. Your dream refers to the dreamer's spiritual conflict with the will of God and that of men. At present, you have attempted spiritual perfection via the teachings of erroneous religious guides, and other human means, both of which have led to deception and oppression, and have open the door for heavy demonic activity within your life. Graciously, God will come to offer salvation and deliverance, via one of God's anointed messengers. This messenger will come to rescue you out of an extremely severe or dire situation, a situation that is the consequence of your choices. Be aware that the stranger within your midst may be that servant. He or she comes to lead the way. Dreamer, give ear, if, or when, you choose to work out your opposition to God, there will be those, of wh ich you've surrounded yourself with, that will mock your spiritual growth, nonetheless, persevere. For, if you choose to do it the way of Jesus, because of your deliverance and freedom, there will be others who will respect your God and acknowledge His Po wer (see Isaiah 40:29-31). Again, you must choose to accept God's leading and guiding. See suggested course of action. If listed, and only if necessary, dreamer may also consider other multiples of this number. First, see Note 6 at the beginning of this category.

44: In addition to one of the following, if listed, and only if necessary, may consider the interpretation for the number 4, as it relates to the repetitiveness of this number (44). Hence, the number 44; is a more intense expression of the nu mber 4, in strength and forcefulness, spiritually, prophetically, and in application. First, see Note 6 at the beginning of this category. With that, this dream has five meanings (choose one). (1) If dreamer is presently experiencing a spiritual struggle within, that is very intensive. Dreamer, the intensity of your struggle, namely inner spiritual warfare because of your anger or rage issues or any other manner of darkness within, is actually the refining and purifying work of the Paraclete; therefore, persevere, for this struggle will cause the emergence of a more divine led wisdom within you. It will also be through these pains that the wisdo m of harmonizing, fear and love of the Lord within your life, will be imparted to you. Due to the intensity of your struggle, one of God's messengers is sent to give you the support needed at this time. Be aware that the new person within your midst may be that messenger. With that said, dreamer, you are encompassed about with righteousness and purity. The in tents and motives of your heart are pure and righteous. You are honorable in the eyes of God. Favorably, dreamer, you will have success overcoming old things; and there will be joy spiritually, as your dream is also an expression of the joy and happiness you will experience serving the Lord. Consequently, you are prepared for any spiritual conflict or evil activity that may come your way. Many will be inspired by your faith in Christ, unpretentiousness, and humility. Moreover, there will be success publicly, regarding some kind of enterprise, as your dream also denotes a company with special status that is given preferential treatment by the federal government because it is owned by socially and economically disadvantaged persons (e.g. small businesses); perhaps development of a market, or investment in new wireless technology, is an option (e.g. li fi). (2) If dreamer is actually expecting an inheritance of some kind, this type of dream is to bring about an awareness of an appointed inheritance of abundant peace, comforts, and sufficient wealth for the dreamer. At some point in the undisclosed future, honor and wealth will be bestowed upon the dreamer, if not already. You are becoming self-sufficient and unrelenting, capable of handling much responsibility, especially when required to make major decisions. Many will be inspired by your wisdom, confidence, and blameless actions. (3) Dreamer, you have learned the Christian values and principles that leads one to reach out and touch others in a loving and graceful manner; ultimately finding yourself promoting the genuine cause of Christ and the good of others. You have an open connection to divine revelation, which will at times be used on a prophetic platform. Properly developed, your link to prophetic revelation can and should be used to help others. If not already, you will inspire others to dream and to make their dreams come true. Dreamer, you are gifted in many areas, and you have access to prophetic wisdom, thus, you are required to be a transformational force in people's lives, via not neglecting the gift that is within you. You will now be led into situations, where you will show up when most needed, and then disappear without a thought of compensation. You will be dispatched on missions, to help believers who are facing urgent needs during a crisis, and/or in an emergency, and to give instant help, as well as, to express God's loving kindness, His grace, mercy, and compassion. You are sent to protect and defend those who obediently love God, and who is loved by God. An angel (perhaps disguised as human, or one, who is a true servant of God, with the Spirit of Truth within) will lead the way. Read, understa nd, and embrace Psalm 147. Altruistic, goodhearted, and generous service to God and others is beneficial at this time. Freely received, freely give. Dreamer, love God so completely that you will never forsake His service for any reason. (4) To the unmarried and if marriage is desired (male or female): A potential spouse is looking carefully at you at present. Your faithfulness and unpretentiousness is beautiful in their sight. An introduction will present itself shortly. The question o f the possibility of relocation may be asked. God will honor the union. Moreover, and if so desired, the union of the groom and bride will result in a literal pregnancy. Continue to have faith in God, which is a resolute trust in the integrity of God a nd in His Word, He will have mercy on you, and grant you the desire of your heart, namely to birth children of your own body, suddenly and very soon. (5) Your dream denotes a virus or inflammation of the liver, or a toxin disease affecting the liver, such as Jaundice or gallstone. If dreamer is ill, or is experiencing health related issues, seek medical attention immediately, your dream is a first step intervention and an alarm. Dreamer is also advised to call for the elders of your church, for it is through their prayers of faith and anointing of oil upon you that sin is forgiven and healing is bestowed[36]. Have faith in this, for it will be by your faith that you will be healed wholly. This is a true saying. See suggested course of action.

45: This number denotes that there is a need for the dreamer to maintain, preserve, and protect special relationships, especially the ones that mean the most, namely your relationship with Jesus, marriage, children, friendships, as well as, maintaining your ministry and education. Further, it is also suggested that you acquire some manner of knowledge regarding the continuance and maintenance of your particular ministry or endeavors, via school, seminars, and workshops. See suggested course of action. If listed, and only if necessary, dreamer may also consider other multiples of this number. First, see Note 6 at the beginning of this category.

In addition, the following is a common word, expression, or usage (e.g. slang or cliché), or a 'probable' that is metaphorically represented by this number:

- .45 caliber pistol

49: This number refers to remission of sins, via only the atoning work of Jesus on the cross. Dreamer needs to understand the cost of your salvation, and to learn to not be carried away by all kinds of strange teachings, or easily remov ed from the Gospel of Jesus Christ. We are not serving an angry God who cannot be embraced or pleased or a God that needs to be appeased via a set of regimented and legalistic rules to prove our dedication to Him, and to prove our holiness and righteousness, all of which are of no value to those who practice such. A deeper understanding of the meaning of the shed Blood of Christ for the remission of your sins, aka atonement, is needed. Read, understand, and embrace, Matthew 6:12 - 15, 18:23-35. Embracing, with a confident and unquestionable belief in the validity of the atoning work of the Cross, knowing that it is enough to justify righteousness within a believer's life. Moreover, by faith, you must deliberately, and purposef ully, offer you, your mind, spirit, and body in a sober, firm, and dignified manner, as a living sacrifice, holy and pleasing to God, as this is a spiritual act of worship. Loving the Lord your God with all your heart, and with all your soul and with all your strength, and it will be good with your soul. Dreamer, it is good for our hearts to be strengthened by God's love, via His grace. For, God's primary identity is love (John 3:16, 1 John 4:7, 16). By His word, God first loved us while we remained in sin, not thinking about Himself, nor desiring to appease Himself, yet He became our propitiation. Therefore, our service should not come from a mind-set of appeasing God, but from a space of gratefulness and love, declaring His worthiness of our praise. Dreamer, we were made alive with Christ even when we were dead in transgressions, it is by grace you have been saved through faith, and this not from yourself, it is the gift of God (Romans 4:16; Ephesians 2:1-10; Hebrews 13:9). With that said, dreamer, God will now separate you from your surroundings that hinder spiritual clarity, and draw you away from any trust in yourself that you might seek your life in Him alone, and confidently entrust yourself to His care. View this separation as a blessing from God and not as an evil thing has happen. The Holy Spirit will lead and guide you to discipline your will, strength, efforts, and pleasures, so that the whole energy of your being will be free, and open to receive the Holy Spirit inwardly. This promise comes by gra ce; and if applicable, is guaranteed to your offspring. Moreover, you must not allow yourself to be annoyed with acts of devotion, for example, family bible study and other quality times, fellowshipping with other believers, church attendance, acknowledgin g God's goodness to you, to others, and the like. See suggested course of action. If listed, and only if necessary, may consider the interpretation for the number 7, as it relates to this number squared; see Note 6 at the beginning of this category.

50: In addition to one of the following, and only if necessary, dreamer may also consider other multiples of this number. First, see Note 6 at the beginning of this category. With that, this dream has three meanings (choose one). (1) Your dream denotes that the Lord your God has chosen you, the dreamer, out of all the peoples on the face of the earth to be His people, to be His treasured possession. The Lord did not set His affection on you and choose you because you were better than other peoples, but it was because the Lord loved you and kept the oath He swore to your forefathers (Deuteronomy 7:1-8). Dreamer, a spark of life remains hidden inside of you, because you are God's child according to grace (the free and unmerited favor and beneficence of God). He wants to balance your understanding of things; thus, effecting wholen ess within your life, for you are now ready to receive the deepest measures of understanding, so that the enemy will no longer be able to manipulate your emotions so easily. Thus, you are beckoned this day to love the Lord your God, to walk in His ways, to embrace His commandments, statutes, and judgments, that you may live and multiply properly; and the Lord your God will bless you in your land. If you need only to believe that the Lord truly loves you, you will begin to walk in His ways and into His purpose for you. Dreamer, if you will accept the Heavenly Father's Words, via the Bible, and store up His principles and His ways and means, within you. Turning your ear to wisdom, and applying your heart to understanding, calling out for insight an d crying aloud for discernment, Jesus will meet you. This, coupled with a lifestyle of prayer and fasting, followed by appropriate application of wisdom, and you will know the Messiah, Christ Jesus, intimately, and find the knowledge of God you need. For the Lord gives wisdom and from His mouth comes knowledge and understanding. Then you will understand what is right and just and fair, every good path. When wisdom enters your heart and knowledge becomes sweet to your soul, discretion will protect you, understanding will guard you, and His Truth will lead you. To deliver you from the ways of wickedness, from demons whose words and ways are perverse, who attempt to cause you to walk in darkness gladly, whose paths are crooked and devious, causing you to leave straight paths (Proverbs 2:1-6, 9-15). The Holy Spirit is with you to help you throughout this entire process. This is one of God's covenant promises to you. Have faith in this. See suggested course of action. (2) Dreamer, you will be used, if not already, to usher others into a totally new and higher level of spiritual awareness. Even amongst the "broken", a spark of life remains hidden, awaiting your particular ministry, your unique way of presenting the gospel. You will appear when needed, and then disappear without thought of anything in return. Dreamer, by fulfilling your part and remaining humble, you will be worthy of your wage. You will eat and do very well, on this side of eternity, and inh erit eternal life. Humility is the key to your success (requisite). Know the full meaning of the word and define your life by it. Additionally, this is your year of restoration, restitution, freedom, and fullness of life. If necessary, see suggested course of action. (3) Your dream denotes one who has redirected your negative impulses, your natural inclinations to sin, especially your sexual desires. You have redirected your negative impulses towards righteous activities (e.g. doing good works), and have desired to make God's will your own will, having your mind and thoughts clinging faithfully to the greatness of God. You now are, decreed as one who is genuinely righteous. This type of spiritual worthiness, after receiving the Lord as your Savior, is by grace, faith, and doing good deeds, in your case, the re-directing of your sinful inclinations, with the help of the Holy Spirit. Moreover, as you were already predestined to be a miracle worker, you have now achieved a level of spiritual balance and purity necessary to, successfully fulfill, the duties of this office. Your prayers are especially effective now, what you decree, God will fulfill. You will begin to walk and grow into a mature spiritual being, enabled to see into the spiritual realm more clearly, going on towards perfection. No matter your hardships, you will never again look back. You have genuinely in words and deeds put away childish things. Dreamer, you will usher others into a totally new and higher level of spiritual awarenes s (see John 21:3-17). You will appear when needed, and then disappear without thought of anything in return. Those, whom you will reach for Christ, will stand before you as their teacher, connecting their thoughts with your thoughts, with love fr om their hearts. By fulfilling your mission and remaining humble, you will be worthy of your wage. Moreover, as already promised, you will eat and do very well, on this side of eternity, and inherit eternal life. Humility is a keyword for you. Know the full meaning of the word and define your life by it. If necessary, see suggested course of action.

In addition, the following is a common word, expression, or usage (e.g. slang or cliché), or a 'probable' that is metaphorically represented by this number:

- Someone who is entering the golden years of their life

51: This number refers to one, namely the dreamer, who is experiencing divine revelation. What you receive should be shared, via preaching, teaching, art, or acting that others might be enlightened. This is your gift to the world.

52: In addition to one of the following, and only if necessary, dreamer may also consider other multiples of this number. First, see Note 6 at the beginning of this category. With that, this dream has five meanings (choose one). (1) A generational curse (or morally objectionable behavior) has been broken or lifted from over, the dreamer. Read Isaiah 58:12. Unfavorable situations and circumstances will now be annulled, and better conditions bestowed. If necessary, see suggested course of action. (2) Your dream refers to a union of husband and wife. If not married, and marriage is desired, you will be married soon. (3) If married, because of the dreamer's unconditional love of God, the dreamer, or if male, your spouse, is either actually pregnant, will become pregnant very shortly, or you two are becoming grandparents. If not pregnant, and you desire children, continue to have faith and hope in God, He will have mercy on you, and grant you the desire of your heart, suddenly and very soon. You will birth a son. (4) To the married male: Learn how to deal with your wife according to understanding. Once you learn her, do not try to change her, and deal with her with according to wisdom, and then she will respond to you with lovingkindness, she will become aroused, and become to you a true "help mate". See suggested course of action. (5) If a literal pregnancy is not an issue or desire, perhaps due to age, then your dream represents a spiritual pregnancy. A spiritual pregnancy denotes a ministry will be birth from within you, the dreamer. You are full of nurturing abilities; thus, you will become, responsible for a few young men and women being born again into the Kingdom of God (see John 3:1-17). You know how to nurture and accept anyone; therefore, many are intended to connect with you, including those, others label as indigents, via your ministry.

In addition, the following is a common word, expression, or usage (e.g. slang or cliché), or a 'probable' that is metaphorically represented by this number:

- 52-week, this is used in the context of share prices and economic data to refer to the highest or lowest point reached in the last year, or in a particular one-year period.

54: Your dream addresses the dreamer's purpose, and it points to expectancy of divine approval and release. Dreamer your purpose and time is upon you. You are chosen and released now, to preach and teach the Gospel of Jesus Christ. Therefore, dreamer is advised to come out from among unbelievers, and to separate yourself from them, says the Lord, for what company has righteousness with unrighteousness, or what sharing of personal thoughts and feelings has light with darkness. Have nothing to do with their sinful and wicked deeds, and I will restore you (see 2 Corinthians 6:14-18). Additionally, dreamer, as painful as this may hurt, the following must also be said, and only if applicable, dreamer your experiences of aloneness, depression, rejection, and/or low self-esteem is influencing your present behavior, without you realizing it. You are not allowing yourself to get close enough to share love, trust, and intimacy qualitatively with no one. Most of the conflicts within your present relationships, including your spiritual one, are provoked because of this. Unconsciously, you are against anything that will help you develop closer friendships, including your relationship with Christ Jesus, to the point of dissolution, divorce, or ruin. As a result, your feelings, thoughts, and memories, together, have prevented you from developing a balanced, discriminating, and an overall lifestyle of wholeness. Favorably, although, your previous lifestyle, your past, was overshadowed by negative experiences, and deferred hopes, God's righteousness dwells with and in you. God will raise you up and sit you amongst His people for the benefit of all within your sphere, help God's people by doing good deeds. You will be considered, and now is, a righteous person (see Romans 8:1), for there is a difference between conviction and condemnation. Dreamer, if you will trust the empowering work of the Holy Spirit, which is beginning to manifest within your life on a conscious level; thus your dream, your emotional and spiritual well-being will be made whole (meditate upon and pray Psalm 51). Moreover, a conscientious and diligent effort on the part of the dreamer, to deeply reflect, on your emotional fears and scars is needed; perhaps some type of Christian counseling may help as well. This coupled with, the refining and purifyi ng work of the Paraclete will cause the emergence of a more divine led wisdom. It will also be through these pains that the wisdom of harmonizing, fear and love of the Lord within your life, will be imparted to you. Fear within this context is the practice of living life on God's terms, in order to receive reward, meaning while hoping for some benefit from your efforts. You respect God but your love for Him is conditional. A tenacious faith in, and acceptance of, all of the Word of God, the good and the not so easily received, and prayer, will lead you into the Light of His Love. Love within this context, is the practice of living life on God's terms, for no other reason or benefit, than to be close to God, and to bless His Holy name for allowing you the honor to know Him, this is called holiness. See suggested course of action. If listed, and only if necessary, dreamer may also consider other multiples of this number. First, see Note 6 at the beginning of this category.

57: Your dream was sent to encourage the dreamer. It implies that the dreamer is a hard worker concerning your duties, missions, and responsibilities. You devote yourself to work, as well as show concern for the betterment of your community at large; and with your organized, efficient approach, things are done resourcefully. You radiate security, and often forfeit your own desires for your family, anyone you consider a responsibility, and for any worthy cause. You will now reap the rewards of such diligence, including rest and graceful surroundings. If applicable, your children will reap the fruits of the blessing of your giving. Moreover, as you are able to handle great responsibility and wealth, and are one who is tolerant, you will experience receiving an act of kindness, monetarily, from someone who is affluent. Additionally, dreamer you are entering into a season within your life that will prepare you spiritually for the visitation of the Lord in your individual life. During this time, you will experience His love and presence, as you've never known it before. For, He is saying to you, "I will teach you godly wisdom". You will receive direct insight of divine truth. You will come to know, without a doubt, that God is the true source of your strength and wisdom, and He is your sufficiency. As a result, a greater love for self, family, and others will begin to manifest, affecting wholeness within your life. From here forward, speaks of God's "weaning" of a righteous person, the dreamer. Dreamer, do not be deceived, with affluence, power, and wealth, comes good and evil. Today, you will need to choose between good and evil; and set "checks and balances" within yourself, because you have innate tendencies to become extreme and will judge others according to your "extremisms". Embracing this side of yourself will cause you to be deemed inappropriate, and delayed at that moment, to be of service to the Kingdom of God. Regrettably, this will lead to you being unhappy, and unable to discern between truth and error, without you realizing your shortsightedness. Therefore, the "checks and balances" are meant to rectify the soul to increase its capacity to receive the blessings of the Lord more fully. Blessings; in this sense, is a state of high honor, spiritual beauty, and great illumination. Henceforth, in accordance with your decision as to how you shall continue, from this day forward, will define your increase or the dwindling thereof, in your future and beyond. Note, if you choose to embrace the positive, this will lead to a great balancing of your theology, resulting in a belief that is complete, with solid attributes, and your inspiration will make for very good teaching. You would make an excellent apologist (witness) for the Kingdom of God. Seriously consider this branch of Christian theology. If necessary, see suggested course of action.

58: Your dream denotes one who is set aside for the priesthood. Dreamer, you are being prepared to carry out the official role, position, or office of a priest (e.g. prophet, pastor, minister, or some type of a very visible cleric). With this office comes spiritual growth and divine illumination, if you have genuinely sought after truth, truth will continue to be revealed to you and lead and guide you. With that said, the following is necessary to say. First, your promotion is predicated upon your understanding of, and continued obedience to, God's directives over your life. Second, pray to God for divine truth, for one should never exalt their thoughts, ideas, feelings, emotions, above God's truth, for, every house is built by someone, but the builder of all things is God (Hebrews 3:2-4). Further, chosen, you are to show forth the praises of Him who has called you out of darkness into His marvelous light (also see 1 Peter 2:9, 10). At present, continue to allow the Paraclete to complete the work of purification and sanctification within you. For those who go forth in tears, shall return rejoicing (Psalm 126:5, 6). Be diligent and patient, everything will be done proper, and in its own time; you will be ordained to a priestly office, and if relevant, your request in another area of your life will be granted. Again, your height of spiritual progress and promotion will be according to your faith and obedience to God's will over your life personally. If necessary, see suggested course of action. If listed, and only if necessary, dreamer may also consider other multiples of this number. First, see Note 6 at the beginning of this category

59: Dreamer, visit the sick and elderly, especially family members, and your visit will remove some of the burden of their sickness, thus lightening their load. Couple this with one of the following (choose one). (1) Unmarried dreamer: Your dream is a sign or indication of an engagement and wedding. This covenant relationship is honored by God; therefore, get married. A potential spouse is looking carefully at you at present. Your faithfulness and unpretentiousness is beautiful in their sight. An introduction will present itself shortly. The question of the possibility of relocation may be asked. Moreover, and if so desired, the union of the groom and bride will result in a literal pregnancy. Continue to have faith in God, which is a resolute trust in the integrity of God and in His Word, He will have mercy on you, and grant you the desire of your heart, namely to birth children of your own body. (2) Married dreamer, your marriage is not defiled. Therefore, deal with your unwarranted jealously and/or doubts. Further, the wife should not usurp authority over her husband; and, the husband must learn to dwell with his wife according to knowledge. See suggested course of action.

60: In addition to one of the following, and only if necessary, dreamer may also consider other multiples of this number. First, see Note 6 at the beginning of this category. The number sixty refers to life cycles, fundamental truths as reflected within the Bible and within reality, pride, and a wedding ring. With that, this dream has two meanings (both may apply). (1) Dreamer, what goes around comes around, and there is nothing new that God does not know, good, bad, or indifferent. Adonai Elohim knows all. Therefore, remember and trust, once again, God's power to support and lift you up when you have fallen, especially due to your own pride, as He has done before, during your negative life cycles, when you've fallen to your very lowest, physically and/or spiritually, unable to raise yourself up. Trust Him to lift you up once again, and then go on and progress from that negative life circle, via daily prayer. Dreamer, prayerfully and faithfully rely on the loving-kindness of God to sustain you, perhaps miraculously, especially in the face of disorder. He will support you, be encourage. Dreamer is also counseled to make different life and spiritual choices, trusting and believing God differently and truer, less superficially, than before. In your service to God and in your relation to worldly experiences, always place God's truth, before you, in all you r choices, life activities, and events. This will keep all things equally accepted or rejected as they relate to God's principles, per the Holy Record. Moreover, dreamer should continuously be in a state of aspiration to achieve higher and higher levels of clinging to God's love and realizing His Will for your life. Additionally, dreamer, visit the sick and elderly, especially family members, and your visit will remove some of the burden of their sickness, thus lightening their load. See suggested course o f action. (2) Your dream is a sign or indication of an engagement and wedding. This covenant relationship is honored by God; therefore, get married. A potential spouse is looking carefully at you at present. Your faithfulness and unpretentiousness is beautiful in their sight. An introduction will present itself shortly. The question of the possibility of relocation may be asked. Moreover, and if so desired, the union of the groom and bride will result in a literal pregnancy. Continue to have faith in God, which is a resolute trust in the integrity of God and in His Word, He will have mercy on you, and grant you the desire of your heart, namely to birth children of your own body. On the other hand, if dreamer is married, perhaps there is a wedding that you will be closely connected and support financially.

62: Your dream refers to one who is redeemed; however, you are going through a refining process, see Proverbs 17:3, 27:21; thus, your dream. Dreamer is strongly urged, at this point in your life, to adhere to God's instructions and principles that guide actions and moral behavior, via His principles, as outlined within Holy Writ. Following godliness is, aimed at making you not only wiser, but also better. Dreamer, it is imperative that you govern your desires, lusts, and pa ssions with wisdom during your refining process. You have a journey to go on, spiritual warfare to fight, and a great work to do. God wants to purify you that you might fulfill the righteous purpose for which you were designed. With that said, as you ha ve been saved from the power of sin, you will now be refined in the "crucible" of adversity. Dreamer, if you allow God's power to break th e residuals of sin within you, you will experience a great deliverance from oppression. Be very aware that your emot ional and/or physical adversities have been allowed by God that you might be humbled and made ready and prepared to render your gifts unto the Lord properly. God will use your sufferings to instill His principles into your mind, and make His ways penetrate your heart. He or she who has suffered in the flesh has ceased from sinning (1 Peter 4:1) that the sacrificial offerings of your worship, service, and financial support to the ministry, might be a sweet smell unto the Lord. Moreover, the refinement process that you are going through (or will go through shortly) is meant to bring honor and glory to the One who died to redeem you. True conversion makes a marvelous change in the heart and life. It alters the mind, judgment, affections, and conversation. When a man is truly converted, it grieves him to think how the time past of his life has been spent (Matthew Henry Concise Commentary). After this, you will become productive and go forth, bearing spiritual fruit, counted amongst those who are sagacious; whose character is faithful, law-abiding, moral, open, scrupulous, sincere, straightforward, trustworthy, upright, reasonable in many situations, and submissive to God. Blessings, joy, protection, and prosperity will be yours. See suggested course of action. If listed, and only if necessary, dreamer may also consider other multiples of this number. First, see Note 6 at the beginning of this category.

65: In addition to one of the following, and only if necessary, dreamer may also consider other multiples of this number. First, see Note 6 at the beginning of this category. With that, this dream has four meanings (choose one). (1) Unmarried dreamer: The year of the Lord's favor is upon you. Immediately you will find favor before God, and He will withhold from you anything causing misery, severe affliction, and/or death. He will provide for you, and bestow a crown of beauty upon you, instead of ashes. You shall receive the oil of gladness, instead of mourning, and you shall receive a garment of praise instead of a spirit of despair. You will be known as righteous; therefore, bless the name of the Lord, for His kindness endures forever. (2) Married couple without children and you desire children: Read Isaiah 54:1-10, Psalm 113:9, it is the meaning of your dream. Husband pray on behalf of your wife, as Isaac did on behalf of his wife, and the Lord will answer your prayer, and your wife will become pregnant (Genesis 25:21). (3) Married couple with children: If you have not "bullied or harassed in any manner" the married without children: The ordeal you think will destroy you, it will not. The current darkness and gloom that surrounds you at present, is intended to elevate you; causing you to stand up and to become an anointed and powerful force within the Kingdom of God. Dreamer, your adversity is affecting a dependable, faithful, loyal, reliable responsible, resourceful, upright, and upstanding spirit within both of you. Do not be confused, you will not be made ashamed. It is, understood on high that at present you don't feel elevated while going through your making season. Yet, this is when you can expect God to come and show Himself strong on your behalf. Dreamer, even in your dilemma, you are to elevate and promote the righteousness of Christ to those around you. You are endowed with the power of God, to cause some to become alive again, from a depressed, inactive, or unused state, those who are broken, and/or who sit in darkness. In you, they will find refuge, because your sou rce is preeminent in God's Will. Someone, a prayer warrior, will come to pray for you. This person is someone you least expect to be so powerful in the realm of prayer; more than likely a male who is very humble and unassuming. During the prayer, you wil l see yourself, spiritually, getting up from a sitting or prostrate position. Let your dream, and the vision during prayer, be your comfort for the endurance. (4) To the married with children: If you have "bullied or harassed in any way or manner" the married without children, your dream implies that you will begin to lose vigor, health, and strength because of grief. Moreover, you are contemptuous in your dealings with others. Dreamer, you have broken or violated an agreement between you and God; thus, any previously established agreement between you and another will be broken or violated. See suggested course of action.

66: This number refers to erroneous beliefs, trickery, guile, deception, and/or idolatry. Your dream denotes one, the dreamer, who is powerful, full of pride, and insolent. You trivialize the honor your ancestors obtained by worshipping and honoring Jesus, and His righteousness, and have made, or are making, yourself a renowned name by that which perpetually ruins good names. You have chosen low or base standards, morals, ethics, principles, tenets, and beliefs; and you use trickery, guile, and deception, to gain notoriety. Thus, there is a defection of the faith, which is in Jesus Christ. You have abando ned the faith, and are now, worshipping false gods and images, and adhering to lies; holding to beliefs, views, and practices that are erroneous, unlawful, toxic, and spiritually and/or physically deadly. Dreamer, because of your unwise and foolish passions, the sharp reproofs of the Word, and the severe censures of men, you are allowing a weakening of your core beliefs, namely a rejection of all or some of the original foundational teachings of Christ and His apostles, to take root within you spiritual ly. You are listening to, and being fooled by demons. Moreover, your lack of an objective critical analysis and judgment of a belief system's infrastructure, its foundation, existence, deity, nature of worship, sacred text, values, attitudes, earthly and eternal benefits and recompense; and whether its beliefs are worthy of consideration or not, is leading you towards dark and erroneous knowledge, the devil's so-called deep secrets. This knowledge is gained through personal experience and through supernatural imparting, which is demonically communicated (1 Timothy 4:1-5). The knowledge gained will not allow you to praise the Lord, only to exalt one's self. This counterfeit image of godliness is excessively concern with outward forms and appearances, especially in religious matters. Your lifestyle choices are, or will become, offensive and repulsive (abominable) in the sight of God and humanity, for your kind of choices leads to desolation. Dreamer, you are forfeiting purpose for foolishness and ruin. Demonic influences will swarm around you, ready to help you in your wicked, evil, despicable, immoral, reprehensible, disreputable, degenerate, infamous, or perverse choices. Dreamer, demons have had thousands of years to master human weaknesses and can rival men and women of God if we are not careful. Favorably, because of grace and the many mercies of God extended to you, your dream is only a warning and not an official declaration. Utilizing the powerful resources of prayer and heartfelt repentance to Jesus and to individuals affected by your actions, in the form of an apology (if possible), is needed. As well, fasting, a changed mindset, serious re-consideration of God's ways and means, and an honest acknowledgement of God's hand within your life, then and only then, can the severe impact of your choices and actions upon your life, be reversed and damages restored (see Ezekiel 33:8-19). To Jesus pray, Psalm 51, this followed by appropriate application of wisdom, can conceivably avert some of the repercussions of your choices; this is what is called leaving a blessing. Dreamer is counseled to seek all kinds of spiritual support now, to perhaps move away from your present environment, definitely walk away from all negativity abruptly. If you do not genuinely, and earnestly, seek help and change, for sure ruin will be your destiny. See suggested course of action. If listed, and only if necessary, may consider the interpretation for the number 6, as it relates to the repetitiveness of this number (66). Hence, the number 66; is a more intense expression of the number 6, in strength and forcefulness, spiritually, prophetically, and in application. First, see Note 6 at the beginning of this category.

67: This dream refers to a promise made you by God, and the fulfillment of that promise made to you. The promise was made when you first invited Christ into your life. It will, very shortly happen. With that, this dream has two meanings (both apply). (1) God's wisdom, care, and guidance, coupled with His divine intervention, has kept you, and will, again, cause your mouth to be filled with laughter, and your tongue with singing. When God reverse your tragedy, you will testify that the Lord has done great things for you, and you will be glad. Your situation will change and He will give you a new song in your heart. You will sing a new song. (2) As well, your dream points to one who was born to be a teacher and a nurturer. You should be teaching the elementary truths of God's word to your own children and/or to those not familiar with the teachings of righteousness, mainly new converts, and infants in Christ. Your diligent teaching will prepare others to spread the gospel o f Jesus Christ; thus, reproducing your teaching ministry and abundantly blessing you. You will receive wages for your diligence, if indeed you are diligent (Luke 10:2-7, 1 Timothy 5:18).

68: In addition to one of the following, and only if necessary, dreamer may also consider other multiples of this number. First, see Note 6 at the beginning of this category. With that, this dream has two meanings (both may apply). (1) Unmarried Female: Your dream signifies a marriage. Your husband is before you at present, or will be, very shortly. Handle the relationship, on God's terms, embracing His ethics, and not yours, as you've previously done before, and things will be in your favor. If necessary, see suggested course of action. (2) Dreamer, because of God's grace, His faithfulness, and His mercy towards you, you will begin to experience a surge of positive feelings, due to restoration, transformation, and a miraculous healing and strengthening, both physically and emotionally. The emotional level is already happening within your inner most feelings and affections, for, God is first healing your broken heart. Now, your burdens, having been dealt with, freedom from your weaknesses is yours. Freedom from bondage, domination by evil, and hardship, is beginning for you. Dreamer, you are asked to give careful thought regarding your bondages and hardships, considering how things are, and have been for you, for your experiences have prepared you for ministry. From this day forward, God will bless you. You will be favored with complete healing, go and sin no more, but go and offer prayers, supplications, and thanksgiving before your Lord and Savior, Jesus Christ, for He is forgiving, compassionate, long-suffering, and full of loving-kindness, restoring more favorable conditions. Additionally, in time, you may find yourself assistant to a high-ranking leader within a ministry, perhaps in the position of personal aide, leadership counselor, associate pastor, or CEO of your individual ministry. As well, there will be clarity an d freedom in the way you communicate yourself to others, especially prophetically. Note, although your life is (will become) very busy and full of concerns; it is advised that you do not forget your personal relationship with Christ, nor neglect the devotions that keep that personal relationship healthy. Nor must you allow yourself to be annoyed with other acts of devotion, e.g. family bible study and other quality times, fellowshipping with other believers, church attendance, acknowledging God's goodness to you, to others, and the like. Therefore, choose good habits and deeds, e.g. good stewardship and commitment to ministry; speak to yourself what is true and good, embrace Philippians 4:8, and choose good nutritional habits that you might remain in good health. These choices will greatly support you in your progress forward towards your transformation and freedom, and help guide you toward, and enable you to fulfill, your purpose. All these blessings are rain. Dreamer, as one perfects him or herself, God helps by sending 'rains of blessings', then situations prosper. The rain is coming!

70: This number refers to God's completed purpose, divine providence, pleasant, peaceful situations, and restoration. Read, understand, and embrace Psalm 30:5, "joy has come". Darkness has ended and the dawn is occurring. Dreamer, the eyes of God are upon your life's state of affairs, from the beginning of the year to the end of the year. Any condition that is upon you at present that seems hopeless or extremely frustrating; you will overcome it. For instance, if you have been diagnosed with a serious or incurable illness, you will be healed and survive to declare the glories of the Lord. Go through your circumstances hopeful and optimistic (Psalm 27:5; 38:1-22). Additionally, since you are endowed with multiple talents that may be expressed through inspirational teaching, preaching, or acting, and have access to prophetic wisdom, you are required to be a transformational force in people's lives, via not neglecting the gift that is within you. Do not say what gift, for this is sin for you, as your dream supposes that you are aware of, at least, one of your gifts (talent, skill). Acknowledging and embracing your gift to help others, in this, you imitate Christ. If listed, and only if necessary, dreamer may also consider other multiples of this number. First, see Note 6 at the beginning of this category.

71: It is time for the dreamer to painfully and eagerly thirst and long for those things by which the soul; is genuinely refreshed, supported, and strengthen. It is suggested that you go away, into a quiet place, away from all the distractions to seriously fast, and deprogram and re-program yourself (Galatians 1:12-24). At this crossroads in your life, you need to count all that you know, to be worthless (Philippians 3:3-9). Subsequently, you will begin to walk and grow into a more mature spiritual being, going on towards perfection, enabled to see into the spiritual realm more clearly. Additionally, no matter the hardships and they may prove grievously; never again look back, but genuinely, in words and deeds, continue to progress forward. By this, your capacity for greater illumination, intellectually and spiritually, will become enlarged, giving you access to more than a few of the gates of wisdom (2 Corinthians 12:2-10). See suggested course of action.

73: This number refers to wisdom. Dreamer you will now be taught divine wisdom. Dreamer, you are the student, another is your teacher, and you are ready. Although, you may be very accomplished, prosperous, and/or prudent, you have need of a teacher at present. God is sending someone into your life to help you carry out your next undertaking, by enlarging your spiritual capacity. Your capacity for greater illumination, intellectually and spiritually, will become enlarged giving you access to more than a few of the gates of wisdom. Your teacher is one who is modest and unassuming in attitude, behavior, and dress. Notwithstanding, great respect towards them is appropriate and required, as well as some form of compensation. You will need to be honest, open, and transparent, to get what you need from him or her. Your undivided attention is required, thus you may need to take a vacation from your normal business and/or ministerial activities. Your dream is to bring about an awareness of this person's coming, and to prepare you to meet them sagaciously. Dreamer, you will receive direct insight of divine truth. You will come to know, without a doubt, that God is the true source of your wisdom, and He is your sufficiency. If necessary, see suggested course of action.

75: This number refers to cleansing, purification, separation, and God's Word. Your dream was sent to bring about awareness. Dreamer, God will now do a cleansing, purifying, and separating of you from people, places, and things, to affect holiness within your life. Dreamer is counseled to steal away, to a quiet place, to separate from people, places, and things to fast, reflect, repair, and mend some heart and/or life issues that you've ignored too long, and to feel and experience God's love. During this time, dreamer is also counseled to immerse yourself in the Holy Bible that you might find the Word of God cleansing and purifying. The Holy Spirit will be with you throughout this entire process. Dreamer, all of these, the cleansing, purifying, separating, and immersion in God's Word, have the same ultimate aim, the rectification of your soul to increase its capacity to receive the blessings of the Lord more fully. Blessings; in this sense, is a state of high honor, spiritual beauty, and great illumination. Then you will be presented, heavily anointed, without any kind of stain or wrinkle, holy and without faults. Dreamer, you will still need to choose between good and evil, exercising your free will, because you have innate tendencies to become excessive regarding immoral impurities. See suggested course of action. If listed, and only if necessary, dreamer may also consider other multiples of this number. First, see Note 6 at the beginning of this category.

76: Dreamer, because of your acumen, courageous and optimistic spirit, faith, humility, and wise leadership, you will be greatly honored. You will rise to a level the anointing of God and your acumen deem you should be. God is with you, and He will keep you wherever you go. Even more, you have the power to change history. If listed, and only if necessary, dreamer may also consider other multiples of this number. First, see Note 6 at the beginning of this category.

In addition, the following is a common word, expression, or usage (e.g. slang or cliché), or a 'probable' that is metaphorically represented by this number:

- Someone needs to leave abruptly, or, to tell somebody who is unwelcome to leave.

77: This number refers to divine providence, spiritual purification, rectification of chaos, and a refinement process happening within the life of the dreamer. During this season of purification, rectification, and refinement, the dreamer will be favored with a sabbatical, including pay. This process of purification, rectification, and refinement, will take some time, be patient, and allow the process. This process will perfect quietness within your soul, restoring a more pleasant and peaceful concentration of the mind on spiritual matters such as achieving closer unity with God. As well, it will create within you a more compassionate and obedient spirit, leaving you more open to divine influence. Dreamer, be encourage, the eyes of God are always upon your life's state of affairs, from the beginning of the year to the end of the year that you may go on to perfection spiritually, being built up in your faith and complete, lacking nothing. You will gain knowledge on how to be moderate in all things, just and fair, and you will become one whom other believers will interact with socially on very personal levels, e.g. business associate, friendship, ministry, or spouse. Note, this sabbatical should be used exclusively for the purpose it was intended. To draw you away from, personal pursuits and to allow time for you to devote yourself and all that you are, to God's glory (e.g. perfect your inborn gift in some way for the glory of God). After your sabbatical, you are asked to emulate Chri st by helping to care for others. You are endowed with multiple talents that may be expressed through inspirational teaching, preaching, acting, or art, and have access to prophetic wisdom; thus, you are required to be a transformational force in other people's lives. By this, you imitate Christ. See suggested course of action. If listed, and only if necessary, may consider the interpretation for the number 7, as it relates to the repetitiveness of this number (77). Hence, the number 77; is a more intense expression of the number 7, in strength and forcefulness, spiritually, prophetically, and in application. First, see Note 6 at the beginning of this category.

78: This number denotes spiritual and/or spiritual life is passing away, due to spiritual weakness, erroneous ideology, or a physical illness. Thus, your dream was sent to warn the dreamer. It implies that the dreamer is in a backsliding downward spiral. Your activities and attitude will lead to spiritual and/or literal death. Favorably, via your dream, Jesus Christ is demonstrating grace (the free and unmerited favor and beneficence of God) by offering you a resurrection from dead works, people, places, and things. First, check your own spiritual life and make sure your salvation is real, see Acts 2:37-40 in the Holy Bible. Subsequently, Jesus will strengthen you emotionally, psychologically, and physically, to go get help for your backsliding and/or illness, via a faith based support group, Christian counseling, healthcare, and/or inpatient. Regarding a physical illness, seek medical attention as soon as possible, and call for the elders of your church, for it is through their prayers of faith and anointing of oil upon you that sin is forgiven and healing is bestowed[36]. Have faith in this, for it will be by your faith that you will be healed wholly. This is a true saying. If you will not choose behaviors, actions, thoughts, and choices that promote life, especially spiritual life, you will begin to experience extreme poverty, at the very least, or you will die, spiritually and perhaps physically. Notions, which presuppose the possibility of an actual loss of your prosperity, or even life itself is not real, must not undermine these warnings, the warnings are real. Further, spiritually and materially bless the people of God, those belonging to "The Way", as we were called in the early church (Acts 9:2) with your words and actions, and not curse.

Pray Psalm 38:1-22. See suggested course of action. If listed, and only if necessary, dreamer may also consider other multiples of this number. First, see Note 6 at the beginning of this category.

In addition, the following is a common word, expression, or usage (e.g. slang or cliché), or a 'probable' that is metaphorically represented by this number:

- A phonograph record, played at 78 revolutions per minute, a former standard speed

79: This number suggest that God is renewing His promises to the dreamer, however, dreamer must acknowledge, especially within, that humility and the fear of the Lord, secures authentic wealth, honor, and life (Proverbs 22:4). Further, dreamer must strive to let go of materialism, and its clearly visible secular intentions within your life (e.g. greed, image, power, or pride). This is not to say that you should put an end to the desire for economic growth. Faith teaches us not to ignore economics, for it benefits the sacred, as well as the mundane (Malachi 3:10, Proverbs 22:4, Luke 16:9). However, dreamer must rather, strive to restore God's divine purpose for your economic growth (1 Timothy 6:17-19); thereby, revealing the spark of holiness that effects true riches. See suggested course of action.

80: In addition to one of the following, and only if necessary, dreamer may also consider other multiples of this number. First, see Note 6 at the beginning of this category. With that, this dream has three meanings (choose one). (1) Unmarried dreamer: Your dream denotes that godly principles that makes for a strong foundation for a good and balanced marriage has been presented, and taught to the dreamer. Dreamer if those principles are wholeheartedly embraced and if so desired; you may marry the potential mate that is before you at present. This marriage will last a very long time, and each spouse will be endowed with the power to sustain the marriage. (2) Married dreamer: Your dream denotes that you are now empowered, via divine providence, to strengthen your marriage, if you choose to do so, please choose to do so. Your marriage will last a very long time, and each spouse will be endowed with the power to sustain the marriage. If necessary, see suggested course of action. (3) Your dream denotes a time when something very important to your future will be decided upon and happen. The dreamer is approaching a critical season in which the state of affairs within your life will become very difficult, painful, and uncertain. This turbulence is purposed to disturb and shake-up your foundation of pleasure, with an intense and life-changing upheaval, breaking up hardened ground that a new foundation may begin. This transition will also include transforming your spiritual concepts (beliefs, ideas, impressions, notions, perceptions, theories, thoughts, and views) into actions that will reunite you with God, for God desires to bring you back into a right relationship with Him. The Spirit of Truth will begin challenging, checking, and threatening, the irregular, illicit, and/or unsafe "thrills" you are accustomed too. For, you have primarily focused your life upon a foundation of personal pleasure; thus, you have settled for a voluptuary type way of life. How can you say, "I have great desire, thus my physical enjoyment, luxury, and sensual gratifications are my primary concerns? This is a characterization of the ungodly or spiritually immature. Weigh: The child thinks that all that appears pleasant and tasty belongs to them and that he or she has the right to partake of any and everything. Consideration of others, and/or of the resulting outcome is unfamiliar to him or her. They will never consider the results of their behavior, nor how their behavior will affect others. This type of consideration is not within a child's mind-set, because he or she is a child. As the immature child takes what they want, when they want it, and believes that it's theirs, and that they do have a right to whatever it is, so does the spiritually immature, do what they want, when they want, and believe that it's OK, using grace as a cover for sin. Unfortunately, spiritual change cannot begin with this kind of expectation and mind-set. Dreamer, rather say, "I have great desire, but what can I do, since my Father in Heaven forbids me from involving myself in such acts". Moreover, action must b e taken on your part to avoid complete disaster or breakdown, e.g. acknowledgment of your denial of illicit sensuous relations, and repentance, or else, all the evils your desires attract will prove very detrimental to you and your family. Consider your dream as God's faithfulness, loving kindness, mercy, and grace (the free and unmerited favor and beneficence of God) towards you. See suggested course of action.

82: Your dream was sent to encourage. Dreamer, because of your humble and submissive faith in God's word, and not your works alone, you are, declared one who is a righteous minister. Planted in the House of the Lord, you will continue to prosper and mature. The same God, who planted you in your ministry, is the same God who will cause you to mature and prosper. You will live and thrive where most things perish, independent of outward circumstances, via divine grace. Your spiritual growth may not be so rapid, however, if you endure, you will become a beautiful picture of a godly man or woman, who in your uprightness, aims to glorify God. On another vein, your dream also represents some type of spiritual privileges and a purification process, God will separate you from people, places, and circumstances that will hinder your growth, view this separation as a blessing from God and not as an evil thing has happen. Under all adversities retain a spirit of joy, continue to make progress in your spiritual life, with gladness, thanksgiving, singing, and then, strength, intense energy, and fertility will be your recompense, and your praise will be a sweet aroma in the nostrils of the Lord. If applicable, this promise is to your generations to come. Come what may, you shall make steady progress and flourish in a very impressive manner; bringing forth fruit, even in your old age. Dreamer, as you age, your anointing to minister, and divine revelations, will always be fresh and edifying. See Psalm 92:12-15. If listed, and only if necessary, dreamer may also consider other multiples of this number. First, see Note 6 at the beginning of this category.

84: Dreamer, a harvest is appointed for you. The Lord your God will restore your prosperity, give you double for what has been lost, and He will have compassion on you; He will fill your mouth with laughter and your lips with shouts of joy. You will experience a great deliverance from oppression, and fruitfulness will be added; therefore, fill your conscience with God's peace. The dark cloud that has hovered over your life will cease, and suddenly, and so overwhelmingly, and so great, will be your joy that it will seem too good to be true, it will be as a dream. Your captivity has been great, and so, great will be your deliverance, for God Himself has wrought it. You will say, "It seems too good to be true". Read Psalm 126, for this is God' sword to you. Dreamer, receive God's power to break the residuals of sin within, and from over, you. If listed, and only if necessary, dreamer may also consider other multiples of this number. First, see Note 6 at the beginning of this category.

86: This number refers to an ordination or promotion. Dreamer, you have been found by God, and scrutinized by some superiors, to be a wise man or woman. As well as, one who has reached the maximum level you are able to attain, with which you are able to fulfill your purpose and work for the Kingdom of God. Thus, you have proven fit to be officially ordained and/or promoted to a senior official appointment. You will be rendering conclusive decisions on dubious matters. Moreover, as you are genuine, tactful, and adaptable, your sensitivity and gentleness will be a great healing force, bringing harmony and support to some. If listed, and only if necessary, dreamer may also consider other multiples of this number. First, see Note 6 at the beginning of this category.

In addition, the following are common words; expressions or usages (e.g. slang or clichés) or a 'probable' that are metaphorically represented by this number:

- To get rid of, or dispose of somebody or something
- To refuse to serve a customer in a restaurant or bar, nightclub

88: In addition to one of the following, if listed, and only if necessary, may consider the interpretation for the number 8, as it relates to the repetitiveness of this number (88). Hence, the number 88; is a more intense expression of the number 8, in strength and forcefulness, spiritually, prophetically, and in application. First, see Note 6 at the beginning of this category. With that, this dream has three meanings (one, two, or all may apply). (1) It denotes some type of ministry that will be birth from within you. You will become, responsible for a few young men and women being born again into the Kingdom of God (see John 3:1-17). You know how to nurture and accept anyone; therefore, many will be drawn to you, including those, others call "ne'er-do-wells", via your ministry. Under your tutelage, those newly born into the Body of Christ will become strong and active, for the cause of the Kingdom of God. They will be known as persons who speak and does that which is good, counted amongst those who are faithful and submissive to God. Dreamer, be willing, obedient, prepared, and in place (accountable to a specific house of worship, church), for the birthing of your ministry and for those who will become born again because of your ministry. (2) Your dream also denotes the fruit of your natural talents, pursuits, and morality is coming into full fruition. Your conduct towards others (for benefit or harm) will be openly manifested before all. You will reap what you have sown. With regard to renewal and heartfelt repentance, dreamer, seeking pardon and expressing sincere feelings of regret and brokenness for having done something awry, or having made bad choices, and/or for having hurt someone, will lift heavy burdens you are carrying, because of you reaping what you've sowed, and release a spirit of renewal (a spiritual revival) within your life. See 2 Corinthians 7:10, 11. (3) Dreamer, there is a struggle within you, between your old nature and your new nature, the leftovers of sin and the new beginnings of grace. Your old nature is resisting everything that is spiritual and is opposing all the suggestions of the Holy Spirit and the ethical urgings of your conscience. This is spiritual circumcision of the heart. Fortunately, you are choosing to side with godly principles and to stand on your convictions. Dreamer, you will have success overcoming old things; there will be joy about your success, publicly. Now, the old has gone, and the new has come (2 Corinthians 5:17). God's providential blessing is upon you to increase. All things will be made beautiful in their own time. Do not boast of your increase, and be very mindful of your words. For example, words used in a patronizing and condescending manner, and/or embracing a judgmental nature, for the universal law: With the same judgments, you judge others, so will you be judged, is still applicable to you. Furthermore, due to the intensity of your struggle, one of God's messengers is sent to give you the support needed at this time. Be aware that the new person within your midst may be that messenger. See suggested course of action. If listed, and only if necessary, dreamer may also consider other multiples of this number. First, see Note 6 at the beginning of this category.

90: Your dream is sent as a word of encouragement to the dreamer. As you have re-directed your negative impulses, your natural inclinations to sin, especially your sexual desires, towards righteous activities (e.g. doing good works), and h ave desired to make God's will your own will, having your mind and thoughts clinging faithfully to the greatness of God. You are now decreed as one who is filled with love and reverence for God, a genuinely righteous person. This type of spiritual worthiness, after receiving the Lord as your Savior, is achieved by doing good works, in your case, the re-directing of your sinful inclinations, and this with the help of the Paraclete. Moreover, as you were already predestined to be a miracle worker, you have now achieved the level of holiness necessary, to successfully, carry out the duties of this office. Your prayers are especially effective, now, what you decree, God will fulfill. You will begin to walk and grow into a mature spiritual being, enabled to see into the spiritual realm more clearly, going on towards perfection. No matter your hardships, you will never again look back. You have, genuinely, in words and deeds put away childish things. Moreover, you will be used, if not alrea dy, to usher others into a totally new and higher level of spiritual awareness. Even amongst the "broken", a spark of life remains hidden, awaiting your particular ministry, your unique way of presenting the gospel. You will appear when needed, and then disappear without thought of anything in return. Those, whom you will reach for Christ, will stand before you as their teacher, connecting their thoughts with your thoughts, with love from their hearts. By fulfilling your mission and remaining humble, you will be worthy of your wage. It is promised that you will eat and do well, on this side of eternity, and inherit eternal life. Note humility is a keyword for you. Know the full meaning of the word and define your life by it. If listed, and only if necessary, dreamer may also consider other multiples of this number. First, see Note 6 at the beginning of this category.

In addition, the following is a common word; expression or usage (e.g. slang or clichés) or a 'probable' that is metaphorically represented by this number:

- A 90° angle

91: Read, understand, and embrace Isaiah 40, 57:10-21, for this is to you. Dreamer, the Lord Almighty, will help you, via emotional and moral support to keep you going. He will renew your energy, particularly through rest, if you will truly rest. This will cause you to feel more energetic. Dreamer, the Lord God will love and care for you, because He values you. God graciously does all this for your comfort and consolation that you faint not under temptation, but lift up your head with hop e. Additionally, he (or she) that shall come will come, and they will not delay. Therefore, dreamer, literally expect someone to come.

94: In addition to one of the following, and only if necessary, dreamer may also consider other multiples of this number. First, see Note 6 at the beginning of this category. With that, this dream has five meanings (one, two, etc., or all may apply). (1) Dreamer, God is going to heal your broken heart. If necessary, see suggested course of action. (2) Dreamer, character traits from ancestors, namely genetic codes and traits, will often trouble and taunt the offspring of a given progenitor, especially generational issues (Exodus 20:5-7). The demons that have so plague your family line, are now visiting (re-visiting) you, namely voices that whisper, you are without value, insignificant, or pointless, and it is the embracing of those voices that will lead to other issues, such as sexual perversion (e.g. adultery, fornication, homosexuality, prostitution, or whorishness), and on to a bleak and desolate atmosphere. This will lead to much sadness, and feelings of being forsaken or abandoned. Favorably, generational curses and issues can stop with you (Jeremiah 31:29, 30; Ezekiel 18:2-14, 20-23). Hence, your Heavenly Father is requiring that you overcome and subdue negative and dark emotions, feelings, behaviors, and/or ideas that have come to influence you, before they overcome you; and leave you desolate. Dreamer, God is not asking you to do something you cannot do. For a surety, vanquishing of dark influences can be done. By faith, you will need to declare some kind of fast and commit to it, for a long period-of-time, to abate the demonically instigated circumstance, you find yourself in now, Matthew 6:16-18. Try abstaining from food and drink (midnight to 6 PM), twice a week, and refrain from words, attitudes, people, places, and things, including music, magazines, videos, TV, or any such things that fuel anger and discont ent, and stir up lustful feelings. This is also known as, faith with works, read, understand, and embrace James 2:14-26. Nonetheless, earnestly pray, God will guide, enable, and answer you as to the type of fast. Additionally, if relevant, forgive your mother and/or father for the darkness (aka curse) they may have perpetuated, for they knew not what they done. Forgiveness is important to your success (Matthew 6:12-15, 8:21-35). See suggested course of action. (3) Your dream also represents some type of spiritual privileges and a purification process, dreamer God will now separate you from people, places, and circumstances that will hinder your growth. View this separation as a blessing from God and not as an evil thing has happen. Under all adversities retain a spirit of joy, and continue to make progress in your spiritual life. Subsequently, dreamer, because of your humble and submissive faith in God's word, you will be declared as one who is a righteous minister. Planted in the House of the Lord, you will continue to prosper and mature. The same God, who plants you in your ministry, is the same God who will cause you to mature and prosper. Further, another benefit of allowing Jesus to have authority of your life; is that independent of outward circumstances, you will live and thrive where most things perish, via divine grace. Dreamer, while your spiritual growth may not be so rapid, if you endure, you will become a beautiful picture of a godly man or woman, who in your uprightness, aims to glorify God. Accordingly, gladness, thanksgiving, singing, then, strength, intense energy, and fertility will be your recompense, and your praise will be a sweet aroma in the nostrils of the Lord. If applicable, this promise is also to your generations to come. Come what may, you shall make steady progress and flourish in a very impressive manner; bringing forth fruit, even in your old age. Dreamer, as you age, your anointing to minister, and divine revelations, will always be fresh and edifying. See Psalm 92:12-15. Therefore, put the spiritual work in and go through what you need to go through now. If necessary, see suggested course of action. (4) Male dreamer: An event or situation that will cause intense fear is coming to discourage and terrify you. This will be in the form of an annoying, difficult, and unpleasa nt person. The trouble this person will cause will become so overwhelming, because they will expose a secret regarding you. This spiritual battle will be great, and will demand your full attention. Although you will walk through this alone, know that Go d will walk you through it. Dreamer, learn wisdom from the situation, for truth do set one free; and go on from there unashamed. Then, suddenly, unexpectedly, and without any warning, all the evil and wickedness that caused you to fear and be troubled, will disappear. It will be as though it was never there. At that point, you will express great joy, and feel extremely happy. Take courage and be strong, knowing that the Lord knows where you are, what's going on, and He cares. See suggested course of action. (5) Male dreamer (unmarried): Your dream denotes that a very attractive and sensual female; one whom the dreamer, may marry, especially before having sex, will enter your life. If necessary, see suggested course of action.

100: Dreamer, there are those amongst you, close significant others, who are diametrically opposed to holiness and have essentially separated themselves from God. It is said of them that their feet descend into death, and they are ultimately responsible for bringing death into their own life's situations. This is also said of you, by some, not most. Favorably, as your dream also references election according to grace, expectancy, God's faithfulness, grace abounding, fullness, full measure, full recompense, full reward, holiness, and redemption of those who have fallen away, a spark of life remains hidden inside of you, and in them, because both, you and they are God's children. There awaits you, and them, a spiritual resurrection, according to God's grace. His grace is abounding towards you, and His promises will come quickly and in full measure. What are His promises to you? Dreamer, recall His promises to you. Expect all of this (spiritual resurrection, grace abounding, His prom ises to you, full measure); therefore, wait on it. Warning, these great blessings, can result in an excessive concern for your image, the false imitations of this world, pride, and vanity. These attributes will keep you from being in the right place, at the right moment, to hear God through the ears of faith. Therefore, humble yourself before the True and Living God and accept His blessings of healing, help, and restoration in a balanced manner. This great favor is shown you because of God's great faithfulness towards you. If listed, and only if necessary, dreamer may also consider other multiples of this number. First, see Note 6 at the beginning of this category. If listed, and only if necessary, may consider the interpretation for the number 10, as it relates to this number squared; see Note 6 at the beginning of this category.

In addition, the following are common words; expressions or usages (e.g. slang or clichés) or a 'probable' that are metaphorically represented by this number:

- One who is truthful, and/or to depict something realistically
- This symbol denotes someone giving 100% of their effort, in a complete manner, as well as, completely well, completely fit, and healthy.
- The optimal location for a business in terms of profitability per unit of area

102: Your dream refers to faith, forgiveness of sins, and healing. According to your faith, it will be done to you. Therefore, start with trusting in the integrity of God. If you believe in your heart that your sins are forgiven, because yo u have asked to Jesus to forgive you of your sins, then all your past sins are forgiven, embrace that. Additionally, your request will be granted, go in peace and be freed from your suffering. Jesus has said, "I tell you the truth, if you have faith and do not d oubt, not only can you do what was done to the fig tree, but also you can say to this mountain, 'Go, throw yourself into the sea,' and it will be done (Matthew 21:18-22, Mark 11:12-14, 20-25). If necessary, see suggested course of action. If listed, and only if necessary, dreamer may also consider other multiples of this number. First, see Note 6 at the beginning of this category.

103: Dreamer, you are one, who is resentful and vindictive, and will "cross the line" with others, and all of this contrariness, is because you've been hurt by one you considered safe, and an authority figure. You profane that which is holy, because you have been wounded by one considered pious, who is not. Consequently, you are now prone to ideas that feed hatred, and you excuse violence. As well, you attempt to convert others to your violent and profane beliefs; thereby, causing you to be a serious threat to others. Further, outwardly, you will change your behavior to suit the circumstances of a particular situation in order to gain an advantage over others. You easily and frequently change and/or alter your beliefs and views, superficially, according to the situation. Dreamer, as long as you seethe in resentment and vindictiveness, just know that God will not ignore those who are hurt by you. Word of Wisdom, there is only one force that can break the power of hatred and resentment within you, and that is the rule of the Holy Spirit. Therefore, a change is vitally needed in the way you behave. Core issue, dreamer, bad things do happen to innocent people and a bad thing happened to you. However, you no longer have to be the bad thing that happens to others. Ask your Heavenly Father to forgive you of your sins, as you forgive those who violated you, and forgive yourself, and no longer will the bad thing hold sway over your entire life. For whom Jesus sets free, is free. By grace (the free and unmerited favor and beneficence of God), prayer, fasting, and change, your life will begin to transform and you will be restored to the person you was intended to be. Weigh, no one person, people, or denomination, hypocrite or not, is the full representation of the Kingdom of God; therefore, no longer allow the enemy to rob you of your intended destiny. It would be wise for you, at this time in your life, to embrace holiness, wholeheartedly, to prevent the practice of greater immoral acts; for such acts are grossly unclean and will defile you spiritually and physically completely. Further, your acts of immorality, will unequivocally lead to you selling your "birthright", just to satisfy the growing lust in your flesh and heart (Genesis 25:29-34; Hebrews 12:14-17). The repercussions of such acts; see Ezekiel 18:24-32, 33:10-13. Dreamer, without holiness no one shall see the Lord. Therefore, look diligently within, and consider the state of great suffering and distress, you are experiencing, and then consider the healing that Jesus is offering you now. Dreamer, respect your time of visitation from the Lord, for it is upon you. You can be made free, pray and ask Jesus for help. When you stand for what is just and right, God will stand with you. Read, understand, and embrace Romans 12:9-21. Additionally, dreamer, if you've been so hurt by another that you feel you are a hopeless cause, even to the point of suicide. You will only take all of your hurt and pain with you; and you will descend into some place that is a thousand times worse than what's going on with you now. Therefore, dreamer, you must choose to overcome your hurt that your soul might be saved. No longer, allow the violation(s) to hold sway over your future and eternal destiny. Note, those who deny the opportunity to change your wicked ways and refuse to treat others with kindness and respect, does not deserve kindness and respect from others. Dreamer, make the choice to serve in a cause larger than your wants and desires and larger than yourself, serve Christ Jesus. See suggested course of action.

106: In addition to one of the following, and only if necessary, dreamer may also consider other multiples of this number. First, see Note 6 at the beginning of this category. With that, this dream has two meanings (choose one). (1) Dreamer grace is being extended to you, via deliverance from the dangers of your fleshly passions, and a verifiable miracle within the area of your mind or head. Moreover, there will be a divine work upon your emotions, and this will manifest within your life in the form of liberality in Christ Jesus, thankfulness, and joy. All this is preparation, that you may become qualified, proven worthy, spiritually, morally, and ethically, for a religious position within an ecclesiastical order. Additionally, there is a need to make a sacrificial offering, financially, to the ministry which, you are connected. Weigh, he, or she who sows sparingly shall reap sparingly; and he or she who sows bountifully shall reap bountifully. Let each man or woman do according as you have purposed in your heart, not grudgingly, or of necessity for God loves a cheerful giver. For, God is able to make all grace abound unto you; that you, having always all sufficiency in everything, may abound unto every good work (2 Corinthians 9:6-8). See suggested course of action. (2) Dreamer will be granted some manner of favor, gratuitously, from a very strong ally, benefactor, defender, or supporter, via an "in-kindness" or grant, or through a pardon or forgiveness of a very large debt (e.g. auto loan, bank loan, college, student loan, or mortgage). With that said, dreamer, give ear, two "favors" will be presented, one sacred, one profane. The key to knowing which favor is sacred, and which is profane. The profane favor will ask you to compromise your beliefs, namely to "gray area" some of God's unequivocal positions on certain tenets. Dreamer, never do you ever compromise your beliefs in Jesus Christ, as the Word of God made flesh, nor do you distort the meanings of His Holy Word, for any manner of favor, for this is akin to spiritual prostitution, aka idolatry. Therefore, consider carefully what is being presented to you. Additionally, there is a need to make a sacrificial offering, financially, to the ministry which, you are connected. Weigh, he, or she who sows sparingly shall reap sparingly; and he or she who sows bountifully shall reap bountifully. Let each man or woman do according as you have purposed in your heart, not grudgingly, or of necessity for God loves a cheerful giver. For, God is able to make all grace abound unto you; that you, having always all sufficiency in every thing, may abound unto every good work (2 Corinthians 9:6-8). If necessary, see suggested course of action.

107: Dreamer, you will blossom in the Kingdom of God. Weigh, as it takes an unrivaled level of confidence to successfully endure mountain top experiences, without imploding, as you are elevated, it will be wise, for you, to periodically take a reflective look within, to check the pride level, within your heart (also see Deuteronomy 6:10 -18). It is counseled that you set up 'mile markers', a type of accountability system for yourself along the way. Do not be deceived, with affluence, power, and wealth, comes good and evil; thus, today, you will need to choose between good and evil; and set "checks and balances" within yourself, because you have innate tendencies to become extreme and will judge others according to your "extremisms". Embracing this side of yourself will cause you to be deemed inappropriate, and delayed at that moment, to be of further service to the Kingdom of God. If necessary, see suggested course of action.

108: Dreamer, God is completely restoring things materially and spiritually within your life and in the lives of those immediately connected to you. Because of your brokenness over your past sins, you have opened the door to contriteness and humility. It is through this door that an act of kindness will come very soon. With that said, dreamer there is a need to understand the unadulterated and full meaning of divine providence, get a bible dictionary, and respect the meaning. For, there is also a need to recognize, acknowledge, and respect divine providence, God's absolute control over the affairs of humankind, and to renounce the belief that humans are in complete control (see Job 9:12, Isaiah 14:27; 43:13). There is a difference between divine providence and the will of humankind. Although you have the power of free choice, you should not think that your accomplishments are purely of your own volition. It is God, who gives you the capability and strength to achieve success. This is especially true of your struggles with your sinful tendencies, whether you manifest as a lack of concern or interest in the things of God, a stubborn resistance to the will of God, or laziness. If it had not been for God's effort s on your behalf, you would not have been able to overcome any negative tendencies. He delivered you. Any achievements you've accomplished, any good deeds you've done, any fulfillment of God's will, was, and still is, dependent upon divine aid and guidance. One merely places his or her hand under the weight carried exclusively by God. Just say and truly believe, "I will exalt you, God, for you have lifted me up". In addition, there is a need to check your theology. There is something missing in your belief system that has affected someone who is very close to you. It has caused them to seek God in other teachers, in other faces, and most are evil. Fortunately, that love one lead astray, because of you, will come home, embracing Jesus. Altruistic, goodhearted, and generous service to God and others is beneficial at this time. This is concerning the dreamer's purpose. Dreamer you are one chosen and released now, to preach and/or teach the Gospel of Jesus Christ. If listed, and only if necessary, dreamer may also consider other multiples of this number. First, see Note 6 at the beginning of this category.

109: Your dream refers to one who needs to, spiritually hear the Word of God, believe and trust it, say amen to it; and then stand still; you will see the salvation of the Lord (Exodus 14:13, 14). For God's power has made a way out of no way for you, and your state of affairs is turning around. Dreamer, there will be a relaxation or slackening of tension in your life, stop, and feel the tension leaving. Those who have charged you falsely, with malicious intent, attacking your good name and reputation will be far from you. Others will become less hostile, as will you. You will be more relaxed, easygoing, and genial. The necessity to be reconciled with others than to always be in opposition has been resolved. Dreamer, you have simply taken the higher ground. You have re-evaluated your life, learned from your mistakes, found new directions in solving problems, pursued healing, sought out encouragement, and figured out what God would like you to change in order to, better fulfill His purpose. Moreover, you have learned the principles and Christian values that encourage one to reach out and touch others in a loving and graceful manner; ultimately finding yourself promoting the genuine cause of Christ and the good of others.

113: Dreamer will be granted some manner of favor, gratuitously, from a very strong ally, benefactor, defender, or supporter, via an "in-kindness" or grant, or through a pardon or forgiveness of a very large debt (e.g. auto loan, bank loan, college, student loan, or mortgage). With that said, dreamer, give ear, two "favors" will be presented, one sacred, one profane. The key to knowing which favor is sacred, and which is profane. The profane favor will ask you to compromise your beliefs, namely to "gray area" some of God's unequivocal positions on certain tenets. Dreamer, never do you ever compromise your beliefs in Jesus Christ, as the Word of God made flesh, nor do you distort the meanings of His Holy Word, for any manner of favor, for this is akin to spiritual prostitution, aka idolatry. Therefore, consider carefully what is being presented to you. Additionally, there is a need to make a sacrificial offering, financially, to the ministry which, you are connected. Weigh, he, or she who sows sparingly shall reap sparingly; and he or she who sows bountifully shall reap bountifully. Let each man or woman do according as you have purposed in your heart, not grudgingly, or of necessity for God loves a cheerful giver. For, God is able to make all grace abound unto you; that you, having always all sufficiency in everything, may abound unto every good work (2 Corinthians 9:6-8). If necessary, see suggested course of action.

119: This number signifies spiritual fulfillment, and that this is the year of the Lord's favor upon your life (also see Isaiah 61:1-62:12). It also refers to the resurgence of something long ago abandoned, forgotten, or neglected. See suggested course of action. If listed, and only if necessary, dreamer may also consider other multiples of this number. First, see Note 6 at the beginning of this category.

120: This number signifies the start of life in the Spirit, and an end of life in the flesh. Dreamer, you have truly sacrificed your flesh that your soul might be saved. With that, the following is necessary to say. There is a divinely appointed period of probation and a season of waiting. This probationary period decreed is a testing by waiting (Acts 7:23-30), and should be earnestly regarded. A probable answer, as to why the probationary period of waiting. Is that you may progress from one state or stage to another, solidifying your spiritual foundation. Further, this probationary season, points to grace, leads to repentance, and ends in revival and renewal. During this season, you are counseled to begin implementing godly principles that will move you toward discipline and humility, namely developing habits of holiness, while embracing faith and love of God. Dreamer, regularly, thank God for His patience, long-suffering, and grace (the free and unmerited favor and benefice of God), while you get things decent and in order. See suggested course of action. If listed, and only if necessary, dreamer may also consider other multiples of this number. First, see Note 6 at the beginning of this category.

122: In addition to one of the following, and only if necessary, dreamer may also consider other multiples of this number. First, see Note 6 at the beginning of this category. With that, this dream has two meanings (choose one). (1) Dreamer grace is being extended to you, via deliverance from the dangers of your fleshly passions, and a verifiable miracle within the area of your mind or head. Moreover, there will be a divine work upon your emotions, and this will manifest within your life in the form of liberality in Christ Jesus, thankfulness, and joy. All this is preparation, that you may become qualified, proven worthy, spiritually, morally, and ethically, for a religious position within an ecclesiastical order. Additionally, there is a need to make a sacrificial offering, financially, to the ministry which, you are connected. Weigh, he, or she who sows sparingly shall reap sparingly; and he or she who sows bountifully shall reap bountifully. Let each man or woman do according as you have purposed in your heart, not grudgingly, or of necessity for God loves a cheerful giver. For, God is able to make all grace a bound unto you; that you, having always all sufficiency in everything, may abound unto every good work (2 Corinthians 9:6-8). See suggested course of action. (2) Dreamer will be granted some manner of favor, gratuitously, from a very strong ally, benefactor, defender, or supporter, via an "in-kindness" or grant, or through a pardon or forgiveness of a very large debt (e.g. auto loan, bank loan, college, student loan, or mortgage). With that said, dreamer, give ear, two "favors" will be presented, one sacred, one profane. The key to knowing which favor is sacred, and which is profane. The profane favor will ask you to compromise your beliefs, namely to "gray area" some of God's unequivocal positions on certain tenets. Dreamer, never do you ever compromise your beliefs in Jesus Christ, as the Word of God made flesh, nor do you distort the meanings of His Holy Word, for any manner of favor, for this is akin to spiritual prostitution, aka idolatry. Therefore, consider carefully what is being presented to you. Additionally, there is a need to make a sacrificial offering, financially, to the ministry which, you are connected. Weigh, he, or she who sows sparingly shall reap sparingly; and he or she who sows bountifully shall reap bountifully. Let each man or woman do according as you have purposed in your heart, not grudgingly, or of necessity for God loves a cheerful giver. For, God is able to make all grace abound unto you; that you, having always all sufficiency in every thing, may abound unto every good work (2 Corinthians 9:6-8). See suggested course of action.

128: First, what your dream references, the dreamer has unequivocally heard before. What God has been speaking to you, and is requiring of you, has been clearly laid-out earlier, there is no doubt or misunderstanding; you know His will, and it leads to only one conclusion; what you have heard on other occasions, at other times, is true, and denial of that truth is unacceptable at this point. Your dream is a third or fourth warning. Dreamer, you've been clearly told to, come out from among unbelievers, and to separate yourself from them, says the Lord, for what company has righteousness with unrighteousness, or what sharing of personal thoughts and feelings has light with darkness. Have nothing to do with their sinful and wicked deeds, and I will welcome you, read, understand, and embrace 2 Corinthians 6:14-18. Unfortunately, at present, concerned with your own interest, you are driven by, and occupied with, sensual appetites, rather than spiritual needs. Your new way is based on exploring alternatives to God's righteous principles, as well as, creating a sense of unity with the wickedness around you. You have adopted a bourgeois mentality, believing yourself above God's word and above the law of the land. This mentality is concerned only with your personal comfort, material wealth, and status, at any expense. You, now, having in yourself nothing that you respect more than power and greed, are willing to sacrifice all, God, principle, family, and friend, to the image or idol of vanity. This mentality sacrifices children, family, and morality to the hollowness of satisfying immoral desires and appetites. All carried out with the hope of finding happiness by pacifying jealously and covetousness. The selling-out of yourself over to immorality, allowing wickedness to prevail in your home, devaluing those you should be protecting and nurturing, while closing your eyes to it all, are all principles based on values that are not only vile, but also increasingly unstable. This way cries out against godly ethics, and its' end offends any sense of godliness. Moreover, your desires, appetites, and attitude are leading to a chaotic and empty life. A life figuratively similar to the condition of ea rth in Genesis 1:2, wasteful, empty, and dark. This type of carnal strain and toil leads to sorrow and spiritual darkness. There is a need to re-connect with God. Favorably, dreamer, because of God's love for you, His abounding grace, and His long-suffering, there is a ray of light, sent by God, purposed to break through the darkness of your state of affairs. This ray of light is a person, anointed and sent, especially to you. Their words and inspiration will be to you, like Genesis 1:3-5 is to Genesis 1:2. Illuminatingly wise, this person will powerfully affect your life, externally and internally. Their inspiration, coupled with you earnestly embracing change, humility, contentedness, integrity, ethicalness, and a renewed faith in God's word and His process, will strengthen you to return in complete heartfelt repentance to Jesus, from a heart of love. By this, the severity of your transgressions becomes partially sweetened; for, when a man or woman genuinely return to God, in complete surrender and humility, your deliberate transgressions become like actual merits, aka "the sweetening" (Luke 7:37-50). Because, the realization of your distance from God, due to your transgressions (Isaiah 59:2-21; Luke 15:11-24), becomes the motivating force to return to God with a passion even greater than that of someone who has never sinned in such a manner, or never left the Father's house, completely converting your present to good (Acts 9:1-30). This is the secret of repentance and returning to God. Go; therefore now, and seek the Lord Jesus, repent and place your hope in Him. Hope, placed in Him, will not deceive. If, you turn and genuinely repent, you will be favored with complete healing, however, go and sin no more. For, if anyone knows the good they ought to do and doesn't do it, it is sin for them (see James 4:17). Therefore, fro m this moment forward, choose good habits and deeds, e.g. good stewardship and commitment to ministry; speak to yourself what is true and good, embracing Philippians 4:8. Authentic repentance, will affect complete restoration of things, materially and spiritually within your life and in the lives of those immediately connected to you; allowing freedom from your weaknesses to be yours. Additionally, dreamer is counseled to also recognize, acknowledge, and respect, God's absolute control over the affairs of humankind, and to renounce the belief that humans are in complete control (see Job 9:12, Isaiah 14:27; 43:13). There is a difference between divine providence and the will of humankind. Moreover, you need to take a short break from doing something. See suggested course of action. If listed, and only if necessary, dreamer may also consider other multiples of this number. First, see Note 6 at the beginning of this category.

129: In addition to one of the following, and only if necessary, dreamer may also consider other multiples of this number. First, see Note 6 at the beginning of this category. With that, this dream has two meanings (one or both may apply). (1) Dreamer is advised to abstain from a judgmental attitude, abusive talking, contentions, revenge, envy, and hatred. As your dream also denotes death; therefore, take heed and abstain from all that you are asked to abstain from, lest you die an early death (Ecclesiastes 7:17). If dreamer embrace change, and subdue your carnal side, then your prayers will be heard on high; moreover, see #2. Nonetheless, see suggested course of action. (2) Dreamer, your prayers have been heard by the Most High. God will give you new insight, a truthful vision, and it shall "come to pass". With that, the following is necessary to say. Dreamer, at present, you've gotten to the point where you're spiritually weak and feel discouraged, feeling that your faith has been in vain; intimidated by the spirit of fear. Read, understand, and embrace Romans 8:15-18, 2 Timothy 1:7. Therefore, do not allow the spirit of fear to frustrate you; only be strong and courageous, for this too will pass. However, dreamer is counseled to re-evaluate your life and figure out, what God would like you to change, that you might better fulfill His purpose within your life. Learn from your mistakes, find new direction in solving problems, pursue healing, and seek out encouragement. Favorably, dreamer, by God's power, a way out of no way will be made for you, and your state of affairs will turn around. Somehow, God will make a way for you. Jesus will come and see about you, thus, keep your faith regarding what you've believed God for; He has promised never to leave you alone. You will experience a miracle. Subsequent, joy will be revealed, rest shall appear, and healing will descend, disease will withdraw, and anxiety, anguish and crying shall pass from you; gladness will happen. If necessary, see suggested course of action.

130: Dreamer, there is an unpleasant person, one who is declared evil and anathema by God, in your midst. This person is threatened with divine punishment. This divine punishment will affect you, your household, and your environment, if they remain within your domain, or closely connected to you in some way. Dreamer, you will not be able to rise above the messenger sent to afflict this divine punishment upon that person, for they will also afflict whomever gets in his or her way. If this person is removed or disconnected from you, the divine punishment intended for them, will follow the person, and not remain within your domain, and cease from touching you. Unfortunately, dreamer your desires of ill-gotten gain and coveting may "trick" you into allowing the person to remain within your domain; therefore, check your level of greed and covetousness, repent, embrace change, and remove the wicked person from before you. If no action is taken to remove this person from before you, you will not be spared the divine punishment, nor its residuals. See suggested course of action. If listed, and only if necessary, dreamer may also consider other multiples of this number. First, see Note 6 at the beginning of this category.

132: Your dream refers to one who is redeemed; however, you are going through a refining process, see Proverbs 17:3, 27:21; thus, your dream. Dreamer is strongly urged, at this point in your life, to adhere to God's instructions and principles that guide actions and moral behavior, via His principles, as outlined within Holy Writ. Following godliness is, aimed at making you not only wiser, but also better. Dreamer, it is imperative that you govern your desires, lusts, and passions with wisdom during your refining process. You have a journey to go on, spiritual warfare to fight, and a great work to do. God wants to purify you that you might fulfill the righteous purpose for which you were designed. With that said, as you have been saved from the power of sin, you will now be refined in the "crucible" of adversity. Dreamer, if you allow God's power to break the residuals of sin within you, you will experience a great deliverance from oppression. Be very aware that your emotional and/ or physical adversities have been allowed by God that you might be humbled and made ready and prepared to rend er your gifts unto the Lord properly. God will use your sufferings to instill His principles into your mind, and make His ways penetrate your heart. He or she who has suffered in the flesh has ceased from sinning (1 Peter 4:1) that the sacrificial offerings of your worship, service, and financial support to the ministry, might be a sweet smell unto the Lord. Moreover, the refinement process that you are going through (or will go through shortly) is meant to bring honor and glory to the One who died to redeem you. True conversion makes a marvelous change in the heart and life. It alters the mind, judgment, affections, and conversation. When a man is truly converted, it grieves him to think how the time past of his life has been spent (Matthew Henry Concise Commentary). Subsequent, you will become productive and go forth, bearing spiritual fruit, counted amongst those who are sagacious; whose character is faithful, law-abiding, moral, open, scrupulous, sincere, straightforward, trustworthy, upright, reasonable in many situations, and submissive to God. Blessings, joy, protection, and prosperity will be yours. See suggested course of action. If listed, and only if necessary, dreamer may also consider other multiples of this number. First, see Note 6 at the beginning of this category.

137: Dreamer, God has made a promise to you. This promise was made when you first invited Christ into your life. However, the fulfillment of that promise made to you is conditional, and it is at hand. The condition is t hat the dreamer must subdue, chasten, and "bind" your ego, that part that fuels your negative desires, such as pride, narcissism, covetousness. Dreamer, God needs you to transition that the promise might be fulfilled, embraced, and maintained. Thus, you need to make a connection between the Light of God, and the steps needed to transition into that realm of Light (a higher spiritual divine knowledge). This higher knowledge will be the source of your wisdom and it ensures happiness. Subsequent, you will become productive and go forth, bearing spiritual fruit, counted amongst those who are sagacious; whose character is faithful, law - abiding, moral, open, scrupulous, sincere, straightforward, trustworthy, upright, reasonable in many situations, and submissi ve to God. Blessings, joy, protection, and prosperity will be yours. See suggested course of action.

144: Your dream comes as a word of encouragement, as this number refers to one of God's "shining stars", His hidden righteous. Dreamer, you are one, whose spiritual life shines as the stars of heaven, and you are a chosen and righteous minister of God. Therefore, as you have always obeyed, continue to work out your salvation with fear and trembling. For it is God who works in you, to will and to act according to His good purpose. Do everything without complaining or arguing, so that you may go on to perfection, blameless and pure, a child of God without fault, in this crooked and depraved generation, in which you shine like the stars in the universe, as you spread the word of life (Philippians 2:12-16). Moreover, you will be a revivalist, if not already, used to usher others into a totally new and higher level of spiritual awareness. You will awaken and stir-up those, who are already, predestined to become born again within the Kingdom of God (see John 3:1-17). Even amongst the "broken", a spark of life remains hidden, awaiting your particular ministry, your unique way of presenting the gospel. Y ou will appear when needed, and then disappear without thought of anything in return. By fulfilling your mission and remaining humble, you will eat and do well on this side of eternity and inherit eternal life; this is a promise to you. Note humility is the key to your success (requisite). Know the full meaning of the word and define your life by it. If listed, and only if necessary, may consider the interpretation for the number 12, as it relates to this number squared; see Note 6 at the beginning of this category.

146: This number refers to God's defense and protection. Protection, especially from the attacks of your enemies, for God's banner over you is love and grace (the free and unmerited favor and beneficence of God), to keep you from danger, harm, and hurt. Dreamer, why then should you be afraid or run from those who would dare to challenge, provoke, taunt, or rise up, in any way, against you? Cannot God deliver, without you cowardly retreating? Dreamer, nothing can be done in heaven, on earth, or in hell, unless God has decreed it to be, and He always will exercise control over it (Lamentations 3:37, 38). No one can do anything to you, nor can anyone have any power or success over you, except what is given him or her from above (also see Psalm 34). This is a well-established great truth, which, if received, can help quiet your spirit when under afflictions. If you trust the King of kings, is not this enough? Moreover, acknowledge Him as Jehovah -Nissi in your life. See suggested course of action. If listed, and only if necessary, dreamer may also consider other multiples of this number. First, see Note 6 at the beginning of this category.

150: Dreamer, your apparent loss of spiritual identity and anger issues has blinded you to God's miraculous wonders within your life. You have become insensitive to His continuous acts of making things happen for you. Consequently, you no longer respect His divine providence, and all of this you do willingly. Dreamer, you have seen and sensed His Power, but you chose not to respect your times of visitation of the Lord. Your disdainfulness wreaked the havoc you have been experiencing within your life. Fortunately, there is one earnestly interceding on your behalf. Because of their urgent and emotional requests on your behalf, God will cause your judgment by afflictions and persecution to abate. He will cause you to return from your self-imposed "exile". Subsequently, within 150 days, the chaos within your life will end. Afterwards, dreamer, do remember His Covenant of peace promised you (refer to a prophecy given you, some time ago); and respect Gods peace, it shall stand until the end of your time. Do not be afraid, there is no need to fear anything anymore. You will not be made ashamed. See suggested course of action. If listed, and only if necessary, dreamer may also consider other multiples of this number. First, see Note 6 at the beginning of this category.

151: This number refers to the rectification of anger. Dreamer, your connection to Jesus will help you to rectify your anger. You are advised to fast for 7 days, declaring your own fast (e.g. abstain from sexual immorality, in addition to other morally wrong issues, abstain from indulgence, vice, and/ or crime). To Jesus pray, Psalm 51, and He will lead you as to the kind of fast. Afterwards, dreamer is counseled to embrace a lifestyle of fasting, perhaps twice a week. Nonetheless, dreamer, deliberately develop habits of holiness, prayer, fasting, theological study, abstinence, sobriety, and separation from people, places, and circumstances that are contrary to your development of clarity, cleanness, and stability. Moreover, acknowledging that anger and fear are parts of your character, and seeking help, via repentance, fasting, prayer, and/or an anger managemen t program, will help determine the root cause of your anger, and possibly your fears. By this, you will be healed emotionally, physically, and spiritually of that which has caused your anger issue. If you are unwilling to acknowledge, challenge, and/o r change you, you will be pursued by one with an unrelenting vendetta against you, and yes, it will be allowed. Further, although the following suggestion may seem small, especially to help overcome anger, consciously putting them into practice can bring you a sense of serenity and happiness, which in itself will lessen your inner anger. Dreamer, anytime you manage to overcome anger, allow that moment to become a source of joy, a moment to be celebrated, and it will become a source of joy in the eyes of God. Remain connected to Jesus. See suggested course of action.

153: Dreamer, you will be used, in the office of revivalist, if not already, to usher others into a totally new and higher level of spiritual awareness. You will awaken and stir-up those, who are already, predestined to become born again within the Kingdom of God (see John 3:1-17). Even amongst the "broken", a spark of life remains hidden, awaiting your particular ministry, your unique way of presenting the gospel. You will appear when needed, and then disappear without thought of anything in return. By fulfilling your mission and remaining humble, you will be worthy of your wage. It is promised that y ou will eat and do well, on this side of eternity, and inherit eternal life. Note humility is the key to your su ccess (requisite). Know the full meaning of the word and define your life by it. Moreover, humbling yourself before the True and Living God and by accepting His blessings of healing, help, and restoration, He will rectify your anger issues. If listed, and only if necessary, dreamer may also consider other multiples of this number. First, see Note 6 at the beginning of this category.

155: This number denotes freedom, holiness, and redemption. Dreamer, because of your prayers and heartfelt repentance to Jesus and man or woman, seeking pardon and expressing sincere feelings of regret and brokenness for having done something awry and/or for having hurt someone, see 2 Corinthians 7:10, 11. This, coupled with humility, and your servant's attitude towards God, His laws and order, to His Word, and to holiness, God is going to bless you with tremendous recompense. He will also send an angel to rescue you out of an extremely severe or dire situation, because of your faith. Be aware that the stranger within your midst may be that angel. He comes to lead the way. Moreover, you will be used, in the office of revivalist, if not already, to usher others into a totally new and higher level of spiritual awareness. You will awaken and stir-up those, who are already, predestined to become born again within the Kingdom of God (see John 3:1-17). Even amongst the "broken", a spark of life remains hidden, awaiting your particular ministry, your unique way of presenting the gospel. You will appear when needed, and then disappear without thought of anything in return. By fulfilling your mission and remaining humble, you will be worthy of your wage. It is promised that you will eat and do well, on this side of eternity, a nd inherit eternal life. Note humility is the key to your success (requisite). Know the full meaning of the word and define your life by it. Additionally, because of your deliverance and freedom from hard things, your oppressor will respect your God and acknowledge His Power (see Isaiah 40:29-31). If listed, and only if necessary, dreamer may also consider other multiples of this number. First, see Note 6 at the beginning of this category.

160: In addition to one of the following, and only if necessary, dreamer may also consider other multiples of this number. First, see Note 6 at the beginning of this category. With that, this dream has five meanings (choose one). (1) It is your season to begin choosing purposeful choices. You are responsible for your unique purpose in life, and all that is invol ve in fulfilling that purpose. You are responsible for planning your actions and your life, around your purpose. You must make calculated decisions as to how you will live your life, and who and what you will allow in your life; and relying on emotions alone is a dangerous, an unreliable route to follow. It will not lead to purpose. Dreamer, do not allow your life to be weighed down with indulgence in sensual relations, useless or profitless activity, licentiousness, wastefulness, drunkenness and the anxieties of life. Be always vigilant and careful, attentively observing negative "triggers" in your life. Questions to journal: who do you want to be and how do you want to live, if not for Jesus, promoting the Kingdom of God? Make an earnest effort to f ind out, learn, and determine, with certainty, how to live your life on God's terms, according to His purpose for you; and what actual ly is required. This usually begins with prayer, joining, attending, and committing to a church, bible study, Sunday school. Also pray that you might be able to escape all that is about to happen, and that you may be able to stand before Adonai Elohim, knowing that the end of days is near. See suggested course of action. (2) It is necessary to say first, dreamer you are Christian, and filled with the Holy Spirit, thus, God will not take His Spirit away from you, nor blot your name out of the Book of Life. However, your dream does speak of one who is angry, dishonest, frustrated, resentful, self-centered, and imprisoned to your own ego, with no sincere intent or desire to change. You have severe mood changes, and are greatly immoral, especially sexually. You also have a tendency to blame others for your personal misfortune. Drunk with power, material possessions, and pride, you put everything before God, worshipping anything but God (spiritual adultery). Your actions have provoked divine punishment. Before reaching this point, you were clearly warned, and reproved; yet, you have not taken care. There will be a decrease in help from the only real true God, including any Word from the Lord regarding you and His hedge will be removed. Your finances will dwindle greatly; you will have to downsize. Your family, friends, mentors, and teachers will le ave from before your face. This "famine" will leave only anxiety, fear, and despair as your food. On another vein, since your frustration with Christianity, God, His principles, and standards was demonically influenced this famine will not be complete ly devastating, according to God's tender mercies and grace (the free and unmerited favor and beneficence of God). All this will create within you a clean heart and restore an upright spirit within you. Pray Psalm 51. See suggested course of action. (3) Although dreamer is unable to bear children, perhaps embarrassed and/or crushed by grief as a result, and always wanting or lacking, dreamer, you are powerful and strong and are well able to do mighty works for the Kingdom of God. God has given you a rare sense of purpose from birth. Ultimately, that purpose is seriously tied to the Word of God. For you, a purposeless existence will cause only frustration and despair. Therefore, you must choose a lifelong commitment to sowing "seeds" that will ultimately uproot and replace the wicked seeds planted by demonic forces some time ago, at an earlier age, perhaps the reason for your inability to bear young. Your seeds should be intentional development of habits of holiness, prayer, fasting, theological study, abstinence, sobriety, and separation from people, places, and circumstances that are contrary to your development of holiness, clarity, and stability. Dreamer, wise choices will bring you authentic joy, happiness, divine purpo se, and miraculous knowledge and power, in due time. Moreover, dreamer, you are under the special protection of the Lord. Have faith in God, and not in state of affairs. God is promising that no longer will hurt be done you, if you respect His pr inciples and precepts, and most importantly reverence Him. In addition, God has persuaded others to be very compassionate, sensitive, and to take care, when dealing or speaking with you. Additionally, dreamer, know that a person, even you, can go from bad to good in one day. That place or thing previously unusable or unprofitable can become suitable for good and/or profitable in some way, or that which is, emptied can be refilled again. Indeed one or all of these situations maybe rectifi ed, if dreamer adheres to wisdom; put works with your faith, see James 2:14-26. For example, proper nutrition, exercise, and rest, can stabilized or cease, some diseases; prudence with finances, can stop constant foreclosure notices, end a cycle of poverty, or any kind of money shortages; and prayer and fasting can push any kind of darkness or demonic force far away from you. See suggested course of action. (4) If dreamer has a chronic illness at present, your dream implies an illness, perhaps a chronic (ongoing) illness, (e.g. cancer, diabetes, heart disease, HIV), will continue for a little while longer, or an illness that will recur, again, and again; if, the appropriate health initiatives, or lifestyle changes, are not, taken. Proper nutrition, exercise, healthy lifestyle choices, and rest, can stabilized or cease, some diseases. Dreamer, your malady may lead to early death if the appropriate lifestyle changes are not heeded. This warning must not be undermined by notions that presuppose, the warning is real, but the possibility of an actual loss of life itself, is not. With that said, if you haven't already, dreamer is encouraged to seek medical attention as soon as possible, and call for the elders of your church, for it is through their prayers of faith and anointing of oil upon you that sin is forgiven and healing bestowed[36]. This is a true saying, thus it is time to have faith in God. Moreover, dreamer it is always a good time to get your house and papers in order (e.g. insurances, bequeaths, untold truths that need to be said), and always a good time to gather family together for prayer, support, wisdom, and truthfulness (Ecclesiastes 12:6). Additionally, dreamer although you may be currently suffering or soon will enter a season of suffering, suffering has a purifying effect in one's life so that after you have suffered you will cease (stop, restrain, refrain, quit, desist) from sin, especially the sin that chronically assails you. This should be your attitude toward sin and it should be so inten se that even in your suffering, your determination remains, I'm done with sin! See 1 Peter 4:1-3. Dreamer, know that a person, can go from bad to good in one day, if wisdom is adhered to. For example, faith, prayer, and fasting do affect deliverance and healing, spiritually and physically, especially when traditional medicine has reached its end. Moreover, proper diet, water, vitamins, prescription medication, exercise, and rest, can stabilized or cease some symptoms, or restore health. The key here is to st op sinning via a complete change of lifestyle choices. See suggested course of action. (5) If you are a preacher, educator, prophet, praise leader, your dream denotes that God will deal with the dreamer; He will mark you with a sign of His displeasure, by way of a trial. He will also strip you of your anointing, and you will no longer inspire. Your works and words have testified against you, for you have proven proud, covetous, false, and oppressive. Dreamer, if you pretend to be a spiritual leader of some sort, and are immoral, your immorality exposes your pretensions for what they are, false. See Philippians 3:1-21. One should regard your dream, with sincere alarm. This warning must not be undermined by notions that presuppose, the warning is real, but the possibility of an actual loss of a God-given ministry, your prosperity, or even life itself is not. Favorably, grace will be shown you via a probationary period. This probationary period decreed might be a proving by trial (e.g. a wilderness experience); by humiliation and servitude (Judges 13:1; Acts 13:21, 22); or by waiting (Acts 7:23-30). This probationary season points to grace, leads to repentance, and ends in revival and renewal. During this season, you are counseled to begin implementing godly principles that will move you toward discipline and humility, while embracing faith and love of God. Thank God for His patience, long-suffering, and grace (the free and unmerited favor and beneficence of God), while you get things decent and in order. Therefore, be earnest to repent, and God will deliver you from death and your feet from stumbling, that you may again walk before God in the light of life (Psalm 56:13). See suggested course of action.

170: In addition to one of the following, and only if necessary, dreamer may also consider other multiples of this number. First, see Note 6 at the beginning of this category. With that, this dream has two meanings (choose one). (1) Your dream was sent to encourage the dreamer. Dreamer, because of your humble and submissive faith in God's word, and not your works alone, you are, declared as one who is a righteous minister, one who lives by faith. Planted in the House of the Lord, you will continue to prosper and mature. The same God, who planted you in your ministry, is the same God who will cause you to mature and prosper. You will live and thrive where most things perish, independent of outward circumstances, via divine grace. Your spiritual growth may not be so rapid, however, if you endure, you will become a beautiful picture of a godly man or woman, who in your uprightness, aims to glorify God. (2) Your dream represents some type of spiritual privileges and a purification process, God will separate you from people, places, and circumstances that will hinder your growth, view this separation as a blessing from God and not as an evil thing has happen. Under all adversities retain a spirit of joy, continue to make progress in your spiritual life, with gladness, thanksgiving, singing, and then, strength, intense energy, and fertility will be your recompense, and your praise will be a sweet aroma in the nostrils of the Lord. If applicable, this promise is to your generations to come. Come what may, you shall make steady progress and flourish in a very impressive manner; bringing forth fruit, even in your old age. Dreamer, as you age, your anointing to minister, and divine revelations, will always be fresh and edifying. See suggested course of action

183: Your dream comes as a stern rebuke. Your dream denotes one whose spirit is without restraint (Proverbs 25:28). Although you, the dreamer, is intended to be one who has the capacity to exemplify empathy, forgiveness, and understanding; one whom people are drawn to for absolution, as well, one who is important to the well-being of others, and important as a leader, promoting in every way the welfare of others, and is powerfully anointed for this. Instead, you live in excess, mischievousness, arrogance, and unruliness, to the point of recklessness, ruin, and desolation. And not only so, but you trample those you consider less than yourself, harmful to those about you. The selling-out of yourself over to immorality, devaluing those, you should be protecting and nurturing, especially the faithful, while closing your eyes to it all, are all principles based on values that are not only vile, but also increasingly unstable. This way cries out against godly ethics, and its' end offends any sense of godliness. Dreamer, you obey no one, and accept no correction. You do not trust in the Lord, nor do you draw near to Him, although He has given you space to repent; instead, you seduced your children to follow you, perpetuating your sins. Sidebar, regarding your condescendingly arrogant attitude towards others, this is why you are uncontrollably spending money wastefully, as well, this is why no healing has manifested in an area you so desire healed. Thus, sin will very soon turn your paradise into chaos, and dishonor the beauty of your name. You are also at risk of fallin g into a state of serious health problems and possibly loss of life. So severe are things that restoration can only be by returning to Christ Jesus wholeheartedly. Dreamer when God hides His face from someone celebrations are turned into moaning and groaning, and the party is exchanged for depression and solitude. Your recklessness can be remedied by prayer and heartfelt repentance to Jesus and to individuals affected by your action. Dreamer, in order to fulfill your commission, to reach many, you will need to, seriously begin reflecting upon your moral weaknesses, especially your lack of self-restraint and arrogance. How you might bring them under subjection to biblical principles, and how you might aspire for a certain level of spiritual purity. You are advised to discipline your body and your sensual desires and to bring them under control. Temperance in all things is your key word. Moreover, adopt a determined resolve, to go no further with an attitude of uncertainty about God, His Word, and Christianity. Rather, become intense and convicted when it comes to defending your beliefs. As well, steel your emotions and thoughts against all that will come against your God. God will lead the way. If not brought under subjection, you will become an object of scorn, derision, laughter, a joke to all who encounters you. Moreover, having proved yourself, many times, morally unclean for God's purposes, you will die before your time, in order for your soul to be saved. See suggested course of action. If listed, and only if necessary, dreamer may also consider other multiples of this number. First, see Note 6 at the beginning of this category.

185: Your dream denotes an intervention of some kind, in some manner or another. Dreamer, God desires to rescue you from darkness. It will not be through some miraculous or cataclysmic means, but rather by a natural course of events. Jesus will strengthen you emotionally, psychologically, and physically, to go get help with your problem via a faith based community, aka a church, a Christian based support group, Christian counseling, healthcare, or inpatient. Embrace the process, and you will be rescued from darkness, and led into God's authentic light. See suggested course of action. If listed, and only if necessary, dreamer may also consider other multiples of this number. First, see Note 6 at the beginning of this category.

200: In addition to one of the following, and only if necessary, dreamer may also consider other multiples of this number. First, see Note 6 at the beginning of this category. With that, this dream has two meanings (choose one). (1) Dreamer, there will be clarity and freedom in the way you communicate yourself to others, especially prophetically. Thus; from this time forward, so speak and act as those who are judged by the law of liberty; see James 2:12, 13. For example, remove condemnation from your message of grace and holiness, see John 3:17, Romans 8:1, 1 John 3:20, 21, for there is a difference between conviction and condemnation. Moreover, take note of this, you should be quick to listen, slow to speak, and slow to anger, see James 1:19-25. The servant of God always experiences a gap between his or her thoughts and deeds. Meaning, before you actually act or speak, there is an instant of time for you to decide, to do, or say, what is wise and good or foolish and evil. Hence, your words should align with your moral stance, and should be seasoned with empathy, compassion, and understanding. For example, you may not agree with another's lifestyle choices, but you do know, and should voice if necessary, that they do have a right to enter into the House of God to repent, pray, and praise Adonai, without being condemned by you or others, see John 3:17. Nonetheless, dreamer, as you perfect yourself, God will help by sending 'rains of blessings', then your situations will prosper. With that said, dreamer, the rains of blessings is coming, get ready! (2) Your dream comes as a message of grace. God wants to balance your understanding of His ways and means, for you are surely being called. Adonai Elohim has need of you in His Kingdom. Dreamer, you are above average in intelligence, and are one who has the courage to stand up for what you believe in, especially those things regarding your spirituality. You sincerely believe that what you believe is truth. However, your truth is insufficient; thus, you are spiritually impoverished (Revelation 3:17 -22). Question to journal, are your beliefs in harmony with God's provision for life on the other side of eternity, in heaven? Dreamer, I invite you to consider the following. Believing and/or encouraging others to approach God the Father, without the essential provision He has provided for humankind to approach Him properly; that provision being Yeshua HaMashiach, is not safe, and causes one to remain spiritually impoverish. Some call God's provision Jesus, Wonderful Counselor, Mighty God, Everlasting Father, Prince of Peace, our atonement, advocate, liberator, propitiator, and our salvation. It is only through this channel that we may hope through faith to conciliate with our Creator, see John 3:16, Acts 2:37-42, 1 Timothy 2:4-7. See suggested course of action.

In addition, the following is a common word; expression or usage (e.g. slang or clichés) or a 'probable' that is metaphorically represented by this number:

- A bicentennial birthday or anniversary

204: Your dream was sent to encourage the dreamer. Dreamer, you are down-to-earth, fair, humble, just, unpretentious, not rude or obscene, and one whom believers may interact with socially on very personal levels (e.g. business associate, friendship, ministry, spouse). If these attributes are not present at this moment, embracing them, at this time, will prove expedient, for, you will be used, if not already, to usher others into a totally new and higher level of spiritual awareness, appearing only, to do God's will and then fade back into obscurity. Even amongst the "broken", a spark of life remains hidde n, awaiting your particular ministry, your unique way of presenting the gospel. You will appear when needed, and then disappear without thought of anything in return. Dreamer, by fulfilling your part and remaining humble, you will be worthy of your wag e. It is promised that you will eat and do well, on this side of eternity, and on the other side. Humility is the key to your success (requisite). Know the full meaning of the word and define your life by it. Additionally, the dreamer will be a recipient of another's help, shortly, and the dreamer may feel free to establish a relationship on some level, with that someone. With that said, dreamer is counseled to start trusting in the integrity of God. If listed, and only if necessary, dreamer may also consider other multiples of this number. First, see Note 6 at the beginning of this category.

216: In addition to one of the following, and only if necessary, dreamer may also consider other multiples of this number. First, see Note 6 at the beginning of this category. With that, this dream has six meanings (one, two, etc. may apply). (1) Unmarried dreamer: Dreamer, if marriage is desired, a potential spouse is looking carefully at you at present. Your faithfulness and unpretentiousness is beautiful in his or her sight. An introduction will present itself shortly. The question of the possibility of relocation may be asked. God will honor the union. Moreover, and if so desired, the union of the groom a nd bride will result in a literal pregnancy. Continue to have faith in God, which is a resolute trust in the integrity of God and in His Word, He will have mercy on you, and grant you the desire of your heart, namely to birth children of your own body, suddenly and very soon. (2) Dreamer, you are encompassed about with righteousness and purity. The intents and motives of your heart are pure and righteous. You are honorable in the eyes of God. Favorably, dreamer, you will have success overcoming ol d things; and there will be joy spiritually, you will experience joy and happiness serving the Lord. Consequently, you are prepared for any spiritual conflict or evil activity that may come your way. Many will be inspired by your faith in Christ, your humility, and your unpretentiousness. (3) Dreamer, you have learned the Christian values and principles that leads one to reach out and touch others in a loving and graceful manner; ultimately finding yourself promoting the genuine cause of Christ and the good of others. Consequently, you have an open connection to divine revelation, which will at times be used on a prophetic platform. Properly developed, your link to prophetic revelation can and should be used to help others. If not already, you will inspire others to dream and to make their dreams come true. Dreamer, you are gifted in many areas, and you have access to prophetic wisdom, thus, you are required to be a transformational force in people's lives, via not neglecting the gift that is within you. You will now be led into situations, where you will show up when most needed, and then disappear without a thought of compensation. You will be dispatched on missions, to help believers who are facing urgent needs during a crisis, and/or in an emergency, and to give instant help, as well as, to express God's loving kindness, His grace, mercy, a nd compassion. You are sent to protect and defend those who obediently love God, and who is loved by God. An angel (perhaps disguised as human, or one, who is a true servant of God, with the Spirit of Truth within) will lead the way. Read, understa nd, and embrace Psalm 147. Altruistic, goodhearted, and generous service to God and others is beneficial at this time. Freely received, freely give. Dreamer, love God so completely that you will never forsake His service for any reason. (4) There will be success publicly, regarding some kind of enterprise, as your dream also denotes a company with special status that is given preferential treatment by the federal government because it is owned by socially and economically disadvantaged persons (e.g. small businesses). With that, dreamer, you will experience a very distinct moment of divine guidance, a "flash" of inspiration. An idea will pop into your head, apparently out of nowhere. It is an idea waiting to be developed. The prophe tic wisdom, via inspired intellect, will allow you to create something, seemingly out of nothing. However, the process of investigating and understanding the implications of this "flash of inspiration", the idea, is on you exclusively. This proce ss is known as, "faith with works" (James 2:17-26). Dreamer, by examining the length and breadth of the inspired idea (aka doing the research), and establishing a thorough understanding of the concept, conclusions can be reached. Conclusions such as, is there a market for your idea? Where is the market located? How should I market my idea? Do I need further education to learn about my idea? Are there investment resources, and so on? When your process is finally complete, an idea will be born and should be ready for market. This idea will prosper you greatly, and it should benefit people, greatly transforming lives. Seize the moment, and capitalize on it, while you have an open link to divine inspiration. (5) If dreamer is actually, at present, experiencing a spiritual struggle within that is very intense. Dreamer, your inner spiritual warfare, is due to your anger or rage issues, and/or some other manner of darkness within. Moreover, the intensity or "heat" of the struggle is actually the refin ing and purifying work of the Paraclete. Therefore, persevere, for your struggle will cause the emergence of a more divine led wisdom within you. It will also be through these pains that the wisdom of harmonizing, fear and love of the Lord within your life, will be imparted to you. Further, due to the intensity of your struggle, one of God's messengers is sent to give you the support needed at this time. Be aware that the new person within your midst may be that messenger. (6) Your dream denotes a virus or inflammation of the liver, or a toxin disease affecting the liver, such as Jaundice or gallstones. Dreamer is advised to seek medical attention.

220: This number refers to one, namely the dreamer, who should embrace the spirit of expectancy, coupled with faith. Dreamer, as the old saying goes; "the spirit of expectation is the breeding ground for your miracle". Expectation is a confident belief or strong hope (faith) that a particular event will happen. It's a divine given mental image of something expected. Read and embrace Hebrews 11:1, 2. Dreamer, do you have a spirit of expectancy? Is what you're expecting within the realm of godliness and logic, not considered outside of God's will, or not considered illogical or irrational by most? Have faith in that. If necessary, see suggested course of action. If listed, and only if necessary, dreamer may also consider other multiples of this number. First, see Note 6 at the beginning of this category.

230: Your dream refers to one who is redeemed; however, you are going through a refining process, see Proverbs 17:3, 27:21; thus, your dream. Dreamer is strongly urged, at this point in your life, to adhere to God's instructions and principles that guide actions and moral behavior, via His principles, as outlined within Holy Writ. Following godliness is, aimed at making you not only wiser, but also better. Dreamer, it is imperative that you govern your desires, lusts, and passions with wisdom during your refining process. You have a journey to go on, spiritual warfare to fight, and a great work to do. God wants to purify you that you might fulfill the righteous purpose for which you were designed. With that said, as you have been saved from the power of sin, you will now be refined in the "crucible" of adversity. Dreamer, if you allow God's power to break the residuals of sin within you, you will experience a great deliverance from oppression. Be very aware that your emotional and/ or physical adversities have been allowed by God that you might be humbled and made ready and prepared to render your gi fts unto the Lord properly. God will use your sufferings to instill His principles into your mind, and make His ways penetrate your heart. He or she who has suffered in the flesh has ceased from sinning (1 Peter 4:1) that the sacrificial offerings of your worship, service, and financial support to the ministry, might be a sweet smell unto the Lord. Moreover, the refinement process that you are going through (or will go through shortly) is meant to bring honor and glory to the One who died to redeem you. True conversion makes a marvelous change in the heart and life. It alters the mind, judgment, affections, and conversation. When a man is truly converted, it grieves him to think how the time past of his life has been spent (Matthew Henry Concise Commentary). After this, you will become productive and go forth, bearing spiritual fruit, counted amongst those who are sagacious; whose character is faithful, law-abiding, moral, open, scrupulous, sincere, straightforward, trustworthy, upright, reasonable in many situations, and submissive to God. Blessings, joy, protection, and prosperity will be yours. See suggested course of action. If listed, and only if necessary, dreamer may also consider other multiples of this number. First, see Note 6 at the beginning of this category.

234: Read, understand, and embrace Revelation 3:15-22, this is to you, now. Thus, your dream comes as a rebuke against quarreling about words, pride, and the love of money. Dreamer, God knows you, and the way that you are. He knows your deeds, that you are neither cold nor hot. So, because you are lukewarm, neither hot nor cold, He is about to spit you out of His mouth. You say, 'I am rich; I have acquired wealth and do not need a thing.' However, you do not realize that you are spiritually wretched, pitiful, poor, blind, and naked. You are counseled to do what it takes, namely earnestly repent, so your shameful nakedness can be covered. Those whom God loves, He rebukes and discipline, so do be earnest, and repent. When Jesus has tried and proven you, you will come forth as gold. In this, you will greatly rejoice, though now for a little while you will have to suffer grief in all kinds of trials. The grief and trails have come so that your faith; of greater worth than gold, which perishes even though refined by fire, may be proved genuine and may result in praise, glory, and honor when Jesus Christ is revealed. So, sincerely do your best to present yourself to God as one approved, who does not need to be ashamed and who correctly handles the word of truth. Avoid godless chatter, because those who indulge in it; will become more and more ungodly, like those who have wandered away from the truth. Don't have anything to do with unlearned, irrational, and unwise and foolish arguments, for they produce quarrels, as you know quite well; and the Lord's servant must not quarrel over theological or spiritual matters; instead, you should strive to be genial, using wisdom to teach, not resentful. Those who oppose you, you must gently instruct, in the hope that God will grant them repentance, leading them to a knowledge of the truth, as He has done for you, and that they will come to their senses and escape from the trap of the devil, who has taken them captive to do his will. If you cleanse yourself from wickedness, you will be an instrument for noble purposes, made holy, useful to the Master and prepared to do any good work. Therefore, flee evil desires, and pursue righteousness, faith, love, and peace, along with those who call on the Lord out of a pure heart. See suggested course of action. If listed, and only if necessary, dreamer may also consider other multiples of this number. First, see Note 6 at the beginning of this category.

240: This number denotes a spirit doubt is overtaking the dreamer. Read, understand, and embrace Matthew 21:21, James 1:5-8. See suggested course of action. If listed, and only if necessary, dreamer may also consider other multiples of this number. First, see Note 6 at the beginning of this category

242: Your dream was sent to encourage the dreamer. Dreamer, the Lord eyes are always upon you, in your difficult situations, distresses, and hardships, that He may help you at the appropriate time. Acknowledge and praise Him as Jehovah Jireh, your provider, and cheerfully trust in God, and obey Him, for the Lord will provide for you. If listed, and only if necessary, dreamer may also consider other multiples of this number. First, see Note 6 at the beginning of this category.

246: Your dream was sent to encourage the dreamer. It implies that the dreamer is a diligent worker concerning your duties, missions, and responsibilities. You devote yourself to work, as well as, show concern for the betterment of your community at large; and with your organized, efficient approach, things are done resourcefully. Dreamer, you radiate security, and will often forfeit your own desires for your family, others, or for any worthy cause. You will now reap the rewards of such diligence, including rest and graceful surroundings. If applicable, your children will reap the fruits of the blessing of your giving. Moreover, as you are able to handle great responsibility and wealth, and are one who is tolerant, you will experience receiving an act of kindness, monetarily, from someone who is affluent. Additionally, dreamer you are entering into a season within your life that will prepare you spiritually for the visitation of the Lord in your individual life. During this time, you will experience His love and presence, as you've never known it before. For, He is saying to you, "I will teach you godly wisdom". You will receive direct insight of divine truth. You will come to know, without a doubt, that God is the true source of your strength and wisdom, and He is your sufficiency. As a result, a greater love for self, family, and others will begin to manifest, affecting wholeness within your life. With all that, the following is necessary to say. Dreamer, do not be deceived, with affluence, power, and wealth, comes good and evil. Today, you will need to choose between good and evil; and set "checks and balances" within yourself, because you have innate tendencies to become extreme and will judge others according to your "extremisms". Embracing this side of yourself will cause you to be deemed inappropriate, and delayed at that moment, to be of service to the Kingdom of God. Regrettably, this will lead to you being unhappy, and unable to discern between truth and error, without you realizing your shortsightedness. Therefore, the "checks and balances" are meant to rectify the soul to increase its capacity to receive the blessings of the Lord more fully. Blessings; in this sense, is a state of high honor, spiritual beauty, and great illumination. Henceforth, in accordance with your decision as to how you shall continue from this day forward, will define your increase or the dwindling thereof, in your future and beyond. Note, if you choose to embrace the positive, this will lead to a great balancing of your theology, resulting in a belief that is complete, with solid attributes, and your inspiration will make for very good teaching. You would make an excellent apologist (witness) for the Kingdom of God. Seriously consider this branch of Christian theology. If listed, and only if necessary, dreamer may also consider other multiples of this number. First, see Note 6 at the beginning of this category.

248: In addition to one of the following, and only if necessary, dreamer may also consider other multiples of this number. First, see Note 6 at the beginning of this category. With that, this dream has two meanings (choose one). (1) Dreamer is one who will hold an important or distinguished position in some organization, and/or you are purposed to found or establish some kind of institution. If necessary, see suggested course of action. (2) Male dreamer: Dreamer is becoming a father, be it biological father, adoptive, stepfather, in-law, or you are one who will raise-up and/or take care of a child. Dreamer is counseled to support and nurture, in the principles and love of the Lord, as this child will reach back to support you greatly. Read, understand, and embrace Proverbs 22:6. If necessary, see suggested course of action.

252: In addition to one of the following, and only if necessary, dreamer may also consider other multiples of this number. First, see Note 6 at the beginning of this category. With that, this dream has two meanings (choose one). (1) Dreamer grace is being extended to you, via deliverance from the dangers of your fleshly passions, and a verifiable miracle within the area of your mind or head. Moreover, there will be a divine work upon your emotions, and this will manifest within your life in the form of liberality in Christ Jesus, thankfulness, and joy. All this is preparation, that you may become qualified, proven worthy, spiritually, morally, and ethically, for a religious position within an ecclesiastical order. Additionally, there is a need to make a sacrificial offering, financially, to the ministry which, you are connected. Weigh, he, or she who sows sparingly shall reap sparingly; and he or she who sows bountifully shall reap bountifully. Let each man or woman do according as you have purposed in your heart, not grudgingly, or of necessity for God loves a cheerful giver. For, God is able to make all grace abound unto you; that you, having always all sufficiency in everything, may abound unto every good work (2 Corinthians 9:6-8). If necessary, see suggested course of action. (2) Dreamer will be granted some manner of favor, from a very strong ally, benefactor, defender, or supporter, via an "in-kind" grant, or through a forgiveness of a very large debt (e.g. auto loan, bank loan, college, student loan, or mortgage), or through a pardon. With that said, dreamer, give ear, two "favors" will be presented, one sacred, one profane. The key to knowing which favor is sacred, and which is profane. The profane favor will ask you to compromise your beliefs, namely to "gray area" some of God's unequivocal positions on certain tenets. Dreamer, never do you ever compromise your beliefs in Jesus Christ, as the Word of God made flesh, nor do you distort the meanings of His Holy Word, for any manner of favor, for this is akin to spiritual prostitution, aka idolatry. Dreamer, you are a Christian soldier, a battle-seasoned Christian, who should know what to do because of your experience and familiarity with Scripture. You also have access to prophetic wisdom; therefore, you have the capacity to discern truth from false. Nurture your gift of discernment; developing it; by which you will be able to discern compromise, regarding ideologies, "isms", and other concerns and issues, pertaining to, contained within, and in accordance with the Bible. You are able to keep with the nature of the Bible.

Therefore, consider carefully what is being presented to you. The lesson is, no matter how personable, powerful, or difficul t a person, or how uncertain or unpopular the choices and issues, always take the next biblical and ethical step, for obedience to God's principles will always prove safer and stronger foundationally. Additionally, there is a need to make a sacrificial of fering, financially, to the ministry which, you are connected. Weigh, he, or she who sows sparingly shall reap sparingly; and he or she who sows bountifully shall reap bountifully. Let each man or woman do according as you have purposed in your heart, not grudgingly, or of necessity for God loves a cheerful giver. For, God is able to make all grace abound unto you; that you, having always all sufficiency in everything, may abound unto every good work (2 Corinthians 9:6-8). See suggested course of action. If listed, and only if necessary, dreamer may also consider other multiples of this number. First, see Note 6 at the beginning of this category.

264: Your dream refers to one who is redeemed; however, you are going through a refining process, see Proverbs 17:3, 27:21; thus, your dream. Dreamer is strongly urged, at this point in your life, to adhere to God's instructions and principles that guide actions and moral behavior, via His principles, as outlined within Holy Writ. Following godliness is, aimed at making you not only wiser, but also better. Dreamer, it is imperative that you govern your desires, lusts, and passions with wisdom during your refining process. You have a journey to go on, spiritual warfare to fight, and a great work to do. God wants to purify you that you might fulfill the righteous purpose for which you were designed. With that said, as you have been saved from the power of sin, you will now be refined in the "crucible" of adversity. Dreamer, if you allow God's power to break th e residuals of sin within you, you will experience a great deliverance from oppression. Be very aware that your emotional and/or physical adversities have been allowed by God that you might be humbled and made ready and prepared to render your gifts unto the Lord properly. God will use your sufferings to instill His principles into your mind, and make His ways penetrate your heart. He or she who has suffered in the flesh has ceased from sinning (1 Peter 4:1) that the sacrificial offerings of your worship, service, and financial support to the ministry, might be a sweet smell unto the Lord. Moreover, the refinement process that you are going through (or will go through shortly) is meant to bring honor and glory to the One who died to redeem you. True conversion makes a marvelous change in the heart and life. It alters the mind, judgment, affections, and conversation. When a man is truly converted, it grieves him to think how the time past of his life has been spent (Matthew Henry Concise Commentary). After this, you will become productive and go forth, bearing spiritual fruit, counted amongst those who are sagacious; whose character is faithful, law-abiding, moral, open, scrupulous, sincere, straightforward, trustworthy, upright, reasonable in many situations, and submissive to God. Blessings, joy, protection, and prosperity will be yours. See suggested course of action. If listed, and only if necessary, dreamer may also consider other multiples of this number. First, see Note 6 at the beginning of this category.

270: This number refers to God's judgment (divine reprimand for folly and sin) because of evil doings. See Lamentations 3:1-5:22. This passage is a picture of your coming dilemmas. Dreamer, because of the Lord's great love, you will not be consumed, for His compassions never fail (Lamentations 3:22). See suggested course of action. If listed, and only if necessary, dreamer may also consider other multiples of this number. First, see Note 6 at the beginning of this category.

280: Dreamer, for a little while, you will be given access to very powerful and prophetic wisdom, use this wisdom to be a transformational force, spiritually, in other people's lives. It is necessary to say, the beginning of wisdom is the fear (deep respect and honor) of God, and to shun evil is understanding, (see Psalm 111:10, Proverbs 1:7, 4:7, 9:10). With that, dreamer, you will experience a very distinct moment of divine guidance, a "flash" of inspiration. An idea will pop into your head, apparently out of nowhere. It is an idea waiting to be developed. The prophetic wisdom, via inspired intellect, will allow you to create something, seemingly out of nothing. However, the process of investigating and understanding the implications of this "flash of inspiration", the idea, is on you exclusively. This process is known as, "faith with works" (James 2:17-26). Dreamer, by examining the length and breadth of the inspired idea (aka doing the research), and establishing a thorough understanding of the concept, conclusions can be reached. Conclusions such as, is there a market for y our idea? Where is the market located? How should I market my idea? Do I need further education to learn about my idea? Are there investment resources, and so on? When your process is finally complete, an idea will be born and should be ready for mark et. This idea will prosper you greatly, and it should benefit people, greatly transforming lives. Seize the moment, and capitalize on it, while you have an open link to divine inspiration. Moreover, selflessness will serve as the vessel that contains all the insight you'll be receiving. An angel (perhaps disguised as human, or one, who is a true servant of God, with the Spirit of Truth within) will help lead the way. If listed, and only if necessary, dreamer may also consider other multiples of this number. First, see Note 6 at the beginning of this category.

284: It is time for the dreamer to earnestly thirst and long for those things, by which the soul is genuinely refreshed, supported, and strengthen. It is suggested that you go away, into a quiet place, away from all the distractions, to seriously fast, and deprogram and re-program yourself (Galatians 1:12-24). At this crossroads in your life, you need to count all that you know, to be worthless (Philippians 3:3-9). Subsequently, you will begin to walk and grow into a more mature spiritual being, going on towards perfection, enabled to see into the spiritual realm more clearly. Additionally no matter, the hardships and they may prove grievously, never again look back, but genuinely, in words and deeds, continue to progress forward. By this, your capacity for greater illumination, intellectually and spiritually, will become enlarged, giving you access to more than a few of the gates of wisdom (2 Corinthians 12:2-10). See suggested course of action. If listed, and only if necessary, dreamer may also consider other multiples of this number. First, see Note 6 at the beginning of this category.

288: Your dream denotes idolatry. Idolatry is "foreign service"; any act that expresses devotion or fanatical admiration to something or someone other than Adonai Elohim, or any particulars of these sorts. This enslavement has made you spiritually irrational and demonically influenced. Moreover, fear is akin to idolatry; for one may exalt the spirit of fear, above God's promised word of protection from all hurt, harm, and danger. Serious fear issues, also makes one spiritually irrational and demonically influenced. Therefore, dreamer is advised to exalt no one, nor your public image of well-being, nor fear or worry, above God, especially to the point of death, even death emotionally or spiritually. Why die needlessly (Ecclesiastes 7:17). Other forms of spiritual idolatry include anger problems. One primary sign that anger maybe manifesting within you is a continual unforgiving heart towards another or a group of persons, a place, or a thing. An unforgiving heart is a most subtle thing that steals its way into your heart almost unknown, but in the sight of God, it is the greatest hindrance to your spiri tual fellowship and communion with a Holy God who answers prayer. This is the one thing, spoken of in the Word that if found in the heart of a believer it will hinder answered prayer and it opens the door to all kinds of sicknesses, even premature death. Idolatry, then, is the forsaking of God's love and the embracing of the world's values and desires. Your dream is challenging you, the dreamer, to confront your dysfunction, one way, or another; and your dream exposes a need of refinement of character, namely in the area dealing with the deeds of the flesh. For example, dishonesty, adultery, sensuality, hostility, feuding, vendettas, grudges, unfriendliness, strife, jealousy, outbursts of anger, disputes, dissensions, discord, factions, cliques, envying, drunkenness, carousing (see 1 Corinthians 6:8-11). Dreamer, a decision to repent, and return, and reject the attitude of foolishness, hypocrisy, and selfishness; and where there would be chaos, genuine peace will abide. Where there is a lack of prudence, wisdom will rule. A simple prayer of repentance is in order. "Jesus, I beg your forgiveness. I know I've broken your heart, I never meant to treat you this way. Heavenly Father, I'll do whatever it takes, to never hurt you again, and I'll lo ve you for the rest of my life". Further, take steps now to avert feeding the growing desires of your carnal nature. Deliberately develop habits of holiness, prayer, fasting, theological study, abstinence, sobriety, and separation from people, places, and circumstances that are contrary to your development of clarity, cleanness, and stability. Dreamer, by acknowledging that idolatry, at its core, is part of your character, and by seeking help, via prayer, fasting, and/or an anger management program, this will help determine the root cause of your idolatry, anger, and your fears. With all that said, dreamer, one, who does understand your situation, is near you. Seek them out, for when at least two agree; that which needs "binding or loosening", will give, and heaven will hear and honor the agreement (Matthew 18:19-20). The Lord is awaiting your agreement with Him (Matthew 9:20-21, Luke 6:19). Dreamer, look to Jesus. Love and forgiveness can and will embrace and restore you, wait for it. For God knows what you need, the burdens you bear, and the pain you feel, dreamer, He knows. You can be healed emotionally, physically, and spiritually. On another vein, he or she, who do not respect the opportunities placed before the m shall have the things that support their peace taken away. Thus, if you are unwilling to acknowledge, challenge yourself, and change, you will be stripped of position, status, and finances, namely of all that 'covers' you, and yes, it will be allowed. See suggested course of action. If listed, and only if necessary, dreamer may also consider other multiples of this number. First, see Note 6 at the beginning of this category.

298: There is a conflict, which needs to be resolved, between the dreamer and another, be it a family member, or fri end, or foe. The core cause of the conflict is your own stubbornness and/or rebelliousness. There is a necessity to be reconcile d with another, rather than to, always be in opposition and/or contrary. Dreamer, you simply need to take the higher ground. Dreamer, if you are truly unaware of the part you've played within the conflict, you are being made aware via your dream. However, deep within, you recognize your own stubbornness, but are unwilling to own up to it. Nonetheless, this conflict really needs to be resolved; you need to heal the wounds that you've made, the war within you and without has to cease. In this, you will learn principles and Christian values that will encourage you to reach out and touch others in a loving and gr aceful manner; ultimately finding yourself promoting the genuine cause of Christ and the good of others. See suggested course of action. If listed, and only if necessary, dreamer may also consider other multiples of this number. First, see Note 6 at the beginning of this category.

300: This type of dream acknowledges that the dreamer is (or will be) in the midst of a personal crisis, as this number denotes a season of change, confliction, noticeable loss of spiritual identity, a mind closed to spiritual realities, the p ower of your words, reconciliation, serenity, teaching, and aging. Dreamer, you are going through a maturing season, so between the mundane and the sacred, beginnings and endings will be constant elements in your life at this time. Not all the changes wi ll be equal in significance, therefore, the diverse kinds of issues and situations, calls for regard in differing degrees. Nonethe less, this season will be marked with many 'turn-arounds', 'changes', and ups and downs, a very tumultuous and troubling season. Favorably, your personal crisis will have a purifying effect upon your life, so that after you have endured for a while, you will cease (stop, restrain, refrain, quit, desist) from sin (1 Peter 4:1-9), especially the sin that chronically assails you. With that said, dreamer, noticeably conflicted, you no longer know who and/or what you truly believe in. God has not changed, you have. Dreamer, you have lost your spiritual identity, and ensnared by your own words, having trusted in oppression, you have closed your mind to spiritual realities that brings mental and emotional clarity, genuine calmness, composure, contentment, mellowness, peacefulness, and tranquility. Unconsciously, you are against anything that will help you develop a closer friendship with Christ Jesus, to the point of ruin, and you will not allow yourself to get close enough to share love, trust, and intimacy qualitatively with others. Dreamer, when a man or woman genuinely return to God, in complete surrender and humility, your deliberate transgressions become like actual merits (Luke 7:37-50). Because, the realization of your distance from God, due to your transgressions (Isaiah 59:2), becomes the motivating force to return to God with a passion even greater than that of someone who has never sinned in such a manner (or never left the Father's house, Acts 9:1-30). Completely converting your present to good, effecting restoration, transformation and a miraculous healing, this is the secret of repentance, returning to God, and serenity. Go; therefore now, and seek the Lord Jesus, repent and place your hope, once again, in Him. Hope, placed in Him, will not deceive. When you have been restored completely, reach back and teach your experience that others might be saved and/or spared the trouble. See suggested course of action. If listed, and only if necessary, dreamer may also consider other multiples of this number. First, see Note 6 at the beginning of this category.

318: Dreamer, don't be afraid to go forward with your plans, for you will be refreshed with restored energy, and will recover all. Remember God in your prosperity, and pay 10% of your earnings to your church. If necessary, see suggested course of action. If listed, and only if necessary, dreamer may also consider other multiples of this number. First, see Note 6 at the beginning of this category.

320: Dreamer, for a little while, you will be given access to very powerful and prophetic wisdom, use this wisdom to be a transformational force, spiritually, in other people's lives. It is necessary to say, the beginning of wisdom is the fear (deep respect and honor) of God, and to shun evil is understanding, (see Psalm 111:10, Proverbs 1:7, 4:7, 9:10). With that, dreamer, you will experience a very distinct moment of divine guidance, a "flash" of inspiration. An idea will pop into your head, apparently out of nowhere. It is an idea waiting to be developed. The prophetic wisdom, via inspired intellect, will allow you to create something, seemingly out of nothing. However, the process of investigating and understanding the implications of this "flash of inspiration", the idea, is on you exclusively. This process is known as, "faith with works" (James 2:17 -26). Dreamer, by examining the length and breadth of the inspired idea (aka doing the research), and establishing a thorough understanding of the concept, conclusions can be reached. Conclusions such as, is there a market for your idea? Where is th e market located? How should I market my idea? Do I need further education to learn about my idea? Are there investment resources, and so on? When your process is finally complete, an idea will be born and should be ready for market. This idea will prosper you greatly, and it should benefit people, greatly transforming lives. Seize the moment, and capitalize on it, while you have an open link to divine inspiration. Moreover, selflessness will serve as the vessel that contains all the insight y ou'll be receiving. An angel (perhaps disguised as human, or one, who is a true servant of God, with the Spirit of Truth within) will help lead the way. If listed, and only if necessary, dreamer may also consider other multiples of this number. First, see Note 6 at the beginning of this category.

345: Dreamer, although your good intentions are (were) to help another with their problems, you have become too involved in their life or business, and have worried much too much. Dreamer, your difficulty in distinguishing between helping and interfering, reflects as bossy, as well as, a dominant, self-righteous, and stubborn attitude. Let it go, and let things be, lest you find yourself adopting a "savior" complex, and find your intentions unwanted, and unappreciated. If necessary, see suggested course of action. If listed, and only if necessary, dreamer may also consider other multiples of this number. First, see Note 6 at the beginning of this category.

348: Your dream denotes one who is set aside for the priesthood. Dreamer, you are being prepared to carry out the official role, position, or office of a priest (e.g. prophet, pastor, minister, or some type of a very visible cleric). With this office comes spiritual growth and divine illumination. If you have genuinely sought after truth, truth will continue to be, revealed to you, and will lead and guide you. With that said, the following is necessary to say. First, your promotion is predicated upon your understanding of, and continued obedience to, God's directives over your life. Second, pray to God for divine truth, f or one should never exalt their thoughts, ideas, feelings, emotions, above God's truth, for, every house is built by someone, bu t the builder of all things is God (Hebrews 3:2-4). Further, chosen, you are to show forth the praises of Him who has called you out of darkness into His marvelous light (see 1 Peter 2:9, 10). At present, continue to allow the Paraclete to complete the work of purification and sanctification within you. For those who go forth in tears, shall return rejoicing (Psalm 126:5, 6). Be diligent and patient, everything will be done proper, and in its own time; you will be ordained to a priestly office, and if relevant, your request in another area of your life will be granted. Again, your height of spiritual progress and promotion will be according to your faith and obedience to God's will over your life personally. If listed, and only if necessary, dreamer may also consider other multiples of this number. First, see Note 6 at the beginning of this category.

364: Your dream was sent to encourage the dreamer. Dreamer, Jesus will give you the power to manifest your potential. God promises to increase the fruit of your hands (e.g. you will get a raise), the desires of your heart, particularly, those healthy, life giving, and enhancing desires, and, if relevant, He will increase your links and lineages, e.g. children and grandchildren, and He will again rejoice over you. If listed, and only if necessary, dreamer may also consider other multiples of this number. First, see Note 6 at the beginning of this category.

368: In addition to one of the following, and only if necessary, dreamer may also consider other multiples of this number. First, see Note 6 at the beginning of this category. With that, this dream has five meanings (one, two, etc., or all may apply). (1) Dreamer, God is going to heal your broken heart. If necessary, see suggested course of action. (2) Dreamer, character traits from ancestors, namely genetic codes and traits, will often trouble and taunt the offspring of a given progenitor, especially generational issues (Exodus 20:5-7). The demons that have so plague your family line, are now visiting (re-visiting) you, namely voices that whisper, you are without value, insignificant, or pointless, and it is the embracing of those voices that will lead to other issues, such as sexual perversion (e.g. adultery, fornication, homosexuality, prostitution, or whorishness), and on to a bleak and desolate atmosphere. This will lead to much sadness, and feelings of being forsaken or abandoned. Favorably, generational curses and issues can stop with you (Jeremiah 31:29, 30; Ezekiel 18:2-14, 20-23). Hence, your Heavenly Father is requiring that you overcome and subdue negative and dark emotions, feelings, behaviors, and/or ideas that have come to influence you, before they overcome you; and leave you desolate. Dreamer, God is not asking you to do something you cannot do. For a surety, vanquishing of dark influences can be done. By faith, you will need to declare some kind of fast and commit to it, for a long period-of-time, to abate the demonically instigated circumstance, you find yourself in now, Matthew 6:16-18. Try abstaining from food and drink (midnight to 6 PM), twice a week, and refrain from words, attitudes, people, places, and things, including music, magazines, videos, TV, or any such things that fuel anger and discontent, and stir up lustful feelings. This is also known as, faith with works, read, understand, and embrace James 2:14 -26. Nonetheless, earnestly pray, God will guide, enable, and answer you as to the type of fast. Additionally, if relevant, forgive your mother and/or father for the darkness (aka curse) they may have perpetuated, for they knew not what they done. Forgiveness is important to your success (Matthew 6:12-15, 8:21-35). See suggested course of action. (3) Your dream also represents some type of spiritual privileges and a purification process, dreamer God will now separate you from people, places, and circumstances that will hinder your growth. View this separation as a blessing from God and not as an evil thing has happen. Under all adversities retain a spirit of joy, and continue to make progress in your spiritual life. Subsequently, dreamer, because of your humble and submissive faith in God's word, you will be declared as one who is a righteous minister. Planted in the House of the Lord, you will continue to prosper and mature. The same God, who plants you in your ministry, is the same God who will cause you to mature and prosper. Further, another benefit of allowing Jesus to have authority of your life; is that independent of outward circumstances, you will live and thrive where most things perish, via divine grace. Dreamer, while your spiritual growth may not be so rapid, if you endure, you will become a beautiful picture of a godly man or woman, who in your uprightness, aims to glorify God. Accordingly, gladness, thanksgiving, singing, then, strength, intense energy, and fertility will be your recompense, and your praise will be a sweet aroma in the nostrils of the Lord. If applicable, this promise is also to your generations to come. Come what may, you shall make steady progress and flourish in a very impressive manner; bringing forth fruit, even in your old age. Dreamer, as you age, your anointing to minister, and divine revelations, will always be fresh and edifying. See Psalm 92:12-15. Therefore, put the spiritual work in and go through what you need to go through now. If necessary, see suggested course of action. (4) Male dreamer: An event or situation that will cause intense fear is coming to discourage and terrify you. This will be in the form of an annoying, difficult, and unpleasa nt person. The trouble this person will cause will become so overwhelming, because they will expose a secret regarding you. This spiritual battle will be great, and will demand your full attention. Although you will walk through this alone, know that Go d will walk you through it. Dreamer, learn wisdom from the situation, for truth do set one free; and go on from there unashamed. Then, suddenly, unexpectedly, and without any warning, all the evil and wickedness that caused you to fear and be troubled, will disappear. It will be as though it was never there. At that point, you will express great joy, and feel extremely happy. Take courage and be strong, knowing that the Lord knows where you are, what's going on, and He cares. See suggested course of action. (5) Male dreamer (unmarried): Your dream denotes that a very attractive and sensual female; one whom the dreamer, may marry, especially before having sex, will enter your life. If necessary, see suggested course of action.

370: Dreamer, as you have re-directed your negative impulses, your natural inclinations to sin, especially your sexual desires, towards righteous activities (e.g. doing good works), and have desired to make God's will your own will, having your mind and thoughts clinging faithfully to the greatness of God. You are now decreed as one who is genuinely righteous. This type of spiritual worthiness, after receiving the Lord as your Savior, is achieved by doing good works, in your case, the re- directing of your sinful inclinations. Anyone who turns away from bad and becomes good will merit the goodness and blessings of the Lord. Blessings in this sense, is being elevated to a state of high honor, spiritual beauty, and great illumination. Hence, dreamer, from this day forward, God's blessings will flow abundantly, producing spiritual growth within you. More of God's blessings are the Gifts of God's grace, anything God freely gives you, absolution, the Holy Spirit, salvation, regeneration, eternal life, health, children, love of family, longevity, necessities, prosperity, and dominion over all that is yours; and all are parts of the supply of grace, and all are sanctified by the Lord, and technically belongs to Him. The result of this supply in your life will be peace. Dreamer, the Lord will manifest tremendous good will, mercy, and love within your life. He will increase the fruit of your land. If listed, and only if necessary, dreamer may also consider other multiples of this number. First, see Note 6 at the beginning of this category.

372: Your dream refers to one who is redeemed; however, you are going through a refining process, see Proverbs 17:3, 27:21; thus, your dream. Dreamer is strongly urged, at this point in your life, to adhere to God's instructions and principles that guide actions and moral behavior, via His principles, as outlined within Holy Writ. Following godliness is, aimed at making you not only wiser, but also better. Dreamer, it is imperative that you govern your desires, lusts, and passions with wisdom during your refining process. You have a journey to go on, spiritual warfare to fight, and a great work to do. God wants to purify you that you might fulfill the righteous purpose for which you were designed. With that said, as you have been saved from the power of sin, you will now be refined in the "crucible" of adversity. Dreamer, if you allow God's power to break the residuals of sin within you, you will experience a great deliverance from oppression. Be very aware that your emotional and/or physical adversities have been allowed by God that you might be humbled and made ready and prepared to render your gifts unto the Lord properly. God will use your sufferings to instill His principles into your mind, and make His ways penetrate your heart. He or she who has suffered in the flesh has ceased from sinning (1 Peter 4:1) that the sacrificial offerings of your worship, service, and financial support to the ministry, might be a sweet smell unto the Lord. Moreover, the refinement process that you are going through (or will go through shortly) is meant to bring honor and glory to the O ne who died to redeem you. True conversion makes a marvelous change in the heart and life. It alters the mind, judgment, affections, and conversation. When a man is truly converted, it grieves him to think how the time past of his life has been spent (Matthew Henry Concise Commentary). After this, you will become productive and go forth, bearing spiritual fruit, counted amongst those who are sagacious; whose character is faithful, law-abiding, moral, open, scrupulous, sincere, straightforward, trustworthy, upright, reasonable in many situations, and submissive to God. Blessings, joy, protection, and prosperity will be yours. See suggested course of action. If listed, and only if necessary, dreamer may also consider other multiples of this number. First, see Note 6 at the beginning of this category.

385: In addition to one of the following, and only if necessary, dreamer may also consider other multiples of this number. First, see Note 6 at the beginning of this category. With that, this dream has two meanings (one or both apply). (1) Your dream refers to a cycle within your life, a cycle that needs to be broken within your life. The dreamer needs to consider your own well-being emotionally, mentally, and spiritually. Think about your personal life cycles, and what have prevented you from developing, growing, expanding, increasing, or becoming all that you can be. What exactly is holding you back?

Dreamer, after thoughtful and earnest consideration, it is suggested that you begin attempting to render those negative life cycles no longer beneficial, and began anew attempting to move forward, using different tactics to overcome unproductive habitual life cycle choices, and for maneuvering through this thing we call life in a more, better way. On a more positive tone, dreamer, you've reached a turning point in your life that will lead to success, and you've been in this space before within one of your positive life cycles. If you embrace the positive, and seize this moment, God will use this season in your life to fortify you spiritually that you may be complete, wanting nothing, having broken your negative life cycles of self-sabotaging spiritual and ministerial progression. Within one year, those negative life cycles and those negative habits and ways of doing things, will have been broken because of the Word of God. Therefore, be encouraged, and stay in the process you're experiencing. You will begin to see the fruit of your labor, if you faint not. (2) Your dream refers to a bride and groom, and the presence of the Lord in the midst of them. If not married, and if desired, you will become a bride or groom, very soon. If married, your dream references your marriage. No matter which, married or unmarried, God is in your midst of your relationship with another. Moreover, in His mercy, the Creator will reveal to you some of the light of His glory, and you will experience His Divine Presence. Glory in this sense is a state of high honor, spiritual beauty, and great illumination.

387: In addition to one of the following, and only if necessary, dreamer may also consider other multiples of this number. First, see Note 6 at the beginning of this category. Even when the Lord knows the works of His people is done in love, faith, zeal, and patience, yet if His eyes observe them committing, or allowing, what is evil, He will rebuke or correct them. Thus, this dream is a rebuke to some, a dire warning to some, and fortunately, encouragement to others. With that, this dream has three meanings (choose one). (1) Married male: Dreamer, if you are a married bishop, elder, minister, pastor, priest, rabbi, or is acting in any ecclesiastical leadership type role. Your dream is a rebuke. You are assenting to, even encouraging, wicked seducers, especially your wife, also known as a prophetess and/or teacher. In allowing her, and others who embrace her corrupt doctrine, to perpetuate heresy, you are therefore the greater seducer. Thus, you are responsible for the spiritual disarray of some of God's faithful, due to erroneous teachings and beliefs. You have the power to restrain your wife; but you do not do it, thus, she and her cohorts have every opportunity of seducing even more of the faithful. This is what Christ ha s against you. Sin will very soon turn your paradise into chaos, and dishonor the beauty of your name. God will bring your deeds to the light; He will show you that He is, according to His title, The Son of God; and that He knows your heart. He will pry into your actions, and like a fire, He will search into everything, and burn up the chaff, which cannot stand His trial. So severe are things that restoration can only be by returning to Christ Jesus wholeheartedly. Your recklessness can be remedied by prayer and heartfelt repentance to Jesus and to individuals affected by your actions, and by rebuking, and putting a stop to the "spirit of jezebel" that has been allowed to reign within your ministry. See suggested course of action. (2) Married female dreamer: If you are a wife of a bishop, elder, minister, pastor, pope, priest, rabbi, or is acting in any ecclesiastical leadership type role. Your dream is a severe and dire warning of coming chastening. Dreamer, you are a woman of power and influence, possibly, also known as a prophetess and/or teacher. However, your pride has deceived you; and you have corrupted the one true religion, with syncretistic[28] ideas, and you harass the followers of God. Your dream pronounces a judgment against your impenitence. Dreamer, you believe in a god of your own making, coupled with outrageous claims you have wholeheartedly embraced from other erroneous guides. You say Adonai Elohim creates imperfect beings and then forces them to rise up to a level of perfection, which by design, they are unable to attain, by torturing them, causing millions to suffer in body and soul. You reason that this is God's only way, a path of pain, torture, and then death. You ask what human being aspires to evolve through this endless agony. You proclaim that God's promises are no more than vague words of doubtful happiness, and implacable laws that promise remote and unknowable joy, under the mask of love of humanity. You say His ways are nothing more than a profound indifference and a hardened selfishness. Further, you believe that God's intolerance of sin and the inherent results of sin, mainly separation from Him, as written within

Holy Writ, and expressed in Christian dogma, are the picture of an angry god, conjured up by angry, unwise, and foolish men. You boast of philosophies, which appeal to the lustful desires of human nature, condoning rebellious, unhealthy, immodest, immoral, indecent, lewd, and lascivious, behavior. Desires that if not checked, can and often do lead to early death, as you have personally witnessed. This is what you call love. You exalt your wisdom above the Creator. While you discredit the Creator's wise and sensible guidelines for living life, on this side of eternity, as healthy, humanly, and sanely as possible; and in harmony with His provision for life on the other side of eternity, in heaven. You respect your truth, while never acknowledging, it is delivered without grace; thus, it is never eno ugh to fill an emaciated soul. Read, understand, and embrace Galatians 5:13-25. See suggested course of action. (3) Your dream was sent as encouragement to one, namely the dreamer, who has kept yourself pure and undefiled from the teachings of heresy that has surrounded you, even within the ministry, with which you are connected. Dreamer, your dream denotes that you have grown wiser and better. Continue to earnestly, desire that your last works might be your best works. There is promise of ample recompense to the persevering, victorious believer; also, knowledge and wisdom will be given that you might continue in the power of God. For now, do not leave your current place of worship, stay right where you are, things will pan out. If necessary, God will give you a door to leave, and lead you to a faith-based community, after things have calmed down, and He will be glorified. If necessary, see suggested course of action.

390: This number refers to one who is chosen by God, namely, the dreamer. Favorably, you will now begin to be used as witness for Christ Jesus to a great number of people. You are gifted for this, because you have a multi-dimensionality that befriends you to many people, no matter their social status. On another vein, you are part of a small group, surviving without compromise, and by faith; unfortunately, you are within an evil setting. Read and understand Revelations 2:1-7, for this is to you. Remember your first love. If necessary, see suggested course of action. If listed, and only if necessary, dreamer may also consider other multiples of this number. First, see Note 6 at the be-ginning of this category.

393: The dreamer is split internally. Your thoughts are ambiguous, and are primarily, discouraging, faithless, fatalistic, and troubling to yourself and others. Dreamer, such dubious thinking will cause you to be fretful, irritable, and fearful of going to Jesus boldly, supposing you're forcing your presence or opinions on Him, or that you are unwelcome in Jesus' sight, all of which, are untrue. Dreamer, although your faults are before you, Jesus loves you. Dreamer, go to God, aware of your own inadequacies, to ask for wisdom, and rest assure that He has wisdom to give, and is generous and liberal enough to give to whomever ask, that includes you. He will not correct or criticize in a harsh manner, for He knows you are seeking wisdom. One may suffer needlessly, because he or she will not ask Jesus for wisdom. Further, regarding God's most Holy Word, do not be hesitant, suspicious, or faithless, about His promises, especially to think that His promises and benefits are limited to a select few, and exclude others. God gives to all men and women; yes you too, and He gives unabatedly. Ask Jesus as often as you need to, regarding all of your emotional concerns, considering how personal His promises are, He will meet you in your needs. There is only one thing required of you, and that is, in your asking, you ask with a believing, steady mind, for it is written, let him (or her) ask in faith, nothing wavering, see James 1:6. See suggested course of action. If listed, and only if necessary, dreamer may also consider other multiples of this number. First, see Note 6 at the beginning of this category.

395: There is a conflict, which needs to be resolved, between the dreamer and another, be it a family member, or friend, or foe. The core cause of the conflict is your own stubbornness and/ or rebelliousness. There is a necessity to be reconcile d with another, rather than to, always be in opposition and/or contrary. Dreamer, you simply need to take the higher ground. Dreamer, if you are truly unaware of the part you've played within the conflict, you are being made aware via your dream. However, deep within, you recognize your own stubbornness, but are unwilling to own up to it. Nonetheless, this conflict really needs to be resolved; you need to heal the wounds that you've made, the war within you and without has to cease. In this, you will learn principles and Christian values that will encourage you to reach out and touch others in a loving and gr aceful manner; ultimately finding yourself promoting the genuine cause of Christ and the good of others. See suggested course of action. If listed, and only if necessary, dreamer may also consider other multiples of this number. First, see Note 6 at the beginning of this category.

400: Dreamer, you will be cleared of blame, guilt, suspicion, and/or doubt. God has heard your plea, He will defend you, and justice will prevail. Therefore, go on and fight for, and excel, in your "calling". You are a natural mediator, perhaps a judge, teacher, or an apologist (one who defends and justifies Christianity), as you are genuine, tactful, and adaptable. Your sensitivity and gentleness will be a great healing force in the lives of others, bringing harmony and support to them, via defending them, by any right means necessary, against the deceit and trickery of the enemy, and by teaching them about simple faith. The simple faith you inherited from your family, a simple faith which is in Jesus Christ (a resolute trust in the integrity of God and in His Word), and in His absolute omnipresence. By this, you advance the cause of God, especially concerning restoration, transformation, and miraculous healings and strengthening, both physically and emotionally. Further, allow these to be the primary focus of you ministry. Additionally, dreamer, be aware, concerning the expectancy of something great, become aware of opportunities, and expect spiritual maturity. If listed, and only if necessary, may consider the interpretation for the number 20, as it relates to this number squared; see Note 6 at the beginning of this category.

402: In addition to one of the following, and only if necessary, dreamer may also consider other multiples of this number. First, see Note 6 at the beginning of this category. This dream refers to a promise made you by God, and the fulfillment of that promise made to you. The promise was made when you first invited Christ into your life. It will, very shortly happen. With that, this dream has two meanings. (1) God's wisdom, care, and guidance, coupled with His divine intervention, has kept you, and will, again, cause your mouth to be filled with laughter, and your tongue with singing. When God reverse your tragedy, you will testify that the Lord has done great things for you, and you will be glad. Your situation will change and He will give you a new song in your heart. You will sing a new song. (2) As well, your dream points to one who was born to be a teacher and a nurturer. You should be teaching the elementary truths of God's word to your own children and/or to those not familiar with the teachings of righteousness, mainly new converts, and infants in Christ. Your diligent teaching will prepare others to sp read the gospel of Jesus Christ; thus, reproducing your teaching ministry and abundantly blessing you. You will receive wages for your diligence, if indeed you are diligent (Luke 10:2-7, 1 Timothy 5:18). If necessary, see suggested course of action.

408: In addition to one of the following, and only if necessary, dreamer may also consider other multiples of this number. First, see Note 6 at the beginning of this category. With that, this dream has two meanings (one or both may apply). (1) Dreamer, because of God's grace, His faithfulness, and His mercy towards you, you will begin to experience a surge of positive feelings, due to restoration, transformation, and a miraculous healing and strengthening, both physically and emotionally. The emotional level is already happening within your inner most feelings and affections, for, God is first healing your broken heart. Now, your burdens, having been dealt with, freedom from your weaknesses is yours. Freedom from bondage, domination by evil, and hardship, is beginning for you. Dreamer, you are asked to give careful thought regarding your bondages and hardships, considering how things are, and have been for you, for your experiences have prepared you for ministry. From this day forward, God will bless you. You will be favored with complete healing, go and sin no more, but go and offer prayers, supplications, and thanksgiving before your Lord and Savior, Jesus Christ, for He is forgiving, compassionate, long-suffering, and full of loving-kindness, restoring more favorable conditions. In time, you may find yourself assistant to a high-ranking leader within a ministry, perhaps in the position of personal aide, leadership counselor, associate pastor, or CEO of your individual ministry. As well, there will be clarity and freedom in the way you communicate yourself to others, especially prophetically. Note, although your life is (will become) very busy and full of concerns; it is advised that you do not forget your personal relationship with Christ, nor neglect the devotions that keep that personal relationship healthy. Nor must you allow yourself to be annoyed with other acts of devotion, e.g. family bible study and other quality times, fellowshipping with other believers, church attendance, acknowledging God's goodness to you, to others, and the like. Therefore, from this moment forward, choose good habits and deeds, e.g. good stewardship and commitment to ministry; speak to yourself what is true and good, embrace Philippians 4:8, and choose good nutritional habits that you might remain in good health. Also, these choices will greatly support you in your progress forward towards your transformation and freedom, and help guide you toward, and enable you to fulfill, your purpose. All these blessings are rain. Dreamer, as one perfects him or herself, God helps by sending 'rains of blessings', then situations prosper. The rain is coming! (2) Unmarried Female: In addition to the previous interpretation, your dream also signifies a marriage. Your husband is before you at present, or will be, very shortly. Handle the relationship, on God's terms, embracing His ethics, and not yours, as you've previously done.

410: This number refers to a one-hour period. Freedom from bondage, domination by evil, and hardship, is beginning for you, within the hour. Therefore, from this moment forward, choose good habits and deeds. Additionally, as your dream denotes a "time frame", see subcategory, Time. If listed, and only if necessary, dreamer may also consider other multiples of this number. First, see Note 6 at the beginning of this category.

412: This number refers to desire and passion. While these emotions may often imply that this is a negative human feeling, in your dream, it denotes the positive desires and passions of a righteous person, namely the dreamer. God will fulfill your passions. Further, you will be respected because of your dedication to, and zeal for, your God and reap the fruit of the blessing of your zeal for the Lord. Blessings; in this sense, is being elevated to a state of high honor, spiritual beauty, and great illumination. Moreover, as you are able to handle great responsibility and wealth, and are one who is tolerant, you will experience receiving an act of kindness, monetarily, from someone who is affluent. Additionally, you must also become a fundraiser for, and giver of, charity. If listed, and only if necessary, dreamer may also consider other multiples of this number. First, see Note 6 at the beginning of this category.

420: Dreamer, there are those amongst you, close significant others, who are diametrically opposed to holiness and have essentially separated themselves from God. It is said of them that their feet descend into death, and they are ultimately responsible for bringing death into their own life's situations. This is also said of you, by some, not most. Favorably, as your dream also references election according to grace, expectancy, God's faithfulness, grace abounding, fullness, full measure, full recompense, full reward, holiness, and redemption of those who have fallen away, a spark of life remains hidden inside of you, and in them, because both, you and they are God's children. There awaits you, and them, a spiritual resurrection, according to God's grace. His grace is abounding towards you, and His promises will come quickly and in full measure. What are His promises to you? Dreamer, recall His promises to you. Expect all of this (spiritual resurrection, grace abounding, His promises to you, full measure); therefore, wait on it. Warning, these great blessings, can result in an excessive concern for your image, the false imitations of this world, pride, and vanity. These attributes will keep you from being in the right place, at the right moment, to hear God through the ears of faith. Therefore, humble yourself before the True and Living God and accept His blessings of healing, help, and restoration in a balanced manner. This great favor is shown you because of God's great faithfulness towards you. If listed, and only if necessary, dreamer may also consider other multiples of this number. First, see Note 6 at the beginning of this category.

425: This number refers to acknowledgement and recognition. Dreamer, you will soon be acknowledged and recognized for something achieved. If listed, and only if necessary, dreamer may also consider other multiples of this number. First, see Note 6 at the beginning of this category.

426: It is time for the dreamer to painfully thirst, and eagerly long, for those things by which, the soul is genuinely refreshed, supported, and strengthen. It is suggested that you go away, into a quiet place, away from all the distractions, to seriously fast, and deprogram and re-program yourself

(Galatians 1:12-24). At this crossroads in your life, you need to count all that you know, to be worthless (Philippians 3:7, 8). Subsequently, you will begin to walk and grow into a more mature spiritual being, going on towards perfection, enabled to see into the spiritual realm more clearly. Additionally, no matter, the hardships and they may prove grievously, never again look back, but genuinely, in words and deeds, continue to progress forward. By this, your capacity for greater illumination, intellectually and spiritually, will become enlarged, giving you access to more than a few of the gates of wisdom (2 Corinthians 12:2-10). See suggested course of action. If listed, and only if necessary, dreamer may also consider other multiples of this number. First, see Note 6 at the beginning of this category.

434: Your dream refers to reaping and sowing, deliverance, remembrance, restoration, and service. Dreamer, it is because of the universal law of reaping and sowing, you have experienced hardship. Favorably, freedom from bondage, domination by evil, and hardship, is beginning for you. Dreamer, you are asked to give careful thought regarding your bondages and hardships, considering how things are, and have been for you, for your experiences are a result of your previous choices. Favorably, your experiences prepared you for ministry, if you choose to learn from your past choices, and choose wiser behavior. If you choose godly wisdom, from this day forward, God will bless you. Therefore, go and offer prayers, supplications, repentance, and thanksgiving before your Lord and Savior, Jesus Christ, for He is forgiving, compassionate, long- suffering, and full of loving-kindness, restoring more favorable conditions. See suggested course of action. If listed, and only if necessary, dreamer may also consider other multiples of this number. First, see Note 6 at the beginning of this category.

438: There is a conflict, which needs to be resolved, between the dreamer and another, be it a family member, or friend, or foe. The core cause of the conflict is your own stubbornness and/ or rebelliousness. There is a necessity to be reconciled with another, rather than to, always be in opposition and/or contrary. Dreamer, you simply need to take the higher ground. Dreamer, if you are truly unaware of the part you've played within the conflict, you are being made aware via your dream. However, deep within, you recognize your own stubbornness, but are unwilling to own up to it. Nonetheless, this conflict really needs to be resolved; you need to heal the wounds that you've made, the war within you and without has to cease. In this, you will learn principles and Christian values that will encourage you to reach out and touch others in a loving and gr aceful manner; ultimately finding yourself promoting the genuine cause of Christ and the good of others. See suggested course of action. If listed, and only if necessary, dreamer may also consider other multiples of this number. First, see Note 6 at the beginning of this category.

444: In addition to one of the following, if listed, and only if necessary, may consider the interpretation for the numbers 4, 44, as they relate to the repetitiveness of this number (444). Hence, the number 444 is a more intense expression of the numbers 4, 44, in strength and forcefulness, spiritually, prophetically, and in application. First, see Note 6 at the beginning of this category. With that, your dream has two meanings (one or both may apply). (1) An undertone of discontent has arisen within the dreamer because you have had to suppress your emotions and words, even when you are right. Dreamer, sometimes it is necessary to keep silent, especially when you are before wicked men and women, for they will watch your words, and turn your words, if they can, to your disadvantage. Dreamer, for sure, there are those around you who are diametrically opposed to holiness and, essentially, have separated themselves from God. It is said of them that their feet descend into death, and they are ultimately responsible for bringing death into their own life. Therefore, it is good for you to be patiently submissive, to God and His ways, and pray for the removal of this wickedness from before you, that you not be a reproach, and for God to enlighten your mind via His Holy Spirit, and fill your heart with His grace. In addition, dreamer, by addressing God and not man, your emotions can easily be softened and subdued. See suggested course of action. (2) Your dream also refers to secularism, resulting in a humanistic belief system, within the life of the dreamer. This belief embraces the teachings that religion and religious persons should have no part in political or civic affairs, or in running public institutions, especially schools. This type of conviction exposes a rejection of God and His moral system. See suggested course of action.

456: In addition to one of the following, and only if necessary, dreamer may also consider other multiples of this number. First, see Note 6 at the beginning of this category. Even when the Lord knows the works of His people is done in love, faith, zeal, and patience, yet if His eyes observe them committing, or allowing, what is evil, He will rebuke or correct them. Thus, your dream is a rebuke to some, a dire warning to some, and fortunately, encouragement to others. With that, your dream has four meanings (choose one). (1) Married male: Dreamer, if you are a married bishop, elder, minister, pastor, priest, rabbi, or is acting in any ecclesiastical leadership type role. Your dream is a rebuke. You are assenting to, even encouraging, wicked seducers, especially your wife, also known as a prophetess and/or teacher. In allowing her, and others who embrace her corrupt doctrine, to perpetuate heresy, you are therefore the greater seducer. Thus, you are responsible for the spiritual disarray of some of God's faithful, due to erroneous teachings and beliefs. You have the power to restrain your wife; but you do not do it, thus, she and her cohorts have every opportunity of seducing even more of the faithful. This is what Christ has against you. Sin will very soon turn your paradise into chaos, and dishonor the beauty of your name. God will bring your de eds to the light; He will show you that He is, according to His title, The Son of God; and that He knows your heart. He will pry into your actions, and like a fire, He will search into everything, and burn up the chaff, which cannot stand His trial. So sever e are things that restoration can only be by returning to Christ Jesus wholeheartedly. Your recklessness can be remedied by prayer and heartfelt repentance to Jesus and to individuals affected by your actions, and by rebuking, and putting a stop to the "spirit of jezebel" that has been allowed to reign within your ministry. See suggested course of action. (2) Married female dreamer: If you are a wife of a bishop, elder, minister, pastor, pope, priest, rabbi, or is acting in any ecclesiastical leadership ty pe role. Your dream is a severe and dire warning of coming chastening. Dreamer, you are a woman of power and influence, possibly, also known as a prophetess and/or teacher. However, your pride has deceived you; and you have corrupted the one true religion, with syncretistic[28] ideas, and you harass the followers of God. Your dream pronounces a judgment against your impenitence. Dreamer, you believe in a god of your own making, coupled with outrageous claims you have wholeheartedly embraced from other erroneous guides. You say Adonai Elohim creates imperfect beings and then forces them to rise up to a level of perfection, which by design, they are unable to attain, by torturing them, causing millions to suffer in body and soul. You reason that this is God's only way, a path of pain, torture, and then death. You ask what human being aspires to evolve through this endless agony. You proclaim that God's promises are no more than vague words of doubtful happiness, and implacable laws that promise remote and unknowable joy, under the mask of love of humanity. You say His ways are nothing more than a profound indifference and a hardened selfishness. Further, you believe that God's intolerance of sin and the inherent results of sin, mainly separation from Him, as written within Holy Writ, and expressed in Christian dogma, are the picture of an angry god, conjured up by angry, unwise, and foolish men. You boast of philosophies, which appeal to the lustful desires of human nature, condoning rebellious, unhealthy, immodest, immoral, indecent, lewd, and lascivious, behavior. Desires that if not checked, can and often do lead to early death, as you have personally witnessed. This is what you call love. You exalt your wisdom above the Creator. While you discredit the Creator's wise and sensible guidelines for living life, on this side of eternity, as healthy, humanly, and sanely as possible; and in harmony with His provision for life on the other side of eternity, in heaven. You respect your truth, while never acknowledging, it is delivered without grace; thus, it is never eno ugh to fill an emaciated soul. Read, understand, and embrace Galatians 5:13-25. See suggested course of action. (3) Dreamer, you have adopted a bourgeois mentality, believing yourself above God's word and above the law of the land. This mentality is concerned only with your personal comfort, material wealth, and status, at any expense. Now, having in yourself nothing that you respect more than power and greed, you are willing to sacrifice all, God, principle, family, and friend, to the image or idol of vanity. Your new way is based on exploring alternatives to God's righteous principles, as well as, creating a sense of unity with the wickedness around you. This mentality sacrifices children, family, and morality, to the hollowness of satisfying immoral desires and appetites. All carried out, with the hope of finding happiness by pacifying jealously and covetousness. The selling-out of yourself over to immorality, devaluing those, you should be protecting and nurturing, especially the faithful, while closing your eyes to it all, are all principles based on values that are not only vile, but also increasingly unstable. This way cries out against godly ethics, and its' end offends any sense of godliness. Dreamer, you obey no one, and accept no correction. You do not trust in the Lord, nor do you draw near to Him, although He has given you space to repent; instead, you seduced your children to follow you, perpetuating your sins. Thus, sin will very soon turn your paradise into chaos, and dishonor the beauty of your name. You are also at risk of falling into a state of serious health problems and possibly loss of life. So severe are things that restoration can only be by returning to Christ Jesus wholeheartedly. Dreamer when God hides His face from someone celebrations are turned into moaning and groaning, and the party is exchanged for depression and solitude. Your recklessness can be remedied by prayer and heartfelt repentance to Jesus and to individuals affected by your actions, and by rebuking and renouncing the "spirit of jezebel", that has attached itself to you. See suggested course of action. (4) Your dream was sent as encouragement to one, namely the dreamer, who has kept yourself pure and undefiled from the teachings of heresy that has surrounded you, even within the ministry, with which you are connected. Dreamer, your dream denotes that you have grown wiser and better. Continue to earnestly, desire that your last works might be your best works. There is promise of ample recompense to the persevering, victorious believer; also, knowledge and wisdom will be given that you might continue in the power of God. For now, do not leave your current place of worship, stay right where you are, things will pan out. If necessary, God will give you a door to leave, and lead you to a faith-based community, after things have calmed down, and He will be glorified. If necessary, see suggested course of action.

468: In addition to one of the following, and only if necessary, dreamer may also consider other multiples of this number. First, see Note 6 at the beginning of this category. With that, this dream has two meanings (choose one). (1) Dreamer, because of God's grace, His faithfulness, and His mercy towards you, you will begin to experience a surge of positive feeling s, due to restoration, transformation, and a miraculous healing and strengthening, both physically and emotionally. The emotional level is already happening within your inner most feelings and affections, for, God is first healing your broken heart. Now, your burdens, having been dealt with, freedom from your weaknesses is yours. Freedom from bondage, domination by evil, and hardship, is beginning for you. Dreamer, you are asked to give careful thought regarding your bondages and hardships, considering how things are, and have been for you, for your experiences have prepared you for ministry. From this day forward, God will bless you. You will be favored with complete healing, go and sin no more, but go and offer prayers, supplications, and thanksgiving before your Lord and Savior, Jesus Christ, for He is forgiving, compassionate, long-suffering, and full of loving-kindness, restoring more favorable conditions. In time, you may find yourself assistant to a high-ranking leader within a ministry, perhaps in the position of personal aide, leadership counselor, associate pastor, or CEO of your individual ministry. As well, there will be clarity and freedom in the way you communicate yourself to others, especially prophetically. Note, although your life is (will become) very busy and full of concerns; it is advised that you do not forget your personal relationship with Christ, nor neglect the devotions that keep that personal relationship healthy. Nor must you allow yourself to be annoyed with other acts of devotion, e.g. family bible study and other quality times, fellowshipping with other believers, church attendance, acknowledging God's goodness to you, to others, and the like. Therefore, from this moment forward, choose good habits and deeds, e.g. good stewardship and commitment to ministry; speak to yourself what is true and good, embrace Philippians 4:8, and choose good nutritional habits that you might remain in good health. Also, these choices will greatly support you in your progress forward towards your transformation and freedom, and help guide you toward, and enable you to fulfill, your purpose. All these blessings are rain. Dreamer, as one perfects him or herself, God helps by sending 'rains of blessings', then situations prosper. The rain is coming! (2) Unmarried female dreamer: Coupled with the previous interpretation, your dream also signifies a marriage. Your husband is before you at present, or will be, very shortly. Handle the relationship, on God's terms, embracing His ethics, and not yours, as you've previously done.

470: Dreamer, you will highly blossom in the Kingdom of God. Moreover, as you are able to handle great responsibility and wealth, and are one who is tolerant, you will experience receiving an act of kindness, monetarily, from someone who is affluent. Even more, you are entering into a season within your life that will prepare you spiritually for the visitation of the Lord in your individual life. During this time, you will experience His love and presence, as you've never known it before. For, He is saying to you, "I will teach you godly wisdom". You will receive direct insight of divine truth. You will come to know, without a doubt, that God is the true source of your strength and wisdom, and He is your sufficiency. As a result, a greater love for self, family, and others will begin to manifest, affecting wholeness within your life. Moreover, if applicable, your children will reap the fruits of the blessing of your giving. On the other hand, words of caution. Dreamer, as it takes an unrivaled level of confidence to successfully endure mountain top experiences, without imploding, as you are elevated, it will be wise, for you, to periodically take a reflective look within, to check the pride level, within your heart (also see Deuteronomy 6:10-18). It is counseled that you set up 'mile markers', a type of accountability system for yourself along the way. Do not be deceived, with affluence, power, and wealth, comes good and evil; thus, today, you will need to choose between good and evil; and set "checks and balances" within yourself, because you have innate tendencies to become extreme and will judge others according to your "extremisms". Embracing this side of yourself will cause you to be deemed inappropriate, and delayed at that moment, to be of further service to the Kingdom of God. Regrettably, this will lead to you being unhappy, and unable to discern between truth and error, without you realizing your shortsightedness. Therefore, the "checks and balances" are meant to rectify the soul to increase its capacity to receive the blessings of the Lord more fully. Blessings; in this sense, is a state of high honor, spiritual beauty, and great illumination. Henceforth, in accordance with your decision as to how you shall continue from this day forward, will define your level of esteem from the Lord, whether little esteem or greatly esteem, in your future and beyond. Further, if you choose to embrace the positive, this will lead to a great balancing of your theology, resulting in a belief that is complete, with solid attributes, and your inspiration will make for very good teaching. If listed, and only if necessary, dreamer may also consider other multiples of this number. First, see Note 6 at the beginning of this category.

480: This type of dream exposes a need of refinement of character, namely in the area dealing with the deeds of the flesh. For example, dishonesty, adultery, sensuality, hostility, feuding, vendettas, grudges, unfriendliness, strife, jealousy, outbursts of anger, disputes, dissensions, discord, factions, cliques, envying, drunkenness, carousing, idolatry (idolatry is "foreign service", any act that expresses devotion or fanatical admiration to something or someone other than Adonai Elohim), or any traits of these sorts, see 1 Corinthians 6:8-11. This also includes a possible belief in, and/or practice of, necromancy. Your dream comes to warn an immoral believer that your activities are illegal. You have deliberately chosen to become enslaved to that which is forbidden by the One True and Living God. Your choices are spiritually forbidden. Further, you compel individuals to follow other gods, and hard-press people to believe what you say. You are one, who is the direct opposite of a born-again, aka a believer, the antithesis of Christ. As a result you will now begin to experience serious mental health issues and will have to be restrained, against your will if needs be. Dreamer, if urged by God, declare a one, two, or three day fast for sanctification purposes; also, wash (bathe) and make yourself, clothing, and personal surroundings clean. If not a day fast, you will need to declare some kind of fast and commit to it, for a period-of-time, to abate this coming influence. Refrain from wickedness and do no one harm, physically, sexually, emotionally, and/or spiritually, any longer. Start treating God's people, your family, and others, with respect. By this, God will pardon your injustices. See suggested course of action. If listed, and only if necessary, dreamer may also consider other multiples of this number. First, see Note 6 at the beginning of this category.

490: This number refers to restoration and blessings within the life of the dreamer. Dreamer, from this day forward, God's blessings will flow abundantly, producing spiritual growth within you. God's blessings: Gifts of God's grace, anything God freely gives you, absolution, the Holy Spirit, salvation, regeneration, eternal life, health, children, love of family, longevity, necessities, prosperity, and dominion over all that is yours; and all are parts of the supply of grace, and all are sanctified by the Lord, and technically belongs to Him. The result of this supply in your life will be peace. If listed, and only if necessary, dreamer may also consider other multiples of this number. First, see Note 6 at the beginning of this category.

492: Your dream was sent to encourage. Dreamer, because of your humble and submissive faith in God's word, and not your works alone, you are, declared as one who is a righteous minister. Planted in the House of the Lord, you will continue to prosper and mature. The same God, who planted you in your ministry, is the same God who will cause you to mature and prosper. You will live and thrive where most things perish, independent of outward circumstances, via divine grace. Your spiritual growth may not be so rapid, however, if you endure, you will become a beautiful picture of a godly man or woman, who in your uprightness, aims to glorify God. Your dream also represents some type of spiritual privileges and a purification process. Dreamer, God will separate you from people, places, and circumstances that will hinder your growth, view this separation as a blessing from God and not as an evil thing has happen. Under all adversities retain a spirit of joy, continue to make progress in your spiritual life, with gladness, thanksgiving, singing, and then, strength, intense energy, and fertility will be your recompense, and your praise will be a sweet aroma in the nostrils of the Lord. If applicable, this promise is to your generations to come. Come what may, you shall make steady progress and flourish in a very impressive manner; bringing forth fruit, even in your old age. Dreamer, as you age, your anointing to minister, and divine revelations, will always be fresh and edifying. See Psalm 92:12-15. If listed, and only if necessary, dreamer may also consider other multiples of this number. First, see Note 6 at the beginning of this category

500: In addition to one of the following, and only if necessary, dreamer may also consider other multiples of this number. First, see Note 6 at the beginning of this category. With that, this dream has two meanings (one or both may apply). (1) Your dream was sent to warn and to urge the dreamer. Dreamer is warned that there are those who have drawn near you, particularly within the past 21 days, or will draw near you, within 21 days, they are diametrically opposed to holiness. Fundamentally, they have separated themselves from Adonai Elohim. They refute archaeological, scientific, and other critical evidence that legitimize ancient biblical history, and debate the existence of a historical Jesus. Therefore, they do not accept Jesus as the Messiah, and they flaunt anti-Christ behavior. Dreamer, the more God allows you to see their emptiness, it is suggested that you be more earnest to tell them to repent. Dreamer is urged to stand on your convictions and strongly advocate prayer and heartfelt repentance to Jesus. That those who are led astray may find in God, grace and healing, refreshment, and a refuge. Notwithstanding, bad company corrupts good manners. If these persons are allowed an entrance into your inner circle of friends, or circle of close associates, they will provoke you to anger, hostility, unforgiving heart, and other emotional burdens that you will have to shoulder. (2) Dreamer, because of your liberal attitude, some type of promotion to leadership is at hand for you, in a secular and/or spiritual arena. However, if you're preoccupied with biting others, because of provocation by those who are the antithesis of Christ, your anointing will begin to wane and your authority to abate, resulting in lost opportunities. Dreamer, God is going to introduce Himself to you, that you may have a more intimate relationship with Him. In order to trust Him you must know Him in an intimate and personal way (Psalm 9:10). To know God is more than just knowing facts about Him, although becoming acquainted with Him through extra-biblical knowledge is good too. To know Him intimately, is to enter into a deeper personal relationship with Him by seeking Him and discovering Him to be a true and living God, who is very trustworthy. You must by faith, deliberately, and purposefully, offer you, your mind, spirit, and body in a sober, firm, and dignified manner, as a living sacrifice, holy and pleasing to God. It is only when you know God in such a personal way that you will come to trust Him wholeheartedly. With a confident and unquestionable belief in the validity of salvation, via the atoning work of the cross, knowing that it is enough to justify righteousness within a believer's life. It will be through this closeness that you will develop your mind to be skilled at searching out, and choosing truth, over evil. Go now, pray, and meditate on Psalm 119:145-152.

501: This number refers to one, the dreamer, who has provoked God with the works of your hands. What could you have possibly done with your hands that would anger God? With your very own hands, you are financing, and endeavoring to put, the wrong person (or people) in power over you. This effort, if carried out to completion, will result in your personal downfall. Giving authority and power to a person (or persons) who do not believe in God, nor in His Son, Jesus Christ, will bring about a spiritual collapse within your life and/or ministry. Dreamer, by supporting godless or atheistic persons, you assist in bringing about your own moral and financial downfall. See suggested course of action. If listed, and only if necessary, dreamer may also consider other multiples of this number. First, see Note 6 at the beginning of this category.

536: Your dream was sent, in the spirit of grace (the free and unmerited favor and beneficence of God), to see if you will yet be worked upon, and change your mindset, or else to leave you inexcusable, in your accusations against God, because of your ruin. Also see Jeremiah 9:7-9; Zechariah 13:9; Malachi 3:3; Matthew 23:37-39; Revelation 3:15-21. Dreamer, you will begin to experience afflictions and troubles. These are intended to purify you from worthless and vain acts of immorality an d to see if the experiences will bring you to prayer and heartfelt repentance to Jesus and man or woman, seeking pardon and expressing sincere feelings of regret and brokenness for having done something awry and/ or for having hurt someone, see 2 Corinthians 7:10, 11. You must be refined from your impurities and purged from your immorality; you must be brightened and bettered. Your growing immorality leaves no other recourse. With the Holy Ghost working like fire, God will purge you that you might be precious in His sight. That you may offer unto the Lord an offering in righteousness, sincerely transformed, and sanctified, a peculiar people. Those, whom God sets apart for Himself must go through a refining process, see Proverbs 17:3, 27:21. You must be tried that your faith may be found to praise and honor the Lord and you able to be presented before the Father without spot or wrinkle. See suggested course of action. If listed, and only if necessary, dreamer may also consider other multiples of this number. First, see Note 6 at the beginning of this category.

546: Although you are gentle and quiet, you lack wisdom and practical understanding. Thus, you are easily deceived or cheated, especially financially. Moreover, your comfort with appearing gentle and quiet, has also kept you spiritually immature. Thus, you are still considered an infant spiritually, not fully acquainted with the teachings about righteousness. You are spiritually, emotionally, and perhaps physically, weak, because you need to submit to, and earnestly embrace, the teachings of the basic truths of God's word. Dreamer, crave pure spiritual milk, the direct words of God imparted to us through the words of others, such as a preacher in a worship service, a Sunday school teacher, and other bible studies. It is through these avenues, the Christian experiences, and God's direct leading, that His deeper mysteries, which are more valuable than any knowledge gotten on one's own, are imparted. Further, respect your present place of worship and the appointed leaders of that place. Do not leave to, aimlessly, wander from place to place, and never allow anyone to deter you from learning God's word via pastors, preachers, and teachers; for faith comes by hearing, see Romans 10:17, and by studiously reading your Bible and other biblical resources. Further, it is not wise to take counsel from within your own head. Always seek counsel from your spiritual leaders and other believers. Deliberate, discuss, and debate with colleagues, experts, and other Christians, for there is wisdom in the counsel of many. See Proverbs 11:14, 15:22, 23. Dreamer, you are encouraged to continue your spiritual journey towards Jesus, and turn not back, for continuing on, Christianity promises a better you, a nd furthermore, you have too much to lose looking back. If necessary, see suggested course of action. If listed, and only if necessary, dreamer may also consider other multiples of this number. First, see Note 6 at the beginning of this category.

562: Dreamer you've reached a fork in the road. Before you choose which path, which course of conduct, to embark upon, you really need to do your research, an objective critical analysis of each particular path's basic values, attitudes, infrastructure, foundation, earthly and eternal benefits and recompense; and whether the particular path is worthy of consideration or not, and journal your findings. Your research should reveal the origin of each path, and which one, will prove a wise decision. Additional, consider, as your dream also denotes your mother, it will also prove sagacious for you to consider your mother's words, her lifestyle, and your upbringing, whether positive or unwise, in some manner. Considering both your critical research and your fostering, then you should decide. See suggested course of action. If listed, and only if necessary, dreamer may also consider other multiples of this number. First, see Note 6 at the beginning of this category.

564: In addition to one of the following, and only if necessary, dreamer may also consider other multiples of this number. First, see Note 6 at the beginning of this category. With that, this dream has six meanings (one, two, etc., or all may apply). (1) Dreamer, God is going to heal your broken heart. If necessary, see suggested course of action. (2) Dreamer, character traits from ancestors, namely genetic codes and traits, will often trouble and taunt the offspring of a given progenitor, especially generational issues (Exodus 20:5-7). The demons that have so plague your family line, are now visiting (re-visiting) you, namely voices that whisper, you are without value, insignificant, or pointless, and it is the embracing of those voices that will lead to other issues, such as sexual perversion (e.g. adultery, fornication, homosexuality, prostitution, or whorishness), and on to a bleak and desolate atmosphere. This will lead to much sadness, and feelings of being forsaken or abandoned. Favorably, generational curses and issues can stop with you (Jeremiah 31:29, 30; Ezekiel 18:2-14, 20-23). Hence, your Heavenly Father is requiring that you overcome and subdue negative and dark emotions, feelings, behaviors, and/or ideas that have come to influence you, before they overcome you; and leave you desolate. Dreamer, God is not asking you to do something you cannot do. For a surety, vanquishing of dark influences can be done. By faith, you will need to declare some kind of fast and commit to it, for a long period-of-time, to abate the demonically instigated circumstance, you find yourself in now, Matthew 6:16-18. Try abstaining from food and drink (midnight to 6 PM), twice a week, and refrain from words, attitudes, people, places, and things, including music, magazines, videos, TV, or any such things that fuel anger and discontent, and stir up lustful feelings. This is also known as, faith with works, read, understand, and embrace James 2:14-26. Nonetheless, earnestly pray, God will guide, enable, and answer you as to the type of fast. Additionally, if relevant, forgive your mother and/or father for the darkness (aka curse) they may have perpetuated, for they knew not what they done. Forgiveness is important to your success (Matthew 6:12-15, 8:21-35). See suggested course of action. (3) Dreamer, you are insincere in your dealings with people, especially by being outwardly friendly but secretly disloyal. All of these behaviors are a sign of a hardened heart or a heart becoming hardened and deep-seated anger. Your behavior opened the door for a demonic instigated situation or issue. Dreamer, your present situation, or issue, whatever "it" is, "it" was demonically instigated, and "it" is spiritually perverse. Dreamer, the Lord Jesus, is asking you to come to Him, come away privately, and ask Him to heal you, come, and ask Him to deliver you; and give Him authority over your life that you might be healed, delivered, and set free. Thus says the Lord, "I will sprinkle clean water on you, and you will be clean; I will cleanse you from all your impurities and from all your idols. I will give you a new heart and put a new spirit in you; I will remove from you your heart of stone and give you a heart of flesh. Dreamer, God knows your thoughts afar off, so genuinely repent. Other than heartfelt repentance to Jesus, no other excuse or weak justification will be heard. See suggested course of action. (4) Your dream also represents some type of spiritual privileges and a purification process, dreamer God will now separate you from people, places, and circumstances that will hinder your growth. View this separation as a blessing from God and not as an evil thing has happen. Under all adversities retain a spirit of joy, and continue to make progress in your spiritual life. Subsequently, dreamer, because of your humble and submissive faith in God's word, you will be declared as one who is a righteous minister. Planted in the House of the Lord, you will continue to prosper and mature. The same God, who plants you in your ministry, is the same God who will cause you to mature and prosper. Further, another benefit of allowing Jesus to have authority of your life; is that independent of outward circumstances, you will live and thrive where most things perish, via divine grace. Dreamer, while your spiritual growth may not be so rapid, if you endure, you will become a beautiful picture of a godly man or woman, who in your uprightness, aims to glorify God. Accordingly, gladness, thanksgiving, singing, then, strength, intense energy, and fertility will be your recompense, and your praise will be a sweet aroma in the nostrils of the Lord. If applicable, this promise is also to your generations to come. Come what may, you shall make steady progress and flourish in a very impressive manner; bringing forth fruit, even in your old age. Dreamer, as you age, your anointing to minister, and divine revelations, will always be fresh and edifying. See Psalm 92:12-15. Therefore, put the spiritual work in and go through what you need to go through now. If necessary, see suggested course of action. (5) Male dreamer: An event or situation that will cause intense fear is coming to discourage and terrify you. This will be in the form of an annoying, difficult, and unpleasant person. The trouble this person will cause will become so overwhelming, because they will expose a secret regarding you. This spiritual battle will be great, and will demand your full attention. Although you will walk through this alone, know that God will walk you through it. Dreamer, learn wisdom from th e situation, for truth do set one free; and go on from there unashamed. Then, suddenly, unexpectedly, and without any warning, all the evil and wickedness that caused you to fear and be troubled, will disappear. It will be as though it was ne ver there. At that point, you will express great joy, and feel extremely happy. Take courage and be strong, knowing that the Lord knows where you are, what's going on, and He cares. See suggested course of action. (6) Male dreamer (unmarried): Your dream denotes that a very attractive and sensual female; one whom the dreamer, may marry, especially before having sex, will enter your life. If necessary, see suggested course of action.

589: Your dream refers to one who needs to spiritually hear the Word of God, say amen to it, believe, trust, and stand still; and you will see the salvation of the Lord. For God's power has made a way out of no way for you, and your state of affairs is turning around. Dreamer, there will be a relaxation or slackening of tension in your life, stop, and feel the ten sion leaving. Those who have charged you falsely, with malicious intent, attacking your good name and reputation will be far from you. Others will become less hostile, as will you. You will be more relaxed, easygoing, and genial. The necessity to be reconciled with others than to always be in opposition has been resolved. Dreamer, you have simply taken the higher ground. You have re-evaluated your life, learned from your mistakes, found new directions in solving problems, pursued healing, sought out encouragement, and figured out what God would like you to change in order to, better fulfill His purpose. Moreover, you have learned the principles and Christian values that encourage one to reach out and touch others in a loving and graceful manner; ultimately finding yourself promoting the genuine cause of Christ and the good of others. If listed, and only if necessary, dreamer may also consider other multiples of this number. First, see Note 6 at the beginning of this category.

600: This number refers to spiritual warfare. Dreamer, do not entangle yourself with affairs, concerns, or situations, so much so that you become hindered, diverted, or drawn away, from your relationship with Jesus, and from the responsibilities of your Christian duties "your calling", because of them. As a Christian, you are a soldier of Jesus Christ; thus, you fight for His cause, and against His enemies, including your own lustful flesh. As a soldier in the army of God, you must be faithful to H im, and persevere in His cause and in your calling. So, avoid worldly entanglements, pray, consult God, and your spiritual leaders, deny self, endure hardness, be self-controlled, and be alert. Read, understand, and embrace, Ephesians 6:10-18, for this is to you now. Moreover, bring every thought, the intents of your mind and will, into obedience of Christ. See suggested course of action. If listed, and only if necessary, dreamer may also consider other multiples of this number. First, see Note 6 at the beginning of this category.

608: Dreamer, you have been blessed with a heart that understands knowledge, and not without reason. One who is given the means to study and teach, the freedom to choose, to move about without limitation, to absorb information and to observe life, and has access to prophetic wisdom, is purposed to be a transformational force in people's lives. The heart of your ministry should focus on teaching about the essence of God, the Blood of Christ, and divine order. If necessary, see suggested course of action. If listed, and only if necessary, dreamer may also consider other multiples of this number. First, see Note 6 at the beginning of this category.

620: Your dream refers to God's great mercies shown the dreamer. Within your life, God has been compassionate towards you, before you sinned, and He is compassionate towards you, after you have sinned. He will yet give you according to your need, demonstrating mercy towards you, so that you do not become too overly distressed because of your sin. Dreamer, God is slow to anger, plenteous in mercy and truth, forgiving sin and pardoning you. Get up, dry your weeping eyes, repent, and keep it moving. See suggested course of action. If listed, and only if necessary, dreamer may also consider other multiples of this number. First, see Note 6 at the beginning of this category.

636: Dreamer grace is being extended to you, via deliverance from the dangers of your fleshly passions, and a verifiable miracle within the area of your mind or head. Moreover, there will be a divine work upon your emotions, and this will manifest within your life in the form of liberality in Christ Jesus, thankfulness, and joy. All this is preparation, that you may become qualified, proven worthy, spiritually, morally, and ethically, for a religious position within an ecclesiastical order. Additionally, there is a need to make a sacrificial offering, financially, to the ministry which, you are connected. Weigh, he, or she who sows sparingly shall reap sparingly; and he or she who sows bountifully shall reap bountifully. Let each man or woman do according as you have purposed in your heart, not grudgingly, or of necessity for God loves a cheerful giver. For, God is able to make all grace abound unto you; that you, having always all sufficiency in everything, may abound unto every good work (2 Corinthians 9:6-8). If necessary, see suggested course of action. If listed, and only if necessary, dreamer may also consider other multiples of this number. First, see Note 6 at the beginning of this category.

641: First, what your dream references, the dreamer has unequivocally heard before. What God has been speaking to you, and is requiring of you, has been clearly laid-out earlier, there is no doubt or misunderstanding; you know His will, and it leads to only one conclusion; what you have heard on other occasions, at other times, is true, and denial of that truth is unacceptable at this point. Your dream is a third or fourth warning. Dreamer, you've been clearly told to, come out from among unbelievers, and to separate yourself from them, says the Lord, for what company has righteousness with unrighteousness, or what sharing of personal thoughts and feelings has light with darkness. Have nothing to do with their sinful and wicked deeds, and I will welcome you, read, understand, and embrace 2 Corinthians 6:14-18. Unfortunately, concerned with your own interest, you are driven by, and occupied with, sensual appetites, rather than spiritual needs. Your new way is based on exploring alternatives to God's righteous principles, as well as, creating a sense of unity with the wickedness around you. You have adopted a bourgeois mentality, believing yourself above God's word and above the law of the land. This mentality is concerned only with your personal comfort, material wealth, and status, at any expense. You, now, having in yourself nothing that you respect more than power and greed, are willing to sacrifice all, God, principle, family, and friend, to the image or idol of vanity. This mentality sacrifices children, family, and morality to the hollowness of satisfying immoral desires and appetites. All carried out with the hope of finding happiness by pacifying jealously and covetousness. The selling-out of yourself over to immorality, allowing wickedness to prevail in your home, devaluing those you should be protecting and nurturing, while closing your eyes to it all, are all principles based on values that are not only vile, but also increasingly unstable. This way cries out against godly ethics, and its' end offends any sense of godliness. Moreover, your desires, appetites, and attitude are leading to a chaotic and empty life. A life figuratively similar to the condition of ea rth in Genesis 1:2, wasteful, empty, and dark. This type of carnal strain and toil leads to sorrow and spiritual darkness. There is a need to re-connect with God. Favorably, because of God's love for you, His abounding grace, and His long-suffering, there is a ray of light, sent by God, purposed to break through the darkness of your state of affairs. This ray of light is a person, anointed and sent, especially to you. Their words and inspiration will be to you, like Genesis 1:3-5 is to Genesis 1:2. Illuminatingly wise, this person will powerfully affect your life, externally and internally. Their inspiration, coupled with you earnestly embracing change, humility, contentedness, integrity, ethicalness, and a renewed faith in God's word and His process, will strengthen y ou to return in complete heartfelt repentance to Jesus, from a heart of love. By this, the severity of your transgressions becomes partially sweetened; for, when a man or woman genuinely return to God, in complete surrender and humility, your deliberate transgressions become like actual merits, aka "the sweetening" (Luke 7:37-50). Because, the realization of your distance from God, due to your transgressions (Isaiah 59:2-21; Luke 15:11-24), becomes the motivating force to return to God with a passion even greater than that of someone who has never sinned in such a manner, or never left the Father's house, completely converting your present to good (Acts 9:1-30). This is the secret of repentance and returning to God. Go; therefore now, and seek the Lord Jesus, repent and place your hope in Him. Hope, placed in Him, will not deceive. If, you turn and genuinely repent, you will be favored with complete healing, however, go and sin no more. For, if anyone knows the good they ought to do and doesn't do it, it is sin for them (see James 4:17). Therefore, from this moment forward, choose good habits and deeds, e.g. good stewardship and commitment to ministry; speak to yourself what is true and good, embracing Philippians 4:8. Authentic repentance, will affect complete restoration of things, materially and spiritually within your life and i n the lives of those immediately connected to you; allowing freedom from your weaknesses to be yours. Additionally, dreamer is counseled to also recognize, acknowledge, and respect, God's absolute control over the affairs of humankind, and to renounce the belief that humans are in complete control (see Job 9:12, Isaiah 14:27; 43:13). There is a difference between divine providence and the will of humankind. Additionally, you need to take a short break from doing something. See suggested course of action. If listed, and only if necessary, dreamer may also consider other multiples of this number. First, see Note 6 at the beginning of this category.

642: Dreamer, you will blossom in the Kingdom of God. Weigh, as it takes an unrivaled level of confidence to successfully endure mountain top experiences, without imploding, as you are elevated, it will be wise, for you, to periodically take a reflective look within, to check the pride level, within your heart (also see Deuteronomy 6:10 -18). It is counseled that you set up 'mile markers', a type of accountability system for yourself along the way. Do not be deceived, with affluence, power, an d wealth, comes good and evil; thus, today, you will need to choose between good and evil; and set "checks and balance s" within yourself, because you have innate tendencies to become extreme and will judge others according to your "extremisms". Embracing this side of yourself will cause you to be deemed inappropriate, and delayed at that moment, to be of further service to the Kingdom of God. If necessary, see suggested course of action. If listed, and only if necessary, dreamer may also consider other multiples of this number. First, see Note 6 at the beginning of this category.

647: This number refers to an anger problem within the dreamer, as well as, God's displeasure at your rebellion and disobedience. Dreamer, you are devious and guilty of cruelly destroying someone spiritually, because of your uncontrolled anger. You will be pursued by one with an unrelenting vendetta against you, and yes, it will be allowed. Nonetheless, dreamer is urged to refrain from wickedness and to do none harm, physically, sexually, emotionally, and/or spiritually, any longer. Start treating God's people, your family, and others, with respect. By this, God will pardon your injustices. Moreover, seek help, via prayer, fasting, and an anger management program. You will need to declare some kind of fast and commit to it, for a period - of-time, to abate this coming influence. See suggested course of action.

666: This dream has two parts both are applicable. (1) This number is one of the secret symbols of ancient paganism, e.g. sorcery, necromancy, Satanism, and is today the syncretistic link between the revival of Spiritism, theosophy, and the last great apostasy. (2) This number refers to arrogance, one who is the antithesis of Adonai Elohim, an antagonist of Jesus Christ, adversarial to His ways and means, as well as, one pretending to be a god, desiring to be worship as such, or at least adulation. This number also points to one who has naively embraced a mélange of ancient religions and syncretistic practices, all of which leads to demonic possession. Dreamer, your lack of an objective critical analysis and judgment of a belief system's infrastructure, its foundation, existence, deity, nature of worship, sacred text, values, attitudes, earthly and eternal bene fits and recompense; and whether its beliefs are worthy of consideration or not, is leading you towards dark and erroneous knowledge, the devil's so-called deep secrets. You will gain this knowledge through personal experience and a supernatural imparting, albeit, demonically communicated. The knowledge gained will lead you to a desolate and dark ominous burning place of pain, emotionally, spiritually, and if not aborted, eternally. Moreover, the knowledge gained will not allow you to praise the Lord, only to exalt one's self. In your state of affairs, godly wisdom is urgently needed. Dreamer, God is giving you time to repent. Read and hear Revelation 2:20-29, for this is to you. See suggested course of action. If listed, and only if necessary, may consider the interpretation for the numbers 6, 66, as they relate to the repetitiveness of this number (666). Hence, the number 666 is a more intense expression of the numbers 6, 66, in strength and forcefulness, spiritually, prophetically, and in application. First, see Note 6 at the beginning of this category.

In addition, the following are common words; expressions or usages (e.g. slang or clichés) or a 'probable' that are metaphorically represented by this number:

- The Antichrist (aka the beast): This is one who is the antithesis of Christ; an antagonist of Jesus Christ, who spreads evil throughout the world, and will be overcome by the second coming of Christ.
- Fallacy, trickery, guile, and/or deception are also connected to this number.

672: See Psalm 42 and 43, and know that Elohim is the lifter of your head and of your downcast soul. You will be vindicated. Only, acknowledge in your heart that there is a God, and His son is Jesus Christ. Moreover, dreamer, you will have to, continually be intentional regarding embracing mental and emotional habits of holiness, for habits are formed by practice or neglect. You must by faith, deliberately, and purposefully, offer you, your mind, spirit, and body in a sober, firm, and dignified manner, as a living sacrifice, holy and pleasing to God. With a confident and unquestionable belief in the validity of salvation, via the atoning work of the cross, knowing that it is enough to justify righteousness within a believer's life. And the Lord God is to be loved with all your heart, and with all your soul and with all your strength. If necessary, see suggested course of action. If listed, and only if necessary, dreamer may also consider other multiples of this number. First, see Note 6 at the beginning of this category.

677: This type of dream exposes a need of refinement of character, namely in the area dealing with the deed s of the flesh. For example, dishonesty, adultery, sensuality, hostility, feuding, vendettas, grudges, unfriendliness, strife, jealou sy, outbursts of anger, disputes, dissensions, discord, factions, cliques, envying, drunkenness, carousing, idolatry (idol atry is "foreign service", any act that expresses devotion or fanatical admiration to something or someone other than Adonai Elohim), or any traits of these sorts (see 1 Corinthians 6:8-11). This also includes a possible belief in, and/or practice of, necromancy. Thus, your dream comes to warn an immoral believer that your activities are illegal. Your choices are spiritually forbidden. You have deliberately chosen to become enslaved to that which is forbidden by the One True and Living God, and you compel individuals to follow other gods, and hard-press people to believe what you say. You are one, who is the direct opposite of a born-again, aka a believer, the antithesis of Christ. As a result you will now begin to experience serious mental health issues and will have to be restrained, against your will if needs be. Dreamer, if urged by God, declare a one, two, or three day fast for sanctification purposes; also, wash (bathe) and make yourself, clothing, and personal surroundings clean. If not a day fast, you will need to declare some kind of fast and commit to it, for a period-of-time, to abate this coming influence. Refrain from wickedness and do no one harm, physically, sexually, emotionally, and/or spiritually, any longer. Start treating God's pe ople, your family, and others, with respect. By this, God will pardon your injustices. See suggested course of action.

678: Dreamer will be granted some manner of favor, from a very strong ally, benefactor, defender, or supporter, via an "in-kind" grant, or through a forgiveness of a very large debt (e.g. auto loan, bank loan, college, student loan, or mortgage), or through a pardon. With that said, dreamer, give ear, two "favors" will be presented, one sacred, one profane. The key to knowing which favor is sacred, and which is profane. The profane favor will ask you to compromise your beliefs, namely to "gray area" some of God's unequivocal positions on certain tenets. Dreamer, never do you ever compromise your beliefs in Jesus Christ, as the Word of God made flesh, nor do you distort the meanings of His Holy Word, for any manner of favor, for this is akin to spiritual prostitution, aka idolatry. Dreamer, you are a Christian soldier, a battle-seasoned Christian, who should know what to do because of your experience and familiarity with Scripture. You also have access to prophetic wisdom; therefore, you have the capacity to discern truth from false. Nurture your gift of discernment; developing it; by which you will be able to discern compromise, regarding ideologies, "isms", and other concerns and issues, pertaining to, contained within, and in accordance with the Bible. You are able to keep with the nature of the Bible. Therefore, consider carefully what is being presented to you. The lesson is, no matter how personable, powerful, or difficult a person, or how uncertain or unpopular the choices and issues, always take the next biblical and ethical step, for obedience to God's principles will always prove safer and stronger foundationally. Additionally, there is a need to make a sacrificial offering, financially, to the ministry which, you are connected. Weigh, he, or she who sows sparingly shall reap sparingly; and he or she who sows bountifully shall reap bountifully. Let each man or woman do according as you have purposed in your heart, not grudgingly, or of necessity for God loves a cheerful giver. For, God is able to make all grace abound unto you; that you, having always all sufficiency in every thing, may abound unto every good work (2 Corinthians 9:6-8). If necessary, see suggested course of action. If listed, and only if necessary, dreamer may also consider other multiples of this number. First, see Note 6 at the beginning of this category.

682: This dream has two meanings and both apply. (1) Your dream was sent as a grave rebuke and serious alarm to the dreamer. The grave rebuke and serious alarm is as follows (choose one). (a) This type of dream reveals the loss of a ministry (or ministries) due to spiritual immaturity and serious neglect, as well as the loss of honor and respect. Dreamer, it is a wicked servant who would bury, discount, disregard, or spurn his or her talents, skills, and/or ministerial responsibilities, blaming your lack of, commitment, faithfulness, knowledge, and stewardship on God, others, or transitory circumstances (Matthew 25:24- 30). Dreamer needs to consider your own well-being, emotionally, mentally, and spiritually. Think about what personal life cycles, denials, fears, failures, experiences, hang-ups, hindrances, lies, and/or rejections, have prevented you from developing, growing, expanding, increasing, and becoming all that you can be. What is lifeless in your life? What exactly is holding yo u back? For sure, it is not God, a person, or thing. You, personally, will have to give an account of your stewardship to Jesus Christ, and your life choices will testify against you. You have been appointed to do certain things within your present fellowship, this is a small thing; do what is expected of you. If no action, commitment, or obligation to ministry, is heeded at this time, you may find yourself similar to the servant spoken of in the parable who buried his gift (Matthew 25:15). Furthe r, if your designated service is given to another, so will the prosperity that is attached to that service, be given to that person also, and for you, jealously will be your recompense. (b) Dreamer, prideful and powerful, you lack Christ-like humility, and is becoming cruel and insensitive. Moreover, at present, concerned with your own interest, you are driven by, and occupied with, sensual carnal appetites, rather than spiritual needs. Your desires, appetites, and attitude are leading to a chaotic and empty life. A life figuratively similar to the condition of earth in Genesis 1:2, wasteful, empty, and dark. This type of carnal strain and toil leads to sorrow and spiritual darkness. There is a need to re-connect with God. (2) Although, your dream is a grave rebuke and a serious alarm to the dreamer, fortunately, there is a ray of light, sent by God, purposed to break through the darkness of your state of affairs. This ray of light is a person, anointed and sent, especially to you. Their words and inspiration will be to you, like Genesis 1:3-5 is to Genesis 1:2. Illuminatingly wise, this person will powerfully affect your life, externally and internally. Their inspiration, coupled with you earnestly embracing change, humility, contentedness, integrit y, ethicalness, and a renewed faith in God's word and His process, will strengthen you to return in complete heartfelt repentance to Jesus, from a heart of love. By this, the severity of your transgressions becomes partially sweetened; for, when a man or woman genuinely return to God, in complete surrender and humility, your deliberate transgressions become like actual merits, aka "the sweetening" (Luke 7:37-50). Because, the realization of your distance from God, due to your transgressions (Isaiah 59:2-21; Luke 15:11-24), becomes the motivating force to return to God with a passion even greater than that of someone who has never sinned in such a manner, or never left the Father's house, completely converting your present to good (Acts 9:1 -30). This is the secret of repentance and returning to God. Go; therefore now, and seek the Lord Jesus, repent and place your hope in Him. Hope, placed in Him, will not deceive. See suggested course of action. If listed, and only if necessary, dreamer may also consider other multiples of this number. First, see Note 6 at the beginning of this category.

700: In addition to one of the following, and only if necessary, dreamer may also consider other multiples of this number. First, see Note 6 at the beginning of this category. Your dream denotes rectification, leadership, and marriage. With that, this dream has four meanings (choose one). (1) A change of direction and attitude is highly recommended. Dreamer, you are encouraged, re-think your views and attitude, regarding the doctrine you are adhering to, and your philosophy, and/or your plans for establishing or joining an institution or organization. Why, because your interpretation of the Word of God has become unrecognizable to those you influence. When those who seek truth, ask Jesus why they do not recognize your philosophy, the words spoken of you are that you are true to yourself. To be true to self or another, is to seek affirmation with respect to condoning your particular sin, while basing your ideas, arguments, and/or beliefs on something that is sacrilegious, profane, illogical, and non-mainstream doctrine or philosophy. Your ideology is without favorable conclusions, thus this dream. You are full of pride. If you persist on perpetuating your self-serving ideology and calling it divinely ordained, you will be stripped and humiliated publicly of shameful acts. Therefore, repent. See suggested course of action. (2) Male Married dreamer: Dreamer, you are purposed to become a shepherd over God's people. Your calling is to give sermons, spread the gospel, and conduct religious services, a cleric of some kind, e.g. bishop, elder, parson, pastor, priest, rabbi, or teacher. A large part of your mission should center on you raising the spirits of your fellow mankind, and establishing yourself as an inspirational person spreading hope. Your gift is to inspire and motivate. Dreamer, therefore, decline the temporary relations of darkness that you might inherit an entrance into paradise having sincerely answered God's request upon your life, and experience the prosperity that is attached to such a calling. Further, for selfless altruism to be complete within your life, you must be refined, polished, and educated in three areas. Weigh the following. (a) A change must occur in your interaction with God. With respect to God, a selfless and consistent humble submission and obedience to His will is needed, (b) a change must occur in your marital relationship, it being the most personal and intense of human interactions. With respect to your marriage, this involves the heart felt practice of regard for, and devotion to, your wife, this means viewing and finding in your spouse, your spiritual helpmate, and (c) a change must occur with yourself. With respect to yourself, selflessness means refining your character, and finding within yourself contentment, especially with God's affirmation. (3) Female Married dreamer: Dreamer, God has given you the task to bring to perfection, the rectification of your husband. You are purposed to rectify your husband's will by elevating him to a new awareness of his innate potential. This is known as, "she who does her husband's will", or a "good woman". Read, understand, and embrace, Proverbs 31:10-:31. Dreamer, you have within you the possibility to make all things which your husband conceives a reality; thus "doing your husband's will", by rectifying, via bringing, leading, or forcing him to abandon a wrong or evil course of life or conduct, and to adopt a right one, namely that which he needs to fulfill purpose. This is your purpose. Unfortunately, while both of you are physically and emotionally able, neither of you is walking in purpose. Consequently, within your life, you are experiencing strong conflict, from within and without; this is your spirits struggling to fulfill purpose. Dreamer is counseled to handle your marriage, on God's terms, embracing His ethics, and not yours, as you've previously done, and then things will begin to improve. See suggested course of action. (4) Unmarried dreamer: If there is a desire to marry, you will marry, very soon, perhaps within seven months. This marriage will prove to be a time of "jubilee" for you. Celebrate for God's blessings are upon you. Moreover, see, interpretation #1 or #2, and glean the wisdom, for this is for you.

709: Your dream was sent to warn the dreamer. As your dream alludes to one who needs to abstain from immorality, and other profane acts, dreamer, you will experience some level of public exposure, for open shame shortly. Therefore, a change is vitally needed in the way you behave. You profane that which is holy, because you have been wounded by one considered pious, who is not. Core issue, dreamer, bad things do happen to innocent people and a bad thing happened to you. However, you no longer have to be the bad thing that happens to others. Ask your Heavenly Father to forgive you of your sins, as you forgive those who violated you, and forgive yourself, and no longer will the bad thing hold sway over your entire life. For whom Jesus sets free, is free. By grace (the free and unmerited favor and beneficence of God), prayer, and change, your life will begin to transform and you will be restored to the person you was intended to be. Weigh, no one person, people, or denomination, hypocrite or not, is the full representation of the Kingdom of God; therefore, no longer allow the enemy to rob you of your intended destiny. It would be wise for you, at this time in your life, to embrace holiness, wholeheartedly, to prevent the practice of greater immoral acts; for such acts are grossly unclean and will defile you spiritually and physically completely. Further, all devotion to sin; reveals a total lack of respect towards God, and all that is sacred. Your acts of immorality, will unequivocally lead to you selling your "birthright", just to satisfy the growing lust in your flesh and heart (Genesis 25:29-34; Hebrews 12:14-17). The repercussions of such acts; see Ezekiel 18:24-32, 33:10-13. Dreamer, without holiness no one shall see the Lord. Therefore, look diligently within, and consider the state of great suffering and distress, you are experiencing, and then consider the healing that Jesus is offering you now. Dreamer, respect your time of visitation from the Lord, for it is upon you. You can be made free, pray and ask Jesus for help. See suggested course of action.

728: In addition to one of the following, and only if necessary, dreamer may also consider other multiples of this number. First, see Note 6 at the beginning of this category. This dream is one of encouragement and validation. With that, this dream has two meanings (choose one). (1) Dreamer, you will now, be led into situations where you will be the agent who ushers God's Presence into the mentality of situations, elevating and promoting the righteousness of Christ to those around you. You will show up when most needed, and then disappear without a thought of compensation, having faith that Jehovah Jireh, will provide for you and them (Genesis 22:13-14). Dreamer, it is your role in life to inspire and motivate others; you are, purposed to raise the spirits of your fellow mankind. You are endowed with the power of God to cause them to become alive again; and there will be restoration within their lives, from depressed, inactive, and unused states, because of your ministry. While you continue to inspire and motive, God will continue to sustain and nourish those, touch by your ministry, while simultaneously allowing each one, the ability to grow and develop independently (see 1 Corinthians 3:6-10, 2 Corinthians 9:9-15). That they might be known as trees of righteousness, the planting of Jehovah, that He may be glorified. Many will be inspired by your humility, wisdom, blameless actions, confidence, and by your faith in Christ Jesus. All of this suggests that the dreamer has a balance of love and respect for the Lord and others. On the other hand, dreamer, you must develop your abilities to communicate more effectively, via studying and research (2 Timothy 2:15), writing your words down, outlining your topics, that you might express yourself clearly and confidently. For your words will motivate others, and you will inspire others to dream and to make their dreams come true. Your words of inspiration will set people free (John 8:32, 36). Moreover, capable and unrelenting, you will handle much responsibility, and will be required to make major decisions. At some point in the undisclosed future, honor and wealth will be bestowed upon the dreamer, if not already. You will be as a tree planted by streams of water, which yields its fruit in season and who leaf does not wither, whatever you do will prosper. (2) Dreamer, at present, there is a struggle within you. Between your old nature and your new nature, the leftovers of sin and the new beginnings of grace (the free and unmerited favor and beneficence of God). The carnal part of you is struggling against the spiritually renewed you. Your old nature is resisting everything that is spiritual and is opposing all the suggestions of the Holy Spirit and the ethical urgings of your conscience. This is spiritual circumcision of the heart. Fortunately, you are choosing to side with godly principles and to stand on your convictions. Dreamer, you will have success overcoming old things; there will be joy about your success, publicly. Now, the old has gone, and the new has come (2 Corinthians 5:17). God's providential blessing is upon you to increase. All things will be made beautiful in their own time. Be mindful of your words and do not boast of your increase. Furthermore, due to the intensity of your struggle, one of God's messengers is sent to give you the support needed at this time. Be aware that the new person within your midst may be that messenger. If necessary, see suggested course of action.

730: The trying times that have brought much frustration, aggravation, and were so troublesome will (or have already) begin to abate. You've weathered a great storm, suffered enormous difficulties, and have not gotten any relief. God has seen your plight. You are now entering into (or you are already experiencing) a rest. Your heavenly Father is protecting you by allowing you to rest from your work; in order to avoid overly cruel and oppressive pressure from the enemy, via those he uses. You will be spiritually concealed, hidden, or kept secret by God, appearing only, to do God's will and then fade back into obscurity. During this sabbatical, peace will again hold sway over your life. Put your trust in Him, and your peace will overflow. Additionally, Jehovah Jireh will provide for all your needs. Now, those that have vexed you will go far from you, for God will make you a threat to them without any effort on your part. Use this "you" time to cultivate your strengths and discipline your weaknesses. If necessary, see suggested course of action. If listed, and only if necessary, dreamer may also consider other multiples of this number. First, see Note 6 at the beginning of this category.

741: In addition to one of the following, and only if necessary, dreamer may also consider other multiples of this number. First, see Note 6 at the beginning of this category. With that, this dream has two meanings (one or both may apply). (1) Your dream was sent as a message of encouragement. Dreamer, your prayers have been heard by the Most High. God will give you new insight, a truthful vision, and it shall "come to pass". Dreamer, although you've gotten to the point where you're spiritually weak and now feel discouraged or troubled, feeling that your faith has been in vain, no longer allow the spirit of fear to intimidate you, only be strong and courageous. Read and understand Romans 8:15, 2 Timothy 1:7. Dreamer, by God's power, a way out of no way will be made for you, and your state of affairs will be turned around. Somehow, God will make a way for you. Jesus will come and see about you. Thus, keep your faith, regarding what you've believed God for; He has promised never to leave you alone. You will experience a miracle. You are encouraged to re-evaluate your life and figure out what changes need to be made to, better fulfill God's purpose within your life. Learn from your mistakes, find new direction in solving problems, pursue healing, and seek out encouragement. Subsequently, joy shall then be revealed, rest shall appear, and healing will descend, disease shall withdraw, anxiety, anguish and crying shall pass from you; gladness will happen. If necessary, see suggested course of action. (2) Dreamer, most importantly, take heed to abstain from a judgmental attitude, abusive talking, contentions, revenge, envy, and hatred. As your dream also denotes death; therefore, take heed and abstain from all that you are asked to abstain from, lest you die an early death (Ecclesiastes 7:17). See suggested course of action.

759: Dreamer is seeking other knowledge and revelations, disciplines that do not support intimacy with Jesus Christ, and do not support meditating on the Word of God (Joshua 1:8), such as meditative disciplines. Disciplines that claim to train the consciousness for a state of perfect spiritual insight and tranquility, which they say is achieved through paths of actions, knowledge, and devotion. Not only is this course or discipline, delivered without grace, it will never be enough to fill an empty soul, nor does it prepare you for eternal life, for it approaches the spiritual realm without the provision that God has provided for man to approach, and reach, true spiritual perfection, and that provision being Jesus the Christ. Moreover, this way opens you up to be deceived regarding your own fallen nature, and to the deception of demons, which are always looking for inroads into our minds, and it is unscriptural. Thus, your seeking has led to you gaining dark and erroneou s knowledge, through personal experiences and through a supernatural imparting, which was demonically communicated. The knowledge you've gained does not allow you to praise the Lord, only to exalt one's self. You have abandoned the faith, and are now adhering to lies. You are embracing beliefs, views, and practices that are erroneous, unlawful, toxic, and spiritually and/or physically deadly. Your choices will not withstand your storms of life. Your conscience will haunt you. Weakened by frequent panic attacks, brought on by your own guilt and the fear of God's retribution, you will begin to crack in your personality. He, wh o carries his or her own accuser, and their own tormentor, always in their bosom, cannot but be afraid on every side (Matthew Henry's Commentary on Job 18:11-21). The only foundation upon which one should wisely establish his or her identity is the principles within the Word of God. Your attitude is leading to a mental and spiritual breakdown, opening the door for demons to run havoc within your life and to bring you down to desolation. You are forfeiting purpose for foolishness and ruin. Demonic influences will swarm around you, ready to help you explore all manner of wickedness, and evil, despicable, immoral, reprehensible, disreputable, degenerate, infamous, and perverse choices. Your lifestyle choices will become offensive and repulsive (abominable) in the sight of God and humanity. Dreamer, demons have had thousands of years to master human weaknesses and can rival men and women of God if we are not careful. Favorably, while your dream is a seriously severe rebuke and warning, because of grace and the many mercies of God extended to you, it is not an official declaration. Dreamer is counseled to seek all kinds of spiritual support now, to possibly avert or turn things around, and perhaps move away from your present environment, definitely walk away from all negativity that is the antithesis of Christ, abruptly. Utilizing the powerful resources of prayer and heartfelt repentance to Jesus is a good place to start. To Jesus pray, Psalm 51, this followed by appropriate application of wisdom, can conceivably avert some of the repercussions of your choices. This coupled with fasting, a changed mindset, serious re-consideration of God's ways and means, and an honest acknowledgement of God's hand within your life, then the severe impact of your choices and actions upon your life, can be reversed and damages repaired (also see Ezekiel 33:12-19). This is what is called leaving a blessing behind. If you do not genuinely seek help and change, for sure ruin will be your destiny's declaration. See suggested course of action. If listed, and only if necessary, dreamer may also consider other multiples of this number. First, see Note 6 at the beginning of this category.

774: Dreamer, hurling insults, you've proven to be a bully and braggart, with tyrannical tendencies. Further, you have violated a trust, a confidence communicated to you. Ruthlessly aggressive, you harbor wicked thoughts, using half-truths, twisting confidences, to gain advantage over some. In doing so you have tainted the faith, which is in Jesus Christ, of him or her whose confidence was violated, you will be found out. Confession to God and seeking forgiveness is required, by this you will be forgiven for all you've done. See suggested course of action. If listed, and only if necessary, dreamer may also consider other multiples of this number. First, see Note 6 at the beginning of this category.

776: Your dream denotes one, namely the dreamer, who needs to come back to the Lord. Fortunately, dreamer, be encouraged, for your dream also denotes that you are willing to do the spiritual work within, to come back to Jesus. See suggested course of action. If listed, and only if necessary, dreamer may also consider other multiples of this number. First, see Note 6 at the beginning of this category.

768: First, what your dream references, the dreamer has unequivocally heard before. What God has been speaking to you, and is requiring of you, has been clearly laid-out earlier, there is no doubt or misunderstanding; you know His will, and it leads to only one conclusion; what you have heard on other occasions, at other times, is true, and denial of that truth is unacceptable at this point. Your dream is a third or fourth warning. With that, dreamer, you've been clearly told to, come out from among unbelievers, and to separate yourself from them, says the Lord, for what company has righteousness with unrighteousness, or what sharing of personal thoughts and feelings has light with darkness. Have nothing to do with their sinful and wicked deeds, and I will welcome you, read, understand, and embrace 2 Corinthians 6:14-18. Unfortunately, concerned with your own interest, you are driven by, and occupied with, sensual appetites, rather than spiritual needs. Your way is based on exploring alternatives to God's righteous principles, as well as, creating a sense of unity with the wickedness around you. You have adopted a bourgeois mentality, believing yourself above God's word and above the law of the land. This mentality is concerned only with your personal comfort, material wealth, and status, at any expense. You, now, having in yourself nothing that you respect more than power and greed, are willing to sacrifice all, God, principle, family, and friend, to the image or idol of vanity. This mentality sacrifices children, family, and morality to the hollowness of satisfying immoral desires and appetites. All carried out with the hope of finding happiness by pacifying jealously and covetousness. The selling- out of yourself over to immorality, allowing wickedness to prevail in your home, devaluing those you should be protecting and nurturing, while closing your eyes to it all, are all principles based on values that are not only vile, but also increasingly unstable. This way cries out against godly ethics, and its' end offends any sense of godliness. Moreover, your desires, appetites, and attitude are leading to a chaotic and empty life. A life figuratively similar to the condition of earth in Genesis 1:2, wasteful, empty, and dark. This type of carnal strain and toil leads to sorrow and spiritual darkness. There is a n earnest need to re-connect with God. Favorably, because of God's love for you, His abounding grace, and His long-suffering, there is a ray of light, sent by God, purposed to break through the darkness of your state of affairs. This ray of light is a person, a nointed and sent, especially to you. Their words and inspiration will be to you, like Genesis 1:3-5 is to Genesis 1:2. Illuminatingly wise, this person will powerfully affect your life, externally and internally. Their inspiration, coupled with you earnestly embra cing change, humility, contentedness, integrity, ethicalness, and a renewed faith in God's word and His process, will strengthen you to return in complete heartfelt repentance to Jesus, from a heart of love. By this, the severity of your transgressions beco mes partially sweetened; for, when a man or woman genuinely return to God, in complete surrender and humility, your deliberate transgressions become like actual merits, aka "the sweetening" (Luke 7:37-50). Because, the realization of your distance from God, due to your transgressions (Isaiah 59:2-21; Luke 15:11-24), becomes the motivating force to return to God with a passion even greater than that of someone who has never sinned in such a manner, or never left the Father's house, completely converting your present to good (Acts 9:1-30). This is the secret of repentance and returning to God. Go; therefore now, and seek the Lord Jesus, repent and place your hope in Him. Hope, placed in Him, will not deceive. If, you turn and genuinely repent, you will be favored with complete healing, however, go and sin no more. For, if anyone knows the good they ought to do and doesn't do it, it is sin for them (see James 4:17). From this moment forward, choose good habits and deeds, e.g. good stewardship and commitment to ministry; speak to yourself what is true and good, embracing Philippians 4:8. Authentic repentance, will affect complete restoration of things, materially and spiritually within your life and in the lives of those immediately connected to you; allowing freedom from your weaknesses to be yours. Additionally, dreamer is counseled to also recognize, acknowledge, and respect, God's absolute control over the affairs of humankind, and to renounce the belief that humans are in complete control (see Job 9:12, Isaiah 14:27; 43:13). There is a difference between divine providence and the will of humankind. See suggested course of action. If listed, and only if necessary, dreamer may also consider other multiples of this number. First, see Note 6 at the beginning of this category.

770: Read Psalm 91:7-16, for God is declaring this word over your life from this moment forward. Dreamer, do not fear (reverence) anything in this world, but reverence only the Almighty God. If you fear (reverence) the Almighty God only, all those who would desire to do you harm, will simply fall to your side. Moreover, there will be an acknowledgement of you winning something in your life, because of the rectification of your soul, and the conquering of sin, within your life. If listed, and only if necessary, dreamer may also consider other multiples of this number. First, see Note 6 at the beginning of this category.

776: This number denotes that there is a need to come back to Jesus, and subsequently, all that has been lost, will come back to you. Unfortunately, this is a final warning, before a weakening of your core beliefs begins to happen, namely a rejection of all or some of the original foundational teachings of

Christ and His apostles. Thus, your dream was sent, in the spirit of grace (the free and unmerited favor and beneficence of God), to see if you will yet be worked upon, and change your mindset, or else to leave you inexcusable, in your accusations against God, because of your ruin (also see Jeremiah 9:7 -9; Matthew 23:37-39; Revelation 3:15-21). See suggested course of action. If listed, and only if necessary, dreamer may also consider other multiples of this number. First, see Note 6 at the beginning of this category.

777: This number refers to God's faithfulness, and to His understanding, and to one who is spiritually concealed, hidden, or kept secret by God (see Romans 11:3-5), appearing only, to do God's will and then to fade back into obscurity. You are down-to-earth, fair, humble, just, unpretentious, not rude, or obscene. If these attributes are not present within you at this moment, a change is coming, via spiritual purification, rectification of chaos, and a refinement process within the life of t he dreamer. That you may go on, complete spiritually, being built up in your faith, lacking nothing. During this season of cleansing, if the process of purification is actually needed, the dreamer will be favored with a sabbatical, including pay. This purification, refinement, and rectification will take some time, be patient, and allow the process. It will perfect a complete quietness within your soul, and a more compassionate and obedient spirit, leaving you more open to divine influence. You wil l gain knowledge on how to be moderate in all things, just and fair, and you will become one whom other believers will interact with socially on very personal levels, e.g. business associate, friendship, ministry, or spouse. This sabbatical should be used exclusively for the purpose it was intended. To draw you away from personal pursuits a nd to allow time for you to devote yourself, and all that you are, to God's glory, e.g. perfect your inborn talent in some way for the glory of God. Dreamer, a spark of life remains hidden inside of you, because you are God's child according to grace (the free and unmerited favor and beneficence of God). He wants to balance your understanding of things; thus, effecting wholeness within your life, for you a re now ready to receive the deepest measures of understanding, and so that the enemy will no longer b e able to manipulate your emotions so easily. The Paraclete is with you to help you throughout this entire process. Moreover, you will be used, if not already, to usher others into a totally new and higher level of spiritual awareness. Even amongst the "broken", a spark of life remains hidden, awaiting your particular ministry, your unique way of presenting the gospel. You will appear when needed, and then disappear without thought of anything in return. In this, you imitate Christ. Dreamer, by fulfil ling your part and remaining humble, you will be worthy of your wage. It is promised that you will eat and do well, on this side of eternity, a nd inherit eternal life. This is your year of total restoration, restitution, freedom, and fullness of life. I n addition, you may also consider the number seven. If listed, and only if necessary, may consider the interpretation for the numbers 7, 77, as they relate to the repetitiveness of this number (777). Hence, the number 777 is a more intense expression of the numbers 7, 77, in strength and forcefulness, spiritually, prophetically, and in application. First, see Note 6 at the beginning of this category.

788: In addition to one of the following, and only if necessary, dreamer may also consider other multiples of this number. First, see Note 6 at the beginning of this category. With that, this dream has two meanings (one or both may apply). (1) Dreamer, because of God's grace, His faithfulness, and His mercy towards you; you will begin to experience a surge of positive feelings, due to restoration, transformation, and a miraculous healing and strengthening, both physically and emotionally. The emotional level is already happening within your inner most feelings and affections, for, God is first healing yo ur broken heart. Now, your burdens, having been dealt with, freedom from your weaknesses is yours. Freedom from bondage, domination by evil, and hardship, is beginning for you. Dreamer, you are asked to give careful thought regarding your bondages and hardships, considering how things are, and have been for you, for your experiences have prepared you for ministry. From this day forward, God will bless you. You will be favored with complete healing, go and sin no more, but go and offer prayers, supplications, and thanksgiving before your Lord and Savior, Jesus Christ, for He is forgiving, compassionate, long-suffering, and full of loving-kindness, restoring more favorable conditions. In time, you will find yourself assistant to a high-ranking leader within a ministry, perhaps in the position of personal aide, leadership counselor, associate pastor, or CEO of your individual ministry. As well, there will be clarity and freedom in the way you communicate yourself to others, especially prophetically. Note, although your life is (will become) very busy and full of concerns; it is advised that you do not forget your personal relationship with Christ, nor neglect the devotions that keep that personal relationship healthy. Nor must you allow yourself to be annoyed with other acts of devotion, e.g. family bible study and other quality times, fellowshipping with other believers, church attendance, acknowledging God's goodness to you, to others, and the like. Therefore, from this moment forward, choose good habits and deeds, e.g. good stewardship and commitment to ministry; speak to yourself what is true and good, embrace Philippians 4:8, and choose good nutritional habits that you might remain in good health. Also, these choices will greatly support you in your progress forward towards your transformation and freedom, and help guide you toward, and enable you to fulfill, your purpose. All these blessings are rain. Dreamer, as one perfects him or herself, God helps by sending 'rains of blessings', then situations prosper. The rain is coming! (2) Unmarried female dreamer: In addition to the previous interpretation, your dream also signifies a marriage. Your husband is before you at present, or will be, very shortly. Handle the relationship, on God's terms, embracing His ethics, and not yours, as you've previously done. If necessary, see suggested course of action.

807: It is time for you, the dreamer, to be refined from your impurities; and purged from your immorality; it is your time to become enlightened and healed. Accordingly, dreamer, you will begin to experience afflictions and troubles, intended to purify you from worthless and vain pursuits, and to bring you to heartfelt repentance. Repentance is seeking pardon for having done something awry, and for having hurt someone, and expressing sincere feelings of regret and brokenness. To Jesus pray, Psalm 51:1-19. To individuals, a phone call or a letter of apology is a good place to start, if appropriate. Moreover, see 2 Corinthians 7:10, 11. God will make that which you think gives you the most pleasure, very difficult and painful, "a bitter pill" to swallow, so to say, as it is with all who live by sensual relations only and not by faith. A pill so bitter, so intensely hostile, and penetratingly unpleasant, that you will become angry, disillusioned, estranged, indifferent, resentful, withdrawn, or even worse. God will allow this, so that when those lustful desires and wants, disappoint, they will draw forth from you "a hallelujah". However, this kind of praise, this kind of "hallelujah", will not be the result of a happy feeling, or will not necessarily come from one who has seen the light. It will be offered through the teeth of pain, it will be broken, and will be offered in spite of emotional numbness. This kind of praise will be offered to Jesus as a pure act of obedience, and as a naked act of your will. It will come from a place deep down, within your heart, beneath the changes and turnarounds of feelings, a nd the vicissitudes of life. This act of praise will be offered in defiance of the darkness, and it will evoke a confession of faith in Jesus who lives above tears, and who calls you to Himself, the One and only Light of the world, and He is the only rescuer fr om the darkness of pain and despair. When one, namely the dreamer, is able to praise Jesus in such circumstances, you are acknowledging that you are not the center of the universe, and that your pain and loss, though personally difficult, was allowed to rectify your faithfulness in God. Like Job looking to God, who appeared to him out of the whirlwind, dreamer, lift up your eyes from yourself to behold the Lord, and find a whole new perspective and peace. Then you will be driven to Him who heals according to your deepest needs, and in whose favor, we find great compassion, genuine comfort, and satisfaction. He does this, in the spirit of grace (the free and unmerited favor and beneficence of God), to see if you will yet be worked upo n, and change your mindset (also see Jeremiah 9:7-9; Zechariah 13:9; Revelation 3:15-21). He wants to restore your soul. Dreamer, be earnest and repent that all may be well you. It is time, and you are able. See suggested course of action. If listed, and only if necessary, dreamer may also consider other multiples of this number. First, see Note 6 at the beginning of this category.

864: Your dream was sent to encourage. Dreamer, because of your humble and submissive faith in God's word, and not in your works alone, you are, declared as one who is a righteous minister. Planted in the House of the Lord, you will continue to prosper and mature. The same God, who planted you in your ministry, is the same God who will cause you to mature and prosper. You will live and thrive where most things perish, independent of outward circumstances, via divine grace. Your spiritual growth may not be so rapid, however, if you endure, you will become a beautiful picture of a godly man or woman, who in your uprightness, aims to glorify God. On another vein, your dream also represents some type of spiritual privileges and a purification process. Dreamer, God will separate you from people, places, and circumstances that will hinder your growth, view this separation as a blessing from God and not as an evil thing has happen. Under all adversities retain a spirit of joy, continue to make progress in your spiritual life, with gladness, thanksgiving, singing, and then, strength, intense energy, and fertility will be your recompense, and your praise will be a sweet aroma in the nostrils of the Lord. If applicable, this promise is to your generations to come. Come what may, you shall make steady progress and flourish in a very impressive manner; bringing forth fruit, even in your old age. Dreamer, as you age, your anointing to minister, and divine revelations, will always be fresh and edifying. See Psalm 92:12-15. If listed, and only if necessary, dreamer may also consider other multiples of this number. First, see Note 6 at the beginning of this category.

873: Dreamer, take refuge in the Most High, for He will deliver you from all accusations that have resulted in you being intensely harassed, hounded, maltreated, persecuted, singled out and/or a loss of favor. Please note that this intense opposition has been instigated by the enemy of your soul using others to do his dirty work, thus vigorous pestering and serious aggravation by the demonically used. Dreamer, know that your struggle is not with mankind, but is spiritual. Read, understand, and embrace, Ephesians 6:10-18, for this is to you now. Therefore, worldly or carnal dealings will not prove very advantageous. Godly wisdom is your best bet. Dreamer, you are instructed to live at peace as much as possible with others, avoiding arguments and conflict, and you are encouraged to take the higher ground by playing the role of peacemaker when disagreements arise. In the midst of discouragement, dreamer is urged to stand up for righteousness and to stand up for truth, and Jesus will always be with you. You can pass this spiritual test. Listen to that still small voice; it will guide you, for it is of God. Moreover, pray after the similitude of Psalm 7:3-17: "Most High, if I have done anything and there is guilt on my hands, if I have done evil to anyone who was at peace with me or without cause have injured, then, forgive me. If listed, and only if necessary, dreamer may also consider other multiples of this number. First, see Note 6 at the beginning of this category.

888: In addition to one of the following, if listed, and only if necessary, may consider the interpretation for the numbers 8, 88 as they relate to the repetitiveness of this number (888). Hence, the number 888; is a more intense expression of the numbers 8, 88 in strength and forcefulness, spiritually, prophetically, and in application. First, see Note 6 at the beginning of this category. This number refers to Jesus Christ, who is the Tree of Life, and it refers to an evangelistic calling on the life of the dreamer, and a wedding. With that, your dream has two meanings (choose one). (1) Your dream is to urge the dreamer to become definite in your dogma (also see 1 Timothy 2:4-7). Dreamer, your natural inclination toward the spiritual, access to prophetic wisdom, and your positive attitude, endows you with a religious zeal that enables you to express yourself through inspirational acting, art, preaching or teaching. It is through these evangelistic tools and the power of God that you are (or will become) a transformational force in people's lives, at least 288+ people. Moreover, as you also have the ability to lead by example, you are chosen, and predestined as a high-ranking cleric. Your family is a chosen people, a royal priesthood, a holy nation, a people belonging to God, that you all may worship and declare the praises of Him who called you out of darkness into His wonderful light. Dreamer, your abilities must be used exclusively for the Kingdom of God, to declare and teach His principles, precepts, and wisdom. You are to teach on confession, eternal life, praise, the resurrection of the saints, and on righteousness, as well as, on the power of godly knowledge. You are to expose idolatry, and to instruct on the futileness of foolishness, lying, pride, sexual immorality, and unreliability. To teach otherwise; will lead you towards emotional dualism, resulting in a humanistic or syncretistic belief system, eventually leaving you an apostate. However, in fulfilling God's will for your life, you will find favor and grace in the eyes of God and man, as is said, "The words of the mouth of the wise find favor". If necessary, see suggested course of action. (2) This number also refers to the physical union of a man and wife (a wedding). Dreamer, if you are unmarried, God has appointed a spouse for you, a religious or civil leader (e.g. politician, representative, or an official of some kind), and that person is very near you at present. As they are sensitive to God's leading right now, so should you be sensitive to God's leading. Moreover, seek out the true and practical meaning of unequally yoked, and you will better understand relationships. If you seek truth, truth will come, by this God is showing His loving kindness towards you. Nonetheless, you will soon be given the opportunity to get married, if you so desire and the marriage will bear righteous fruit. Go forth in confidence, that your union will be honored by God.

911: Your dream denotes distress, an "SOS", an emergency call for help. The dreamer needs help emotionally, spiritually, and/or physically, and suddenly. Your inner person is asking for help, even if you will not admit that you need it. Do you sense your need for help, especially from other believers or another in general? Do you sense your need for any kind of help? God uses people to help people. Interdependence means mutual dependence, reciprocal dependency, and mutual reliance. This happens when two or more people rely on one another for their needs. According to the Bible, the church and humankind ar e an interdependent group of people whose need for one another is often greater than we perceive. Read, understand, and embrace Matthew 18:19-20, by this, dreamer is encouraged to humble yourself and ask for help from someone nearby (e.g. your church, a neighbor, friend, close relative, a hospital emergency room). Call someone, because you need help, especially spiritually! See suggested course of action.

937: This dream is a message of grace that you may be clean, for you are surely, called to be one of God's ministers. Although you are gentle and quiet, you lack wisdom and practical understanding. Thus, you are easily deceived or cheated, especially financially. Moreover, your comfort with appearing gentle and quiet, has also kept you spiritually immature. Thus, you are still considered an infant spiritually, not fully acquainted with the teachings about righteousness. You are spiritually, emotionally, and perhaps physically, weak, because you need to submit to, and earnestly embrace, the teachings of the basic truths of God's word. Dreamer, crave pure spiritual milk, the direct words of God imparted to us through the words of others, such as a preacher in a worship service, a Sunday school teacher, and other bible studies. It is through these avenues, the Christian experiences, and God's direct leading, that His deeper mysteries, which are more valuable than any knowledge gotten on one's own, are imparted. Further, respect your present place of worship and the appointed leaders of that place. Do not leave to, aimlessly, wander from place to place, and never allow anyone to deter you from learning God's word via pastors, preachers, and teachers; for faith comes by hearing, see Romans 10:17, and by studiously reading your Bible and other biblical resources. Further, it is not wise to take counsel from within your own head. Always seek counsel from your spiritual leaders and other believers. Deliberate, discuss, and debate with colleagues, experts, and other Christians, for there is wisdom in the counsel of many. See Proverbs 11:14, 15:22, 23. Dreamer, you are encouraged to continue your spiritual journey towards Jesus, and turn not back, for continuing on, Christianity promises a better you, and furthermore, you have too much t o lose looking back. If necessary, see suggested course of action.

999: Dreamer, you are fated for the blessings of God to be within your life, however, there is a darkness that is prevailing within your life now that is preventing these blessings from being manifested; it needs dealing with. Therefore, God is extending His mercy and forgiveness towards you, because He knows why you do what you do, even if you don't. Your soul is buried underneath the pain of violations, contempt, and lustful malice, therefore; be earnest and repent. Your malice may be concealed by deception, but your wickedness will be exposed in the assembly. Thus, your dream was sent, in the spirit of grace (the free and unmerited favor and beneficence of God), to see if you will yet be worked upon, and change your mindset, or else to leave you inexcusable, in your accusations against God, because of your ruin (also see Jeremiah 9:7 -9; Matthew 23:37-39; Revelation 3:15-21). Dreamer, a malicious person disguises him or herself with their lips, but in their heart, they harbor deceit. Though your speech is charming, abominations fill your heart (Proverbs 26:24-28). Your choices are so negative that they have made you desolate emotionally, physically, and spiritually. Unfortunately, as a result, you will experience a physical illness due to an abomination within your life, as your sin is one that leads to early death. Dreamer, repentantly pray Psalm 38:1-22, looking reflectively within, as to why you do what you do, and then seek available resources for help, support, and accountability. Know yourself; and resist those detrimental urges via a serious commitment to a lifestyle of prayer and fast ing; humbly submitting your negative inclinations to Christ and to His principles. Dreamer, the strength and resistance you draw upon to resist those dark urges when you're before people, use that same level of resistance and control when no one is looking or suspects you, and your urges will abate See suggested course of action. If listed, and only if necessary, may consider the interpretation for the numbers 9, 99 as they relate to the repetitiveness of this number (999). Hence, the number 999 is a more intense expression of the numbers 9, 99 in strength and forcefulness, spiritually, prophetically, and in application. First, see Note 6 at the beginning of this category.

In addition, the following is a common word, expression, or usage (e.g. slang or cliché), or a 'probable' that is metaphorically represented by this number:

- A distress signal, an "SOS", an emergency call for help

1000: It is time for the dreamer to, qualitatively enjoy the prosperity you already have, humble yourself, and be content. Do you eat well, thank God and live truthfully before Him, and before your family. Further, if applicable, spend quality time enjoying your family also. Make sure your family is happy that you may rest emotionally, physically, and spiritually, and wh en the time comes that you may have a proper burial. As well, this number denotes completeness, the blessings of the Lord, full stature, one approaching maturity, mature service, and mature judgment. Blessings; in this sense, is a state of high honor, spiritual beauty, and great illumination. If listed, and only if necessary, dreamer may also consider other multiples of this number. First, see Note 6 at the beginning of this category.

1007: This type of dream exposes a need of refinement of character, namely in the area dealing with the deeds of the flesh. For example, dishonesty, adultery, sensuality, hostility, feuding, vendettas, grudges, unfriendliness, strife, jealousy, outbursts of anger, disputes, dissensions, discord, factions, cliques, envying, drunkenness, carousing, idolatry (idolatry is "foreign service", any act that expresses devotion or fanatical admiration to something or someone other than Adonai Elohim), or any traits of these sorts, see 1 Corinthians 6:8-11. This also includes a possible belief in, and/or practice of, necromancy. Elohim knows all. Thus, your dream comes to rebuke and warn an immoral believer that your activities are illegal. You have deliberately chosen to become enslaved to that which is forbidden by the One True and Living God. Your choices are spiritual ly forbidden. Moreover, you compel individuals to follow other gods, and hard-press people to believe what you say. You are one, who is the direct opposite of a born-again, aka a believer, the antithesis of Christ. As a result you will now begin to experience serious mental health issues and will have to be restrained, against your will if needs be. However, if dreamer would genuinely, in deed, refrain from wickedness and no longer do harm, physically, sexually, emotionally, and/or spirituall y, to anyone, and start treating God's people, your family, and others, with respect, by this God will pardon your injustices. Additionally, dreamer, will need to declare a one, two, or three day fast for sanctification purposes; also, wash (bathe) and make yourself, clothing, and personal surroundings clean. If not a day fast, you will need to declare some kind of fast and commit to it, for a period-of-time, to abate this coming influence. Dreamer is counseled to seek God, as to the way you should go. See suggested course of action.

1031: This dream refers to a promise made you by God, and the fulfillment of that promise made to you. The promise was made when you first invited Christ into your life. It will, very shortly happen. With that, this dream has two meanings (one or both may apply). (1) Dreamer, God's wisdom, care, and guidance, coupled with His divine intervention, has kept you, and will, again, cause your mouth to be filled with laughter, and your tongue with singing. When God reverse your tragedy, you w ill testify that the Lord has done great things for you, and you will be glad. Your situation will change and He will give you a new song in your heart. You will sing a new song. (2) As well, your dream points to one who was born to be a teacher and a nurturer. You should be teaching the elementary truths of God's word to your own children and/or to those not familiar with the teachings of righteousness, mainly new converts, and infants in Christ, via the Holy Bible. Your diligent teaching will prepare others to spread the gospel of Jesus Christ; thus, reproducing your teaching ministry and abundantly blessing you. You will receive wages for your diligence, if indeed you are diligent (Luke 10:2-7, 1 Timothy 5:18).

1071: This number refers to absolution and inheritance. Dreamer, there is forgiveness for your sins, and it is imperative that you extend this same forgiveness to others for their wrongs committed against you. For, if you forgive others, your heavenly Father will also forgive you. Moreover, they that are in Christ, and live according to t he Spirit, are free from condemnation. Please note there is a difference between conviction and condemnation. Albeit, you are included in that number, they that are in Christ, in that when you heard the word of truth, the gospel of your salvation, having believed, you were marked in Him with a seal; that seal being the Holy Spirit. Whom, is a deposit guaranteeing your inheritance until the redemption of those who are God's possession (see, Ephesians 1:13, 14). Christ has given you the Holy Spirit, and this makes you a joint heir with Him. The inheritance is the Kingdom of God with all its blessings now, both on this side of eternity, and forever in heaven. God's blessings: Gifts of God's grace, anything God freely gives you, absolution, the Holy Spirit, salvation, regeneration, eternal life, health, children, love of family, longevity, necessities, prosperity, and dominion over all that is yours; and all are parts of the supply of grace, and all are sanctified by the Lord, and technically belongs to Him. The result of this supply in your life will be peace. If listed, and only if necessary, dreamer may also consider other multiples of this number. First, see Note 6 at the beginning of this category.

1090: This number refers to sanctification. Sanctification is needed within the dreamer's life. Dreamer, you are to bear fruit that defines how different you are from those who are of the kingdom of darkness; therefore, a distinction demonstrated, within your life, is expected. Dreamer, there is a difference between the sacred and the profane. Hence, there is a need for you to set aside a day, as sacred, dedicated wholly unto the Lord. Read, understand, and embrace Romans 14:4-6. If you do so, you will know the Lord in His process of sanctification for you. Jehovah-Mekaddishkem, via the Paraclete will cleanse you from corruption, and purify you from sin, resulting in a detachment of your affections from the world and its defilements. T his process will effect sanctification and holiness within you. For this is the will of God, your sanctification. Dreamer, it is not His will that you should perish but that you would come to heartfelt repentance to Jesus and man or woman. Repentance is seeking pardon and expressing sincere feelings of regret and brokenness for having done something awry and/or for having hurt someone. To Jesus pray, Psalm 51. To individuals, a phone call or a letter of apology is a good place to start, if appropriate. This coupled with prayer and fasting, followed by appropriate application of wisdom, and Jesus will meet you, thus saving you from eternal separation from Him and heaven, and preparing you for ministry. Subsequently, you, having been cleansed and purified by the Holy Spirit, will be able to use your gifts exclusively for the Kingdom of God, throwing yourself into your work as God has given you, for you are called to be set apart and sanctified; and not without divine purpose. His purpose is to sanctify you for salvation, and for you to go on to ministering to believers. If listed, and only if necessary, dreamer may also consider other multiples of this number. First, see Note 6 at the beginning of this category.

1098: Your dream denotes one whose spirit is without restraint (Proverbs 25:28). Although you (the dreamer) is intended to be one who has the capacity to exemplify empathy, forgiveness, and understanding; one whom people are drawn to for absolution, as well, one who is important to the well-being of others, and important as a leader, promoting in every way the welfare of others, and is powerfully anointed for this. Instead, you live in excess, mischievousness, arrogance, and unruliness, to the point of recklessness; and not only so, but trample those you consider less than yourself, harmful to thos e about you. Sidebar, regarding your condescendingly arrogant attitude towards others, this is why you are uncontrollably spending money wastefully. Further, this is why no healing has manifested in an area you so desire healed. Dreamer, in order to fulfill your commission, to reach many, you will need to, seriously and earnestly begin reflecting upon your moral weaknesses, especially your lack of self-restraint and arrogance. How you might bring them under subjection to biblical principles, and how you might aspire for a certain level of spiritual purity. You are advised to discipline your body and your sensual desires and to bring them under control. Temperance in all things is your key word. Prepare yourself at this time, via a solemn consecration[35]. Moreover, adopt a determined resolve, to go no further with an attitude of uncertainty about God, His Word, and Christianity. Rather, become intense and convicted when it comes to defending your beliefs. As well, steel your emotions and thoughts against all that will come against your God. God will lead the way. Nevertheless, if you do no not bring under subjection your excess, mischievousness, arrogance, and unruliness, you will become an object of scorn, derision, laughter, a joke to all who encounter you. Moreover, having proved yourself, many times, morally unclean for God's purposes, you will die before your time, in order for your soul to be saved. See suggested course of action. If listed, and only if necessary, dreamer may also consider other multiples of this number. First, see Note 6 at the beginning of this category.

1174: Dreamer will be granted some manner of favor, gratuitously, from a very strong ally, benefactor, defender, or supporter, via an "in-kindness" or grant, or through a pardon or forgiveness of a very large debt (e.g. auto loan, bank loan, college, student loan, or mortgage). With that said, dreamer, give ear, seriously consider, and remember. There will be two "favors", presented, one sacred, one profane. The key to knowing which favor is sacred, and which is profane. The profane favor will ask you to compromise your beliefs, namely to "gray area" some of God's unequivocal positions on certain tenets. Dreamer, never do you ever compromise your beliefs in Jesus Christ, as the Word of God made flesh, nor do you distort the meanings of His Holy Word, for any manner of favor, for this is akin to spiritual prostitution, aka idolatry. Therefore, consider carefully what is being presented to you and the requirements or demands, read the small print. Additionally, there is a need to make a sacrificial offering, financially, to the ministry which, you are connected. Weigh, he, or she who sows sparingly shall reap sparingly; and he or she who sows bountifully shall reap bountifully. Let each man or woman do according as you have purposed in your heart, not grudgingly, or of necessity for God loves a cheerful giver. For, God is able to make all grace a bound unto you; that you, having always all sufficiency in everything, may abound unto every good work (2 Corinthians 9:6-8). If necessary, see suggested course of action. If listed, and only if necessary, dreamer may also consider other multiples of this number. First, see Note 6 at the beginning of this category.

1224: Dreamer is reacting in a "temper tantrum" and rebellious manner, because you disagree with certain spiritual principles. This is not good. Dreamer, you may not like God's ways and means, but you do have to accept and surrender to them all. For, your human understanding of, and reaction to, spiritual realities is oftentimes crudely green. Dreamer, at this crossroad in your life, it is counseled that you do as the apostle Paul, and count all that you know, all that has brought yo u to this point, to be worthless (Philippians 3:8). Your dream has come to let you know that there is still hope and time for you to recognize the wrong in what you're doing, feel the regret about your past actions, and change your ways and habits. Dreamer, God knows your thoughts afar off, so genuinely and earnestly repent. Take words to Jesus, "'I have sinned, and I have done wrong and acted wickedly". Other than prayer and heartfelt repentance to Jesus, no other excuse or weak justification will be heard. Moreover, ask Jesus for wisdom and for the courage to apply it. See suggested course of action. If listed, and only if necessary, dreamer may also consider other multiples of this number. First, see Note 6 at the beginning of this category.

1234: Your dream is sent as a message of grace that you may be clean, for you are surely, called to be one of God's ministers. Dreamer is counseled to respect your present place of worship and the appointed leaders of that place. Do not leave to, aimlessly, wander from place to place, and never allow anyone to deter you from learning God's word via pastors, preachers, and teachers; for faith comes by hearing, see Romans 10:17, and by studiously reading your Bible and other biblical resources. Further, it is not wise to take counsel from within your own head. Always seek counsel from your spiritual leaders and other believers. Deliberate, discuss, and debate with colleagues, experts, and other Christians, for there is wisdom in the counsel of many. See Proverbs 11:14, 15:22, 23. Dreamer, you are encouraged to continue your spiritual journey towards Jesus, and turn not back, for continuing on, Christianity promises a better you, and furthermore, you have too much to lose looking back. Therefore, dreamer, crave pure spiritual milk, the direct words of God imparted to us through the words of others, such as a preacher in a worship service, a Sunday school teacher, and other bible studies. It is through these avenues, the Christian experiences, and God's direct leading, that His deeper mysteries, which are more valuable than any knowledge gotten on one's own, are imparted. If necessary, see suggested course of action. If listed, and only if necessary, dreamer may also consider other multiples of this number. First, see Note 6 at the beginning of this category

1335: This number denotes a time of trouble is approaching. See suggested course of action. If listed, and only if necessary, dreamer may also consider other multiples of this number. First, see Note 6 at the beginning of this category.

1644: This number represents God's divine power, freedom, and spiritual growth. Dreamer, the essential key to your spiritual health, personal growth, and wholeness, is prayer and bible study that is holistic, meaning well rounded, deeply personal, relevant, and applied to the mundane aspects of your life, as well as to the spiritual. This is, loving the Lord your God with all your soul and might. By this, your level of communication and reasoning will become clearer, and more centered, taking you beyond your limitations. Through prayer, bible study, and by God's divine power, you will surpass your previous level of living that kept you in the shadows angry and jealously. A greater status awaits you (also see Joshua 1:8, 9). Dreamer, in order to warrant this great degree of revelation, it has been necessary for you to go through the hardships you have gone through that your knowledge, coupled with experience, will affect wholeness. If listed, and only if necessary, dreamer may also consider other multiples of this number. First, see Note 6 at the beginning of this category.

1742: Dreamer, although you are amongst widespread corruption, dishonesty, adultery, sensuality, hostility, feuding, vendettas, grudges, unfriendliness, strife, jealousy, outbursts of anger, disputes, dissensions, discord, factions, cliques, envying, drunkenness, carousing, idolatry (idolatry is "foreign service", any act that expresses devotion or fanatical admiration to something or someone other than Adonai Elohim). Including necromancy and other acts of these sorts (see 1 Corinthians 6:8- 11). You are called to be a light unto the nations, and to stand up for righteousness. Even, in the midst of discouragement, continue to do what's right, and know that the cause that you represent is right, the highest realm of ministry is reserve for you, and your dream is one confirmation of that. The dreamer has been chosen by God, and approved by man, to be set aside and ordained as a ministerial leader. Dreamer, you have fulfilled all requirements for righteousness and you have a clear conscience. You have been found of good reputation, full of the Spirit, and wise; thus, you will be officially ordained. Yo u are to carry out the official role of that of a bishop, elder, evangelist, pastor, preacher, superintendent, or teacher. Dreamer, the way the ordination will be carried out may not be to your liking; nonetheless, do not attribute (or call) that which is of Go d, unclean (e.g. confusion, erroneous, out of order, unlawful, weak, wicked, or any other attributes of the unregenerate). Do not consider your ordination as unofficial or a small thing, for it is of God, for you are sent to nations. In addition, you hav e access to prophetic insight; enabling you to discern between true and false. Your wisdom will be a transformational force in many people's lives. Dreamer, if you accept your Heavenly Father's Words and store up His commands within you, turning your ear to wisdom and applying your heart to understanding, calling out for insight and crying aloud for discernment. Looking for it as for silver and searching for it as for hidden treasure, then you will know the fear of the Lord and find the knowledge of God you seek. For the Lord gives wisdom and from His mouth comes knowledge and understanding. Then you will understand what is right and just and fair – every good path. When wisdom enters your heart and knowledge becomes sweet to your soul, discretion will protect you, and understanding will guard you. To deliver you from the ways of wickedness, and from people whose words are perverse, who leave the straight paths to walk in darkness gladly, whose paths are crooked and who are devious in their ways (Proverbs 2:1-6, 9-15). This wisdom will also help you discern authorized prophets, teachers, preachers, pastors, from illegal ones, as well as the many other various forms of syncretism.

Angels will protect you along the way, and the Holy Spirit will lead and guide into all truth. This is one of God's covenant promises to you. Additional, if relevant, a son will be born from you. God will strengthen. If listed, and only if necessary, dreamer may also consider other multiples of this number. First, see Note 6 at the beginning of this category.

1981: This number signifies a start of life in the Spirit, and an end of life in the flesh. You have truly sacrificed your flesh that your soul might be saved. This number also refers to a divinely appointed period of probation and a season of waiting. This probationary period decreed is a testing by waiting (Acts 7:23-30), and should be earnestly regarded. A probable answer, as to why the probationary period of waiting is that you may progress from one state or stage to another, solidifying your spiritual foundation. Nonetheless, this probationary season point to grace, leads to repentance, and ends in revival and renewal. During this season, you are counseled to begin implementing godly principles that will move you toward discipline and humility, while embracing faith and love of God. Regularly, thank God for His patience, long-suffering, and grace (the free and unmerited favor and beneficence of God), while you get things decent and in order. See suggested course of action.

2000: Dreamer, as "free-will" is, you can delay your spiritual resurrection. If you deliberately choose to embrace a belief that is not according to the teachings of Christ, His apostles, and mainstream Christianity, you will remain spiritually imma ture and dead having choose oppression rather than freedom, forfeiting purpose for foolishness. Notwithstanding, spiritual wholeness can be yours right now, ending in a resurrection of the soul, if you choose by faith, to embrace the teachings of Jesus Christ. Dreamer is strongly urged to return to ideals that are holy, wise, well judged; ways that are in keeping with the nature of the Bible, ways pertaining to, contained within, and are in accordance with the Bible; ways that are scriptural. See suggested course of action. If listed, and only if necessary, dreamer may also consider other multiples of this number. First, see Note 6 at the beginning of this category.

2016: This number denotes a time of trouble is approaching. Dreamer, you are one who flaunts antichrist type persona. You, intentionally going against your better judgment, do not accept Jesus as the Messiah nor as your personal Savior, and you refute all critical evidence that legitimize biblical history. Dreamer, you are heavily influenced demonically. You have li ved in luxury and self-indulgence, using the money of those who do not dispute your words. Your money will testify against you. You will weep and wail because of the misery that is coming upon you. Graciously, dreamer, the more God allows you to see your emptiness, the more earnest you should be to repent, via prayer and fasting, that you may find in Him grace and healing, refreshment, and a refuge. See suggested course of action. If listed, and only if necessary, dreamer may also consider other multiples of this number. First, see Note 6 at the beginning of this category.

2018: Dreamer, although you are amongst widespread corruption, dishonesty, adultery, sensuality, hostility, feuding, vendettas, grudges, unfriendliness, strife, jealousy, outbursts of anger, disputes, dissensions, discord, factions, cliques, envying, drunkenness, carousing, idolatry (idolatry is "foreign service". Any act that expresses devotion or fanatical admiration to something or someone other than Adonai Elohim), necromancy, and other acts of these sorts (see 1 Corinthians 6:8-11), you are called to be a light unto the nations, and to stand up for righteousness. Even, in the midst of discouragement, continue to do what's right, and know that the cause that you represent is right, the highest realm of ministry is reserve for you, and your dream is one confirmation of that. The dreamer has been chosen by God, and approved by man, to be set aside and ordained as a ministerial leader. Dreamer, you have fulfilled all requirements for righteousness and you have a clear conscience. You have been found of good reputation, full of the Spirit, and wise; thus, you will be officially ordained. You are to carry ou t the official role of that of a bishop, elder, evangelist, pastor, preacher, superintendent, or teacher. Dreamer, the way the ordination will be carried out may not be to your liking; nonetheless, do not attribute (or call) that which is of God, unclean (e.g. confusion, erroneous, out of order, unlawful, weak, wicked, or any other attributes of the unregenerate). Do not consider your ordination as unofficial or a small thing, for it is of God, for you are sent to nations. In addition, you have access to prophetic insight;

enabling you to discern between true and false. Your wisdom will be a transformational force in many people's lives. Dreamer, if you accept your Heavenly Father's Words and store up His commands within you, turning your ear to wisdom and applying your heart to understanding, calling out for insight and crying aloud for discernment. Looking for it as for silver and searching for it as for hidden treasure, then you will know the fear of the Lord and find the knowledge of God you seek. For the Lord gives wisdom and from His mouth comes knowledge and understanding. Then you will understand what is right and just and fair – every good path. When wisdom enters your heart and knowledge becomes sweet to your soul, discretion will protect you, and understanding will guard you. To deliver you from the ways of wickedness, and from peopl e whose words are perverse, who leave the straight paths to walk in darkness gladly, whose paths are crooked and who are devious in their ways (Proverbs 2:1-6, 9-15). This wisdom will also help you discern authorized prophets, teachers, preachers, pastors, from illegal ones, as well as the many other various forms of syncretism. Angels will protect you along the way, and the Holy Spirit will lead and guide into all truth. This is one of God's covenant promises to you. Additional, if relevant, a son will be born from you. God will strengthen. If listed, and only if necessary, dreamer may also consider other multiples of this number. First, see Note 6 at the beginning of this category.

2398: Your dream comes as a stern rebuke. Your dream denotes one whose spirit is without restraint (Proverbs 25:28). Although you (the dreamer) is intended to be one who has the capacity to exemplify empathy, forgiveness, and understanding; one whom people are drawn to for absolution, as well, one who is important to the well-being of others, and important as a leader, promoting in every way the welfare of others, and is powerfully anointed for this. Instead, you live in excess, mischievousness, arrogance, and unruliness, to the point of recklessness; and not only so, but trample those you consider less than yourself, harmful to those about you. Sidebar, regarding your condescendingly arrogant attitude towards others, this is why you are uncontrollably spending money wastefully. Further, this is why no healing has manifested in an area you so desire healed. Dreamer, in order to fulfill your commission, to reach many, you will need to, seriously and earnestly begin reflecting upon your moral weaknesses, especially your lack of self-restraint and arrogance. How you might bring them under subjection to biblical principles, and how you might aspire for a certain level of spiritual purity. You are advised to discipline your body and your sensual desires and to bring them under control. Temperance in all things is your key word. Prepare yourself at this time, via a solemn consecration[35]. Moreover, adopt a determined resolve, to go no further with an attitude of uncertainty about God, His Word, and Christianity. Rather, become intense and convicted when it comes to defending your beliefs. As well, steel your emotions and thoughts against all that will come against your God. God will lead the way. Nevertheless, if you do no not bring under subjection your excess, mischievousness, arrogance, and unruliness, you will become an object of scorn, derision, laughter, a joke to all who encounter you. Moreover, having proved yourself, many times, morally unclean for God's purposes, you will die before your time, in order for your soul to be saved. See suggested course of action. If listed, and only if necessary, dreamer may also consider other multiples of this number. First, see Note 6 at the beginning of this category.

3213: Dreamer, be aware that there is one or some amongst you; that accuses you of hypocrisy and wrongdoings. Their accusations, has caused, or will cause, an extremely severe emotional situation, that will lead to a physical illness, within your life. Favorably, angels are encamped about you. Your Heavenly Father has sent angels to rescue you out of an extremely severe situation, because of your faith. Be aware that the strangers within your midst may be those angels. They have come to lead the way. Moreover, dreamer is counseled to live your life in such a way that the accusations of some will prove to be untruths. If you are living correct, you will be justified with benefits. Because of your deliverance and freedom from hard things, your oppressor will respect your God and acknowledge His Power within your life (also, see Isaiah 40:29-31). If listed, and only if necessary, dreamer may also consider other multiples of this number. First, see Note 6 at the beginning of this category.

4000: Dreamer, choose this day who you will serve, Christ or antichrist. You cannot serve both, for you will love one and hate the other. These two opposing forces will never integrate. Dreamer, your dream has come to set life and death soberly before you, and if you will not choose beliefs, tenets, principles, behaviors, actions, thoughts, and choices that promot e life, you will spiritually implode. To the dreamer it is said, for you to remember your Creator, before your days of trouble come and time has caught up with you (Ecclesiastes 12:1-7). Further, no dead philosophy, or any other lifeless "ism" will come to life to tell you truth, nor will a dead person come to life to tell you of what he or she has seen. For, if the "ism" did contain a spark of life, or if the dead did come back to tell you of what he or she is experiencing, you would not believe the tea ching, nor would you believe the dead. For, relationship with Christ, appeals to people not by half-truths or lies, or ghosts or frightful apparitions; it appeals to your reason, your conscience, and your hopes. God's Holy Spirit leads to genuine truth. Dreamer, if you will not hear the Son of God and the warnings of the Scriptures, there is nothing, which you will, or can, hear; you will never be persuaded, and one can never escape the place of torment. See suggested course of action. If listed, and only if necessary, dreamer may also consider other multiples of this number. First, see Note 6 at the beginning of this category.

5000: Dreamer, be encouraged, you are anointed, and will be ordained and set apart for a high purpose, namely consecrated to do the work of a priest, e.g. one who has the authority to perform or administer various religious rites. Prepare yourself at this time, via a solemn consecration[35]. By spiritually preparing, and thus able to do what you are called to do, according to the Messiah's leading and guiding, via the Paraclete, you will be happy, prosper, and be in safety. Nonetheless, your dream announces that the dreamer will be clothed formally in ecclesiastical garments, ordained as a clergy. You will be rendering conclusive decisions on dubious matters. Moreover, as you are genuine, tactful, and adaptable, your sensitivity and gentleness will be a great healing force, bringing harmony and support to many. The dreamer will begin to see the omnipotent Hand of God within your life's circumstances. Therefore, from this moment forward, if not already, become seriously vested in your set place of worship, submissive to the head leadership (e.g. pastor, bishop, elder). One thing is for sure; you are hi ghly favored and blessed of God. If listed, and only if necessary, dreamer may also consider other multiples of this number. First, see Note 6 at the beginning of this category.

5754: Dreamer, you will receive a prophetic confirmation regarding a divine inspired endeavor you will undertake, and it will be unique. You are advised to take hold, now, of any and everything that provides inspiration and foundation for your unique endeavor (e.g. go to school, read articles, or topics relevant to your ideas, do an apprenticeship, and research thoroughly your ideas). Express yourself clearly, thoroughly, and boldly, in you thought, speech, and actions. Write your vision down, that you may articulate it to others properly, for the vision will happen, suddenly and quickly. Prepare a good proposal, name your product, and write down all the details and specifics. Give it your best that it may be acceptable to any reputable financial entity, benefactor, or merit a grant of some kind. Perhaps, hire a grant writer. That which you will need to fulfill your aims, surely, you will have. Dreamer, you will receive help, namely "seed money", for your business venture. This help will come in the early stages of your endeavor's development. If you choose not to seize the opportunity, at this time, to educate yourself fully regarding your endeavor, you will remain drunk-and-disorderly spiritually, forfeiting purpose for foolishness. See suggested course of action. If listed, and only if necessary, dreamer may also consider other multiples of this number. First, see Note 6 at the beginning of this category.

5758: Dreamer, by earnestly and genuinely embracing ethical, honorable, and moral principles, God is extending grace to you, giving you enough time and the emotional ability, to end, renounce, and terminate your horrible treatment of the indigent, and your personal perverseness, namely your deliberate deviating from what is good, and your stubborn unruliness and resistance to guidance or discipline. Dreamer, use God's extended grace, via prayer and fasting, to rectify and correct your sins and your wickedness, by doing what is right, and by being kind to the oppressed, as well as, compensating those you have cheated and wronged, that your prosperity may continue. See suggested course of action. If listed, and only if necessary, dreamer may also consider other multiples of this number. First, see Note 6 at the beginning of this category.

5770: This number denotes spiritual rains in their proper time, providing harvest and blessings (physical and spiritual), given the dreamer, by God, in loving-kindness. Dreamer, this season in your life, will be one of blessings, favor, and goodness. With that, dreamer, remain pleasant and peaceful, and in due time you will reap and be blessed. To be blessed: Gifts of God's grace, anything God freely gives you, absolution, the Holy Spirit, salvation, regeneration, eternal life, health, children, love of family, longevity, necessities, prosperity, and dominion over all that is yours; and all are parts of the supply of grace, and all are sanctified by the Lord, and technically belongs to Him. The result of this supply in your life will be peace. If listed, and only if necessary, dreamer may also consider other multiples of this number. First, see Note 6 at the beginning of this category.

5778: Dreamer, although you are amongst widespread corruption, dishonesty, adultery, sensuality, hostility, feuding, vendettas, grudges, unfriendliness, strife, jealousy, outbursts of anger, disputes, dissensions, discord, factions, cliques, envying, drunkenness, carousing, idolatry (idolatry is "foreign service", any act that expresses devotion or fanatical admiration to something or someone other than Adonai Elohim). This also includes necromancy, and other acts of these sorts (see 1 Corinthians 6:8-11). You are called to be a light unto the nations, and to stand up for righteousness. Even, in the midst of discouragement, continue to do what's right, and know that the cause that you represent is right, the highest re alm of ministry is reserve for you, and your dream is one confirmation of that. The dreamer has been chosen by God, and approved by man, to be set aside and ordained as a ministerial leader. Dreamer, you have fulfilled all requirements for righteousness and you have a clear conscience. You have been found of good reputation, full of the Spirit, and wise; thus, you will be officially ordained. You are to carry out the official role of that of a bishop, elder, evangelist, pastor, preacher, superintendent, or teacher. Dreamer, the way the ordination will be carried out may not be to your liking; nonetheless, do not attribute (or ca ll) that which is of God, unclean (e.g. confusion, erroneous, out of order, unlawful, weak, wicked, or any other attributes of the unregenerate). Do not consider your ordination as unofficial or a small thing, for it is of God, for you are sent to nations. In addition, you have access to prophetic insight; enabling you to discern between true and false. Your wisdom will be a transformational force in many people's lives. Dreamer, if you accept your Heavenly Father's Words and store up His commands within you, turning your ear to wisdom and applying your heart to understanding, calling out for insight and crying aloud for discernment. Looking for it as for silver and searching for it as for hidden treasure, then you will know the fear of the Lord and find the knowledge of God you seek. For the Lord gives wisdom and from His mouth comes knowledge and understanding. Then you will understand what is right and just and fair – every good path. When wisdom enters your heart and knowledge becomes sweet to your soul, discretion will protect you, and understanding will guard you. To deliver you from the ways of wickedness, and from people whose words are perverse, who leave the straight paths to walk in darkness gladly, whose paths are crooked and who are devious in their ways (Proverbs 2:1-6, 9-15). This wisdom will also help you discern authorized prophets, teachers, preachers, pastors, from illegal ones, as well as the many other various forms of syncretism. Angels will protect you along the way, and the Holy Spirit will lead and guide into all truth. This is one of God's covenant promises to you. Additional, if relevant, a son will be born from you. God will strengthen. If listed, and only if necessary, dreamer may also consider other multiples of this number. First, see Note 6 at the beginning of this category.

6000: In addition to one of the following, and only if necessary, dreamer may also consider other multiples of this number. First, see Note 6 at the beginning of this category. This number denotes deception perpetrated by one who is secretly against Christ. To determine whom the dream is referring to, either the dreamer or another, what context was the number used? Was the dreamer number 6000, or was someone else? Did the dreamer give or receive 6000 of anything or did another? With that, this dream has two meanings (choose one). (1) If dreamer was the giver of, or specifically connected to, the number, in any way, your dream refers to the dreamer. If dream is for the dreamer, you are one who flaunts antichrist type persona. You, intentionally going against your better judgment, do not accept Jesus as the Messiah nor as your personal Savior, and you refute all critical evidence that legitimize biblical history. Dreamer, you are heavily influenced demonically, with a primary purpose, to lead astray others into a dark and oppressive level of spirituality. Dreamer, the cries of an innocent person against you, has reached the ears of the Lord Almighty. You are an oppressor of God's people. You have lived in luxury and self-indulgence, using the money of those who do not dispute your words. Your money will testify against you. You will weep and wail because of the misery that is coming upon you. Graciously, dreamer, the more God allows you to see your emptiness, the more earnest you should be to repent that you may find in Him grace and healing, refreshment, a nd a refuge. If you have been fortunate enough, to have been favored with the truth of God; and have seen His hand in your life, and have tasted of His benefits that He has caused to pass before you, why would you walk away or deviate from that. In doing so, you forfeit wisdom for folly. See suggested course of action. (2) If dreamer was the receiver of, or another was specifically connected to the number, in some way, your dream refers to another, and their negative influential effects upon the dreamer. If, another, someone is deceiving the dreamer. Dreamer, you should break-off the relationship, on all levels, with that someone, for they are against Christ and His Kingdom (aka antichrist). This person is against the Lord Jesus Christ, a sinner by choice, and you are deceived, being led to think otherwise. The fruit of their behavior is akin to false teachers or deceivers who, by pretending they care about the underprivileged, lead men away from the truth. Their ideas have opened a dark gate that will lead you, and others, to demonic oppression, or demon possession, and possible suicide. Renounce the relationship, and change your mind about that person that you may have life. Repent, and God will deliver you from devastation and your feet from stumbling, that you may walk before God in the light of life (Psalm 56:13). See suggested course of action.**7000:** Dreamer, you have kept the charge given you by God, regarding the administration of His church. When most went astray from God, some having become corrupt, stealing the offerings and committing adultery and fornication with each other. Consequently, in this great and final order of God, the highest realm of ministry is reserved for you. Dreamer, you will enter God's sanctuary and shall come near to God's table to minister to His people, covered with His anointing, and have great peace, and you will prosper, in this season of your life. You will be far from oppression, and this will be sweetness to you r soul. This is your inheritance in Christ, and this promise to you is final. As this promise is final to you, so is God's promise of divine reprimand for folly and sin to those who went astray. However, a few will still yet minister in the "outer court", as they do have a genuine belief in Jesus Christ. Dreamer, you will see God's judgment upon, and the guaranteed justice of, those who went astray, and an outcome they're not expecting. Since you will see justice handed down, do not say, "God is not fair by allowing this or that to happen". Your expressed disapproval of justice handed down by God will not be tolerated. If listed, and only if necessary, dreamer may also consider other multiples of this number. First, see Note 6 at the beginning of this category.

8515: Dreamer, you are going to experience a difficult situation, causing intense sadness and distress, heartrending. Unfortunately, your refusal to embrace healthy and self-affirming choices, and a victim mentality, all are leading you towards this difficult situation, yet you are a survivor. Favorably, this situation is allowed to provoke an extreme transformation within you, driving you to a higher level of purpose, and affecting a healthy and balanced self-esteem. Subsequently, it will be with this energy that you will become a great healing force, bringing tremendous harmony and support to others, dedicating your life to bettering other victims, and giving of your own time and resources to help the unfortunate cope. Yours will be a great walk of faith. Dreamer, while we know that there is a natural cause and effect in the world, for example, moral delinquency affects, not only the guilty, but the innocent as well. Where would the innocent be, without compassion, and inspiring others, like you, to care for people who can never repay you? Yours is the path of trailblazers, enacting new laws, defending the needy, leaving hope and inspiration in your trail, giving second chances, and free-flowing forgiveness, demonstrating compassion, even after one has sinned. You will rebuild desolate lives. Adonai will be your Lord, and He will bless you double for your trouble. The banner over your ministry should be, "You're not heavy; you are my brother, you are my sister". If necessary, see suggested course of action. If listed, and only if necessary, dreamer may also consider other multiples of this number. First, see Note 6 at the beginning of this category.

8819: You will be sent to those whose ideas, arguments, and/or beliefs are base. Their arguments, ideas, and beliefs are illogical, non-mainstream, and without favorable conclusions. Your responsibility is to usher God's Presence in and magnify the Lord. This you do, when you proclaim His goodness and His truth. You are a vessel of God's glory, and a possessor of the truth needed for the place and situation at hand, the greater the truth, the greater your authority, the greater your success. Moreover, know that there are angels about you to protect and uphold you in case that's needed, therefore, do not be afraid of people faces, their positions, titles, wealth, nor of the place or circumstances. You are equipped to handle your, and God's, business. Have faith in this.

10,000: Dreamer, you have been found diligent and sincere in your thoughts and expectations, regarding the cause of Christ. Therefore, expect a greater revelation of divine grace (the free and unmerited favor and beneficence of God). Moreover, if your difficulties increase know that God's encouragements will increase in proportion. Remain courageous and unbendable. He will send angels, soldiers of the armies of the Lord, to rescue you out of extremely severe situations, because of your faith. Be aware that the strangers within your midst may be those angels. If listed, and only if necessary, may consider the interpretation for the numbers 10, 100, as they relate to this number squared; see Note 6 at the beginning of this category.

12,000: In addition to one of the following, and only if necessary, dreamer may also consider other multiples of this number. First, see Note 6 at the beginning of this category. With that, this dream has three meanings (choose one). (1) This number refers to the Lord's mighty army. Dreamer, although enemies surround you, do not be afraid or deceived, for those who are for you, are far more than those who are against you. Look through your spiritual eyes by faith, namely, consider clearly, and you will see those who are with you (2 Kings 6:17, 18). Moreover, you will not have to fight any battle that is before you at present. Stand still and see the deliverance the Lord will effect on your behalf. Do not be afraid; do not be discouraged, the Lord is with you (2 Chronicles 20:17). (2) Unmarried dreamer: If so desired, your dream denotes that there will be a literal wedding, and it is honored by the Lord. Dreamer, your marriage will prove to be a time of "jubilee" for you. Therefore, go and prepare for your wedding in peace. (3) Married dreamer, do rekindle things within your marriage, with emphasis on marriage and fidelity. Dreamer, be confident and trusting, you and your spouse, will fulfill your God given responsibility within your marriage, and both of you will fulfill your covenant relationship with Jesus. If relevant, dreamer, God has granted mercy to you and has deemed your marriage worthy to merit children. If desired, you will very soon give birth to your own children. Celebrate for God's blessings are upon you.

144,000: This number refers to a righteous person, namely the dreamer, who is leading a holy and humble life. Dreamer, you are free, saved, and declared righteous by grace (the free and unmerited favor and beneficence of God). Jesus loves you just the way you are. Therefore, from this time forward, so speak and act as those who are going to be judged by the law of liberty, see James 2:12, 13, and even more, thank God for you and for who you are becoming. Dreamer, you will be used, if not already, to usher others, particularly those who are presently at odds with you and other Christians, int o a totally new and higher level of spiritual awareness and selflessness, leading to a relationship with Jesus Christ. Dreamer, even amongst the "broken", a spark of life remains hidden, awaiting your particular ministry, your unique way of presenting the gospel. You will appear when needed, and then disappear without thought of anything in return. By fulfilling your mission and remaining humble, you will be worthy of your wage. Moreover, it is promised that you will eat and do very well, on this side o f eternity, and inherit eternal life. Note humility is the key to your success (requisite). Know the full meaning of the word and defin e your life by it. If listed, and only if necessary, dreamer may also consider other multiples of this number. First, see Note 6 at the beginning of this category.

Suggested Course of Action

Question to consider and journal, did your dream depict any symbols that alludes to, the dreamer will make the necessary changes, spiritually, emotionally, and/or physically to affect a more positive outcome? If changes are initiated, your dreams will change.

Consider and journal the following questions. The questions will help you determine; the issue at hand, how you feel about it, and what may have instigated it. What context did your number(s) appear within your dream? Was there addition, multiplication, or subtraction activity? Were others involved? If yes, who and in what manner were they involved? Keep in mind that the others represent a character trait, quality, or talent within you. Did anyone get hurt emotionally, physically, or was disturbed in any way? How did you feel, and what was your reaction to the number activity? Was it agitating, confusing, dangerous, disturbing, frustrating, peace with the situation, happy, joyful, life threatening, safe, scary, or unsure? What was your reaction to the number activity? Your reaction to the activity, or the circumstances, reveals your attitude regarding t his information about yourself. Where did the activity occur, the place and background setting? For more information, see index or relevant category and subcategory for other particulars within your dream.

In view of your dream's context, and the primary symbols, what does your dream reveal about you, your ethics, intents, mental state, and motives? You will need to earnestly look within and consider that the sum of your answers is a reflection of where you are emotionally, physically, and/or spiritually, and a reflection of who you are becoming. Dreamer, consider seriously your observations. If what was revealed prevail, will it sabotage any good that's happening at present within your life? Will it build or destroy, strengthen or weaken, enlighten or blind? If you lack wisdom, ask Je sus for wisdom. He gives wisdom to all, generously, no matter who you are and what you've done; wisdom is available (see James 1:5-8, Proverbs 2:1-6, 10). Hence, if, by just asking, you may get wisdom, one may suffer needlessly, because you will not ask Jesus for wisdom.

With everything stated, dreamer, if you are here, prayer and heartfelt repentance to Jesus and man or woman is needed. A seeking pardon and expressing sincere feelings of regret and brokenness for having done something awry and/or for having hurt someone; see 2 Corinthians 7:10, 11. Dreamer must make a complete turn-round; a change has to come, lest you find yourself in ruin. Ask, and God will grant you the power to make a change.

Now, pray (See Prayer of Deliverance, pg. 897)

Specific Meaning

If, you have a very real connection with numbers, e.g. accountant, actuary, banking, computer codes, economist, fiscal operations, lottery, mathematician, statistician, tax preparer, stock market, teacher, or any other activity dealing with numbers. These dreams are usually about the anxieties that overwhelm your mind during the day. They are an inner release mechanism, which helps provide you with emotional balance and the maintaining of your sanity. These sorts of dreams, are not significant, and do not warrant special attention.

Note: If an audit, hacking, illegal activity, insider trading, IRS, FBI, stock market crash, or any other negative activity that is not good, was highlighted within your dream. This is a literal warning signal that something is wrong, and serious repercussions can result, in the physical realm, perhaps there may be potential for incarceration. Dreamer, the details, kept within context of your dream, should be relevant to your life, and closely resemble your real-life situations. Meaning it can actually occur during your awaked state. This will help you narrow down the specifics needed to support and steer you clear of possible mishaps. However, if your dream was inundated with symbols that are not easily linked to your life activitie s, then the spiritual implications (the interpretation) should be heeded.

Odors, Scents, Perfumery, Fragrances, Incense, and Aromas
(any property detected by the olfactory system)

And Jehovah smelled the sweet savor; and Jehovah said in his heart, I will not again curse the ground any more for man's sake, for that the imagination of man's heart is evil from his youth; neither will I again smite any more everything living, as I have done. (Genesis 8:21 ASV)

So he came near and kissed him. And Isaac smelled the smell of his garments and blessed him and said, "See, the smell of my son is as the smell of a field that the LORD has blessed! (Genesis 27:27 ESV)

…better than the fragrance of cologne. (Cologne should be named after you.) No wonder the young women love you! (Song of Solomon 1:3 GW)

Dead flies cause the ointment of the apothecary to stink (Ecclesiastes 10:1 Darby)

Then the king Nebuchadnezzar fell upon his face, and worshipped Daniel, and commanded that they should offer an oblation and sweet odors unto him (Daniel 2:46 ASV)

But thanks be to God, who in Christ always leads us in triumphal procession and through us spreads the fragrance of the knowledge of him everywhere. For we are the aroma of Christ to God among those who are being saved and among those who are perishing, to one a fragrance from death to death, to the other a fragrance from life to life. (2 Corinthians 2:14-16 ESV)

And when he had taken the book, the four beasts and four and twenty elders fell down before the Lamb, having every one of them harps, and golden vials full of odours, which are the prayers of saints. Revelation 5:8 (KJV)

And another angel came and stood over the altar, having a golden censer; and there was given unto him much incense, that he should add it unto the prayers of all the saints upon the golden altar, which was before the throne. And the smoke of the incense, with the prayers of the saints, went up before God out of the angel's hand. And the angel taketh the censer; and he filled it with the fire of the altar, and cast it upon the earth: and there followed thunders, and voices, and lightings, and an earthquake. And the seven angels that had the seven trumpets prepared themselves to sound. (Revelation 8:3-6 ASV)

This category deals with aroma, fragrance, smells, olfaction, and the faculty that enables us to distinguish scents. Some short descriptions of types, phrases, and other processes and particulars, connected in some way to this category are, for example, aroma, bad stench, foul smell, fragrance, good smell, incense, perfumes, sweet smells. Also, see category content list, or index.

All Symbols and Referents, Notes (1, 2, 3, etc.), Suggested Course of Action, and Specific Meaning offer guidance toward a more comprehensive interpretation.

Notes

1. Unless otherwise noted elsewhere, if, in your everyday living, your awaked state, as part of your lifestyle, work, or ministerial activities, or a special event. You have a very real connection with any aroma, fragrance, incense, perfumery, scents, a container for burning incense, especially one that is swung on a chain in a religious ritual, or any activity that includes smells.

811

For example, maker or user of censers, chef, coroner embalmer, medical examiner, mortician, perfumer, scent shop, your dream is not significant and does not warrant special attention.

Otherwise noted, this dream of odors may be a Prophetically Simple Dream (see Chapter One: The 60th Part of Prophecy). Whereas, the dreamer is encouraged, for example, if an aroma, fragrance, or perfume was introduced to you within your dream, to adopt the unique aroma, fragrance, or perfume as your own signature brand (e.g. a perfume brand name), especially if you are part of the science, technology, expertise, or specialist in the areas of scents. Did you formulate something, for example, mixing certain substances to produce a new fragrant or perfume. Dreamer, consider it not strange for someone, who is involved in some manner of activity or the science of aromas, odors, scents, or one who creates and/ or sells perfumes, to receive inspirations regarding scents via their dreams that might prove beneficial to the dreamer and to mankind. The details, kept within context of your dream, should be relevant to your life, and closely resemble your real-life situations. Meaning it can actually occur during your awaked state. It is suggested that you seize the opportunity your dream is presenting to fulfill the purpose for which it was sent. Also, see Specific Meaning: at the end of this category, section entitled, Note (Specific Meaning).

Otherwise noted, this dream of odors may be a Prophetically Simple Dream (see Chapter One: The 60th Part of Prophecy). For example, if dreamer actually knows what an actual "Odor of Death" smells like, and you work in an arena where you are exposed to such an odor, or if an accident, e.g. an explosion, perhaps caused by a chemical reaction, was highlighted within your dream, this is a precautionary warning. See Specific Meaning at the end of this category, section entitled, Note (Specific Meaning).

Otherwise noted, this dream of odors may be a Real-Time Dream (see Chapter One, Chalom, Ordinary Dreams). Whereas, your dream "picked up" on activity, connected with some kind of odor that is going on within your space, while you were asleep, in real time, the actual time it was happening, disquieting your olfactory modality. The events in this type of dream are actually happening in real time, and are for the most part, influenced by substantive stimuli. If, after thoroughly checking your space, to make sure your environment is safe, e.g. making sure no fire is smoldering, or making sure that no poisonousness or odorousness fumes are spreading, basically if no alarm is determined, then this dream is not significant, and does not warrant special attention. It was just a strong odor at the time, e.g. body odor; then perhaps a bath is warranted.

Otherwise noted, per your lifestyle, if your dream closely resembled real life situations, meaning it can actually occur during your awaked state, this dream may be an Ordinary Dream, resulting from your daily activities (see Chapter One, Chalom). These sorts of dreams are usually about your routine, mundane activities or anxieties that overwhelm your mind during the day. They are an inner release mechanism, which helps provide you with emotional balance and the maintaining of your sanity. These dreams are not significant, and do not warrant special attention.

2. Probables: As odors are frequently demonstrated in many, and very personal ways; for example, in religious rituals, where incense, a substance that produces a fragrant odor is burned, Leviticus 10:1, 16:12; Numbers 16:17, 18, 46; 2 Chronicles 26:19, or the smell of a certain dish to a chef. Does a certain aroma remind you of your favorite dish? Does a particular fragrance remind you of your favorite perfume? Thus, could the odor depicted be a possible probable (see Chapter One, section entitled, Probables)? Hence, dreamer may also consider your own personal and special associations with various odors, and/or the actions or activities connected to certain odors. As long as, the interpretation is kept within the principles of spiritual boundary markers, landmarks, and property lines, (see Chapter One, section entitled, Spiritualizing Boundary Markers, Landmarks, and Property Lines).

3. Determine who your dream is for you or another. If odor originated from dreamer, no matter how, or if it was said that the dream was for the dreamer, then, dreamer should presume your dream is for you. Subsequent, see following relevant subcategory, the interpretation is about and for you.

    Did the odor actually originate from another, no matter how? Does dreamer know someone whose life activities or physical being is similar to that which stood out the most within your dream? Could it be that person? Was it said, within your dream that the dream was for another? If you sense that your dream is for or about another, the question as to why you have been made privy to this information, and how do you factor into the equation, should be seriously considered along with necessary actions. Perhaps the dreamer is being made aware of the plight of someone, and you are to get involved (see Chapter One, Are You Ready to Hear the Messages in Your Dreams, section entitled, The 10% for others).

    If your dream is for, or about another:

    Dreams that reference others and the revelation within those dreams, is not given haphazardly to any individual, but only to those with the ability, and influence to do something with the information; this is also prophecy. If person(s) is unknown, the person(s) will be introduced to dreamer shortly. If person(s) are known, in your awaked life, unless otherwise noted, the person(s) represents him or herself. With that, depending upon the type of smell that originated from the person, good or bad, dreamer needs to discern between the sacred and the profane, between truth and error, or between good and bad, and/or how did the odor issue from another? The dreamer is counseled to make a sagacious decision as to whether or not to allow this type of person(s) to become connected to you, and your life. The lesson is, no matter how personable, powerful, or difficult a person, or how uncertain or unpopular the choices and issues, always take the next biblical and ethical step, for obedience to God's Word and to His principles will always prove safer and stronger foundationally.

    Note: If your dream has attributes that indicate that your dream is about you, and other attributes that indicate that your dream is about another, dreamer should consider that your dream is about you and another. For example, did another spray perfume on dreamer? Did dreamer attempt to cover the odor of another? Did dreamer smell exactly like another? Did someone embalm another? An answer of yes to one of these, or similar, questions, indicates that your dream is about the dreamer and another. Therefore, while your dream is about the dreamer, the dreamer should expect the role and/or influential effects of another, also plays a part in your interpretation.

    More questions to consider. Why has the person been allowed within your life, and/or how did they get there? Again, if unable to answer the questions now, this denotes that the person, represented within your dream, will enter your life shortly. If their activity, within your dream, has proven positive, via the interpretation, this someone will prov e, unwittingly, to be a very strong ally, benefactor, defender, and supporter. God has sent this someone into your life to help you carry out your next endeavor by enlarging your spiritual capacity. Allow the strength of that person's character to guide, help, and support you. On the other hand, if his or her presence and/or activity, within your dream, proven negative, via the interpretation, for sure, this person will prove to be a very strong and formidable challenge for you, perhaps unto death. If negative, this dream is a dire warning. Take steps accordingly to struggle against, or to cut off, adverse and unfavorable relationships. Remember certain personalities are all encompassing, affecting everything, cataclysmic, contagious, deadly, harmful, infectious, predatory, and/or venomous. Symbolically meaning that if allowe d to continue or prosper within your life, serious harm or death to the dreamer may result. Idolize no one, especially beyond the warning of the Lord, and we are definitely not to lay our lives down for no one. Although, you will need all kinds of outside support to recover from this person's domination, again, no longer, allow that particular person's influence within your life to continue or thrive, especially if negative, end it abruptly. Then again, this person maybe allowed within your life, because of the dreamer's unwillingness to abstain from immorality after having been asked to abstain from such by God, see 1 Corinthians 6:9-20, Galatians 5:19-21, or the dreamer's self-righteous behavior, or a lack of a balanced and honest view of your own personality. In this case, this person will affect self-awareness within the life of the dreamer, exposing the negative traits of your personality, especially those traits, which cause you to follow, or to be so easily misled, and/or your wrong beliefs; no matter, this type of mentality needs reckoning with. Graciously, all of this will restore the dreamer to his or her right place with God, opening your eyes to see how far you've strayed from God (1 Corinthians 5:4-7; James 5:20).

4. Consider all the people, places, backgrounds, and activity highlighted within your dream.

Known (in your awaked life) person, animal, place, or organization within your dream:

Unless otherwise noted elsewhere, people, animals, places, backgrounds that are actually known by the dreamer in your awaked life, indicates a part of you that you recognize within yourself on some level or another. Question to journal, if dreamer seriously considers all the particulars, what stood out the most, what features, or character traits stood out the most. For example, color, size, happiness, loving, peacefulness, encouraging, irrational, leader, liar, passionate, neglected, poor, run-down, unwise, upscale, vengeful. Write down (journal) the particular highlighted within your dream. The attribute or activity highlighted is for a reason. Since the attribute written down is a part of you, namely the dreamer's nature, demeanor, and/or lifestyle, an honest assessment is very important for truth sake. Happy note, considering that other people's attributes, within dreams, also represent attributes of your own personality, causes one to look at another in a better light. According to your capacity to embrace self-awareness and a rectification of mind, body, and spirit, God will begin to enhance, make better, more attractive, sanctify, diminish, and make pure and free from sin and guilt, this part of you.

Otherwise noted, if the person, animal, place, or background within your dream is actually known by the dreamer, in your awaked life, this person, animal, place, or background may represent him or herself, or itself.

Unknown in your awaked life or although known, was unseen, invisible, or only talked about - person, animal, place, or organization within your dream:

Unless otherwise noted elsewhere, if you did not recognize, the person, place, thing, they, or it, was not seen, invisible, or only talked about within your dream, this indicates an attribute or activity within your life that you are unfamiliar with, or are in denial about, or you refuse to acknowledge it, but it does exists. Question to journal, if dreamer seriously considers all the particulars, what stood out the most, what features, or character traits stood out the most. For example, color, size, happiness, loving, peacefulness, encouraging, irrational, leader, liar, passionate, neglected, poor, run-down, unwise, upscale, vengeful. Write down (journal) the particular highlighted within your dream. The attribute or activity highlighted is for a reason. Although, on some conscious level, you are aware of a certain behavior or attribute within you, you have chosen to filter out or simply ignore certain information about yourself that contradicts your view of yourself and/or your preconceived notions of others and of the world around you. Possibly protecting yourself, emotionally and psychologically, from a situation, which you are unable to cope with at this time, or you lack control over; then again, perhaps the dreamer has an exaggerated or unrealistic view of yourself. No matter the reason, right now a question is before you, via your dream. Do you want to know this part of yourself? According to your ability to handle self-awareness, God will begin to reveal this side of you to you. Why, He wants to balance your understanding of things; thus, effecting wholeness within your life, so that the enemy will no longer be able to manipulate your emotions so easily. The Holy Spirit is with you to help you throughout this entire process, listen to Him. Now, in your life, this activity or attribute needs reckoning with, somehow or some way.

Otherwise noted, (known or unknown), if the person, place or thing that initiated (or was a recipient of) the action or activity within your dream was not seen, invisible, or only talked about within your dream, this may indicate that the dreamer does not recognize the influential effects another has within your life, or upon your attitude.

If more than one person (known or unknown):

Consider what the group had in common. What behavior, character trait, feature, action, or activity, stood out the most? For example, were they argumentative, authoritative, beautiful, criminal minded, dancing, difficult, dressed unusual, enigmatic, fighting, focused, flirty, helpful, hurtful intentions, powerful, promiscuous, quiet, secretive, seemed unreal, unassuming? That which was highlighted and noted is what you need to focus on at present.

If the attribute or quality is a desirable or positive one, allow the strength of that attribute to help you overcome some manner of immorality or irreverence within your life and/or to help you to become better, productively, for the Kingdom of God in some manner. If the attribute is an undesirable or negative one, take steps accordingly to struggle against the growing desires of the carnal side of you. If applicable, get help and support via prayer, fasting, and a Christian based support group.

For dreams of the dead see following note.

Did you smell an odor of death? While the dead has nothing to do with the living (Ecclesiastes 9:4-6), it may be considered what character trait did that person represent to the dreamer, while the person was actually alive, what character feature stood out the most. With that trait noted, dreamer may consider that the trait noted, is within the dreamer, and that trait is no longer useful or needed for the progression of your spiritual walk, on this side of heaven. Dreamer, it is suggested that you render that trait (good or bad) obsolete, and began anew attempting to move forward, using different tactics to overcome unproductive habitual life cycle choices, and for maneuvering through this thing we call life in a more, better way. See category, Death, and/or other relevant categories.

5. In addition to the following interpretations, see index or relevant categories for more information. For example, if embalmment was done in some way, see category, Death; if colors was highlighted, see category, Colors. Kept within context of your dream and the interpretation, the additional symbols are perhaps relevant. It will be within the sum of all the symbols that you will find a more thorough interpretation.

6. While the fluctuations of odors are extensive and deep in variations, and mystifying in their stimulating effect, yet biblically, odors are either pleasing or disturbing aromas. Thus, while the extensiveness of odors is great, this category will deal with only two variations of odors, good and pleasing, or bad, disturbing, or foul. It is suggested that the dreamer see also, other relevant research, via a Bible concordance, Bible illustrated dictionary, encyclopedia, or internet, to seek biblical guidelines for metaphorical meanings of a particular odors, scents, perfumery, fragrances, incense, or aromas. Having done your research you should be able to determine some basic behaviors your Lord and Savior wants you to focus on.

Symbols and Referents

Smell is intangible, yet very intuitive. Odors are generally interposed within dreams for the purpose of, revealing the condition of your heart and/or soul or spirit; for odors permeates virtually all aspects of life, even going beyond that which spiritual. Although heart and soul are often used interchangeably, in this case they are separate. According to the Bible, your heart (aka your mind, feelings, and intuitions) is fundamentally your far-reaching ways of thinking and behaving, the depth and breadth of your values, the seat of your conscience, the seat of your faculty of reason, your personal sense of right and wrong, and your choices thereof; therefore, you are designated, according to your heart. According to your heart, you are deemed pure, upright and righteous, pious and good, or wicked, as the imagination of mankind's heart is evil from youth, contaminating your whole life and character. In this, the heart must be changed and regenerated before one can willingly obey God. Matters of the heart, see, Genesis 8:21, 20:5- 6; 1 Kings 3:12; Psalm 11:2, 24:4-5, 51:10-14, 78:72; Ecclesiastes 8:11; Ezekiel 11:19, 36:26-27; Matthew 5:8, 12:34, 15:18; Luke 8:15; Romans 2:14-15, et al. On the other hand, biblically, the soul or spirit, (Strong's 5315: "*nephesh*" meaning soul, and *betseth naphshah*, Genesis 35:18 "as her soul was in departing, for she died), is a vital principle within you; the soul animates the body. The soul is a living thing, compared to the body, which is a non-living thing; the soul enters the body and the body borrows life from the soul. The soul is a spiritual or immaterial part of humanity, regarded as immortal. The soul can exist separate from, and is independent of, the body. The body goes back to dust and becomes a non-living thing once again, and the soul goes on living. As the soul is the seat of your appetites, desires, emotions, and passions, what lives on is every aspect of your life, your memories, relationships, pains, pleasures, wisdom, and knowledge. The soul by itself cannot do good deeds, and a body without a soul can't do good deeds. You can only be rewarded once you're back together soul and body. The "smell" is the connection of the physical and spiritual, our connection to the soul. Matters of the soul or spirit; see Ecclesiastes 8:8; Luke 10:20, 24:37-39; Acts 7:59; 1 Corinthians 5:5; 6:20, 7:34; Hebrews 1:14, 12:23, et al.

Since thoughts, behaviors, and beliefs come from either a place of positive or unwise ways of thinking and behaving, memories, relationships, pains, pleasures, appetites, desires, and emotions, these types of dreams often expose the condition of your heart, mind, and the possible destination of your soul. Hence, odors within dreams figuratively reveal what's in your heart and the condition of your soul. Consequent, it is from your heart, mind, and soul that the pleasing and fragrant odors of holiness permeate your life, or the displeasing aroma of profaneness that alters the goodness of life and creates atmospheres of faithlessness, fear, distrust, and death, is smelled. For we are the aroma of Christ to God among those who are being saved and among those who are perishing, to the one a fragrance from death to death, to the other a fragrance from life to life (2 Corinthians 2:14-16 ESV).

In addition to the varied meanings of odors, other common words, expressions, usages, (e.g. slang or clichés), or a 'probable' that are metaphorically represented by any of the following are also considered.

Category Content: If not listed see index, perchance, for your specific type of odors, scents, perfumery, fragrances, incense, or aromas type dream.

- Aromas or scents of foods, flowers, gardens, herbs, and spices, see category Agriculture
- Bad, dirty, disturbing, stench, foul, stink, or some other unpleasant odor or an "Odor of Death", including the diverse variations of these odors
- Good, clean, lovely, sweet, or some other pleasantly fragrant smelling odor or the "Odor of Sanctity", including the diverse variations of these odors
- Incense or Censers (substance that produces an odor when burned or a container for burning incense, especially one that is swung on a chain in a religious ritual)
- Perfume

BAD, DIRTY, DISTURBING, STENCH, FOUL, STINK, OR SOME OTHER UNPLEASANT ODOR OR AN "ODOR OF DEATH", INCLUDING THE DIVERSE VARIATIONS OF THESE ODORS:

This dream has four meanings (choose one). (1) Dreamer, all of your morally objectionable behavior, namely in the area dealing with the deeds of the flesh; examples of deeds of the flesh are dishonesty, adultery, sensuality, hostility, feuding, vendettas, grudges, unfriendliness, strife, jealousy, outbursts of anger, disputes, dissensions, discord, factions, cliques, envying, drunkenness, carousing, idolatry, or any traits of these sorts (see 1 Corinthians 6:8-11). This also includes a possible belief in, and/or practice of, necromancy. It is beneath this kind of negativity, your disobedient spirit, bad character, and unwise choices, choices that clearly lack forethought; that your soul is suffering, and consequent, your self-imposed alienation, depression, homelessness, aimlessness, and/or some other crisis within. Dreamer, whenever your collective actions, and soul, grow heavy from sinful pursuits, there emerges from deep within you a stench, symbolically likened to the "odor of death". When you are in denial, embracing anger, dishonesty, sacrilege, and other depravity, and the consequences of your behaviors began to tear your life apart, and your world implodes. When your tears fall hopelessly to the ground and disappear beneath the sullenness of your conscience, and all around you is nothing but desolation and barrenness, and the blood of others is on your hands, and the stench of it all emerges for all to smell, there is yet redeeming grace, there is still hope for you. Dreamer, yes, evilness is punished, but favorably, God is slow to anger; and because of His amazing grace, mercy, and compassion, there is still yet a grace waiting for you, to lay hold of and to embrace. Dreamer, the disturbing and unpleasant odor injected in to your dream is a sign that the Creator is awakening inside of you the need for self-contemplation and change; that you might emit a sweet smell, an aroma well pleasing to God. And this change solely depends on you, starting now. Dreamer, taking ownership of what your warning dream is revealing to you about you, and working from that point, via prayer, fasting, earnest and diligent self-examination. Also including, persistent practice of truthfulness, and in embracing the fruits of the spirit (see Galatians 5:22-26), and respecting candid support from family and friends, and Christian counseling, all this will help truth inwardly begin to emerge; at a pace, you'll be able to "wrap your mind around" comfortably. This followed by appropriate application of wisdom, can conceivably avert self-deception and denial, and the repercussions thereof. Dreamer you shall love the LORD your God with all your heart, soul and might. Read, understand, and embrace Deuteronomy 6:4-9, this is to you. See suggested course of action. (2) Dreamer, hardness of heart evidences itself by, "light" views, partial acknowledgment, partial confession of sin, stifling convictions of conscience; shunning reproof, pride and conceit; ingratitude; unconcern about the word and ordinances of God; inattention to divine Providence, shunning reproof, and a general ignorance of divine things. This is the condition of your heart and soul. Dreamer, the process of salvation begins in the heart by the believing reception of the testimony of God, while the rejection of that testimony hardens the heart. Read, understand, and embrace Psalm 95:7, 8, and Proverbs 28:14. See suggested course of action. (3) If dreamer actually knows what an actual "Odor of Death" smells like, your dream denotes a serious and life threatening illness within the dreamer, or within one closely connected to the dreamer, see Notes 1, 3. On some level, you already know something is seriously wrong with your health or the health of another. Dreamer, while it is acknowledged that no one lives forever, for there is no human that has power over the spirit to retain the spirit, neither hath he or she has power over the day of death (Ecclesiastes 8:8). It is highly suggested that you seek medical attention as soon as possible, and call for the elders of your church, for it is through their prayers of faith and anointing of oil upon you that sin is forgiven and spiritual healing is bestowed, and perhaps physical healing also[36]. Have faith in this, for it will be by your faith that you might be healed wholly. This is a true saying. Further, God has appointed someone, possibly a relative, to help you through this difficult time. Also, see Specific Meaning at the end of this category, section entitled, Note (Specific Meaning). See suggested course of action. (4) If dreamer is actually familiar with a particular unpleasant odor, e.g. the smell of same sex persons intimately coming together, or the smell of "crack or meth" houses, etc., your dream warns that when there is a bad stench within one's life, one is compelled to remove, and not cover, the source of the offending odor. Dreamer, your reality of God is based on emotions and personal preconceptions, due to the pain of rejection, abuse, and/or other emotional and physical violations, of your past or recent present. The violation(s) has affected your "approach pattern" to all your relationships. Examples of the violation are abuse, assault, bullying, kidnapping, molestation, rape, stalked, or being held prisoner. This has left you internally inconsistent and disordered, fraught with uncertainty, doubt, suspicion, and secret hidden sins. Unfortunately, your paradigm is "gridded" through the emotions of fear and rejection. Paradigm shift, the diabolical entity, having possessed the person(s) who committed the literal act, was sent to rob, steal, and destroy a quality of life that has been destined you, to keep you from living that life abundantly, happily, and in peace. The demon's mission is to get you to entertain, embrace, and live out the negative results of your particular violation, with a hope to oppress, persecute, and bring you into bondage of an ungodly and unprofitable lifestyle. Desiring that the unfavorable consequences of that ungodly and unprofitable lifestyle; will cost you your emotional sanity, possibly your life, and ultimately your soul. Dream er; oftentimes, bad things happen to innocent and good people. A bad thing happened to you, and you are good and innocent. Dreamer, at your very core, you want to know love and trust, but you cannot "touch it" or receive it, because you do not believe you are lovable or trustworthy. Compassionately, the Lord is creating a miracle in your life. This miracle will stop the effects of your violation from playing a significant role in your life, enabling you to move forward with your life and to ma ke good decisions. However, the miracle's success depends upon your willingness to be healed and set free; for one will always have the choice to say no, or perhaps sabotage their progress. First, recognize and respect your time of visitation from the Lord, for it is upon you, as well as the work of His Hand upon your life. If you lack wisdom ask God for wisdom; and He will give you wisdom. For the Lord gives wisdom and from His mouth comes knowledge and understanding. Then you will understand what is right and just and fair, every good path. When wisdom enters your heart and knowledge becomes sweet to your soul, discretion will protect you, understanding will guard you, and His Truth will lead you. To deliver you from the ways of wickedness, and from demons whose words and ways are perverse, who causes you to walk in darkness gladly, whose paths are crooked and devious, causing you to leave straight paths (Proverbs 2:1-6, 9-15). This is one of God's covenant promises to you. Have faith in this. Further, with much fortitude choose not to perpetuate the desolation. Dreamer, go and separate yourself from anyone and anything that hinders your clarity and emotional stability. Moreover, if relevant, go, and continue your education, the Lord will help you in your endeavors. Dreamer, if you do not respect the work of the Lord within your life, and the opportunities He is offering you, to be set free, spiritually, emotionally and physically. You will have nothing to work with, but your body, namely, deviant sexual promiscuousness, and all that comes with that manner of behavior, including loss of life and soul. See suggested course of action.

GOOD, CLEAN, LOVELY, SWEET, OR SOME OTHER PLEASANTLY FRAGRANT SMELLING ODOR OR THE "ODOR OF SANCTITY" including the diverse variations of these odors:

This dream has four meanings (one, two, or all may apply). (1) Dreamer, it has been declared, that the Lord has smelled a pleasing aroma emanating from your life; consequently, that which has caused you much misery and/or severe affliction within your life, will now cease. Further, there will be a relaxation or slackening of tension in your life, stop, and feel the ten sion leaving. Those who have charged you falsely, with malicious intent, attacking your good name and reputation will be far from you. Others will become less hostile, as will you. You will be more relaxed, easygoing, and genial. The necessity to be reconciled with others than to always be in opposition has been resolved. Dreamer, you have simply taken the higher ground. You have re-evaluated your life, learned from your mistakes, found new directions in solving problems, pursued healing, sought out encouragement, and figured out what God would like you to change in order to, better fulfill His purpose. You hav e learned the principles and Christian values that encourage one to reach out and touch others in a loving and graceful manner; ultimately finding yourself promoting the genuine cause of Christ and the good of others. Moreover, spiritually mature, you are a very peaceful and poised individual; now, prepared, you will be honored publicly. (2) The dreamer has the capacity to spearhead a new dawn, giving birth to a new generation that will usher in an age of mass revivals, with primary emphasis on a personal and saving relationship with Christ Jesus. That you might fulfil your purpose, a profound and insightful wisdom, previously unknown to you, will begin to emerge from deep within you, as well as, new emotions, and other nice results, will come forth. Dreamer will be infused with an "Odor of Sanctity", producing for you a good name, an honorable reputation, and an overall life emitting an agreeable fragrance, according to God's will. (3) Male dreamer only: Your dream implies one, namely the male dreamer, who will trouble the kingdom of darkness. Dreamer, you are definitely a force spiritually, not to be underestimated. Similar to Moses, you have the capacity to usher in a time of revival and deliverance for God's people, call ed for such times as these. You will cause the dishonorable and non-believer to break their agreement with death and choose to live, and cause the believer to remember once again the blood sacrifice of Jesus. Further, there will be miraculous healings, because of your ministry. Additionally, a female (wife, mother, daughter, sister, niece, cousin) will greatly support you and your ministry, she will be there as a voice of wisdom, and as encouragement. (4) Unmarried dreamer, if so desired, your dream also implies love. The love between a man and woman, leading to a lasting marriage, honored by God, and to children. Read and embrace Song of Songs 1, this is to you and your sweetheart.

INCENSE OR CENSERS (substance that produces a fragrant odor when burned or a container for burning incense, especially one that is swung on a chain in a religious ritual):

This dream has four meanings (choose one). (1) If dreamer is actually considered a spiritual or religious leader, e.g. bishop, deacon, deaconess, elder, evangelist, minister, overseer, pastor, pope, preacher, priest, rabbi, superintendent, teacher, or any cleric or ecclesiastical leader type role. Dreamer, if the incense or censer gave off a bad, disturbing, foul stench, or some other unpleasant odor, including the diverse variations of these odors. Read, understand, and embrace Leviticus 10:1-3, this is to you. See suggested course of action. (2) If dreamer is actually considered a spiritual or religious leader, e.g. bishop, deacon, deaconess, elder, evangelist, minister, overseer, pastor, pope, preacher, priest, rabbi, superintendent, teacher, or any cleric or ecclesiastical leader type role. Dreamer, if the incense or censer gave off a good, lovely, pleasant odor or some other fragrance, including the diverse variations of these odors. Your dream denotes that the dreamer's ministry will begin to flow within the realm of miraculous phenomena. Demons will submit to you in Jesus' name. For you have been anointed, and given high authority, to overcome all the powers and schemes of the enemy, nothing will harm you. If demonic possession is the case, it should be noted, exorcism (commanding demons and all unclean spirits to leave a person in the name of Jesus the Christ) was practiced by the disciples as part of Christ's instructions, see Matthew 10, Mark 9:38, Luke 11:18, 19, Acts 16, 19:11-16. Dreamer, you will need to "exorcise" the demon out of others and pray for them to be filled with the Holy Spirit, thus preventing the demon from re-entering them later (Matthew 12:43-45). However, do not rejoice that demonic spirits submit to you, but rejoice that your name is written in heaven. Even more, those who will listen to you will also listen to Jesus; those who reject you will also reject Jesus. Moreover, dreamer, you are anointed to become a healer, and will begin to sense the healing power of God within your hands. You will begin to sense a feeling of heat within your hands, and have probably experience this once or twice before, when you've prayed for another. Nonetheless, you have authority in Jesus name, your heavenly Father watches over you, and you have His ear. (3) Your dream denotes a transition within the life of the dreamer, and good health and strength to make the changeover. This transition will affect within you a far-reaching hope, profoundly greater faith, and a more intense love for all things Jesus, including His people; allow it. Dreamer, as you have done well serving your present place of worship, the leadership, and members, especially by making them bett er and greater qualitatively. By this you have open the door for you to become a leader, namely a CEO of your own ministry. God will send someone to help you along the way. He or she will lead and guide you to where you need to be. This relationship wi ll be an "equal partner" or "friendship" type relationship, in other words they will not be head over you. You will always be respect ed as a lead person. Moreover, dreamer you have been blessed with a great understanding of spiritual knowledge, and not without reason. One who is given the means to study and teach and has access to prophetic wisdom, is purposed to be a transformational force in people's lives. Your power of speech and wisdom will convert souls to the Kingdom of God. Your time of missions is upon you. You are sent to those who are spiritually "asleep". You are counseled to focus your ministry on God's providence over life. Primarily, the wisdom, care, and guidance He has provided His people, for He always guards over His chosen; thus, He watches over His people. You must continue to encourage others, and encourage yourself too, that the feeling of rest and serenity that comes with trust in God's divine providence is available right now, and that it would be wise of them to put their trust in God now. This, coupled with, contentment, and theirs, and your, peace will overflow. Those who will listen and adhere will begin to experience the blessings spoken of in Leviticus 26:4-13, tell them this. In particular, (verse 6 GW), "I will bring peace to your land. You will lie down with no one to scare you". Moreover, you (the dreamer) will be leaving your present church, and you will experience a mega-ministry. You will become friends with major leaders, but not covenant partners with them. You will (or should) remain attached to your present church and come back to rest there. Shortly thereafter, because of your diligence and honorable service, you will be given the opportunity to take a sabbatical rest, covered by the Lord's grace. (4) Dreamer, God will rescue, or has rescued, you from a powerful enemy, one who is/was too strong for you. This person confronted you during a very hard time in your life, but the Lord was your support (2 Samuel 22: 17-25). A "hallelujah" is in order. Further, now, you will begin to experience a miraculous increase in divine knowledge, and wisdom. This knowledge and wisdom will be imparted to you to be used exclusively for interpreting the gospel of Jesus Christ to others, and for the edifying of the Body of Christ; the body of believers. Your optimistic and generous personality, coupled with your strong desire to uplift humanity is leading you into situations where you will be able to express your desire to serve others. You will be provided with the resources to carry out your vision, and will become established, expect this. Additionally, in your present business or personal dealings, you will be satisfied and take delight in your goals. If you are involved in any situation that is competitive, you will triumphant. This dream also confirms that you're in order for heaven.

PERFUME:

This dream has three meanings (choose one). (1) The smell of cheap or bad smelling perfume, is liken to putting perfume on a corpse, therefore, see category, Death (Embalmment). Also, see suggested course of action of this category. (2) The smell of fragrant perfume implies spiritual growth, divine illumination, and some type of promotion or confirmation, on some level or another within a ministry. Nevertheless, dreamer, your height of spiritual progress and promotion will be according to your faith and obedience to God's will over your life personally. The following is necessary for you to hear, understand, and heed. If you want to approach and worship the Holy One by way of inspirational music, praise and worship ministry, teaching, or preaching, you should come before Him in a sense of appropriateness. Meaning you should aspire for some level of truthfulness, modesty, and reliability. No other is responsible for this discipline within your life but you; therefore, deal with an existing situation that hinders your approach to God with some level of purity (Leviticus 11:45, 1 Peter 1:13-2:3). Therefore, prepare your mind for action; be self-controlled; set your hope fully on the grace to be given you when Jesus Christ is revealed, and no longer conform to your carnal desires (see 1 Peter 1:13-16). (3) Your dream is additional proof of something you have believed God for is correct (e.g. for a spouse, rectification of an attitude of anger, frustration, discontent, or for a healing of unbelief, or a healing of your faith level, or a healing of physical health, or for any hindrances to your spiritual clarity that you have recognized). You will receive what you have believed God for, all this long time. In addition, if unmarried, and you so desire, you will meet a potential spouse in about 50 days.

Suggested Course of Action

If you are here, your heart and soul is suffering beneath the immoral ways of your thinking and behaving, and the depth and breadth of your syncretistic ideas. All of which are disturbing aromas. And when there is a bad stench, it too touches the soul. Therefore, your heart and soul can no longer handle the smell of your lifestyle. Dreamer, you are being compelled to remove the source of the offending odor and "air out your room", sort to say. Your emotional and spiritual health is in jeopardy.

Question to consider and journal, did your dream depict any symbols that alludes to, the dreamer will make the necessary changes, spiritually, emotionally, and/or physically to affect a more positive outcome? If changes are initiated, your dreams will change. Nevertheless, in keeping with the fact that olfactory property is a sensation of the heart (aka your mind, feelings, and intuitions), and soul (that spiritual or immaterial part of humanity, regarded as immortal), permeating virtually all aspects of your life, revealing the condition of your heart and soul. Hence, there is a need to seriously, reflect on your emotions, and your soul; your faculty of reason, your personal sense of right and wrong, and your choices, for you are designated according to your heart. Favorably, as an individual is refreshed upon smelling a pleasant fragrance; likewise, your heart and soul be can refreshed, for, no sin is beyond Adonai Elohim ability to forgive. Read, understand, and embrace Psalm 23, and Romans 5:20. Utilizing the powerful tools of prayer, fasting, and embracing studiousness to God and to His Word, all these are pleasant and fragrant aromas; they please, refresh and warm the soul, and they will calm you down. It is this refreshing that will cause the Light of God to shine forth in your life.

Jesus came to cleanse all sin: "Truly I tell you, people can be forgiven all their sins" (Mark 3:28 NIV). When you recognize your sin, and then deeply cry out to God for deliverance, with much fasting and prayer, He will hear you, forgive you, and sanctify you. Dreamer, you are ask to start over again, and begin loving the Lord your God with all your heart, with all your soul, and with all your strength, and if applicable, to studiously teach your children, to do so as well (Deuteronomy 6:3 -7). If you lack wisdom, ask Jesus for wisdom. He gives wisdom to all men generously, no matter who you are and what you've done; wisdom will be given you (James 1:5-8). Therefore, no longer say, "I don't know His truth", simply open your bible, and study what's before your eyes. Focusing on one verse per day, this is a start. Further, in the genuineness of your heart, set Christ as Lord. Dreamer, you are precious in the sight of God. Further, choosing to speak and practice God's unadulterated truth, without second-guessing it, or double mindedness, always emits a pleasant fragrance.

Now, pray (See Prayer of Deliverance, pg. 897)

Specific Meaning

If you have a very real connection with any agriculture activity, these sorts of dreams are usually about your routine, munda ne activities or anxieties that overwhelm your mind during the day. They are an inner release mechanism, which helps provide you with emotional balance and the maintaining of your sanity. These dreams are not significant, and do not warrant special attention.

Per your lifestyle, if your dream closely resembled real life situations, meaning it can actually occur during your awaked state, this dream may be an Ordinary Dream, resulting from your daily activities (see Chapter One, Chalom). These sorts of dreams are usually about your routine, mundane activities or anxieties that overwhelm your mind during the day. They are an inner release mechanism, which helps provide you with emotional balance and the maintaining of your sanity. These dreams are not significant, and do not warrant special attention.

Note: If, you have a very high chance of formulating a new aroma, fragrance, or perfume, and you sense that, your dream is some type of divine inspiration regarding development, then go, and start formulating, brand mark, and marketing your divine sent inspiration. For God does give originative inspiration, via dreams, and it is meant to prosper your life. It is advisable for you to; prayerfully determine the unique details and specifics needed for your product creation, write down all the details and specifics. Prepare a good proposal, name your product, and give it your best that it may be acceptable to any reputable financial entity, benefactor, or merit a grant of some kind. That which you will need to fulfill your aims, surely, you will have. It is suggested that you seize the opportunity your dream is presenting to fulfill the purpose for which it was sent.

If dreamer actually knows what an actual odor of death, smells like perhaps due to your work in an arena where you are exposed to such an odor. Coroner, Embalmer, Medical Examiner, Mortician, or any sort of professional that deals in death, might consider an "Odor of Death", coming from a specific area, e.g., a specific part of a body, within a dream, as a clue pointing to a possible death determination. Dreamer, the details, kept within context of your dream, should be relevant to your life, and closely resemble your real-life situations. Meaning it can actually occur during your awaked state. This will help you narrow down the specifics needed to support you. However, if your dream was inundated with symbols not easily linked to your life activities, then you should heed the spiritual implications (the interpretation).

A crime investigator, or any sort of professional of this kind, that actually knows what an actual odor of death smells like. The dreamer may consider his or her (specific) dream as a clue given to assist in finding facts, needed to support a prevaili ng or pressing situation or investigation. Example, crime investigator might consider an odor of death from inside a building or within a garden, as a clue pointing towards the direction of a possible homicide crime scene, the victim, and/or the perpetrator. Dreamer, the details, kept within context of your dream, should be relevant to your life, and closely resemble your real-life situations. Meaning it can actually occur during your awaked state. This will help you narrow down the specifics needed to support and steer you in the right direction. However, if your dream was inundated with symbols not easily linked to your life activities, then you should heed the spiritual implications (the interpretation).

If an accident, e.g. an explosion, perhaps caused by a chemical reaction, was highlighted within your dream, this is a precautionary warning. There may be potential for an accident. The dreamer may consider his or her (specific) dream as a clue given to assist in finding facts, needed to support a prevailing, pressing, or dangerous situation. Example, if t wo chemicals are combined, this may result in a bad side effect, consequently lawsuits, or again, perhaps some kind of explosion. This will help you narrow down the specifics needed to support you or to steer you clear of possible mishaps. Dreamer, the d etails, kept within context of your dream, should be relevant to your life, and closely resemble your real-life situations. Meaning it can actually occur during your awaked state. However, if your dream was inundated with symbols not easily linked to you r life activities, then you should heed the spiritual implications (the interpretation).

PEOPLE

A creature of a more exalted kind was wanting yet, and then was man designed. Conscious of thought, of more capacious breast, for empire formed, and fit to rule the rest. (Blavatsky, translated by John Dryden)

Then God said, "Let us make man in our image, after our likeness". And God created man in his own image, in the image of God created he him, male and female created he them. And the Lord God made man from the dust of the earth, breathing into him the breath of life: and man became a living soul. This is the book of the generations of Adam. In the day that God crea ted man, in the likeness of God made he him; male and female created he them, and blessed them, and called their name Adam, in the day when they were created. (Genesis 1:26, 27; 2:7; 5:1-2 ASV)

What is man, that you have made him great, that your attention is fixed on him, that your hand is on him every morning, and t hat you are testing him every minute? What is man, that he may be clean? And how may the son of woman be upright? (Job 7:17-18; 15:14 BBE)

For he did not make the angels rulers over the world to come, of which I am writing, but a certain writer has given his witne ss, saying, what is man that you keep him in mind? What is the son of man that you consider him? You made him a little lower than the angels; you gave him a crown of glory and honor, and made him ruler over all the works of your hands: You put all things under his feet. For in making man the ruler over all things, God did not put anything outside his authority, though we do not see everything under him now. But we see him who was made a little lower than the angels, even Jesus, crowned with glory and honor, because he let himself be put to death so that by the grace of God he might undergo death for all men. And because the children are flesh and blood, he took a body himself and became like them. Because of this, it was necessary for him to be m ade like his brothers in every way, so that he might be a high priest full of mercy and keeping faith in everything to do with God, making offerings for the sins of the people. For having been put to the test himself, he is able to give help to others when they are tested. (Hebrews 2:5-9, 14, 17-18 BBE)

The relationship of God to His people is more than His calling; they also call Him their God. The relationship does not come through church attendance or good deeds. It is a deliberate choice to follow God alone. 2 Corinthians 6:16, Mark 8:38 both indicate that a choice has to be made. When we make that choice to embrace God, He embraces us as well. Then we truly are His people. (gotquestions.org, paraphrased)

This category deals with any living or extinct member of the family Hominidae; any group of human beings, characterized by superior intelligence, articulate speech, and erect carriage, aka people, living and deceased. Some short descriptions of types, phrases, and other processes and particulars, connected in some way to this category are, for example, humanity, humankind, mankind, man, woman, male, female, baby, children, kin, friend, foe, brother, sister, nations, the races, the masses. Also, see category content list, or index.

All Symbols and Referents, Notes (1, 2, 3, etc.), Suggested Course of Action, and Specific Meaning offer guidance toward a more comprehensive interpretation.

Notes

1.   Unless otherwise noted elsewhere, if, in your everyday living, your awaked state, as part of your lifestyle, work, or ministerial activities, or a special event, you have a very real connection with any activity involving people. For example, spiritual leader, human resource or social worker, counselor, law enforcement or judicial system officer, celebrity, paparazzi, politician,

or any activity or business involved in, or pertaining, to people, your dream is not significant and does not warrant special attention.

Otherwise noted, this dream of people may be a Prophetically Simple Dream (see Chapter One: The 60ᵗʰ Part of Prophecy). Whereas, the dreamer is encouraged to educate, invent, or create something. For example, if dreamer received a unique message to educate people, or if dreamer invented something, or was inspired to create or upgrade something within your dream, that would benefit the masses. If dreamer actually entertains or minister to a great number of people, or you work in an arena where you are exposed to the collective masses. If you are part of the science, technology, expertise, or specialist in the areas of counting, documenting, moving, motivating people, etc. Dreamer, consider it not strange for someone, who is involved in some manner of activity that involves people, to receive inspirations regarding the collective masses via their dreams that might prove beneficial to the dreamer and to mankind. The details, kept within context of your dream, should be relevant to your life, and closely resemble your real-life situations. Meaning it can actually occur during your awaked state. It is suggested that you seize the opportunity your dream is presenting to fulfill the purpose for which it was sent. Skip interpretation and go prepare, do, or learn. Also, s ee Specific Meaning at the end of this category, section entitled, Note (Specific Meaning).

Otherwise noted, this dream of people may be a Prophetically Simple Dream (see Chapter One: The 60ᵗʰ Part of Prophecy). For example, if dreamer actually entertains or ministers to a great number of people, and you work in an arena where you are exposed to the collective masses. If an unfortunate mishap, especially one causing damage or injury, happened within your dream, e.g. perhaps an incident caused by a terrorist or insane gunman, was highlighted within your dream, this is a precautionary warning. See Specific Meaning at the end of this category, section entitled, Note (Specific Meaning).

Otherwise noted, this dream of people may be a Real-Time Dream (see Chapter One, Chalom, Ordinary Dreams). Whereas, your dream "picked up" on activity, connected with persons, going on within your space, while you were asleep, in real time, the actual time it was happening, disquieting your senses. The events in this type of dream are actually happening in real time, and are for the most part, influenced by substantive stimuli. For example, a party going on next door at your neighbors or on another vein, someone was breaking into your personal space unlawfully. If, after handling an unwelcome situation, or thoroughly checking your space, to make sure your environment is safe, e.g. making sure no break-in, or any other unwelcome activity is happening within your environment. Other than, a situation that needed handling, basically, if no alarm is determined then this dream is not significant, and does not warrant special attention. It was just loud people noise at the time you were asleep.

Otherwise noted, per your lifestyle, if your dream closely resembled real life situations, meaning it can actually occur during your awaked state, this dream may be an Ordinary Dream, resulting from your daily activities (see Chapter One, Chalom). These sorts of dreams are usually about your routine, mundane activities or anxieties that overwhelm your mind during the day. They are an inner release mechanism, which helps provide you with emotional balance and the maintaining of your sanity. These dreams are not significant, and do not warrant special attention.

2. Probables: As people present, and are frequently viewed, in many, and very personal ways; for example, does a hungry child or homeless person remind you of a particular missionary journey? Does a celebrity remind you of years gone by? Does a certain personality remind you of a major historical event? Is a certain ruler synonymous with corruption, traitorous, racists, and/or times that were very arduous? For example, slavery, the holocaust, indentured importees, Native Americans, thus, could people or persons depicted be a possible probable (see Chapter One, section entitled, Probables)? Hence, dreamer may also consider your own personal and special associations with various people groups or persons, as long as

the interpretation is kept within the principles of spiritual boundary markers, landmarks, and property lines, (see Chapter One, section entitled, Spiritualizing Boundary Markers, Landmarks, and Property Lines).

3. Determine who your dream is for you or another. Always, considering yourself first, reflecting on your present behaviors. Ask yourself, why am I dreaming about this now? What is this dream revealing about me? Have I taken on new attributes? Has anyone commented on my present behaviors as being untypical of me? Has my ministry changed for the better or for the worse? What about my beliefs, doctrine, or philosophy, are they still based on Holy Writ? Is there something I need to know about those I am ministering to or serving?

    Remember your actions and emotions within your dream. Was the dreamer walking with someone, talking with some, preaching, counseling, leading others, a coordinator, or director of a major event involving the masses? Was the dreamer entertaining a group of soldiers? Was the dreamer a stripper? Was the dreamer another race? Was the dreamer introduced to yourself? Unless otherwise noted elsewhere, an answer of yes, to one or more of these, or similar questions, is a good indicator that your dream is about you, the dreamer. What happened to you in your dream? How did things end? In light of your dream, via the relevant interpretation, do you believe that your choices will enhance or endanger your well-being, safety, and/or happiness, if so, how and why? Is spiritual or physical death a possibility? For example, are you "morphing" into someone else that is not good person? Are you "angry" at another, perhaps seeking revenge? See following relevant subcategory, the interpretation is about and for you.

    Was paparazzo the cause of some mishap? Was someone else leading you in any way? Did another in any way, coordinate, plan, or sponsor a major entertaining event? Did another have an issue with the dreamer? Was the person depicted within your dream your spouse, child, supervisor, pastor, or friend? Unless otherwise noted elsewhere, an answer of yes, to one or more of these, or similar questions, is a good indicator that your dream is about another and their role, and/or influential effects, within the life of the dreamer. Does someone find fault with you ministerial support to God's church, and/or His people? Are you dealing with someone, who truly believes in their heart that they will not have to give an account of their service to Heavenly Father? Is another enhancing your spiritual and/or literal prosperity, or are they responsible for the dwindling thereof? Do you know someone whose life activities or physical being is similar to that which stood out the most within your dream? Could it be that person? If you sense that your dream is for or about another, the question as to why you have been made privy to this information, and how do you factor into t he equation, should be seriously considered along with necessary actions. Perhaps the dreamer is being made aware of the plight of someone, and you are to get involved (see Chapter One, Are You Ready to Hear the Messages in Your Dreams, section entitled, The 10% for others).

    If your dream is for, or about another:

    Dreams that reference others and the revelation within those dreams, is not given haphazardly to any individual, but only to those with the ability, and influence to do something with the information; this is also prophecy. With that, journal the following questions, and if unable to answer the questions now, this denotes that the person, represented within your dream, will enter your life shortly. Are you entering into a personal relationship with someone? Do you not know or understand what you're looking at, especially certain behaviors, when learning about this person? Has someone new entered your life or maybe you've just begun opening up to someone not so new, and have started listening to their advice, accepting their assistance, or are you supporting or enabling someone? Are you in denial regarding the toxicity of one of your present relationships, particularly a spouse, family member, or friend? Are you anxious, concerned, frightened, and/or troubled by recent changes in your behavior, especially because of someone's influence upon your life at present? Have you allowed someone to convince you to deceive another? Have you recently become aware of (or is being made aware of, via your dream) certain undesirable behaviors within you towards another? Are you trying to cut ties with one that is bad company? Have you just joined (or re-joined) a church, fellowship, or social group?

Note: If your dream has attributes that indicate that your dream is about you, and other attributes that indicate that your dream is about another, dreamer should consider that your dream is about you and another. For example, was dreamer asking for help from a friend? Were you (the dreamer) a supervisor, and another was given your position? Was encouraging others to follow someone? Was dreamer supporting an opposing team? Was dreamer at the table with others of like-mindedness? Thus indicating that your dream is about the dreamer, and another; therefore, while your dream is about the dreamer, the dreamer should expect the role and/or influential effects of another, also plays a part in your interpretation. For example, dreamer may have been emotionally wounded, violated, hurt, by another, and now that hurt has bred bitterness and an unforgiving spirit within the dreamer. From which now the dreamer needs deliverance, again, see relevant interpretation.

More questions to consider. Why has the person been allowed within your life, and/or how did they get there? Again, if unable to answer the questions now, this denotes that the person, represented within your dream, will enter your life shortly. If their activity, within your dream, has proven positive, via the interpretation, this someone will prov e, unwittingly, to be a very strong ally, benefactor, defender, and supporter. God has sent this someone into your life to help you carry out your next endeavor by enlarging your spiritual capacity. Allow the strength of that person's character to guide, help, and support you. On the other hand, if his or her presence and/or activity, within your dream, proved negative, via the interpretation, for sure, this person will prove to be a very strong and formidable challenge for you, perhaps unto death. If negative, this dream is a dire warning. Take steps accordingly to struggle against, or to cut off, adverse and unfavorable relationships. Remember certain personalities are all encompassing, affecting everything, cataclysmic, contagious, deadly, harmful, infectious, predatory, and/or venomous. Symbolically meaning that if allowed to continue or prosper within your life, serious harm or death to the dreamer may result. Idolize no one, especially beyond the warning of the Lord, and we are definitely not to lay our lives down for no one. Then again, this person maybe allowed within your life, because of the dreamer's unwillingness to abstain from immorality after having been asked to abstain from such by God, see 1 Corinthians 6:9-20, Galatians 5:19-21, or the dreamer's self-righteous behavior, or a lack of a balanced and honest view of your own personality. In this case, this person will affect self-awareness within the life of the dreamer, exposing the negative traits of your personality, especially those traits, which cause you to follow, or to be so easily misled, and/or your wrong beliefs; no matter, this type of mentality needs reckoning with. Graciously, all of this will restore the dreamer to his or her right place with God, opening your eyes to see how far you've strayed from God (1 Corinthians 5:4-7; James 5:20). The lesson is, no matter how personable, powerful, or difficult a person, or how uncertain or unpopular the choices and issues, always take the next biblical and ethical step, for obedience t o God's principles will always prove safer and stronger foundationally. Although, you will need all kinds of outside support to recover from this person's domination, no longer, allow that particular person's influence within your life to continue or thrive, especially if negative, end it abruptly.

4. Consider all the people, places, backgrounds, and activity highlighted within your dream.
Known (in your awaked life) person, animal, place, or organization within your dream:
Unless otherwise noted elsewhere, people, animals, places, backgrounds that are actually known by the dreamer in your awaked life, indicates a part of you that you recognize within yourself on some level or another. Question to journal, if dreamer seriously considers the person, animal, place, or background attributes, what character traits stood out the

most, or what features stood out the most. For example, age, color, height, size, happiness, considerate, loving, let you be yourself, peacefulness, encourager, irrational, leader, liar, mentor, passionate, personable, neglected, poor, run-down, sage, shyster, unwise, upscale, vengeful. Write down (journal) the particular highlighted within your dream. The attribute or activity highlighted is for a reason. Since the attribute written down is a part of you, namely the dreamer's nature, demeanor, and/or lifestyle, an honest and unbiased assessment is very important for truth sake. Happy note, considering that other people's attributes, within dreams, also represent attributes of your own personality, causes one to look at another in a better light. According to your capacity to embrace self-awareness and a rectification of mind, body, and spirit, God will begin to enhance, make better, more attractive, sanctify, diminish, and make pure and free from sin and guilt, this part of you.

Otherwise noted, if the person, animal, place, or background within your dream is actually known by the dreamer, in your awaked life, this person, animal, place, or background may represent him or herself, or itself.

Unknown in your awaked life or although known, was unseen, invisible, or only talked about - person, animal, place, or organization within your dream:

Unless otherwise noted elsewhere, if you did not recognize, the person, place, thing, they, or it, was not seen, invisible, or only talked about within your dream, this indicates an attribute or activity within your life that you are unfamiliar with, or are in denial about, or you refuse to acknowledge it, but it does exists. Question to journal: what character trait, feature, action, or activity, stood out the most? For example, age, color, gender, height, size, happiness, considerate, loving, let you be yourself, peacefulness, encourager, irrational, leader, liar, mentor, passionate, person able, neglected, poor, run-down, sage, shyster, unwise, upscale, vengeful. Although, on some conscious level, you are aware of a certain behavior or attribute within you, you have chosen to filter out or simply ignore certain information about yourself that contradicts your view of yourself and/or your preconceived notions of others and of the world around you. Possibly protecting yourself, emotionally and psychologically, from a situation, which you are unable to cope with at this time, or you lack control over; then again, perhaps the dreamer has an exaggerated or unrealistic view of yourself. No matter the reason, right now a question is before you, via your dream. Do you want to know this part of yourself? According to your ability to handle self-awareness, God will begin to reveal this side of you to you. Why, He wants to balance your understanding of things; thus, effecting wholeness within your life, so that the enemy will no longer be able to manipulate your emotions so easily. The Paraclete is with you to help you throughout this entire process, listen to Him. Now, in your life, this activity or attribute needs reckoning with, somehow or someway.

Otherwise noted, (known or unknown), if the person, place or thing that initiated (or was a recipient of) the action or activity within your dream was not seen, invisible, or only talked about within your dream, this may indicate that the dreamer does not recognize the influential effects another has within your life, or upon your attitude.

If more than one person (known or unknown):

Consider what the group had in common. What behavior, character trait, feature, action, or activity, stood out the most? For example, were they argumentative, authoritative, beautiful, criminal minded, dancing, difficult, dressed unusual, enigmatic, fighting, focused, flirty, helpful, hurtful intentions, powerful, promiscuous, quiet, secretive, seemed unreal, unassuming? What about age, color, height, size, happiness, considerate, loving, let you be yourself, peacefulness, encourager, irrational, leader, liar, mentor, passionate, personable, neglected, poor, run-down, sage, shyster, unwise, upscale, vengeful, death. That which was highlighted and noted is what you need to focus on at present.

If the attribute or quality is a desirable or positive one, allow the strength of that attribute to help you overcome some manner of immorality or irreverence within your life and/or to help you to become better, productively, for the Kingdom of God in some manner. If the attribute is an undesirable or negative one, take steps accordingly to struggle against the growing desires of the carnal side of you. If applicable, get help and support via prayer, fasting, and a Christian based support group.

    For dreams of the dead see following note:

    Did you see many dead people? Unless, otherwise noted, most referents within this category include people who are living and deceased.

5. In addition to the following interpretations, see index or relevant categories for more information. For example, if preaching was involved in some way, see category: Talking. If clothing was involved in some way, see category, Clothing. Kept within context of your dream and the interpretation, the additional symbols are perhaps relevant. It will be within the sum of all the symbols that you will find a more thorough interpretation.

6. Since the following list is not extensive, dreamer is encouraged to seek biblical guidelines and other relevant research to determine the metaphorical meaning of your particular people, depicted within your dream, via a Bible concordance, Bible illustrated dictionary, encyclopedia, or internet. Having done your research you should be able to determine some basic behaviors or attributes your Lord and Savior wants you to focus on.

Symbols and Referents

Most dreams of people generally imply, coupled with the relevant interpretation; that every person that appears within your dream is supposed to represent an aspect of yourself. Try to think about what aspect this could be. It can be something you admire and wish to emulate and incorporate into your own personality, or it could be a more negative characteristic that you may dislike intensely in your waking life, both of which, are telling you something about yourself, your beliefs, judgments, and attitudes.

In addition to the varied meanings of people, other common words, expressions, usages, (e.g. slang or clichés), or a 'probable' that are metaphorically represented by any of the following are also considered (this section is an addendum at the end of the category).

Category Content - If not listed see index, perchance, for other specifics, relating to people dreams.

- Ambassador, Chancellor, Dictator, King, Legislator, Monarch, Oppressor, Politician, President, Prime Minister, Queen, or Tyrant (any nation's ruler, leader, head of state, civil authority, or any one engaged in government and civil administration, living and deceased)
    - Dictator, Oppressor, or Tyrant (cruel and oppressive dictator)
- Business partner, leader, employer, supervisor, see one of the following categories: Working, Work Places, or Sitting
- Celebrity (actors, other famous people, big-name, historical, illustrious, notable, widely known people who are highly esteemed, those very public figures, usually with status, power, and/or finances, living and deceased)
- Classmate(s)
- Co-worker(s), see category, Working (Co-workers)
- Dead people, see category, Death
- Educators, Facilitators, Students, see category, Working
- Elderly person (senior citizens, aged, living and deceased)
- Family (biological, adopted, step, maternal and paternal, husband, wife, children, parents, grandparents, siblings, nephews, nieces, aunts, uncles, cousins, in-laws, and ex-spouse)
    - Aunt or Uncle (biological, adopted, in-law); Children, babies (children, grandchildren, great-grands, biological, adopted, step, in-law); Daughter or Daughter-in-law (biological, adopted, step-daughter, in-law); Son or Son-in-law (biological, adopted, step-son,

in-law); Cousin (biological, adopted, in-law); Nephew or Niece (biological, adopted, in-law); Parents, progenitors (biological, adopted, step-parent, in-law); Father (biological, adopted, stepfather, in-law, or one who reared, or took care of you as his child); Grandparent(s), great-grands (paternal and material, grandfather, or grandmother, biological, adopted, step-grandparents, in-laws, or one who you consider a grandparent, great- grandparent); Mother (biological, adopted, step-mother, in-law, or one who reared, or took care of, you as her child); "Church Mother" (a term of address, and a title of respect, for a senior clergywoman, who is a respected spiritual leader, and is looked upon as a sagacious and understanding leader, whose instructions, reproofs, and corrections are heeded); Siblings (brother or sister, biological, adopted, step-sibling, in-law, or spiritual brothers and sisters); Spiritual Brothers and Sisters (aka Believers, Christians, Saints, those of "The Way"); Spouse or Ex- spouse (husband or wife, if relevant, may also see one of the following categories: The Body, Chasing, Cheating, or Divorce); Husband or Ex- husband; Wife or Ex-wife

- Friends, Girlfriend, or Boyfriend (or someone who was depicted as friendly)
  - Ex-friends or Ex-girlfriend or Ex-boyfriend or Enemy
- Law Officers (attorneys, judges, police), see one of the following categories: Chasing, or Working, Work Places)
- Midget (markedly small in stature), see category, Abating (Dwarf)
- Models or Mannequins (persons who wear clothes to display fashions, or one who poses for a photographer, painter, or sculptor)
- Neighbor or Neighborhood (a literal neighbor, or if one was depicted as a neighbor)
- Parables of People (a parable is any short moral story, to convey a religious message)
- Physician or Psychiatrist or Healer or Health Aides (any health care provider), see one of the following categories: Chasing, or Working, Work places
- Soldiers or Branches of the Armed Forces
  - All Branches: United States Special Operations (SOF, those component forces of the military services specifically organized, trained, and equipped to conduct and support special operations, e.g. Navy SEAL, Green Beret, et.al.); Air and Space (Air Force); Land (Army, Marine); Sea (Navy, Coast Guard)
- Spiritual or Religious Leaders (e.g. bishop, deacon, deaconess, elder, evangelist, minister, overseer, pastor, pope, preacher, priest, rabbi, superintendent, teacher, or any cleric or ecclesiastical leader type role)
- You, the dreamer
- Youth (young people)

AMBASSADOR, CHANCELLOR, DICTATOR, KING, LEGISLATOR, MONARCH, OPPRESSOR, POLITICIAN, PRESIDENT, PRIME MINISTER, QUEEN, OR TYRANT (any nation's ruler, leader, head of state, civil authority, or any one engaged in government and civil administration, living and deceased):

For dictator, oppressor, tyrant, see following subcategory, dictator, tyrant, oppressor. First, it is suggested that dreamer, journal two or three of the very public attributes the governmental official is primarily known for, it will be within the su m of those attributes that you will find what you need to, primarily focus on, concerning your character. Dreamer, the governmental official's public and historical persona, and other symbols within your dream, once noted, should begin to revea l attributes that are inherent within you. With that noted, this dream has four meanings (choose one). (1) If governing official is recognized by dreamer in your awaked life, either, through biography, history, news, or personal. A nation's ruler, leade r, head of state, or civil authority, character is oftentimes revealed via biographical, historical, or information reported in a newspaper or some other publication.

For example, some are known for their friendship with God, as King David, or for their wisdom, as King Solomon. On a more contemporary vein, President Richard Nixon pushed Congress to provide funding for school lunches beyond the reimbursement program, declaring, "The time has come to end hunger in America". President Barack Obama was the USA first president of African descent; thus, inspiring other young African Americans to reach, and he was also the first to initiate a health care endeavor for the entire nation, preceding all others. With that, questions to consider. How is the government leader, within your dream, character designated, via biography, history, news, or personal? What is his or her historical significance? What do the attributes of the governing official have to do with the dreamer? It is the dreamer's prerogative to search out those attributes, and to consider how they relate to you. Again, it is suggested that the dreamer journal, three or more of the widely known distinguishing attributes the governing official is primarily known for; it will be within the sum of those attributes noted, that you will find what your dream is exposing about you; thus, the meaning of your dream. Those distinguishing features journaled are inherent within the dreamer, and will begin to manifest publicly. Those features will begin to arise upon the stage of your life, and appear, and be made public, for honor or dishonor. Thus, dreamer is encourage to heed this dream, and perhaps privately prepare, physically, mentally, emotionally, and spiritually, for any positive character traits or attributes, that was revealed, namely those traits that you've journaled, it will be those traits that will begin to arise within you, leading to you becoming a very public figure. Dreamer is also counseled to deal privately with any negative character traits, whether physically, mentally, emotionally, and/or spiritually, that was revealed within your dream, before you are publicly exposed. Nonetheless, the governmental official historical and very public persona; namely his or her designated character also is within the dreamer. This, coupled with other symbols within your dream, once noted, should begin to unfold the subject matter and/or issue at hand. If necessary, see suggested course of action. (2) Unknown governing official: if governing official is unknown to the dreamer in your awaked life, but was very benevolent and philanthropic, within your dream, this denotes that the dreamer is one, who is very strong and fierce. You are on your way to becoming very affluent, as well as, a great and mighty man or woman of God; a high ruler (e.g. leading activist, Christian dignitary, senior cleric, church head, president, prime minister, head of state, political ruler). To you, this dream is encouragement. You are one who has a proper amount of self-respect. Your behavior is exemplary, living a life of integrity, and can be trusted. You are anointed, charismatic, and have a following to prove it. You also try to live out what you preach; having the necessary emotional qualities to virtuously deal with stress, grief, loss, risk, and other difficulties, authoritatively, knowledgeable, and skillfully. You're deeply profound and fiercely loyal to God, His people, and to family. (3) Unknown governing official: if governing official is unknown to the dreamer in your awaked life, but was very malign, harmful in influence, or spoke unfavorably about others, within your dream, this denotes that the dreamer is one who embraces the negative aspects of your personality, namely those demonstrated by the official within your dream. To you, this dream is a stern rebuke. Moreover, you have an exaggerated opinion of your personal worth and abilities and show a lack of humility. You're conceited, egotistical, vain, and possibly sexually immoral (e.g. adultery or fornication). You use your influence to force others to do what you say; this is akin to witchcraft (aka rebellion). You are aggressive, intense, and violent. Dreamer, the more God allows you to see your emptiness, it is suggested that you be more earnest to repent, for this dream is to warn a rebellious person, in the spirit of grace. To see if you will yet be worked upon, and change your mindset, or else to leave you inexcusable, in your accusations against God, because of your ruin (e.g. continually plundered, seized, and disfavored, also see Jeremiah 9:7-9; Zechariah 13:9; Matthew 23:37-39; Revelation 3:15-21). See suggested course of action. (4) If dreamer is not a member of a faith based community, e.g. a church, synagogue, etc., at present, the governing official within your dream, known or unknown, in your awaked life; this dream is a summons, as this is your appointed time for change. Your time to be about your heavenly Father's business is now. He has need of you; it is time for you to begin starting your ministry, first, quietly building a strong infrastructure; researching what is needed to initiative your endeavor, embracing ethicalness, integrity, perseverance, to the end. Dreamer, there is a set assembly, assigned to help you fulfill your purpose, therefore, find your church, and abide there, until. As well, genuinely heed the counsel of the overseers of the ministry. By heeding counsel, you will gain God's favor and be a light unto others. Dreamer, the counsel of the Lord makes wise and pleases the sincere of heart and coverts the soul (Psalm 19:7-14). God will cause you to be well known, celebrated, and full of joy, and if relevant happily married. Thus, do not be indecisive about the matter or long in deciding a church. With that stated, the following is necessary to say. Dreamer, refrain from all boasting or you will experience a downfall, which will "arduously" lead you to your destined place, see Proverbs 16:18. Dreamer, you speak and/or write arrogantly about your accomplishments, possessions, and pilgrimages. This is what the Lord says, to male or female, "Let not the wise man boast of his wisdom or the strong man boast of his strength or the rich man boast of his riches. But let him who boasts boast about this: That he understands and knows me, that I am the Lord, who exercises kindness, justice, and righteousness on earth, for in these I delight", declares the Lord (Jeremiah 9:23, 24; 1 Corinthians 1:31). Unfortunately, if you continue without change, expecting different results, you will be made a fool of, resulting in you acting insanely. Choosing to remain powerless, in spite of spiritual help, makes it easier for the enemy of our soul to subjugate. Evil spirits always lie-in-wait for those who are willing to be in denial, or even slightly deceived, just to remain justified in purposelessness. Pray, God will guide you as to what He has need of from you. See suggested course of action.

Dictator, Oppressor, or Tyrant (cruel and oppressive dictator): If oppressor is highly recognized throughout history, news, or biography, as a cruel and oppressive tyrant; e.g., those that are widely known for their atrocities committed against those they had rule over, such as Duvalier "Papa Doc", Franco, Hitler, Idi Amin Dada "Big Daddy", Mussolini, et.al. Religiously, Jim Jones was responsible for a mass suicide in Jonestown, Guyana, and UFO religious millenarian cult leaders Marshall Applewhite and Bonnie Nettles were responsible for a mass suicide, in San Diego, California. Biblically, Queen Jezebel is recorded as a cruel queen. An example of a true radical feminist, she usurps the authority of her husband, and uses her husband's position and power to persecute and kill the true prophets of God; and so ruled over Israel with her bullying 'Quee n Bee' behavior. She was a great patroness of fornication, witchcraft, and idolatry, fostering the worship of Baal, via the false prophets of Baal. Dreamer, this type of dream is sent to warn an immoral believer, and to expose a need of refinement of character, especially in the area dealing with the deeds of the flesh and rebellion. Dreamer, you have not considered the reality of the repercussions of your unwise choices. You emanate anger and rage, perpetuate violence, and possibly promote indecent practices, and other odious traditions, under the guise of Christianity. You do that which is evil in the sight of the Lord, proving yourself fierce, cruel, merciless, unprincipled, and oppressive, very much like the demons you worship. You cause division amongst innocent people, and with premeditation, you intentionally attempt to destroy God's emissaries reputations because of their truths spoken to you. Are you not afraid to speak against God, His ways and means, and His people? Dreamer, is nothing sacred? Do you think the detestable things you are speaking, promoting, and perpetuating are of little consequence, and of little importance to God, His ways, His Kingdom, His people (the Body of Christ)? Did you not exp ect that God would resent it, and take it as an affront to Himself personally? It is a dangerous thing to offend Christ. You show yourself presumptuous, when you do not fear to speak evil of the Lord and His people. You dishonor God, His truth, His Kingdom, His church, and continually provoke God to anger. Thus, the anger of the Lord is, kindled against you. Now, He will deal with you harshly. The dreamer will begin to experience a loss of divine favor and authority, and an event or situation that will cause intense fear is coming to discourage and terrify you. This will be in the form of an annoying, difficult, and unpleasant person, one you've disdained, and treated in a harsh and oppressive manner, in the past. The trouble this person will cause will become so overwhelming stressful, because they will expose a secret regarding you. You will begin to experience some mental health issues, and will probably have to be restrained, against your will if needs be. You will also experience a loss of divine favor and authority. Additionally, a third of the people that adhere to such practices as you do, will all die of the same illness, a third will fall away (becoming apostates) because of a lack of saving knowledge, and a third will "pull up stakes" with a stigma attached to their name. The dreamer will find him or herself within one of these three categories. When these things begin to happen, if not already, you will know that the Lord has spoken. Dreamer, you take great risk, when you have no fear of promoting and perpetuating ideology and behavior that is clearly adversarial to God, per Holy Writ. For, all scripture is inspired by God and is useful to teach us what is true and to make us realize what is awry in our lives. It corrects us when we are wrong and teaches us to do what is right (2 Timothy 3:16). Dreamer, those who truly love Jesus, regards certain actions, characteristics, and behaviors as destructive to the church, family, society, self, and soul. Dreamer, turn from your wicked ways, and dump your darken ideology, and encourage others to do so as well. Moreover, as He knows your thoughts afar off, repent. Take words to Jesus, "'I have sinned, and I have done wrong and acted wickedly". Other than heartfelt repentance to Jesus and a change in your beliefs, behavior, and choices, no other excuse or weak justification will be heard. See suggested course of action.

In addition, the following is a common word, expression, or usage (e.g. slang or cliché), or a 'probable' that is metaphorically represented by politician:

- Figuratively, denotes one who is a schemer who tries to gain advantage in an organization in sly or underhanded ways.

CELEBRITY (actors, other famous people, big-name, historical, illustrious, notable, widely known people who are highly esteemed, those very public figures, usually with status, power, and/or finances, living and deceased):

This dream has two meanings (choose one). (1) Actors: To dream of actors, this choice has two parts (choose one). (a) If dreamer was an actor, the dreamer is counseled to deal with hypocrisy within your life. Dreamer, hypocrisy is a heavy and unnecessary burden. Such an attitude will cause God to relent on His promises to approve you in any of your endeavors. Any genuine praise you would receive because of service to the King's Kingdom will be halted. Dreamer, presenting a more realistic and truthful image of yourself will gain you the respect and support you need to go forward in your endeavors, as well as, diminish the embarrassment that comes when the masquerade is over. God, and God alone is to be worship", for God has said, "I am the Lord: that is my name: and my glory will I not give to another" (Isaiah 42:8). If no abandonment of hypocrisy occurs, your choices will possibly lead you to be counted amongst those illustrated in Matthew 7:21 -23. Dreamer, is it wise to forfeit the eternality of heaven, for that which is an illusion of piety, especially after having been warned? Receive God's message in simple childlike faith, trusting that by it you will be saved (Matthew 18:3-5, 7-9). See suggested course of action. (b) To see a famous actor represents a person, personally known by the dreamer, who is hypocritical. If more than one actor, dreamer has surrounded yourself with persons who are very insincere, shallow, and vain; thus, like kind has attracted like kind. Nonetheless, their insincerity will cause feelings of resentment and rejection within the dreamer, resulting in an offense th at will be difficult to overcome. You are warned to investigate what you may be committing to with another(s), especially regarding legal commitments or any commitment involving you. Further, dreamer, do not invest your feelings too deep, lest you reap an emotional state that you will find it very hard to forgive. Read, understand, and embrace, Romans 2:1 -5, Matthew 6:12. See suggested course of action. (2) A dream of a famous person, other than an actor, points to the gist of their publicly known talents and/or other attributes. First, it is suggested that dreamer, journal the talents the celebrity is primarily k nown for, it will be within those talents, you will find what you need to, primarily focus on, concerning your gifting. Those tal ents and/or other qualities are inherent within the dreamer, and will begin to manifest publicly. The talents and/or other tra its attributed to the celebrity will begin to arise upon the stage of the dreamer's life, and appear, and be made public, for hon or or dishonor. Thus, dreamer is encourage to heed this dream, and perhaps privately prepare, physically, mentally, emotionally, and spiritually, for any positive talents or character attributes, via your dream, that will eventually be revealed and begin to arise within you, leading you to becoming a very public figure and prosperous. On the other hand, dreamer is counseled to deal privately with any negative traits that were exposed within your dream, before you are publicly exposed. Examples, a singer, while known for his or her great talent, may also be known publicly as a prima donna, or on another vein, for his or her great inspiration to others, as well as, their great commitment to love and family. A notable comedian, may not only be known for his or her comedic prowess, but may also be known publicly for his or her drug addiction and resultant downfall. A well - known public figure may be known for his or her "ethical" appearance on TV, but is also exposed as a sexual abuser of people. Further, the gist of one's biography may state that he or she is a charismatic leader, visionary, provocative thinker, and entrepreneur, but now, that same famous person is primarily known as mentally unstable, eccentric, or a con. A retired Superior Court Judge, and TV personality, frequently used his courtroom series to highlight his "troubled-youth-turned-success-story", as a way of motivating and inspiring youth. In sum and substance, he's known for his inspirational and positive messages to young people; highlighting that there's no adversity that they can't pick themselves up from and overcome. Another celebrity judge, known for her trademark wit and wisdom, is well known as a no-nonsense fact-finder, incisive decision-maker, and overall tough and strict adjudicator; highlighting a need for zero tolerance for foolishness. Nevertheless, it will be within the sum of the talents and qualities of the celebrity depicted within your dream, that you will find the meaning of your dream. Question to consider, what does the qualities of the celebrity have to do with you? It is the dreamer's prerogative to search out those qualities, and to consider how they relate to you, and deal with what is going to be exposed about you. See suggested course of action.

CLASSMATE (living and deceased):

This dream denotes that there is a life lesson, having been previously learned by the dreamer, which needs to be brought back to memory, revisited, and resuscitated. Dreamer will need to remember and journal, what endeared and linked you and your classmate(s) to each other. Particularly, the shared behavior during the year(s) you two were in school. You will also need to journal the actions that were highlighted within your dream. The shared behavior "back then", coupled with the actions highlighted within your dream, it will be within the sum of these attributes that you will find what your dream is revealing concerning the life lesson(s) needing to be remembered at this time in your life. It will be these same choices that the dre amer will need to focus on, namely what lesson you previously learned from embracing those attributes and/or activities, be it wise or naive behavior. For example, did you two (or group) encourage each other to, not quit but to continue and see projects or activities through to the end, which most times ended positively, or were you two (or group) "partners in crime", wit h your behavior mostly ending negatively, e.g. juvenile delinquency. Dreamer, the behaviors that stood out the most, that endeared and linked you two (or group) together did during that season in your life, and the resulting consequences of those choices. What life lessons did you learn from all of that at that time? What stands out the most in your memory, is what the dreamer is asked to bring to memory, and to utilize the lessons learned, in a pressing situation now within your life. See suggested co urse of action.

ELDERLY PERSON (senior citizens, aged, living and deceased):

This dream has two meanings (choose one). (1) If elderly person(s), within your dream, is actually known by the dreamer in your awaked life, this dream denotes that there is one, or some, who is before you, who is giving you advice, and/or is imparting some manner of knowledge to you; either, through counsel, teaching, or preaching. Dreamer is encouraged to heed their words, for they are giving you godly and wise counsel. With that, dreamer, God's wisdom is first pure, then peaceable, gentle, and easy to be entreated, full of mercy and good fruits, without partiality, and without hypocrisy (James 3:17). It is first pure, meaning unadulterated by worldly attitudes. Dreamer by comparing every word of counsel, and every thought, with the Word of God, this will give you a peace that only wisdom can afford. (2) If elderly person(s), within your dream, is not kn own, by the dreamer, this dream denotes that one, or some, who are before you, giving you advice; their counsel is not wise, their wisdom comes not from above, but is earthly, sensual, and devilish (James 3:15, 16). You are counseled not to heed their counsel or advice. Dreamer, when we lack the wisdom of God that we need for life's struggles, God's promise is this: But if any man (or woman) among you is without wisdom, let him or her make their request to God, who gives freely to all without an unkind word, and it will be given to him or her (James 1:5). Everyone has access to this wisdom, but we must first realize where it comes from, and acknowledge the source, that we might tap into this wisdom and obtain it, or we too, will be duped by worldly wisdom. If necessary, see suggested course of action.

FAMILY (biological, adopted, step, maternal and paternal, husband, wife, children, parents, grandparents, siblings, nephews, nieces, aunts, uncles, cousins, in-laws, and ex-spouse):

Unless otherwise noted elsewhere, living and deceased. Family generally denotes attributes, characteristics, and generational issues that are familiar, or "akin", to the dreamer. Dreamer, character traits from ancestors, namely genetic codes and trai ts, will often trouble and taunt the offspring of a given progenitor, especially generational issues (Exodus 20:5-7). These spirits attempt to "bend" the personality, as early as possible with regards to age, towards a certain direction, oftentimes towards a way that is desolate and wicked, for it is Satan's scheme to kill and make desolate all; thus, to keep some from rising up and leading their generation to Christ (see the birth of Moses, Exodus 1:15-2:10). Favorably, generational issues, especially if negative, can stop with you (Jeremiah 31:29, 30; Ezekiel 18:2-14, 20-23). Couple this with one of the following.

Aunt or Uncle (biological, adopted, in-law): This dream has two meanings (choose one). (1) If your aunt or uncle is actually alive, this dream denotes that the Lord your God has chosen you, the dreamer, out of all the peoples on the face of the earth to be His people, as His treasured possession. The Lord did not set His affection on you and choose you because you were better than other peoples, but it was because the Lord loved you and kept the oath He swore to your forefathers (Deuteronomy 7:1-8). Therefore, dreamer, choose this day, "this moment", whom you will serve. God has set before you this day, this moment, life and good, and death and evil. Thus, you are beckoned from this moment on to love the Lord your God, to walk in His ways, to embrace His commandments, statutes, and judgments, that you may live and multiply properly; and the Lord your God will bless you in your land. If you need only to believe that the Lord truly loves you, dreamer, you will begin to walk in His ways in obedience and on into His purpose for you. If necessary, see suggested course of action. (2) If aunt or uncle is actually no longer living, dreamer does not believe that he or she is one of God's beloved ones, nor do you believe that others genuinely love you. You call positive affirmations from others, especially when others express that they love you, you call this "fake"; and you call negative expressions, and most are imagined slights, meaning the discourteous acts are only in your head and not actual, you call this "real". Your beliefs are twisted; there is a measure of disorder in your belief system. Moreover, it is time for the dreamer to restrain or get yourself under control morally (also see 1 Corinthians 6:9, 10). By this, your views of yourself, God, and others will become clearer and realistic. Nonetheless, if you continue in your negative mindset, you will eventually walk away from the genuine love of God and others. If, in your heart you turn away so that you will not hear nor heed this dire warning, but be drawn away, and worship other gods, and serve them, it is denounced against you this day, this moment, you will not fare well. Dreamer, if it seems evil to you, for you to believe that the Lord and others genuinely love you, and if it seems evil to you to serve the Lord, choose for yourself this day, this moment, whom you will serve, and to not choose, is to choose evil (Deuteronomy 30:16-20, Joshua 24:15). Dreamer, don't allow the hurts and pains of life, and your naive and unwise choices, to cause you to miss the real thing that's facing you now. That real thing is Jesus. See suggested course of action.

Children, babies (children, grandchildren, great-grands, biological, adopted, step, in-law): First, if applicable, see subcategory, Daughter or Son. Other than that, this dream has three meanings (choose one). (1) To a literal parent or grandparent (biological, adopted, stepparent, in-law): Question, was the child hurting within your dream? This dream may reveal a physical condition or an emotional problem of a child. For example, a parent may find out within a dream that his o r her adult child is returning home sick. In the parent's dream, the parent realizes that their child has come home, looking smaller in stature, and emaciated, and is need of rest. Then suddenly the child is out of bed and regular size again. This denotes that the child will come home for rest and recuperation. Fortunately, according to the dream, the child recovers ful ly. On a more serious note, if you sense that your dream is about your child, dreamer, and that your child might be in dire need, per your dream; then you are to get involved immediately. This dream is a first step intervention and an alarm. Is your child in an abusive relationship? Is your child in a dangerous environment? Is someone too young to be pregnant? Is child abuse, molestation, or rape suspected? Have authorities been notified? Establishing a safe environment, alerting the law and other pertinent individuals is strongly recommended. Dreams that are about the safety of your children or grandchildren and the revelation within those dreams, are not given haphazardly. But only to those with the ability, and influence to, truly do something with the information. Jesus will strengthen you emotionally, psychologically, and physically to go get help. If you suspect child abuse, you must contact the appropriate authorities. Remove yourself and your children or grandchildren from the unsafe environment and contact the proper authorities immediately (e.g. police, child, and/or adult protective services). Dreamer, if you were abused as a child and now, you have placed your child or grandchild in harm's way, often the identical situation; feigning denial, go talk to God, and ask Him to help you emotionally and mentally, to do what it takes to keep your child safe, from the same violation. Allow the darkness of the violation to stop with you. Moreover, if you suspect that yo ur abuser is still harming others, please report it. You may also check with your local department of human services for reporting procedures. Medical, legal, and psychological intervention, are likely necessary. Children or grandchildren should never be left in abusive situations. Abuse of, or sex with, a child, teen, or incapacitated adult, is never justifiable; it is always wrong. Jesus says, it's better for you to sink to the bottom of the sea, tied to cement (Mark 9:42-48), than for anyone to perpetrate such acts against others. Molestation, rape, or any unwanted sexual activity or attention forced upon a child, teen, or even a psychological, physically weaker, incapacitated adult (consensual or not) is a sad reality, but it is not beyond God's ability to overcome. God can redeem and restore. We praise Him "who is able to do immeasurably more than all we ask or imagine, according to His power that is at work within us" (Ephesians 3:20). The "more than we can imagine" includes forgiveness and healing. Question, can you be forgiven if you have sexually abused a child? Yes[34]. God is gracious and merciful. No sin is beyond His ability to forgive (Romans 5:20). Jesus came to cleanse all sin: "Truly I tell you, people can be forgiven all th eir sins" (Mark 3:28). When you recognize your sin, acknowledge that it is evil, and then genuinely and deeply cry out to God for deliverance, with much fasting and prayer, He will hear you, forgive you, and sanctify you. Often, abusers have been abused themselves. In addition to God's forgiveness, you may require professional help and accountability support for, stopping certain behaviors, healing from past wounds, and seeking forgiveness from those, you have injured. See suggested course of action. (2) If dreamer is a literal parent or grandparent (biological, adopted, step-parent, in-law), dreams of your children, grandchildren, or babies in general, primarily highlight that part of your personality, reasoning, and behaviors that are spiritually immature, and possibly emotional and psychological immaturity is also apparent, due to severe violations, hurts, and/ or rejections, from early childhood until now. Moreover, children or grandchildren also point to a part of your personal ity that is identical to that literal child's personality at present. Dreamer, while your dream points to spiritual immaturity, it presupposes Jehovah's restoration of the dreamer; thus, you are being made aware that healing and wholeness is available right now, via prayer. Journal the actions and behavior of the child, this will point to a possible issue within you that hinders spiritual growth. For example, is your child, or grandchild, in your awaked life, a rebellious sort? What other particulars was highlighted? Dreamer, ask God for healing and freedom from past traumas that have hindered spiritual, emotional, and/or psychological maturity. Note, authentic freedom, and wholeness, come with responsibility. Your responsibility is to become self-aware, and to make an earnest effort to forgive those who violated, hurt, and/or rejected you. Dreamer, your violations, hurts, and/or rejections were demonically influenced, in an attempt to "bend" your personality, as early as possible, towards a certain direction, towards a way that is desolate and wicked. For it is Satan's scheme to kill and make desolate; thus, to keep you from fully experiencing a life fated you by God, a life of freedom and abundance, and to prevent you from raising up and leading your generation to Christ (see the birth of Moses, Exodus 1:15-2:10). Dreamer, your soul is buried underneath the pain of past violations, and this has distorted your reasoning. The pain of rejection, abuse, and/or other emotional and physical violations, of your past, has affected your "approach pattern" to all your relationships. Dreamer, when our hearts are painfully torn apart, broken, or troubled, God can take those disappointments, those trials and tragedies, and make them door of hope. For no, one has an experience to give to another until God has given them their own experience. Therefore, dreamer, question not, His absolute goodness in His dealings with you, but ask, what are you to glean from it. See the Lord's providence behind all the events in your life. Fortunately, your perspective on the nature of God is in the process of change and you will begin to experience a paradigm shift; this will cause you to view God differently. Not as a God of curses and blessings, but as a righteous and just God who is full of mercy and grace (the free and unmerited favor and beneficence of God), and healing will begin. Additionally, dreamer, as painful as this may hurt the question needs to be asked. How and when do you stop allowing the effects of your past violations to stop playing a significant part in your life? Dreamer, by faith, began to embrace and trust your reasoning, thoughts, and emotions to Jesus, that a very personal relationship with Him may emerge, and that healing and wholeness may begin. Consider this dream as God's faithfulness, loving kindness, mercy, and grace towards you. See suggested course of action. (3) Non-parent, this choice has two parts (choose one). (a) If child appeared to be yours, this dream denotes an innate ministry within the dreamer that needs to be initiated by the dreamer soon; this is your personal ministry(s), and your possibilities are endless. On another note, if child (depicted as yours) was in danger of possible los s of life, due to neglect or abuse, this dream is a dire warning to the dreamer; you are akin to the unprofitable servant referenced in Matthew 25:24-30. Did dreamer attempt to save the child's life? If so, you were trying to rectify the situation, as saving the child would be spiritually equivalent to you abandoning a wrong or evil course of life or conduct and choosing to follow a right one. If so, grace is extended for you to become expedient in the things the Lord has commissioned for you to do on this side of eternity that you may be considered a good and faithful servant when entering heaven. Nonetheless, dreamer, God knows your thoughts afar off, so genuinely repent. Take words to Jesus, "'I have sinned, and I have done wrong and acted wickedly". Other than prayer and heartfelt repentance to Jesus, no other excuse or weak justification will be heard. Moreover, ask Jesus for wisdom and for the courage to apply it. See suggested course of action. (b) If child belonged to another, this dream i s about another who may possibly need your help. Ask yourself, what would you do if a literal baby were in that condition depicted within your dream? For example, if you saw or sensed, someone so neglect or abused a baby or children to the point of possible loss of life, would you try to rectify the situation or save the child? Would you hide the incident? Would you call the police or other appropriate authorities? Would you handle the situation without involving the authorities? Would you take the baby? What were your actions within your dream? To determine the symbolic equivalents to responses: You trying to rectify the situation or saving the child would be spiritually equivalent to you mentoring and leading another to abandon a wrong or evil course of life or conduct, and to adopt a right one. You hiding the incident would be spiritually equivalen t to you feigning support or pretending that a ministry is something that it is not. Calling the police is figurative of intercessory prayer for a ministry. Taking the baby denotes taking over a ministry. Handling the situation without involving authori ties is equivalent to you attempting to get a ministry off the ground according to your own ideas, understanding, perspective, and reasoning abilities, without dependence upon God. Just observing is equivalent to doing nothing. Journal your answers, and then determine the ministry this dream is referring to, considering any new ministry you are involved with or you are trying to help get underway, and react appropriately. See suggested course of action.

Daughter or Daughter-in-law (biological, adopted, stepdaughter, in-law): This dream deals with a good, bad, or no longer living daughter, thus it has three meanings (choose one). (1) If dreamer considers your daughter a godly, and/or goodly, and wise daughter, one whom you are endeared, or if a daughter was depicted as behaving well in your dream, a good daughter is symbolic of fear of the Lord. Fear within this context is the practice of living life on God's terms in order to receive reward, meaning while hoping for some benefit from your efforts. You respect God but your love for Him is conditional. Dreamer, a tenacious faith in, and acceptance of, all of the Word of God, the good and the not so easily received, and prayer, will lead you into the deeper Light of His Love. Additionally, dreamer is encouraged to embark upon a ministry, and the focal point of your ministry should be geared towards empowerment, encouraging positive self-esteem, and/or or uplifting others in some way, particularly females. (2) If dreamer considers your daughter, a bad, evil, and/or foolish daughter, one whom you are not endeared, or if a daughter was depicted as behaving badly or naughtily in your dream. This child is a mirror reflection of you and your attitude towards others. The dreamer's actions or reactions to that child within your dream, denotes your convictions regarding this side of your personality and the effort you are willing to invest in yourself, and in your soul, to change. Nonetheless, a conscientious and diligent effort on the part of the dreamer to deal with your emotional fears and scars and some type of Christian counseling is needed at this time. See suggested course of action. (3) If daughter is deceased, see category, Death, Dying, and the Dead (Dead).

Son or Son-in-law (biological, adopted, stepson, in-law): This dream deals with a good, bad, or no longer living son, thus it has three meanings (choose one). (1) If dreamer considers your son, a godly, and/or goodly, and wise son, one whom you are endeared, or if a son was depicted as behaving well in your dream, a good son is symbolic of love of the Lord. Love within this context is the practice of living life on God's terms for no other reason or benefit than to be close to God, this is called holiness. God will raise you up and sit you amongst His people. You will receive the benefits of participating in a local church (community, support, proper ordination, honor, respect, edification, accountability, and proper burial). Moreover, visit and fellowship with those who are glad and sincere of heart. (2) If dreamer considers your son, a bad, evil, and/or foolish son, one whom you are not endeared, or if a son, was depicted as behaving badly or naughtily in your dream; this child is a mirror reflection of you and your attitude towards God, His authority, as well as, towards your spiritual leaders, and the people of God. The dreamer's actions or reactions to that child within your dream, denotes your convictions regarding this side of your personality and the effort you are willing to invest in yourself, and in your soul, to change. See suggested course of action. (3) If son is deceased, see category, Death, Dying, and the Dead (Dead).

Cousin (biological, adopted, in-law): This dream has two meanings (choose one). Question, does dreamer know the cousin depicted within your dream, in your awaked life? (1) If cousin is unknown, the dreamer is encouraged to consider the activities and/or behaviors that were highlighted within your dream. Journal those behaviors and/or activities, and consider how do they relate to you, and then somehow deal with what is being exposed about you. For, it is within the sum of the attributes journaled that you will discover what you are embracing. The behavior highlighted will begin to take prominence within your life, and be made public. Dreamer, what you do (or have done) in secret will begin to manifest publicly, for honor or dishonor. Thus, dreamer is encourage to heed this dream, and perhaps privately prepare, physically, mentally, and spiritually, for any positive or unwise character traits that may be made manifest publicly. Additionally, dreamer, be warned, because of an association (e.g. a friend, social, or business relationship, or some kind of connection with others), or some kind of union (e.g. engagement, or the state of being joined, united, or linked) with another. If necessary, see suggested course of action. (2) If cousin is actually known in your awaked life, dreamer, first, journal, two, or three very prominent attributes; in your opinion, that "stands-out" when you consider your cousin's person, couple this with the following. Dreamer, you have become linked to, and thus, have begun to embrace, certain attributes, attitudes, or activities that are primarily common to the cousin, within your dream; e.g. polite, sagacious, prudent, or partying, drug or alcohol abuse, foolhardiness, sexual perversion. The reason why dreamer has so easily embraced these attributes is because these attributes are akin to you, passed down within your family, the behaviors or activities are generational; thus like kind has attracted like kind. Nonetheless, it will be within the sum of the attributes journaled that you will discover what you are embracing. These character traits and/or activities will begin to take prominence within your life, and be made public. Dreamer, what you do (or have done) in secret will begin to manifest publicly, for honor or dishonor. Thus, dreamer is encourage to heed this dream, and perhaps privately prepare, physically, mentally, and spiritually, for any positive character traits that may be made manifest publicly for honoring, namely to bestow honor or rewards upon you. On the other hand, dreamer is counseled to deal privately with any negative character traits or activities that may be exposed, before you are publicly exposed and designated dishonorable. If necessary, see suggested course of action.

Nephew or Niece (biological, adopted, in-law): This dream denotes that a choice between wisdom and naiveté needs to be made regarding your lifestyle choices (e.g. spirituality, living conditions, prudence, and/or sexuality). Dreamer, wisdom, and folly advertise similar want ads. Both broadcast that they are deeply mysterious, meaningful, and fun. However, wisdom exalts God and leads to spiritual maturity and genuine joy, while folly cheapens and runs down life, bringing upon the head God's asperity and early death (also see Ecclesiastes 2:13, 1 Corinthians 6:12). The one, calls for open commitment, the other offers secret and illicit relations and a sensual, secular knowledge. Depending on your choice, wisdom or folly, the Lord or the angel of death, soon will visit you. Therefore, be observant and pray, thus, found by God, mindful of Him. Pray for truth a nd wisdom inwardly, and for the courage to apply it, God will grant wisdom. If, by just asking, you might get wisdom, one may suffer needlessly, because he or she will not ask Jesus for it. Ask Jesus as often as you need to, regarding all of your life choices start praying at least three time's daily, morning, afternoon, and evening (tithing God 10% of your day, via 2 hours and 40 minutes of pray and meditation on His Word, bible study, Joshua 1:8, 9). Again, petition God for the courage and sensibility to choose and apply His wisdom within your life, thereby averting God's asperity. By this, He will answer your most personal prayers, and cause others to fix, repair, and renew things around your living quarters. Moreover, seeing the blood, the angel of death will pass over you. If necessary, see suggested course of action.

Parents, progenitors (biological, adopted, step-parent, in-law, living and deceased): As "good" parents denote wisdom, understanding, and leadership, dreamer is counseled to give heed to their sayings; that your paths will be plain, and by taki ng, and holding fast to instruction, you will avoid stumbling, Proverbs 1:8,9. With that, also see one of the following.

Father (biological, adopted, stepfather, in-law, or one who reared, or took care of you as his child): This dream has four meanings (choose one). (1) If dreamer considers your father, a godly, and/ or goodly, and wise father, one whom you are endeared, and he is actually alive at the time of this dream. Dreamer, for a little while, you will be given access to very powerful and prophetic wisdom, use this wisdom to be a transformational and benevolent force, in o ther people's lives, and as charity begins at home, let your benevolence start with your father. It is necessary to say, the beginning of wisdom is the fear (deep respect and honor) of God, and to shun evil is understanding, (see Psalm 111:10, Proverbs 1:7, 4:7, 9:10). With that, dreamer, you will experience a very distinct moment of divine guidance, a "flash" of inspiration. An idea will pop into your head, apparently out of nowhere. It is an idea waiting to be developed. The prophetic wisdom, via inspired intellect, will allow you to create something, seemingly out of nothing. However, the process of investigating and understanding the implications of this "flash of inspiration", and how your inspiration should benefit yourself, family, and others, i s on you exclusively. This process is known as, "faith with works" (James 2:17-26). Dreamer, by examining the length and breadth of the inspired idea (aka doing the research), and establishing a thorough understanding of the concept, conclusions can be r eached. Conclusions such as, is there a market for your idea? Where is the market located? How should I market my idea? Do I need further education to learn about my idea? Are there investment resources, and so on? When your process is finally complete, an idea will be born and should be ready for market. This idea will prosper you greatly, and it should benefit people, greatly transforming lives. Seize the moment, and capitalize on it, while you have an open link to divine inspiration. Moreover, selflessness will serve as the vessel that contains all the insight you'll be receiving. An angel (perhaps disguised as human, or one, who is a true servant of God, with the Spirit of Truth within) will help lead the way. (2) If dreamer considers your f ather, a bad, evil, and/or foolish father, or an absentee father, one whom you are not endeared, and he is actually alive at the time of this dream. Dreamer, there are two types of leadership and wisdom, godly and worldly, or good and bad. This type of fa ther, within a dream, denotes secular, sensual, bad leadership and wisdom. Dreamer is caution against keeping bad company, those who adhere to worldly and/or bad wisdom. The way of evil men may seem pleasant but it is an evil way, and their way will end badly. Dreamer, if you love God and your soul, avoid the way of the wicked, bad, and evil people. Keep at a great distance; you can never be too far enough away from them and their ways. Dreamer, although, the saints will not be perfect until they reach heaven, the way of sin is as darkness. The way of the righteous is light; Christ is their Way, and He is the Light. The way of the wicked is dark, therefore dangerous; they fall into sin, and know not how to avoid it. They fall into trouble, but ne ver seek to know why God contends with them, nor what will be the end of their choices; this is their way, and you are counseled to shun or avoid this way, at all costs. Dreamer, attentively hearing the Word of God, is a good sign of the work of grace beginning in your heart. Moreover, there is in the Word of God a proper remedy for all the problems of your soul. Dreamer, keep your heart with all diligence, set a strict guard upon your choices, and keep yourself from doing hurt to people, and f rom getting hurt by avoiding trouble. Thus you will be enabled to put away a self-willed heart and perverse words; your eyes will be turned from beholding vanity, looking straight forward, and walking by the rule of God's word, treading in the steps of your Lord and Master. The Lord, will forgive your past, and enable you to follow Him more closely this second time. Read Proverbs 4:1-24. See suggested course of action. (3) Father is deceased: If endeared father, is actually no longer living, this dream denotes one, namely the dreamer, who is adhering to irrelevant and/or obsolete religious paradigms. Dreamer, you need a paradigm shift, a fundamental change in the basic concepts and practices of your leadership traditions and thinking. Your debates are over fundamentals that are no longer relevant or applicable to those you are leading. While God never changes, His word is contextually progressive. Therefore, dreamer needs to look again at your leadership traditions and your wisdom, and make the relevant changes to fit the context of this time and age. Dreamer, update, or the "shift" that's happening within those you are leading will happen without you, for you will, and can, be replaced. See suggested course of action. (4) Fat her is deceased: If dreamer considers your father, a bad, evil, and/or foolish father, or absentee father, one whom you are not endeared, and this person is actually no longer living. This dream denotes that the secular wisdom and bad leadership practices that the dreamer has adhered to is changing. Your way of thinking and operating, as you know it, is about to "come to an end". There will be major changes (significant in scope, extent, and effect) in your normal, everyday habits, and in y our way of operating, functioning, and thinking. The changes are a result of your prayers. You've asked God for a change; a change is coming. Pay close attention to shifts within your relationships with others and in your beliefs. Keep what is goo d, toss what is bad, know the difference, and understand God's hand within all your situations. Dreamer, resolve to vigorously to prevent being stuck in a negative and self-sabotaging mind-set for many years. Choose good deeds and habits that will lead to the fulfilment of your God given purpose. While it is easier said than done, it is necessary to say; one cannot grow or go forward stuck in the past. Do not lose today holding on to yesterday; let it go. See suggested course of action.

Grandparent(s), great-grands (paternal and material, grandfather, or grandmother, biological, adopted, step - grandparents, in-laws, or one who you consider a grandparent, great-grandparent, living or deceased): This dream has two meanings (choose one). (1) If dreamer is literally a religious leader (e.g. bishop, deacon, deaconess, elder, evangelist, m inister, overseer, pastor, pope, preacher, priest, rabbi, superintendent, teacher, or any cleric or ecclesiastical type role), this dream denotes that the dreamer is a respected spiritual leader, who is looked upon as a sagacious and understanding leader, and whose instructions, reproofs, and corrections are heeded. With that said, the following is necessary to say, dreamer, you too must heed instruction, as well as, reproof and correction from those who are considered your spiritual leaders. For your spiritual leaders love you, as you love those you are leading, thus, both, you, and your leaders, are embracing godly wisdom. Therefore, dreamer, heed the wisdom that is before you, via your spiritual leaders, that happiness may be your end. Moreover, continue desiring to embrace God wholly and to subdue your carnal nature, putting an end to (or con trolling) negative desires and passions, for religious purposes. It is counseled that you use (if not already doing) the principles of discipline and abstinence, via fasting, prayer, and/or reading and meditating on the Holy Bible in solitude, daily. Not for study only, or to fill your head with trivia, but that you might as a believer and a spiritual leader, observe to do according to w hat is written therein; and that you might understand the Word and have it in you when occasion calls for you to know th e Word. For the principles of discipline and abstinence, helps to control and put an end to ungodly desires and passions, and your occasion, your present situation, is calling for godly wisdom. He or she, who will humble them self shall be exalted. Additionally, read Proverbs 4:1-13. (2) Dreamer, do not entangle yourself with affairs, concerns, or situations, so much so that you become hindered, diverted, or drawn away, from your relationship with Jesus, and from the responsibilities of your Christian duties "your calling", because of them. As a Christian, you are a soldier of Jesus Christ; thus, you fight for His cause, and against His enemies, including your own lustful flesh. As a soldier in the army of God, you must be faithful to Him, and persevere in His cause and in your calling. So, avoid worldly entanglements, pray, consult God, and your spiritual leaders, deny self, endure hardness, be self-controlled, and be alert. If necessary, see suggested course of action.

Mother (biological, adopted, stepmother, in-law, or one who reared, or took care of, you as her child): This dream has four meanings (choose one). (1) If dreamer considers your mother, a godly, and/ or goodly, and wise mother, one whom you are endeared, and she is actually alive at the time of this dream. This dream was sent to encourage, as this dream denotes wisdom. As godly wisdom yields an abundance of fruit, and the dreamer is indeed embracing godly wisdom, it is accepted that the dreamer is endowed with the ability to apply your experiences, understanding, insight, common sense, and studious knowledge, prudently, to all situations that are presented before you. This dream also suggests that sophistication and formality is needed to be successful in your endeavor at hand, as wisdom and understanding is often embraced by clergy, judges, government officials; those in positions of authority, particularly with regards to promotion or sponsorship. Moreov er, this dream also refers to one who is abiding in the presence and secret place of the Father, and it refers to one, the dreamer, who is wholly beautiful, meaning spiritually and physically. Read Psalm 91, this is God's word to you. Additionally, the dreamer will be healed and cleansed in your personal life and/or ministry. (2) If dreamer considers your mother, a bad, evil, and/or foolish mother, or an absentee mother, one whom you are not endeared, and she is actually alive at the time of this dream. Dreamer, there are two types of wisdom, godly and good or worldly and bad. This type of mother, within a dream, denotes secular, sensual, bad wisdom. Dreamer, this is your time to rectify a major weakness, flaw, and/or defect in your understanding of spiritual things, and a time to repent; thus, this dream. Dreamer, you have a lack of understanding of the Word of God, to the point of peril. You are one who moves from place to place, church to church, ministry to ministry, witho ut a known destination and without purpose. As a result of wandering, you've lost (or is losing) the willingness and ability to listen, think, concentrate, speak, and/or write on the truths, principles, and precepts of God, in a coherent manner. Your reasoning is secular, sensual, and bad. Moreover, you've allowed others to trample upon the truths of th e Gospel taught you, to appear tolerant. So much so, that this has caused a confusion of mind. Your attitude of tolerance has now put you in the hands of cruel and wicked leaders, and amongst the nefarious rich. Those who are hostile towards the truth o f God's Word, who spread beliefs based on the premise that sensual desires are our primary concern. Their beliefs and doctrine are snares, hastening judgment and a shameful death. Read, understand, and embrace, Daniel 3:1-30, and have faith in God. Dreamer, where there is a lack of understanding of God's Nature, His Word, His intentions; and a lack of trust in the integrity of God and in His goodwill towards humankind, genuine godly truth can be, and often is, twisted. Thus, this dream highlights, and s uggests rectification of, chaos and waywardness within your life. The Lord can deliver you, if you would but, with bold faith, seek Him while He may be found, and call upon Him while He is near. Recognize and respect your time of visitation from the Lord, for it is upon you. See suggested course of action. (3) Mother is deceased: If endeared mother is actually no longer living, this dream denotes that the dreamer is adhering to irrelevant and/or obsolete paradigms. Namely spiritual fundamentals that are no longer relevant or applicable, especially to those you are guiding, if you are a spiritual leader of some sort. Fortunately, your way of thinking and operating spiritually, as you know it, is about to "come to an end". By way of this dream, the Cr eator is letting you know there will be a renewal within your mind, body, and soul; anticipate this. There will be a flash of insi ght, a sudden awareness, recognition, or realization of new ways of looking at spiritual ideals. This personal revival will reconnect and reunify, your intellect to your spirituality, as well as revive and restore faith and prayer within your life. Instead o f worshiping God primarily from the perspective of your head (intellect), namely from your own understanding, you will ag ain worship Him with your whole heart, mind, body, and soul. (4) Mother is deceased: If dreamer considers your mother, a bad, evil, and/or foolish mother, or absentee mother, one whom you are not endeared, and this person is actually no longer living. Two things (both may apply). (a) Dreamer, there is a major defect in a legal document, a plan, or a theory, which you are closely connected to, therefore, it is suggested that you closely review, read the fine print, and get a good understanding o f the big picture, and again closely review the fine details. (b) Dreamer, your negative way of understanding spiritual concepts, principles, and ideas, and the ungodly wisdom that you've adhered to in the past is changing, especially your way of reasonin g, which has only led to an imbalance mentally, as well as, depression, prayerlessness, and faithlessness. Your way of thinking and operating, as you know it, is about to "come to an end". With that said, dreamer, it is written, If you lack wisdom ask God for wisdom; and He will give you wisdom (James 1:5). For the Lord gives wisdom and from His mouth comes knowledge and understanding. Then you will understand what is right and just and fair, every good path. When wisdom enters your heart and knowledge becomes sweet to your soul, discretion will protect you, understanding will guard you, and His Truth will lead you. To deliver you from the ways of wickedness, and from demons whose words and ways are perverse, who causes you to walk in darkness gladly, whose paths are crooked and devious, causing you to leave straight paths (Proverbs 2:1-6, 9-15). This is one of God's covenant promises to you. Have faith in this. If necessary, see suggested course of action.

"Church Mother" (a title of respect and term of address for a senior clergywoman, who is a respected spiritual leader, and is looked upon as a sagacious and understanding leader, whose instructions, reproofs, and corrections are heeded). This dream is sent to encourage. Dreamer you are one who is skilled through long experience, in your functions of nourishing and protecting believers, via counseling, guidance, intercessory prayers, and fasting. You are one who voluntarily offers help or sympathy in times of trouble, one who demonstrates mercy, and truly loves his or her neighbor. You are the proverbial "Good Samaritan" (Luke 10:25-37). You have learned to handle much; therefore, much will be given you. You will live to testify of God's great love, everlasting kindness, and of His great faithfulness. With that, the following is necessary for you to hear, understand, and heed. This dream also denotes that it is time, if not already, for dreamer to start a ministry initiative. Including endeavors, aimed at a devotion to human welfare, and other humanitarian values. For, the dreamer has naturally been given big goals that involve building a better world and giving back to it what it has given you. Additionally, write y our vision down, that you may articulate it to others properly, for the vision will happen, suddenly and quickly. Prepare a good proposal, name your ministry, and write down all the details and specifics. Give it your best that it may be acceptable to a ny reputable financial entity, benefactor, or merit a grant of some kind. Perhaps, hire a grant writer. That which you will need to fulfill your aims, surely, you will have. Often, an individual starts his or her endeavors of service to the Kingdom of God without leadership or community support. Some examples of altruistic or "acts of kindness" services to others is to offer, without though of receiving anything in return, free medical services, and give charity to the poor, (see Ben Sira 29). Offer hospitality to strangers, help families bury their dead, via religious services, help with marriage ceremonies, and/or help a person make peace with his or her family member, fellow humankind, or their Maker.

Siblings (brother or sister, biological, adopted, stepsibling, in-law, or spiritual brothers and sisters): This dream denotes love, or it denotes conflict, disagreement, and/or hatred. Additionally, the dreamer's actions or reactions to your brother or sister within your dream, is a mirror reflection of your character. Couple this with one of the following (choose one). (1) If a loving, kind, peaceful, and/or amicable relationship was depicted between you and your sibling, God's power has made a way out of no way for you, and your state of affairs is turning around. Dreamer, there will be a relaxation or slackening of ten sion in your life. STOP, and feel the tension leaving! Those who have charged you falsely, with malicious intent, attacking your good name and reputation will be far from you. Others will become less hostile, as will you. You will be more relaxed, easygoing, and kind. The necessity to be reconciled with others than to always be in opposition has been resolved. Dreamer, you have simply taken the higher ground. You have re-evaluated your life, learned from your mistakes, found new directions in solving problems, pursued healing, sought out encouragement, and figured out what God would like you to change in order to, better fulfill His purpose. Moreover, you have learned the principles and Christian values that encourage one to reach out and touch others in a loving and graceful manner; ultimately finding yourself promoting the genuine cause of Christ and the good of others. (2) If dreamer was at odds with, in a disagreement with, or there was some manner of conflict with your sibling, or if you killed and/or hated your sibling, this type of dream denotes jealously, brokenness, and spiritual murder. Spiritual murder is a premeditated attempt to cruelly, destroy someone's reputation or an attempt to destroy someone's personal relationship with Christ, because of jealously. First, it is important to understand that conflict between you and your sibling(s), be it emotional or physical conflict; is not part of God's plan for your life. However, God can ultimately use t he situation to bring about His will. The following are a few principles that may be applied to a broken sibling relationship. You are to love your brother or sister in a way that reflects the agape love of Christ, see 1 John 4:7, 8. You are not to judge your brother or sister, but to show kindness, treating your sibling the way you want to be treated, see Ephesians 4:37-32, Luke 6:37-49. This means that you should not only respond gracefully in the face of your siblings' anger or accusations, but also go o ut of the way, "take the higher ground", to serve him or her. For, Jesus likens a close family relationship to the bond He shares with everyone who believes in Him. In fact, Jesus' bond with believers is even stronger, since it is not marred by jealousy, ange r, frustration, or disagreements. Thus, dreamer, you are instructed to live at peace with your family, avoiding arguments and conflict, and you are encouraged to take the higher ground by playing the role of peacemaker when disagreements arise within your family. See suggested course of action.

Spiritual Brothers and Sisters (aka Believers, Christians, Saints, those of "The Way"): Question, was there a peaceful or hostile relationship or environment depicted? (1) If peaceful, harmonious, and good relations were depicted between the brothers and/or sisters (aka believers, Christians, the saints) within Christianity, or the church. Read, understand, and embrace Psalm 133, for this is about you, and to you. Further, this part has three meanings (choose one). (a) Dreamer, God will rescue, or has rescued, you from a powerful enemy, one who is/was too strong for you. This person confronted you during a very hard time in your life, but the Lord was your support (2 Samuel 22: 17-25). A "hallelujah" is in order. That which has caused you much misery and/or severe affliction within your life, will now cease. Further, there will be a relaxation or slackening of tension in your life, stop, and feel the tension leaving. Those who have charged you falsely, with malicious intent, attacking your good name and reputation will be far from you. Others will become less hostile, as will you. You will be more relaxed, easygoing, and genial. The necessity to be reconciled with others than to always be in opposition has been resolved. Dreamer, you have simply taken the higher ground. You have re-evaluated your life, learned from your mistakes, found new directions in solving problems, pursued healing, sought out encouragement, and figured out what God would like you to change in order to, better fulfill His purpose. You have learned the principles and Christian values that encourage one to reach out and touch others in a loving and graceful manner; ultimately finding yourself promoting the genuine cause of Christ and the good of others. Moreover, spiritually mature, you are a very peaceful and poised individual; now, prepared, you will be honored publicly. (b) The dreamer has the capacity to spearhead a new dawn, giving birth to a new generation that will usher in an age of mass revivals, with primary emphasis on a personal and saving relationship with Christ Jesus. That you might fulfil your purpose, a profound and insightful wisdom, previously unknown to you, will begin to emerge from deep within you, as well as, new emotions, and other nice results, will come forth. Now, you will begin to experience a miraculous increase in divine knowledge, and wisdom. This knowledge and wisdom will be imparted to you to be used exclusively for interpreting the gospel of Jesus Christ to others, and for the edifying of the Body of Christ; the body of believers. Your optimistic and generous personality, coupled with your strong desire to uplift humanity is leading you into situations where you will be able to expr ess your desire to serve others. You will be provided with the resources to carry out your vision, and will become established, expect this. This dream also confirms that you're in order for heaven. (c) If dreamer is actually considered a spiritual o r religious leader, e.g. bishop, deacon, deaconess, elder, evangelist, minister, overseer, pastor, pope, preacher, priest, rabbi, superintendent, teacher, or any cleric or ecclesiastical leader type role. Dreamer, your dream denotes that the dreamer's ministry will begin to flow within the realm of miraculous phenomena. Demons will submit to you in Jesus' name. For you have been anointed, and given high authority, to overcome all the powers and schemes of the enemy, nothing will harm you. If demonic possession is the case, it should be noted, exorcism (commanding demons and all unclean spirits to leave a person in the name of Jesus the Christ) was practiced by the disciples as part of Christ's instructions, see Matthew 10, Mark 9:38, Luke 11:18, 19, Acts 16, 19:11-16. Dreamer, you will need to "exorcise" the demon out of others and pray for them to be filled with the Holy Spirit, thus preventing the demon from re-entering them later (Matthew 12:43-45). However, do not rejoice that demonic spirits submit to you, but rejoice that your name is written in heaven. Even more, those who will listen to you will also listen to Jesus; those who reject you will also reject Jesus. Moreover, dreamer, you are anointed to become a healer, a nd will begin to sense the healing power of God within your hands. You will begin to sense a feeling of heat within your hands, and have probably experience this once or twice before, when you've prayed for another. Nonetheless, you have authority in Jesus name, your heavenly Father watches over you, and you have His ear. (2) If hostile, unharmonious, and bad relations were depicted between the brothers and/or sisters (aka believers, Christians, the saints) within Christianity, or the church. Dreamer, all of your morally objectionable behavior, namely in the area dealing with the deeds of the flesh; examples of deeds of the flesh are dishonesty, adultery, sensuality, hostility, feuding, vendettas, grudges, unfriendliness, strife, jealousy, outbursts of anger, disputes, dissensions, discord, factions, cliques, envying, drunkenness, carousing, idolatry, or any traits of these sorts (see 1 Corinthians 6:8-11). This also includes a possible belief in, and/or practice of, necromancy. It is beneath this kind of negativity, your disobedient spirit, bad character, and unwise choices, choices that clearly lack forethought; that your soul is suffering, and consequent, your self-imposed alienation, depression, homelessness, aimlessness, and/or some other crisis within. Dreamer, whenever your collective actions, and soul, grow heavy from sinful pursuits, this creates a breach deep within your soul, and you begin to view good and peaceful relationships, especially those of the Body of Christ from a very negative space. You start to call positive affirmations from others, especially when others express that they love you, you call this "fake"; and you call negative expressions, and most are imagined slights, meaning the discourteous acts are only in your head and not actual, you call this "real". Your beliefs are twisted; there is a measure of disorder in your belief system. When you are in denial, embracing anger, dishonesty, sacrilege, and other depravity, and the consequences of your behaviors began to tear your life apart, and your world implodes. When your tears fall hopelessly to the grou nd and disappear beneath the sullenness of your conscience, and all around you is nothing but desolation and barrenness, there is yet redeeming grace, the re is still hope for you. Dreamer, yes, evilness is punished, but favorably, God is slow to anger; and because of His amazing grace, mercy, and compassion, there is still yet a grace waiting for you, to lay hold of and to embrace. Your dream is a sign that the Creator is awakening inside of you the need for self-contemplation and change. And this change solely depends on you, starting now. Dreamer, taking ownership of what your warning dream is revealing to you about you, and working from that point, via prayer, fasting, earnest and diligent self-examination. Also including, persistent practice of truthfulness, and in embracing the fruits of the spirit (see Galatians 5:22-26), and respecting candid support from family and friends, and Christian counseling, all this will help truth inwardly begin to emerge; at a pace, you'll be able to "wrap your mind around" comfortably. This followed by appropriate application of wisdom, can conceivably avert self-deception and denial, and the repercussions thereof. Dreamer you shall love the Lord your God with all your heart, soul and might. Read, understand, and embrace Deuteronomy 6:4-9, this is to you. For, Jesus likens a congenial relationship to the bond He shares with everyone who believes in Him. See suggested course of action.

Spouse or Ex-spouse (husband or wife): This dream has two meanings (choose one). (1) Husband or Ex-husband: This choice has three parts (choose one). (a) If dreamer is a still with your husband, at present, this dream refers to intimate human love between a husband and wife. Dreamer, your husband is beckoning you to come to him. Absence of intimacy, spiritual fecundity, passion, romance, sexual love, adventure, and other aspects of human love, and/or separation, makes will power weak and temptation strong. See also 1 Corinthians 7:3-5, 33, 34. Moreover, if no children and children are desired, dreamer, heeding your spouse's gestures of love, will cause your marriage to merit children, born of you and your spouse's strength. (b) If there were, in any way, accusations, fighting, struggling, violence, conflict, contestation, or dispute, within your dream, with your present husband. This dream denotes that the dreamer has authoritative and submissiveness issues, as well, you are expressing behaviors that are not pleasing to God, nor to your husband. Dreamer, you are too angry, and too strong. Your actions are that of a woman desirous of changing sexes. The Lord your God forbids the confusing of the relationships of the sexes, women must not be virile, or very domineering, as to usurp authority over a male who has authority over you (e.g. husband, father, pastor, or male supervisor), nor must men be effeminate or figuratively emasculated by a female. Dreamer, as disobedience in small matters shows great contempt of God's principles, so obedience in small matters shows a very great regard for them. Daughter, obey him that has rule over you, namely your husband. Like Sarah, who obeyed Abraham, you are her daughter if you do what is right and do not give way to fear. Hence, read, understand, and embrace 1 Peter 3:1-6. Notwithstanding, dreamer, if you do not gain control over your antagonistic and domineering attitude, standing before the Lord improperly, you will begin to experience a loss of glory (glory in this sense is divine admiration, praise, prosperity, succe ss, triumph, and/or respect of your husband and of others) within your life. Dreamer, heeding the message of your dream and earnestly dealing with your authority and anger issues, via prayer and fasting, by this your expression towards God and other s, will begin to soften. See suggested course of action. (c) Ex-husband: Dreamer, noticeably conflicted, you no longer know who and what you truly believe in. God has not changed, you have. Unconsciously, you will not allow yourself to get close enoug h to share love, trust, and intimacy qualitatively with Jesus, nor with others. Having trusted in oppression so long, you are ensnared by your own words, and having closed your mind to spiritual realities that bring genuine calmness, composure, contentment, mellowness, peacefulness, and tranquility, you have lost your spiritual identity. Dreamer, if you continue in this emotional upheaval, you will miss the real thing, namely an authentic relationship, once it comes along. Dreamer, when one genuinely return to God, in complete surrender and humility, your deliberate transgressions become like actual merits (Luke 7:37-50). Because, the realization of your distance from God, due to your transgressions (Isaiah 59:2), becomes the motivating force to return to God with a passion even greater than that of someone who has never sinned in such a manner (or never left the Father's house, Acts 9:1-30). Completely converting your present to good, effecting restoration, transformation and a miraculous healing, this is the secret of repentance, returning to God, and serenity. Go; therefore now, and seek the Lord Jesus, repent and place your hope in Him. Hope, placed in Him, will not deceive. See suggested course of action. (2) Wife or Ex-wife: This choice has three parts (choose one). (a) If dreamer is a still with your wife, at present, this dream denotes that the wherewithal needed by the dreamer, to create, nourish, and enhance all facets of your life, is available to you. All tha t you need, to take something from the state of potential, develop it, and bring it to actualization through creative abilities, and to accomplish your goals, is within you and your wife's reach, but only working as a team. Dreamer, all the blessings a husband receives is connected to the worth of his wife. For there is no blessing in one's home without the wife's honor. When a husband honors and loves his wife, he is handling his primary responsibility of maintaining peace, spiritually and naturally. The worth of a man is largely dependent on how he treats his wife, not just in public but also behind closed doors. This is honorable in the eyes of God. Then blessings come. The benefits of honoring your wife will begin to manifest even more within your life starting now (Proverbs 12:14, 18:20). Dreamer, the benefits of honorable choices are, but not limited to, the dreamer will be successful in your endeavors, especially after practical planning and effort. Dreamer, receive the affirmati on, validation, and encouragement your dream is meant to impart. (b) If there were, in any way, fighting, struggling, violence, conflict, contestation, dispute, accusations, within your dream, with your present wife. Dreamer, since it is the very shortcomings and imperfections of your wife that allow you to grow into something larger than yourself; you will come to discover that it is precisely those dimensions of your wife, that challenges you to transcend your ego and become the person you are capable of becoming. Thus, your wife is the perfect candidate to refine and sublimate the crudeness within you, and restore you to your innate spiritual potential. Therefore, dreamer is counseled to heed the advice of your wife, namely, regarding a pressing situation that is before you at present. Although your wife is standing "toe to toe" with you, she is acting in the spirit of a prophetess that you might rise to the level your acumen deem you should be. The ordeal you think will destroy you, the current darkness and gloom that surrounds you at present, is intended to elevate you; causing you to stand up and become an anointed and powerful force within the Kingdom of God. Thus, God is using your wife as "helpmate" and prophetess to support you standing up and becoming that powerful force within the Kingdom of God, b y any right means necessary. Dreamer, your adversity, and contention are affecting a dependable, faithful, loyal, reliable, responsible, resourceful, upright, and upstanding spirit within you, and within your wife. Therefore, listen to your wife. Do not be confused, you will not be made ashamed. It is, understood on high that at present you don't feel elevated while going throug h your making season. Yet, this is when you can expect God to come and show Himself strong on your behalf. Additionally, the husband is ultimately responsible for his wife's happiness and hence the husband is primarily responsible for peace within your marriage. The husband needs to initiate the giving, especially when it comes to giving honor, for there is no blessing in on e's home without the wife's honor. All the blessings a husband receives are in the merit of his wife. When a husband honors and loves his wife, she will respond in kind, and the frustration and tension will dissolve, especially when she senses, and sees consistent, deep-rooted changes in you. Dreamer, the following are some examples of attitudes and behaviors that do not honor your wife, nor promote peace within a marriage, dreamer, you may have never cussed your wife, but every time you've been very critical of every penny your wife spends, and every time you've been overly stingy and tight with money that was a form of cruelty. Every time you don't give her your full attention or been abrupt when she spoke or asked for your help, tha t was harshness. Once you begin to look within, you may begin to see a husband who is generous with his time, attention, and money with everyone who needs you, except for your wife. Consequently, seeking honor and recognition from outside your marriage, sometimes even from strangers, while simultaneously ignoring your wife's needs. This is also cruelty. Perhaps these actions seem like common flaws, but it is suggested that you stop blaming your wife and start looking inwardly. You will beg in to see how responsible you are for the conflict, contestation, dispute, or accusations within your marriage, and how so much of her misbehavior and complaining are, simply a response to your complete misunderstanding of what she needs from you. With that said, dreamer; needs to give honor to your wife. See suggested course of action. (c) Unmarried male, your wife is before you, for this dream signifies a marriage. Moreover, in several months, you will go through a remarkable transformatio n. Your view on marital and family dynamics will change. You will truly regret the pain you've caused others, especially family members and significant others, when you begin to understand that the problems within your life have all stemmed from your flawed thinking and lack of knowledge. Further, you will no longer doubt the ability of people to change, no matter how low they have fallen. Therefore, dreamer, become deeply grateful to the Almighty God, for giving you the challenges you needed to bring you to the person you are becoming, and begin putting forth a personal and sincere effort to change. Once you do, you will feel God guiding you to be the best person, husband, and family man you can be. Additionally, this is necessary to say, to a potential husband of the covenant of marriage. Dreamer, when you receive your wife, on your wedding day, veiled and then unveiled, you are saying that you will love, cherish, and respect not only the 'her', which was revealed to you, but als o those elements of her personality that are hidden or "veiled" from you. Moreover, as you are bound to her in marriage, you are committing to creating a space within yourself for her, for all time; remembrance of this has the power to bathe your marriage in the loving light of God's presence. If necessary, see suggested course of action.

FRIENDS, GIRLFRIEND, OR BOYFRIEND (or someone who was depicted as friendly, unless otherwise noted, living and deceased):

This dream denotes one who is set aside for the priesthood. Dreamer, you are being prepared to carry out th e official role, position, or office of a priest (e.g. prophet, pastor, minister, or some type of a very visible cleric). With this office co mes spiritual growth and divine illumination, if you have genuinely sought after truth, truth will continue to be revealed to you and lead and guide you. With that said, the following is necessary to say. First, your priestly promotion is predicated upon your understanding of, and continued obedience to, God's directives over your life. Second, pray to God for divi ne truth, for one should never exalt his or her thoughts, ideas, feelings, or emotions, above God's truth, for, every house is built by someone, but the builder of all things is God (Hebrews 3:2-4). Further, chosen, you are to show forth the praises of Him who has called you out of darkness into His marvelous light (see 1 Peter 2:9, 10). Continue to allow the Paraclete to complete the work of purification and sanctification within you. For those who go forth in tears, shall return rejoicing (Psalm 126:5, 6). Be diligent and patient, everything will be done proper, and in its own time; you will be ordained to a priestly office, and if relevant, your request in another area of your life will be granted. Again, your height of spiritual progress and promoti on will be according to your faith and obedience to God's will over your life personally. See suggested course of action.

Ex-friends, Ex-girlfriend, Ex-boyfriend, or Enemy (or someone who was depicted as an ex, or unfriendly, or as an enemy): This dream comes as a rebuke. Dreamer, you live in excess, mischievousness, and unruliness, to the point of recklessness; and not only that, but you also blame your lack of commitment, sagacious choices, and stewardship on others. I f you are Christian, you also blame your lack of relationship with Christ, faithfulness, and/or anointing on others. Moreover, dreamer, you are harmful to those about you; trampling on those you consider less than yourself, taking advantage of their spiritual and natural poverty, necessity, and inability to help themselves, making them poorer and needier than they were before connecting with you, while you give nothing in return (especially in the form of service). You are an enemy to God's people; therefore, God will become your enemy. With that said, it is suggested that dreamer begin to embrace the direct Word of God imparted to us through the words of others, such as a preacher in a worship service, a Sunday school teacher, and other bible studies, so that by it you may grow up in your salvation and mature emotionally. Read Luke 6:27-49. See suggested course of action.

MODELS OR MANNEQUINS (persons who wear clothes to display fashions, or one who poses for a photographer, painter, or sculptor):

This dream has two meanings (choose one). (1) If dreamer was a model or mannequin, dreamer will serve as a role model to females (if female models were depicted) or to males (if male models were depicted within your dream), or to both, to teach the proper way to conduct oneself righteously. Do not hide but reveal your righteousness for the sake of women or men within your sphere of influence. (2) If dreamer saw models or mannequins, dreamer will be taught the deeper things of God from one of His preferred or model teachers. Remain under their tutelage and never discredit their appointment as a teacher sent to you. A wise man or woman will increase their learning; the unwise and foolish is opposite. If necessary, see suggested course of action.

NEIGHBOR OR NEIGHBORHOOD (a literal neighbor, or if one was depicted as a neighbor, unless otherwise noted, living and deceased):

This dream has two meanings (choose one). (1) To dream of a neighbor or neighborhood, dreamer you have been found by God, willing and obedient to Him and to His cause. Because of this, you will recover all that was lost because of your youth and/or bad, unwise, and foolish decisions and choices (e.g. family, fertility, finances, friends, health, honor, job, respect, or reputation). Question to journal: what have you lost, and desire God to rectify or restore? The righteous desires of your heart will now begin to manifest within your life. You will receive double, and you will live your life more peaceful and abundant than before and to its fullest, financially, happiness, love, and respect. If illness is a concern at present, you will recover from this, and live; all this because of your sense of duty and respect to others. You are one who voluntarily offers help and empathy, in times of trouble, one who demonstrates mercy, and truly loves his or her neighbor. You are the proverbial "Good Samaritan" (Luke 10:25-37). You have learned to handle much; therefore, much will be given you. You will live to testify of God's great love, everlasting kindness, and of His great faithfulness. (2) To dream of a neighborhood from your past, e.g. childhood, see category, Numbers (Past).

PARABLES OF PEOPLE (a parable is any short moral story, to convey a religious message):

and he took up a parable... "I will open my mouth in a parable; I will utter dark sayings from of old" (Psalm 78:2). Thus, the Holy Spirit has given us parables. Dreamer, an open and receptive heart is necessary for hearing and for better understandin g the parables, for they reveal the psychological, emotional, and spiritual root of problems and convey a religious message, giving spiritual insight, because while seeing you do not see and while hearing you do not hear, nor do you understand. Thus, Jesus uses parables to lead your mind towards heavenly concepts, and spiritual order. That the parable might help you understand what Jesus wants you to focus on; the image borrowed from the visible world is accompanied by a truth from the invisible (spiritual) world, they shed a unique light on the work of the Holy Spirit within your life. Although, the following parables seem simple, the messages they convey are deep, and central to the leading and guiding of the Paraclete. Question to journal, what lesson are you to learn from the parable. The dreamer is encouraged to seek biblical guidelines for recognizing the symbolic meaning of the parable depicted within your dream. See also, other relevant research to determine the metaphorical meaning of your particular parable, via a Bible concordance, Bible illustrated dictionary, encyclopedia, or internet. Having done your research you should be able to determine some basic truths your Lord and Savior wants you to focus on. While there are many parables, the following are just a few; again, dreamer is encouraged to seek biblical guidelines for your particular parable. A few parables are as such, the prophet Nathan, for instance, told the famous parable of the ri ch man's theft of the poor man's sheep, see 2 Samuel 12:1-15. The parable of two builders, see Matthew 7:24-27, Luke 6:47-49. The parable of the children in the marketplace, see

Matthew 11:16-20, Luke 7:31-35. The parable of a rich man and an unfaithful steward, see Matthew 18:23-35, Luke 16:1-18. The parable of the agreed wages of the vineyard workers, see Matthew 20:1-16. The parable of two sons, see Matthew 21:28-32. The parable of the wicked tenants who abused and slew the property superintendents, see Matthew 21:33-46. The parable of the ten virgins, see Matthew 25:1-13. The parable of a moneylender and two debtors, see Luke 7:41-50. The parable of the Good Samaritan, see Luke 10:25-37. The parable of a friend in need asking a neighbor for support, see Luke 11:5-13. The parable of the arrogant guest, see Luke 14:7-14. The parable of a king preparing for war, see Luke 14:31-33. The parable of the rich man and Lazarus, the beggar, see Luke 16:19-31. The parable of a judge and a widow pleading for justice, see Luke 18:1-8. The parable of those who think they are righteous, see Luke 18:9-14, et.al. See suggested course of action.

SOLDIERS OR BRANCHES OF THE ARMED FORCES:

Read, understand, and embrace Ephesians 6:10-17. With that, this dream has two meanings (choose one). (1) Soldier(s): First, as soldier(s) are frequently demonstrated in many, and very personal ways; for example, does a particular soldier remind you of a particular person, place, or situation? Thus, could a soldier be a possible probable, see Note (2) of this category. Hence, dreamer may also consider your own personal and special associations with soldiers and/or soldiering. Other than that, this dream denotes one, namely the dreamer, whose mission is to serve, via some manner of guidance and/or protection. You will show up to protect and defend those who obediently love God, and who is loved by God. You will be dispatched on missions, to help believers who are facing urgent needs during a crisis, and/or in an emergency, and to give instant help. Y our mission, behavior, and words, will be prophetic, usually beneficent, and sometimes punitive, depending on the nature of your mission. Dreamer, you are a solider of God, and your primary concern is to be a champion of the cause of Christ, to protect, spread truth, advocate integrity, build courage, and to help strengthen, as well as, to encourage the recipients to express God's loving kindness, His grace, mercy, and compassion, to others. With that said, dreamer, altruistic, goodhearted, and generous service to God and others is beneficial at this time. Some examples of altruistic service or "acts of kindness" to others are, provide a child with necessities, such as food, clothing, shelter, toys, medical equipment. Visit the sick, provide free med ical services, and give charity to the poor, (see Ben Sira 29). Offer hospitality to strangers, help families bury their dead, via religious services, help with marriage ceremonies, and/or help a person make peace with his or her family member, fellow humankind, or their Maker. Provide free roadside assistance and emergency mechanical help, or freely help with structural problems in private homes. All of these, and more, are examples of acts of service. Moreover, often an individual starts th e initiative of service without leadership or community support. Thus, God will give you the necessary tools, courage, strength, and wherewithal, to do it. Dreamer, love God so completely that you will never forsake His service for any reason. (2) Branches of the Armed Forces: Air Force, Army, Coast Guard, Marine, and Navy: To dream you joined (or was signing up to join) one of the branches of the US Armed forces. [37]The U.S. Armed Forces are made up of five armed service branches: Air Force, Army, Coast Guard, Marine, and Navy. The five primary branches of the Armed Forces operate in four fields of operations, sea, land, air, and space. While each branch operates in more than one field of operation, this reference will d eal with the primary field of operation for each, according to their badge. Question to journal, which branch was highlighted within your dream? With that, consider one of the following:

All Branches: United States Special Operations (SOF, those component forces of the military services specifically organized, trained, and equipped to conduct and support special operations, e.g. Navy SEAL, Green Beret, et.al.): To dream you are part of a military special operations team. This dream denotes that the dreamer, who is, or will be, introduced secr etly into a pseudo religious group, deep undercover. The purpose for this mission undercover, is for dreamer to stealthily learn the mentality, and mechanics, of the group beliefs, that you, might know how to, strategically introduce the mentality of Christ within the group, with hopes of saving some of its members from eternal damnation. Note, do not reveal your religious beliefs. Begin noting all erroneous beliefs within this group. Any beliefs that contradict the inspired word of God, includ ing His provision for humankind to be save; namely belief and faith in Jesus Christ as Savior, God incarnate, and their beliefs on grace without works. Then, after a long while, wisely and cautiously begin pointing out the errors of the group's belief system to certain others you are led to, by Holy Spirit. Do not be afraid of their status, words, or any other characteristic, that might be intimidating. Stay focus and remember your mission.

Air and Space (Air Force): Now, you will begin to experience a miraculous increase in divine knowledge, and wisdom. This knowledge and wisdom will be imparted to you to be used exclusively for interpreting the gospel of Jesus Christ to others, and for the edifying of the Body of Christ; the body of believers. Dreamer, you are one who is (or will be) a highly esteeme d ruler. Chosen from birth, you have (or should have) stepped into your destiny. Your spiritual strength, tenacity, knowledge, and voice will be used as instruments of God; penetrating the soul of those who listen, affecting conversion. You will appoint times for rejoicing, and declare sacred assemblies, asserting that no one work, and these days will be a memorial before God. You will appoint fellowship offerings. You will also oversee great ceremonies for great men of God. Your voice will be used as an instrument of righteousness; coming against those who would attempt to oppress you and others. Your words will cause enemies to turn on themselves. By all this, you will be remembered by the Lord your God and rescued from your enemies. You are called to a high calling; withdraw not your hand when that day is officially upon you. He will send angels, soldiers of the armies of the Lord, to rescue you out of extremely severe situations, because of your faith. Warning, if you "morph" into something wicked, your headship will be taken violently and dishonorably away from you, and given to another, one more powerful than yourself (1 Samuel 15:22-16:1).

Land (Army, Marine): This dream denotes one, the dreamer, whose calling is to give sermons, spread the gospel, and conduct religious services, a cleric of some kind (e.g. bishop, evangelist, minister, missionary, parson, pastor, preacher, priest, rabbi, teacher). A large part of your mission should center on you raising the spirits of your fellow mankind, and establish ing yourself as an inspirational person spreading hope. Your gift is to inspire and motivate. He will send angels, soldiers of the armies of the Lord, to rescue you out of extremely severe situations, because of your faith.

Sea (Navy, Coast Guard): This dream comes as a reminder. God is sending you to all nations and kinds of people; and you are asked to make disciples of all nations, see Matthew 28:18-20. You are to put on the armor of God that you might be ready at all times with everything you need. Read, understand, and embrace, Ephesians 6:10-18, for this is to you now. This is especially important that you might be ready to fend off the opposition from demonic forces who don't want to see people saved by the gospel of Christ. Not only must you be prepared to fight opposition; you must also know the people group you are ministering to, understanding, especially psychologically, the lost condition of the people around you, will help you understand them that you might make good, strong, and consistent disciples. You will skillfully help develop minds at searching out truth, train disciples, refresh many spiritually, and encourage others to faithfully join religious organizatio ns (e.g. churches, Christian colleges, Christian and faith based support groups) for mutual help and support in building close relationships with other brothers and sisters in Christ, and with close significant others as well. Prayer and the presentin g of the unadulterated gospel of Jesus Christ are essential. Although, to those who are perishing, the message of the cross is foolishness, to you, it is the power of God (1 Corinthians 1:18); thus, be encourage, with Jesus before you, you will be able to penetrate the darkest of minds for the Kingdom of God. Be strong soldier. He will send angels, soldiers of the armies of the Lord, to rescue you out of extremely severe situations, because of your faith.

SPIRITUAL OR RELIGIOUS LEADERS (e.g. bishop, deacon, deaconess, elder, evangelist, minister, overseer, pastor, pope, preacher, priest, rabbi, superintendent, teacher, or any cleric or ecclesiastical leader type role), unless otherwise noted, living and deceased:

This dream has two meanings (choose one). (1) Primarily, spiritual and religious leaders symbolize a unique leadership quality within you, namely the title held by the particular leader depicted within your dream. Hence, this dream denotes one, the dreamer, whose calling is to give sermons, spread the gospel, and conduct religious services and observances. A larg e part of your mission should center on you raising the spirits of your fellow mankind; establishing yourself as an inspirational perso n spreading hope. Your gift is to inspire and motivate. Dreamer, you are that spiritual leader and you're on the right track, pursuing, growing, and going towards your purpose God has destined for you. Dreamer, patiently and contentedly continue on the track you are on, you will get there. For, you are purposed to do whatever that cleric is "ordained and titled" to do (e.g. builder, laying-on-of-hands for divine healing, preaching, teaching, or perhaps as an exorcist, casting out demons). The dreamer, already chosen and approved by God, will be, in the near future, if not already, approved by man, to be set aside an d ordained as a ministerial leader. You have been found of good reputation, full of the Spirit, and wise. You will be officially ordained. Dreamer, the way the ordination will be carried out may not be to your liking; nonetheless, do not attribute (or c all) that which is of God, unclean (e.g. confusion, erroneous, out of order, unlawful, weak, wicked, or any other attributes of th e unregenerate). Do not consider your ordination as unofficial or a small thing, for it is of God and His kindness towards you. (2) Dreamer if that cleric actually has a dishonorable reputation on any level, in any matter, small or large, or some deceptive, delusory, fraudulent, misleading, unethical, or abominable behavior was depicted within your dream by that person. Those negative traits are within the dreamer, and if not dealt with and brought into submission, you too will be known as a dishonorable cleric, and find yourself also disgracing the Name of Jesus and the church. Thus, if you've gotten off track, meaning, you are, at present, engage in behaviors that do not affect clarity, wholeness, and godliness within the life of a believer. You are to consider this dream a warning. Dreamer, begin again embracing your first acts of love and obedience towards Christ and His cause. See suggested course of action.

YOU, THE DREAMER:

This dream has three meanings (choose one). (1) If this meaning is chosen, the dreamer is already aware that you have the following ability. The dreamer has the ability to remove yourself from situations, emotionally and mentally, while actually being physically present. You hide within yourself. While this ability has proven advantageous in some situations, where th e state of things, circumstances, affairs, were too overwhelming for the dreamer to handle emotionally. This same ability has kept you from becoming emotionally vested, fully, in the people and things of God. Dreamer, you must, now, somehow learn how to transition into actually "being present", emotionally and mentally, and to begin to "touch" your life activities, as well as, to "touch" the lives of the people you are sent to minister to, via your ministry. Dreamer is encourage to earnestly desire, to learn how to "touch" love, and know it, in all of its forms (e.g. agape, philia, storge, and eros), without twisting its meanings or distorting its purposes. Dreamer, read, understand, and embrace, 1 Corinthians 9:19-23; that perhaps like Paul, via "touching lives", you might become able to feel what others are feeling, and empathically use their own feelings, conscience, beliefs, and ways and means, to minister the truth of your Lord and Savior Jesus, Christ to them. This transition will deepen your understanding of the love of Christ for His people. See suggested course of action. (2) This dream was sent to affect self- awareness, and possibly wholeness, never experienced, within the life of the dreamer. This dream alludes to how the dreamer perceives him or herself, how God perceives you, and/or how others perceive you. A dream of you, meeting you, seeing you, talking to you, reading about you, hearing about you, exposes who you secretly are, what you are striving to accomplish, your personality, your secret, innermost longings, your motivations, your spiritual urges, and your heart's desires. Moreover, this type of dream gives you a peek at some hidden talents you may, or may not, have. Questions to journal, did dreamer readily recognize that you were the one being depicted within your dream? If not, why did you not recognize you? How did dreamer come to recognized that it was you being depicted within your dream? What were the behaviors, actions, or activities of the dreamer within your dream, and what were your first and last impressions you had of yourself within your dream? Were you bewildered? Were you in agreement with, or were you at odds, with the person that proved to be you? Your answers to these questions, reveals your level of self-awareness, namely, how you view yourself, a better idea of how the world sees you, your reaction to that information, and what might need to happen to effect, perhaps, wholeness within you. Dreamer, although you may not be aware of how you perceive yourself, and at times our perception of who we are, does not match how God perceives us; favorably, a rectification of that perception will now begin to happen within you. That you might see yourself as God sees you. Most importantly, this rectification process will teach the dreamer to; learn not to be afraid of darkness, but to stand bold in its face, for the greater one lives within you, and that spirit of fear that has intimidated you, and kept you from embracing who you truly are in Christ, will flee. Read, understand, and embrace Romans 8:15, 2 Timothy 1:7. Dreamer, while your weaknesses maybe legitimate, you unknowingly deny the truth of His report, "Therefore, there is now no condemnation for those who are in Christ Jesus"; as well, "His grace is sufficient". There is a difference between conviction and condemnation. Dreamer, think on these things (see Romans 7:7-8:17; 2 Corinthians 12:7-10; Philippians 1:6; 4:8). Take great care and heed God's warnings. Dreamer, you are on the brink of promotion and celebrity, and you are being watched by heaven and others. Hence, you are called to exhibit faith by steadfast obedience, determination, confidence, fortitude, thanks, and love. The genuineness of your faith is judged by your response to hardships and opposition engendered by your identification with Christ, and by your inner temptations to sin. Be encouraged, take comfort, and believe (see John 14:1-4). No other affirmation will be sent. (3) If dreamer was displaying a talent, known or unknown, to yourself, perhaps dreamer should consider learning, embracing, and move forward with the talent depicted within your dream. The talents that we use to, get along in the world, will in some instances, protect us from it. Thus, out of obedience to your calling, by displaying your talent, at the right place and at the right time, this will keep you from being in the wrong place at the wrong time. If necessary, see suggested course of action.

YOUTH (YOUNG PEOPLE), unless otherwise noted, living and deceased:

Dreamer, God is completely restoring things materially and spiritually within your life and in the lives of those immediately connected to you. Read, understand, and embrace Isaiah 40:31. With that, because of your brokenness over your past sins, you have opened the door to contriteness and humility. It is through this door that an act of kindness will come very soon. Additionally, dreamer there is a need to understand the unadulterated and full meaning of divine providence, get a bible dictionary, and respect the meaning. Dreamer, recognize, acknowledge, and respect divine providence, God's absolute control over the affairs of humankind, and to renounce the belief that humans are in complete control (see Job 9:12, Isaiah 14:27; 43:13). There is a difference between divine providence and the will of humankind. Although you have the power of free choice, you should not think that your accomplishments are purely of your own volition. It is God, who gives you the capability and strength to achieve success. This is especially true of your struggles with your sinful tendencies, whether they manifest as a lack of concern or interest in the things of God, a stubborn resistance to the will of God, or laziness. If it had not been for God's efforts on your behalf, you would not have been able to overcome any negative tendencies. He delivered you. Any achievements you've accomplished, any good deeds you've done, any fulfillment of God's will, was, and still is, dependent upon divine aid and guidance. One merely places his or her hand under the weight carried exclusively by God. Just say and truly believe, "I will exalt you, God, for you have lifted me up" (Psalm 30:1). Further, altruistic, goodhearted, and generous service to God and others is beneficial at this time. In addition, there is a need to check your theology. There is something missing in your belief system that has affected someone who is very close to you. It has caused them to seek God in other teachers, in other faces, and most are evil. Fortunately, that love one lead astray, because of you, will come home, embr acing Jesus. If necessary, see suggested course of action.

Suggested Course of Action

Question to consider and journal, did your dream depict any symbols that alludes to, the dreamer will make the necessary changes, spiritually, emotionally, and/or physically to affect a more positive outcome? If changes are initiated, your dreams will change.

Questions to journal, in view of your dream's context, and the primary symbols, what does your dream reveal about you, your ethics, intents, mental state, and motives? What was your reaction to the people, person, or situation? Were you angry, concerned, confused, defensive, fearful, happy, helpful, pleased, shocked, unconcerned, or ready to get out of someone's presence? Your reaction to the activity, or the circumstance, reveals your attitude regarding this information about yourself. You will need to earnestly look within and consider that the sum of your answers is a reflection of where you are emotionally, physically, and/or spiritually, and a reflection of who you are becoming. Therefore, take into account your entire dream's context and remember, dreams are, for the most part, warnings. People and situations do, and can, change for the good, especially with the help of God. Change is the key word. There is a lesson to learn, please be attentive, and give ear to what God is trying to convey to you, and encourage yourself. Along with prayer and fasting, seek counsel from spiritual leaders.

That stated, dreamer, if you are here, you are entering a time of preparation, and grounding for ministry, thus, your dream is a call to alter your thinking in some manner, in order to become more self-aware of certain negative aspects of your own personality, because they are hampering your spiritual growth and making life harder for you. First, there is need to remember your identity in Christ, and re-attempt to live consistent with that identity, via God's principles, precepts, and truths. Second, there is a need to know or remember who you are uniquely. Your secret identity, private conversations, and your private expressions, all expose who you truly are; this is where you feel most comfortable, this is your authentic self. Ear nest self-contemplation, will give you a look at your deeper motives, and a deeper look into what motivates you. Hint: you attract people and situations to you that match your personal magnetism. If you've lost that unique identifier that is you, then you have lost you. Considerations to ponder, dreamer, how you view yourself, is what you value. If you view yourself primarily as a sexual object, you value sexual immorality. If you view yourself as a financial survivor, you value material gain. If you view yourself as a child of God, one who is secure in Christ, whom God promises to care for in this life and in the life to come, and as one who is called to the high honor of representing God in this world, then you will live consistent with your identity in Ch rist. You will value God, self, and others. Is it time to change your paradigm of you?

Jesus said that "the good man {humankind} brings good things out of the good stored up in him, and the evil man {humankind} brings evil things out of the evil stored up in him" (Matthew 12:35). That being said, dreamer, if your true intent is on glorifying God, doing His will, reaping prosperity, experiencing genuine joy, and most importantly inheriting eternal l ife, you will have to practice restricting yourself in all things (weaning yourself from sensual appetites). This includes your diet, activities, relationships, associations, friendships, partying, and your lack of Christian fellowship. Dreamer, in the recti fication of your character, in order to reach an acceptable level of proficiency in ministry, you must bring your appetites and sensual desires under subjection, sacrificing fleshy satisfaction, especially during this time within your life of preparation and grounding. You will need to lay aside every obstacle that hinders you and causes you to forfeit God's principles, inclu ding laziness; that you might reach the point where you are capable of accomplishing your mission, and learn contentment. Moreover, see Luke 3:4-6, 10-14. Dreamer, when you begin to pursue your issues, in a manner consistent with your purpose, with a vital drive toward the fulfillment of your goals, sacrificing many sensual urges for the Kingdom's sake, mindful to observe rules, while accomplishing your pursuits. You will begin to experience confidence, sincerity, truthfulness, a willin gness to serve God, and an active trust that God will give you the power to accomplish your objectives in life.

Now, pray (See Prayer of Deliverance, pg. 897)

Specific Meaning

If, you have a very high chance that you will be dealing with people on some minor or major level, dreams of this sort, for the most part, are ordinary dreams, resulting from your daily activities (see Chapter One, Chalom). These sorts of dreams are usually about your routine, mundane activities or anxieties that overwhelm your mind during the da y. They are an inner release mechanism, which helps provide you with emotional balance and the maintaining of your sanity. These dreams are not significant, and do not warrant special attention.

Note: Dreamer, consider this question; did you invent or create something within your dream? Did you receive a unique idea? Could you be receiving inspiration, via your dream, regarding an idea, or possible creation of something, that would benefit the masses or enhance living conditions of others; especially, if you have a very real connection with any activity involving the betterment of mankind, human resources, the ability to change or initiate humanitarian initiatives or laws, or missions. Your dream may very well be a divine sent inspiration. Therefore, consider it not strange for someone, who is involved in some manner of activity that involves people, to receive inspirations regarding the collective masses, via their dreams, that might prove beneficial to the dreamer and to mankind. Per chapter one, sometimes the most meaningless dream will help change your life in ways you would have never thought, especially entrepreneurially and enterprisingly. Throughout history, humankind has received life changing insight and guidance from their dreams. Most of the time the information acquired within dreams exceeds that which we could obtain during our normal, analytical, waking state of mind. With that said, via your dream, dreamer you have miraculously been given big goals that involve building a better world and giving back to it what it has given you. Therefore, write your vision down, that you may articulate it to others properly, for the visio n will happen. Prepare a good proposal, name your inspiration, and write down all the details and specifics, an d brand mark it. Give it your best that it may be acceptable to any reputable financial entity, benefactor, or merit a grant of some kind. Perhaps, hire a grant writer. That which you will need to fulfill your aims, surely, you will have. Your dream should closely resembled real life situations. Meaning it can actually occur during your awaked state.

If, there is a very high propensity for an accident, mishap, misunderstanding, due to disgruntle persons, or some other dangers, because of crowds. A dream of this sort should be received as a precautionary warning, to prevent serious harm to yourself, and/or others. Be careful. Do not assume that you're safe or it's ok, caution should be heeded at this time. If an unfortunate mishap, especially one causing damage or injury, happened within your dream, e.g. perhaps an incident caused by a terrorist or insane gunman, was highlighted within your dream, this is a precautionary warning. The mishap, kept within context of the dream, should be relevant to your everyday working life and/or closely resemble real life situations. Meaning it can actually occur during your awaked state. This will help you narrow down the specifics, and avoid danger.

If another had the accident, you are being made aware of the plight of someone, the person highlighted within your dream, and you are to get involved (see Chapter One, Are You Ready to Hear the Messages in Your Dreams, section entitled, The 10% for others). There may be potential for a serious accident. Did you know the individual within your dream? If not, God will bring them to your attention. Where did the accident occur? What kind of accident was it? Dreamer, the details, kept within context of your dream, should be relevant to the person's life, and/or closely resemble real life situations. Meaning it can actually occur during your awaked state. If you sense your dream is for or about another, namely the person highlighted within the dream, the question as to why you have been made aware of this information, and how do you factor into the equation, should be seriously considered, along with necessary actions. Call the person, and warn them of your concerns. Your warnings will help them narrow down the specifics needed to steer them clear of possible trouble. However, if your dream was inundated with symbols that are not easily linked to your life activities, then the spiritual implications (th e interpretation) should be heeded.

VEHICLES AND MODES OF TRANSPORTATION

And Rebekah arose, and her damsels and they rode upon the camels,
and followed the man (Genesis 24:60-66 KJV)

"Give them this order: 'Take wagons with you from Egypt for your children and
your wives. Bring your father, and come back. (Genesis 45:19 GW)

They brought these gifts to the LORD: six freight wagons and twelve oxen, one wagon
from every two leaders and one ox from each leader. (Numbers 7:3 GW)

And the donkey said to Balaam, "Am I not your donkey, on which you have ridden all your life long
to this day? Is it my habit to treat you this way?" And he said, "No" (Numbers 22:21-33 ESV)

And David smote them from the twilight even unto the evening of the next day: and there escaped not
a man of them, save four hundred young men, who rode upon camels and fled (1 Samuel 30:17 KJV)

The Arameans fled from Israel, and David killed 700 chariot drivers
and 40,000 horsemen. (2 Samuel 10:18 GW)

The appearance of the wheels and their work was like unto a beryl: and they four had one likeness;
and their appearance and their work was as it were a wheel within a wheel (Ezekiel 1:16 ASV)

…heralds were permitted to compel any person, or to press any horse, boat, ship, or other vehicle that
they might need, for the quick transmission of the king's commandments. It was to this custom that
our Savior refers. Rather, says he, than resist a public authority, requiring your attendance and aid for a
certain distance, go peaceably twice the distance. (Barnes' Notes on the New Testament Matthew 5:41)

Say to the daughter of Zion, "Behold, your king is coming to you, humble, and mounted
on a donkey, and on a colt, the foal of a beast of burden"(Matthew 21:5 ESV)

In addition, sitting in his chariot Acts 8:28 His carriage, his vehicle. (Barnes' Notes on the New Testament)

And I saw, and behold, a white horse, and he that sat thereon had a bow; and there was given
unto him a crown: and he came forth conquering, and to conquer. And another horse came forth,
a red horse, and behold, a black horse, and behold, a pale horse (Revelation 6:2-9 ASV)

This category deals with any modes of transportation. Any vehicle that can be pushed by a person, or ridden or drawn via an animal; however, now, are usually propelled by an internal combustion engine, or electricity, or is powered by propellers or jets. Some short descriptions of types, phrases, and other processes and particulars, connected in some way to this category are, for example, airplane, animals, bicycle, boat, car, caravan, chariot, hearse, helicopter, motorcycle, RV, spacecraft, su bway, taxi, tractor, train truck. While the designs of some vehicles, modes of transportations have changed considerably over the years, others have remained the same (e.g. airplane, bicycle, boat, helicopter, train, wagons). Also, see category content l ist, or index.

All Symbols and Referents, Notes (1, 2, 3, etc.), Suggested Course of Action, and Specific Meaning offer guidance toward a more comprehensive interpretation.

Notes

1. Unless otherwise noted elsewhere, if, in your everyday living, your awaked state, as part of your lifestyle, work, or ministerial activities, or a special event, you have a very real connection with any activity involving vehicles, modes of transportation. For example, astronaut, auto auctioneer, dealer, or mechanic, bus or van driver, cab d river, captain of a ship, pilot, racecar driver, traveler, or any activity or business involved in dealing with any vehicles, modes of transportation, your dream is not significant and does not warrant special attention.

    Otherwise noted, this dream may be a Prophetically Simple Dream (see Chapter One: The 60th Part of Prophecy). Whereas, the dreamer is warned to stop any reckless or dangerous activities that is related to the handling of some type of vehicle; you should cease any daredevil or impetuous activity, especially if this is a thing within the dreamer's life. If any of the preceding is happening, or was depicted within your dream, this dream is a first step intervention and an alarm. Skip interpretation and re-consider your activity as harmful, hurtful, or life threatening, at present. Handle the situation wisely, by first thanking God for the warning, for Adonai Elohim knows all. Also, see Specific Meaning at the end of this category, section entitled, Note (Specific Meaning).

    Otherwise noted, this dream of vehicles, modes of transportation may be a Prophetically Simple Dream (see Chapter One: The 60th Part of Prophecy). Did you invent something? Whereas, the dreamer is encouraged, for example, to learn a new vehicle, or if a uniquely new mode of transportation was introduced to you within your dream, to create or invent a new style of vehicle, or to initiate a new way of handling or driving a vehicle, and to adopt the new inspiration as your own signature style. For example, name the style after you. See Specific Meaning at the end of this category, section entitled, Note (Specific Meaning)

    Otherwise noted, per your lifestyle, if your dream closely resembled real life situations, meaning it can literally occur during your awaked state, this dream may be an Ordinary Dream, resulting from your daily activities (see Chapter One, Chalom). These sorts of dreams are usually about your routine, mundane activities or anxieties that overwhelm your mind during the day. They are an inner release mechanism, which helps provide you with emotional balance and the maintaining of your sanity. These dreams are not significant, and do not warrant special attention.

2. Probables: As vehicles, modes of transportation are frequently demonstrated in many, and very personal ways; for example, does a Dodge Omni remind you of your first car? Does a 1965 Buick Electra remind you of your family car? Was working at the Auto Train in Sanford, Florida your first job? Does travel by camel remind you of your ancestors? Thus, could the mode of transportation depicted be a possible probable (see Chapter One, section entitled, Probables)? Hence, dreamer may also consider your own personal and special associations with various vehicles, modes of transportation, as long as the interpretation is kept within the principles of spiritual boundary markers, landmarks, and property lines, (see Chapter One, section entitled, Spiritualizing Boundary Markers, Landmarks, and Property Lines).

3. Determine who your dream is for you or another. Always, considering yourself first, reflecting on your present behaviors. Ask yourself, why am I dreaming about this now? What is this dream revealing about me? Have I taken on new attributes? Has anyone commented on my present behaviors as being untypical of me? Has my ministry changed for the better or for the worse? What about my beliefs, doctrine, or philosophy, are they still based on Holy Writ? Is there something I need to know about those I am ministering to or serving?

    Remember your actions and emotions within your dream. Was the dreamer a pilot, a primary driver? Did the dreamer fix the vehicle? Was the dreamer an auto sales representative? Did the dreamer cause an accident, crash, or did you run out of gas? Was the dreamer the director of traffic? Unless otherwise noted elsewhere, an answer of yes, to one or more of these, or similar questions, is a good indicator that your dream is about you, the dreamer. What happened to you in your dream? How did things end? In light of your dream, via the relevant interpretation, do you believe that your choices will enhance or endanger your well-being, safety, and/or happiness, if so, how and why? Do you believe that your belief system will strengthen or weaken you spiritually in any way, if so, how and why? Is spiritual or physical death a possibility? See following relevant subcategory, the interpretation is about and for you.

Was someone else the dealer or seller of vehicles in any way? Did another have an issue with the mode of transportation? Was another the director of traffic? Did another, in any way, drive, control, or handled the vehicle? Was another responsible for the vehicle breakdown, crash, or impound of the vehicle? Unless otherwise noted elsewhere, an answer of yes, to one or more of these, or similar questions, is a good indicator that your dream is about another and their role, and/or influential effects, within the life of the dreamer. Does someone find fault with you lifestyle or life choices? Are you dealing with someone, who truly believes in their heart that they will not have to give an account of their attitude towards you? Are they enhancing your spiritual and/or literal prosperity, or are they responsible for the dwindling thereof? Do you know someone whose life activities or physical being is similar to that which stood out the most within your dream? Could it be that person? If you sense that your dream is for or about another, the question as to why you have been made privy to this information, and how do you factor into the equation, should be seriously considered along with necessary actions. Perhaps the dreamer is being made aware of the plight of someone, and you are to get involved (see Chapter One, Are You Ready to Hear the Messages in Your Dreams, section entitled, The 10% for others).

If your dream is for, or about another:

Dreams that reference others and the revelation within those dreams, is not given haphazardly to any individual, but only to those with the ability, and influence to do something with the information; this is also prophecy. With that, journal the following questions, and if unable to answer the questions now, this denotes that the person, represented within your dream, will enter your life shortly. Are you entering into a personal relationship with someone? Do you not know or understand what you're looking at, especially certain behaviors, when learning about this person? Has someone new entered your life or maybe you've just begun opening up to someone not so new, and have started listening to their advice, accepting their assistance, or are you supporting or enabling someone? Are you in denial regarding the toxicity of one of your present relationships, particularly a spouse, family member, or friend? Are you anxious, concerned, frightened, and/or troubled by recent changes in your behavior, especially because of someone's influence upon your life at present? Have you allowed someone to convince you to deceive another? Have you recently become aware of (or is being made aware of, via this dream) certain undesirable behaviors within you towards another? Are you trying to cut ties with one that is bad company? Have you just joined (or re-joined) a church, fellowship, or social group?

Note: If your dream has attributes that indicate that your dream is about you, and other attributes that indicate that your dream is about another, dreamer should consider that your dream is about you and another. For example, were you, the dreamer, the owner of the vehicle, but was not the driver? Did someone wreck the dreamer's car? Was dreamer teaching another how to drive or operate a vehicle? Was dreamer asking for help with fixing their vehicle? Was dreamer a member of a nomadic tribe, e.g. Bedouins? Thus indicating that your dream is about the dreamer, and another; therefore, while your dream is about the dreamer, the dreamer should expect the role and/or influential effects of another, also plays a part in your interpretation. For example, dreamer may be a taxi driver, but having been robbed, is now apprehensive about your job. From which now the dreamer needs deliverance from fear, again, see relevant interpretation.

More questions to consider. Why has the person been allowed within your life, and/or how did they get there? Again, if unable to answer the questions now, this denotes that the person, represented within your dream, will enter your life shortly. If their activity, within your dream, has proven positive, via the interpretation, this someone will prove, unwittingly, to be a very strong ally, benefactor, defender, and supporter. God has sent this someone into your life to help you carry out your next endeavor by enlarging your spiritual capacity. Allow the strength of that person's character to guide, help, and support you. On the other hand, if his or her presence and/or activity, within your dream, proved negative, via the interpretation, for sure, this person will prove to be a very strong and formidable challenge for you, perhaps unto death. If negative, this dream is a dire warning. Take steps accordingly to struggle against, or to cut off, adverse and unfavorable relationships. Remember certain personalities are all encompassing, affecting everything, cataclysmic, contagious, deadly, harmful, infectious, predatory, and/or venomous. Symbolically meaning that if allowed to continue or prosper within your life, serious harm or death to the dreamer may result. Idolize no one, especially beyond the warning of the Lord, and we are definitely not to lay our lives down for no one. Then again, this person maybe allowed within your life, because of the dreamer's unwillingness to abstain from immorality after having been asked to abstain from such by God, see 1 Corinthians 6:9-20, Galatians 5:19-21, or the dreamer's self-righteous behavior, or a lack of a balanced and honest view of your own personality. In this case, this person will affect self-awareness within the life of the dreamer, exposing the negative traits of your personality, especially those traits, which cause you to follow, or to be so easily misled, and/or your wrong beliefs; no matter, this type of mentality needs reckoning with. Graciously, all of this will restore the dreamer to his or her right place with God, opening your eyes to see how far you've strayed from God (1 Corinthians 5:4-7; James 5:20). The lesson is, no matter how personable, powerful, or difficult a person, or how uncertain or unpopular the choices and issues, always take the next biblical and ethical step, for obedience to God's principles will always prove safer and stronger foundationally. Although, you will need all kinds of outside support to recover from this person's domination, no longer, allow that particular person's influence within your life to continue or thrive, especially if negative, end it abruptly.

4. Consider all the people, places, backgrounds, and activity highlighted within your dream.

   Known (in your awaked life) person, animal, place, or organization within your dream:

   Unless otherwise noted elsewhere, people, animals, places, backgrounds that are literally known by the dreamer in your awaked life, indicates a part of you that you recognize within yourself on some level or another. Question to journal, if dreamer seriously considers the person, animal, place, or background attributes, what character traits stood out the most, or what features stood out the most. For example, age, color, height, size, happiness, considerate, loving, peacefulness, encourager, irrational, leader, liar, mentor, passionate, neglectful, poor, run-down, sage, shyster, unwise, upscale, vengeful. Write down (journal) the particular highlighted within your dream. The attribute or activity highlighted is for a reason. Since the attribute written down is a part of you, namely the dreamer's nature, demeanor, and/or lifestyle, an honest and unbiased assessment is very important for truth sake. Happy note, considering that other people's attributes, within dreams, also represent attributes of your own personality, causes one to look at another in a better light. According to your capacity to embrace self-awareness and a rectification of mind, body, and spirit, God will begin to enhance, make better, more attractive, sanctify, diminish, and make pure and free from sin and guilt, this part of you.

   Otherwise noted, if the person, animal, place, or background within your dream; is literally known by the dreamer, in your awaked life, this person, animal, place, or background may represent him or herself, or itself.

Unknown in your awaked life or although known, was unseen, invisible, or only talked about - person, animal, place, or organization within your dream:

Unless otherwise noted elsewhere, if you did not recognize, the person, place, thing, they, or it, was not seen, invisible, or only talked about within your dream, this indicates an attribute or activity within your life that you are unfamiliar with, or are in denial about, or you refuse to acknowledge it, but it does exists. Question to journal: what character trait, feature, action, or activity, stood out the most? For example, age, color, height, size, happiness, considerate, loving, let you be yourself, peacefulness, encourager, irrational, leader, liar, mentor, passionate, personable, neglected, poor, run-down, sage, shyster, unwise, upscale, vengeful. Although, on some conscious level, you are aware of a certain behavior or attribute within you, you have chosen to filter out or simply ignore certain information about yourself that contradicts your view of yourself and/or your preconceived notions of others and of the world around you. Possibly protecting yourself, emotionally and psychologically, from a situation, which you are unable to cope with at this time, or you lack control over; then again, perhaps the dreamer has an exaggerated or unrealistic view of yourself. No matter the reason, right now a question is before you, via your dream. Do you want to know this part of yourself? According to your ability to handle self-awareness, God will begin to reveal this side of you to you. Why, He wants to balance your understanding of things; thus, effecting wholeness within your life, so that the enemy will no longer be able to manipulate your emotions so easily. The Paraclete is with you to help you throughout this entire process, listen to Him. Now, in your life, this activity or attribute needs reckoning with, somehow or someway.

Otherwise noted, (known or unknown), if the person, place or thing that initiated (or was a recipient of) the action or activity within your dream was not seen, invisible, or only talked about within your dream, this may indicate that the dreamer does not recognize the influential effects another has within your life, or upon your attitude.

If more than one person (known or unknown):

Consider what the group had in common. What behavior, character trait, feature, action, or activity, stood out the most? For example, were they argumentative, authoritative, beautiful, criminal minded, dancing, difficult, dressed unusual, enigmatic, fighting, focused, flirty, helpful, hurtful intentions, powerful, promiscuous, quiet, secretive, seemed unreal, unassuming? What about age, color, height, size, happiness, considerate, loving, let you be yourself, peacefulness, encourager, irrational, leader, liar, mentor, passionate, personable, neglected, poor, run -down, sage, shyster, unwise, upscale, vengeful, death. That which was highlighted and noted is what you need to focus on at present.

If the attribute or quality is a desirable or positive one, allow the strength of that attribute to help you overcome some manner of immorality or irreverence within your life and/or to help you to become better, productively, for the Kingdom of God in some manner. If the attribute is an undesirable or negative one, take steps accordingly to struggle against the growing desires of the carnal side of you. If applicable, get help and support via prayer, fasting, and a Christian based support group.

5. In addition to the following interpretations, see index or relevant categories for more information. For example, if an accident was in involved in some way, see category, Accidents, if pursuing was highlighted, see category, Chasing. Kept within context of your dream and the interpretation, the additional symbols are perhaps relevant. It will be within the sum of all the symbols that you will find a more thorough interpretation.

6. Since the following list is not extensive, dreamer is encouraged to seek biblical guidelines and other relevant research to determine the metaphorical meaning of your particular vehicle or mode of transportation activity, depicted within your dream, via a Bible concordance, Bible illustrated dictionary, encyclopedia, or internet. Having done your research you should be able to determine some basic behaviors or attributes your Lord and Savior wants you to focus on.

Symbols and Referents

Most dreams of vehicles or modes of transportation generally imply, coupled with the relevant interpretation, the type of lifestyle dreamer is embracing, your modus operandi (mode or state of operating, living, or lifestyle), your manner of living that reflects your values and attitudes, and what that particular lifestyle may be leading to. As well, this dream may be sent as an alarm, especially if vehicle was in a bad condition.

In addition to the varied meanings of vehicles, modes of transportation, other common words, expressions, usages, (e.g. slang or clichés), or a 'probable' that are metaphorically represented by any of the following are also considered (this section is an addendum at the end of the category or subcategory).

Category Content - If not listed see index, perchance, for your specific type of vehicle, mode of transportation dream.

- Accidents, see category, Accidents
- Airplane or Helicopter
  - Airplane or Helicopter crashed, see category, Accidents (Airplane); Flying, Airplane, or Helicopter, see category, Flying (Airplane); Flying in an Airplane or Helicopter, or taking off, see category, Flying (Airplane)
- Automobile, Vehicles (two, three, or four wheeled vehicle; usually propelled by an internal combustion engine or by electricity)
  - Car; Farming Vehicles (e.g. farm truck, harvester, mower, plough, tractor); Herse (or any vehicle carrying a coffin to a church or a cemetery); Motorcycle, motored bike (a motored vehicle with two wheels); Public Transportation (Airplane or Helicopter, see category, Flying [Airplane]; Ambulance or Medical Airplane, e.g. Mercy Flight or Medical Bus, Bus Stop/Stations, Taxi Stand/Stations, Train or Rail Stops/Stations [a place on a bus, taxi, or train route where they stop to take on passengers and/or discharge passengers]; Motor Coach, Regional Transit Bus, Double Decker, or Taxi [e.g. Greyhound, Regional Transit System, Trailways, Yellow Taxi]; School Bus; Train, Tram Car, Trolley, Street Car, or Subway (vehicles that run on, or use, rails); Truck or SUV (tractor trailer, semi, and rig – [a truck consisting of a tractor and trailer together], or a SUV, [a four-wheel drive car built on a truck chassis]; Recreational Vehicles (any recreational vehicles equipped with living quarters while traveling, e.g. RV, camper, motorhome, or a caravan); Work Vehicles (any vehicle used for work purposes)
- Bicycle or Cart (one, two, or three, wheeled vehicle that can be pedaled, pushed, or pulled by a person)
- Boat, Ship (cruise ship, ferryboat, ocean liner, any watercraft, good condition, or in need of repairs, e.g. broke-down, capsized, dented, impounded, unworkable, or sinking)
- Caravan, Carriage, Chariot, Wagons, or Animals (a mode of transportation pulled by camels, horses, or mules, or riding on an animal)
- Cleaning or Washing Vehicle, see category Cleaning, Washing
- Hot Air Balloon, see category, Ascending (Hot air balloon)
- Intoxicated and operate a vehicle, see category, Drinking
- Rocket, Spacecraft, or Spaceship
- Tires or Wheels (good condition or bad condition, e.g. flat, damaged, dented, unusable)
  - Rims (of tires or wheels)
- Sitting in a vehicle, see category, Sitting
- Vehicle (someone in any mode of transportation) pursuing you or vice versa, see category, Chasing, Running, Following, or Stalking
- Walking, see category, Walking

AUTOMOBILE, VEHICLES (two, three, or four-wheeled vehicle; usually propelled by an internal combustion engine or by electricity):

As this dream gives you a glimpse into the way you operate within your lifestyle, your general patterns of behavior, your habits, your "ways and means", your "MO" modus operandi (mode or state of operating, living, or lifestyle), so to speak. Consider and journal the following two cites. (1) The type of car denotes what your life choices, your "MO", may be leading too. (2) If the condition of the automobile, vehicle within your dream was bad (broke-down, dented, impounded, or unworkable), this denotes changes in your "MO", changes often happening without warning or in a short space of time. Couple your journaled notes, with one of the following.

Car: The bigger the car, the more energy you are expending living out your daily life experiences, albeit, positive or unwisely. With that, this dream has four meanings (choose one). (1) The dreamer trusts in secondary causes. The following is a very basic explanation of first and secondary causes. The first cause is that which receives neither its power nor the exercise of its power from another; God alone is first cause. A second cause receives both its power and the use of it from the first cause; all creatures [and resources] are secondary causes (Christian Philosophy, Louis de Poissy). God is the first (or primary) cause of everything. He miraculously created, "creatio ex nihilo" (creation out of nothing), John 1:3. From this act of God comes secondary causes and their purposes, "creatio ex materia" (creation out of some pre-existent matter), Genesis 1:2-2, 2 Peter 3:5. With this very basic explanation stated, the following is made easier to present. This is for you, the dreamer. You are trusting only in secondary causes. Examples, you need healing. You may testify with words that God heals and can heal miraculously (first cause). But with your heart you believe your healing can only come through a doctor's medicine (secondar y cause); except now your illness is incurable and you need a miracle (a miraculous act of God, something out of nothing, per se). Another example, perhaps, you stand before a judge, desiring a certain outcome. While you confess that God has said the charges will be dropped; and you say God controls men, and answers prayer, inwardly you fear an undesirable outcome, so you do that which you know; you take the plea (secondary cause). This is where you truly put your faith, in secondary causes. You say you have faith in God, which is a resolute trust in the integrity of God and in His Word, but with your heart you only trust in others or things that can be used as a source of help or information, for example, a reserve supply of money, your o wn ability to find solutions to your problems. While these attributes are certainly commendable, and have worked for you in the past, they are purely secondary causes and should be recognized as such. Be it physical, emotional, or physical, dreamer, yo u need a miracle that only God can create, hence, put your faith in God, and Him alone. (2) Dreamer, subconsciously (your mental activity just below the level of awareness) you are giving up on God's love, His grace, and His mercy; believing no help can, or will, come from Him regarding you, because of your personal shortcomings, e.g. you've not obey ed completely, an order from the Lord, or that minor flaw in your character. Thus, your present state is a result of an overall feeling of worthlessness, due to your own personal weaknesses. Dreamer, while your weaknesses maybe legitimate, do not deny the truth of God's report, "Therefore, there is now no condemnation for those who are in Christ Jesus"; as well, "His grace is sufficient". Romans 8:1, 2 Corinthians 12:9, upon these two scriptures and similar others, base your ideas of God's mercy regarding personal weaknesses. There is a difference between conviction and condemnation. All insinuations that God does not care, one way or the other, about your everyday living (bills, clothing, emotional well -being, family, finances, food, health care, political situations, safety, shelter, transportation, violence, war) are conceived without grace. Moreover, "dethroning" God from His providential sovereignty (the wisdom, care, and guidance provided by God) over your life, within your heart, coupled with your hasty and inconsiderate verdicts on His divine procedures, denies His Power. Thus, your love for Jesus is dwindling, and this gradual loss of love for Christ is festering within you like a cancer. You have stopped asking why, or for what reason this or that happened, but you need to go further and ask the deeper questions, seeking to understand why God allowed this or that, and what is the lesson to be learned, what is He revealing to you in His providential dealings with you. Dreamer, question not, His absolute goodness in His dealings with you, but ask, what are you to glean from it. See the Lord's providence behind all the events in your life, and change your paradigm. For, though apparently absent, He really is present, and He has promised never to leave you. Additionally, the dreamer will experience spiritual progression and growth suddenly. See suggested course of action. (3) Dreamer, distinguish yourself from those that live without God, by having satisfaction in God's power alone, over people, places, and things; in your personal relationship with Him; and in His revelation of Himself to you, and know that the difference between the sacred and the profane is confidence in God (also see Psalm 20:7, 8). Further, it is not for us to dictate what the procedure of infinite love and wisdom should be. We often don't see the providence of God behind events in our lives, but we must trustingly rely upon, and make, His providence in all the events of our life, our foundation, and trust. He wants you to make Him the complete center of your faith, not people, places, things, or ideas. If you are an unbeliever, God will save you via the born again experience (see John 3:1-17, Acts 2:37-40) and you will be made clean. So that, having been justified by grace (the free and unmerited favor and beneficence of God), you have hope for eternal life. See suggested course of action. (4) Bad condition of car (broke-down, dented, impounded, or unworkable): Your lifestyle as you know it is about to "come to an end", and/ or be legally changed. There will be major changes (significant in scope, extent, or effect) in your normal, everyday, habits, and in your way of operating and functioning. Favorably, if relevant, you will be rescued legally from that which is potentially dangerous to your personal relationship with Christ and your health. The changes are a result of your prayers. You've asked God for a change; a change is coming. Pay close attention to shifts within your relationships with others. Keep what is good, toss what is bad, know the difference, and understand God's hand within all the situations. Allow God, not you, to handle His business of keeping His promises to you, namely, "I will give you rest" and "M y peace I leave with you". If necessary, see suggested course of action.

Farming Vehicles (e.g. farm truck, harvester, mower, plough, or tractor): This dream has two meanings (choose one). (1) This dream denotes one, the dreamer, whose calling is to give sermons, spread the gospel, and conduct religious services, a cleric of some kind (e.g. bishop, evangelist, minister, missionary, parson, pastor, preacher, priest, rabbi, or teacher). A large part of your mission should center on you raising the spirits of your fellow mankind, and establishing yourself as an inspirational person spreading hope. Your gift is to inspire and motivate. Unfortunately, although you are prosperous, and physically prepared, you are not walking in your purpose. Thus, you are experiencing strong inner conflict. This is your inner man struggling to fulfill purpose. There is a need to reflect on your behavior, if it's correct or appropriate, especially a s it relates to your spiritual health. This is also the time to reflect on your ministry, does it properly consider others, and on your prosperity (or the dwindling thereof). This dream also implies a time to consider your physical health, perhaps go get a physical check-up, via a physician. (2) Bad condition of farming vehicle (broke-down, dented, impounded, or unworkable): Dreamer, a change of life choices direction and attitude is highly recommended. Re-think your views and attitude, regarding the doctrine you are adhering to, and your philosophy, and/or your plans for establishing or joining an institution or organization. Why, because your interpretation of the Word of God has become unrecognizable to those you influence. When those who seek truth, ask Jesus why they do not recognize your teachings, the words spoken of you are that you are true to yourself. To be true to self or another, is to seek affirmation with respect to condoning your particular sin, while basing your ideas, arguments, and/or beliefs on something that is sacrilegious, profane, illogical, and non-mainstream doctrine or philosophy. Your ideology is without favorable conclusions, thus this dream. You are full of pride. If you persist on perpetuating your self-serving ideology and calling it divinely ordained, you will be publicly humiliated, stripped, and replaced, because of shameful acts. See suggested course of action.

Herse (or any vehicle carrying a coffin to a church or a cemetery): This dream has two meanings (choose one). (1) This dream denotes false security; see Isaiah 28:14 -18, which is leading to spiritual death. Spiritual death is when we think that we do not need God. It is when you embrace and live out the ideology of, "what good is it whether one is righteous or wicked if both paths lead to the same end, or I will not be one who serves God simply for what I can get out of it, I won't serve Him at all". The important point is that spiritual death is when we refuse to seek out and have fellowship with the one true and living God. Spiritual death is a separation from Adonai Elohim. There is nothing emptier than the emptiness one feel inside, in their hour of darkness, in their hour of reckoning, when they realize that ultimately the paths of the righteous and wicked do not lead to the same end. Spiritual death is what can, and often does, lead to eternal death. If we physically die while we are separated from God, that condition will be permanent, it will last for all eternity. The truth is that there is life after death, and if you do not want to live with, and in, God's presence while you are on this earth, God will not force you to live with Him forever, on the other side of eternity. Also, read and understand Galatians 5:19-21, for this speaks of spiritual death. See suggested course of action. (2) Bad condition of hearse or any vehicle carrying a coffin to a church or a cemetery (broke-down, dented, impounded, or unworkable): A hearse depicted in this condition, within your dream, denotes that your lifestyle choices are unequivocally leading to desolation, a departure from abundant life, and physical death. See suggested course of action.

Motorcycle, motored bike (a motored vehicle with two wheels): This dream has two meanings (choose one). (1) Dreamer, your prayers have been heard by the Most High. God will give you new insight, a truthful vision, and it shall "come to pass". Dreamer, although you are discouraged or troubled, and you've gotten to the point where you're spiritually weak and feel discouraged, feeling that your faith has been in vain, do not allow the spirit of fear to intimidate you, only be strong and courageous. Read and understand Romans 8:15, 2 Timothy 1:7. Dreamer, by God's power, a way out of no way will be made for you, and your state of affairs will turn around, and suddenly. Somehow, God will make a way for you. Jesus will come and see about you, for He has promised never to leave you alone. Therefore, keep your faith, regarding what you've believed God for; and you will experience a miracle. With that said, dreamer, you are advised to re-evaluate your life and figure out what changes are needed, so that you might better fulfill God's purpose within your life. Learn from your mistakes, find new direction in solving problems, pursue healing, and seek out wise counsel and encouragement. Ask the important and right questions. Deliberate, discuss, and debate with colleagues, experts, and other Christians, for there is wisdom in the counsel of many. See Proverbs 11:14, 15:22, 23. Listen attentively, become moderate in your business affairs, and allow humility, joy, and purity to be that, which intercedes on your behalf. Then shall joy be revealed, rest shall appear, and healing shall descend, disease shall withdraw, anxiety, anguish, and crying shall pass from you; and gladness will happen. Only, abstain from a judgmental attitude, abusive talking, contentions, revenge, envy, and hatred. As your dream also denotes death; therefore, take heed and abstain from all that you are asked to abstain from, lest you die an early death (Ecclesiastes 7:17). See suggested course of action. (2) Bad condition of motorcycle, motored bike (broke-down, dented, impounded, or unworkable): Dreamer, hurling insults, you've proven to be a bully and braggart, with tyrannical tendencies. Further, you have violated a trust, a confidence communicated to you. Ruthlessly aggressive, you harbor wicked thoughts, using half-truths, twisting confidences, to gain advantage over some. In doing so you have tainted the faith, which is in Jesus Christ, of him or her whose confidence was violated, you will be found out. Confession to God and seeking forgiveness is required, by this you will be forgiven for all you've done. See suggested course of action.

Public Transportation (ambulance, double-decker, medical airplane, medical bus, motor coach, regional transit bus, school bus, street car, subway, taxi, train, tram car, trolley, any vehicle carrying passengers, used for public transport. For example, Amtrak, Greyhound, Mercy Flight, Regional Transit System, Trailways, Yellow Taxi, Uber, including places on a bus, taxi, or train route where they stop to take on passengers and/or discharge passengers):

Public Transportation Vehicle was in bad condition of public transportation vehicle: Ambulance, Medical Airplane, Medical Bus, Motor Coach, Regional Transit Bus, Double Decker, Taxi, or School Bus (broke-down, dented, impounded, or unworkable): This dream implies some manner of decadence, excessive and immoral activities involving, for example, sex, drugs, or alcohol, within the life of the dreamer. Thus, this dream comes to alert the dreamer of the approaching consequences of your choices. Dreamer, a high level of leadership demands great personal sacrifice of rights and freedoms and requires the subduing of your passions. "To whom much is given, much is required". Dreamer, flee immorality, per this dream implications of decadence within you. Dreamer, you must bring your appetites, lusts, and sensual desires under subjection, sacrificing fleshy satisfaction for the cause of God. You will have to practice restricting yourself in all things; this includes your activities, associations, friendships, and diet (see Psalm 119:9). Fate will put you in a position for some le vel of public exposure, either for honoring, because you sincerely choose to apply the truths of God's word to your life, or for open shame, due to a lack of self-restraint. Thus, prepare to become a public figure on some level or another. Dreamer, of your own free will, you made a public profession of following Christ Jesus; thus, you need to walk according to that commitment, cautiously, refraining from all forms of evil, and approaches towards it, because many eyes are upon you. They watch your character, for error, faltering, stumbling; for any type of dishonor or violation, and surely, you have a great deal to lose. Before you are the possible loss of distinction, honor, reputation, and life. Dreamer, a lifestyle change and commitment is needed to turn things around that you might live to declare the goodness of Jehovah-Rapha; the Lord God heals (Psalm 147:1-3, Luke 7:50). See suggested course of action.

Ambulance or Medical Airplane, e.g. Mercy Flight or Medical Bus: This dream is a first step intervention and an alarm to the dreamer, as it points to serious health concerns. Your dream denotes that the dreamer is engaging in some manner of unhealthy life choices and habits, which will result in a serious health related issues, if, the appropriate lifestyle changes, are not, taken, at this time. Dreamer, your physical health, and life, are something that should be valued, as well as, your spiritual life. There are many bitter and poisonous consequences of immorality and carnality. One bad habit (e.g. drug, alcohol, sexu al addictions) can ruin all hope for life. Read, understand, and embrace, Romans 8:13, Galatians 5:19-21, this is to you. Dreamer, your behavior and choices will bring disease, a physical rottenness in the flesh, and perhaps bring great dishonor to you, an d your home, if not already. Your behavior is irresponsible, and if not diligently avoided, will usher you into the path of darkness, and your attitude and unwise choices will prove to your disadvantage, even to the point of being exposed openly. Therefore, flee immorality, for this principle is a hedge of protection to the dreamer, against, perhaps a chronic illness, e.g. AIDS, diabetes, heart disease, HIV, lung cancer. With that said, dreamer you are warned to restrain and get your flesh under control. Your dream is one of God's ways of calling you back unto Him that you might be saved, and to see if you will yet be worked upon, and change your mindset; or else to leave you inexcusable, in your accusations against God, because of your ruin. Thus, neglect not the purity of your covenant relationship with Christ, for God desires to bring you back into a right relationship with Him. Return to ideals and life choices that are holy, wise, well judged, disciplined, and healthy. This will lead you back to Christ. See suggested course of action.

Bus Stop/Stations, Taxi Stand/Stations, Train or Rail Stops/Stations (a place on a bus, taxi, or train route where they stop to take on passengers and/or discharge passengers): This dream denotes that your appointment for Kingdom business is upon you, and you are prepared, ready, and willing. Moreover, the contentment that one feels when you have fulfilled a desire, need, or expectation is coming. Wait for it, for it will surely come, and that very soon, again, I say wait. Couple this with one of the following, as this dream also has two parts (one or both may apply). (1) This dream denotes atonement and it denotes one, the dreamer, who is overcoming some major difficulties in your spiritual and temporal life. For, you are a Christian soldier, a battle-seasoned Christian, who knows quickly what to do because of your experience and familiarity with Scripture, and your strong belief that the atoning work of Jesus on the cross, is enough to justify righteousness within a believer's life; therefore, you are ready to fight. Hence, no matter the issue at present, you will triumph; there will be a successful ending of your struggles. (2) This dream symbolizes a unique leadership quality within you. Hence, this dream denotes one, the dreamer, whose calling is to give sermons, spread the gospel, and conduct religious services and observances. A large part of your mission should center on you raising the spirits of your fellow mankind; and establishing yourself as an inspirational person spreading hope. Your gift is to inspire and motivate. Dreamer, you are that spiritual leader and you're on the right track, pursuing, growing, and going towards your purpose God has destined for you. Dreamer, patiently and contentedly continue on the track you are on, you will get there. For, you are purposed to lead, preach, and teach. The dreamer, already chosen and approved by God, will be, in the near future, if not already, approved by man, to be set aside an d ordained as a ministerial leader. You have been found of good reputation, full of the Spirit, and wise. You will be officially ordained. Dreamer, the way the ordination will be carried out may not be to your liking; nonetheless, do not attribute (or c all) that which is of God, unclean (e.g. confusion, erroneous, out of order, unlawful, weak, wicked, or any other attributes of the unregenerate). Do not consider your ordination as unofficial or a small thing, for it is of God and His kindness towards you.

Motor Coach, Regional Transit Bus, Double Decker, or Taxi (e.g. Greyhound, Regional Transit System, Trailways, Yellow Taxi): Your ministry will be anointed and endowed to reach and save multitudes of people from uncomfortable situations; namely, circumstances where they feel confused, overwhelmed, and/or desolate. Moreover, you will expose extreme and irrational beliefs, counterfeits, and perversions within Christendom that are being introduced by all venues of public communications; effecting reformation, refreshing, reconciliation, and reunions. It will be through your mastery of illustrating God's truths that many will come together in unity; worshipping Jesus as Messiah. Moreover, prepare for public honoring.

School Bus: This dream suggests that the dreamer must become skilled at analyzing, discerning, and judging truth, so that little escapes your observation and deep understanding. A greater development of your mind for searching out truth is needed. Get involve in a search for wisdom and become a leader on whatever it is you are focusing on. Pursue knowledge with vigor. If you have been contemplating some kind of educational pursuit, now is the time to act upon that stirring within you. That you might advance personally, your life requires some manner of formal educational pursuit (GED, advance degree), thus the educational stirring within you. Dreamer, you are well capable to study and learn really deep and difficult subjects, and to search for hidden fundamentals. In addition, regularly, attend worship services, bible study, and Sunday school withi n your church, and go school, or a theological college, or be self-taught, by earnest, studious, and serious research, via a Bible concordance, Bible illustrated dictionary, encyclopedia, and internet, and networking with others who are wise and knowledgeable within the area of your pursuit. Having done your research, you should be able to discern truth from error, regarding ideologies, "isms", and other concerns and issues, pertaining to, contained within, and in accordance with the Bibl e. You will be able to keep with the nature of the Bible and its times and people. Again, go to school. If necessary, see suggested course of action.

Train, Tram Car, Trolley, Street Car, or Subway (vehicles that run on, or use, rails): This dream has three meanings (choose one). (1) This dream refers to one who is redeemed; however, you are going through a refining process, see Proverbs 17:3, 27:21; thus, this dream. As you have been saved from the power of sin, you will now be refined in the "crucible" of adversity. Dreamer is strongly urged, at this point in your life to earnestly, adhere to God's instructions and principles that guide your actions and moral behavior, via His principles, as outlined within Holy Writ. Dreamer, it is imperative that you govern your desires, lusts, and passions with wisdom during your refining process. For, following godliness is aimed at making you not only wiser, but also better. You have a journey to go on, spiritual warfare to fight, and a great work to do. God w ants to purify you that you might fulfill the righteous purpose for which you were designed. Dreamer, if you allow God's power to break the residuals of sin within you, you will experience a great deliverance from oppression. Be very aware that your emotional and/ or physical adversities have been allowed by God that you might be humbled and made ready and prepared to render your gifts unto the Lord properly. God will use your sufferings to instill His principles into your mind, and make His ways penetrate your heart. He or she who has suffered in the flesh has ceased from sinning (1 Peter 4:1) that the sacrificial offerings of your worship, service, and financial support to the ministry, might be a sweet smell unto the Lord. Moreover, the refinement process that you are going through (or will go through shortly) is meant to bring honor and glory to the One who died to redeem you. True conversion makes a marvelous change in the heart and life. It alters the mind, judgment, affection s, and conversation. When a man is truly converted, it is very grievous to him, to think how the time past of his life has been spent, (Matthew Henry Concise Commentary). After this, you will become productive and go forth, bearing spiritual fruit, counted amongst those who are sagacious; whose character is faithful, law-abiding, moral, open, scrupulous, sincere, straightforward, trustworthy, upright, reasonable in many situations, and submissive to God. Blessings, joy, protection, and prosperity will be yours. If necessary, see suggested course of action. (2) Subway: Your unbelief in, or disagreement with, God, His Word, and/or with your church mores', such as rituals, practices, attendance, pecuniary efforts, has led to you rejecting authentic worship of God. Consequently, you now participate in a simulated worship of humanistic or superstitious ideas that are in direct conflict with Holy Writ. Dreamer you have chosen not to conform to mainstream Christianity; you are now looking to someone or something else, other than Jesus as Savior and Lord. You are as one who is expecting another messiah, deliverer. Your new way is based on exploring alternatives to God's righteous principles, as well as, creating a sense of unity with the wickedness around you. You have chosen not to see God's unfailing love, but instead have chosen to trust in fallacy. Moreover, covetousness has caused you to defile yourself, even to the point of sexual immorality to satisfy your lu sts. Therefore, servitude to the master of darkness is forced or imposed upon you, and you have conformed to his ways. This recklessness can be remedied by repentance. Dreamer, you are advised to re-think your views and attitude, regarding the doctrine you are adhering to, and your philosophy, and/or your plans for establishing or joining an i nstitution or organization. Dreamer is strongly urged to return to ideals that are holy, wise, and well judged. Expressions and beliefs that are, in kee ping with the nature of the Bible, ways pertaining to, contained within, and are in accordance with the inspired scripture. This will lead you back to Christ. Neglect not the purity of your covenant relationship with Christ, for God desires to bring you back into a right relationship with Him. This dream is one of God's ways of calling you back unto Him that you might be saved. See suggested course of action. (3) Bad condition of train, tramcar, trolley, streetcar, or subway (broke-down, dented, impounded, or unworkable): This dream denotes that the dreamer actions are in total disregard of God's pri nciples, precepts, and ways. Your behavior hinders the sanctification process, reckoning you as a rebellious child of God. You disagree with t he Word of God, and you take a "hard" stance against it. This type of attitude is preventing you from achieving your goals, having forfeited purpose for foolishness. There is a need for repentance. Dreamer, a character, and lifestyle change can occur through prayer and heartfelt repentance to Jesus. To Jesus pray, Psalm 51, this coupled with prayer, fasting, and follow-thru with appropriate application of wisdom, can conceivably avert some of the repercussions of your choices. This is known as leaving a blessing behind. Unfortunately, until you own up to your rebellious behavior, repent, and become submissive, obedient, and useful within God's Kingdom again, you will begin to decrease, and become weaken in spirit and body. In addition, your actions and behavior, that which is secret, and previously known only to a few, will become public information. See suggested course of action.

Truck or SUV (tractor-trailer, semi, and rig - a truck consisting of a tractor and trailer together, or a SUV, a four-wheel drive car built on a truck chassis): This dream has two meanings (choose one). (1) The dreamer is split internally. Your thoughts are ambiguous, and are primarily, discouraging, fatalistic, faithless, and troubling to yourself and others. Dreame r, your dubious thinking has caused you to be fretful, irritable, and fearful of going to Jesus boldly, supposing you're forcing your presence or opinions on Him, or that you are unwelcome in Jesus' sight, all of which, are untrue. Dreamer, although your faults are before you, and some perhaps legitimate, Jesus loves you. Thus, dreamer is counseled to go to Jesus, aware of your own inadequacies, to ask for guidance and wisdom, and rest assure, that He has wisdom to give, and is generous and liberal enough to give to whomever ask, that includes you. He will not correct or criticize in a harsh manner, for He knows yo u are seeking guidance and wisdom. One may suffer needlessly, because he or she will not ask Jesus for wisdom, and for the courage to apply that wisdom within your own life. Further, regarding God's most Holy Word, do not be hesitant, suspicious, or faithless, about His promises, especially to think that His promises and benefits are limited to a select few, and exclude others. God gives to all men and women; yes you too, and He gives unabatedly. Dreamer, ask Jesus as often as you need to, regarding all of your emotional concerns. Considering how personal His promises are, He will meet you in your needs. Finally, there are two things required of you. Read, understand, and embrace Philippians 4:8, this is to you, and, in your asking, Je sus for anything, ask with a believing, steady mind, for it is written, let him (or her) ask in faith, nothing wavering, see James 1:6. See suggested course of action. (2) Bad condition of truck or SUV vehicle (broke-down, dented, impounded, or unworkable): This dream denotes false worship. Dreamer, you have rejected authentic worship of God, and now participate in a simulated worship of humanistic or superstitious ideas that are in direct conflict with the inspired written Word of God. You are rejecting Christianity's core system of beliefs and practices (also see John 3:16-21; 1 Corinthians 10:1-23; Hebrews 12:14; Revelation 20:1-15). Because of your beliefs and practices, you are unable to overcome your present predicament, for your wisdom only leads to shadows and desolation. See suggested course of action.

Recreational Vehicles (any recreational vehicles equipped with living quarters while traveling, e.g. RV, camper, motorhome, or a caravan): This dream has two meanings (choose one). (1) This dream is a message of grace that you may be clean, for you are surely, called to be one of God's ministers. Dreamer, respect your present place of worship and the appointed leaders of that place. Do not leave to, aimlessly, wander from place to place, church-to-church, doctrinal belief to another doctrinal belief, and never allow anyone to deter you from learning God's word via pastors, preachers, and teachers. For faith comes by hearing, see Romans 10:17; and a living faith by obedience to God's word, via studiously studying your Bible and other biblical resources, and by attending church services regularly. Further, it is not wise to take counsel from within your own head. Thus, always seek counsel from your spiritual leaders and other believers. Deliberate, discuss, and debate with colleagues, experts, and other Christians, for there is wisdom in the counsel of many. See Proverbs 11:14, 15:22, 23. Dream er, you are encouraged to continue your spiritual journey towards Jesus, and turn not back, for continuing on, Ch ristianity promises a better you, and furthermore, you have too much to lose looking back. Therefore, dreamer, crave the direct words of God imparted to us through the words of others, such as a preacher in a worship service, a Sunday school teacher, and other bible studies. It is through these avenues, the Christian experiences, and God's direct leading, that His deeper mysteries, which are more valuable than any knowledge gotten on one's own, are imparted. See suggested course of action. (2) Bad condition of recreational vehicle (broke-down, dented, impounded, or unworkable): Dreamer is reacting in a "temper tantrum" and rebellious manner, because you disagree with certain spiritual principles. This is not good. Dreamer, you may not like God' s ways and means, but you do have to accept and surrender to them all. For, your human understanding of, and reaction to, spiritual realities is oftentimes crudely green. Dreamer, at this crossroad in your life, it is counseled that you do as the apostle Paul, and count all that you know, all that has brought you to this point, to be worthless (Philippians 3:8). This dream has come to let you know that there is still hope and time for you to recognize the wrong in what you're doing, feel the regret about your past actions, and change your ways and habits. Dreamer, God knows your thoughts afar off, so genuinely repent. Take words to Jesus, "'I have sinned, and I have done wrong and acted wickedly". Other than prayer and heartfelt repentance to Jesus, n o other excuse (or weak justification) will be heard. Moreover, ask Jesus for wisdom and for the courage to apply it. Se e suggested course of action.

Work Vehicles (any vehicle used for work purposes): This dream has two meanings (choose one). (1) The dreamer needs to consider someone, one that might be before you now, to be of importance and valuable to your process, project, or team, and you need to include him or her in the loop, in the process, on the project, and on the team. (2) Bad condition of work vehicle (broke-down, dented, impounded, or unworkable): Dreamer, your attitude of insubordination and waywardness has led to a more secular and worldly mind-set. The comfort, security, and over all ease afforded you by Christ, will now have to be worked for with difficulty. Further, hidden secret sin will be exposed in a very public way. For God humbles the high- minded that your paths might be righteous. Additionally, it is suggested that you concern yourself with the spiritual well -being of others. Listen, you will hear their cry. See suggested course of action.

BICYCLE OR CART (one, two, or three, wheeled vehicle that can be pedaled, pushed, or pulled by a person):

This dream has two meanings (choose one). (1) Dreamer will be given the resources needed to complete your endeavor whatever that might be, subsequently presenting you with the opportunity to progress spiritually and naturally. One thing however, as this dream also denotes spiritual and emotional immaturity, it will be wholly up to the dreamer to seize the opportunities God is putting before you to advance you in some manner. The conditions, which must be complied with in order to receive from the Kingdom of God, are that you must have faith, be perceptive, be prepared, and remain humble; hence, an earnest effort to, spiritually and emotionally mature is of great importance at this time, lest you forfeit purpose, choosing to remain immature. Spiritual and emotional maturity will cause you to begin to experience God's benevolence speedily, via His servants. Additionally, there is a need to remember that your reputation and life were given back to you because of His grace, mercy, and love for you. It is absolutely nothing you have done. Give God all the glory, and glorify not yourself this time. If necessary, see suggested course of action. (2) Bad condition of bicycle or cart (broke-down, dented, impounded, or unworkable): This dream implies that the dreamer is refusing to pay attention to the alarms, danger signs, and warning bells, you have been receiving, forewarning of imminent danger, physically and spiritually. You have previously been extensively warned, and now warned via this dream. Dreamer you show a lack of knowledge that prevents one from perishing; you have been very unwise in your words and deeds. You have not "invested" in that which illuminates the mind, body, and soul, spiritually and physically. You have despised the Word of God, and have trusted in oppression and perversity. Rebelliously, you are unwilling to hear the instructions of the Lord. You tell those who speak truth to you, do not speak truth, but tell me smooth things, and teach me lies and illusions. I don't want to hear no more about the Holy One of Israel (Isaiah 9-13). Consequently, danger is approaching, even near your doors. The beginning, development, arrival, or manifestation of something large (significant in scope, extent, or effect) is about to happen within your life, in a threatening way. This re buke is only a precursor of even worse judgments that will come later, if you do not abandoned and change your ways. God is not condemning you, He's holding out His Hand of Hope, giving you an opportunity to start anew. Let the wicked forsake his (or her) way, God wants to pardon (Isaiah 55:7-13, Matthew 7:17-23, Luke 6:43-45). Dreamer, if you earnestly change your ways, you will be healed from your present condition and pardoned from the guilt previously mentioned. Dreamer, humbly seek to restore your relationship with God. For the door to God allows for only the humble of spirit to enter. Prayer and repentance is the first step. See suggested course of action.

BOAT, SHIP (cruise ship, ferryboat, ocean liner, any watercraft, good condition, or in need of repairs, e.g. broke-down, capsized, dented, impounded, unworkable, or sinking):

This dream has two meanings (one or two may apply). (1) This dream denotes a ministry that is being divinely inspired within the dreamer's spirit, be encourage you will prosper in your endeavors. Dreamer, you are one whose calling is to give sermons, spread the gospel, and conduct religious services, a cleric of some kind (e.g. bishop, evangelist, minister, missionary, parson, pastor, preacher, priest, rabbi, or teacher). A large part of your mission should center on you raising the spirits of your fellow mankind, and establishing yourself as an inspirational person spreading hope. With that, dreamer, recall the size of the boa t. The size of the boat symbolically denotes the potential capacity of your ministry, and the dreamer's ability to handle, effectively, those you touch, via your ministry. Big boat denotes, dreamer has good potential towards, and the wherewithal t o, successfully handle, a large to "mega" size ministry; a small boat denotes, dreamer has good potential to successfully handle, a "modest" size ministry. (2) Question, was boat in good condition, or in need of repairs, e.g. broke-down, dented, impounded, unworkable, or sinking? Thus, this choice has two parts (choose one). (a) Good condition of boat, e.g. beautiful, clean: Dreamer, God will raise you up and sit you amongst His people for the benefit of all within your sphere, help God's people by doing good deeds. However, during this time of "raising you up", there will be quick turnovers in your interests and relationships, and perhaps jobs; favorably, along with these changes will come business, power, and money, people will elect you to lead. As well, these changes will give you a multi-dimensionality that will befriend you to people of every "walk of life". Suggestion, perhaps dreamer may attached a humanitarian effort to your ministry, e.g. build rent-free, mortgage-free, housing for God's people, or use your organizing ability, to become a child advocate, on behalf of abused, abandoned, neglected, and at-risk children, perhaps becoming a foster care parent, or support the agencies and individuals who work on these children behalf. Maybe serve the indigent on some level of another. Notwithstanding, initiate some effort that promotes human welfare and/or social reforms, with a primary focus on God's love towards His people. Further, dreamer has the wherewithal within to become a primary catalysts that keeps family and friends coming together (e.g. some kind of regular reunions), and to become one who is good at resolving conflict, bringing peace, hope, and joy to many. You will be considered, and now is, a righteous person (see Romans 8:1). (b) Bad condition of boat, e.g. boat, broke-down, capsized, dented, impounded, unworkable, or sinking: Three things (one, two, or all may apply). (I) Your individual ministry, as you know it, is ending. There will be distress, disappointment, and disconcert over a major issue (significant in scope, extent, or effect), coupled wit h concerns regarding finances; the larger the water vessel the greater the issue and/ or nuisance (refer back to boat size withi n your dream). See suggested course of action. (II) This dream warns that pride goes before destruction and a haughty spirit before a fall, see Proverbs 16:18. Dreamer, those that are of a prideful arrogant spirit, that think more of themselves than what is appropriate, and who look down on others condescendingly, offends God. You will be humbled, either by distress in some manner or by heartfelt repentance to Jesus and to individuals affected by your actions, in the form of an apology (if possible), its' your choice. Nonetheless, God will humble the proud, for this is His way. See suggested course of action. (III) Dreamer, give contributions to those who live uprightly, according as you've prospered, and do not resent the giving of the gift when you make it, nor attach any requisites. Moreover, do not turn your face away from the poor man, and the face of God will not be turned away from you. Help a poor man for the commandment's sake, and because of his need do not send him away empty; (see Ben Sira 29). Dreamer, no one can serve two masters, for either he (or she) will hate the one and love the other, or they will be devoted to the one and despise the other, see Matthew 6:24, Luke 16:13. You cannot serve God and mammon (at its most basic level, the word mammon means riches or wealth, but it implies an idea of personified wealth gained with avarice, often taking on a deified nature). This warning, challenges the dreamer to appropriate wealth according to the commandments of the Most High, for this is an example of the principle reaping what you sow or "measure for measure". Allow this attitude to become part of your conduct, your "MO" sort to say, that your character might become full of love and generosity. In the words of Jesus, "Stop storing up treasures for yourselves on earth, where moths and rust destroy and where thieves break in and steal. But keep on storing up treasures for yourselves in heaven, where moths and rust do not destroy and where thieves do not break in and steal, because where your treasure is, there your heart will be also" (Matthew 6:19-21 ISV). Moreover, "Bring the entire tithe into the storehouse that there may be food in my house. So, put me to the test in this right now", says the Lord of the Heavenly Armies, "and see if I won't throw open the windows of heaven for you and pour out on you blessing without measure. In addition, I'll prevent the devourer from harming you, so that he does not destroy the crops of your land. Nor will the vines in your fields drop their fruit", says the Lord of the Heavenly Armies. "Then all the nations will call you blessed, for you will be a land of delight," says the Lord of the Heavenly Armies" (Malachi 3:10-12 ISV). See suggested course of action.

CARAVAN, CARRIAGE, CHARIOT, WAGONS, OR ANIMALS (a mode of transportation pulled by camels, horses, or mules, or riding on an animal):

This dream denotes that the dreamer is deliberately provoking someone, by mocking or poking fun at their lifestyle, often in an aggressive or "bullying" manner. While the dreamer is actually embracing the same attributes of the one you're bullying. You're not much different from the one you're aggressively mocking. Read, understand, and embrace Romans 2:1, 14:13, James 4:11, 5:9. With that said, also, see category, Animals. The negative characteristics attributed to the particular ani mal highlighted within your dream; the dreamer is embracing in your lifestyle; those negative attributes reflect your values and attitude. It is suggested as a course of action that the dreamer stop judging, mocking, and/or making fun of another and jud ge you. If counsel is not adhered, very soon, your actions will lead to a violent provocation, with you, the dreamer, on the losing end of the battle. By "checking" and judging yourself, you will become able to embrace the positive attributes of the same animal, if there are indeed positive attributes. FYI, the one you're mocking has already embraced the positive characteristics of the animal highlighted or have begun to turn from the negative attributes. See suggested course of action.

ROCKET, SPACECRAFT, OR SPACESHIP:

This dream has two meanings (choose one). (1) The dreamer desires freedom, or an escape, from a set of regimented rules and restrictions imposed upon your physical and/or spiritual life by an organization or place, or you desire freedom from a person. Dreamer, whatever you have asked for from God, namely that which initiated the desire to be free from some place, person you are involved with, or circumstance, it is the right thing. Your desires will be granted you; and this will result in your freedom, literally, emotionally, and spiritually. Suddenly, and without warning to anyone, you will be removed from that person, place, or circumstance that you seek to escape from; persons will look for you, and it will be as if you disappeared. (2) Bad condition of spacecraft (broke-down, dented, impounded, or unworkable): Although dreamer "voices" a desire to be free from some place, person you are involved with, or circumstance, there is no real desire to be delivered; therefore, dreamer w ill not be removed. Dreamer, you've only feign a desire for deliverance, while in your heart, you've chosen to remain a victim. Hence, until you own up to your victim mentality, and genuinely desire to be free, and repent from exalting someone, place, o r circumstance, above Almighty God. Until you seek God's wisdom and guidance via Jesus, and become obedient to His leading and guiding you, you will begin to decrease, and become weaken in spirit and body, and things will deteriorate, and it will b e allowed. See suggested course of action.

TIRES OR WHEELS (good condition or bad condition, e.g. flat, damaged, dented, or unusable):

This dream has two meanings (one or two may apply). (1) Dreams of tires generally point to the dreamer's attitude, behaviors, and life choices that are affecting your overall comfort and safety in your everyday living. Do your life choices promote a peaceful, self-supporting, independent type lifestyle? If not, the Lord gives wisdom and from His mouth comes knowledge and understanding. Then you will understand what is right and just and fair, every good path (Proverbs 2:1-6, 9-15). Dreamer, although your faults are before you, and some perhaps legitimate, Jesus loves you. Thus, dreamer is counseled to go to Jesus, aware of your own inadequacies, to ask for guidance and wisdom, and rest assure, that He has wisdom to give, and is generous and liberal enough to give to whomever ask, that includes you. He will not correct or criticize in a harsh manner, for He knows you are seeking guidance and wisdom. One may suffer needlessly, because he or she will not ask Jesus for wisdom, and for the courage to apply that wisdom within your own life. (2) Question, was tires/wheels in good condition, or in bad condition, e.g. flat, damaged, dented, unusable? Thus, this choice has two parts (choose one). (a) Good condition of tires/wheels: This dream was sent to encourage. Dreamer, you are "faring" very well in your life, and you are making life a nd financial adjustments wisely; therefore allow contentment to be the "wheels", sort to say, that maneuvers you through this thing we call life. Read, understand, and embrace, Hebrews 13:5, 1 Timothy 6:6-12, Luke 3:14, this is to you. With that said, the following is necessary for you to heed. Dreamer; do not allow anyone to "deflate" or lessen the importance of your self- confidence, and never do you ever feign a pseudo-humility by allowing yourself to be victimize. For, although you have a quiet and gentle spirit, you lack a practical wisdom and understanding of people; thus, you are easily deceived and cheated, especially financially. Hence, it will take for you, an unrivaled level of healthy self-confidence to continue growing spiritually and emotionally; and to become self-supporting and independent. Allow God's "strong" wisdom to lead the way. You are counseled to incorporate some of the "strong" and practical wisdom in the Book of Proverbs, and to make the wisdom, that which keeps your life "moving" in a good direction, a part of your life. (b) Bad condition of tires/wheels, e.g. flat, damaged, dented, unusable: Dreamer, you are internally inconsistent and disordered, because of a violent violation in your past or recent present; examples of the violation are abuse, assault, bullying, kidnapping, molestation, rape, stalked, being held prisoner. The diabolical entity, having possessed the person(s) who committed the literal act, was sent to rob, steal, and destroy a quality of life that has been fated you, to keep you from living that life abundantly, happily, and in peace. The demon's mission is to get you to entertain, embrace, and live out the negative results of your particular violation, with a h ope to oppress, persecute, and bring you into bondage of an ungodly and unprofitable lifestyle. Desiring that the unfa vorable consequences of that ungodly and unprofitable lifestyle; will cost you your emotional sanity, possibly your life, and ultimat ely your soul. Hence, instead of you moving towards, and thus fulfilling, your divine purpose, and reaching a pinnacle in your life, thereby with, you will prosper, you have begun to listen to, and be fooled by, demons. Having listened and embraced their lies, you have begun to decrease and fall, eventually running amok your life, literally crashing. Dreamer; oftentimes, ba d things happen to innocent and good people. A bad thing happened to you, and you are good and innocent. Compassionately, the Lord is creating a miracle in your life. This miracle will stop the effects of your violation from playing a significant role i n your life, enabling you to move forward with your life. However, the miracle's success depends upon your willingness to be healed and set free; for one will always have the choice to say no, or perhaps sabotage their progress. First, recognize and respect your time of visitation from the Lord, for it is upon you, as well as the work of His Hand upon your life. With fortitude, choose not to be a victim, nor to perpetuate the desolation. Dreamer, go and separate yourself from anyone and anything that hinders your clarity and emotional stability; literally stop what you're doing. Additionally, and if applicable, go, and conti nue your education, the Lord will help you in your endeavor. Dreamer, if you do not respect the work of the Lord within your life, and the opportunities He is offering you, to be set free, spiritually, emotionally and physically. You will have nothing to work with, but your body, namely deviant sexual promiscuousness, and all that comes with it, including physical death; having forfeited purpose, reasonable resources, and wise counsel that has surrounded you. For, your kind of choices, at present, leads to begging, early death, homelessness, homosexuality, imprisonment, poverty, and/or prostitution. Working with and using your intellect (mind) and/or strength, and good ethics, for your livelihood, will always out last the use of your body immorally for sustenance, and these choices makes life easier. Dreamer is counseled to seek all kinds of spiritual support n ow, to possibly avert or turn things around. Again, if you are in a negative place, move away from your present environment, definitely you should run away from all negativity abruptly. If you do not genuinely seek

871

help and change, for sure ruin wil l be your destiny. Utilizing the powerful resources of prayer and heartfelt repentance to Jesus is needed. Repentance is seeking pardon and expressing sincere feelings of regret and brokenness for having done something wrong and/or for having hurt someone. To Jesus pray, Psalm 51, this followed by appropriate application of wisdom, can conceivably avert some of the repercussions of your choices. If you lack wisdom ask God for wisdom; and He will give you wisdom. This coupled with fasting, a changed mindset, serious re-consideration of God's ways and means, and an honest acknowledgement of God's hand within your life, then the severe impact of your choices and actions upon your life, can be reversed and damages repaired (also see Ezekiel 33:12-19). This is what is called leaving a blessing behind. See suggested course of action.

Rims (of tires or wheels): This dream has six meanings (one, two, etc., or all may apply). (1) Dreamer, God is going to heal your broken heart. If necessary, see suggested course of action. (2) Dreamer, character traits from ancestors, namely genetic codes and traits, will often trouble and taunt the offspring of a given progenitor, especially generational issues (E xodus 20:5-7). The demons that have so plague your family line, are now visiting (re-visiting) you, namely voices that whisper, you are without value, insignificant, or pointless, and it is the embracing of those voices that will lead to other issues, such as sexual perversion (e.g. adultery, fornication, homosexuality, prostitution, or whorishness), and on to a bleak and desolate atmosphere. This will lead to much sadness, and feelings of being forsaken or abandoned. Favorably, generational curses and issues can stop with you (Jeremiah 31:29, 30; Ezekiel 18:2-14, 20-23). Hence, your Heavenly Father is requiring that you overcome and subdue negative and dark emotions, feelings, behaviors, and/or ideas that would influence you, before they overcome you; and leave you desolate. Dreamer, God is not asking you to do something you cannot do. For a surety, vanquishing of the coming influence can be done. Dreamer, the Lord Jesus, is asking you to come to Him, come away privately, and ask Him to heal you, come, and ask Him to deliver you; and give Him authority over your life that you might be healed, delivered, and set free. Thus says the Lord, "I will sprinkle clean water on you, and you will be clean; I will cleanse you from all your impurities and from all your idols. I will give you a new heart and put a new spirit in you; I will remo ve from you your heart of stone and give you a heart of flesh. See suggested course of action. (3) Dreamer, you are insincere in your dealings with people, especially by being outwardly friendly but secretly disloyal. All of these behaviors are a sign of a hardened heart or a heart becoming hardened and deep-seated anger. Your behavior opened the door for a demonic instigated situation or issue. Dreamer, your present situation, or issue, whatever "it" is, "it" was demonically instigated, and "it" is spiritually perverse. By faith, you will need to declare some kind of fast and commit to it, for a long period-of-time, to abate the demonically instigated circumstance, you find yourself in now, Matthew 6:16-18. Try abstaining from food and drink (midnight to 6 PM), twice a week, and refrain from words, attitudes, people, places, and things, including music, magazines, videos, TV, or any such things that fuel anger and discontent, and stir up lustful feelings. This is also known as, faith with works, re ad, understand, and embrace James 2:14-26. Nonetheless, earnestly pray, God will guide, enable, and answer you as to the type of fast. Dreamer, God knows your thoughts afar off, so genuinely repent. Other than heartfelt repentance to Jesus, no other excuse or weak justification will be heard. Additionally, if relevant, forgive your mother and/or father for the darkness (aka curse) they may have perpetuated, for they knew not what they done. Forgiveness is important to your success (Matthew 6:12-15, 8:21-35). See suggested course of action. (4) This dream also represents some type of spiritual privileges and a purification process. Dreamer God will now separate you from people, places, and circumstances that will hinder your growth. View this separation as a blessing from God and not as an evil thing has happen. Under all adversities retain a spirit of joy, and continue to make progress in your spiritual life. Subsequently, dreamer, because of your humble and submissive faith in God' s word, you will be declared as one who is a righteous minister. Planted in the House of the Lord, you will continue to prosper and mature. The same God, who plants you in your ministry, is the same God who will cause you to mature and prosper. Further, another benefit of allowing Jesus to have authority of your life; is that independent of outward circumstances, you will live and thrive where most things perish, via divine grace. Dreamer, while your spiritual growth may not be so rapid, if you endure, you will become a beautiful picture of a godly man or woman, who in your uprightness, aims to glorify God. Accordingly, gladness, thanksgiving, singing, then, strength, intense energy, and fertility will be your recompense, and your praise will be a sweet aroma in the nostrils of the Lord. If applicable, this promise is also to your generations to come. Come what may, you shall make steady progress and flourish in a very impressive manner; bringing forth fruit, even in your old age. Dreamer, as you age, your anointing to minister, and divine revelations, will always be fresh and edifying. See Psalm 92:12-15. Therefore, put the spiritual work in and go through what you need to go through now. If necessary, see suggested course of action. (5) Male dreamer: An event or situation that will cause intense fear is coming to discourage and terrify you. This will be in the form of an annoying, difficult, and unpleasant person. The trouble this person will cause will become so overwhelming, because they will expose a secret regarding you. This spiritual battle will be great, and will demand your full attention. Although you will walk through this alone, know that God will walk you through it. Dreamer, learn wisdom from th e situation, for truth do set one free; and go on from there unashamed. Then, suddenly, unexpectedly, and without any warning, all the evil and wickedness that caused you to fear and be troubled, will disappear. It will be as though it was ne ver there. At that point, you will express great joy, and feel extremely happy. Take courage and be strong, knowing that the Lord knows where you are, what's going on, and He cares. See suggested course of action. (6) Male dreamer (unmarried): This dream denotes that a very attractive and sensual female; one whom the dreamer, may marry, especially before having sex, will enter your life. If necessary, see suggested course of action.

Suggested Course of Action

Question to consider and journal, did your dream depict any symbols that alludes to, the dreamer will make the necessary changes, spiritually, emotionally, and/or physically to affect a more positive outcome? One hint as to whether or not you will deal with your issues and/or respond righteously; is, was the condition of the vehicle fixed? If fixed, t his is a good clue as to whether you will respond to God positively. If changes are initiated, your dreams will change

Nevertheless, if you are here, first things first, dreamer it is acknowledged that your struggles with your life choices and issues are real, and it really has been hard living your life, but a change can come. While there's nothing more frustrating than having genuinely tried to "straighten out" your life, and make the right choices, just to find yourself starting all over aga in, and again, and again, reaping the same negative results. Further, because of emotional scarring and/or insecurities resulting fro m past difficult situations, you may not have the ability to work through challenging circumstances at this time and to make th e best decisions; favorably, the Lord wants to be the difference.

You may ask what good is it to try to get back on track, to choose life, if ultimately your efforts will always prove empty. What good is it whether one is righteous or wicked if both paths eventually lead to the same end? If all roads lead to the same end, why be righteous? Why sacrifice for others, or why not "live it up" while one is alive. It would seem that faithfulnes s is not nearly as important as one's own happiness, even if this happiness is only short-lived and, in the end, futile. It is within this context that, the Lord wants to be the difference. We must understand the reality of death and of hell, mentally, emotionally, physically, spiritually, and eternally. While certain life choices are easier on the mind, emotions, feelings, and desires, and other choices, primarily wise and prudent choices, require much more energy to maintain. The life choices that always lead t o ruin, creates death and hell on this side of eternity. Those choices will never have you consider eternity. Question to consider, why live in deathlike and hellish situations, and then die, and take all that with you. Dreamer, you must consider life on t he other side of this life also. Thus, dreamer this moment, God is placing before you, life, and good, death, and evil, and He is asking that you choose life (Deuteronomy 30:15-20). Yes, once again, and again, and again, until you begin to maintain, for you will eventually maintain, if you don't give up. For an upright man (or woman), after falling seven times, will get up again: but trouble is the downfall of the evil

(Proverbs 24:16 BBE). Nevertheless, the issue of eternal life will not be forced upon anyone who desires to remain in sin. Dreamer, it is when we think that we do not need God or that God does not care, that we remain in a negative life cycle, aka that merry-go-around. It is when you embrace and live out the ideology of, "what good is it whether one is righteous or wicked if both paths lead to the same end, or I'm not serving God simply for what I can get out of it. Therefore, God is merely a means to an end"; it is this kind of thinking that keeps you from maintaining a genuine lifestyle of comfortability and ease. Regrettably, this in turn can, and often do, result in emotional emptiness, and you rejecting the love, authority, and instructions of God. A spirit of apathy towards your personal relationship with Christ is a bad frame o f mind. In time, your carnal nature will dominantly reign over your spiritual side. Carnality always opens the door for someone, under the influence of evil, to run amok your life, both physically and spiritually until you are unable to recover.

It is suggested that you re-examine your choices, write down the good versus the wicked, the sacred versus the profane, those that promote life, and those that bring about death, and allow God to be the difference. For, there are character trai ts within you that you need to render obsolete, and began anew attempting to move forward, using different tactics to overcome unproductive habitual life cycle choices, and for maneuvering through this thing, we call life in a more, better way. Dreamer, it is time for you to make that leap to love God, to truly learn of His ways and means, and to learn to follow His plan for your life. If you can do this, you can live forever in His paradise (heaven), and experience peace on this side of heaven.

Compassionately, grace (the free and unmerited favor and beneficence of God) is extended that you may change your heart. God is giving you the opportunity to turn things around spiritually and emotionally, and He will turn things around literally; however, you will have to choose to allow the opportunity, for you still have free will; thus, the choice is yours. Free will is the expression of you choosing to participate in the divine acts of God; albeit, you are only merely placing your han d under the weight carried exclusively by God. Thus, you are not being asked to do something you cannot do, or to do it alone. Moreover, dreamer is strongly urged to return to ideals that are holy, wise, well judged; ways that are in keeping with the nature of the Bible, ways pertaining to, contained within, and are in accordance with the Bible; way s that are scriptural. This will lead you back to Christ.

God has not given up on you. He has provided a way for you to defeat negative life choices. This solution is given to us in John 3:16. Those who follow Him experience blessings now in the present age and in the age to come, eternal life.

Now, pray (See Prayer of Deliverance, pg. 897)

Specific Meaning

If, in your everyday living (your waking state), as part of your lifestyle or work related activities, you have a very specia l relationship with any mode of transportation (e.g. a bus drive, mechanic, car dealership salesman or owner, pilot, animal rider or trainer, vacationer). Dreams of this sort, for the most part, are ordinary dreams, resulting from your daily activities (see Chapter One, Chalom). These sorts of dreams are usually about your routine, mundane activities or anxieties that overwhelm your mind during the day. They are an inner release mechanism, which helps provide you with emotional balance and the maintaining of your sanity. These dreams are not significant, and do not warrant special attention.

Note: Dreamer, consider this question, did you create something within your dream? Did you receive a unique idea? Could you be receiving inspiration, via your dream? Regarding an idea, or possible creation of something, that would benefit the masses, via an enhancement of a mode of travel; especially if you are an enthusiast, or have a connection with any activi ty involving vehicles or modes of travel. Your dream may very well be a divine sent inspiration. Therefore, consider it not strange for someone, who is involved in some manner of activity that involves vehicles or modes of travel, to receive inspirations regarding the collective masses, via their dreams, that might prove beneficial to the dreamer and to mankind. Per chapter one, sometimes the most meaningless dream will help change your life in ways you would have never thought, especially entrepreneurially and enterprisingly. Throughout history, humankind has received life changing insight and guidance from their dreams. Most of the time the information acquired within dreams exceeds that which we could obtain during our normal, analytical, waking state of mind. With that said, via your dream, dreamer you have miraculously been given big goals that involve building a better world and giving back to it what it has given you. Therefore, write your vision down, that yo u may articulate it to others properly, for the vision will happen. Prepare a good proposal, name your inspiration, and write down all the details and specifics, and brand mark it. Give it your best that it may be acceptable to any reputable financia l entity, benefactor, or merit a grant of some kind. Perhaps, hire a grant writer. That which you will need to fulfill your aims, surely, you will have. Your dream should closely resemble real life situations. Meaning it can actually occur during your awaked state.

If, there is a very high propensity for an accident, a dream of this sort should be received as a precautionary warning, to prevent serious harm to yourself, and/or others. For example, is dreamer a racecar driver or motocross competitor? Be careful. Do not assume that you're safe or it's ok, caution should be heeded at this time. If an unfortunat e mishap, especially one causing damage or injury, happened within your dream, e.g. perhaps a serious racing accident was depicted within your dream; this is a precautionary warning. The accident, kept within context of the dream, should closely resemble real life situations. Meaning it can actually occur during your awaked state. This will help you narrow down the specifics, and avoid danger.

If vehicle was damaged in anyway within the dream, this may also be heeded as an alert or warning in the physical realm, to prevent serious harm to driver and/or passengers. The dreamer may consider his or her dream as a clue given that may be needed to support a prevailing situation. For example, if any kind of distraction caused an accident, e.g. cell phone, dri ving while under the influence, yelling at children, driver might consider being more mindful and consider safety when operating a vehicle. Possibly, the person in the dream who caused the accident may need the safety reminder. If another had the accident, perhaps you are being made aware of the plight of someone, particularly the person highlighted within your dream, and you are to get involved (see Chapter One, Are You Ready to Hear the Messages in Your Dreams, section entitled, The 10% for others). There may be potential for a serious accident. Did you know the individual within your dream? Where did the accident occur? What kind of accident was it? Dreamer, the details, kept within context of your dream, should closely resemble real life situations. Meaning it can actually occur during your awaked state. If you sense your dream is for or about another, namely the person highlighted within the dream, the question as to why you have been made aware of this information, and how do you factor into the equation, should be seriously considered, along with necessary actions. Call the person, and warn them of your concerns. Your warnings will help them narrow down the specifics needed to steer them clear of possible trouble. Nonetheless, the mishap, kept within context of the dream, should be relevant to your lifestyle and closely resemble your real-life situations. Meaning it can literally occur during your awaked state. This will help you narrow down the specific area of concern. However, if your dream was inundated with symbols that are not specifically related to your everyday life, job, and/or responsibilities, then the spiritual implications should be heeded.

WEATHER

(the state of the atmosphere with regard to temperature, cloudiness, rainfall, wind, and other meteorological conditions)

"Have you entered the storehouses of the snow, or have you seen the storehouses of the hail, which I have reserved for the time of trouble, for the day of battle and war? What is the way to the place where the light is distributed, or where the east wind is scattered upon the earth? Who has cleft a channel for the torrents of rain and a way for the thunderbolt, to bring rain on a land where no man is, on the desert in which there is no man, to satisfy the waste and desolate land, and to make the ground sprout with grass? Has the rain a father, or who has begotten the drops of dew? From whose womb did the ice come forth, and who has given birth to the frost of heaven? The waters become hard like stone, and the face of the deep is frozen". (Job 38:22-30 ESV)

He who is watching the wind will not get the seed planted, and he who is looking at the clouds will not get in the grain (Ecclesiastes 11:4 BBE)

Son of man, say to her, you are a land on which no rain or thunderstorm has come in the day of wrath. (Ezekiel 22:24 BBE)

Daniel said, "I was looking in my vision by night, and behold the four winds of heaven were stirring up the great sea. Daniel 7:2

...and the rain descended, and the floods came, and the winds blew Matthew 7:25 (ASV)

For as in a thunderstorm the bright light is seen from one end of the sky to the other, so will the Son of man be when his ti me comes. Luke 17:24 (BBE)

This category deals with the atmospheric conditions that comprise the state of the atmosphere in terms of temperature, wind, clouds, and precipitation. Some short descriptions of types, phrases, and other processes and particulars, connected in some way to this category are, for example, climate, cloudy, elements, fall, hurricanes, rain, seasons, spring, summer, tornadoes, violent or severe weather, winter. Also, see category content list, or index.

All Symbols and Referents, Notes (1, 2, 3, etc.), Suggested Course of Action, and Specific Meaning offer guidance toward a more comprehensive interpretation.

Notes

1. Unless otherwise noted elsewhere, if, in your everyday living, your awaked state, as part of your lifestyle, work, or ministerial activities, or a special event, you have a very real connection with any activity involving any science that deals with the phenomena of the atmosphere, especially weather and weather conditions. For example, atmospheric physic, climatology, forecaster, meteorology, or any disciplines of the atmospheric sciences, your dream is not significant and does not warrant special attention.

   Otherwise noted, on occasion, one may experience an Oneirovatic or "OV" dream (see Chapter One, "The 60th Part of Prophecy", section entitled – Other Prophetic Dreams). This type of dream should be regarded as a vision and received as a precautionary warning. For example, to dream that you "see or forecasted" a disastrous weather event headed toward your location, and that it may prove catastrophic in nature, e.g. hurricane, tsunami. This type of dream bares insight into the life of those who may seriously be affected by the coming event. The dreamer is being warned to be extra cautious regarding the location "pin-pointed", especially if dreamer lives within or near the location depicted, because of a high chance for personal harm. Dreamer is also urged to take cover somewhere, evacuate, and/or to strongly advise, or warn others, to do the same, due to possible disastrous issues related to, perhaps violent weather conditions, especially if this is a common issue within that area. Your dream should closely resemble real life situations, with the dream events literally being capable of happening. If you sense that your dream is a vision, the question as to why you have been made aware of this information, and how do you factor into the equation, should be seriously considered, along with necessary actions. Dreamer, you are meant to get involved. If possible, how can you ease the situation? Dreams that reference others and the revelation within those dreams, is not given haphazardly to any individual, but only to those with the ability, and influence to do something with the information; this is also prophecy. Skip interpretation, Jesus will strengthen you emotionally, psychologically, and physically to seek help and support in your endeavors, and possibly how to help others.

Otherwise noted, this dream of weather may be a Prophetically Simple Dream (see Chapter One: The 60th Part of Prophecy). Whereas, the dreamer is encouraged, for example, to learn, and/or invent or devise a new weather instrument, or to initiate a new way of determining weather, especially if a uniquely new device, or way, was introduced to you within your dream, and to adopt the new style as your own signature style (e.g. name the style after you). Did you invent something? See Specific Meaning at the end of this category, section entitled, Note (Specific Meaning).

Otherwise noted, per your lifestyle, if your dream closely resembled real life situations, meaning it can literally occur during your awaked state, this dream may be an Ordinary Dream, resulting from your daily activities (see Chapter One, Chalom). These sorts of dreams are usually about your routine, mundane activities or anxieties that overwhelm your mind during the day. They are an inner release mechanism, which helps provide you with emotional balance and the maintaining of your sanity. These dreams are not significant, and do not warrant special attention.

2. Probables: As weather is frequently demonstrated in many, and very personal ways; for example, does dreamer live in region that is known for its inclement weather? Does a particular season remind you of a particular place or environment? Thus, could the weather depicted be a possible probable (see Chapter One, section entitled, Probables)? Hence, dreamer may also consider your own personal and special associations with the various seasons of the year, as long as the interpretation is kept within the principles of spiritual boundary markers, landmarks, and property lines, (see Chapter One, section entitled, Spiritualizing Boundary Markers, Landmarks, and Property Lines).

3. Determine who your dream is for you or another. Always, considering yourself first, reflecting on your present behaviors. Ask yourself, why am I dreaming about this now? What is this dream revealing about me? Have I taken on new attributes? Has anyone commented on my present behaviors as being untypical of me? Has my ministry changed for the better or for the worse? What about my beliefs, doctrine, or philosophy, are they still based on Holy Writ? Is there something I need to know about those I am ministering to or serving?

Remember your actions and emotions within your dream. Was the dreamer a weather forecaster, was the dreamer in a storm, or preparing for a storm? Were dark clouds over your head? Did inclement weather flood your house? Unless otherwise noted elsewhere, an answer of yes, to one or more of these, or similar questions, is a good indicator that your dream is about you (the dreamer). What happened to you in your dream? How did things end? In light of your dream, via the relevant interpretation, do you believe that your choices will enhance or endanger your well-being, safety, and/or happiness, if so, how and why? Do you believe that your belief system will strengthen or weaken you spiritually in any way, if so, how and why? Is spiritual or physical death a possibility? Are you teaching a "twisted" message, perpetuating hate towards others? See following relevant subcategory, the interpretation is about and for you.

Was someone else a weather forecaster? Did dreamer see another on a raft, preparing for a storm? Did inclement weather flood another's home? Did dreamer see others in a storm? Was the sun shining directly on someone? Unless otherwise noted elsewhere, an answer of yes, to one or more of these, or similar questions, is a good indicator that your dream is about another and their role, and/or influential effects, within the life of the dreamer. Does dreamer know someone whose life activities or physical being is similar to that which stood out the most within your dream, thus leading to storms in that person's life? Could it be that person? If you sense that your dream is for or about another, the question as to why you have been made privy to this information, and how do you factor into the equation, should be seriously considered along with necessary actions. Perhaps the dreamer is being made aware of the plight of someone, and you are to get involved (see Chapter One, Are You Ready to Hear the Messages in Your Dreams, section entitled, The 10% for others).

If your dream is for, or about another:

Dreams that reference others and the revelation within those dreams, is not given haphazardly to any individual, but only to those with the ability, and influence to do something with the information; this is also prophecy. With that, journal the following questions, and if unable to answer the questions now, this denotes that the person, represented within your dream, will enter your life shortly. Are you entering into a personal relationship with someone? Do you not know or understand what you're looking at, especially certain behaviors, when learning about this person? Has someone new entered your life or maybe you've just begun opening up to someone not so new, and have started listening to their advice, accepting their assistance, or are you supporting or enabling someone? Are you in denial regarding the toxicity of one of your present relationships, particularly a spouse, family member, or friend? Are you anxious, concerned, frightened, and/or troubled by recent changes in your behavior, especially because of someone's influence upon your life at present? Have you allowed someone to convince you to deceive another? Have you recently become aware of (or is being made aware of, via this dream) certain undesirable behaviors within you towards another? Are you trying to cut ties with one that is bad company? Have you just joined (or re-joined) a church, fellowship, or social group?

Note: If your dream has attributes that indicate that your dream is about you, and other attributes that indicate that your dream is about another, dreamer should consider that your dream is about you and another. For example, were you and another preparing for a storm? Did inclement weather affect your neighborhood, or town? Did you and another get caught in a storm? Thus indicating that your dream is about the dreamer, and another; therefore, while your dream is about the dreamer, the dreamer should expect the role and/or influential effects of another, also plays a part in your interpretation. For example, dreamer may not have heeded evacuation notices prior to a hurricane, and now is responsible for the loss of clients in a nursing the dreamer owned. From which now the dreamer needs to rebuild your life, again, see relevant interpretation.

More questions to consider. Why has the person been allowed within your life, and/or how did they get there? Again, if unable to answer the questions now, this denotes that the person, represented within your dream, will enter your life shortly. If their activity, within your dream, has proven positive, via the interpretation, this someone will prove, unwittingly, to be a very strong ally, benefactor, defender, and supporter. God has sent this someone into your life to help you carry out your next endeavor by enlarging your spiritual capacity. Allow the strength of that person's character to guide, help, and support you. On the other hand, if his or her presence and/or activity, within your dream, proved negative, via the interpretation, for sure, this person will prove to be a very strong and formidable challenge for you, perhaps unto death. If negative, this dream is a dire warning. Take steps accordingly to struggle against, or to cut off, adverse and unfavorable relationships. Remember certain personalities are all encompassing, affecting everything, cataclysmic, contagious, deadly, harmful, infectious, predatory, and/or venomous. Symbolically meaning that if allowed to continue or prosper within your life, serious harm or death to the dreamer may result. Idolize no one, especially beyond the warning of the Lord, and we are definitely not to lay our lives down for no one. Then again, this person maybe allowed within your life, because of the dreamer's unwillingness to abstain from immorality after having been asked to abstain from such by God, see 1 Corinthians 6:9-20, Galatians 5:19-21, or the dreamer's self-righteous behavior, or a lack of a balanced and honest view of your own personality. In this case, this person will affect self-awareness within the life of the dreamer, exposing the negative traits of your personality, especially those traits, which cause you to follow, or to be so easily misled, and/or your wrong beliefs; no matter, this type of mentality needs reckoning with. Graciously, all of this will restore the dreamer to his or her right place with God, opening your eyes to see how far you've strayed from God (1 Corinthians 5:4-7; James 5:20). The lesson is, no matter how personable, powerful, or difficult a person, or how uncertain or unpopular the choices and issues, always take the next biblical and ethical step, for obedience to God's principles will always prove safer and stronger foundationally. Although, you will need all kinds of outside support to recover from this person's domination, no longer, allow that particular person's influence within your life to continue or thrive, especially if negative, end it abruptly.

4. Consider all the people, places, backgrounds, and activity highlighted within your dream.

Known (in your awaked life) person, animal, place, or organization within your dream:

Unless otherwise noted elsewhere, people, animals, places, backgrounds that are literally known by the dreamer in your awaked life, indicates a part of you that you recognize within yourself on some level or another. Question, if dreamer seriously considers the person, animal, place, or background attributes, what character traits stood out the most, or what features stood out the most? For example, age, color, height, size, happiness, considerate, loving, let you be yourself, peacefulness, encourager, irrational, leader, liar, mentor, passionate, personable, neglected, poor, run-down, sage, shyster, unwise, upscale, vengeful. Write down (journal) the particular highlighted within your dream. The attribute or activity highlighted is for a reason. Since the attribute written down is a part of you, namely the dreamer's nature, demeanor, and/or lifestyle, an honest and unbiased assessment is very important for truth sake. Happy note, considering that other people's attributes, within dreams, also represent attributes of your own personality, causes one to look at another in a better light. According to your capacity to embrace self-awareness and a rectification of mind, body, and spirit, God will begin to enhance, make better, more attractive, sanctify, diminish, and make pure and free from sin and guilt, this part of you.

Otherwise noted, if the person, animal, place, or background within your dream; is literally known by the dreamer, in your awaked life, this person, animal, place, or background may represent him or herself, or itself.

Unknown in your awaked life or although known, was unseen, invisible, or only talked about - person, animal, place, or organization within your dream:

Unless otherwise noted elsewhere, if you did not recognize, the person, place, thing, they, or it, was not seen, invisible, or only talked about within your dream, this indicates an attribute or activity within your life that you are unfamiliar with, or are in denial about, or you refuse to acknowledge it, but it does exist. Question, what character trait, feature, action, or activity, stood out the most? For example, age, color, height, size, happiness, considerate, loving, let you be yourself, peacefulness, encourager, irrational, leader, liar, mentor, passionate, personable, neglected, poor, run - down, sage, shyster, unwise, upscale, vengeful. Although, on some conscious level, you are aware of a certain behavior or attribute within you, you have chosen to filter out or simply ignore certain information about yourself that contradicts your view of yourself and/or your preconceived notions of others and of the world around you. Possibly protecting yourself, emotionally and psychologically, from a situation, which you are unable to cope with at this time, or you lack control over; then again, perhaps the dreamer has an exaggerated or unrealistic view of yourself. No matter the reason, right now a question is before you, via your dream. Do you want to know this part of yourself? According to your ability to handle self-awareness, God will begin to reveal this side of you to you. Why, He wants to balance your understanding of things; thus, effecting wholeness within your life, so that the enemy will no longer be able to manipulate your emotions so easily. The Paraclete is with you to help you throughout this entire process, listen to Him. Now, in your life, this activity or attribute needs reckoning with, somehow or someway.

Otherwise noted, (known or unknown), if the person, place or thing that initiated (or was a recipient of) the action or activity within your dream was not seen, invisible, or only talked about within your dream, this may indicate that the dreamer does not recognize the influential effects another has within your life, or upon your attitude.

If more than one person (known or unknown):

Consider what the group had in common. What behavior, character trait, feature, action, or activity, stood out the most? For example, were they argumentative, authoritative, beautiful, criminal minded, dancing, difficult, dressed unusual, enigmatic, fighting, focused, flirty, helpful, hurtful intentions, powerful, promiscuous, quiet, secretive, seemed unreal, unassuming? That which was highlighted and noted is what you need to focus on at present.

If the attribute or quality is a desirable or positive one, allow the strength of that attribute to help you overcome some manner of immorality or irreverence within your life and/or to help you to become better, productively, for the Kingdom of God in some manner. If the attribute is an undesirable or negative one, take steps accordingly to struggle against the growing desires of the carnal side of you. If applicable, get help and support via prayer, fasting, and a Christian based support group.

For dreams of the dead see following note.

Did someone die because of weather conditions? While the dead has nothing to do with the living (Ecclesiastes 9:4- 6), it may be considered what character trait did that person represent to the dreamer, while the person was literally alive, what character feature stood out the most. With that trait noted, dreamer may consider that the trait noted, is within the dreamer, and that trait is no longer useful or needed for the progression of your spiritual walk, on this side of heaven. Dreamer, it is suggested that you render that trait (good or bad) obsolete, and began anew attempting to move forward, using different tactics to overcome unproductive habitual life cycle choices, and for maneuvering through this thing we call life in a more, better way. See category, Death, and/or other relevant categories.

5. In addition to the following interpretation, see index or relevant category for more information. For example, if a boat capsized, see category, Accidents. If broken branches were everywhere, see category, Agriculture. If broken bones, or perhaps a wall or ceiling was crumbling, falling down, or leaking, see categories, the Body and/or Buildings, and relevant subcategories. If air pressure or category of type of storm (e.g. category 5), see category, Numbers. Kept within context of your dream and the interpretation, the additional symbols are perhaps relevant. It will be within the sum of all the symbols that you will find a more thorough interpretation.

6. Since the following list is not extensive, dreamer is encouraged to seek biblical guidelines and other relevant research to determine the metaphorical meaning of your particular types of weather activity, depicted within your dream, via a Bible concordance, Bible illustrated

dictionary, encyclopedia, or internet. Having done your research you should be able to determine some basic behaviors or attributes your Lord and Savior wants you to focus on.

Symbols and Referents

Most dreams of weather, coupled with the relevant interpretation, are generally sent as an alarm to the dreamer, signaling the occurrence of some undesirable event, outside of the dreamer's control or resulting from the dreamer's behavior and choices. In addition to the varied meanings of weather, other common words, expressions, usages, (e.g. slang or clichés), or a 'probable' that are metaphorically represented by any of the following are also considered (this section is an addendum at th e end of the category or subcategory).

Category Content - If not listed see index, perchance, for your specific type of weather dream.

- Avalanche, see category, Landforms
- Blizzard or Snow (ice storm, snowstorm, snow bank, glacier, or snow covered)
- Clouds (bright and clear clouds, clouds clear and then come back with rain, cloudy, dark ominous clouds, also "Dark clouds over head")
- Cyclone, Hurricane, Thunder and Lightning, Lightning, without the sound of thunder, Tornado, or Typhoon
- Dew
- Flood, Tidal Wave, Torrent, Tsunami
- Fog, Night Midst
- Hail (rain of ice pellets)
- Monsoons, Winds (wind that changes direction with the seasons)
- Rain
- Sleet (mixture of snow and rain)
- Seasons (winter, spring, summer, and fall; one of the natural periods into which the year is divided by the equinoxes, or atmospheric conditions during a certain time of year)
- Sunny, see subcategory, (Summer)
- Weather Forecasting

BLIZZARD OR SNOW (ice storm, snowstorm, snow bank, glacier, or snow covered):

This dream has two meanings (choose one). (1) Blizzard: Your dream refers to one who is unhappy, disliked, devoid of genuine spirituality, unable to discern between truth and error, and you do not realize that you are these things. Dreamer, although your behavior has been immoral and shameful, even horrible, and yes the Lord disapproves, genuinely owning up to your offenses, without justifications, will allow healing and restoration to begin in your life. The immoral and shameful behavior: your truths are deceitful and worthless, leading to destruction. Your justifications are weak excuses, unstable, leading to trouble. The Lord detests lying lips, but He delights in men (and women) who are truthful (Proverbs 12:22). The more God allows you to see your emptiness, it is suggested that you be more earnest to repent that you may find Him to be grace and healing, refreshment, and a refuge. Question to consider, dreamer if after God has examined you, would it turn out well for you? If not, it is time to make it so that all might be well. Hence, your dream is to warn a rebellious person, in the spirit of grace (the free and unmerited favor and beneficence of God). To see if you will yet be worked upon, and change your mindset, or else to leave you inexcusable, in your accusations against God, because of your ruin (e.g. continually plundered, seized, and disfavored, also see Jeremiah 9:7-9; Zechariah 13:9; Matthew 23:37-39; Revelation 3:15-21). (2) Snow, snow bank, glacier, or snow covered: God sees a fresh desire for divine knowledge rising up within you. Do you see this desire within you? It's a desire for a more balanced view of spiritual things, a balance between heart and intellect. He will manifest Himself to you. Additionally, although you cannot see your way right now, God is making a way for you, creating streams of peace, causing you to go forth in serenity. For your part, He is challenging you by asking some very penetrating questions. Questions to journal: Can God be trusted? Do you believe in the goodness of the Lord for your life? Can God do immeasurably more than you can ask or imagine? Do you have faith in God, which is a resolute trust in the integrity of God and in His Word? Do you know your divine purpose and/or gifting? Do you like the things that life is showing you? Have you've gotten what you'v e been hoping for, or gotten your heart's desire? Are there any open doors "opportunities" for your desire? Are you content? Will you trust God to make a way of peace and serenity for you? Your capacity to answer these questions honestly, and not in an approved or fittingly manner, signifies your depth of God, and depth of spirituality and self-awareness. If you were unable to answer at least four of the questions, or most of your answers were, "I don't know", this indicates spiritual unawareness, a lack of faith, and/or prideful words of criticism. If you've found yourself unable to answer most, or none, of the questions, this reveals a lack of studiousness in knowing the things and nature of God; for your lifestyle inhibits you from learning, progressing, and becoming skilled at what God has called you to do, as well as, your ability to proselytize. This type of attitude is spiritually poisonous to the believer, and can lead to a rejection of all or some of the original foundational teachings o f Christ and His apostles. If you've found yourself answering "no" to most, or all, of the questions, this is indicative of never-ending complaining, whining, and overall unconstructive thinking. Quiet yourself within and hear God's quiet voice. It is here where you will begin to become aware of what God is saying to you about you and how might the negativity within be remedied. This can include but is not limited to, a lack of tithe paying and general giving, receipt of disability support, when no legitima te disability is present, cheating on taxes, using others for gain, receiving government help when not qualified, and of course stealing. Kept within context of your dream and the interpretation, deceit and unfaithfulness may be an area of relevance regarding your attitude problem. See suggested course of action.

CLOUDS (bright and clear clouds, clouds clear and then come back with rain, cloudy, dark ominous clouds; also "Dark clouds over head"):

This dream has three meanings (choose one). (1) Bright and clear clouds: Dreamer, you have reached the end of a refining process, see Proverbs 17:3, 27:21. Moreover, as this dream is figurative of the Shekinah, a glow of the Light of God's Goodness. The Creator, via this dream, is expressing His nearness to the dreamer, to make known His thoughts and feelings regarding you. Dreamer, God's opinion of, and high regard for you, is as if there is no fault. The prosperity of your soul, your lifestyle, and choice of friends, God takes great delight in. So impressive are you, you will be honored, notable, and weigh ted with goods, property, and money, as well as given some level of authority (if not already). His love towards you, and delight in you, is no small matter. "For I know the plans I have for you," declares the Lord, "plans to prosper you and not to harm you, plans to give you hope and a future" (Jeremiah 29:11 NIV). In His mercy, the Creator will reveal to you some of the light of His glory. Glory in this sense is a state of honor, spiritual beauty, and greater illumination. You will experience instantaneo us knowledge, according to your aptitude for knowledge, understanding, and maturity level. This experience will create within you a greater capacity for spiritual ideals, and a better spirit. Dreamer, you will genuinely experience His Divine Presence, His Shekinah, if you remain diligent and don't give up on your spiritual journey. In all this, glorify God's loving Hand upon your life, which is worthy of praise, and continue giving Him the honor. Further, a negative lifestyle cycle that needs to be broken wi thin your life, experiencing the glory of God's Shekinah, a glow of the Light of God's Goodness, will heal this too, as well; you will be healed of a present sickness. Additionally, bright and clear clouds, also denotes one who is under godly and ethical leaders hip be it civil or religious. Dreamer is under the authority of moral, God-fearing, very conscientious, and ethical leadership; therefore, remain in your present place of worship. (2) Clouds clear and then come back with rain: As this symbol denotes physical death is imminent and perhaps even spiritual death. This dream has come to set life and death soberly before you, the dreamer, and if you will not choose behaviors, actions, thoughts, and choices that promote life, you will die physically, and this before your time, (Ecclesiastes 7:17). To the dreamer it is said, for you to remember your Creator, before your days of trouble come and time has caught up with you (Ecclesiastes 12:1-7). Further, no dead philosophy, or any other lifeless "ism" will come to life to tell you truth, nor will a dead person, come to life, to tell you of what he or she has seen. For, if the "ism" did contain a spark of life, or if the dead did come back to tell you of what he or she experienced, you would not believe th e teaching, nor would you believe the dead. For, relationship with Christ, appeals to people not by half-truths or lies, or ghosts or frightful apparitions; it appeals to your reason, your conscience, and your hopes. God's Holy Spirit leads to truth. Additionally, about your dream, dreamer death is not only physical, but also it denotes a spiritual separation from God, a place of torment, aka "Tartarus", which is also death. Dreamer, if you will not hear the Son of God and the warnings of the Scriptures, there is nothing, which you will or can hear, you will never be persuaded, and will never escape the place of torment. See suggested course of action. (3) Dark ominous clouds (also "Dark clouds over head"): This dream has two parts (one or both may apply). (a) This dream denotes one, namely the dreamer, who is under very ungodly, unethical, and demonically led leadership, be it civil or religious. Dreamer is under the authority of immoral, unscrupulous, unprincipled, and unconscionable leadership. Dreamer needs to make a decision as to remain under this type of leadership or leave. The Lord will make a way for you to leave; if you would but leave, it's your choice. (b) This dream denotes one, who is the antithesis of Christ; in that you pretend to be a god or you naively embrace a mélange of ancient religions and syncretistic practices, which leads to demonic possession. Dreamer, your lack of an objective critical analysis and judgment of a belief system's infrastructure, its foundation, existence, deity, nature of worship, sacred text, values, attitudes, earthly and eternal benefits and recompense; and whether its beliefs are worthy of consideration or not, has led you towards dark and erroneous knowledge, the devil's so-called deep secrets. As a result, you are now an advocate of a type of worship that is in direct conflict with Holy Writ. You view spirituality from a secular, dark perspective; the source of your knowledge is limited to tools instigated by devils. You have forsaken godliness, and now believe in something akin to Spiritism. You worship with spiritists and witches, and have attributed your prosperity to the power of demons. Further, your manner of service is to exert control and power over others, via deceptive means, primarily for your advantage. You often herald peace when there is none, pointing people down a road of possible catastrophe. You hard-press people, including your family, to believe what you say and compel individuals to follow false gods. You do not pursue by faith, the righteousness that only comes from the Lord, and is unable to acknowledge God's providence on any level. A change has come. The prosperity God has provided you will begin to abate and your anarchy will be exposed. Turn back to God, seek forgiveness, and tangibly, if applicable, participate in the turning back of your children to God that He may leave a blessing, out of the abundance of His mercies and compassions. Only, if dreamer would earnestly resist unruliness within your nature, it will flee. Nonetheless, one thing is for sure; you can no longer pursue perverseness and continue as before. You will now begin reap the fruit of your choices. See suggested course of action.

CYCLONE, HURRICANE, THUNDER AND LIGHTNING, LIGHTNING, WITHOUT THE SOUND OF THUNDER, TORNADO, OR TYPHOON:

This dream has three meanings (choose one). (1) Dreamer has lacked wisdom in your choices and behavior. Therefore, this dream was sent. Read, embrace, and fully understand Proverbs 1:20-33, this is to you. See suggested course of action. (2) Lightning (without the sound of thunder, no stormy weather): Dreamer, you are the redeemed, and know that this is who you are. You are not considered a fool, nor a wicked and lazy servant, nor unclean, by the Lord, Jesus Christ. Further, any present evil and/or wickedness that have caused you to fear and/or be troubled, will suddenly disappear. It will be as though it was never there. Take courage and be strong, knowing that the Lord knows who you are, where you are, what's going on, and He will take care of you, for you are His and He cares. (3) Thunder and Lightning (only, no stormy weather): This dream is an alarm to assemble yourself to God at the door of the church. Simply put, you need to go to church. Every Christia n should be faithfully attending and supporting a fundamental, faith-based, Holy Bible believing church. Revelation 2:1, 8, 12, 18, 3:1, 7, 14, references churches; thus, this lets us know that God has ordained churches, and not without purpose. Hebrews 10:25, sheds light on the reasons for participation in the local church. The church is a place of edification, protection, and fellowship. The ultimate reason why we should participate in a local church, it is specifically charged by God for us to do so. Allow God's wisdom to be greater than your own. See suggested course of action.

DEW:

This dream was sent to greatly, encourage the dreamer, and it denotes two things (one or both may apply). (1) To see dew, especially in the morning, denotes physical and spiritual healing and deliverance within the life of the dreamer, as well as, one who is a purposed to be a healer, namely the dreamer. Dreamer, you may lay hands on one who is sick. Have faith and they will be healed. (2) This dream implies the dreamer is one who is a just and righteous person; you exemplify the religious ideals of Jesus. You also take joy in justice (Proverbs 21:15). You are also disciplined, educated, refined, and sophisticated. I f a leader, you rule justly and righteously. Take comfort and rest in this encouragement.

FLOOD, TIDAL WAVE, TORRENT, TSUNAMI:

This type of dream is sent to warn an immoral believer, namely the dreamer, to expose a need of refinement of character, especially in the area dealing with the deeds of the flesh. Dreamer, you have not considered the reality of the repercussions of your unwise choices. You emanate anger and rage, perpetuate violence, and possibly promote all kinds of indecent practices, sexual perversions, and other odious traditions, under the guise of Christianity. You dishonor God, His truth, His Kingdom, His church, and continually provoke God to anger. You do that which is evil in the sight of the Lord, proving yourself fierce, cruel, merciless, unprincipled, and oppressive, very much like the demons you worship. You cause division amongst innocent people and intentionally and with premeditation attempt to destroy God's prophet's reputation because of their truth spoken to you. Are you not afraid to speak against God, and His ways and means and His people? Dreamer, is nothing sacred? Do you think the detestable things you are speaking, promoting, and perpetuating are small, are of little consequence, and are of little importance to God, His ways, His Kingdom, His people (the Body of Christ)? You show yourself presumptuous, when you do not fear to speak evil of the Lord and His people. It is a dangerous thing to offend Christ. Did you not expect that God would resent it, and take it as an affront to Himself personally? Further, you take great risk, when you have no fear of promoting and perpetuating ideology that is clearly "adversarial" to God, per Holy Writ. For, all scripture is inspired by God and is usef ul to teach us what is true and to make us realize what is wrong in our lives. It corrects us when we are wrong and teaches us to do what is right (2 Timothy 3:16). Dreamer, those who truly love Jesus, regards certain actions, characteristics, and behaviors as destructive to the church, family, society, self and soul. The harshness of the Lord is kindled against you; you will now begin to experience a change in your favor given from the Lord. An event or situation that will cause intense fear is coming to discourage and terrify you. This will be in the form of an annoying, difficult, and unpleasant person, one you've disdained, treated in a harsh and oppressive manner, in the past. The trouble this person will cause; will become so overwhelming, because they will expose a secret regarding you, and you will begin to experience a loss of authority. Additionally, a third of the people that adhere to such practices as you do, will all die of the same illness, a third will fall away (becoming apostates) because of a lack of saving knowledge, and a third will "pull up stakes" with a stigma attached to their name. The dreamer will find him or herself within one of these three categories. Another repercussion, you will also begin to experience serious mental health issues and will have to be restrained, against your will if needs be. When these things begin to happen, if not already, you will know that the Lord has spoken. Dreamer, turn from your wicked ways, and dump your darken ideology, and enlighten and encourage others to do so as well. Moreover, as He knows your thoughts afar off, repent. Take words to Jesus, "'I have sinned, and I have done wrong and acted wickedly". Other than heartfelt repentance to Jesus and a change in your beliefs, behavior, and choices, no other excuse (or weak justification) will be heard. See suggested course of action.

FOG, NIGHT MIDST:

This dream denotes one who has been led away into error and sin. You have been led away from God's truth, into error, and have been greatly deceived. Dreamer, you have been too easily led astray from God and from the truth of His word because of the lust of your flesh; thus, you are willing to give up eternal happiness for temporary pleasures of today. Hence, this dream was sent as a dire warning to the dreamer, it is to warn a rebellious person, in the spirit of grace, to see if you will yet be worked upon, and change your mindset. Or else to leave you inexcusable, in your accusations against God, because of your ruin (e.g. continually plundered, seized, and disfavored). Dreamer, your belief system has changed. Having turned, you now look to heretical ideology to be your strength and satisfaction, rather than the Lord God. You have become weak-willed, and in so doing, you are no longer faithful to the Creator of this world. You are actively involved in t he immorality of your surroundings, which has its primary focus on spiritual separation from the Lord and His truth. Dreamer, your attempt to fuse or cause a union between different systems of thoughts or beliefs (especially in religion or philosophy), will be publicly manifested in your life, and dreamer may or may not be able to handle the "fall out". Christ warns plainly against embracing and/or spreading heretical doctrines, teachings that oppose truth (see Romans 11:20-24). You will definitely be an outcast and possibly labeled a heretic by many. Thus, sin will very soon turn your paradise into chaos, and dishonor the beauty of your name. When God hides His face from someone, celebrations are turned into moaning and groaning, and the party is exchanged for depression and solitude. You will be rejected and shown disapproval by the ones with whom you have committed spiritual fornication. You will bribe them to come to you from everywhere; but no one will run after you for your favors, and no compensation will be given you. Instead of receiving pay, you will give payment and none will be given to you. This is done, in spite of the fact that God has dealt with you according to His grace. Dreamer, embracing or adopting the sensual, soothing, flattering philosophies, beliefs, and doctrines, of those who oppose divine truth will prevent you from becoming a true follower of Christ. Their "opinions" come not from God, and do lead to sin. They don't really abide in Him, and possibly, they were never a part of The Body of Christ; for they feign to be a part of, or connected to, God's people. Nonetheless, and consequently, dreamer, a literal and spiritual exile has been officially decided upon, regarding you, by the divine council in heaven and this will be enforced by a civil, criminal, or religious court on earth. So severe are things that restoration can only be by returning to Christ Jesus wholeheartedly. This recklessness can be remedied by returning to Chris t Jesus, via prayer and heartfelt repentance to Jesus and to individuals affected by your actions, and by rebuking and renouncing the "spirit of jezebel", that has attached itself to you. See suggested course of action.

HAIL (rain of ice pellets):

Dreamer, low self-esteem and feelings of insignificance, has caused you to act very corruptly. Thus, your difficult state of affairs, at present, is a result of your own malicious plots against innocent persons, your handling of people indiscriminate ly and unwisely, and/or your own conceit. You will be held accountable for all your actions, before God and man. Actually, you are reaping what you have sown, and your present difficult state bears witness of this. Excessive pride, not caring about yo ur spiritual well-being, and not caring about how you treat others, coupled with your suggestive behavior, will always leave you humiliated and in bondage. Although your way may seem hard, you can endure the repercussions of this universal law. You are counseled to go to a quiet place; and re-think your actions, motives, and behaviors. Practice the golden rule, the rule of conduct that advises people to treat others in the same manner as they wish to be treated themselves. As well, align your ideology with faithful biblical values and love, and study your bible. Go to church and forsake not the gathering of yourself together with other mainstream Christians. Avoid persons, places, or things that do not promote moral and ethical living, a balanced and healthy self-esteem, and emotional and spiritual clarity. You personally, must learn to choose the good over the bad. Then, after many days, you will be reinstated into God's favor. This process may take up to three years. Invest the time. If you choose to invest the time, you will begin to do great works for the Kingdom of God, for you are chosen for such times as these. See suggested course of action.

MONSOONS, WINDS (wind that changes direction with the seasons):

This dream has four meanings (one, two, or three may apply). (1) This dream denotes a waning of love for Christ Jesus, and a caution. Dreamer, although you have the power of free choice, you should not think that your accomplishments are purely of your own volition. Truthfully, it is God, who gives you the capability and strength to achieve success. This is especially true of your struggles with your sinful tendencies, whether they manifest as a lack of concern or interest in the things of God, a stubborn resistance to the will of God, or laziness. If it had not been for God's efforts on your behalf, you would not have been able to overcome any negative tendencies. He delivered you. Any achievements you will accomplish, or have accomplished, any good deeds you've done, any fulfillment of God's will, was, and still is, dependent upon divine aid and guidance. One merely places his or her hand under the weight carried exclusively by God. Therefore, do not claim credit for your achievements. See suggested course of action. (2) This dream denotes a "coming to God". Hence, God will save you from all your uncleanness that you might know God is God, and honor and glorify Him whose power is the power, and whose rule will endure eternally, and that you might know your God ordained destiny, and again begin to love all things Jesus. Drea mer, because of God's grace, His faithfulness, and His mercy towards you; now, your burdens, having been dealt with, freedom from your weaknesses is yours. You will be favored with complete healing, go and sin no more. For, if anyone knows the good they ought to do and doesn't do it, it is sin for them (see James 4:17). Therefore, from this moment forward, choose good habits and deeds, e.g. good stewardship and commitment to ministry, develop an authentic and reverent love for Christ, speak to yourself what is true and good, embracing Philippians 4:8, and choose good nutritional habits that you might remain in good health. These choices will help you progress forward towards your transformation and freedom, enhance your love for Jesus, and help guide you toward, and enable you to fulfill, your purpose. All these blessings are rain. Dreamer, as one perfects him or herself, God helps by sending 'rains of blessings', then situations prosper. The rain is coming! As well, there will be clarity and freedom in the way you communicate yourself to others, especially prophetically. Thus; from this time forward, so speak and act as those who are judged by the law of liberty; see James 2:12, 13. For example, remove condemnation from your message of grace and holiness, see John 3:17, Romans 8:1, 1 John 3:20, 21, for there is a difference between conviction and condemnation. Moreover, take note of this, you should be quick to listen, slow to speak, and slow to anger, see James 1:19-25. If necessary, see suggested course of action. (3) This dream denotes one who is headed towards his or her chosen destiny. Dreamer, you are endowed with multiple talents that may be expressed through inspirational teaching, preaching, or acting, and you have access to prophetic wisdom, thus, you are required to be a transformational force in people's lives, via not neglecting the gift that is within you. Do not say what gift, for this is sin for you and it exposes your lack of love for Jesus, similar to the servant's attitude spoken of in the parable of Matthew 25:15. As, this dream supposes that you are aware of, at least, one of your gifts (talent, skill), you are advised to acknowledge and embrace your gift to help others, in this, you i mitate and reverence Christ. You will now be led into situations, where you will show up when most needed, and then disappear without a thought of compensation. You will be dispatched on missions, to help believers who are facing urgent needs during a crisis, and/or in an emergency, and to give instant help, as well as, to express God's loving kindness, His grace, mercy, and compassion. You are sent to protect and defend those who obediently love God, and who is loved by God. Altruistic, goodhearted, and generous service to God and others is beneficial at this time. Dreamer, love God so completely that you will never forsake His service for any reason. Often, an individual starts the initiative of service without leadership or commun ity support. Some examples of altruistic service or "acts of kindness" to others are, provide a child with necessities, such as food, clothing, shelter, toys, medical equipment. Visit the sick, provide free medical services, and give charity to the poor, (see Ben Sira 29). Offer hospitality to strangers, help families bury their dead, via religious services and/or financial support, help with marriage ceremonies, and/or help a person make peace with his or her family member, fellow human, or their Maker. Provide free roadside assistance and emergency mechanical help, or freely help with structural problems in private homes that they might see Christ. All of these, and more, are examples of service to the Kingdom of God. God will give you the necessary to ols, courage, strength, and wherewithal, to do whatever needs to be done. Additionally, respect cautionary advice about something imminent (especially imminent danger or other unpleasantness), remain thankful, and become aware and tap into the intuitive insight you are (or will be) receiving. An angel (perhaps disguised as human, or one, who is a true servant of God, with the Spirit of Truth within) will lead the way. If necessary, see suggested course of action. (4) Wind blowing over a land: This dream may be considered a forewarning, giving the dreamer ample time (a grace period), to change his or her mind and ways. This dream denotes one who will experience horror, and be in astonishment, because of the emptiness and desolation within you. It is your character, especially your great pretense, which has led you here. Dreamer, you've practiced the act of giving a false appearance, and lying, so long that you are unable to separate truth from false. Even when you desire to tell the truth, you are unable too. This has prevented wholeness, and, as hypocrisy does, has led to your spiritual desolation. How does a man or woman embrace truth inwardly, when they do not know the path to truth, or are unable to embrace truth? Taking ownership of what your warning dream is revealing to you about you, and working from that point, via prayer, fasting, diligent self-examination, persistent practice of truthfulness, candid support from family and friends, and/or Christian counseling, will help truth inwardly begin to emerge; at a pace, you'll be able to "wrap your mind around" comfortably. This followed by appropriate application of wisdom, can conceivably avert self-deception and the repercussions thereof. This is what is called leaving a blessing behind. See suggested course of action.

RAIN:

Dreamer, as a man or woman perfects him or herself, God helps by sending rain, 'a rain of blessings', then situations prosper. Couple this with one of the following three (choose one). (1) If dreamer is an educator of some sort, a spiritual or secula r teacher, this dream implies spiritual growth, divine illumination, and some type of promotion or confirmation on a prophetic level. Hence, dreamer will now begin to experience a supernatural increase in divine knowledge and wisdom. This knowledge and wisdom will be imparted to you to be used exclusively for interpreting the gospel of Jesus Christ to others, and for the edifying of the Body of Christ; the body of believers. Your height of spiritual progress and promotion will be according to your faith and obedience to God's will over your life personally. (2) If dreamer is a leader of some sort, spiritual or secular, this dream points to one, namely the dreamer, who is independent, strong, curious, and a great leader. Yours is the path of great leaders who has the power to change history. You are powerful and strong, and know what to do with your authority. You see yourself a match for all you meet. Dreamer, this is your time, your season of influence. In six years, if you seize the mom ent now to prepare, you will become a great leader. You will be sent to leaders, who when they had power abused it, and because none opposed them, they withheld not themselves from doing wrong. Their power will be taken from them and given to you. Further, your witness of Christ's death, burial, and resurrection is sustenance to many and your service is a covering for others. Additionally, if exercised, your artistic abilities will give us all a glimpse of heaven. (3) This dream was sent to encourage, no matter your status or duties in life. It implies one who is purifying him or herself morally, by dealing with the sin issues in your life, no matter how seemingly insignificant. You have begun, again, to listen to the Paraclete within you, instead of relyin g on your emotions and opinions. This is good. Dreamer, the state of affairs in your life at present, may not be to your liking; but God allows them. God is using your situations to work things out for your good. Therefore, do not attribute (or call) that which is of God, unclean (e.g. confusion, erroneous, out of order, unlawful, weak, wicked, or any other attributes of the unregenerate). No matter how difficult or how uncertain the issues always take the next biblical, ethical, and most informed step, for obedience is better than sacrifice. If necessary, see suggested course of action.

Sleet (mixture of snow and rain): Dreamer, rain and snow, are like joy and pain, one is set over against the other, for balance. Therefore, testify gratefully of God's beneficent hand upon your life, sing of His mercy and grace (the free and unmerited favor and beneficence of God) shown you, and be content wherever you find yourself now. This too shall pass. Dreamer, question not, His absolute goodness in His dealings with you, but ask, what are you to glean from it. See the Lord's providence behind all the events in your life, and change your paradigm. Make the best of your circumstances, and learn from them, instead of complaining and murmuring. For, complaining and murmuring, do not affect recovery, it only delays it. Additionally, read, understand, and embrace Psalm 118, Isaiah 55:6-12. See suggested course of action.

SEASONS (winter, spring, summer, and fall; one of the natural periods into which the year is divided by the equinoxes, or atmospheric conditions during a certain time of year):

Naturally, the four seasons (winter, spring, summer, and fall) have a huge impact on how we lead our daily lives. This ranges from the activities we take part in, the food we eat, the drinks we drink, and the clothes we wear. As it is in our temporal life, so it is in our spiritual life. The spiritual seasons of our life have very big impacts on how we live out our lives, how we view and feel about family, friends, foes, work, retirement, youth, and old age, life in general, and about our God. Spiritual life seasons also affect our purpose.

Winter: To dream that it is winter denotes that it is time for the dreamer to deal with the need to follow the subtle whispers of your body's desire to slow down and go deep within, to become more self-aware. Dreamer, it is time to return to stillness, to enter into a state of rest, to create time for reflection on the next steps in your life, and to, spiritually r e-connect with Jesus. Dreamer is counseled to steal away, and reflect, repair, and mend some heart and/or life issues that you've ignored, and if sickness is your weakness, take time to heal. With that said, unfortunately, this season in your life will p rove to be the hardest season of all; yet it is the most hopeful. For, weak and fragile life issues will die off, and only that which is strong will remain, to effect restoration, and a spark of life does remain, hidden deep within the very cold times. Question s to journal, dreamer, will you create time, now, to slow down and rest? Do you take time to take care of your body? Are you ill? Have you seen doctors? Dreamer, just because you can do something, does it mean you have to do it? Are you too busy doing the Lord's work to rest? Would God have you serve Him in a state where you are too impaired or sick to serve Him? How submissive are you to God's will? If you took advantage of rest and quietness, now, how would it affect your personal level of faith, patience, love, endurance, and health today? The benefits can, and often do, result in encouragement, greater faith, endurance, and healing. Again, dreamer steal away, to reflect, repair, and mend some heart and/or life issues that you've ignored, and if ill, take time to heal. If necessary, see suggested course of action.

Spring: To dream that it is spring denotes that there awaits you, the dreamer, a physical, emotional, and spiritual, time of growth, renewal, revival, resuscitation, resurrection, and hope, according to God's grace, in all aspects of your life. Although, you have lacked courage, boldness, and/or enthusiasm, and may have been weak in spirit; thus, unfit for service, you will be healed, restored, and strengthened by the grace of God. Your mind will become clearer, clever, and quick, and you will be graced with the ability and vision to accomplish a great deal in a short period-of-time. The dreamer has looked inward, and has become enlighten, and now is endowed with the ability to apply studious knowledge, your experiences, understanding, insight, and common sense, prudently to all situations that are presented before you during this season in your life. Moreover, as godly wisdom yields an abundance of fruit, and the dreamer is indeed embracing godly wisdom, via you service to others, now, embrace the "seeds of potential" given you by God that your fruit may be greatly abundant. Life growth is your key. Begin t o embrace optimism and hopefulness, and become fueled by the opportunities of giving and receiving that will begin to take place in your life. Again, the dreamer will be healed and cleansed in your personal life and/or ministry. Read Psalm 103:1-5, and let this be your praise to God. Additionally, questions to journal, does dreamer have projects and/or prior ities unfinished or "setting on the shelf" that you may need to look at again? Note, one or two projects, and/or priorities that you can take off "the shelf", look at again, and finish. Consider what gifting do you have inside of you that need to be explored, practiced, or used. What is needed to bring your initiative to fruition? Can you supply the need? Are there resources, sponsors availabl e to support you? Note, how can you handle the obstacles? Dreamer, it is not too late to finish unfinished pr ojects, and again, dreamer, embrace the "seeds of potential" given you by God, during this season in your life, that your fruit may be greatly abundant.

Summer (sunshine, sunny weather): To dream that it is summer denotes that dreamer will experience events that will result in a spiritual and emotional transformation within you; thus, dreamer is entering into a season of transition and chan ge. Dreamer, during this season in your life, you will begin to experience lots of movement, within your everyday life, in the form of new opportunities, new growth, transition, and change. Dreamer has divine permission to explore new opportunities. Moreover, dreamer is counseled to nurture and/or cultivate old relationships left unattended, new relationships that are beginning to emerge, as well as other things that are beginning to happen or occur because of new opportunities, growth, transition, and change. Along with this, on the other hand, you must also begin to "weed -out" people, places, and things that hinder your spiritual and emotional growth and clarity. Additionally, during this season in your life, you will begin to attract to yourself the people and material resources needed to manifest the highest and best use of all that you are, in service to God and humanity. This can be achieved via a network of relationships and will be maximized through intimacy and harmony with God. Key, you must be at peace with God, at peace with yourself, and at peace with others to maximize the power that is available to you during this season in your life. With that said, dreamer exploring, nurturing, and cultivating, new opportunities and experiences, will oftentimes expose limitations on how one handles transitions and change. If transition and change comes easy, and is welcomed, your transitions and changes will be full of exciting new experiences. If transition and change is hard, your transformations and changes will prove very demanding, difficult, and frustrating. The frustrations may cause you to feel resentful and even rebellious. It is counseled that you keep an optimistic and flexible outlook. As well, the quality of your transitions and changes will depend on how well you know yourself and how comfortable you are with exactly who you are. Questions to journal, dreamer, if you took advantage of opportunities to connect or re-connect with family or friends how would it affect your personal level of spiritual growth or maturity. How would it reflect who you are via your transformatio ns and changes? Consider, re-connecting with a family member, or with an old friend, and/or with a new friend you've recently met. If necessary, see suggested course of action.

Fall (autumn): To dream that it is fall denotes that the dreamer is entering into a season where you will begin to reap what you sown. You will begin to experience, the goodness or "not so good" of what you've sown. Read and understand 2 Corinthians 9:6, 7. Harvest and change are key. If you've sown good things, according to biblical principles, you will begin to experience great change, celebrations, and productivity. Dreamer will also begin to experience a "falling away" of things no longer useable, making way for the new. On the other hand, if dreamer begins to experience "not so good" reaping because of negative sowing. Dreamer is counseled that through, 'thought-out' and wise choices, personal commitment to strong biblical principles, hard work, and a strong commitment to becoming the very best version of you, via belief in yourself; you can achieve, again, your God-given right to experience joy, love, and health, and become who you were gifted to be. Therefore, use the power of your God-given intelligence, strength, and energy to think on and embrace ways to better yourself, and to organize specific plans on how to both, serve God and others. Additionally, considerations to journal, write three "new opportunities to sow" or three opportunities for new growth, you may have over looked, wasn't ready for at the time, or just didn't know they were opportunities at the time they were presented to you. Plus, write the name of the person(s) or resource(s) connected to those opportunities. It is not too late to begin again. Pray that your opportunities be not lost, but redeemed, and, that God will give you the strength, power, and resolve to nurture and cultivate, again, your opportunities, and the relationships connected to them. If necessary, see suggested course of action.

WEATHER FORECASTING:

This dream has two meanings (choose one). (1) Question, what was forecasted? If a hurricane was forecasted, see subcategory (Cyclone), if strong winds, see subcategory (Monsoons). Whatever the interpretation, dreamer has spoken the situation, circumstance, into manifestation. If necessary, see suggested course of action. (2) Per Note 1 of this category: This type of dream may be regarded as a vision and received as a precautionary warning. For example, to dream that you "see or forecasted" a disastrous weather event headed toward your location, and that it may prove catastrophic in nature, e.g. hurricane. This type of dream bares insight into the life of those who may be seriously affected by the coming event. The dreamer is being warned to be extra cautious regarding the location pinpointed, especially if dreamer lives within or near the location depicted, because of a high chance for personal harm. Dreamer is also urged to take cover somewhere and/or to strongly advise, or warn others, to do the same, due to possible disastrous issues related to violent weather conditions, especially if this is a common issue within that area. Your dream should closely resemble real life situations, with the dre am events literally being capable of happening. If you sense that your dream is a vision, the question a s to why you have been made aware of this information, and how do you factor into the equation, should be seriously considered, along with necessary actions. Dreamer, you are meant to get involved. If possible, how can you ease the situation? Dreams that reference others and the revelation within those dreams, is not given haphazardly to any individual, but only to those with t he ability, and influence to do something with the information; this is also prophecy; see Specific Meaning at the end of this category.

Suggested Course of Action

Question to consider and journal, did your dream depict any symbols that alludes to, the dreamer will make the necessary changes, spiritually, emotionally, and/or physically to affect a more positive outcome? If changes are initiated, your dreams will change.

Nonetheless, dreamer, God utilizes meteorological elements (herein symbolically) to intervene in our lives, to limit the chaotic that we might reach outside of our human knowledge, outside of ourselves, and into the spiritual realm. Hence, read, understand, embrace Job: 38:1-3, 22-30; 40:1-14. Although your dream is a strong rebuke and convicts, and while your weaknesses maybe legitimate, never again deny the truth of God's report. "Therefore, there is now n o condemnation for those who are in Christ Jesus"; as well, "His grace is sufficient". There is a difference between conviction and condemnatio n. Moreover, take great care and heed God's warnings, and think on these things, see Romans 7:7-8:17; 2 Corinthians 12:7-10; Philippians 1:6; 4:8.

Reach outside of your human knowledge, outside of yourself. The following are a few toxic beliefs that can keep you under the umbrella of self-condemnation; thus, keeping you from experiencing and enjoying your life in a spirit of wholeness. It would be wise for you to allow each transitional experience, each life change, to teach you how to deal with life issues more successfully than you've perhaps, done before. That your strength may become strong, and that you may continue to grow and mature in your relationship with Christ, and learn from one or more of the toxic beliefs following.

I am not enough: Release the limiting and toxic belief of you not being enough, "good enough", "smart enough", "rich enough", or "beautiful enough". Remind yourself as often as possible that, who you are, is more than enough.

I've lost my purpose in life: Your purpose isn't something that you will ever lose since your purpose is part of who you are. Your purpose is in your heart, it is within you. And, as long as you are still breathing and living on this planet, your purpose will be living as well. So stop denouncing purpose, and look for your purpose within Christ, and He will show it to you within yourself, because that's where you'll find your purpose.

It's too late for me to pursue my dreams. Time can be a very misleading thing. If what you want to accomplish will take you five years to do, from today, and you feel like that's too long. Weigh, in five years you will be five years older, with, or without the accomplishment. Since, you are going to be five years older anyway; you might as well start today, and even though you are five years older, you will have accomplished what you wanted. Now you have something to celebrate on your birthday, five years later! If you here today, God is saying, it's not too late to reignite your passion, for life and for love. It's not too late to set a new intention and dream another dream.

I will never be a fully functioning person, not after all that I've been through: You and your past are not one; release the limiting belief that the story of your past has to be the story of your life. Question, how long will your past, and, if rel evant, the violations of your past, hold sway over your future, and perhaps your eternal destiny? You must look for ways to turn your wounds into wisdom and your difficulties into opportunities. Make your life story worth telling, and read and begin embracin g Philippians 4:8.

I lack the necessary formal education: Never allow the absence of a high school, college, or university degree to keep you from pursuing your dreams. You are able, as others have before you, to move forward in life, maneuvering around limitations. If you are truly passionate about something, and if you know in your heart that you are meant to do that work, with or without a degree, you'll find a way to make it happen.

I am all alone: While you may live alone, without children and/or without family near or far. You are never alone. For, God has said, "Never will I leave you; never will I forsake you". So we say with confidence, The Lord is my helper; I will not be afraid. What can man do to me (ref. Hebrews 13:6)? You never were; you never will be. Neither, should you feel that you are alone. In a world full of people, you will never be all alone, unless you choose to "think" otherwise. Feelings of loneliness often lead to suicidal thoughts. If this is true, those feelings are not of God. Therefore, p urpose to think on things that are true, and "reach out and touch somebody's hand, and make this world a better place if you can" (Diana Ross). Tear down all the fortresses and/or walls you have built to hide and numb yourself. Remove all the barriers between you and ever yone else and allow yourself to be fully seen. Reveal yourself to those around you and allow yourself to be truly loved. Get comforta ble with your perfect imperfections and never deny your vulnerability.

I can't be happy until I get there: Many people think that if they were only in some other place, or some other time, or had some other job; they would be happy. How many people postpone their happiness because they wait for something magical to happen to them? Happiness is not a destination, happiness is not people, places or things; happiness is from God and it grows deep within you, until it manifests without. So release the idea about happiness being somewhere in the future.

I can't be happy unless I'm in a relationship: Never do you ever, give your power to be happy to anyone else; never make authentic happiness dependent on another person, place, or thing. Your happiness is not dependent on external things or on other people. You become vulnerable and can be easily hurt when your feelings of security and happiness depend on the behavior and actions of other people.

Last, release the limiting and toxic belief that you can't be trusted, and that the people around you can't be trusted, and that life itself can't be trusted. To the pure, all things are pure, but to those who are corrupted and do not believe, nothing is pure. Read and understand Titus 1:15. Perception is in the eye of the beholder. For instance, to the untrustworthy, all pe ople are untrustworthy, to a thief, all are thieves, everybody steals; to a liar, everybody lies. To not be able to trust anyone, not even yourself, says more about who you are, and how you perceive yourself, than it does about others. While no one is perfect, not everybody "blunders" in the same way you do. Some people can be trusted to the utmost, and would never steal from anyone. Some people are very honest. While those same people do have flaws, "untrustworthy" may not be one of them. Finally, dreamer, people can and do change, sometimes in one day. We all come into this imperfect world, born into imperfect families, and are imperfect versions of ourselves. Not one of us is without a story or two about dysfunction, economic hardships, medical limitations, self-esteem challenges and more. Taking good care of yourself, healing your emotional wounds, and unconditionally loving yourself, will bring you closer to your resurrection, resuscitation, renewal, revival, and hope. Remember, it's never too late.

Now, pray (See Prayer of Deliverance, pg. 897)

Specific Meaning

If, you live in an area that has a very high chance of disastrous weather, and you are especially connected with any activity involving weather and weather conditions, see Note 1.

Note: Dreamer, consider this question, did you create something within your dream? Did you receive a unique idea? Could you be receiving inspiration, via your dream, regarding an idea, or possible creation of something, that would benefit the masses? If dreamer was given an idea, within your dream, to learn and/or devise a new weather instrument, or to initiate a new way of determining weather, especially if you are an enthusiast, or have a connection with any activity involving weather. Your dream may very well be a divine sent inspiration, especially if a unique new device, or way, was introduced to you within your dream. Dreamer is encouraged to adopt the new style as your own signature style (e.g. name the style after you). Moreover, consider it not strange for someone, who is involved in some manner of activity that involves the weather, to receive inspirations regarding the collective masses, via their dreams, that might prove beneficial to the dreamer and to mankind. Per chapter one, sometimes the most meaningless dream will help change your life in ways you would have never thought, especially entrepreneurially and enterprisingly. Throughout history, humankind has received life changing insight and guidance from their dreams. Most of the time the information acquired within dreams exceeds that which we could obtain during our normal, analytical, waking state of mind. With that said, via your dream, dreamer you have miraculously been give n big goals that involve building a better world and giving back to it what it has given you. Therefore, write your vision down, that you may articulate it to others properly, for the vision will happen. Prepare a good proposal, name your inspiration, and write down all the details and specifics, and brand mark it. Give it your best that it may be acceptable to any reputable financial entity, benefactor, or merit a grant of some kind. Perhaps, hire a grant writer. That which you will need to fulfill your aims, surely, you will have. Your dream should closely resemble real life situations. Meaning it can actually occur during your awaked state.

If, there is a very high propensity that approaching weather may prove catastrophic in nature, a dream of this sort should be received as a precautionary warning, to prevent serious harm to yourself, and/or others. Be careful, perhaps evacuate. Do not assume that you're safe or it's ok, caution should be heeded at this time, especially if a weather condition, causing damage or injury, happened within your dream. This is a precautionary warning. The weather condition, kept within context of the dream, should closely resemble real life situations. Meaning it can actually occur during your awaked state. This will help you narrow down the specifics, and avoid danger. However, if your dream was inundated with symbols that are not specifically related to your everyday life, job, and/or responsibilities, then the spiritual implications should be heeded.

1   History of Honey Baked Hams, John Harry Hoenselaar | http://bluwiki.com/go/Honey_Baked_Ham_coupons

2   Chalom: Strong's Talking Greek & Hebrew Dictionary: Hebrew Strong's Number: 2472—chalom, khal-ome'; from (H2492); (chalam); a dream: dream (-er).

3   https://livingwisdom.kabbalah.com/dreams

4   http://www.betemunah.org/dreams.html#_Toc371852888

5   Hazon: The Brown-Driver-Briggs Hebrew and English Lexicon (p. 303), Wilson's Old Testament Word Studies, by William Wilson (p. 277) |
    http://biblehub.com/hebrew/2377.htm

6   Zohar II, 199b Recurring Dream

7   Abraham's dream: Genesis chapter 15

8   R. Berekiah, Brachot 55

9   Talmud, Berachot 55b–57b | http://www.chabad.org/library/article_cdo/aid/1076083/jewish/Dreams.htm

10 http://www.ravkooktorah.org/MIKETZ63.htm

11 https://www.theatlantic.com/health/archive/2014/02/new-research-says-there-are-only-four-emotions/283560/

12 Expositional constancy is a term used to convey to us that the use of symbolism and idioms in Scripture is consistent. The meaning of the word is most often defined by the first use in the Bible, which is another term of Biblical interpretation called "Law of First Mention. This definition remains consistent throughout the Bible. A good way to apply this principal to your hermeneutics is to see how a word or idiom in the passage you're studying is defined and used throughout the Bible and apply that definition to the current passage.
    http://www.ephesians611.com/expositional-consistancy

13 Hermeneutics 101: Interpret Scripture with Scripture. "Scripture interprets Scripture" is the principle of Regula Fidei from the perspective of Sola Scriptura. A correct interpretation of the Bible will always be consistent with the rest of the Scriptures. Therefore, it is essential for us as students of the Bible to interpret a passage in light of what the rest of the Scriptures say on the topic. Summary: The idea that we can use scripture to interpret other scripture is a common theme throughout Hermeneutics. Ultimately, it is simply the idea that we can use scripture to shed light on other passages within the Bible. No one passage stands alone. All Scripture is to be compared together. Difficult passages will be explained by clear passages. Any interpretation of a passage will be based on another passage. Each passage should be placed in its proper context. We cannot take a verse by itself, or even a piece of a verse, and then build a doctrine. We must take the complete passage. Our interpretation cannot contradict another passage. Our interpretation must be built by all passages- allowing Scripture to interpret itself. The scope and significance of one passage is to be brought out by relating it to others. http://studiesinscripture.com/biblical-interpretation/ http://1peter315. blogspot.com/2009/05/hermeneutics-101-interpret-scripture.html http://hermeneutics.stackexchange.com/ questions/79/what-does-it-mean-that-scripture-interprets-scripture
    http://www.bible-researcher.com/packer1.htm: Interpreting Scripture by Scripture

14 Chabad.org/library/article_cdo/aid/1076083/Jewish/Dreams.htm: In the words of the Talmud, "All dreams follow the mouth". Therefore, if one doesn't have his dream interpreted, it will not be fulfilled.

15 https://en.wikipedia.org/wiki/Sleep#Stages; https://en.wikipedia.org/wiki/Dream http://encyclopedia2. thefreedictionary.com/dream; https://www.verywell.com/the-four-stages-of-sleep-2795920 http://www. ehealthmd.com/library/insomnia

16 Dreams in the Bible: The Secret Language of God; www. abarim-publications.com/dictionary; https:llenim. wikipedia.org/wiki/dream- question

17 http://www.iloveulove.com/spirituality/kabbalah/kabbadreams.htm

18 Déjà Vu: French pronunciation: [de.ʒa.vy]) from French, literally "already seen", is the phenomenon of having the strong sensation that an event or experience currently being experienced has already been experienced in the past. Déjà vu is a feeling of familiarity, and déjà vécu (the feeling of having "already lived through" something) is a feeling of recollection. How Déjà Vu Works:
    http://science.howstuffworks.com/science-vs-myth/deja-vu5.htm
    Dream Déjà Vu | https://www.psychologytoday.com/blog/dream-factory/201410/dream-d-j-vu https:// en.wikipedia.org/wiki/D%C3%A9j%C3%A0_vu Déjà vu, https://en.wikipedia.org/wiki/Dream#D.C3.A9j.C3.A0_vu, https://exemplore.com/dreams/Dreams-and-Deja-Vu-Dreams-Really-Do-Come-

19   *Zohar* text: Zohar II, 200a

20   Duane A. Garrett, feasts-and-festivals-of-Israel: Israel's festivals were communal and commemorative as well as theological and typological. They were communal in that they drew the nation together for celebration and worship as they recalled the common origin and experience of the people. They were commemorative in that they kept alive the story of what God had done in the exodus and during the sojourn. They were theological in that the observance of the festivals presented the participants with lessons on the reality of sin, judgment, and forgiveness, on the need for thanksgiving to God, and on the importance of trusting God rather than hoarding possessions. They were typological in that they anticipated a greater fulfillment of the symbolism of the feasts. It is not surprising that each of the major feasts is in some way alluded to in the New Testament. On the other hand, the festivals could become meaningless rituals and were subject to the criticism of the prophets (Isaiah 1:13, 14). Duane A. Garrett, aka John R. Sampey, Professor of Old Testament Interpretation at The Southern Baptist Theological Seminary. http://www.biblestudytools.com/dictionaries/bakers-evangelical-dictionary/feasts-and-festivals-of-israel.html

21   The Catholic Encyclopedia, Volume V. Published 1909. Souvay, Charles. "Interpretation of Dreams"

22   Moses in the Midrash - Midrash Rabba is part of a collection of rabbinic teachings on the Torah and Megillot. Midrash is a Hebrew word referring to a method of exegesis of a Biblical text. The term "midrash" can also refer to a compilation of Midrashic teachings, in the form of legal, exegetical, or homiletical commentaries on the Tanakh (Jewish Bible). According to the Pardes system of exegesis, understanding of Biblical text in Judaism is divided among peshat (simple meaning), remez (hints, clues), derash (interpretation) and sod ("secret"). The Midrash concentrates somewhat on remez, but mostly on derash. Midrashic exegesis was the interpretation methodology of choice for certain authors of the New Testament | http://www.jewishagency.org/jewish-culture/content/25365

23   http://www.aish.com/jl/48936097.html

24   http://www.nephos.com/patriapage73.htm

25   Brachot 55, an un-interpreted dream is like an unread letter | http://talmud-daily.livejournal.com/326803.html

26   The Zohar says that the interpretation of a dream is actually more important than the dream itself. Hence, it behooves you to make every effort to find the right person to interpret your dream. It should be someone who truly loves and cares for you, or it should be a spiritual person who possesses a love for all mankind, because the interpretation will color the dream's influence in your life.

27   http://www.iloveulove.com/spirituality/kabbalah/kabbadreams.htm

28   Syncretism consists of the blending of two or more disparate or contradictory religious belief systems into a new system. Often, melding practices of various schools of thought, and thus asserting an underlying unity allowing for an inclusive approach to other faiths, basically, the fusion of diverse religious beliefs and practices. Instances of religious syncretism—as, for example, Gnosticism, a religious dualistic system that incorporated elements from the Oriental mystery religions, such as a blending of Judaism, Christianity, and Greek religious philosophical concepts—which were particularly prevalent during the Hellenistic period (c. 300 BC–300 AD). Manichaeism, a dualistic religion, combined elements of Christianity, Zoroastrianism, and Buddhism, and Sikhism (a religion that combined elements of Islam and Hinduism). The Abrahamic religions, Christian religions, or any system that exhibits an exclusivist approach, affirms that an incompatible belief corrupts the original religion, rendering it no longer true. https://en.wikipedia.org/wiki/Syncretism

29   Interpreters: It is written that there were 24 interpreters of dreams in Jerusalem during the time of the Second Temple (approximately 2000 years ago). If a person told his dream to all 24 interpreters, the dreamer might very well receive 24 different interpretations. Remarkably, the sages teach us, all 24 interpretations could actually play themselves out in the physical world. Namely, the act of interpreting dramatically impacts and influences the dream's expression in the physical world | http://www.iloveulove.com/spirituality/kabbalah/kabbadreams.htm

30   Setting the Captives Free Deliverance Manual, Bev Tucker, www.bjtucker49@gmail.com

31   While the loaf of barley represented Gideon to the Midianite dream interpreter, because Gideon was a miller by trade; so, supporting the belief that dreams can be specific to you with regard to your job related activities.

32   Pastor Alma M. Perry, hishabitationfellowship.com

33   The Path of Duty, Arthur Pink, May 1944 | http://www.gracegems.org/Pink2/path_of_duty.htm

34   https://www.gotquestions.org/sexual-abuse.html

35   Solemn consecrations: What is a solemn consecration? First, what a consecration is not, this is not a fast (abstaining from certain foods, as for religious or medical reasons). A solemn consecration is the beginning

of a new lifestyle, spiritually. Consecration marks the beginning and confirmation of full spiritual maturity, so set your anniversary date. God is calling you to a higher and new spiritual level; therefore, draw closer to Him. Consecration, is a private and personal, or public, dedicatory sacrifice. It is a dedication to initiate or discipline, to train up, to accomplish, to confirm, a setting (of gems), to be properly set apart, i.e. dedication of a priest, to purity from defilement, to be hallowed, pious, sacred, sure, holy (Strong's Greek & Hebrew Dictionary). Symbolically a consecration is new wine poured into new wineskins, new cloth sewn into a new garment, (Matthew 9:16-17, Mark 2:21-22). The symbols convey a growing, and stretching, a process and preparation that has led to a spiritual capacity that is now able to contain (or handle) the amazing and miraculous things that the Lord has prepared, namely the new wine, and the new cloth, without one bursting or tearing. (Sidebar) Bursting, or tearing, denotes one who is unable to apprehend and embrace the changes, vicissitudes, and the spiritual revolution within, that resulted from Jesus' teachings, especially spiritual truths that expose foolishness and man-made traditions. Thus, one violently pursues their own plans, while denying the miraculous works of Jesus, aka a "bursting or tearing", rendering one unable to make that leap of faith towards authentic spiritual progression. Nonetheless, the spiritually ready are the new wineskins, and are the new garments. The process that has created the "new" is called salvation and sanctification, simply put; this is the act of delivering from sin or saving from evil. The initial act was done at the cross. Hence, for believers to approach consecrating themselves to God; they have already learned that their union with Christ in death and in His resurrection is done; they have fully connected with Him in His death, burial, and resurrection. No longer are they conformed to the pattern of this world, but have been transformed by the renewing of their mind, able to test and approve what God's will is, His good, pleasing and perfect will (Romans 12:1, 2, 1 Peter 2:9, 10). Only those that have fully connected with Him in death, burial, and resurrection are asked to present their bodies as instruments unto God; therefore, a sanctifying process happens before consecration. From this place, that is the sanctifying process, we are to count ourselves dead to sin, self, the law, and the world, and alive to God in the risen Christ (Romans 6:4-18). We are now ready for consecration. What is expected of the person embarking upon a solemn consecration? People who are truly desirous of living consecrated lives, will have to be intentional regarding embracing mental and emotional habits of holiness, for habits are formed by practice or neglect. You must by faith, deliberately, and purposefully, offer you, your mind, spirit, and body in a sober, firm, and dignified manner, with a confident and unquestionable belief in the validity of your salvation, and the atoning work of the Cross, as a living sacrifice, holy and pleasing to God, as this is a spiritual act of worship. And the Lord your God is to be loved with all your heart, and with all your soul and with all your strength. Afterward, there is a need to, apprehend by faith, and to declare, that God accepts you, accepts your talents, accepts your efforts, and accepts the spirit for which they are presented, definitively. Therefore, resolve exactly what are your talents and efforts, e.g. preacher, teacher, healer, writer, singer, poet, whatever your endowments, see Matthew 25:14, parable of the talents), write them down, and present them to God, with a mindset that, as you've been diligent with what you've been given, He accepts, and is ok, with what you have presented. The fact that God receives what you present is proof that a sanctifying and purification process has happened, and a perfecting, via a consecration, is beginning. Moreover, faith comes with a statement that says, "God has accepted what I have presented." This is faith with works, believing that He accepts. It is necessary that your faith is alive, for what will be the practical outcome of all your presenting, if you do not believe that God accepts what you give? Further, solemn consecration demands great personal sacrifice of rights and freedoms and requires the subduing of your appetites and passions. For it written, to whom much is given, much is required, (see Luke 12:48), also in another place it is written. For, though I was free from all men, I made myself a servant to all, so that more might have salvation. And to the Jews I was as a Jew, so that I might give the good news to them; to those under the law, I was the same, not as being myself, under the law, but so that I might give the good news to those under the law. To those without the law I was as one without the law, not as being without law to God, but as under law to Christ, so that I might give the good news to those without the law. To the feeble, I was as one who is feeble, so that they might have salvation: I have been all things to all men, so that some at least might have salvation. And I do all things for the cause of the good news, so that I may have a part in it. Do you not see that in a running competition all take part, but only one gets the reward? So let your minds be fixed on the reward. And every man who takes part in the sports has self-control in all things. Now they do it to get a crown, which is of this world, but we for an eternal crown. So then I am running, not uncertainly; so I am fighting, not as one who gives blows in the air: But I give blows to my body, and keep it under control, for fear that, after having given the good news to others, I myself might not have God's approval. (1 Corinthians 9:19-27 BBE). Additionally, every consecration in biblical times was accompanied by rubbing or anointing with oil the person or object to be consecrated. The priests were anointed with oil, and by this rite, they were hallowed, as well as objects. God's part in our unfolding drama is to guide us; our part is simply to follow and to obey. Keep these words, which I say to you this day, deep in your hearts, teaching them to your children with all care, talking of them when you are at rest in your house or walking by the way, when you go to sleep and when you get up. Let them be fixed as a sign on your hand, and marked on your brow. Have them lettered on the pillars of your houses and over the doors of your towns (Deuteronomy 6:5-9). We can be assured that our Lord and Savior has our ultimate good in mind even when we do not understand the details, we know that all things work together for the good of those who love God, those whom He has called according to his plan (Romans 8:29).

36   The Prayer of Faith, the Elders, the Anointing Oil (James 4:14-16): Is any sick among you; call for the Elders, anointing of oil, and the prayer of faith. The Elders: Is any sick among you, let him call for the elders. This was also a Jewish maxim. Rabbi Simeon, in Sepher Hachaiyim, said, "What should a man do who goes to visit the sick? Answer. He, who studies to restore the health of the body, should first lay the foundation in the health of the soul. The wise men have said, "No healing is equal to that which comes from the word of God and prayer. When sickness or disease enters into a man's family, let him apply to a wise man, who will implore mercy on his behalf". (See Schoettgen). Anointing of oil: It was the practice of the Jews to apply oil as a means of healing, and that James refers to this custom; as well, Luke 10:34, refers to this custom in the case of the wounded man ministered to by the Good Samaritan. And that Mark 6:13 also refers to this custom, when they cast out many devils, and anointed with oil many that were sick, and healed them, is evidence that oil was used for healing. In Midrash Koheleth, fol. 73, 1, it is said: "Chanina, son of the brother of the Rabbi Joshua, went to visit his uncle at Capernaum; he was taken ill; and Rabbi Joshua went to him and anointed him with oil, and he was restored". They had, therefore, recourse to this as a natural remedy; and we find that the disciples used it also in this way to heal the sick, not exerting the miraculous power but in cases where natural means were ineffectual. Note, regarding the oil, it is the opinion of many commentators that it might have been done symbolically, in order to prepare the way for a miraculous cure. In short, anointing the sick with oil, in order to their recovery, was a constant practice among the Jews; (see Lightfoot and Wetstein). Prayer of faith: Who is able to implore mercy and forgiveness of sins, on another's behalf, to offer up prayers to God on another's behalf? It is written that God will often make these (the calling of elders, anointing of oil, and the prayer of faith) the means of a sick person's recovery and the forgiveness of his (or her) sins, see James 5:14, 15. James very properly sends all such as is sick to the elders of the Church, who have power with God through the great Mediator, Jesus that they might pray for them. James desires them to use prayer and faith, while looking to God for an exceptional blessing. However, there are often cases where faith and prayer are both ineffectual; because God sees, it will be prejudicial to the person's salvation, to be restored to life. Therefore, all faith and prayer on such occasions should be exerted on this ground, if it be most for thy glory, and the eternal good of this person's soul, let him or her be restored; if otherwise, Lord, pardon, purify him or her, and take him or her to thy glory. For, it will always be the Lord, who shall raise him or her up, and not the elders, no matter how faithfully and fervently they have prayed. (Loosely taken from Adam Clarke's Commentary)

37   http://www.military.com/join-armed-forces/us-military-overview.html

Now, pray

Lord Jesus, because of your kindness that is eternal, I humbly ask you to come into my life and I ask you to forgive me of my sins. I ask you to forgive my iniquity and the iniquity of all my ancestors. We have sinned against you, but today, I repent for my entire ancestral line. We have committed the sins of (name the prominent sin), and I repent for all occult activity on either my father or mother's family line, and I place the Blood of Jesus Christ between all generational sin and myself, on both my mother and father's family line. I ask that the Blood of Jesus cleanse my family's bloodline all the way back to Adam. I break the authority of all ungodly covenants, vows, pronouncements, oaths, agreements, contracts, alliances, hexes, all blood covenants, and curses between me and my mother and father's lines. Lord, I ask that all patterns of sin, doubt, ungodly belief systems, and hereditary diseases, in my life and my family, be destroyed. I ask you to forgive and to cleanse me. Purge from my spirit, soul, and body all iniquity. I now command all iniquity residing in my bones, my organs, my blood, my DNA, and my genetic code to leave my body, now in Jesus Name. I cancel any curse that resulted from these iniquities. I declare that the righteousness of God is being established in my life, with all the blessings of God released, to me, and my family, in Jesus Name. Father, you said if I would come to you, you would not cast me away. So, I come to you now, and surrender every area of my life to you. I invite you to be Lord of my mind, my thoughts, my soul, my body, and my spirit. I ask you to be Lord over my emotions and all my feelings, to be Lord of my will and all decisions. I ask you to be Lord of my family and all my relationships. I ask you to be Lord of my time and my possessions; Lord of my word; Lord of my entertainment, and Lord over my relationship with you. I thank you for being my Lord and Savior, in Jesus Name. Moreover, Father I thank you for forgiving me. Lord, in Jesus' Name, I cover myself with the Blood of Jesus. I pray a hedge of protection around me, my family, my finances, and all that I own and that is within my sphere of influence. I pray you would bring to remembrance all that is pertinent for my deliverance. I bind every strongman in Jesus's Name. I ask that every gift of the Holy Spirit be made available to me as need be. I call in Warrior Angels to remove every evil spirit to the abyss, and I seal them there by the power of the Blood and Name of Jesus. I forbid them to return me and to any member of my family. Father I give you all the praise and glory for what is done in my life. Amen.

Canyon (see Landforms, Valley) 679
Car, Car Dealership (see Buildings, Storage Facilities or Vehicles, Automobile Vehicles) 509, 860
Carport (see Buildings, Storage Facilities) 509
Carwash (see Buildings, Storage Facilities) 509
Caravan (see Vehicles) 860
Cards (see Games, Tabletop Games) 183
Cardinal Directions 541
Carnival (see Parades) 188
Carriage (see Vehicles, Caravan) 860
Carrots (see Agriculture, Food, Foodstuff) 281
Cart (see Vehicles, Bicycle) 860
Carving (see Cutting) 123
Cashier, cash handler (see Working, Work Places, Accountant) 258
Casket (see Sleeping, Asleep or Bury) 213, 281
Cassette player (see Music, Stereo) 701
Casino (see Buildings, Hotel) 508
Castle (see Buildings, Residential Buildings) 509
Castration (see Body, Sexuality) 428
Cataclysmic (see Landforms) 679
Catastrophe (see Landforms, Cataclysmic) 679
Caterer (see Working, Work Places, Foodservice) 258
Caterpillar (see Animals, Insects) 351
Cathedral (see Buildings, Religious Buildings) 509
Cats (see Animals, Felines) 351
Cattle (see Animals) 351
Catwalk (see Walking, Pathway) 243
Causeway (see Walking, Pathway) 243
Cave (see Landforms) 679
Cavity (see Ascending and Descending, Baptize) 72
CD player (see Music, Stereo) 701
Ceilings (see Buildings) 508
Celebrations 553
Celebrity (see People, Celebrity) 828
Cellar (e.g. root cellar, storm cellar, see Agriculture, Agricultural Structures) 280
Censers (see Odors, Incense) 816
Centaur (see Animals, Monsters, Mythological or Legendary Creatures) 352
Centipedes (see Animals, Worms) 352
CEO (see Working, Work Places) 258
Cereal Grasses, Grains (see Agriculture, Food, Foodstuff) 280

CFO (see Working, Work Places, Accountant) 258
Chair (see Sitting) 205
Chancellor (see People, Ambassador) 828
Channel (see Bodies of Water, Canal) 679
Chapel (see Buildings, Religious Buildings) 509
Chariot (see Vehicles, Caravan) 860
Chasing 53, 93
Cheap, cheapen (see Abating, to discount) 54
Cheating 53, 104
Checkers (see Games, Tabletop Games) 183
Cheeks (see Body, Head) 427
Cheering (see Clapping, Applaud) 109
Cheerleader (see Games) 183
Chef (see Working, Work Places, Foodservice) 258
Chess (see Games, Tabletop Games) 183
Chest (see Body, Breasts or Chest) 426
Chicken Coop (see Agriculture, Agricultural Structures) 280
Children (grandchildren, biological, adopted, step, in-law, see People, Family) 75, 828
Chimes (see Music, Percussion Instruments) 701
Chin (see Body, Head) 427
Chipmunk (see Animals, Rodents, Burrowing Animals, Weasels) 352
Chiseling (see Cutting, Sculpt) 123
Choking (see Body, Head) 427
Chop (see Cutting) 123
Choreograph (see Dancing) 132
Chorus (see Music, Singing) 701
Christians (see People, Family, Siblings) 829
Church (see Ascending or Buildings, Religious Buildings) 65, 509
Church Mother (see People, Family, Mother) 829
Cider (see Agriculture, Food, Foodstuff) 281
Cigarettes, Cigars (see Drinking) 143
Circus Rides (see Ascending and Descending) 72
Circumcised, circumcision (see Body, Sexuality) 428
Cistern (see Bodies of Water, Dam) 679
Citadel (see Buildings, Military Buildings) 508
City (see Walking) 242
Claimant (see Divorce) 138
Clapping 53, 109
Clarinet (see Music, Wind Instruments) 701
Classmate (see People) 828

Classroom (see Working, Work Places, Educator) 258

Clavichord (see Music, Stringed Instruments) 701

Cleaning 53, 112

Cleft (see Landforms) 679

Clergy, Cleric, Clergy Garments (see Chasing or Clothing, Ecclesiastical or People, Spiritual or Religious Leaders) 94, 570, 829

Clerk (see Working, Work Places, CEO) 258

Climbing (see Ascending, Lower elevation to a higher one) 65

Clinic (see Buildings, Health Care Facility) 508

Cloak (see Clothing, Hats) 570

Cloister (see Buildings, Residential Buildings) 509

Closet (see Drinking, Intoxicated) 143

Cloth (see Falling, Rope) 152

Clothing (see Blood) 75, 565

Clouds (see Ascending, Body in Heaven or Falling or Weather 65, 152, 881

Co-Worker (see Working, Work Places) 258

Coals (see Walking, Fire) 242

Coast Guard (see People, Soldiers) 829

Coat (see Clothing) 570

Coastline (see Landforms) 679

Cobwebs (see Animals, Spiders) 352

Cocaine (see Drinking, Intoxicated) 143

Cold 53, 177

College (see Working, Work Places, Educator) 258

Colors, Coloring (applying color) 592

Communications, Communication Devices 608

Communication Towers (see Communications) 613

Community Hall (see Buildings) 508

Complaining (see Talking) 232

Compliments (see Talking) 232

Computer (Laptop, PC, Tablet, see Cutting, Chopped or Communications) 123, 613

Con (see Cheating) 105

Concert, Concert Hall (see Buildings, Arts and Entertainment Facilities) 507

Concourse (see Buildings, Vestibule) 509

Condominium (see Buildings, Residential Buildings) 509

Conflict, Contestation 53, 157

Confused (see Emotions, Fear) 661

Conspire (see Talking) 232

Construction Site (see Working, Work Places, Manufacturing) 258

Consulate (see Buildings, Residential Buildings) 509

Continent (see Landforms) 679

Contract (agreement between two people) 620

Contractions (see Labor)

Convention Center (see Buildings, Community Hall) 508

Cook (see Working, Work Places, Foodservice) 258

Copper (see Currency, Precious Metals) 625

Cord (see Ascending) 65

Cornerstone (see Standing, Standing Stones) 221

Cornet (see Music, Wind Instruments) 701

Coroner (see Death) 641

Corporal Punishment (see Fighting, Whipping) 159

Corpse (see Death) 641

Correspondences (see Communications, Mail) 613

Corridor (see Buildings, Entryways) 508

Cottage (see Buildings, Residential Buildings) 509

Counter Tops (see Buildings, Kitchen) 508

Counting (see Numbers) 712

Coupon sale (see Abating, to discount) 54

Courtroom (see Sitting, Place) 205

Cousin (biological, adopted, in-law, see People, Family) 829

Cove (see Landforms, Cave) 679

Cow (see Animals, Cattle) 351

Cowshed (see Agriculture, Agricultural Structures) 280

Coyote (see Animals, Canines) 351

Crater (see Ascending and Descending, Baptize) 72

Credit Cards (see Currency) 625

Creek (see Bodies of Water, River) 679

Crevice (see Landforms, Cleft) 679

Criminals (see Chasing or Working, Work Places) 94, 258

Crippled (see Body, Limbs) 428

Crops (see Agriculture) 280

Cross, Crucifix (see Agriculture, Trees) 282

Cruel and Inhumane Treatment (see Divorce) 138

Cruise ship (see Vehicles, Boat) 860

Friends, Friendly, Ex-friend (see Chasing or People) 94, 829
Frogs (see Animals) 351
Frost 53, 177
Frozen 53, 177
Fruit (see Agriculture, Food, Foodstuff) 280
Frustrated (see Emotions, Anger) 661
Funeral (see Death) 642
Furrow (see Landforms, Valley) 679

G

Gambling (see Games) 183
Games (something played for fun or competition) 53, 182
Gangster (see Chasing, Criminal) 94
Garage (see Buildings, Storage Facilities) 509
Garbage Can (see Buildings, Waste Yard) 509
Garbage Dump (see Buildings, Waste Yard) 509
Garden, gardening, gardener, nurseryman (see Agriculture) 281
Garden of Eden (see Agriculture, Garden) 281
Gargoyles (see Animals, Monsters, Mythological or Legendary Creatures) 352
Gas station (see Buildings, Storage Facilities) 509
Gate (see Buildings, Entryways) 508
Gatekeeper (see Working, Work Places, Doorkeeper) 258
Gazelle (see Animals, Deer) 351
Gehenna (see Realms of the Dead)
Gems (see Cutting, Cut or Currency, Stones) 123, 625
Genital System (see Body, Sexuality) 428
Genocide (see Fighting) 159
Genuflect (see Bowing) 85
Gerbil (see Animals, Rodents, Burrowing Animals, Weasels) 352
Geyser (see Bodies of Water, River) 679
Ghosts (see Chasing, Demon) 94
Giant (see Chasing or Body) 94, 427
Gift, gift cards (see Currency, Gift) 625
Giraffe (see Animals) 351
Girlfriend, Ex-girlfriend (see People, Friends) 829
Glacier (see Weather, Blizzard) 881
Glass (see Buildings, Windows) 509
Glasshouse (see Agriculture, Agricultural Structures) 280
Gloves (see Clothing, Jewelry) 570
Gnats (see Animals, Insects) 351

Goat (see Animals) 351
God 65, 85, 94, 232, 613
Gold (see Colors, Primary Colors or Currency, Precious Metals) 596, 625
Gong (see Music, Percussion Instruments) 701
Google (see Communications, Mail) 613
Gossiping (see Talking) 232
Grafting (see Agriculture, Cuttings) 280
Grains (see cereal grasses)
Granary (see Agriculture, Agricultural Structures) 280
Grandchildren (see Children)
Grandparent (biological, adopted, step, in-laws, or one who you consider a grandparent, see People, Family) 829
Grandparent's Day (see Celebrations, Parent's Day) 557
Grasshopper (see Animals, Insects) 351
Grave, Graveyard (see Death) 642
Gravies (see Agriculture, Food, Foodstuff) 280
Gray (see Colors) 596
Greed (see Emotions, Hatred) 662
Green (see Colors, Secondary Colors) 596
Green Beret (see People, Soldiers) 829
Greenhouse (see Agriculture, Agricultural Structures) 280
Greyhound (see Bus)
Griffin (see Animals, Felines, winged lion, aka griffon, gryphon) 351
Groaning (see Emotions, Crying) 661
Ground (see Agriculture) 281
Groundhog (see Animals, Rodents, Burrowing Animals, Weasels) 352
Groves (see Agriculture, Crops) 280
Guard (see Standing, Standing Apart) 221
Guest House (see Hotel)
Guitar (see Music, Stringed Instruments) 701
Guilty or Not Guilty (see Fighting) 159
Guinea Pig (see Animals, Rodents, Burrowing Animals, Weasels) 352
Gulf (see Bodies of Water, Ocean) 679
Gulley (see Bodies of Water, Canal) 679
Gum (chewing gum, see Body, Head) 427
Gym, Gymnasium (see Games, Sports or Working, Work Places, Educator) 183, 258

H

Hack (to chop or cut) (see Cutting) 123
Hacked (into a computer) (see Cutting) 123
Hades (see Realms of the Dead)

907

Identity Theft (see Cheating, Stolen ID) 105
Idols (see Bowing, before an adversary) 85
Ignored (see Emotions, Hatred) 662
Illegal immigrant (see Working, Work Places, Criminal) 258
Illicit lover (see Adultery)
Illness (see Body, Sickness) 428
In-laws (see People, Family) 829
Incapacitated (see Accidents) 57
Incarceration (see Buildings, Jail) 508
Incense 811
Indignant Estrangement (see Divorce) 138
Indignation (see Emotions, Anger) 661
Inheritance (see Currency, Gift) 625
Injured (see Accidents) 57
Inn (see Hotel)
Inoculation (see Body) 428
Insanity (see Emotions, Fear) 661
Insects (see Animals) 351
Insider trading (see Working, Work Places, Criminal) 258
Inspecting (see Walking) 243
Instagram (see Communications, Television) 613
Intercom (see Communications, Telephone) 613
Internet (see Communications, Computer) 613
Intestine (see Body, Excretory System) 426
Intimidated (see Emotions, Anger) 661
Intoxicated (see Drinking) 143
Investigator (see Working, Work Places, Judicial) 258
Invisible, invisible entity (see Chasing) 94
Irreconcilable Differences (see Divorce) 138
Island (see Landforms) 679
Isthmus (see Landforms, Island) 679

J

Jackal (see Animals, Canines) 351
Jacket (see Clothing) 570
Jail (see Buildings) 508
Janitorial (see Working, Work Places, Butler) 258
Jaws (see Cheeks)
Jealousy (see Emotions, Hatred) 662
Jesus 65, 75, 85, 94, 232, 613
Jewelry 565
Joke (see practical joke)
Joy (see Emotions) 657

Judge (see Chasing, Officer or Working, Work Places, Judicial) 94, 258
Jump Rope (see Games, Children Games) 183
Junior High (6th – 9th grades, see Working, Work Places, Educator) 258

K

Kangaroos (see Animals, Marsupials) 352
Keyboard, digital keyboard (see Music, Electronic Instruments) 701
Kidneys, kidney stones (see Body, Excretory System) 426
Killer, Killing (see Chasing, Criminal) 53, 94, 157
Kindergarten (see Working, Work Places, Educator) 258
King (see People, Ambassador) 828
Kiosks (see Buildings, Market Facilities) 508
Kissing (see Emotions, Love) 662
Kitchen (see Buildings) 508
Kitchen-Island (see Buildings, Kitchen) 508
Kite (see Flying) 172
Kittens (see Animals, Larvae) 351
Kneeling 53, 84
Knees (see Body, Limbs) 428
Knife (see Cutting) 123
Knocked-out (see Fighting, Boxing) 159
Kotex (see Blood, Women's monthly) 75

L

Labor (see Pregnancy, Birth Pains) 195
Labs (see Drinking, Winepress) 150
Lacerate (see Cutting) 123
Ladder (see Ascending or Falling) 65, 152
Ladybugs (see Animals, Insects) 351
Lake (see Bodies of Water) 679
Lamb (see Animals, Sheep) 352
Landforms 674
Landlord (see Working, Work Places, CEO) 258
Landmines (see Agriculture, Plant) 281
Landslide (see Landforms, Earthquake) 679
Language (speaking another language, see Talking) 232
Lap (see Sitting) 205
Laptop (see Computer)
Larceny (see Cheating, Thievery) 105
Larvae (see Animals) 351
Late, Lateness (see Numbers, Time) 712
Laughter (see Emotions) 657
LaVenta Monument (see Standing, Standing Stones) 221

Mercy Flight (see Vehicles, Automobile Vehicles) 860

Mermaids (see Animals, Monsters, Mythological or Legendary Creatures) 352

Meth (see Drinking, Intoxicated) 143

Metro Station (see Buildings, Storage Facilities) 509

Mice (see Animals, Rodents, Burrowing Animals, Weasels) 352

Michelangelo (see Currency, Stones) 625

Middle School (see Junior High) Midget (see Abating) 54

Midnight (see Numbers, Time) 712

Migrant (see Agriculture, Farm Worker) 280

Milk (see Agriculture, Food, Foodstuff) 280

Mill (see Working, Work Places, Manufacturing) 258

Millipedes (see Animals, Worms) 352

Military Buildings (see Buildings) 508

Mining, Mineshaft (see Working, Work Places, Manufacturing) 258

Minister (see People, Spiritual or Religious Leaders) 829

Mink (see Animals, Rodents, Burrowing Animals, Weasels) 352

Minotaur (see Animals, Monsters, Mythological or Legendary Creatures) 352

Mirror (see Buildings, Windows) 509

Miscarriage (see Pregnancy, Infant Loss) 195

Mites (see Animals, Parasites) 352

Mobile phones (aka cell phone, see Communications, Telephone) 613

Mobster (see Chasing, Criminal) 94

Models (persons display fashions, see People, Friends) 829

Mole (see Animals, Rodents, Burrowing Animals, Weasels) 352

Molester, Molestation (see Chasing, Criminal or Body, Sexuality) 94, 428

Monarch (see People, Ambassador) 828

Monastery (see Buildings, Residential Buildings) 509

Monet (see Currency, Stones) 625

Money 75, 620

Moneychanger (see Working, Work Places, Accountant) 258

Monkeys (see Animals) 351

Monthly cycle (see Blood, Woman's monthly) 75

Monsoons (see Weather) 881

Monsters (see Chasing, Demon or Animals) 94, 352

Monument (see Standing, Standing Stones) 221

Moon (see Cardinal Directions) 546

Mopping (see Cleaning) 113

Morgue (see Death, Grave) 642

Morning (see Numbers, Time) 712

Mortician (see Death, Coroner) 641

Mosque (see Buildings, Religious Buildings) 509

Mosquitoes (see Animals, Parasites) 352

Motel (see Hotel)

Mother (biological, adopted, step-mother, in-law, or one who reared, or took care of, you as her child, see People, Family) 829

Mother's Day (see Celebrations, Parent's Day) 557

Motorcycle, motored bike (see Vehicles, Automobile Vehicles) 860

Motorhome (see Vehicles, Automobile Vehicles) 860

Mound (see Landforms, Hill) 679

Mountain (see Ascending and Descending, Going up and down or Landforms) 72, 152, 679

Mouth (see Body, Head) 427

Movie, Movie Theatre (see Buildings, Arts and Entertainment Facilities or Communications, Television) 507, 613

Mower (see Vehicles, Automobile Vehicles) 860

Mt. Rushmore (see Standing, Standing Stones) 221

Mule (see Animals, Horse) 351

Murder, Murderer (see Chasing, Criminal) 94

Murmuring (see Talking, Complaining) 232

Museum (see Buildings, Arts and Entertainment) 507

Music, Musical Instruments 701

Musical Chairs (see Games) 183

Mutilate (see Cutting) 123

Mythological Creatures (see Animals, Monsters, Mythological or Legendary Creatures) 352

N

Nail Technician (see Working, Work Places, Manufacturing) 258

Nails (see Body, Limbs) 428

Naked (see Body) 428

Napping (see Sleeping) 213

Navy (see People, Soldiers) 829